FEDERAL INCOME TAXATION

EDITORIAL ADVISORY BOARD

FEDERAL INCOME TAXATION

Tenth Edition

WILLIAM A. KLEIN
Professor of Law
University of California, Los Angeles

JOSEPH BANKMAN
Professor of Law
Helen L. Crocker Faculty Scholar
Stanford University

LITTLE, BROWN AND COMPANY
Boston New York Toronto London

Tenth Edition

Library of Congress Catalog Card No. 94-75306

ISBN 0-316-47622-6

FOURTH PRINTING

MV-NY

Published simultaneously in Canada
by Little, Brown & Company (Canada) Limited

Printed in the United States of America

SUMMARY OF CONTENTS

CONTENTS

4

PERSONAL DEDUCTIONS, EXEMPTIONS, AND CREDITS **473**

5

ALLOWANCES FOR MIXED BUSINESS AND PERSONAL OUTLAYS 523

8

CAPITAL GAINS AND LOSSES 829

ACKNOWLEDGMENTS

We are grateful for permission to reprint passages from the following:

S. Terkel, Working: People Talk about What They Do All Day and How They Feel about What They Do. Copyright © 1972, 1974 by Studs Terkel, reprinted by permission of Pantheon Books, a division of Random House, Inc.

Fullerton and Goodman, The Economic Recovery Tax Act of 1981: Implications for Charitable Giving, 16 Tax Notes 1027 (1982). Copyright © 1982, reprinted by permission of Tax Analyst, publisher of Tax Notes. All rights reserved.

EDITORIAL NOTICE

The original author of this casebook was Boris I. Bittker of Yale Law School, who has earned the admiration and affection of generations of teachers and students. Much of his original structure and choice of materials remains in the current edition. Bittker was joined in later editions by Lawrence M. Stone, who kept the book current and added important ideas and materials. Neither Bittker nor Stone has been involved in recent revisions, but the current authors are deeply indebted to them for the many wise choices and valuable insights that have survived.

All omissions from cases and other materials, except omissions of footnotes, are indicated either by substitution of new material in brackets or, more often, by an ellipsis (. . .). Thus, omissions of citations, as well as omissions of text, are generally indicated by the insertion of the ellipsis. Citations have been excised ruthlessly on the theory that for the most part they are of no use to students and that the rare student who might have some interest in them can easily look them up in the original report. There is no notation of omitted footnotes, and all footnotes, including those in cases and other materials, are numbered consecutively from the beginning of each chapter.

FEDERAL INCOME TAXATION

1

INTRODUCTION

A. THE IMPORTANCE OF INCOME TAXES

1. Some Data

As can be seen from Table 1-1,[1] in 1993, income taxes, corporate and individual, were expected to produce 54.4 percent of total federal revenues and represented 10.6 percent of GNP. If one removes social insurance taxes and contributions and looks only at the so-called general revenues, income taxes are 86.3 percent of the total.

TABLE 1-1
Sources of Federal Revenue for 1994 (Estimated)

Source	*Amount (bil.)*		*Percentage of total*		*Percentage of GDP**	
Income taxes	$680.3		54.6		10.3	
Individual income taxes		$560.0		44.9		8.5
Corporation income taxes		120.3		9.7		1.8
Social insurance taxes and contributions	465.0		37.3		7.1	
Excise taxes	51.4		4.1		0.8	
Other	49.7		4.0		0.8	
Total	$1,246.4		100.0		19.0	

* GDP stands for gross domestic product.

1. Budget of the United States Government, Fiscal Year 1993, pp. 6, 11 (1993).

The federal individual income tax burden is widely shared. In 1988, the number of tax returns was 83 million, and over half of these were joint returns of husbands and wives. The statistics in Table 1-2 reveal that the most important revenue source is the middle-income taxpayer.[2] Low-income people cannot afford to and, generally speaking, do not pay income taxes. High-income people probably could afford to pay more, though the point is hotly debated, but there are relatively few of them. The adoption in 1993 of an increase in the top rates of individual income taxation should result in a small shift of the total burden to high-income taxpayers.

Income taxes are also an important source of revenue for state and local governments. In 1988, of a total of $435.7 billion in tax collections at this level, the individual income tax produced $88.4 billion (10.0 percent), and the corporate income tax produced $23.7 billion (2.7 percent).[3]

2. Effects on the Law

The income tax is important not only because of its central role in financing government but also, and of special interest to lawyers, because of the ways in which it affects so many other branches of law.

TABLE 1-2
Income and Tax Liability by Adjusted Gross Income (AGI)* for 1988

AGI class	*Number of returns (mil.)*	*Aggregate AGI (bil.)*	*Tax (bil.)*	*Effective rate (percentage)*
Under $11,000	35.7	$143.2	$5.9	4.1
$10,000 to $50,000	60.6	1,572.1	151.4	9.6
$50,000 to $200,000	15.1	1,131.8	178.5	15.8
$200,000 and over	0.8	409.1	97.1	23.7

* This label is described infra page 49.

2. See Statistical Abstract of the United States 1991, at 326 (U.S. Dep't of Commerce, Bureau of the Census). More recent data show a significant compression of the effective rate. A Joint Committee on Taxation summary of the distributional effects of the Omnibus Budget Reconciliation Act of 1990 shows anticipated effective rates for the years 1991–1995 varying from 13.1 percent for taxpayers with adjusted gross income under $10,000 to 26.8 percent for taxpayers with adjusted gross income over $200,000. The bulk of revenue continues to come from middle-income taxpayers. For example, over one-half of total revenue is expected to come from taxpayers earning between $20,000 and $75,000. Joint Committee Summary of Distributional Effects, By Income Category, Budget Reconciliation (H.R. 5825), reprinted as special supplement to Tax Notes (October 29, 1990).

3. Id. at 284.

The tax lawyer, perhaps above all else, is a planner — a person who advises clients on how to shape their transactions so as to minimize their tax liability. Lawyers who do not specialize in tax law must know at least enough about it to recognize when a tax specialist must be consulted. Tax considerations may play a key role in transactions ranging from the sale, lease, or encumbrance of property; to the dissolution of a marriage; to the choice between the partnership and the corporate form of business organization; to the form of compensation in an employment agreement; to the settlement of a claim for damages for personal injuries; and so on. By the same token, the practitioner or the legal scholar who wants to understand economic and legal institutions such as the sale and leaseback method of financing the purchase of property, the family-controlled charitable foundation, or the use of limited partnerships must understand the tax reasons for the use of such devices. For good or ill, the federal income tax has played a role in legal history ranking in importance with the invention of the trust and the corporation and the development of the doctrine of respondeat superior.

The income tax has had this kind of impact not just because of the amount of money involved but also because it is a complex system of rules that presents many opportunities for adjustment of conduct to achieve desirable tax results. The property tax (which in 1990 produced revenues of $156 billion for state and local government) and the general sales tax (which produced $178 billion) are based on much simpler concepts and rules and consequently produce far less business for lawyers, relative to the amounts involved, than the income tax. Most lawyers will end their careers in total ignorance of customs duties and federal taxes on alcohol and tobacco, but a lawyer might better be ignorant of the rule against perpetuities, the parol evidence rule, or the requisites of negotiability than of the federal income tax.

3. Economic Consequences

The income tax has also had a substantial effect on the allocation of resources in our economy, on the ways in which people invest their time and their money; indeed, it has affected our lives in the broadest sense. For example, the deductions for interest payments and for property taxes[4] and the nontaxation of imputed income[5] encourage people (especially those with high incomes) to buy homes rather than rent apartments. At one time, very substantial and quite unique provisions benefited the oil industry,[6] thereby encouraging the production of oil

4. See infra pages 511-518.
5. See infra page 117.
6. See infra pages 677-681.

and reducing the price of gasoline; even today, the tax laws treat the oil industry more favorably in some respects than other industries. It is by no means implausible to suppose that low-price gasoline and encouragement of home ownership have been important elements in the shift of populations to the suburbs and in the problems of pollution and of energy management. Other kinds of tax provisions may have had effects that most people would view as more benign — for example, the deduction for charitable contributions, which seems to have played a significant role in raising the level of support for private colleges and universities, museums and symphony orchestras, and organized religion.

Much of the complexity of the present tax laws is attributable to provisions designed to encourage particular kinds of economic activity. Many people think that the use of the tax system in this way is likely to be, at best, less effective than reliance on direct subsidies. As special incentive provisions proliferate, the efficacy of each may be diminished. But Congress seems to have become addicted. For example, in recent years we have witnessed the addition of incentive provisions for investment in low-income housing, in pollution control, in the removal of barriers to the handicapped and elderly, in the creation of employee stock ownership plans, in preservation of certain historical structures, in job creation, and so forth. Congress has reduced business taxes by billions of dollars with provisions increasing deductions for investments in plant and equipment. Economists differ in their views of many of the economic effects of such provisions, but one effect is clear: Incentive provisions contribute substantially to the complexity of the law and to the need for tax advice in planning business and other activities.

B. HISTORY

The preceding observations about the magnitude of the tax and its effects on the legal system and on the economy raise the question, how did we get where we are? A serious effort to answer that question is well beyond the scope of this book, but it will be useful to summarize briefly some of the major events in the history of taxation in the United States, from the slow and difficult birth of the income tax in the pre-1913 period to its explosive growth in recent decades. This account should convey some sense of the forces at play in the adoption of the tax and of the ways in which it has developed and is likely to develop in the future.

From the time of the Jefferson administration until the Civil War, customs receipts, or tariffs (whose burden Jefferson thought was borne by the rich), were the backbone of the federal tax system. The tariffs not only produced revenues but protected developing industries, mostly in the North. During the War of 1812, customs receipts declined and revenue needs were met by the imposition of various excise taxes, but these were repealed shortly after that war ended. During the Civil War, customs receipts once again were unable to carry the load, and Congress levied an income tax. The 1864 version imposed a tax of 5 percent on income from $600 to $5,000, of 7.5 percent on income from $5,000 to $10,000, and of 10 percent on income above $10,000. By comparison with the present law, the statute then was almost unbelievably short and simple. The Confederacy also employed an income tax.

After the Civil War, the federal income tax was repealed and customs receipts again became a basic source of federal revenue, but they were never again to be the dominant source that they once had been. Federal excises on tobacco and liquor together produced almost as much as, and sometimes even more than, the tariff during the next half-century. Throughout the 1870s and 1880s, moreover, agrarian and labor groups called for reductions in the tariff and for a revival of the income tax. Leading the opposition were eastern businessmen, for whom the income tax meant "confiscation," "spoliation," and "communism." Throughout this period the Republican Party was able to hold the fort, but the task became more difficult as the Democratic Party gradually emerged from its handicap as the party of secession and finally became impossible when the Populist movement gained strength from the panic of 1893.

In 1894, during Cleveland's second administration, a federal income tax, based largely on the Civil War statute, was passed by Congress after a bitter struggle, a notable feature of which was the oratory of William Jennings Bryan. A tax of 2 percent was imposed on individual incomes over $4,000 and on the entire income of business corporations. In 1894 eggs sold for twenty cents a dozen and round steak for twelve cents a pound,[7] and the average annual earnings of nonfarm employees was $420.[8] Adjusted to take account of inflation (by applying the Consumer Price Index[9]) the $4,000 threshold of 1894 would have been a $65,957 threshold in 1990. Thus, the income tax was a tax on the well-to-do and might be thought to reflect a "soak the rich" philosophy. This observation may help explain the intensity of the opposition. The adoption of the tax was a victory for egalitarianism and a reflection of the rising Democratic and Populist voting power. Beyond that, it was a victory of the South and the Middle West over the Northeast, part of

7. See U.S. Department of Commerce, Historical Statistics of the United States, Colonial Times to 1970, at 213 (1975).

8. Id. at 165.

9. See id. at 210-211; Statistical Abstract, supra note 2, at 468.

the same sectional movement that produced the Interstate Commerce Act in 1887 and the Sherman Act in 1890.

The victory of the Democrats and the Populists was soon to be snatched away, however, by the Supreme Court. The tax became law on August 28, 1894, to take effect as of January 1, 1895, and by January 29, 1895, the Supreme Court had agreed to hear a test case challenging its constitutionality. Pollock v. Farmers' Loan & Trust Co., 157 U.S. 429, aff'd on rehearing, 158 U.S. 601 (1895). The attack was based on the theory that a tax on rental income and on dividends and interest was in effect a tax on the underlying property interest and as such violated the prohibition on unapportioned "direct" taxes in Article I, section 9, clause 4, of the Constitution, which provides: "No Capitation, or other direct, Tax shall be laid, unless in Proportion to the Census or Enumeration herein before directed to be taken." The Court heard argument, involving several notable attorney-orators, for five days. The public interest was intense. After a rehearing, the Court, in a five-to-four decision, sustained the constitutional challenge to the imposition of the tax on rents, dividends, and interest and further held that since the provisions taxing those receipts were inseparable from the other provisions of the law, the entire law was invalid.

After Pollock v. Farmers' Loan & Trust Co., advocates of an income tax turned their efforts to amendment of the Constitution. But William McKinley's victories in 1896 and 1900 over William Jennings Bryan, the candidate of the Democrats and the Populists, reflected the temper of the times. Not even the financial demands of the Spanish-American War were enough to restore the tax. Within a few more years, however, the tide had turned again, with even such eminent Republicans as Theodore Roosevelt and William Howard Taft announcing their support for the tax.

In 1909 President Taft helped to defeat efforts, of Democrats and of insurgent Republicans who had followed Roosevelt, to challenge the Supreme Court decision in *Farmers' Loan & Trust Co.* by enacting another income tax. In return for his efforts, Taft extracted from the opponents of individual income taxation their support for a corporation income tax and for a congressional resolution proposing a constitutional amendment to permit an individual income tax with a tax on all types of income. The congressional resolution adopted the following language: "The Congress shall have the power to lay and collect taxes on incomes, from whatever source derived, without apportionment among the several States, and without regard to any census or enumeration." The corporate tax was adopted in 1909. It produced revenues that year of a paltry $21 million,[10] but the avalanche had begun.

10. Historical Statistics, supra note 7, at 1109.

In this renewed struggle over income taxation, the feelings of some of the opponents were, as before, intense. They spoke of confiscation, of discouragement of thrift and hard work, of encouragement of profligacy by government, and of radicalism, socialism, and un-Americanism. But the proponents prevailed, and by early 1913 the proposed constitutional amendment had been ratified by thirty-six states and had become the sixteenth amendment.

Congress reacted quickly, adopting in 1913 a tax law modeled after the 1894 act. Like its 1894 predecessor, the 1913 tax was imposed only on the well-to-do, but the rates were modest. There was an exemption of $3,000 for an individual and of an additional $1,000 for a married person living with his or her spouse.[11] The rate was 1 percent with a "surtax" ranging from 1 percent on net income from $20,000 to $50,000 up to 6 percent on that part of net income exceeding $500,000. History has proved, however, that the opponents' fears of vastly increased burdens over time were by no means attributable solely to paranoia.

Before proceeding with data on later developments, it seems useful to stop and speculate on the effect of the historical background on the shaping of the terms of the tax. History reveals a tax that was opposed with great fervor, and, one must suppose, with a sense of high principle, by most of those people on whom it was imposed. The top government officials and the judges who were called on to interpret and apply the law no doubt shared many of the attitudes of its opponents. Much of the early development of the tax law seems consistent with the notion that they begrudgingly accepted their defeat and did all they could to encourage and adopt interpretations shaping the tax as narrowly as possible regardless that such interpretations might produce illogical and unfair outcomes. As time passed, as the importance of the tax grew, and as people became more familiar with it, administrators and courts seem to have become more aware of sound tax theories, less begrudging and narrow in their approach to interpretation of the law, and more receptive to principles designed to produce sensible, logical elaboration. Some significant features of the present law, however, remain in place, as relics of the earlier era. And over the years, as Congress has increasingly used the income tax to achieve nontax objectives, much of the income tax's potential appeal to one's sense of fairness has been undermined.

Returning to the facts, the income tax in 1913 was a relatively small contributor to total federal revenues, well behind customs duties and

11. Since 1894, the Consumer Price Index had risen by only about 14 percent, and average annual earnings of fully employed employees was still only $663. The married-couple threshold of $4,000 was equivalent after adjustment for inflation to $52,760 in 1990.

excise taxes.[12] The revenue needs created by World War I changed that, leading to "the discovery of how easily and quickly large sums or revenue could be raised through the income tax."[13] The reach of the tax was broadened by reducing personal exemptions and its impact was increased by raising rates, with individual rates reaching a maximum of 77 percent in 1918. The tax rates had become significantly progressive.[14] Despite the lowering of exemptions, the major burden of the tax fell on people with high incomes. "For the years 1917 to 1919, although less than 1 percent of the returns reported income over $20,000, that group paid an average of 70 percent of the income taxes."[15] In 1913, revenue from the income tax was $28.3 million. By 1920 it had risen to $1.1 billion and remained at roughly that level until the beginning of World War II.[16]

Following World War I, as federal expenditures declined and budget surpluses arose, rates were gradually reduced, reaching a maximum individual rate of 24 percent. In this decade, as in more recent years, the debate over rates revolved around predictions about incentive effects and theories (and rhetoric) of justice and fairness in society.

With the thirties came the depression, and with the depression came budget deficits and demands in Congress to balance the budget by increasing taxes. Part of the response was to increase rates (to a maximum of 63 percent in 1932 and 79 percent in 1936) and part was to eliminate "loopholes" (that is, cleverly designed strategies and schemes that use the rules to achieve results that seem unexpected, or unintended, and unwarranted). Inevitably, as the process of closing loopholes and dealing with the increasingly complex nature of the country's economic system continued, the law became more and more complex.

With World War II came a dramatically increased need for revenue and a correspondingly dramatic increase in income taxes. Exemptions were reduced, with the result that between 1940 and 1944, "those paying some income tax rose from 7.1 to 64.1 percent of the population."[17] The maximum individual rate rose (in 1944) to 94 percent. With that rate of taxation, there was, of course, an intense incentive to find ways to avoid taxes by exploiting existing rules or by seeking special treatment

12. See J. Witte, The Politics and Development of the Federal Income Tax 79-80 (1985). This book is an excellent source of facts and analysis and is relied on heavily in the account that follows in text.

13. Id. at 81.

14. A progressive rate structure is one under which rates rise as income rises. Thus, high-income taxpayers pay a higher *proportion* of their income as taxes than do lower-income taxpayers. See discussion infra page 35.

15. Witte, supra note 12, at 86.

16. See Historical Statistics, supra note 7, at 1107, 1110.

17. Witte, supra note 12, at 125.

from Congress, and the tendency of the tax laws to become more and more complex continued.

In the years immediately following World War II, rates were reduced only slightly, to a maximum of 91 percent, which remained in effect until 1964.[18] There were Treasury surpluses in 1948, 1949, and 1950,[19] but any prospect of tax reduction was frustrated by the beginning of the Korean War in 1950.

In 1954 a substantially revised tax code was adopted. While it was a "reform" enactment in that it eliminated some unwarranted tax benefits, it followed the pattern of most post-World War II legislation in bestowing tax benefits on a variety of groups. Perhaps the most significant provision was one allowing "accelerated depreciation," which increased deductions for the cost of plant and equipment and other assets used in a business.[20] This provision reflected at least a tentative acceptance by Congress of the notion that the tax system should be used to control specific aspects of economic behavior (in this case, to stimulate investment) — a notion that, in the next three decades, played an increasingly important role in shaping the law. At the same time, it was plain that members of Congress had become well aware of the possibilities for gaining political support by rewarding their constituents, and contributors to their campaigns, with favored tax treatment in the form of deductions, exclusions, favorable tax accounting rules, credits, etc. (For a sense of the nature of these special provisions, see the Tax Expenditure Budget, infra page 24.) The inclination of members of Congress to use the tax system to encourage certain kinds of economic behavior (e.g., investment in factories and equipment or in research and development) and to respond to the claims of specific industries (e.g., mining and timber) and groups of individuals (e.g., the blind and the elderly) put Congress at odds with many objective tax experts who had become concerned with the "erosion" of the tax base — that is, with the proliferation of provisions designed to provide benefits to particular industries, activities, or groups. These observers argued that in order for the income tax to be fair, administrable, and consistent with economic rationality, virtually no exclusions or deductions should be allowed other than those required to arrive at an economically sound measure of income. The proponents of this kind of broad-based tax fought a losing battle (with some exceptions) during most of the history of the tax laws, but increasingly so in the sixties and seventies.

Congressional commitment to use of the tax system to "stimulate" the economy was dramatically demonstrated in 1962 with the adoption of the Investment Tax Credit (ITC). The ITC provided a credit (that

18. With the exception of 1952 and 1953 when the maximum rate was 92 percent.
19. Id. at 136.
20. See infra page 57.

is, an amount subtracted from the amount of tax due) equal to a percentage of amounts invested in productive equipment. It was designed to encourage investment, not to generate an accurate measure of income. Like accelerated depreciation, it results in big tax reductions. In 1985 it accounted for a tax reduction, and revenue loss, of $24 billion; in the same year accelerated depreciation, officially titled Accelerated Cost Recovery System (ACRS), cost $28 billion.[21] The ITC and accelerated depreciation, along with various other similar provisions designed to benefit particular kinds of investments, not only reduced revenues, and the tax burdens of business investors, but also gave rise to the "tax shelter" industry. The phrase "tax shelter" has no universally accepted definition; roughly, it refers to investments by passive investors (that is, people who do not take any active part in running the businesses in which their assets are used), where a dominant, or at least a substantial, motive for the investment is a reduction of taxes on the investors' incomes from fees, salaries, and other such sources. For example, a doctor with a high income from her medical practice might buy railroad boxcars to be rented to the railroads. One of the principal attractions of such an investment has been that in the early years of ownership, because of the ITC and the deductions for accelerated depreciation and interest (on the funds borrowed to finance the investment), the investor would show a loss for tax purposes — that is, a tax loss — even if an economically realistic analysis would show a profit. Tax shelters became increasingly important as the years passed. A tax shelter "industry" arose; that is, a substantial number of people devoted their efforts to organizing and selling tax shelter investments. Despite various limitations imposed by Congress (see infra page 711), the industry flourished.

Tax shelters are a product of congressional generosity with provisions favoring investment, but the generosity was extended to individual circumstances as well. For example, one of the most important sources of "erosion" of the tax base is the rule (made a part of the Code in 1954) that exempts from taxation amounts an employer contributes to a pension fund for the benefit of an employee. This is, as we will see (infra page 396), a plain departure (for better or worse) from broad-based tax under which everyone is taxed on everything they earn. It can be thought of as a subsidy to saving for retirement. The cost of the subsidy in 1987 was $59 billion (see Tax Expenditure Budget, infra page 26). Other benefits for individuals abound, including the deduction for interest on home-mortage debt; the exclusion from income of various noncash benefits received from an employer (e.g., medical insurance); the extra personal exemption for people over age 65; and an exclusion from income of $125,000 of any gain on the sale of a personal residence by a person over age 55.

21. See Tax Expenditure Budget figures, infra page 26.

Thus, a pattern can be seen. Many objective observers argued for a broad-based tax and restraint in the use of the tax system for stimulating particular economic activities. Individual members of Congress found almost irresistible the temptation to use the tax system to reward their constituents and to engage in logrolling to that end. Congress was constrained by the need to raise revenue. This need from time to time combined with embarrassment over the more outrageous tax avoidance opportunities to produce some genuine tax reform. But for the most part, the reform was piecemeal and pusillanimous. Thus, for example, Congress showed some willingness to attack tax shelters, thereby denying to individuals relatively modest tax savings from the use of accelerated depreciation and the ITC. At the same time, it has continued to accept the huge tax savings of corporations taking advantage of the same provisions.[22] And for the most part the record has been one of increasing use of the tax system to provide benefits for particular investments and activities, and an increasingly complex set of rules, with substantial compliance costs.[23]

During the period from 1960 to the present, revenues from the income tax have steadily risen, from $4.9 billion in 1960; to $103.7 billion in 1970; to $308.7 billion in 1980; and to $601.4 billion in 1990.[24] The maximum individual rate was reduced in 1964 to 77 percent and in 1965 to 70 percent. In 1969 the maximum rate for earned income (that is income from wages, salaries, etc. as opposed to interest, dividends, and other income from property) was reduced to 50 percent (beginning in 1972), and in 1981 the maximum individual rate on all income became 50 percent.[25] Thus, one sees a rejection of use of a

22. A good example of congressional timorousness and the complex, patchwork results that flow from it, is the alternative minimum tax, described more fully infra page 735. Much publicity had been given to the fact that a relatively small number of wealthy individuals had used various tax-benefit provisions to reduce their taxable incomes to zero, so that they paid no tax. The congressional solution was not to repeal the offensive provisions that were the source of this outcome. Rather, it was to list certain of such provisions (but not all) and to add back to income the amounts excluded under these provisions. The income figure thus derived was subjected to a tax at a modest rate. The result is that some wealthy individuals are penalized for using provisions, such as accelerated depreciation, to save a few million dollars in tax, while major corporations use the same provisions, with full congressional approval, to save many billions of dollars in tax.

23. See Slemrod and Sorum, The Compliance Cost of the U.S. Individual Income Tax System, 37 Nat'l Tax J. 461 (1984):

> [I]n 1982 [the compliance] cost [for state and federal income tax returns] was between $17 and $27 billion, or from five to seven percent of the revenue raised by the federal and state income tax systems combined. Between 1.8 and 2.1 billion hours of taxpayer time were spent on filing tax returns, and between $3.0 and $3.4 billion was spent on professional tax assistance.

24. The figures for 1960 and 1970 are from Historical Statistics, supra note 7, at 1107 and for 1980 and 1990 from Statistical Abstract, supra note 2, at 316.

25. The maximum corporation rate (applicable to incomes above $100,000) went from 52 percent in 1960 to 48 percent in 1970 to 46 percent in 1980.

highly progressive rate structure and, correspondingly, of use of the income tax to reduce disparities in income and wealth. This change seems to have been the product in part of a shift in philosophy or ideology away from an egalitarian ideal, in part a reflection of concern for the adverse incentive effects of high marginal rates, and in part a reaction to the reality that many high-income people avoided paying the top rates by investing in "tax shelters" (real estate, oil and gas ventures, etc.).

In 1981, under the leadership of President Ronald Reagan, stimulation of investment became the rallying cry (as it had in 1961 under President John Kennedy). An increase in depreciation deductions (ACRS) yielded billions of dollars of tax reduction to business firms (and, despite the reduction in the maximum individual rates, substantially increased the lure of tax shelters). As previously stated, by 1985 the year's revenue cost of accelerated depreciation had reached $28 billion. The result of this and previous congressional action is vividly revealed in the data in Table 1-3,[26] showing the decline, since 1950, in the role of the corporation income tax, and in Table 1-4,[27] showing the increase, since 1977, in tax losses reported by limited partnerships (the form used by most tax shelters). Also, in 1981, as previously indicated, the maximum individual rate was reduced to 50 percent for income from all sources. Proponents of the 1981 tax reductions argued that they would stimulate investment and other economic activity, thereby increasing the national income and the government's share of that income and producing a balanced budget. Unfortunately, that scenario (referred to by opponents as "voodoo economics") did not unfold. Investment over the next five years remained sluggish (increasing at a rate of less than 2 percent per year), and the budget deficit (and the foreign trade deficit) rose to unprecedented levels.

In 1986 there was a significant, though partly illusory and possibly temporary, reversal of the trend toward serving special interests. It was as if members of Congress said to themselves, "enough is enough." The consensus was that there should be "reform" but neither an increase nor a decrease in total revenue (a principle referred to as "revenue neutrality"). With considerable fanfare, Congress adopted a tax bill that included the most important set of changes in decades, one that, according to its backers, represented a victory for fairness and simplicity. Much of the content of this bill will be examined throughout the rest of this book and cannot effectively be summarized here, but a brief description seems appropriate. Among the most important features was

26. Reproduced from Joint Committee on Taxation, Study of 1983 Effective Tax Rates of Selected Large U.S. Corporations 25 (1985).

27. Testimony of Ronald A. Pearlman, Assistant Secretary (for Tax Policy) of the Treasury, Hearing before the Subcommittee on Oversight of the House Committee on Ways and Means, 99th Cong., 1st Sess. 29 (1986).

TABLE 1-3
Federal Government Receipts, 1950–1983
[By major category, as percent of total receipts*]

Fiscal year	*Individual income taxes*	*Corporation income taxes*	*Social insurance taxes and contributions*	*Excise taxes*	*All other receipts*
1950	39.9	26.5	11.1	19.1	3.4
1952	42.2	32.1	9.8	13.4	2.6
1954	42.4	30.3	10.3	14.3	2.8
1956	43.2	28.0	12.5	13.3	3.0
1958	43.6	25.2	14.1	13.4	3.7
1960	44.0	23.2	15.9	12.6	4.2
1962	45.7	20.6	17.1	12.6	4.0
1964	43.2	20.9	19.5	12.2	4.2
1966	42.4	23.0	19.5	10.0	5.1
1968	44.9	18.7	22.2	9.2	5.0
1970	46.9	17.0	23.0	8.1	4.9
1972	45.7	15.5	25.4	7.5	6.0
1974	45.2	14.7	28.5	6.4	5.2
1976	44.2	13.9	30.5	5.7	5.8
1978	45.3	15.0	30.3	4.6	4.8
1980	47.2	12.5	30.5	4.7	5.1
1981	47.7	10.2	30.5	6.8	4.8
1982	48.2	8.0	32.6	5.9	5.3
1983	48.1	6.2	34.8	5.9	5.0

* Components may not total 100.0 percent due to rounding.
Source: Office of Management and Budget, Federal Government Finances: 1985 Budget Data, February, 1984.

TABLE 1-4
Limited Partnership Losses

	Limited partnerships		
Year	*Percent of all partnerships*	*Net income*	*Number of partners*
1983	15.2	$−18.7	5,434,870
1982	14.9	−17.5	4,709,723
1981	14.3	−15.7	4,176,572
1980	12.3	−9.4	3,620,036
1979	10.5	−5.7	2,352,378
1978	9.6	NA	NA
1977	8.3	−3.6	1,542,107

a reduction in rates for both individuals and corporations, with the maximum individual rate dropping to 28 percent for some people and 33 percent for others[28] and the maximum rate for most corporations dropping to 34 percent (39 percent for some). At the same time, individual exemptions were increased, with the effect that the threshold at which taxes became payable was raised. The reduction and leveling of the maximum tax rates reflected an historic shift away from a progressive income tax. Many supported the bill for precisely that reason; others supported it in the belief that the reduced rates would lead to increased work effort and greater national prosperity.

The lowering of rates and increase in exemptions required, and was used as a justification for, a long list of revenue-raising provisions. Some of these eliminated tax benefits that, a year earlier, most knowledgeable people would have supposed were so firmly embedded in the law, and so important to politically powerful interest groups, that change would have been unthinkable.

Most of the tax benefits eliminated were benefits enjoyed by investors. One important provision eliminated the credit given to purchasers of certain forms of business property (the Investment Tax Credit, or ITC); another provision eliminated the favorable tax treatment of capital gain. And in what some people saw as a mortal blow to the activities of certain real estate promoters and investors (and a heavy blow to construction workers, lumber suppliers, etc.), the bill substantially reduced the depreciation (ACRS) deduction for real estate and virtually shut down the tax shelter industry by sharply limiting deductions for "passive losses." Among the important changes affecting individual taxpayers were the elimination of the deduction for interest on consumer debt (other than debt secured by personal residences) and the denial of charitable deductions for many low-income taxpayers. There were hundreds of other changes.

The reduction in tax preferences on capital investment reduced the influence of the tax law on particular investment decisions, but increased the overall tax on capital investment. Supporters of the bill argued that the reduced influence of taxes on investment decisions would lead to more efficient allocation of productive assets. Others argued that the overall increase in taxes on income and gain from capital would discourage investment and encourage consumption. It is not surprising that the question of the actual effect of the bill on investment remains controversial.

In many areas, complexity was reduced. Many low-income taxpayers were taken off the tax rolls by the increase in exemptions. The crackdown on tax shelters similarly will reduce waste of human resources

28. In some circumstances, however, the maximum rate under the 1986 act was as high as 49.5 percent, or even higher, because of phaseouts of deductions and exemptions.

devoted to planning tax-motivated investments and to resolving disputes between the government and taxpayers over the more aggressive of such ventures. In other areas, however, the act increased the complexity of the tax law.

One final aspect of the bill deserves mention: The 1986 act accomplished a substantial shift from taxes imposed on individuals to taxes imposed on "business." Anyone with a serious concern for tax policy must always keep in mind the reality that tax burdens can only be borne by people, not by "business" or by "corporations." Imposing a heavier tax burden on "business," while reducing direct taxes on individuals, does not in reality reduce the burden on individuals. It is instead a substitution of indirect or hidden taxes for direct or visible ones. Proponents of the 1986 legislation relied on the idea that shifting part of the individual tax burden from individuals to business firms was going to make individuals better off. In doing so, they revealed their ignorance or their dishonesty. In fact, all they did was encourage the illusion that it is possible to get something (individual tax reduction) for nothing. Beginning around 1966, by a series of changes in the law, Congress had gradually reduced the revenue from the corporation income tax. In doing so, it shifted the tax burden from indirect, or hidden, taxes to direct, or visible, taxes. In 1986 there was a reversal of that trend; we moved from visible taxes toward hidden taxes; from taxes that we cannot help but notice to taxes that we can easily forget. In the long run, the big spenders may have had the last laugh.[29]

Many hoped that, after 1986, Congress would leave the substantive tax law alone and turn its attentions elsewhere. Instead, Congress has continued to legislate in the area, albeit at a slower pace. The Revenue Act of 1987, among other changes, limited the deduction allowed for interest on home equity loans and the ability of certain taxpayers to use the installment method to report income. The Technical and Miscellaneous Revenue Act of 1988 contained hundreds of minor changes that, in the aggregate, materially affect the taxation of pensions, employee benefits, and other sources of income.

The Omnibus Budget Reconciliation Act of 1990 increased the marginal rate on high-income individuals to 31 percent. Other measures of the act also enhanced the progressivity of the tax law. For example, the act reduced the itemized deductions claimed by high-income individuals and increased the earned income credit available to low-income individuals. On the other hand, the act imposed a maximum rate on capital gains of 28 percent, thus reintroducing the historic preference given to

29. It is ironic that the change in the direction of hidden taxes came with the support of President Reagan. When he was governor of California, Reagan had opposed withholding of individual income taxes on the ground that, in his view, taxes ought to be noticeable: they ought to hurt.

this form of income. A substantial portion of the expected revenue raised by the act will come from increased excise taxes on motor fuels, tobacco, alcohol, airfares, and telephone service.

In 1993 Congress, responding to the proposals of newly elected President Bill Clinton, again raised the top individual tax rate, this time to 39.6 percent. The top corporate rate was raised from 34 to 35 percent. At the other end of the income spectrum, the 1993 act increased the earned income credit, which provides cash payments to low-income earners. The effect of the increased rates and, especially, of the imposition of the top bracket on both single persons and married couples at an income level above $250,000, was to increase the amount of the "marriage penalty." A variety of other changes were responses primarily to increasing concern for budget deficits and the consequent focus on the need to increase revenue. Collectively, these changes (including an increase in the tax on gasoline) produced what was probably the largest tax increase in history.

C. THEORY AND POLICY

We turn now to this set of questions: Why is "income" an appealing base for taxation? How should "income" be defined? What are the principles or goals that should guide us in establishing the contours of the tax? What are the most serious kinds of problems we can expect to encounter? What can be said about the economic and other effects of the tax? What are the alternatives?

1. Why "Income"?

The amount, or concept, that forms the basis on which the tax is imposed is income — by which we mean, at least as a first approximation, something like the accounting concept of net income (receipts less allowances for the costs of producing those receipts). As we will see, that basic concept has been substantially modified, for better or worse, by the rules that have developed over time and that now define the statutory concept "taxable income" (see description infra page 50). For now, a vague notion corresponding to net income is sufficient. The question to be considered is why we tax people according to that concept. Why is the tax not based instead on wages, or consumption, or the size of one's house, or the number of years one has spent in school? Why don't we use a "head tax" — a tax of equal dollar amount on everyone, or at least on every able-bodied adult?

The answer to these questions seems to depend on two propositions. The first is that we think it fair that people should be taxed according to their ability to pay, according to their capacity to contribute to the costs of national defense, relief of poverty, public parks, and so forth. The second proposition is that income, depending on how it is defined, is a good measure of, or surrogate for, ability to pay. It is vital, however, for those seeking to understand the problems of income taxation, to recognize that income is merely a measure of ability and, no matter how it is defined, by no means a perfect measure. The use of income as the measure of the more subtle and more fundamental capacity we are trying to identify is a compromise reflecting our determination not just to find a fair measure of ability but also to use a measure that is reasonably objective.

In some ways a property tax might be a superior measure of ability to pay. A millionaire who loses money (has a negative income) in a given year, or even over a long period of time, may have more ability to pay than a person who earns a modest salary and has no wealth. Unfortunately, a property tax raises difficult problems of valuation (for the tax authorities) and liquidity (for the taxpayer), as well as some potentially perverse effects on incentives to save and invest. Moreover, it is reasonable to assume that in most years individuals with large property holdings will receive substantial income from the property, so a tax on income will have effects similar to a tax on the property. Notwithstanding its flaws, property taxation is used in most states, but at the federal level it has never been considered a serious alternative to the income tax.

Both the income tax and the property tax offer reasonably objective measures of ability to pay. In doing so, they reflect the judgment that we do not want a system that requires government officials to make more subjectively based judgments about how much people can afford to pay. If we could trust government officials to do that fairly, compassionately, and unobtrusively, the results would be far closer to ideal than those of the present system. But we know from experience that we cannot trust government officials to behave that way. Moreover, the financial cost of a subjective, personalized system would probably be intolerable. So we adopt an objective standard that we think corresponds as closely as any objective standard can to the underlying standard of ability.

With an income tax, if we understand what we have done, we are aware that since income is not a perfect measure of taxpaying capacity there will be aspects of an income tax that may be deeply troubling. For example, people have become increasingly aware in recent years of the value of the services that one performs at home for oneself and one's family. Economists refer to that value as "imputed income" and have argued that an income tax that does not take account of such benefits is seriously defective. (See infra page 117.) But imputed income is not part of the objective measure that is thought of as "income" by most people. Moreover, tax experts have conceded the impracticality of measuring imputed income, and there has never been any serious prospect of including it in taxable returns.

The problems of using income as the measure of ability may be even more fundamental than those associated with measurement limits. What about an untapped ability to earn? Of course, there are very good reasons for not trying to impose taxes on untapped ability to pay. There are very good reasons, that is, for taxing income rather than ability in a broader sense. The point is not that we should tax untapped ability but rather that the income tax may not satisfy our yearnings for perfect justice. One must be prepared to accept the idea that there are many problems with income taxation that similarly reflect deviations between the concept of income and that perfectly fair and just standard for allocating burdens that an income tax, albeit imperfectly, attempts to respond to, but that income seems nonetheless to be the best practical, objective standard available.

It is a slight digression, but worth noting here, that there are other possible objective measures of ability besides income. In recent years many people have argued that it would be better to tax people on the basis of their consumption rather than their income. We will examine this alternative shortly (infra page 31).

2. The "Definition" of Income

Throughout the history of income taxation in the United States, people have sought to capture the meaning of the concept of income in a sentence or two. One should not be surprised that these efforts have been frustrating and ultimately not only futile but mischievous. As has been suggested, *income* is only a word used to refer to a subtle, complex concept. It is a manageable surrogate for a less concrete, more amorphous concept, ability to pay. It is true that *income* has a meaning independent of the tax system; that is the basis for its appeal to objectivity. We do not want to adopt the attitude that for tax purposes income means whatever we want it to mean or that it means nothing other than ability. But even outside the tax system the word refers to a complex set of ideas that can be summarized briefly for some purposes but not for others. For example, income might be thought of as receipts less expenses. But that definition requires that we define expenses and, in doing so, resolve complex problems such as how to account for wear and tear on investments in plant and equipment, how to account for inventories, etc. For tax purposes, to the degree to which we think we have the freedom to do so, we will want to define *income* in ways that promote the objectives of income taxation, which objectives in turn reflect our underlying system of values. "At bottom, . . . every tax structure, whether on the books or projected, is an assemblage of value judgments on scores of issues that plausibly could have been decided differently," and it is silly to suppose that "value judgments can be plucked out of a definition."[30] The value judgments underlying the income tax are reflected in the goals that are next discussed, and it is only by reference to those goals that we can soundly and sensibly generate and appraise the myriad rules that provide the meaning of "income."

3. The Goals for a Good Income Tax

Before people can effectively analyze whether particular provisions of the tax law are good or bad they must establish a list of criteria. Over the years, tax scholars have proposed many such lists. They have differed in detail but reflect common themes. At this point in our study of the income tax law it is well to keep things simple; we can introduce more subtle ideas as we reach concrete problems. For now, it is enough to identify three basic goals: (a) fairness, (b) administrative feasibility, and (c) soundness of economic effects, or economic rationality. Each of these will be considered in turn, but first we must dispose of an often-cited but spurious criterion — revenue-raising potential. It is true, of course, that a key objective of an income tax is to raise revenue, but that observation tells us nothing about whether an income tax is better than some other revenue-raising alternative or whether particular provisions are good or bad. If we were interested only in revenue we might, for example, allow no deductions from gross receipts; we might tax gross income rather than net. But the consensus among tax experts is that that would be unfair and would produce unsound economic results. Or we could entirely abandon the notion of taxing income and meet our revenue needs simply by printing money (as we have done to some significant degree in recent years).[31] The fact that we could rely exclusively on the printing press to meet our revenue needs tells us nothing about whether that is a sensible approach.

It is frequently claimed that one vital goal of a good tax system is *fairness.* Fairness is sometimes divided into two categories, *horizontal equity* and *vertical equity.* The principle of horizontal equity is sometimes

30. Bittker, The Tax Expenditure Budget: A Reply to Professors Surrey and Hellmuth, 22 Nat'l Tax J. 538, 542 (1969).

31. This method of raising revenue has one great virtue. It minimizes costs of administration and enforcement by the government and of compliance by taxpayers (keeping records and preparing returns).

said to be that people who are "similarly situated" should be taxed alike. This statement seems to have little, if any, content; it leaves open the essential question of what is meant by "similarly situated." The possibly more meaningful ethical proposition underlying the concept of horizontal equity is that people in the same economic circumstances should bear the same tax burden. Though this statement itself is obviously laden with ambiguity and uncertainty, it may point us in the right direction. It does lend support to the further principle that people with the same income should, all else equal, pay the same tax. Again, we are left with essential questions: what do we mean by "income" and by "all else equal." But again we may be moving in the right direction. We may have laid an ethical foundation for the conclusion, for example, that if one person earns $18,000 per year and receives from her employer, without cost, an automobile worth $2,000 per year, for her personal use, while another earns $20,000 and must pay for her automobile out of her own pocket, the two should pay the same tax — all else equal. We might conclude that the tax burdens should not be the same, however, if, for example, one person had incurred substantial, unavoidable medical expenses and the other had not.

Vertical equity refers to the relative amounts of taxes paid by people with different incomes. The rate structure of our income tax reflects adoption of a principle of vertical equity called *progressivity,* which means that as one's income rises the *proportion* of income that one pays as a tax rises. (The mechanics of progressivity and some of its implications are described infra page 35.) The philosophic underpinning of progressivity is the notion that our free-market, private-property system of economic organization has many virtues (mainly, that it maximizes productivity and partly that it promotes individual freedom) but that justice requires a more equal distribution of rewards than what we get with this system. In other words, progressivity is designed to reduce the inequalities of income associated with our largely free-market system. Why do we want to do this? This book is not the place for anything even approaching a thorough examination of that question, but a very brief heuristic response may be helpful. That response begins with a woman described in Studs Terkel's fascinating and valuable book, Working (1974). Terkel begins his depiction with this introduction (at 289):

> She is a sparrow of a woman in her mid-forties. She has eighteen grandchildren. "I got my family the easy way. I married my family." She has worked in factories for the past twenty-five years: "A punch press operator, oven unloader, sander, did riveting, stapling, light assembly. . . ." She has been with one company for twenty-one years, ARMCO Corporation.
>
> During the last four years she has worked in the luggage division of one of the corporation's subsidiaries.

Terkel then presents the woman's own account of her job and her life (at 289-293):

> The tank I work at is six-foot deep, eight-foot square. In it is pulp, made of ground wood, ground glass, fiberglass, a mixture of chemicals and water. . . .
>
> In forty seconds you have to take the wet felt out of the felter, put the blanket on — a rubber sheeting — to draw out the excess moisture, wait two, three seconds, take the blanket off, pick the wet felt up, balance it on your shoulder — there is no way of holding it without it tearing all to pieces, it is wet and will collapse — reach over, get the hose, spray the inside of this copper screen to keep it from plugging, turn around, walk to the hot dry die behind you, take the hot piece off with your opposite hand, set it on the floor — this wet thing is still balanced on my shoulder — put the wet piece on the dry die, push this button that lets the dry press down, inspect the piece we just took off, the hot piece, stack it, and count it — when you get a stack of ten, you push it over and start another stack of ten — then go back and put your blanket on the wet piece coming up from the tank . . . and start all over. Forty seconds. We also have to weigh every third piece in that time. It has to be within so many grams. We are constantly standing and moving. If you talk during working, you get a reprimand, because it is easy to make a reject if you're talking.
>
> A thirty-inch luggage weighs up to fifteen pounds wet. The hot piece weighs between three to four pounds. The big luggage you'll maybe process only four hundred. On the smaller luggage, you'll run maybe 800, sometimes 850 a day. All day long is the same thing over and over. That's about ten steps every forty seconds about 800 times a day.
>
> We work eight straight hours, with two ten-minute breaks and one twenty-minute break for lunch. If you want to use the washroom, you have to do that in that time. By the time you leave your tank, you go to the washroom, freshen up a bit, go into the recreation room, it makes it very difficult to finish a small lunch and be back in the tank in twenty minutes. . . .
>
> The job I'm doing is easier than the punch presses I used to run. . . .
>
> I guess my scars are pretty well healed by now, because I've been off on medical leave for two, three months. Ordinarily I usually have two, three burn spots. It's real hot, and if it touches you for a second, it'll burn your arm. Most of the girls carry scars all the time.
>
> We had two or three serious accidents in the last year and a half. . . .
>
> I have arthritis in the joints of some of my fingers. Your hands handling hot pieces perspire and you end up with rheumatism or arthritis in your fingers. Naturally in your shoulder, balancing that wet piece. You've got the heat, you've got the moisture because there's steam coming out. You have the possibility of being burnt with steam when the hot die hits that wet felt. You're just engulfed in a cloud of steam every forty seconds. . . .
>
> It's very noisy. . . . I've lost a certain percentage of my hearing already. I can't hear the phone in the yard. The family can.

> In the summertime, the temperature ranges anywhere from 100 to 150 degrees at our work station. . . .
>
> I attended a conference of the Governor's Commission on the Status of Women. Another lady went with me. We were both union officers. Most of the women there were either teachers or nurses or in a professional field. When they found out we were from labor, their attitude was cold. You felt like a little piece of scum. . . .
>
> I hope I don't work many more years. I'm tired. I'd like to stay home and keep house. We're in hopes my husband would get himself a small hamburger place and a place near the lake where I can have a little garden and raise my flowers that I love to raise.

Terkel does not tell us how much the woman earned from her job, but one can imagine that the pay was low. With the image of Terkel's factory worker in mind, think of the corporate executives, the singers, the movie stars, and the athletes who earn millions of dollars a year. Then ask yourself, where is the justice in that? The point of the story about the factory worker is not that people like her necessarily work harder or at more onerous jobs than people who are highly paid. Nor can we assume that low-income people generally are kinder, more considerate, more loving, or in other ways more deserving than high-income people. The point is simply that, based on our common experience, it is not reasonable to assume that observable disparities in income can be adequately explained by differences in effort, in the psychic costs of the job, or in other measures of deservedness. It may be, of course, that the factory worker in the excerpt had a chance to go to school and ultimately earn big money and that she turned down the chance because she lacked ambition or determination or a willingness to defer gratification. People who lack ambition or determination or an ability to defer gratification may deserve the low incomes they wind up with. But if you think that generally it is not such factors that lead to differences in income, if you think the differences are more likely to result from genetic make-up or lack of education or opportunity, or other such factors, then you may share the sentiments of those who are uneasy with disparity in the distribution of income. You may sense that there is an argument for redistribution of income, and that may lead you to favor benefits for the poor and the near-poor and a progressive tax on income.

A second general goal of a good system of income taxation is *administrative feasibility*. One important part of this goal is that the government's cost of enforcement and the taxpayer's cost of compliance should be as low as possible. Another important part of the goal of administrative feasibility is objectivity. Objectivity implies, for example, that we should not tax imputed income from services performed for oneself since it seems virtually impossible to impose a tax on such economic benefits without requiring government officials to be subjective and intrusive. To some degree objectivity conflicts with fairness (since it means that we may need arbitrary rules and that we must ignore certain sources of income) and with minimization of enforcement and compliance costs (since objectivity may require detailed rules that will require long forms, expert advice, etc.).

The third major goal of income tax policy is *sound economic effects,* or *economic rationality.* This criterion embodies a number of related ideas. At the most modest, and perhaps the most sensible, level, this criterion requires simply that in appraising a tax provision we should consider carefully its economic effects. This means, for one thing, that we should try to be sure that we have not produced unintended perverse incentives. For example, the value of parking supplied to an employee by an employer generally is not included in income. The result may be that more people drive to work than would do so if that benefit were taxable. The increased driving may create congestion, air pollution, urban sprawl, etc. Maybe not; and maybe parking is part of the cost of earning a living and cannot properly be treated as a taxable benefit. But we should at least give the matter some serious thought. Another aspect of the goal of soundness of economic effects has to do with the increasing reliance on the income tax to provide incentives for various kinds of special activities and investments. Many observers have questioned the soundness of this use of the tax system and have argued that generally a direct subsidy program would be better than the more indirect (and more hidden) benefit granted by an exclusion, a deferral, a deduction, or a credit. (This idea is pursued in connection with the discussion of the tax expenditure budget, infra page 24.)

At one time tax experts often relied (and some still do) on an economic criterion of neutrality, or compatibility with the free-market system. This form of economic criterion rests on the assumptions, first, that a free-market, perfectly competitive, entirely unregulated economic system produces an ideal allocation of resources and, second, that the economy of the United States has those characteristics. Given the assumptions, it can be demonstrated that any tax rule that alters choices that would be made without a tax system wastes resources — creates a "deadweight loss" — since it induces people to use resources in less valuable ways than they otherwise would. In recent years, economists have increasingly recognized that the second assumption is unrealistic and that as a result the principle of economic neutrality has little to offer as a general guide to income tax policy[32] (though perhaps it is still a useful tool for economists for other purposes and the notion of

32. This conclusion is associated with the problem of second best. See Lipsey and Lancaster, The General Theory of Second Best, 24 Rev. Econ. Studies 11 (1956), which is generally credited as originating the idea that once the economy deviates from the ideal of unregulated perfect competition, it is not clear whether a move in the direction of that ideal will improve the allocation of resources.

"deadweight loss," in a limited application, can be helpful (see infra page 34)).

A final criterion is worth mentioning even though it is probably redundant with the three that have already been discussed. This criterion is reflected in the phrase "*old taxes are good taxes,*" which reminds us that it is one thing to say that we never should have adopted a provision in the first place and quite another to say that it should be repealed, especially without transition rules designed to protect any legitimate reliance interests that may have arisen. For example, the deduction for interest paid on home mortgages may be a bad idea. It may be unfair to renters, it may encourage overinvestment in housing and reduce investment in productive capacity, etc. But people may have bought their houses in reliance on the deduction. It seems unrealistic to suggest that they should have planned on the possibility that the deduction might be repealed; most individual home buyers probably don't think that way. (By the same token, many business taxpayers probably do take account of the possibility of repeal of tax provisions favorable to them.) A repeal of the deduction could be drafted to apply prospectively, with interest on loans incurred before the change in the law continuing to be deductible. But even that would not entirely protect reliance interests since nondeductibility of the interest on new loans would adversely affect the price at which a person could sell a house and that might seem unfair for a person who had recently bought and was forced by changing circumstances to sell. The problem suggested by this example is one of general importance in the tax system.

A final aspect of tax policy deserves very brief mention. Economists have argued that an income tax can be used to promote economic stability by adjusting revenue to the need for economic stimulation or dampening. In recent years there has been a general decline in confidence in our ability to use any part of the tax system (and other economic tools) successfully for this purpose. In any event, this goal is relevant to aggregate or "macro" phenomena and not to the kinds of policy issues that are presented in this book.

4. The Tax Expenditure Budget

In recent years tax experts have increasingly referred to a concept called the "tax expenditure budget," under which certain tax benefits are equated with direct subsidies. The general approach is to identify various exclusions (such as interest on state and local bonds), deductions (such as the deduction for charitable contributions), deferrals (such as for employer payments to pension plans), and credits (such as the child-care credit or the credit for investment in new equipment) that are seen as departures from a neutral concept of income taxation; then to figure out the cost of these special provisions;[33] and then to attribute these costs to various budget functions. The government now regularly publishes tax expenditure data. See Table 1-5.[34] You cannot expect at the beginning of the study of the income tax law to understand many of the individual references in this table, but you may be able to gain some sense of how the law has developed and you should be aware of the availability of the data so that you can go back to it later.

The tax expenditure budget depends on the notion that there is a natural, neutral, or normal income tax and that it is possible to identify departures without great difficulty or dissent. That proposition is not beyond debate. For example, it is not clear why the deduction for medical expenses is regarded as an expenditure for health and welfare while the deduction for alimony is not an expenditure for marriage or divorce; or why neither the exclusion for scholarships nor the nontaxation of the benefit of an education at a public university is on the list; or why imputed income from home ownership is not included; or why the deduction for contributions to educational institutions is a subsidy to education while the deduction for contributions to churches is not a subsidy to religion. The point is that there is much legitimate debate over and genuine uncertainty about the proper contours of an income tax and that the tax expenditure budget largely ignores the debate and denies the uncertainty.[35] Despite all the debate, there does seem to be substantial agreement that most of the items on the published lists deserve to be there — that they achieve some purpose, thought by some people to be desirable, other than the measurement of net income. And it does seem clear that the tax expenditure budget has proved to be an extremely valuable tool for exposing tax policy issues.

5. Incidence and Incentive Effects

The incidence of a tax is its ultimate burden. For example, if a tax is imposed on the manufacture of refrigerators and the manufacturer is able to raise prices and pass the tax on to consumers, then it is said that the tax has been shifted and the incidence is on consumers rather

33. Traditionally, and in the table that follows, the cost is stated in terms of revenue lost. In the calculation by the Office of Management and Budget for the Administration's annual budget, the amount presented is the estimated outlays that would be required to provide an equal after-tax income to the taxpayer. Budget of the United States Government, Fiscal Year 1992, Part Three, p. 22.

34. This version excludes all items with a cost of less than $1 billion. It is taken from Statistical Abstract, supra note 2, at 320. Other versions have more detail and project costs several years into the future.

35. There is also considerable uncertainty about the dollar amounts, which are based on the assumption, among others, that conduct would remain the same if the law were changed (i.e., that an increase in the tax on gain from the sale of property would not reduce the number of sales or the amount realized).

TABLE 1-5
Revenue Losses Estimates for Selected "Tax Expenditures" by Function: 1994
[In billions of dollars. For years ending Sept. 30. Represents tax expenditures of $1 billion or more.]

Description	*Amount*
National defense:	
Exclusion of benefits and allowances to Armed Forces personnel	2.0
International affairs:	
Exclusion of income earned abroad by United States citizens	1.4
Inventory property sales source rules exception	3.9
Natural resources and environment:	
Exclusion of interest on state and local IDB for pollution control and sewage and waste disposal facilities	1.2
Commerce and housing credit:	
Exclusion of interest on—	
Life insurance savings	10.3
State and local housing bonds for owner-occupied housing	1.7
State and local debt for rental housing	1.1
Exclusion of capital gains on home sales for persons age 55 and over	4.7
Deductibility of—	
Mortgage interest on owner-occupied homes	45.5
Property tax on owner-occupied homes	13.7
Carryover basis of capital gains at death	12.4
Accelerated depreciation of machinery and equip.	15.2
Reduced rates on the first $75,000 of corporate incomes	3.2
Education:	
Deductibility of—	
Charitable contributions (education)	2.0
Other charitable contributions other than education and health	12.9
Credit for child and dependent care expenses	2.8

than on manufacturers. To determine the incidence of a tax, or the burden or effect of particular provisions of a tax system, one must compare the world with the tax or provision and the world without it. Economists have devoted an enormous amount of thought and writing to questions of incidence and in doing so have discovered problems that have proved to be largely intractable. To begin with, it is by no means easy, if, indeed, it is possible, to generate a sound meaning of incidence, taking account of short-term and long-term effects, heterogeneity of

TABLE 1-5
Continued

Description	*Amount*
Health:	
Exclusion of employer contributions for medical insurance premiums and medical care	36.7
Deductibility of medical expenses	3.5
Exclusion of interest on State and local debt for private nonprofit health facilities	1.8
Deductibility of charitable contributions (health)	1.6
Social Security and medicare:	
Exclusion of social security and railroad retirement benefits	28.0
Income security:	
Exclusion of workers' compensation benefits	4.1
Net exclusion of pension contributions and earnings:	
Employer plans	55.3
Individual Retirement Accounts	6.2
Keoghs	3.0
Exclusion of other employee benefits:	
Premiums on group term life insurance	2.2
Additional exemption for elderly and blind	1.6
Veterans benefits and services:	
Exclusion of veterans disability compensation	1.6
General purpose fiscal assistance:	
Exclusion of interest on public purpose State and local debt	14.0
Deductibility of nonbusiness State and local taxes other than on owner-occupied homes	25.7
Tax credit for corporations receiving income from doing business in United States possessions	3.9

Source: Joint Committee on Taxation, 103d Cong., 1st Sess., Estimates of Federal Tax Expenditures for Fiscal Years 1994-1998, prepared for the Committee on Ways and Means and the Committee on Finance (1993).

taxpayers, and other problems. Beyond that is the even more difficult problem of trying to imagine what the world would be like without a particular tax or even without a particular provision of a tax law, considering that a change in the tax law would require either a change in outlays or reliance on some other means of finance, or both. A leading economist has said, "The basic problem with tax incidence is that it attempts to undertake a type of analysis that is both empirically difficult and theoretically impossible."[36] Even if this conclusion is not dispositive, it should serve as a warning about simple generalities or confident

36. Thurow, The Economics of Public Finance, 28 Nat'l Tax J. 185, 187 (1975).

conclusions concerning tax burdens and should suggest why further discussion of the topic is not appropriate in this book. We will stick to some basic observations about incidence-related issues.

First, it is generally assumed that the burden of the individual income tax, so far as it falls on income from wages, salaries, and other earnings from services, is, for the most part, not shifted from the individuals on whom it is imposed. If shifting generally does occur, much of the virtue (or vice) of the income tax as a device for distributing burdens according to ability to pay tends to disappear and much of the discussion of the structure of the tax begins to seem misguided. Tax experts have not been willing to admit of that possibility and have even produced some plausible (though not unshakable) theories to support their assumption of no shifting. With respect to income from investments, it does seem plain that certain types of shifting of benefits and burdens does occur. For example, we will see in Chapter 2 (Section I) that the benefits granted to holders of state and local bonds are partially shifted to state and local taxpayers and, possibly, to other investors.

Second, it seems generally to be recognized by economists who have examined the problem thoughtfully that the incidence of the corporation income tax is wholly uncertain (disregarding the question, adumbrated at the beginning of this section, of whether the concept of incidence is so complex and beyond our capacity to examine, either empirically or theoretically, as to be meaningless).

Third, all realistic tax systems, including the income tax, have complex, often disturbing, effects on incentives to work and to save. As a device for describing, at the simplest level, the forces at work, consider two possible taxes: (a) an "investment tax," meaning a tax falling only on income from investments, and (b) an "income tax," meaning a tax on income from all sources, including income from investments and income from wages, salaries. Compared with an investment tax, the aggregate effects of an individual income tax on incentives to work are uncertain. One presumed effect of the tax is to stifle the incentive to work — to encourage people to work less and substitute leisure for income — because of the decreased reward for their efforts; this is called the *substitution effect.* Another presumed effect is to induce people to work harder to replace the income that has been taken by the tax; this is called the *income effect.* Theory cannot tell us how powerful these contradictory effects are or which of them dominates, and the empirical studies have been largely inconclusive. This does not, however, deter some people from asserting that the income tax has destroyed incentives and that the rates must be lowered or others from asserting the opposite.

Fourth, it is clear that one unfortunate effect of an income tax is a disturbing labor-supply trade-off. Suppose that an employer is willing to pay a worker $20 per hour for overtime work and that the worker is taxed at a rate of 40 percent. The worker will take home only $12 per hour. Suppose that the worker would be happy to work for a take-home pay of $15 per hour, but not for less. The employment will not occur, even though the employer thinks the worker's time was worth $20 per hour and the worker's leisure is worth to him or her only $15 per hour. This distortion of the market system is an inevitable effect of an income tax.

Fifth, to the extent that the tax system favors one type of investment over another, money and other resources will be shifted from the unfavored type of investment to the favored type. This kind of important economic effect is easy to predict and to observe.

Sixth, as investments shift in response to tax incentives, before-tax rates of return will be altered. For example, because of the exemption from taxation of interest on state and local bonds, the rate of return on these bonds is less than the rate of return on taxable bonds. (See infra pages 279-280.) The individual who invests in the tax-exempts accepts a lower rate of before-tax return because that return is not subject to tax. The before-tax reduction in return on the investment in the tax-exempts — that is, the difference between the return on the tax-exempts and the higher forgone return on taxable bonds that the taxpayer might have bought — is a form of self-imposed tax, often called a *putative tax.*[37] This is a widespread phenomenon.

Finally, to the extent that before-tax rates of return fall in response to the effects of a tax provision, and a putative tax arises, any lack of fairness (horizontal equity) associated with treating one source or use of income better than another is reduced or eliminated. For example, if a person buys tax-exempt bonds and pays a putative tax, that putative burden must be taken into account before asserting that the person has been treated more favorably than other people with income that is directly taxed. Failure to take account of the notion of putative taxes, and their effect on fairness, is a serious error in tax policy discussion and one that is all too common among experts as well as among nonexperts.

6. Inflation

Our present income tax system does not make adjustments, in any systematic way, for the effects of inflation. Inflation gives rise to at least three serious problems. The first of these is *bracket creep,* which is the increase in tax rates that occurs solely as a result of inflation. To illustrate, suppose that our tax law initially provides that at an income of

37. For example, if taxable bonds yield 14 percent and tax-exempt bonds of comparable quality yield 10 percent, a person investing $1,000 in tax-exempts earns $100 per year and forgoes an additional $40 that could have been earned by investing in taxable bonds. The forgone $40 is the putative tax.

$25,000 a person's marginal rate of taxation (see infra page 35) is 15 percent and that at an income of $50,000 the marginal rate is 30 percent. Now suppose that ten years pass and inflation reduces the value of money by half. A person currently earning $50,000 is in the same real economic position as a person earning $25,000 ten years earlier. There will be many more people earning $50,000 now than earlier. (The higher we go on the real income ladder, the fewer people we find.) If there is no automatic adjustment that lowers the rates to take account of the economic reality, then even without any increase in real (that is, inflation-adjusted) income, people will be paying higher percentages of their real incomes as taxes. Government revenues will increase (in real terms) with none of the unpleasant political consequences associated with explicit increases in rates. In recent years, Congress has from time to time reduced nominal rates, but the effect has been merely to restore to taxpayers some of the windfalls resulting from bracket creep. In 1981, Congress added §1(f) and §151(f),[38] which require increases in the standard deduction, in the deduction for personal exemption, and in the rate schedule dollar-amount brackets, to reflect increases in the Consumer Price Index.

A second serious problem attributed to inflation has to do with deductions for the cost of investments in productive property. Suppose that a taxpayer builds a factory with an expected useful life of forty years. In calculating his or her tax liability, the taxpayer cannot treat the entire cost of that factory as an offset to current receipts. Instead, the taxpayer must offset some portion of the cost against current receipts and some portion against receipts in future years, through an allowance traditionally called depreciation and now labeled, in the Code, accelerated cost recovery system (ACRS). (See infra page 57.) This allowance or deduction is based on original, or historical, cost rather than on the present value or replacement value of the asset. Taxpayers have complained that the effect of the use of original cost is to overstate their income and deprive them of funds to replace assets at the end of their useful lives. Congress has responded to this and other arguments of business taxpayers by increasing allowances for depreciation (or, if you will, cost recovery), through provisions that concentrate deductions in the early lives of assets, but this is at best an awkward and inaccurate solution to the inflation problem.

A third problem of inflation has to do with gains on the disposition of property, especially property held for a long period of time. Often, much of the gain realized on such disposition is attributable to inflation; it does not represent a real economic gain. There is certainly some appeal in the notion that a person who has realized such gains has not

38. All section references are to the Internal Revenue Code of 1986, unless otherwise noted.

realized any true economic increment that should be taxed. On the other hand, it is plain that a person who has had such gains is better off than one who has made another investment, on which there has been no gain at all. Most gain on the disposition of property held for investment or for productive use for more than a year falls in a special category called *capital gain.* Before 1987, a portion of such gain was excluded from income. This special tax treatment may have mitigated some of the effects of inflation but, again, only in an awkward and inaccurate way.

7. Income versus Consumption

In recent years scholars (and some legislators) have devoted considerable attention to the possibility of basing personal taxation on consumption, or expenditure, rather than income. The idea behind a consumption-based personal tax is that people would be taxed on what they took out of the pot rather than what they put in or, more precisely, on the wealth they consumed but not on the wealth they created and set aside (in private investments) for their own or someone else's future consumption. Though there is little likelihood that a pure consumption tax will replace our present income tax in the foreseeable future, that alternative is worthy of brief examination for the light it sheds on the mechanics of the present system and on some of the important policy issues arising under it.

At one time, many experts thought that a consumption tax would be hopelessly difficult to administer because of problems of measuring consumption outlays. In an article published in 1974, however, Professor William D. Andrews of Harvard Law School demonstrated that this fear was unfounded both conceptually and practically and that, apart from other possible virtues, the consumption tax would probably (depending on the form it took) be easier to compute than an income tax.[39] As he showed, a consumption tax is simply an income tax with a deduction for savings in any form and with the inclusion in the tax base of amounts drawn down from savings and used for consumption. The effects may best be demonstrated by reference to a feature added to our present law in 1981, the *individual retirement account* (IRA). Amounts set aside in an IRA for retirement are currently deductible in computing

39. A Consumption-Type or Cash Flow Personal Income Tax, 87 Harv. L. Rev. 1113. See also J. Pechman, ed., What Should Be Taxed: Income or Expenditure? (1980); Klein, Timing in Personal Taxation, 6 J. Legal Studies 461 (1977); Warren, Would a Consumption Tax Be Fairer Than an Income Tax?, 89 Yale L.J. 1081 (1980); Warren, Fairness and a Consumption-Type or Cash Flow Personal Income Tax, 88 Harv. L. Rev. 931 (1975); Andrews, Fairness and the Personal Income Tax: A Reply to Professor Warren, 88 Harv. L. Rev. 947 (1975).

the amount subject to taxation and amounts withdrawn from the IRA account are included in income in the year of withdrawal. For example, if a taxpayer earns $40,000 each year and contributes $2,000 to an IRA, the amount subject to income taxation is $38,000 (assuming no other deductions). Later, if the taxpayer earns $10,000 and withdraws from the IRA a retirement benefit of, say, $5,000, the amount subject to income taxation is $15,000. This is entirely consistent with a consumption tax and entirely inconsistent with a straightforward income tax. If one simply imagines a vastly expanded IRA account, with no limits on the amount or purpose of contributions to the account and with no limits on the time of or reasons for withdrawal, one has a consumption tax.

In fact, the IRA is not the first, only, or most important consumption-based feature of our present income tax system. For example, amounts contributed by an employer to a qualified pension plan are not included in the employee's income until paid out of the plan to the employee even if the employer contribution creates a vested (nonforfeitable) right in the employee and is therefore equivalent economically to a payment to the employee followed by a payment by the employee into the plan. Such a plan is equivalent, in effect, to an involuntary IRA. More fundamentally, our present tax system has the characteristics of a consumption tax in its nontaxation of unrealized appreciation. Unrealized appreciation is gain that has not yet been converted into money or other property — for example, the gain in the value of an apartment building that is held for investment but that has not yet been sold. Unrealized appreciation is a plain economic increment, and many tax experts believe that the failure to tax it creates a severe problem of fairness in the tax system (because people with one kind of gain, unrealized, are not taxed, while people with another kind of gain, realized, are taxed) or of economic distortion (because people are encouraged to invest in assets whose returns take the form of unrealized appreciation), or some of each. There seem to be compelling reasons of administrative feasibility for the failure to tax unrealized appreciation, but that is not to deny the difficulties created by that failure. Given the widespread deviation between the broad-based income tax that seems to be required by considerations of fairness and the income tax as it is and perhaps must be, Professor Andrews was able to argue with great force that we would be better off to go the whole way and adopt a consumption base. One of the advantages of doing so would be that tax administration would be vastly simplified in many ways, largely because the entire cost of all investments would be recovered in a tax sense (that is, deducted) in the year of purchase and there would be no deductions in respect of such investments in later years. Among other things, there would no longer be any depreciation or other such cost-recovery deduction, since the entire cost of productive assets would be deducted at the time of purchase.

The consumption tax is sometimes compared with a sales tax. This comparison is likely to be misleading, since the consumption tax is imposed on individuals, rather than transactions, and therefore can be adjusted to individual circumstances. Most notably, it is generally assumed that a consumption tax, like the income tax and unlike the sales tax, would be progressive.

One basic and interesting feature of a consumption tax is that it has effects similar to those of an income tax with an exclusion for, or zero rate of tax on, returns from investments. For example, consider a person who is taxed under an income tax at a rate of 40 percent; who earns $1,000 and pays $400 tax on that amount; and who invests the remaining $600 at 10 percent to produce an annual income of $60.[40] Under the present income tax, this person would pay a tax of $24 on the $60, leaving $36 after tax. It is sometimes argued that the person has been doubly taxed — once on the earnings and then on the earnings from those earnings — and that this is unfair and bad for the economy. If this conclusion is accepted, the income of $60 should not be taxed and the taxpayer's net after tax should be $60. Under a consumption tax, if the person earning $1,000 saves the $1,000, that amount is not taxed and is fully available for investment. If it is invested at 10 percent, the annual income will be $100. If this amount is spent, the tax will be $40 and the amount available to spend after tax will be $60. Thus, to repeat, the consumption tax (under certain simplifying assumptions) has the same effect as an income tax under which the "double tax" is avoided by not taxing the income from investments; both leave an after-tax spendable amount of $60. There are, of course, proponents of the income tax who reject the double-tax argument. Their view is that a person whose income from saving is taxed is not doubly taxed at all, but is simply taxed separately on two separate sources of income.

Other theorists have taken a different approach, arguing that the earnings (the $60 in the initial version of the above example) on the invested after-tax savings (the $600) merely equate the value of presently available consumption ($600) with the value of future consumption ($660 one year later); in other words, the future $660 is equivalent in satisfaction to the present $600. Consequently, the argument goes, if we want to treat people equally we should compare the present values of their consumption and should disregard (that is, not impose a tax on) the return ($60) on the investment. The response some people have offered to this argument is that future consumption is not ordinarily less desirable than present consumption and that the return from saving is simply a windfall to those who happen to want to defer some portion

40. Technically, if the tax is to be imposed on the amount of the consumption ($60), rather than the amount of the income ($100), and if the amount of the tax is to be $40, the rate must be 67 percent, but the effect is the same as that of an income tax of 40 percent on $100.

of their consumption into the future.[41] One may find these arguments wholly inconclusive, but if one accepts the notion that people prefer present consumption, and concludes that therefore we should not impose a levy on the returns from investments, then the consumption tax has considerable appeal since its effects, as demonstrated above, are at least roughly comparable to such a system of income taxation.

The adoption of a consumption tax would affect investment in two ways. The higher after-tax rate of return under a consumption tax would tend to encourage people to save (a substitution effect). At the same time, to the extent that people save to achieve a certain target (such as an amount of money they consider sufficient to buy a house or to provide adequate resources for retirement), the higher rate of return would permit a lower amount of saving to reach the target (an income effect). On balance, most experts believe that the substitution effect will dominate, and that the adoption of a consumption tax would increase aggregate investment.[42] It is also important to bear in mind the implication of increased aggregate investment — namely, that the present generation of taxpayers would be induced to reduce its own level of consumption, and to save and invest the amount of that reduction, in order that future generations can consume (or have the opportunity to consume) more. You may or may not find this an appealing prospect, depending in part on your present age.

8. Tax Policy and Public Opinion

In 1982, the income tax was rated the "worst-tax — that is, the least fair" by 36 percent of those polled in an annual survey on government and taxes, compared with the local property tax (30 percent), the state sales tax (14 percent), and the state income tax (11 percent).[43] It is not surprising in view of what political candidates constantly tell them that most Americans feel the federal tax system is unfair.[44] It is also not

41. For a more complete development of these arguments, see W. Klein, Policy Analysis of the Federal Income Tax 39-43, 61-67 (1976).

42. The effect of a consumption tax on investment is discussed in Klein, supra note 41, at 94-99.

43. U.S. Advisory Commission on Intergovernmental Relations, Changing Public Attitudes on Governments and Taxes, Eleventh Annual Public Opinion Poll 4 (1982). The federal government nonetheless scored ahead of state and local governments on the question, "From which level of government do you feel you get the most for your money?" — 35 percent for federal, 28 percent for local, and 20 percent for state governments, with 20 percent saying, "don't know." See Witte, supra note 12, at 362-364. A recent study reports that in a poll of 380 adults, "On average, 14 percent indicated they paid 'far too much,' 54 percent 'too much,' 28 percent 'about right,' and only 5 percent indicated they paid too little in taxes." Kinsey, Grasmick, and Smith, Framing Justice: Taxpayer Evaluations of Personal Tax Burdens, 25 Law and Soc'y Rev. 845 (1991).

44. Roper Opinion Poll, Hearing before the Senate Committee on Finance, 95th Cong., 2d Sess. (July 27, 1978).

surprising that the same public generally likes the exemptions, deductions, and exclusions in the existing income tax system; prefers tax reduction two-to-one over tax simplification; and greatly underestimates the taxes paid by persons in higher brackets and overestimates the taxes paid by themselves.[45] And one study concluded that "except for a relatively small elite, the very notion of a *progressive* tax [is] beyond grasp."[46]

D. THE RATE STRUCTURE, PROGRESSION, AND MARGINAL RATES

A *progressive* income tax is one with rates that rise as income rises. Under a progressive rate structure the tax on a person with a high income is not just a greater *amount* than the tax on a person with a lower income; it is a greater *proportion* of income. Progression is accomplished primarily by a schedule of rates with increasing *marginal rates* — that is, with increases in rates that apply only to increments in income. For example, suppose the rates are 15 percent on the first $20,000 of income and 25 percent on all income above that amount. A person with income of $30,000 would pay 15 percent on the first $20,000, or $3,000, plus 25 percent on the next $10,000, or $2,500, for a total of $5,500. The marginal rate for such a person is 25 percent; it is the rate applicable to the last, and the next, increment to income. Progression is also accomplished by exempting a certain amount of income from taxation (in effect applying a zero rate to that amount).

During most of the history of the income tax in this country, the rate structure for individuals was characterized by a large number of rates and a big difference between the highest and the lowest rate. For example, in 1986, for married couples there were fourteen rates applicable to various levels of income, with a range from 11 percent to 50 percent (plus a zero rate on income that is not subject to taxation because of personal exemptions, the zero bracket amount (now the standard deduction), and a credit for earned income). The 1986 act brought a radical change, effective in 1988. There were further, more modest changes in 1990 and 1993. In 1994 there were nominally four brackets: 15 percent, 28 percent, 31 percent, and 36 percent. In addition, however, there was a "surtax" on the top bracket, for people with incomes over $250,000, creating a fifth bracket of 39.6 percent. Moreover, the benefits of the personal exemption and certain itemized deductions

45. Id. See Witte, supra note 12, at 347-352.

46. W. Blum and H. Kalven, The Uneasy Case for Progressive Taxation, Introduction to paperback edition, at x (1963).

(explained at page 520) are phased out as adjusted gross income exceeds a certain threshold amount. See §151(d). The phaseout has the effect of creating an additional tax bracket, since the taxpayer loses a tax benefit (and thus pays more tax) for each additional dollar earned above the threshold amount. The significance of the phaseout depends on the number of personal exemptions and itemized deductions claimed. For a married couple filing a joint return with two personal exemptions, the phaseout may transform the 31 percent rate into about a 33 percent rate. Similar phaseouts of other benefits (notably, the earned income credit for low-income people) create their own effective marginal tax rates.[47]

It is important to recognize that it is the marginal rate that is relevant for purposes of tax planning and for understanding incentive effects. For example, suppose a couple with an income of $25,000 and a marginal rate of 15 percent contemplates a gift of $100 to charity. They are permitted to deduct such gifts in calculating the amount of their income subject to taxation. By making the gift they would reduce their taxable income by $100 and save $15 in taxes. Their net cost would be $85. For a couple with a taxable income of $125,000 and a marginal rate of 33 percent, the net cost of a $100 gift is $67.

47. For example, under §469 (adopted in 1986), taxpayers are generally denied a deduction for "passive losses." See description infra page 711. In certain special circumstances, taxpayers with incomes below $100,000 are allowed to deduct $25,000 of such losses, but for each dollar that income rises above $100,000 the amount of such losses that can be deducted is reduced by 50 cents. §469(i). Thus, the entire deduction is phased out when income reaches $150,000. In the income range from $100,000 to $150,000 the effect of the phase-out is to increase taxable income by 50 percent. This has the same effect as increasing the marginal rate by 50 percent of the normal rate — that is, by 50 percent of 31 percent, or 15.5 percent, to a total of 46.5 percent.

Various other provisions of the Code also have the effect of increasing the marginal rate and may operate cumulatively to raise the effective marginal rate above 50 percent. For example, medical expenses are deductible only to the extent that they exceed 7.5 percent of adjusted gross income, and casualty losses are deductible only to the extent that they exceed 10 percent of adjusted gross income. The effect of each of these provisions is that as income rises the deduction diminishes. To illustrate the potential results when combined with the effect of the phaseout of the passive activity loss (PAL), imagine a person with adjusted gross income of $100,000, medical expenses of $20,000, a casualty loss of $15,000, and a PAL of $25,000. Suppose that income rises by $1,000. The effects are as follows:

AGI	*$100,000*	*$101,000*
Deductions:		
Medical	12,500	12,425
Casualty	5,000	4,900
PAL	25,000	24,500
Taxable	57,500	59,175
Tax (31%)	17,825	18,344
Increase:		
Income		1,000
Tax		519
Effective marginal tax rate		51.9%

Several other aspects of a progressive rate structure deserve brief attention. First, since increased marginal rates apply only to increments of income and do not exceed 100 percent, a person is never worse off by earning more money. The popular expression, "I can't afford to earn more money because it will throw me into a higher bracket," reflects ignorance of the mechanics of progression. (There is a very minor exception, resulting from the use of tax tables, under which the tax liabilities are provided for $50 increments of taxable income.)

Second, some analysts have asserted (especially in the past when maximum marginal rates were higher and tax shelters were more readily available than now) that high marginal rates cannot be taken seriously because wealthy people are able to avoid the high rates by using such avoidance techniques as investing in tax-exempt bonds or in real estate. There are several reasons why the attitude reflected in such comments is misguided. For one thing, some wealthy taxpayers may avoid part of the burden of the high rates, but some do not. Moreover, taxpayers who invest in tax shelters are responding to incentives that are for the most part deliberately created by Congress, and usually they must accept a lower before-tax rate of return than they could earn on other investments; they pay a putative tax (see supra page 279). Thus, it is misleading to suggest (as many economists do in their studies of tax burden and tax expenditures) that the entire amount of tax-sheltered income escapes tax burden. And finally, even if it were true that no one is currently subject to high marginal rates, it would still be important to ask whether they ought to be.

Third, the number of high-income people is relatively small and, consequently, the revenue that can be raised from a "soak the rich" income tax is modest. This reality is reflected in Table 1-2 supra. This is not to say that progression is a bad idea or even that it is not worth the trouble it may cause. It is only to say that progression does not produce as much revenue as one might imagine.[48] The people to look to for revenue are middle-income taxpayers because there are so many of them and, in the aggregate, they have so much money. This means that we must be very careful with broad-based tax reductions such as increases in the deduction for personal exemptions (see infra page 520).

48. The amounts are not, however, insignificant by any means. In 1979 the rates rose to a maximum of 70 percent on taxable income above $215,400 (married couples) or $108,300 (unmarried). The rates rose above 49 percent at $60,000 (married) and $41,500 (unmarried). In that year, according to a calculation by the Tax Foundation, Inc., the total revenue from the individual income tax was $219,919 million, of which $6,565 (2.99 percent) was generated by the 70 percent rate and $27,369 (12.45 percent) by the various rates above 49 percent. The number of returns with income taxed at rates above 49 percent was 1,810,000, of a total of 74,228,000, or 2.43 percent. Tax Foundation, Inc., 26 Monthly Tax Features 3 (1982).

Fourth, because of the operation of the progressive rate structure, a person whose income fluctuates widely from year to year will, over a number of years, pay more taxes than a person with the same total income whose income is steady from year to year and who, consequently, is able to take full advantage of the bottom of the rate structure (and of the personal exemptions and of the standard deduction or itemized deductions) each year. The seeming unfairness of this disparity in treatment can be mitigated by "averaging" provisions. Such provisions were introduced into our income tax in 1964 but were repealed in 1986.[49]

E. RATE SCHEDULES, THE TAXABLE UNIT, AND THE MARRIAGE PENALTY

Among tax theorists, "taxable unit" means that individual, or group of individuals, who is, or are, treated as a taxpaying unit in the sense that they must aggregate their income for purposes of calculating the tax payable. Theorists have examined at length the question whether the unit should be the individual; husband and wife; husband, wife, and children; all people in the household; or some other possibility. While that kind of inquiry seems meaningful for some purposes, it is unfortunately not one that is properly framed for a person seeking to understand the present rules of the federal income tax. Those rules do not reflect the kind of logical, coherent approach implicit in the notion of a taxable unit. To some significant extent, the present rules can be understood only by reviewing their history. The historical development is presented later in this book. (See infra page 763.) For the present, it is enough to recognize that the rules governing how taxes are affected by the relationships of people to one another are reflected in the four rate schedules and in the rules for applying them[50] and, to a lesser extent, in the exemptions[51] and certain other provisions.[52] We will see that the rate-schedule rules produce a "marriage penalty" and a seemingly perverse work incentive for married "secondary" workers.

49. It turned out that the people who benefited most from averaging were not people like farmers, fishers, actors, and writers, whom Congress had in mind when averaging was adopted, but young doctors and other people whose incomes rose rapidly, but steadily, in the early years of their careers. In any event, the need for averaging declined when the top marginal rates were reduced in 1986.

50. §1.

51. §151.

52. E.g., §21 (child-care credit); §71 (alimony); and §221 (deduction for two-earner married couples).

Married people[53] are permitted to file a "joint return," which means a return on which they aggregate their income and deductions so that it does not matter who earned what. The rate schedule for such returns provides the lowest rates of the four schedules provided in the Code. This rate schedule is also available to "surviving spouses"[54] but not to single-sex couples, who might wish to marry but are not permitted to do so.

Another rate schedule is for "heads of households"[55] and is somewhat less favorable than the one for married couples. Very roughly, a head of household is an unmarried person with a dependent living with him or her. The thought behind the semifavorable rate schedules is that a head of household has financial burdens similar to those of married couples and should get part of the benefits available to them.

Next is the schedule for "unmarried individuals,"[56] commonly referred to as single people. The rate schedule for such people is less favorable than the one for heads of household.

Finally, there is the least favorable schedule of all, for married people filing separate returns. For reasons explained in Chapter 7B, there is a special rate schedule for married persons filing separate returns. With this rate schedule, the filing of separate returns generally will result in increased aggregate taxes and only rarely will result in reduced aggregate taxes.[57]

Apart from married people who file jointly (as almost all do) and who aggregate their income, taxpayers are not required to include in their income the income of relations, dependents, or members of their households. In other words, the taxable unit is the individual, except that we take account of a deceased spouse (in the provision for a surviving spouse), of dependents (in the provision for heads of households), and various other family attributes. To demonstrate the significance of the basic rule that each individual is a separate taxpayer, consider a hypothetical family consisting of a husband, a wife, and a fifteen-year-old daughter. Suppose that the daughter is entitled each year to the income of $25,000 from a trust set up for her by her grandmother. The child would file her own return. The parents' return would not reflect the $25,000 income of the child (except possibly if some of that income were used to discharge their obligation of support). Moreover, if all the $25,000 were put aside for the child and the parents supplied more

53. "Marriage" has a special statutory definition. §143.

54. Defined in §2(a).

55. Defined in §2(b).

56. This is a residual category — that is, one including anyone who is not married, a surviving spouse, or a head of household. §1(c).

57. Even if filing separately would increase total liability, the spouses might want to do so if, for example, they are separated and cannot find one another or are unable to cooperate in filing jointly.

than half her support, they would be entitled to claim a deduction for her as a dependent[58] and they could deduct her medical expenses,[59] to the extent allowable.[60]

The relationship between the rate schedules for married people, heads of households, single people, and married people filing separately, and the rules relating to their availability, produce two important effects. First, married single-earner couples are better off than they would be under a system with one schedule for all, since they have the advantage of the most favorable rate. On the other hand, two-earner married couples may be worse off than if they had remained single because of the requirement that they file jointly (or use the unfavorable schedule for separate returns of married people). This is true because if they were single each would use a less-favorable rate schedule, but since they would be filing two returns they would get two separate starts at the bottom of the rate schedule. Married couples filing jointly have only one start at the bottom of their rate schedule, albeit that is a more favorable schedule. Moreover, the top rate (39.6 percent) applies both to married couples and to single persons as income exceeds $250,000. The result is the infamous "marriage penalty" — that is, the added tax paid by two people who have roughly the same earnings and who marry one another.

For example, in 1993 two single persons with taxable incomes of $300,000 would pay a tax of $99,572 each, or a total of $199,144. If they were married their tax liability would be $214,128, an increase of $14,984. If the incomes were $115,000 each, the total if single (ignoring the effect of phaseouts) would be $62,244, while the total if married would be $68,328, a difference of $5,984. If the two single persons had been heads of households, the disparity would be even greater: $29,558 for the twosome with incomes of $300,000 each and $7,833 for the twosome with incomes of $115,000 each. There is also a marriage penalty, for lower income people, arising from the operation of the earned income credit (described infra page 521). The result may be a marriage penalty, in 1994, of as much as $3,109 in the case of two heads of households with incomes of $11,000 each! This aspect of the marriage penalty affects only lower income people, because the earned income credit is phased out as income rises above certain levels. Indeed, it is the phaseout that produces the penalty.

A final point worth noting about the rate-structure rules is that the secondary worker in a married couple is subject to tax rates determined by the income of the primary worker. The "secondary worker" is the person whose income is lower and whose commitment to working is

58. §151.
59. §213.
60. §213(a).

generally less than that of the primary worker. In our society, the secondary worker is most often the wife rather than the husband. The secondary worker's income will be thought of as the marginal income, since it is more likely that the couple would consider sacrificing this income than the income of the primary worker. Thus, the marginal rates that must be taken into account by married secondary workers, mostly women, are the relatively high rates resulting from the fact that the primary worker's (husband's) income uses up the lower rates. This effect is magnified by the fact that the wife's alternative of providing services in the home, rather than working outside the home, results in "imputed" income, which is not taxed at all. Also, one must bear in mind that for secondary workers the social security tax is a significant burden.[61]

Both the marriage penalty and the disincentive for secondary workers would be eliminated by a system with only one rate schedule and a rule making each individual taxable on his or her own income.

F. COMPLIANCE AND ADMINISTRATION

Our income tax relies on initial self-assessment, which means that once each year each individual or entity subject to the tax makes a calculation of the amount of tax owed. The calculation is based on information supplied by the taxpayer on forms, sometimes called tax "returns," devised and provided by the Internal Revenue Service. The Internal Revenue Service, often called the Service, or the IRS, is a branch of the Treasury Department, is headed by a person called the Commissioner of Internal Revenue, and is responsible for the administration of the tax laws. The Service makes available some limited amount of assistance in preparing returns, but no government approval or other involvement is required before a return is filed. Before the taxpayer files the annual return, some amount approximating the tax owed will probably have been paid to the government either through withholding from wages by an employer[62] or by special quarterly returns for estimated taxes for people whose income is from sources not subject to withholding (like income from self-employment) or for whom the

61. For further discussion and citations of recent economic studies of the effects on labor-force participation, see Gann, Abandoning Marital Status as a Factor in Allocating Tax Burdens, 59 Tex. L. Rev. 1, 39-46 (1980). For an earlier presentation of similar observations, see Blumberg, Sexism in the Code: A Comparative Study of Income Taxation of Working Wives and Mothers, 21 Buffalo L. Rev. 49 (1971). But recall the prior discussion (supra page 25) of the barriers to studies of incidence and economic effects.

62. §3402.

amount withheld is less than the amount of tax that will be payable.[63] When the annual return is filed, the taxpayer takes a credit against the tax computed on that return for any taxes paid by withholding or as estimated tax and will be entitled to a refund of any overpayment or must pay the amount of any shortfall.

A person who fails to file an income tax return may be subject to both civil and criminal penalties.[64] There is no statutory limit on the time within which the civil penalties must be sought[65] and a six-year limitation on criminal prosecution.[66] The risk of being caught for failure to file is high, in large part because employers and other payors of income are required to file "information" returns,[67] reporting wages, dividends and interest, and various other kinds of payments and benefits.

The Service reviews all income tax returns for computational error and selects a relatively small number of them for a more complete review, called an audit. Some returns are selected for audit at random, but most are selected on the basis of some evidence, either in the return itself or from some other source (e.g., information returns), indicating a greater-than-average probability of error.

The Service ordinarily has only three years to assert a "deficiency"[68] — that is, to assert that the taxpayer owes more tax by virtue of an error in the return. The amount owed is called an "underpayment," and the taxpayer must pay interest on all underpayments.[69] The interest rate is set quarterly and is equal to the rate on U.S. Treasury short-term obligations plus 3 percent.[70] Taxpayers also must pay a penalty equal to 20 percent of the amount of any underpayment due to negligence,[71] but "the sort of conduct typically found subject to the negligence penalty is reckless and intentional."[72] A penalty equal to 20 percent of the amount of any underpayment is levied on taxpayers who substantially understate their income tax.[73] A substantial understatement is one that exceeds the greater of 10 percent of the proper tax or $5,000, but the amount of the understatement is reduced by amounts attributable to

63. §§6015, 6153.
64. The basic provisions are §6651(a) (civil) and §7201 (criminal).
65. §6501(c)(3).
66. §6531.
67. §§6031-6058.
68. §6501(a). The period is extended to six years if the taxpayer omits from gross income more than "25 percent of the amount of the gross income stated in the return." §6501(e). See also §6229(c)(2) (similar rule for partnerships).
69. §6601.
70. §6621.
71. §6662(a), (c).
72. Asimow, Civil Penalties for Inaccurate and Delinquent Tax Returns, 23 U.C.L.A. L. Rev. 637, 650 (1976).
73. §6662(a), (d).

treatment for which there was "substantial authority"[74] and amounts "with respect to which the relevant facts affecting the item's tax treatment are adequately disclosed."[75] The penalty "may" be waived by the Service if the taxpayer demonstrates "reasonable cause" and "good faith."[76] Finally, a 20 percent penalty is levied on any underpayment attributable to overvaluation of property (for example, in the case of a gift of property to charity);[77] that penalty is doubled in cases of gross overvaluation. An underpayment that fits within more than one of the above categories (for example, an understatement that is substantial and negligent) is subject to only one 20 percent penalty. There is also a penalty of 5 percent per month, not to exceed 25 percent, for failure to file a return and 0.5 percent per month, not to exceed 25 percent, for failure to pay a tax shown on a return when it is due or for failure to pay, within 10 days, a tax assessed and demanded by the IRS.[78] Notwithstanding the seemingly inclusive array of penalty provisions, in the ordinary case of underpayment, all the taxpayer stands to lose, in addition to the amount of the tax owed, is interest on that amount.

An error may be attributable to what is loosely referred to as "fraud." An underpayment attributable to fraud subjects the taxpayer to a civil penalty of 75 percent of the amount of the fraudulent underpayment.[79] While fraud seems to be a familiar concept and one that could sensibly be applied to a large number of taxpayer returns, in fact the courts have developed a narrow definition and even the civil penalty is imposed only in "cases of highly flagrant behavior."[80] Criminal fraud, or, to be more precise, any "willful attempt to evade or defeat any tax imposed by this title or the payment thereof,"[81] is a felony carrying a penalty of not more than $100,000 ($500,000 for corporations) or five years in prison, or both. As with civil fraud, however, criminal fraud penalties are used only to "punish highly culpable conduct . . . [in] cases involv[ing] large amounts of income and deficiencies, patterns of conduct stretching over several years, and particularly reprehensible forms of

74. See Regs. §1.6661-3(a)(2), stating that "a position with respect to the tax treatment of an item that is arguable but is *fairly unlikely* to prevail in court would satisfy a reasonable basis standard [applicable to the imposition of a negligence penalty under §6653(a)], but not the substantial authority standard." Emphasis supplied. What, if anything, does "fairly" add to "unlikely"?

75. §6662(d). For items "attributable to a tax shelter," however, the disclosure exception does not apply and the substantial authority exception applies only to taxpayers who "reasonably believed that the tax treatment of [the] item . . . was more likely than not" proper. §6662(d).

76. §6664(c).

77. §6662(c), (h). The penalty also applies to certain valuation misstatements on sales between related taxpayers.

78. §6651(a). The penalty percentages for failure to file are increased to 15 percent and 75 percent if the failure is "fraudulent." §6651(f).

79. §6663.

80. Asimow, supra note 72, at 645.

81. §7201.

concealment."[82] There is no statutory limit on the time within which the civil fraud penalties may be sought.[83] For criminal prosecution the statute of limitations is six years.[84]

Questions of tax fraud seldom arise in the materials in this book and in most tax practices. There is a specialized segment of the bar that represents people in peril of, or charged with, criminal tax offenses. The more pervasive compliance questions confronting practitioners relate to doubtful issues. For example, a "gift" is not includable in income[85] and need not be reported on one's tax return, but tips and other such payments in recognition of the performance of services are includable. Suppose that a surgeon performs a life-saving operation and the grateful patient presents to her a gift certificate for $500. What are the obligations of the surgeon and of his or her lawyer? Often it is said that taxpayers are entitled to call the close ones in their own favor; that there is no obligation to bring the decision to exclude to the attention of the Service; and that all the taxpayer needs is a "reasonable basis" for his or her decision or "some realistic possibility of success if the matter is litigated."[86] It may be more accurate to say that if there is a

82. Asimow, supra note 72, at 646.
83. §§6501(c)(2), 6671.
84. §6531.
85. §102. See infra pages 130-139.
86. The "reasonable basis" standard had been approved by the ABA Standing Committee on Ethics and Professional Responsibility in 1965 in Formal Opinion 65-314. It was replaced by the "some realistic possibility of success" standard in 1985 in Formal Opinion 85-352. In its report on the adoption of the new standard, the Committee noted that some lawyers had interpreted the reasonable basis standard "to support the use of any colorable claim on a tax return to justify exploitation of the lottery of the tax return audit selection process." Despite its disapproval of the "colorable claim" interpretation, the Committee concluded that "sufficient doubt has been created regarding the validity of the [reasonable basis] standard so as to erode its effectiveness as an ethical guideline," a conclusion requiring, in its view, that the standard should be "restated." The restatement is as follows (emphasis supplied):

> [A] lawyer may advise reporting a position on a return even where the lawyer believes the position probably will not prevail, there is no "substantial authority" in support of the position, and there will be no disclosure of the position in the return. However, the position to be asserted must be one which the lawyer in good faith believes is warranted in existing law or can be supported by a good faith argument for an extension, modification or reversal of existing law. This requires that there is some realistic possibility of success if the matter is litigated. In addition, in his role as advisor, the lawyer should refer to potential penalties and other legal consequences should the client take the position advised.

In the Report of the Special Task Force on Formal Opinion 85-352, 39 Tax Law. 635, 638 (1986) it is said that "a position having only a 5% or 10% likelihood of success, if litigated, should not meet the new standard."

On October 8, 1992, the IRS issued proposed regulations governing practice before the IRS. Under the proposal a practitioner may not sign a return as a preparer, advise a client to take a position, or prepare a portion of a return on which a position is taken, unless

> (i) The practitioner determines that there is a realistic possibility of the position being sustained on its merits . . . ; or

reasonable basis for the taxpayer decision, the taxpayer who decides an issue in his or her own favor is not guilty of a crime, even though the taxpayer knows that the government would undoubtedly dispute the taxpayer's decision if it became aware of it and would probably prevail if the issue were tested in court. If the decision is close to fraud, the government's basis for asserting fraud may be undercut if the taxpayer "red flags" the issue (that is, voluntarily makes some note of the issue as part of the return). A lawyer cannot countenance criminal conduct on the part of a client, even if the client is willing to run the risk of criminal prosecution. A lawyer should never advise a client to take a tax position that would not be defensible if all the facts were known; in other words, a lawyer cannot countenance lying or concealment, no matter how remote the chance of detection. But a lawyer is not barred by any canon of ethics from advising a client of the possibilities for making claims based on weak but "reasonable" grounds. If the lawyer has personal moral qualms against doing so, it may be his or her duty to advise the client of those qualms and also to suggest that other lawyers might limit themselves to providing purely legal advice. As an expert in taxation, the lawyer might simply advise the client of the most favorable position for which there is a reasonable basis; of the probability that that position would be sustained if challenged; of the alternatives; and of the consequences to the taxpayer if the matter is challenged and the taxpayer loses. Of course, just as the lawyer is not required to represent murderers, rapists, or drug traffickers, he or she is not required to represent or assist those taxpayers who seek always to take the most aggressive possible position — who seek always to shift as much as possible of the tax burden from their own shoulders to the shoulders of those who, for one reason or another, are unwilling to push to the limits.

Problems of professional responsibility in tax practice are more subtle and complex than the foregoing remarks might suggest,[87] but it does

---

> (ii) The position is not frivolous and the practitioner advises the client to adequately disclose the position.

"Realistic possibility" is defined as follows:

> A position is considered to have a realistic possibility of being sustained on its merits if a reasonable and well-informed analysis by a person knowledgeable in the tax law would lead such a person to conclude that the position has approximately a one in three, or greater, likelihood of being sustained on its merits. The authorities described in [Regs.] §1.6662-4(d)(3)(iii) of the substantial understatement penalty regulations may be taken into account for purposes of this analysis. . . .

Violation of the proposed standard subjects a practitioner to disbarment or suspension from practice before the Service. The force of the rules may be diminished by a provision that "only violations of this section that are willful, reckless, or a result of gross incompetence will subject a practitioner to suspension or disbarment."

87. For a fascinating and valuable treatment of some of the issues, see Cooper, The Avoidance Dynamic: A Tale of Planning, Tax Ethics, and Tax Reform, 80 Colum. L. Rev.

seem clear that clients are entitled to know the consequences of their actions and to make their own decisions if they want to. What is troubling about this is that the odds are heavily in favor of aggressive taxpayer reporting postures — that is, in favor of reliance on any favorable position for which there is a "reasonable basis." This is true largely because of the "audit lottery" — the fact that because of the limited enforcement resources of the IRS, the chances of an audit of the return and of a challenge to the item in question are small. In addition, the consequences of losing are, in many situations, by no means onerous. This situation has led one scholar[88] to conclude:

> The most surprising fact that emerges from the theoretical models and the relevant tax law is that *anyone* complied with the income tax law in the past decade whenever fraud penalties could have been avoided. The most rudimentary cost-benefit analysis . . . reveals [that] . . . if the sanction structure is to have any deterrent effect, a probability of punishment of less than 100 percent requires that the sanction must be greater than the amount of the cheater's benefit. During the past decade, while aggregate audit probabilities were typically closer to 2 percent than 100 percent, interest rates on understated tax liabilities were often less than market rates.

What if the taxpayer files a return thinking that it is correct and later discovers a mistake? If the mistake is one that becomes evident only because of events that have occurred after the close of the year for which the return was filed, the remedy is to make an adjustment in the year in which the true facts appear. If, however, the mistake was plainly an error at the time of reporting — in other words, if, on the basis of the facts existing at the time the return was filed, the return was in error — then the remedy is to file an amended return. An amended return is simply a new version of the original return, changed to correct the error. Claims for refunds of overpayments, made by an amended return or otherwise, must be filed within the general three-year statute of limitations period.[89] Naturally, if the error is in the favor of the government and the taxpayer is entitled to a refund, he or she can refrain from claiming the refund, but is unlikely to do so if the amount is significant. That leaves the question whether the taxpayer is obligated to file an amended return if the error is in his or her favor and the tax paid was less than what was owed. We assume here that we are talking about errors — sometimes redundantly called "innocent" errors—and not about willful misrepresentation. There is no explicit

1553 (1980). See generally B. Wolfman and J. Holden, Ethical Problems in Federal Tax Practice (2d ed. 1985).

88. Graetz, Can the Income Tax Continue to Be the Major Revenue Source?, in J. Pechman, ed., Options for Tax Reform 39, 58 (1984).

89. §6511(a).

statutory penalty for failure to file an amended return.[90] It may be that the only legal consequence of failing to file an amended return is that, if the error is later discovered and payment made, the taxpayer will owe greater interest on the underpayment. On the other hand, it can be argued that the amount owed is a debt and that taxpayers have as much moral obligation to pay their debts to the government (that is, to their fellow citizens) as they have to pay their just debts to anyone else (even though the creditor may not realize that the amount is due).

If a taxpayer's return is audited and the taxpayer and the employee who initially reviews the return for the IRS cannot agree on one or more items, there are opportunities for review at higher levels within the IRS. Most disputes are ultimately settled within the IRS, often after considerable bargaining and with compromise on both sides. If the taxpayer and the IRS cannot reach agreement, the IRS will order the taxpayer to pay the deficiency, plus interest and any applicable penalties, and the taxpayer must either do so or go to court. Three different options are available to the taxpayer for judicial review. One option is to decline to pay the tax and file a petition for review with the *Tax Court*[91] (formerly the Board of Tax Appeals). The Tax Court is available only if the tax has not been paid as of the date of the petition. (The tax can be paid thereafter to stop the running of interest.) Tax Court judges have tax backgrounds and try only tax cases. There are no jury trials in the Tax Court. Tax Court judgments are reviewable by the federal circuit courts of appeals in the circuit where the taxpayer resides[92] and ultimately by the Supreme Court (but only on certiorari). If the taxpayer loses, the tax must be paid with interest to the date of payment, so an important factor in deciding whether to follow the Tax Court route is the current interest rate charged by the government on deficiencies, as compared with what the taxpayer must pay or can earn elsewhere.

The second option is to pay the tax and sue for a refund in the federal *district court* where the taxpayer resides.[93] The judge in the district court is not likely to be a tax expert and a jury trial is available. Appeal is, as usual, to the circuit courts of appeals, with the possibility of review by the Supreme Court on certiorari.

The final option is to pay the tax and sue for a refund in the United States Court of Federal Claims.[94] Its decisions are reviewable by the United States Court of Appeals for the Federal Circuit[95] and by the

90. But see Regs. §§1.451-1(a), 1.461-1(a) (taxpayer "should" file amended return to report items of income and expense erroneously reported in prior year).
91. §§6213, 7441.
92. §7482(b).
93. §7422; 28 U.S.C. §§1346(a)(1), 1402(a)(1).
94. 28 U.S.C. §1491.
95. 28 U.S.C. §1295.

Supreme Court (on certiorari). If an issue is first litigated by a taxpayer who obtains a favorable legal ruling in the Claims Court, and that ruling is upheld on appeal, all other taxpayers may then take their cases to that court and foreclose the possibility of a conflict among the circuits. By contrast, if a taxpayer wins a favorable ruling in a court of appeals in a circuit other than the Federal Circuit, the government is free to litigate that issue with other taxpayers in other circuits.[96]

In the past, tax suits could take the form of personal actions against the tax "collector," which explains why some old tax cases bear the names of individuals as defendants. The real party in interest was the government, and the nominal involvement of an individual as defendant is of no importance in interpreting the decisions.

G. SOME TAX TERMINOLOGY AND CONCEPTS

1. The Tax Base and Calculation of the Tax Payable

Tax base is not part of the specialized vocabulary of the Internal Revenue Code. It refers to a general concept used by lawyers and economists to describe the amount that is to be taxed under whatever system of taxation one adopts — that is, the amount to which the appropriate tax rate is applied. Under a sales tax the base is sales; under a consumption tax the base is consumption or expenditure.[97] Under general theories of income taxation the base is, of course, income or perhaps, at a somewhat higher level of sophistication, disposable income, meaning the amount available to pay taxes after appropriate allowances for the basic costs of staying alive and well. Under the present tax, which, of course, is the subject of this book, the tax base is a specialized, technically defined amount called *taxable income,* a statutory[98] term that is narrower than one would expect if one started with the notion that disposable income is the appropriate base. The narrowness is in large part attributable to Code provisions that treat favorably various actions such as making gifts to charity or acquiring and holding buildings, machinery, and other assets for profit-making purposes.

Taxable income, then, is the "bottom line." The top line or starting point is another term of art, *gross income.* Gross income is defined by an

96. See 4 B. Bittker, Federal Taxation of Income, Estates, and Gifts ¶115.7, at 115-142 (1981).

97. See supra page 31.

98. §63.

elaborate set of rules found in the Internal Revenue Code, the case law, and other sources of tax law. The statutory centerpiece is §61. Read it. It consists of a general, all-inclusive description of what is to be included, plus a list of nonexclusive exemplars. For most individuals the major items covered will be wages, salaries, interest, dividends, and rents. Note that item 2 on the list is "gross income derived from a business." This is a bit misleading. It is understood to mean amounts received by a taxpayer ("gross receipts") after subtraction of the cost of any goods that had been acquired by the taxpayer and ultimately sold (possibly after some transformation) to generate those returns. Sections 71 to 85 list various items that are included in gross income but require special treatment. These sections also, however, identify certain receipts, such as child-support payments,[99] that are excluded from gross income. Sections 101 to 127 exclude from gross income a number of receipts such as interest on state and local bonds[100] (sometimes called *municipal bonds*) and tort recoveries for personal injuries.[101]

The result of the various statutory and other exclusions is that there is a substantial difference between any generally accepted economic concept of gross income and the tax concept. Chapter 2 is devoted to an elaboration of the tax concept. The table of contents for that chapter provides some sense of the kinds of issues that will be considered.

Once a taxpayer's gross income has been determined, the next step is to calculate *adjusted gross income,* or *AGI,* another statutorily defined amount or concept that is arrived at by deducting (subtracting) from gross income a set of items listed in §62. At this point you should give §62 a once-over-lightly reading. Most of what is listed will be, at best, barely comprehensible. It's like reading a foreign language. That is a problem in any field that has developed its own terminology; even though the words are familiar, their meaning in the specialized context is not. You will become familiar with tax terminology as you work your way through this book. If the §62 list seems to you to lack coherence, don't worry; you may be right. Certainly the items lack any clear nexus. The most important item on the list is the first, which may be thought of as the costs of producing business income. These allowances must be made in order to move from total receipts to net income. Item 10, on the other hand, is alimony, which seems to be a personal rather than a business allowance. The closest one can come to a general concept of the meaning of AGI is that it is designed "to reflect the amount available to an individual taxpayer to pay for food, lodging, shelter, and other elements of the cost of living."[102] The items listed in §62 are by no

99. §71(b).
100. §103.
101. §104(a)(2).
102. B. Bittker, Federal Taxation of Income, Estates and Gifts ¶2.1.3, at 2-6 (1981).

means all of the deductions allowable in arriving at taxable income. They are only what may be thought of as the first-stage allowances. The issue presented by §62 and the concept of adjusted gross income explain why certain items are deducted at this stage rather than at the next stage. Consideration of that issue is best deferred until we have examined the next step.

The next step is to move from AGI to *taxable income.* This involves deducting (a) the amount of the personal exemptions of the taxpayers and their dependents, if any, plus (b) either (i) the standard deduction or (ii) "itemized" deductions. The deduction for personal exemptions is $2,000 per person in 1989, with adjustments for inflation thereafter.[103] The standard deduction is $5,000 for a married couple or surviving spouse, $4,400 for a head of household, and $3,500 for a single person, with an extra amount — $600 for married people and $750 for single people — for taxpayers over age 65.[104] The function of the standard deduction is to relieve people with modest incomes of the nuisance of keeping track of outlays covered by the itemized deduction, and of filing a somewhat complex return, and to ensure that people with incomes below a certain level pay no tax. The itemized deductions that may be claimed only by taxpayers who forgo the standard deduction include mortgage interest, state income and property taxes, casualty losses above 10 percent of AGI, medical expenses above 7.5 percent of AGI, charitable contributions, and certain business expenses of employees above 2 percent of AGI.[105]

The net figure arrived at by deducting from AGI the personal exemptions and either the standard deduction or the itemized deductions is, as previously stated, called taxable income. It is this figure that is

103. §151. For example, in 1989 a married couple with two dependent children would be entitled to four personal exemptions (one each for the husband and wife and one for each of the children) for a total of $8,000. In 1992, with the inflation adjustment, the exemption amount had increased to $2,300.

104. §63. The standard deduction replaces the zero bracket amount (ZBA) that had been in effect for a number of years and accomplished the same objectives in a confusing way. For a person who may be claimed as a dependent by another taxpayer, the standard deduction is limited to the greater of $500 or the person's earned income. §63(c)(5). In 1992, with the inflation adjustment, the standard deduction had increased to $6,000 for married couples, $5,250 for heads of households, and $3,600 for single persons.

105. The concept of AGI has three functions. First, AGI is used to separate those deductions that can be claimed by all taxpayers, regardless whether they claim the standard deduction, from those that cannot. Essentially, one must choose between the standard deduction and certain other deductions (mostly personal) but not between the standard deduction and those deductions allowable in arriving at AGI. Second, AGI is for some tax policy purposes considered a better measure of income than is taxable income. Thus, it is used in shaping the rule for deduction of medical expenses, where the amount deductible is the excess of such expenses over 7.5 percent of AGI. §213(a). Similarly, AGI is used in calculating the maximum amount that can be deducted for contributions to charity. §170(b). Third, people using tax statistics in analysis of tax and economic policy issues find AGI to be more useful for many purposes than taxable income, since AGI corresponds more closely to economic income.

used in the rate schedule to arrive at the amount of the tax. The rate schedules are set forth in §1 of the Code.

Ultimately taxpayers will arrive at an amount of tax that they owe, either from a tax table or from a rate schedule. That is almost the end of the process, but not quite. The final step is to offset the tax with any credits that may be available and to determine whether a minimum tax must be paid. A credit is a direct offset to the tax. It is to be contrasted with a deduction, which reduces taxable income and thereby reduces the tax payable by the amount of the deduction multiplied by the relevant rate of tax. For example, there is a credit for "expenses for household and dependent care services necessary for gainful employment," sometimes referred to (somewhat inaccurately) as the child-care credit.[106] Consider a couple with both spouses working; with two children, ages 7 and 9; with AGI of $50,000; and with child-care expenses of $4,800 (the maximum that can be taken into account). Their credit is 20 percent of the amount of the expenses, or $960. The amount of tax that they owe is reduced by this amount so they save the full amount of the credit. Suppose that, instead of a credit, they were allowed a deduction for the $4,800 of expenses and that their marginal tax rate is 33 percent. Their taxable income would be reduced by the $4,800 deduction and their tax would be reduced by $1,584. If their income were higher and their tax rate rose, the deduction would become more valuable. The credit, on the other hand, would remain a constant dollar amount.[107] Other credits are found at §§21 to 41. The most important, and most obviously appropriate, is the credit for the amount of tax withheld from wages.[108]

Finally, there is an alternative minimum tax for individuals, in §55.[109] The tax is imposed on a special base at a rate of 26 percent of the first $175,000 and 28 percent on amounts above $175,000. The special base is AGI plus various "preferences" and exclusions, reduced, for individuals, by certain non-§62 deductions. This tax is in lieu of, and is payable only if it is greater than, the tax computed under the normal rules. There is also a counterpart for corporations: a 20 percent minimum tax on tax preferences.

The calculation of tax is illustrated in Table 1-6.

2. Capital Gain

During most of the history of our income tax, capital gain was taxed at a lower rate than was other income. The preferred treatment was

106. §21.

107. In fact, the rate of the credit for child-care expenses is reduced from 30 percent to 20 percent as AGI rises from $10,000 to $30,000. §21(a)(2).

108. §31.

109. For further discussion of §55, see infra page 735.

TABLE 1-6
Illustration of an Individual's Tax Base and Calculation of Tax Payable by Single Person, 1992

	Financial picture	*Tax picture*		
	Receipts	*Gross income*		
Salary	$55,000	$55,000		
Dividends	10,000	10,000		
Interest on state bonds	9,000	excluded		
Rent received	8,000	8,000		
Total:	$82,000		$73,000	(Gross)
Less:	*Outlays*	*§62 Deductions*		
Depreciation on rental unit	—	$ 4,000		
Interest paid on loan on rental unit	3,000	3,000		
Alimony	6,000	6,000		
Subtotal to subtract:	−$ 9,000		−13,000	(§62)
Adjusted Gross Income (AGI):			$60,000	
		Non-§62 deductions		
Less:				
Interest paid on debt on personal residence	$ 5,000	$ 5,000		
Contributions to charities	2,000	2,000		
State income and property taxes	4,000	4,000		
Subtotal to subtract:	−$11,000		−$11,000	(non-§62)
Net cash flow	$62,000			
Personal exemption			− 2,300	
Taxable income			$46,700	
Tax (§1(c))*			$10,288	

* Single person, 1992 rate schedule: $3,218 on the first $21,450 plus $7,070 on the excess over $21,450. The brackets are adjusted each year to take account of inflation.

eliminated by the 1986 act but was reintroduced in attenuated form by the 1990 act. Currently, capital gain of non-corporate taxpayers is subject to a maximum rate of 28 percent—11.6 percentage points less than the maximum rate on other forms of income; capital gain recognized on common stock in certain start-up corporations is taxed at a maximum rate of 14 percent. The definition of capital gain depends on a large and complex body of law; efforts to transform gain from ordinary income into capital gain gave rise to an even larger and more complex body of law. Capital losses can be used only to offset capital gain, except that individuals may use up to $3,000 of capital losses to offset ordinary income. This means that it is important in some instances to be able to distinguish between capital gain and loss and ordinary gain and loss. The distinction is explored in detail in Chapter 8. Briefly, capital gain or loss is gain or loss from the "sale or exchange of a capital asset."[110] "Capital asset" is statutorily defined as "property," with a number of exceptions — most notably for "inventory" or "property held by the taxpayer primarily for sale to customers in the ordinary course of his trade or business."[111] For example, an individual who has bought a house for use as a personal residence has acquired a capital asset and gain on sale of the house will be capital gain. (Any loss is capital loss but is not deductible, even as an offset against capital gain from other sources, because it is considered a personal expense.) The house is property and is not within any of the exceptions. Similarly, a person who invests in a corporation, like IBM or AT&T, by buying common stock or bonds issued by the corporation, has acquired a capital asset. Gain on the sale of a capital asset held for one year or less is short-term capital gain. Gain from the sale of a capital asset held for more than a year is long-term capital gain. Gains and losses, short term and long term, are netted out. Before 1987 a portion (in 1986, 60 percent) of any net long-term gain was deducted from gross income, so the effective tax rate was lower than the tax rate on ordinary income. There is a disadvantage on the loss side. Capital loss, above $3,000, as indicated above, can be used only to offset capital gain. Net short-term gain has been taxed as ordinary income.

3. Tax Accounting

Methods. The rules of accounting for income tax purposes follow the basic approaches of nontax accounting, though they differ in some important respects. The two basic methods of tax accounting, which are familiar to nontax accounting, are the *cash receipts and disbursements method,* or *cash method,* and the *accrual method.* Under the cash method, speaking very generally, amounts are treated as income when received in cash (or cash equivalent) and are deductible when paid. Under the accrual method, subject to some important exceptions, items are included in gross income when earned, regardless whether payment has been received, and items of expense are deductible when the obligation to pay is incurred, regardless when payment is made. For example, suppose that an accountant, *A,* performs services in connection with the law practice of a lawyer, *L.* The services are performed on December

110. §1222.
111. §1221.

5, 1989; three days later *L* receives a bill for $500; *L* does not dispute his obligation to pay the full amount but does not pay until January 10, 1990. If *A* and *L* both use the cash method, *L* is entitled to a deduction (if otherwise allowable) in 1990, and *A* should report the item as income in the same year, since 1990 is the year of payment by *L* and of receipt by *A*. If both *A* and *L* used the accrual method, *L* would be entitled to the deduction in 1989, when the obligation was incurred, and *A* would include the $500 in income in 1989, when it was earned.[112] Most individuals use the cash method (because it is simple), and most businesses use the accrual method (because it more accurately reflects economic realities).

The cash method: capital costs. An important limitation on the cash method is that the costs of capital investments may not be deducted when the cash outlay is made, but only as the asset is used or when it is sold, exchanged, or abandoned. For example, suppose a farmer who uses the cash method buys forty acres of farm land, to be used in his farming business, for $40,000. The $40,000, which is called a capital expenditure, may not be deducted at the time of the purchase. Generally speaking, capital expenditures are amounts spent for assets that have a useful life of more than a year. In the case of land, a record is kept of the cost and gain or loss is computed, and reported for tax purposes, on disposition of the land. Suppose the farmer buys a tractor for $10,000. Again, the $10,000 outlay is a capital expenditure and cannot be treated as a current expense. Instead, a record is kept of the amount of the outlay and a portion is deducted each year as the tractor is used. The annual deduction is called depreciation of — under the present tax law — the ACRS (accelerated cost recovery system) deduction. (See infra page 57.)

The cash method: constructive receipt. Another limitation on the cash method is the doctrine of constructive receipt. A right to a payment is treated as if received when the taxpayer had an unrestricted right to receive cash, even if the cash was not in fact taken. For example, if your pay envelope is available at your employer's office at the end of the year, you are treated as having received the pay even if you did not in fact pick up the envelope. Similarly, if you have money in a passbook savings account on which interest is earned, you are taxable on the amount credited to your account during the year even if you do not withdraw any money from the account. You are treated as if you received the cash that you could have withdrawn. As in other areas of law, the word "constructive" is used by courts to pretend that something

112. Under rules added to the Code in 1984, the deduction for *L* in 1989 would be allowed under the accrual method, but the result would depend not only on principles of accrual accounting but also on the fact that the obligation meets the requirements of §461(h)(4) (the "all events" test) and §461(h)(2)(a)(i) (the "economic performance" test).

is so when in fact it is not so, in order to reach a result that seems compelled by common sense. The advantage of the use of the fiction is that one can pretend that the basic rule (here, the cash method) remains simple and unsullied. All the complexity is associated with defining the scope of the fiction.

The cash method: cash equivalence and economic benefit. Another limitation on the cash method is the doctrine that people are treated as if they had received cash when they receive valuable property or rights.[113] For example, suppose your employer offers to pay you for your services by transferring to you ownership of a computer you have been using. You accept the offer. The computer is not cash. It is called a cash equivalent or economic benefit, and you are treated as if you had received cash equal to its fair market value. Or suppose you are an athlete who has just signed a contract with a sports team. Part of the contract requires that the team deposit at a bank in an escrow account a sum of money to be paid to you next year. The money, once transferred to the bank, is immune from the claims of the team and its creditors. You cannot demand the money this year, so there is no constructive receipt. You have income this year, nonetheless, because the amount in the escrow account is fully protected; it is "as good as gold." It is a cash equivalent or economic benefit.[114]

Annual accounting. Tax liabilities are computed on an annual, as opposed to a transactional, basis. To illustrate, suppose that a business firm, *F*, performs work under a contract in 1986 and in doing so incurs current expenses of $50,000. Suppose further that there is a substantial dispute as to whether *F* is entitled to any payment for its work, so no income is accrued in 1986. In 1987, the work is completed (at no further cost), the dispute is settled, and *F* collects $50,000. The proper accounting for tax purposes, even for an accrual method taxpayer, is to deduct all the expenses in 1986, when incurred, and to report all the income in 1987. The deduction in 1986 may do the firm no good if it has no other income. That does not matter. The point is that each year must be closed out for tax accounting purposes at the end of the year on the basis of the information then available. The firm must report the entire $50,000 as income in 1987,[115] even though the transaction as a whole produced no profit and regardless whether the deduction in 1986 pro-

113. The terms *cash equivalent* and *economic benefit* are assumed here to be interchangeable. Some people draw a distinction in which cash equivalence refers only to certain promises to pay received from the other party to an exchange. All other noncash benefits (including promises to pay of third parties) are referred to as economic benefits. The distinction is little used. In fact, the courts and commentators often seem unable to recognize the obvious distinction between constructive receipt, on the one hand, and cash equivalence or economic benefit, on the other hand.

114. For further elaboration, see infra pages 372-395.

115. For tax purposes, the $50,000 is not considered to have been earned in 1986 because of the uncertainty about entitlement.

duced a tax benefit. If the deduction produced no tax benefit in 1986, this system of accounting obviously produces an unfair outcome.[116] There are provisions of the Code that give relief from this unfairness (here, most notably, a provision for carrying forward the loss from 1986 to 1987),[117] but these are relief provisions; they leave in place the general principle of annual accounting.

4. Realization and Recognition

Realization and recognition are important terms of art in tax law. A gain or loss is said to be realized when there has been some change in circumstances such that the gain or loss *might be* taken into account for tax purposes. A gain or loss is said to be recognized when the change in circumstances is such that the gain or loss *is* taken into account. Thus, where there is realization there may or may not be recognition, but where there is recognition there must have been realization. For example, suppose a taxpayer, *T*, buys a house for use as a personal residence and over time the house rises in value, but *T* does not sell. There has been a gain, but the gain is not realized. Now suppose that *T* does sell the house, at a gain. The gain is realized. Ordinarily the gain would also be recognized and taken into account for tax purposes, but there is a special provision[118] that permits nonrecognition if *T* invests in another personal residence within two years. Thus, the gain has been realized; if the proceeds are reinvested in another personal residence within two years, the gain is not recognized until the new house is sold (and the proceeds in turn not reinvested within two years).

For another example, suppose *T* buys shares of common stock (that is, a portion of the ownership interest) in *ABC* Corporation for $1,000 and the value of the *ABC* shares (which, let us assume, are publicly traded at prices regularly reported in the newspapers) rises to $2,500. The gain of $1,500 is not realized. Now suppose that *ABC* Corporation is acquired by *XYZ* Corporation in a transaction in which *T* receives shares of *XYZ* stock in return for the *ABC* shares, and that the *XYZ* shares received by *T* are worth $2,500. As a result of the exchange of the *ABC* shares for the *XYZ* shares, *T* will have realized a gain of $1,500. That gain must be recognized unless the two corporations have taken advantage of special provisions of the Code[119] under which recognition can be avoided (until the *XYZ* shares are sold).

116. The hypothetical facts are based on Burnet v. Sanford & Brooks Co., 282 U.S. 359 (1931) (infra page 194), in which the taxpayer argued unsuccessfully that the outcome was not constitutionally permissible under the sixteenth amendment, since the transaction did not produce any net gain.

117. §172.

118. §1034.

119. See §354. See infra page 471.

5. Recovery of Cost, Depreciation, and Basis

Suppose *T* is a retail seller of widgets. In a particular year, *T* buys 1,000 widgets for $10 each and sells them all for $15 each. Obviously *T* has a profit (assuming no expenses other than the cost of the widgets) of $5,000, which is arrived at simply by deducting her cost of $10,000 from her receipts of $15,000. Since the federal income tax is a tax on the net income of $5,000, not on the gross receipts of $15,000, *T* must be allowed to recover her cost of $10,000 in arriving at the taxable amount.

Now suppose *T* decides to manufacture widgets and buys widget-making machinery at a cost of $100,000. Assume that there are no other expenses. *T* makes the widgets and starts selling them. For tax purposes, how does she take account of the cost incurred in buying the machinery? One possibility would be to provide that the proceeds of sales are not taxable until *T* has taken in $100,000 and all proceeds thereafter are fully taxable as profit. That would be a very extreme form of "cash method" accounting. It is not allowed. What *T* must do instead is recover her investment by taking a deduction (against gross receipts) traditionally called *depreciation,*[120] but now called (in the Code) the *accelerated cost recovery system* (ACRS) amount or, more simply, cost recovery.[121] Under ACRS, the cost of the machine is spread out over a number of years (less than the expected life) according to formulas provided in the Code. The effect of the formulas is to bunch the deductions in the early years of the use of the machine.[122] This treatment is accelerated in comparison with normal methods of accounting, under which the amount of the allowance is designed to correspond better to the actual decline in the value of the asset and under which costs are spread out over a period roughly equivalent to the expected useful life of the asset. Often these normal methods of accounting are used by publicly owned corporations in reporting profits to investors even though accelerated methods have been used for tax purposes. The reason is simple: The tax method produces a larger deduction and a correspondingly smaller profit, a profit that is less than the realistic amount in most cases.

ACRS applies only to tangible property like buildings and equipment. For intangible property (like patents), the cost must be deducted over the realistic expected life of the asset. Generally, an equal amount is deducted each year;[123] this is called the *straightline* method. For example, if an intangible asset costs $100,000 and has an expected life of ten years, the deduction is $10,000 each year, even though this may not be

120. See §167.
121. §168.
122. See infra pages 669-673.
123. §167(b),(c).

consistent with the actual pattern of decline in the value of the asset over time. In common usage, in the case of an intangible asset the process of spreading deductions over time is called *amortization* (as compared with depreciation, the term used for tangible assets). In the tax law, however, the deduction in the case of intangibles is called "depreciation." See §167. The word "amortization" is generally applied in the tax Code and parlance to both tangibles and intangibles and is used to describe deductions under special provisions that allow rapid write-offs or permit the write-off of assets that one would normally assume do not decline in value.[124]

The tax law uses the term "basis" in dealing with recovery of the cost of an investment.[125] "Basis" is an economic and tax concept. It can be thought of as a record of the cost of an investment — of the amount that one looks to in calculating the deduction for depreciation (cost recovery) or amortization and in determining, on disposition, the amount of any gain or loss. The basis of *T*'s widget-making machinery immediately after she buys it is its cost of $100,000. If she were to sell it at that time for $110,000, her taxable gain would be $10,000, the difference between the proceeds of sale ($110,000) and her basis ($100,000).[126]

Suppose that *T* keeps the machinery and operates it for one year and that on her tax return for that year she claims a depreciation (cost recovery) deduction of $20,000. For tax accounting purposes, then, she has recovered that much of her investment. It is as if she had sold that portion of the machinery. All that remains invested is $80,000. In other words, since $20,000 has been "written off" against income, since it has been recovered through the ACRS deduction, her unrecovered cost or investment is now $80,000. That $80,000 is called her *adjusted basis.*[127] Adjusted basis in this case is cost less the ACRS deduction. If *T* were now to sell the machinery for $95,000 her taxable gain would be $15,000 — the difference between the proceeds of sale and the adjusted basis.[128]

Now consider something that is a bit more tricky and sometimes puzzles people. Suppose *T* buys a commercial building for $20,000. (To simplify, ignore ACRS deductions.) Suppose the building rises in value to $50,000. Since *T* has not sold the building, her gain is not "realized" and she is not required (or permitted) to take it into account for tax purposes. At this point suppose the building is destroyed by fire. The insurance proceeds are, let us assume, $40,000. What is *T*'s gain or loss

124. See, e.g., §169 (amortization of pollution-control facilities over sixty-month period) and §248 (amortization of corporate organizational expenditures).

125. See §102.

126. See §1001.

127. §1016(a)(2).

128. §1001(a). See also §61(a)(3).

for tax purposes? Under §1001(a), *T* has a gain of $20,000. This is as it should be. It is true that by virtue of the fire *T* has suffered an economic loss of $10,000. But *T* had properly refrained from reporting the increase in value from $20,000 at the time of purchase to $50,000 at the time of the fire. *T* started out with an investment of $20,000 and *T* now has $40,000; so *T* now must (belatedly) report and pay a tax on the $20,000 increase in her wealth.

Consider this related problem: Suppose that *E* is an employee of IBM and that as a year-end bonus *E* receives shares of IBM common stock with a market value of $10,000. Suppose that the tax law is such that *E* is permitted to, and does, exclude the value of this bonus from his gross income for tax purposes. What is *E*'s basis for the shares? Obviously it must be zero. For tax purposes, *E* acted as if he had not received the shares in the first instance, so if *E* later sells them the entire amount received is gain that is subject to taxation.

So much for business and investment assets. What about personal assets? Suppose *P* has a car that she bought three years ago for $3,000 and has used solely for personal purposes. Now suppose *P* sells it for $1,400. *P* has never written off any part of the cost for tax purposes. So does she have a loss of $1,600 that can be deducted on her tax return? The answer must be no. The decline in value of $1,600 was in the nature of a personal expense and should be no more an offset to *P*'s income than any other personal expense. But suppose that instead of selling the car *P* kept it and it is destroyed by fire (with no insurance and no salvage value). Does *P* have a loss? Certainly. It may be deductible in part under §165(c)(3) as a "casualty" loss. (See infra page 476.) What is the amount of the loss that is taken into account for tax purposes? $1,400, not $3,000. The other $1,600 of decline in value was attributable not to a casualty (the fire) but, as indicated before, to simple personal consumption.

Finally, there are special rules governing the basis of property acquired by gift or inheritance. Speaking very broadly, the basis of property inherited from a decedent is the fair market value of that property at the time of decedent's death.[129] As for lifetime gifts, for purposes of computing gain, there is a *substituted* basis — that is, the donee takes the same basis that the donor had.[130] The same rule applies for purposes of computing loss, except that if the market value of the property at the time of transfer was lower than the donor's basis then the donee's basis for purposes of computing loss is the value at the time of transfer.[131] This last rule is designed to prevent one person from shifting a

129. §1014.
130. §1015(a).
131. Id.

potential loss to another by making a gift. The basis of property acquired by gift may be increased in certain circumstances by the amount of any federal gift tax paid by virtue of the gift.[132]

6. Entities

A *sole proprietor* is a person who owns a business solely and directly — no partners or other co-owners and no use of a corporation or other such legal device. All items of income and expense of the business are treated for tax purposes as items of income and expense of the sole proprietor. There are separate forms on which these items may be netted out, but the use of these forms does not negate the direct relationship between the sole proprietor and each and every one of the transactions occurring in his or her business.

A *partnership* is a combination of two or more people who have agreed to carry on a business for profit as co-owners. The partnership is to some extent reified for tax purposes: "It" files a tax return. (That is, some person files a tax return covering the joint activities of the partners.) On the partnership tax return, income and expenses are netted out, but the partnership pays no tax. (That is, the partners' jointly held funds are not used to pay a tax.) Instead, the partners report on their individual tax returns their pro rata share of whatever net profit or loss was calculated by the partnership. This treatment of partners and partnerships is sometimes called *pass-through* taxation. The partnership is also sometimes referred to as a *conduit* for tax purposes. The pass-through feature is critical to groups of people who pool their resources to invest in *tax shelters,* which are investments that, because of special tax accounting rules (like the ACRS deductions), produce a loss for tax purposes even though profitable in an economic sense. The loss is passed through to the partner/investors and is used by them to offset income from other sources (such as a medical practice or an acting career).

A *trust* is a legal device by which one person, the trustee, holds and invests property for the benefit of another person, the beneficiary. The rules for taxation of trusts are too complex for development here. It is enough for now to say that the general effect is to achieve a pass-through or conduit result, but since there may be a delay between the time income is earned and the time when a beneficiary becomes entitled to it, and since the identity of the beneficiary may be undetermined, the trust may be required to pay a tax, which is generally treated like a withholding tax paid by an employer on the wages of an employee but is sometimes the final tax on the income.

132. §1015(d).

Corporations, which are legal devices for organizing economic activity, are treated as separate taxpaying entities. They compute the amount of their income, for the most part, according to the same rules as those applicable to the business activities of individuals and pay a tax based on a special rate schedule with rates of 15 percent on the first $50,000, 25 percent on the next $25,000, and 34 percent on amounts above $75,000, but with the benefit of the rates below 34 percent phased out as income rises above $100,000.[133] Payments of income by a corporation to its shareholders are called dividends[134] and are treated as income of the shareholders.[135] Thus, distributed income is doubly taxed, once at the corporate level and again at the individual level, while income that is retained is subject only to the corporate tax. When a corporation retains income, if the amount is wisely invested, the value of the corporation and of its common shares should rise (all other things equal). Thus, retained income should result in an increase in shareholder wealth in the form of increased share values. Such gain is not realized; it is not taxed until the shares are sold. Shareholders, unlike partners, cannot take into account their pro rata share of corporate losses. Losses can be used only by the corporation to offset income in other years.[136]

H. DEFERRAL AND ITS VALUE

In recent years, as interest rates have risen, taxpayers have found it increasingly advantageous to find ways to defer their tax liability to future years. The advantage of deferral is simple: A tax liability deferred from the present to the future gives the taxpayer the use in the

133. §11. The phaseout is accomplished by applying a rate of 39 percent, instead of 34 percent, until the benefit ($11,750) is recovered (at an income of $335,000). Thus, the effective rate schedule is:

$0-50,000	15%
$50,000-75,000	25%
$75,000-100,000	34%
$100,000-335,000	39%
above $335,000	34%

134. See §316.

135. §61(a)(7). Technically, income (or, to be more precise, "earnings and profits," a statutory concept similar to income) is an accounting concept, not a medium of payment, and a dividend is that portion of any payment (normally in cash) that does not exceed income.

136. Certain corporations are permitted to elect, under Subchapter S of the Code (§§1361 to 1379), to be taxed on a conduit or pass-through basis, in which case the corporation pays no tax and all net gains and losses are taken into account pro rata by the shareholders on their individual returns. In other words, the tax treatment of these corporations is essentially the same as that of partnerships.

interim of the amount that would otherwise have been paid presently in taxes. The advantage of deferral is far greater than the untutored may suspect (except for those who, from grammar school years, may recall the miracle of compound interest). Consider this illustration:

T is a high-income taxpayer subject to a marginal rate of 40 percent. Assume that he is permitted to set aside from his income, in a retirement fund, $10,000, without paying any tax on that amount and that, in addition, the earnings on that $10,000 from the present to whenever it is drawn out on retirement are not taxed. In other words, *T* has received the income, in cash; he has the cash to use, but taxation is deferred until retirement on both the $10,000 and the earnings on it. Suppose *T* invests the $10,000 for ten years at 10 percent, compounded annually, and then retires. By that time, the $10,000 will have increased to $25,937. If *T* then pays a tax at the rate of 40 percent, he will have $15,562 left to spend. In contrast, suppose that the law is different, that there is no special provision for deferral and that *T* must pay taxes on any money that he earns and wants to set aside for retirement as well as on the earnings on the amount set aside. In other words, assume normal current taxation rather than deferral. The $10,000 would be reduced by taxes to $6,000 and that $6,000, if invested to produce interest at the rate of 10 percent per year, would earn, after tax, only 6 percent. At the end of ten years, at 6 percent, the $6,000 would have increased to $10,745. This amount would be tax paid and fully spendable, but it is still only 69 percent of what is available with deferral. As the number of years of deferral increases, the gap between the two amounts becomes even more dramatic. If the number of years to retirement is twenty rather than ten, the relative after-tax amounts are $40,365 with deferral and $19,243 without.

Another way of looking at deferral is to calculate the present value of a future payment. Suppose, for example, that your client, *C*, wants to know what is saved by pushing a tax of $10,000 five years into the future, assuming a tax rate of 40 percent. One way to approach answering that question is to ask what amount must be set aside today to pay $10,000 in five years, assuming some reasonable rate of return on the amount set aside. Suppose *C* tells you she can earn 8 percent after tax (compounded annually) on her investments. With this interest rate, the amount to be set aside is $6,805. This means that a tax of $10,000 to be paid five years hence is financially equivalent to a tax of $6,805 to be paid today. That $6,805 is the *present value* of the $10,000 future amount, at 8 percent.

It is important to bear in mind, however, that if the deferral of tax can be achieved only by a deferral of a receipt of a taxable amount, any gain from the deferral of the tax must be measured against the loss from the deferral of the receipt. In other words, if tax liabilities are discounted to present value, corresponding receipts must also be discounted. The objective of tax deferral is to defer the tax without affecting the timing of receipts, or without affecting the present value of receipts. It is also worth noting that a comparison of the same investment with and without deferral of tax may be misleading in that a taxpayer who is currently taxable may choose to invest so as to take advantage of other tax benefits, such as investment in tax-exempt bonds.

The process of calculating the present value of a future amount is called *discounting to present value* and the present value is sometimes redundantly called the discounted present value.[137]

Table 1-7 gives relationships between present and future amounts. Present values can be derived by multiplying the future amount by the appropriate number. Thus, for the present value of $1 ten years hence, at 10 percent, the multiplier is 0.386. The present value of $10,000 ten years hence, at 10 percent, is 0.386 ($10,000) or $3,860. The present value of $25,907 ten years hence, at 10 percent, is 0.386 ($25,907) or about $10,000 (these figures are slightly inaccurate because of rounding off in the table).

The same table can be used to calculate future amounts, simply by dividing by the appropriate number rather than multiplying by it. For example, the future value of $10,000 ten years hence, at 10 percent, is $10,000 ÷ 0.386, which equals $25,905 (again slightly inaccurate due to rounding).

In case you want to make some rough calculations of present or future amounts or figure out interest rates, and don't have access to a table or a pocket calculator, you can use a convenient rule of thumb — the "rule of 72." This rule holds that (roughly) an amount doubles within the number of years determined by dividing 72 by the interest rate. Thus, at 12 percent, compounded annually, $1 will be worth $2

137. The algebraic formulas for the relationships between present and future value are simple. For computing future value,

$$FV = PV(1 + r)^n,$$

where FV is future value (or future amount), PV is present value (or amount), r is the interest rate, and n is the number of years. Thus, in the first example, in which $10,000 is invested at 15 percent for ten years,

$$FV = \$10{,}000(1.15)^{10} = \$40{,}456.$$

To determine present value, we do a minor transposition, and the formula is

$$PV = \frac{FV}{(1 + r)^n}.$$

Thus, using the same numbers,

$$PV = \frac{\$40{,}456}{(1.15)^{10}} = \$10{,}000.$$

TABLE 1-7
Present Value of $1: What a Dollar at End of Specified Future Year Is Worth Today

Year	*3%*	*4%*	*5%*	*6%*	*7%*	*8%*	*10%*	*12%*	*15%*	*20%*	*Year*
1	.971	.962	.952	.943	.935	.926	.909	.893	.870	.833	1
2	.943	.925	.907	.890	.873	.857	.826	.797	.756	.694	2
3	.915	.889	.864	.840	.816	.794	.751	.712	.658	.579	3
4	.889	.855	.823	.792	.763	.735	.683	.636	.572	.482	4
5	.863	.822	.784	.747	.713	.681	.620	.567	.497	.402	5
6	.837	.790	.746	.705	.666	.630	.564	.507	.432	.335	6
7	.813	.760	.711	.665	.623	.583	.513	.452	.376	.279	7
8	.789	.731	.677	.627	.582	.540	.467	.404	.327	.233	8
9	.766	.703	.645	.592	.544	.500	.424	.361	.284	.194	9
10	.744	.676	.614	.558	.508	.463	.386	.322	.247	.162	10
11	.722	.650	.585	.527	.475	.429	.350	.287	.215	.135	11
12	.701	.625	.557	.497	.444	.397	.319	.257	.187	.112	12
13	.681	.601	.530	.469	.415	.368	.290	.229	.163	.0935	13
14	.661	.577	.505	.442	.388	.340	.263	.205	.141	.0779	14
15	.642	.555	.481	.417	.362	.315	.239	.183	.123	.0649	15
16	.623	.534	.458	.394	.339	.292	.218	.163	.107	.0541	16
17	.605	.513	.436	.371	.317	.270	.198	.146	.093	.0451	17
18	.587	.494	.416	.350	.296	.250	.180	.130	.0808	.0376	18
19	.570	.475	.396	.331	.277	.232	.164	.116	.0703	.0313	19
20	.554	.456	.377	.312	.258	.215	.149	.104	.0611	.0261	20
25	.478	.375	.295	.233	.184	.146	.0923	.0588	.0304	.0105	25
30	.412	.308	.231	.174	.131	.0994	.0573	.0334	.0151	.00421	30
40	.307	.208	.142	.0972	.067	.0460	.0221	.0107	.00373	.000680	40
50	.228	.141	.087	.0543	.034	.0213	.00852	.00346	.000922	.000109	50

in six years (72 ÷ 12). By the same token, if the interest rate is 12 percent, the right to receive $2 six years from now is presently worth $1. And if $1 invested today yields $2 in six years, the return is 12 percent per year.

As the materials in this book unfold, it will become clear just how important is an understanding of the relationships between present and future value. Deferral is a major phenomenon in tax analysis.

I. THE SOURCES OF FEDERAL TAX LAW IN A NUTSHELL

Taxes are imposed only by statute. Although the lawyer who fails to look beyond the statute will often err, the statute should almost always be the starting point.

At the same time, some parts of federal tax law, especially where statutory pronouncements were absent, vague, or confused, have been influenced by judicial doctrines of a common law character, created by the courts as case after case came before them. In these areas, the lawyer must be attuned to the judiciary's signals even more than to those of Congress. Moreover, the detail of the statute is often deceptive, since the courts may exercise their traditional power to disregard form for substance and to hold that an arrangement that complies with the literal terms of the statute is not within its spirit, just as a deed absolute on its face may be shown to be a mortgage. One of the fascinations of federal tax law is the interplay between the detail of a statute and the creative spirit of the courts; and even the tax attorney who cannot pause to enjoy this interplay must understand it to survive.

The statute is, of course, the Internal Revenue Code of 1986. The prior Codes were enacted in 1939 and in 1954 and were frequently amended.

Although the congressional debates ordinarily do not illuminate technical problems of federal taxation, there are occasional exceptions, and then recourse to the Congressional Record is necessary. The committee reports, on the other hand, are frequently helpful, and it is common for the courts to rely heavily on them.[138] They are prepared by technicians on the staff of the Joint Committee on Taxation. That committee

138. Since 1939, the reports of the House Ways and Means Committee, the Senate Finance Committee, and the conference committees have been reprinted in the Internal Revenue Bulletin, which is published weekly by the Internal Revenue Service and compiled into semiannual volumes. The congressional reports for the period 1913-1939 were reprinted together in a separate number of the bulletin: 1939-1 (Part 2) C.B.

is composed of representatives of the House Ways and Means Committee and the Senate Finance Committee, who are assisted by a kind of legislative civil service of tax experts.[139] Because of the profusion of technical detail and because some members of the committee may know little of the content of the committee's reports (and this is a fortiori true of the members of Congress who do not serve on the tax committees), it might be said that the reports are not evidence of the "intent" of Congress unless we apply the doctrine of respondeat superior. However, the same might be said of the statutes themselves (as well as many other complex statutes) since many members of Congress, including some on the tax committees, do not understand the technical detail of the statutes and instead rely on the representations of the "technicians" regarding

139. The preparation of the committee report is described as follows in R. Blough, The Federal Taxing Process 75-76 (1952):

> Preparation of the Committee report is ordinarily in the hands of the Chief of Staff of the Joint Committee [on Taxation] and his staff members. The report is customarily divided into two parts. The first is a discussion in non-technical language of the need for the legislation, what the bill provides, and the anticipated impact on various groups of taxpayers. Among the tax staffs this section of the report is referred to as the 'guff'. Despite this derisive label, the section is very important. The latter part of the Committee report is a technical explanation of what each section of the bill provides. The Legislative Counsel [of the Treasury] and the Treasury tax staff participate in the preparation of the technical section.

In recent years, the Joint Committee Staff has published a General Explanation of tax acts after their enactment. This is a compilation of the various committee reports — House, Senate, and Conference — into one report that reflects the final legislation. The General Explanation is an interesting and useful document, nicely described in the following passage from Michael Livingston, Congress, the Courts, and the Code: Legislative History and the Interpretation of Tax Statutes, 69 Texas L. Rev. 819, 884-885 (1991) (footnotes omitted):

> A notable example of post-enactment legislative history in the General Explanation, commonly known as the "Blue Book" [because its cover is blue], written by the Joint Committee on Taxation staff after a major tax bill [has been enacted]. While primarily a collation of the previous committee reports, the Blue Book also contains some materials not found in the committee reports. These materials are not officially part of the legislative history, and a debate persists as to their authority. Courts have cited the Blue Book on various occasions. . . . The consensus appears to be that the Blue Book has some authority, but less than the actual committee reports.
>
> I am not so sure. If the legislative history is largely an exercise in writing regulations, are the staff's later efforts necessarily worse than their earlier ones? . . .
>
> I recommend that the Blue Book be treated in a manner similar to the committee reports themselves. Where the Blue Book adds explanatory material, it should be as persuasive as similar material in the committee reports. (This is a relatively rare occurrence.) Where the Blue Book specifies detailed applications of the statute, it should be entitled to a presumption of correctness, but should not be followed if it is inconsistent with the underlying provision. This would discourage the use of the Blue Book to "strong-arm" interpretations not otherwise supported by the statute.
>
> In taking this position, I am aware of the constitutional difficulties in consulting post-enactment history.

the contents of the statute and the committee reports. The importance of the committee reports increases with the complexity of the statute since difficult drafting problems frequently are "taken care of" in the committee report.[140]

Occasionally, though more rarely, the courts refer to the hearings before the House and Senate Committees as an aid to construction. Although some of the oral testimony is quite diffuse, interested public and private individuals and groups often present closely reasoned memoranda in support of their positions. If a proposal is accepted, modified, or rejected by the committee after it has been explained by testimony or memorandum, the presentation may be a clue to the meaning of the committee's action and, by extension, to the meaning of the action of Congress. The hearings are printed by the committees in limited quantities, however, and are to be found in only a few libraries.[141]

Second only to the statute and the legislative materials in importance are the Treasury Regulations. Code §7805 authorizes the Secretary of the Treasury or his delegate to prescribe "all needful rules and regulations for the enforcement" of the Code. In addition, the secretary is authorized to issue regulations to cover more specific areas — e.g., under §3 to prescribe tax tables for individuals, and under §472 to set rules governing use of the last-in-first-out method of accounting for inventories. Perhaps most interesting are §§1501 to 1505, giving to the Treasury the authority to prescribe by regulations the conditions under which consolidated returns may be filed by one or more affiliated corporations and pursuant to which virtually a separate tax code has been promulgated by regulation. Regulations issued under these sections are of a quasi-legislative character; Congress has chosen to delegate to the Treasury authority it might have exercised itself. Other regulations interpret the statute for the guidance of the taxpayers and the staff of the Internal Revenue Service. During recent years the Congress has increasingly intervened in the Treasury's regulation function. Regulations or rulings dealing with fringe benefits, travel and entertainment, deduction of expenses of commuting to work, treatment of deferred compensation, and imputed interest on related party transactions have been blocked either by formal legislation or by agreement with congressional committees.[142] Whatever their function or origin, regulations are

140. Occasionally, the Committee Report is used to direct the Treasury to modify, institute, or abandon a regulation or other administrative practice. Often these directions, the result of understandings between Treasury staff and the committees, are followed by the Internal Revenue Service. Some view this as abuse of the process; others as an efficient way of doing business.

141. On use by the judiciary of inaccessible legislative history as an aid to the construction of statutes, see Justice Jackson, concurring, in United States v. Public Utilities Commission, 345 U.S. 295, 319 (1953).

142. See Parnell, Congressional Interference in Agency Enforcement: The IRS Experience, 89 Yale L.J. 1360 (1980).

issued from time to time in the form of Treasury Decisions (T.D.), which are compiled at irregular intervals as a systematic series of regulations.

The current regulations bear the key numeral "1" if related to the income tax provisions of the Code; "20" or "25" if related to the estate or gift tax provisions, respectively. Thus, "Regs. §1.170-1" denotes a regulation having to do with §170 (income tax consequences of charitable contributions); "Regs. §20.2041-1" is concerned with §2041 (estate tax treatment of powers of appointment); "Regs. §25.2512-1," with §2512 (value of property in computing gift tax). There are other series for more specialized subjects. Changes in the regulations are issued as Treasury Decisions. The Administrative Procedure Act requires proposed regulations (with certain exceptions) to be published in the Federal Register to permit interested parties to file their objections or suggestions for consideration before adoption.[143] The proposed regulations are prepared by the Service in consultation with the Treasury staff.

Regulations, whether of a legislative or an interpretive character, can serve a useful function only if both administrators and taxpayers can rely on them. Seldom are regulations, of either kind, overturned by the courts, but occasionally a regulation, especially one of the interpretive type, is invalidated. It is impossible to generalize beyond saying that a regulation that was issued soon after enactment of the statute it interprets and that has been adhered to consistently by the government will command great respect from the courts, but that if contemporaneity and consistency are lacking, the courts will be less constrained to accept the regulation. Reenactment of a statute may carry an implication of congressional approval of an interpretive regulation.[144] Another problem in this area is whether a proper interpretive regulation in time takes on the force of law so that only Congress, and not the Treasury, may alter it. The Treasury may ordinarily amend an interpretive regulation if the new interpretation is to be given prospective force only, and there may also be power to apply it retroactively. Retroactive application may be withheld by the Treasury itself, however, as wise administration, pursuant to its power, conferred by §7805(b), to prescribe the extent to which regulations and rulings shall be applied prospectively only.

In addition to the regulations, which are issued by authority of the Secretary of the Treasury, a steady supply of rulings, instructions, releases, and other lesser pronouncements flows from the Internal Rev-

143. 5 U.S.C. §553.

144. It is hard to assess the importance of the reenactment rule in this area. It may be only a handkerchief covering something already covered by a blanket if the court would have upheld the regulation whether the statute had been reenacted or not; but it may be crucial if the court thinks the regulation when issued was either debatable or demonstrably wrong but that it gained authority as a result of silent acquiescence by Congress.

enue Service. Not bearing the imprimatur of the secretary, these documents are less authoritative than the regulations, but they are of great importance in the day-to-day administration of the tax laws, and often they are persuasive to the courts. The most important are Revenue Rulings (Rev. Rul.) and Revenue Procedures (Rev. Proc.). Revenue Rulings are opinions on matters of law arising in particular fact settings. Often they are based on requests by taxpayers for advice about a specific legal issue with which they are confronted. Revenue Procedures are statements describing procedures affecting the rights or duties of taxpayers or other information. Both Revenue Rulings and Revenue Procedures are published by the government currently in the weekly Internal Revenue Bulletin (I.R.B.) and permanently (every six months) in the Cumulative Bulletins (Cum. Bull.). Earlier versions of Revenue Rulings and Revenue Procedures were designated "I.T." (rulings to taxpayers on income tax matters), "G.C.M." (General Counsel Memorandum), and "Mim." (Mimeograph). Also of importance is advice given to taxpayers in "private letter rulings" (Ltr. Rul.), sometimes referred to as "private rulings" or "letter rulings." These rulings are issued (in letter form) to taxpayers in response to requests for advice about their own specific fact situations. Some of these ultimately are developed into Revenue Rulings, which set forth the official position of the IRS on which all taxpayers are entitled to rely. In the case of a letter (private) ruling that has not become a Revenue Ruling, the government is not bound to follow the legal position that it adopts except as it is applied to the individual taxpayer to whom the advice is directed. Letter rulings are published by commercial publishers.[145] While letter rulings lack precedential force,[146] they are useful to practitioners in determining the position the IRS has adopted.

As we have seen, tax litigation may begin in the Tax Court, in the various federal district courts, or in the Claims Court. The opinions of the Tax Court fall into two categories: "regular" decisions, which are published by the court itself, and "memorandum" decisions, which are not officially reported but are published commercially by Prentice-Hall, Inc., and by Commerce Clearing House. The opinions of the district courts, Claims Court, courts of appeals, and Supreme Court are, of course, to be found in the regular federal reports, but the tax cases decided by these courts are also separately published by Prentice-Hall, Inc., in the series American Federal Tax Reports (cited as A.F.T.R.) and by Commerce Clearing House in the series United States Tax Cases (cited as U.S.T.C.). These sets also contain a few district court opinions in tax cases that are not to be found in the Federal Supplement. A few opinions on federal tax claims are handed down by federal courts sitting

145. Letter rulings first became public information in 1976 with the adoption of §6110.
146. Section 6110(j)(3). See Rev. Proc. 79-45, 1979-2 C.B. 508, §17.01.

in bankruptcy and by state courts passing on probate or receivership matters.

When the service loses a case in the Tax Court, it often announces, in the Internal Revenue Bulletin, whether it acquiesces (acq. or A) or does not acquiesce (nonacq. or NA) in the decision. Acquiescence operates as advice to the staff of the Service on whether to rely on the decision in the disposition of other cases. Nonacquiescence indicates that the Service, whether it appeals the decision or not, will not accept the principle enunciated in it in disposing of other cases (though of course the decision is binding as to the taxpayer in the case itself, unless reversed on appeal), and that it may litigate the same issue when it arises again. Because decisions of the Tax Court are reviewed by thirteen courts of appeals, the government may eventually succeed in obtaining a reversal of the Tax Court, even though the decision in the nonacquiesced case was affirmed by a court of appeals; indeed, the principal way for the Treasury to get a conflict among the circuits (as a basis for a petition for certiorari) when the Tax Court decides in favor of the taxpayer is to stick to its guns and relitigate the same issue in one or more other cases. After announcing its nonacquiescence, the Treasury may be discouraged by a series of losses in the courts of appeals, or it may reconsider its views for other reasons and substitute an acquiescence for nonacquiescence.[147]

Another administrative practice related to litigation is based on the Treasury's power, already mentioned, to prescribe the extent to which its rulings and regulations will be applied prospectively only. When a judicial decision in the government's favor overrules earlier cases or conflicts with rulings that had been extensively relied on by taxpayers, the Treasury sometimes announces that a new regulation or ruling, issued to conform to the judicial decision, will not be applied retroactively.

J. SELECTED BIBLIOGRAPHY

1. Introduction to the Law

M. Chirelstein, Federal Income Taxation: A Law Student's Guide to the Leading Cases and Concepts (6th ed. 1991), is everything that its subtitle promises. Most students will find it extremely helpful. There is

147. The Tax Court will normally apply the rule of the Court of Appeals with jurisdiction over an appeal in the particular case before it even if it disagrees with the Court of Appeals. Golsen v. Commissioner, 54 T.C. 742 (1970).

a hornbook, M. Rose and J. Chommie, Federal Income Taxation (1988). Also interesting, though dated, are J. Sneed, The Configurations of Gross Income (1969), and even more dated, R. Magill, Taxable Income (rev. ed. 1945). For more complete study of particular subject matter, the treatises or services listed below should be consulted.

2. Treatises

B. Bittker and L. Lokken, Federal Taxation of Income, Estates and Gifts (1989), is thorough and readable. Research Institute of America (R.I.A.), Federal Tax Coordinator 2d (looseleaf), is more complete but still generally quite readable. J. Mertens, Law of Federal Income Taxation (various dates, with looseleaf updates), is comprehensive but often too much so. Tax planning topics are covered effectively in B.N.A.'s series, Tax Management Portfolios. On corporate/shareholder taxation, see B. Bittker and J. Eustice, Federal Income Taxation of Corporations and Shareholders (1993, with current supplements). On partnership taxation, see A. Willis, J. Pennell, and P. Postlewaite, Partnership Taxation (4th ed. 1989 looseleaf); W. McKee, W. Nelson, and R. Whitmire, Federal Taxation of Partnerships and Partners (1990, looseleaf). On the taxation of pensions and profit-sharing (including the treatment of deferred compensation), see R. Osgood, The Law of Pensions and Profit-Sharing (1984).

3. Services

Prentice-Hall, Federal Taxes, and Commerce Clearing House, Federal Tax Reporter, are complete, current multivolume reference works and include citations of all relevant authorities, organized by Code sections; citators ("shepardizing" the authorities); indexes of articles; and brief explanations of Code provisions and the most salient cases, rulings, and other authorities interpreting those provisions.

4. History

An excellent historical analysis (with emphasis on political forces and process), with thoughtful presentations of data, is found in J. Witte, The Politics and Development of the Federal Income Tax (1985). S. Ratner, American Taxation (1942), is a standard account of taxation as a social force in American history. E. Seligman, The Income Tax (2d ed. 1914), is a study of the history and theory of income taxation, at home and abroad, by a scholar whose influence on federal income taxation in its early days was very great. R. Paul, Taxation in the United States (1954), follows Ratner and Seligman for the early period, but it is an indispensable account of the economic and political background of federal taxation from 1932 on, made more spirited by the author's own role as advisor and official of the Treasury Department from 1937 to 1944. Another useful work is R. Blakey and G. Blakey, The Federal Income Tax (1940), which summarizes each Revenue Act from 1913 to 1939.

Legislative development of the tax law may be traced through W. Barton, Federal Tax Laws Correlated (1968); J. Seidman, Legislative History of Federal Income and Excess Profits Tax Laws, 1939-1953 (1954); and J. Seidman, Legislative History of Federal Income Tax Laws, 1861-1938 (1938).

5. Policy, Theory, and Reform

For an excellent bibliography, see Nacev, A Bibliography of the Literature on Tax Policy, 30 Tax Notes no. 30, §2 (March 10, 1986).

Important works abound, including L. Lindsey, Growth Experiment: How the New Tax Policy Is Transforming the U.S. Economy (1990) (an economist argues that the tax reductions and reforms of the Reagan era had good economic effects); H. Aaron, H. Galper, and J. Pechman, eds., Uneasy Compromise: Problems of a Hybrid Income-Consumption Tax (1988) (papers and comments from a Brookings Institute conference on current policy issues, including taxes in general equilibrium analysis, effects of taxes on organizational form, the interest deduction, savings and investment incentives, indexing for inflation, and the alternative minimum tax); J. Pechman, Federal Tax Policy (5th ed. 1987) (a readable presentation of the problems of tax policy, by a stalwart, savvy liberal tax reformer); D. Bradford, Untangling the Income Tax (1986) (useful description of basic income tax policy issues and of economic (public finance) theory relevant to those issues; written by a sophisticated economist for serious but unsophisticated readers); H. Aaron and H. Galper, Assessing Tax Reform (1985) (two well-known economists offer indictment of current system and proposals for reform); C. Clotfelter, Federal Tax Policy and Charitable Giving (1985) (economic study of the effects of federal taxes on charitable giving); J. Pechman, Who Paid the Taxes, 1966-85 (1985) (further development and updating of the author's well-known work on tax burden and distribution of income); C. Steuerle, Taxes, Loans, and Inflation (1985) (analysis of alleged distorting effect of individual and corporate taxes on investment decisions; argument for broad-based, low-rate income tax); S. Surrey and P. McDaniel, Tax Expenditures: From Idea to Ideology (1985) (traces the development of the uses of the tax expenditure concept and its impact on tax policy and legislation and on judicial decisions); J. Witte, The Politics and Development of the Federal Income Tax (1985) (useful examination of the historical development of the income tax, with political analysis and interesting data); Treasury Department Report to the President, Tax Reform for Fairness, Simplicity, and Economic Growth (1984) (referred to as Treasury I, after it was supplanted by a more politically acceptable document, this document effectively expresses the goals of tax reform and offers a comprehensive set of proposals and reasons for those proposals; a remarkable publication coming, as it did, from the Treasury Department under President Reagan and Secretary Regan); J. Pechman, ed., Options for Tax Reform (1984) (survey by lawyers and economists of substantive, compliance, and legislative issues, for Brookings Institution conference; good summary in the introduction); A. Auerbach, The Taxation of Capital Income (1983); M. Feldstein, Inflation, Tax Rules, and Capital Formation (1983); M. Feldstein, Capital Taxation (1983) (effect of taxation on behavior of individual investors and business firms; incidence); M. McIntyre, F. Sander, and D. Westfall, eds., Readings in Federal Taxation (2d ed. 1983) (good collection of tax policy articles and other materials, for law students); H. Aaron and J. Pechman, eds., How Taxes Affect Economic Behavior (1981) (economists reporting and discussing studies of how taxation affects labor supply, investment, corporation finance, stock prices, capital formation, housing, saving, and charitable contributions); H. Aaron and M. Boskin, eds., The Economics of Taxation (1980) (economists again, on distribution of tax burdens, the concept of tax expenditures, the tax base, treatment of the family, and other topics); J. Pechman, ed., What Should Be Taxed: Income or Expenditure? (1980) (papers and debate by economists and lawyers on income versus consumption as tax base, including problems of implementation); C. McClure, Must Corporation Income Be Taxed Twice? (1979) (study by author plus his report of discussion by economists and lawyers); J. Pechman, ed., Comprehensive Income Taxation (1977) (excellent discussions of basic tax policy issues including definition of income, personal deductions, employee benefits, capital gain, homeowner preferences, and treatment of the family); U.S. Treasury, Blueprints for Basic Tax Reform (1977) (a remarkably lucid and thoughtful report on basic issues, with a proposal for a consumption-based tax); W. Klein, Policy Analysis of the Federal Income Tax (1976) (text and readings on basic issues and tools of analysis, for law students); S. Surrey, Pathways to Tax Reform (1973) (excellent presentation of the theory for the tax expenditure budget and arguments for limiting use of the income tax to accomplish nontax objectives, by a leading tax professor and former Treasury official (during the 1960s)); B. Bittker, C. Galvin, R. Musgrave, and J. Pechman, A Comprehensive Tax Base? A Debate (1968) (republishing, with some new material, a famous debate in the Harvard Law

Review over the Comprehensive Tax Base (CTB), a tax-reform concept labeled and attacked by Bittker and defended by the faithful); Report of the Royal Commission on Taxation (Canada 1966) (an excellent review of basic issues, with proposals for reform); W. Blum and H. Kalven, The Uneasy Case for Progressive Taxation (1953) (a classic work by two law professors, drawing on economics and philosophy; tightly written with brilliant analysis); H. Simons, Personal Income Taxation (1938) (another classic, still valuable for those interested in the problem of how broad the income tax base should be).

Statistics can be found in the Treasury Department's annual compilation of information from tax returns, Statistics of Income. Additional information may be found in the Annual Reports of the Secretary of the Treasury and of the Commissioner of Internal Revenue; the Statistical Abstract of the United States and a supplement to it, Historical Statistics of the United States; the biennial publication, Facts and Figures on Government Finance (Tax Foundation, Inc.) (a handy source of data summarized from more complete sources and including information on state and local taxes and on federal taxes other than the income tax); and another biennial publication, Significant Features of Fiscal Federalism (Advisory Commission on Intergovernmental Relations).

2

SOME CHARACTERISTICS OF INCOME

As we have already seen (supra pages 19-24), it is unrealistic to suppose that we can describe in a sentence or two what "income," for purposes of our federal income tax system, is or ought to be. The ideal must be defined by applying to myriad, subtly varying fact situations the often conflicting goals of a good tax system. The reality is defined by a vast amount of statutory, judicial, and administrative material, which this chapter attempts, in a summary fashion, to reflect. Still, pithy definitions are widely discussed[1] and cited as authority. These definitions do have some content; they reflect an approach or an ideal and as such seem to have had an effect on the development of the law as well as on how people think about what the law ought to be.

At one extreme is a concept reflected in the widely quoted statement from Eisner v. Macomber, 252 U.S. 189, 207 (1920) (infra page 286), "'Income may be defined as the gain derived from capital, from labor, or from both combined.' . . ." As we will see, this is a narrow definition. For example, it excludes windfalls, so that a person who works to earn money is taxed on it, while a person who finds the same amount lying in the street would not be. Eisner v. Macomber explicitly draws on dictionary definitions. Its plain language or strict constructionist approach appeals to a desire for objectivity, for reliance on some standard that is external to the tax system and does not call for value judgments by administrators and judges, and perhaps not even by legislators. But the narrowness of the definition produces unfairness (because people with similar ability to pay are not taxed similarly) or economic distortion

1. See Goode, The Economic Definition of Income in Comprehensive Income Taxation 1, 3-10 (J. Pechman ed. 1977); Wueller, Concepts of Taxable Income, 53 Pol. Sci. Q. 83, 557 (1938).

(because some kinds of gain-producing activities are favored over others).[2]

At the other extreme is the more broadly encompassing idea found in a later Supreme Court decision, Commissioner v. Glenshaw Glass Co., 348 U.S. 426 (1955) (infra page 126), where the Court stated (at 429-430) that "Congress applied no limitations as to the source of taxable receipts, nor restrictive labels as to their nature." A more elaborate, and perhaps even broader, version of this approach is reflected in a formula by economist Henry Simons, which has become a touchstone or rallying call of tax theorists and reformers:

> Personal income may be defined as the algebraic sum of (1) the market value of rights exercised in consumption and (2) the change in the value of the store of property rights between the beginning and the end of the period in question.

H. Simons, Personal Income Taxation 50 (1938).[3]

This definition is widely thought to be the foundation for what Professor Bittker labeled the comprehensive tax base (CTB).[4] The Simons definition and the CTB reflect an understandable yearning for uniformity. They fail to take account, however, of the requirements of administrative feasibility and for that and other reasons are far removed not only from our present tax system but also, as Professor Bittker pointed out, from any tax system that reasonable people might propose. For example, the Simons definition would require taxation of unrealized appreciation, imputed income, and the value of government services

2. To the extent that a tax rule produces distortion it tends not to produce unfairness. That is, where a tax rule encourages people to engage in particular kinds of activities, normally they will be forced to accept lower returns in those activities. They pay a "putative" tax. (See supra page 29.) To that extent the unfairness (to others) of the favorable treatment is reduced or eliminated.

3. This definition is based on a similar one by another economist, R. M. Haig, and is often referred to as the Haig-Simons definition. An elaboration of it is found in the following passage from a Canadian study, defining a person's "economic power" (tax base) as:

> 1. The market value of the goods and services used up by the tax unit during the year to satisfy its own wants (consumption).
> 2. The market value of the goods or services given to other tax units during the year (gifts).
> 3. The change over the year in the market value of the total net assets held by the tax unit (current saving = change in net worth = change in wealth). This may be either a positive or a negative figure in any time period.

3 Report of the Royal Commission on Taxation 23 (Can. 1966).

4. Bittker, A "Comprehensive Tax Base" as a Goal of Income Tax Reform, 80 Harv. L. Rev. 925 (1967). This article became the focal point of an extensive and continuing debate among lawyers and economists interested in tax policy and tax reform. A series of direct responses, appearing in the Harvard Law Review, plus some additional commentary, are collected in B. Bittker, C. Galvin, R. Musgrave, and J. Pechman, A Comprehensive Income Tax Base? (1968).

such as an education at a state-supported low-tuition university. And it would not countenance use of the tax system to encourage or reward activities thought by Congress to be meritorious.

In the early days of the income tax, the narrow definition of Eisner v. Macomber, or at least the attitudes revealed by that definition (see supra page 75), seem to have had a significant impact on the development of the law. Definitions, approaches, and attitudes have changed, but much of what we find in the present law can best be understood as relics of the era in which the Eisner v. Macomber approach held sway.

A. NONCASH BENEFITS

"Gross income includes income realized in any form, whether in money, property, or services." Regs. §1.61-l(a). "[I]f services are paid for in property, the fair market value of the property taken in payment must be included in income as compensation." Regs. §1.61-2(d)(1). One can easily appreciate the need to include noncash benefits in income if the outcomes under a contrary rule are imagined. Although not all taxpayers could readily barter work for noncash benefits, many could — for example, a lawyer might draft a will for a carpenter in exchange for work on her home or the employees of a supermarket might accept part of their pay in groceries. To the extent that some people could take advantage of such arrangements more freely than others, tax burdens to some degree would, at least initially, fall in a haphazard manner, depending on the practicality of compensation in kind in a particular kind of activity. That would violate the goal of fairness. As people responded by moving to tax-favored jobs, the wages in such jobs would tend to fall. Industries providing such jobs would, for no good reason, tend to benefit as compared with industries that did not. That would violate the goal of economic rationality. Moreover, people would be encouraged to take compensation in the form of goods and services instead of taking it in cash and spending the cash on goods and services that they might value more highly; again, that would violate the goal of economic rationality — it would be wasteful.

On the other hand, taxing noncash benefits raises problems of administrative feasibility or practicality. Often it is difficult to know whether a noncash benefit (e.g., life insurance or free air travel) has any significant value to the taxpayer and, if so, how much. Sometimes it may be best, for reasons of practicality, to wait until some later time to impose the tax (e.g., where the benefit consists of an item of property that will not be sold until some time in the future and whose present value is uncertain). Sometimes it may be difficult to separate the business from the personal aspects of such noncash benefits as the use of a well-furnished office or a company limousine.

The cases and other materials that follow in this section reveal how the law has reacted to the competing dictates of fairness, economic rationality, and practicality. One background factor must be kept in mind: Use of noncash benefits may make enforcement difficult. The amounts involved tend to be modest; the Service (IRS) has bigger fish to fry. Cheating is often difficult to detect. Taxpayers begin to realize that they can get away with certain kinds of cheating — for example, with not reporting the value of the personal use of a company car. They may rely on that disturbing but common defense, "everyone is doing it." The Service must ever be alert to the dangers inherent in enforcement policies that tend to encourage such attitudes, not so much because the amounts may grow over time (if they do, the Service can crack down), but because of adverse effects on general taxpayer morale and because, after a sufficiently long period of nonenforcement, taxpayers may begin to rely on, and to feel that they are entitled to continue to enjoy, the tax benefits they have claimed; and Congress may agree. One should always be careful, however, to distinguish between cheating that one can get away with (and that the Service knows people are getting away with) and permissible conduct. Tax cheating may not be a mortal sin. It's certainly not as serious a moral transgression as murder or robbery. But it *is* cheating; it is contrary to law; it does mean that the cheaters fail to bear their fair share of the total burden; and it is, simply, wrong.

We begin our study of noncash benefits with a case involving an annuity. An *annuity* is a form of contract under which a payment is made now in return for a payment, or series of payments, to be made in the future. People speak of "buying" an annuity, usually from an insurance company. Commonly, as in our first case, the purchaser makes a single payment in return for the seller's promise to make fixed payments to the annuitant, for life, beginning at the time the annuitant retires. People can buy annuities, often called annuity policies, for themselves — that is, with themselves as annuitants. In the following case, however, the payment to the insurance company for the policy is made by an employer with the later payments from the insurance company to be made to an employee. The insurance company has the use of the money paid for the policy from the date of receipt until the time when payments are made. It can earn interest (or other returns) on this money and therefore can afford to, and will, agree to pay out a total amount that is expected (based on the amount of time until the insurance company must make the first payment and the annuitant's life expectancy) to be greater than the amount paid in initially. The tax problem might be seen as one of deciding whether to impose a tax at the time the employer makes the payment to the insurance company, plus an additional tax on payments received by the annuitant in excess of the amount originally taxed,[5] or to wait and tax the entire amount of payments received by the annuitant on retirement. In other words, we can see the issue as one of timing or deferral — as one of when to impose the tax. Alternatively, we can focus more directly and more intently on the year in which the employer buys the policy and on the appropriateness of imposing a tax in that year, taking into account various attributes of the benefit received (though in doing so we must remember that we are talking not about permanent exclusion or exemption, but rather about a benefit that will be included in income in some later year if it is not included in the year of receipt). In other words, we can see the issue essentially as one of whether to impose a tax in the year the benefit is bestowed. For purposes of our initial inquiry into the nature of income for tax purposes, the latter perspective, the "whether" approach, seems more suitable. Timing questions are pursued more directly and more fully in the next chapter.

1. Retirement Benefits

UNITED STATES v. DRESCHER

179 F.2d 863 (2d Cir. 1950), cert. denied, 340 U.S. 821 (1950)

Before L. Hand, Chief Judge, and Swan and Clark, Circuit Judges.
Swan, Circuit Judge. . . .

[Plaintiff] was an officer and director of Bausch & Lomb Optical Company, and in each of the taxable years the Company purchased from an insurance company at a cost of $5000 a single premium annuity contract naming him as the annuitant. The taxes in dispute resulted from the Commissioner's including such cost as additional compensation received by the plaintiff in the year when the annuity contract was purchased. The district court awarded the plaintiff judgment. . . .

The facts are not in dispute. In 1936 the Optical Company inaugurated a plan to provide for the voluntary retirement at the age of 65 of its principal officers then under that age. There were five such, of whom Mr. Drescher was one. He was born April 28, 1894. Pursuant to this plan and in "recognition of prior services rendered," the Company purchased on December 28, 1939, and on the same date in 1940, a single premium, non-forfeitable annuity contract which named Mr. Drescher as the annuitant. Each policy was issued by Connecticut General Life Insurance Company and was delivered to the Optical Company which retained possession of it. It was the Company's intention, and so understood by the annuitant, that possession of the policy should be retained until the annuitant should reach the age of 65. The premium paid for each policy was $5000. The amount of such payment was

5. We return later to the method of taxing this excess. See infra page 179.

deducted by the Company in its tax return for the year of payment as part of the compensation paid to Mr. Drescher during that year. His salary as an officer was not reduced because of the purchase of the annuity contract, and he was not given the option to receive in cash the amounts expended by the Company for the premium payments. In filing income tax returns Mr. Drescher reported on the cash basis; the Optical Company on the accrual basis.

By the terms of the policy the Insurance Company agrees to pay the annuitant, commencing on December 28, 1958, a life income of $54.70 monthly under the 1939 policy and $44.80 monthly under the 1940 policy, with a minimum of 120 monthly payments. If the annuitant dies before receiving 120 monthly payments, the rest of them are payable to the beneficiary named in the policy. Each policy gives the annuitant an option to accelerate the date when monthly payments shall commence, but this option must be exercised by the annuitant in writing and endorsed on the policy. Consequently so long as the Optical Company retains possession of the policy the annuitant cannot exercise the option. If the annuitant dies before December 28, 1958, or before the acceleration date if he has exercised the option to accelerate monthly income payments, a death benefit is payable to the beneficiary designated by him (his wife). The policy reserves to him the right to change the beneficiary. The policy declares that "Neither this contract nor any payment hereunder may be assigned, and the contract and all payments shall be free from the claims of all creditors to the fullest extent permitted by law." The policy has no cash surrender, salable, or loan value, and does not entitle the annuitant to a distribution of surplus.

This case is governed by the provisions of the Internal Revenue Code as they existed in 1939 and 1940. The appellant contends that the contracts are taxable to the annuitant in the year of purchase by the employer because §22(a) [1939 Code; now §61(a)] sweeps into gross income "compensation for personal service, of whatever kind and in whatever form paid, . . . and income derived from any source whatever." The taxpayer . . . cites Treasury rulings to the effect that retirement annuity contracts purchased for an employee gave rise to taxable income only as the annuitant received payments under the contract; and that the entire amount of each annuity payment was includible in gross income for the year of its receipt if he had made no contribution toward the purchase of the annuity. . . .

Whether we should construe the statute in accord with these Treasury rulings if the matter were res integra, we need not say. In this court the question of construction is not res integra because of our decision in Ward v. Commissioner, 2 Cir., 159 F.2d 502. That case involved a single premium annuity contract delivered to the annuitant and assignable by him. We there held that "the petitioner became taxable in 1941 upon whatever value was, by the delivery of the policy to him in that year, then unconditionally placed at his disposal. . . . This was the then assignable value of the policy." 159 F.2d page 504. We then considered whether it was error to value the policy in the amount of the premium paid for it. We recognized that the assignable value of the policy in 1941 might be less than the single premium paid for it, but as the purchaser had offered no proof that it was we held that the Tax Court was right in treating "cost to the purchaser as the assignable value of the policy when received by the taxpayer." 159 F.2d page 505.

As we shall not overrule the *Ward* case, the question is narrowed to determining whether the present case is distinguishable because the plaintiff's policies are nonassignable and were retained in the possession of the employer. We do not think these facts are sufficient to distinguish the cases with respect to taxability of the contracts, although they may affect the value of the rights the respective annuitants acquired. It cannot be doubted that in 1939 the plaintiff received as compensation for prior services something of economic benefit which he had not previously had, namely, the obligation of the insurance company to pay money in the future to him or his designated beneficiaries on the terms stated in the policy. That obligation he acquired in 1939 notwithstanding the employer's retention of possession of the policy and notwithstanding its non-assignability. The perplexing problem is how to measure the value of the annuitant's rights at the date he acquired them. The taxpayer contends that they then had no present value, while the appellant argues that their value was equal to the premium paid by the employer. We are unable to accept either contention.

The prohibition against assignment does not prove complete absence of present value. The right to receive income payments which accrued to the plaintiff when the Optical Company received each contract represented a present economic benefit to him. It may not have been worth to him the amount his employer paid for it; but it cannot be doubted that there is a figure, greater than zero although less than the premium cost, which it would have cost him to acquire identical rights. Likewise, the assurance that any beneficiary named by him at the time the contract was executed, or substituted by him at a later date, would in the event of his death receive the cost of each contract, plus interest after a few years, conferred a present economic benefit on him. Whatever present value the life insurance feature had to him is clearly taxable. . . . Another element of value inheres in the possibility that the annuitant could realize cash by contracting with a putative third person to hold in trust for him any payments to be received under the annuity contract. True, the promisee would run the risk that the annuitant might die before becoming entitled to any payment, in which event they would be payable to the beneficiary designated in the policy, but by exercising the reserved power to change the beneficiary the annuitant could designate his promisee. The power to make such a contract based on the policy may well have had some present value. No proof was offered as to this. . . . On the other hand, it seems clear that the policy was worth less to the annuitant than the premium paid because the employer's retention of possession precluded him from exercising the privilege of accelerating the date of annuity payments since the insurance company's approval had to be endorsed upon the policy. The granting of this privilege must have been one of the factors taken into account in fixing the premium — at least, we may so assume in the absence of evidence. Hence deprivation of ability to exercise the privilege would decrease the value of the policy to the annuitant below its cost to the employer.

None of the authorities relied on by the parties is precisely in point on the issue of valuation. In Hackett v. Commissioner, 1 Cir., 159 F.2d 121, although the policy was non-assignable, the value to the annuitant was measured by the cost of the premium. As already stated, that basis is inapplicable here, for retention of the policy by the employer cut off the acceleration privilege. The same distinction exists with respect to the partially assignable policy involved in Oberwinder v. Commissioner, 8 Cir., 147 F.2d 255. And the tax treatment of the assignable policy in that case, as well as of those involved in the *Ward* case . . . , affords little guidance to a correct valuation here. Likewise, the cases holding free from taxation a non-assignable promise to pay money at a future date do not assist us, since they rest decision on taxability — here concluded by the *Ward* case — rather than on valuation. But it is unnecessary on the present appeal to determine the precise valuation of the policies.

. . . [T]he burden of proving by how much he was overtaxed was on the plaintiff. . . . He relied upon the terms of the contract to prove that it had no present value whatever. But for reasons already stated we are satisfied that the 1939 policy had some present value and since he did not prove that such value was less than $5,000 the judgment in his favor cannot stand. . . .

Judgment reversed and cause remanded.

Clark, Circuit Judge (dissenting in part).

I agree that the judgment must be reversed, but do not share in the view that some amount less than the $5000 expended by the employer for this taxpayer in each of the years in question may be found to be the value of the annuity and hence the amount of additional compensation for which he is to be taxed. For the contrary seems to me well supported in reason and well established by the authorities cited in the opinion, some directly in point and some with, I suggest, immaterial variations of fact. In the light of modern conditions of life, the satisfying of the highly natural and indeed burning desire of most men of middle age to obtain security for their old age and for their widows at death seems so clearly an economic benefit that I wonder it has been questioned as much as it has. Nor do I see the need to support this conclusion by looking for some highly theoretical possibility of turning this benefit into immediate dollars and cents any more than in the case where an employee is furnished living quarters or meals. Just as the latter are valued as additional compensation, though not assigned or assignable, so I think this highly valuable security is a purchased benefit for these company executives. Consequently the making of nice distinctions in either taxability or the amount thereof between assignable or accelerable annuities or their delivery or retention by the company — after careful forethought and advice of its attorneys with naturally an eye on both pension and tax possibilities — seems to me improper, when the general purpose to make adequate retirement provisions for these employees was made so clear. . . .

Hence for any issues here involved I do not think it is important to discover what reasons impelled the employer to make the slightly differing provisions from those before this court in Ward v. Commissioner, 2 Cir., 159 F.2d 502, 505. Perhaps the employer may have had the prescience to foresee these tax problems which are troubling my brothers and did trouble the court below and may result in at least postponement, if not non-collectibility, of most, if not all, of the tax on the additional return provided by the employer for these executives. Perhaps, rather, the employer was providing only for a surer provision "free from the claims of all creditors to the fullest extent permitted by law" for this taxpayer and his wife. So in retaining possession of the policies and cherishing the present intent not to permit acceleration of the annuities, the employer may have had in mind a way of both securing the purchased services to the retirement age in normal cases and guarding against unusual situations due to disability or other special cause. In any event the fact is that the employer purchased at the going insurance rate those contracts which for the parties fulfilled the conditions desired.[6] Actually they would return to the annuitant, or to his widow, total amounts at least well in excess of the premiums paid and increasing yet more the longer he lived. The parties got just what they paid for in the insurance market, and its cost price is the additional compensation the executive received. The two features stressed in the opinion, namely, the nonassignability and the present non-accelerability of the annuities, may add to their usability for the particular purpose, but would seem not to change the basis of value. Perhaps, indeed, they render the contracts more desirable not only to the employer, but also to the annuitant's wife, as making the security provisions less easily impaired, and thus have a special appeal to a husband solicitous of his wife's future. At least, I do not see what basis we have for thinking they adversely affect values of provisions for a particular purpose, viz., security. If, in fact, these conditions do affect the amount of the premium, as the opinion rather naturally assumes, then all the more is the bargain

6. This was a tightly controlled corporation, so much so that the executives receiving the annuities and their families owned approximately 35 percent of the voting stock, while the older officers and directors owned approximately 57 percent. Hence there was never a sharp divergency of interest between these executives and their employer.

of the parties to be respected as made; even the annuitant would doubtless be interested in a maximum return though it be strictly limited to himself or his wife. It seems to me that there is being set up some premise, not found in any of the precedents, of a fictitious partly-impaired transferability which is now somehow to be given a value in place of the wholly practical values set upon these contracts in the insurance market itself.

Of the cases, Hackett v. Commissioner, 1 Cir., 159 F.2d 121, seems directly in point and Judge Mahoney's opinion wholly persuasive as to both the meaning of the statute and the value to be set upon a nonassignable annuity contract. The suggested ground of distinction, that here retention of the policy by the employer cut off the acceleration privilege, cannot be accepted, since there does not appear to have been any such privilege in the annuity there considered; for no mention of the fact, or allusion of any kind to it, is made by the court. The same is true in Oberwinder v. Commissioner, 8 Cir., 147 F.2d 255, which also appears to be on all fours with this case. Similar results were reached in Hubbell v. Commissioner, 6 Cir., 150 F.2d 516, 161 A.L.R. 764, and by this court in Ward v. Commissioner, supra; for the reasons I have stated, the fact that the annuities in these cases were assignable should not make their purchase price any more accurate a gauge of their value than is the purchase price here. A like conclusion has been reached with respect to insurance premiums, . . . and amounts deposited in the federal Civil Service Retirement Fund . . . ; while no case supporting a lesser valuation has been discovered. True, in the *Ward* case we spoke of the failure of the taxpayer "to show that the contract was not worth as much as it cost." Surely there is nothing in this record to suggest anything different. Here there was even an official of the insurance company to testify to the somewhat ordinary nature of these contracts. That the parties actually got the particular provisions they desired for their purposes does not at all suggest that the policies were overpriced.

Hence unless these benefits are now taxed, this small group of top executives will be given a tax advantage not accruing to less fortunate or less well-advised persons. Such taxation should not be confused or rendered abortive by directions for valuation impossible of execution in any realistic way.

NOTES AND QUESTIONS

1. *What's at stake in* Drescher? Since the court holds that Drescher was taxable on some amount (likely to be close to the $5,000 paid by his employer, Bausch & Lomb for the annuity policy) he is treated for tax purposes as if he had received in cash the amount included in income, and had used the cash to buy the policy. This means that he has an investment in the policy and, as was suggested in the descriptive

paragraph immediately preceding the case, this investment is taken into account later, when he starts collecting the annuity payments. The portion of the payment that represents the return of Drescher's investment will be nontaxable. That is, he will be entitled to an exclusion to take account of the fact that a tax has already been imposed. In contrast, had Drescher won, he would have paid no tax at the time of his employer's purchase of the annuity contract and, for tax purposes, would have had no investment (or, in tax language, "basis") in the policy. Consequently, the entire amounts later received would have been taxable; there would have been no exclusion.

Why should Drescher care whether or not he is able to defer recognition of income until he starts collecting payments under the policy? The answer lies in the fact that deferral reduces the present value of the tax burden. See description of deferral at page 61 above and in Note 3.

2. *Was the valuation issue real?* (a) The court in *Drescher* ruled that, because of the company-imposed restrictions on acceleration, the value of the annuities to the taxpayer might be less than the $5,000 cost of the annuities to Bausch & Lomb. Is it reasonable to believe that a company would pay $5,000 for an annuity and then, by restricting acceleration, "mar" the annuity so that its value to an employee was only, say, $4,500? Would not such a company be better off by paying the employee $4,750 cash in lieu of the annuity? Or by leaving the acceleration provisions intact?

(b) Does the fact that Drescher was an officer and director of Bausch & Lomb, and one of only five individuals who received annuities, tell us anything about the likelihood that the annuity was worth less to Drescher than it cost Bausch & Lomb?

3. *Calculating the amount of the tax benefit.* Suppose that Drescher's marginal tax rate was 35 percent (combined state and federal). The result of this decision is that he would have been liable for a tax of $1,750 by virtue of receiving the policy, assuming it is valued at $5,000. If he had won the case, he would have been able to retain and invest that $1,750 until the tax in fact became due. Assume that the full amount of the tax became due at retirement twenty years later and that at that time his tax rate was still 35 percent. He would then pay the $1,750 tax. In the meantime, however, if he had invested that amount at, say, 6 percent per year (after tax), the $1,750 would have grown to $5,612.[7] His gain would be $3,862 ($5,612 minus $1,750). That $3,862 would be the after-tax benefit of the deferral that he sought.

The $3,862 is the future-value gain — that is, the amount by which Drescher would be ahead at the end of twenty years. The present value of that amount (still assuming an interest rate of 6 percent) is $1,204.

7. Using the table on page 64, the amount is $1,750 ÷ 0.312 = $5,608, which is slightly inaccurate due to rounding off in the table.

Viewing the same benefit from a different perspective, if Drescher pays the tax at the time the annuity is purchased, the amount of the tax is $1,750, and that, of course, is its present value (that is, the dollar value of the burden). If the $1,750 is not payable until twenty years later, the present value is only $546, which is $1,204 less than $1,750.

These calculations may be summarized as follows.

A. Future Value Perspective

1939	Tax if $5,000 included in income	$1,750
1939	Savings if no present tax	1,750
1939	Savings set aside (the "fund")	1,750
1959	Value of the fund if invested at 6 percent (after tax)	5,612
1959	Tax payable on the $5,000 if not taxed in 1939	1,750
1959	Net after-tax fund	3,862
	Present value in 1939	$1,204

B. Present Value Perspective

1939	Tax if $5,000 included in income	$1,750
1939	Amount that must be set aside (at 6 percent) to pay a tax of $1,750 in 1959 (i.e., present value of future tax)	546
	Savings	$1,204

4. *An accounting perspective.* The issue in *Drescher* can be viewed in a somewhat different perspective, as a problem of accounting. Drescher was a cash-method taxpayer. (See supra page 53.) If he had used the accrual method, it is plain that he would have been taxable in the year in which Bausch & Lomb bought the policy, since that was the year when he earned the benefit and his rights had become fixed and determinable. See Regs. §1.446-1(c)(1)(ii). The advantage of the accrual method is accuracy, while the advantage of the cash method is simplicity.

5. *Bausch & Lomb's deduction.* The $5,000 cost of the annuity was properly deducted by Bausch & Lomb as a business expense in the year of purchase. Presumably that deduction reduced the amount of tax paid by Bausch & Lomb. A victory for the taxpayer in *Drescher* would have left the government with a tax regime under which the cost of employer-held annuities was currently deductible but the value of the annuities was not currently included in income.

6. Drescher *today.* (a) *Drescher* is presented at this point in the casebook because it introduces some basic problems in determining taxable income. The valuation issue introduced in the case appears again and again in the casebook (and in the tax law). The holding in *Drescher* is not important, nor is it important at this point to know whether the

retirement plan at issue in *Drescher* would receive similar treatment today. Nonetheless, the following summary of present law may be helpful.

(b) Under present law employers may set up "qualified" pension and profit-sharing plans to provide retirement benefits for their employees. Contributions by the employer to the plan are deductible by it as such contributions are made. Employees are not taxed until they later begin to receive payments, on retirement. There is no tax on the earnings generated by amounts contributed to, and held for investment in, the plan, except that those earnings increase the benefits received by the employees and ultimately are taxed to them, as they receive payments on retirement. From the perspective of the employee, the tax on the amount paid into the qualified plan and on the earnings on those amounts is deferred until retirement and, as we have seen (supra page 86), this can result in greatly increased after-tax benefits. The combination of immediate deduction of the cost to the employer and deferred recognition of income of the employee is the result that the parties in *Drescher* sought to achieve. But the tax benefits of qualified plans, under present law, are limited to plans meeting a number of conditions, one of which is that the plan cannot discriminate in favor of highly paid employees. In other words, Congress has conditioned tax deferral for retirement benefits on nondiscrimination. Drescher benefited from a plan that covered only highly paid employees. Such a plan would fail the nondiscrimination test and would not constitute a "qualified" pension or profit-sharing plan. Qualified plans are examined in more detail at page 395.

(c) Deferred compensation may take the form of an unsecured promise by the employer to make a payment in a future year. Such "mere" promises to pay are not income to the employee or deductible by the employer until the year of payment. The fact that the employer may be financially stable, and the obligation fixed and unequivocal, is irrelevant. Drescher, of course, received more than a mere promise to pay. He received a nonforfeitable right to an annuity purchased from a third party. Thus, under present law, as under the decision in *Drescher,* he would not be allowed to defer taxation of the value of the policy under the rule relating to mere promises to pay. Unsecured promises to pay are considered further at pages 381-385.

(d) Employee deferred-compensation benefits that amount to more than a mere promise to pay, but are not excluded from income under some specific section of the Code (such as the section that governs qualified plans), are now covered by §83 and §403. These provisions are considered further at pages 407-410.

7. *Enforcement.* (a) How would the Service find out that a taxpayer like Drescher had become entitled to an annuity? If an employer regards such a payment as taxable, then, under present law, it may be required

to withhold tax and report the amount on the employee's annual statement of income and of tax withheld (the "W-2" form). Under §3402, withholding is required on "wages," which are defined in §3401(a) as "all remuneration . . . for services performed by an employee for his employer, including the cash value of all remuneration paid in any medium other than cash," with various exceptions, none of which is relevant to the issue considered here. If the employer treats the benefit as income and withholds taxes (from the employee's salary), an employee who wants to treat the benefit as nontaxable will be required to claim an exclusion and offer some sort of explanation on his or her return, thereby bringing the matter to the attention of the person in the Service who might examine that return. But what if the employer considers that the amount is not current remuneration and does not report or withhold on it? Nothing will show up on the taxpayer's current return, unless the employee chooses to report the amount. Now how will the Service become aware of the matter?

(b) Because employers who fail to withhold the prescribed amounts are liable for an employee's taxes, pro tanto, if the employee fails to pay them (§§3403, 3402(d)), the Supreme Court in Central Illinois Public Service Co. v. United States stated that "the employer's obligation to withhold must be precise and not speculative." 435 U.S. 21, 31 (1978). On this theory, the Court ruled that an employer was not required to withhold taxes on amounts paid to reimburse employees for certain lunches, even though the amounts constituted income to the employees, because the Service rulings on the withholding obligation had been ambiguous. Id. at 32.

8. *Burden of proof.* As the last paragraph of the *Drescher* majority opinion indicates, the burden of proof is on the taxpayer. The same is true, with some exceptions, in Tax Court proceedings. See Tax Court Rule 142. To the same effect, it is sometimes said that a presumption of correctness attaches to the Commissioner's determination of a deficiency. See 4 B. Bittker, Federal Taxation of Income, Estates and Gifts ¶115.4, at 115-133 (1981).

QUESTIONS

1. What if Drescher had had a right under his contract with Bausch & Lomb to take either cash ($5,000) or the annuity policy? See the discussion of the doctrine of constructive receipt (supra page 54). As a practical matter, does it seem likely that Drescher could have bargained for cash or some other noncash benefit?

2. Suppose that the retirement annuities in *Drescher* were part of a standard fringe benefits package that was granted to all management employees. Would this fact make it more or less likely that the annuities

were worth less to Drescher than the $5,000 cost to Bausch & Lomb?

3. Suppose again that retirement annuities were part of a standard fringe benefits package. In that case, disregarding tax considerations, it seems reasonable to assume that most employees would consider the value of the benefits to be at least as high as the cost to the employer. Otherwise, why would the employer not pay cash? Would it be practical (administratively feasible) to allow a particular employee like Drescher to argue that the annuity he received was worth less to him? Do our notions of fairness suggest that Drescher should be allowed to make that argument?

4. The court in *Drescher* held that the amount to be included in income was the value of the annuities to Drescher, rather than the cost to Bausch & Lomb. What if Bausch & Lomb had been able to buy the policy for $5,000 because of its bargaining position with the insurance company, but the same policy would have cost Drescher $5,300 if he had bought it himself?

5. Suppose that the policy had been assignable and that Drescher had proved that the most he could have gotten by assignment was $4,500. Would it not seem odd that a possibility of assignment would support a lower valuation?

6. Suppose that, instead of buying a retirement annuity, Bausch & Lomb had paid $5,000 toward the cost of the college education for Drescher's children. Might it be reasonable to assume that the benefit was worth less to Drescher than the amount paid? If so, would it be reasonable to allow Drescher to pay tax on that lesser value? If so, what amount should Bausch & Lomb be allowed to deduct?

2. Food and Lodging

Although in *Drescher* the issue was now or later, in the next case it is now or never. In other words, the question next considered is strictly one of whether to tax, with no aspect of the when-to-tax question. As in *Drescher,* we are again confronted with a problem of valuation, but there is a new problem as well — namely, an overlap between business and personal aspects of a taxpayer's life.

BENAGLIA v. COMMISSIONER

36 B.T.A. 838 (1937), acq. 1940-1 C.B. 1

FINDINGS OF FACT

The petitioners are husband and wife, residing in Honolulu, Hawaii, where they filed joint income tax returns for 1933 and 1934.

The petitioner has, since 1926 and including the tax years in question, been employed as the manager in full charge of the several hotels in Honolulu owned and operated by Hawaiian Hotels, Ltd., a corporation of Hawaii, consisting of the Royal Hawaiian, the Moana and bungalows, and the Waialae Golf Club. These are large resort hotels, operating on the American plan. Petitioner was constantly on duty, and, for the proper performance of his duties and entirely for the convenience of his employer, he and his wife occupied a suite of rooms in the Royal Hawaiian Hotel and received their meals at and from the hotel.

Petitioner's salary has varied in different years, being in one year $25,000. In 1933 it was $9,625, and in 1934 it was $11,041.67. These amounts were fixed without reference to his meals and lodging, and neither petitioner nor his employer ever regarded the meals and lodging as part of his compensation or accounted for them.

Opinion

Sternhagen, J.

The Commissioner has added $7,845 each year to the petitioner's gross income as "compensation received from Hawaiian Hotels, Ltd.," holding that this is "the fair market value of rooms and meals furnished by the employer." In the deficiency notice he cites article 52 [53], Regulations 77,[8] and holds inapplicable Jones v. United States, 60 Ct. Cls. 552; I.T. 2232; G.C.M. 14710; and G.C.M. 14836. The deficiency notice seems to hold that the rooms and meals were not in fact supplied "merely as a convenience to the hotels" of the employer.

From the evidence, there remains no room for doubt that the petitioner's residence at the hotel was not by way of compensation for his services, not for his personal convenience, comfort or pleasure, but solely because he could not otherwise perform the services required of him. The evidence of both the employer and employee shows in detail what petitioner's duties were and why his residence in the hotel was necessary. His duty was continuous and required his presence at a moment's call. He had a lifelong experience in hotel management and operation in the United States, Canada, and elsewhere, and testified that the functions of the manager could not have been performed by one living outside the hotel, especially a resort hotel such as this. The

8. ["Where services are paid for with something other than money, the fair market value of the thing taken in payment is the amount to be included as income. . . . When living quarters such as camps are furnished to employees for the convenience of the employer, the ratable value need not be added to the cash compensation of the employees, but where a person receives as compensation for services rendered a salary and in addition thereto living quarters, the value to such person of the quarters furnished constitutes income subject to tax." — Eds.]

demands and requirements of guests are numerous, various, and unpredictable, and affect the meals, the rooms, the entertainment, and everything else about the hotel. The manager must be alert to all these things day and night. He would not consider undertaking the job and the owners of the hotel would not consider employing a manager unless he lived there. This was implicit throughout his employment and when his compensation was changed from time to time no mention was ever made of it. Both took it for granted. The corporation's books carried no accounting for the petitioner's meals, rooms, or service.

Under such circumstances, the value of meals and lodging is not income to the employee, even though it may relieve him of an expense which he would otherwise bear. In Jones v. United States, supra, the subject was fully considered in determining that neither the value of quarters nor the amount received as commutation of quarters by an Army officer is included within his taxable income. There is also a full discussion in the English case of Tennant v. Smith, H.L. (1892) App. Cas. 150, III British Tax Cases 158. A bank employee was required to live in quarters located in the bank building, and it was held that the value of such lodging was not taxable income. The advantage to him was merely an incident of the performance of his duty, but its character for tax purposes was controlled by the dominant fact that the occupation of the premises was imposed upon him for the convenience of the employer. The Bureau of Internal Revenue has almost consistently applied the same doctrine in its published rulings.

The three cases cited by the respondent, Ralph Kitchen, 11 B.T.A. 855; Charles A. Frueauff, 30 B.T.A. 449; and Fontaine Fox, 30 B.T.A. 451, are distinguishable entirely upon the ground that what the taxpayer received was not shown to be primarily for the need or convenience of the employer. Of course, as in the *Kitchen* case, it can not be said as a categorical proposition of law that, where an employee is fed and lodged by his employer, no part of the value of such perquisite is income. If the Commissioner finds that it was received as compensation and holds it to be taxable income, the taxpayer contesting this before the Board must prove by evidence that it is not income. In the *Kitchen* case the Board held that the evidence did not establish that the food and lodging were given for the convenience of the employer. In the present case the evidence clearly establishes that fact, and it has been so found.

The determination of the Commissioner on the point in issue is reversed.

Reviewed by the Board.

Judgment will be entered under Rule 50.

MURDOCK, J., concurs only in the result.

ARNOLD, J., dissenting.

I disagree with the conclusions of fact that the suite of rooms and meals furnished petitioner and his wife at the Royal Hawaiian Hotel were entirely for the convenience of the employer and that the cash salary was fixed without reference thereto and was never regarded as part of his compensation.

Petitioner was employed by a hotel corporation operating two resort hotels in Honolulu — the Royal Hawaiian, containing 357 guest bed rooms, and the Moana, containing 261 guest bed rooms, and the bungalows and cottages in connection with the Moana containing 127 guest bed rooms, and the Waialae Golf Club. His employment was as general manager of both hotels and the golf club.

His original employment was in 1925, and in accepting the employment he wrote a letter to the party representing the employer, with whom he conducted the negotiations for employment, under date of September 10, 1925, in which he says:

> Confirming our meeting here today, it is understood that I will assume the position of general manager of both the Royal Waikiki Beach Hotel (now under construction) and the Moana Hotel in Honolulu, at a yearly salary of $10,000.00, payable monthly, together with living quarters, meals, etc., for myself and wife. In addition I am to receive $20.00 per day while travelling, this however, not to include any railroad or steamship fares, and I [am] to submit vouchers monthly covering all such expenses.

While the cash salary was adjusted from time to time by agreement of the parties, depending on the amount of business done, it appears that the question of living quarters, meals, etc., was not given further consideration and was not thereafter changed. Petitioner and his wife have always occupied living quarters in the Royal Hawaiian Hotel and received their meals from the time he first accepted the employment down through the years before us. His wife performed no services for the hotel company.

This letter, in my opinion, constitutes the basic contract of employment and clearly shows that the living quarters, meals, etc., furnished petitioner and his wife were understood and intended to be compensation in addition to the cash salary paid him. Being compensation to petitioner in addition to the cash salary paid him, it follows that the reasonable value thereof to petitioner is taxable income. Cf. Ralph Kitchen, 11 B.T.A. 855; Charles A. Frueauff, 30 B.T.A. 449.

Conceding that petitioner was required to live at the hotel and that his living there was solely for the convenience of the employer, it does not follow that he was not benefited thereby to the extent of what such accommodations were reasonably worth to him. His employment was a matter of private contract. He was careful to specify in his letter accepting the employment that he was to be furnished with living quarters, meals, etc., for himself and wife, together with the cash salary, as compensation for his employment. Living quarters and meals are necessities which he would otherwise have had to procure at his own expense. His contract of employment relieved him to that extent. He has been enriched to the extent of what they are reasonably worth.

The majority opinion is based on the finding that petitioner's residence at the hotel was solely for the convenience of the employer and, therefore, not income. While it is no doubt convenient to have the manager reside in the hotel, I do not think the question here is one of convenience or of benefit to the employer. What the tax law is concerned with is whether or not petitioner was financially benefited by having living quarters furnished to himself and wife. He may have preferred to live elsewhere, but we are dealing with the financial aspect of petitioner's relation to his employer, not his preference. He says it would cost him $3,600 per year to live elsewhere.

It would seem that if his occupancy of quarters at the Royal Hawaiian was necessary and solely for the benefit of the employer, occupancy of premises at the Moana would be just as essential so far as the management of the Moana was concerned. He did not have living quarters or meals for himself and wife at the Moana and he was general manager of both and both were in operation during the years before us. Furthermore, it appears that petitioner was absent from Honolulu from March 24 to June 8 and from August 19 to November 2 in 1933, and from April 8 to May 24 and from September 3 to November 1 in 1934 — about 5 months in 1933 and 3½ months in 1934. Whether he was away on official business or not we do not know. During his absence both hotels continued in operation. The $20 per day travel allowance in his letter of acceptance indicates his duties were not confined to managing the hotels in Honolulu, and the entire letter indicates he was to receive maintenance, whether in Honolulu or elsewhere, in addition to his cash salary.

At most the arrangement as to living quarters and meals was of mutual benefit, and to the extent it benefited petitioner it was compensation in addition to his cash salary, and taxable to him as income.

The Court of Claims in the case of Jones v. United States, relied on in the majority opinion, was dealing with a governmental organization regulated by military law where the compensation was fixed by law and not subject to private contract. The English case of Tennant v. Smith, involved the employment of a watchman or custodian for a bank whose presence at the bank was at all times a matter of necessity demanded by the employer as a condition of the employment.

The facts in both these cases are so at variance with the facts in this case that they are not controlling in my opinion.

Smith, Turner, and Harron agree with this dissent.

NOTES

1. *The Board's reasoning.* The Board of Tax Appeals (now the Tax Court), though conceding that Benaglia was "relieve[d] of an expense which he would otherwise bear," reasoned that the meals and lodging were "imposed upon him for the convenience of the employer" and that therefore their value was not income to him. If this were a case of first impression decided according to modern principles (embodied in *Glenshaw Glass* and in the Simons definition, supra page 76), the best response to that argument might be the classic demurrer, "I understand everything but the 'therefore.'" In fact, the "convenience of the employer" test appeared as early as 1919 (see O.D. 265, 1 C.B. 71), and its present-day version (see discussion of §119 infra) may be thought of as one of the relics of the narrow, strict constructionist spirit of Eisner v. Macomber. Thus, with this case we begin to learn that exclusions are far easier to permit in the first place than they are to get rid of once taxpayers have come to rely on them.

2. *"Slippery slope"?* Is the rule applied in *Benaglia* one that creates a serious "slippery slope" problem? That is, is it the kind of rule that leads to wholesale avoidance as employers and employees find ways to take advantage of it? Or is it self-limiting?

3. *The statutory treatment.* Section 119, adopted in 1954, ended a relatively unrestrained period of administrative and judicial development (or bungling) of the "convenience of the employer" doctrine regarding meals and lodging. When Congress intervenes in such a situation, it may confirm some prior practices and curtail others; and it will usually create new issues. In this instance, both these results occurred. Is it now necessary to determine whether meals or lodging are "intended as compensation"? Even though §119 provides that the terms of an employment contract or state statute are not "determinative," are they significant in deciding whether the meals or lodging are excluded by §119? Lodging is excluded only if the employee "is required to accept such lodging on the business premises of his employer as a condition of his employment." Does this automatically ensure that the lodging was furnished "for the convenience of the employer"? These are only a sample of some of the issues that have been the subject of the profuse litigation under §119. Section 119 is an example of how a seemingly minor provision in terms of revenue and general applicability can foster an inordinate amount of judicial interpretation and administrative complexity, not to mention congressional intervention (§119 was amended twice in 1978). The brief and selective survey that follows provides some sense of the nature of the litigation.

(a) *"Furnished."* In Commissioner v. Kowalski, 434 U.S. 77 (1977), the Court, resolving a conflict among the circuits, held that meal allowance payments to state highway patrol troopers were income within the contemplation of §61 and were not excludable under §119 because the statutory language exempts only meals that are "furnished," which means that the employer must supply the meals themselves, not cash with which to buy meals. Is there any sense to such a limitation? If not, perhaps one can understand the unwillingness of some judges (and justices) to apply the language literally. On the other hand, if the entire exclusion under §119 makes no sense, should the courts interpret the various elements of the statute so as to limit the exclusion as much as possible? Even with a conflict among the circuits, should the Supreme Court be spending its time on a case such as *Kowalski?* The Commissioner's petition for writ of certiorari (at page 7) noted that fifteen states were currently making payments to 10,301 police troopers in the amount of about $10 million annually and that there were "2,193 cases involving this issue presently pending administratively in the Internal Revenue Service with $4,518,573 in taxes at stake."

Though perhaps not relevant to the decision, it is interesting that in *Kowalski* the taxpayer's wages were $8,746 and the meal allowance was an additional $1,698, or 19.4 percent of the cash wages. The meal allowance was included in income by the state for purposes of computing pension benefits. 434 U.S. at 81.

One might have supposed that *Kowalski* would have settled the controversy over cash versus in-kind benefits. In Sibla v. Commissioner, 611 F.2d 1260 (9th Cir. 1980), however, the court allowed a fireman to exclude from his income the amounts that he paid (about $3 a day) to participate in an obligatory organized mess at the station house. The court distinguished *Kowalski* on the ground that in that case the taxpayer received cash that he was free to spend wherever he wished or not to spend at all. The court conceded that its language was inconsistent with the "language" of *Kowalski* (more precisely, its expressed rationale), but argued that the Supreme Court could not have meant what it said, only what it held. On the other hand, in Phillips v. Commissioner, T.C. Mem. 1986-503, the court held nondeductible the cost of a firefighter's meals at the station house where the firefighter's union, rather than the employer (as in *Sibla*), organized the mess, but in Christey v. United States, 841 F.2d 809 (8th Cir. 1988), the court permitted much the same tax outcome as is achieved through exclusion by allowing a deduction of meal expenses incurred by state police troopers who, like Kowalski, were restricted in their choice of restaurants and were on call while eating. The court held that the district court finding, that the meal expenses were "ordinary and necessary" business expenses under §162(a), was not clearly erroneous.

(b) "*Meals.*" In Tougher v. Commissioner, 51 T.C. 737 (1969), aff'd per curiam, 441 F.2d 1148 (9th Cir.), cert. denied, 404 U.S. 856 (1971), the Tax Court held that "meals" did not include groceries bought by an employee of the Federal Aviation Administration (FAA) for himself and his family from the commissary maintained by the FAA at Wake Island, where he was employed. On the other hand, in Jacob v. United States, 493 F.2d 1294 (3d Cir. 1974), the court held that "meals" did include groceries supplied to the executive director of a medical institute who was required to live with his family on the institute premises. Toilet tissue, soap, and other nonfood items were also held to be excludable as an integral part of meals and lodging. After *Kowalski,* supra, the taxpayer in *Tougher* would lose on the "furnished" issue since he was reimbursed for groceries he bought from the commissary. Why should it matter whether the system used by the employer requires the employee to pay for the groceries rather than allowing him or her to select "free" groceries that it makes available (while presumably reducing his salary)? In other words, what reason is there for holding that statutory use of the word "furnished" means that the employer must actually make the selection of the items that the employee is to receive? See Rev. Rul. 68-579, 1968-2 C.B. 61, holding that lodging includes utilities when furnished by the employer but not when the employee contracts directly with the utility and is reimbursed.

(c) "*Business premises of the employer.*" The circuits have split on what constitutes "business premises of the employer" for state police. United States v. Barrett, 321 F.2d 911(5th Cir. 1963), held that every state road and highway, and evidently adjacent restaurants as well, constitute the business premises of their employer, the state. Accord: United States v. Keeton, 383 F.2d 429 (10th Cir. 1967); United States v. Morelan, 356 F.2d 199 (8th Cir. 1966). Contra: Wilson v. United States, 412 F.2d 694 (1st Cir. 1969). In *Kowalski,* supra, the Supreme Court did not reach the "business premises" issue because it was able to dispose of the case on the basis of the "furnished" language.

In Lindeman v. Commissioner, 60 T.C. 609 (1973), acq., the business premises of a beachfront hotel were held to include a house across the street from it occupied by the hotel's manager and his family. But in Commissioner v. Anderson, 371 F.2d 59 (6th Cir. 1966), cert. denied, 387 U.S. 906 (1967), a house that was two blocks away from the employer's motel and was occupied by its manager was held not to be part of the employer's business premises. Official residences of the governors of the states, and presumably the White House, also qualify under §119. Rev. Rul. 75-540, 1975-2 C.B. 53. Taking the idea a step further, the Court of Claims permitted exclusion for the "White House" of the U.S. Jaycees (U.S. Junior Chamber of Commerce v. United States, 334 F.2d 660 (1964)) and the Tokyo residence of the president of a Japanese subsidiary of Mobil Oil (Adams v. United States, 585 F.2d 1060 (1977)).

(d) "*Convenience of the employer.*" In most cases, the requisite employer's convenience is established by proof that the employee is "on call" outside of business hours. See Rev. Rul. 71-411, 71-2 C.B. 103. See also Setal v. Commissioner, 20 T.C.M. 780 (1961), holding that meals and lodging furnished by a mining company at a company town in a mountainous area of California were provided for the "convenience of the employer" because the closest alternative facilities were sixty-seven miles away by roads that were hazardous in winter; the same facts established that the lodging was a required condition of employment within the meaning of §119(2).

Examine Regs. §1.119-1(a)(2) and the examples in Regs. §1.119-1(f). Can the results in the examples be reconciled with the statute? Try to imagine the administrative process by which the regulations were adopted. It is safe to assume that there was heavy input by organizations representing affected employees. The distinctions that seem to be required by the statutory language might be difficult to explain to these employees. Where does that leave the Treasury when it comes to drafting regulations? And what does it tell us about §119?

(e) "*Employee.*" Section 119's exclusion is for "an employee," which rules out self-employed persons such as farmers who own and operate their own farms. But a person may be treated as the employee of a corporation even if she or he owns all the shares of that corporation. In J. Grant Farms, Inc. v. Commissioner, 49 T.C.M. 1197 (1985), Mr. Grant had since 1949 owned and operated a farm. In 1976 he formed a corporation, all of whose shares were owned by himself and his wife. Mr. Grant transferred or leased to the corporation all of the assets used in the farming business and the corporation formally became the operator of the farm. The corporation hired Mr. Grant as its employee in the role of manager of the farm, and he continued to manage and operate the farm as he had been doing in the past. One of the assets transferred to the corporation was the house in which the Grants and their children lived; the house thus became a business asset of the corporation instead of a personal asset of the Grants. The corporation (remember, it was owned and controlled by the Grants) required Mr. Grant to live in the house as a condition of his employment, and the Tax Court found that there were sound business reasons for this requirement. Accordingly, the corporation was allowed deductions for depreciation and utility costs for the house, and Mr. Grant was not required to include any amount in his gross income by virtue of its use by himself and his family. Note that before the farming business was incorporated the Grants did not have income for tax purposes by virtue of their use of their house. (See discussion of imputed income from home ownership infra page 117.) The advantage of incorporation was that because the house became a business asset of the corporation rather than a personal asset of the Grants, a deduction for depreciation, utility costs, and maintenance costs became available. Section 119 was important in this context because without it the value of the use of the house would have become taxable to Mr. Grant as a form of noncash compensation to him as an employee of the corporation.

4. *Political issue.* In an era when Congress seems to be searching for additional sources of revenue, why does the §119 exclusion survive? Is it the power of unions representing hotel workers and other such beneficiaries of the provision? Is that enough?

QUESTIONS

1. The Commissioner sought to tax Benaglia on the $7,800 annual "retail" value of the employer-provided food and lodging. Assume that the current ("out-of-pocket") cost of the food and lodging to the hotel was only $3,000. Assume further that employees most similar to Benaglia (in income, family composition, location, and the like) spent an average of $3,600 a year on food and lodging. What are the merits of taxing Benaglia on the following amounts?

(a) The retail value of the benefit ($7,800)
(b) The probable cost of alternative arrangements ($3,600)
(c) The current cost of the benefit to the hotel ($3,000)
(d) $0

2. Suppose that in a document discovered by the government and introduced into evidence at trial, Benaglia wrote that the sumptuous accommodations and free meals provided by the hotel were worth $4,600 to him, $1,000 more than the cost of alternative arrangements he would have made, but $3,200 less than their retail value. Suppose that in that same document Benaglia had revealed that he had rejected an offer to manage a hotel in Chicago in favor of his position in Hawaii. The Chicago job promised similar responsibilities, free food and lodging, and an additional $2,000 in cash salary. The Chicago job did not, of course, promise the weather of the Hawaiian job, and in the document Benaglia stated that the latter feature of the Hawaiian job was worth at least $1,000 a year to him. Should Benaglia be taxed on the $4,600 value he placed on the food and lodging? If so, should he be taxed on the $1,000 value he placed on the Hawaiian weather?

3. In *Benaglia,* the meals and lodging were provided in a hotel that was, at the time, one of the most luxurious in the world, located on the then-uncrowded, paradisiacal beach at Waikiki. Suppose, instead, that Benaglia was paid a reasonably good salary to manage a refuge for destitute seamen, located in a bad part of town, and was required to live there in a small, spartan apartment. Which of the alternatives discussed in Question 1 should be the touchstone of taxation? The retail value of the accommodations? The cost to the employer? The cost of alternative accommodations? Nothing?

4. (a) Assume that a corporate executive, *E*, has been living and working in Columbus, Ohio, where he rents a house for $12,000 per year. His employer wants to move him to its Los Angeles office. To rent a house in Los Angeles that is comparable to the one in Columbus (apart from the weather) *E* must pay $30,000 per year. The employer pays him an extra $18,000 as a "housing allowance" to induce him to move to Los Angeles. This added amount plainly is taxable under present law. Should it be? Should we compare *E* with other taxpayers in Los Angeles or with other taxpayers in Columbus?

(b) Suppose that instead of paying *E* a housing allowance, the employer buys a house and leases it to *E* for $12,000 per year. Comparable houses rent for $30,000. Should *E* be taxed on the difference between his rent and the rent of comparable houses?

(c) Suppose the employer decides that to promote its own image it wants *E* to live in a lavish house in the best part of town. It buys such a house and leases it to *E* for $12,000. Comparable houses rent for $60,000 per year. Should *E* be taxed on the difference between his $12,000 rent and the rent of comparable houses? Between the $12,000 rent and the $30,000 it would have taken to rent a house in Los Angeles comparable to the house *E* occupied in Columbus? Should nothing be included in his income by virtue of the transaction?

5. Review your responses to Questions 1 through 4. What general rule on employer-provided food and lodging seems most sensible?

6. Wagner & Metro is a large New York City law firm. There are many restaurants located within a few blocks of the law firm, but those restaurants are usually crowded and noisy at lunch time. The law firm has found that the billable hours of its associates increase if it provides lunch to them on its business premises. The firm provides a buffet lunch for associates each day. It deducts the cost. The associates are encouraged but not required to take advantage of the buffet lunch, and most of them do. May the associates exclude the value of such meals under §119?

7. Sally is a police officer who is on duty from 8 A.M. to 4 P.M. each day. Her employment contract requires that she remain on duty, available for calls and to the public, during her lunch break. The police department reimburses Sally for lunch expenses up to a maximum of $5 per day. A city ordinance setting out the terms of employment for police officers states that the meals are provided as "a working condition and not part of an officer's compensation." Must Sally include in her gross income the amount of her reimbursements?

8. What effect do you imagine §119 has on the way employees are compensated?

9. Carla, a contestant on a quiz show, wins a new car. The producer of the show received the car free from the manufacturer because of the advertising value to the manufacturer. The ordinary dealer cost of the

car was $20,000 and the "sticker" price was $25,000. Carla tried to sell the car, but the best offer she got was $19,000 and she decided to keep it. Plainly there was a valid business reason for using a car, rather than cash, as a prize on the show, just as in *Benaglia* there was a valid business reason for providing food and lodging. Does it follow that Carla should not be taxed on the value of the car? If not, what amount should be taxed?

3. Other Fringe Benefits

Fringe benefits are noncash benefits provided free, or at a below-market price, by an employer to an employee. Among the most important of such benefits are life insurance, medical insurance and payments, discounts on merchandise, parking, company cars, airline travel, club memberships, and tuition remissions. In many cases these benefits are a substitute for cash; they relieve employees of expenses they would otherwise incur and are intended as compensation. Yet all too often they have not been taxed, which explains in part why it is that over the years they became an increasingly important part of employee compensation. Fringe benefits raise problems of valuation, of enforcement, and of political acceptance.

The problems of valuation are similar to those we have already examined in this chapter. The value of a particular benefit to the person receiving it may depend on the circumstances of that person. Consider, for example, airline employees who are permitted to fly free, or at reduced cost, on their employers' flights. Is it fair to include in income the amount that ordinary passengers would be required to pay for the same flight? Even if employees are required to fly on a standby basis? Or what about life insurance supplied to a single person with no dependents? Or a government-owned limousine that drives the Commissioner of Internal Revenue from home to the office in the morning, to meetings around town during the day, and back home at night? Is it relevant that the limousine has a reading lamp and a telephone?

Problems of enforcement are associated with the fact that the individual items are often small and the information on which the tax outcome depends is easy to falsify. For example, suppose an employer supplies an employee with the free use of a car. The employee is supposed to include in income the value of his or her personal use of the car. Until recently, many employees simply ignored the matter; they reported no income at all. Others relied on unrealistic claims that their personal use was a small part of the total use. The Service, understandably concerned about deployment of limited resources, was lax in enforcement. As word of this reality got around, abuse increased. Ultimately it became clear that some action was required. Revenue was being lost. Perhaps more important was the effect on the morale of taxpayers who were compensated in cash and paid for their cars out of after-tax dollars and even on the morale of those who were cheating (on the "don't be dumb, everyone's doing it" theory) but felt uncomfortable about it. But there was resistance to change: No matter how unjustified a tax break may be, if people have relied on it for long enough they will resent giving it up and, if asked to do so, will complain to their representatives in Congress about how they are being unjustly treated, about the adverse economic effects of the proposed change and, in general, about how nobody respects or appreciates them. This is the problem of political acceptance.

Through the years, some fringe benefits were excluded as a result of the Service's inaction (e.g., parking supplied or paid for by an employer and air travel by airline employees) or acquiescence (e.g., tuition remission). Others were excluded by express statutory provisions, including $50,000 worth of group term life insurance (§79), medical insurance and payments (§§105(b), 106), and dependent care assistance (§129). Not until 1984 was there a set of rules providing comprehensive coverage of fringe benefits. The rules adopted in that year, now found in §132, are described below.

HOUSE REPORT ON THE TAX REFORM ACT OF 1984: FRINGE BENEFIT PROVISIONS

H.R. Rep. No. 432, pt. 2, 98th Cong., 2d Sess. 1590-1608 (1984)

B. Reasons for Change

In providing statutory rules for exclusion of certain fringe benefits for income and payroll tax purposes, the committee has attempted to strike a balance between two competing objectives.

First, the committee is aware that in many industries, employees may receive, either free or at a discount, goods and services which the employer sells to the general public. In many cases, these practices are long established, and have been treated by employers, employees, and the IRS as not giving rise to taxable income. Although employees may receive an economic benefit from the availability of these free or discounted goods or services, employers often have valid business reasons, other than simply providing compensation, for encouraging employees to avail themselves of the products which they sell to the public. For example, a retail clothing business will want its salespersons to wear, when they deal with customers, the clothing which it seeks to sell to the public. . . .

The second objective of the committee's bill is to set forth clear boundaries for the provision of tax-free benefits. . . .

C. Explanation of Provisions

1. overview

Under the bill, certain fringe benefits provided by an employer are excluded from the recipient employee's gross income for Federal income tax purposes and from the wage base (and, if applicable, the benefit base) for purposes of income tax withholding, FICA [Federal Insurance Contribution Act, the act requiring payments for Social Security retirement benefits], FUTA [Federal Unemployment Tax Act], and RRTA [Railroad Retirement Tax Act].

The excluded fringe benefits are those benefits that qualify under one of the following five categories as defined in the bill: (1) a no-additional-cost service, (2) a qualified employee discount, (3) a working condition fringe, (4) a de minimis fringe, and (5) a qualified tuition reduction. Special rules apply with respect to certain parking or eating facilities provided to employees, on-premises athletic facilities, and demonstration use of an employer-provided car by auto salespersons. Some of the exclusions under the bill apply to benefits provided to the spouse and dependent children of a current employee, to former employees who separated from service because of retirement or disability (and their spouses and dependent children), and to the widow(er) of a deceased employee (and the dependent children of deceased employees). . . .

Any fringe benefit that does not qualify for exclusion under the bill (for example, free or discounted goods or services which are limited to corporate officers) and that is not excluded under another statutory fringe benefit provision of the Code is taxable to the recipient under Code sections 61 and 83, and is includible in wages for employment tax purposes, at the excess of its fair market value over any amount paid by the employee for the benefit.

2. no-additional-cost service (sec. 502 of the bill and new code sec. 132(b))

General Rule

Under this category, the entire value of any no-additional-cost service provided by an employer to an employee for the use of the employee (or of the employee's spouse or dependent children) is excluded for income and employment tax purposes. . . .

To qualify under this exclusion, the employer must incur no substantial additional cost in providing the service to the employee, computed without regard to any amounts paid by the employee for the service. For this purpose, the term cost includes any revenue forgone because the service is furnished to the employee rather than to a non-employee. In addition, the service provided to the employee must be of the type which the employer offers for sale to nonemployee customers in the ordinary course of the line of business of the employer in which the employee is performing services.

Generally, situations in which employers incur no additional cost in providing services to employees are those in which the employees receive, at no substantial additional cost to the employer, the benefit of excess capacity which otherwise would have remained unused because nonemployee customers would not have purchased it. Thus, employers that furnish airline, railroad, or subway seats or hotel rooms to employees working in those lines of business in such a way that nonemployee customers are not displaced, and telephone companies that provide telephone service to employees within existing capacity, incur no substantial additional cost in the provision of these services to employees, as this term is used in the bill.

Line of Business Limitation

To be excluded under this category, a service must be the same type of service which is sold to the public in the ordinary course of the line of business of the employer in which the employee works. . . .

Under this limitation, for example, an employer which provides airline services and hotel services to the general public is considered to consist of two separate lines of business. As a consequence, the employees of the airline business of the employer may not exclude the value of free hotel rooms provided by the hotel business of the employer, and vice versa. The purpose of the line of business limitation is to avoid, to the extent possible, the competitive imbalances and inequities which would result from giving the employees of a conglomerate or other large employer with several lines of business a greater variety of tax-free benefits than could be given to the employees of a small employer with only one line of business. . . .

Definition of Employee

The bill provides that, with respect to a line of business of an employer, the term employee means (1) an individual who is currently employed by the employer in that line of business; (2) an individual who separated from service with the employer in that line of business by reason of retirement or disability; and (3) a widow or widower of an individual who died while employed by the employer in that line of business or of an individual who had separated from service with the employer in that line of business by reason of retirement or disability. The bill also provides that any use (e.g., of a standby airline flight) by the spouse or a dependent child of the employee (as so defined) is to be treated as use by the employee. These definitions are relevant both for purposes of eligibility for the exclusion under the bill and for purposes of defining nonemployee customers.

Examples

As an illustration of the no-additional-cost service category of excludable benefits, assume that a corporation which operates an airline as its only line of business provides all of its employees (and their spouses and dependent children) with free travel, on the same terms to all employees, as stand-by passengers on the employer airline if the space taken on the flight has not been sold to the public shortly before departure time. In such a case, the entire fair market value of the free travel is excluded under the no-additional-cost service rule in the bill. . . .

3. QUALIFIED EMPLOYEE DISCOUNT (SEC. 502 OF THE BILL AND NEW CODE SEC. 132 (C))

General Rule

Under the bill, certain employee discounts allowed from the selling price of qualified goods or services of the employer are excluded for income and employment tax purposes, but only if the discounts are available to employees on a nondiscriminatory basis (see description below of the nondiscrimination rules of the bill). The exclusion applies whether the qualified employee discount is provided through a reduction in price or through a cash rebate from a third party.

The exclusion is not available for discounts on any personal property (tangible or intangible) of a kind commonly held for investment or for discounts on any real property. Thus, for example, the exclusion does not apply to discounts on any employee purchases of securities, gold coins, residential or commercial real estate, or interests in mineral-producing property (regardless of whether a particular purchase is made for investment purposes). This limitation is provided because the committee does not believe that favorable tax treatment should be provided when noncash compensation is provided in the form of property which the employee could typically sell at close to the same price at which the employer sells the property to its nonemployee customers. . . .

Line of Business Limitation

To qualify under this exclusion, the goods or services on which the discount is available must be those which are offered for sale by the employer to nonemployee customers in the ordinary course of the employer's line of business in which the employee works. . . .

Amount of Exclusion

General rule. Under the bill, an employee discount is excluded only up to a specified limit. In the case of merchandise, the excludable amount of the discount is limited to the selling price of the merchandise, multiplied by the employer's gross profit percentage. The discount exclusion for a service may not exceed 20 percent of the selling price, regardless of the actual gross profit percentage. . . .

4. WORKING CONDITION FRINGE (SEC. 502 OF THE BILL AND NEW CODE SEC. 132(D))

General Rules

Under the bill, the fair market value of any property or services provided to an employee of the employer is excluded for income and employment tax purposes to the extent that the costs of the property or services would be deductible as ordinary and necessary business expenses (under Code secs. 162 or 167) if the employee had paid for such property or services. The nondiscrimination rules applicable to certain other provisions of Title V of the bill do not apply as a condition for exclusion as a working condition fringe. . . .

Examples

By way of illustration, the value of use by an employee of a company car or airplane for business purposes is excluded as a working condition fringe. (However, use of a company car or plane for personal purposes is not excludable. Merely incidental personal use of a company car, such as a small detour for a personal errand, might qualify for exclusion as a de minimis fringe.) As another example, assume the employer subscribes to business periodicals for an employee (e.g., a brokerage house buys a financial publication for its brokers). In that case, the fair market value of the subscriptions is an excluded working condition fringe, since the expense could have been deducted as a business expense if the employee had directly paid for the subscription.

Examples of other benefits excluded as working condition fringes are those provided by an employer primarily for the safety of its employees, if such safety precautions are considered ordinary and necessary business expenses. . . .

5. DE MINIMIS FRINGE (SEC. 502 OF THE BILL AND NEW CODE SEC. 132(E))

General Rules

Under the bill, if the fair market value of any property or a service that otherwise would be a fringe benefit includible in gross income is so small that accounting for the property or service would be unreasonable or administratively impracticable, the value is excluded for income and employment tax purposes. The nondiscrimination rules applicable to certain other provisions of the bill do not apply as a condition for exclusion of property or a service as a de minimis fringe, except for subsidized eating facilities (as described below). . . .

To illustrate benefits which generally are excluded from income and employment taxes as de minimis fringes (without regard to the aggregation rule) include the typing of personal letters by a company secretary, occasional personal use of the company copying machine, monthly transit passes provided at a discount not exceeding $15, occasional company cocktail parties or picnics for employees, occasional supper money or taxi fare because of overtime work, traditional holiday gifts of property with a low fair market value, occasional theatre or sporting event tickets, and coffee and doughnuts furnished to employees. . . .

7. ATHLETIC FACILITIES (SEC. 502 OF THE BILL AND NEW CODE SEC. 132(H)(5))[9]

In general, the fair market value of any on-premises athletic facility provided and operated by an employer for its employees, where substantially all the use of the facility is by employees of the employer (or their spouses or dependent children), is excluded under the bill for income and employment tax purposes. The athletic facility need not be in the same location as the business premises of the employer, but must be located on premises of the employer and may not be a facility for residential use. Examples of athletic facilities are swimming pools, gyms, tennis courts, and golf courses.

The exclusion for certain employer-provided athletic facilities does not apply to the providing of memberships in a country club or similar facility unless the facility itself is owned and operated by the employer and satisfies the employee-use and other requirements for the exclusion. Thus, where no exclusion is available under this provision, the fair market value of such country club membership is includible in the income of the employee who is provided with membership, and is deductible to the extent permitted by present-law sections 162 and 274.

A nondiscrimination requirement is not provided in the bill as a condition for this exclusion, because present law (Code sec. 274) denies a deduction to the employer for costs attributable to a facility which is primarily for the benefit of officers, owners, or highly compensated employees.

8. NONDISCRIMINATION RULES

To qualify under the bill for the exclusions for no-additional-cost services, qualified employee discounts, . . . or eating facilities, or quali-

9. [This provision is now found in §132(j)(4) — Eds.]

fied tuition reductions, the benefit must be available on substantially the same terms to each member of a group of employees which is defined under a reasonable classification set up by the employer that does not discriminate in favor of officers, owners, or highly compensated employees (the "highly compensated group"). If the availability of the fringe benefit does not satisfy this nondiscrimination test, the exclusion applies only to those employees (if any) who receive the benefit and who are not members of the highly compensated group. For example, if an employer offers a 20-percent discount (which otherwise satisfies the requirements for a qualified employee discount) to rank-and-file employees and a 35-percent discount to the highly compensated group, the entire value of the 35-percent discount (not just the excess over 20 percent) is includible in gross income and wages of the members of the highly compensated group who make purchases at a discount. . . .

Also of some relevance to fringe benefits is §280F, added in 1984 and amended in 1985 and 1986, which substantially limited the cost recovery deduction (ACRS) and investment credit for "luxury" automobiles. In justifying the original House version of this provision, the House Report on the Tax Reform Act of 1984, H.R. Rep. No. 432, 98th Cong., 2d Sess. 1387 (1984), states that "the investment incentives afforded by the investment credit and ACRS should be directed to capital formation, rather than to subsidize the element of personal consumption associated with the use of very expensive automobiles." Do you think that an executive who drives an expensive car, strictly for business, receives a benefit that should be taxed? What about an executive who flies first class or who stays at first-class hotels while on business trips?

NOTES

1. *Qualified transportation fringes.* Under §132(f), added to §132 in 1992, an employee may exclude from income, as a de minimis fringe benefit, employer-provided parking (including parking near carpool pick-up locations) or mass transit passes, or employer reimbursement for the cost of parking or mass transit. The maximum value that may be excluded per month per employee is $155 in the case of parking and $60 in the case of mass transit passes. Both amounts are to be adjusted upward to reflect inflation, beginning in 1994.

2. *Valuation: the regulations.* The Treasury has now published regulations on fringe benefits. Regs. §1.61-21 and §1.132-1 to -8. These regulations include rules for valuation of certain fringe benefits, most

significantly the personal use of employer-provided aircraft and automobiles. The basic valuation rule is that the amount to be included is "fair market value." Regs. §1.61-21(b). Special optional "safe-harbor" valuation formulas are provided, however, for aircraft and automobiles, and it can be expected that most employers and employees will use these formulas. For automobiles there is a table that provides an "annual lease value" based on the value of the automobile. Regs. §1.61-21. There is a special rule for situations in which the personal use of the automobile is commuting and "for bona fide noncompensatory reasons, the employer requires the employee to commute to and/or from work in the vehicle" (e.g., so that the vehicle can be used on emergency calls at night or to keep the vehicle safe from thieves and vandals). In this situation, the value is treated as $3 per round trip. Regs. §1.61-21(f). For aircraft, the formula consists of the Standard Industry Fare Level (SIFL), plus a terminal charge, multiplied by a factor based on the weight of the aircraft.[10] Regs. §1.61-21(g). The regulations respond to the particular circumstances of a variety of employment situations and contain myriad special rules for those circumstances. While the rules are lengthy and detailed, individual employers and employees will generally be able to focus on the relatively few rules relevant to them. A reading of the regulations will provide a good sense of the interplay between the need to impose fair tax burdens and prevent tax avoidance and the need to have common-sense, workable rules.

3. *Cafeteria plans.* A "cafeteria plan" is a plan under which an employee may choose among a variety of noncash nontaxable benefits or may choose to take cash (which is, of course, taxable). In other words, an employee may in effect elect to reduce his or her taxable salary and take noncash benefits instead. This makes it possible for an employer to provide nontaxable fringe benefits to those employees who want them without being unfair to employees who have no need for them. For example, suppose an employer has two employees, each earning $35,000 a year. One employee has children and pays $5,000 a year to baby-sitters while he is at work. The other employee has no children. Under a cafeteria plan, the employer can allow the employee with children to take his compensation in the form of $30,000 worth of taxable salary and $5,000 worth of child-care payments (nontaxable under §129). Meanwhile, the other employee can elect to take the entire $35,000 in salary; all of this is taxable, but he is no worse off than he would be if there were no cafeteria plan. The employer is allowed to deduct the full $35,000 for each employee.

10. For the first half of 1993, the terminal charge was $30.62 and the SIFL was $.1675 per mile for the first 500 miles, $.1277 per mile for miles between 501 and 1,500, and $.1228 per mile for miles over 1,500. Rev. Rul. 93-95, I.R.B. 1993-19.

Section 125 expressly authorizes cafeteria plans. Were it not for that provision, the doctrine of constructive receipt would result in an employee being taxed on the cash that he or she could have taken, even if a nontaxable benefit were chosen instead. In other words, without §125, cafeteria plans in which there was an option to take cash would not be tax effective. (It would still be possible to have plans under which the only alternatives were various nontaxable fringe benefits.) Section 125 greatly increases the potential use of nontaxable fringe benefits by removing the element of employee envy that would restrain an employer from offering fringe benefits for which some employees have no use.

Section 125 limits the fringe benefits that can be included in a cafeteria plan and imposes a nondiscrimination rule. The permissible benefits include group-term life insurance (up to $50,000) (§79), accident and health insurance (§106), and dependent care (§129).

The Treasury has issued proposed regulations for cafeteria plans. Proposed Regs. §1.125-1. Perhaps the most interesting and controversial of the proposals is a "use-it-or-lose-it" rule. Under this rule, if, for example, an employee elects at the beginning of the year to take $5,000 worth of child-care reimbursement instead of the same amount of cash compensation or other benefits, any part of the $5,000 not used for child care will be lost to the employee. The unused portion cannot at the end of the year be paid out to the employee as additional taxable compensation or carried forward to the next year. There is an exception allowing a change in election of benefits or cash during the year on account of, and consistent with, a change in family status (e.g., marriage, divorce, or death of a child). The rationale offered by the Treasury in support of the use-it-or-lose-it rule is that nontaxable benefits under cafeteria plans are supposed to be in the nature of insurance. Why so? There is some evidence in testimony by Treasury officials before Congress of concern about the substantial loss of revenue associated with increasing use of cafeteria plans. Were it not for this concern, would it not make sense, as long as one is prepared to accept §125, to go one step further and allow all taxpayers simply to deduct amounts spent for child care or for the other benefits available under cafeteria plans? Is the congressional interest in imposing rules of nondiscrimination under §125 a persuasive argument against such a suggestion?

4. *Employer deduction.* One of the barriers to taxing employees on fringe benefits is that often the value to each employee is small and difficult to determine — for example, the value of meals supplied to employees at a company cafeteria. One way to respond to this problem is to ignore the income to the employees but deny the employer a deduction for the amount of the subsidy — that is, the amount by which the cost of the meals exceeds the payments received from employees. The effect is to treat the employer, for taxpaying purposes, as a sur-

rogate for the employees. Another possibility is to impose a special tax on the amount of the subsidy, using a rate intended to approximate the rate at which the employees would be taxed. One problem with this approach is that it may be difficult to explain to people why one person should be denied a deduction, or pay a tax, because another person may have income. Another is that the denial of a deduction is ineffective when the employer is not taxable (either because it shows a loss for tax purposes or because it is a governmental, charitable, or other nontaxable entity).

5. *Benefits from other than employer.* Suppose that a school principal receives unsolicited sample books from the publishers. Even if the books could be sold, it would not seem proper to include the value of the books in the gross income of the principal. After all, they are not items for personal consumption, nor do they provide the wherewithal to acquire consumption items, except by trade or barter. And even if the value of the books were included in income, an offsetting deduction for the same amount, as a business expense (§162), might seem appropriate. Accordingly, exclusion seems sensible. On the other hand, if the books are sold, the proceeds surely should be included in income. If the taxpayer gives the books to a charity (e.g., the school's library) and claims their value as a deduction, it is as if they had been sold and the proceeds given to charity. Any amount allowed as a charitable deduction should be included in income. It was so held in Haverly v. United States, 513 F.2d 224 (7th Cir.), cert. denied, 423 U.S. 912 (1975). In Rev. Rul. 70-498, 1970-2 C.B. 6, the Service ruled that sample books (received by a book reviewer for a newspaper) would be taxable only if the taxpayer donated them to charity and claimed a deduction for that donation.

QUESTIONS

What tax treatment is required by §132 in each of the following situations?

1. *F,* a flight attendant in the employ of *A,* an airline company, and *F*'s spouse decide to spend their 1993 annual vacation in Europe. *A* has a policy whereby any of its employees, along with members of their immediate families, may take a number of personal flights annually for a nominal charge, on a standby basis. *F* and *F*'s spouse take advantage of this policy and fly to and from Europe. See Regs. §1.132-2(b)(5).

2. *P* is the president of *C,* a corporation that has its executive offices situated in New York City. *P* is planning a week-long business trip to Los Angeles and will fly there and back on *C*'s corporate jet. *P*'s spouse intends to accompany *P* on the round trip flight for personal reasons.

3. *B* is an officer in the employ of *C,* a manufacturing company. *C*

provides personalized financial planning services to all of its officers without charge.

4. Corporation *F* provides brokerage and financial planning services to customers. *F* offers those same services to employees at a 20 percent discount. The 20 percent discount represents *F*'s profit margin on the services. Thus, after taking account of the discount, the services are offered to employees at *F*'s cost. See Regs. §132(c)(1)(B).

5. The facts are the same as in Question 4 except that the services are also available to the employee's spouse, parents, and children.

6. The facts are the same as in Question 4 except that the services are offered at a 50 percent discount and the 50 percent discount represents *F*'s profit margin on the services. Thus, after taking account of the discount, the services are offered to employees at cost.

7. *S,* a senior vice president of *D,* a retail department store, purchases a refrigerator from *D*'s appliance department. *D* has a policy whereby all employees are entitled to a 20 percent discount from the ticketed sales price of any item sold by the store so long as the resulting sales price, on average, approximately covers *D*'s costs. See §132(c), Regs. §1.132-3(c).

8. The facts are the same as in Question 7 except that *D*'s profit margin on ticketed items is only 10 percent, so the resultant sales price does not cover *D*'s costs.

9. The facts are the same as in Question 7 except that *S* and all other employees are entitled to a 50 percent discount from the ticketed sale price. The 50 percent discount represents *D*'s profit margin, so that the goods are sold to employees at cost.

10. The facts are the same as in Question 7 except that the discount is available only to *S* and other officers of *D*.

11. *M* is a maintenance worker employed by *C,* a manufacturing corporation. While changing a light fixture, *M* falls from a ladder and sustains several minor cuts and bruises. *M* receives first aid from an on-site emergency health unit maintained by *C*. Such services are available to all of *C*'s employees who either are injured or become ill while working on the job. See §132(e)(1).

12. The facts are the same as in Question 11. In addition, based on the recommendation of health unit personnel, *C* sends *M* home and pays for the cab fare. Such payment is pursuant to company policy whereby *C* will pay the cost of an injured or ill employee's transportation home.

13. *A,* an assistant manager in the employ of *D,* a department store, is occasionally required to work overtime to help mark down merchandise for special sales. On those occasional instances, *D* pays for the actual cost of *A*'s evening meal. Such payment is pursuant to company policy whereby *D* will pay the actual, reasonable meal expense of a management-level employee when such an expense is incurred in connection

with the performance of services either before or after such an employee's regular business hours.

14. *E*, an executive employed by *M*, a multinational corporation, has been promoted to president of *S*, one of *M*'s foreign subsidiaries. The country in which *S* is located has been beset by terrorist activity. Major targets of such activity are Americans who are employed by American-owned corporations doing business in that country. In order to protect these employees, the American corporations have instituted a number of security measures. For example, a heavily guarded residential compound has been established within which all American employees and their families must live. Additionally, residents traveling outside the compound are always accompanied by armed security personnel.

15. *S*, a senior partner of *L*, a law firm, is provided free parking by the law firm. This benefit is provided by *L* to all partners, associates, and other employees. The parking privilege has a value of $75 per month. See §132(f), Regs. §1.132-1(b).

16. The facts are the same as in Question 15 except that *S* is given a choice of whether to accept parking or $75 a month and *S* accepts the parking.

17. The facts are the same as in Question 15 except that the parking is available only to partners and associates of the law firm.

18. *A* is an associate in the employ of *L*, a prominent law firm located in a large city. In order to encourage participation in community activities and local society, *L* pays its associates' membership fees for various local clubs and organizations. *A*, taking advantage of this policy, joins a prestigious country club.

19. *A*, an attorney in the employ of *C*, a corporation, works at *C*'s national headquarters. *C* maintains an on-site gymnasium which is available to all employees during normal business hours. *A* uses the gymnasium each working day.

4. Economic Effects: An Example

Suppose an employer is willing to provide employees with parking during working hours at the place of employment, which costs the employer $50 per month. Suppose further that the parking is worth only $40 per month to a particular employee (who would take the bus or join a carpool if a payment of more than $40 were required). Suppose, finally, that the employer is willing either to provide the parking or pay the employee $50 per month. Either way, the employer will spend and will be able to deduct $50, so even after tax effects are accounted for, the employer is indifferent concerning the two options. The question is, what are the economic effects of a tax system under which the employee is taxed on the cash payment but not on the noncash benefit (the parking)?

First, assume that there is no income tax at all; assume, that is, a no-tax world. Plainly the employee would choose the $50 cash, with which he or she could buy goods or services worth that amount to him or her. If the employer were to provide the parking, it would be paying $50 for a benefit worth only $40 to the employee. There would be a waste of $10. But that won't happen.

Next assume that we have an income tax system under which the cash payment is taxable but parking is not, and suppose that the combined state and federal marginal tax rate of the employee is 40 percent. Now, if the employee takes the cash, he or she will pay a tax of $20 and will have only $30 left. If, on the other hand, the employee takes the parking, there will be no tax; the net benefit will be the $40 value of the parking. So the employee will take the parking, worth only $40 to him or her, despite the fact that it costs the employer $50 to provide it. There appears to be a waste of $10. Economists call this a "deadweight loss."

So far we have established that a tax system with an exclusion of the value of the parking seems to produce a perverse outcome. The next question is, what about a tax system that taxes the employee on the employer's cost of the parking? Suppose, then, that there is an income tax but that the employer's cost of the parking is included in the employee's income. In this situation there will be no distortion (no deadweight loss). The employee can take either the parking or the cash. Either way, the tax will be $20. So we can forget about the tax; it is a constant. Since the tax is a constant, the employee will take the cash. There will be no deadweight loss.

Another way of arriving at the same result is to observe that if both cash and parking are taxed, the employee can take the parking (worth $40, but valued for tax purposes at $50) and pay a tax of $20, leaving a net benefit of $20, or take the cash ($50) and pay the tax of $20, leaving a net benefit of $30. The employee will choose cash and the employer will not supply a noncash benefit whose cost is higher than its value to the employee.

Suppose that the employee is taxed only on the $40 value of the parking, rather than its cost of $50. If that is the rule, again the result is no distortion, but the demonstration gets a bit more difficult. If the employee takes the parking, the value of the benefit is $40 and the tax is $16. The net benefit is $24. If the cash is taken, the benefit is $50 and the tax is $20 for a net benefit of $30. The cash will be chosen and there will be no distortion. To put that another way, if the cash is taken, the tax rises by $4 but the value of the benefit rises by $10. The relative difficulty of analysis arises from the fact that two variables change at the same time. But the result is the same.

Of course, Congress might decide, despite all this, that parking benefits should be tax free because it wants to encourage commuting by private automobile (perhaps as an aid to the automobile industry), because it wants to encourage the use of land for parking lots, or for some other such reason. Comparison of the world with taxes with an imaginary world without taxes may be helpful in identifying and describing the economic consequences of taxes, but it is an unreliable guide to tax policy. What is important is that members of Congress and their advisors be clear in our own minds about what they are doing with the tax system. In the case of parking, it is reasonable to suppose that under the present rule (excluding the value of parking from the employee's income) employees whose parking is free may use parking space that is worth less to them than its market value (that is, its value to others) and that this would not happen under a rule that treats the value of the parking as income subject to taxation. We can also expect that under the rule excluding the value of parking there will be greater use of private automobiles for commuting to work than there would be under a rule including that value. It is difficult to imagine that in this era of concern for traffic congestion, air pollution, and energy conservation Congress would consciously adopt a provision with that kind of economic incentive.[11] What we see, then, is a good example of how rules with presumably undesirable economic effects can become part of our tax law unless we are alert to those effects.

The possibility of undesirable economic effects of employer-provided free parking is not just the idle speculation of ivory-tower intellectuals. Professor Donald C. Shoup presents the following data:

> An astonishing number of cars park free at work even in central business districts where parking is most expensive. For example, in 1974, slightly over half the 100,000 cars commuting to downtown Los Angeles parked free, although the market price of parking averaged $35 a month; in 1976, almost half the 140,000 cars commuting to downtown Washington, D.C. parked free, although the market price of parking averaged $50 a month. Nationwide, 90 percent of the labor force commutes to work in private vehicles, and 75 percent of them park free in employer-paid, offstreet parking spaces.

Cashing Out Parking, 36 Transportation Q. 351 (1982).

Professor Shoup goes on to cite two studies of the effect of free parking. One study compared two similar groups of government employees in downtown Los Angeles and found that among the group

11. The federal government has, however, provided most of the funds for construction of urban freeways, and local governments have in various ways encouraged development of both the suburbs and (more recently) of downtown shopping and business areas, actions that seem to have encouraged the use of private automobiles.

that paid for parking 40 percent drove to work alone, while in the group that did not pay, 72 percent did so. The other study found that in Ottawa, Canada, when the government stopped providing free parking to its employees the number driving to work alone fell by 20 percent. After an interesting discussion of the effects of free parking on the transportation system, urban form, air quality, fuel consumption, and fairness, Professor Shoup proposes that we allow employers to offer tax-free cash in lieu of free parking. This, he claims, "would encourage ridesharing by eliminating free parking's almost irresistible invitation to drive to work alone." Id. at 352. Section 132(f)(5), which allows an employer to offer $60.00 a month tax-free in mass transit assistance in lieu of free parking is a step in the right direction. See discussion on page 107 supra.

One should be cautious, however, about the foregoing analysis of free parking and its implications. It rests in part on an unstated assumption that the choice of whether to drive to work and pay for parking or take mass transit (or carpool) is a personal rather than a business decision. That assumption is not free from doubt. See infra page 592. For many employers the cost of supplying parking is small — for example, a manufacturing firm with a plant at the outskirts of a small town, with parking in a large, open lot. Presumably if free parking were treated as a taxable benefit, the amount included in the income of the employees of such a firm would be trivial. If that is so, why is it that a person who works in a central business district should be taxed on the much higher value of free parking in an underground parking lot of a building owned and occupied by the employer? or in a space rented in a garage next door to the building occupied by the employer? And what about employees who live in areas without adequate mass transit, and whose work schedules prohibit carpooling? Maybe parking should be considered a cost of earning income and, as such, as a proper deduction in arriving at net income. If so, exclusion of free parking would be the correct treatment and taxation would be considered a burden or penalty. Suppose that an associate in a law firm drives to work and thereafter uses her automobile to drive to court and that the firm pays for the parking near the court building. Should that free parking be treated as part of the associate's income? If, so, should there be an offsetting deduction as a business expense? Suppose we know that if the value of the parking near the court building were included in the associate's income, with no offsetting deduction, she would take public transportation. Would you characterize a rule excluding the value of the parking from income as a "subsidy" or "encouragement" to the use of private transportation? When a manufacturer is allowed to deduct the cost of raw materials, is that a "subsidy" to the use of those raw materials? What, if anything, is different about the use of an automobile by our hypothetical associate?

5. Interest-Free Loans

A common problem in tax law is that transactions may be structured (consciously or not) in ways that do not fully reflect the underlying economic reality, with the result that, if the form of the transaction is respected, appropriate tax treatment is not achieved. In these situations it is often necessary to imagine a putative transaction that adequately reflects the economic reality and to tax the parties as if their transaction had followed the putative form. This process is reflected in the treatment of interest-free loans, where it may be necessary to tax the lenders as if they had received interest income, and borrowers as if they had paid it, even though in fact they did not.

Suppose that Peggy is a doctor with a high income; that she has a son, Sam, who is about to go to college and needs $15,000 a year for his tuition and expenses; and that she has $200,000 invested in a savings account on which she earns $15,000 a year. Peggy can, of course, leave the $200,000 in the savings account, collect the $15,000 in interest, and turn it over to Sam, but then she must pay tax, at her marginal rate, on that $15,000. Suppose instead that she withdraws the $200,000 from her savings account and lends it to Sam, interest free. Sam then puts the money into a savings account and collects the $15,000 interest, on which he pays tax at his relatively low rate. It seems fair to say that if the interest-free-loan route is followed, Peggy's and Sam's positions are not much different, except for taxes, than they would be if Peggy had kept the money, earned the interest herself, and given the $15,000 to Sam. Either way, Peggy accomplishes her objective of supporting Sam in college. It is hard to imagine, in this kind of case, why a parent would make use of the interest-free loan except for tax considerations. In other words, the interest-free loan is a clever tax-avoidance scheme. It is a scheme that many taxpayers caught on to in the early 1980s. In 1984, Congress, with the enactment of §7872, deprived the scheme of its tax advantage. The technique adopted in §7872 is, in effect, to tax the interest-free loan transaction as if the loan had been made at arm's length, with provision for interest at the "applicable federal rate" (which is likely to be higher than what Peggy can earn on a safe investment). Thus, if Peggy makes the interest-free loan to Sam, Peggy is treated as having received interest from Sam and is taxed on that interest. §7872(a)(1). She is then treated as having returned the interest to Sam as a nontaxable gift. Sam is treated as having paid the interest and can claim a deduction for the amount paid, and thereby offset the interest he earns, subject to §163(d), which limits the interest deduction to the amount of interest earned. In fact, §7872 is not applied often to parent-child loans; once it was adopted people stopped making such loans and returned to using more normal financial arrangements. Because interest-free loans were used to shift income to a family member in a lower tax bracket, our discussion of this technique, and the legislative reaction, might be deferred until our discussion of income shifting in Chapter 7. We cover this topic here because the use of interest-free loans provides a good example of the varied and often hidden nature of noncash benefits. In the above hypothetical, the hidden benefit went to the family member who made the loan, who was relieved of responsibility for providing for college education for her son. Since the mother owns the principal of $200,000 it is the mother, as a practical matter, who earns the interest of $15,000, which she gives to her son. The focus in this chapter is on the fact that the mother earns, but attempts to hide, income. The focus in Chapter 7 is on the effort to shift income from parent to child.

B. IMPUTED INCOME

People may use their property or their own services to provide benefits directly to themselves or to members of their households — for example, when they occupy houses that they own, when they care for their own children, or when they prepare their own tax returns. The benefits they derive are not part of any commercial transaction. Experts refer to these kinds of benefits as "imputed income." That terminology may cause some confusion since the ordinary person probably does not think of the benefits as "income" and generally they are not in fact treated as income for tax purposes. Nonetheless, it can be demonstrated that failure to include these benefits in income produces serious problems of fairness and economic rationality. As one might guess, the reason why we seem to be stuck with these problems is that inclusion of the benefits in the calculation of individual income is assumed to be impractical.

1. Property

(a) The best and most significant example of imputed income from property is the owner-occupied home. The imputed income is simply the rental value of that home. It is the same kind of benefit that we examined in *Benaglia* (supra page 89, involving the manager of the Royal Hawaiian Hotel). An illustration will reveal this similarity and will uncover a complexity arising from the fact that a home in this era is not just a source of personal benefit but an investment as well.

To begin, imagine that there are two taxpayers, *A* and *B*, each earning $50,000 per year. Each inherits $100,000, which is received tax free. §102(a). *A* invests the $100,000 in U.S. Treasury bonds that pay her $8,000 per year. She continues to live in a modest apartment. Her income will be $58,000; there is no deduction for rent, since it is a personal expense. See §262.

B uses his $100,000 to buy a house next door, and virtually identical, to *A*'s. He figures that in the first year he will earn a return of $5,000 in the form of the rent that he saves plus $3,000 from the increase in value he expects. His return, like *A*'s, will be 8 percent. But his income for tax purposes will be only his $50,000 salary. The $8,000 return on the investment in the house will escape taxation. The $5,000 rental value is imputed income. It is never taxed. The other $3,000, the increase in value of the house, is unrealized income (see supra page 56) and is taxed only on ultimate sale of the house, if at all (see §121).

This is unfair to *A*. *B*'s and *A*'s economic positions are essentially the same; each has essentially the same ability to pay. But *A* is taxed on $58,000 while *B* is taxed on only $50,000. To the extent of the $5,000 imputed rental income, this unfairness is associated with the failure to include the $5,000 rental value in *B*'s income — or to allow *A* a deduction for her rental payment. So far, however, the facts are unrealistic in one important respect. *A* earns an 8 percent taxable return, while *B* earns an 8 percent untaxed return. People like *A* will soon awaken to reality and will begin to emulate *B*. They will buy houses, which will drive up the price and drive down the rate of return. As this happens, the after-tax return to people like *B* will fall. The after-tax difference between people like *A* and *B* will diminish. Moreover, any claim of unfairness by *A* can be blunted by pointing out that she was entirely free to make the same kind of investment made by *B* — or to make some other tax-favored investment. Even if fairness is not a problem, however, we will find that we have encouraged investment in owner-occupied housing — without any prior conscious, deliberate consideration of the wisdom of doing so.

(b) While *A* may be free to pursue the tax advantage seized by *B*, there are others who may not have the same option unless they borrow. For example, imagine a taxpayer, *C*, with a salary of $58,000 and no inheritance. Suppose that *C* is able to borrow $100,000 to buy a house just like *B*'s, at an interest rate of 8 percent or $8,000 per year. If *C* is allowed to deduct the amount of interest paid, her position will be the same as *B*'s. Her income subject to taxation will be $50,000 ($58,000 less the $8,000 interest payment), and she will have imputed income of $5,000 plus unrealized gain of $3,000. But then *A* may have further cause for complaint of unfairness. Both *B* and *C* now are treated better than *A* (though, again, only because *A* has not had the wit to engage in effective tax planning). Or perhaps the effect of the tax incentives on investment behavior will tend to eliminate any unfairness, but only at the cost of questionable economic effects. Many economists in recent years have argued that the trouble with our economy is in part attributable to the fact that the tax system has induced people to invest in housing when they should invest instead in the tools of production. "Sound farfetched? A tortured argument by someone pushing a tax reform scheme? Not a bit. Merely a way of showing the effect of the tax system on behavior." Baldwin, Where Will the Money Come From?, Forbes, Sept. 14, 1981, at 150, 153.

(c) Often it is asserted that the treatment of homeowners (the deductibility of interest, plus the deductibility of property tax, and the nontaxation of imputed income) discriminates against renters. It is worth noting, however, that the tax system may, in some circumstances, provide significant tax benefits to landlords, mainly in the form of deductions for "cost recovery" that may be unrelated to economic reality (see supra page 56). Presumably these tax benefits to some significant degree are passed through to tenants in the form of lower rents (though to some significant extent the tax benefits may simply drive up the price of land and existing buildings). If people who rent to others are entitled to these deductions, then if we were to tax homeowners on their imputed income, should we not allow them offsetting cost recovery deductions? That is, if *B* is treated as his own landlord, is he not entitled to the same deductions that are available to other landlords? For homeowners whose cost of buying their homes is close to the present market value, the result could be an imputed loss rather than imputed income.

(d) The reason people usually give for not taxing imputed income from home ownership is that it would be impractical to do so because of problems of valuation. What would be wrong with including in income an amount equal to a percentage of the value of the house? The critical issue then would be the value of the house itself rather than its rental value. We do value houses for purposes of local property taxes and seem to think that the results are tolerable despite all the obvious problems.

(e) It should be clear that the kind of benefit that people derive from their investments in their principal residences will also be derived from their investments in vacation homes, in yachts, and in a wide variety of consumer durables. If one were intent on taxing the imputed income from ownership of principal residences, would it follow that we must also tax the imputed income from all these other investments, or at least those of any significant size? Where would you draw the line?

(f) A recent phenomenon of some importance in the marketing and ownership of resort developments is the "time share." There are many variations, but essentially what happens in time-sharing is that a number of individuals buy shares in a particular unit (an apartment, condominium apartment, hotel room, or what have you), with each owner entitled to use the unit for a given period of time. For example, a particular unit at a resort might be divided into fifty shares, with fifty separate owners each entitled to use the unit for one week (and two weeks set aside for maintenance). It is interesting to speculate on why this kind of arrangement might be attractive to an investor as compared with simply renting a unit when it is wanted. The time-share approach may produce economies to users by virtue of the fact that there are no vacancies or rental costs, but there are corresponding disadvantages to the user in being pinned down to a particular resort and time (though in some time-share plans there is flexibility as to the time of use). But it is not unreasonable to assume that tax considerations play an important role. Ownership of a time-share provides on a reduced level the kinds of imputed income available in greater amount to the more affluent people who can afford to own the year-round use of vacation homes.

(g) A point made in connection with the initial discussion of owner-occupied housing deserves emphasis. The person who borrows to invest in a personal residence relies on a combination of two tax rules: (1) the nontaxation of imputed income and (2) the deductibility of the interest payment. On the tax return, the favored tax position shows up simply as the interest deduction, and much of the discussion of the tax bias in favor of home ownership focuses on this aspect of the phenomenon. But the bias could be ended by taxing the imputed income. If the imputed income were taxed, the interest deduction would be entirely justified since the interest would be the cost of producing taxable income. Thus, the tax benefit at issue in the case of debt-financed personal residences is part of a broader category of benefits achieved by taxpayers who borrow money to invest in tax-favored investments. For all such debt-financed investments, one must ask whether it would be appropriate to disallow the interest deduction and thereby limit the advantages of the tax-favored investment to those taxpayers who can afford to acquire them without borrowing.

2. Services

(a) Suppose that a nurse works overtime to earn enough money so he can afford to hire someone to paint his house. Obviously, the nurse will pay income tax on the amount earned in the overtime work. If, on the other hand, the nurse decides to forgo the overtime work and stay home and paint his own house, the value of the time he devotes to the project will not count as income. The benefit of the services that one performs for oneself is called imputed income, and the failure to tax that benefit produces the same kinds of problems encountered in connection with imputed income from home ownership. First, there is unfairness: The nurse who performs services for others, as a nurse, and uses his wages to hire housepainting services will pay more tax than an otherwise similar person who does not work overtime and instead performs housepainting services for himself. Second, there is economic distortion or malallocation: The nurse may put in time as a housepainter even though, disregarding taxes, his time is more valuable when he works as a nurse and even though he would rather work overtime as a nurse than paint his house. The tax system reduces the value *to him* (though not to others) of his time as a nurse but does not similarly reduce the value to him of his time as a housepainter (for himself), which means that he may choose to paint his house even though his productivity as a nurse is greater than his productivity painting his house.[12]

This does not mean that we should tax the imputed income. Indeed, overwhelming considerations of practicality, privacy, public comprehension, and enforcement make any suggestion that we tax such benefits seem patently unsound. But to conclude that the benefit should not be taxed is not to deny that nontaxation offends principles of fairness and of economic rationality.

(b) It may be difficult to take seriously problems arising from such services as painting one's house, shining one's shoes, or filling one's gas tank. There is, however, another set of services that cannot be dismissed so readily: the services performed essentially full time for the members of one's household, usually by women — in other words, the services of homemakers.[13] These services raise an important tax issue because they are of substantial value and are not evenly distributed among households. Again, we find problems both of fairness and of unfortunate economic effects. Imagine, for example, two couples, each with two children. With the first couple, one spouse works and earns $40,000 while the other stays at home and performs services in caring for the

12. Suppose for example that the nurse can earn $20 per hour as a nurse; that is the value that society places on his services. If his tax rate is, say, 40 percent, he nets only $12 per hour. Suppose that a housepainter would charge $15 per hour, which is, again, the value that society places on those services. Assume that the nurse can do the housepainting job just as efficiently as the housepainter and has no aversion to the work (or at least no more aversion than to overtime nursing). The nurse will be better off to do his own housepainting than to work as a nurse and hire a housepainter, and will presumably wind up doing the housepainting job for himself. Thus, a $20-per-hour person performs a $15-per-hour job even though there is ample demand for the $20-per-hour services. There is a $5-per-hour deadweight loss.

13. In recent years nontax law has increasingly taken account of the value of the services of homemakers. For example, in In re Marriage of Lieb, 80 Cal. App. 3d 629, 145 Cal. Rptr. 763 (1978), the court reduced an ex-husband's support obligation by the amount of the ex-wife's imputed (putative) income from services provided to the man with whom she was living. See Blumberg, Cohabitation without Marriage: A Different Perspective, 28 U.C.L.A. L. Rev. 1125, 1162 (1981).

children, cleaning the house, preparing the meals, etc. With the second couple, both spouses work, with one earning $40,000 and the other earning $10,000, and a housekeeper is hired at a cost of $8,000. The second couple has a true economic advantage over the first of only $2,000, but for tax purposes its income is greater by $10,000. To the extent that it is taxed on the extra $8,000, the second couple is treated unfairly as compared with the first. And the effect may be to induce the secondary worker in the second household to stay home and provide services to the household rather than take a job where his or her services may be more valuable to society. One solution to this set of problems would be to tax the imputed income of the first couple, but that possibility is universally dismissed as impractical. The second possibility is to allow a deduction for the second couple for the costs of hiring household services from outsiders. Section 21 (the credit for child and household care) moves in this direction, as does §129 (allowing tax-free employer reimbursement for child-care expenses), combined with §125 (allowing employers to offer employees a choice between tax-free benefits and cash). See supra page 109. Deductions and credits for child-care services are considered more fully in Chapter 5C (infra page 576).

(c) Another important source of imputed income from services has received relatively little attention from tax experts but has begun to be more widely recognized in the context of marital dissolution. This is the value of services that one performs for oneself in creating "human capital." A good example is that of the person who devotes many years to the study of medicine. During the period of training, such a person forgoes income that could have been earned in some other activity in order to develop a skill of considerable financial value. The prospective doctor is not wasting time; the time is being used in a valuable way. The return is the ultimate ability to practice medicine, which is an intangible asset whose value can far exceed that of tangible assets. (For further discussion of the tax problems arising from human capital, see Chapter 3G, page 429.)

3. Psychic Income and Leisure

Closely related to the phenomenon of imputed income is that of psychic income and leisure. Imagine, for example, two taxpayers with the same salary. One enjoys playing chess, engaging in intellectual discourse, reading, and bird-watching. The other is happy only while sailing a yacht or traveling abroad. Both manage to enjoy life to the same degree; their "psychic income" is the same. But the cost of achieving similar happiness is higher for the second taxpayer than for the first. The tax system does not, and obviously cannot, take account of the possible difference in the two taxpayers' ability to pay.

Similarly, imagine two taxpayers with the same incomes, one who earns that income working two days a week and another who works six. Apart from the possibility of taxing the first person's untapped ability to pay, one might think it appropriate, in the interests of fairness, to take account of the value of the first person's leisure, of the psychic income that it produces. Since we do not, the tax system distorts economic choice: It taxes earnings but does not tax the benefit of the leisure that one "buys" by not working, and to that extent makes the trade-off between leisure and work different for the individual than it is for society. (See supra page 28.)

QUESTIONS

1. Which, if any, of the following raise issues of imputed income?
(a) buying a car
(b) buying a tuxedo
(c) renting a tuxedo
(d) buying a washing machine
(e) repairing one's own car
(f) enjoyment of leisure
(g) enjoyment of work

2. In what way does the nontaxation of imputed income from housing create problems of fairness? Of economic development?

3. Is a rent deduction for people who do not own their own homes a good solution to the problems created by the nontaxation of the imputed income from owner-occupied housing?

4. Suppose the tax rate on earned income is lowered and a special tax is added to the price of leisure-time activities such as sporting events, concerts, movies, and nonbusiness travel. Would these two changes be a sensible way to reduce the problems caused by the nontaxation of the psychic value of leisure?

4. Drawing the Line

The Revenue Ruling produced below is concerned with a problem of economic benefit, or noncash benefit, rather than with a problem of imputed income. Its function at this point in the book is to permit exploration of the distinction between imputed income and noncash benefits. The taxpayers in the ruling perform services for strangers, not themselves or members of their households. But the difference may not be so clear in other situations.

REVENUE RULING 79-24

1979-1 C.B. 60

Facts

Situation 1. In return for personal legal services performed by a lawyer for a housepainter, the housepainter painted the lawyer's personal residence. Both the lawyer and the housepainter are members of a barter club, an organization that annually furnishes its members a directory of members and the services they provide. All the members of the club are professional or trades persons. Members contact other members directly and negotiate the value of the services to be performed.

Situation 2. An individual who owned an apartment building received a work of art created by a professional artist in return for the rent-free use of an apartment for six months by the artist.

Law

The applicable sections of the Internal Revenue Code of 1954 and the Income Tax Regulations thereunder are 61(a) and 1.61-2, relating to compensation for services.

Section 1.61-2(d)(1) of the regulations provides that if services are paid for other than in money, the fair market value of the property or services taken in payment must be included in income. If the services were rendered at a stipulated price, such price will be presumed to be the fair market value of the compensation received in the absence of evidence to the contrary.

Holdings

Situation 1. The fair market value of the services received by the lawyer and the housepainter are includible in their gross incomes under section 61 of the Code.

Situation 2. The fair market value of the work of art and the six months fair rental value of the apartment are includible in the gross incomes of the apartment-owner and the artist under section 61 of the Code.

QUESTIONS

1. Suppose that Betty owns the right, under a time-share (see supra page 119), to the use of an apartment at the beach for a week in July

and exchanges that right for the right of another time-share owner, Stan, to the use of an apartment at a ski resort for a week in December. Should each person report income by virtue of the exchange? How much? What about deductions?

2. Suppose that two couples exchange babysitting services on weekends. Should both report income? See Regs. §1.6045-1(a)(4) ("taxable barter does not include arrangements that provide solely for the informal exchange of similar services on a noncommercial basis").

3. Suppose that one couple joins a cooperative day care center that maintains a limited professional staff and requires each parent to supply two hours of day care a week. Parents who do not wish to supply day care may buy out of the obligation for $50 a month. However, parents are encouraged to provide child care and not buy their way out of the obligation. Should parents who provide child care pay tax on $50 of monthly income?

4. Attorney Ann joins a barter club. In return for services as an attorney, Ann receives credits that she can use to obtain other professional services, such as carpentry or dentistry. Taxable? See Rev. Rul. 80-52, 1980-1 C.B. 100, holding people taxable on credits earned in a barter club. Section 6045, added in 1982, requires information returns to the IRS from "barter exchanges."

5. One hundred people pool their resources and buy land in Colorado, where they set up a commune. They perform various tasks for each other according to their skills. Any income for tax purposes?

6. A bank offers its customers the option of earning interest on the money in their checking accounts or of receiving free checking services. Any income to the customers who take the free checking services? The Service has never sought to tax the value of such services. Would you concur in that practice if you were Commissioner?

NOTE

Commissioner v. Minzer, 279 F.2d 338 (5th Cir. 1960), held an insurance agent taxable on the normal commission payable on a policy on his own life issued by a company he represented, without regard to whether he paid the full premium to the company and received the company's check for his customary commission or simply deducted the commission at the outset. Similar results have been reached in cases involving real estate brokers (see United States v. Allen, 551 F.2d 208 (8th Cir. 1977); Williams v. Commissioner, 64 T.C. 1085 (1975)) and a stockbroker (see Kobernat v. Commissioner, 31 T.C.M. 593 (1972)). On the other hand, Rev. Rul. 66-167, 1966-1 C.B. 20, holds that an executor is not taxable on a statutory fee that he waived, in a timely manner, where his son was the beneficiary.

C. WINDFALLS AND GIFTS

1. Punitive Damages

COMMISSIONER v. GLENSHAW GLASS CO.

348 U.S. 426 (1955)

Mr. Chief Justice WARREN delivered the opinion of the Court.

This litigation involves two cases with independent factual backgrounds yet presenting the identical issue. The two cases were consolidated for argument before the Court of Appeals for the Third Circuit and were heard en banc. The common question is whether money received as exemplary damages for fraud or as the punitive two-thirds portion of a treble-damage antitrust recovery must be reported by a taxpayer as gross income under §22(a) of the Internal Revenue Code of 1939 [the predecessor of §61 of the 1954 Code]. In a single opinion, 211 F.2d 928, the Court of Appeals affirmed the Tax Court's separate rulings in favor of the taxpayers. . . .

The facts of the cases were largely stipulated and are not in dispute. So far as pertinent they are as follows:

Commissioner v. Glenshaw Glass Co. The Glenshaw Glass Company, a Pennsylvania corporation, manufactures glass bottles and containers. It was engaged in protracted litigation with the Hartford-Empire Company, which manufactures machinery of a character used by Glenshaw. Among the claims advanced by Glenshaw were demands for exemplary damages for fraud and treble damages for injury to its business by reason of Hartford's violation of the federal antitrust laws. In December, 1947, the parties concluded a settlement of all pending litigation, by which Hartford paid Glenshaw approximately $800,000. Through a method of allocation which was approved by the Tax Court, 18 T.C. 860, 870-872, and which is no longer in issue, it was ultimately determined that, of the total settlement, $324,529.94 represented payment of punitive damages for fraud and antitrust violations. Glenshaw did not report this portion of the settlement as income for the tax year involved. The Commissioner determined a deficiency claiming as taxable the entire sum less only deductible legal fees. As previously noted, the Tax Court and the Court of Appeals upheld the taxpayer.

Commissioner v. William Goldman Theatres, Inc. William Goldman Theatres, Inc., a Delaware corporation operating motion picture houses in Pennsylvania, sued Loew's, Inc., alleging a violation of the federal antitrust laws and seeking treble damages. After a holding that a violation had occurred, William Goldman Theatres, Inc. v. Loew's, Inc., 150 F.2d 738, the case was remanded to the trial court for a determination of damages. It was found that Goldman had suffered a loss of profits equal to $125,000 and was entitled to treble damages in the sum of $375,000. William Goldman Theatres, Inc. v. Loew's, Inc., 69 F. Supp. 103, aff'd, 164 F.2d 1021, cert. denied, 334 U.S. 811. Goldman reported only $125,000 of the recovery as gross income and claimed that the $250,000 balance constituted punitive damages and as such was not taxable. The Tax Court agreed, 19 T.C. 637, and the Court of Appeals, hearing this with the *Glenshaw* case, affirmed. 211 F.2d 928.

It is conceded by the respondents that there is no constitutional barrier to the imposition of a tax on punitive damages. Our question is one of statutory construction: are these payments comprehended by §22(a)?

The sweeping scope of the controverted statute is readily apparent:

Sec. 22. Gross Income

> (a) *General Definition.* "Gross income" includes gains, profits, and income derived from salaries, wages, or compensation for personal service . . . of whatever kind and in whatever form paid, or from professions, vocations, trades, businesses, commerce, or sales, or dealings in property, whether real or personal, growing out of the ownership or use of or interest in such property; also from interest, rent, dividends, securities, or the transaction of any business carried on for gain or profit, *or gains or profits and income derived from any source whatever.* . . .

(Emphasis added.)

This Court has frequently stated that this language was used by Congress to exert in this field "the full measure of its taxing power." Helvering v. Clifford [309 U.S. 331]; Helvering v. Midland Mutual Life Ins. Co., 300 U.S. 216, 223; Douglas v. Willcuts, 296 U.S. 1, 9; Irwin v. Gavit [infra page 188]. Respondents contend that punitive damages, characterized as "windfalls" flowing from the culpable conduct of third parties, are not within the scope of the section. But Congress applied no limitations as to the source of taxable receipts, nor restrictive labels as to their nature. And the Court has given a liberal construction to this broad phraseology in recognition of the intention of Congress to tax all gains except those specifically exempted. . . . Thus, the fortuitous gain accruing to a lessor by reason of the forfeiture of a lessee's improvements on the rented property was taxed in Helvering v. Bruun [infra page 301]. Cf. Robertson v. United States, 343 U.S. 711; Rutkin v. United States, 343 U.S. 130; United States v. Kirby Lumber Co. [infra page 235]. Such decisions demonstrate that we cannot but ascribe content to the catchall provision of §22(a), "gains or profits and income derived from any source whatever." The importance of that phrase has been too frequently recognized since its first appearance in the Revenue

Act of 1913 to say now that it adds nothing to the meaning of "gross income."

Nor can we accept respondents' contention that a narrower reading of §22(a) is required by the Court's characterization of income in Eisner v. Macomber, 252 U.S. 189, 207 [infra page 286], as "the gain derived from capital, from labor, or from both combined."[14] The Court was there endeavoring to determine whether the distribution of a corporate stock dividend constituted a realized gain to the shareholder, or changed "only the form, not the essence," of his capital investment. Id., at 210. It was held that the taxpayer had "received nothing out of the company's assets for his separate use and benefit." Id., at 211. The distribution, therefore, was held not a taxable event. In that context — distinguishing gain from capital — the definition served a useful purpose. But it was not meant to provide a touchstone to all future gross income questions. . . .

Here we have instances of undeniable accessions to wealth, clearly realized, and over which the taxpayers have complete dominion. The mere fact that the payments were extracted from the wrongdoers as punishment for unlawful conduct cannot detract from their character as taxable income to the recipients. Respondents concede, as they must, that the recoveries are taxable to the extent that they compensate for damages actually incurred. It would be an anomaly that could not be justified in the absence of clear congressional intent to say that a recovery for actual damages is taxable but not the additional amount extracted as punishment for the same conduct which caused the injury. And we find no such evidence of intent to exempt these payments. . . .

Reversed.

Mr. Justice DOUGLAS dissents.

Mr. Justice HARLAN took no part in the consideration or decision of this case.

NOTES AND QUESTIONS

1. *The holding.* As previously indicated (supra page 76), the thrust of this case is in the language, "But Congress applied no limitations as to the source of taxable receipts, nor restrictive labels as to their nature."

14. The phrase was derived from Stratton's Independence, Ltd. v. Howbert, 231 U.S. 399, 415, and Doyle v. Mitchell Bros. Co., 247 U.S. 179, 185, two cases construing the Revenue Act of 1909, 36 Stat. 11,112. Both taxpayers were "wasting asset" corporations, one being engaged in mining, the other in lumbering operations. The definition was applied by the Court to demonstrate a distinction between a return on capital and "a mere conversion of capital assets." Doyle v. Mitchell Bros. Co., supra, at 184. The question raised by the instant case is clearly distinguishable.

The case is consistent with the broad definition of income that is reflected in the Simons formulation (supra page 76) and is favored by most modern tax experts. The facts of the case nicely illustrate the appeal of that definition. As the Court argues, it would be anomalous indeed to tax a recovery of lost profits but not a treble-damages windfall arising from the same events. Similarly, it would offend one's sense of fairness to tax wages a person earns by hard work but not money a person happens to find lying on the street. See Cesarini v. United States, 296 F. Supp. 3 (N.D. Ohio 1969), aff'd per curiam, 428 F.2d 812 (6th Cir. 1970), holding that $4,467 in old currency discovered in a piano, which had been bought for $15 at an auction, was income in the year it was discovered. See Regs. §1.61-14. Is there any argument in principles of taxation other than fairness for excluding windfalls? Are windfalls "income" as that word is normally used outside the tax system?[15] Examine the language of §22(a) of the 1939 Code, quoted in the Court's opinion. Can you make a "strict constructionist" or "plain language" argument for exclusion? Bear in mind, this is a tax code that we interpret, not a constitution. Is there virtue in a "government of laws," even if the laws produce results we would not otherwise find appealing?

2. *Taxation and antitrust policy.* The punitive portion of an antitrust treble-damages award is intended to encourage private actions of the sort initiated by the plaintiffs in *Glenshaw Glass.* Should the punitive portions of the awards be excluded from gross income in order to promote, or avoid undercutting, the policies of the antitrust laws? If the punitive award is not a large enough incentive, would it be preferable to increase it and make the enlarged amount taxable, or retain the current amount and make it tax free? To focus the issue, think about an award of $1 million as the punitive portion of damages received (under the present system, without augmentation for tax effects) by two different corporations, *A* Corp., which is taxable at a rate of 34 percent, and *B* Corp., which is not taxable (because of losses carried forward from earlier years or because it is a not-for-profit corporation).

3. *Personal injury recoveries.* In a footnote, the Court attempts to reconcile its holding with the rule that damages for personal injury had been excluded, for many years, by administrative rulings. These rulings and their implications are considered further infra at pages 210-217. It does seem plain, however, that the administrative rulings are consistent with the Eisner v. Macomber definition of income, on which the earlier ones expressly relied.

15. Suppose that last year you earned $20,000 as a law clerk and won $5,000 in a lottery and someone now asks you, "How much did you earn last year?" What would you say? Suppose the question is, "What was your income last year?"

2. Gift: The Basic Concept

COMMISSIONER v. DUBERSTEIN

363 U.S. 278 (1960)

Mr. Justice BRENNAN delivered the opinion of the Court.

These two cases concern [§102(a)] which excludes from the gross income of an income taxpayer "the value of property acquired by gift." . . .

No. 376, Commissioner v. Duberstein. The taxpayer, Duberstein, was president of the Duberstein Iron & Metal Company, a corporation with headquarters in Dayton, Ohio. For some years the taxpayer's company had done business with Mohawk Metal Corporation, whose headquarters were in New York City. The president of Mohawk was one Berman. The taxpayer and Berman had generally used the telephone to transact their companies' business with each other, which consisted of buying and selling metals. The taxpayer testified, without elaboration, that he knew Berman "personally" and had known him for about seven years. From time to time in their telephone conversations, Berman would ask Duberstein whether the latter knew of potential customers for some of Mohawk's products in which Duberstein's company itself was not interested. Duberstein provided the names of potential customers for these items.

One day in 1951 Berman telephoned Duberstein and said that the information Duberstein had given him had proved so helpful that he wanted to give the latter a present. Duberstein stated that Berman owed him nothing. Berman said that he had a Cadillac as a gift for Duberstein, and that the latter should send to New York for it; Berman insisted that Duberstein accept the car, and the latter finally did so, protesting however that he had not intended to be compensated for the information. At the time Duberstein already had a Cadillac and an Oldsmobile, and felt that he did not need another car. Duberstein testified that he did not think Berman would have sent him the Cadillac if he had not furnished him with information about the customers. It appeared that Mohawk later deducted the value of the Cadillac as a business expense on its corporate income tax return.

Duberstein did not include the value of the Cadillac in gross income for 1951, deeming it a gift. The Commissioner asserted a deficiency for the car's value against him, and in proceedings to review the deficiency the Tax Court affirmed the Commissioner's determination. It said that "The record is significantly barren of evidence revealing any intention on the part of the payor to make a gift. . . . The only justifiable inference is that the automobile was intended by the payor to be remuneration for services rendered to it by Duberstein." The Court of Appeals for the Sixth Circuit reversed. 265 F.2d 28.

No. 506, Stanton v. United States. The taxpayer, Stanton, had been for approximately 10 years in the employ of Trinity Church in New York City. He was comptroller of the Church corporation, and president of a corporation, Trinity Operating Company, the church set up as a fully owned subsidiary to manage its real estate holdings, which were more extensive than simply the church property. His salary by the end of his employment there in 1942 amounted to $22,500 a year. Effective November 30, 1942, he resigned from both positions to go into business for himself. The Operating Company's directors, who seem to have included the rector and vestrymen of the church, passed the following resolution upon his resignation:

> *BE IT RESOLVED* that in appreciation of the services rendered by Mr. Stanton . . . a gratuity is hereby awarded to him of Twenty Thousand Dollars, payable to him in equal instalments of Two Thousand Dollars at the end of each and every month commencing with the month of December, 1942; provided that, with the discontinuance of his services, the Corporation of Trinity Church is released from all rights and claims to pension and retirement benefits not already accrued up to November 30, 1942.

The Operating Company's action was later explained by one of its directors as based on the fact that,

> Mr. Stanton was liked by all of the Vestry personally. He had a pleasing personality. He had come in when Trinity's affairs were in a difficult situation. He did a splendid piece of work, we felt. Besides that . . . he was liked by all of the members of the Vestry personally.

And by another:

> [W]e were all unanimous in wishing to make Mr. Stanton a gift. Mr. Stanton had loyally and faithfully served Trinity in a very difficult time. We thought of him in the highest regard. We understood that he was going in business for himself. We felt that he was entitled to that evidence of good will.

On the other hand, there was a suggestion of some ill-feeling between Stanton and the directors, arising out of the recent termination of the services of one Watkins, the Operating Company's treasurer, whose departure was evidently attended by some acrimony. At a special board meeting on October 28, 1942, Stanton had intervened on Watkins' side and asked reconsideration of the matter. The minutes reflect that "resentment was expressed as to the 'presumptuous' suggestion that the action of the Board, taken after long deliberation, should be changed." The Board adhered to its determination that Watkins be separated from employment, giving him an opportunity to resign rather than be discharged. At another special meeting two days later it was revealed that Watkins had not resigned; the previous resolution terminating his services was then viewed as effective; and the Board voted the payment of six months' salary to Watkins in a resolution similar to that quoted in regard to Stanton, but which did not use the term "gratuity." At the meeting, Stanton announced that in order to avoid any such embarrassment or question at any time as to his willingness to resign if the Board desired, he was tendering his resignation. It was tabled, though not without dissent. The next week, on November 5, at another special meeting, Stanton again tendered his resignation which this time was accepted.

The "gratuity" was duly paid. So was a smaller one to Stanton's (and the Operating Company's) secretary, under a similar resolution, upon her resignation at the same time. The two corporations shared the expense of the payments. There was undisputed testimony that there were in fact no enforceable rights or claims to pension and retirement benefits which had not accrued at the time of the taxpayer's resignation, and that the last proviso of the resolution was inserted simply out of an abundance of caution. The taxpayer received in cash a refund of his contributions to the retirement plans, and there is no suggestion that he was entitled to more. He was required to perform no further services for Trinity after his resignation.

. . . The trial judge, sitting without a jury, made the simple finding that the payments were a "gift," and judgment was entered for the taxpayer. The Court of Appeals for the Second Circuit reversed. 268 F.2d 727. . . .

The exclusion of property acquired by gift from gross income under the federal income tax laws was made in the first income tax statute passed under the authority of the Sixteenth Amendment, and has been a feature of the income tax statutes ever since. The meaning of the term "gift" as applied to particular transfers has always been a matter of contention. Specific and illuminating legislative history on the point does not appear to exist. Analogies and inferences drawn from other revenue provisions, such as the estate and gift taxes, are dubious. . . . The meaning of the statutory term has been shaped largely by the decisional law. With this, we turn to the contentions made by the Government in these cases.

First. The Government suggests that we promulgate a new "test" in this area to serve as a standard to be applied by the lower courts and by the Tax Court in dealing with the numerous cases that arise.[16] We

16. [The government's test would have generally ruled out gift treatment for transfers from employers to employees.—Eds.]

reject this invitation. We are of opinion that the governing principles are necessarily general and have already been spelled out in the opinions of this Court, and that the problem is one which, under the present statutory framework, does not lend itself to any more definitive statement that would produce a talisman for the solution of concrete cases. The cases at bar are fair examples of the settings in which the problem usually arises. They present situations in which payments have been made in a context with business overtones — an employer making a payment to a retiring employee; a businessman giving something of value to another businessman who has been of advantage to him in his business. In this context, we review the law as established by the prior cases here.

The course of decision here makes it plain that the statute does not use the term "gift" in the common-law sense, but in a more colloquial sense. This Court has indicated that a voluntary executed transfer of his property by one to another, without any consideration or compensation therefor, though a common-law gift, is not necessarily a "gift" within the meaning of the statute. For the Court has shown that the mere absence of a legal or moral obligation to make such a payment does not establish that it is a gift. Old Colony Trust Co. v. Commissioner, 279 U.S. 716, 730. And, importantly, if the payment proceeds primarily from "the constraining force of any moral or legal duty," or from "the incentive of anticipated benefit" of an economic nature, Bogardus v. Commissioner, 302 U.S. 34, 41, it is not a gift. And, conversely, "[w]here the payment is in return for services rendered, it is irrelevant that the donor derives no economic benefit from it." Robertson v. United States, 343 U.S. 711, 714. A gift in the statutory sense, on the other hand, proceeds from a "detached and disinterested generosity," Commissioner v. LoBue, 351 U.S. 243, 246 [infra page 402]; "out of affection, respect, admiration, charity or like impulses." Robertson v. United States, supra, at 714. And in this regard, the most critical consideration, as the Court was agreed in the leading case here, is the transferor's "intention." Bogardus v. Commissioner, 302 U.S. 34, 43. "What controls is the intention with which payment, however voluntary, has been made." Id., at 45 (dissenting opinion).

The Government says that this "intention" of the tranferor cannot mean what the cases on the common-law concept of gift call "donative intent." With that we are in agreement, for our decisions fully support this. Moreover, the *Bogardus* case itself makes it plain that the donor's characterization of his action is not determinative — that there must be an objective inquiry as to whether what is called a gift amounts to it in reality. 302 U.S., at 40. It scarcely needs adding that the parties' expectations or hopes as to the tax treatment of their conduct in themselves have nothing to do with the matter. . . .

Second. The Government's proposed "test," while apparently simple and precise in its formulation, depends frankly on a set of "principles" or "presumptions" derived from the decided cases, and concededly subject to various exceptions; and it involves various corollaries, which add to its detail. Were we to promulgate this test as a matter of law, and accept with it its various presuppositions and stated consequences, we would be passing far beyond the requirements of the cases before us, and would be painting on a large canvas with indeed a broad brush. The Government derives its test from such propositions as the following: That payments by an employer to an employee, even though voluntary, ought, by and large, to be taxable; that the concept of a gift is inconsistent with a payment's being a deductible business expense; that a gift involves "personal" elements; that a business corporation cannot properly make a gift of its assets. The Government admits that there are exceptions and qualifications to these propositions. We think, to the extent they are correct, that these propositions are not principles of law but rather maxims of experience that the tribunals, which have tried the fact of cases in this area have enunciated in explaining their factual determinations. Some of them simply represent truisms: it doubtless is, statistically speaking, the exceptional payment by an employer to an employee that amounts to a gift. Others are overstatements of possible evidentiary inferences relevant to a factual determination on the totality of circumstances in the case: it is doubtless relevant to the over-all inference that the transferor treats a payment as a business deduction, or that the transferor is a corporate entity. But these inferences cannot be stated in absolute terms. Neither factor is a shibboleth. The taxing statute does not make nondeductibility by the transferor a condition on the "gift" exclusion; nor does it draw any distinction, in terms, between transfers by corporations and individuals, as to the availability of the "gift" exclusion to the transferee. The conclusion whether a transfer amounts to a "gift" is one that must be reached on a consideration of all the factors.

Specifically, the trier of fact must be careful not to allow trial of the issue whether the receipt of a specific payment is a gift to turn into a trial of the tax liability, or of the propriety, as a matter of fiduciary or corporate law, attaching to the conduct of someone else. . . . The major corollary to the Government's suggested "test" is that, as an ordinary matter, a payment by a corporation cannot be a gift, and, more specifically, there can be no such thing as a "gift" made by a corporation which would allow it to take a deduction for an ordinary and necessary business expense. As we have said, we find no basis for such a conclusion in the statute; and if it were applied as a determinative rule of "law," it would force the tribunals trying tax cases involving the donee's liability into elaborate inquiries into the local law of corporations or into the peripheral deductibility of payments as business expenses.

Third. Decision of the issue presented in these cases must be based ultimately on the application of the fact-finding tribunal's experience with the mainsprings of human conduct to the totality of the facts of each case. The nontechnical nature of the statutory standard, the close relationship of it to the data of practical human experience, and the multiplicity of relevant factual elements, with their various combinations, creating the necessity of ascribing the proper force to each, confirm us in our conclusion that primary weight in this area must be given to the conclusions of the trier of fact. . . .

This conclusion may not satisfy an academic desire for tidiness, symmetry and precision in this area, any more than a system based on the determinations of various fact-finders ordinarily does. But we see it as implicit in the present statutory treatment of the exclusion for gifts, and in the variety of forums in which federal income tax cases can be tried. If there is fear of undue uncertainty or overmuch litigation, Congress may make more precise its treatment of the matter by singling out certain factors and making them determinative of the matter, as it has done in one field of the "gift" exclusion's former application, that of prizes and awards. Doubtless diversity of result will tend to be lessened somewhat since federal income tax decisions, even those in tribunals of first instance turning on issues of fact, tend to be reported, and since there may be a natural tendency of professional triers of fact to follow one another's determinations, even as to factual matters. But the question here remains basically one of fact, for determination on a case-by-case basis.

One consequence of this is that appellate review of determinations in this field must be quite restricted. Where a jury has tried the matter upon correct instructions, the only inquiry is whether it cannot be said that reasonable men could reach differing conclusions on the issue. . . . Where the trial has been by a judge without a jury, the judge's findings must stand unless "clearly erroneous." Fed. Rules Civ. Proc., 52 (a). . . .

Fourth. A majority of the Court is in accord with the principles just outlined. And, applying them to the *Duberstein* case, we are in agreement, on the evidence we have set forth, that it cannot be said that the conclusion of the Tax Court was "clearly erroneous." It seems to us plain that as trier of the facts it was warranted in concluding that despite the characterization of the transfer of the Cadillac by the parties and the absence of any obligation, even of a moral nature, to make it, it was at bottom a recompense for Duberstein's past services, or an inducement for him to be of further service in the future. We cannot say with the Court of Appeals that such a conclusion was "mere suspicion" on the Tax Court's part. To us it appears based in the sort of informed experience with human affairs that fact-finding tribunals should bring to this task.

As to *Stanton,* we are in disagreement. To four of us, it is critical here that the District Court as trier of fact made only the simple and unelaborated finding that the transfer in question was a "gift." To be sure, conciseness is to be strived for, and prolixity avoided, in findings; but, to the four of us, there comes a point where findings become so sparse and conclusory as to give no revelation of what the District Court's concept of the determining facts and legal standard may be. . . . Such conclusory, general findings do not constitute compliance with Rule 52's direction to "find the facts specially and state separately . . . conclusions of law thereon." While the standard of law in this area is not a complex one, we four think the unelaborated finding of ultimate fact here cannot stand as a fulfillment of these requirements. It affords the reviewing court not the semblance of an indication of the legal standard with which the trier of fact has approached his task. For all that appears, the District Court may have viewed the form of the resolution or the simple absence of legal consideration as conclusive. While the judgment of the Court of Appeals cannot stand, the four of us think there must be further proceedings in the District Court looking toward new and adequate findings of fact. In this, we are joined by Mr. Justice Whittaker, who agrees that the findings were inadequate, although he does not concur generally in this opinion.

Accordingly, in No. 376, the judgment of this Court is that the judgment of the Court of Appeals is reversed, and in No. 546, that the judgment of the District Court of Appeals is vacated, and the case is remanded to the District Court for further proceedings not inconsistent with this opinion.

It is so ordered.

Mr. Justice HARLAN concurs in the result in No. 376. In No. 546, he would affirm the judgment of the Court of Appeals for the reasons stated by Mr. Justice Frankfurter.

Mr. Justice WHITTAKER, agreeing with *Bogardus* that whether a particular transfer is or is not a "gift" may involve "a mixed question of law and fact," 302 U.S., at 39, concurs only in the result of this opinion.

Mr. Justice DOUGLAS dissents, since he is of the view that in each of these two cases there was a gift under the test which the Court fashioned nearly a quarter of a century ago in Bogardus v. Commissioner, 302 U.S. 34.

[Mr. Justice BLACK concurred in *Duberstein* and dissented in *Stanton,* on the ground that the trial court's finding in each case was "not clearly erroneous."]

[Mr. Justice FRANKFURTER said that "in the two situations now before us the business implications are so forceful that I would apply a presumptive rule placing the burden upon the beneficiary to prove the payment wholly unrelated to his services to the enterprise" and that the Court's emphasis on the fact-finding tribunal's "experience with the mainsprings of human conduct" would set them "to sail on an illimitable ocean of individual beliefs and experiences." He concluded that Duberstein was properly taxed, and that Stanton's payment should have been taxed because it was not "sheer benevolence but in the nature of a generous lagniappe, something extra thrown in for services received though not legally nor morally required to be given."]

NOTES AND QUESTIONS

1. *Aftermath.* (a) On the remand of the *Stanton* case, the district court made detailed findings of fact and again concluded that the payments to Stanton were gifts. 186 F. Supp. 393 (E.D.N.Y. 1960). On appeal the Court of Appeals affirmed on the ground that the findings were not "clearly erroneous," Chief Judge Lumbard concurring because of the restricted character of appellate review, although he thought a "contrary inference should have been drawn from the undisputed basic facts." 287 F.2d 876, 877 (2d Cir. 1961).

(b) Section 102(c), added in 1986, alters the result in *Stanton* by a categorical rule precluding gift treatment in the case of any transfer by an employer to an employee. There is, however, a modest and carefully circumscribed exclusion for "employee achievement awards." See §74(c).

2. *Analysis.* (a) The Court says that it cannot find any "specific and illuminating legislative history." Accordingly, it interprets "gift" in the "colloquial sense." In other words, it adopts a "plain language" approach to the statute. From there, it defines "gift" by reference to a state of mind. What is the required state of mind? In a case like *Stanton,* whose state of mind counts? How does the trier of fact find that state of mind?

(b) Would an inquiry into the policy reasons for excluding gifts from gross income have been useful? Henry Simons argued that gifts ought to be included in income because "surely it is hard to defend exclusion of certain receipts merely because one has done nothing or given nothing in return." Personal Income Taxation 135 (1938). Simons would not have allowed a deduction for the donor. Id. at 136. Simons's position seems insufficiently sensitive to notions of the family or household as an economic unit, though such notions may be more relevant to modest transfers bordering on support than to substantial transfers of wealth. When one thinks of gifts, the classes of people who are the typical donees would no doubt be family members or the needy. Does this observation suggest an interpretation of "gift" that would be consistent with the plain language approach and also might make some sense in terms of rational tax policy? Under such an interpretation, what would the outcome be on the *Duberstein* and the *Stanton* facts?

(c) People who are supported by members of their family do not have gross income in the amount of the support they receive. This rule is without express statutory authority; it is simply part of the definition of "income" and has never been questioned by the Service or by tax theorists. Often it may be difficult to distinguish between support payments and gifts — for example, where a parent buys an automobile for his or her child. Does this help explain the gift exclusion? If so, how does it bear on the decision in *Duberstein?*

3. *Congressional reaction and the payor's deduction for business gifts.* Section 274(b), added in 1962, allows persons such as Berman, in the *Duberstein* case, to deduct as an ordinary and necessary business expense the first $25 of any business gift. That section seems to accept implicitly the notion that there can be "business gifts" — that is, transfers that, though business motivated for the transferor, are gifts to the transferee. Of course, if the business motivation is strong enough, the transfer will not be a gift, the transferee will be required to treat item received as an addition to adjusted gross income, and §274(b)'s limitation will not operate to deny a deduction to the transferor. Where the item is treated as a gift to the transferee and, under §274(b) the deduction is denied to the transferor, the net effect can be thought of as a form of surrogate taxation, where the tax burden of one person (here, the transferor) is increased to offset what is regarded as an improper tax benefit to another person (here, the payee).

In a case like *Duberstein,* for example, suppose you start with the notion that Berman's cost in presenting the Cadillac to Duberstein is properly regarded as a business expense for Berman and income to Duberstein. Suppose the cost was $10,000 and that both Berman and Duberstein pay tax at a rate of 40 percent. Berman should be entitled to a deduction of $10,000, which will reduce his tax liability by $4,000. Duberstein should have income of $10,000, which will increase his tax liability by $4,000. Now suppose that for some reason we decide that we cannot tax Duberstein on the value of the automobile. Duberstein's tax payments will decline by $4,000 (compared with what we think to be the correct result). We might then deny a deduction to Berman. His tax payments will then increase by $4,000 (compared with the correct result). The Treasury then comes out whole. Duberstein escapes taxation, but Berman is taxed as his surrogate. Berman might claim that he has been treated unfairly, but one's sympathy for this claim may be diminished by the knowledge that he can adjust the amount of the benefit he is willing to confer on Duberstein to take account of the tax detriment to himself and the tax benefit to Duberstein. Surrogate taxation may be especially appealing where an employer supplies a benefit that is particularly difficult to allocate among employees (e.g., the use of athletic facilities). See supra page 110. But note the importance of the relative tax rates of the person who should be taxed and the surrogate. Consider, for example, what the surrogate would be in the *Stanton* case. The net effect of surrogate taxation is that the Treasury will collect the proper amount of tax, or close to the proper amount, in most, but not all, cases. To achieve the proper tax result in all cases, one must tax the proper person (a result now achieved under §102(c) for transfers like those in *Stanton,* involving transfers from employers to employees).

4. *Later development: §83.* Section 83 was adopted after the decision in *Duberstein,* with different, more sophisticated kinds of transactions in mind. Would it make a difference in a case like *Duberstein?* Under the decision in *Duberstein* is it possible for a transfer of property to be a "gift" within the meaning of §102 and still be made "in connection with the performance of services" within the contemplation of §83? If so, which provision governs?

QUESTIONS

1. While away from home on a business trip, Ellen eats at an airport coffee shop. Ellen knows that she is unlikely to ever eat at the coffee shop again. Nonetheless, after lunch, Ellen leaves a dollar tip for the waiter. Under the rules set forth in *Duberstein,* is the waiter taxable on the tip? (The problem of tips is examined further in the next case, Olk v. Commissioner. For the present, focus exclusively on *Duberstein.*)

2. Under current law, a gift is not treated as income to the donee and, with the exception of small business gifts (discussed in Note 4 supra), a gift does not generate a deduction for the donor. Suppose the law were changed so that gifts were income to the donee and deductible by the donor.

(a) How might such a regime be justified?

(b) How do you suppose such a regime would affect tax revenues?

3. Suppose that the current tax treatment of gifts is changed so that gifts are included in the gross income of the donee, but are not deductible by the donor. What arguments can you make in favor of, or in opposition to, such a regime?

UNITED STATES v. HARRIS

942 F.2d 1125 (7th Cir. 1991)

ESCHBACH, Senior Circuit Judge.

David Kritzik, now deceased, was a wealthy widower partial to the company of young women. Two of these women were Leigh Ann Conley and Lynnette Harris, twin sisters. Directly or indirectly, Kritzik gave Conley and Harris each more than half a million dollars over the course of several years. For our purposes, either Kritzik had to pay gift tax on this money or Harris and Conley had to pay income tax. The United States alleges that, beyond reasonable doubt, the obligation was Harris and Conley's. In separate criminal trials, Harris and Conley were convicted of willfully evading their income tax obligations regarding the money,[17] and they now appeal.

Under Commissioner v. Duberstein, 363 U.S. 278 (1960), the donor's intent is the "critical consideration" in distinguishing between gifts and income. We reverse Conley's conviction and remand with instructions to dismiss the indictment against her because the government failed to present sufficient evidence of Kritzik's intent regarding the money he gave her. We also reverse Harris' conviction. The district court excluded as hearsay letters in which Kritzik wrote that he loved Harris and enjoyed giving things to her. These letters were central to Harris' defense that she believed in good faith that the money she received was a nontaxable gift, and they were not hearsay for this purpose.

We do not remand Harris' case for retrial, however, because Harris had no fair warning that her conduct might subject her to criminal tax liability. Neither the tax code, the Treasury Regulations, nor Supreme Court or appellate cases provide a clear answer to whether Harris owed any taxes or not. The closest authority lies in a series of Tax Court decisions — but these cases *favor* Harris' position that the money she received was not income to her. Under this state of the law, Harris could not have formed a "willful" intent to violate the statutes at issue. For this reason, we remand with instructions that the indictment against Harris be dismissed. The same conclusion applies to Conley, and provides an alternative basis for reversing her conviction and remanding with instructions to dismiss the indictment.

Insufficiency of the Evidence as to Conley

Conley was convicted on each of four counts for violating 26 U.S.C. §7203, which provides,

> Any person . . . required . . . to make a [tax] return . . . who willfully fails to . . . make such return . . . shall, in addition to other penalties provided by law, be guilty of a misdemeanor. . . .

17. Harris was sentenced to ten months in prison, to be followed by two months in a halfway house and two years of supervised release. She was also fined $12,500.00 and ordered to pay a $150.00 special assessment. Conley was sentenced to five months in prison, followed by five months in a halfway house and one year supervised release. She was also fined $10,000.00 and ordered to pay a $100.00 assessment.

Conley was "required . . . to make a return" only if the money that she received from Kritzik was income to her rather than a gift. Assuming that the money was income, she acted "willfully," and so is subject to criminal prosecution, only if she knew of her duty to pay taxes and "voluntarily and intentionally violated that duty." Cheek v. United States—U.S.—(1991). The government met its burden of proof if the jury could have found these elements beyond a reasonable doubt, viewing the evidence in the light most favorable to the government.

The government's evidence was insufficient to show either that the money Conley received was income or that she acted in knowing disregard of her obligations. "Gross income" for tax purposes does not include gifts, which are taxable to the donor rather than the recipient. §§61, 102(a), 2501(a). In Commissioner v. Duberstein, 363 U.S. 278 (1960), the Supreme Court stated that in distinguishing between income and gifts the "critical consideration . . . is the transferor's intention." A transfer of property is a gift if the transferor acted out of a "detached and disinterested generosity, . . . out of affection, respect, admiration, charity, or like impulses." Id. By contrast, a transfer of property is income if it is the result of "the constraining force of any moral or legal duty, constitutes a reward for services rendered, or proceeds from the incentive of anticipated benefit of an economic nature."

Regarding the "critical consideration" of the donor's intent, the only direct evidence that the government presented was Kritzik's gift tax returns. On those returns, Kritzik identified gifts to Conley of $24,000, $30,000, and $36,000 for the years 1984-6, respectively, substantially less than the total amount of money that Kritzik transferred to Conley. This leaves the question whether Kritzik's other payments were taxable income to Conley or whether Kritzik just underreported his gifts. The gift tax returns raise the question, they do not resolve it.[18]

This failure to show Kritzik's intent is fatal to the government's case. Without establishing Kritzik's intent, the government cannot establish that Conley had any obligation to pay income taxes. Further, Conley

18. Our discussion assumes that the gift tax returns were admissible as evidence because the parties have not raised the issue. We note, however, that the returns appear on their face to be hearsay. The government used the returns (out of court statements) to prove that Kritzik's gifts were the amount that he reported (that is, to prove the truth of the matter asserted). . . .

Along these lines, the United States tried to present direct evidence of Kritzik's intent in the form of an affidavit that he provided IRS investigators before his death. In the affidavit, Kritzik stated that he regarded both Harris and Conley as prostitutes. But Kritzik had an obvious motive to lie to the investigators—he could have been subject to civil or criminal penalties for failure to pay gift taxes if he failed to shift the tax burden to the sisters. The District Court was correct to exclude this affidavit under the hearsay rule and under the confrontation clause. In general, evidentiary difficulties such as this will often be insurmountable in trying to prove a willful tax violation that hinges on the intent of a dead person. The civil remedies available to the IRS will almost always lead to surer justice in such cases than criminal prosecution.

could not have "willfully" failed to pay her taxes unless she knew of Kritzik's intent. Even if Kritzik's gift tax returns proved anything, the government presented no evidence that Conley knew the amounts that Kritzik had listed on those returns. Absent proof of Kritzik's intent, and Conley's knowledge of that intent, the government has no case.

The government's remaining evidence consisted of a bank card that Conley signed listing Kritzik in a space marked "employer" and testimony regarding the form of the payments that Conley received. The bank card is no evidence of Kritzik's intent and even as to Conley is open to conflicting interpretations — she contends that she listed Kritzik as a reference and no more. As to the form of payments, the government showed that Conley would pick up a regular check at Kritzik's office every week to ten days, either from Kritzik personally or, when he was not in, from his secretary. According to the government, this form of payment is that of an employee picking up regular wages, but it could just as easily be that of a dependent picking up regular support checks.

We will "not permit a verdict based solely upon the piling of inference upon inference." United States v. Balzano, 916 F.2d 1273, 1284 (7th Cir. 1990). . . .

The Admissibility of Kritzik's Letters

Harris was convicted of two counts of willfully failing to file federal income tax returns under §7203 (the same offense for which Conley was convicted) and two counts of willful tax evasion under §7201. At trial, Harris tried to introduce as evidence three letters that Kritzik wrote, but the District Court excluded the letters as hearsay. The District Court also suggested that the letters would be inadmissible under Fed. R. Evid. 403 because the possible prejudice from the letters exceeded their probative value. We hold that the letters were not hearsay because they were offered to prove Harris' lack of willfulness, not for the truth of the matters asserted. We further hold that the critical nature of the letters to Harris' defense precludes their exclusion under Rule 403, and so reverse her conviction.

The first of the letters at issue was a four page, handwritten letter from Kritzik to Harris, dated April 4, 1981. In it, Kritzik wrote that he loved and trusted Harris and that, "so far as the things I give you are concerned — let me say that I get as great if not even greater pleasure in giving than you get in receiving." Def. Ex. 201, p. 2. He continued, "I love giving things to you and to see you happy and enjoying them." Id. In a second letter to Harris of the same date, Kritzik again wrote, "I . . . love you very much and will do all that I can to make you happy," and said that he would arrange for Harris' financial security. Def. Ex.

202, p. 3. In a third letter, dated some six years later on May 28, 1987, Kritzik wrote to his insurance company regarding the value of certain jewelry that he had "given to Ms. Lynette Harris as a gift." Kritzik forwarded a copy of the letter to Harris.

These letters were hearsay if offered for the truth of the matters asserted — that Kritzik did in fact love Harris, enjoyed giving her things, wanted to take care of her financial security, and gave her the jewelry at issue as a gift. But the letters were not hearsay for the purpose of showing what Harris believed, because her belief does not depend on the actual truth of the matters asserted in the letters. Even if Kritzik were lying, the letters could have caused Harris to believe in good faith that the things he gave her were intended as gifts. . . . This good faith belief, in turn, would preclude any finding of willfullness on her part. . . .

The Tax Treatment of Payments to Mistresses

Our conclusion that Harris should have been allowed to present the letters at issue as evidence would ordinarily lead us to remand her case for retrial. We further conclude, however, that current law on the tax treatment of payments to mistresses provided Harris no fair warning that her conduct was criminal. Indeed, current authorities favor Harris' position that the money she received from Kritzik was a gift. We emphasize that we do not necessarily agree with these authorities, and that the government is free to urge departure from them in a *non*criminal context. But new points of tax law may not be the basis of criminal convictions. For this reason, we remand with instructions that the indictment against Harris be dismissed. Although we discuss only Harris' case in this section, the same reasoning applies to Conley and provides an alternative basis for dismissal of the indictment against her.

Again, the definitive statement of the distinction between gifts and income is in the Supreme Court's *Duberstein* decision, which applies and interprets the definition of income contained in §61. But as the Supreme Court described, the *Duberstein* principles are "necessarily general." It stated, "'One struggles in vain for any verbal formula that will supply a ready touchstone. The standard set up . . . is not a rule of law; it is rather a way of life. Life in all its fullness must supply the answer to the riddle.'" Id., quoting Welch v. Helvering, 290 U.S. 111 (1933). Along these lines, Judge Flaum's concurrence properly characterizes *Duberstein* as "eschew[ing] . . . [any] categorical, rule-bound analysis" in favor of a "case-by-case" approach.

Duberstein was a civil case, and its approach is appropriate for civil cases. But criminal prosecutions are a different story. These must rest on a violation of a clear rule of law, not on conflict with a "way of life".

If "defendants [in a tax case] . . . could not have ascertained the legal standards applicable to their conduct, criminal proceedings may not be used to define and punish an alleged failure to conform to those standards." United States v. Mallas, 762 F.2d 361, 361 (4th Cir. 1985). . . .

We do not doubt that *Duberstein*'s principles, though general, provide a clear answer to many cases involving the gift versus income distinction and can be the basis for civil as well as criminal prosecutions in such cases. We are equally certain, however, that *Duberstein* provides no ready answer to the taxability of transfers of money to a mistress in the context of a long term relationship. The motivations of the parties in such cases will always be mixed. The relationship would not be long term were it not for some respect or affection. Yet, it may be equally clear that the relationship would not continue were it not for financial support or payments.

Usually, a tax decision by the Supreme Court does not stand by itself. Treasury Regulations add specifics to broad principles, and federal cases apply the broad principles and prevailing regulations to the facts of particular cases. But these usual sources of authority are silent when it comes to the tax treatment of money transferred in the course of long term, personal relationships. No regulations cover the subject, and we have found no appellate or district court cases on the issue.

The most pertinent authority lies in several civil cases from the Tax Court, but these cases *favor* Harris' position. At its strongest, the government's case against Harris follows the assertions that Harris made, but now repudiates, in a lawsuit she filed against Kritzik's estate. According to her sworn pleadings in that suit, "all sums of money paid by David Kritzik to Lynette Harris . . . were made . . . in pursuance with the parties' express oral agreement." Government Exhibit 22, p. 4. As Harris' former lawyer testified at her trial, the point of this pleading was to make out a "palimony" claim under the California Supreme Court's decision in Marvin v. Marvin, 18 Cal. 3d 660, 134 Cal. Rptr. 815, 557 P.2d 106 (1976). Yet, the Tax Court has likened *Marvin*-type claims to amounts paid under antenuptial agreements. Under this analysis, these claims are *not* taxable income to the recipient:

> In an antenuptial agreement the parties agree, through private contract, on an arrangement for the disposition of their property in the event of death or separation. *Occasionally, however, the relinquishment of marital rights is not involved. These contracts are generally enforceable under state contract law. See Marvin v. Marvin, 18 Cal. 3d 660 [134 Cal. Rptr. 815], 557 P.2d 106 (1976).* Nonetheless, transfers pursuant to an antenuptial agreement are generally treated as gifts between the parties, because under the gift tax law the exchanged promises are not supported by full and adequate consideration, in money or money's worth.

Green v. Commissioner, T.C. Memo 1987-503 (emphasis added). We do not decide whether *Marvin*-type awards or settlements are or are not taxable to the recipient. The only point is that the Tax Court has suggested they are not. Until contrary authority emerges, no taxpayer could form a willful, criminal intent to violate the tax laws by failing to report *Marvin*-type payments. Reasonable inquiry does not yield a clear answer to the taxability of such payments.

Other cases only reinforce this conclusion. Reis v. Commissioner, T.C. Memo 1974-287 is a colorful example. The case concerned the tax liability of Lillian Reis, who had her start as a 16 year old nightclub dancer. At 21, she met Clyde "Bing" Miller when he treated the performers in the nightclub show to a steak and champagne dinner. As the Tax Court described it, Bing passed out $50 bills to each person at the table, on the condition that they leave, until he was alone with Reis. Bing then offered to write a check to Reis for any amount she asked. She asked for $1,200 for a mink stole and for another check in the same amount so her sister could have a coat too.

The next day the checks proved good; Bing returned to the club with more gifts; and "a lasting friendship developed" between Reis and Bing. For the next five years, she saw Bing "every Tuesday night at the [nightclub] and Wednesday afternooons from approximately 1:00 P.M. to 3:00 P.M. . . . at various places including . . . a girl friend's apartment and hotels where [Bing] was staying." He paid all of her living expenses, plus $200 a week, and provided money for her to invest, decorate her apartment, buy a car, and so on. The total over the five years was more than $100,000. The Tax Court held that this money was a gift, not income, despite Reis' statement that she "earned every penny" of the money. Similarly, in Libby v. Commissioner, T.C. Memo 1969-184 (1969), the Tax Court accorded gift treatment to thousands of dollars in cash and property that a young mistress received from her older paramour. And in Starks v. Commissioner, T.C. Memo 1966-134, the Tax Court did the same for another young woman who received cash and other property from an older, married man as part of "a very personal relationship."

The Tax Court did find that payments were income to the women who received them in Blevins v. Commissioner, T.C. Memo 1955-211, and in Jones v. Commissioner, T.C. Memo 1977-329. But in *Blevins*, the taxpayer was a woman who practiced prostitution and "used her home to operate a house of prostitution" in which six other women worked. Nothing suggested that the money at issue in that case was anything other than payments in the normal course of her business. Similarly in *Jones*, a woman had frequent hotel meetings with a married man, and on "*each* occasion" he gave her cash (emphasis added). Here too, the Tax Court found that the relationship was one of prostitution, a point that was supported by the woman's similar relationships with other men.

If these cases make a rule of law, it is that a person is entitled to treat cash and property received from a lover as gifts, as long as the relationship consists of something more than specific payments for specific sessions of sex. What's more, even in *Blevins*, in which the relationship was one of raw prostitution, the Tax Court rejected the IRS' claim that a civil fraud penalty should be imposed. Nor was a fraud penalty applied in *Jones*, the other prostitution case, although there the issue apparently was not raised. The United States does not allege that Harris received specific payments for specific sessions of sex, so *Reis, Libby,* and *Starks* support Harris' position.

Judge Flaum argues in his concurrence that these cases turn on their particular facts and do not make a rule of law. Fair enough (although the cases do cite each other in a manner that suggests otherwise). We need not decide this issue. We only conclude that a reasonably diligent taxpayer is entitled to look at the reported cases with the most closely analogous fact patterns when trying to determine his or her liability. When, as here, a series of such cases favors the taxpayer's position, the taxpayer has not been put on notice that he or she is in danger of crossing the line into criminality by adhering to that position. . . .

Besides Harris' prior suit, the United States also presented evidence regarding the overall relationship between Harris and Kritzik. Testimony showed that Harris described her relationship with Kritzik as "a job" and "just making a living." She reportedly complained that she "was laying on her back and her sister was getting all the money," described how she disliked when Kritzik fondled her naked, and made other derogatory statements about sex with Kritzik.

This evidence still leaves Harris on the favorable side of the Tax Court's cases. Further, this evidence tells us only what Harris thought of the relationship. Again, the Supreme Court in *Duberstein* held that the *donor's* intent is the "critical consideration" in determining whether a transfer of money is a gift or income. Commissioner v. Duberstein, 363 U.S. 278, 285 (1960). If Kritzik viewed the money he gave Harris as a gift, or if the dearth of contrary evidence leaves doubt on the subject, does it matter how mercenary Harris' motives were? *Duberstein* suggests that Harris' motives may not matter, but the ultimate answer makes no difference here. As long as the answer is at least a close call, and we are confident that it is, the prevailing law is too uncertain to support Harris' criminal conviction.

Finally, the evidence showed Harris to be a thief and to have evaded her tax obligations regarding *other* money. The thievery occurred when Kritzik offered to pay for extensive remodelling of a house that he had bought for Harris. Harris inflated the bills that she submitted to him for payment by more than a hundred thousand dollars, and funnelled her "profit" through a paper corporation that she had set up. The law is clear that embezzled or fraudulently obtained funds are income to the recipient. . . . But the government has relied on Harris' theft only to illustrate the nature of Harris' relationship with Kritzik, not as an independent criminal act. Along these lines, the government failed to request a jury instruction on point and failed to refer to any embezzled or misappropriated amounts in the indictment. The issue is waived. Similarly, the government presented evidence that, even apart from the money that she received from Kritzik, Harris willfully failed to file returns in 1984. Again, however, the government has not argued this point as an alternative basis for affirming the relevant count of Harris' conviction. The government based its case on the gift/income distinction, and its case must stand or fall on that distinction.

In short, criminal prosecutions are no place for the government to try out "pioneering interpretations of tax law." United States v. Garber, 607 F.2d 92, 100 (5th Cir. 1979) (en banc). The United States has not shown us, and we have not found, a single case finding tax liability for payments that a mistress received from her lover, absent proof of specific payments for specific sex acts. Even when such specific proof is present, the cases have not applied penalties for civil fraud, much less criminal sanctions. The broad principles contained in *Duberstein* do not fill this gap. Before she met Kritzik, Harris starred as a sorceress in an action/adventure film. She would have had to be a real life sorceress to predict her tax obligations under the current state of the law.[19]

Conclusion

For the reasons stated, we reverse Harris and Conley's convictions and remand with instructions to dismiss the indictments against them.

Flaum, Circuit Judge, concurring.

19. Harris and Conley have already served most of the sentences under the convictions that we now reverse. This is an injustice, and requires at least a brief explanation.

To be released pending appeal of a criminal conviction, a defendant must show "by clear and convincing evidence that the person is not likely to flee or pose a danger to the safety of any other person" *and* "that the appeal is not for the purpose of delay and raises a substantial question of law or fact likely to result in reversal or an order for a new trial." 18 U.S.C. §3143(b).

This is an exacting standard. Harris and Conley's counsel performed well, but failed in their petitions for release pending appeal to draw the Court's attention to the unique nature of Harris and Conley's convictions under the prevailing tax cases. In Orders dated September 25, 1990 and October 26, 1990, the Court denied those petitions. We vacated those Orders on May 10, 1991, the day after oral argument, and ordered Harris and Conley's immediate release.

In the future, counsel who believe that the Court should have granted a petition for release can assist the Court by renewing the petition in their main appellate briefs. Also, this Court's warnings to counsel against the "buckshot" approach of raising as many issues as possible . . . are particularly applicable to motions for release pending appeal. Finally, the district courts can assist us by stating in detail their reasons for denying a petition for release pending appeal, especially in a case like the present one in which the defendants posed no danger to the community and apparently negligible threat of flight. Necessarily, a district court's thorough knowledge of the merits of a case puts it in a better position to evaluate petitions for release than our Court, at least until the issues have been fully presented to the Court through briefing and oral argument.

The majority has persuasively demonstrated why Leigh Ann Conley's conviction is infirm and why the district court abused its discretion in excluding the Kritzik letters. I therefore join that portion of its opinion.

I further agree that Lynnette Harris' conviction must be reversed as well. . . .

I am troubled, however, by the path the majority takes to reach this result, and thus concur only in the court's judgment with respect to the reversal of Harris' conviction. I part company with the majority when it distills from our gift/income jurisprudence a rule that would tax only the most base type of cash-for-sex exchange and categorically exempt from tax liability all other transfers of money and property to so-called mistresses or companions. After citing several decisions of the tax court, the majority concludes that a person "is entitled to treat cash and property received from a lover as gifts, as long as the relationship consists of something more than specific payments for specific sessions of sex." I respectfully disagree. In Commissioner v. Duberstein, 363 U.S. 278 (1960), the font of our analysis of the gift/income distinction, the Supreme Court expressly eschewed the type of categorical, rule-bound analysis propounded by the majority. See id. at 289 ("while the principles urged by the Government may, in nonabsolute form as crystallizations of experience, prove persuasive to the trier of facts in a particular case, neither they, nor any more detailed statement than has been made, can be laid down as a matter of law"). The Court counseled instead that in distinguishing gifts from income we should engage in a case-by-case analysis, the touchstone of which is "the 'transferor's intention.'" Id. at 285-86 (quoting Bogardus v. Commissioner, 302 U.S. 34 (1937)). After reading *Duberstein*, a reasonable taxpayer would conclude that payments from a lover were taxable as income if they were made "in return for services rendered" rather than "out of affection, respect, admiration, charity or like impulses." Id. at 285 (quoting Robertson v. United States, 343 U.S. 711 (1952)).

Viewed in this light, I suggest that the bulk of the tax court cases cited by the majority offer no more than that the transferors in those particular cases harbored a donative intent. In my view, one cannot convincingly fashion a rule of law of general application from such a series of necessarily fact-intensive inquiries. That other taxpayers were found to have a donative intent does not bear on whether Harris had a duty to pay taxes on the monies she received from Kritzik. Whether Harris had such a duty is, under *Duberstein*, a question of Kritzik's intent, a question whose answer can be found only upon analysis of her particular circumstances. If Kritzik harbored a donative intent, then Harris was not obligated to pay taxes on his largess; if, however, he did not — if he was paying Harris for her services — then she was under a duty to do so.

It appears that the majority at once agrees and disagrees with this analysis. The majority acknowledges that *Duberstein's* principles "though general, provide a clear answer to many cases involving the gift versus income distinction and can be the basis for civil as well as criminal prosecutions in such cases." The majority is "equally certain," however, that "*Duberstein* provides no ready answer to the taxability of transfers of money to a mistress in the context of a long-term relationship." It takes this view because tax court cases have characterized similar payments made to other mistresses and companions as gifts rather than income. While apparently nodding to *Duberstein*, the majority contends that the state of the law is such that no reasonable mistress or companion could *ever*, with sufficient certainty, conclude that the payments she received were income rather than gifts and hence taxable.

How the majority can agree that the focal point of our inquiry is properly the transferor's intent and yet establish what amounts to a rule of law effectively preempting such inquiries I find perplexing. Putting aside this problem, I am unpersuaded by the majority's argument that *Duberstein's* guidance is categorically no guidance at all. Consider the following example. *A* approaches *B* and offers to spend time with him, accompany him to social events, and provide him with sexual favors for the next year if *B* gives her an apartment, a car, and a stipend of $5,000 a month. *B* agrees to *A*'s terms. According to the majority, because this example involves a transfer of money to a "mistress in the context of a long-term relationship," *A* could never be charged with criminal tax evasion if she chose not to pay taxes on *B*'s stipend. I find this hard to accept; what *A* receives from *B* is clearly income as it is "in return for services rendered." 363 U.S. at 285. To be sure, there will be situations — like the case before us — where the evidence is insufficient to support a finding that the transferor harbored a "cash for services" intent; in such cases, criminal prosecutions for willful tax evasion will indeed be impossible as a matter of law. That fact does not, however, condemn as overly vague the analysis itself.

I am thus prompted to find Harris' conviction infirm because of the relative scantiness of the record before us, not because mistresses are categorically exempt from taxation on the largess they receive. Simply put, the record before us does not establish beyond a reasonable doubt that Kritzik's intent was to pay Harris for her services, rather than out of affection or charitable impulse. As the majority relates, the record does contain evidence showing that Harris thought their relationship to be of the "cash-for-services" kind. Such evidence is, in my view, probative — to some degree — of Kritzik's intent. . . . But not sufficiently so to support a criminal conviction. Absent even a scintilla of direct evidence of Kritzik's intent, I cannot conclude, on the basis of

Harris' perception of the relationship alone, that the government proved the nature of Kritzik's payments to be income rather than gift beyond a reasonable doubt.

NOTES

1. *The Stakes in* Harris. A government victory in *Harris* would have increased income tax revenue by the amount of tax due on the income; there would have been no offsetting deduction for the payor, Kritzik. (A government victory would, however, lessen the gift tax liability due the government from Kritzik's estate.) In contrast, cases involving business-related transfers usually involve a tradeoff for the government. If the transfers do not constitute gifts, they are taxable to the recipient but generally deductible by the payor. As noted supra page 135, if the two parties are in the same tax bracket, tax revenues will not be affected by whether the transfer is characterized as a gift or a business payment.

2. *Criminal tax evasion. Harris* is a criminal tax case; it is the only such case in this casebook. The statutes under which Harris was convicted, §7201 and §7203, apply to "willful" failures to pay tax or file a return, respectively. In order to obtain a conviction, the government had to prove not only that the transfers constituted income to Harris but that Harris *knew* the transfers constituted income and willfully failed to file returns or pay tax due. The mens rea requirement for the crime is knowledge or intent. Note that there is no mens rea required for civil tax liability. (Or, to put the matter somewhat differently, the tax law is in general a strict liability statute.) An individual who receives income is liable for tax on that income regardless of whether she realizes she has income or, for that matter, realizes she must pay tax on that income.

Would the court have reached a similar decision if the issue had been solely one of civil tax liability?

3. *Transfers in and out of marriage.* Had Kritzik and Harris married, the transfers of money to Harris would have been tax-free under §1041, discussed infra in Chapter 3F. The tax law would not inquire as to the motives for the marriage or the transfers. Because Kritzik and Harris were not married, the taxability of the transfers hinged on the application of the "detached and disinterested generosity" test of *Duberstein.*

4. *Taxes and morality.* Relationships like the one in *Harris* may be inherently exploitative. It may be that the tax law does not want to make it easy for couples to structure this kind of relationship in a tax-favored manner. Certainly, at the extreme, the tax law would not want to exempt wages from prostitution.

On the other hand, transfers may be made between two same-sex individuals who live in a committed relationship and cannot legally marry, or between two individuals in a committed relationship who choose not to marry. Assume the low-wage earner in the couple wants to assure himself the right to support payments in the event the relationship ends. He cannot rely on alimony: It is reserved for transfers incident to the breakup of a marriage. He could perhaps establish a right to "palimony" by insisting on a contract that assured him support in the event of a breakup. The consideration for the contract might include the services he provides to the relationship. Would the receipt of property pursuant to such a contract be taxable? Should it be taxable? See Green v. Commissioner, T.C. Memo 1987-503 (transfers pursuant to private contractual arrangements in marriage-like relationship treated as gifts).

3. Gift: Dealers' "Tokes"

OLK v. UNITED STATES

536 F.2d 876 (9th Cir.), cert. denied, 429 U.S. 920 (1976)

Before Goodwin and Sneed, Circuit Judges, and Van Pelt, District Judge.

Sneed, Circuit Judge.

This is a suit to obtain a refund of federal income taxes. The issue is whether monies, called "tokes" in the relevant trade, received by the taxpayer, a craps dealer employed by Las Vegas casinos, constitute taxable income or gifts within the meaning of §102. . . . The taxpayer insists "tokes" are non-taxable gifts. If he is right, he is entitled to the refund for which this suit was brought. The trial court in a trial without a jury held that "tokes" were gifts. The Government appealed and we reverse and hold that "tokes" are taxable income.

I. The Facts

There is no dispute about the basic facts which explain the setting in which "tokes" are paid and received. The district court's finding with respect to such facts which we accept are, in part, as follows:

> In 1971 plaintiff was employed as a craps dealer in two Las Vegas gambling casinos, the Horseshoe Club and the Sahara Hotel. The basic services performed by plaintiff and other dealers were described at trial. There are four persons involved in the operation of the game, a boxman and three dealers. One of the three dealers, the stickman, calls the roll of the dice and then collects them for the next shooter. The other two dealers collect losing bets and pay off winning bets under the supervision of the boxman. The boxman is the casino employee charged with direct super-

> vision of the dealers and the play at one particular table. He in turn is supervised by the pit boss who is responsible for several tables. The dealers also make change, advise the boxman when a player would like a drink and answer basic questions about the game for the players.
>
> Dealers are forbidden to fraternize or engage in unnecessary conversation with the casino patrons, and must remain in separate areas while on their breaks. Dealers must treat all patrons equally, and any attempt to provide special service to a patron is grounds for termination.
>
> At times, players will give money to the dealers or place bets for them. The witnesses testified that most casinos do not allow boxmen to receive money from patrons because of their supervisory positions, although some do permit this. The pit bosses are not permitted to receive anything from patrons because they are in a position in which they can insure that a patron receives some special service or treatment.
>
> The money or tokes are combined by the four dealers and split equally at the end of each shift so that a dealer will get his share of the tokes received even while he is taking his break. Uncontradicted testimony indicated that a dealer would be terminated if he kept a toke rather than placed it in the common fund.
>
> Casino management either required the dealers to pool and divide tokes or encouraged them to do so. Although the practice is tolerated by management, it is not encouraged since tokes represent money that players are not wagering and thus cannot be won by the casino. Plaintiff received about $10 per day as his share of tokes at the Horseshoe Club and an average of $20 per day in tokes at the Sahara. . . .

Additional findings of fact by the district court are that the taxpayer worked as a stickman and dealer and at all times was under the supervision of the boxman who in turn was supervised by the pit boss. Also the district court found that patrons sometimes give money to dealers, other players or mere spectators at the game, but that between 90-95% of the patrons give nothing to a dealer. No obligation on the part of the patron exists to give to a dealer and "dealers perform no service for patrons which a patron would normally find compensable." Another finding is that there exists "no direct relation between services performed for management by a dealer and benefit or detriment to the patron."

There then follows two final "findings of fact" which taken together constitute the heart of the controversy before us. These are as follows:

> 17. The tokes are given to dealers as a result of impulsive generosity or superstition on the part of players, and not as a form of compensation for services.
>
> 18. Tokes are the result of detached and disinterested generosity on the part of a small number of patrons.

These two findings, together with the others set out above, bear the unmistakable imprint of Commissioner v. Duberstein [supra page 130] particularly that portion of the opinion which reads as follows:

> The course of decision here makes it plain that the statute does not use the term "gift" in the common-law sense, but in a more colloquial sense. . . .

II. Finding Number 18 Is a Conclusion of Law

The position of the taxpayer is simple. The above findings conform to the meaning of gifts as used in section 102 of the Code. *Duberstein* further teaches, the taxpayer asserts, that whether a receipt qualified as a non-taxable gift is "basically one of fact," . . . and appellate review of such findings is restricted to determining whether they are clearly erroneous. Because none of the recited findings are clearly erroneous, concludes the taxpayer, the judgment of the trial court must be affirmed.

We could not escape this logic were we prepared to accept as a "finding of fact" the trial court's finding number 18. We reject the trial court's characterization. The conclusion that tokes "are the result of detached and disinterested generosity" on the part of those patrons who engage in the practice of toking is a conclusion of law, not a finding of fact. . . .

III. Finding Number 18 and Other Conclusions of Law Based Thereon Are Erroneous

Freed of the restraint of the "clearly erroneous" standard, we are convinced that finding number 18 and all derivative conclusions of law are wrong. "Impulsive generosity or superstition on the part of the players" we accept as the dominant motive. In the context of gambling in casinos open to the public such a motive is quite understandable. However, our understanding also requires us to acknowledge that payments so motivated are not acts of "detached or disinterested generosity." Quite the opposite is true. Tribute to the gods of fortune which it is hoped will be returned bounteously soon can only be described as an "involved and intensely interested" act.

Moreover, in applying the statute to the findings of fact, we are not permitted to ignore those findings which strongly suggest that tokes in the hands of the ultimate recipients are viewed as a receipt indistinguishable, except for erroneously anticipated tax differences, from wages. The regularity of the flow, the equal division of the receipts, and the daily amount received indicate that a dealer acting reasonably would come to regard such receipts as a form of compensation for his services. The manner in which a dealer may regard tokes is, of course, not the touchstone for determining whether the receipt is excludable from gross income. It is, however, a reasonable and relevant inference well-grounded in the findings of fact.

Our view of the law is consistent with the trend of authorities in the area of commercial gratuities as well as with the only decision squarely in point, Lawrence E. Bevers, 26 T.C. 1218 (1956), and this Circuit's view of tips as revealed in Roberts v. Commissioner, 176 F.2d 221 (9th Cir. 1949). Generalizations are treacherous but not without utility. One such is that receipts by taxpayers engaged in rendering services contributed by those with whom the taxpayers have some personal or functional contact in the course of the performance of the services are taxable income when in conformity with the practices of the area and easily valued. Tokes, like tips, meet these conditions. That is enough.

The taxpayer is not entitled to the refund he seeks.

Reversed.

NOTES

1. *Ordinary tips.* Ordinary tips are includable in income on the theory that they are payments for services rendered. See Regs. §1.61-2(a)(1). The problem with tips is enforcement. Section 6053, enacted in 1982, contains complex and stiff rules requiring employer information returns on actual or putative tip income in the case of restaurants and cocktail lounges employing more than ten persons. The apparent burdensomeness of the reporting requirement is testimony to the seriousness of the Service's enforcement problems.

More unusual payments, analogous (at least) to tips, have led to clever, but unsuccessful, arguments. For example, United States v. McCormick, 67 F.2d 867 (2d Cir. 1933), cert. denied, 291 U.S. 662 (1934), holds that "contributions" received by a city clerk after marriage ceremonies from bridegrooms who were fearful of being accused of stinginess were taxable; and see Regs. §1.61-2(a)(1), to the effect that "marriage fees and other contributions received by a clergyman for services" are taxable. See also Miller v. Commissioner, 327 F.2d 846 (2d Cir.), cert. denied, 379 U.S. 816 (1964) (distributions from a Christmas fund contributed by members of a club for its employees held taxable).

2. *Surviving spouses.* Poyner v. Commissioner, 301 F.2d 287 (4th Cir. 1962), referred to by the court in *Olk,* was one of many cases involving payments by corporations to the surviving spouses of deceased executives, with the recipient claiming gift and the corporation claiming a deductible expense. Relying on the wording of the corporate resolution authorizing the payment, which resolution began "in recognition of the services," the Tax Court had ruled that the payment was not a gift. The Court of Appeals reversed, relying on pre-*Duberstein* Tax Court precedent (301 F.2d at 291-292):

> The clearest formulation appears in Florence S. Luntz, 29 T.C. 647, 650 (1958) where the Tax Court listed the following as the five factors to be considered:
>
> > (1) the payments had been made to the wife of the deceased employee and not to his estate; (2) there was no obligation on the part of the corporation to pay any additional compensation to the deceased employee; (3) the corporation derived no benefit from the payment; (4) the wife of the deceased employee performed no services for the corporation; and (5) the services of her husband had been fully compensated.
>
> The stipulated facts directly respond to every one of the five factors, and in each instance the response is favorable to the widow. This being so, we see no justification for the Tax Court's finding that "there is no solid evidence that they [the directors authorizing the payments] were motivated in any part by the widow's needs or by a sense of generosity or the like." . . . The only evidence on which the Tax Court specifically relies for its contrary finding is the wording of the authorizing corporate resolutions. . . .
>
> The Supreme Court in *Duberstein* did not destroy the authority of the earlier Tax Court cases and the guides enunciated in them for discovering motivation.

The appeal of this kind of benefit was reduced considerably by the adoption, in 1962, of §274(b), which limits the deduction for gifts to $25. See supra page 138. Would it still be possible for separate triers of fact to find a gift in the case of a surviving spouse and nongift in the case of the corporate payor? How would you advise a corporate client on the drafting of a resolution authorizing a payment to a surviving spouse, assuming that management is determined to assure the corporation a deduction?

3. *Prizes, awards, scholarships, and fellowships.* Before 1954, the forerunner of §102 was relied on by the courts and the Service to provide a broad exclusion for scholarships and fellowships and a limited exclusion for prizes and awards. The 1954 act added provisions that modified and attempted to clarify the existing law in this area but, at least in the case of scholarships and fellowships, left enough uncertainty to generate a seemingly endless stream of litigation (e.g., over whether a graduate student's or an intern's stipend was compensation for services rather than a fellowship). The 1986 act excised that portion of the provision relating to prizes and awards (§74) that allowed a limited exclusion. In doing so it left in place a rule requiring inclusion of such benefits in gross income (with a few minor exceptions relating to charitable contributions).[20]

20. The 1986 act also added §74(c), which provides a narrowly circumscribed exclusion for certain noncash awards to employees for length of service or for safety achievements.

The 1986 act also drastically modified the provision relating to scholarships and fellowships (§117), leaving only a limited exclusion for scholarships provided to degree candidates. The limited exclusion is for that portion of a scholarship that is required to be used for tuition, fees, books, and supplies and for equipment required for courses. The new law retained the previous rule that the exclusion does not apply to any portion of a scholarship that represents payment for teaching, research, or other services. This rule has given rise to disputes between students (who proved to be an exceptionally litigious lot) and the Service in the past and will no doubt continue to do so in the future, but the stakes will be much smaller (because the exclusion is more limited). Does the distinction between a "pure" scholarship and one that requires the performance of services seem to you to be consistent with sound principles of taxation? Why should there be any exclusion at all for scholarships? Are they like gifts? (And if so, so what?) Or does the exclusion reflect the notion that a tuition remission has no significant value? If it is fair to exclude tuition scholarships from gross income, should students who work their way through school, and pay full tuition, be allowed a deduction for their tuition payments? Should students who pay relatively low tuition at state universities and colleges be required to include in income the value of the subsidy they receive? What about the argument that scholarship students generally receive barely enough for survival and therefore should not be expected to pay taxes?

4. *Bequest.* Under §102, bequests are excluded from income along with gifts. Problems have arisen in distinguishing between bequests and belated compensation for services rendered to the decedent during his or her lifetime. In Wolder v. Commissioner, 493 F.2d 608 (2d Cir.), cert. denied, 419 U.S. 828 (1974), a "bequest" to a lawyer pursuant to a formal agreement under which he rendered legal services without charge was held to be income. On the other hand, in McDonald v. Commissioner, 2 T.C. 840 (1943), a bequest "in appreciation" of services as the decedent's nurse, dietitian, secretary, and driver during his declining years was held to be excluded under §102.

A payment received in settlement of a will contest by a person claiming rights as an heir has been held to be a bequest within the contemplation of §102. Lyeth v. Hoey, 305 U.S. 188 (1938).

5. *Welfare.* Welfare payments and various other government payments, such as those for relief of disaster (Rev. Rul. 76-144, 1976-1 C.B. 17) and for victims of crime (Rev. Rul. 74-74, 1974-1 C.B. 18), have been treated by the Service as excludable not under §102 but rather as not within the contemplation of §61. The label attached is payments "for the general welfare," or something similar. Should these exclusions be thought of as "subsidies" or "tax expenditures"? Do they reflect an improper use of the tax system to achieve nontax goals?

Unemployment payments were also excluded (Rev. Rul. 76-63, 1976-1 C.B. 14), but now, under §85, are fully includable.

6. *Social security.* Before 1983, the entire amount of social security retirement benefits was excluded from income, by long-standing IRS fiat. See Rev. Rul. 70-217, 1970-1 C.B. 13. Under current law, the treatment of social security benefits depends on the taxpayer's adjusted gross income, augmented by one-half the benefits received, tax-exempt interest and other items. §86. Married couples filing joint returns with adjusted gross income (augmented by items stated above) less than $32,000 may continue to exclude social security benefits from taxation. Married couples with adjusted gross income in excess of $32,000 but below $44,000 must take into income the lesser of one-half of social security benefits or one-half the amount by which adjusted gross income exceeds $32,000. The treatment of benefits received by married couples with adjusted gross income between $44,000 and about $60,000 is computationally somewhat complex. Essentially, as adjusted gross income rises above $44,000, the couple must take into income 85 percent of the amount of social security benefits. The obvious intent behind all this complexity is to phase out the exclusion as income rises.

7. *Alimony versus gift.* The special rules relating to alimony, child support, and property settlement payments are considered later (infra page 420). Generally, alimony payments are deductible by the payor and taxable to the recipient, while child support and property settlement payments are not deductible by the payor and are not income to the payee. Under the law of many states, the obligation to pay alimony terminates on the remarriage of the person entitled to receive such payments. Rev. Rul. 82-155, 1982-2 C.B. 36, considers two situations in which alimony payments were continued despite the fact that the recipient had remarried and the payor's legal obligation to make those payments had terminated. In one situation, the payor was unaware of the remarriage; the ruling holds that the payment is taxable to the recipient under §61 but the payor is not entitled to a deduction. In the other situation, the payor knew of the termination of the legal obligation and decided to continue payments anyway; the ruling holds that those payments were excludable from the income of the recipient under §102.

QUESTIONS

1. Is the result in the *Olk* case consistent with the goals of a good tax system? Is it consistent with *Duberstein?* What is the significance under *Duberstein* of the fact, cited as relevant by the court, that "tokes in the hands of the ultimate recipient are viewed as a receipt indistinguishable . . . from wages"?

2. (a) Orthopedic surgeon Sandy successfully performs a difficult operation on accident victim Wendy. Therapist Teresa helps Wendy recover the full use of her damaged muscles. Wendy pays her bill and then, unexpectedly, offers both Sandy and Teresa free use of her ski

condominium. Sandy and Teresa each accept Wendy's offer and each spends two weeks at the condominium. Suppose that Sandy and Teresa ask your advice on whether they must, or should, report the value of their use of the condominium as income. What do you say?

(b) The facts are the same as in Question 2(a) except that instead of giving the use of the condominium, Wendy gives Sandy and Teresa each a check for $2,000. Are Sandy and Teresa taxable on the amounts they received? Is it important to know whether Wendy claimed a deduction for the payments as medical expenses? Suppose Wendy did deduct the payments as medical expenses, that the deduction was challenged by the IRS, and that the Tax Court, after observing that Wendy's opinion about the nature of the payments is irrelevant, upheld the IRS's denial of the deduction. Would these additional facts relating to the deduction by Wendy strengthen or weaken Sandy's and Teresa's claim that the payments were gifts?

3. Phyllis is a wealthy woman who grew up in a small town. She learns that the factory that is the principal employer in the town pays wages so low that its employees can eke out only a meager existence. She wants to help these hardworking people and enters into an arrangement with the factory owner under which each employee receives at Christmas a bonus equal to 25 percent of the wages he or she earned in the preceding twelve months. Is the bonus excludable from gross income under §102? What if the same bonus is paid every year for ten years?

4. Transfer of Unrealized Gain

The following case is not part of our examination of gifts and windfalls as they affect the concept of income for tax purposes. Instead, it illustrates the effects of a gift transaction. The principal purpose of putting the case here is to introduce the concept of basis, which we will examine at various points in these materials and which is vital to an understanding of income taxation. But the case may also be thought of as an illustration of what might be called a "surrogate" taxpayer — a person who is taxed on the income of another person. As such, the case is another example of the conflict between fairness (which argues in this setting for taxing the person to whom the income accrued) and practicality (which argues here for taxing the person who realizes the income).

The present statutory background of the case is this: Section 61(a)(3) includes in gross income "gains from dealings in property." Section 1001 provides that the amount of the gain is the "excess of the amount realized . . . over the adjusted basis." The adjusted basis is the basis, defined under §1012 as "cost" (with certain exceptions), "adjusted as provided in section 1016." However, there is an exception in §1015 for property acquired by gift. Where gift property is sold by the donee for an amount greater than the donor's basis, the donee's basis (which word is used in §1015 to refer to adjusted basis) is the same as the donor's basis — in other words, the donee takes a "substituted basis" (§7701(a)(42)) from the donor. (Tax experts often use the word "basis" to refer to the original or cost basis or the adjusted basis, whichever is appropriate, and commonly use the phrase "carryover basis" to refer to what the code now calls "substituted basis.") The same basic statutory scheme was in effect at the time the case arose. The taxpayer challenged its application on constitutional grounds.

TAFT v. BOWERS

278 U.S. 470 (1929)

Mr. Justice McReynolds delivered the opinion of the Court. . . .

Abstractly stated, this is the problem:

In 1916 *A* purchased 100 shares of stock for $1,000, which he held until 1923 when the fair market value had become $2,000. He then gave them to *B* who sold them during the year 1923 for $5,000. The United States claim that under the Revenue Act of 1921 *B* must pay income tax upon $4,000, as realized profits. *B* maintains that only $3,000 — the appreciation during her ownership — can be regarded as income; that the increase during the donor's ownership is not income assessable against her within intendment of the Sixteenth Amendment.

The District Court ruled against the United States; the Circuit Court of Appeals held with them. . . .

We think the manifest purpose of Congress expressed in [§1015] was to require the petitioner to pay the enacted tax.[21]

The only question subject to serious controversy is whether Congress had power to authorize the exaction.

It is said that the gift became a capital asset of the donee to the extent of its value when received and, therefore, when disposed of by her no part of that value could be treated as taxable income in her hands.

The Sixteenth Amendment provides —

21. [Before the enactment of the predecessor of §1015, the Service had ruled that the basis to the donee of property received by gift was its fair market value at the time of the transfer. In 1921 the House Committee on Ways and Means reported: "This rule has been the source of serious evasion and abuse. Taxpayers having property which has come to be worth far more than it cost give such property to wives or relatives by whom it may be sold without realizing a gain unless the selling price is in excess of the value of the property at the time of the gift." To cure this practice, Congress enacted what is now the first clause of §1015(a). At the same time, it endorsed the administrative rule for pre-1921 gifts. §1015(c). See H.R. Rep. No. 350, 67th Cong., 1st Sess., 1939-1 (Pt. 2) C.B. 175. — Eds.]

> The Congress shall have power to lay and collect taxes on incomes from whatever source derived, without apportionment among the several States, and without regard to any census or enumeration.

Income is the thing which may be taxed — income from any source. The Amendment does not attempt to define income or to designate how taxes may be laid thereon, or how they may be enforced.

Under former decisions here the settled doctrine is that the Sixteenth Amendment confers no power upon Congress to define and tax as income without apportionment something which theretofore could not have been properly regarded as income.

Also, this Court has declared — "Income may be defined as the gain derived from capital, from labor, or from both combined, provided it be understood to include profit gained through a sale or conversion of capital assets." Eisner v. Macomber, 252 U.S. 189, 207 [infra page 286]. The "gain derived from capital," within the definition, is "not a gain accruing to capital, nor a growth or increment of value in the investment, but a gain, a profit, something of exchangeable value proceeding from the property, severed from the capital however invested, and coming in, that is, received or drawn by the claimant for his separate use, benefit and disposal." United States v. Phellis, 257 U.S. 156, 169.

If, instead of giving the stock to petitioner, the donor had sold it at market value, the excess over the capital he invested (cost) would have been income therefrom and subject to taxation under the Sixteenth Amendment. He would have been obliged to share the realized gain with the United States. He held the stock — the investment — subject to the right of the sovereign to take part of any increase in its value when separated through sale or conversion and reduced to his possession. Could he, contrary to the express will of Congress, by mere gift enable another to hold this stock free from such right, deprive the sovereign of the possibility of taxing the appreciation when actually severed, and convert the entire property into a capital asset of the donee, who invested nothing, as though the latter had purchased at the market price? And after a still further enhancement of the property, could the donee make a second gift with like effect, etc.? We think not.

In truth the stock represented only a single investment of capital — that made by the donor. And when through sale or conversion the increase was separated therefrom, it became income from that investment in the hands of the recipient subject to taxation according to the very words of the Sixteenth Amendment. By requiring the recipient of the entire increase to pay a part into the public treasury, Congress deprived her of no right and subjected her to no hardship. She accepted the gift with knowledge of the statute and, as to the property received, voluntarily assumed the position of her donor. When she sold the stock she actually got the original sum invested, plus the entire appreciation and out of the latter only was she called on to pay the tax demanded.

The provision of the statute under consideration seems entirely appropriate for enforcing a general scheme of lawful taxation. . . .

The power of Congress to require a succeeding owner, in respect of taxation, to assume the place of his predecessor is pointed out by United States v. Phellis, 257 U.S. 156, 171:

> Where, as in this case, the dividend constitutes a distribution of profits accumulated during an extended period and bears a large proportion to the par value of the stock, if an investor happened to buy stock shortly before the dividend, paying a price enhanced by an estimate of the capital plus the surplus of the company, and after distribution of the surplus, with corresponding reduction in the intrinsic and market value of the shares, he was called upon to pay a tax upon the dividend received, it might look in his case like a tax upon his capital. But it is only apparently so. In buying at a price that reflected the accumulated profits, he of course acquired as a part of the valuable rights purchased the prospect of a dividend from the accumulations — bought "dividend on," as the phrase goes — and necessarily took subject to the burden of the income tax proper to be assessed against him by reason of the dividend if and when made. He simply stepped into the shoes, in this as in other respects, of the stockholder whose shares he acquired, and presumably the prospect of a dividend influenced the price paid, and was discounted by the prospect of an income tax to be paid thereon. In short, the question whether a dividend made out of company profits constitutes income of the stockholder is not affected by antecedent transfers of the stock from hand to hand.

There is nothing in the Constitution which lends support to the theory that gain actually resulting from the increased value of capital can be treated as taxable income in the hands of the recipient only so far as the increase occurred while he owned the property. And Irwin v. Gavit, 268 U.S. 161, 167 [infra page 188], is to the contrary.

The judgments below are affirmed.

NOTES AND QUESTIONS

1. *Gift versus compensation.* The stock received by the taxpayer in this case was plainly a gift. As such it was excluded from income under §102(a). If the transfer had been compensatory, the basis rule would have been different. For example, suppose that *L* (a lawyer) performs services for *C* (a client) and bills *C* for $2,000. *C* admits she owes the $2,000 but offers to pay by transferring to *L* shares of stock of IBM that *C* had bought for $1,000 and that presently are worth $2,000. *L* accepts, and the shares are transferred. *L* has income of $2,000, and

her basis for the shares is $2,000. The basis is arrived at under §1012, which refers to "cost"; "cost" has a special meaning for tax purposes. The results are, as they should be, the same as they would be if *C* had paid *L* $2,000 cash and *L* had used the cash to buy the shares. If *L* subsequently sells the shares for $5,000, she will have a gain for tax purposes of $3,000. By virtue of the transfer of the shares to *L, C* has a taxable gain of $1,000, just as if she had sold the shares and paid *L* cash. Would it be better in this situation to follow the approach used in the case of gifts? That is, would it be sensible to ignore the gain on the stock at the time of the transfer from *C* to *L* and tax *L* on $4,000 gain at the time of sale? Would your answer be different if the property transferred were not shares of stock of a publicly traded corporation but rather property that was difficult to value (for example, a work of art)?

2. *Pity the donee?* The taxpayer made the following argument (278 U.S. at 474): "The person acquiring property can never tell what liability he assumes in the way of income tax if any basis entirely foreign to him can be arbitrarily adopted for determining his gain." How would you respond? Is it relevant that Ms. Taft, the donee, happened to be the daughter of the donor? Is this relationship a surprising element in the case? Why should the donee's basis not be zero?

3. *Estoppel?* The Court says that Ms. Taft "accepted the gift with knowledge of the statute." Would the result be different in another case if the taxpayer were able to prove total ignorance of the statute? What if the taxpayer were six months old at the time of the gift?

4. *Tax the donor?* Would it be better to tax the gain (or allow a deduction for the loss) on property at the time of a transfer by gift? In other words, should such a transfer be a recognition event? See §84, treating the transfer of appreciated property to a political organization as a sale. See also §644, taxing a trust at the donor's rates where property is sold by the trust within two years of the transfer to it.

5. *Broader implications.* In *Taft,* the taxpayers (there were two cases, consolidated) relied heavily on Eisner v. Macomber's definition of income, but they lost. See supra page 160. This case therefore can be seen as a limitation on, or partial rejection of, the concept of income for which *Macomber* is authority and symbol. (Note, by the way, that where a tax case is to be referred to by one of two names in its caption, the name used should be that of the taxpayer, e.g., Macomber, not that of the tax collector, e.g., Eisner, since the tax collector's name is likely to appear in many cases.)

6. *Adjustment for gift tax.* Section 1015(d) provides an upward adjustment of the donee's basis to reflect any federal gift tax paid by the donor.[22] For gifts made before 1977 the adjustment is for the entire

22. The gift tax is a tax on the act of transfer by gift and is imposed on the donor

amount of the gift tax paid by the donor, but the basis as adjusted may not exceed the value of the property at the time of the gift. For post-1977 gifts, the adjustment is limited to the gift tax attributable to the net appreciation in the value of the gift property. §1016(d)(6). The congressional rationale for the adjustment is that the gift tax is part of the cost of the property. The post-1977 rule reflects a sense that the prior rule was too generous, but, in any event, the congressional rationale is unsatisfactory. See 2 B. Bittker, Federal Income, Estate and Gift Taxation ¶41.3.23 (1981). The adjustment perhaps reflects the fact that the gift tax may have been excessive since that tax is based on the full value of the property instead of the value reduced by the liability for a future income tax. See discussion of the §691 adjustment for estate taxes, infra Note 8.

7. *Transfers at death.* Under §1014, the basis of property acquired by reason of death is the fair market value on the date of death or, at the election of the executor or administrator under §2032, on the optional valuation date (six months after death). For simplicity we will, as most practitioners do, sometimes use "date-of-death" value to refer to whichever date is applicable. The effect of §1014 is that the basis is either "stepped up" or "stepped down" from the decedent's basis to the date-of-death value. What we encounter in practice is mostly stepped-up basis, because of inflation and because holders of property will find it profitable to sell their loss property before death, to take advantage of a deduction for the loss, and to retain their gain property, enabling their heirs to take advantage of the step-up. Most objective observers regard the step-up as a disturbing tax gap. It is true, of course, that the full value of the property will be subject to an estate tax, but that is not a satisfactory justification for failing to apply the income tax, for two reasons. First, conceptually the estate tax is a tax on a transfer; it has nothing to do with gain or loss associated with the property transferred. Second, and more substantively, the estate tax does not fill the gap left by the income tax's step-up because it applies without regard to previously unrealized appreciation. Thus, a person who sells property before death pays an income tax on any gain plus an estate tax on the property remaining in the estate after payment of the tax. Both taxes are collected, though the estate tax is imposed on an amount reduced by the income tax payment. An otherwise identical person who holds on to the property until death pays only the estate tax, though on a larger amount, because the estate has not been reduced by the income tax.

The effect of §1014 is to encourage people to hold on to appreciated property until death, which results in some degree of immobility of

---

with secondary liability on the donee if the donor does not pay. For the most part, the gift tax, and the estate tax (which is a tax on the act of transfer by reason of death), should be thought of as entirely separate from, and not relevant to, the income tax.

capital, which economists find troubling. The fact that a person must hold on to the property until death does not necessarily mean that that person will be unable to enjoy the benefit of its increased value. Often, the owner will be able to borrow against the appreciation, and loans do not result in recognition of gain, even when they exceed basis. (See infra page 232.) The proceeds of the loan can be used for any purpose, including consumption, and the property can be sold to pay off the loan after death has produced a stepped-up basis, so that the sale will not generate taxable income. At the same time, the loan obligation will reduce the value of the estate for estate tax purposes.

In 1970, Stanley Surrey (Harvard Law School professor and, from 1961 to 1969, Assistant Secretary of the Treasury for Tax Policy) and Jerome Kurtz (tax practitioner, formerly Tax Legislative Counsel and later Commissioner of Internal Revenue) wrote (perhaps with hyperbole) that "the failure of the income tax to reach the appreciation in value of assets transferred at death" is "the most serious defect in our federal tax structure today." Reform of Death and Gift Taxes: The 1969 Treasury Proposals, The Criticisms, and a Rebuttal, 70 Colum. L. Rev. 1365, 1381.

In 1976 Congress enacted §1023, which provided for a substituted basis for property acquired by reason of death. This reform later was postponed and ultimately was repealed, with a grandfather clause to protect reliance interests.

8. *Income in respect of a decedent.* Although §1014(a) relieves from taxation income or gain that had not been realized at the time of decedent's death (see supra page 163), under §691, income or gain that had been *earned,* in an accrual accounting sense, before death is subject to a different set of rules. See §1014(c). Such income is called "income in respect of a decedent," a term that is used in §691 but is not defined anywhere in the Code. The application of §691 may be illustrated as follows. In 1986, *L,* a lawyer, bills a client $10,000 for services but, before collecting, dies. *L*'s executor collects the $10,000 for the estate in 1987. Three tax returns must be considered. First, there is the final income tax return of the decedent *L* for 1986. Second, there is the estate tax return — that is, the return on which the amount of the estate tax is calculated. Third, there is the income tax return of the estate for 1987.

If *L* were an accrual-method taxpayer (which would be unusual), the $10,000 fee would be reported on his 1986 return. Suppose that his marginal tax rate is 40 percent. The tax would be $4,000. Since the $10,000 was reported as income on *L*'s 1986 return, it would not be treated as income of the estate when collected by it in 1987, so it would not affect the 1987 income tax return of the estate. For estate tax purposes, the right to collect the $10,000 would be an asset of the estate, but it would be offset by the tax liability of $4,000, so the item would increase the size of the estate by only $6,000. Suppose that the estate tax marginal rate is 30 percent. The estate tax attributable to the item would be $1,800. The total of the income tax ($4,000) and the estate tax ($1,800) would be $5,800. As applied to these facts, accrual accounting is an accurate method of accounting and the result, with a total tax of $5,800, is the accurate (though to some people perhaps distasteful) result, given the basic rules embodied in the income tax and the estate tax.

Now suppose (more realistically) that *L* is a cash-method taxpayer. For purposes of his 1986 tax return, his executor is permitted to continue to use the cash method. Consequently, *L*'s 1986 income tax return will not include the $10,000 item of earned income. Under §691, however, that item must be reported as income by the estate, on its 1987 income tax return. But the estate must also include the full value of the item — $10,000 — in the estate for the purpose of computing the estate tax. Assume again that the marginal estate tax rate for the estate is 30 percent. It will pay an estate tax of $3,000 on the item. This $3,000 becomes a deduction on the income tax return of the estate. §691(c). Thus, the net amount by which the item increases the income of the estate, for purposes of its income tax return, is $7,000. If the income tax rate of the estate is the same as *L*'s rate, 40 percent, the tax attributable to the item will be $2,800. The total taxes paid by the estate will be the $3,000 estate tax and the $2,800 income tax, or $5,800. This is the same as the result arrived at under the "accurate" method. The identity of result depends, however, on the fact that the income tax rate of the estate was hypothesized to be the same as the income tax rate of the decedent.

Instead of collecting the $10,000 itself, the estate might, in certain circumstances, assign that right to a beneficiary of the estate. In that case, the beneficiary would include the $10,000 in his or her income in the year of collection, with a deduction for the amount of the estate tax attributable to the item.

Income in respect of a decedent is not limited to items of income from the performance of services or to items of ordinary income. Suppose, for example, that before his death *L* had contracted to sell a piece of property but that delivery and payment had not occurred at the date of death. Any gain realized on the transaction would be taxed under the same system of rules applicable to the $10,000 income from performance of services, except that the gain would be capital gain.

Income in respect of a decedent does not, however, include gain on assets owned by the decedent and not subject to any contract for sale at the date of death; if it did, there would be nothing left of the §1014 stepped-up basis at death. Suppose, for example, that at the time of his death in 1986, *L* owned a house, in which he lived, with a basis of $10,000. Suppose that in 1987 *L*'s executor sells the house for $115,000.

Here §1014(a) controls. The basis of the house for the purpose of determining gain or loss on sale by the executor in 1987 is the fair market value at the date of death (or alternative valuation date). Suppose that that value was $100,000. In that case, the executor, on the income tax return of the estate for 1987, would report a capital gain of $15,000.

QUESTIONS

1. Suppose *A* purchases stock for $1,000 and gives the stock to his son, *B*, at a time when the fair market value of the stock is $2,500.

(a) How much gain does *B* recognize if he sells the stock for $3,500?

(b) How much gain does *B* recognize if he sells the stock for $1,500?

2. Suppose *C* purchases stock for $2,000 and gives the stock to her daughter, *D*, at a time when the fair market value of the stock is $1,000. What amount of gain or loss (if any) is recognized by *D* on a sale for the following amounts?

(a) $2,500

(b) $500

(c) $1,500

3. During the next four years, Ernesto's daughter, Ana, will require $80,000 for college tuition and expenses. In each of the following settings, advise Ernesto as to the best means of transferring wealth to his daughter so that she may go to college. Ernesto is in the maximum marginal tax bracket and Ana has no income.

(a) Ernesto has a single asset, stock with a basis of $20,000 and a fair market value of $80,000.

(b) Ernesto has a single asset, stock with a basis of $120,000 and a fair market value of $80,000.

(c) Ernesto has stock with a basis of $20,000 and a fair market value of $80,000, plus $80,000 in a savings account.

(d) Ernesto has stock with a basis of $20,000 and a fair market value of $80,000, plus stock with a basis of $120,000 and a fair market value of $80,000.

(e) The facts are the same as in (a) except that Ernesto is 88 years old and is in poor health.

D. RECOVERY OF CAPITAL

Income includes interest, rents, dividends, and other returns *on* one's capital or cost or investment. It also includes gains from the sale (or other disposition) of that capital. But it does not include returns or recoveries *of* one's capital. The materials in this section are concerned with the recovery-of-capital exclusion, which has always been a part of fundamental tax doctrine. The rules tend to reflect the ever-present conflict between practicality and accuracy.

If a taxpayer buys one hundred shares of common stock of a corporation for $1,000 and later sells forty of those shares for $700, the tax calculation is simple. Since the shares are homogeneous, the total cost is allocated equally among them. Thus, the cost of the forty shares that were sold is $400, and the gain for tax purposes is $300. But suppose that the taxpayer buys one hundred acres of land for $1,000, that forty acres are wooded and sixty acres are tillable, and that the forty wooded acres are sold for $700. It is not reasonable to assume that the value of wooded acres is necessarily the same as the value of tillable acres. An allocation of the total cost will require judgment based on experience. Despite the difficulties, an allocation of cost will be required. Suppose, for example, that experts determine that at the time of purchase, the wooded acres had been worth $450 and the tillable acres had been worth $550. The gain on the sale of the wooded acres for $700 would then be $250. See Regs. §1.61-6 and cases cited in Heiner v. Mellon, 304 U.S. 271, 275 n.3 (1938).

At some point, however, the uncertainties in calculating the relative values of what has been sold and what has been retained may be so great as to require some other sort of solution. In other words, at some point practicality may require some sacrifice of accuracy. For example, suppose you invest $1 million in a gold mine and start to mine and sell the gold. Ultimately, all the gold will be mined and the mine will be worthless. Unfortunately, no one may be able to provide a reasonably accurate estimate of the amount of gold to be mined. So how do you recover the $1 million investment? One possibility that Congress hit on early in the development of the tax law was to allow a deduction for a percentage of the sales price of the gold. For example, if the applicable percentage were 5 percent and if, in a given year, the taxpayer sold $300,000 worth of gold, she or he would be entitled to a deduction (called percentage depletion) of $15,000 to reflect the cost of the sales. In Stanton v. Baltic Mining Co., 240 U.S. 103 (1916), a taxpayer argued that this allowance was inadequate and that the resulting tax was unconstitutional. The Court rejected this argument. While the opinion can be read as authorizing a tax on gross receipts, the better view seems to be that "because of the uncertainties [in calculating the cost of the ore that has been mined] no direct allowance for depletion need be made, any loss on account of the working of the mine being allowed if, and when, the mine is sold." R. Magill, Taxable Income 351 (rev. ed. 1945).

We must always be mindful, however, of what accuracy requires and of the significance of its sacrifice. An accurate measure of income is one that properly reflects the difference between one's total economic resources at the beginning and at the end of the relevant time period. If, for example, at the beginning of the taxable year a taxpayer puts $1,000 into an ordinary savings account at a bank, and the bank pays interest of 8 percent, at the end of the year the account should have risen in value to $1,080. The accurate measure of income is the $80 increment and that amount is in fact treated as income for tax purposes. This is true without regard to whether the $80 is in fact withdrawn and without regard to what label is attached by the bank to any amount that is in fact withdrawn. Suppose, however, that the $1,000 is invested instead in an annuity policy (see supra page 79), that the value of that policy rises to $1,080 by the end of the year, that the terms of the policy provide that the $80 increase in value (the interest equivalent) cannot be withdrawn but that an equivalent amount of the original $1,000 can be withdrawn, and that for tax purposes the $80 increment is ignored and the withdrawal of $80 is treated as a recovery of a part of one's original $1,000 investment rather than as income. The result will be an understatement of income in an economic sense. Investments in annuities will be treated more favorably than investments in savings accounts, which will produce unfairness and distortion of economic choice. The unfairness and distortion are clear and dramatic in this instance. Congress ultimately eliminated the possibility of a tax-free withdrawal (see §72(e)), but it failed to eliminate the basic source of the problem — the failure to tax the earnings on annuities until those earnings are withdrawn.

1. Sales of Easements

INAJA LAND CO. v. COMMISSIONER

9 T.C. 727 (1947), acq. 1948-1 C.B. 2

[In 1928 the taxpayer paid $61,000 for 1,236 acres of land on the banks of the Owens River in Mono County, California, together with certain water rights, for use primarily as a private fishing club. In 1934, the City of Los Angeles constructed a tunnel nearby and began to divert "foreign waters" into the Owens River upstream from the taxpayer's property. These foreign waters contained "concrete dust, sediment, and foreign matter," which adversely affected the fishing on taxpayer's preserve and, by substantially increasing the flow of water, caused flooding and erosion. In 1939, after the taxpayer threatened legal action, a settlement was reached under which the city paid the taxpayer $50,000 to "release and forever discharge" the city from any liability for the diversion and for an easement to continue to divert foreign waters into the Owens River. In settling its claim, the taxpayer incurred attorneys' fees and costs of $1,000.]

Leech, Judge.

The question presented is whether the net amount of $49,000 received by petitioner in the taxable year 1939 under a certain indenture constitutes taxable income under [§61(a)], or is chargeable to capital account. The respondent contends: (a) That the $50,000, less $1,000 expenses incurred, which petitioner received from the city of Los Angeles under the indenture of August 11, 1939, represented compensation for loss of present and future income and consideration for release of many meritorious causes of action against the city, constituting ordinary income; and, (b) since petitioner has failed to allocate such sum between taxable and nontaxable income, it has not sustained its burden of showing error. Petitioner maintains that the language of the indenture and the circumstances leading up to its execution demonstrate that the consideration was paid for the easement granted to the city of Los Angeles and the consequent damage to its property rights; that the loss of past or future profits was not considered or involved; that the character of the easement rendered it impracticable to attempt to apportion a basis to the property affected; and, since the sum received is less than the basis of the entire property, taxation should be postponed until the final disposition of the property. . . .

Upon this record we have concluded that no part of the recovery was paid for loss of profits, but was paid for the conveyance of a right of way and easements, and for damages to petitioner's land and its property rights as riparian owner. Hence, the respondent's contention has no merit. Capital recoveries in excess of cost do constitute taxable income. Petitioner has made no attempt to allocate a basis to that part of the property covered by the easements. It is conceded that all of petitioner's lands were not affected by the easements conveyed. Petitioner does not contest the rule that, where property is acquired for a lump sum and subsequently disposed of a portion at a time, there must be an allocation of the cost or other basis over the several units and gain or loss computed on the disposition of each part, except where apportionment would be wholly impracticable or impossible. . . . Petitioner argues that it would be impracticable and impossible to apportion a definite basis to the easements here involved, since they could not be described by metes and bounds; that the flow of the water has changed and will change the course of the river; that the extent of the flood was and is not predictable; and that to date the city has not released the full measure of water to which it is entitled. In Strother v. Commissioner, 55 Fed.(2d) 626, the court says: " . . . A taxpayer . . . should not be charged with gain on pure conjecture unsupported by any foundation of ascertainable fact." See Burnet v. Logan [infra page 358].

This rule is approved in the recent [case of] Raytheon Prod. Corp. [v. Commissioner, 144 F.2d 110 (1st Cir.), cert. denied, 323 U.S. 779 (1944)]. Apportionment with reasonable accuracy of the amount received not being possible, and this amount being less than petitioner's cost basis for the property, it can not be determined that petitioner has, in fact, realized gain in any amount. Applying the rule as above set out, no portion of the payment in question should be considered as income, but the full amount must be treated as a return of capital and applied in reduction of petitioner's cost basis. Burnet v. Logan [supra].

Reviewed by the Court.

NOTES AND QUESTIONS

1. *All or nothing at all?* Given the difficulty of allocating basis or cost, why not treat the entire $49,000 as gain? What about some sort of arbitrary rule of allocation? What justification, if any, is there for in effect allocating the entire basis, up to the amount received, to the interest conveyed? Rev. Rul. 70-510, 1970-2 C.B. 159, covering a situation remarkably similar to that in *Inaja,* follows the same allocation-of-basis rule. No explanation is given.

2. *Drawing the line.* The 1,236 acres owned by the taxpayer included 419 acres of "rocky hill lands." Suppose that this part of the property had been sold for $2,000. How would gain or loss be determined? See Introductory Note supra page 166. See also Williams v. McGowan, infra page 913 (taxpayer selling hardware business is treated as selling various individual assets, not one aggregate asset, and must allocate price among the various components to determine tax consequences, where the sale of some assets produces ordinary gain or loss and the sale of others produces capital gain or loss).

3. *Effect in later years.* Suppose that in a later year Inaja sells the entire property for $25,000. What tax consequences? Suppose that in 1939 the city had paid Inaja $65,000 instead of $49,000 (net). What tax result in that year and in a later year when the entire property is sold for $25,000?

4. *The forgone income issue.* (a) What characteristics of the transaction justify treatment of the $50,000 as payment for part of the taxpayer's property rather than rent or the like? Is it possible for a payment to be for "loss of profits" and still be proceeds from the sale of a capital asset?

(b) Suppose that negotiations between the city and Inaja had reached a point where the city offered to pay a fee of $2,500 a year forever for the discharge and easement, but Inaja was more interested in a lump-sum payment. Suppose that at this point a financial expert pointed out that for an annual interest cost of $2,500 the city could issue a bond for $50,000 and use the proceeds to pay off Inaja and that an agreement was thereupon reached under which Inaja received the $50,000 instead of the $2,500 per year. Plainly, the $2,500 per year would have been fully taxable — there would be no recovery-of-cost offset. Does it follow that the $50,000 should be fully taxable? Why?

(c) What if Inaja had agreed to sell to the city gravel to be used in constructing the city's pipeline? There has been considerable litigation over such sales, which raise an issue of capital gain versus ordinary income tied up with the issue of recovery of cost. Depending on the terms of the sale, the transaction might be treated as a sale of a part of the taxpayer's property, in which case some portion of total basis must be allocated to the sale and the gain will be capital gain. Or the transaction might be treated as a lease of a right to use the property, in which case there is no allowance for recovery of cost and the proceeds are ordinary income. The line between the two kinds of transactions can be a fine one, bordering on the metaphysical. See Estate of Walker v. Commissioner, 464 F.2d 75 (3d Cir. 1972) (because taxpayer retained an "economic interest" and because title to any sand removed did not pass until actually removed by "purchaser," taxpayer had not sold all of its interest in the sand deposit but instead had "leased" the right to remove sand, for which ordinary income was received); Rhodes v. United States, 464 F.2d 1307 (5th Cir. 1972) (selling taxpayer was entitled to capital-gain treatment from "sale" of clay deposits, where taxpayer was guaranteed a minimum price, even though the actual price payable could be much higher in the event that more clay was removed).

2. Life Insurance

Basic analysis. Section 101(a) excludes "amounts received . . . under a life insurance contract, if such amounts are paid by reason of the death of the insured." This exclusion applies to all types of life insurance policies. As to some of these, the exclusion results in a reasonably accurate reporting of income in the aggregate (as explained below), though not in individual cases. As to others, the result is a substantial underreporting in the aggregate as well as inaccuracy in individual cases. To understand these tax effects one must understand the two basic elements of life insurance policies — (1) mortality protection or "pure" insurance and (2) savings — and how they work.

Let us begin with the pure insurance element — the simple protection against mortality losses. One example of this kind of insurance is trip insurance covering air travel. These policies pay off if the insured dies as a result of an airplane crash. Suppose that a person pays $5 for $50,000 of such coverage. If the plane crashes and the insured dies, the beneficiary receives the $50,000, which can be thought of as consisting of a $5 recovery of cost plus a mortality gain of $49,995. The entire amount is excluded under §101(a). On the other hand, if the plane arrives safely at its destination, the insured loses his or her gamble with the insurance company. There is a $5 mortality loss, for which there is no deduction. In this lottery with life there will be those who gain, financially, and those who do not. In individual cases, where death occurs, large gains will escape taxation. In the aggregate, however, the amounts paid out will equal the amounts paid in (disregarding the amounts diverted to cover the costs and profits of the insurer). Since the premiums are not deductible, the tax effect in the aggregate is roughly accurate: In the aggregate, the amount received is a recovery of capital and no gain escapes taxation (assuming that we disregard the value of the peace of mind acquired by the purchase of the policies).

The same analysis applies to other types of "term" insurance, under which a premium is paid in return for protection against death for a defined, relatively short, term or period of time. For example, depending on age, a person might be able to buy $50,000 worth of protection for one year for, say, $1,000. Again, if the person dies during the year, there is a mortality gain — in this case $49,000 — that is excluded under §101(a). If the person lives out the year, there is a mortality loss of $1,000, which is not deductible. If the insurance company sells enough policies and makes the proper calculations of life expectancy, it will be subject to virtually no risk. Assuming a large enough number of insured people, the number of deaths should be such that the amount collected in premiums will cover the amounts paid out in benefits, plus the company's cost of operation and its profit. This observation is a reflection of the idea previously expressed — that in the aggregate there is no gain or loss (disregarding the insurance company's costs and profits) and that consequently the tax effect is accurate in the aggregate but not in individual cases (except in an expected, or ex ante, sense). Individual policies of one-year term insurance are widely sold. Far more common are one-year term policies for groups of people such as employees of a particular firm; these policies are called group-term life insurance.

So far, however, we have seen only part of the picture. We have ignored the savings element that is found in many forms of life insurance and the exclusion from taxation of the accumulated earnings on that savings element. An extreme example of a savings element is found in the single-premium life insurance policy. Suppose, for example, that an insurance policy calls for a single initial payment of $25,000 by the insured in return for a payment by the insurance company of $100,000 at death, whenever it occurs. Here, both in the aggregate, and in individual cases, the amounts paid out will be four times the amounts paid in. How can the insurance company afford to do that? Obviously, because it is able to invest the $25,000 and earn enough to make the required payments (plus covering its costs and profits). The returns on investment earned by the insurance company essentially benefit the people who have bought the policies. The insurance company is not required to pay a tax on such returns, on the theory that they are set aside as reserves for payment to policyholders. Nor are those returns taxed to the policyholders. While this kind of policy has a large savings element, it also includes protection against mortality risk. For insureds who die early there will be a mortality gain (to the beneficiary) and for those who outlive their life expectancies there will be a mortality loss. Even for those in the latter category, there will be an overall gain; the proceeds will still be $100,000 on an investment of $25,000. But the mortality loss reduces what would otherwise be a larger investment gain.[23] In any event, if we wanted to tax returns on the savings element while preserving the rule that mortality gains and losses were to be ignored, we would be confronted with the difficult task of separating the two elements of the proceeds.

The single-premium policy is, as previously suggested, just an extreme example. Other forms of insurance also have substantial savings elements, and the result is that the amounts paid out, in the aggregate, will exceed the amounts paid in as premiums. These other policies have many names, such as whole life, ordinary life, endowment, and level-premium term. They are all varying combinations of term insurance and a savings element.[24] The greater the savings element, the greater the aggregate tax avoidance. Consider, for example, a level-premium term policy. For a simple one-year term policy the premium will rise each year as the insured gets older and the probability of death increases. Suppose that a policy is offered that provides for a level yearly premium for ten years. In order to be able to afford to offer such a level premium, an insurance company obviously must charge a premium that exceeds the one-year pure term cost in the early years of the policy. The excess over true cost is the savings element, or reserve, which is used, in effect, to help meet the higher costs in the later years of the

23. Suppose that there are three people, Alice, Bob, and Carol, each of whom has a life expectancy of 14.5 years and each of whom buys, for $25,000, a single-premium life insurance policy with a death benefit of $100,000. The interest rate at which $25,000 grows to $100,000 in 14.5 years is 10 percent. Suppose that Alice dies exactly at the end of 14.5 years. For her, the $100,000 proceeds includes her $25,000 plus an investment gain of $75,000. There is no mortality gain or loss. Bob dies the day after he buys his policy. The $100,000 paid on his policy includes a mortality gain of $75,000 and no investment gain. Carol lives twenty-five years. If she had invested her $25,000 at 10 percent for that time it would have grown to $271,000. Since she collects only $100,000 on the policy, she has an investment gain of $246,000 and a mortality loss of $171,000. The numbers may be summarized as follows:

	Life span	*Investment grows to*	*Death benefit*	*Investment gain or loss*	*Mortality gain or loss*
Alice	14.5 yrs	$100,000	$100,000	$ 75,000	-0-
Bob	-0-	25,000	100,000	-0-	$ 75,000
Carol	25 yrs	271,000	100,000	246,000	(171,000)

24. For a good description of various types of insurance policies, see Joint Committee on Taxation, Tax Reform Proposals: Taxation of Insurance Products and Companies (September 20, 1985).

policy. If the premium is to remain level not just for ten years but for the entire life of a young insured, the savings element in the early years will have to be even greater. As with the single premium policy, proceeds in individual cases will include mortality gains and losses plus returns on the savings element. In the aggregate, the amounts paid out will exceed the amounts paid in. Yet because of §101(a), nothing will be taxed. Note that in *all* cases some return on savings will escape taxation. It is true that people who live long enough may pay more in premiums than their beneficiaries receive in proceeds. This may suggest that in such cases there has been no gain for tax purposes, but that is not so. All that will have happened is that the mortality loss has exceeded the investment gain. The investment gain has still provided a benefit: lower total premiums than would have been paid with simple one-year renewable term insurance. Even though total premiums over time exceed total proceeds, if a savings element has decreased the amount that would otherwise have been paid in premiums, a return *on* investment will have escaped tax. Where premiums exceed proceeds, this kind of escape from taxation does not depend on §101(a). There is no tax even if the policy is of the sort that not only pays the covered amount at death, but also, in lieu of the payment at death, pays the covered amount at some specified age (e.g., 65), if the insured lives to that age. See §72(e)(1)(B).[25]

Some data. The importance of the failure to tax the "inside interest buildup" (that is, earnings, or increase in the savings element) in annuities and insurance policies and the impact of that failure on the fairness of the system is suggested by the data in Table 2-1 (taken from Treasury Department Report to the President, Tax Reform for Fairness, Simplicity, and Economic Growth, vol. 2, p. 282 (1984)).

With the elimination in 1986 of many forms of tax-favored investment, the allure of life insurance (especially the single-premium life insurance policy), and the promotional activities of insurance companies, increased noticeably.

25. Suppose, for example, that at age 45 Edith buys an "endowment" policy for which the premium is $500 per year for twenty years (until she is age 65). Suppose the policy provides that if she dies at any time during the twenty-year term of the policy, her beneficiary is to receive $10,000, but if she is still alive at the end of the twenty years, she is entitled to a cash payment of $10,000 (the endowment). Suppose it turns out that she lives for twenty years and collects the $10,000. No tax will be payable. This result ignores economic reality; it ignores the value of the insurance on Edith's life during the twenty-year term of the policy. Actuaries can readily figure out the relative amounts of each annual premium allocable to current life insurance and to the endowment (the savings element). (If they could not, insurance companies could not sell such policies and stay in business for long.) Suppose that the cost of the insurance element over the twenty years was $6,000 and the amount allocated to the savings element was $4,000. In this case, Edith has had a gain of $6,000 on her savings account with the insurance company and should be taxed on it at some time. She has also spent $6,000 on life insurance, but that is not a deductible outlay, any more than it would have been if she had separately bought term insurance and put money aside in a savings account.

TABLE 2-1
Distribution of Ownership of Cash-Value Life Insurance Policies and the Annual Inside Interest Buildup[a] by Economic Income—1983

Family income	*Families with cash-value life insurance policies percentage*	*Average annual economic inside buildup*[b]
$0– $ 9,999	13	$ 85
$10,000– $14,999	25	110
$15,000– $19,999	33	135
$20,000– $29,999	41	190
$30,000– $49,999	53	310
$50,000– $99,999	68	520
$100,000–$199,999	78	1,240
$200,000 or more	70	3,050
All families	42	$ 355

Source: Treasury estimates. Office of the Secretary of the Treasury, November 29, 1984; Office of Tax Analysis
a. Includes annuities.
b. For those with policies.

Policy questions. Why is it that Congress allows returns on investments with insurance companies to escape taxation while investments with banks or in mutual funds are taxed? Consider the two elements of tax avoidance — the deferral and the ultimate exemption — in the case of the single-premium policy. Each year, as the insured gets older, the policy increases in value. Would it be appropriate to tax this annual increment or allocate the insurance company's investment income each year to policyholders based on the company's calculations of amounts required for necessary reserves for future payments? Is the policyholder's gain more like the increase in the value of farm land held for investment or like the annual interest earned on a savings account? (Note that, because of commissions and other costs, if a life insurance policy is cashed in too soon after its purchase, the insured person generally will lose money. Life insurance is not a good short-term investment.) If annual taxation of policyholders is not sensible, would it be appropriate to tax the insurance company on the investment returns set aside for policyholders? What about the exclusion at death?

Assuming that the annual increments in the value of a life insurance policy should not be taxed each year, is the gain like the gain that escapes taxation under §1014 or like the gain that is taxable under §691? (See supra pages 163-166.)

Life insurance might also be compared with qualified pension plans. When an employer has adopted a qualified pension plan and sets aside money that is to be used to pay a pension to an employee, the employer deducts the amount set aside. In effect, that money is treated as if it had been paid as a salary or as wages to the employee. The employee, however, is not required to report the amount as income. That exclusion is equivalent to the receipt and simultaneous deduction of the amount by the employee. In other words, it is as if the employee had earned income and had received a deduction by putting it into a pension trust. Thereafter, the employee is not taxed on amounts earned by the pension trust, but amounts ultimately received as pension payments are fully taxed. In short, from the perspective of the employee, the system is, in effect, one of deduction of the investment, tax-free buildup, and taxation on ultimate receipt. But as was demonstrated earlier (see Chapter 1C7, page 31), the financial result of this system is equivalent to that of a system in which there is no initial deduction, but the income earned on the investment is entirely free of tax (both as it accumulates and when it is received), and that is the tax treatment of the savings element in life insurance. So one way to think about how life insurance should be taxed is to ask whether there are reasons to afford it the same favorable tax treatment as we afford qualified pension plans.

Tax planning (avoidance) implications. The single-premium insurance policy, as we have just seen, is obviously a good device for avoiding taxes on the returns on one's investment. But suppose that the taxpayer lacks the $25,000. Such a taxpayer is analogous to the person who observes that his or her neighbor is enjoying tax-free imputed income from home ownership but lacks the money to buy a house. The solution that this analogy suggests is to borrow the $25,000. Assuming that the interest on the loan is deductible, the effect is to reduce income subject to tax by the amount of that interest. Meanwhile, the gain generated by the investment of the borrowed funds in the insurance policy is tax free. Taxable income is transformed into tax-free gain, in a process sometimes called "tax arbitrage." For example, suppose that a woman wants to buy $100,000 worth of coverage for the benefit of her child; that the cost of a single-premium $100,000 policy for a woman her age is $25,000; and that her marginal tax rate (combined state and federal) is 40 percent. She might borrow the $25,000 (perhaps from the insurance company) at an interest cost of, say, 10 percent. If her $2,500 annual interest payment is deductible, her after-tax cost is only $1,500. Essentially, she will have transformed a nondeductible payment of an insurance premium into a deductible payment of interest; the government will pay 40 percent of the cost of her coverage. Her insurance policy will increase in value each year (by more than the $1,500 net cost, if she chooses policies wisely), but that gain will be tax free if she holds the policy until death.[26]

26. If, as this example assumes, the loan is still outstanding at the time of death, the

Does that sound too good to be true? In its simplest form, it is. Congress caught on many years ago and provided in §264(a)(2) that the interest paid on indebtedness "incurred or continued to purchase or carry a single premium life insurance, endowment, or annuity contract" is not deductible. The barrier presented by §264(a)(2) can be avoided (though not completely) by use of policies with relatively large savings elements that avoid categorization as "single premium" policies. See §264(b) and (c). Since 1987, however, tax avoidance has been constrained by the disallowance, in §163(h), of deductions for "personal" interest (see infra page 511).

In the 1970s, some insurance companies began to offer new policies known as "flexible premium" or "universal life" policies. These policies had large savings elements in relation to their term, or "pure," insurance amount. Competitors offering only traditional policies complained, and, after certain administrative responses by the Service, Congress reacted (in 1982, with further limitations in 1984 and 1986) by limiting the types of policies that qualify for the §101(a) exclusion to those with a reasonable relationship between the savings and the pure insurance elements. The congressional handiwork is contained in §§101(f) and 7702, which rely on concepts familiar to actuaries and beyond the grasp of most of the rest of us. The lesson to be learned from this story is that people in the insurance industry are aware of the tax advantage associated with the savings elements of life insurance; it should not be surprising that some people in the industry would seek to make money by devising new kinds of life insurance policies that push that advantage to, or beyond, the limits of congressional tolerance.

Life insurance (especially single premium) for a while enjoyed a substantial boom among seekers of tax-favored investments. It was one of the few "tax shelters" left after the 1986 act. The tax attractiveness of a single-premium life insurance policy arose from the fact that as the policy increased in value, the insured was permitted to withdraw amounts equal to the increase and to treat these withdrawals as nontaxable recoveries of the initial investment, until that investment was exhausted. The rule was different for annuities. See infra page 188. Some insurance companies aggressively promoted policies designed to appeal to people with little interest in life insurance but a strong interest in tax shelters. In 1988 Congress substantially restricted the opportunity to use life insurance for tax avoidance purposes by treating payments under certain "single premium" life insurance policies, and loans against such policies, as income, includable in gross amount and subject to an

insurance company will subtract the loan amount from the proceeds otherwise due and pay the beneficiary the net amount of $75,000. The fact that the beneficiary receives only the net amount of coverage would not mitigate the tax advantage: the policy has combined tax-free interest buildup with tax-deductible interest payments.

additional 10 percent penalty. See §7702A. In the case of ordinary endowment policies (other than a "modified endowment policy"), however, loans against the policy are nontaxable and cash distributions are taxable only to the extent that they exceed the policyholder's investment in the contract. See §72(e)(5).

Employee coverage. Suppose that a corporation buys one-year term insurance on the life of one of its key executives, with itself as the beneficiary. Here the premium seems to be part of the cost of doing business and should be deductible like any other business expense (under §162). But §264(a)(1) expressly denies the deduction. Correspondingly, the proceeds, if any, are excluded under §101(a). On the other hand, if the beneficiary under the policy on the life of the executive were his or her spouse, or if the corporation were to buy group-term life insurance for its employees, §264(a)(1) would not apply and the premiums would be deductible (as a form of compensation to such employees). The premiums would be taxable to the executive or other employees, except for the portion allocable to the first $50,000 of group-term coverage. See §79.

Transferees. The exclusion in §101(a)(1) generally is not available to a person who acquired the policy for valuable consideration. For many such people there will be no statutory basis for deduction of premiums and for some, even if there is such a basis in §162, deduction will be barred by §264(a)(1).

The congressional rationale for the §101(a)(2) limitation was that the exclusion might "result in abuse by encouraging speculation on the death of the insured." S. Rep. No. 1622, 83d Cong., 2d Sess. 14 (1954). Consistently with this rationale, certain policies that were transferred for consideration remain eligible for the exclusion — policies transferred to a person with a substituted, or carryover, basis (e.g., a successor corporation in a tax-free merger or a corporation resulting from a tax-free incorporation of a partnership) and transfers to the insured or to his or her partner, partnership, or corporation. Both these exceptions were enacted to overrule adverse judicial decisions. No exemption from the "transfer for valuable consideration" restriction is needed for transfers of insurance policies by gift or bequest, since no consideration is paid for such transfers.

Benefits for the terminally ill. Under Proposed Reg. §1.7702-2(d), the statutory exclusion for "benefits paid by reason of death" is defined, generally, to include benefits paid to terminally ill patients. An individual qualifies as "terminally ill" if, notwithstanding appropriate medical treatment, death is expected to occur within 12 months. Prop. Reg. §1.7702(e). The purpose of the proposed regulation is to allow persons with diseases such as AIDS to receive insurance money without incurring a substantial tax burden.

3. Annuities and Pensions

Basic analysis: annuities. An annuity is an amount paid at regular intervals. It will often take the form of an amount to be paid for the life of the annuitant, though not all annuities are for life. To illustrate, suppose that *A* is 62 years old, has just retired, and has $100,000 to invest. She goes to an insurance company seeking a fixed payment from it for as long as she lives. Her life expectancy is about twenty years. See Regs. §1.72-9. What should an insurance company be willing to pay her each year? Because the insurance company will have the $100,000 to invest, plainly it can afford to pay more than $5,000 per year ($100,000 divided by twenty years). How much more depends on how much it expects to earn on the $100,000. Suppose that it calculates that it can afford to pay $9,000 per year (which implies an interest rate of about 6.4 percent). If *A* lives her life expectancy, no more and no less, she will collect $180,000. The question is, how do we tax the $9,000 annual payment that she receives?

One possibility, an investment-first rule, would be to treat each payment as a tax-free recovery of capital until the entire $100,000 investment is recovered and then treat all payments as income. That is the approach of the *Inaja Land Co.* case, supra page 168, and of Burnet v. Logan, infra page 358. It would be the best *A* could hope for. It was once allowed generally, but is too favorable and is permitted now only for unsecured promises by individuals to pay so-called "private annuities" (see Lloyd v. Commissioner, 33 B.T.A. 903 (1936)). At the other extreme, under an income-first rule, all payments could be treated as income to the extent of any income set aside for the policyholder by the insurance company in its policyholder reserves. Thus, the early payments would be largely income;[27] as time passed, more and more of

27. The position of the insurance company would be comparable to that of a bank that has loaned $100,000 on a long-term loan to finance the purchase of a home and will receive fixed monthly payments throughout the term of the loan to cover interest and to "amortize" (that is, pay off in increments) the principal amount. In the early years of such a loan, most of each payment is interest, but some is principal. As the principal sum of the debt is slowly reduced, the amount of interest owed is reduced correspondingly, and for each succeeding payment the interest portion declines and the principal portion rises until the loan is finally repaid.

Thus, assuming payments of $9,000 per year for twenty years, the amounts of interest and principal are as follows:

Year	*Interest*	*Principal*	*Balance*
1	$6,395	$2,605	$97,395
2	6,228	2,772	94,623
3	6,051	2,949	91,674
—	—	—	—
18	1,527	7,473	16,410
19	1,049	7,951	8,459
20	541	8,459	-0-

each payment would be a recovery of capital; for people who lived out their life expectancies exactly, capital would be fully recovered at death and all income would be taxed; for others there would be mortality gains and losses. This approach would be roughly consistent with the treatment of distributions by corporations (all distributions are dividend income to the extent of accumulated earnings and profits) and trusts (all distributions are income to the extent of previously undistributed accumulations of income). See supra pages 60-61. It might still be more favorable than the treatment of amounts held in a savings account, where interest is taxed as earned, without regard to whether it is withdrawn. Again, however, the income-first rule has not been adopted in the Code. Which of the two possibilities seems fairer?

In fact, the rule under §72 requires the calculation of an "exclusion ratio." §72(b). The ratio is simply the investment in the contract (here, $100,000) divided by the expected return ($180,000), or 55.55 percent. This ratio is applied to each payment received. Thus, of each $9,000, 55.55 percent, or $5,000, would be treated as a nontaxable recovery of investment and the remaining $4,000 would be treated as income. If *A* dies before twenty years pass, she will not recover, for tax purposes, the entire amount of her investment. In that case, she is entitled, in her final income tax return, to a deduction for the portion of her investment not recovered by the time of her death through the operation of the exclusion ratio. §72(b)(3). If she lives more than twenty years, she will have recovered her entire investment in the contract and after that has occurred the entire amount of each $9,000 payment received is included in gross income. §72(b)(2). This is the rule for annuities whose payments begin after December 31, 1986. For annuities whose payments began before that date, the rule (from the law as it stood before the 1986 act) is that the exclusion ratio applies for as long as the payments last, even if that means total exclusions of more than the investment in the contract. Correspondingly, if death occurs, and payments end, before recovery of the investment in the contract, there is no deduction for the unrecovered basis. In recent years deferred annuities, because of their substantial tax advantage, have become an important product for insurance companies and an important tax-reduction tool for individuals. Insurance companies have enhanced the attraction of deferred annuities by designing them so that investors can choose the type of investment (for example, a choice from among a number of different mutual funds, including common stock funds, bond funds, etc.) and, thus, can choose a "variable" return, or buildup in value, dependent on their investment choice. Moreover, investors can be allowed to change their minds from time to time (for example, switching from one type of mutual fund to another).

Suppose that *A* had paid the $100,000 to the insurance company long before her retirement and, thus, long before any payments to her were called for under the contract. Under this arrangement, called a "deferred annuity," the insurance company would have had the benefit of investment of the $100,000 for a longer period of time, and it could afford to make larger payments beginning on *A*'s retirement at age 62. The increase in value before *A*'s retirement would not be taxed to *A* before retirement, so that increase would not affect her investment in the contract for tax purposes (which would, therefore, still be $100,000). For example, if the $100,000 had been paid to the insurance company twelve years before retirement and if it had grown in value at the rate of 6 percent a year, it would roughly double, to $200,000, by the time of retirement. Thus, the insurance company could afford to double the annual payment, to $18,000. The expected return would then be $360,000, and the exclusion ratio would be 27.77 percent ($100,000 divided by $360,000). The treatment of deferred annuities is obviously favorable to taxpayers: the value of the annuitant's investment increases each year as the payment dates approach, but tax on that increase is deferred until the payments are received.

The favorable rules governing annuities have given rise to a number of tax planning strategies. For example, a taxpayer might invest in a deferred annuity and then borrow the increase in value of the annuity. In the past, such loans did not trigger recognition of gain except to the extent that the amount of the loan exceeded the investment in the contract. If the amount of the loan did not exceed the investment, no tax would be due on the loan or on the increase in the value of the investment until payments began. Today, under §72(e), a taxpayer who receives a loan against an annuity policy will recognize income equal to the lesser of the amount of the loan or the increase in the value of the policy. Moreover, under §72(q), taxpayers who are under the age of 59½ generally must pay a penalty tax equal to 10 percent of the amount of the income otherwise recognized.

Section 72(q) applies not just to amounts received by loan but to any "premature distribution." A premature distribution includes any distribution that is not part of a series of substantially equal periodic payments for life. Absent §72(q), a taxpayer might purchase a deferred annuity that did not pay out for the annuitant's lifetime but that instead provided only a few annual payments beginning at a designated future date. Such an annuity would offer tax-deferred savings and a quick withdrawal of the investment at maturity; it would be much like a bond issued by a corporation or certificate of deposit issued by a bank. Under §72(q), unless the recipient is age 59½ or older, the distributions on such nonperiodic annuities are subject to the 10 percent penalty tax. For people over 59½, and for younger people who do not need access to their savings until they reach that age, the deferred annuity offers a tax-favored alternative to direct investment in a mutual fund or savings account. The tax advantage cannot be achieved without some cost. The insurance companies that sell annuities charge fees for their services. Still, in many situations deferred annuities will produce better long-run returns than will direct investments that are essentially identical except for tax consideration. The annuity with an underlying investment in a mutual fund and a direct investment in the same mutual fund are, financially, "perfect substitutes," with different tax characteristics. Taxpayers are therefore encouraged to engage in what is sometimes called "tax arbitrage," which means that they will select the tax-favored investment over the direct investment as long as the tax saving exceeds the fees paid to achieve that tax saving. The fees, by the way, should probably be regarded as a "deadweight loss" — though insurance companies and their representatives certainly do not view them that way. A question that emerges from these observations is, if Congress is willing to allow people to escape tax on their investments, why not let them do so directly so they can save the administrative costs of an intermediary? The answer to that question is more likely to be found by examination of the exercise of political influence by insurance companies and their agents than by study of criteria for good tax rules.

Pensions. The tax treatment of pensions is essentially the same as the tax treatment of annuities. See §§402(a), 403(a). In applying §72 to pensions one must remember, however, that amounts contributed toward the pension by the employer and not treated at the time of the contribution as income of the employee are not part of the employee's "investment in the contract" for purposes of the §72(b) exclusion ratio. For example, suppose that an employer sets up a "qualified" pension plan (described more fully infra page 395), and each year for ten years contributes $5,000 to the trustee of the plan. This $5,000 is not treated as income to the employee because of the special rules applicable to qualified plans. (Despite the nontaxation of the employee, the employer is entitled to deduct the $5,000 as compensation. See §404(a). And all earnings on amounts invested and held by the pension plan trustee are nontaxable.) Suppose that in addition to the employer contribution of $5,000 per year, the employer withholds from the employee's wages and transfers into the plan an additional $3,000. This is usually called an employee "contribution" even though the employee is given no choice. This $3,000 contribution would be treated as taxable to the employee.[28] At the end of the ten years suppose the employee retires and starts to collect her pension. Her investment in the contract is $30,000, the amount on which she has already been taxed. The $50,000

28. Neither the employee contribution nor the employer contribution is subject to Social Security (FICA) tax. Nor are amounts received as a pension. See §3121(a)(2)(A), (3).

contributed by the employer was not taxed to her and is therefore not an amount that she is, or should be entitled to, recover tax free.

As is perhaps obvious, employee contributions are not treated as favorably as employer contributions. The best explanation (though not an excuse) for plans that require mandatory employee contributions seems to be money illusion. Employers may feel that employees are attracted by higher nominal salaries even though part of the wage or salary is withheld for a pension. Suppose, for example, that the employee's salary is $53,000 and that $3,000 is withheld for the employee's "contribution" to the pension plan. The employee would be better off financially if the employer reduced the salary to $50,000 and paid the $3,000 into the plan as an employer contribution. But employers may fear that employees will fail to understand this and will seek other jobs where the nominal salary is higher.[29]

Variable annuities. "Normal" annuities call for payments that are fixed at the time of issuance of the contract and in effect reflect a fixed rate of interest guaranteed by the company. The Code also expressly provides for a form of annuity, called a variable annuity, under which the payments to the annuitant depend on the investment experience of a "segregated assets account" held by the company for such policyholders. §801(g).

Down the slippery slope. The basic rules of taxation of annuities and insurance companies create an opportunity for tax-free accumulation of income on investments with insurance companies, and §801(g) extended this tax avoidance opportunity to people who were unwilling to invest their assets in a safe but dull and (they thought) relatively low-return form of investment. But there was still a group of people not willing to sign up — people who thought the investment policies of insurance companies were too stodgy and wanted to make investment decisions themselves. The next step, therefore, was to create a separate investment account for each "policyholder." The account was held by a bank, as custodian, and the policyholder was allowed to select investments from an approved list. The policyholder had the right to cash in the annuity, which resulted in liquidation of the investment account and payment of the proceeds to the policyholder. The net effect was a private investment portfolio with a tax-free accumulation of income, plus the opportunity to take an annuity in the future. This kind of plan

29. Another possibility that achieves the same tax objective as the $8,000 employer contribution with a salary reduction to $50,000 has been available since 1980 under §401(k): The employer can leave the salary at $53,000, contribute $5,000 to the plan, and give the employee an option to reduce his or her salary by $3,000 and have that amount contributed to the plan on his or her behalf. Without §401(k) the employee would be taxable on the $3,000 that could have been taken in cash, under the doctrine of constructive receipt (see supra page 54). Under §401(k), the $3,000 employee contribution is excluded from the employee's gross income, so the employee is taxed on $50,000.

was approved by a private letter ruling in 1965. One can easily imagine the joy of "insurance" purveyors and the anguish of tax reformers. The Service, after reflecting on the matter for twelve years, decided that it no longer approved of such arrangements. In Rev. Rul. 77-85, 1977-1 C.B. 12, it ruled that it would consider the policyholder to be the owner of the custodial accounts and therefore taxable on the income received by the custodian. Holders of existing contracts were excluded from the coverage of the ruling unless they made additional contributions to their accounts. This ruling, together with action by the SEC and state regulatory agencies, had the effect of foreclosing further sales of such policies, and in Investment Annuity, Inc. v. Blumenthal, 609 F.2d 1 (D.C. Cir. 1979), cert. denied, 446 U.S. 981 (1980), it was held that §7421 (barring actions for injunction against "assessment or collection of any tax") barred judicial intervention on behalf of potential sellers seeking to challenge the ruling.

4. Gains and Losses from Gambling

The basic rule. With gambling we are again confronted with a situation in which, in the aggregate, proceeds equal investments (again, disregarding costs and profits). Here, however, we tax more than aggregate income: All gains are taxable, but losses (both for professional and amateur gamblers) are deductible only to the extent of gains. See §165(d). Accuracy in the aggregate would require either that net gains be ignored (as with life insurance) or that net losses be fully deductible (as with most other gain-seeking activities). It may be that the aggregate overtaxation (the aggregate failure to allow full cost recovery) reflects a moral condemnation of gambling, though in the case of state-sponsored lotteries, legal betting on horse racing, and other such lawful forms of gambling, this position seems difficult to defend. Or it may be that gambling is a sport, or some such personal activity, in which losses are the cost of having fun and gains are pure windfalls. To many purchasers of lottery (or "numbers") tickets, however, their regular purchases may be a special means of saving — the only way the person has any reasonable likelihood of accumulating enough money for a costly item of consumption or for a truly meaningful binge of some sort.

Enforcement. Since gambling is a cash business, enforcement is a problem. For relatively large transactions, §3402(q) requires that the race track or other payor withhold taxes at a rate of 20 percent. How would a taxpayer prove losses to offset such highly visible gains? In Parchutz v. Commissioner, 1988-327 T.C. Memo, the court had this to say about evidence of race-track gambling losses:

> Gambling loss tickets are of slight, if any, evidentiary weight where no corroboration is offered of petitioner's own testimony that each ticket was

> purchased by him. . . . In the instant case, petitioner offered only his own uncorroborated testimony that the losing tickets were his. We have no way of knowing whether petitioner purchased these tickets or received them from acquaintances at the track or acquired them by resorting to stooping, i.e., stooping down and picking up the discarded stubs of other bettors. . . . Moreover, the credibility of petitioner's testimony that he purchased each of the losing tickets has been undermined since some of the losing tickets were purchased during a two-week period within the first two months of 1982, when he was confined to a hospital and unable to go to the track.

What is "gambling"? In Jasinski v. Commissioner, 37 T.C.M. 1 (1978), the court gave short shrift to a taxpayer argument that the purchase of the subordinated debentures (corporate debt obligations) of a company in precarious financial condition amounted to gambling and that the ultimate loss should therefore be available to offset interest income from the bonds instead of being treated as a capital loss. Precisely what is the difference between a person who legally bets the horses (but only after spending many hours studying all available information) and a person who trades in the commodities market?

The preceding cases and materials on recovery of cost have focused on judicial and legislative reactions to problems of practicality. The case that follows is concerned with the somewhat more perplexing question of what we mean, for tax purposes, by a "recovery of capital."

5. Recovery of Loss

CLARK v. COMMISSIONER

40 B.T.A. 333 (1939), acq. 1957-1 C.B. 4

LEECH, J.

This is a proceeding to redetermine a deficiency in income tax for the calendar year 1934 in the amount of $10,618.87. The question presented is whether petitioner derived income by the payment to him of an amount of $19,941.10, by his tax counsel, to compensate him for a loss suffered on account of erroneous advice given him by the latter. The facts were stipulated and are so found. The stipulation, so far as material, follows:

> 3. The petitioner during the calendar year 1932, and for a considerable period prior thereto, was married and living with his wife. He was required by the Revenue Act of 1932 to file a Federal Income Tax Return of his income for the year 1932. For such year petitioner and his wife could have filed a joint return or separate returns.
>
> 4. Prior to the time that the 1932 Federal Income Tax return or returns of petitioner and/or his wife were due to be filed, petitioner retained

experienced tax counsel to prepare the necessary return or returns for him and/or his wife. Such tax counsel prepared a joint return for petitioner and his wife and advised petitioner to file it instead of two separate returns. In due course it was filed with the Collector of Internal Revenue for the First District of California.

5. Thereafter on or about the third day of February, 1934, a duly appointed revenue agent of the United States audited the aforesaid 1932 return and recommended an additional assessment against petitioner in the sum of $34,590.27, which was subsequently reduced to $32,820.14. This last mentioned sum was thereafter assessed against and was paid by petitioner to the Collector of Internal Revenue for the First District of California.

6. The deficiency of $32,820.14 arose from an error on the part of tax counsel who prepared petitioner's 1932 return. The error was that he improperly deducted from income the total amount of losses sustained on the sale of capital assets held for a period of more than two years instead of applying the statutory limitation required by Section 101(b) of the Revenue Act of 1932.

7. The error referred to in paragraph six above was called to the attention of the tax counsel who prepared the joint return of petitioner and his wife for the year 1932. Recomputations were then made which disclosed that if petitioner and his wife had filed separate returns for the year 1932 their combined tax liability would have been $19,941.10 less than that which was finally assessed against and paid by petitioner.

8. Thereafter, tax counsel admitted that if he had not erred in computing the tax liability shown on the joint return filed by the petitioner, he would have advised petitioner to file separate returns for himself and his wife, and accordingly tax counsel tendered to petitioner the sum of $19,941.10, which was the difference between what petitioner and his wife would have paid on their 1932 returns if separate returns had been filed and the amount which petitioner was actually required to pay on the joint return as filed. Petitioner accepted the $19,941.10.

9. In his final determination of petitioner's 1934 tax liability, the respondent included the aforesaid $19,941.10 in income.

10. Petitioner's books of account are kept on the cash receipts and disbursements basis and his tax returns are made on such basis under the community property laws of the State of California.

The theory on which the respondent included the above sum of $19,941.10 in petitioner's gross income for 1934, is that this amount constituted taxes paid for petitioner by a third party and that, consequently, petitioner was in receipt of income to that extent. The cases of Old Colony Trust Co. v. Commissioner, 279 U.S. 716; United States v. Boston & Maine Railroad, 279 U.S. 732, are cited as authority for his position. Petitioner, on the contrary, contends that this payment constituted compensation for damages or loss caused by the error of tax counsel, and that he therefore realized no income from its receipt in 1934.

We agree with petitioner. The cases cited by the respondent are not applicable here. Petitioner's taxes were not paid for him by any person — as rental, compensation for services rendered, or otherwise. He paid his own taxes.

When the joint return was filed, petitioner became obligated to and did pay the taxes computed on that basis. . . . In paying that obligation, he sustained a loss which was caused by the negligence of his tax counsel. The $19,941.10 was paid to petitioner, not qua taxes . . . , but as compensation to petitioner for his loss. The measure of that loss, and the compensation therefor, was the sum of money which petitioner became legally obligated to and did pay because of that negligence. The fact that such obligation was for taxes is of no moment here.

It has been held that payments in settlement of an action for breach of promise to marry are not income. . . . Compromise payments in settlement of an action for damages against a bank on account of conduct impairing the taxpayer's good will by injuring its reputation are also not taxable. . . . The same result follows in the case of payments in settlement for injuries by libel and slander. . . . Damages for personal injury are likewise not income. . . .

The theory of those cases is that recoupment on account of such losses is not income since it is not "derived from capital, from labor or from both combined." . . . And the fact that the payment of the compensation for such loss was voluntary, as here, does not change its exempt status. . . . It was, in fact, compensation for a loss which impaired petitioner's capital.

Moreover, so long as petitioner neither could nor did take a deduction in a prior year of this loss in such a way as to offset income for the prior year, the amount received by him in the taxable year, by way of recompense, is not then includable in his gross income. . . .

Decision will be entered for the petitioner.

PROBLEM AND QUESTIONS

The problem presented by this case is more subtle and more puzzling than may appear at first blush. The following hypothetical and the questions based on it are designed to help sort out the issues.

Suppose that on December 29, 1992, Tom picks up his pay envelope containing $300. When he arrives home he finds that there is a hole in his pocket and no pay envelope. He retraces his steps and cannot find it. He reports his loss to the police but they offer him no encouragement. He checks with the police again on December 31 and still there is no encouragement.

1. What are the income tax consequences for 1992? (a) Is the $300 excludable from income? (b) May Tom deduct the $300 as a loss? (See §165(c)(3); disregard the limitations in §165(h).)

2. Assume that Tom was entitled to and claimed a deduction of $300 in 1992 but that in 1993 he once more retraces his steps and, by a stroke of remarkable good fortune, finds his lost pay envelope with the $300 still in it. (a) Should he file an amended return for 1992? See supra page 46. (b) Assuming that it would not be appropriate to file an amended return for 1992, should he treat the $300 as income in 1993? Your intuition no doubt tells you that he should. That intuition is sound and is consistent with rules referred to as the "tax benefit doctrine," which is considered later in this chapter.

3. Assume again that in 1993 he finds his lost pay envelope with the $300, but that in 1992 he had not been entitled to and did not claim a loss deduction. How should he treat the $300 in 1993? The *Clark* case provides the answer to this question. Is that answer correct? Is it not clear that Tom is better off than an otherwise identical person who does not find his pay envelope in 1993? To achieve fairness, if Tom can exclude the $300, should that other person not be allowed a deduction? When?

4. Assume, as in Note 3, that Tom was not entitled to and did not claim a deduction in 1992 and in 1993 he finds a pay envelope with $300 but it is someone else's rather than his own. Assume further that efforts to find the owner prove unavailing and Tom is advised by a lawyer in 1993 that he is entitled to treat the $300 as his own. Must he report that amount as income? See *Glenshaw Glass*, supra page 126. Can you reconcile your answer to this question with your answer to the questions in Note 3? What would Henry Simons (see supra page 76) say?

5. Suppose that Tom was entitled to a deduction in 1992 but neglected to claim it. (a) He finds his $300 in 1993. Should he include it in income? (b) He finds his $300 in 1996, after the statute of limitations has run on 1992. Now, how should he treat the $300?

6. Claims in Property Divided over Time

While continuing to reconsider problems of recovery of cost, we now turn to the question of how to allocate cost between two people with claims in property divided over time.

IRWIN v. GAVIT

268 U.S. 161 (1925)

Mr. Justice Holmes delivered the opinion of the Court. . . .

The question is whether the sums received by the plaintiff under the will of Anthony N. Brady in 1913, 1914 and 1915, were income and [taxable. The taxpayer (plaintiff in this case), E. Palmer Gavit, was

Brady's son-in-law and the father of Marcia Gavit, who was six years old when Brady died. Brady left property in trust with part of the income to be used for Marcia's support and part to be paid quarterly to the taxpayer, but with his interest to terminate on the earlier of his death, Marcia's death, or Marcia's reaching age twenty-one. Thus, the maximum term of the taxpayer's income interest was fifteen years. He argued that the amounts he received were payments of a bequest of property, measured by the income of the property, and, as bequests, were not taxable to him. The lower courts agreed.]

The statute in Section II, A, subdivision 1, provides that there shall be levied a tax "upon the entire net income arising or accruing from all sources in the preceding calendar year to every citizen of the United States." If these payments properly may be called income by the common understanding of that word and the statute has failed to hit them it has missed so much of the general purpose that it expresses at the start. Congress intended to use its power to the full extent. Eisner v. Macomber [infra page 286]. By B. the net income is to include "gains or profits and income derived from any source whatever, including the income from but not the value of property acquired by gift, bequest, devise or descent." By D. trustees are to make "return of the net income of the person for whom they act, subject to this tax," and by E. trustees and others having the control or payment of fixed or determinable gains, &c., of another person, who are required to render return on behalf of another are "authorized to withhold enough to pay the normal tax." The language quoted leaves no doubt in our minds that if a fund were given to trustees for *A* for life with remainder over, the income received by the trustees and paid over to *A* would be income of *A* under the statute. It seems to us hardly less clear that even if there were a specific provision that *A* should have no interest in the corpus, the payments would be income none the less, within the meaning of the statute and the Constitution, and by popular speech. In the first case it is true that the bequest might be said to be of the corpus for life, in the second it might be said to be of the income. But we think that the provision of the act that exempts bequests assumes the gift of a corpus and contrasts it with the income arising from it, but was not intended to exempt income properly so-called simply because of a severance between it and the principal fund. No such conclusion can be drawn from Eisner v. Macomber [supra]. The money was income in the hands of the trustees and we know of nothing in the law that prevented its being paid and received as income by the donee.[30]

The Courts below went on the ground that the gift to the plaintiff was a bequest and carried no interest in the corpus of the fund. We do not regard those considerations as conclusive, as we have said, but if it were material a gift of the income of a fund ordinarily is treated by

30. [The Court applied the provision that is now §102(b)(1). The result reached by the Court is now embodied in §102(b)(2), adopted in 1942. — Eds.]

equity as creating an interest in the fund. Apart from technicalities we can perceive no distinction relevant to the question before us between a gift of the fund for life and a gift of the income from it. The fund is appropriated to the production of the same result whichever form the gift takes. Neither are we troubled by the question where to draw the line. That is the question in pretty much everything worth arguing in the law. . . . Day and night, youth and age are only types. But the distinction between the cases put of a gift from the corpus of the estate payable in instalments and the present seems to us not hard to draw, assuming that the gift supposed would not be income. This is a gift from the income of a very large fund, as income. It seems to us immaterial that the same amounts might receive a different color from their source. We are of opinion that quarterly payments, which it was hoped would last for fifteen years, from the income of an estate intended for the plaintiff's child, must be regarded as income within the meaning of the Constitution and the law. It is said that the tax laws should be construed favorably for the taxpayers. But that is not a reason for creating a doubt or for exaggerating one when it is no greater than we can bring ourselves to feel in this case.

Judgment reversed.

Mr. Justice SUTHERLAND, dissenting.

By the plain terms of the Revenue Act of 1913, the value of property acquired by gift, bequest, devise, or descent is not to be included in net income. Only the income derived from such property is subject to the tax. The question, as it seems to me, is really a very simple one. Money, of course, is property. The money here sought to be taxed as income was paid to respondent under the express provisions of a will. It was a gift by will, — a bequest. . . . It, therefore, fell within the precise letter of the statute; and, under well settled principles, judicial inquiry may go no further. The taxpayer is entitled to the rigor of the law. There is no latitude in a taxing statute — you must adhere to the very words. . . .

The property which respondent acquired being a bequest, there is no occasion to ask whether, before being handed over to him, it had been carved from the original corpus of, or from subsequent additions to, the estate. The corpus of the estate was not the legacy which respondent received, but merely the source which gave rise to it. The money here sought to be taxed was not the fruits of a legacy; it was the legacy itself. . . .

With the utmost respect for the judgment of my brethren to the contrary, the opinion just rendered, I think without warrant, searches the field of argument and inference for a meaning which should be found only in the strict letter of the statute.

Mr. Justice BUTLER concurs in this dissent.

NOTES

1. *Explanation.* The arguments in *Gavit* seem legalistic, and the underlying economics may be unclear. The following hypothetical, and the discussion of it, is intended to reveal the underlying economic issues. The explanation is in large part relevant to other problems arising throughout the remainder of the book, so careful study is especially important.

G dies. His will directs his executor to take $100,000 in cash and transfer it to a trustee, *T*. The trustee, by provisions contained in the trust instrument, is directed to buy a bond for $100,000, which has a face value of $100,000 and an interest rate of 8 percent, and matures at the end of nine years. (Assume that 8 percent is the market rate of interest at the time on such bonds, so that the face value and the market value are identical.) Thus, the borrower (that is, the obligor) agrees to pay $8,000 at the end of the first year, $8,000 at the end of the second year, and so forth. At the end of the ninth year the borrower will pay $8,000 interest plus the $100,000 principal.

Assume that the trustee is directed to pay the $8,000 interest each year to *A* for nine years and to pay the $100,000 principal to *B* when received from the borrower at the end of the ninth year.

At the inception the value of *A*'s interest is $49,975 (using the 8 percent rate) and the value of *B*'s interest is $50,025. The total of the two interests must equal the total value of the trust property since there are no other interests.

A's term of years may be viewed as the right to a series of payments. Thus,

The Right to:	*At the End of:*	*Is Presently Worth:*
$8,000	1 year	$7,407
8,000	2 years	6,859
8,000	3 years	6,351
8,000	4 years	5,880
8,000	5 years	5,445
8,000	6 years	5,041
8,000	7 years	4,668
8,000	8 years	4,322
8,000	9 years	4,002
		Total: $49,975

What if *A* immediately sells his interest to *C* for $49,975? *C* will receive $8,000 each year, but plainly that is not *C*'s net income. The $8,000 is partly a return of *C*'s initial investment — a recovery of capital. His income for tax purposes is only the difference between what he will receive ($8,000 × 9 = $72,000) and what he paid out ($49,975), or $22,025. He is permitted to amortize the $49,975. See supra page 58.

C can deduct \$49,975 ÷ 9, or \$5,553, each year. See §167(a)(2), (c). But see §167 (denying an amortization deduction where the remainder interest is held by a related party).

What about *A*? If he does not sell to *C*, can he similarly deduct \$5,553 per year? The answer is no. As a donee or legatee of a term of years *A* is treated as if he had no investment. See §273. His basis is zero and the entire \$8,000 per year is taxable. The entire basis (in this case \$100,000) will ultimately go to *B*. (If *B* sells out before the end of the nine years, his basis will be less than \$100,000 and part of the potential total basis may never be recovered. See infra page 875.)

It should be apparent that as time passes and *A*'s term declines in value, *B*'s remainder increases in value. (Remember, the total value of the two interests will always equal the total value of the trust property.) Assuming no change in the value of the trust property, here is what happens:[31]

		A's Term	*B's Remainder*	*Change*
Start		\$49,975	\$ 50,025	—
End of year	1	45,973	54,027	\$4,002
	2	41,651	58,349	4,322
	3	36,983	63,017	4,668
	4	31,942	68,058	5,041

31. For those who like graphs:

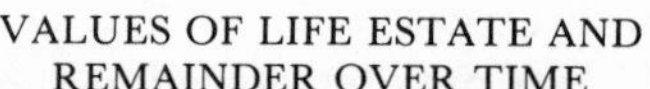

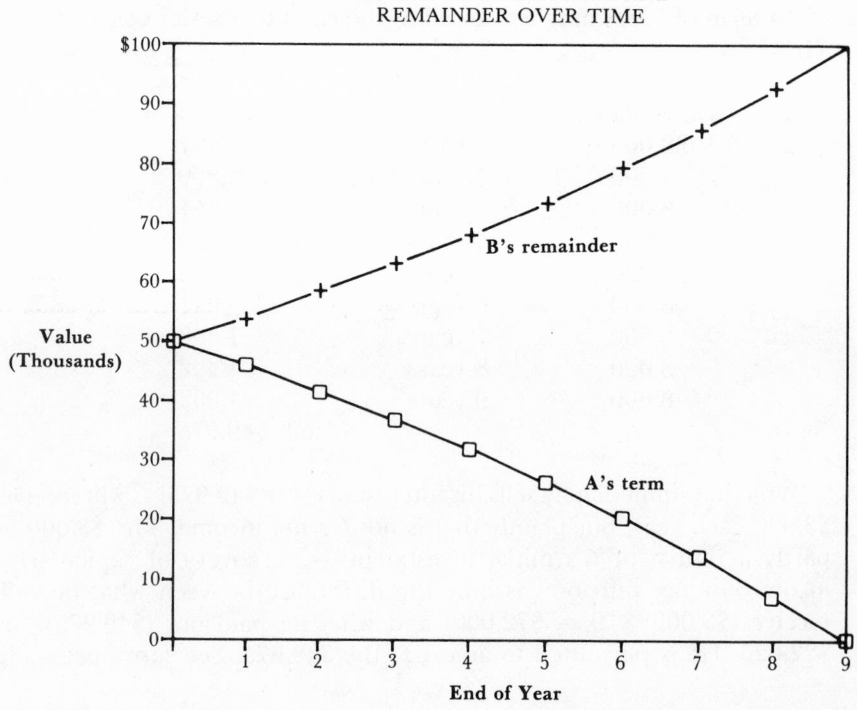

5	26,497	73,503	5,445
6	20,617	79,383	5,880
7	14,266	85,734	6,351
8	7,407	92,593	6,859
9	-0-	100,000	7,407

It could be argued, then, that *B* has income of $4,002 at the end of year 1, $4,322 at the end of year 2, and so forth, and that *A* has suffered corresponding declines that should be offset against the $8,000 he receives. But we have already seen that *A* is allowed no such deduction. Correspondingly, *B* is not charged with income each year, and when the trustee collects the principal of the bond ($100,000) at the end of the nine years and pays it to *B*, *B* will have no gain or loss at that time.

Note that the decline in the value of *A*'s interest is only $4,002 in the first year and rises to $7,407 in the ninth year. Recall that *C*, a purchaser of *A*'s interest, would be allowed a straightline amortization deduction of $5,553 each year. Thus, it is clear that straightline amortization is too rapid. It allows a deduction in the early years greater than the true decline in economic value and thus results in an underreporting of true economic income in those years. The effect is to defer recognition of some income to the later years when the $5,553 deduction is lower than the true decline in economic value.

2. *Legalisms.* Suppose that in the hypothetical in Note 1, *G*'s will had provided that the trustee should "pay to *A* from the trust corpus a lump sum of $72,000 in annual installments of $8,000 per year for nine years and accumulate all income for distribution, along with the remaining corpus, to *B* at the end of the nine years." This is the kind of possible disposition that seems to have caused the Court some concern. It is plain under present law that the result would be no different than if the disposition had been "$8,000 of income to *A* for nine years, remainder to *B*." It seems equally plain that this approach, ignoring the language used and focusing on the availability of income, is a sensible one. Otherwise taxpayers would be given too much freedom to manipulate tax results. In fact, the language establishing the trust at issue in *Gavit* plainly conveyed to the taxpayer an income interest. The taxpayer's argument was simply that this interest was a "bequest" excludable under the forerunner of §102.

E. ANNUAL ACCOUNTING AND ITS CONSEQUENCES

The issues and principles to be examined in this section have traditionally been thought of as stemming from problems of "accounting," and because of the tradition it is convenient to accept the categorization. Otherwise, these issues and principles might have been treated as part of the broader problems of recovery of cost (or capital or investment) that we have just examined or as part of the still broader problems of timing and recognition that are taken up later. Begin by reviewing the discussion of annual, versus transactional, accounting supra at pages 55-56.

1. The Use of Hindsight

BURNET v. SANFORD & BROOKS CO.

282 U.S. 359 (1931)

Mr. Justice STONE delivered the opinion of the Court. . . .

From 1913 to 1915, inclusive, respondent, a Delaware corporation engaged in business for profit, was acting for the Atlantic Dredging Company in carrying out a contract for dredging the Delaware River, entered into by that company with the United States. In making its income tax returns for the years 1913 and 1916, respondent added to gross income for each year the payments made under the contract that year, and deducted its expenses paid that year in performing the contract. The total expenses exceeded the payments received by $176,271.88. The tax returns for 1913, 1915, and 1916 showed net losses. That for 1914 showed net income.

In 1915 work under the contract was abandoned, and in 1916 suit was brought in the Court of Claims to recover for a breach of warranty of the character of the material to be dredged. Judgment for the claimant, 53 Ct. Cls. 490, was affirmed by this Court in 1920. . . . It held that the recovery was upon the contract and was "compensatory of the cost of the work, of which the government got the benefit." From the total recovery, petitioner received in that year the sum of $192,577.59, which included the $176,271.88 by which its expenses under the contract had exceeded receipts from it, and accrued interest amounting to $16,305.71. Respondent having failed to include these amounts as gross income in its tax returns for 1920, the Commissioner made the deficiency assessment here involved, based on the addition of both items to gross income for that year.

The Court of Appeals ruled that only the item of interest was properly included, holding, erroneously as the government contends, that the item of $176,271.88 was a return of losses suffered by respondent in earlier years and hence was wrongly assessed as income. Notwithstanding this conclusion, its judgment of reversal and the consequent elimination of this item from gross income for 1920 were made contingent upon the filing by respondent of amended returns for the years 1913 to 1916, from which were to be omitted the deductions of the related items of expenses paid in those years. Respondent insists that as the Sixteenth Amendment and the Revenue Act of 1918, which was in force in 1920, plainly contemplate a tax only on net income or profits, any application of the statute which operates to impose a tax with respect to the present transaction, from which respondent received no profit, cannot be upheld.

If respondent's contention that only gain or profit may be taxed under the Sixteenth Amendment be accepted without qualification, . . . the question remains whether the gain or profit which is the subject of the tax may be ascertained, as here, on the basis of fixed accounting periods, or whether, as is pressed upon us, it can only be net profit ascertained on the basis of particular transactions of the taxpayer when they are brought to a conclusion.

All the revenue acts which have been enacted since the adoption of the Sixteenth Amendment have uniformly assessed the tax on the basis of annual returns showing the net result of all the taxpayer's transactions during a fixed accounting period, either the calendar year, or, at the option of the taxpayer, the particular fiscal year which he may adopt. . . .

That the recovery made by respondent in 1920 was gross income for that year within the meaning of these sections cannot, we think, be doubted. The money received was derived from a contract entered into in the course of respondent's business operations for profit. While it equalled, and in a loose sense was a return of, expenditures made in performing the contract, still, as the Board of Tax Appeals found, the expenditures were made in defraying the expenses incurred in the prosecution of the work under the contract, for the purpose of earning profits. They were not capital investments, the cost of which, if converted, must first be restored from the proceeds before there is a capital gain taxable as income. . . .

That such receipts from the conduct of a business enterprise are to be included in the taxpayer's return as a part of gross income, regardless of whether the particular transaction results in net profit, sufficiently appears from the quoted words of §213(a) and from the character of the deductions allowed. Only by including these items of gross income in the 1920 return would it have been possible to ascertain respondent's net income for the period covered by the return, which is what the statute taxes. The excess of gross income over deductions did not any the less constitute net income for the taxable period because respondent, in an earlier period, suffered net losses in the conduct of its business which were in some measure attributable to expenditures made to produce the net income of the later period. . . .

But respondent insists that if the sum which it recovered is the income defined by the statute, still it is not income, taxation of which without apportionment is permitted by the Sixteenth Amendment, since the particular transaction from which it was derived did not result in any net gain or profit. But we do not think the amendment is to be so narrowly construed. A taxpayer may be in receipt of net income in one year and not in another. The net result of the two years, if combined in a single taxable period, might still be a loss; but it has never been supposed that that fact would relieve him from a tax on the first, or that it affords any reason for postponing the assessment of the tax until the end of a lifetime, or for some other indefinite period, to ascertain more precisely whether the final outcome of the period, or of a given transaction, will be a gain or a loss.

The Sixteenth Amendment was adopted to enable the government to raise revenue by taxation. It is the essence of any system of taxation that it should produce revenue ascertainable, and payable to the government, at regular intervals. Only by such a system is it practicable to produce a regular flow of income and apply methods of accounting, assessment, and collection capable of practical operation. It is not suggested that there has ever been any general scheme for taxing income on any other basis. The computation of income annually as the net result of all transactions within the year was a familiar practice, and taxes upon income so arrived at were not unknown, before the Sixteenth Amendment. . . . It is not to be supposed that the amendment did not contemplate that Congress might make income so ascertained the basis of a scheme of taxation such as had been in actual operation within the United States before its adoption. While, conceivably, a different system might be devised by which the tax could be assessed, wholly or in part, on the basis of the finally ascertained results of particular transactions, Congress is not required by the amendment to adopt such a system in preference to the more familiar method, even if it were practicable. It would not necessarily obviate the kind of inequalities of which respondent complains. If losses from particular transactions were to be set off against gains in others, there would still be the practical necessity of computing the tax on the basis of annual or other fixed taxable periods, which might result in the taxpayer being required to pay a tax on income in one period exceeded by net losses in another. . . .

NOTES AND QUESTIONS

1. *Relationship with recovery-of-cost principles.* How can the decision in this case be reconciled with the decision in Clark v. Commissioner, supra page 185?

2. *Implications. Sanford & Brooks* is often cited for the proposition that our income tax system uses annual, as opposed to transactional, accounting. Transactional accounting as a general proposition would pre-

sent the practical problem of separating out the costs of and returns from separate transactions. For example, in *Sanford & Brooks* it would require allocation of the taxpayer's general overhead cost (e.g., the salary of its president and the costs of its headquarters facilities) among all of its projects. At the time of the decision in *Sanford & Brooks* such allocation would probably have been considered a daunting task. In the current era accountants are more familiar with the required techniques. In fact, allocations of overhead and other such costs among various projects are now required for the purpose of determining the costs of assets that a taxpayer produces for itself. See §263A, which is described infra page 623.

3. *Relief from harshness: whose job?* The Court's insistence on strict application of annual accounting produces a harsh, basically unfair outcome in this case. Should the Court have figured out some device for providing relief? Or is the problem one that should be left to Congress? Consider the forms of relief from the harshness of annual accounting that are described in the following note and in the rest of this section.

4. *Loss carryovers.* The harshness of annual accounting is mitigated by the provision in §172 for net operating loss (NOL) carryovers. ("Carryover" includes carryback to earlier years and carryforward to later years.) The losses that may be carried over are primarily losses incurred in a trade or business. There is a separate provision for carryover of capital losses, in §1212. In United States v. Foster Lumber Co., 429 U.S. 32, 42 (1976), the Supreme Court described the policy objectives of §172 as follows:

> [In Libson Shops v. Koehler, 353 U.S. 382, 386 (1957)] the Court said that the net operating loss carryover and carryback provisions
>
> > were enacted to ameliorate the unduly drastic consequences of taxing income strictly on an annual basis. They were designed to permit a taxpayer to set off its lean years against its lush years, and to strike something like an average taxable income computed over a period longer than one year.
>
> There were, in fact, several policy considerations behind the decision to allow averaging of income over a number of years. Ameliorating the timing consequences of the annual accounting period makes it possible for shareholders in companies with fluctuating as opposed to stable incomes to receive more nearly equal tax treatment. Without loss offsets, a firm experiencing losses in some periods would not be able to deduct all the expenses of earning income. The consequence would be a tax on capital, borne by shareholders who would pay higher taxes on net income than owners of businesses with stable income. Congress also sought through allowance of loss carryovers to stimulate enterprise and investment, particularly in new businesses or risky ventures where early losses can be carried forward to future more prosperous years.

Under the original version of §172, enacted in 1918, the NOL could be carried over to the one immediately preceding year and the one immediately succeeding year. Over time, the carryover period has bit by bit been extended. Since 1981 the period ordinarily is three years back and fifteen years forward. For individuals, the losses that can be carried over are primarily business losses, as distinguished from losses attributable to investments, unused non-§62 deductions, and deductions for personal dependency exemptions. In general, §172 fulfills the policy objectives stated by the Court in *Foster Lumber.* However, §172 contains some technical provisions that produce results inconsistent with those objectives.

5. *Accounting for long-term contracts.* Taxpayers who perform work under long-term contracts for construction or the manufacture of property must account for profit under the percentage-of-completion method. See §460. Under this method, a portion of the gross contract price is included in income as work progresses, with the portion determined on the basis of cost of work performed. See Regs. §1.451-3. In earlier years, an alternative method of accounting for long-term contracts, the completed contract method, was also available. Under this method, the taxpayer was permitted to ignore all costs and all items of revenue associated with a particular contract until the contract was completed. This method was considered too favorable to taxpayers (many of them in the defense industry) and, beginning in 1986, was phased out.

6. *Capital expenditures.* If a taxpayer buys a barge or a truck, the cost is treated as a capital expenditure. Such costs are spread out over the years and are recovered through ACRS or, in earlier times, the depreciation deduction. See supra page 57. The outlays at issue in *Sanford & Brooks,* by contrast, are not capital expenditures; they were not the cost of acquiring an asset that is expected to contribute to generating income over future years. The income in *Sanford & Brooks* was generated — it was *earned* (though payment was not received)—in the year in which the outlays occurred. Ordinarily an accrual method taxpayer reports income in the year in which it is earned and this results in a matching of income and expenses. In *Sanford & Brooks,* however, the taxpayer did not use the accrual method. Moreover, because of the uncertainty about collection, even if the taxpayer had used the accrual method, the amount earned probably would not have been accrued (that is, treated as current income and reported on that year's tax return). Nonetheless, in a situation like that in *Sanford & Brooks* the accounting theory is that matching is achieved, if at all, not by holding off on deducting the expenses but by accruing the income. The holding of the case is that if the taxpayer suffers as a result of the fact that matching does not occur in this way, it is just tough luck for the taxpayer.

7. *Mitigation of the statute of limitations: §§1311-1314.* Relief from the harsh effects of the statute of limitations is provided in certain limited

circumstances under the complex provisions of §§1311-1314. Roughly, a year that is closed by the statute of limitations may be reopened, either by the taxpayer or by the government, to correct errors (e.g., failure of the taxpayer to claim a deduction or to include an item in income) that arose because the taxpayer or the government picked the wrong year or the wrong person. For example, suppose the government in 1993 asserts that a taxpayer's bad-debt deduction for 1992 was unjustified. The issue is litigated and the court in 1994 enters a final judgment in favor of the government on the ground that the deduction should have been taken in 1991. Thus, it becomes clear that in its 1991 return the taxpayer had failed to claim a deduction to which it was entitled and therefore overpaid its taxes. By 1994, the statute of limitations has run on 1991, but it had not run in 1993 when the government first asserted its position with respect to 1992. Under §1311, the taxpayer is permitted to correct the error for 1991 by recalculating its 1991 tax to take account of the bad-debt deduction and will be entitled to a refund of the overpayment (without interest).

8. *Unprofitable transactions.* In Bowers v. Kerbaugh-Empire Co., 271 U.S. 170 (1925), distinguished by the Court, the taxpayer borrowed funds from a German bank. The lender transmitted marks to its New York representative, which converted the marks into dollars and advanced the dollars to the taxpayer. The taxpayer agreed to repay the loan in marks or in their equivalent in gold coin of the United States. The loan funds were invested in a business venture that failed and were lost in the years 1913 to 1918. In 1921, the taxpayer paid off the loan balance with dollars at the then much lower rate of exchange, so the amount paid was $685,000 less than the amount received. The Court held that the difference between the dollars received by the taxpayer and the amount paid in 1921 was not income (271 U.S. at 175):

> The transaction here in question did not result in gain from capital and labor, or from either of them, or in profit gained through the sale or conversion of capital. The essential facts set forth in the complaint are the loans in 1911, 1912, and 1913, the loss in 1913 to 1918 of the moneys borrowed, the excess of such losses over income by more than the item here in controversy, and payment in the equivalent of marks greatly depreciated in value. The result of the whole transaction was a loss. . . . When the loans were made and notes given, the assets and liabilities of defendant in error were increased alike. The loss of the money borrowed wiped out the increase of assets, but the liability remained. The assets were further diminished by payment of the debt. The loss was less than it would have been if marks had not declined in value; but the mere diminution of loss is not gain, profit, or income.

It is quite plain, for reasons explained later (see infra page 232), that in the normal case the discharge of the debt in 1921 for $685,000 less than the amount previously received (as a nontaxable loan) results in income in that amount in that year. Here, the Court in effect allowed the taxpayer, without benefit of any statutory device such as §172, to offset the income in 1921 with the losses of the earlier years because the funds initially borrowed (received) had been invested and produced those losses. In other words, the Court used transactional, as opposed to annual, accounting. It does not appear, however, that the Court was aware in this early case that it was thus violating fundamental principles of tax accounting and the case, though never expressly overruled, has not been followed. See United States v. Kirby Lumber, infra page 235.

PROBLEMS

1. Aerospace Corp. was formed in 1994, and in the same year was awarded a ten-year government contract, which was its only source of business. At the end of 1994, its books showed a loss on the contract of $30,000 and a net taxable loss of the same amount. In 1995, Aerospace Corp. showed a profit on the contract of $30,000 (still its only source of business) and a net taxable income of the same amount. Aerospace Corp. did not elect or qualify for the special accounting methods for long-term contracts. Must Aerospace Corp. pay tax on the $30,000 income in 1995? See §172(b)(1)(A)(ii), (c).

2. Would your answer to Problem 1 change if Aerospace's $30,000 net income in 1995 were attributable to sales to other companies, rather than to profits on the government contract?

3. In 1994, Bob earned a salary of $60,000 as an associate of a large law firm and had no other income. He had a deduction for personal exemptions of $4,000 and itemized nonbusiness deductions of $16,000, so his taxable income for 1994 was $40,000. In 1995, Bob again earned $60,000 as an associate in the law firm, but also suffered an ordinary (that is, noncapital) loss of $80,000 from his wholly owned business. His deduction for personal exemptions was $6,000 and his itemized nonbusiness deductions were $15,000. How much, if any, of the 1995 loss can Bob carry back against his 1994 income? (Assume Bob had no income in 1992 and 1993 so that no portion of the 1995 loss could be carried back to those years.) See §172(c), (d)(3) and (4).

4. Xenon Corp.'s adjusted taxable income for the years 1989-1994, before the application of §172, is shown below:

1989	*1990*	*1991*	*1992*	*1993*	*1994*
$600	$400	$700	($3,000)	$700	$700

The $3,000 loss for 1990 is a net operating loss. Disregarding any special elections, how is the 1990 NOL allocated to the other years?

2. Claim of Right

NORTH AMERICAN OIL CONSOLIDATED v. BURNET

286 U.S. 417 (1932)

Mr. Justice BRANDEIS delivered the opinion of the Court.

The question for decision is whether the sum of $171,979.22 received by the North American Oil Consolidated in 1917, was taxable to it as income of that year.

The money was paid to the company under the following circumstances. Among many properties operated by it in 1916 was a section of oil land, the legal title to which stood in the name of the United States. Prior to that year, the Government, also claiming the beneficial ownership, had instituted a suit to oust the company from possession; and on February 2, 1916, it secured the appointment of a receiver to operate the property, or supervise its operations, and to hold the net income thereof. The money paid to the company in 1917 represented the net profits which had been earned from that property in 1916 during the receivership. The money was paid to the receiver as earned. After entry by the District Court in 1917 of the final decree dismissing the bill, the money was paid, in that year, by the receiver to the company. United States v. North American Oil Consolidated, 242 Fed. 723. The Government took an appeal (without supersedeas) to the Circuit Court of Appeals. In 1920, that Court affirmed the decree. 264 Fed. 336. In 1922, a further appeal to this Court was dismissed by stipulation. 258 U.S. 633.

The income earned from the property in 1916 had been entered on the books of the company as its income. It had not been included in its original return of income for 1916; but it was included in an amended return for that year which was filed in 1918. Upon auditing the company's income and profits tax returns for 1917, the Commissioner of Internal Revenue determined a deficiency based on other items. The company appealed to the Board of Tax Appeals. There, in 1927, the Commissioner prayed that the deficiency already claimed should be increased so as to include a tax on the amount paid by the receiver to the company in 1917. The Board held that the profits were taxable to the receiver as income of 1916; and hence made no finding whether the company's accounts were kept on the cash receipts and disbursements basis or on the accrual basis. 12 B.T.A. 68. The Circuit Court of Appeals held that the profits were taxable to the company as income of 1917, regardless of whether the company's returns were made on the cash or on the accrual basis. 50 F.(2d)752. This Court granted a writ of certiorari. 284 U.S. 614.

It is conceded that the net profits earned by the property during the receivership constituted income. The company contends that they should have been reported by the receiver for taxation in 1916; that if not returnable by him, they should have been returned by the company for 1916, because they constitute income of the company accrued in that year; and that if not taxable as income of the company for 1916, they were taxable to it as income for 1922, since the litigation was not finally terminated in its favor until 1922.

First. The income earned in 1916 and impounded by the receiver in that year was not taxable to him, because he was the receiver of only a part of the properties operated by the company. Under Sec. 13(c) of the Revenue Act of 1916 [and its successors], receivers who "are operating the property or business of corporations" were obliged to make returns "of net income as and for such corporations," and "any income tax due" was to be "assessed and collected in the same manner as if assessed directly against the organization of whose business or properties they have custody and control."[32] . . . The regulations of the Treasury Department have consistently construed these statutes as applying only to receivers in charge of the entire property or business of a corporation; and in all other cases have required the corporations themselves to report their income. . . . That construction is clearly correct. The language of the section contemplates a substitution of the receiver for the corporation; and there can be such substitution only when the receiver is in complete control of the properties and business of the corporation. Moreover, there is no provision for the consolidation of the return of a receiver of part of a corporation's property or business with the return of the corporation itself. It may not be assumed that Congress intended to require the filing of two separate returns for the same year, each covering only a part of the corporate income, without making provision for consolidation so that the tax could be based upon the income as a whole.

Second. The net profits were not taxable to the company as income of 1916. For the company was not required in 1916 to report as income an amount which it might never receive. See Burnet v. Logan [infra page 358]. Compare Lucas v. American Code Co., 280 U.S. 445, 452; Burnet v. Sanford & Brooks Co. [supra page 194]. There was no constructive receipt of the profits by the company in that year, because at

32. [The current equivalent of this provision is §6012(b)(3). — Eds.]

no time during the year was there a right in the company to demand that the receiver pay over the money. Throughout 1916 it was uncertain who would be declared entitled to the profits. It was not until 1917, when the District Court entered a final decree vacating the receivership and dismissing the bill, that the company became entitled to receive the money. Nor is it material, for the purposes of this case, whether the company's return was filed on the cash receipts and disbursements basis, or on the accrual basis. In neither event was it taxable in 1916 on account of income which it had not yet received and which it might never receive.

Third. The net profits earned by the property in 1916 were not income of the year 1922 — the year in which the litigation with the Government was finally terminated. They became income of the company in 1917, when it first became entitled to them and when it actually received them. If a taxpayer receives earnings under a claim of right and without restriction as to its disposition, he has received income which he is required to return [that is, report on his or her tax return], even though it may still be claimed that he is not entitled to retain the money, and even though he may still be adjudged liable to restore its equivalent. . . . If in 1922 the Government had prevailed, and the company had been obliged to refund the profits received in 1917, it would have been entitled to a deduction from the profits in 1922, not from those of any earlier year. . . .

Affirmed.

NOTES AND QUESTIONS

1. *The stakes.* While ordinarily the taxpayer seeks to defer the taxation of income, here the taxpayer argues for taxation in the earliest possible year. The explanation is that in 1916 the tax rate was 2 percent; in 1917 it was 6 percent plus an excess profits tax ranging from 20 percent to 60 percent; and in 1922 it was 12.5 percent, with no excess profits tax.

2. *The receivership.* The Court viewed the receiver, appointed in 1916, as a custodian of funds and not as a substitute operator of the business. Such a receiver, who is not in control of the taxpayer's entire business, was not required to file a return for the taxpayer. (For the present rule, which is to the same effect, see §6012(b)(3).) What, if anything, would be wrong with taxing the receiver? If the receiver had invested the funds and earned interest on the investment, how should that interest have been treated?

3. *The proper taxable year.* (a) There was no finding as to whether the taxpayer was on the cash or the accrual method of accounting. Under §446(a), "taxable income shall be computed under the method of accounting on the basis of which the taxpayer regularly computes his income in keeping his books." Section 446(b) provides an exception

where the method used by the taxpayer "does not clearly reflect income." Assume that the taxpayer was on the accrual method. (For a brief description, see supra page 53.) What was it that stood in the way of taxation in 1916, the dispute or the receivership?

(b) If the latter, can the result be reconciled with principles of accrual accounting?

(c) If the former, why was the receipt taxable in 1917, when the dispute was still alive?

(d) Could the taxpayer have protected itself from liability in 1917 by treating the receipt as a trust fund pending outcome of the appeal — for example, by depositing it in a special account and labeling it as a trust fund on its books? No, per Commissioner v. Alamitos Land Co., 112 F.2d 648 (9th Cir.), cert. denied, 311 U.S. 679 (1940), and Rev. Rul. 55-137, 1955-1 C.B. 215. See also Commissioner v. Brooklyn Union Gas Co., 62 F.2d 505 (2d Cir. 1933), acq. (amount under dispute but received before final judicial determination taxable despite the fact that taxpayer was required to post bond to secure repayment if dispute ultimately were resolved against it).

4. *The "claim of right" doctrine.* (a) *North American Oil* is often cited for its statement (in the final paragraph of the opinion) of the "claim-of-right" doctrine:

> If a taxpayer receives earnings under a claim of right and without restriction as to its disposition, he has received income which he is required to return [i.e., report], even though it may still be claimed that he is not entitled to retain the money, and even though he may still be adjudged liable to restore its equivalent.

(b) In Illinois Power Co. v. Commissioner, 792 F.2d 683 (7th Cir. 1986), the taxpayer, an electric company, was ordered by the Illinois Commerce Commission to raise its rates. The Commission made it clear, however, that its purpose was to discourage the consumption of electricity and that the taxpayer would not be allowed to keep the extra revenue resulting from the increase, or any interest on it. The money was not, however, kept in any separate account or trust. The IRS argued that the money was taxable under *North American Oil.* The court, in rejecting this position, likened the taxpayer to "a custodian, . . . with no greater beneficial interest in the revenues collected than a bank has in the money deposited with it." Generalizing, the court stated, "The underlying principle is that the taxpayer is allowed to exclude from his [sic] income money received under an unequivocal contractual, statutory, or regulatory duty to repay it, so that he really is just the custodian of the money." Thus, in this case there was no dispute; the taxpayer never claimed a right to the funds at issue. Note that during the time the power company held the money, it earned interest on that money. How should that interest be taxed?

UNITED STATES v. LEWIS

340 U.S. 590 (1951)

Mr. Justice Black delivered the opinion of the Court.

Respondent Lewis brought this action in the Court of Claims seeking a refund of an alleged overpayment of his 1944 income tax. The facts found by the Court of Claims are: In his 1944 income tax return, respondent reported about $22,000 which he had received that year as an employee's bonus. As a result of subsequent litigation in a state court, however, it was decided that respondent's bonus had been improperly computed; under compulsion of the state court's judgment he returned approximately $11,000 to his employer. Until payment of the judgment in 1946, respondent had at all times claimed and used the full $22,000 unconditionally as his own, in the good faith though "mistaken" belief that he was entitled to the whole bonus.

On the foregoing facts the Government's position is that respondent's 1944 tax should not be recomputed, but that respondent should have deducted the $11,000 as a loss in his 1946 tax return. . . . The Court of Claims, however, relying on its own case, Greenwald v. United States, 102 Ct. Cl. 272, 57 F. Supp. 569, held that the excess bonus received "under a mistake of fact" was not income in 1944 and ordered a refund based on a recalculation of that year's tax. 117 Ct. Cl. 336, 91 F. Supp. 1017. We granted certiorari, 340 U.S. 903, because this holding conflicted with many decisions of the courts of appeals, see, e.g., Haberkorn v. United States, 173 F.2d 587, and with principles announced in North American Oil v. Burnet [supra page 201].

In the *North American Oil* case we said:

> If a taxpayer receives earnings under a claim of right and without restriction as to its disposition, he has received income which he is required to return, even though it may still be claimed that he is not entitled to retain the money, and even though he may still be adjudged liable to restore its equivalent.

286 U.S. at 424. Nothing in this language permits an exception merely because a taxpayer is "mistaken" as to the validity of his claim. Nor has the "claim of right" doctrine been impaired, as the Court of Claims stated, by Freuler v. Helvering, 291 U.S. 35, or Commissioner v. Wilcox, 327 U.S. 404. The *Freuler* case involved an entirely different section of the Internal Revenue Code, and its holding is inapplicable here. 291 U.S. at 43. . . .

Income taxes must be paid on income received (or accrued) during an annual accounting period. Cf. [§§441, 451(a), and 446(a)]; and see Burnet v. Sanford & Brooks Co. [supra page 194]. The "claim of right" interpretation of the tax laws has long been used to give finality to that period, and is now deeply rooted in the federal tax system. . . . We see no reason why the Court should depart from this well-settled interpretation merely because it results in an advantage or disadvantage to a taxpayer.[33]

Reversed.

Mr. Justice DOUGLAS, dissenting.

The question in this case is not whether the bonus had to be included in 1944 income for purposes of the tax. Plainly it should have been because the taxpayer claimed it as of right. Some years later, however, it was judicially determined that he had no claim to the bonus. The question is whether he may then get back the tax which he paid on the money.

Many inequities are inherent in the income tax. We multiply them needlessly by nice distinctions which have no place in the practical administration of the law. If the refund were allowed, the integrity of the taxable year would not be violated. The tax would be paid when due; but the Government would not be permitted to maintain the unconscionable position that it can keep the tax after it is shown that payment was made on money which was not income to the taxpayer.

NOTES AND QUESTIONS

1. *Equity consideration.* Why did Justice Douglas think that an adjustment for 1944 would be more equitable? After all, the taxpayer did receive the full $22,000 in 1944. In 1946 he discovered that he was $11,000 less well off than he had thought. Why is his economic setback any different from an investment loss or a casualty loss in 1946?

2. *Scope of the doctrine.* Suppose a bank erroneously credits your account with interest on December 31. You discover this on January 1 of the following year and have the bank make the correction. Must you include the erroneous interest in income for the first year and take a deduction in the later year? What if you withdraw the interest on December 31 of the first year (with or without knowledge of the error) and repay it in the following year?

3. *Congressional reaction: §1341.* (a) Congress apparently agreed that the result in cases like *Lewis* was inequitable and provided relief in §1341. It retained the notion that the proper starting point was a deduction in the year of repayment rather than a reopening of the earlier year. But it provided that if the deduction exceeds $3,000, the tax is the lesser of

33. It has been suggested that it would be more "equitable" to reopen respondent's 1944 tax return. While the suggestion might work to the advantage of this taxpayer, it could not be adopted as a general solution because, in many cases, the three-year statute of limitations would preclude recovery. [§6511(a).]

the amount determined by claiming a deduction in the ordinary manner or by forgoing the deduction and claiming a credit in the year of repayment for the tax that would have been saved by excluding the item in the earlier year. The effect of the latter alternative is the same as allowing the taxpayer to reopen the earlier year, except for the interest on the overpayment. If §1341 had been the law in 1946, Lewis would have reduced his tax bill for 1946 by the "tax cost" of including the item in 1944. Why is the taxpayer allowed to choose the better of two alternatives? A taxpayer who paid little or no tax when the item was included in gross income is permitted, under §1341, to deduct it from the later year's income, even though the tax saving from the deduction in that later year exceeds the tax cost of the earlier inclusion. Would Justice Douglas have found that unconscionable?

(b) While Congress's objective in enacting §1341 may have been to achieve equity, it was not content simply to provide the courts with a broad, vague mandate to accomplish that objective. The statute applies to items as to which it "*appeared* that the taxpayer had an *unrestricted right*" in one year and as to which a repayment is made in a subsequent year "because it was *established after* the close of such prior taxable year" that the taxpayer did not have such an unrestricted right (emphasis added). The IRS has ruled that restorations do not qualify under §1341 if based on "mere errors," such as in arithmetic, or on "subsequent events," such as a refund pursuant to a contractual right. Rev. Rul. 68-153, 1968-1 C.B. 371. Nor does it believe that the repayment by an embezzler of his embezzled gains qualifies. Rev. Rul. 65-254, 1965-2 C.B. 50. The rulings are based on the theory that §1341 applies only where amounts are held under a "semblance" of a right — i.e., a claim that is somewhere between "absolutely no right" (embezzled funds) and a situation where the repayment is made to the payee based on a "non-challengeable" obligation to make such repayment (e.g., a refund based on a contractual right merely contingent upon subsequent events). The ruling that an embezzler cannot invoke §1341 because he or she does not have an "unrestricted right" to the embezzled funds was upheld in McKinney v. United States, 574 F.2d 1240 (5th Cir. 1978), cert. denied, 439 U.S. 1072 (1979), and in Yerkie v. Commissioner, 67 T.C. 388 (1976). In each of these cases the taxpayer restored part of the embezzled funds when the embezzlement was discovered. The IRS did not dispute the taxpayer's right to a deduction for the restoration but denied the right to invoke §1341(a)(5)(B). As an alternative to their claims for relief under §1341, the taxpayers sought unsuccessfully to establish that they were in the trade or business of embezzlement and therefore should be entitled to carry the undeducted portion of the losses back to earlier years under §172. This position was rejected, even though, in McKinney's case, the taxpayer established that he had devoted about half of his working time to the embezzlement scheme and that the one in question was his third.

(c) Do the limitations found in §1341 make sense? If not, why were they imposed? Is it likely that Congress addressed itself to a specific problem and (as is often the case) failed to consider that the specific problem was part of a more general problem? Or does §1341 simply reflect caution or timidity? Why might the Service be hostile to the statute and interpret it narrowly?

3. The Tax Benefit Doctrine

ALICE PHELAN SULLIVAN CORP. v. UNITED STATES

381 F.2d 399 (Ct. Cl. 1967)

COLLINS, Judge.

Plaintiff, a California corporation, brings this action to recover an alleged overpayment in its 1957 income tax. During that year, there was returned to taxpayer two parcels of realty, each of which it had previously donated and claimed as a charitable contribution deduction. The first donation had been made in 1939; the second, in 1940. Under the then applicable corporate tax rates [18 and 24 percent respectively], the deductions claimed ($4,243.29 for 1939 and $4,463.44 for 1940) yielded plaintiff an aggregate tax benefit of $1,877.49.

Each conveyance had been made subject to the condition that the property be used either for a religious or for an educational purpose. In 1957, the donee decided not to use the gifts; they were therefore reconveyed to plaintiff. Upon audit of taxpayer's income tax return, it was found that the recovered property was not reflected in its 1957 gross income. The Commissioner of Internal Revenue disagreed with plaintiff's characterization of the recovery as a nontaxable return of capital. He viewed the transaction as giving rise to taxable income and therefore adjusted plaintiff's income by adding to it $8,706.93 — the total of the charitable contribution deductions previously claimed and allowed. This addition to income, taxed at the 1957 corporate tax rate of 52 percent, resulted in a deficiency assessment of $4,527.60. After payment of the deficiency, plaintiff filed a claim for the refund of $2,650.11, asserting this amount as overpayment on the theory that a correct assessment could demand no more than the return of the tax benefit originally enjoyed, i.e., $1,877.49. The claim was disallowed.

This court has had prior occasion to consider the question which the present suit presents. In Perry v. United States, 160 F. Supp. 270, 142 Ct. Cl. 7 (1958) (Judges Madden and Laramore dissenting), it was recognized that a return to the donor of a prior charitable contribution gave rise to income to the extent of the deduction previously allowed. The court's point of division — which is likewise the division between the instant parties — was whether the "gain" attributable to the recovery was to be taxed at the rate applicable at the time the deduction was first claimed or whether the proper rate was that in effect at the time of recovery. The majority, concluding that the Government should be entitled to recoup no more than that which it lost, held that the tax liability arising upon the return of a charitable gift should equal the tax benefit experienced at the time of donation. Taxpayer urges that the *Perry* rationale dictates that a like result be reached in this case.

The Government, of course, assumes the opposite stance. Mindful of the homage due the principle of stare decisis, it bids us first to consider the criteria under which judicial reexamination of an earlier decision is justifiable. We are referred to Judge Davis' concurring opinion in Mississippi River Fuel Corp. v. United States, 314 F.2d 953, 958, 161 Ct. Cl. 237, 246-247 (1963), wherein he states that:

> The question is not what we would hold if we now took a fresh look but whether we should take that fresh look. A court should not scrutinize its own prior ruling — putting constitutional adjudication, which has its own standards, to one side — merely because, as now constituted, it might have reached a different result at the earlier time. Something more is required before a reexamination is to be undertaken: (a) a strong, even if not yet firm, view that the challenged precedent is probably wrong; (b) an inadequate or incomplete presentation in the prior case; (c) an intervening development in the law, or in critical comment, which unlocks new corridors; (d) unforeseen difficulties in the application or reach of the earlier decision; or (e) inconsistencies in the court's own rulings in the field. Where these or like reasons for reopening are lacking, respect for an existing precedent is counselled by all those many facets of stability-plus-economy which are embodied in the principle of stare decisis. . . .

Judged in light of the above-listed criteria, reexamination is claimed to be warranted. In expanding its position on this point, the Government begins by recommending consideration of the views of the *Perry* dissent. Stress is placed upon the point therein noted, namely, that the "balancing" technique adopted by the court in *Perry* — though equitable — was otherwise without legal foundation. The dissent viewed the majority result as going beyond the recognized limits of either statutory or judge-made law. Like expressions of disagreement have been voiced elsewhere. . . .

As additional ground in support of reconsideration, the Government mentions that *Perry* was decided on a ground which neither of its parties had argued and which we, in later decisions, are said to have abandoned. The Government contrasts the principle of taxation adopted in *Perry* with that reflected in such later decisions as California & Hawaiian Sugar

Ref. Corp. v. United States, 311 F.2d 235, 159 Ct. Cl. 561 (1962), and Citizens Fed. Sav. & Loan Ass'n v. United States, 290 F.2d 932, 154 Ct. Cl. 305 (1961). These last cited cases are said to contradict *Perry* because they sanction taxation of "recovered" deductions at the tax rate prevailing in the later year, that is, the year of recovery. The foregoing considerations express sufficient reason to relinquish our deference to precedent in order to examine anew the issue which this case presents.

A transaction which returns to a taxpayer his own property cannot be considered as giving rise to "income" — at least where that term is confined to its traditional sense of "gain derived from capital, from labor, or from both combined." Eisner v. Macomber [infra page 286]. Yet the principle is well engrained in our tax law that the return or recovery of property that was once the subject of an income tax deduction must be treated as income in the year of its recovery. . . . The only limitation upon that principle is the so-called "tax-benefit rule." This rule permits exclusion of the recovered item from income so long as its initial use as a deduction did not provide a tax saving. . . . But where full tax use of a deduction was made and a tax saving thereby obtained, then the extent of saving is considered immaterial. The recovery is viewed as income to the full extent of the deduction previously allowed.[34]

Formerly the exclusive province of judge-made law, the tax-benefit concept now finds expression both in statute and administrative regulations. Section 111 of the Code accords tax-benefit treatment to the recovery of bad debts, prior taxes, and delinquency amounts.[35] Treasury regulations have "broadened" the rule of exclusion by extending similar treatment to "all other losses, expenditures, and accruals made the basis of deductions from gross income for prior taxable years.". . .

Drawing our attention to the broad language of this regulation, the Government insists that the present recovery must find its place within the scope of the regulation and, as such, should be taxed in a manner consistent with the treatment provided for like items of recovery, i.e., that it be taxed at the rate prevailing in the year of recovery. We are compelled to agree.

Ever since Burnet v. Sanford & Brooks Co. [supra page 194], the concept of accounting for items of income and expense on an annual basis has been accepted as the basic principle upon which our tax laws are structured. "It is the essence of any system of taxation that it should

34. The rationale which supports the principle, as well as its limitation, is that the property, having once served to offset taxable income (i.e., as a tax deduction) should be treated, upon its recoupment, as the recovery of that which had been previously deducted. . . .

35. [Section 111 has now been amended to provide a broad tax-benefit rule. — Eds.]

produce revenue ascertainable, and payable to the government, at regular intervals. Only by such a system is it practicable to produce a regular flow of income and apply methods of accounting assessment, and collection capable of practical operation." 282 U.S. at 365. To insure the vitality of the single-year concept, it is essential not only that annual income be ascertained without reference to losses experienced in an earlier accounting period, but also that income be taxed without reference to earlier tax rates. And absent specific statutory authority sanctioning a departure from this principle, it may only be said of *Perry* that it achieved a result which was more equitably just than legally correct.[36]

Since the taxpayer in this case did obtain full tax benefit from its earlier deductions, those deductions were properly classified as income upon recoupment and must be taxed as such. This can mean nothing less than the application of that tax rate which is in effect during the year in which the recovered item is recognized as a factor of income. We therefore sustain the Government's position and grant its motion for summary judgment. Perry v. United States, supra, is hereby overruled, and plaintiff's petition is dismissed.

NOTES AND QUESTIONS

1. *Analysis.* (a) For purposes of discussion, assume the following facts: The fair market value of the property donated in 1939 and 1940 was $8,700 and this was the amount deducted. The basis was $2,000 and the tax saved was $1,900. In 1957, the fair market value of the property, which was returned to the taxpayer, was $12,000. The Commissioner's position was that the amount to be included in income in 1957 was $8,700, with a resulting tax of $4,500. The taxpayer's position was that it should pay an additional tax of $1,900 in 1957. What are the arguments for including in the taxpayer's income for 1957:

(i) nothing,
(ii) $8,700, or
(iii) $12,000?

36. This opinion represents the views of the majority and complies with existing law and decisions. However, in the writer's personal opinion, it produces a harsh and inequitable result. Perhaps, it exemplifies a situation "where the letter of the law killeth; the spirit giveth life." The tax-benefit concept is an equitable doctrine which should be carried to an equitable conclusion. Since it is the declared public policy to encourage contributions to charitable and educational organizations, a donor, whose gift to such organizations is returned, should not be required to refund to the Government a greater amount than the tax benefit received when the deduction was made for the gift. Such a rule would avoid a penalty to the taxpayer and an unjust enrichment to the Government. However, the court cannot legislate and any change in the existing law rests within the wisdom and discretion of the Congress.

What is the argument for increasing the taxpayer's tax liability in 1957 by $1,900?

(b) Suppose that the taxpayer had enjoyed no tax benefit from the deductions in 1939 and 1940 (for example, because other deductions were sufficient to eliminate any tax liability). How would your answers to part (a) of this question change?

(c) Do you agree with the court that the decision in the *Perry* case was so plainly in error as to require overruling? Do you agree with the view expressed in footnote 36 that the result reached by the court is "harsh and inequitable"?

(d) Suppose that at the time of the gift the property was worth $9,000 and that the taxpayer valued its reversion at $300 and deducted only $8,700. Does that approach seem sound? If so, what is the proper tax result when the property is recovered under the terms of the reversion, assuming it was worth $12,000 at that time?

2. *Tax benefit and annual accounting.* The tax-benefit doctrine, discussed and relied on by the court, is a limitation on the broader rule that taxes are accounted for on an annual rather than a transactional basis (see supra page 55). The doctrine has two aspects, one inclusionary and one exclusionary. In *Alice Phelan Sullivan Corp.* we see the inclusionary aspect: The taxpayer is required to include in income a recovery of property previously given to charity because the gift in the prior year had been deducted. Similar situations arise where there have been deductions for bad debts, taxes, losses by theft, worthless assets, expropriation losses, or other calamities and later, to the surprise and delight of the taxpayer, there is a recovery of part or all of the amount written off. The phrase "tax benefit doctrine" is used in its inclusionary sense to describe the rule that recoveries in such situations must be included in income. More frequently, however, and somewhat confusingly, the same phrase is used in its exclusionary sense to refer to a limitation on the general principle of taxation — namely, the idea, now embodied in §111, that if (or to the extent that) the taxpayer received no "tax benefit" from the deduction, the recovery need not be included in income. (It is worth noting, by the way, that even if a deduction was of no tax benefit in the year it was taken, the taxpayer may have enjoyed a benefit in another year by reason of an operating-loss or capital-loss carryover. The broader the scope of these carryovers, and the longer the period to which they apply, the more frequently will a deduction produce a tax benefit in some year.)

In Hillsboro National Bank v. Commissioner, 460 U.S. 370 (1983), the taxpayer had been allowed, under §164(e), to deduct certain taxes that were imposed on its shareholders but that it paid. In a later year the taxes were refunded directly to the shareholders, and the Commissioner sought to require that the taxpayer restore to income the amount previously deducted. While the Court ultimately based its decision on an interpretation of §164(e), it began with an examination of the tax benefit doctrine, about which it had this to say:

> The taxpayers and the Government . . . propose different formulations of the tax benefit rule. The taxpayers contend that the rule requires the inclusion of amounts *recovered* in later years, and they do not view the events in these cases as "recoveries." The Government, on the other hand, urges that the tax benefit rule requires the inclusion of amounts previously deducted if later events are inconsistent with the deductions; it insists that no "recovery" is necessary to the application of the rule. Further, it asserts that the events in these cases are inconsistent with the deductions taken by the taxpayers. We are not in complete agreement with either view.
>
> An examination of the purpose and accepted applications of the tax benefit rule reveals that a "recovery" will not always be necessary to invoke the tax benefit rule. The purpose of the rule is not simply to tax "recoveries." On the contrary, it is to approximate the results produced by a tax system based on transactional rather than annual accounting. . . . It has long been accepted that a taxpayer using accrual accounting who accrues and deducts an expense in a tax year before it becomes payable and who for some reason eventually does not have to pay the liability must then take into income the amount of the expense earlier deducted. . . . The bookkeeping entry cancelling the liability, though it increases the balance sheet net worth of the taxpayer, does not fit within any ordinary definition of "recovery." . . .
>
> The basic purpose of the tax benefit rule is to achieve rough transactional parity in tax, . . . and to protect the Government and the taxpayer from the adverse effects of reporting a transaction on the basis of assumptions that an event in a subsequent year proves to have been erroneous. Such an event, unforeseen at the time of an earlier deduction, may in many cases require the application of the tax benefit rule. We do not, however, agree that this consequence invariably follows. Not every unforeseen event will require the taxpayer to report income in the amount of his earlier deduction. On the contrary, the tax benefit rule will "cancel out" an earlier deduction only when a careful examination shows that the later event is indeed fundamentally inconsistent with the premise on which the deduction was initially based. That is, if that event had occurred within the same taxable year, it would have foreclosed the deduction. In some cases, a subsequent recovery by the taxpayer will be the only event that would be fundamentally inconsistent with the provision granting the deduction. In such a case, only actual recovery by the taxpayer would justify application of the tax benefit rule. . . . A court must consider the facts and circumstances of each case in the light of the purpose and function of the provisions granting the deductions.

After examining the purpose of §164(e), the Court concluded that the taxpayer should not have been required to recognize income when the taxes were refunded to its shareholders because the taxpayer itself had received no payment.

F. RECOVERIES FOR PERSONAL AND BUSINESS INJURIES

1. Damages for Personal Injury in General

SOLICITOR'S OPINION 132

1-1 C.B. 92 (1922)

The question presented is whether the following receipts constitute income within the meaning of the sixteenth amendment and the statutes enacted thereunder: (1) Damages for alienation of affections; (2) damages for slander or libel of personal character; and (3) money received by a parent in consideration of the surrender of his right to the custody of his minor child.

All of these items relate to personal or family rights, not property rights, and accordingly may be treated together. Nor is there a material distinction between payment under an agreement of the parties and payment pursuant to a judgment of a court.

It is held in Solicitor's Memorandum 957 that money recovered as damages in libel proceedings is subject to income tax, and in Solicitor's Memorandum 1384, that damages for alienation of a wife's affections are not exempt from income tax under [§104(a)(2), relating to "damages received . . . on account of personal injuries or sickness"]. Both of these rulings, however, were made prior to the decision of the Supreme Court in Eisner v. Macomber [infra page 286]. Solicitor's Memorandum 1384 correctly held that the exemption contained in [§104(a)(2)] does not include damages for alienation of affections, but the question is really more fundamental, namely, whether such damages received by a lawyer for libel of his professional reputation constitute income. Business libel may be distinguished from ordinary defamation of character and is not here under consideration. The ruling in Solicitor's Memorandum 957, however, was not limited but apparently applied to libel generally.

In Stratton's Independence v. Howbert (231 U.S. 399) and in Eisner v. Macomber [supra], the Supreme Court defined income as "the gain derived from capital, from labor, or from both combined. . . ." In other words, without gain of some sort no income within the meaning of the sixteenth amendment can be said to be realized.

In the light of these decisions of the Supreme Court it must be held that there is no gain, and therefore no income, derived from the receipt of damages for alienation of affections or defamation of personal character. In either case the right invaded is a personal right and is in no way transferable. While a jury endeavors roughly to compute the amount of damage inflicted, in the very nature of things there can be no correct estimate of the money value of the invaded rights. The rights on the one hand and the money on the other are incomparable things which can not be placed on opposite sides of an equation. If an individual is possessed of a personal right that is not assignable and not susceptible of any appraisal in relation to market values, and thereafter receives either damages or payment in compromise for an invasion of that right, it can not be held that he thereby derives any gain or profit. It is clear, therefore, that the Government can not tax him on any portion of the sum received. This also applies to money received in consideration of the surrender of the custody of a minor child. Holding otherwise would be equivalent to treating as chattels the wife whose affections were alienated and the child whose custody was surrendered. . . .

NOTES AND QUESTIONS

1. *In search of a theory.* The rule adopted in Sol. Op. 132 is now embodied in §104(a)(2). What is, or should be, the theory in support of the exclusion in §104(a)(2)? Consider a case in which a young lawyer is injured in an automobile accident, loses the use of his legs, and recovers $1 million, no significant portion of which is for lost earnings. (a) Is the best theory for exclusion of the $1 million that there was a "disposition" but no gain because the value of what the taxpayer lost equals the amount that he received? See §1001(a). What is the lawyer's basis for what he lost? (b) Or should the theory be that any gain is offset by a corresponding loss in an economic, if not in a tax, sense? If so, should a taxpayer who is unable to recover for such a loss because the wrongdoer is insolvent or because the loss resulted from his or her own negligence be allowed a deduction? (c) What about the notion that the psychic (or other intangible) benefits that the taxpayer has lost could have been enjoyed tax free and that the monetary substitute should therefore be tax free? If that is the rationale, what about the fact that a person who works for a living (particularly at an arduous job) sacrifices the physical and psychic benefits of leisure? Again, what about the person who recovers nothing? Or the person who was born with a disability? (d) What if the injured person had been a professional athlete and his recovery was mostly for loss of earnings? In this situation, what is the theory or rationale for exclusion?

2. *Authority.* Sol. Op. 132 relies on Eisner v. Macomber's definition of income. Would the result be different under *Glenshaw Glass* (supra page 126)? Can the notions underlying *Glenshaw Glass* be reconciled with Sol. Op. 132 and §104(a)(2)? See footnote 14 of *Glenshaw Glass,* supra page 128.

3. *Limits.* The §104(a)(2) exclusion does not apply to recoveries for loss of business profits or to recoveries for loss of, or damage to, business assets; those recoveries are taxable, though a recovery for the loss of, or damage to, a business asset may call for an offset of the taxpayer's adjusted basis in that asset and may be treated as capital gain. See Raytheon Production Corp. v. Commissioner, 144 F.2d 110 (1st Cir.), cert. denied, 323 U.S. 779 (1944), where the entire amount of a recovery for injury to goodwill was held to be taxable because the taxpayer had failed to establish that it had any basis in that goodwill. (Goodwill is the value of a business above the value of its physical assets, stemming from favorable attitudes by its customers, a smoothly working team of experienced and carefully selected workers, and other such intangibles.) At the same time, it is plain that where a person sustains a "personal injury," §104(a)(2) excludes from taxation the full amount of a damages award based on that injury, including recoveries for loss of earnings.

2. Business versus Personal Injuries

ROEMER v. COMMISSIONER

716 F.2d 693 (9th Cir. 1983)

Alarcon, Circuit Judge.

Paul F. Roemer Jr. (Roemer) and Marcia E. Roemer appeal a decision of the United States Tax Court upholding a determination of deficiencies for their 1975 taxable year. Marcia E. Roemer is a party solely because she signed a joint income tax return with her spouse.

We must decide whether the defamation of an individual constitutes a personal injury for purposes of I.R.C. §104(a)(2) (personal injury damages excludable from gross income). As we disagree with the tax court's treatment of the lump-sum award of damages in a defamation suit, we reverse.

Facts

Paul F. Roemer Jr. started his own insurance business in 1952 in Oakland, California, where he had lived all his life. In order to build clientele, Roemer became a member of numerous social, civic and professional organizations. By the mid-1960's, he enjoyed an excellent personal and professional reputation in the community. His gross annual income had risen to approximately $300,000 (about one-half of which represented his net income).

In 1965, Roemer applied for an agency license from Penn Mutual Life Insurance Company (Penn Mutual). In the course of reviewing Roemer's application, Penn Mutual requested a credit report from Retail Credit Company (Retail Credit). Retail Credit prepared the report and sent it to Penn Mutual and other insurance companies.

The credit report was grossly defamatory. Roemer's honesty was questioned. In addition, the report falsely stated that Roemer neglected his clients' affairs, that he was recently fired from his position as president of an insurance firm, and that he intentionally defaced property belonging to others. Roemer demanded a retraction of the report. Retail Credit's purported retraction, however, contained further defamatory innuendoes. Roemer was denied agency licenses to sell life insurance by Penn Mutual and other companies as a direct result of Retail Credit's report. His general reputation in the community where he resides and works also suffered because most of his clients were also his friends.

Roemer brought an action in a California court for libel under section 45 of the California Civil Code. Section 45 provides as follows:

> Libel is a false and unprivileged publication by writing, printing, picture, effigy, or other fixed representation to the eye, which exposes any person to hatred, contempt, ridicule, or obloquy, or which causes him to be shunned or avoided, or which has a tendency to injure him in his occupation.

In his complaint for libel Roemer alleged that the defendant's defamatory publication was done "with intent to damage his reputation, and to injure him in his business profession and occupation." Roemer's attorney argued to the jury that in fixing damages the jury should consider that prior to the defamation the plaintiff had an excellent character and that his reputation in both the insurance industry and his personal life was excellent. In closing argument, the jury was told that Roemer had lost $136,000 in prospective income as the result of the libel. The jury found that Retail Credit had committed libel and awarded Roemer compensatory damages of $40,000 and punitive damages of $250,000.[37] The judgment was upheld on appeal in Roemer v. Retail Credit Co., 44 Cal. App. 3d 926, 119 Cal. Rptr. 82 (1975). At trial the only defense was that of a qualified privilege claimed by the

37. [The Tax Court opinion provides the following information on Roemer's net recovery (79 T.C. 398, 403 n.2):

Compensatory damages	$ 40,000	
Punitive damages	250,000	
Interest and costs	85,601	
		$375,601

defendant under California Civil Code, section 47, subdivision 3 (a communication, without malice, between interested persons is privileged and therefore not defamation).

The jury was not asked to specify whether the damages were awarded as compensation for injury to Roemer's personal or professional reputation, nor did the jury allocate the award between Roemer's personal injury and his economic loss. The jury was instructed, however, that in determining the amount of actual or compensatory damages, it could "take into consideration the grief, anguish, mental suffering, mortification and humiliation which Plaintiff has undergone and suffered by reason of the Defendant's publication." The jury was also told that in awarding general and compensatory damages it could consider "the prominence of the Plaintiff in the community in which he lives, his social standing, his family status or any mental suffering proximately resulting from the defamation."

On Roemer's 1975 federal tax return, he reported $16,020 of the damages awarded in the defamation action as income. The Commissioner of Internal Revenue determined that the entire judgment received by Roemer should have been included in gross income with a deduction for all costs and attorneys' fees and assessed a deficiency of $32,980 against Roemer. The tax court, in an opinion by Judge Dawson reviewed by the court with three judges dissenting, upheld the Commissioner's determination. The tax court ruled that: (1) the compensatory damages were not excludable from gross income under §104(a)(2), because the taxpayer had failed to establish that the compensatory damages were received for injury to his personal reputation; (2) the punitive damages were also includable in gross income, since the tax court found that the compensatory damages were intended to reimburse the taxpayer for injury to his professional reputation; (3) both the compensatory and the punitive damages were taxable as ordinary income. . . .

A. COMPENSATORY DAMAGES

1. *Tax Treatment of Personal Injury Damages*

Section 61(a) defines gross income as "all income from whatever source derived." All realized accessions to wealth are presumed to be taxable income, unless the taxpayer can demonstrate that an acquisition is specifically exempted from taxation. Commissioner v. Glenshaw Glass

---

Less:		
Attorney's fees	220,710	
Costs	7,751	
		228,461
Net to Petitioner		$147,140

— Eds.]

Co. [supra page 126] (Congress intended to tax all gains except those specifically exempted).

Since 1918 Congress has expressly excluded from gross income tort damages received on account of personal injuries.[38] Revenue Act of 1918, §213(b)(6), 40 Stat. 1066. An individual who wins a personal injury suit usually is given a lump-sum award that includes an amount for items that ordinarily would be taxable, such as lost income. Although it might be logical to allocate a lump-sum award between its excludable and taxable components, the Commissioner has long excluded from income the entire monetary judgment. See Sol. Op. 132 [supra page 214] (rights invaded and money value are incomparable, cannot tax any portion of sum received). The rationale behind the exclusion of the entire award is apparently a feeling that the injured party, who has suffered enough, should not be further burdened with the practical difficulty of sorting out the taxable and nontaxable components of a lump-sum award. Note, Taxation of Damages Recoveries from Litigation, 40 Cornell L.Q. 345, 346 (1955).

The dispositive issue on this appeal is whether Roemer's lump-sum recovery of damages in his defamation action against Retail Credit is excludable from gross income under §104(a)(2) as damages received "on account of personal injuries." The tax court found that the defamatory statements predominantly resulted in a loss of income to Roemer caused by damage to his professional reputation. The court held that damages received in a defamation action are includable in gross income to the extent that they are measured by the effect on an individual's professional reputation. Damages are excludable from gross income to the extent a taxpayer can show that the damages, including amounts for lost income, were received for an injury to the individual's personal reputation.

Whether the tax court drew a proper distinction between personal reputation and professional reputation for purposes of §104(a)(2) is a question of law subject to de novo review on appeal. . . . This court may modify or reverse a decision of the tax court that is not in accordance with the law. §7482(c)(1). We reverse because we have concluded that the tax court's analysis of this matter confuses a personal injury with its

38. It was thought that there was no gain and therefore no income as income was then defined by the Supreme Court. Eisner v. Macomber, 252 U.S. 189, 207 (1920) (income is gain derived from capital or labor). . . . The Supreme Court later made it clear that the *Eisner* definition of income was not exclusive and that other realized accessions to wealth may be taxable income. Commissioner v. Glenshaw Glass Co. [supra] (punitive damages for fraud and antitrust violations are taxable income). Since there is no tax basis in a person's health and other personal interests, money received as compensation for an injury to those interests might be considered a realized accession to wealth. Nevertheless, Congress in its compassion has retained the exclusion (now codified at §104(a)(2)).

consequences and illogically distinguishes physical from nonphysical personal injuries.

When an individual recovers damages for a physical personal injury, the lump-sum award is not allocated between the personal aspects of the injury and the economic loss occasioned by the personal injury, nor is the taxpayer precluded from use of §104(a)(2) when the predominant result of the injury is a loss of income. However, when the injury is nonphysical, as is defamation, the majority of the tax court would require the taxpayer to allocate an award between the excludable and the otherwise taxable components of the damages. 79 T.C. at 405-06.

The relevant distinction that should be made is between personal and nonpersonal injuries, not between physical and nonphysical injuries. Section 104(a)(2) states that damages received on account of personal injuries are excludable; it says nothing about physical injuries. "[T]he words of statutes — including revenue acts — should be interpreted where possible in their ordinary, everyday senses." Crane v. Commissioner, 331 U.S. 1, 6 (1947). The ordinary meaning of a personal injury is not limited to a physical one. Indeed, the Service has long said that certain nonphysical injuries are personal injuries and that all damages received for nonphysical personal injuries are excludable from gross income. Sol. Op. 132 [supra page 214] (damages for alienation of affections, defamation of personal character, and surrender of child custody rights are damages for invasion of personal rights and not income).

Since the damages at issue here were awarded to the taxpayer after the trial of a defamation action,[39] we must look to the nature of the tort of defamation to determine whether the award should have been reported as gross income. See Woodward v. Commissioner, 397 U.S. 572 (1970) (characterization of stock appraisal litigation expenses depends on the origin of the claim litigated); Raytheon Production Corp. v. Commissioner, 144 F.2d 110, 113 (1st Cir. 1944) (analysis of antitrust damages; "In lieu of what were the damages awarded?"), cert. denied, 323 U.S. 779 (1944).

2. *The Tort of Defamation*

Since there is no general federal common law of torts (Erie Railroad Co. v. Tompkins, 304 U.S. 64, 78 (1938)) nor controlling definitions in the tax code, we must look to state law to analyze the nature of the claim litigated. United States v. Mitchell, 403 U.S. 190, 197 (1971) (quoting Burnet v. Harmel, 287 U.S. 103, 110 (1932) (state law creates legal interests; federal law determines when and how to tax). In order

39. We note in passing that we do not have here the problem, as in some settlement awards, of determining whether or not the settlement was on account of personal injuries by looking at the intent of the payor. . . .

to determine the nature of Roemer's claim, we must analyze the defamation action as it developed in state law. . . .

[T]he law of defamation in California is an unhappy tangle of illogical rules derived from its haphazard historical development. Although the civil code has been extensively amended, the definitions of defamation and its component torts of libel and slander have basically remained as they were when enacted in 1872. Cal. Civ. Code §§44, 45, 46 (West 1982). In California, tort actions continue the common law courts' emphasis on the effects of the defamation. There are a myriad of rules for when and what sort of damages may or must be proved with the applicable rules varying according to the form of the defamatory statements made (oral or written) and the content of the statements. . . .

There is nevertheless a unifying theme to defamation law as evidenced by the fact that the California defamation statutes appear in the Civil Code at "Division 1. Persons. Part 2. Personal Rights." The first statute in part 2, section 43 of the Civil Code, recognizes a general personal right to be protected from defamation. In contrast, California law also provides for related torts of disparagement or trade libel that will remedy an attack on the quality of the plaintiff's products or services. See, e.g., Gudger v. Manton, 21 Cal. 2d 537, 541, 134 F.2d 217, 220 (1943) (citing Rest. Torts, §624, for definition of slander of title, also known as disparagement of title); Erlich v. Etner, 224 Cal. App. 2d 69, 73, 36 Cal. Rptr. 256, 258 (1964) (citing Rest. Torts, §§626, 627, for definition of trade libel).

It is sometimes difficult to draw the line between disparagement and defamation. For example, the same statement may attack a person's character as well as disparage a property interest. Such a plaintiff has a choice of actions under California law. He or she may file a defamation action for the attack on his or her personal character or a disparagement action for the attack on a property or business interest, or both the defamation and the disparagement actions. Rosenberg v. Penney Co., 30 Cal. App. 2d 609, 620-621, 86 F.2d 696, 702-703 (1939) (statements concerning goods may also reflect on the honesty of the seller). However difficult it may be to decide whether a disparagement or a defamation suit is appropriate in any given situation, defamation concerns the person of the plaintiff, while disparagement concerns the plaintiff's goods. Shores v. Chip Steak Co., 130 Cal. App. 2d 627, 630, 279 F.2d 595, 597 (1955) (libel concerns person or reputation of plaintiff, trade libel relates to plaintiff's goods).

Although there are different types of defamation actions (libel or slander) depending on the form of the defamatory statements, all defamatory statements attack an individual's good name. This injury to the person should not be confused with the derivative consequences of the defamatory attack, i.e., the loss of reputation in the community and any resulting loss of income. The nonpersonal consequences of a personal injury, such as a loss of future income, are often the most persuasive means of proving the extent of the injury that was suffered. The personal nature of an injury should not be defined by its effect. . . .

So, too, a defamatory attack on one's character should not be confused with the damage to a person's reputation that flows from that injury. Frequently, as a result of defamatory statements attacking one's character, the individual suffers an impairment of his or her relationships with others. While some of these relationships may be personal and some may be professional, all of the harm that is done flows from the same personal attack on the defamed individual. The evidence presented in the state court demonstrated that Roemer suffered an impairment of both his personal and professional relationships as a result of Retail Credit's report that falsely attacked his good name. The evidence is uncontradicted that Roemer received damages as the result of filing an action for defamation.

Since, as discussed above, the defamation of an individual is a personal injury under California law, the compensatory damages received by Roemer in his defamation suit against Retail Credit are excludable from gross income under §104(a)(2), as would be the compensatory damages received on account of any personal injury.

B. PUNITIVE DAMAGES

Normally, an amount awarded for punitive damages is includable in gross income as ordinary income. Commissioner v. Glenshaw Glass Co. [supra page 126]. . . . Nevertheless, the Commissioner liberally interprets §104(a)(2) to exclude punitive damages as well as all compensatory damages where there has been a personal injury. Rev. Rul. 75-45, 1975-1 C.B. 47. Therefore, according to the Commissioner's own interpretation, the punitive damages received by Roemer on account of his §104(a)(2) personal injury (the defamation) are excludable from gross income. . . .

CONCLUSION

As we find that Roemer's defamation suit was brought to remedy a personal injury and that the award should not be differentiated on the basis of the resulting damage to his personal life and his professional career, all of Roemer's compensatory damages are excludable from gross income under §104(a)(2) and the decision of the tax court is reversed.

UNITED STATES v. BURKE

112 S. Ct. 1867 (1992)

Justice BLACKMUN delivered the opinion of the Court.

In this case we decide whether a payment received in settlement of a backpay claim under Title VII of the Civil Rights Act of 1964, 78 Stat. 253, as amended, 42 Stat. §2000e et seq., is excludable from the recipient's gross income under §104(a)(2) of the federal Internal Revenue Code, 26 U.S.C. §104(a)(2), as "damages received . . . on account of personal injuries."

I

The relevant facts are not in dispute. In 1984, Judy A. Hutcheson, an employee of the Tennessee Valley Authority (TVA), filed a Title VII action in the United States District Court for the Eastern District of Tennessee alleging that TVA had discriminated unlawfully in the payment of salaries on the basis of sex. . . .

The complaint alleged that TVA had increased the salaries of employees in certain male-dominated pay schedules, but had not increased the salaries of employees in certain female-dominated schedules. In addition, the complaint alleged that TVA had lowered salaries in some female-dominated schedules. . . .

[In settlement of the claim,] TVA agreed to pay $4,200 to Hutcheson and a total of $5,000,000 for the other affected employees, to be distributed under a formula based on length of service and rates of pay. Id., at 70-71, 76-77. Although TVA did not withhold taxes on the $4,200 for Hutcheson, it did withhold, pursuant to the agreement, federal income taxes on the amounts allocated to the other affected employees. . . .

Respondents filed claims for refund for the taxes withheld from the settlement payments. The Internal Revenue Service (IRS) disallowed those claims. Respondents then brought a refund action in the United States District Court for the Eastern District of Tennessee, claiming that the settlement payments should be excluded from their respective gross incomes under §104(a)(2). . . . The District Court ruled that, because respondents sought and obtained only backwages due them as a result of TVA's discriminatory underpayments rather than compensatory or other damages, the settlement proceeds could not be excluded from gross income. . . .

The United States Court of Appeals for the Sixth Circuit, by a divided vote, reversed. 929 F.2d 1119 (1991). . . .

We granted certiorari to resolve a conflict among the Courts of Appeals concerning the exclusion of Title VII backpay awards from gross income under §104(a)(2).

II

A

The definition of gross income under the Internal Revenue Code sweeps broadly. Section 61(a) provides that "gross income means all income from whatever source derived," subject only to the exclusions specifically enumerated elsewhere in the Code. . . . There is no dispute that the settlement awards in this case would constitute gross income within the reach of §61(a).

The question, however, is whether the awards qualify for special exclusion from gross income under §104(a), which provides in relevant part that "gross income does not include — (2) the amount of any damages received . . . on account of personal injuries or sickness. . . ."

Neither the text nor the legislative history of §104(a)(2) offers any explanation of the term "personal injuries." Since 1960, however, IRS regulations formally have linked identification of a personal injury for purposes of §104(a)(2) to traditional tort principles: "The 'term damages received (whether by suit or agreement)' means an amount received . . . through prosecution of a legal suit or action based upon tort or tort type rights, or through a settlement agreement entered into in lieu of such prosecution." §1.104-1(c) (1991). . . .

A "tort" has been defined broadly as a "civil wrong, other than breach of contract, for which the court will provide a remedy in the form of an action for damages." See W. Keeton, D. Dobbs, R. Keeton & D. Owen, Prosser and Keeton on the Law of Torts 2 (1984). Remedial principles thus figure prominently in the definition and conceptualization of torts. . . .

For example, the victim of a physical injury may be permitted, under the relevant state law, to recover damages not only for lost wages, medical expenses, and diminished future earning capacity on account of the injury, but also for emotional distress and pain and suffering. . . . Similarly, the victim of a "dignitary" or nonphysical tort such as defamation may recover not only for any actual pecuniary loss (e.g., loss of business or customers), but for "impairment of reputation and standing in the community, personal humiliation, and mental anguish and suffering." Gertz v. Robert Welch, Inc., 418 U.S. 323, 350 (1974). . . . Furthermore, punitive or exemplary damages are generally available in those instances where the defendant's misconduct was intentional or reckless. . . .

We thus agree with the Court of Appeals' analysis insofar as it focused, for purposes of §104(a)(2), on the nature of the claim underlying respondents' damages award. . . . Respondents, for their part, agree that this is the appropriate inquiry, as does the dissent. In order to come within the §104(a)(2) income exclusion, respondents therefore must show that Title VII, the legal basis for their recovery of backpay, redresses a tort-like personal injury in accord with the foregoing principles. We turn next to this inquiry.

B

Title VII of the Civil Rights Act of 1964 makes it an unlawful employment practice for an employer "to discriminate against any individual with respect to his compensation, terms, conditions, or privileges of employment, because of such individual's race, color, religion, sex, or national origin." 42 U.S.C. §2000e-2(a)(1). . . .

It is beyond question that discrimination in employment on the basis of sex, race, or any of the other classifications protected by Title VII is, as respondents argue and this Court consistently has held, an invidious practice that causes grave harm to its victims. The fact that employment discrimination causes harm to individuals does not automatically imply, however, that there exists a "tort-like personal injury" for purposes of federal income tax law.

Indeed, in contrast to the tort remedies for physical and nonphysical injuries discussed above, Title VII does not allow awards for compensatory or punitive damages; instead, it limits available remedies to backpay, injunctions, and other equitable relief. . . . An employee wrongfully discharged on the basis of sex thus may recover only an amount equal to the wages the employee would have earned from the date of discharge to the date of reinstatement, along with lost fringe benefits such as vacation pay and pension benefits; similarly, an employee wrongfully denied a promotion on the basis of sex, or, as in this case, wrongfully discriminated against in salary on the basis of sex, may recover only the differential between the appropriate pay and actual pay for services performed, as well as lost benefits. . . .

Notwithstanding a common-law tradition of broad tort damages and the existence of other federal antidiscrimination statutes offering similarly broad remedies, Congress declined to recompense Title VII plaintiffs for anything beyond the wages properly due them — wages that, if paid in the ordinary course, would have been fully taxable. Thus, we cannot say that a statute such as Title VII,[40] whose sole remedial focus

40. Respondents contend that Congress' recent expansion of Title VII's remedial scope supports their argument that Title VII claims are inherently tort-like in nature. Under the Civil Rights Act of 1991, victims of intentional discrimination are entitled to a

is the award of backwages, redresses a tort-like personal injury within the meaning of §104(a)(2) and the applicable regulations.

Accordingly, we hold that the backpay awards received by respondents in settlement of their Title VII claims are not excludable from gross income as "damages received . . . on account of personal injuries" under §104(a)(2). The judgment of the Court of Appeals is reversed. . . .

Justice SCALIA, concurring in the judgment. [omitted]

Justice O'CONNOR, with whom Justice THOMAS joins, dissenting.

The Court holds that respondents, unlike most plaintiffs who secure compensation after suffering personal injury, must pay tax on their recoveries for alleged discrimination because suits under Title VII of the Civil Rights Act of 1964, do not involve "tort type rights." This is so, the Court says, because "Congress declined to recompense Title VII plaintiffs for anything beyond the wages properly due them." I cannot agree. In my view, the remedies available to Title VII plaintiffs do not fix the character of the right they seek to enforce. The purposes and operation of Title VII are closely analogous to those of tort law, and that similarity should determine excludability of recoveries for personal injury under 26 U.S.C. §104(a)(2). . . .

NOTES

1. *Title VII damages.* The Court in *Burke* held that causes of action under Title VII, as it existed during the taxable year in question, more closely resembled contract claims than tort claims. In 1991, Title VII was amended to give victims of intentional discrimination the right to a jury trial to recover damages for pain and suffering, as well as punitive damages. Thus, under the standard laid down by the Court in *Burke*, claimants who now sue under Title VII should find their awards tax-free under §104. *Burke* is an important decision because it affirms the *Roemer* court's interpretation of §104: that tort-like claims produce tax-free compensatory damages. The fact that the damages may reflect lost wages, which would normally be taxable, is irrelevant. *Burke* also illustrates one of the problems with the *Roemer* court's interpretation: the somewhat arbitrary exercise of distinguishing between claims brought in tort and contract.

---

jury trial, at which they may recover compensatory damages for "future pecuniary losses, emotional pain, suffering, inconvenience, mental anguish, loss of enjoyment of life, and other nonpecuniary losses," as well as punitive damages. See Pub. L. 102-166, 105 Stat. 1073. Unlike respondents, however, we believe that Congress' decision to permit jury trials and compensatory and punitive damages under the amended act signals a marked change in its conception of the injury redressable by Title VII, and cannot be imported back into analysis of the statute as it existed at the time of this lawsuit. . . .

2. *Payments for release of claims based on right of privacy.* In Roosevelt v. Commissioner, 43 T.C. 77 (1964), Franklin D. Roosevelt, Jr., received about $18,000 from Dore Schary under a contract relating to the play *Sunrise at Campobello,* based on the life of Roosevelt's father. Roosevelt claimed that he had been paid to release Schary from any claims based on a right of privacy and that consequently the amount received was excludable under §104(a)(2). The court rejected this argument and held the $18,000 taxable, partly on the basis that it doubted whether Roosevelt would have been entitled to any damages if the play had been produced without his consent. Other courts have reached the same result in similar cases. See Starrels v. Commissioner, 304 F.2d 574 (9th Cir. 1962), relying in part on the notion that the taxpayer had received the payments in advance of, and for consenting to, the alleged invasion of privacy. See also Ehrlich v. Higgins, 52 F. Supp. 805, 809 (S.D.N.Y. 1943):

> If the contrary principle were recognized, there would be suits for refunds by each of the actresses in Hollywood upon the ground that, although each is paid a salary for personal services in the production of films, the real value which the producer obtains from the contract is the right to produce before the public the representation so made, and that the payments are really damages in prospect for the violation of the right of personal privacy. The revenue laws do not contain any such loophole.

3. *Jury instructions.* If a jury reduces the amount of an award for lost earnings, to take account of the excludability of the award, the payor benefits, at the expense of the Treasury (that is, at the expense of the citizenry at large). If the jury does not reduce the award to take account of excludability, the plaintiff (payee) benefits, again at the expense of the Treasury. How should the jury be instructed, if at all, on the taxability of the award? Should it be instructed that the amount of earnings lost by the plaintiff is the after-tax amount? These issues were confronted in the context of a Federal Employers' Liability Act case in Norfolk & Western Railroad v. Liepelt, 444 U.S. 490 (1980), where the Court held that the jury should have been instructed both as to the probable effects of taxes on the plaintiff's wages and as to the excludability of the award.

4. *Punitive damages.* The court in *Roemer* found that because the taxpayer had suffered a personal injury he could exclude compensatory damages from income under §104. The court also allowed the taxpayer to exclude punitive damages arising from the same personal injury. This latter holding was consistent with Rev. Rul. 75-47, which held that punitive damages arising from personal injuries fell within the ambit of §104.

In Rev. Rul. 84-104, the Service revoked Rev. Rul. 75-47 and held that punitive damages were taxable, whether or not they were attributable to a personal injury. According to Rev. Rul. 84-104, punitive damages are meant to punish the wrongdoer rather than compensate the victim. The holding in Rev. Rul. 84-104 seems to reflect a recovery-of-capital theory similar to that found in Sol. Op. 132. Punitive damages go beyond restoration of capital or compensation for injury and, under this theory, ought to be taxed.

The Service's attempt to tax punitive damages generated litigation that often ended up with taxpayer victories. In 1989, Congress amended §104(a)(2) to exclude from its (exclusionary) ambit punitive damages arising out of nonphysical injury or sickness. As a result of this legislation, punitive damages arising out of nonphysical injury or sickness are now taxable.

The treatment of punitive damages arising out of physical injury or sickness is still unclear. The 1989 amendment does not explicitly address the tax treatment of these sorts of damages, and there are no reported cases on this issue for years after the effective date of the amendment. On the one hand, the Service has not modified Rev. Rul. 84-104, which states that these awards, too, ought to be taxed. On the other hand, in the few reported cases explicating section 104 as it existed before the 1989 amendment, the Service was unsuccessful in its attempt to tax punitive damages arising out of physical injuries. See Horton v. Commissioner, 100 T.C. — (1993) (Punitive damages for injuries suffered in explosion nontaxable under §104). Moreover, by holding that punitive damages arising out of nonphysical injuries or sickness are taxable, the 1989 amendment suggests, by negative inference, that punitive damages arising out of physical injuries or sickness qualify for nontaxation under §104.

QUESTION

Section 104 excludes from gross income amounts received on account of personal injuries. The court in *Roemer* struggled with the proper definition of the phrase "personal injury." What are the merits of the following definitions of that phrase, as a matter of judicial interpretation?

(a) Personal injury means a physical injury.

(b) Personal injury does not include an injury that occurs while performing work, or in connection with work.

(c) Personal injury does not include an injury that causes damages to business profit or results in the loss of profit, salary, or wage.

(d) Personal injury means an injury that is classified as a personal injury under state law.

(e) Personal injury includes all physical injuries and all nonphysical injuries that do not arise in a business context and that do not cause damage to business property or profit.

3. Deferred Payments and Structured Settlements

In 1983, Congress codified an earlier revenue ruling and added to §104(a)(2) the language that reads "and whether as a lump sum or periodic payments." Under that provision, as amended, a tort victim who is able to defer current payment in return for a series of later payments can exclude the entire amount of the later payments as recovery for personal injury. The complete exclusion is available even though the deferred payments will invariably contain an interest component.

The nontaxation of the interest component creates an incentive for tort victims to structure settlements to provide deferred periodic payments. Suppose that a person, *P*, has suffered an injury from a defective product and has sued the manufacturer and the manufacturer has offered to settle for $1 million (plus legal fees), which *P* considers fair and is prepared to accept. But *P* does not plan to spend the money right away; what she would like to do is to invest the $1 million at 10 percent for one year and use the $100,000 interest income, plus the $1 million principal, to purchase a business at the end of the year. If she accepts $1 million and invests the money for one year at 10 percent, she will, of course, be taxable on the interest. Instead, *P* may ask the manufacturer to pay her $1,100,000 in one year. As noted in the preceding paragraph, under §104(a)(2), the entire amount will be nontaxable.

In some circumstances the tax advantage to the tort victim may be offset by a disadvantage to the tortfeasor. Suppose, for example, that the tortfeasor is an individual who cannot deduct the amount to be paid and suppose, again, that the amount of the agreed-upon current settlement is $1 million. If the tortfeasor holds the $1 million for payment a year later, she or he will be able to earn $100,000 (assuming, again, an interest rate of 10 percent). But suppose that the tortfeasor is taxable at a rate of 40 percent. After paying tax on the interest, the tortfeasor will be left with the original $1,000,000 that she or he was willing to pay, plus the $60,000 interest after tax, or a total of $1,060,000. Presumably this is all that the tortfeasor will be willing to pay at the end of a year. If the victim is also taxable at a rate of 40 percent, the net effect will be the same as if the victim had accepted the $1 million at the beginning of the year, invested it to earn $100,000, and paid the tax of $40,000. The tortfeasor could then be said to have paid the tax as a surrogate for the victim, but there is no loss to the Treasury.

A similar result (surrogate taxation) is achieved where the tortfeasor is, for example, a business firm and is allowed to deduct the payment. That result is achieved by denying any deduction to the tortfeasor (for either the $1 million or the $100,000) until the payment is actually made. See §461(h)(2)(C)(ii). Delay of the deduction of the entire amount has the same economic effect as denying a deduction for the interest, so the tortfeasor will, again, be willing to pay only $1,060,000.[41]

Deferral of the deduction and surrogate taxation can be avoided, however, if the business tortfeasor enters into a somewhat complex set of transaction with an insurance company, which in turn transacts with another company that specializes in "structured settlements" (that is, settlements providing for deferred payments). Consequently, deferred payments are now commonly used to settle tort cases involving large sums of money. The victim might prefer to take an immediate payment and invest it herself or himself, but the tax advantage of deferred payment — the ability to avoid tax on interest earned on the lump sum amount — provides a powerful incentive to use the somewhat complex, costly, and restrictive structured settlement technique.

4. Medical Expenses and Other Recoveries and Benefits

Medical expenses, including premiums paid for medical insurance, are deductible only to the extent that in the aggregate they exceed, for the taxable year, 7.5 percent of adjusted gross income. §213. Recoveries under an individual's medical insurance policy are excluded, even if those recoveries exceed the cost of medical care (for example, where the insured has two policies covering the same outlay and is permitted to recover under both). See §104(a)(3). Assuming that the premium was not deducted (as part of expenses in excess of 7.5 percent of adjusted gross income), this rule of no deduction of premiums/no income from payments is consistent with the rule for taxation of life insurance; in the aggregate, disregarding insurance company costs and profits, nondeductible payments equal nontaxable benefits. There is an exception

41. If the tortfeasor makes an immediate payment of $1 million, it will deduct that amount. Assuming a tax rate of 40 percent, its net cost will be $600,000. Assume that it would be willing to set aside that amount for payment, with interest, to the victim at the end of one year. At the end of the year, the $600,000 will have grown, with interest, to $660,000, but a tax of $24,000 will be due on the $60,000 interest, so the net amount available will be $636,000. At the time it makes the payment, the tortfeasor will be entitled to deduct the amount of the payment. Suppose it makes a payment of $1,060,000. It would then have a tax saving of $424,000. When this $424,000 is added to the $636,000, the tortfeasor winds up in the same position as if it had paid the $1,000,000 at the outset. The point is that the victim winds up with only $1,060,000, so surrogate taxation is achieved.

for payments received in reimbursement of expenses previously deducted. See §104(a), initial flush language. This rule simply takes account of the fact that in retrospect the deduction was unjustified. It is a kind of tax-benefit rule.

Where an employer pays the premiums on the employee's medical insurance, the amount is deductible by the employer but is not included in the employee's income. See §§106 and 162. Similarly, if an employer does not take out insurance and instead adopts a plan under which it pays or reimburses employee medical expenses itself, the payments (or reimbursements) are not taxable to the employee. §105(b). Again, there is an exception for reimbursements of amounts previously deducted. Thus, if an employer pays an employee, say, $28,500 per year in salary and the employee uses $3,500 of that money to buy medical insurance, the full $28,500 received by the employee will be included in his or her income, and there will be no offsetting deduction for the outlay for insurance except to the extent that it (together with other medical-expense outlays for the year) exceeds 7.5 percent of adjusted gross income. If the employer pays only $25,000 as salary to the employee and uses the extra $3,500 to buy medical insurance for that employee, the $3,500 does not enter into the employee's income. This opportunity for paying for medical insurance (and medical expenses) out of before-tax dollars is not available to the self-employed, but self-employed people are allowed to deduct 25 percent of the amount they pay for medical insurance, under a provision scheduled to expire at the end of September 1990. §162(*l*).

The exclusion for employer-provided medical care extends to an employee's spouse or dependents. See Regs. §1.106-1. The definition of *dependent* is set forth in §152 and discussed infra page 520. The exclusion does not apply to coverage that might be offered by an employer to a nondependent partner in an unmarried couple.

The opportunity to pay for employee medical insurance with before-tax dollars presumably increases the amounts that are spent on this benefit and may help doctors maintain a tolerable standard of living (in the short run) or provide opportunities for more people to make a living as doctors (in the longer run). If the tax system is to provide benefits for doctors, what about lawyers? They were late getting into the act, but in 1976 Congress enacted §120, excluding employer payments for benefits under any "group legal services plan." As originally enacted, this provision would have expired at the end of 1981, at which point reconsideration, based on experience, was supposed to occur, but in 1981 the expiration date was extended through 1984, in 1984 it was extended through 1985, in 1986 was extended through 1987, and in 1988 was extended through 1988, but with a limitation of $70 worth of insurance, and in 1989 was again extended, through September 1990.

What about plumbers? Alas, they have been ignored. Why so? Are medical and legal services more vital to individual welfare than indoor plumbing?

Section 104(a)(1) excludes workers' compensation. Section 105(c) excludes certain payments from employer insurance (or plans) for permanent physical injuries. No matter how misguided these exclusions may be, they are at least rules of general application. Far more troublesome are the exclusions for members of special groups such as veterans of the armed forces, the Coast and Geodetic Survey, and the Public Health Service. §104(a)(4), (b). Recoveries under disability insurance policies financed by taxpayer (rather than employer) payments are excluded under §104(a)(3); but the premiums are not deductible.

G. TRANSACTIONS INVOLVING LOANS AND "INCOME FROM DISCHARGE OF INDEBTEDNESS"

The ideas presented in this section relate to an aspect of tax doctrine often referred to as "income from discharge of indebtedness." See §61(a)(12). We will see that the issues are more disparate than that simple phrase seems to suggest, but there is enough of a nexus to justify deference to the traditional rubric.

1. Loan Proceeds Are Not Income

The rule. Before examining the rules relating to income from the discharge of indebtedness, we must take notice of another basic rule of tax law (which is not spelled out in any express provision of the Code) — namely, that loan proceeds are not included in gross income and loan repayments are not deductible. This rule applies both to recourse loans (that is, loans on which the borrower is personally liable) and to nonrecourse loans (as to which the lender's only recourse in case of default is against the property pledged as security for the loan). The rule also applies without regard to the nature and tax attributes of the property used as security for the loan.[42]

The rationale. The rationale usually given for the exclusion of loan proceeds is that they do not improve one's economic condition because they are offset by a corresponding liability; in other words, the loan

42. But see §72(e)(4)(A), treating loans against annuity policies as income to the extent of earned increments in the value of the policy. See supra page 182. See also §77, giving the taxpayer an election to treat crop loans from the Commodity Credit Corporation as income.

does not increase net worth. This rationale requires exclusion regardless of the security for the loan, the probable source of repayment, or the use of the funds. Is the rationale sound? Examine the following hypotheticals. Do you think that in any or all of them gain should be recognized when the loan proceeds are received, bearing in mind that if the proceeds are included in income, any repayment should be a deductible outlay?

(a) *A* earns a good salary and over the years is able to save, out of her after-tax earnings, $50,000. She invests this $50,000 in common stock of IBM. At a time when the stock is still worth $50,000, she decides to take a trip around the world and borrows $25,000, nonrecourse, pledging the IBM shares as security for the loan.

(b) *B* saves $25,000 out of after-tax earnings and uses this, together with $75,000 borrowed from a bank, to buy for $100,000 a house that he occupies as a personal residence. The house is mortgaged to secure the loan.

(c) *C* saves $10,000 out of after-tax earnings and invests it in the common stock of *XYZ* Computer Co. The stock rises in value to $100,000, at which point *C* borrows $50,000 from a bank, nonrecourse, pledging the stock as collateral. What if the loan were with recourse?

(d) *D* has just completed a surgical residency and is about to begin her practice, in which she expects that she will soon be earning over $100,000 a year. She borrows $25,000 from a bank and uses it to pay the initial expenses of establishing her practice (rent, wages paid to assistants, telephone bills, stationery, etc.).

(e) *E*'s circumstances are the same as *D*'s except that *E* uses the $25,000 for a trip around the world with her husband.

(f) *F* owns property with a basis of $10,000 and a highly uncertain fair market value. He is able to convince a financier to lend him $50,000, for one year, nonrecourse, on the security of the property. He believes the property is worth only $40,000 and does not expect to repay the loan when it is due, though he retains a glimmer of hope that the property will rise in value and that it will be worth his while to repay the loan, when due, so as to retain the property, sell it, and increase his gain.

Relation to accounting method. As an aside, note that the rule that loan proceeds and repayments are not taken into account in computing income applies both to cash-method and to accrual-method taxpayers. If the cash method were pushed to its extreme (which it is not), all loan proceeds would be included in income and repayments would be deducted. If the loan proceeds were invested in a business or other income-producing asset, and, to repeat, if the cash method were pushed to its extreme, the full cost of that asset would be deducted currently (just as would the cost of an asset bought with one's own funds). The effect of such an accounting system would be to tax people only on consumption expenditures. See supra page 31.

2. True Discharge of Indebtedness

The notion that a person can have income from the discharge of indebtedness may not be intuitively obvious to a person who is not versed in tax law, but it is a matter of pure tax logic and is not debatable. The task of the student is to master the logic — a task that becomes especially challenging in contexts in which the loan transaction is tied to an investment in and disposition of property.

Suppose that *T* borrows $50,000 for three years, at 8 percent per year, and uses the money to finance a trip around the world. He returns from his trip six months later and finds that interest rates have risen drastically in his absence. In the meantime, he has inherited some money and offers to pay off the loan for $45,000. The bank accepts, since it can lend the $45,000 at a rate higher than the 8 percent that it is entitled to receive from *T*. *T* received $50,000 and paid no tax on that amount. He now repays only $45,000. He is $5,000 ahead on the loan transaction and must pay tax on that gain. Think about what his situation would have been if he had not paid off the loan early. He would have held onto his $45,000 and could have invested it. Presumably he could have earned more than the 8 percent he would have been required to pay on his loan. The difference could be thought of as his profit from having borrowed money on terms that turned out to be favorable. This profit would have been realized over the remaining term of the loan. Instead, when *T* pays off the loan, the profit from the favorable loan is realized in a lump sum without waiting.

One's intuition may be misled by the fact that in settling the debt *T* laid out $45,000. It is easy to forget the $50,000 that was previously received and not treated as income. But the net cash flow is clear: $50,000 in, $45,000 out, leaving a net gain of $5,000. What has *T* to show for it? Presumably memories of a $50,000 trip around the world. He saved $5,000 not because the trip was worth less than $50,000 (though it may have been) but rather because he entered into a loan transaction that turned out well for him. For tax purposes one should separate the loan transaction from the transaction in which the proceeds of the loan were used. The tax consequences of the use of the funds should be accounted for independently, according to the requirements of annual accounting. Thus, if the $50,000 had been embezzled by *T*'s travel agent and *T* had never taken the trip, the loss presumably would be deductible, at least in part, in the year in which it occurred, according to rules affecting the use of the funds, not the source of the funds. See §165(c)(3), discussed infra pages 476, 482. For purposes of tax accounting, this is a separate item from the income from discharge of the indebtedness. Unfortunately, the leading case on discharge of indebtedness (*Kirby Lumber,* presented immediately below) distinguished, instead of rejecting outright, an earlier case (*Kerbaugh-Empire*) that mistakenly applied a transactional approach, tying the treatment of the loan discharge to a loss on the use of the proceeds.

UNITED STATES v. KIRBY LUMBER CO.

284 U.S. 1 (1931)

Mr. Justice Holmes delivered the opinion of the Court.

In July, 1923, the plaintiff, the Kirby Lumber Company, issued its own bonds for [$12,000,000] for which it received their par value.[43] Later in the same year it purchased in the open market [$1,000,000 face amount] of the same bonds at [$862,000], the difference of price being [$138,000]. The question is whether this difference is a taxable gain or income of the plaintiff for the year 1923. By the Revenue Act of 1921, gross income includes "gains or profits and income derived from any source whatever" [§61(a), 1954 Code] and by the Treasury Regulations . . . that have been in force through repeated reenactments, "If the corporation purchases and retires any of such bonds at a price less than the issuing price or face value, the excess of the issuing price or face value over the purchase price is gain or income for the taxable year." . . . We see no reason why the Regulations should not be accepted as a correct statement of the law.

In Bowers v. Kerbaugh-Empire Co., 271 U.S. 170, the [taxpayer] had borrowed money repayable in marks or their equivalent for an enterprise that failed. At the time of payment the marks had fallen in value, which so far as it went was a gain for the [taxpayer] and it was contended by the [Service] that the gain was taxable income. But the transaction as a whole was a loss, and the contention was denied. Here there was no shrinkage of assets and the taxpayer made a clear gain. As a result of its dealings it made available [$138,000 worth of] assets previously offset by the obligation of bonds now extinct. We see nothing to be gained by the discussion of judicial definitions. The [taxpayer] has realized within the year an accession to income, if we take words in their plain popular meaning, as they should be taken here. Burnet v. Sanford & Brooks Co. [supra page 194].

Judgment reversed.

43. [Generally, it has been assumed these proceeds were cash. The bonds were in fact issued in exchange for Kirby Lumber Co.'s outstanding preferred stock that had large dividend arrearages on them. Bittker, Income from Cancellation of Indebtedness: A Historical Footnote to the *Kirby Lumber* case, 4 J. Corp. Tax. 124 (1977). — Eds.]

NOTES AND QUESTIONS

1. *Theory. Kirby Lumber* and its progeny are aptly described in the following passages from 1 B. Bittker, Federal Taxation of Income, Estates and Gifts ¶¶6-31 to 6-32 (1981):

> A particularly troublesome legacy of the above passage has been the tendency of some courts to read *Kirby Lumber* as holding that the *freeing of assets* on the cancellation of indebtedness, rather than the cancellation itself, results in a taxable gain. In actuality, income results from the discharge of indebtedness because the taxpayer has received more than is paid back, not because assets are freed of offsetting liabilities on the balance sheet. . . .
>
> Since borrowed funds are obviously worth their face amount and assets acquired on credit in an arm's-length transaction are also worth what the buyer agrees to pay, a taxpayer who ultimately pays back less than he received enjoys a financial benefit whether the funds were invested successfully, lost in a business venture, spent for food and clothing, or given to a charity. Were we blessed with perfect foresight, it would be possible to exclude borrowed funds from gross income only to the extent of the ultimate repayment and to tax at the outset the amount that will not be repaid. In the absence of perfect prevision, however, a second-best solution is required. One alternative would be to tax the entire amount borrowed and to allow deductions only when, as, and if the debt is repaid. But since most loans are in fact paid in full and taxing the receipt would impose a heavy front-end burden on debt financing of investment projects, a better alternative is the existing system of excluding the borrowed funds from gross income when received and requiring the taxpayer to account for any gain if he succeeds in settling the debt for less than the amount due.
>
> [T]he tax treatment of below-face debt discharges would have been much simplified if it had been based at the outset on the fact that borrowed funds are excluded from gross income because of the assumption that they will be repaid in full and on the simple corollary that a tax adjustment is required when this assumption proves erroneous, regardless of the use to which the taxpayer put the borrowed funds. Unfortunately, *Kerbaugh-Empire* linked the tax treatment of the debt discharge to the fate of the borrowed funds, and *Kirby Lumber* carried forward this idea by distinguishing rather than repudiating *Kerbaugh-Empire*, seeming thereby to sanction an open-ended inquiry into the debtor's financial history in order to determine whether the discharge of the debt generated a "clear gain."

In Vukosovich, Inc. v. Commissioner, 790 F.2d 1409 (9th Cir. 1986), the taxpayer, relying on *Kerbaugh-Empire,* argued that it was not required to recognize income from discharge of indebtedness because it had suffered a loss on the transaction in which the borrowed funds had been invested. The government conceded that if *Kerbaugh-Empire* were still good law, the taxpayer's argument had merit, but argued that the case had in effect been overruled by later Supreme Court decisions. The Ninth Circuit agreed with the government, citing United States v. Kirby Lumber (supra), Commissioner v. Tufts (infra page 256), and Burnet v. Sanford & Brooks (supra page 194) (rejecting transactional accounting).

2. *Child support and other obligations.* Does a noncustodial parent realize income from discharge of indebtedness when he or she fails to make legally required child-support payments? If so, when? What about a person who fails to pay a judgment in a personal injury case? Should it matter that the debtor in these situations never received cash or other property as a consequence of incurring the debt? Or is it enough that such a person is better off than a similarly situated person who pays the debt?

3. Relief Provision

Insolvent debtors. Section 108 contains elaborate rules relating to discharge of the indebtedness of insolvent debtors. Generally, these rules reflect the notion, previously embodied in judicially developed doctrine, that one should not hit a person who is down, or cannot squeeze blood from a turnip, or both. If, at the time of discharge, taxpayer was insolvent or was the debtor in a proceeding under the Bankruptcy Act, the income from discharge of indebtedness is excluded, but certain tax attributes (e.g., the net operating loss carryover) must be reduced so that in effect the income will show up later if all goes well and the taxpayer has profits that would otherwise escape taxation. See §108(b).

Solvent farmers. The relief provided under §108 for insolvent debtors is also available to solvent farmers for "qualified farm indebtedness," which is debt incurred in the operation of a farm by a person who, during the three preceding taxable years, derived more than 50 percent of his or her annual gross receipts from farming. §108(g). This relief for farmers is a vestige of a general relief provision for solvent debtors that was repealed by the 1986 act.

Adjustment of purchase money debt. Section 108(d)(5) provides that the reduction of debt incurred to purchase property and owed to the seller is treated as a reduction in sale price, rather than income to the purchaser.

4. Misconceived Discharge Theory

Suppose that *X* borrows $10,000 from her parents to finance her law school education and that on graduation, in a spirit of love, affection, and pride, they cancel the debt. That might be thought of as a discharge of debt, but the benefit to *X* is not income for tax purposes because it was received as a gift. See §102(a).

Suppose that *Y* borrows $10,000 from a bank to finance her law school education and that on her graduation, her proud, loving parents pay the debt for her. As with *X,* there is no income for tax purposes because of §102(a). Moreover, although from *Y*'s perspective the debt has, in a sense, been canceled, from the perspective of the bank it has been paid in full. This is not a true discharge of debt case, or at least it is not the same kind of case as *Kirby Lumber,* where a debt was discharged for less than the amount that was owed. The best way to grasp the tax consequences of the transaction is to compare it with a gift of $10,000 cash to *Y* from her parents and use of that money by *Y* to pay the debt.

Finally, suppose that *Z* borrowed $10,000 to finance her law school education and that her employer pays the debt on her behalf as a Christmas bonus for her good work during the few months following her graduation. *Z* plainly has income of $10,000. Again, however, "discharge of indebtedness" does not seem to be an apt theory, since the debt has been paid in full. The transaction should be viewed for tax purposes as if the employer had paid *Z* a cash bonus of $10,000 and she had used her money to pay her debt. The tax should be imposed under §61(a)(1), not §61(a)(12). "Indirect payment" or "economic benefit" might best capture the essence of the transaction. Regardless of the theory, or semantics, the correct tax result should be clear. But the theory might be relevant to other issues, such as the availability of relief under §108. See supra page 237.

ZARIN v. COMMISSIONER

916 F.2d 110 (3d Cir. 1990)

COWEN, Circuit Judge.

David Zarin ("Zarin") appeals from a decision of the Tax Court holding that he recognized $2,935,000 of income from discharge of indebtedness resulting from his gambling activities, and that he should be taxed on the income. . . . After considering the issues raised by this appeal, we will reverse.

I

Zarin was a professional engineer who participated in the development, construction, and management of various housing projects. A resident of Atlantic City, New Jersey, Zarin occasionally gambled, both in his hometown and in other places where gambling was legalized. To facilitate his gaming activities in Atlantic City, Zarin applied to Resorts

International Hotel ("Resorts") for a credit line in June, 1978. Following a credit check, Resorts granted Zarin $10,000 of credit. Pursuant to this credit arrangement with Resorts, Zarin could write a check, called a marker,[44] and in return receive chips, which could then be used to gamble at the casino's tables.

Before long, Zarin developed a reputation as an extravagant "high roller" who routinely bet the house maximum while playing craps, his game of choice. Considered a "valued gaming patron" by Resorts, Zarin had his credit limit increased at regular intervals without any further credit checks, and was provided a number of complimentary services and privileges. By November, 1979, Zarin's permanent line of credit had been raised to $200,000. Between June, 1978, and December, 1979, Zarin lost $2,500,000 at the craps table, losses he paid in full.

Responding to allegations of credit abuses, the New Jersey Division of Gaming Enforcement filed with the New Jersey Casino Control Commission a complaint against Resorts. Among the 809 violations of casino regulations alleged in the complaint of October, 1979, were 100 pertaining to Zarin. Subsequently, a Casino Control Commissioner issued an Emergency Order, the effect of which was to make further extensions of credit to Zarin illegal.

Nevertheless, Resorts continued to extend Zarin's credit limit through the use of two different practices: "considered cleared" credit and "this trip only" credit.[45] Both methods effectively ignored the Emergency Order and were later found to be illegal.[46]

By January, 1980, Zarin was gambling compulsively and uncontrollably at Resorts, spending as many as sixteen hours a day at the craps table.[47] During April, 1980, Resorts again increased Zarin's credit line without further inquiries. That same month, Zarin delivered personal checks and counterchecks to Resorts which were returned as having been drawn against insufficient funds. Those dishonored checks totaled $3,435,000. In late April, Resorts cut off Zarin's credit.

Although Zarin indicated that he would repay those obligations, Resorts filed a New Jersey state court action against Zarin in November, 1980, to collect the $3,435,000. Zarin denied liability on grounds that

44. A "marker" is a negotiable draft payable to Resorts and drawn on the marker's bank.

45. Under the "considered cleared" method, Resorts would treat a personal check as a cash transaction, and would therefore not apply the amount of the check in calculating the amount of credit extended Zarin. "This trip only" credit allows Resorts to grant temporary increases of credit for a given visit, so long as the credit limit was lowered by the next visit.

46. On July 8, 1983, the New Jersey Casino Control Commission found that Resorts violated the Emergency Order at least thirteen different times, nine involving Zarin, and fined Resorts $130,000.

47. Zarin claims that at the time he was suffering from a recognized emotional disorder that caused him to gamble compulsively.

Resort's claim was unenforceable under New Jersey regulations intended to protect compulsive gamblers. Ten months later, in September, 1981, Resorts and Zarin settled their dispute for a total of $500,000.

The Commissioner of Internal Revenue ("Commissioner") subsequently determined deficiencies in Zarin's federal income taxes for 1980 and 1981, arguing that Zarin recognized $3,435,000 of income in 1980 from larceny by trick and deception. After Zarin challenged that claim by filing a Tax Court petition, the Commissioner abandoned his 1980 claim, and argued instead that Zarin had recognized $2,935,000 of income in 1981 from the cancellation of indebtedness which resulted from the settlement with Resorts.

Agreeing with the Commissioner, the Tax Court decided, eleven judges to eight, that Zarin had indeed recognized $2,935,000 of income from the discharge of indebtedness, namely the difference between the original $3,435,000 "debt" and the $500,000 settlement. *Zarin v. Commissioner*, 92 T.C. 1084 (1989). Since he was in the seventy percent tax bracket, Zarin's deficiency for 1981 was calculated to be $2,047,245. With interest to April 5, 1990, Zarin allegedly owes the Internal Revenue Service $5,209,033.96 in additional taxes. Zarin appeals the order of the Tax Court.

II

The sole issue before this Court is whether the Tax Court correctly held that Zarin had income from discharge of indebtedness.[48] Section 108 and section 61(a)(12) of the Code set forth "the general rule that gross income includes income from the discharge of indebtedness." §108(e)(1). The Commissioner argues, and the Tax Court agreed, that pursuant to the Code, Zarin did indeed recognize income from discharge of gambling indebtedness.

Under the Commissioner's logic, Resorts advanced Zarin $3,435,000 worth of chips, chips being the functional equivalent of cash. At that time, the chips were not treated as income, since Zarin recognized an obligation of repayment. In other words, Resorts made Zarin a tax-free loan. However, a taxpayer does recognize income if a loan owed to another party is cancelled, in whole or in part. I.R.C. §§61(a)(12), 108(e). The settlement between Zarin and Resorts, claims the Commissioner, fits neatly into the cancellation of indebtedness provisions in the Code.

48. Subsequent to the Tax Court's decision, Zarin filed a motion to reconsider, arguing that he was insolvent at the time Resorts forgave his debt, and thus, under section 108(a)(1)(B), could not have income from discharge of indebtedness. He did, not, however, raise that issue before the Tax Court until after it rendered its decision. The Tax Court denied the motion for reconsideration. By reason of our resolution of this case, we do not need to decide whether the Tax Court abused its discretion in denying Zarin's motion.

Zarin owed $3,435,000, paid $500,000, with the difference constituting income. Although initially persuasive, the Commissioner's position is nonetheless flawed for two reasons.

III

Initially, we find that sections 108 and 61(a)(12) are inapplicable to the Zarin/Resorts transaction. Section 61 does not define indebtedness. On the other hand, section 108(d)(1), which repeats and further elaborates on the rule in section 61(a)(12), defines the term as any indebtedness "(A) for which the taxpayer is liable, or (B) subject to which the taxpayer holds property." §108(d)(1). In order to bring the taxpayer within the sweep of the discharge of indebtedness rules, then, the IRS must show that one of the two prongs in the section 108(d)(1) test is satisfied. It has not been demonstrated that Zarin satisfies either.

Because the debt Zarin owed to Resorts was unenforceable as a matter of New Jersey state law,[49] it is clearly not a debt "for which the taxpayer is liable." §108(d)(1)(A). Liability implies a legally enforceable obligation to repay, and under New Jersey law, Zarin would have no such obligation.

Moreover, Zarin did not have a debt subject to which he held property as required by section 108(d)(1)(B). Zarin's indebtedness arose out of his acquisition of gambling chips. The Tax Court held that gambling chips were not property, but rather, "a medium of exchange within the Resorts casino" and a "substitute for cash." Alternatively, the Tax Court viewed the chips as nothing more than "the opportunity to gamble and incidental services. . . ." *Zarin*, 92 T.C. at 1099. We agree with the gist

49. The Tax Court held that the Commissioner had not met its burden of proving that the debt owed Resorts was enforceable as a matter of state law. *Zarin*, 92 T.C. at 1090. There was ample evidence to support that finding. In New Jersey, the extension of credit by casinos "to enable [any] person to take part in gaming activity as a player" is limited. N.J. Stat. Ann. §5:12-101(b) (1988). Under N.J. Stat. Ann. §5:12-101(f), any credit violation is "invalid and unenforceable for the purposes of collection. . . ." In Resorts Int'l Hotel, Inc. v. Salomone, 178 N.J. Super. 598, 429, A.2d 1078 (App. Div. 1981), the court held that "casinos must comply with the Legislature's strict control of credit for gambling purposes. Unless they do, the debts reflected by players' checks will not be enforced. . . ." Id. at 607, 429 A.2d at 1082.

With regards to the extension of credit to Zarin after the Emergency Order of October, 1979, was issued, Resorts did not comply with New Jersey regulations. The Casino Control Commission specifically stated in 1983 "that Resorts was guilty of infractions, violations, improprieties, with the net effect that [Zarin] was encouraged to continue gambling long after, one, his credit line was reached, and exceeded; two, long after it became apparent that the gambler was an addicted gambler; three, long after the gambler had difficulty in paying his debts; and four, Resorts knew the individual was gambling when he should not have been gambling." Appendix at 325-326. It follows, therefore, that under New Jersey law, the $3,435,000 debt Zarin owed Resorts was totally unenforceable.

of these characterizations, and hold that gambling chips are merely an accounting mechanism to evidence debt.

Gaming chips in New Jersey during 1980 were regarded "solely as evidence of a debt owed to their custodian by the casino licensee and shall be considered at no time the property of anyone other than the casino licensee issuing them." N.J. Admin. Code tit. 19k, §19:46-1.5(d) (1990). Thus, under New Jersey state law, gambling chips were Resorts' property until transferred to Zarin in exchange for the markers, at which point the chips became "evidence" of indebtedness (and not the property of Zarin).

Even were there no relevant legislative pronouncement on which to rely, simple common sense would lead to the conclusion that chips were not property in Zarin's hands. Zarin could not do with the chips as he pleased, nor did the chips have any independent economic value beyond the casino. The chips themselves were of little use to Zarin, other than as a means of facilitating gambling. They could not have been used outside the casino. They could have been used to purchase services and privileges within the casino, including food, drink, entertainment, and lodging, but Zarin would not have utilized them as such, since he received those services from Resorts on a complimentary basis. In short, the chips had no economic substance.

Although the Tax Court found that theoretically, Zarin could have redeemed the chips he received on credit for cash and walked out of the casino, *Zarin*, 92 T.C. at 1092, the reality of the situation was quite different. Realistically, before cashing in his chips, Zarin would have been required to pay his outstanding IOUs. New Jersey state law requires casinos to "request patrons to apply any chips or plaques in their possession in reduction of personal checks or Counter Checks exchanged for purposes of gaming prior to exchanging such chips or plaques for cash or prior to departing from the casino area." N.J. Admin. Code tit. 19k, §19:45-1.24(s) (1979) (currently N.J. Admin. Code tit. 19k, §19:45-1.25(o) (1990) (as amended)). Since his debt at all times equalled or exceeded the number of chips he possessed, redemption would have left Zarin with no chips, no cash, and certainly nothing which could have been characterized as property.

Not only were the chips non-property in Zarin's hands, but upon transfer to Zarin, the chips also ceased to be the property of Resorts. Since the chips were in the possession of another party, Resorts could no longer do with the chips as it pleased, and could no longer control the chips' use. Generally, at the time of a transfer, the party in possession of the chips can gamble with them, use them for services, cash them in, or walk out of the casino with them as an Atlantic City souvenir. The chips therefore become nothing more than an accounting mechanism, or evidence of a debt, designed to facilitate gambling in casinos where the use of actual money was forbidden. Thus, the chips which Zarin held were not property within the meaning of §108(d)(1)(B).

In short, because Zarin was not liable on the debt he allegedly owed Resorts, and because Zarin did not hold "property" subject to that debt, the cancellation of indebtedness provisions of the Code do not apply to the settlement between Resorts and Zarin. As such, Zarin cannot have income from the discharge of his debt.

Instead of analyzing the transaction at issue as cancelled debt, we believe the proper approach is to view it as disputed debt or contested liability. Under the contested liability doctrine, if a taxpayer, in good faith, disputed the amount of a debt, a subsequent settlement of the dispute would be treated as the amount of debt cognizable for tax purposes. The excess of the original debt over the amount determined to have been due is disregarded for both loss and debt accounting purposes. Thus, if a taxpayer took out a loan for $10,000, refused in good faith to pay the full $10,000 back, and then reached an agreement with the lendor that he would pay back only $7000 in full satisfaction of the debt, the transaction would be treated as if the initial loan was $7000. When the taxpayer tenders the $7000 payment, he will have been deemed to have paid the full amount of the initially disputed debt. Accordingly, there is no tax consequence to the taxpayer upon payment.

The seminal "contested liability" case is N. Sobel, Inc. v. Commissioner, 40 B.T.A. 1263 (1939). In *Sobel,* the taxpayer exchanged a $21,700 note for 100 shares of stock from a bank. In the following year, the taxpayer sued the bank for recision, arguing that the bank loan was violative of state law, and moreover, that the bank had failed to perform certain promises. The parties eventually settled the case in 1935, with the taxpayer agreeing to pay half of the face amount of the note. In the year of the settlement, the taxpayer claimed the amount paid as a loss. The Commissioner denied the loss because it had been sustained five years earlier, and further asserted that the taxpayer recognized income from the discharge of half of his indebtedness.

The Board of Tax Appeals held that since the loss was not fixed until the dispute was settled, the loss was recognized in 1935, the year of the settlement, and the deduction was appropriately taken in that year. Additionally, the Board held that the portion of the note forgiven by the bank "was not the occasion for a freeing of assets and that there was no gain. . . ." Id. at 1265. Therefore, the taxpayer did not have any income from cancellation of indebtedness.

There is little difference between the present case and *Sobel.* Zarin incurred a $3,435,000 debt while gambling at Resorts, but in court, disputed liability on the basis of unenforceability. A settlement of $500,000 was eventually agreed upon. It follows from *Sobel* that the settlement served only to fix the amount of debt. No income was realized or recognized. When Zarin paid the $500,000, any tax consequence dissolved.[50]

50. Had Zarin not paid the $500,000 dollar settlement, it would be likely that he would

Only one other court has addressed a case factually similar to the one before us. In United States v. Hall, 307 F.2d 238 (10th Cir. 1962), the taxpayer owed an unenforceable gambling debt alleged to be $225,000. Subsequently, the taxpayer and the creditor settled for $150,000. The taxpayer then transferred cattle valued at $148,110 to his creditor in satisfaction of the settlement agreement. A jury held that the parties fixed the debt at $150,000, and that the taxpayer recognized income from cancellation of indebtedness equal to the difference between the $150,000 and the $148,110 value affixed to the cattle. Arguing that the taxpayer recognized income equal to the difference between $225,000 and $148,000, the Commissioner appealed.

The Tenth Circuit rejected the idea that the taxpayer had any income from cancellation of indebtedness. Noting that the gambling debt was unenforceable, the Tenth Circuit said, "The cold fact is that taxpayer suffered a substantial loss from gambling, the amount of which was determined by the transfer." Id. at 241. In effect, the Court held that because the debt was unenforceable, the amount of the loss and resulting debt cognizable for tax purposes were fixed by the settlement at $148,110. Thus, the Tenth Circuit lent its endorsement to the contested liability doctrine in a factual situation strikingly similar to the one at issue.[51]

The Commissioner argues that *Sobel* and the contested liability doctrine only apply when there is an unliquidated debt; that is, a debt for which the amount cannot be determined. . . . Since Zarin contested his liability based on the unenforceability of the entire debt, and did not dispute the amount of the debt, the Commissioner would have us adopt the reasoning of the Tax Court, which found that Zarin's debt was liquidated, therefore barring the application of *Sobel* and the contested liability doctrine. *Zarin*, 92 T.C. at 1095 (Zarin's debt "was a liquidated amount" and "[t]here is no dispute about the amount [received].").

We reject the Tax Court's rationale. When a debt is unenforceable, it follows that the amount of the debt, and not just the liability thereon, is in dispute. Although a debt may be unenforceable, there still could

---

have had income from cancellation of indebtedness. The debt at that point would have been fixed, and Zarin would have been legally obligated to pay it.

51. The Commissioner argues that the decision in *Hall* was based on United States Supreme Court precedent since overruled, and therefore *Hall* should be disregarded. Indeed, the *Hall* court devoted a considerable amount of time to *Bowers v. Kerbaugh-Empire Co.*, 271 U.S. 170 (1926), a case whose validity is in question. We do not pass on the question of whether or not *Bowers* is good law. We do note that *Hall* relied on *Bowers* only for the proposition that "'a court need not in every case be oblivious to the net effect of the entire transaction.'" United States v. Hall, 307 F.2d at 242, quoting Bradford v. Commissioner, 233 F.2d 935, 939 (6th Cir. 1956). *Hall's* reliance on *Bowers* did not extend to the issue of contested liability, and even if it did, the idea that "Courts need not apply mechanical standards which smother the reality of a particular transaction," Id. at 241, is hardly an exceptional concept in the tax realm. See Commissioner v. Tufts, 461 U.S. 300 (1983); Hillsboro Nat'l Bank v. Commissioner, 460 U.S. 370 (1983).

be some value attached to its worth. This is especially so with regards to gambling debts. In most states, gambling debts are unenforceable, and have "but slight potential. . . ." United States v. Hall, 307 F.2d 238, 241 (10th Cir. 1962). Nevertheless, they are often collected, at least in part. For example, Resorts is not a charity; it would not have extended illegal credit to Zarin and others if it did not have some hope of collecting debts incurred pursuant to the grant of credit.

Moreover, the debt is frequently incurred to acquire gambling chips, and not money. Although casinos attach a dollar value to each chip, that value, unlike money's, is not beyond dispute, particularly given the illegality of gambling debts in the first place. This proposition is supported by the facts of the present case. Resorts gave Zarin $3.4 million dollars of chips in exchange for markers evidencing Zarin's debt. If indeed the only issue was the enforceability of the entire debt, there would have been no settlement. Zarin would have owed all or nothing. Instead, the parties attached a value to the debt considerably lower than its face value. In other words, the parties agreed that given the circumstances surrounding Zarin's gambling spree, the chips he acquired might not have been worth $3.4 million dollars, but were worth something. Such a debt cannot be called liquidated, since its exact amount was not fixed until settlement.

To summarize, the transaction between Zarin and Resorts can best be characterized as a disputed debt, or contested liability. Zarin owed an unenforceable debt of $3,435,000 to Resorts. After Zarin in good faith disputed his obligation to repay the debt, the parties settled for $500,000, which Zarin paid. That $500,000 settlement fixed the amount of loss and the amount of debt cognizable for tax purposes. Since Zarin was deemed to have owed $500,000, and since he paid Resorts $500,000, no adverse tax consequences attached to Zarin as a result.

In conclusion, we hold that Zarin did not have any income from cancellation of indebtedness for two reasons. First, the Code provisions covering discharge of debt are inapplicable since the definitional requirement in I.R.C. section 108(d)(1) was not met. Second, the settlement of Zarin's gambling debts was a contested liability. We reverse the decision of the Tax Court and remand with instructions to enter judgment that Zarin realized no income by reason of his settlement with Resorts.

Stapleton, Circuit Judge, dissenting.

I respectfully dissent because I agree with the Commissioner's appraisal of the economic realities of this matter.

Resorts sells for cash the exhilaration and the potential for profit inherent in games of chance. It does so by selling for cash chips that entitle the holder to gamble at its casino. Zarin, like thousands of others, wished to purchase what Resorts was offering in the marketplace. He chose to make this purchase on credit and executed notes evidencing his obligation to repay the funds that were advanced to him by Resorts. As in most purchase money transactions, Resorts skipped the step of giving Zarin cash that he would only return to it in order to pay for the opportunity to gamble. Resorts provided him instead with chips that entitled him to participate in Resorts' games of chance on the same basis as others who had paid cash for that privilege.[52] Whether viewed as a one or two-step transaction, however, Zarin received either $3.4 million in cash or an entitlement for which others would have had to pay $3.4 million.

Despite the fact that Zarin received in 1980 cash or an entitlement worth $3.4 million, he correctly reported in that year no income from his dealings with Resorts. He did so *solely* because he recognized, as evidenced by his notes, an offsetting obligation to repay Resorts $3.4 million in cash. . . . In 1981, with the delivery of Zarin's promise to pay Resorts $500,000 and the execution of a release by Resorts, Resorts surrendered its claim to repayment of the remaining $2.9 million of the money Zarin had borrowed. As of that time, Zarin's assets were freed of his potential liability for that amount and he recognized gross income in that amount. . . .[53]

The only alternatives I see to this conclusion are to hold either (1) that Zarin realized $3.4 million in income in 1980 at a time when both parties to the transaction thought there was an offsetting obligation to repay or (2) that the $3.4 million benefit sought and received by Zarin is not taxable at all. I find the latter alternative unacceptable as inconsistent with the fundamental principle of the Code that anything of commercial value received by a taxpayer is taxable unless expressly excluded from gross income.[54] Commissioner v. Glenshaw Glass Co.,

52. I view as irrelevant the facts that Resorts advanced credit to Zarin solely to enable him to patronize its casino and that the chips could not be used elsewhere or for other purposes. When one buys a sofa from the furniture store on credit, the fact that the proprietor would not have advanced the credit for a different purpose does not entitle one to a tax-free gain in the event the debt to the store is extinguished for some reason.

53. This is not a case in which parties agree subsequent to a purchase money transaction that the property purchased has a value less than thought at the time of the transaction. In such cases, the purchase price adjustment rule is applied and the agreed-upon value is accepted as the value of the benefit received by the purchaser; see e.g., Commissioner v. Sherman, 135 F.2d 68 (6th Cir. 1943); N. Sobel, Inc. v. Commissioner, 40 B.T.A. 1263 (1939). Nor is this a case in which the taxpayer is entitled to rescind an entire purchase money transaction, thereby to restore itself to the position it occupied before receiving anything of commercial value. In this case, the illegality was in the extension of credit by Resorts and whether one views the benefit received by Zarin as cash or the opportunity to gamble, he is no longer in a position to return that benefit.

54. As the court's opinion correctly points out, this record will not support an exclusion under §108(a) which relates to discharge of debt in an insolvency or bankruptcy context. Section 108(e)(5) of the Code, which excludes discharged indebtedness arising from a "purchase price adjustment" is not applicable here. Among other things, §108(e)(5) necessarily applies only to a situation in which the debtor still holds the property acquired in the purchase money transaction. Equally irrelevant is §108(d)'s definition of "indebt-

348 U.S. 426 (1955); United States v. Kirby Lumber Co., supra. I find the former alternative unacceptable as impracticable. In 1980, neither party was maintaining that the debt was unenforceable and, because of the settlement, its unenforceability was not even established in the litigation over the debt in 1981. It was not until 1989 in this litigation over the tax consequences of the transaction that the unenforceability was first judicially declared. Rather than require such tax litigation to resolve the correct treatment of a debt transaction, I regard it as far preferable to have the tax consequences turn on the manner in which the debt is treated by the parties. For present purposes, it will suffice to say that where something that would otherwise be includable in gross income is received on credit in a purchase money transaction, there should be no recognition of income so long as the debtor continues to recognize an obligation to repay the debt. On the other hand, income, if not earlier recognized, should be recognized when the debtor no longer recognizes an obligation to repay and the creditor has released the debt or acknowledged its unenforceability.

In this view, it makes no difference whether the extinguishment of the creditor's claim comes as a part of a compromise. Resorts settled for 14 cents on the dollar presumably because it viewed such a settlement as reflective of the odds that the debt would be held to be enforceable. While Zarin should be given credit for the fact that he had to pay 14 cents for a release, I see no reason why he should not realize gain in the same manner as he would have if Resorts had concluded on its own that the debt was legally unenforceable and had written it off as uncollectible.[55]

I would affirm the judgment of the Tax Court.

NOTES

1. The dissent in *Zarin* and the majority opinion in the Tax Court decision in that case treated the forgiveness of Zarin's debt as income under the holding of *Kirby Lumber*, supra page 235. The majority in *Zarin* ruled for the taxpayer on the basis of a judicially created "contested liability" doctrine, under which the amount of a disputed debt is held to be the amount for which the debt is settled. In the majority's view, there was never a valid debt for $2,935,000, so there could be no

---

edness" relied upon heavily by the court. Section 108(d) expressly defines that term solely for the purposes of §108 and not for the purposes of §61(a)(12).

55. A different situation exists where there is a bona fide dispute over the amount of a debt and the dispute is compromised. Rather than require tax litigation to determine the amount of income received, the Commission treats the compromise figure as representing the amount of the obligation. I find this sensible and consistent with the pragmatic approach I would take.

relief from cancellation of indebtedness income when the debt was settled for $500,000.

Central to the majority's holding in *Zarin* was the fact that New Jersey law cast doubt on the enforceability of debts incurred by compulsive gamblers such as Zarin. Suppose that such debts were clearly enforceable under state law. Is it clear then that Zarin would have recognized income equal to the difference between the debt incurred and the settlement amount? Does someone who borrows approximately $3.4 million from a casino, loses the sum in a matter of hours, and settles the debt for $500,000 have $2,900,000 of income? The Tax Court opinion indicated that at the time the debt was incurred, Zarin was gambling twelve to sixteen hours a day, seven days a week, and wagering $15,000 on each roll of the dice. Is that relevant? Why do you suppose the casino allowed Zarin to gamble with its money (or chips)?

2. One of the dissents in the Tax Court case held that Zarin qualified for the exclusion from relief from indebtedness income under §108(d)(5). As noted supra page 236, that provision treats the reduction of debt incurred to purchase property as a reduction in the purchase price of property. This argument was rejected by the majority of the judges in both the Tax Court and the Third Circuit on the grounds that the chips did not represent property. Is there any good reason why §108(d)(5) should not cover debt incurred to purchase services?

3. Zarin did not invoke §108(a)(1)(B), which provides that a taxpayer does not recognize income from discharge of indebtedness if, at the time of the discharge, she or he was insolvent. The opinion in the case does not explain why Zarin could not or did not invoke §108(a)(1)(B).

DIEDRICH v. COMMISSIONER

457 U.S. 191 (1982)

Chief Justice Burger delivered the opinion of the Court.

We granted certiorari to resolve a circuit conflict as to whether a donor who makes a gift of property on condition that the donee pay the resulting gift tax receives taxable income to the extent that the gift tax paid by the donee exceeds the donor's adjusted basis in the property transferred. 454 U.S. 813 (1981). The United States Court of Appeals for the Eighth Circuit held that the donor realized income. 643 F.2d 499 (1981). We affirm.

I

In 1972 petitioners Victor and Frances Diedrich made gifts of approximately 85,000 shares of stock to their three children, using both a direct transfer and a trust arrangement. The gifts were subject to a condition that the donees pay the resulting federal and state gift taxes. There is no dispute concerning the amount of the gift tax paid by the donees. The donors' basis in the transferred stock was $51,073; the gift tax paid in 1972 by the donees was $62,992. . . .

II

A

Pursuant to its Constitutional authority, Congress has defined "gross income" as income "from whatever source derived," including "[i]ncome from discharge of indebtedness." §61 (1976).[56] This Court has recognized that "income" may be realized by a variety of indirect means. In Old Colony Tr. Co. v. Commissioner, 279 U.S. 716 (1929), the Court held that payment of an employee's income taxes by an employer constituted income to the employee. Speaking for the Court, Chief Justice Taft concluded that "[t]he payment of the tax by the employer was in consideration of the services rendered by the employee and was a gain derived by the employee from his labor." Id., at 729. The Court made clear that the substance, not the form, of the agreed transaction controls. "The discharge by a third person of an obligation to him is equivalent to receipt by the person taxed." Ibid. The employee, in other words, was placed in a better position as a result of the employer's discharge of the employee's legal obligation to pay the income taxes; the employee thus received a gain subject to income tax.

The holding in *Old Colony* was reaffirmed in Crane v. Commissioner, 331 U.S. 1 (1947). In *Crane* the Court concluded that relief from the obligation of a nonrecourse mortgage in which the value of the property exceeded the value of the mortgage constituted income to the taxpayer. The taxpayer in *Crane* acquired depreciable property, an apartment building, subject to an unassumed mortgage. The taxpayer later sold the apartment building, which was still subject to the nonrecourse mortgage, for cash plus the buyer's assumption of the mortgage. This Court held that the amount of mortgage was properly included in the amount realized on the sale, noting that if the taxpayer transfers subject to the mortgage, "the benefit to him is as real and substantial as if the mortgage

56. The United States Constitution provides that Congress shall have the power to lay and collect taxes on income "from whatever source derived." Art. I, §8, cl. 1; Amendment XVI.

In Helvering v. Bruun [infra page 301], the Court noted: "While it is true that economic gain is not always taxable as income, it is settled that the realization of gain need not be in cash derived from a sale of an asset. Gain may occur as a result of exchange of property, *payment of the taxpayer's indebtedness, relief from a liability*, or other profit realized from the completion of a transaction." (Emphasis supplied.)

were discharged, or as if a personal debt in an equal amount had been assumed by another." Id. at 14. Again, it was the "reality," not the form, of the transaction that governed. Ibid. The Court found it immaterial whether the seller received money prior to the sale in order to discharge the mortgage, or whether the seller merely transferred the property subject to the mortgage. In either case the taxpayer realized an economic benefit.

B

The principles of *Old Colony* and *Crane* control.[57] A common method of structuring gift transactions is for the donor to make the gift subject to the condition that the donee pay the resulting gift tax, as was done in each of the cases now before us. When a gift is made, the gift tax liability falls on the donor under §2502(d).[58] When a donor makes a gift to a donee, a "debt" to the United States for the amount of the gift tax is incurred by the donor. Those taxes are as much the legal obligation of the donor as the donor's income taxes; for these purposes they are the same kind of debt obligation as the income taxes of the employee in *Old Colony,* supra. Similarly, when a donee agrees to discharge an indebtedness in consideration of the gift, the person relieved of the tax liability realizes an economic benefit. In short, the donor realizes an immediate economic benefit by the donee's assumption of the donor's legal obligation to pay the gift tax.

An examination of the donor's intent does not change the character of this benefit. Although intent is relevant in determining whether a gift has been made, subjective intent has not characteristically been a factor in determining whether an individual has realized income. Even if intent were a factor, the donor's intent with respect to the condition shifting the gift tax obligation from the donor to the donee was plainly to relieve the donor of a debt owed to the United States; the choice was made because the donor would receive a benefit in relief from the obligation to pay the gift tax.[59]

57. Although the Commissioner has argued consistently that payment of gift taxes by the donee results in income to the donor, several courts have rejected this interpretation. . . .

It should be noted that the *gift* tax consequences of a conditional gift will be unaffected by the holding in this case. When a conditional "net" gift is given, the gift tax attributable to the transfer is to be deducted from the value of the property in determining the value of the gift at the time of transfer. . . .

58. "The tax imposed by section 2501 shall be paid by the donor."

Section 6321 imposes a lien on the personal property of the donor when a tax is not paid when due. The donee is secondarily responsible for payment of the gift tax should the donor fail to pay the tax. §6324(b). The donee's liability, however, is limited to the value of the gift. Ibid. This responsibility of the donee is analogous to a lien or security. Ibid.

59. The existence of the "condition" that the gift will be made only if the donee assumes the gift tax consequences precludes any characterization that the payment of the

Finally, the benefit realized by the taxpayer is not diminished by the fact that the liability attaches during the course of a donative transfer. It cannot be doubted that the donors were aware that the gift tax obligation would arise immediately upon the transfer of the property; the economic benefit to the donors in the discharge of the gift tax liability is indistinguishable from the benefit arising from discharge of a preexisting obligation. Nor is there any doubt that had the donors sold a portion of the stock immediately before the gift transfer in order to raise funds to pay the expected gift tax, a taxable gain would have been realized. §1001. The fact that the gift tax obligation was discharged by way of a conditional gift rather than from funds derived from a pregift sale does not alter the underlying benefit to the donors.

C

Consistent with the economic reality, the Commissioner has treated these conditional gifts as a discharge of indebtedness through a part gift and part sale of the gift property transferred. The transfer is treated as if the donor sells the property to the donee for less than the fair market value. The "sale" price is the amount necessary to discharge the gift tax indebtedness; the balance of the value of the transferred property is treated as a gift. The gain thus derived by the donor is the amount of the gift tax liability less the donor's adjusted basis in the entire property. Accordingly, income is realized to the extent that the gift tax exceeds the donor's adjusted basis in the property. This treatment is consistent with §1001 of the Internal Revenue Code, which provides that the gain from the disposition of property is the excess of the amount realized over the transferor's adjusted basis in the property.

III

We recognize that Congress has structured gift transactions to encourage transfer of property by limiting the tax consequences of a transfer. See, e.g., §102 (gifts excluded from donee's gross income). Congress may obviously provide a similar exclusion for the conditional gift. Should Congress wish to encourage "net gifts," changes in the income tax consequences of such gifts lie within the legislative responsibility. Until such time, we are bound by Congress' mandate that gross income includes income "from whatever source derived." We therefore hold that a donor who makes a gift of property on condition that the donee pay the resulting gift taxes realizes taxable income to the extent

taxes was simply a gift from the donee back to the donor.

A conditional gift not only relieves the donor of the gift tax liability, but also may enable the donor to transfer a larger sum of money to the donee than would otherwise be possible due to such factors as differing income tax brackets of the donor and donee.

that the gift taxes paid by the donee exceed the donor's adjusted basis in the property.

The judgment of the United States Court of Appeals for the Eighth Circuit is affirmed.

[The dissenting opinion of Mr. Justice Rehnquist is omitted.]

NOTES AND QUESTIONS

1. *The amount of the gain.* (a) At the end of the opinion the Court states that the amount of gain to be taxed is the excess of "the gift taxes paid by the donee [over] the donor's adjusted basis in the property." Is this formula for computing the amount of gain consistent with the theory of the case? See the last two sentences of Part IIB of the Court's opinion. Consider the following hypothetical facts: *P* owns 1,000 shares of common stock with a basis of $15,000 and a fair market value of $100,000. She transfers the shares to *C*, who agrees to pay the gift tax of $20,000. Under the *Diedrich* formula the gain recognized is $5,000. What would the gain have been if *P* had sold enough shares to pay the tax herself? What if the basis of the shares had been $25,000? The Court's reasoning in *Diedrich* seems to suggest that *P* should be allowed to claim a loss of $5000. Regs §1.1001-1(e), however, hold otherwise.

(b) By way of comparison, in the case of a transfer to a charitable organization that is part sale and part gift (that is, where the transfer is for an amount less than the fair market value of the property), the basis of the property is allocated between the portion deemed to have been sold and the portion deemed to have been given. §1011(b). For example, suppose that *T* transfers to a charitable organization property with a basis of $20 and a fair market value of $100, in return for a payment of $20. The transaction is treated as if *T* had sold $20 worth, or one-fifth, of the property and had given the other $80 worth. Thus, one-fifth of the basis, or $4, is allocated to the sale and *T* has a taxable gain of $16. *T* will also be entitled to a charitable deduction of $80, to the extent allowed by §170.

2. *Theory.* What is the correct result and the most sensible theory in each of the following hypotheticals?

(a) Parent, *P*, transfers to child, *C*, shares of stock with a value of $10,000 and a basis of $1,000. No gift tax is payable. *P* tells *C* that *C* is free to do what she wants with the property. *C* sells the shares. See questions supra page 161.

(b) *P* transfers the shares to *C* and tells *C* to sell the shares for her and use the proceeds to pay *P*'s $10,000 bill at the country club.

(c) *P* transfers the shares to *C* and tells *C* that she can do as she wishes with them provided that she pays *P*'s $10,000 bill at the country club.

(d) Same as (c) except that *C* must pay *P*'s $10,000 debt to the United States Treasury for income taxes.

3. *Donor's liability.* As the court in *Diedrich* points out, the gift tax is imposed on the donor. Would the result have been different if the tax had been imposed on the donee? Would it matter whether the donee had funds with which to pay the tax without selling any of the shares?

4. *Time of recognition.* In Estate of Weeden v. Commissioner, 685 F.2d 1160 (9th Cir. 1982), the taxpayer near the end of 1968 made a gift of property subject to an obligation on the part of the donees to pay the gift tax, which exceeded the donor's basis in the property. The donees paid the tax in 1969. The court held that the gain should be recognized in 1969, pointing out that the donor remained personally liable for the tax until paid, that he was a cash-basis taxpayer, and that what he had received from the donees was only an unsecured promise to pay, which it said was not "the equivalent of cash." (The same result might now be reached under §453, relating to installment sales (see infra page 364).)

5. *The* Crane *case.* In simplified form, the facts of *Crane*, discussed by the Court, were as follows: *T* inherited property with a fair market value of $250,000 but subject to a debt of $250,000. *T* held the property for a number of years, during which she claimed depreciation deductions of $30,000. Then she sold the property, still subject to the $250,000 debt, for $2,500. The Court held that her gain for tax purposes was $32,500, not $2,500. In a sense, she was taxed not only on the net cash she received ($2,500), but also on the $30,000 deduction that in retrospect was unwarranted. The logic of this result depends on the interplay between the taxpayer's original basis in the property, the depreciation deduction she claimed, and the effect of the ultimate disposition. This logic will be examined in detail in the next case (Commissioner v. Tufts) and the notes and questions following it.

6. *The* Old Colony *case.* The facts of *Old Colony,* a leading case relied on by the Court in *Diedrich,* were simple. In 1918, Mr. William M. Wood earned and received, as president of the American Woolen Company, salary and commissions of approximately $1 million. The company decided to pay his income tax liability of approximately $680,000, though it had no obligation to do so. The Court held that Mr. Wood was taxable on the $680,000 as well as the $1 million. Putting aside the possibility of gift, which the Court easily rejected, the result is obviously correct. At the time the case arose there was no withholding tax, but the $680,000 is comparable to withheld taxes and it is plain that the income subject to taxation is the full amount earned before withholding, not the net amount after withholding. What is interesting about *Old Colony,* by the standards of the present day, is that it was litigated at all, especially all the way to the Supreme Court. The taxpayer relied on a very narrow definition of "income" and emphasized that the $680,000 payment had been made by the corporation not in fulfillment of any contractual obligation but voluntarily (apparently out of sympathy for

the plight of its president, whose expectations of earning enough to be able to lead a comfortable life had been frustrated by the imposition of an income tax on his $1 million earnings).

7. *Substance and form in tax law.* It is worth emphasizing that the analytic technique encountered in this note, and in *Diedrich* — the technique of reconstructing or restating a transaction to fully and accurately reflect its underlying economic reality — is encountered throughout tax (and other) law. Sometimes (though not here) it may be difficult to determine what the reality is or how it may best be fit into the descriptive modes with which we are familiar.

5. Transfer of Property Subject to Debt

The *Diedrich* case is a relatively simple instance of an assumption of debt in connection with a transfer of property. We turn now to somewhat more complex instances of that phenomenon.

Before turning to the next case, it will be helpful to explain some basic tax principles in the context of a simple example. These principles are explained again, and developed further, in other examples in the notes following the case.

Suppose *T* buys commercial property (land and building) for $2 million using her own funds, and that she rents the property out for a net of $300,000 a year after all expenses. The $300,000 will be *T*'s cash in pocket each year, but it will not be her income for tax purposes. For tax purposes she will be allowed a deduction called ACRS (for accelerated cost recovery system), sometimes called depreciation, which is intended as an allowance for the decline in the value of the building due to wear and tear and obsolescence. See supra page 56. The deduction may not be consistent with economic reality; it is allowed even if in fact there is no decline in the value of the property. Suppose that the ACRS deduction is $100,000 per year and that this deduction is taken, against the income of $300,000, each year for five years. Each year the taxable income will be $200,000, and *T*'s basis in the property will be reduced by the amount of the ACRS deduction ($100,000). At the end of the fifth year the total reduction in basis will be $500,000, and the remaining, or adjusted, basis will be $1.5 million. If the ACRS deduction is consistent with economic reality, the property will have declined in value to $1.5 million, and if it is sold at that price there will be no gain or loss. Assume, however, that the property has not declined (or risen) in value and that at the end of the five years it is sold for $2 million. The gain for tax purposes will be $500,000, which is the difference between the amount realized, $2 million, and the adjusted basis, $1.5 million.[60]

60. These facts may be summarized as follows:

See §1001(a). The $500,000 corresponds to the difference between the total amount of cash that *T* has received as rent ($1.5 million) and the total amount of income she has reported ($1 million) in connection with the ownership of the property. It can also be thought of as the amount by which the ACRS deduction exceeded the economic decline in the value of the property.

Now suppose that instead of using her own funds, *T* borrows the $2 million that she invests in the property, that the lender takes a mortgage on the property in that amount, and that the interest on the loan is at a rate of 10 percent or $200,000 per year. Suppose that the loan is nonrecourse, which means that in the event of default the lender can foreclose on the mortgage but has no recourse against *T* personally. We have already seen (see supra pages 232-233) that the amount *T* receives by loan is not included in her income. Nonetheless, her basis in the property will be $2 million. Regardless of the formalities of the entire transaction, she is treated as if she had received the $2 million in cash (a nontaxable receipt) and had then invested what is now her $2 million in the property (an investment giving rise to basis). Suppose again that *T* receives rent net of expenses of $300,000 per year for five years and that each year she takes an ACRS deduction of $100,000 and a deduction for the interest payment of $200,000, so that her taxable income each year is zero. At the end of the fifth year her basis in the property is $1.5 million.[61] Suppose that at the end of the fifth year she abandons

---

	(a) *One year*	*(b)* *Five years cumulative*	*(c)* *End of fifth year*
1. Purchase price	$2,000,000	—	—
2. Net annual rent	300,000	$1,500,000	—
3. ACRS	100,000	500,000	—
4 Taxable income	200,000	1,000,000	—
5. Sale price	—	—	$2,000,000
6. Adjusted basis[a]	—	—	1,500,000
7. Gain	—	—	500,000

a. 1(a) minus 3(b).

61. These facts may be summarized as follows:

	(a) *One year*	*(b)* *Five years cumulative*	*(c)* *End of fifth year*
1. Purchase price	$2,000,000	—	—
2. Loan proceeds	2,000,000	—	—
3. Net cash outlay	-0-	—	—
4. Net annual rent	300,000	$1,500,000	—
5. ACRS	100,000	500,000	—
6. Interest paid	200,000	1,000,000	—
7. Net cash	100,000[a]	500,000	—
8. Taxable income	-0-	-0-	—
9. Sale price	—	—	$2,000,000

the property, which is taken by foreclosure by the lender. What tax consequences to *T*? Note that she has received $500,000 over the five years of her ownership of the property and has paid no tax. She ought to be taxable on an additional $500,000. But what is the proper theory?

COMMISSIONER v. TUFTS

461 U.S. 300 (1983)

Justice BLACKMUN delivered the opinion of the Court.

Over 35 years ago, in Crane v. Commissioner, 331 U.S. 1 (1947), this Court ruled that a taxpayer, who sold property encumbered by a nonrecourse mortgage (the amount of the mortgage being less than the property's value), must include the unpaid balance of the mortgage in the computation of the amount the taxpayer realized on the sale. The case now before us presents the question whether the same rule applies when the unpaid amount of the nonrecourse mortgage exceeds the fair market value of the property sold.

I

On August 1, 1970, respondent Clark Pelt, a builder, and his wholly owned corporation, respondent Clark, Inc., formed a general partnership. The purpose of the partnership was to construct a 120-unit apartment complex in Duncanville, Tex., a Dallas suburb. Neither Pelt nor Clark, Inc., made any capital contribution to the partnership. Six days later, the partnership entered into a mortgage loan agreement with the Farm & Home Savings Association (F&H). Under the agreement, F&H was committed for a $1,851,500 loan for the complex. In return, the partnership executed a note and a deed of trust in favor of F&H. The partnership obtained the loan on a nonrecourse basis: neither the partnership nor its partners assumed any personal liability for repayment of the loan. Pelt later admitted four friends and relatives, respondents Tufts, Steger, Stephens, and Austin, as general partners. None of them contributed capital upon entering the partnership.

The construction of the complex was completed in August 1971. During 1971, each partner made small capital contributions to the part-

10. Loan discharge	—	—	2,000,000
11. Net cash	—	—	-0-
12. Adjusted basis[b]	—	—	1,500,000
13. Gain	—	—	500,000

a. 2(a) minus 4(a).
b. 1(a) minus 5(b).

nership; in 1972, however, only Pelt made a contribution. The total of the partners' capital contributions was $44,212. In each tax year, all partners claimed as income tax deductions their allocable shares of ordinary losses and depreciation. The deductions taken by the partners in 1971 and 1972 totalled $439,972. Due to these contributions and deductions, the partnership's adjusted basis in the property in August 1972 was $1,455,740.

In 1971 and 1972, major employers in the Duncanville area laid off significant numbers of workers. As a result, the partnership's rental income was less than expected, and it was unable to make the payments due on the mortgage. Each partner, on August 28, 1972, sold his partnership interest to an unrelated third party, Fred Bayles. As consideration, Bayles agreed to reimburse each partner's sale expenses up to $250; he also assumed the nonrecourse mortgage.

On the date of transfer, the fair market value of the property did not exceed $1,400,000. Each partner reported the sale on his federal income tax return and indicated that a partnership loss of $55,740 had been sustained.[62] The Commissioner of Internal Revenue, on audit, determined that the sale resulted in a partnership capital gain of approximately $400,000. His theory was that the partnership had realized the full amount of the nonrecourse obligation.[63]

Relying on Millar v. Commissioner, 577 F.2d 212, 215 (C.A.3), cert. denied, 439 U.S. 1046 (1978), the United States Tax Court, in an unreviewed decision, upheld the asserted deficiencies. 70 T.C. 756 (1978). The United States Court of Appeals for the Fifth Circuit reversed. 651 F.2d 1058 (1981). That court expressly disagreed with the *Millar* analysis, and, in limiting Crane v. Commissioner, supra, to its facts, questioned the theoretical underpinnings of the *Crane* decision. We granted certiorari to resolve the conflict. . . .

II

Section 752(d) of the Internal Revenue Code of 1954 specifically provides that liabilities incurred in the sale or exchange of a partnership interest are to "be treated in the same manner as liabilities in connection with the sale or exchange of property not associated with partnerships." Section 1001 governs the determination of gains and losses on the

62. The loss was the difference between the adjusted basis, $1,455,740, and the fair market value of the property, $1,400,000. On their individual tax returns, the partners did not claim deductions for their respective shares of this loss. In their petitions to the Tax Court, however, the partners did claim the loss.

63. The Commissioner determined the partnership's gain on the sale by subtracting the adjusted basis, $1,455,740, from the liability assumed by Bayles, $1,851,500. . . .

disposition of property. Under §1001(a), the gain or loss from a sale or other disposition of property is defined as the difference between "the amount realized" on the disposition and the property's adjusted basis. Subsection (b) of §1001 defines "amount realized." "The amount realized from the sale or other disposition of property shall be the sum of any money received plus the fair market value of the property (other than money) received." At issue is the application of the latter provision to the disposition of property encumbered by a nonrecourse mortgage of an amount in excess of the property's fair market value.

A

In Crane v. Commissioner, supra, this Court took the first and controlling step toward the resolution of this issue. Beulah B. Crane was the sole beneficiary under the will of her deceased husband. At his death in January 1932, he owned an apartment building that was then mortgaged for an amount which proved to be equal to its fair market value, as determined for federal estate tax purposes. The widow, of course, was not personally liable on the mortgage. She operated the building for nearly seven years, hoping to turn it into a profitable venture; during that period, she claimed income tax deductions for depreciation, property taxes, interest, and operating expenses, but did not make payments upon the mortgage principal. In computing her basis for the depreciation deductions, she included the full amount of the mortgage debt. In November 1938, with her hopes unfulfilled and the mortgagee threatening foreclosure, Mrs. Crane sold the building. The purchaser took the property subject to the mortgage and paid Crane $3,000; of that amount, $500 went for the expenses of the sale.

Crane reported a gain of $2,500 on the transaction. She reasoned that her basis in the property was zero (despite her earlier depreciation deductions based on including the amount of the mortgage) and that the amount she realized from the sale was simply the cash she received. The Commissioner disputed this claim. He asserted that Crane's basis in the property, under . . . §1014, was the property's fair market value at the time of her husband's death, adjusted for depreciation in the interim, and that the amount realized was the net cash received plus the amount of the outstanding mortgage assumed by the purchaser.

In upholding the Commissioner's interpretation of [§1014], the Court observed that to regard merely the taxpayer's equity in the property as her basis would lead to depreciation deductions less than the actual physical deterioration of the property, and would require the basis to be recomputed with each payment on the mortgage. 331 U.S., at 9-10. The Court rejected Crane's claim that any loss due to depreciation belonged to the mortgagee. The effect of the Court's ruling was that the taxpayer's basis was the value of the property undiminished by the mortgage. Id., at 11.

The Court next proceeded to determine the amount realized under . . . §1001(b). In order to avoid the "absurdity," see 331 U.S., at 13, of Crane's realizing only $2,500 on the sale of property worth over a quarter of a million dollars, the Court treated the amount realized as it had treated basis, that is, by including the outstanding value of the mortgage. To do otherwise would have permitted Crane to recognize a tax loss unconnected with any actual economic loss. The Court refused to construe one section of the Revenue Act so as "to frustrate the Act as a whole." Ibid.

Crane, however, insisted that the nonrecourse nature of the mortgage required different treatment. The Court, for two reasons, disagreed. First, excluding the nonrecourse debt from the amount realized would result in the same absurdity and frustration of the Code. Id., at 13-14. Second, the Court concluded that Crane obtained an economic benefit from the purchaser's assumption of the mortgage identical to the benefit conferred by the cancellation of personal debt. Because the value of the property in that case exceeded the amount of the mortgage, it was in Crane's economic interest to treat the mortgage as a personal obligation; only by so doing could she realize upon sale the appreciation in her equity represented by the $2,500 boot. The purchaser's assumption of the liability thus resulted in a taxable economic benefit to her, just as if she had been given, in addition to the boot, a sum of cash sufficient to satisfy the mortgage.

In a footnote, pertinent to the present case, the Court observed:

> Obviously, if the value of the property is less than the amount of the mortgage, a mortgagor who is not personally liable cannot realize a benefit equal to the mortgage. Consequently, a different problem might be encountered where a mortgagor abandoned the property or transferred it subject to the mortgage without receiving boot. That is not this case.

Id., at 14, n.37.

B

This case presents that unresolved issue. We are disinclined to overrule *Crane*, and we conclude that the same rule applies when the unpaid amount of the nonrecourse mortgage exceeds the value of the property transferred. *Crane* ultimately does not rest on its limited theory of economic benefit; instead, we read *Crane* to have approved the Commissioner's decision to treat a nonrecourse mortgage in this context as a true loan. This approval underlies *Crane*'s holdings that the amount of the nonrecourse liability is to be included in calculating both the basis and the amount realized on disposition. That the amount of the loan exceeds the fair market value of the property thus becomes irrelevant.

When a taxpayer receives a loan, he incurs an obligation to repay that loan at some future date. Because of this obligation, the loan proceeds do not qualify as income to the taxpayer. When he fulfills the obligation, the repayment of the loan likewise has no effect on his tax liability.

Another consequence to the taxpayer from this obligation occurs when the taxpayer applies the loan proceeds to the purchase price of property used to secure the loan. Because of the obligation to repay, the taxpayer is entitled to include the amount of the loan in computing his basis in the property; the loan, under §1012, is part of the taxpayer's cost of the property. Although a different approach might have been taken with respect to a nonrecourse mortgage loan,[64] the Commissioner has chosen to accord it the same treatment he gives to a recourse mortgage loan. The Court approved that choice in *Crane,* and the respondents do not challenge it here. The choice and its resultant benefits to the taxpayer are predicated on the assumption that the mortgage will be repaid in full.

When encumbered property is sold or otherwise disposed of and the purchaser assumes the mortgage, the associated extinguishment of the mortgagor's obligation to repay is accounted for in the computation of the amount realized.[65] . . . Because no difference between recourse and nonrecourse obligations is recognized in calculating basis,[66] *Crane*

64. The Commissioner might have adopted the theory, implicit in Crane's contentions, that a nonrecourse mortgage is not true debt, but, instead, is a form of joint investment by the mortgagor and the mortgagee. On this approach, nonrecourse debt would be considered a contingent liability, under which the mortgagor's payments on the debt gradually increase his interest in the property while decreasing that of the mortgagee. . . . Because the taxpayer's investment in the property would not include the nonrecourse debt, the taxpayer would not be permitted to include that debt in basis. . . .

We express no view as to whether such an approach would be consistent with the statutory structure and, if so, and *Crane* were not on the books, whether that approach would be preferred over *Crane's* analysis. We note only that the *Crane* Court's resolution of the basis issue presumed that when property is purchased with proceeds from a nonrecourse mortgage, the purchaser becomes the sole owner of the property. . . .

65. In this case, respondents received the face value of their note as loan proceeds. If respondents initially had given their note at a discount, the amount realized on the sale of the securing property might be limited to the funds actually received. See Commissioner v. Rail Joint Co., 61 F.2d 751, 752 (C.A.2 1932) (cancellation of indebtedness); Fashion Park, Inc. v. Commissioner, 21 T.C. 600, 606 (1954) (same). See generally J. Sneed, The Configurations of Gross Income 319 (1967) ("[I]t appears settled that the reacquisition of bonds at a discount by the obligor results in gain only to the extent the issue price, where this is less than par, exceeds the cost of reacquisition").

66. The Commissioner's choice in *Crane* "laid the foundation stone of most tax shelters," Bittker, Tax Shelters, Nonrecourse Debt, and the *Crane* Case, 33 Tax. L. Rev. 277, 283 (1978), by permitting taxpayers who bear no risk to take deductions on depreciable property. Congress recently has acted to curb this avoidance device by forbidding a taxpayer to take depreciation deductions in excess of amounts he has at risk in the investment. . . . §465(a) [see infra page 712]. Real estate investments, however, are exempt

teaches that the Commissioner may ignore the nonrecourse nature of the obligation in determining the amount realized upon disposition of the encumbered property. He thus may include in the amount realized the amount of the nonrecourse mortgage assumed by the purchaser. The rationale for this treatment is that the original inclusion of the amount of the mortgage in basis rested on the assumption that the mortgagor incurred an obligation to repay. Moreover, this treatment balances the fact that the mortgagor originally received the proceeds of the nonrecourse loan tax-free on the same assumption. Unless the outstanding amount of the mortgage is deemed to be realized, the mortgagor effectively will have received untaxed income at the time the loan was extended and will have received an unwarranted increase in the basis of his property.[67] The Commissioner's interpretation of §1001(b) in this fashion cannot be said to be unreasonable.

C

The Commissioner in fact has applied this rule even when the fair market value of the property falls below the amount of the nonrecourse obligation. Treas. Reg. §1.1001-2(b); Rev. Rul. 76-111, 1976-1 Cum. Bull. 214. Because the theory on which the rule is based applies equally in this situation, . . . we have no reason, after *Crane,* to question this treatment.[68]

---

from this prohibition. §465(c)(3)(D). Although this congressional action may foreshadow a day when nonrecourse and recourse debts will be treated differently, neither Congress nor the Commissioner has sought to alter *Crane's* rule of including nonrecourse liability in both basis and the amount realized.

67. Although the *Crane* rule has some affinity with the tax benefit rule; . . . the analysis we adopt is different. Our analysis applies even in the situation in which no deductions are taken. It focuses on the obligation to repay and its subsequent extinguishment, not on the taking and recovery of deductions. . . .

68. Professor Wayne G. Barnett, as amicus in the present case, argues that the liability and property portions of the transaction should be accounted for separately. Under his view, there was a transfer of the property for $1.4 million, and there was a cancellation of the $1.85 million obligation for a payment of $1.4 million. The former resulted in a capital loss of $50,000, and the latter in the realization of $450,000 of ordinary income. Taxation of the ordinary income might be deferred under §108 by a reduction of respondents' bases in their partnership interests. [Deferral under §108 was broadly available at the time this case was decided. It is now available only for insolvent debtors and farmers and the relief mechanism is slightly different from the one applied under the now-repealed provision referred to by the Court. — Eds.]

Although this indeed could be a justifiable mode of analysis, it has not been adopted by the Commissioner. Nor is there anything to indicate that the Code requires the Commissioner to adopt it. We note that Professor Barnett's approach does assume that recourse and nonrecourse debt may be treated identically.

The Commissioner also has chosen not to characterize the transaction as cancellation of indebtedness. We are not presented with and do not decide the contours of the cancellation-of-indebtedness doctrine. We note only that our approach does not fall within certain prior interpretations of that doctrine. . . .

In the context of a sale or disposition of property under §1001, the extinguishment of the obligation to repay is not ordinary income; instead, the amount of the canceled

Respondents received a mortgage loan with the concomitant obligation to repay by the year 2012. The only difference between that mortgage and one on which the borrower is personally liable is that the mortgagee's remedy is limited to foreclosing on the securing property. This difference does not alter the nature of the obligation; its only effect is to shift from the borrower to the lender any potential loss caused by devaluation of the property. If the fair market value of the property falls below the amount of the outstanding obligation, the mortgagee's ability to protect its interests is impaired, for the mortgagor is free to abandon the property to the mortgagee and be relieved of his obligation.

This, however, does not erase the fact that the mortgagor received the loan proceeds tax-free and included them in his basis on the understanding that he had an obligation to repay the full amount. . . . When the obligation is canceled, the mortgagor is relieved of his responsibility to repay the sum he originally received and thus realizes value to that extent within the meaning of §1001(b). From the mortgagor's point of view, when his obligation is assumed by a third party who purchases the encumbered property, it is as if the mortgagor first had been paid with cash borrowed by the third party from the mortgagee on a nonrecourse basis, and then had used the cash to satisfy his obligation to the mortgagee.

Moreover, this approach avoids the absurdity the Court recognized in *Crane*. Because of the remedy accompanying the mortgage in the nonrecourse situation, the depreciation in the fair market value of the property is relevant economically only to the mortgagee, who by lending on a nonrecourse basis remains at risk. To permit the taxpayer to limit his realization to the fair market value of the property would be to recognize a tax loss for which he has suffered no corresponding economic loss. Such a result would be to construe "one section of the Act . . . so as . . . to defeat the intention of another or to frustrate the Act as a whole." 331 U.S., at 13.

In the specific circumstances of *Crane*, the economic benefit theory did support the Commissioner's treatment of the nonrecourse mortgage as a personal obligation. The footnote in *Crane* acknowledged the limitations of that theory when applied to a different set of facts. *Crane* also stands for the broader proposition, however, that a nonrecourse loan should be treated as a true loan. We therefore hold that a taxpayer must account for the proceeds of obligations he has received tax-free and included in basis. Nothing in either §1001(b) or in the Court's prior

---

debt is included in the amount realized, and enters into the computation of gain or loss on the disposition of property. According to *Crane*, this treatment is no different when the obligation is nonrecourse: the basis is not reduced as in the cancellation-of-indebtedness context, and the full value of the outstanding liability is included in the amount realized. Thus, the problem of negative basis is avoided.

decisions requires the Commissioner to permit a taxpayer to treat a sale of encumbered property asymmetrically, by including the proceeds of the nonrecourse obligation in basis but not accounting for the proceeds upon transfer of the encumbered property. . . .

Justice O'CONNOR, concurring.

I concur in the opinion of the Court, accepting the view of the Commissioner. I do not, however, endorse the Commissioner's view. Indeed, were we writing on a slate clean except for the *Crane* decision, I would take quite a different approach — that urged upon us by Professor Barnett as amicus.

Crane established that a taxpayer could treat property as entirely his own, in spite of the "coinvestment" provided by his mortgagee in the form of a nonrecourse loan. That is, the full basis of the property, with all its tax consequences, belongs to the mortgagor. That rule alone, though, does not in any way tie nonrecourse debt to the cost of property or to the proceeds upon disposition. I see no reason to treat the purchase, ownership, and eventual disposition of property differently because the taxpayer also takes out a mortgage, an independent transaction. In this case, the taxpayer purchased property, using nonrecourse financing, and sold it after it declined in value to a buyer who assumed the mortgage. There is no economic difference between the events in this case and a case in which the taxpayer buys property with cash; later obtains a nonrecourse loan by pledging the property as security; still later, using cash on hand, buys off the mortgage for the market value of the devalued property; and finally sells the property to a third party for its market value.

The logical way to treat both this case and the hypothesized case is to separate the two aspects of these events and to consider, first, the ownership and sale of the property, and, second, the arrangement and retirement of the loan. Under *Crane,* the fair market value of the property on the date of acquisition — the purchase price — represents the taxpayer's basis in the property, and the fair market value on the date of disposition represents the proceeds on sale. The benefit received by the taxpayer in return for the property is the cancellation of a mortgage that is worth no more than the fair market value of the property, for that is all the mortgagee can expect to collect on the mortgage. His gain or loss on the disposition of the property equals the difference between the proceeds and the cost of acquisition. Thus, the taxation of the transaction in *property* reflects the economic fate of the *property.* If the property has declined in value, as was the case here, the taxpayer recognizes a loss on the disposition of the property. The new purchaser then takes as his basis the fair market value as of the date of the sale. See, e.g., United States v. Davis, 370 U.S. 65 (1962); Gibson Products Co. v. United States, 637 F.2d 1041, 1045, n.8 (C.A.5 1981) (dictum);

see generally Treas. Reg. §1.1001-2(a)(3), 26 C.F.R. §1.1001-2(a)(3) (1982); B. Bittker, 2 Federal Income Taxation of Income, Estates and Gifts, ¶41.2.2., at 41-10 – 41-11 (1981).

In the separate borrowing transaction, the taxpayer acquires cash from the mortgagee. He need not recognize income at that time, of course, because he also incurs an obligation to repay the money. Later, though, when he is able to satisfy the debt by surrendering property that is worth less than the face amount of the debt, we have a classic situation of cancellation of indebtedness, requiring the taxpayer to recognize income in the amount of the difference between the proceeds of the loan and the amount for which he is able to satisfy his creditor. 26 U.S.C. §61(a)(12). The taxation of the financing transaction then reflects the economic fate of the loan.

The reason that separation of the two aspects of the events in this case is important is, of course, that the Code treats different sorts of income differently. A gain on the sale of the property may qualify for capital gains treatment, §§1202, 1221 (1976 ed. and Supp. V),[69] while the cancellation of indebtedness is ordinary income, but income that the taxpayer may be able to defer. §§108, 1017 (1976 ed. Supp. V). Not only does Professor Barnett's theory permit us to accord appropriate treatment to each of the two types of income or loss present in these sorts of transactions, it also restores continuity to the system by making the taxpayer-seller's proceeds on the disposition of property equal to the purchaser's basis in the property. Further, and most important, it allows us to tax the events in this case in the same way that we tax the economically identical hypothesized transaction.

Persuaded though I am by the logical coherence and internal consistency of this approach, I agree with the Court's decision not to adopt it judicially. We do not write on a slate marked only by *Crane.* The Commissioner's longstanding position, Rev. Rul. 76-111, 1976-1 C.B. 214, is now reflected in the regulations. Treas. Reg. §1.1001-2, 26 C.F.R. §1.1001-2 (1982). In the light of the numerous cases in the lower courts including the amount of the unrepaid proceeds of the mortgage in the proceeds on sale or disposition, . . . it is difficult to conclude that the Commissioner's interpretation of the statute exceeds the bounds of his discretion. As the Court's opinion demonstrates, his interpretation is defensible. . . .

NOTES AND QUESTIONS

1. *Debt and basis.* (a) Perhaps the most significant doctrine reflected in *Tufts* is that the cost basis of property under §1012 is the full cost of

69. [Section 1202 was repealed in 1986. After 1987, capital gain is no longer taxed at a favorable rate, but there are still important differences between capital gain and loss and ordinary gain and loss. See infra page 829. — Eds.]

the property, including any part of that cost paid for with borrowed funds, regardless of whether the loan is made by the seller or by a third party, or is an existing debt assumed by the purchaser, and regardless of whether the loan is with or without recourse. In other words, when property is acquired subject to debt, the buyer is treated as if he or she had received cash equal to the amount of the debt and had used that cash to buy the property. The basis thus established is important in determining the depreciation deduction to which the taxpayer is entitled.

(b) As the court in *Tufts* points out, because the taxpayer in *Crane* inherited the property, her basis was determined under §1014 rather than under §1012.[70] The Court in *Crane* reasoned, however, that what she inherited was the property, worth $250,000, and not just the equity, worth nothing, and that therefore her basis under §1014 was $250,000 rather than zero. Thus, inherited property is treated the same as purchased property in that basis is determined with reference to the value of the property, not the value of the taxpayer's equity.

2. *Taking debt into account on disposition of property.* (a) The Court in *Tufts* requires the taxpayer to recognize income upon the disposition of the apartment complex. The following simplified version of the facts in the case should help illuminate the logic behind that aspect of the decision. Assume Tufts put up $45,000 of his own funds and used $1,850,000 of borrowed funds to acquire an apartment complex for $1,895,000. Tufts deducted $440,000 depreciation and then "sold" the complex for a nominal sum (which we will ignore). Tufts' total dollar loss, then, was $45,000. His prior tax loss, however, was $440,000. Clearly, something is amiss here. Tufts deducted $440,000 depreciation but lost only the cash contribution of $45,000. In order for the tax consequences to match the economic consequences, the taxpayer must, in effect, "give back" the $395,000 of depreciation that represented a loss he did not incur.

The Court in *Tufts* reaches the correct result (as to income recognized) by including the buyer's assumption of the nonrecourse debt as part of the sales proceeds. The taxpayer is thus treated as having received $1,850,000 upon sale of the property. The depreciation reduced the taxpayer's basis in the property from $1,895,000 (the invested loan proceeds plus the $45,000 of the taxpayer's own funds) to $1,455,000 (basis less depreciation). The difference between that basis and the

70. It could be argued, however, that since Mrs. Crane took the property subject to a debt equal in amount to its full market value, in effect she bought the property and her basis should be determined under §1012. The result is the same either way on the *Crane* facts. The theory (§1014 versus §1012) could matter, however, in the unusual case where the property is subject to a contingent debt, which may not create basis (see Albany Car Wheel Co. v. Commissioner, 40 T.C. 831 (1963), aff'd per curiam, 333 F.2d 653 (2d Cir. 1964); but see United States v. Davis, infra page 411, holding that basis can be determined by reference to the value of the property received).

$1,850,000 sales proceeds yields a gain of $395,000. There is a nice symmetry to the way the Court derives the proper result: If nonrecourse debt is treated as cash for the purposes of determining basis, perhaps it should be treated as cash for the purposes of determining sales proceeds.

The approach favored in Justice O'Connor's concurrence reaches the same result (as to amount recognized), but by a different means. Under that approach, property is treated as sold for its fair market value. If property purchased with, and secured by, a nonrecourse loan declines in value to zero and is abandoned (or foreclosed upon by the lender, or deeded over to the lender in lieu of foreclosure) the sales proceeds are zero. The taxpayer recognizes no property gain and, depending on the basis of the property at the time the proposed is disposed of, may well recognize a loss. The taxpayer does, however, recognize cancellation of indebtedness income equal to the difference between the amount of outstanding debt secured by the property and its fair market value at time of disposal. The intuition behind this "bifurcated" approach is that the taxpayer has not repaid the full amount it has borrowed and must recognize cancellation of indebtedness income under *Kirby Lumber*, supra page 230. The bifurcated approach is discussed in more detail in Note 5, infra.

(b) While the dictates of logic are clear, the language of the Code, at least in the case of nonrecourse debt, is not. The relevant provisions are §§61(a)(3), 61(a)(12), and 1001(a) and (b). Section 61(a)(12) does not quite fit because it focuses on the debt alone and not on the transfer of property. Moreover, in the case of many transfers subject to debt there will be no reason to suppose that there is a gain from a favorable loan, such as was encountered in *Kirby Lumber* (supra page 235). (See discussion of bifurcation, at Note 5 infra.) Application of §1001 (with §61(a)(3)) requires that an assumption of debt by the transferee of the property be treated as an "amount realized," which requires a strained interpretation of that language, but that is the approach taken by the Court in *Tufts*. This approach seems to foreclose the application of §108 and the treatment of any portion of the gain as ordinary income (which is the possibility associated with bifurcation). But see, as to recourse debt, Note 5, infra.

3. *Basis and tax shelters.* The rule that the cost of property for purposes of determining basis includes amounts paid with borrowings was a critical element in the development of "tax shelters" — that is, investments entered into largely for the sake of their tax benefits. The tax benefits depended also on the fact that depreciation and other deductions often exceed any allowance that would be consistent with economic reality. Thus, investments that were in fact profitable economically might show losses for tax purposes. Before the adoption in 1986 of the "passive loss" limitations (see infra page 711), those losses could be used

to offset, or "shelter," income from other sources (such as compensation for services as a doctor, a lawyer, a movie star, or an athlete). Tax shelters will be examined at some length, after we have examined deductions, but a simple illustration, which merely extends the analysis in Note 2(a), may be helpful here. Suppose that *S* is a surgeon earning $300,000 per year. He has saved $100,000, which he uses to buy an office building that is worth $1 million and is subject to a mortgage of $900,000. Suppose that the rents from the building are just equal to the interest and all other expenses, but that *S* is entitled to depreciate the building at a rate of $50,000 per year. He will show a loss of $50,000 a year on his investment, even if (as is likely in many instances) the property is not in fact declining in value. Before 1987, the $50,000 loss could have been deducted on his personal income tax return and thus would have "sheltered" $50,000 of income from his medical practice. In other words, he would have received $50,000 of income tax-free because of the tax loss. Suppose that he kept the building for three years and then sold it, subject to the $900,000 mortgage, for $100,000 — the amount he initially invested. His basis would be $850,000 (for the land and building), so he would have a gain for tax purposes of $150,000, which is, as it should be, precisely equal to the deductions he had taken in earlier years. He would come out even except that he would have had the advantage of deferral and of long-term capital gain treatment of the $150,000 gain.

4. *Borrowing against appreciation.* Suppose that *T* buys property for $10,000 cash; the property rises in value to $100,000; *T* then borrows $60,000, nonrecourse on the security of the property. It is plain at this point that *T* has "locked in" gain to the extent of $50,000; the worst that can happen is that the property will decline in value to $60,000 or less and will be taken over by the lender in settlement of the debt, in which case *T* is still $50,000 ahead. Thus, a strong argument can be made that *T* has taxable gain of $50,000 at the time of borrowing the $60,000 or, more generally, that gain should be recognized to the extent that loans exceed basis. But that is not the law; *T* is not taxed in the year in which the property is encumbered by the loan in excess of basis. This being so, when the property is later transferred, the earlier loan proceeds must be treated as proceeds of sale. If, for example, the property were transferred later in return for a cash payment of $20,000, with the purchaser assuming the debt, the proceeds must be treated as $80,000 and the gain to be recognized must be $70,000. Or if the property declined in value to $60,000 or less and were taken by the lender in settlement of the debt, the gain to be recognized would be $50,000 — the amount of gain that was previously received in a cash-flow sense but was not recognized for tax purposes. See Woodsam Associates v. Commissioner, 198 F.2d 357 (2d Cir. 1952), where the court rejected the taxpayer's argument that a tax should have been

imposed in the year when money was borrowed nonrecourse in an amount in excess of basis (a year for which taxes could not be collected because of the statute of limitations) and therefore could not be taxed in the year in which the property was abandoned to the lender. See also Malone v. United States, 326 F. Supp. 106 (N.D. Miss. 1971), aff'd per curiam, 455 F.2d 502 (5th Cir. 1972) (where property with a basis of $13,500, a fair market value of $52,000, and a mortgage of $32,000 was transferred by gift, the donor realized a gain of $18,500); Estate of Levine v. Commissioner, 72 T.C. 780 (1979), aff'd, 634 F.2d 12 (2d Cir. 1980) (same result). The tax principles reflected in these cases are essentially the same as those we have already examined. In the situations examined earlier, basis was reduced by depreciation deductions below the amount of the loan. The depreciation deduction was allowed because it was assumed, for tax purposes, that the debt would be repaid and that the taxpayer should therefore be treated as having made an investment that includes any borrowed funds. In the case of the borrowing in excess of basis, the gain is ignored on the assumption that the debt will be repaid. When the repayment assumption turns out to be unwarranted, an appropriate tax adjustment must be made.

5. *Bifurcation.* (a) Suppose that *T* many years ago borrowed at 5 percent to buy the house that he occupies as a personal residence; that the loan balance is $100,000 with many years left until it is repaid; and that the present rate on such loans is 12 percent. Suppose further that *T* wants to sell the house and has found a buyer who is willing either to pay $200,000 in cash for the house and assume the $100,000 mortgage, or to pay $280,000 cash for the house unencumbered. Suppose that *T*'s basis in the house is $160,000. If *T* sells subject to the mortgage, the gain is the difference between the proceeds of $300,000 (the cash plus the amount of the mortgage assumed by the buyer) and the basis ($160,000), or $140,000. All of this is treated as capital gain. Suppose that *T* decides to pay off the loan and accept the all-cash offer of $280,000, and that the lender is willing to take $80,000 in settlement of the loan. *T* will have ordinary income of $20,000 on discharge of the loan indebtedness and $120,000 capital gain on the sale of the house.[71] Table 2-2 summarizes this hypothetical.

(b) The above hypothetical illustrates a more general theory that where property is transferred in settlement of a debt there may be two separate kinds of gain: (i) gain from paying off a favorable loan at a

71. Suppose that the buyer borrows $80,000, at current market rates, to help finance the purchase. Of each payment the buyer makes on the loan a larger portion will be deductible interest and a smaller portion nondeductible repayment of debt than if the buyer had assumed the $100,000 loan to *T*. Thus, in the all-cash alternative, a present detriment to *T* ($20,000 of ordinary income) is offset by future benefits to the buyer (of each payment, a higher portion is deductible interest as opposed to nondeductible repayment of principal).

TABLE 2-2
Illustration of Bifurcation Problem

Face amount of loan	$100,000
Present value of loan	80,000
Price of house, unencumbered	280,000
Price of house, with loan	300,000
Effects on seller	
(a) Sale subject to loan	
Proceeds	$300,000
Basis	160,000
Capital gain	$140,000
(b) Sale for cash	
(i) House	
Proceeds	$280,000
Basis	160,000
Capital gain	$120,000
(ii) Debt	
Face amount	$100,000
Payment to discharge	80,000
Income	$ 20,000

TABLE 2-3
Gain on Transfer of Encumbered Property

Taxpayer	*A*	*B*	*C*
(a) Debt discharged	$100	$100	$100
(b) Basis	70	70	70
(c) Fair market value	100	70	90
(d) Type of gain			
(i) Debt-discharge	-0-	30	10
(ii) Property disposition	30	-0-	20

reduced price (as in *Kirby Lumber*) and (ii) gain from the disposition of the property. The latter might be treated in some circumstances as capital gain while the former is ordinary income (under §61(a)(12)). This suggests the possibility that gain should be divided, or bifurcated. The following hypothetical (based on 1 B. Bittker and L. Lokken, Federal Taxation of Income Estates and Gifts ¶6.4.3 (1989)) illustrates the concept: Each of three taxpayers, *A*, *B*, and *C*, transfers property with an adjusted basis of $70 and subject to a debt of $100. The fair market value of the properties is, respectively, $100, $70, and $90. The amounts of each of the two types of gain, debt discharge and property disposition, are indicated in Table 2-3.

As can be seen from the table, *A*'s basis in the property is $70, and it is worth $100. He has a gain of $30 because of the difference between the value of the property and its basis. The property is worth enough to fully satisfy the debt, so there is no reduction in the debt and no debt-discharge income. For *B*, there is no gain in the property and the gain of $30 is entirely attributable to the lender's acceptance of property worth $70 in settlement of a debt of $100. Why would the lender accept property worth $70 in satisfaction of a debt of $100? Perhaps for the reason suggested in the hypothetical in 5(a): Interest rates have risen since the debt was made, so that the lender would just as soon have $70 today (that would be lent out at current, higher rates) than continue to receive lower than market interest rates under the present loan and wait for the eventual repayment of $100. Most likely, though, the lender accepts the property in satisfaction of the debt because it has no choice. The loan is nonrecourse and secured only by the property. If the property is only worth $70, it is unrealistic to think that the borrower will ever repay the full $100 debt. With *C* we simply have a combination of the two elements. In each case the correct result should be clear if one simply imagines the taxpayer selling the property for cash for its fair market value and using the cash to pay off the debt. That is how the transactions should be viewed if accurate tax results are to be achieved.

An argument in favor of bifurcation in *Tufts,* offered by Professor Wayne G. Barnett (of Stanford Law School), was treated respectfully by the majority (footnote 57) and with enthusiasm by Justice O'Connor in her concurring opinion, but was rejected by the Court on the ground that it had not been accepted by the Commissioner.

One commentator has objected to bifurcation in the case of nonrecourse debt, arguing that in the case of such debt the borrower does not have a fixed obligation to repay and therefore cannot have income from discharge of indebtedness. Moreover, with a nonrecourse debt the borrower is unconcerned about the value of the property once the property is taken by the lender in satisfaction of the debt; yet differences in the value of the property would be significant under bifurcation. Once the nonrecourse debt is incurred, says this commentator, the lender becomes "a co-owner of an equity in the property, up to the amount of the mortgage debt." (Lurie, New Ghosts for Old: *Crane* Footnote 37 Is Dead (Or Is It?), 20 Tax Notes 3, 4 (1983).) If this view is accepted, who should be entitled to any depreciation deduction that may be allowable in respect of the property?

What is perhaps most interesting and important is that bifurcation is *the rule* with respect to transactions in which property is transferred to a creditor in satisfaction of *recourse* debt. See Regs. §1.1001-2(a)(2), (b), and Ex. 8; Rev. Rul. 90-16, 1990-1 Cum. Bull. 12; Danenberg v. Commissioner, 73 T.C. 370 (1979). What is the significance of the Court's failure in *Tufts* to note the use of bifurcation in the case of such transactions? Professor Deborah A. Geier answers:

> A thoughtful parsing of both the *Tufts* decision and the supporting briefs reveals that the Court was not likely aware that the bifurcated approach controlled in the case of recourse debt and was not likely aware that it was cementing *different* approaches in the *Tufts* situation depending on whether the debt involved in the transaction is recourse or nonrecourse.

Tufts and the Evolution of Debt-Discharge Theory, 1 Florida Tax Rev. 115, 120 (1992). Professor Geier goes on to argue that there is no good reason for the "collapsed" approach that is used for nonrecourse debt. In *Tufts,* however, the property was not transferred to the creditor in satisfaction of the debt. Instead, the property was transferred to a third person who assumed the debt. Should this matter?

6. *A statutory solution.* Section 357, enacted in 1954, provides a statutory solution to the problem of transfers of excessively mortgaged property to a corporation. Ordinarily, where property is transferred to a corporation that is controlled by the transferor(s), no gain or loss is recognized. See §351, examined infra page 470. Under §357(c), however, gain is recognized to the extent that encumbrances on the property exceed its basis. The same result had been reached by judicial ruling in a case arising before 1954. Simon v. Commissioner, 285 F.2d 422 (3d Cir. 1960). A similar result is reached under §311(c) where a corporation transfers encumbered property to its shareholders.

H. ILLEGAL INCOME

GILBERT v. COMMISSIONER

552 F.2d 478 (2d Cir. 1977)

LUMBARD, Circuit Judge.

The taxpayer Edward M. Gilbert appeals from a determination by the tax court that he realized taxable income on certain unauthorized withdrawals of corporate funds made by him in 1962. We reverse.

Until June 12, 1962, Gilbert was president, principal stockholder, and a director of the E. L. Bruce Company, Inc., a New York corporation which was engaged in the lumber supply business. In 1961 and early 1962 Gilbert acquired on margin [that is, in large part with borrowed money] substantial personal and beneficial ownership of stock in another lumber supply company, the Celotex Corporation, intending ultimately to bring about a merger of Celotex into Bruce. To this end, he persuaded associates of his to purchase Celotex stock, guaranteeing them against loss, and also induced Bruce itself to purchase a substantial number of Celotex shares. In addition, on March 5, 1962, Gilbert granted Bruce an option to purchase his Celotex shares from him at cost. By the end of May 1962, 56% of Celotex was thus controlled by Gilbert and Bruce, and negotiations for the merger were proceeding; agreement had been reached that three of the directors of Bruce would be placed on the board of Celotex. It is undisputed that this merger would have been in Bruce's interest.

The stock market declined on May 28, 1962, however, and Gilbert was called upon to furnish additional margin [that is, individual funds] for the Celotex shares purchased by him and his associates. Lacking sufficient cash of his own to meet this margin call, Gilbert instructed the secretary of Bruce to use corporate funds to supply the necessary margin. Between May 28 and June 6 a series of checks totalling $1,958,000 were withdrawn from Bruce's accounts and used to meet the margin call. $5,000 was repaid to Bruce on June 5. According to his testimony in the tax court, Gilbert from the outset intended to repay all the money and at all times thought he was acting in the corporation's best interests as well as his own. He promptly informed several other Bruce officers and directors of the withdrawals; however, some were not notified until June 11 or 12.

On about June 1, Gilbert returned to New York from Nevada, where he had been attending to a personal matter. Shortly thereafter he consulted with Shearman, Sterling & Wright, who were outside counsel to Bruce at the time, regarding the withdrawals. They, he, and another Bruce director initiated negotiations to sell many of the Celotex shares to Ruberoid Company as a way of recouping most of Bruce's outlay.

On June 8, Gilbert went to the law offices of Shearman, Sterling & Wright and executed interest-bearing promissory notes to Bruce for $1,953,000 secured by an assignment of most of his property. The notes were callable by Bruce on demand, with presentment and notice of demand waived by Gilbert. The tax court found that up through June 12 the net value of the assets assigned for security by Gilbert substantially exceeded the amount owed.

After Gilbert informed other members of the Bruce board of directors of his actions, a meeting of the board was scheduled for the morning of June 12. At the meeting the board accepted the note and assignment but refused to ratify Gilbert's unauthorized withdrawals. During the meeting, word came that the board of directors of the Ruberoid Company had rejected the price offered for sale of the Celotex stock. Thereupon, the Bruce board demanded and received Gilbert's resignation and decided to issue a public announcement the next day regarding his unauthorized withdrawals. All further attempts on June 12 to arrange a sale of the Celotex stock fell through and in the evening Gilbert flew to Brazil, where he stayed for several months. On June 13 the market price of Bruce and Celotex stock plummeted, and trading in those shares was suspended by the Securities and Exchange Commission.

On June 22 the Internal Revenue Service filed tax liens against Gilbert based on a [claim of tax liability of] $1,720,000 for 1962. Bruce, having failed to file the assignment from Gilbert because of the real estate filing fee involved,[72] now found itself subordinate in priority to the IRS and, impeded by the tax lien, has never since been able to recover much of its $1,953,000 from the assigned assets.[73] For the fiscal year ending June 30, 1962, Bruce claimed a loss deduction on the $1,953,000 withdrawn by Gilbert. Several years later Gilbert pled guilty to federal and state charges of having unlawfully withdrawn the funds from Bruce.

On these facts, the tax court determined that Gilbert realized income when he made the unauthorized withdrawals of funds from Bruce, and that his efforts at restitution did not entitle him to any offset against this income.

The starting point for analysis of this case is James v. United States, 366 U.S. 213 (1961), which established that embezzled funds can constitute taxable income to the embezzler.

> When a taxpayer acquires earnings, lawfully or unlawfully, without the consensual recognition, express or implied, of an obligation to repay and without restriction as to their disposition, "he has received income which he is required to return, even though it may still be claimed that he is not entitled to the money, and even though he may still be adjudged liable to restore its equivalent." . . .

Id. at 219.

The Commissioner contends that there can never be "consensual recognition . . . of an obligation to repay" in an embezzlement case. He reasons that because the corporation — as represented by a majority of the board of directors — was unaware of the withdrawals, there cannot have been *consensual* recognition of the obligation to repay at the time the taxpayer Gilbert acquired the funds. Since the withdrawals were not authorized and the directors refused to treat them as a loan to Gilbert,

72. When attempting to file in the New York County Clerk's office on June 13 or 14, Bruce was told that it would have to pay a mortgage tax of at least $10,000 because the assignment included real property. Since the net value of the real property was negligible, Bruce sought to perfect only the personal property portion, but the clerk still demanded the mortgage tax on the ground that the real property assignment and the personal property assignment were contained in the same document.

73. As of the date of trial in the tax court, less than $500,000 had been raised through sales of the assigned assets. Pursuant to an agreement reached between Bruce and the government in 1970, 35% of these proceeds have been paid over to the government pending the outcome of this lawsuit.

the Commissioner concludes that Gilbert should be taxed like a thief rather than a borrower.

In a typical embezzlement, the embezzler intends at the outset to abscond with the funds. If he repays the money during the same taxable year, he will not be taxed. See James v. Commissioner, supra at 220; Quinn v. Commissioner, 524 F.2d 617, 624-625 (7th Cir. 1975); Rev. Rul. 65-254, 1965-2 Cum. Bul. 50. As we held in Buff v. Commissioner, 496 F.2d 847 (2d Cir. 1974), if he spends the loot instead of repaying, he cannot avoid tax on his embezzlement income simply by signing promissory notes later in the same year. See also id. at 849-850 (Oakes, J., concurring).

This is not a typical embezzlement case, however, and we do not interpret *James* as requiring income realization in every case of unlawful withdrawals by a taxpayer. There are a number of facts that differentiate this case from *Buff* and *James*. When Gilbert withdrew the corporate funds, he recognized his obligation to repay and intended to do so.[74] The funds were to be used not only for his benefit but also for the benefit of the corporation; meeting the margin calls was necessary to maintain the possibility of the highly favorable merger. Although Gilbert undoubtedly realized that he lacked the necessary authorization, he thought he was serving the best interests of the corporation and he expected his decision to be ratified shortly thereafter. That Gilbert at no time intended to retain the corporation's funds is clear from his actions.[75] He immediately informed several of the corporation's officers and directors, and he made a complete accounting to all of them within two weeks. He also disclosed his actions to the corporation's outside counsel, a reputable law firm, and followed its instructions regarding repayment. In signing immediately payable promissory notes secured by most of his assets, Gilbert's clear intent was to ensure that Bruce would obtain full restitution. In addition, he attempted to sell his shares of Celotex stock in order to raise cash to pay Bruce back immediately.

When Gilbert executed the assignment to Bruce of his assets on June 8 and when this assignment for security was accepted by the Bruce board on June 12, the net market value of these assets was substantially more than the amount owed. The Bruce board did not release Gilbert from his underlying obligation to repay, but the assignment was nonetheless valid and Bruce's failure to make an appropriate filing to protect itself against the claims of third parties, such as the IRS, did not relieve

74. Quinn v. Commissioner, relied on by the Commissioner, involved taxation of funds received without any contemporaneous recognition of the obligation to repay, and it is therefore distinguishable from the present case.

75. If Gilbert had been intending to abscond with the $1,953,000, it is difficult to see how he could have hoped to avoid detection in the long run. Since his equity in the corporation itself was worth well over $1,953,000, it would have been absurd for him to attempt such a theft.

Gilbert of the binding effect of the assignment. Since the assignment secured an immediately payable note, Gilbert had as of June 12 granted Bruce full discretion to liquidate any of his assets in order to recoup on the $1,953,000 withdrawal. Thus, Gilbert's net accretion in real wealth on the overall transaction was zero: he had for his own use withdrawn $1,953,000 in corporate funds but he had now granted the corporation control over at least $1,953,000 worth of his assets.

We conclude that where a taxpayer withdraws funds from a corporation which he fully intends to repay and which he expects with reasonable certainty he will be able to repay, where he believes that his withdrawals will be approved by the corporation, and where he makes a prompt assignment of assets sufficient to secure the amount owed, he does not realize income on the withdrawals under the *James* test. When Gilbert acquired the money, there was an express consensual recognition of his obligation to repay: the secretary of the corporation, who signed the checks, the officers and directors to whom Gilbert gave contemporaneous notification, and Gilbert himself were all aware that the transaction was in the nature of a loan. Moreover, the funds were certainly not received by Gilbert "without restriction as to their disposition" as is required for taxability under *James;* the money was to be used solely for the temporary purpose of meeting certain margin calls and it was so used. For these reasons, we reverse the decision of the tax court.

NOTES AND QUESTIONS

1. *Analysis.* The court says, "In a typical embezzlement, the embezzler intends at the outset to abscond with the funds." That may well be true, but in many instances the embezzler fully intends to repay, as soon as his or her horse, lottery ticket, or high-tech stock investment pays off. If misfortune becomes evident within two weeks and an embezzler confesses, and promises repayment, are the proceeds of the embezzlement nontaxable?

2. *The special status of embezzlers.* The decision of the Supreme Court in James v. United States, relied on by the court in *Gilbert,* overruled an earlier decision of the Court in Commissioner v. Wilcox, 327 U.S. 404 (1946), in which it had held that embezzled funds were not income because of the obligation to restore the funds to the victim. This decision was at odds with a later decision in Rutkin v. United States, 343 U.S. 130 (1952), in which the Court held an extortionist liable for tax on the amount extorted, but the *Rutkin* Court had expressly refused to overrule *Wilcox. James* was thought to have laid to rest the confusion and inconsistency created by the *Rutkin-Wilcox* distinction. Does the *Gilbert* decision revive the confusion and uncertainty to some degree?

3. *Dirty business?* Is it unseemly for the government, by taxing the proceeds of an embezzlement, to share in the profits of an illegal activity? This was the view expressed by Judge Martin T. Manton of the Second Circuit Court of Appeals in a concurring opinion in Steinberg v. United States, 14 F.2d 564, 569 (1926). Judge Manton also expressed his dismay over the thought of the government allowing deductions for bribes. In an O. Henry ending, Judge Manton was convicted in 1939 of accepting bribes of more than $66,000 over a three-year period when he was senior circuit judge of the Second Circuit and in 1948, after his death, was held liable for fraud penalties for failing to report the bribes on his tax returns. 7 T.C.M. 937.

4. *Borrowing versus swindling.* A taxpayer who purports to borrow funds, or to receive them as investments, may in fact be a swindler. The line between the two possibilities may in some instances be difficult to draw. See In re Diversified Brokers Co., 487 F.2d 355 (8th Cir. 1973) (receipts in "Ponzi" pyramiding scheme treated as loans to corporate borrower rather than as embezzled funds); Moore v. United States, 412 F.2d 974 (5th Cir. 1969) (money received in complex scheme involving purported purchase of equipment that did not exist held to be the fruits of a swindle, not a loan). Would it be best in situations of this sort to wait and see how a person uses the funds, instead of examining the circumstances of receipt?

5. *Nontax objectives.* The use of selective tax enforcement to punish political enemies is plainly intolerable. But what about selective enforcement against "known" crime figures who cannot be convicted of other crimes? Al Capone, the Chicago mob leader who was reportedly guilty of a host of serious crimes, was ultimately sent to jail for tax evasion. Is it wrong to use the tax system deliberately to punish people like Capone?

6. *Adding injury to injury.* As the *Gilbert* case illustrates, the taxes collected from an embezzler (or other wrongdoer) by the IRS generally will come from funds that otherwise would be returned (or paid) to the victim; generally the IRS's claim for taxes comes before the victim's claim for recovery of the stolen money.[76]

An interesting example of the IRS attitude toward victims of embezzlement is found in Letter Ruling 8604003. The embezzler, a bank employee, had disguised his defalcation by making false book entries showing wage payments (in amounts reaching a total of about $1 million). As part of his scheme he paid social security taxes (FICA) and

76. Under §6321 the United States has a lien for unpaid taxes after demand for the tax owed. The lien is against all the property of the taxpayer, which, in the case of an embezzler, will include the embezzled funds. This lien will take priority over any claim of the victim unless the victim is able to file a judgment lien (that is, obtain a judgment against the embezzler and then file a lien on the embezzled funds) before the IRS files its lien. See §6323. As a practical matter, the IRS will be able to file its lien before the victim will be able to file its lien.

withholding taxes. The bank, on discovering that it had been victimized, sought to recover the taxes. The IRS refused. It defended this result by arguments in the alternative. On the one hand, it reasoned, if the amounts were wages to the embezzler, the taxes were properly withheld. On the other hand, if the wage payments and the corresponding tax payments were unauthorized, then the bank did not make any payments, the embezzler did; so the bank is not entitled to a recovery on the theory of a mistaken payment. Moreover, the IRS is entitled to keep the money as long as the amount does not exceed what the embezzler owes. As far as the IRS is concerned, once money is stolen, that money belongs to the thief and the thief must pay his or her taxes before returning anything to the victim.

I. INTEREST ON STATE AND MUNICIPAL BONDS

1. Basic Concepts

Section 103 exempts from taxation the interest on certain state, municipal, and other such bonds. This exemption serves as a good model of some general tax principles.

One of the most important observations to be made about tax-exempt bonds is that the holders of such bonds pay what may be called a "putative" tax. Tax-exempt bonds pay a lower rate of interest than taxable bonds because people buying tax-exempts are willing to accept a lower rate in order to obtain the exemption. The relationship between the taxable and the tax-exempt rate varies from time to time, but the tax-exempt rate is always lower than the taxable rate. Suppose that the interest rate on taxable bonds is 10 percent and the rate on comparable tax-exempts is 8 percent. A taxpayer in the 20 percent marginal tax bracket should then be indifferent between taxable and tax-exempt alternatives. If such a person were to invest $100,000 in a taxable bond the annual interest earned would be $10,000 and the tax would be $2,000, leaving a net return after tax of $8,000, which is the same as the return on an investment of the same amount in a tax-exempt. The $2,000 of additional pretax interest that the investor forgoes by investing in the tax-exempt may be thought of as a putative tax. The federal government loses $2,000 of tax that it would have received if the investor had bought a taxable bond, but the state or local entity that issued the tax-exempt bond saves $2,000, the difference between the interest it pays ($8,000) and the interest it would have to pay if the interest were taxable to the recipient ($10,000). There is simply a shift from the federal to the state or local treasury. The investor receives no windfall; there is no violation of either horizontal or vertical equity. The putative tax is equal in amount to the actual tax that is avoided. One might object that if funds are in effect to be shifted from federal to state or local coffers, the federal government should be allowed to decide on the kinds of projects or activities on which the money is to be spent and on the total amount that is to be made available. But the lack of control from Washington is precisely the reason why some people like the exemption. And if controls are thought to be desirable, they can be imposed as a condition for qualifying bonds for exemption, as recent legislative development has amply demonstrated. See §§103(b), 141-150.

The picture changes, however, when purchasers have incomes such that their marginal rates are greater than the spread between the tax-exempt and the taxable rate (in our hypothetical 20 percent). For a person taxed at a marginal rate of 30 percent, if the taxable rate is 10 percent and the tax-exempt rate is 8 percent, then on an investment of $100,000, the after-tax return on the taxable investment will be $7,000 while the after-tax return on the tax-exempt investment will be $8,000. Such an investor pays a putative tax of $2,000 by buying a tax-exempt instead of an actual tax of $3,000 on a taxable investment and therefore saves $1,000 in taxes by buying the tax-exempt. The putative tax is at a rate of only 20 percent, while the nominal rate is 30 percent. The federal government loses $3,000, while the state or local government gains only $2,000. Since most individual investors are in fact in the higher brackets, many analysts argue that the exemption is an inefficient method of federal subsidy to state and local government and that it confers indefensible benefits on investors. As to the latter objection (windfalls to investors), however, one should add the qualification that horizontal equity among *investors* is not the issue, since tax-exempt investment is equally available to all high-bracket investors. One should be concerned only about the effects of the exemption on vertical equity and on horizontal equity between investors and people with incomes from salaries. Suppose, for example, that two taxpayers, Adele and Bernardo, both have inherited $1 million. Adele invests in U.S. Treasury bonds that pay 10 percent or $100,000 per year. She pays an income tax of $28,000 on this amount, and has no other income, so she is left with a spendable $72,000. Bernardo invests his $1 million in state general obligation bonds that pay 8 percent or $80,000, and he, too, has no other income. He pays no tax so his spendable amount is the full $80,000. If Adele were to complain about her treatment relative to that of Bernardo, it might be sufficient to respond that she is free to sell her Treasury bonds and buy state bonds. But now let's add another taxpayer, Carlos, who earns $100,000 in salary and has no investments. He pays tax at a rate of 28 percent, or $28,000, and is left with $72,000.

When he complains of his treatment relative to that of Bernardo, there is no easy answer.

These observations about the effects of the exemption of interest on state and municipal bonds are relevant to other tax-favored investments. Investors in certain kinds of real estate projects, in oil and gas drilling ventures, and in various other kinds of tax shelters generally have been forced to accept a lower before-tax rate of return than they could have earned in fully taxed investments (though the complexity of tax shelter investments makes clear-cut comparisons with taxable alternatives difficult). Such investors have paid a putative tax. Similarly, investors in the common stock of corporations that have paid little tax could expect to earn no greater return than investors in the common stock of corporations that have been heavily taxed. The lightly taxed corporations pay a putative tax. Generally, tax subsidies do not raise problems of horizontal equity, but they do raise problems of vertical equity and of efficiency.

2. Limitations on Exempt Status

Increasingly over the past two decades, state and local governments used their ability to borrow at low rates to finance projects having little or nothing to do with traditional governmental activities. The most important manifestation of this trend was the "industrial revenue bond" (IRB),[77] a bond whose proceeds were used to finance private investment, generally in an effort to lure industry to a community (in competition, often, with other communities offering the same financial incentive). The payment of interest and principal on such bonds is solely the responsibility of the user of the property bought or built with the proceeds; the local government unit that is the purported borrower is strictly an intermediary, with no financial risk. The use of IRBs is described in the following excerpt from testimony by Alice Rivlin, then Director of the Congressional Budget Office (Recent Trends in the Use of Tax-Exempt Bonds for Private Purposes, Hearings on the Administration's Fiscal Year 1983 Budget Proposal before the Senate Committee on Finance, 97th Cong., 2d Sess. pt. 3, at 65 (March 1, 1982)):

> Industrial revenue bonds (IRBs) are the primary mechanism for providing tax-exempt financing for private investment in plant and equipment. Since state and local governments issue these bonds, their interest income is exempt from federal taxation, making it possible for businesses to benefit from below-market interest rates. With IRBs, a government issuer transfers its tax-exempt status to a private borrower, and the federal

77. Also sometimes referred to as industrial development bonds (IDBs).

government gives up revenues to subsidize the borrowing costs of private industry. Generally, the only backing for the bonds is the credit of the borrowing firm or the revenue from the facility financed. If the borrower defaults, the bondholder bears the loss, so that, regardless of how many IRBs a state or local government issues, its credit rating is unaffected. Consequently, the normal motivation to limit the number of bond issues is lacking.

IRBs may be used to finance a wide variety of facilities without regard to issue size. These include pollution control equipment, airport and port facilities, sports facilities, convention or trade show facilities, and land for industrial parks. IRBs may also be used to finance plant and equipment for other unspecified private business purposes, but these issues may not exceed $10 million. These so-called "small issues," which are used to finance a wide variety of facilities from manufacturing plants, to doctors' offices, to country clubs, account for the largest share of all tax-exempt bonds floated for private purposes.

Small Issues

As of 1970, most states used small issue IRBs only for manufacturing and closely related facilities. By the mid-1970s, however, state and local officials, brokers, bankers, and businessmen realized that federal law made virtually any enterprise eligible for small issue IRB financing. One state legislature after another began to pass laws relaxing or entirely removing the restrictions that earlier had confined the use of the bonds. Today, 48 states use small issues, and more than half of these states put no restrictions on the use of the proceeds.

Small issues are particularly advantageous to large, geographically dispersed corporations, since the dollar limit on issue size applies not to the firm, but to facilities within an incorporated county or municipality. Large retail chains are probably in the best position to use IRBs because single stores usually can be financed well within the $10 million capital expenditure limit. Based on listings in Moody's Bond Record, the largest single user of small issue IRBs in the past five years was K-Mart, which financed some 100 stores with $240 million in tax-exempt bonds. Other large users during the same period were Hospital Corporation of America ($70 million), Kroger ($55 million), Weyerhauser Corporation ($52 million), and McDonald's Hamburgers ($43 million).

Between 1975 and 1980, small issue sales increased from $1.3 billion to $8.4 billion. Preliminary indications are that in 1981 small issue sales increased by 25 percent to $10.5 billion and represented nearly 19 percent of all new long-term tax-exempt bond issues.[78]

78. [The volume of tax-exempt bonds used to finance "private activities" (a category broader than, but including, IDBs) increased from $6.2 billion in 1976 to $44.0 billion in 1982, while the share of such bonds in total state and local borrowings rose from 21 percent in 1975 to 51.7 percent in 1982. House Report on the Tax Reform Act of 1986, H.R. Rep. No. 432, 98th Cong., 2d Sess. 1683 (1984). In 1988, the total of all state and local debt was $735 billion, while the total of all federal debt was $2,836 billion. Statistical Abstract of the United States, 1991, at 321. — Eds.]

As this description suggests, Congress had imposed limitations on the use of tax-exempt financing for private purposes. Substantial additional limitations were imposed in 1984 and 1986. These limitations are based on the purpose for which the proceeds are used and require specific provisions defining permissible purposes. The result is that the law, once simple, has become detailed and complex. See §§103, 141-150. Exemption continues to be available, without limit, for bonds whose proceeds are used for traditional governmental purposes such as financing schools, roads, and sewers. All other bonds are called "private-activity bonds" and are not exempt unless they fit within a specific exception. One major exception is for "exempt-facility bonds." These include bonds used to finance airports, docks and wharves, mass commuting facilities, water and sewage disposal facilities, qualified hazardous waste facilities, and certain electric and gas facilities. Other categories of private-activity bonds that qualify for exemption include qualified mortgage bonds (for financing home purchases by middle- and low-income people) and qualified veterans' mortgage bonds, qualified small-issue (not more than $1 million) bonds, and bonds used for certain charitable purposes. The income on certain private-activity bonds, though exempt from the regular tax, may be subject to the alternative minimum tax (see infra page 735).

In addition to the purpose-related limitations, there is an overall, or aggregate, dollar volume limit, or "cap," on most categories of newly issued private-activity bonds for which exemption is available. Beginning in 1988, the limit in each state is the greater of (1) $50 per resident or (2) $150 million. The states may allocate the total among their subdivisions and agencies. If they fail to do so, the allocation is made according to rules set forth in the Code (§146).

There are also rules designed to prevent "arbitrage" — that is to prevent a state or local government from borrowing at tax-exempt rates and investing in taxable obligations with the expectation of profiting on the spread in interest rates. §148. It is easier to describe the problem than to prescribe a solution. A state or local government, with no intention of engaging in arbitrage, may issue bonds for an exempt purpose and collect the proceeds before it is ready to spend those proceeds. In the interim the proceeds will, of course, be invested at the highest available rate. The question presented is at what point this process calls for the application of the arbitrage rules.

3. Constitutional Barrier?

In South Carolina v. Baker, 103 S. Ct. 1355 (1988), the Court upheld Code §103(j)(1) (added by the 1986 act) and thereby rejected the notion that there is a constitutional barrier to the imposition of a federal income tax on the interest earned on obligations issued by a state or one of its instrumentalities.

4. Tax Arbitrage

Tax-exempt bonds offer a good vehicle for describing a general tax strategy called "arbitrage" and to examine its effects. Suppose an individual taxpayer, *T*, has taxable income from a salary of $90,000 per year, pays tax at a marginal rate of 33 percent, and has no investments. *T* borrows $100,000 at 10 percent, or $10,000, per year, and uses the loan proceeds to buy tax-exempt bonds that pay 9 percent, or $9,000, per year. Suppose that the annual $10,000 interest payment is deductible (in fact, under §265(2), it is not). The transaction — the loan and the investment — would cost *T* $1,000 before taxes (the difference between the interest paid and the interest received), but the $10,000 deduction would reduce *T*'s taxes by $3,300, so *T* would be ahead by $2,300. The tax savings arise, of course, because *T*'s interest expense is deductible, while *T*'s interest income is tax-exempt.

The transaction described above would not have changed *T*'s net asset position. The $100,000 investment in the tax-exempt bond would be offset by the $100,000 loan liability, so net assets would still be zero. *T* could be thought of as having "bought" an asset (the borrowed funds) in one market (the taxable market) and as having "sold" a virtually identical asset (the funds loaned to the state or local government) in another market (the tax-exempt market) with the sole objective of taking advantage of the differing tax regimes in the two markets. Assuming that the loan and the investment are of the same duration, it is plain that the transaction would not have taken place but for its tax effects. That is tax arbitrage.

If permitted to do so, the states might also engage in purely tax-motivated transactions involving the interplay between taxable and tax-exempt obligations. For example, a state might issue its tax-exempt bonds at an interest rate of 9 percent and invest the proceeds in Treasury bonds paying 10 percent. This would be another form of tax arbitrage and, again, as we have just seen, is not permitted.

Now we are ready to consider some of the possible economic consequences of arbitrage. Suppose that arbitrage by issuers of state and local bonds is prohibited. There is a limited need for funds for the purposes for which tax-exempt bonds can be issued, so the supply of such bonds is limited. Now suppose we repeal §265(2) and allow a deduction for interest incurred on loans whose proceeds are used to purchase tax-exempt bonds. More people would now be able to buy such bonds. The demand would increase. The probable effect would be that investors would compete for the bonds by accepting lower and lower interest rates until only people in the highest marginal tax brackets would be willing to buy them and all the advantage of the tax exemption would be eliminated. In other words, the putative tax discussed above (page 275) would equal the actual tax that would be avoided and the effect of the exemption would be to reduce state and local borrowing costs by the full amount of the revenue lost by the U.S. Treasury. Some tax experts argue that this would be a good thing and that §265(2) should be repealed.

Suppose we retain the §265(2) restrictions on purchasers, but allow state and local governments to engage in arbitrage. Presumably they would issue more and more tax-exempt bonds and buy more and more U.S. Treasury (or other taxable) bonds. As they did so, the rate the states and local governments would be required to pay on the bonds they issued would rise and the rates paid on taxable bonds would fall until the two rates would be the same and all the advantage of arbitrage would be eliminated. Taxpayers could then buy tax-exempt bonds without paying any putative tax.

Suppose we allow both purchasers and issuers to engage in arbitrage. The arbitrage of purchasers would tend to increase demand and price; the arbitrage of issuers would tend to increase supply and decrease price. The final outcome, or equilibrium position, would be difficult to predict, but fortunately we need not worry about that. What is important, for people who want to understand the workings of the tax system, is a general understanding of the process of arbitrage.

One final point: The proposition that state and local governments should be allowed to engage in arbitrage may seem so dangerous and so inconsistent with the purposes of exemption as to be unthinkable, and it probably is. But thinking the unthinkable may cast light on underlying principles. Consider two hypothetical states, *A* and *B*. *A* relies heavily on borrowing and by virtue of doing so in effect receives a large subsidy from the U.S. Treasury in the form of reduced interest costs attributable to the exemption from federal income taxation of the interest it pays on its obligations. *B* does not borrow at all. Its citizens, believing that borrowing is unfair to future generations, are proud of their pay-as-you-go tradition. *B* receives no benefits from the U.S. Treasury comparable to *A*'s interest-rate subsidy. If we were prepared to allow arbitrage (with, perhaps, a dollar limit on total debt), we could allow *B* to obtain the same subsidy that *A* receives — a possibility that seems to have some appeal to a sense of fairness and that recognizes the importance of allowing states to adopt the fiscal policies they prefer without unwarranted interference from the federal government. But if we were prepared to allow *B* to obtain a subsidy by engaging in arbitrage, would it not be more effective for the federal government simply to write out a check and save all the transactions costs? If so, what are the implications for the treatment of *A*?

5. U.S. Treasury Bonds

Section 135, added by the 1988 act, exempts from taxation the interest on certain U.S. Treasury savings bonds if the proceeds of the redemption of the bonds do not exceed tuition and fees for higher education for the taxpayer and her or his spouse or dependents. The exclusion is phased out as income rises above $40,000 ($60,000 for a joint return), with the phaseout levels to be adjusted for inflation. There is no tracing of funds, so even if other funds are in fact used to pay the education expenses, the exemption is available. One may wonder why education is singled out, as compared, for example, with medical expenses or the down payment on a house.

3

PROBLEMS OF TIMING

A. GAINS AND LOSSES FROM INVESTMENT IN PROPERTY

1. Origins

We have already examined briefly the concepts of realization and recognition. See supra page 56. Here we explore the problems arising in connection with those concepts, problems that reflect a conflict between the goals of fairness and economic rationality on the one hand and practicality on the other.

Taxpayer *A* buys for $10,000 land that rises in value by $1,000 during the year. The land is not sold, so the gain is not realized and is not taxed. Taxpayer *B* buys for $10,000 similar land that also rises in value; he sells for a profit of $1,000. The profit is taxable, even if *B* reinvests the $1,000, along with the $10,000, in other land. Taxpayer *C* receives a salary of $1,000, which he invests, along with $10,000 previously saved, in land. The $1,000 salary is taxable. Fairness and economic rationality argue for taxing as earned (in an accrual accounting sense) the $1,000 gain of each of these three taxpayers. Practicality, however, is generally thought to argue for nontaxation of *A*'s gain, largely because that gain may be difficult to measure and because *A* may not have easy access to cash with which to pay a tax.

Our first case, Eisner v. Macomber, is famous for its now-disparaged definition of income. See supra page 75. The case is also important, however, for its enthusiastic adoption of the requirement, as a condition for taxing gain, that the gain be "realized" — that is, that there be something more than a mere increase in value. The Court holds, in fact, that the realization requirement is embedded in the sixteenth amendment. This use of the Constitution to constrain congressional action in shaping a tax code is not consonant with modern theories of the proper role of the judiciary and the Constitution in regulating matters of economic policy. The present-day Court would no doubt decide the case differently. Still, study of the case is important not only because of its contribution to the concept of income, and as a part of the history of taxation and of attitudes toward taxation in this country, but also because of the insights it offers into problems of realization and recognition.

EISNER v. MACOMBER

252 U.S. 189 (1920)

Mr. Justice PITNEY delivered the opinion of the court.

This case presents the question whether, by virtue of the Sixteenth Amendment, Congress has the power to tax, as income of the stockholder and without apportionment, a stock dividend made lawfully and in good faith against profits accumulated by the corporation since March 1, 1913.

It arises under the Revenue Act of September 8, 1916, c.463, 39 Stat. 756, et seq., which, in our opinion . . . plainly evinces the purpose of Congress to tax stock dividends as income.[1]

[In 1916, the taxpayer, Mrs. Myrtle H. Macomber, owned 2,200 shares of the common stock of Standard Oil Company of California. Each of her shares had a "par value" of $100 per share. In the era in which this case arose, par value was a significant financial and accounting concept; generally, it reflected the amount initially paid to the company for each share, or at least a minimum amount that could be paid; in the aggregate, the amounts paid as par value were labeled, on the company's books, "capital" or "capital stock," with any excess paid, over par value, called "capital surplus" or "paid in surplus" or something of the sort. The company over the years had earned profits substantially in excess of the amounts paid out as dividends on the common stock. Such retained earnings are recorded on the books of a company under a heading such as "earned surplus." By strict accounting convention,

1. TITLE I. INCOME TAX *Part I. On Individuals.* Sec. 2(a) That, subject only to such exemptions and deductions as are hereinafter allowed, the net income of a taxable person shall include gains, profits, and income derived . . . , also from interest, rent, dividends, securities, or the transaction of any business carried on for gain or profit, or gains or profits and income derived from any source whatever: *Provided,* That the term "dividends" as used in this title shall be held to mean any distribution made or ordered to be made by a corporation, . . . out of its earnings or profits accrued since March first, nineteen hundred and thirteen, and payable to its shareholders, whether in cash or in stock of the corporation, . . . which stock dividend shall be considered income, to the amount of its cash value.

the company must show on its books assets corresponding in value to the par value plus the earned surplus (though this book value might be different from market value). Generally, dividends can be paid only to the extent of the earned surplus. In 1916, the company declared a 50 percent stock dividend. This meant that the company issued to each and every existing shareholder one new share for each two old shares, without cost to the shareholders. Accordingly, Mrs. Macomber received 1,100 new shares to add to her 2,200 original shares. The issuance of the new shares required a bookkeeping adjustment by the company: For each new share issued, the par value of that share, $100, was transferred from the earned surplus account to the par value, or capital, account. That amount of earned surplus (undistributed profits) was then said to have been "capitalized." In some instances such an adjustment might improve the credit-worthiness of the company by limiting its freedom to pay dividends, though lenders of large sums can bargain for contractual limitations on dividend payments. Otherwise, the adjustment is purely a matter of changing bookkeeping labels. It has no effect whatsoever on underlying economic values or on operations.

According to the record in the case (at pages 4-5), the market value of Mrs. Macomber's shares before the stock dividend was $360 to $382 per share and after the stock dividend was $234 to $268 per share. In other words, the price of each share fell by about 30 to 35 percent, so that Mrs. Macomber's wealth was not significantly altered by the stock dividend. This is what one would expect, since the total value of the company, and her pro rata share of that total value, both remained the same. (Modern studies confirm the hypothesis that stock dividends do not increase wealth.)

The government sought to impose a tax on Mrs. Macomber based on the par value of the new shares, rather than the market value. However, of the amounts transferred by the company from earned surplus to capital, only 18.07 percent had arisen after the imposition of an income tax in 1913, and it was only this portion of the total that the government claimed to be taxable. Accordingly, the amount the government included in income was 18.07 percent of $100 multiplied by 1,100 shares, or $19,877.]

[In Towne v. Eisner, 245 U.S. 418,] we rejected the reasoning of the District Court, saying (245 U.S. 426):

> Notwithstanding the thoughtful discussion that the case received below we cannot doubt that the dividend was capital as well for the purposes of the Income Tax Law as for distribution between tenant for life and remainderman. What was said by this court upon the latter question is equally true for the former. "A stock dividend really takes nothing from the property of the corporation, and adds nothing to the interests of the shareholders. Its property is not diminished, and their interests are not

> increased. . . . The proportional interest of each shareholder remains the same. The only change is in the evidence which represents that interest, the new shares and the original shares together representing the same proportional interest that the original shares represented before the issue of the new ones." Gibbons v. Mahon, 136 U.S. 549, 559, 560. In short, the corporation is no poorer and the stockholder is no richer than they were before. . . .

. . . We ruled at the same term, in Lynch v. Hornby, 247 U.S. 339, that a cash dividend extraordinary in amount, and in Peabody v. Eisner, 247 U.S. 347, that a dividend paid in stock of another company, were taxable as income although based upon earnings that accrued before adoption of the Amendment. In the former case, concerning "corporate profits that accumulated before the Act took effect," we declared (pp. 343-344):

> Just as we deem the legislative intent manifest to tax the stockholder with respect to such accumulations only if and when, and to the extent that, his interest in them comes to fruition as income, that is, in dividends declared, so we can perceive no constitutional obstacle that stands in the way of carrying out this intent when dividends are declared out of a preexisting surplus. . . . Congress was at liberty under the Amendment to tax as income, without apportionment, everything that became income, in the ordinary sense of the word, after the adoption of the Amendment, including dividends received in the ordinary course by a stockholder from a corporation, even though they were extraordinary in amount and might appear upon analysis to be a mere realization in possession of an inchoate and contingent interest that the stockholder had in a surplus of corporate assets previously existing. . . .

The Sixteenth Amendment must be construed in connection with the taxing clauses of the original Constitution and the effect attributed to them before the Amendment was adopted. In Pollock v. Farmers' Loan & Trust Co., 158 U.S. 601, under the Act of August 27, 1894, c.349, §27, 28 Stat. 509, 553, it was held that taxes upon rents and profits of real estate and upon returns from investments of personal property were in effect direct taxes upon the property from which such income arose, imposed by reason of ownership; and that Congress could not impose such taxes without apportioning them among the States according to population, as required by Art. I, §2, cl. 3, and §9, cl. 4, of the original Constitution.

Afterwards, and evidently in recognition of the limitation upon the taxing power of Congress thus determined, the Sixteenth Amendment was adopted, in words lucidly expressing the object to be accomplished:

> The Congress shall have power to lay and collect taxes on incomes, from whatever source derived without apportionment among the several States, and without regard to any census or enumeration.

As repeatedly held, this did not extend the taxing power to new subjects, but merely removed the necessity which otherwise might exist for an apportionment among the States of taxes laid on income. . . .

A proper regard for its genesis, as well as its very clear language, requires also that this Amendment shall not be extended by loose construction, so as to repeal or modify, except as applied to income, those provisions of the Constitution that require an apportionment according to population for direct taxes upon property, real and personal. This limitation still has an appropriate and important function, and is not to be overridden by Congress or disregarded by the courts.

In order, therefore, that the clauses cited from Article I of the Constitution may have proper force and effect, save only as modified by the Amendment, and that the latter also may have proper effect, it becomes essential to distinguish between what is and what is not "income," as the term is there used; and to apply the distinction, as cases arise, according to truth and substance, without regard to form. Congress cannot by any definition it may adopt conclude the matter, since it cannot by legislation alter the Constitution, from which alone it derives its power to legislate, and within whose limitations alone that power can be lawfully exercised.

The fundamental relation of "capital" to "income" has been much discussed by economists, the former being likened to the tree or the land, the latter to the fruit or the crop; the former depicted as a reservoir supplied from springs, the latter as the outlet stream, to be measured by its flow during a period of time. For the present purpose we require only a clear definition of the term "income," as used in common speech, in order to determine its meaning in the Amendment; and, having formed also a correct judgment as to the nature of a stock dividend, we shall find it easy to decide the matter at issue.

After examining dictionaries in common use (Bouv. L.D.; Standard Dict.; Webster's Internat. Dict.; Century Dict.), we find little to add to the succinct definition adopted in two cases arising under the Corporation Tax Act of 1909 (Stratton's Independence v. Howbert, 231 U.S. 399, 415; Doyle v. Mitchell Bros. Co., 247 U.S. 179, 185) — "income may be defined as the gain derived from capital, from labor, or from both combined," provided it be understood to include profit gained through a sale or conversion of capital assets, to which it was applied in the *Doyle* case (pp. 183, 185).

Brief as it is, it indicates the characteristic and distinguishing attribute of income essential for a correct solution of the present controversy. The Government, although basing its argument upon the definition as quoted, placed chief emphasis upon the word "gain," which was extended to include a variety of meanings; while the significance of the next three words was either overlooked or misconceived. "*Derived — from — capital*"; — "the *gain — derived — from — capital,*" etc. Here we have the essential matter: *not* a gain *accruing to* capital, not a *growth* or *increment* of value in the investment; but a gain, a profit, something of exchangeable value *proceeding from* the property, *severed from* the capital however invested or employed, and *coming in,* being "*derived,*" that is, *received or drawn by* the recipient (the taxpayer) for his *separate* use, benefit and disposal; — *that is* income derived from property. Nothing else answers the description.

The same fundamental conception is clearly set forth in the Sixteenth Amendment — "incomes *from* whatever *source derived*" — the essential thought being expressed with a conciseness and lucidity entirely in harmony with the form and style of the Constitution.

Can a stock dividend, considering its essential character, be brought within the definition? To answer this, regard must be had to the nature of a corporation and the stockholder's relation to it. We refer, of course, to a corporation such as the one in the case at bar, organized for profit, and having a capital stock divided into shares to which a nominal or par value is attributed.

Certainly the interest of the stockholder is a capital interest, and his certificates of stock are but the evidence of it. They state the number of shares to which he is entitled and indicate their par value and how the stock may be transferred. . . . Short of liquidation, or until dividend declared, he has no right to withdraw any part of either capital or profits from the common enterprise; on the contrary, his interest pertains not to any part, divisible or indivisible, but to the entire assets, business, and affairs of the company. Nor is it the interest of an owner in the assets themselves, since the corporation has full title, legal and equitable, to the whole. The stockholder has the right to have the assets employed in the enterprise, with the incidental rights mentioned; but, as stockholder, he has no right to withdraw, only the right to persist, subject to the risks of the enterprise, and looking only to dividends for his return. If he desires to dissociate himself from the company he can do so only by disposing of his stock.

For bookkeeping purposes, the company acknowledges a liability in form to the stockholders equivalent to the aggregate par value of their stock, evidenced by a "capital stock account." If profits have been made and not divided they create additional bookkeeping liabilities under the head of "profit and loss," "undivided profits," "surplus account," or the like. None of these, however, gives to the stockholders as a body, much less to any one of them, either a claim against the going concern for any particular sum of money, or a right to any particular portion of the assets or any share in them unless or until the directors conclude that dividends shall be made and a part of the company's assets segregated from the common fund for the purpose. The dividend normally is payable in money, under exceptional circumstances in some other divisible property; and when so paid, then only (excluding, of course, a possible advantageous sale of his stock or winding-up of the company) does the stockholder realize a profit or gain which becomes his separate property, and thus derive income from the capital that he or his predecessor has invested.

In the present case, the corporation had surplus and undivided profits invested in plant, property, and business, and required for the purposes of the corporation, amounting to about $45,000,000, in addition to outstanding capital stock of $50,000,000. In this the case is not extraordinary. The profits of a corporation, as they appear upon the balance sheet at the end of the year, need not be in the form of money on hand in excess of what is required to meet current liabilities and finance current operations of the company. Often, especially in a growing business, only a part, sometimes a small part, of the year's profits is in property capable of division; the remainder having been absorbed in the acquisition of increased plant, equipment, stock in trade, or accounts receivable, or in decrease of outstanding liabilities. . . .

A "stock dividend" shows that the company's accumulated profits have been capitalized, instead of distributed to the stockholders or retained as surplus available for distribution in money or in kind should opportunity offer. Far from being a realization of profits of the stockholder, it tends rather to postpone such realization, in that the fund represented by the new stock has been transferred from surplus to capital, and no longer is available for actual distribution.

The essential and controlling fact is that the stockholder has received nothing out of the company's assets for his separate use and benefit; on the contrary, every dollar of his original investment, together with whatever accretions and accumulations have resulted from employment of his money and that of the other stockholders in the business of the company, still remains the property of the company, and subject to business risks which may result in wiping out the entire investment. Having regard to the very truth of the matter, to substance and not to form, he has received nothing that answers the definition of income within the meaning of the Sixteenth Amendment. . . .

We are clear that not only does a stock dividend really take nothing from the property of the corporation and add nothing to that of the shareholder, but that the antecedent accumulation of profits evidenced thereby, while indicating that the shareholder is the richer because of an increase of his capital, at the same time shows he has not realized or received any income in the transaction.

It is said that a stockholder may sell the new shares acquired in the stock dividend; and so he may, if he can find a buyer. It is equally true that if he does sell, and in doing so realizes a profit, such profit, like any other, is income, and so far as it may have arisen since the Sixteenth Amendment is taxable by Congress without apportionment. The same would be true were he to sell some of his original shares at a profit. But if a shareholder sells dividend stock he necessarily disposes of a part of his capital interest, just as if he should sell a part of his old stock, either before or after the dividend. What he retains no longer entitles him to the same proportion of future dividends as before the sale. His part in the control of the company likewise is diminished. Thus, if one holding $60,000 out of a total $100,000 of the capital stock of a corporation should receive in common with other stockholders a 50 per cent stock dividend, and should sell his part, he thereby would be reduced from a majority to a minority stockholder, having six-fifteenths instead of six-tenths of the total stock outstanding. A corresponding and proportionate decrease in capital interest and in voting power would befall a minority holder should he sell dividend stock; it being in the nature of things impossible for one to dispose of any part of such an issue without a proportionate disturbance of the distribution of the entire capital stock, and a like diminution of the seller's comparative voting power — that "right preservative of rights" in the control of a corporation. Yet, without selling, the shareholder, unless possessed of other resources, has not the wherewithal to pay an income tax upon the dividend stock. Nothing could more clearly show that to tax a stock dividend is to tax a capital increase, and not income, than this demonstration that in the nature of things it requires conversion of capital in order to pay the tax. . . .

We have no doubt of the power or duty of a court to look through the form of the corporation and determine the question of the stockholder's right, in order to ascertain whether he has received income taxable by Congress without apportionment. But, looking through the form, we cannot disregard the essential truth disclosed; ignore the substantial difference between corporation and stockholder; treat the entire organization as unreal; look upon stockholders as partners, when they are not such; treat them as having in equity a right to a partition of the corporate assets, when they have none; and indulge the fiction that they have received and realized a share of the profits of the company which in truth they have neither received nor realized. We must treat the corporation as a substantial entity separate from the stockholder, not only because such is the practical fact but because it is only by recognizing such separateness that any dividend — even one paid in money or property — can be regarded as income of the stockholder. Did we regard corporation and stockholders as altogether identical, there would be no income except as the corporation acquired it; and while this would be taxable against the corporation as income under appropriate provisions of law, the individual stockholders could not be separately and additionally taxed with respect to their several shares even when divided, since if there were entire identity between them and the company they could not be regarded as receiving anything from it, any more than if one's money were to be removed from one pocket to another.

Conceding that the mere issue of a stock dividend makes the recipient no richer than before, the Government nevertheless contends that the new certificates measure the extent to which the gains accumulated by the corporation have made him the richer. There are two insuperable difficulties with this: In the first place, it would depend upon how long he had held the stock whether the stock dividend indicated the extent to which he had been enriched by the operations of the company; unless he had held it throughout such operations the measure would not hold true. Secondly, and more important for present purposes, enrichment through increase in value of capital investment is not income in any proper meaning of the term.

The complaint contains averments respecting the market prices of stock such as plaintiff held, based upon sales before and after the stock dividend, tending to show that the receipt of the additional shares did not substantially change the market value of her entire holdings. This tends to show that in this instance market quotations reflected intrinsic values — a thing they do not always do. But we regard the market prices of the securities as an unsafe criterion in an inquiry such as the present, when the question must be, not what will the thing sell for, but what is it in truth and in essence.

It is said there is no difference in principle between a simple stock dividend and a case where stockholders use money received as cash dividends to purchase additional stock contemporaneously issued by the corporation. But an actual cash dividend, with a real option to the stockholder either to keep the money for his own or to reinvest it in new shares, would be as far removed as possible from a true stock dividend, such as the one we have under consideration, where nothing of value is taken from the company's assets and transferred to the individual ownership of the several stockholders and thereby subjected to their disposal.

Upon the second argument,[2] the Government, recognizing the force of the decision in Towne v. Eisner, supra, and virtually abandoning the contention that a stock dividend increases the interest of the stockholder or otherwise enriches him, insisted as an alternative that by the true construction of the Act of 1916 the tax is imposed not upon the stock dividend but rather upon the stockholder's share of the undivided profits previously accumulated by the corporation; the tax being levied as a matter of convenience at the time such profits become manifest

2. [Eisner v. Macomber was argued in 1919 and reargued by order of the Court in 1920. — Eds.]

through the stock dividend. If so construed, would the act be constitutional?

That Congress has power to tax shareholders upon their property interests in the stock of corporations is beyond question; and that such interest might be valued in view of the condition of the company, including its accumulated and undivided profits, is equally clear. But that this would be taxation of property because of ownership, and hence would require apportionment under the provisions of the Constitution, is settled beyond peradventure by previous decisions of this court.

The Government relies upon Collector v. Hubbard (1870), 12 Wall. 1, 17, which arose under §117 of the Act of June 30, 1864, c.173, 13 Stat. 223, 282, providing that "the gains and profits of all companies, whether incorporated or partnership, other than the companies specified in this section, shall be included in estimating the annual gains, profits, or income of any person entitled to the same, whether divided or otherwise."

The court held an individual taxable upon his proportion of the earnings of a corporation although not declared as dividends and although invested in assets not in their nature divisible. Conceding that the stockholder for certain purposes had no title prior to dividend declared, the court nevertheless said (p.18):

> Grant all that, still it is true that the owner of a share in a corporation holds the share with all its incidents, and that among those incidents is the right to receive all future dividends, that is, his proportional share of all profits not then divided. Profits are incident to the share to which the owner at once becomes entitled provided he remains a member of the corporation until a dividend is made. Regarded as an incident to the shares, undivided profits are property of the shareholder, and as such are the proper subject of sale, gift, or devise. Undivided profits invested in real estate, machinery, or raw material for the purpose of being manufactured are investments in which the stockholders are interested, and when such profits are actually appropriated to the payment of the debts of the corporation they serve to increase the market value of the shares, whether held by the original subscribers or by assignees.

In so far as this seems to uphold the right of Congress to tax without apportionment a stockholder's interest in accumulated earnings prior to dividend declared, it must be regarded as overruled by Pollock v. Farmers' Loan & Trust Co., 158 U.S. 601, 627, 628, 637. Conceding Collector v. Hubbard was inconsistent with the doctrine of that case, because it sustained a direct tax upon property not apportioned among the States, the Government nevertheless insists that the Sixteenth Amendment removed this obstacle, so that now the *Hubbard Case* is authority for the power of Congress to levy a tax on the stockholder's share in the accumulated profits of the corporation even before division by the declaration of a dividend of any kind. Manifestly this argument must be rejected, since the Amendment applies to income only, and what is called the stockholder's share in the accumulated profits of the company is capital, not income. As we have pointed out, a stockholder has no individual share in accumulated profits, nor in any particular part of the assets of the corporation, prior to dividend declared.

Thus, from every point of view, we are brought irresistibly to the conclusion that neither under the Sixteenth Amendment nor otherwise has Congress power to tax without apportionment a true stock dividend made lawfully and in good faith, or the accumulated profits behind it, as income of the stockholder. The Revenue Act of 1916, in so far as it imposes a tax upon the stockholder because of such dividend, contravenes the provisions of Article I, §2, cl. 3, and Article I, §9, cl. 4, of the Constitution, and to this extent is invalid notwithstanding the Sixteenth Amendment.

Judgment affirmed.

Mr. Justice HOLMES, dissenting. . . .

I think that the word "incomes" in the Sixteenth Amendment should be read in "a sense most obvious to the common understanding at the time of its adoption." . . . For it was for public adoption that it was proposed. McCulloch v. Maryland, 4 Wheat. 316, 407. The known purpose of this Amendment was to get rid of nice questions as to what might be direct taxes, and I cannot doubt that most people not lawyers would suppose when they voted for it that they put a question like the present to rest. I am of opinion that the Amendment justifies the tax. . . .

Mr. Justice DAY concurs in this opinion.

Mr. Justice BRANDEIS, dissenting, delivered the following opinion, in which Mr. Justice CLARKE concurred.

Financiers, with the aid of lawyers, devised long ago two different methods by which a corporation can, without increasing its indebtedness, keep for corporate purposes accumulated profits, and yet, in effect, distribute these profits among its stockholders. One method is a simple one. The capital stock is increased; the new stock is paid up with the accumulated profits; and the new shares of paid-up stock are then distributed among the stockholders pro rata as a dividend. If the stockholder prefers ready money to increasing his holding of the stock in the company, he sells the new stock received as a dividend. The other method is slightly more complicated. Arrangements are made for an increase of stock to be offered to stockholders pro rata at par and, at the same time, for the payment of a cash dividend equal to the amount which the stockholder will be required to pay to the company, if he avails himself of the right to subscribe for his pro rata of the new stock.

If the stockholder takes the new stock, as is expected, he may endorse the dividend check received to the corporation and thus pay for the new stock. In order to ensure that all the new stock so offered will be taken, the price at which it is offered is fixed far below what it is believed will be its market value. If the stockholder prefers ready money to an increase of his holdings of stock, he may sell his right to take new stock pro rata, which is evidenced by an assignable instrument. In that event the purchaser of the rights repays to the corporation, as the subscription price of the new stock, an amount equal to that which it had paid as a cash dividend to the stockholder.

Both of these methods of retaining accumulated profits while in effect distributing them as a dividend had been in common use in the United States for many years prior to the adoption of the Sixteenth Amendment. They were recognized equivalents. Whether a particular corporation employed one or the other method was determined sometimes by requirements of the law under which the corporation was organized; sometimes it was determined by preferences of the individual officials of the corporation; and sometimes by stock market conditions. Whichever method was employed the resultant distribution of the new stock was commonly referred to as a stock dividend. . . .

It is conceded that if the stock dividend paid to Mrs. Macomber had been made by the more complicated method . . . , that is, issuing rights to take new stock pro rata and paying to each stockholder simultaneously a dividend in cash sufficient in amount to enable him to pay for this pro rata of new stock to be purchased — the dividend so paid to him would have been taxable as income, whether he retained the cash or whether he returned it to the corporation in payment for his pro rata of new stock. But it is contended that, because the simple method was adopted of having the new stock issued direct to the stockholders as paid-up stock, the new stock is not to be deemed income, whether she retained it or converted it into cash by sale. If such a different result can flow merely from the difference in the method pursued, it must be because Congress is without power to tax as income of the stockholder either the stock received under the latter method or the proceeds of its sale; for Congress has, by the provisions in the Revenue Act of 1916, expressly declared its purpose to make stock dividends, by whichever method paid, taxable as income. . . .

It surely is not clear that the enactment exceeds the power granted by the Sixteenth Amendment. And, as this court has so often said, the high prerogative of declaring an act of Congress invalid, should never be exercised except in a clear case. "It is but a decent respect due to the wisdom, the integrity and the patriotism of the legislative body, by which any law is passed, to presume in favor of its validity, until its violation of the Constitution is proved beyond all reasonable doubt." Ogden v. Saunders, 12 Wheat. 213, 270.

Mr. Justice CLARKE concurs in this opinion.

NOTES AND QUESTIONS

1. *Introduction.* The government sought to justify the taxation of Mrs. Macomber's stock dividend on at least three related grounds. First, the government argued that the distribution of the stock dividend increased Mrs. Macomber's wealth. Second, the government argued that the company's accumulation of profits increased Mrs. Macomber's wealth and that part of that increase was realized through the distribution of the stock dividend. Finally, the government argued that the company's accumulation of profits increased Mrs. Macomber's wealth and that the increase in wealth could be taxed at any time. Broadly construed, the last argument would allow an annual tax on all property appreciation, whether or not such appreciation had been realized in the form of a sale or a cash distribution.

Most of the Court's opinion deals with the first two arguments, which are explored in Notes 2 and 3. The larger question raised by the case — the possibility of an annual tax on unrealized appreciation — is discussed in Note 4.

2. *Analysis of stock dividends.* (a) If the government had prevailed in Eisner v. Macomber, what effect do you suppose the decision would have had on the policies of corporations on the issuance of stock dividends? What do you suppose Justice Brandeis, who, in his days as a practitioner, had been an expert on matters of this sort, would have advised his corporate clients? If he had been asked how to advise Congress on the advisability of taxing stock dividends, what do you suppose he would have said?

(b) One reason often given for issuing stock dividends is to reduce the price of the shares to facilitate trading. For example, if the value of one share rose to $10,000, many people who wished to invest a lesser amount would be precluded from doing so. Can you think of any devices by which this problem might be solved, other than issuing stock dividends? Another reason sometimes given for issuing stock dividends is to provide shareholders with tangible evidence of the success of the corporation. Wouldn't a piece of parchment entitled "declaration of success," with a gold seal and a blue ribbon, do just as well?

(c) The Court refers to the fact that if Mrs. Macomber had sold her dividend shares she would have reduced her fractional voting power (control) in the company. How important do you suppose this would have been to her?

3. *Dipping into capital.* (a) In the era in which this case arose, many people thought (some still do) that it was highly imprudent, and even immoral, to "dip into capital." A decent person was supposed to live on income and preserve or enhance capital. But what is capital? Suppose that Mrs. Macomber had been held taxable and had been forced to sell some of her shares to pay the tax. Would that have impaired her capital? What if the dividend had been in cash? Imagine a prudent investor, *P*,

who a year ago bought 100 shares of common stock, at $10 per share, in each of three corporations, *X*, *Y*, and *Z*. Each corporation earns $1 per share. Corporation *X* retains its earnings, and the value of *P*'s shares rises to $11 each, or a total of $1,100. Corporation *Y* also retains all its earnings, but it issues a 10 percent stock dividend, so *P* winds up with 110 shares worth $10 each, or a total of $1,100. Corporation *Z* pays a cash dividend of $100 and issues no stock dividend, so *P* winds up with shares worth $1,000 and cash of $100, or a total of $1,100. The facts are summarized in Table 3-1.

TABLE 3-1

	X	*Y*	*Z*
Cost	$1,000	$1,000	$1,000
Amount earned	100	100	100
New value	1,100	1,100	1,100
Dividend:			
Cash	-0-	-0-	100
Stock (value)	-0-	100	-0-
Value of shares after dividend	1,100	1,100	1,000
Cash in hand	-0-	-0-	100
Total wealth	$1,100	$1,100	$1,100

How much is *P* entitled to spend if she wants to avoid impairing her capital but is willing to sell shares? What would Justices Pitney and Brandeis have said? Would your answers be different if the shares had risen in value not because of current earnings but because of (i) a discovery of an extremely promising oil field or (ii) a rise in the value of stocks in general due to improvement in the economy?

(b) Suppose that Mrs. Macomber's shares had been worth $300 each and that the company had paid a cash dividend of $100, after which the shares were worth $200 each. Would the $100 distribution be taxable, assuming that the company had an earned surplus in excess of that amount? See §§61(a)(7) and 316(a). Is this fair? Would it matter whether she had bought the shares the day before the declaration of the dividend?

4. *Policy: taxing unrealized appreciation.* (a) What are the objections to taxing shareholders on amounts earned by the corporation, regardless of distribution? This is how partners are taxed. In a partnership, the decision whether to distribute profits is one that is made by a majority of the partners, but in the absence of an agreement to the contrary, any partner can withdraw from the partnership (and be paid his or her pro rata share of the value of the partnership) at any time. Should this freedom to withdraw matter? If so, what if the partnership agreement makes withdrawal very costly? If the law were to provide for

taxation of shareholders on corporate profits regardless of distribution of dividends, how do you suppose corporations would adjust?

(b) Another possibility would be to tax people like Mrs. Macomber on their "paper" profits — that is, on the unrealized appreciation in the market value of their shares of stock — with a corresponding deduction for unrealized losses. The principal objections to taxing unrealized gains have been (i) the potential difficulties of valuation and (ii) the fact that the taxpayer might have difficulty raising the cash to pay the tax. How forceful are these objections as applied to Mrs. Macomber and people like her? Would it have been difficult to value the appreciation in her holdings? Do you think she would have found it difficult to obtain the cash to pay the tax?

(c) The principle that unrealized appreciation should not be taxed is no longer thought to be embedded in the Constitution, but it is thoroughly embedded in present tax rules. Those rules, which will be examined in the remainder of this chapter, create serious problems of tax fairness, or equity, of economic incentive, and of administration. The problem of horizontal equity is illustrated by comparison of a person whose wealth increases by $100,000 from receipt of a salary, and who must pay a tax on that amount, with a person whose wealth increases by the same amount through a rise in the value of her property holdings and who pays no tax on that increase. The discrepancy in tax treatment is particularly disturbing where the property can easily be sold or can serve as collateral for a loan. Nontaxation of appreciation may also distort investment decisions. At the margin, taxpayers will prefer investments that produce gain in the form of unrealized appreciation. Finally, the current regime raises serious definitional issues: At what point has appreciation been realized? As you read the cases in this chapter you may find it useful to think about how a regime that taxed unrealized appreciation might simplify the law.

5. *The present law.* The rule of Eisner v. Macomber is now embodied in §305(a), with limitations in §305(b). The most easily understood limitation is that a stock dividend is taxable if the shareholder had the option to take cash or other property in lieu of that dividend. §305(b)(1). Other rules in §305(b) cover situations in which the distribution results in some change in the nature of the shareholder's initial investment or proportional interest.

6. *Basis and holding period.* Under Regs. §1.307-1(a), the taxpayer's total basis of the old shares is allocated between the old and the new shares in accordance with relative fair market values after the distribution of the stock dividend. In a case like *Macomber* (where the new shares were identical to the old shares), this means simply that the total basis is allocated equally to all shares, so each share, old and new, winds up with the same basis. The holding period is important in distinguishing between long-term and short-term capital gains. See infra page

832. The rule, under §1223(5), is that the new shares will be deemed to have been acquired at the time when the old shares were acquired.

7. *Statutory provisions ignoring the decision.* Despite the assertion in the penultimate paragraph of the majority opinion of Eisner v. Macomber that "what is called the stockholder's share in the accumulated profits of the company is capital, not income," Congress requires the U.S. shareholders of foreign personal holding companies and of certain other foreign corporations to report their proportionate share of corporate income even though it is accumulated by the corporation rather than distributed to them. The relevant provisions are §551 (foreign personal holding companies) and §951 (controlled foreign corporations). For an extensive discussion of the constitutional validity of requiring shareholders to report their shares of undistributed corporate income, see Whitlock's Estate v. Commissioner, 59 T.C. 490, 506 et seq. (1972) (upholding constitutionality of §951), 494 F.2d 1297 (10th Cir. 1974) (aff'g on this issue). Under §1366, the undistributed income of so-called S corporations is also taxed directly to the shareholders, but this result is elective rather than compulsory. And under §1256, certain taxpayers are required to "mark to market" (that is, "treat as sold for . . . fair market value") at the end of the year various publicly traded options.

Also of relevance are §83 (taxing the gain on property previously transferred for services, on the occurrence of events such as the lapse or cancellation of certain restrictions) and §84 (treating the donation of appreciated property to a political organization as a sale by the contributor on the date of transfer). See also Regs. §1.471-4 (elective valuation of inventories at cost or market, whichever is lower) and §1.471-5(c) (security dealers allowed to value their inventory of securities at market value), both of which allow unrealized depreciation, and the latter, unrealized appreciation as well, to be taken into account each year.

8. *The constitutional issue.* As to the impact of the constitutional "realization" concept, see Surrey, The Supreme Court and the Federal Income Tax: Some Implications of the Recent Decisions, 35 Ill. L. Rev. 779, 782 (1941): "Each succeeding opinion paid its respects to the principle of realization which was the core of the Court's pronouncement in Eisner v. Macomber, but went on to a result which never matched the rigor of that pronouncement." Does the case that follows, Helvering v. Bruun, retreat from the "rigor" of Eisner v. Macomber? See also J. Sneed, The Configurations of Gross Income 125 (1967), suggesting that whatever "rusty remnant" of Eisner v. Macomber remains "be consigned to the junk yard of judicial history."

9. *The "realization" concept today.* Notwithstanding general rejection of the constitutional principle of Eisner v. Macomber, the realization requirement remains important in our tax law. We do not generally tax

unrealized gains in property values, perhaps because annual property appraisals are difficult; or because the taxpayer may not have the money to pay the tax on such gains; or because unrealized gains in one year may turn into unrealized losses in another year. The income tax depends on "transactions" or "taxable events" and is not a tax on "income" as defined by economists.

2. Development: Tenant Improvements

HELVERING v. BRUUN

309 U.S. 461 (1940)

Mr. Justice ROBERTS delivered the opinion of the Court.

The controversy had its origin in the petitioner's [the tax collector's] assertion that the [taxpayer/lessor] realized taxable gain from the forfeiture of a leasehold, the tenant having erected a new building upon the premises. The court below held that no income had been realized. . . .

The Board of Tax Appeals made no independent findings. The cause was submitted upon a stipulation of facts. From this it appears that on July 1, 1915, the respondent, as owner, leased a lot of land and the building thereon for a term of ninety-nine years.

The lease provided that the lessee might, at any time, upon giving bond to secure rentals accruing in the two ensuing years, remove or tear down any building on the land, provided that no building should be removed or torn down after the lease became forfeited, or during the last three and one-half years of the term. The lessee was to surrender the land, upon termination of the lease, with all buildings and improvements thereon.

In 1929 the tenant demolished and removed the existing building and constructed a new one which had a useful life of not more than fifty years. July 1, 1933, the lease was cancelled for default in payment of rent and taxes and the respondent regained possession of the land and building.

The parties stipulated

> that as at said date, July 1, 1933, the building which had been erected upon said premises by the lessee had a fair market value of $64,245.68 and that the [lessor's] unamortized cost of the old building, which was removed from the premises in 1929 to make way for the new building, was $12,811.43, thus leaving a net fair market value [net "gain"] as at July 1, 1933, of $51,434.25, for the aforesaid new building erected upon the premises by the lessee.

On the basis of these facts, the petitioner determined that in 1933 the respondent realized a net gain of $51,434.25. The Board overruled his determination and the Circuit Court of Appeals affirmed the Board's decision.

The course of administrative practice and judicial decision in respect of the question presented has not been uniform. In 1917 the Treasury ruled that the adjusted value of improvements installed upon leased premises is income to the lessor upon the termination of the lease. The ruling was incorporated in two succeeding editions of the Treasury Regulations. In 1919 the Circuit Court of Appeals for the Ninth Circuit held in Miller v. Gearin, 258 F. 225, that the regulation was invalid as the gain, if taxable at all, must be taxed as of the year when the improvements were completed.

The regulations were accordingly amended to impose a tax upon the gain in the year of completion of the improvements, measured by their anticipated value at the termination of the lease and discounted for the duration of the lease. Subsequently the regulations permitted the lessor to spread the depreciated value of the improvements over the remaining life of the lease, reporting an aliquot part each year, with provision that, upon premature termination, a tax should be imposed upon the excess of the then value of the improvements over the amount theretofore returned.

In 1935 the Circuit Court of Appeals for the Second Circuit decided in Hewitt Realty Co. v. Commissioner, 76 F.2d 880, that a landlord received no taxable income in a year, during the term of the lease, in which his tenant erected a building on the leased land. The court, while recognizing that the lessor need not receive money to be taxable, based its decision that no taxable gain was realized in that case on the fact that the improvement was not portable or detachable from the land, and if removed would be worthless except as bricks, iron, and mortar. . . .

This decision invalidated the regulations then in force.

In 1938 this court decided M. E. Blatt Co. v. United States, 305 U.S. 267. There, in connection with the execution of a lease, landlord and tenant mutually agreed that each should make certain improvements to the demised premises and that those made by the tenant should become and remain the property of the landlord. The Commissioner valued the improvements as of the date they were made, allowed depreciation thereon to the termination of the leasehold, divided the depreciated value by the number of years the lease had to run, and found the landlord taxable for each year's aliquot portion thereof. His action was sustained by the Court of Claims. The judgment was reversed on the ground that the added value could not be considered rental accruing over the period of the lease; that the facts found by the Court of Claims did not support the conclusion of the Commissioner as to the value to be attributed to the improvements after a use throughout the term of the lease; and that, in the circumstances disclosed, any enhancement in the value of the realty in the tax year was not income realized by the lessor within the Revenue Act.

The circumstances of the instant case differentiate it from the *Blatt* and *Hewitt* cases; but the petitioner's contention that gain was realized when the respondent, through forfeiture of the lease, obtained untrammeled title, possession and control of the premises, with the added increment of value added by the new building, runs counter to the decision in the *Miller* case and to the reasoning in the *Hewitt* case.

The respondent insists that the realty, — a capital asset at the date of the execution of the lease, — remained such throughout the term and after its expiration; that improvements affixed to the soil became part of the realty indistinguishably blended in the capital asset; that such improvements cannot be separately valued or treated as received in exchange for the improvements which were on the land at the date of the execution of the lease; that they are, therefore, in the same category as improvements added by the respondent to his land, or accruals of value due to extraneous and adventitious circumstances. Such added value, it is argued, can be considered capital gain only upon the owner's disposition of the asset. The position is that the economic gain consequent upon the enhanced value of the recaptured asset is not gain derived from capital or realized within the meaning of the Sixteenth Amendment and may not, therefore, be taxed without apportionment.

We hold that the petitioner was right in assessing the gain as realized in 1933.

We might rest our decision upon the narrow issue presented by the terms of the stipulation. It does not appear what kind of a building was erected by the tenant or whether the building was readily removable from the land. It is not stated whether the difference in the value between the building removed and that erected in its place accurately reflects an increase in the value of land and building considered as a single estate in land. On the facts stipulated, without more, we should not be warranted in holding that the presumption of the correctness of the Commissioner's determination has been overborne.

The respondent insists, however, that the stipulation was intended to assert that the sum of $51,434.25 was the measure of the resulting enhancement in value of the real estate at the date of the cancellation of the lease. The petitioner seems not to contest this view. Even upon this assumption we think that gain in the amount named was realized by the respondent in the year of repossession.

The respondent can not successfully contend that the definition of gross income in [§61(a) of the 1986 Code] is not broad enough to embrace the gain in question. That definition follows closely the Sixteenth Amendment. Essentially the respondent's position is that the

Amendment does not permit the taxation of such gain without apportionment amongst the states. He relies upon what was said in Hewitt Realty Co. v. Commissioner, supra, and upon expressions found in the decisions of this court dealing with the taxability of stock dividends to the effect that gain derived from capital must be something of exchangeable value proceeding from property, severed from the capital, however invested or employed, and received by the recipient for his separate use, benefit, and disposal. He emphasizes the necessity that the gain be separate from the capital and separately disposable. These expressions, however, were used to clarify the distinction between an ordinary dividend and a stock dividend. They were meant to show that in the case of a stock dividend, the stockholder's interest in the corporate assets after receipt of the dividend was the same as and inseverable from that which he owned before the dividend was declared. We think they are not controlling here.

While it is true that economic gain is not always taxable as income, it is settled that the realization of gain need not be in cash derived from the sale of an asset. Gain may occur as a result of exchange of property, payment of the taxpayer's indebtedness, relief from a liability, or other profit realized from the completion of a transaction. The fact that the gain is a portion of the value of property received by the taxpayer in the transaction does not negative its realization.

Here, as a result of a business transaction, the respondent received back his land with a new building on it, which added an ascertainable amount to its value. It is not necessary to recognition of taxable gain that he should be able to sever the improvement begetting the gain from his original capital. If that were necessary, no income could arise from the exchange of property; whereas such gain has always been recognized as realized taxable gain.

Judgment reversed.

THE CHIEF JUSTICE concurs in the result in view of the terms of the stipulation of facts.

Mr. Justice MCREYNOLDS took no part in the decision of this case.

NOTES AND QUESTIONS

1. *The original lease transaction.* When Mr. Bruun leased the land in 1915, did he have rental income in the amount of the present value of the expected future rental payments to be made during the entire term of the lease? Why?

2. *The events of 1929.* When the tenant in 1929 tore down the old building and constructed the new one, why did Bruun not have income for tax purposes in an amount equal to the difference between the value of the new building and his basis in the old one? Apart from taxes, is

it likely that the construction of the building increased the value of his investment? Why?

3. *Buildings intended as rent.* (a) Suppose that the owner of land agrees to allow a tenant to occupy the land "rent free" for ten years if the tenant constructs a building with an expected life of twenty years, a value at the completion of construction of $400,000, and an expected value at the end of the ten-year lease of $200,000. If income is realized in this situation, when and how much? Which of the possibilities discussed by the Court in *Bruun* makes most sense? See Regs. §1.61-8(c). Cf. Code §109.

(b) If an owner of land enters into a lease under which an oil company is permitted to drill for oil, in return for a royalty on any oil that is discovered and sold, does the landowner have income at the time the oil company constructs a rig and begins drilling? When oil is found? Why?

4. *The events of 1933.* The Court holds that Bruun realized a big chunk of income in 1933. (a) Does this accord with economic reality? Though the tenant no doubt added considerable value to the property by constructing the new building in 1929, presumably this added value was not reflected in the rent, since the lease did not require the tenant to build and the cost was borne by the tenant. Thus, as of 1929, presumably the rental value of the property, with its new building, was higher than the amount of rent that the tenant was required to pay to Bruun. (b) If so, why do you suppose that the tenant "threw up" the lease in 1933? (c) What do you suppose had happened to the value of the land? (d) If the value of the land fell, does it follow that Bruun had a loss in a tax sense? See §1001(a). (e) Even if he did have a loss, was it realized? See Trask v. Hoey, 177 F.2d 940 (2d Cir. 1949) (lessor taxed on fair market value at the time of forfeiture of tenant's improvements but can claim no offsetting loss for decline in value of lessor's improvements; taxable gain or loss with respect to lessor's improvements will be realized only on a disposition of the property).

5. *Realization doctrine.* (a) Where does this case leave Eisner v. Macomber (on which the taxpayer heavily relied) and the constitutional doctrine of realization adopted in that case? (b) Considering the reasons that might be given for the result in *Macomber,* and for the requirement of realization in general, does Mr. Bruun seem to have a stronger or a weaker case for nonrealization than Mrs. Macomber? (c) The Court in *Bruun* says, "it does not appear . . . whether the building was readily removable from the land." The building was in Kansas City, Missouri, where, one presumes, buildings have basements and are firmly attached to the ground. Note the interesting discussion of the nature of the taxpayer's stipulation as to the amount of gain at issue. What's this all about? If you had represented Bruun, how would you have written the stipulation?

6. *Statutory relief.* Congress ultimately accepted the arguments for nontaxation in cases like *Bruun.* See §§109 and 1019. Note that the effect of the statutory relief is not to exclude or exempt income but to defer or postpone its recognition. Suppose, for example, that in 1933, when the property was abandoned by the tenant, the building was worth $50,000 and had a ten-year remaining life and that Mr. Bruun was able to lease the property to a new tenant for $7,000 per year net of all expenses, beginning in 1933. Disregard any unrecovered cost of the demolished building. Under the decision in the case, Bruun would have income of $50,000 in 1933. This means that he would have a basis in the building of $50,000; for tax purposes it is as if he had received $50,000 in cash and had used that money to buy the building. Thus, he would have been entitled to a depreciation deduction. If we assume that he would have used straightline depreciation, the deduction would have been $5,000 per year. Thus, the income to be reported from the new rental of the property for the period 1933 through 1942 would have been $2,000 per year, or a total of $20,000. The total income would have been $50,000 in 1933 from the abandonment plus the $20,000 from 1933 through 1942 from the rental, or a total of $70,000. If §§109 and 1019 had been applied, there would have been no income from the abandonment in 1933. Since Bruun paid nothing for the building, his basis in it would have been zero, so there would have been no depreciation deduction. His rental income would therefore have been $7,000 per year or a total of $70,000 over the ten-year term of the new lease. Table 3-2 summarizes this illustration.

TABLE 3-2
Illustration of Mr. Bruun's Income under *Bruun* and under §§109 and 1019

Outcome under Bruun	
Income from abandonment in 1933	$50,000
Income from rental, 1933-1942	20,000
Total	$70,000
Outcome under §§109 and 1019	
Income from abandonment in 1933	$ -0-
Income from rental, 1933-1942	70,000
Total	$70,000

3. Losses

Introductory Note

Interest rates rose steadily during the 1960s and 1970s. Thrift institutions such as banks or savings and loans continued to make home loans during this period, albeit at increasingly high interest rates. In return for its loan, the thrift would receive an IOU from the borrower in the form of a note secured by a mortgage on real property. The combination of note and security interest is sometimes referred to simply as a mortgage. These mortgages constituted the primary assets of any thrift institution.

The rise in interest rates reduced the value of existing mortgages held by thrift institutions. To understand why this is so, imagine that a thrift institution had made a $100,000 loan in 1965 at 7 percent annual interest. Assume somewhat unrealistically that the loan required the borrower to make interest payments only for thirty years and then to repay the full amount of the principal. In 1980, the thrift would hold an asset—the mortgage—that amounted to a promise to repay $100,000 in fifteen years and in the meantime to pay interest of $7,000 a year. The prevailing interest rate on home loans in 1980, however, was approximately 14 percent. No one in 1980 would pay $100,000 for a debt obligation that provided only 7 percent interest. Why invest at 7 percent when you could make a similar investment at 14 percent? The then-current fair market value of the 7 percent mortgage might be as low as $60,000. The $40,000 difference between the purchase price ($60,000) and the amount the owner of the mortgage hoped to collect on repayment ($100,000) would offset the low interest received in the intervening years.

By 1980, when the events at issue in *Cottage Savings* took place, the fair market value of mortgages held by the nation's thrift institutions had declined by over a trillion dollars. By selling mortgages and buying similar mortgages, or swapping mortgages, the thrifts hoped to reap huge tax losses without substantially altering their asset portfolios. The impetus for sales and swaps grew stronger in late 1981, when thrift regulators held that, for accounting purposes, a thrift that sold mortgages at a loss and purchased similar mortgages was not required to recognize a loss in the year of exchange. Instead, the thrift could amortize the loss over the life of the exchanged loans. The accounting treatment of losses was important because federal regulators used accounting income and loss to determine the amount of cash a thrift must have on hand to meet obligations. Accounting income and loss was, and is, also thought to affect stock price.

The promise of recognizing a tax loss without suffering a loss for accounting purposes triggered the sale of billions of dollars of mortgage obligations. How did the thrifts arrange to buy, sell, or swap mortgages? In some cases, buyers and sellers contacted each other directly. In general, however, sellers were, and are, put in contact with buyers through specialists whose business is to provide a market for mortgage obligations. These specialists or traders earn a commission on each sale. The commission is expressed by the gap between a "buy" price and a "sell" price. Thus, a trader in mortgage obligations may offer a seller $99,500 for a mortgage with a principal amount of $100,000, a thirty-year term and an interest rate of 9 percent. The trader may then sell the same mortgage for $100,500. The "buy" price for a mortgage with these characteristics will be 99.5 and the "sell" price 100.5.

As it happened, nearly all of the trading in mortgage obligations was handled by a single firm—Salomon Brothers. In the early and mid-1980s, a small number of traders were reported to have earned (in the aggregate) nearly a billion dollars in profit for that company—and millions for themselves. The creation and operation of the market in mortgage obligations is described in Michael Lewis's hilarious and informative book, Liar's Poker.

COTTAGE SAVINGS ASSOCIATION v. COMMISSIONER

111 S. Ct. 1503 (1991)

Justice MARSHALL delivered the opinion of the Court.

The issue in this case is whether a financial institution realizes tax-deductible losses when it exchanges its interests in one group of residential mortgage loans for another lender's interests in a different group of residential mortgage loans. We hold that such a transaction does give rise to realized losses.

I

Petitioner Cottage Savings Association (Cottage Savings) is a savings and loan association (S&L) formerly regulated by the Federal Home Loan Bank Board (FHLBB). Like many S&L's, Cottage Savings held numerous long-term, low-interest mortgages that declined in value when interest rates surged in the late 1970's. These institutions would have benefited from selling their devalued mortgages in order to realize tax-deductible losses. However, they were deterred from doing so by FHLBB accounting regulations, which required them to record the losses on their books. Reporting these losses consistent with the then-effective FHLBB accounting regulations would have placed many S&L's at risk of closure by the FHLBB.

The FHLBB responded to this situation by relaxing its requirements for the reporting of losses. In a regulatory directive known as "Memorandum R-49," dated June 27, 1980, the FHLBB determined that S&L's need not report losses associated with mortgages that are exchanged for "substantially identical" mortgages held by other lenders.[3] The FHLBB's acknowledged purpose for Memorandum R-49 was to facilitate transactions that would generate tax losses but that would not substantially affect the economic position of the transacting S&L's.

This case involves a typical Memorandum R-49 transaction. On December 31, 1980, Cottage Savings sold "90% participation" in 252 mortgages to four S&L's. It simultaneously purchased "90% participation interests" in 305 mortgages held by these S&L's.[4] All of the loans involved in the transaction were secured by single-family homes, most in the Cincinnati area. The fair market value of the package of participation interests exchanged by each side was approximately $4.5 million. The face value of the participation interests Cottage Savings relinquished in the transaction was approximately $6.9 million.

On its 1980 federal income tax return, Cottage Savings claimed a reduction for $2,447,091, which represented the adjusted difference between the face value of the participation interests that it traded and the fair market value of the participation interests that it received. As permitted by Memorandum R-49, Cottage Savings did not report these losses to the FHLBB. After the Commissioner of Internal Revenue disallowed Cottage Savings' claimed deduction, Cottage Savings sought a redetermination in the Tax Court. The Tax Court held that the deduction was permissible.

3. Memorandum R-49 listed 10 criteria for classifying mortgages as substantially identical.

The loans involved must:

1. involve single-family residential mortgages,
2. be of similar type (e.g., conventionals for conventionals),
3. have the same stated terms to maturity (e.g., 30 years),
4. have identical stated interest rates,
5. have similar seasoning (i.e., remaining terms to maturity),
6. have aggregate principal amounts within the lesser of 2½% or $100,000 (plus or minus) on both sides of the transaction, with any additional consideration being paid in cash,
7. be sold without recourse,
8. have similar fair market values,
9. have similar loan-to-value ratios at the time of the reciprocal sale, and
10. have all security properties for both sides of the transaction in the same state.

Record, Exh. 72-BT.

4. By exchanging merely participation interest rather than the loans themselves, each party retained its relationship with the individual obligors. Consequently, each S&L continued to service the loans on which it had transferred the participation interests and made monthly payments to the participation-interest holders. See 90 T.C. 372, 381 (1988).

On appeal by the Commissioner, the Court of Appeals reversed. 890 F.2d 848 (C.A.6 1989). The Court of Appeals agreed with the Tax Court's determination that Cottage Savings had realized its losses through the transaction. See id., at 852. However, the court held that Cottage Savings was not entitled to a deduction because its losses were not "actually" sustained during the 1980 tax year for purposes of §165(a). See 890 F.2d at 855.

Because of the importance of this issue to the S&L industry and the conflict among the Circuits over whether Memorandum R-49 exchanges produce deductible tax losses, we granted certiorari. We now reverse.

II

Rather than assessing tax liability on the basis of annual fluctuations in the value of a taxpayer's property, the Internal Revenue Code defers the tax consequences of a gain or loss in property value until the taxpayer "realizes" the gain or loss. The realization requirement is implicit in §1001(a) of the Code, which defines "[t]he gain [or loss] from the sale or other disposition of property" as the difference between "the amount realized" from the sale or disposition of the property and its "adjusted basis." As this Court has recognized, the concept of realization is "founded on administrative convenience." Helvering v. Horst, 311 U.S. 112, 116 (1940). Under an appreciation-based system of taxation, taxpayers and the Commissioner would have to undertake the "cumbersome, abrasive, and unpredictable administrative task" of valuing assets on an annual basis to determine whether the assets had appreciated or depreciated in value. See 1 B. Bittker & L. Lokken, Federal Taxation of Income, Estates and Gifts ¶5.2, pp. 5-16 (2d ed. 1989). In contrast, "[a] change in the form or extent of an investment is easily detected by a taxpayer or an administrative officer." R. Magill, Taxable Income 79 (rev. ed. 1945).

Section 1001(a)'s language provides a straightforward test for realization: to realize a gain or loss in the value of property, the taxpayer must engage in a "sale or other disposition of [the] property." The parties agree that the exchange of participation interests in this case cannot be characterized as a "sale" under §1001(a); the issue before us is whether the transaction constitutes a "disposition of property." The Commissioner argues that an exchange of property can be treated as a "disposition" under §1001(a) only if the properties exchanged are materially different. The Commissioner further submits that, because the underlying mortgages were essentially economic substitutes, the participation interests exchanged by Cottage Savings were not materially different from those received from the other S&L's. Cottage Savings, on the other hand, maintains that *any* exchange of property is a "disposition of property" under §1001(a), regardless of whether the property exchanged is materially different. Alternatively, Cottage Savings contends that the participation interests exchanged were materially different because the underlying loans were secured by different properties.

We must therefore determine whether the realization principle in §1001(a) incorporates a "material difference" requirement. If it does, we must further decide what that requirement amounts to and how it applies in this case. We consider these questions in turn.

A

Neither the language nor the history of the Code indicates whether and to what extent property exchanged must differ to count as a "disposition of property" under §1001(a). Nonetheless, we readily agree with the Commissioner that an exchange of property gives rise to a realization even under §1001(a) only if the properties exchanged are "materially different." The Commissioner himself has by regulation construed §1001(a) to embody a material difference requirement:

> Except as otherwise provided . . . the gain or loss realized from the conversion of property into cash, *or from the exchange of property for other property differing materially either in kind or in extent,* is treated as income or as loss sustained.

Treas. Reg. §1.1001-1 (1990) (emphasis added). Because Congress has delegated to the Commissioner the power to promulgate "all needful rules and regulations for the enforcement of [the Internal Revenue Code]," §7805(a), we must defer to his regulatory interpretations of the Code so long as they are reasonable. . . .

We conclude that Treasury Regulation §1.1001-1 *is* a reasonable interpretation of §1001(a). Congress first employed the language that now comprises §1001(a) of the Code in §202(a) of the Revenue Act of 1924, ch. 234, 43 Stat. 253; that language has remained essentially unchanged through various reenactments. And since 1934, the Commissioner has construed the statutory term "disposition of property" to include a "material difference" requirement. As we have recognized, "'Treasury regulations and interpretations long continued without substantial change, applying to unamended or substantially reenacted statutes, are deemed to have received congressional approval and have the effect of law.'" United States v. Correll, 389 U.S. 299, 305-306 (1967), quoting Helvering v. Winmill, 305 U.S. 79, 83 (1938).

Treasury Regulation §1.1001-1 is also consistent with our landmark precedents on realization. In a series of early decisions involving the tax effects of property exchanges, this Court made clear that a taxpayer realizes taxable income only if the properties exchanged are "materially" or "essentially" different. . . . Because these decisions were part of the "contemporary legal context" in which Congress enacted §202(a) of the 1924 Act, . . . and because Congress has left undisturbed through subsequent reenactments of the Code the principles of realization established in these cases, we may presume that Congress intended to codify these principles in §1001(a). . . . The Commissioner's construction of the statutory language to incorporate these principles certainly was reasonable.

B

Precisely what constitutes a "material difference" for purposes of §1001(a) of the Code is a more complicated question. The Commissioner argues that properties are "materially different" only if they differ in economic substance. To determine whether the participation interests exchanged in this case were "materially different" in this sense, the Commissioner argues, we should look to the attitudes of the parties, the evaluation of the interests by the secondary mortgage market, and the views of the FHLBB. We conclude that §1001(a) embodies a much less demanding and less complex test.

Unlike the question *whether* §1001(a) contains a material difference requirement, the question of *what constitutes* a material difference is not one on which we can defer to the Commissioner. For the Commissioner has not issued an authoritative, prelitigation interpretation of what property exchanges satisfy this requirement. Thus, to give meaning to the material difference test, we must look to the case law from which the test derives and which we believe Congress intended to codify in enacting and reenacting the language that now comprises §1001(a). . . .

We start with the classic treatment of realization in Eisner v. Macomber [page 286]. In *Macomber*, a taxpayer who owned 2,200 shares of stock in a company received another 1,100 shares from the company as part of a pro rata stock dividend meant to reflect the company's growth in value. At issue was whether the stock dividend constituted taxable income. We held that it did not, because no gain was realized. . . . We reasoned that the stock dividend merely reflected the increased worth of the taxpayer's stock, . . . and that a taxpayer realizes increased worth of property only by receiving "something of exchangeable value *proceeding from* the property." . . .

In three subsequent decisions—United States v. Phellis, [257 U.S. 156 (1921)]; Weiss v. Stearn, [265 U.S. 242, (1924)]; and Marr v. United States, [268 U.S. 536 (1925)]—we refined *Macomber*'s conception of realization in the context of property exchanges. In each case, the taxpayer owned stock that had appreciated in value since its acquisition. And in each case, the corporation in which the taxpayer held stock had reorganized into a new corporation, with the new corporation assuming the business of the old corporation. While the corporations in *Phellis* and *Marr* both changed from New Jersey to Delaware corporations, the original and successor corporations in *Weiss* both were incorporated in Ohio. In each case, following the reorganization, the stockholders of the old corporation received shares in the new corporation equal to their proportional interest in the old corporation.

The question in these cases was whether the taxpayers realized the accumulated gain in their shares in the old corporation when they received in return for those shares stock representing an equivalent proportional interest in the new corporations. In *Phellis* and *Marr*, we held that the transactions were realization events. We reasoned that because a company incorporated in one State has "different rights and powers" from one incorporated in a different State, the taxpayers in *Phellis* and *Marr* acquired through the transactions property that was "materially different" from what they previously had. . . . In contrast, we held that no realization occurred in *Weiss*. By exchanging stock in the predecessor corporation for stock in the newly reorganized corporation, the taxpayer did not receive "a thing really different from what he theretofore had." Weiss v. Stearn, supra, 265 U.S., at 254. As we explained in *Marr*, our determination that the reorganized company in *Weiss* was not "really different" from its predecessor turned on the fact that both companies were incorporated in the same State. . . .

Obviously, the distinction in *Phellis* and *Marr* that made the stock in the successor corporations materially different from the stock in the predecessors was minimal. Taken together, *Phellis, Marr,* and *Weiss* stand for the principles that properties are "different" in the sense that is "material" to the Internal Revenue Code so long as their respective possessors enjoy legal entitlements that are different in kind or extent. Thus, separate groups of stock are not materially different if they confer "the same proportional interest of the same character in the same corporation." Marr v. United States, 268 U.S., at 540. However, they *are* materially different if they are issued by different corporations, id., at 541; United States v. Phellis, supra, 257 U.S., at 173, or if they confer "differen[t] rights and powers" in the same corporation, Marr v. United States, supra, 268 U.S., at 541. No more demanding a standard than this is necessary in order to satisfy the administrative purposes underlying the realization requirement in §1001(a). . . . For, as long as the property entitlements are not identical, their exchange will allow both the Commissioner and the transacting taxpayer easily to fix the appreciated or depreciated values of the property relative to their tax bases.

In contrast, we find no support for the Commissioner's "economic substitute" conception of material difference. According to the Commissioner, differences between properties are material for purposes of the Code only when it can be said that the parties, the relevant market (in this case the secondary mortgage market), and the relevant regulatory body (in this case the FHLBB) would consider them material. Nothing in *Phellis, Weiss,* and *Marr* suggests that exchanges of properties must satisfy such a subjective test to trigger realization of a gain or loss.

Moreover, the complexity of the Commissioner's approach ill serves the goal of administrative convenience that underlies the realization requirement. In order to apply the Commissioner's test in a principled fashion, the Commissioner and the taxpayer must identify the relevant market, establish whether there is a regulatory agency whose views should be taken into account, and then assess how the relevant market participants and the agency would view the transaction. The Commissioner's failure to explain how these inquiries should be conducted further calls into question the workability of his test.

Finally, the Commissioner's test is incompatible with the structure of the Code. Section 1001(c) provides that a gain or loss realized under §1001(a) "shall be recognized" unless one of the Code's nonrecognition provisions applies. One such nonrecognition provision withholds recognition of a gain or loss realized from an exchange of properties that would appear to be economic substitutes under the Commissioner's material difference test. This provision, commonly known as "like kind" exception, withholds recognition of a gain or loss realized "on the exchange of property held for productive use in a trade or business or for investment . . . for property of like kind which is to be held either for productive use in a trade or business or for investment." §103(a)(1). If Congress had expected that exchanges of similar properties would *not* count as realization events under §1001(a), it would have had no reason to bar recognition of a gain or loss realized from these transactions.

C

Under our interpretation of §1001(a), an exchange of property gives rise to a realization event so long as the exchanged properties are "materially different"—that is, so long as they embody legally distinct entitlements. Cottage Savings' transactions at issue here easily satisfy this test. Because the participation interests exchanged by Cottage Savings and the other S&L's derived from loans that were made to different obligors and secured by different homes, the exchanged interests did embody legally distinct entitlements. Consequently, we conclude that Cottage Savings realized its losses at the point of the exchange.

The Commissioner contends that it is anomalous to treat mortgages deemed to be "substantially identical" to the FHLBB as "materially different." The anomaly, however, is merely semantic; mortgages can be substantially identical for Memorandum R-49 purposes and still exhibit "differences" that are "material" for purposes of the Internal Revenue Code. Because Cottage Savings received entitlements different from those it gave up, the exchange put both Cottage Savings and the Commissioner in a position to determine the change in the value of Cottage Savings' mortgages relative to their tax bases. Thus, there is no reason not to treat the exchange of these interests as a realization event, regardless of the status of the mortgages under the criteria of Memorandum R-49.

III

Although the Court of Appeals found that Cottage Savings' losses were realized, it disallowed them on the ground that they were not sustained under §165(a) of the Code. Section 165(a) states that a deduction shall be allowed for "any loss sustained during the taxable year and not compensated for by insurance or otherwise. Under the Commissioner's interpretation of §165(a),

> To be allowable as a deduction under section 165(a), a loss must be evidenced by closed and completed transactions, fixed by identifiable events, and, except as otherwise provided in section 165(h) and §1.165-11, relating to disaster losses, actually sustained during the taxable year. Only a bona fide loss is allowable. Substance and not mere form shall govern in determining a deductible loss.

Treas. Reg. §1.165-1(b).

The Commissioner offers a minimal defense of the Court of Appeals' conclusion. The Commissioner contends that the losses were not sustained because they lacked "economic substance," by which the Commissioner seems to mean that the losses were not bona fide. We say "seems" because the Commissioner states the position in one sentence in a footnote in his brief without offering further explanation. The only authority the Commissioner cites for this argument is Higgins v. Smith, 308 U.S. 473 (1940).

In *Higgins*, we held that a taxpayer did not sustain a loss by selling securities below cost to a corporation in which he was the sole shareholder. We found that the losses were not bona fide because the transaction was not conducted at arm's length and because the taxpayer retained the benefit of the securities through his wholly owned corporation. . . . Because there is no contention that the transactions in this case were not conducted at arm's length, or that Cottage Savings retained de facto ownership of the participation interests it traded to the four reciprocating S&L's, *Higgins* is inapposite. In view of the Commissioner's failure to advance any other arguments in support of the Court of Appeals' ruling with respect to §165(a), we conclude that, for purposes of this case, Cottage Savings sustained its losses within the meaning of §165(a).

IV

For the reasons set forth above, the judgment of the Court of Appeals is reversed, and the case is remanded for further proceedings consistent with this opinion.

So ordered.

Justice Blackmun, with whom Justice White joins . . . dissenting. . . .

The exchanges, as the Court acknowledges, were occasioned by the Federal Home Loan Bank Board's (FHLBB) Memorandum R-49 of June 27, 1980, and by that Memorandum's relaxation of theretofore-existing accounting regulations and requirements, a relaxation effected to avoid placement of "many S&L's at risk of closure by the FHLBB" without substantially affecting the "economic position of the transacting S&L's." . . . But the Memorandum, the Court notes, also had as a purpose "the facilit[ation of] transactions that would generate tax losses. . . ." I find it somewhat surprising that an agency not responsible for tax matters would presume to dictate what is or is not a deductible loss for federal income tax purposes. I had thought that that was something within the exclusive province of the Internal Revenue Service, subject to administrative and judicial review. Certainly, the Bank Board's opinion in this respect is entitled to no deference whatsoever. . . .

That the mortgage participation partial interests exchanged in these cases were "different" is not in dispute. The materiality prong is the focus. A material difference is one that has the capacity to influence a decision. . . .

The application of this standard leads, it seems to me, to only one answer—that the mortgage participation partial interests released were not materially different from the mortgage participation partial interests received. Memorandum R-49, as the Court notes, . . . lists 10 factors that, when satisfied, as they were here, serve to classify the interests as "substantially identical." These factors assure practical identity; surely, they then also assure that any difference cannot be of consequence. Indeed, nonmateriality is the full purpose of the Memorandum's criteria. The "proof of the pudding" is in the fact of its complete accounting acceptability to the FHLBB. Indeed, as has been noted, it is difficult to reconcile substantial identity for financial accounting purposes with a material difference for tax accounting purposes.

This should suffice and be the end of the analysis. Other facts, however, solidify the conclusion: The retention by the transferor of 10% interests, enabling it to keep on servicing its loans; the transferor's continuing to collect the payments due from the borrowers so that, so far as the latter were concerned, it was business as usual, exactly as it had been; the obvious lack of concern or dependence of the transferor with the "differences" upon which the Court relies (as transferees, the taxpayers made no credit checks and no appraisals of collateral . . .); the selection of the loans by computer programmed to match mortgages in accordance with the Memorandum R-49 criteria; the absence of even the names of the borrowers in the closing schedules attached to the agreements; Centennial's receipt of loan files only six years after its exchange; the restriction of the interests exchanged to the same State; the identity of the respective face and fair market values; and the application by the parties of common discount factors to each side of the transaction—all reveal that any differences that might exist made no difference whatsoever and were not material. This demonstrates the real nature of the transactions, including nonmateriality of the claimed differences.

We should be dealing here with realities and not with superficial distinctions. As has been said many times, and as noted above, in income tax law we are to be concerned with substance and not with mere form. When we stray from that principle, the new precedent is likely to be a precarious beacon for the future.

I respectfully dissent on this issue.

NOTE

In response to the decision in *Cottage Savings*, the Treasury issued a proposed regulation on the important issue of when a modification in the terms of a debt instrument is treated as a "sale or other disposition" of the original obligation, triggering recognition of gain or loss and, in some cases, of income from cancellation of indebtedness. Prop. Reg. §1.1001-3. The proposed regulation covers a wide variety of possible modifications. In general, the key is whether a "significant modification" has occurred in yield, timing or amounts of payments, the obligor, or the nature of the instrument. Some of the rules are specific. For example, if the interest rate is changed by more than ¼ of one percent, the change is significant and a recognition event has occurred, but in the case of a variable-rate obligation, a change in the rate resulting from a change in the index used to compute the rate is not a modification. §1.1001-3(e)(1). An extension of the final maturity date is significant if it is greater than the lesser of five years or 50 percent of the original term. §1.1001-3(e)(2). Other rules are stated more generally. For example, a change in the collateral is "a significant modification if a substantial portion of the collateral is released or replaced with other property," but not where fungible property is replaced by similar property (for example, "government securities of a particular type and rating"). §1.1001-3(e)(3)(iv).

QUESTIONS

1. Is the loss in a case like *Cottage Savings* properly claimed under §165 or under §1001? What is the role of each of these provisions?

2. Before the swap described in *Cottage Savings*, had the taxpayer experienced a true economic loss on the loans that it swapped? If so, when was that loss incurred?

3. If the taxpayer had a true economic loss (with or without the swap), why did the FHLBB not require that the loss be recognized for nontax accounting purposes?

4. Given that the FHLBB did not require recognition of loss at the time of the swap, why was the loss recognized for tax purposes?

5. What is the legal test for recognition of loss? What is meant by "legal entitlements"? Is it fair to describe the test as "formalistic"? If so, what is the advantage, if any, of such a test?

PROBLEMS

1. Joe and Barbara are both cotton dealers and are business acquaintances of one another. Each is in the business of buying cotton from farmers and selling it to manufacturers. Recently each bought large quantities of cotton and stored it in a warehouse in the town where both of them live. The cotton was all grown in the same area and is considered to be identical in grade and quality. The end of the year is approaching. The price of cotton has fallen and Joe and Barbara both have substantial unrealized losses on the cotton they hold in storage. Joe and Barbara both believe that the price of cotton will rise in a month or so and would like to avoid selling, but each has large gains from transactions earlier in the year and would like to be able to deduct their losses. Will each of them be entitled to recognize his or her loss if they swap their cotton holdings?

2. Susan and Josh are both dealers in high-priced, high-performance, "exotic" sports cars. Susan has her showroom and office in New York City, and Josh has his showroom and office in Miami. Two years ago Machorari Automobile Company, which is located in Italy, announced that it had plans to build a new sports car, to be called the Streaker, and that it would take orders at $500,000 each, with $100,000 payable

on placing the order. Only thirty of the cars were to be built. Susan and Josh each placed orders. Machorari's cars are essentially hand made. When an order is placed, a particular car is assigned to the buyer. Susan was assigned Streaker No. 13 and Josh was assigned Streaker No. 14. The cars were recently finished, paid for by Susan and Josh, and shipped to them. Unfortunately, a mistake was made in the shipping and Susan's Streaker No. 13 was shipped to Miami while Josh's Streaker No. 14 was shipped to New York. Susan and Josh each have documents establishing their ownership of their cars. The cars are as close to being identical as cars can be when they are not made on an assembly line. Demand is so intense that the cars can be sold without effort for $750,000. Susan has several potential buyers in New York at that price. In Miami, several people have come to Josh's showroom with suitcases full of cash ($750,000), seeking to buy a Streaker. Certain modifications must be made, however, before the cars can meet federal regulations and be sold. The modifications will take several months. Josh calls Susan and suggests that they swap titles, which can be accomplished easily, so they don't need to ship cars to each other. If they do so, must they recognize their gain at the time of the swap? Would it matter if the colors of the cars were different and colors were of great importance to particular buyers?

4. Express Nonrecognition Provisions

Basic rules. (a) Taxpayer *A* is a lawyer who receives $50,000 as a contingent fee in a personal injury case. This is in addition to his normal income from his law practice. The fee is taxed at a rate of 40 percent (combined federal and state), leaving $30,000 for *A*. *A* invests the $30,000 in shares of common stock of Exxon Corporation.

(b) Long ago *B* bought shares of stock of Texaco for $10,000. She sells those shares for $60,000, pays a tax of $20,000 on the gain, and invests the remaining $40,000 in shares of Exxon.

(c) Long ago *C* bought shares of stock of Texaco for $10,000. He swaps them for shares of stock of Exxon worth $60,000. Is the swap a taxable event? See §§1001(c) and 1031(a).

(d) Long ago *D* bought *X* Farm for $10,000 and has held it as an investment. He swaps *X* Farm for *Y* Farm, worth $60,000. Is the swap a taxable event? See §1031(a).

(e) Long ago *E* bought *M* Farm for $10,000 and has held it as an investment. She sells it for $60,000 and uses the proceeds to buy *N* Farm the next week. Is the sale a taxable event?

(f) Long ago *F* bought a house for $10,000 and has used it as a personal residence. He sells it for $60,000, which he invests a year later in another house that he occupies as a personal residence. Is the receipt of the $60,000 a taxable event? See §1034.

Rationale? Consider the following arguments for nonrecognition: (a) Gain should not be recognized if the transaction does not generate cash with which to pay the tax. (b) Gain or loss should not be recognized if the transaction is one in which the gain or loss is or might be difficult to measure — that is, in which there is or might be a serious problem of valuation. (c) Gain or loss should not be recognized if the nature of the taxpayer's investment does not significantly change. (d) Gain should not be recognized (but loss should be) in order to encourage (or avoid discouraging) mobility of capital (that is the movement of investments from less valuable to more valuable uses).

The first and second of these arguments respond to the goal of practicality or administrative feasibility. The third seems to respond to the goal of fairness; it compares the taxpayer who sells and reinvests, or who swaps, with an otherwise similar taxpayer who holds on to an existing investment, though it ignores comparisons with taxpayers who sell and reinvest, or who swap, in taxable transactions. The fourth argument responds to economic goals.

Is it possible to reconcile the outcomes in the hypotheticals (a) through (f) by reference to these rationales?

REVENUE RULING 82-166

1982-2 C.B. 190

Issue

Does an exchange of gold bullion held for investment for silver bullion held for investment qualify for nonrecognition of gain under section 1031(a) of the Internal Revenue Code?

Facts

An individual taxpayer, who is not a dealer in gold or silver bullion, purchased gold bullion in the cash market and held it as an investment. In 1980, after the gold bullion had appreciated in value, the taxpayer exchanged the gold bullion for silver bullion of equal total fair market value. A gain was realized by the taxpayer as a result of the exchange. The taxpayer holds the silver bullion as an investment.

Law and Analysis

Section 1031(a) of the Code provides that no gain or loss is recognized upon an exchange of property held for productive use in trade or business or for investment solely for property of a like kind to be held either for productive use in trade or business or for investment.

Section 1.1031(a)-1(b) of the Income Tax Regulations provides that as used in section 1031(a) of the Code, the words "like kind" have reference to the nature or character of the property and not to its grade or quality. One kind or class of property may not, under that section, be exchanged for property of a different kind or class.

Rev. Rul. 79-143, 1979-1 C.B. 264, holds that the exchange of United States $20 gold coins (numismatic-type coins) for South African Krugerrand gold coins (bullion-type coins) does not qualify for nonrecognition of gain under section 1031(a) of the Code because the numismatic-type coins and the bullion-type coins represent totally different types of underlying investment and thus are not property of like kind. The bullion-type gold coins, unlike the numismatic-type gold coins, represent an investment in gold on world markets rather than in the coins themselves.

In this case, the values of the silver bullion and the gold bullion are determined solely on the basis of their metal content. Although the metals have some similar qualities and uses, silver and gold are intrinsically different metals and primarily are used in different ways. Silver is essentially an industrial commodity. Gold is primarily utilized as an investment in itself. An investment in one of the metals is fundamentally different from an investment in the other metal. Therefore, the silver bullion and the gold bullion are not property of like kind.

Holding

The taxpayer's exchange of gold bullion for silver bullion does not qualify for nonrecognition of gain under section 1031(a) of the Code.

JORDAN MARSH CO. v. COMMISSIONER

269 F.2d 453 (2d Cir. 1959)

Before Hincks, Lumbard and Moore, Circuit Judges.

Hincks, Circuit Judge.

. . . The transactions giving rise to the dispute were conveyances by the petitioner in 1944 of the fee of two parcels of property in the city of Boston where the petitioner, then as now, operated a department

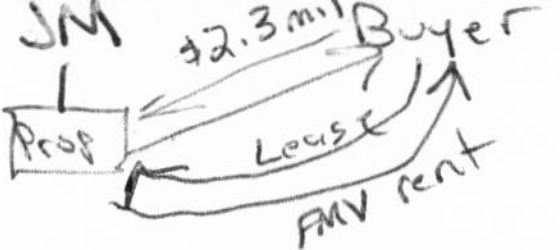

store. In return for its conveyances the petitioner received $2,300,000 in cash which, concededly, represented the fair market value of the properties. The conveyances were unconditional, without provision of any option to repurchase. At the same time, the petitioner received back from the vendees leases of the same properties for terms of 30 years and 3 days, with options to renew for another 30 years if the petitioner-lessee should erect new buildings thereon. The vendees were in no way connected with the petitioner. The rentals to be paid under the leases concededly were full and normal rentals so that the leasehold interests which devolved upon the petitioner were of no capital value.

In its return for 1944, the petitioner, claiming the transaction was a sale under [§1002], sought to deduct from income the difference [$2,500,000] between the adjusted basis of the property [$4,800,000] and the cash received [$2,300,000]. The Commissioner disallowed the deduction, taking the position that the transaction represented an exchange of property for other property of like kind. Under [§1031(a)] such exchanges are not occasions for the recognition of gain or loss; and even the receipt of cash or other property in the exchange of the properties of like kind is not enough to permit the taxpayer to recognize loss [§1031(c)]. Thus the Commissioner viewed the transaction, in substance, as an exchange of a fee interest for a long term lease, justifying his position by [Regs. §1.1031(a)-1(c)], which provides that a leasehold of more than 30 years is the equivalent of a fee interest. . . .

Upon this appeal, we must decide whether the transaction in question here was a sale or an exchange of property for other property of like kind within the meaning of [§1031(a) and (c)]. If we should find that it is an exchange, we would then have to decide whether the Commissioner's regulation, declaring that a leasehold of property of 30 years or more is property "of like kind" to the fee in the same property, is a reasonable gloss to put upon the words of the statute. The judge in the Tax Court felt that Century Electric Co. v. Commissioner, 8 Cir., 192 F.2d 155, certiorari denied 342 U.S. 954, was dispositive of both questions. In the view which we take of the first question, we do not have to pass upon the second question. For we hold that the transaction here was a sale and not an exchange.

The controversy centers around the purposes of Congress in enacting [§1031(a)], dealing with non-taxable exchanges. The section represents an exception to the general rule, stated in [§1002], that upon the sale or exchange of property the entire amount of gain or loss is to be recognized by the taxpayer. The first Congressional attempt to make certain exchanges of this kind non-taxable occurred in Section 202(c), Revenue Act of 1921. Under this section, no gain or loss was recognized from an exchange of property unless the property received in exchange had a "readily realizable market value." In 1924, this section was amended to the form in which it is applicable here. Discussing the old section the House Committee observed:

> The provision is so indefinite that it cannot be applied with accuracy or with consistency. It appears best to provide generally that gain or loss is recognized from all exchanges, and then except specifically and in definite terms those cases of exchanges in which it is not desired to tax the gain or allow the loss. This results in definiteness and accuracy and enables a taxpayer to determine prior to the consummation of a given transaction the tax liability that will result.

[Committee Reports on Rev. Act of 1924, reprinted in 1939-1 C.B. (Pt. 2) 250.] Thus the "readily realizable market value" test disappeared from the statute. A later report, reviewing the section, expressed its purpose as follows:

> The law has provided for 12 years that gain or loss is recognized on exchanges of property having a fair market value, such as stocks, bonds, and negotiable instruments; on exchanges of property held primarily for sale; or on exchanges of one kind of property for another kind of property; but not on other exchanges of property solely for property of like kind. In other words, profit or loss is recognized in the case of exchanges of notes or securities, which are essentially like money; or in the case of stock in trade; or in case the taxpayer exchanges the property comprising his original investment for a different kind of property; *but if the taxpayer's money is still tied up in the same kind of property* as that in which it was originally invested, he is not allowed to compute and deduct his theoretical loss on the exchange, nor is he charged with a tax upon his theoretical profit. The calculation of the profit or loss is deferred until it is realized in cash, marketable securities, or other property not of the same kind having a fair market value.

[House Ways and Means Committee Report, reprinted in 1939-1 C.B. (Pt. 2) 564 (emphasis supplied).]

These passages lead us to accept as correct the petitioner's position with respect to the purposes of the section. Congress was primarily concerned with the inequity, in the case of an exchange, of forcing a taxpayer to recognize a paper gain which was still tied up in a continuing investment of the same sort. If such gains were not to be recognized, however, upon the ground that they were theoretical, neither should equally theoretical losses. And as to both gains and losses the taxpayer should not have it within his power to avoid the operation of the section by stipulating for the addition of cash, or boot, to the property received in exchange. These considerations, rather than concern for the difficulty of the administrative task of making the valuations necessary to compute gains and losses, were at the root of the Congressional purpose in enacting [§1031(a) and (c)]. Indeed, if these sections had been intended to obviate the necessity of making difficult valuations, one would have expected them to provide for nonrecognition of gains and losses in all exchanges, whether the property received in exchanges were "of a like kind" or not of a like kind. And if such had been the legislative objective [§1031(b)], providing for the recognition of gain from exchanges not wholly in kind, would never have been enacted.

That such indeed was the legislative objective is supported by Portland Oil Co. v. Commissioner, 1 Cir., 109 F.2d 479. There Judge Magruder, in speaking of a cognate provision [§351(a), providing for the nonrecognition of gain or loss on the transfer of property to a corporation controlled by the transferor] said:

> It is the purpose of [§351(a)] to save the taxpayer from an immediate recognition of a gain, or to intermit the claim of a loss, in certain transactions where gain or loss may have accrued in a constitutional sense, but where in a popular and economic sense there has been a mere change in the form of ownership and the taxpayer has not really "cashed in" on the theoretical gain, or closed out a losing venture.

In conformity with this reading of the statute, we think the petitioner here, by its unconditional conveyances to a stranger, had done more than make a change in the *form of ownership:* it was a change as to the quantum of ownership whereby, in the words just quoted, it had "closed out a losing venture." By the transaction its capital invested in the real estate involved had been completely liquidated for cash to an amount fully equal to the value of the fee. This, we hold, was a sale — not an exchange within the purview of [§1031].

The Tax Court apparently thought it of controlling importance that the transaction in question involved no change in the petitioner's possession of the premises: it felt that the decision in Century Electric Co. v. Commissioner, supra, controlled the situation here. We think, however, that that case was distinguishable on the facts. For notwithstanding the lengthy findings made with meticulous care by the Tax Court in that case, 15 T.C. 581, there was no finding that the cash received by the taxpayer was the full equivalent of the value of the fee which the taxpayer had conveyed to the vendee-lessor, and no finding that the leaseback called for a rent which was fully equal to the rental value of the premises. Indeed, in its opinion the Court of Appeals pointed to evidence that the fee which the taxpayer had "exchanged" may have had a value substantially in excess of the cash received. And in the *Century Electric* case, the findings showed, 15 T.C. at 585, that the taxpayer-lessee, unlike the taxpayer here, was not required to pay "general state, city and school taxes" because its lessor was an educational institution which under its charter was exempt from such taxes. Thus the leasehold interest in *Century Electric* on this account may well have had a premium value. In the absence of findings as to the values of the properties allegedly "exchanged," necessarily there could be no finding of a loss. And without proof of a loss, of course, the taxpayer could not prevail. Indeed, in the Tax Court six of the judges expressly based their concurrences on that limited ground. . . .

In ordinary usage, an "exchange" means the giving of one piece of property in return for another — not, as the Commissioner urges here, the return of a lesser interest in a property received from another. It seems unlikely that Congress intended that an "exchange" should have the strained meaning for which the Commissioner contends. For the legislative history states expressly an intent to correct the indefiniteness of prior versions of the Act by excepting from the general rule "specifically and in definite terms those cases of exchanges in which it is not desired to tax the gain or allow the loss."

But even if under certain circumstances the return of a part of the property conveyed may constitute an exchange for purposes of [§1031], we think that in this case, in which cash was received for the full value of the property conveyed, the transaction must be classified as a sale. . . .

Reversed.

QUESTIONS

1. Is the result reached in Rev. Rul. 82-166 consistent with the rationale for §1031 relied on by the court in *Jordan Marsh?* Does the result make sense to you? What if the taxpayer had exchanged the gold bullion for gem-grade diamonds?

2. If the government had prevailed in *Jordan Marsh,* how should the $2.3 million have been treated? See §1031(c) and (d). How should the "rent" payments have been treated? What about treating the $2.3 million as a loan and treating the rent as repayments with interest? Would that be consistent with economic reality?

3. If the taxpayer in *Jordan Marsh* had received $1 million in cash, and the business bargain had been equalized by a lower annual rent, would the court have found that the transaction was an "exchange" within the meaning of §1031(a)? If so, would the exchange have been for property of a "like kind"? See Regs. §1.1031(a)-1(c) (leasehold for thirty years exchanged for fee; held, qualified); Century Electric Co. v. Commissioner, cited supra in *Jordan Marsh* (exchange of fee for ninety-five-year leasehold plus cash qualifies); Standard Envelope Manufacturing Co. v. Commissioner, 15 T.C. 41 (1950) (fee for twenty-five-year leasehold; held, not qualified).

NOTES

1. *Involuntary conversions.* Section 1033 provides for nonrecognition where property is compulsorily or involuntarily converted (e.g., by theft,

destruction, or condemnation) and is replaced with property that is "similar or related in service or use." Nonrecognition of gain is mandatory where there is a direct conversion. Where the taxpayer receives cash and then buys the replacement property, nonrecognition is optional. The period in which replacement must occur is generally two years. Note the contrasts with §1031. Under §1033, (a) the replacement property must be "similar or related in service or use" as opposed to "like kind" (but see §1033(g), allowing reliance on the "like kind" standard in the case of certain conversions of real property); (b) if cash is received, the taxpayer has two years in which to find replacement property; and (c) if cash is received, the taxpayer may choose to recognize gain; and (d) losses are recognized.

2. *Sale of taxpayer's principal residence.* Under §1034, gain on a sale of the taxpayer's principal residence is not recognized if the proceeds of the sale are invested in a new principal residence within two years before or after the sale of the old residence.

When §1034 entered the Code in 1951, its purpose was explained by the House Committee on Ways and Means as follows (H.R. Rep. No. 586, reprinted in 1951-2 C.B. 357, 377):

> [The proposed provision] amends the present provisions relating to a gain on the sale of a taxpayer's principal residence so as to eliminate a hardship under existing law which provides that when a personal residence is sold at a gain the difference between its adjusted basis and the sale price is taxed as a capital gain. The hardship is accentuated when the transactions are necessitated by such facts as an increase in the size of the family or a change in the place of the taxpayer's employment. In these situations, the transaction partakes of the nature of an involuntary conversion. Cases of this type are particularly numerous in periods of rapid change such as mobilization or reconversion. For this reason the need for remedial action at the present time is urgent. . . .
>
> This special treatment is not limited to the "involuntary conversion" type of case, where the taxpayer is forced to sell his home because the place of his employment is changed. While the need for relief is especially clear in such cases, an attempt to confine the provision to them would increase the task of administration very much.

Section 121 provides that a person age 55 or older may exclude from gross income, on a once-in-a-lifetime elective basis, up to $125,000 of any gain realized on the sale or exchange of a principal residence ($62,500 in the case of married individuals filing separate returns). The exclusion applies only where the individual has owned and occupied the property as a principal residence for three out of the five years immediately preceding the sale.

3. *Other nonrecognition provisions.* Other nonrecognition provisions are found in §§1036-1042 and in other parts of the Code (e.g., §351 (non-

recognition on certain transfers of property to a corporation in exchange for its common stock or other securities) and §721 (nonrecognition on certain transfers of property by partners to partnership)).

5. "Boot" and Basis

"Boot." "Boot" is the word used by tax practitioners to refer to money, and property other than money, that, under a provision like §1031, is transferred as part of the like-kind exchange but is not like-kind property. The transfer of boot will affect basis and may result in the recognition of gain. For example, if a farmer exchanges a farm for another farm and receives some cash and a tractor to boot (that is, in addition), the amount of the money plus the value of the tractor is the boot. The transaction qualifies for nonrecognition despite the boot, but if there is *gain*, it *is recognized to the extent of* the *boot*. See §1031(b). Thus, the amount of *gain recognized* is the *lesser* of the amount of *gain realized* or the amount of the *boot*. See also §1031(c), relating to loss situations. Note that if there is no gain to be recognized, the boot is not taxable; it is the *gain* that is recognized (and taxable), to the extent of boot, not the boot itself. For example, suppose that *S* exchanges *X* Farm, with a basis of $10,000, for *Y* Farm, which is worth $100,000, and that in addition *S* receives $15,000 cash and a tractor worth $8,000, or a total of $123,000 in property and cash. His total *gain* would be $113,000, the difference between his proceeds ($123,000) and his basis ($10,000). Of this realized gain of $113,000, $23,000, the fair market value of the boot, would be *recognized*. The remaining $90,000 gain would not be recognized. What amount of gain or loss would be recognized if the basis for *X* Farm had been $110,000? $130,000?

Basis. Section 1031(d) sets forth the rule for determining the basis of property received in an exchange covered by §1031. Generally, there will be a "substituted" basis (see §7701(a)(42)) — that is, the basis for the property received will be the same as the basis of the property relinquished. The rule becomes more complicated when there is boot. The calculation of basis when there is boot to account for can be made by following the directions in §1031(d) mechanically, but the following principles should explain why those directions produce a correct result. First, in a simple exchange of like-kind properties with no boot, the property received must take on the basis of the property relinquished so that when the property received is ultimately disposed of in a recognition transaction, any previously unrealized gain or loss will be recognized (except as that gain or loss is changed by changes in the value of the property received, subsequent to the like-kind exchange). For example, if *S* exchanges *X* Farm, with a basis of $10,000, for *Y* Farm, worth $100,000, and there is no boot, and no gain is recognized, *S*'s basis for *Y* Farm must be $10,000 so that if it is later sold for $100,000 the previously unrecognized gain of $90,000 will be recognized.

Second, when gain is recognized because of boot, basis must be increased in the amount recognized so that that gain will not be taxed again; the basis of the like-kind property received plus the basis of the boot must therefore equal the basis of the original property plus the amount of gain recognized. For example, if *S* exchanges his *X* Farm, with a basis of $10,000, for *Y* Farm, worth $100,000, and receives $15,000 cash to boot, he must recognize his gain to the extent of the $15,000, and his basis must be increased by that amount. The basis of the property received plus the basis of the cash must therefore be $25,000.

Third, of the total basis thus calculated, a portion equal to the fair market value of the boot must be allocated to that boot, with the remainder being allocated to the like-kind property received. Thus, in the immediately preceding example, $15,000 of the total basis must be allocated to the cash (which always must receive a basis equal to its face amount). If the boot had consisted of a tractor worth $15,000, rather than cash, $15,000 of basis would be allocated to the tractor; because there is no justification for attaching nonrecognition basis attributes to the tractor, *S* is treated as if he had received cash equal to the tractor's fair market value and had used that cash to buy the tractor.

Fourth, if boot is *paid*, rather than received, the amount of the boot is added to basis. See Regs. §1.1031(d)-1(a). For example, if *T* owns *Y* farm, with a basis of $10,000, and exchanges it, plus $15,000 cash, for *X* farm, in an exchange that qualifies under §1031, *T*'s basis in the *X* farm will be $25,000.

The rules described above can be expressed algebraically. Where *A* is the original basis, *B* is the amount of gain recognized, and *C* is the total basis to be allocated between the like-kind property received and the boot,

$$(1)\ A + B = C$$

Where *D* is the portion of the basis allocated to the boot (which always receives a basis equal to its fair market value (FMV), so *D* is the fair market value of the boot) and *E* is the new, or substituted, basis of the like-kind property received,

$$(2)\ C - D = E.$$

Thus, if there is no boot (*B* and *D* are both zero), the like-kind property received will have the same basis as the property surrendered ($E = A$). If there is boot, the first step is to increase the original basis by the amount of the gain recognized to determine the total basis to be allocated (see equation (1) above). Then the boot receives a basis equal to its fair market value (D = FMV) and the basis left for the like-kind property received (E) is the total basis (C) reduced by the basis allocated to the boot (D), so $E = C - D$. If the gain recognized is equal to the amount of the boot ($B = D$), then the basis of the like-kind property received equals the basis of the like-kind property surrendered.[5]

With these principles in mind, compute the basis of the like-kind property received in the hypothetical in the above paragraph entitled "Boot," under each of the four basis assumptions.

6. Division of Property by Unrelated Co-Owners

REVENUE RULING 56-437

1956-2 C.B. 507

The conversion, for the purpose of eliminating a survivorship feature, of a joint tenancy in capital stock of a corporation into a tenancy in common is a nontaxable transaction for federal income tax purposes. Likewise, the severance of a joint tenancy in stock of a corporation [under a partition action instituted under a Colorado statute, similar to those in force elsewhere], compelling partition and the issuance of two separate stock certificates in the names of each of the joint tenants, is a nontaxable transaction. In each case there was no sale or exchange and the taxpayers neither realized a taxable gain nor sustained a deductible loss.

REVENUE RULING 79-44

1979-1 C.B. 265

Issues

Is the transfer of interests in real property held by tenants in common that results in the conversion of two jointly owned parcels into two individually owned parcels a nontaxable partition or an exchange under section 1001(a) of the Internal Revenue Code of 1954?

If the transfer is an exchange, does it qualify for treatment as a like-kind exchange under section 1031 of the Code?

5.

$$A + B = C \quad (1)$$
$$C - D = E \quad (2)$$
$$C = D + E \quad (3)$$
$$A + B = D + E \quad (1) + (3)$$

If $B = D$,

Then $A = E$.

Facts

Two unrelated individuals, *A* and *B*, neither of whom are dealers in real estate, respectively owned undivided one-half interests in two separate parcels of land as tenants in common. Both parcels were used in the taxpayers' business of farming. One parcel was subject to a mortgage for which *A* and *B* were each personally liable in the face amount of 1,000*x* dollars.

A and *B* rearranged their interests so that each owned 100 percent of a separate parcel. At the time of the transaction, each parcel had a fair market value of 2,000*x* dollars and an adjusted basis of 100*x* dollars. *A* received the parcel subject to the mortgage and *B* received the remaining parcel, which was free of debt. *B* also executed a promissory note to *A* in the amount of, and with a fair market value of, 500*x* dollars to compensate *A* for taking the property subject to the mortgage. *A* and *B* continued to use the parcels in their respective businesses of farming.

Law and Analysis

Section 1001(a) of the Code provides that gain from the sale or other disposition of property shall be the excess of the amount realized therefrom over the adjusted basis in section 1011 for determining gain.

Section 1001(c) of the Code provides that the entire amount of the gain shall be recognized unless an exception provided in subtitle A of the Code applies.

Section 1031(a) of the Code provides that no gain shall be recognized if property held for productive use in trade or business or for investment is exchanged solely for property of a like kind to be held either for productive use in trade or business or for investment. . . .

Holding

The transfer of interests in real property held by tenants in common that resulted in the conversion of two jointly owned parcels into two individually owned parcels is an exchange under section 1001(a) of the Code.

Because the property interests that were exchanged are like-kind property that were being used in the taxpayers' business of farming and have continued to be so used after the exchange, the provisions of section 1031 of the Code apply. Under section 1031, *A* will recognize the gain realized from the exchange, but not in excess of the fair market value of the note received from *B*. *B* will not recognize any of the gain realized from the exchange.

NOTES AND QUESTIONS

1. For the purpose of analysis of Rev. Rul. 79-44, it may be helpful to use a diagram like the following:

START

A ½ B ½		A ½ B ½	
Farm 1		*Farm II*	
FMV	$2,000	FMV	$2,000
Debt	1,000	Debt	0
Basis	100	Basis	100
Unrealized gain:	$1,900	Unrealized gain:	$1,900

DISAGGREGATION and TRANSACTION

A			B	
½ *Farm I*		←	½ *Farm I*	
FMV	$1,000		FMV	$1,000
Debt	500		Debt	500
Basis	50		Basis	50
½ *Farm II*		→	½ *Farm II*	
FMV	$1,000		FMV	$1,000
Debt	0		Debt	0
Basis	50		Basis	50
		←	*B's $500 note*	
			FMV	$500

FINISH

A		B	
Farm I		*Farm II*	
FMV	$2,000	FMV	$2,000
Debt	1,000	Debt	0
Basis	?	Basis	?
B's $500 note		*Debt to A*	
FMV	$500	FMV	$500
Basis	500		

2. *A* and *B*, unrelated individuals, own as tenants in common 100 shares of *X* Corp. common stock. Its fair market value is $100,000 and its basis, for *A* and *B* together, is $30,000. *A* and *B* divide the shares by sending the certificate for 100 shares to *X* Corp. and directing *X* Corp. to issue fifty shares to each of them as individuals. What amount of gain, if any, is realized by *A* and by *B* as a result of the transaction? What is the basis of the shares held by each?

3. *C* and *D*, unrelated individuals, own as tenants in common 100 shares of common stock of *Y* Corp., with a fair market value of $100,000 and a basis of $30,000, and 100 shares of common stock of *Z* Corp. with a fair market value of $100,000 and a basis of $40,000. They rearrange their ownership so that *C* owns all the *Y* shares and *D* owns all the *Z* shares.[6] What amount of gain, if any, is realized and recognized by each individual? What is the basis for the shares held by each? To check the correctness of your determination of basis, calculate the amount of gain that would be recognized by *C* and *D* if they were to sell the shares they wind up with after the exchange, assuming no change in market value. The total amount recognized by both upon the ultimate sale, plus the total gain previously recognized on the exchange, should equal the total gain that would have been recognized if the shares had been sold before the exchange.

4. (a) *E* and *F*, unrelated individuals, own as tenants in common and hold for investment two office buildings, *X* Building and *Y* Building. *X* Building is worth $2 million and *Y* Building is worth $1 million, and both are unencumbered. *X* Building has a total basis of $100,000, and *Y* Building has a total basis of $150,000. *E* and *F* decide to go their separate ways and, to that end, to rearrange their ownership so that

6. The following presentation of the facts may be helpful:

BEFORE

	C and D *100 Y shares*	*C and D* *100 Z shares*
Fair market value	$100	$100
Basis	30	40
Unrealized gain	70	60

DISAGGREGATION and TRANSACTION

	C		*D*
	50 Y shares		*50 Y shares*
Fair market value	$50	⟵	$50
Basis	15		15
	50 Z shares		*50 Z shares*
Fair market value	$50	⟶	$50
Basis	20		20

each will own one building outright. *E* takes *X* Building and *F* takes *Y* Building, and *E* executes a promissory note, secured by a first mortgage on *X* Building, to *F* for $500,000. What amount of gain, if any, is recognized by each individual? (Disregard the installment method, described infra page 364.) What is the basis of the property held by each?

(b) In Rev. Rul. 79-44, supra, what is the amount of gain recognized by *A* and what is the basis of *A* and of *B* in the property held by each after the exchange? See Regs. §1.1031(d)-2, Ex. 2. Suppose that before exchanging their interests in the two properties, *A* and *B* had borrowed $500,000 on the security of the unencumbered property and had used that money to pay off half of the debt on the encumbered property. If they had then made the exchange described in the ruling, what would the tax consequences have been? What does your answer to this question suggest to you about the soundness of the ruling? About the potential value of sophisticated tax advice?

7. Three-Party Transactions and Substance versus Form in Tax Matters

Section 1031 is an important element in the planning of transactions involving farms and real estate investments. Many transactions have taken the form of complex three-party or four-party exchanges. By its terms, §1031 (unlike §§1033 and 1034) would seem to be available only in the relatively unusual circumstance where owners of two like-kind properties happen to want to swap with one another, but it has been extended beyond that situation, in a series of cases dealing with complex, multiparty transactions. These cases offer valuable insights into a basic problem in tax, and other, law — the problem of distinguishing between substance and form and of deciding when outcomes should be governed by form and when by substance.

Suppose that *S* (seller) owns the *X* Farm, which has risen in value because of its potential for residential real estate development. *B* (buyer) offers to buy the farm for $1 million in cash. *S* would be happy to sell and use the proceeds to buy a bigger and better farm, but his basis is only $10,000 and he can't stand the thought of sharing any of his gain with the Treasury. (He has held the farm so long that he thinks of it as entirely his, almost as part of his person. He has come to think of himself as a person worth $1 million and has forgotten, or never recognized, that for years he has managed to escape tax on his gradual increase in wealth.) *R*, a real estate broker, who will earn a commission of $60,000 if the sale is made, proposes that the tax barrier to the transaction can be avoided if the parties are prepared to pay a modest fee for a lawyer to construct a somewhat complex, and obviously artificial, legal arrangement. Following *R*'s advice, *S* finds another farm, the *Y* Farm, whose owner, *O*, is willing to sell for $1 million. The lawyer then devises the following transaction: *B* will buy the *Y* Farm for $1 million cash. Since *B* does not want to be stuck with that farm, there will be a previous agreement between *S* and *B* that will require *S* to swap the *X* Farm for the *Y* Farm once *B* has acquired the *Y* Farm. *S*, *B*, and *O* all follow the plan. *B* buys the *Y* Farm from *O* for $1 million and swaps it with *S* for the *X* Farm. *S* winds up with the *Y* Farm, *B* with the *X* Farm, and *O* with $1 million. *S* is so happy that he scarcely quibbles over the $70,000 that he must borrow in order to be able to pay $60,000 to *R* and $10,000 to the lawyer. The relationships and transactions may be depicted as in Figure 3-1.

(a) What is the substance of the transactions? Bear in mind that *B* never wanted the *Y* Farm. He wanted to buy the *X* Farm for cash and bought the *Y* Farm only to help *S* exchange his farm for another farm he wanted. In fact, his purchase of the *Y* Farm is contingent on *S*'s agreement to swap the *X* Farm for it. In the end, *B* winds up paying out cash and owning the *X* Farm. If tax considerations had played no role in the transactions, the easy, natural way for the three parties to have accomplished their objective would have been for *B* to pay $1 million for the *X* Farm and for *S* to use the $1 million to buy the *Y* Farm. We know as much not just from logic but from experience as well. Thus, one might argue that while the form of the transaction was a swap, the substance was a sale for cash and a reinvestment of the cash (though perhaps that is true to some degree of all swaps). Beyond that, the argument for granting relief under §1031 is weakened by the fact that the calculation of the gain to *S* is not a problem and cash was available to him. Given the substance versus form issue and the policy considerations, will the effort to achieve nonrecognition succeed? Many tax lawyers, if confronted with this question, in the absence of any authority on which to rely, might predict that it would not. The Service is quite capable of seeing through artificially devised transactions and taxing them according to their underlying substance. And the courts often uphold the Service in this kind of effort. But not always, and the three-corner exchange is one instance where they did not. See, e.g., Alderson v. Commissioner, 317 F.2d 790 (9th Cir. 1963), where the court held in favor of the taxpayer even though he had initially agreed

FIGURE 3-1
Illustration of Three-Party Transactions under §1031 (part I).

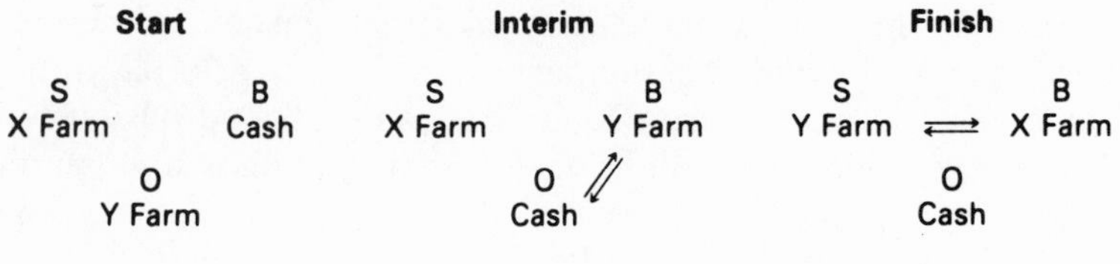

Start
S — X Farm
B — Cash
O — Y Farm

Interim
S — X Farm
B — Y Farm
O — Cash

Finish
S — Y Farm ⇄ B — X Farm
O — Cash

to sell for cash and later modified the agreement to follow the three-corner-exchange model.

(b) One explanation for why taxpayers prevailed in the three-corner-exchange cases may be seen by considering the following slightly modified form of our hypothetical transaction. Suppose that *S* was adamant in refusing to sell unless he could be assured of nonrecognition under §1031. *S* finds *O*'s *Y* Farm and offers to swap his *X* Farm for *O*'s *Y* Farm. *O* is anxious to sell for cash; he does not want *S*'s farm. So *O* finds *B*, who does want *S*'s farm. *O* then enters into an agreement with *B* under which *B* agrees that if *O* acquires the *X* Farm, *B* will buy it from *O* for $1 million cash. *O* and *S* thereupon swap farms, and *O* sells the *X* Farm to *B*. (See Figure 3-2.) Now, from *S*'s perspective, what is the substance? Is the net effect of this transaction any different from the one initially hypothesized? Formally, perhaps the most significant difference is that in the modified form *S* does not agree to swap with *B* before *B* has the *Y* Farm. *S* has no connection with the cash transaction between *B* and *O*. Does this make the case for nonrecognition by *S* seem stronger? Should §1031 be construed to require ownership of the properties by both parties to the swap for some substantial period following the swap? Should it be construed to be inapplicable in any situation in which it is clearly contemplated, or required by the terms of the arrangement viewed in its entirety, that the property initially owned by the taxpayer is to be purchased at some point for cash?

(c) In Biggs v. Commissioner, 69 T.C. 905 (1978), aff'd, 632 F.2d 1171 (5th Cir. 1980), the court allowed nonrecognition in a situation involving convolutions even more strained than those involved in the typical, "straightforward" three-corner exchange of the sort described above. The Service argued, in effect, that the taxpayer had failed to follow the transactional form that had been approved for three-corner exchanges. The court conceded the point but concluded that the transaction was in substance equivalent to the approved form of the three-corner exchange and that therefore the taxpayer was entitled to nonrecognition treatment. In explaining the basis for its conclusion the court stated (69 T.C. at 913):

> The purpose of section 1031 (and its predecessors) was to defer recognition of gain or loss on transactions in which, although in theory the

FIGURE 3-2
Illustration of Three-Party Transactions under §1031 (part II).

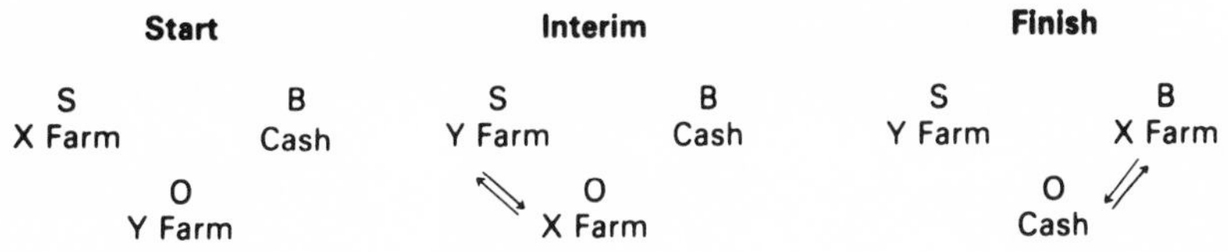

Start		Interim		Finish	
S X Farm	B Cash	S Y Farm	B Cash	S Y Farm	B X Farm
O Y Farm		O X Farm		O Cash	

> taxpayer may have realized a gain or loss, his economic situation is in substance the same after, as it was before, the transaction. Stated otherwise, if the taxpayer's money continues to be invested in the same kind of property, gain or loss should not be recognized.

If that is indeed the purpose of the provision, how might it be amended to permit the objective to be achieved without forcing people to adopt convoluted forms? Would such a change be sensible?

It is worth noting that in support of the statements quoted above, the *Biggs* opinion cites H.R. Rep. 704, 73d Cong., 2d Sess. (1934), 1939-1 C.B. (Pt. 2) 554, 564. The report contains language similar to that used by the court but goes on to say:

> The Treasury Department states that its experience indicates that this provision does not in fact result in tax avoidance. If all exchanges were made taxable, it would be necessary to evaluate the property received in exchange in thousands of horse trades and similar barter transaction each year, and for the time being, at least, claims for theoretical losses would probably exceed any profits which could be established. The committee does not believe that the net revenue which could thereby be collected, particularly in these years, would justify the additional administrative expense.

(d) What if, in our initial example, *S* could not find property that he wanted by the time *B* insisted on acquiring the *X* Farm? Is there a way of structuring the transaction so that *S* can find suitable property later and still achieve nonrecognition under §1031? That is the issue presented in the next case.

STARKER v. UNITED STATES

602 F.2d 1341 (9th Cir. 1979)

Before GOODWIN and ANDERSON, Circuit Judges and JAMESON, District Judge.

GOODWIN, Circuit Judge.

T. J. Starker appeals from the dismissal, on stipulated facts, of his tax refund action. We affirm in part and reverse in part.

I. FACTS

On April 1, 1967, T. J. Starker and his son and daughter-in-law, Bruce and Elizabeth Starker, entered into a "land exchange agreement" with Crown Zellerbach Corporation (Crown). The agreement provided that the three Starkers would convey to Crown all their interests in 1,843 acres of timberland in Columbia County, Oregon. In consideration for this transfer, Crown agreed to acquire and deed over to the Starkers other real property in Washington and Oregon. Crown agreed to provide the Starkers suitable real property within five years or pay any outstanding balance in cash. As part of the contract, Crown agreed to add to the Starkers' credit each year a "growth factor," equal to six per cent of the outstanding balance.

On May 31, 1967, the Starkers deeded their timberland to Crown. Crown entered "exchange value credits" in its books: for T. J. Starker's interest, a credit of $1,502,500; and for Bruce and Elizabeth's interest, a credit of $73,000.

Within four months, Bruce and Elizabeth found three suitable parcels, and Crown purchased and conveyed them pursuant to the contract. No "growth factor" was added because a year had not expired, and no cash was transferred to Bruce and Elizabeth because the agreed value of the property they received was $73,000, the same as their credit.

Closing the transaction with T. J. Starker, whose credit balance was larger, took longer. Beginning in July 1967 and continuing through May 1969, Crown purchased 12 parcels selected by T. J. Starker. Of these 12, Crown purchased 9 from third parties, and then conveyed them to T. J. Starker. Two more of the 12 (the Timian and Bi-Mart properties) were transferred to Crown by third parties, and then conveyed by Crown at T. J. Starker's direction to his daughter, Jean Roth. The twelfth parcel (the Booth property) involved a third party's contract to purchase. Crown purchased that contract right and reassigned it to T. J. Starker. . . .

In their income tax returns for 1967, the three Starkers all reported no gain on the transactions, although their bases in the properties they relinquished were smaller than the market value of the properties they received. They claimed that the transactions were entitled to nonrecognition treatment under section 1031. . . .

The Internal Revenue Service disagreed, and assessed deficiencies of $35,248.41 against Bruce and Elizabeth Starker and $300,930.31 plus interest against T. J. Starker. The Starkers paid the deficiencies, filed claims for refunds, and when those claims were denied, filed two actions for refunds in the United States District Court in Oregon.

In the first of the two cases, Bruce Starker v. United States (*Starker I*), 75-1 U.S. Tax Cas. (CCH) ¶8443 (D. Or. 1975), the trial court held that this court's decision in Alderson v. Commissioner, 317 F.2d 790 (9th Cir. 1963), compelled a decision for the taxpayers. Bruce and Elizabeth Starker recovered the claimed refund. The government appealed, but voluntarily dismissed the appeal, and the judgment for Bruce and Elizabeth Starker became final.

The government, however, did not capitulate in T. J. Starker v. United States (*Starker II*), the present case. The government continued to assert that T. J. Starker was not entitled to section 1031 nonrecognition. According to the government, T. J. Starker was liable not only for a tax on his capital gain, but also for a tax on the 6 per cent "growth factor" as ordinary income (interest or its equivalent).

The same trial judge who heard *Starker I* also heard *Starker II*. Recognizing that "many of the transfers here are identical to those in *Starker I*," the court rejected T. J. Starker's collateral-estoppel argument and found for the government. The judge said:

> I have reconsidered my opinion in *Starker I*. I now conclude that I was mistaken in my holding as well in my earlier reading of *Alderson*. Even if *Alderson* can be interpreted as contended by plaintiff, I think that to do so would be improper. It would merely sanction a tax avoidance scheme and not carry out the purposes of §1031.

T. J. Starker v. United States, 432 F. Supp. 864, 868, 77-2 U.S. Tax Cas. (CCH) ¶9512 (D. Or. 1977). Judgment was entered for the government on both the nonrecognition and ordinary income (interest) issues, and this appeal followed.

T. J. Starker asserts that the district court erred in holding that: (a) his real estate transactions did not qualify for nonrecognition under I.R.C. §1031; (b) the government was not collaterally estopped from litigating that issue; and (c) the transactions caused him to have ordinary income for interest, in addition to a capital gain.

II. Collateral Estoppel . . .

d. Conclusion on Collateral Estoppel

The government, having lost its case against this taxpayer's son based on the same contract to transfer the same family lands, decided not to pursue an appeal in that case, but instead to pursue this taxpayer. Although T. J. Starker's transactions involving three of the parcels differed in a relevant way from those of his son, the legal issues and facts surrounding the other nine are so similar that collateral estoppel applies. Except as to the Bi-Mart, Timian, and Booth properties, the government should have been held collaterally estopped by *Starker I* from relitigation of the applicability of I.R.C. §1031 in *Starker II*.

III. Timian, Bi-Mart, and Booth Properties

As to the Timian, Bi-Mart, and Booth properties, the facts of *Starker I* are so different from those of this case that the entire issue of the applicability of section 1031 to them was properly before the district court in *Starker II*. The court therefore correctly went to the merits of the litigants' arguments as they pertained to these parcels. We now turn to those arguments.

As with the other nine parcels T. J. Starker received, none of these three properties was deeded to him at or near the time he deeded his timberland to Crown. T. J. Starker admits that he received no interest in these properties until a substantial time after he conveyed away title to his property. Thus, the question whether section 1031 requires simultaneity of deed transfers is presented as to all three. In addition, each of these parcels presents its own peculiar issues because of the differing circumstances surrounding their transfers.

A. TIMIAN AND BI-MART PROPERTIES

The Timian property is a residence. Legal title to it was conveyed by Crown at T. J. Starker's request to his daughter, Jean Roth, in 1967. T. J. Starker lives in this residence, and pays rent on it to his daughter. The United States argues that since T. J. Starker never held legal title to this property, he cannot be said to have exchanged his timberland for it. Furthermore, the government contends, because the property became the taxpayer's personal residence, it is neither property "held for investment" nor of a like kind with such property under the meaning of the Code. On the other hand, the taxpayer argues that there was, in economic reality, a transfer of title to him, followed by a gift by him to his daughter.

The Bi-Mart property, a commercial building, was conveyed by Crown to Roth in 1968. The government raises the same issue with regard to the Bi-Mart property: since T. J. Starker never had title, he did not effect an exchange. T. J. Starker points out, however, that he expended substantial time and money in improving and maintaining the structure in the three months prior to the conveyance of the property to his daughter, and he emphasizes that he controlled and commanded its transfer to her.

We begin our analysis of the proper treatment of the receipt of these two properties with a consideration of the Timian residence. T. J. Starker asserts that the question whether such property can be held "for investment" is unsettled. We disagree. It has long been the rule that use of property solely as a personal residence is antithetical to its being held for investment. Losses on the sale or exchange of such property cannot be deducted for this reason, despite the general rule that losses from transactions involving trade or investment properties are deductible. Treas. Regs. §1.165-9(a); see Shields v. Commissioner, 1978-120 T.C.M. (CCH) Dec. 35,064(M). A similar rule must obtain in construing the term "held for investment" in section 1031. 3 J. Mertens, Law of Federal

Income Taxation §20.26 (1972); see Boesel v. Commissioner, 65 T.C. 378, 389 (1975); Rev. Rul. 59-229, 1959-2 Cum. Bull. 180. Thus, nonrecognition treatment cannot be given to the receipt of the Timian parcel.

Moreover, T. J. Starker cannot be said to have received the Timian or Bi-Mart properties in exchange for his interest in the Columbia County timberland because title to the Timian and Bi-Mart properties was transferred by Crown directly to someone else, his daughter. Under an analogous nonrecognition provision, section 1034 of the Code, the key to receiving nonrecognition treatment is maintaining continuity of title. Under section 1034, if title shifts from the taxpayer to someone other than the taxpayer's spouse, nonrecognition is denied. Marcello v. Commissioner, 380 F.2d 499 (5th Cir. 1967); Boesel v. Commissioner, supra. [W]e find similar reasoning compelling here. Although in some cases a father and his daughter may be seen as having an identity of economic interests (cf. McWilliams v. Commissioner, 331 U.S. 694, 699 (1947)), that unity is not sufficient to make transfer of title to one the same as transfer of title to the other. T. J. Starker has not shown that he has any legally cognizable interest in the Timian or Bi-Mart properties that would entitle him to prevent Jean Roth from exercising full ownership rights. In case of a disagreement about the use or enjoyment of these properties, her wishes, not his, would prevail. In these circumstances, T. J. Starker cannot be said to have "exchanged" properties under section 1031, because he never received any property ownership himself.

B. BOOTH PROPERTY

The Booth property is a commercial parcel, title to which has never been conveyed to T. J. Starker. The transfer of this property to him was achieved in 1968 by Crown's acquiring third parties' contract right to purchase the property, and then reassigning the right to T. J. Starker. In addition to emphasizing the lack of simultaneity in the transfers, the government points here to the total lack of deed transfer.

An examination of the record reveals that legal title had not passed by deed to T. J. Starker by the time of the trial. He continued to hold the third-party purchasers' rights under a 1965 sales agreement on the Booth land. That agreement notes that one of the original transferors holds a life interest in the property, and that legal title shall not pass until that life interest expires. In the meantime, the purchasers are entitled to possession, but they are subject to certain restrictions. For example, they are prohibited from removing improvements and are required to keep buildings and fences in good repair. Under the agreement, a substantial portion of the purchase price must be invested, with a fixed return to be paid to the purchaser of the life interest. Should any of these conditions fail, the agreement provides, the sellers may elect, inter alia, to void the contract.

Despite these contingencies, we believe that what T. J. Starker received in 1968 was the equivalent of a fee interest for purposes of section 1031. Under Treas. Regs. §1.1031(a)-1(c), a leasehold interest of 30 years or more is the equivalent of a fee interest for purposes of determining whether the properties exchanged are of a like kind. Under the assigned purchase rights, Starker had at least the rights of a long-term lessee, plus an equitable fee subject to conditions precedent. If the seller's life interest lasted longer than 30 years, the leasehold interest would be the equivalent of a fee; the fact that the leasehold might ripen into a fee at some earlier point should not alter this result. Thus, we hold that what T. J. Starker received in 1968 was the equivalent of a fee.

This does not solve the riddle of the proper treatment of the Booth parcel, however. Since the taxpayer did not receive the fee equivalent at the same time that he gave up his interest in the timberland, the same issue is presented as with the nine parcels on which the government was estopped, namely, whether simultaneity of transfer is required for nonrecognition treatment under section 1031.

The government's argument that simultaneity is required begins with Treas. Reg. §1.1002-1(b). That regulation provides that all exceptions to the general rule that gains and losses are recognized must be construed narrowly:

> . . . Nonrecognition is accorded by the Code only if the exchange is one which satisfies both (1) the specific description in the Code of an excepted exchange, and (2) the underlying purpose for which such exchange is excepted from the general rule.

There are two problems, however, with applying this regulation to section 1031.

First, the "underlying purpose" of section 1031 is not entirely clear. The legislative history reveals that the provision was designed to avoid the imposition of a tax on those who do not "cash in" on their investments in trade or business property. Congress appeared to be concerned that taxpayers would not have the cash to pay a tax on the capital gain if the exchange triggered recognition. This does not explain the precise limits of section 1031, however; if those taxpayers sell their property for cash and reinvest that cash in like-kind property, they cannot enjoy the section's benefits, even if the reinvestment takes place just a few days after the sale. Thus, some taxpayers with liquidity problems resulting from a replacement of their business property are not covered by the section. The liquidity rationale must therefore be limited.

Another apparent consideration of the drafters of the section was the difficulty of valuing property exchanged for the purpose of measuring gain or loss. Section 1031(a) permits the taxpayer to transfer the basis of the property he or she gives up to the property he or she receives, thus deferring the valuation problem, as well as the tax, until the property received is sold or otherwise disposed of in a transaction in which gain or loss is recognized.

But this valuation rationale also has its limits. So long as a single dollar in cash or other non-like-kind property ("boot") is received by the taxpayer along with like-kind property, valuation of both properties in the exchange becomes necessary. In that case, the taxpayer is liable for the gain realized, with the maximum liability being on the amount of cash or other "boot" received, under I.R.C. §1031(b). To compute the gain realized, one must place a value on the like-kind property received. Moreover, the nonrecognition provision applies only to like-kind exchanges, and not to other exchanges in which valuation is just as difficult. Therefore, valuation problems cannot be seen as the controlling consideration in the enactment of section 1031.

In addition to the elusive purpose of the section, there is a second sound reason to question the applicability of Treas. Regs. §1.1002-1: the long line of cases liberally construing section 1031. If the regulation purports to read into section 1031 a complex web of formal and substantive requirements, precedent indicates decisively that the regulation has been rejected. See Biggs v. Commissioner, 69 T.C. 905, 913-914 (1978). We therefore analyze the Booth transaction with the courts' permissive attitude toward section 1031 in mind.

Two features of the Booth deal make it most likely to trigger recognition of gain: the likelihood that the taxpayer would receive cash instead of real estate, and the time gap in the transfers of the equivalents of fee title.

In assessing whether the possibility that T. J. Starker might receive cash makes section 1031 inapplicable, an important case is Alderson v. Commissioner, 317 F.2d 790 (9th Cir. 1963). There, this court held that a "three corner" exchange qualified for nonrecognition treatment. The taxpayer and Alloy entered into an agreement for the simple cash sale of the taxpayer's property, but later amended the agreement to provide that Alloy would purchase another parcel to effect a swap with the taxpayer. This amendment did not totally eradicate the possibility that the cash transaction would take place; it provided, in the words of the court, that "if the exchange was not effected by September 11, 1957, the original escrow re the purchase for cash would be carried out." 317

F.2d at 791. The exchange was effected when reciprocal deeds were recorded. Said the court:

> True, the intermediate acts of the parties could have hewn closer to and have more precisely depicted the ultimate desired result, but what actually occurred on September 3 or 4,957, was an exchange of deeds between the petitioners and Alloy which effected an exchange of the Buena Park property for the Salinas property.

Alderson v. Commissioner, 317 F.2d at 793.

The court stressed that, although at the time the contract was amended there was a possibility that a cash sale would take place, there was from the outset no intention on the part of the taxpayer to sell his property for cash if it could be exchanged for other property of a like kind. Thus, *Alderson* followed Mercantile Trust Co. of Baltimore v. Commissioner, 32 B.T.A. 82 (1935), a case in which the taxpayer could have required the other party to the exchange to pay cash if that other party was unable to purchase an identified parcel that the taxpayer desired. In *Mercantile Trust,* the taxpayer succeeded in getting nonrecognition treatment by virtue of its intention to get other property, rather than cash, if possible.

Coastal Terminals, Inc. v. United States, 320 F.2d 333 (4th Cir. 1963), held similarly. There, a "three corner" exchange was effected, with both the taxpayer and the other party to the exchange maintaining until the closing the option to cancel the exchange and bring about a cash sale instead. Citing *Alderson* with approval, the court noted that the taxpayer intended to sell the property for cash only if it was unable to locate a suitable piece of property to take in exchange. Because an exchange took place, nonrecognition treatment was granted.

The Fifth Circuit has indicated its agreement with this approach in Carlton v. United States, 385 F.2d 238 (5th Cir. 1967). There, the taxpayers gave General Development Corporation (General) an option to purchase their property for cash, but maintained the right to require General to acquire land and transfer it to them in lieu of cash. From the outset, the taxpayers intended to get suitable property, and not cash, in return. As it turned out, at the closing, General transferred to the taxpayers a contract right to purchase two parcels, and enough cash to purchase them, in exchange for the taxpayers' land. Because of the form of payment, section 1031 was held not to apply. But the court noted that the government agreed that had the taxpayers followed the original plan, with General acquiring title and then transferring it to the taxpayers, the section would have applied.

Thus, the mere possibility at the time of agreement that a cash sale might occur does not prevent the application of section 1031. Even in cases such as *Coastal Terminals,* where the taxpayers had the contract right to opt for cash rather than property, a preference by the taxpayers for like-kind property rather than cash has guaranteed nonrecognition despite the possibility of a cash transaction.

In this case, the taxpayer claims he intended from the very outset of the transaction to get nothing but like-kind property, and no evidence to the contrary appears on the record. Moreover, the taxpayer never handled any cash in the course of the transactions. Hence, the *Alderson* line of cases would seem to control.

The government contends, however, that *Alderson* and other precedents of its type are distinguishable. It points out that in those cases, there may have been a possibility of a receipt of cash at the time of the exchange *agreement,* but there was no possibility of receiving cash at the time the taxpayer *transferred* the property pursuant to the agreement. This difference in timing, says the commissioner, renders the *Alderson* line of cases inapplicable.

At least one appellate decision indicates, however, that title may not have to be exchanged simultaneously in order for section 1031 to apply. In Redwing Carriers, Inc. v. Tomlinson, 399 F.2d 652 (5th Cir. 1968), the government argued successfully that mutual transfers of trucks that occurred "at or about" the same time were in fact an "exchange" under section 1031. In *Redwing Carriers,* the taxpayer was attempting to deduct a loss in the purchase of new trucks to replace old trucks; the government disallowed recognition of the loss on the ground that section 1031(c) applied. To keep its replacement transactions outside the scope of the section, a parent corporation transferred its old trucks to a subsidiary, bought new trucks for cash, and had the subsidiary sell the old trucks to the manufacturer for cash. The court viewed the transactions as a whole, and disallowed the loss under section 1031. Some lack of simultaneity was apparently "tolerated" by the commissioner and the court. As the court explained, the transfers to the subsidiary by the parent and to the parent by the manufacturer took place "at or about" the same time. 399 F.2d at 655. Nonetheless, the government urges this court to distinguish *Redwing Carriers,* and *Alderson* and its kin, on the ground that the transfers of title in T. J. Starker's case were separated by a "substantial" period of time. We decline to draw this line.

The government also argues that the contract right to receive property or cash was not "like" title to property, because it was like cash. It asks us to impose a "cash equivalency" test to determine whether section 1031 applies. One flaw in this argument is that title to land is no more or less equivalent to cash than a contract right to buy land. The central concept of section 1031 is that an exchange of business or investment assets does not trigger recognition of gain or loss, because the taxpayer in entering into such a transaction does not "cash in" or "close out" his or her investment. To impose a tax on the event of a deed transfer upon a signing of an exchange agreement could bring about the very result section 1031 was designed to prevent: "the inequity . . . of forcing a taxpayer to recognize a paper gain which was still tied up in a continuing investment of the same sort." Jordan Marsh Co. v. Commissioner, 269 F.2d 453, 456 (2d Cir. 1959).

Against this background, the government offers the explanation that a contract right to land is a "chose in action," and thus personal property instead of real property. This is true, but the short answer to this statement is that title to real property, like a contract right to purchase real property, is nothing more than a bundle of potential causes of action: for trespass, to quiet title, for interference with quiet enjoyment, and so on. The bundle of rights associated with ownership is obviously not excluded from section 1031; a contractual right to assume the rights of ownership should not, we believe, be treated as any different than the ownership rights themselves. Even if the contract right includes the possibility of the taxpayer receiving something other than ownership of like-kind property, we hold that it is still of a like kind with ownership for tax purposes when the taxpayer prefers property to cash before and throughout the executory period, and only like-kind property is ultimately received.

The metaphysical discussion in the briefs and authorities about whether the "steps" of the transactions should be "collapsed," and the truism that "substance" should prevail over "form," are not helpful to the resolution of this case. At best, these words describe results, not reasons. A proper decision can be reached only by considering the purposes of the statute and analyzing its application to particular facts under existing precedent. Here, the statute's purposes are somewhat cloudy, and the precedents are not easy to reconcile. But the weight of authority leans in T. J. Starker's favor, and we conclude that the district court was right in *Starker I*, and wrong in *Starker II*. Thus, on the merits, the transfer of the timberland to Crown triggered a like-kind exchange with respect to the Booth property.

IV. Six Per Cent "Growth" Factor

The next issue presented is whether the 6 per cent "growth factor" received by T. J. Starker was properly treated as capital gain or as ordinary income. The government successfully argued below that this amount should be treated as ordinary income because it was disguised interest. The taxpayer, on the other hand, contends that the 6 per cent "growth" provision merely compensated him for timber growth on the Columbia County property he conveyed to Crown.

The taxpayer's argument is not without some biological merit, but he was entitled to the 6 per cent regardless of the actual fate of the timber on the property. He retained no ownership rights in the timber, and bore no risk of loss, after he conveyed title to Crown. We agree with the government that the taxpayer is essentially arguing "that he conveyed $1,502,500 to a stranger for an indefinite period of time [up to five years] without any interest." The 6 per cent "growth factor" was "compensation for the use or forbearance of money," that is, for the use of the unpaid amounts owed to Starker by Crown. Therefore, it was disguised interest. . . .

V. Timing of Inclusion

Our final task, having characterized the proper nature of T. J. Starker's receipts, is to decide in which years they are includable in income. The Timian and Bi-Mart properties do not qualify for nonrecognition treatment, while the other 10 properties received do qualify. In this situation, we believe the proper result is to treat T. J. Starker's rights in his contract with Crown, insofar as they resulted in the receipt of the Timian and Bi-Mart properties, as "boot," received in 1967 when the contract was made. We hold that section 1031(b) requires T. J. Starker to recognize his gain on the transaction with Crown in 1967, to the extent of the fair market values of the Timian and Bi-Mart properties as of the dates on which title to those properties passed to his appointee.

We realize that this decision leaves the treatment of an alleged exchange open until the eventual receipt of consideration by the taxpayer. Some administrative difficulties may surface as a result. Our role, however, is not necessarily to facilitate administration. It is to divine the meaning of the statute in a manner as consistent as possible with the intent of Congress and the prior holdings of the courts. If our holding today adds a degree of uncertainty to this area, Congress can clarify its meaning.

As to the disguised interest, the district court erred in holding T. J. Starker liable for ordinary income in 1967. As a taxpayer reporting on the cash method, T. J. Starker was not liable for taxes on interest income until that interest was received. Although receipt may be actual or constructive, Crown's liability for the "growth factor" did not commence until after 1967 had expired. Had suitable properties been found for T. J. Starker in 1967 (as was the case with Bruce and Elizabeth), Crown would have owed T. J. Starker no "growth factor" at all. Therefore, the government should not have assessed an ordinary income tax on the "growth factor" in 1967. The proper years of inclusion would have been those in which the taxpayer received the interest. To the extent T. J. Starker paid the ordinary tax for 1967, he was entitled to his refund.

VI. Conclusion

We affirm the judgment of the district court in part, and reverse it in part. We remand for a modified judgment consistent with this opinion.

Vacated and remanded.

NOTES AND QUESTIONS

1. *Aftermath.* (a) The *Starker* case is valuable as an illustration of tax planning for like-kind exchanges and of the problem of substance versus form and statutory interpretation in tax cases. Its specific results, however, have been altered by Congress.

(b) Section 1031 was amended in 1984 by the addition of §1031(a)(3), which is addressed specifically to the problem raised by *Starker.* Section 1031(a)(3) provides that nonrecognition is available if, and only if, after property has been relinquished by the taxpayer, the like-kind property is *identified* within 45 days thereafter and is *received* within the earlier of (a) 180 days or (b) the due date of the taxpayer's return. Thus, delayed three-corner exchanges are permitted, but the transaction in the *Starker* case itself would not be entitled to nonrecognition treatment under §1031 because the new time limits were exceeded. What effect on behavior do you suppose §1031(a)(3) will have in situations such as the one in *Starker?* Do you suppose that the taxpayer in that case could have arranged the transaction to meet the requirements of §1031(a)(3)? Do those requirements seem to you to be too harsh? too generous?

(c) Note that while delayed exchanges are permitted, §1031 still requires an "*exchange.*" A person relinquishing property is not permitted to receive cash even if the cash is reinvested within the time limits specified in §1031(a)(3). That is all well and good if the person relinquishing the property is willing to rely on the promise of the person to whom the property is transferred. If, however, the transferor insists, for example, that the agreed amount be paid into an escrow account, protected from the claims of the transferee's creditors, the "exchange" requirement may not be met.

(d) Section 453 provides that in the case of installment sales (that is, sales with delayed payments), gain ordinarily is not recognized until cash is received. See discussion infra page 364. In 1980, §453 was amended to extend its coverage to situations like the one in *Starker.* The effect of the application of §453 to cases like *Starker* is that if cash (rather than like-kind property) is ultimately received, gain is recognized in the year of such receipt, not (as the court in *Starker* ruled) in the year in which the taxpayer's property was relinquished.

2. *"Metaphysical discussion."* Just before its examination of the 6 percent "growth factor," the court in *Starker* says that "metaphysical discussion" of substance versus form is "not helpful." Do you agree that an inquiry into substance is necessarily metaphysical? Is it relevant to ask how the transaction would have been structured if tax effects had not been relevant? Why is it not helpful to recognize that the form of the transactions in *Starker* was patently convoluted; that the only plausible explanation for the convolution was tax avoidance; and that the effect of the transaction was — and the normal, natural way to accomplish the obvious objectives of the parties would have been — a sale for cash and a reinvestment of the cash proceeds?

It is important to repeat that courts can, and often do, look through the form of transactions and tax them according to their substance. The decision in *Starker* and even the earlier decisions in the less aggressive three-corner exchange cases are, in fact, questionable, even surprising, ones. By no means should one assume that in tax planning one can achieve by clever manipulation of forms what one cannot achieve directly. One should be aware of the dangers of being a pettifogger and of being "too clever by half." Moreover, it is also useful to bear in mind at all times the "pig theory," which derives from the Wall Street adage, "you can make money as a bull, you can make money as a bear, but you can't make money as a pig." The *Starker* scheme, pushing to the limit §1031 and its questionable extension to permit three-corner exchanges, seems at least borderline piggish.

3. *Accounting method.* T. J. Starker was, like most individuals, a cash-method taxpayer. Would the result have been different if he had been on the accrual method?

4. *Trading up.* Suppose that many years ago, *T* bought commercial property consisting of land with an office building, for $500,000, and it is now worth $1 million. A debt of $400,000 that *T* incurred in initially acquiring the property has been fully paid off; *T* owns the property free and clear. Over the years, *T* has claimed the maximum depreciation deductions on the building; her remaining basis in the property is $100,000 and current depreciation deductions are negligible. Rental receipts greatly exceed expenses, plus the limited depreciation deduction; the property generates a good cash return, but it is ordinary income. *T* has substantial income from other sources, dislikes paying income taxes on returns on the property, and does not need the cash she gets from it. This is precisely the kind of situation that attracts the attention and the energies of real estate agents. Suppose that a real estate agent finds another office-building property, worth $4 million, and arranges for *T* to enter into a three-corner like-kind exchange in which she winds up owning that $4 million property, subject to a debt of $3 million. In other words, *T* uses her original property as a 25 percent down payment for the $4 million property. Her basis will be

$3.1 million — the original $100,000 plus the additional $3 million borrowed and invested. See Regs. §1.1016-2(a). This means that she will be entitled to a substantial deduction for depreciation, which may shelter the income from the property. This kind of transaction takes advantage of §1031's nonrecognition rule, but a complete tax analysis requires that one take account of the effects of the addition of the debt. That debt produces both financial leverage and tax leverage. Financial leverage is the advantage (or disadvantage) of borrowing at a given rate and investing at a higher (or lower) rate. Tax leverage, in this example, is the advantage of using borrowed funds (sometimes called OPM, for other people's money) to generate basis, which in turn generates deductions (here, for depreciation). Because of the debt, the new investment is more risky than the old one; it is essentially a different kind of investment for that reason, which means that understanding the pure tax effects, or even the effects of nonrecognition under §1031, requires a complex analysis that can best be developed with computer models. For an excellent illustration of such analysis, see Anderson, Winokur, and Mullin, Tax Planning: The Missing Quantitative Dimension, 31st U.S.C. Tax Institute ¶400 (1981). It is worth noting, by the way, that in some circumstances tax effects comparable to those achieved by *T* in the trade-up three-corner exchange (that is, increased depreciation deductions from an increased amount of investment, financed with borrowed funds) can be achieved more simply by borrowing money to construct a new building on one's presently owned property.

B. RECOGNITION OF LOSSES

The following Revenue Ruling is concerned with the loss side of the timing issue. When the ruling states that costs at issue are "capitalized," it means that those costs are treated as the price of acquiring an asset as opposed to an expense of current operations. Thus, there is no current deduction for those costs; instead the taxpayer keeps track of them in a "capital" account. In this instance, the asset is like land in that it does not decline in value with the passage of time the way an asset like a truck or a building would. Thus, the capitalized cost (which for tax purposes is called basis) is taken into account only on disposition of the asset.

REVENUE RULING 84-145

1984-2 C.B. 47

Issue

Has a domestic commercial air carrier, subject to the regulations of the Civil Aeronautics Board (CAB), sustained a deductible loss under section 165(a) of the Internal Revenue Code because of a devaluation of its route authorities resulting from the enactment of the Airline Deregulation Act of 1978, Pub. L. No. 95-5004, 95th Cong., 2d Sess. (October 24, 1978) (the Deregulation Act)?

Facts

The taxpayer, a commercial air carrier, is engaged in the interstate and international transportation of passengers, mail, and property. The taxpayer is subject to the Federal Aviation Act of 1958, as amended, (the Act), which regulates the economic aspects of air transportation. The Act established the CAB and granted it authority to issue regulations that govern interstate and international air transportation. Pursuant to this authority, the CAB granted taxpayer the rights to service several cities. These rights were represented by route authorities.

In order to obtain a route authority to service a particular geographic location, the taxpayer had to apply to the CAB. The CAB would issue a permanent certificate authorizing the whole route or any part of the route authority covered by the taxpayer's application, if it found the taxpayer fit, willing, and able to perform the transportation properly and to conform to the law, rules, regulations, and requirements of the CAB and if it found that the transportation was required by the public convenience and necessity. The application of this standard to the taxpayer and other carrier applicants resulted in the CAB granting a limited number of route authorities to any one destination. The application process was highly competitive, and the taxpayer typically incurred considerable expense in its efforts to prevail in the awarding of a route authority.

Rev. Rul. 56-600, 1956-2 C.B. 171, and Rev. Rul. 67-113, 1967-1 C.B. 55, require air carriers to keep the costs they incur in the acquisition and development of air routes in separate capital accounts. These costs remain capitalized until the routes are abandoned. In the years prior to 1979, the taxpayer capitalized the costs it incurred in obtaining permanent air route authorities from the CAB.

The Deregulation Act changed the standards the CAB used to grant route authorities. The air transportation offered by a carrier no longer needed to be required by the public convenience and necessity. Under the new standard, the air transportation needed merely to be consistent with the public convenience and necessity. However, from the date of enactment until December 31, 1981, when the new standard became fully effective, carriers in order to obtain new route authorities were still obligated to obtain certificates issued by the CAB authorizing the carrier to fly the routes. Under the Deregulation Act, as fully effective after December 31, 1981, most of the CAB's control over domestic routes terminated.

When the Deregulation Act became fully effective on December 31, 1981, the exclusiveness of route authorities considerably lessened because restrictions on entry into a particular market was significantly reduced. Under the new law, commercial air carriers must still obtain the CAB's permission to operate in a specific market, but they are no longer required to show anything other than that they are not unfit to provide the service. Thus, it is now relatively easy for all commercial air carriers to obtain route authorities from the CAB. In the instant situation, although the taxpayer continued its normal operations, the value of its route authorities declined substantially because its right to operate in a particular market was affected by the potential for increased competition for other commercial air carriers.

Law and Analysis

Section 165(a) of the Code provides that there shall be allowed as a deduction any loss sustained during the taxable year and not compensated by insurance or otherwise.

Section 1.165-1(d) of the Income Tax Regulations provides that to be allowable as a deduction under section 165(a) of the Code, a loss must be evidenced by closed and completed transactions, fixed by identifiable events, and actually sustained during the taxable year. Only a bona fide loss is allowable.

In Reporter Publishing Co., Inc. v. Commissioner, 201 F.2d 743 (10th Cir.), cert. denied, 345 U.S. 993 (1953), the court held that the taxpayer, a newspaper publisher, did not sustain a deductible loss as a result of a decision of the Supreme Court of the United States that held that the by-laws of the Associated Press, which granted the taxpayer an exclusive right to Associated Press services in its community, violated the Sherman Anti-Trust Act. Although the value of the membership in the Associated Press was reduced because of the Supreme Court's decision, it was not eliminated because the taxpayer retained the same rights to receive all the services it received before the decision.

In Consolidated Freight Lines v. Commissioner, 37 B.T.A. 576 (1938), aff'd, 1011 F.2d 813 (9th Cir. 1939), 1939-2 C.B. 206, cert. denied, 308 U.S. 562 (1939), the lowest court denied a deduction for the cost of certificates of convenience and necessity that a motor carrier claimed had no value because a new law was enacted that repealed the monopolistic characteristics of the old law under which the certificates were issued. The United States Court of Appeals for the Ninth Circuit held that a monopoly was not granted by the certificates but rather sprang from the provisions of the old law. The certificates were merely a means by which a carrier might take advantage of the monopoly that was conferred by the statute. The monopoly, not the certificates themselves, was the thing destroyed by the repeal of the old law.

In the instant situation, the taxpayer did not sell or abandon as completely worthless its route authorities. Although the value of its route authorities was substantially reduced after the Deregulation Act became law, the mere diminution in value of the operating rights does not constitute the elimination or abandonment of a completely worthless asset. In addition, there was no closed and completed transaction fixed by identifiable events because the taxpayer's operating rights remained unchanged even though more competition was introduced.

Holding

A commercial air carrier subject to the regulations of the CAB did not sustain a deductible loss of its capitalized costs under section 165(a) of the Code because of the devaluation of its route authorities that resulted when the Deregulation Act became fully effective on December 31, 1981.

QUESTIONS

1. Suppose an air carrier called Firstair spent $1 million to acquire the authority to operate flights between two cities. The $1 million was a capitalized cost, so Firstair's basis in the route authority is $1 million. From the time it acquired the route authority until the time of deregulation, Firstair operated six flights a day on the route. Shortly after deregulation, because of competition, it reduced the number of its flights to two per day and has been operating at that level for several years, with no prospect of increase. Two of the current competitors for flights between the two cities did not begin operation until after deregulation. They spent nothing on acquiring the authority to fly the route. Can Firstair deduct some or all of its investment in the route authority?

2. Pamela bought a grocery store three years ago. She paid fair market value of $100,000 for fixtures and equipment, and $200,000 for goodwill. The building was leased under a twenty-year lease, on which she was substituted as tenant. A year after she bought the store,

a large chain opened a supermarket near her store and her business suffered markedly. Three months ago Pamela realized that she was not making enough to cover her operating costs and has reduced store hours to minimize her losses. As a result of ACRS deductions, her basis in the fixtures and equipment is now $80,000. For the past two months, she has tried to sell the store. The best offer she has received so far is $40,000, from a wholesale dealer in used fixtures and equipment. Is she permitted to claim a loss deduction for the $200,000 investment in goodwill?

3. Do the same considerations that argue for nonrecognition of unrealized gains also argue for nonrecognition of unrealized losses? Given the current realization rules for taxation of gain, what is the strongest argument for nonrecognition of unrealized losses?

4. Is Revenue Ruling 84-145 consistent with the judicially developed doctrines relating to gains that you have studied earlier in this chapter?

5. Is the situation described in the ruling one that seems to call for congressional relief? Assume that you represent the taxpayer and have been asked to draft a new code provision allowing the deduction at issue. What language would you offer?

C. ORIGINAL ISSUE DISCOUNT AND RELATED RULES

The rules on original issue discount (OID) provide that to the extent that a "debt instrument" does not provide for current payment of an adequate amount of interest, interest must be accrued (that is, included currently in income) by the obligee regardless whether the obligee is a cash-method or accrual-method taxpayer. See §§1272-1275. The obligor is entitled to deduct the amount that the obligee is required to accrue. The OID rules apply to debt instruments issued for cash or for property, with certain exceptions for relatively small transactions. The concept of original issue discount (OID) refers to the unstated interest in a deferred payment. When a bond is sold for cash, the OID is the difference between the issue price (that is, the price at which the bond is sold) and the redemption price (the price required to be paid by the issuer/borrower when the term of the loan ends and the bond must be paid off (redeemed)). For example, suppose that a bond is issued (sold) for $600,000 and that it is to be redeemed five years later for $1 million, with no interest payments in the interim. The amount of the OID is the difference between the redemption price ($1 million) and the issue price ($600,000), or $400,000. §1273(a). This amount is treated as interest earned ratably over the five-year term of the loan with semiannual compounding. The amount of interest to be reported by the lender and deducted by the borrower each year is shown below:

Redemption price	$1,000,000
Issue price	600,000
OID	400,000
Term	5 years

Annual interest amounts:		New basis (end of year):
Year 1	$64,540	$664,540
Year 2	71,482	736,022
Year 3	79,171	815,193
Year 4	87,687	902,880
Year 5	97,120	1,000,000
Total	$400,000	

Here the effect of the OID rules is to treat the purchaser of the bond as if she had simply placed the $600,000 issue price in a bank or money market account that paid interest at a rate sufficient to generate the redemption price in five years. Each year the amount in the account would rise and the interest income would increase.

Section 1275(a)(1)(A) provides that "the term 'debt instrument' means a bond, debenture, note, or certificate or other evidence of indebtedness." The OID rules provide an economically accurate reporting of income and deductions. The main purpose of their adoption was to prevent the tax avoidance that occurred when an accrual-method obligor deducted accrued interest while the cash-method obligee reported no interest income.

The application of the OID concept in the above example of a sale of a bond for cash is relatively simple and straightforward since there is no question about the amount of the original issue discount: It is simply the difference between the price paid for the bond at the time of issuance and the redemption price. Where a promissory obligation is issued in return for property, the application of the OID rules is more complex because there is no readily determinable issue price. The counterpart of the receipt and payment of an issue price is the transfer of property; the value of the property often will be difficult to determine. The approach of the OID rules, therefore, is to apply discount rates to the expected payments. In other words, the issue price is determined by discounting the expected payments to present value. Obviously, the key element in the process is the selection of an appropriate interest rate. The Code calls for the Treasury to publish periodically interest rates for obligations of various durations. §1274(d). These interest rates, called the "applicable federal rates," are based on the current rates paid on U.S. Treasury obligations. If the amount of interest stated by the parties is adequate, as compared with the applicable federal rate, then that stated rate is accepted in determining the amount of interest deducted by the obligor and reported by the obligee. Otherwise, the applicable federal rate is used.

To illustrate, assume that on January 1 of year 1, *T* buys an apartment building for an amount stated to be $5 million. *T* pays no cash but instead executes a promissory note for $5 million, due ten years later, with interest payable at the rate of 8 percent per year. Assume that the annualized "applicable federal rate" at the time the note is issued is 10 percent.[7] The payments of $400,000 per year for nine years, plus $5,400,000 in the tenth year, are discounted to present value using the 10 percent rate. The result is a present value, or "imputed principal amount" (§1274(b)(1)), of $4,385,543, which is treated as the issue price. The difference between this amount and the $5,000,000 redemption price is $614,457, which is the OID. A portion of this total amount of OID must be reported each year along with the $400,000 annual cash payment called for in the obligation.

How much OID is recognized each year? In the first year, the total interest earned on the note is equal to the present value of the amount owed ($4,385,543) multiplied by the applicable federal rate of 10 percent. That comes to $438,554. The stated interest is only $400,000, so the OID is the difference, $38,554. This $38,554, along with the $400,000 cash payment, is reported as income by the holder of the obligation and is deducted by the obligor in the first year. The $38,554 has not in fact been paid, however, and is in effect added to the principal amount owed, which produces a principal amount at the beginning of the second year of $4,424,097 (with an error of $1 due to rounding). (The same result is reached by discounting the remaining payments to present value.) The interest on the debt in the second year is equal to the new principal amount ($4,424,097) multiplied by the applicable federal rate of 10 percent, or $442,410. Again, the stated interest is $400,000, so the OID is $42,410. These numbers and the corresponding numbers for the remaining years are shown in Table 3-3.

The OID concept is also applied to rents, under §467. To illustrate, suppose Lessor agrees to rent property to Lessee for three years in return for a single payment of $1 million at the end of the three-year term. Before the adoption of §467, an accrual-method lessee might accrue and treat as a deduction each year one-third of the total amount due at the end of the three years. At the same time, a cash-method

7. The rates published by the Treasury include rates with a slight upward adjustment that may be used for compounding on an annual, rather than semiannual, basis to achieve the same annual result that would be reached using the semiannual rate with semiannual compounding.

TABLE 3-3

Year	*Value of debt obligation*[a]	*Total interest earned*	*Annual stated interest*	*Annual OID*[b]	*Principal payment*
1	$4,385,543	$438,554	$400,000	$38,554	
2	4,424,098	442,410	400,000	42,410	
3	4,466,507	446,651	400,000	46,651	
4	4,513,158	451,316	400,000	51,316	
5	4,564,474	456,447	400,000	56,447	
6	4,620,921	462,092	400,000	62,092	
7	4,683,013	468,301	400,000	68,301	
8	4,751,315	475,131	400,000	75,131	
9	4,826,446	482,645	400,000	82,645	
10	4,909,091	490,909	400,000	90,909	$5,000,000

a. Principal and interest payments discounted at applicable federal rate of 10 percent.
b. This amount is added to principal.

lessor would not include any amount in income until the $1 million was received. Section 467 is intended to put an end to such mismatching. Here is how it would work on the hypothetical facts.

First, one computes the present value of the $1 million payment at the end of the third year, using 110 percent of the applicable federal rate. Assume that the applicable federal rate is 9.09 percent and that 110 percent of that rate is therefore (almost) 10 percent. The present value (with semiannual compounding) is $746,237. One then computes (on a computer) the annual rent, payable at the end of each year, that would have the same present value. That annual rental amount, which turns out to be $301,389, is called the "constant rental amount." See §467(e)(1). The lessee is allowed to deduct, and the lessor is required to include in gross income, this $301,389 at the end of each year. Because that amount of rent is not in fact paid, however, it is treated as if it were a loan from the lessor to the lessee, and unstated interest must be attributed to the parties. Thus, at the end of the first year, the lessee is treated as owing $301,389 and at the end of the second year is treated as owing interest on this amount (again, at 110 percent of the applicable federal rate, compounded semiannually). The interest at the end of the second year is $30,889. In addition, at the end of the second year, lessee is treated as owing the second year's rent of $301,389. In the third year, interest continues to accrue on the first year's unpaid rent (plus the unpaid interest on that rent) and begins to accrue on the second year's unpaid rent. Thus, the total interest at the end of the third year is $64,944. The constant rental amounts, the interest, and the total amounts to be included in income by the lessor and deducted by the lessee are as follows:

Year	*Rent*	*Interest*	*Total*
1	$301,389	—	$ 301,389
2	301,389	30,889	332,278
3	$301,389	64,944	366,333
Total	$904,167	$95,833	$1,000,000

There are also rules for taxation of "market discount." These rules do not alter the normal rules on timing of recognition of gain. Their purpose and function was to prevent the conversion of ordinary income into capital gain. To illustrate their operation, suppose a bond was issued many years ago and bears interest at a rate of 3 percent on a face value of $1,000 (this being the amount that must be paid at maturity), with four years to maturity. If the present market rate of interest is 12 percent, the present value of the bond is $727. A buyer of such a bond would receive annual interest payments of $30. These would be taxable as received as ordinary income. At maturity, the buyer would receive $1,000 and would report a gain of $273. This $273 is called "market discount"; under §§1276 and 1278 the gain is treated as ordinary income, rather than as capital gain (which is the way it was treated before the adoption of these provisions in 1984). If the bond is sold before the maturity date, a ratable portion of the market discount (determined on a linear daily basis) is treated as ordinary income.

There are exceptions to the application of the OID rules, including exceptions for sales of principal residences, sales of farms for less than $1 million, and sales for payments totaling less than $250,000. §1274(c)(3). In these situations, where the OID rules do not apply, §483 applies. Section 483 does not affect the timing of the recognition of the imputed interest income, but ensures that that income is treated as ordinary income rather than as capital gain. In other words, §483 determines the character or nature of the gain from certain sales transactions, whereas the OID rules determine not just the character of the gain but the time of its recognition. For example, suppose that a personal residence with a basis of $400,000 is sold for a single payment of $1 million to be made at the end of five years, and that the applicable federal rate is 10 percent. At the time of sale the present value of the future payment is $620,921 and the "unstated interest" is the difference between that present value amount and the $1 million payment, or $379,079. When the $1,000,000 is collected at the end of five years, the seller will report a total gain of $600,000, the difference between the basis, $400,000, and the amount received, $1 million. Of the $600,000, $379,079 is reported as ordinary interest income and the remaining $220,921 is reported as capital gain.

D. OPEN TRANSACTIONS, INSTALLMENT SALES, AND DEFERRED SALES

1. Open Transactions

The case that follows, Burnet v. Logan, has little if any remaining importance for the rule it adopts. See infra page 361, Note 3. The case continues to be of interest, however, because it establishes what one may think of as one end of a spectrum of possible recovery-of-basis rules and because of its discussion of the justification for the approach it adopts.

BURNET v. LOGAN

283 U.S. 404 (1931)

Mr. Justice McReynolds delivered the opinion of the Court.

[The facts in the case are complicated and confusing. The following simplified and modified version of the facts reveals the essence of the transaction and the issues raised.

Mrs. Logan, the taxpayer, owned 1,000 shares of stock of Andrews and Hitchcock Mining Company. Her basis in these shares was $180,000. Andrews and Hitchcock owned the right to a part of the ore mined from a rich iron deposit. In 1916 Youngstown Sheet & Tube Company bought all the shares of Andrews and Hitchcock owned by Mrs. Logan and her fellow shareholders. As consideration for the purchase, Youngstown made a cash payment and agreed to make additional payments in the future based on the amount of ore that it would receive as a result of its acquisition of the Andrews and Hitchcock rights in the iron mine. There was considerable uncertainty about what the amount of the future payments would turn out to be.

Mrs. Logan's share of the cash payment was $120,000. The government estimated that she would receive future payments, based on the amount of ore going to Youngstown, of $9,000 per year for twenty-five years, with a present value of $100,000.

The position taken by the government was that in 1916 Mrs. Logan sold her shares for $220,000 (the cash of $120,000 plus the present value of the promise of future payments, $100,000) and should have reported a gain of $40,000. In other words, the government claimed that the transaction was a "closed transaction" in 1916. Mrs. Logan would then have a basis of $100,000 in the right to receive the future payments and, according to the government, would be allowed to recover this basis at the rate of $4,000 per year over the twenty-five years in which she expected to receive payments.

Mrs. Logan argued for "open transaction" treatment. There were two separate aspects to her position. The first was that the promise to make future payments did not have an ascertainable value in 1916 and should be ignored in that year. The second aspect of Mrs. Logan's tax position was that she should be allowed to recover her entire basis before reporting any gain. Thus, she claimed that she was not required to report any gain in 1916, since she received only $120,000 in cash and her basis was $180,000, and that she was not required to treat any of the future payments from Youngstown as income until the total of such payments had exceeded her remaining basis ($60,000).

The Court, without separating the two aspects of Mrs. Logan's position, held in her favor. Its opinion follows.]

The 1916 transaction was a sale of stock — not an exchange of property. We are not dealing with royalties or deductions from gross income because of depletion of mining property. Nor does the situation demand that an effort be made to place according to the best available data some approximate value upon the contract for future payments. This probably was necessary in order to assess the mother's estate. As annual payments on account of extracted ore come in they can be readily apportioned first as return of capital and later as profit. The liability for income tax ultimately can be fairly determined without resort to mere estimates, assumptions and speculation. When the profit, if any, is actually realized, the taxpayer will be required to respond. The [total] consideration for the sale [realized by all the shareholders] was $2,200,000.00 in cash and the promise of future money payments wholly contingent upon facts and circumstances not possible to foretell with anything like fair certainty. The promise was in no proper sense equivalent to cash. It had no ascertainable fair market value. The transaction was not a closed one. Respondent might never recoup her capital investment from payments only conditionally promised. Prior to 1921, all receipts from the sale of her shares amounted to less than their value on March 1, 1913. She properly demanded the return of her capital investment before assessment of any taxable profit based on conjecture.

"In order to determine whether there has been gain or loss, and the amount of the gain if any, we must withdraw from the proceeds an amount sufficient to restore the capital value that existed at the commencement of the period under consideration." Doyle v. Mitchell Bros. Co., 247 U.S. 179, 184, 185. . . . Ordinarily, at least, a taxpayer may not deduct from gross receipts a supposed loss which in fact is represented by his outstanding note. . . . And, conversely, a promise to pay indeterminate sums of money is not necessarily taxable income. "Generally speaking, the income tax law is concerned only with realized losses, as with realized gains." Lucas v. American Code Co., 280 U.S. 445, 449.

From her mother's estate, Mrs. Logan obtained [by inheritance] the right to [additional payments from Youngstown Steel by virtue of the mother's ownership of Andrews and Hitchcock stock]. The value of this [right] was assumed [for estate tax purposes] to be $277,164.50. . . . Some valuation — speculative or otherwise — was necessary in order to close the estate. It may never yield as much, it may yield more. If a sum equal to the value thus ascertained had been invested in an annuity contract, payments thereunder would have been free from income tax until the owner had recouped his capital investment.[8] We think a like rule should be applied here. The statute definitely excepts bequests from receipts which go to make up taxable income. . . .

The judgments below are affirmed.

REVENUE RULING 70-63

1970-1 C.B. 36

A taxpayer's delinquency in payment of his county real estate taxes resulted in the "tax sale" of the property by the county. Under the laws of that jurisdiction, the delinquent taxpayer is entitled to redeem the "tax title" within two years from the date of the tax sale.

Held, the "tax sale" under these circumstances is not a closed and completed transaction that gives rise to a gain or loss inasmuch as there is no identifiable taxable event before the expiration of the redemption period. Held further, the tax sale of the property by the county is not a "payment" of taxes by the owner of the realty inasmuch as the property involved was "sold" by the county for the *nonpayment* of taxes. There being no payment of taxes on the property by means of the tax sale, a deduction for taxes paid is not allowable. . . .

NOTES AND QUESTIONS

1. *The "open transaction."* Burnet v. Logan is said to stand for the "open transaction" concept or doctrine — the notion that where the total value of the consideration to be received by a taxpayer is sufficiently uncertain (not "equivalent to cash" because of "no ascertainable fair market value") gain is not recognized until the payments actually received exceed basis. The key sentence in the opinion is, "The transaction was not a closed one." The case may be compared with Inaja Land Co. v. Commissioner, supra page 168, where the taxpayer sold an easement affecting a river that crossed its property and the court treated the entire proceeds as a recovery of basis. There the uncertainty related to what was sold, and in Burnet v. Logan it related to what was received. In both cases the courts adopted a "wait and see" attitude. This is highly

8. [This was the rule for annuities before 1934. — Eds.]

favorable to the taxpayer, much more so in an era of high interest rates than in the era of low interest rates when these cases were decided.

The taxpayer had another, unused string to her bow in Burnet v. Logan. Even if the value of the expected payments in the case had been ascertainable, the taxpayer might have argued that the transaction should not result in recognition or gain because what she received was a "mere" promise to pay, which is not treated as a receipt for cash-method taxpayers. For example, if a lawyer performs services for a client and the client agrees to pay $1,000 to the lawyer next year, the lawyer (assuming she or he uses the cash method) is not required to report the $1,000 until received. If, on the other hand, the promise to pay takes the form of negotiable promissory notes, such notes generally are considered "property," the value of which must be included in income (just as the value of the annuity policy received by the taxpayer in the *Drescher* case (supra page 79) was included in his income). See Note 3, infra.

2. *Three possible approaches.* Consider three possible approaches to recognition of gain or loss and recovery of basis where property has been sold in return for the right to a series of cash payments (installments) to be received in the future. For present purposes, let us assume that each installment payment is to bear interest at the market rate, so we need not be concerned about the rules relating to unstated interest or original issue discount. (1) One possible rule for recovery of basis is the *open transaction* approach. In Burnet v. Logan this was combined with a rule under which all payments received were treated as recovery of basis until the full amount of the basis was recovered and then all payments are treated as gain. Thus, the case may be said to reflect a *basis first* rule. (2) A second possibility is to determine the *present value* of the expected payments and treat this sum as if it were cash received on the date of the sale. Gain or loss is then determined by comparing this amount with basis.[9] This is the *closed transaction* approach. (3) A third possibility is to use an open transaction approach but to allocate some portion of basis to each expected payment received, so that some portion of the gain or loss is recognized as each payment is received. This is the approach of the *installment method,* discussed infra at page 364.

What are the advantages of and objections to each approach? What are the circumstances to which each approach may be best suited?

3. *The present rule.* (a) In 1980, Congress expanded the availability of the installment method of reporting, under which gain or loss is reported as payments are received. See infra page 364. In explaining the

9. If the payments bear interest at the market rate, the present value will be equal to the total stated amount of the payments, before interest.

revised rules, the Senate Finance Committee Report (No. 96-1000, 96th Cong., 2d Sess. (1980)) had this to say:

> The creation of a statutory deferred payment option for all forms of deferred payment sales significantly expands the availability of installment reporting to include situations where it has not previously been permitted. By providing an expanded statutory installment reporting option, the Committee believes that in the future there should be little attempt to obtain deferred reporting. In any event, the effect of the new rules is to reduce substantially the justification for treating transactions as "open" and permitting the use of the cost-recovery method sanctioned by Burnet v. Logan [supra page 358]. Accordingly, it is the Committee's intent that the cost-recovery method not be available in the case of sales for a fixed price (whether the seller's obligation is evidenced by a note, contractual promise, or otherwise), and that its use be limited to those rare and extraordinary cases involving sales for a contingent price where the fair market value of the purchaser's obligation cannot reasonably be ascertained.

(b) Even before 1980, the Regulations relating to gain or loss on disposition of property had provided that "only in rare and extraordinary cases will property be considered to have no fair market value." Regs. §1.1001-1(a).

(c) In Warren Jones Co. v. Commissioner, 524 F.2d 788 (9th Cir. 1975), the taxpayer sold a building by land sale contract for $153,000, receiving $20,000 in cash and a contract calling for payment of the balance, $133,000, over fifteen years. In the year of sale, the taxpayer received $24,000, and since it had a basis of $61,913.34, it deferred reporting gain until it recovered its basis. Evidence was presented that the $133,000 contract could have been sold in the marketplace for only $76,980. The Tax Court held that the taxpayer properly deferred reporting gain, that the contract was not "property (other than money)" under §1001(b), and that it was not the equivalent of cash since with a fair market value of $76,980, it could not be sold for anywhere near its $133,000 face amount. The circuit court reversed, interpreting the legislative history of §1001(b) to mean that Congress intended to establish a definite rule that if the fair market value received in an exchange can be ascertained, the fair market value must be reported as the amount realized, rejecting the argument that cash equivalency close to face amount of an obligation was an element to be considered in determining whether fair market value could be ascertained. The court reasoned that §453, providing for installment reporting and discussed infra page 364, was Congress's way of providing relief from the rigors of §1001(b). Compare material on economic benefit and cash equivalents in Chapter 2A.

(d) Cf. Bolles v. Commissioner, 69 T.C. 342 (1977), where members of the Piper family agreed in 1969 to an exchange offer of their shares of Piper Corp. stock for Bangor Punta Corp. stock if Bangor Punta could acquire more than half of the Piper Corp. outstanding shares, with the consideration to be determined by a third party. During 1969, Bangor Punta had not acquired the requisite number of shares and the final price had not been set by the third party. The court, following Burnet v. Logan, held that due to the contingencies involved, the rights had no ascertainable fair market value and the taxpayer need not recognize any gain from receipt of the rights in 1969. Should the reason for deferral in this case be the lack of ascertainable value or the inappropriateness of the time to tax, given the substantial contingencies still unresolved? Can't everything be valued if necessary?

4. *The capital gain issue.* Under present law, whenever we are confronted with deferred payments we must be concerned about unstated interest (§483) or original issue discount (OID). In the era before 1987, when the tax on long-term capital gain was substantially lower than the tax on ordinary income, the §483 and OID rules had the important effect of ensuring that the interest element in any deferred payment was treated as ordinary income rather than as capital gain. They still have that effect, but the consequences are different and less important. Before §483 and the OID rules were adopted, and to some extent even now, judicially developed rules relating to open versus closed transactions affected the characterization of gain as ordinary or capital and the timing of the recognition of gain. If, as in Burnet v. Logan, a transaction was treated as open, payments received were treated as nontaxable recovery of basis until basis was exhausted and, if, as in that case, the transaction involved the sale of a capital asset, all subsequent payments were treated as capital gain. Thus, the seller had two advantages, maximum deferral and maximum capital gain treatment.

If the transaction had been treated as closed, the seller not only would have lost the advantage of deferral but also could have lost some of the benefit of capital gain treatment. For example, in Waring v. Commissioner, 412 F.2d 800 (3d Cir. 1969), the taxpayer in 1946 had in effect sold a license to use the name "Waring" on the Waring blender, in return for royalties. In his 1946 tax return, he treated the transaction as closed. He valued the right to the royalties at $300,000, deducted his basis of $93,000, and reported a capital gain of $207,000. This meant that his basis for the right to receive the royalties became $300,000. As royalties were received in subsequent years, he treated them as recovery of capital, reducing basis.[10] By the end of 1952, all the basis was ex-

10. Note that the taxpayer treated the initial sale as a closed transaction. The result was that he had a basis of $300,000 in the right to receive the royalty payments. The standard treatment then would have been to amortize this basis over the expected duration

hausted and at that point all subsequent payments were treated as ordinary income (since they were not received as a result of a "sale or exchange"). In time, Waring obviously realized that he would have been better off if, in 1946, he had treated the transaction as open, under Burnet v. Logan. If he had done so, after recovery of basis, all payments would have been treated as capital gain as long as he received them. In 1960 and 1961, he filed returns claiming capital gain treatment for the royalties received in those years; his position was that his original decision to treat the transaction as closed was an error as to a continuing transaction and that he was entitled to correct that error as it affected years not closed by the statute of limitations. Unfortunately for him, open-transaction treatment depends on the taxpayer's ability to establish that the value of the rights received is not ascertainable. In light of the fact that in 1946 his accountant had valued the rights at $300,000, the court had little difficulty in concluding that no error had been made in treating the transaction as closed in 1946.

2. The Installment Method

The installment method (§§453, 453A, and 453B) is a set of accounting rules that permit nonrecognition of gain in transactions involving the sale of property. The principal congressional objective in allowing this method is to provide relief from the harshness of an obligation to pay taxes when the taxpayer has not received cash with which to pay those taxes, but the benefits are enjoyed by many taxpayers who have no problem of cash availability but who prefer, as do most taxpayers, to pay taxes later rather than sooner.

The basic approach. The basic approach is simple. First, the rules relating to unstated interest (§483) or OID (original issue discount) are applied. The installment method applies to what remains. See Regs. §15a.453-1(b)(2)(ii). For purposes of illustration, let us assume that all payments bear interest at an adequate rate; thus, we can focus on the amount of the payment, before interest, and illustrate the installment method without concern for the interest element in any total amount

---

of the payments. For example, if that expected duration was ten years, the taxpayer should have deducted $30,000 per year. Instead, he was allowed to follow the basis-first approach of Burnet v. Logan, allocating basis to the payments thereafter received until all of his basis was recovered, with subsequent payments fully taxed. That basis-first approach was justified in Burnet v. Logan by the difficulty of determining the duration and amount of the payments. In *Waring,* however, the valuation difficulties were not considered too serious to prevent treating the original transaction as closed. That being so, it seems inconsistent to use basis-first cost recovery, which can be thought of as a form of open transaction treatment. In other words, in *Waring* the open transaction issue arises not just once but twice. The first time, we get closed transaction treatment and the second time we get open transaction treatment on the same facts.

received. The taxpayer computes a ratio of gain to total expected payments and applies this ratio to each payment. See §453(c). For example, suppose a taxpayer sells property with a basis of $100,000 in return for a total stated amount of $300,000 in the form of payments to be received at the end of each of the subsequent five years of $30,000, $60,000, $30,000, $60,000, and $120,000 (plus adequate interest on each payment). Since the basis is $100,000 and the total to be received is $300,000, two-thirds of each payment received is treated as gain; the other one-third is a recovery of basis. For the results, see Table 3-4.

The taxpayer is permitted to elect not to use the installment method. See §453(d). In that case, the transaction is treated as closed and gain is recognized at the outset in an amount equal to the difference between the fair market value of the installment payments and the basis (except for the highly unlikely possibility that the taxpayer can establish the right to open-transaction treatment).

A loophole closed. Here is a nice example of a substance-versus-form issue. Suppose that *M* holds property with a basis of $100,000 and wants to sell it now for its fair market value of $300,000 and receive cash from the prospective buyer, *B* (perhaps because *B* is not trustworthy). *M* wants to defer the recognition of gain. She sells the property to her daughter, *D*, for a total of $300,000, in the form of five annual payments of $60,000 over the next five years. *D* sells the property to *B* for $300,000 cash. *D* has no gain since her basis is her purchase price of $300,000. She holds the $300,000 in an interest-bearing account and at the end of each year, for five years, pays $60,000 plus the interest earned in that year. If the form of the transaction is respected, *M*'s gain is deferred even though there is no justification for deferral (since cash was paid and is in the family). The IRS might challenge the transaction using a substance-versus-form approach, but that is often difficult to do. Section 453(e) closes the potential loophole by requiring *M* to treat the $300,000 as an amount realized by her at the time it is received by *D*.

Limitation. The installment method is not available for sales of personal property under a revolving credit plan, for sales of publicly traded

TABLE 3-4
Basis: $100,000

Year	*Amount received*	*Gain recognized*	*Basis used*	*Basis remaining*
1	$ 30,000	$ 20,000	$ 10,000	$ 90,000
2	60,000	40,000	20,000	70,000
3	30,000	20,000	10,000	60,000
4	60,000	40,000	20,000	40,000
5	120,000	80,000	40,000	-0-
Totals	$300,000	$200,000	$100,000	—

property, or for sales of inventory items by dealers in real or personal property. §453(b)(2), (k)(1). There is an interesting exception for sellers of time-share units and residential lots. §453(l). They are permitted to use the installment method, but when payment is received they must pay the government interest on the amount of tax deferred. Thus, any cash-flow problems are solved, but the tax advantage of deferral is eliminated. The advantage of deferral has been described as equivalent to an interest-free loan from the government (in the amount of the tax); here the loan is no longer interest free. A similar approach is taken with respect to sales of all nonfarm property where the sales price is greater than $150,000. See §453A. If the aggregate face amount of the installment obligations arising from such sales exceeds $5 million, tax that is deferred on the excess is subject to an interest charge.

In the case of certain installment obligations, if a taxpayer uses the obligation to secure a loan, the loan is treated as payment of the installment obligation. §453A(d). The installment method does not apply to recapture gain (§453(i)), nor does it apply for purposes of computing the alternative minimum tax (§56(a)(6)).

Permissible consideration. Since the installment method is designed to provide relief where the taxpayer has not received cash, it is not available where the consideration received is thought to be the equivalent of cash. Thus, demand notes and publicly tradable debt obligations are treated the same as cash payments (in an amount equal to their fair market value). See §453(f)(4). The fact that a promise to pay is guaranteed does not, however, transform that promise into a "payment" that must be treated as cash. See §453(f)(3). This rule extends to guarantees by banks in the form of standby letters of credit. (Regs. §15a.453-1(b)(3)(iii) defines a "standby letter of credit" as a "non-negotiable non-transferable (except with the evidence of indebtedness which it secures) letter of credit, issued by a bank or other financial institution, which serves as a guarantee of the evidence of indebtedness which is secured by the letter of credit.")

Sales with contingent payments. In Burnet v. Logan, since the amount of the payments to be received was contingent on the output of a mine, the total consideration was uncertain. In this situation, how does one apply the installment method? How does one allocate basis to the payments? The regulations provide different solutions for three different situations. Regs. §15a.453-1(c). First, if it is possible to determine a maximum amount that may be paid, basis is allocated by treating that maximum as the selling price (that is, the amount to be received by the seller). Second, where a maximum selling price cannot be determined, but it is possible to determine a maximum period of time over which payments will be made, basis is allocated in equal annual amounts over that time period. Third, if it is not possible to determine either a maximum price or a maximum time period (as, for example, in Burnet v. Logan), basis is recovered in equal annual amounts over a period of fifteen years.

3. Deferred Sales

ALSTORES REALTY CORP. v. COMMISSIONER

46 T.C. 363 (1966)

Hoyt, Judge.

[Alstores Realty Corp. entered into a transaction to buy from Steinway & Sons a warehouse with a fair market value of $1 million. Alstores paid $750,000 and granted Steinway a two-and-one-half year right of occupancy, which the court found to be worth $250,000. Alstores claimed that its purchase price was simply the $750,000 that it had paid and that that was all there was to the matter. The Commissioner claimed that Alstores had agreed to pay Steinway $1 million and had then agreed to lease the property back to Steinway for two-and-one-half years for $250,000, which reduced the amount changing hands to $750,000. The court upheld the position of the Commissioner, ruling that the $250,000 was income at the time the transaction was closed and that Alstores was entitled to treat its purchase price as $1 million. In a companion case, Steinway & Sons v. Commissioner, 46 T.C. 375 (1966), the court held that Steinway's proceeds of sale were $1 million and that it was entitled to deduct the $250,000 rent by amortizing it over the term of the lease.]

[Alstores] here argues that, although in form there may have been a sale and leaseback, in substance there was a conveyance of a *future interest* with Steinway reserving to itself, or carving out, a term of 2½ years in a portion of the property. Hence, Steinway in substance retained its right to occupancy not as a lessee of petitioner, but as a legal owner of a reserved term for years. This approach is supported by Kruesel v. United States, an unreported case (D. Minn. 1963, 12 A.F.T.R.2d 5701, 63-2 U.S.T.C. par. 9714).

Although at first blush petitioner's argument is an appealing one, we conclude that it must be rejected. . . . Steinway did not in form or substance reserve an estate for years.

An analogous situation was presented in McCulley Ashlock, 18 T.C. 405 (1952). There the building in question was subject to a lease to a third party at the time it was purchased by the taxpayer. The contract of sale provided that the buyer would pay $40,000 cash but the seller was to retain "possession" of the premises and all the rights to the rental income from the lessee until the expiration of the primary term of the existing lease (about 28 months from date of the sale contract). The

Commissioner determined that the rent received by the seller subsequent to conveyance of title to the taxpayer purchaser was really taxable income to the taxpayer purchaser. We rejected the Commissioner's approach in that case, holding that the seller had reserved an ownership interest in the property (an estate for years) and that the rents received were income to the seller for occupancy of what was still his property — not income to the purchaser, who did not then have a present legal ownership interest but only a future interest. The essence of our reasoning in the *Ashlock* case was as follows (pp. 411-412):

> Here, the trustees [the sellers of the property] not only retained the rents legally but they also retained control and benefits of ownership. Under the contract of sale on April 18, 1945, the trustees specifically agreed to pay property taxes, insurance premiums, and "all normal maintenance items and expenses," so that the property would be delivered to . . . [the buyer] in the present condition except for normal wear and tear. Furthermore, the June 11, 1945, agreement stated that in the event that the property was damaged or destroyed, any loss of income during the period of repair or reconstruction would be the trustees' loss. It further provided that insurance proceeds would be devoted to restore and repair the property, except in the event of total destruction petitioner would have the option of rebuilding the premises or compensating the trustees for unpaid rent. Thus the trustee bore the risks of ownership of the rents and managed the property. Larger expenses or a cessation of rents were risks incurred by the trustees. . . .

The same factors which we looked to in *Ashlock* in deciding in favor of the purchaser, analyzed in the factual posture of the instant case, dictate the opposite result here. [Alstores] assumed control of the premises and the benefits of ownership. [Alstores] specifically agreed to pay for and supply to Steinway, the seller, heat, electricity, and water. The space-occupancy agreement stated that in the event the property was damaged or destroyed and Steinway's occupancy was thereby destroyed or impaired the burden of loss would be upon [Alstores] (with [Alstores] agreeing to pay Steinway 6¼ cents per square foot per month for space so affected). It is clear in the instant case that the buyer bore the risks and burdens of ownership during the term of the space-occupancy agreement. Such was not the case in McCulley Ashlock, supra, nor apparently in Kruesel v. United States, supra, relied upon by petitioner.

Furthermore, the rights of Steinway, the seller, as occupant were not those of a holder of a legal estate for years but were specifically limited to those of a lessee. The standard terms and conditions of a New York Real Estate Board form lease were imposed. For example, Steinway could not alter or improve the building nor sublet or assign its interest without the consent of petitioner.

Of key significance in this case is the fact that [Alstores] was required to pay to Steinway 6¼ cents per square foot per month for space which Steinway was entitled to occupy but which it may have been unable to occupy by reason of an act of God or the fault of [Alstores], or which it may have elected to vacate during the last one-half year of the space occupancy agreement. This arrangement is entirely inconsistent with the theory that Steinway had a reserved estate for years; why would [Alstores], the alleged remainderman, be required to make payments to Steinway, the alleged owner of an estate for years, as a result of nonoccupancy by the latter? What we really have here is a provision for reimbursement of prepaid rent in the event the tenant is denied (or, during the last one-half year of the term, elects abandonment of) its right of unfettered occupancy, the prepaid rent being in the form of the value of the property received by [Alstores] in excess of the $750,000 cash paid therefor.

[Alstores] emphasizes the fact that it received no cash rental payments at any time; it merely purchased real estate for cash. This is partly true, but one need not receive cash to have received income. . . .

Possibly the result in the instant case would be different if the parties had in fact *intended* to carve out a reserved term for years in Steinway and had structured their transaction in that form. . . . We do not agree with [Alstores], however, that to hold that there was a sale of the fee and a simultaneous leaseback here is to exalt form over substance. The so-called space-occupancy agreement placed the two parties' rights, obligations, and risks as they would be allocated in a typical lease arrangement. Hence, the arrangement was a lease in substance as well as in form.

NOTES AND QUESTIONS

1. *Analysis* (a) At the time of purchase, Alstores's interest in the property was worth $750,000. If all else remains equal, two and one-half years later its interest should be worth $1 million. The $250,000 difference could be treated as income at the time of purchase (as it was in this case), at the time when Steinway's two-and-one-half year right of occupancy expired, or ratably over the two-and-one-half year term of Steinway's occupancy. If gain were not recognized in any of these ways, Alstores's basis would be the $750,000 it paid. Part of that would be allocated to the building and part to the land. Some of the gain would then show up during the time that Alstores used the building, since its depreciation deductions would be lower than they would have been if the $250,000 gain had been recognized and the total basis had been $1 million. The rest of the gain would show up on ultimate sale of the property. Which of the possibilities makes most sense? Which is most

consistent with Eisner v. Macomber (supra page 286) and Helvering v. Bruun (supra page 301) (and §109)?

(b) If the court had accepted Alstores's position that it bought only a future interest, how should Steinway be taxed? Should its basis be allocated between the interest retained and the interest sold? If so, how should Steinway recover the portion of its basis allocated to the interest retained?

(c) Could the parties to the actual transaction in *Alstores,* without making any significant changes in the underlying economic substance of the transaction, have structured it as a sale of a future interest? In other words, is the decision one that permits legal formalities to control tax effects?

(d) Is the $750,000 payment analogous to a loan from Alstores to Steinway, to be "paid" by a transfer of the property two-and-one-half years later, with the $250,000 increment in value constituting interest (rather than rent) during the two-and-one-half-year period between the payment of the $750,000 to Steinway and the transfer of possession to Alstores? If so, how should Alstores and Steinway be treated?

2. *A variation.* The *Alstores* technique of deferred ownership transfer has been used in real estate tax-shelter financing. In Ellison v. Commissioner, 80 T.C. 378 (1983), the taxpayers bought an apartment complex with the seller reserving the right to the first $500,000 of rent up to a certain date. As the parties had anticipated, the $500,000 was received by the seller within five-and-one-half months after the closing. The court adopted the *Alstores* view of the transaction, holding that the amount received by the seller was rent to the buyers (taxpayers) and was in effect used by them to pay part of the purchase price. The court said (80 T.C. at 383-384):

> [W]hen the form is peeled away, it becomes apparent that, in substance, the reserved rents were earned by [the taxpayers] and were used to pay part of the consideration for the purchases. . . .
>
> Certainly, if the buyers had simply collected the rent and then paid it over to the sellers as part of the purchase price, there would be no question that the rent was income to the buyers. This, in substance, was what happened, because the buyers owned, controlled, and managed (through agents) the apartments when they produced the rental income.

To the taxpayers' argument that the sellers bore the risk that the rents collected might not reach $500,000, the court responded that on the facts that risk was "very slight."

The taxpayers relied in part on Thomas v. Perkins, 301 U.S. 655 (1937), involving a transaction with an economic structure and substance similar to that in *Alstores* and *Ellison* but relating to an oil and gas venture, where the Supreme Court held that amounts received by the transferors of "oil production payments," consisting of the right to share in the proceeds of the sale of any oil up to a maximum dollar amount, were the income of the transferors. The *Ellison* court said that the rule in Thomas v. Perkins had been applied in subsequent decisions only to transactions involving depletable minerals and had been "limited if not repealed" by §636(b), enacted in 1969, which has no bearing on *Ellison.*

The court distinguished Heminway v. Commissioner, 44 T.C. 96 (1965), acq. 1966-2 C.B. 5, where a taxpayer bought his sister's interest in the shares of a family corporation, with the sister reserving a life interest in the dividends. The dividends were held to be taxable to the sister. In *Ellison,* the court said that *Heminway* was not apposite because the reserved interest in that case was "subject to the substantial contingencies of the profitability of the company, the decision of its management to pay dividends or not pay them, and how long [the sister] would live." 80 T.C. at 391.

3. *Prepayments and interest-free loans.* (a) Suppose a college charges tuition of $8,000 per year but offers to accept lesser amounts for prepayments. For example, suppose the college accepts $7,400 in lieu of an $8,000 tuition payment due one year later. If the college invests the money at 10 percent it will earn $740 and will be $140 ahead. The $740 interest earned by the college would show up as its income, but that is a matter of indifference to it, since it is exempt from taxation. How is the payor treated? How should the payor be treated to prevent tax avoidance? Might the prepayment be treated as a "loan" within the meaning of §7872? If so, is it a loan described in §7872(c)(1)(D)?

(b) The following type of plan has become popular in recent years. A college or university allows a person (usually a parent) to prepay tuition for a designated person (usually the payor's child), with a refund (without interest) to another designated person if the first designated person does not attend the college or university. To illustrate, suppose tuition at Ivy College is currently $10,000 per year and that Maria pays $18,000 for four years of tuition at Ivy for her son, Sam, who will not be old enough to attend college for another ten years. If Sam does not attend the college, the $18,000 is to be paid to Mario, Maria's brother. On similar facts, the IRS, in Private Letter Ruling 8901027, ruled that no income would be taxed to Maria or Sam during the ten years between the time Maria paid the $18,000 and the time Sam is expected to begin college. If Sam does attend Ivy, he (not Maria) will have income each year (for four years) in an amount equal to the difference between the tuition charged by Ivy at the time and one-quarter of the $18,000. For example, if the tuition is $12,000, he will have income each year of $7,500 ($12,000 less $4,500).

E. CONSTRUCTIVE RECEIPT AND RELATED DOCTRINES

1. Basic Principles

Review the discussion of constructive receipt, economic benefit, and cash equivalence, supra pages 54-55. A key to understanding some of the subtler aspects of the doctrine of constructive receipt is to remember that constructive receipt results in taxation of amounts that are set aside or available — amounts to which the taxpayer has a legal claim — not amounts that would have been available if the taxpayer had made some other deal. The following case nicely illustrates this point.

AMEND v. COMMISSIONER

13 T.C. 178 (1949), acq., 1950-1 C.B. 1

BLACK, Judge.

We have two taxable years before us for decision, 1944 and 1946. . . .

In each of the taxable years there is one common issue and that is whether the doctrine of constructive receipt should be applied to certain payments which petitioner received from the sale of his wheat. There is no controversy as to the amounts which petitioner received or as to the time when he actually received them. Petitioners, being on the cash basis, returned these amounts as part of their gross income in the years when petitioner actually received them. . . .

In applying the doctrine of constructive receipt, the Commissioner relies upon Regulations 111, section 29.42-2. . . .[11]

In Loose v. United States, 74 Fed. (2d) 147, the rule providing for the taxation of income constructively received is stated as follows:

> the strongest reason for holding constructive receipt of income to be within the statute is that for taxation purposes income is received or realized when it is made subject to the will and control of the taxpayer and can be, except for his own action or inaction, reduced to actual possession. So viewed, it makes no difference why the taxpayer did not

11. "Sec. 29.42-2. *Income Not Reduced to Possession.* Income which is credited to the account of or set apart for a taxpayer and which may be drawn upon by him at any time is subject to tax for the year during which so credited or set apart, although not then actually reduced to possession. To constitute receipt in such a case the income must be credited or set apart to the taxpayer without any substantial limitation or restriction as to the time or manner of payment or condition upon which payment is to be made, and must be made available to him so that it may be drawn at any time, and its receipt brought within his own control and disposition. . . ."

> reduce to actual possession. The matter is in no wise dependent upon what he does or upon what he fails to do. It depends solely upon the existence of a situation where the income is fully available to him. . . .

Respondent, in his brief, relies upon the *Loose* case, from which the above quotation is taken, and several other cases which deal with the doctrine of constructive receipt. Needless to say, each of those cases depends upon its own facts. In the *Loose* case, for example, interest coupons had matured prior to the decedent's death. The decedent had not presented them for payment because of his physical condition. It was held that, even though the decedent had not cashed them, the interest coupons represented income to him in the year when they matured, under the doctrine of constructive receipt.

It seems clear to us that the facts in the instant case do not bring it within the doctrine of Loose v. United States, supra, and the other cases cited by respondent dealing with constructive receipt.

In discussing the situation which we have in the instant case, we turn our attention first to the contract of sale which petitioner made of his 1944 wheat crop to Burrus. The testimony was that 1944 was a bumper wheat crop year and that petitioner produced and harvested about 30,000 bushels, some of which was lying out on the ground and some of which was stored on the farm. Petitioner, through his attorney in fact, Paul Higgs, sold his wheat to Burrus for January 1945 delivery at $1.57 per bushel. It was the understanding that petitioner would ship his wheat to Burrus at once and that Burrus would pay him for it in January of the following year. The contract was carried out. Some time during the month of August 1944, after August 2, petitioner shipped the 30,000 bushels to Burrus. Burrus received it, put it in its elevator, and paid petitioner for it by check dated January 17, 1945.

Respondent's contention seems to be based primarily on the fact that petitioner could have sold Burrus the wheat at the same price for immediate cash payment in August 1944 and that although he did not do so, he should be treated in the same manner as if he had and the doctrine of constructive receipt should be applied to the payments received. We do not think the doctrine of constructive receipt goes that far. Porter Holmes, who was the manager of the Burrus Panhandle Elevator in Amarillo at the time of the 1944 transaction, testified at the hearing. He testified that it was the usual custom of Burrus to pay cash for wheat soon after it was delivered and that the transaction between Burrus and petitioner for January 1945 delivery and settlement was unusual and that he telephoned the manager at Dallas, Texas, for authority to make the deal that way and secured such authority and the deal was made. He testified that when Burrus' check for $40,164.08 was mailed to petitioner January 17, 1945, it was done in pursuance of the contract. So far as we can see from the evidence, petitioner had no legal right to demand and receive his money from the sale of his 1944 wheat until in January 1945. Both petitioner and Burrus understood that to be the contract. Such is the substance of the testimony of both petitioner, who was the seller of the wheat, and Holmes, who acted for the buyer. Such also is the testimony of Paul Higgs, who represented the seller in the negotiations for the sale. During 1944 all that petitioner had in the way of a promise to pay was Burrus' oral promise to pay him for that wheat in January 1945. Burrus was a well known and responsible grain dealer and petitioner testified that he had not the slightest doubt that he would receive his money in January 1945, as had been agreed upon in the contract. Such a situation, however, does not bring into play the doctrine of constructive receipt. See Bedell v. Commissioner, 30 Fed. (2d) 622, wherein the court said:

> While, therefore, we do not think that the case is like a promise to pay in the future for a title which passes at the time of contract, we would not be understood as holding by implication that even in that case the profit is to be reckoned as of the time of sale. If a company sells out its plant for a negotiable bond issue payable in the future, the profit may be determined by the present market value of the bonds. But if land or a chattel is sold, and title passes merely upon a promise to pay money at some future date, to speak of the promise as property exchanged for the title appears to us a strained use of language, when calculating profits under the income tax. . . . [I]t is absurd to speak of a promise to pay in the future as having a "market value," fair or unfair. . . .

The doctrine that a cash basis taxpayer can not be deemed to have realized income at the time a promise to pay in the future is made was reiterated by the Circuit Court of Appeals for the Eighth Circuit in the more recent case of Perry v. Commissioner, 152 Fed. (2d) 183. In that case it was stated:

> These cases seem to be predicated upon the fact that in a contract of sale of property containing a promise to pay in the future, but not accompanied by notes or other unqualified obligations to pay a definite sum on a day certain, the obligation to pay and the obligation to pass title both being in the future, there is an element of uncertainty in the transaction and the promise has no "market value," fair or unfair. This theory is supported by the decision of the Supreme Court in Lucas v. North Texas Co. . . .

The Commissioner in the instant case is not contending that Burrus' contract to pay petitioner for his wheat in January 1945 had a fair market value equal to the agreed purchase price of the wheat when the contract was made in August 1944. What he is contending is that petitioner had the unqualified right to receive his money for the wheat in

1944; that all he had to do to receive his money was to ask for it; and that, therefore, the doctrine of constructive receipt applies as defined in section 29.42-2, Regulations 118.

For reasons already stated, we do not think the Commissioner's determination to this effect can be sustained. If petitioner had begun this method of selling his wheat in 1944, when he had a bumper crop, there might be reason to doubt the bona fides of the contract, but what we have said about the 1944 transaction between Burrus and petitioner is based upon the finding that the contract between Burrus and petitioner was bona fide in all respects, though it was initiated by petitioner, and each party was equally bound by its terms. Petitioner did not begin this method of selling his wheat in 1944 — he began it in 1942 and continued it through 1946. No doubt his taxes were more in some years and less in others than they would have been if petitioner had sold and delivered his wheat for cash in the year when it was produced. To illustrate this we need only point out that under the method which petitioner used he reported income in 1945 upon which he paid a tax of $2,672.64. His wife Eva also reported income and paid a tax of about the same amount. By treating petitioner's proceeds from the sale of his 1944 wheat as constructively received in 1944, the Commissioner determined over-assessments as to each petitioner for 1945 and deficiencies against each petitioner for 1944.

Petitioner was asked at the hearing why he adopted the manner of selling his wheat which has been detailed in our findings of fact. His answer was as follows:

> Well, that had been my practice, to handle that wheat that way since 1942 and I have handled my wheat that way, '42, '43, '44, '45, '46, '47 and into 1948. It is still my practice to do that and there have been some years in that interval that I would certainly have paid less income had I handled it the other way, but that is a semi-arid country and we are uncertain about our wheat crops and our expenses are always pretty well set and we know they are going to be high and we need our own protection to carry part of this wheat forward. . . .
>
> As I have already explained, it's been a matter of making my income more uniform and even; about five of those years had it all been set back and sold in the year that it was supposed to have been sold in, my income tax would have been less and in the other two it would have been more. I merely emphasize that to show the consistency of my policy and not as a matter of paying any tax.

Whether the reasons advanced by petitioner in his testimony quoted above are good or bad as a business policy, we do not undertake to decide. The question we think we have to decide is whether the contracts detailed in our findings of fact were bona fide arm's-length transactions and whether under them the petitioner had the unqualified right to receive the money for his wheat in the year when the contracts were made and whether petitioner's failure to receive his money was of his own volition. Our conclusion, as already stated, is that the contracts were bona fide arm's-length transactions and petitioner did not have the right to demand the money for his wheat until in January of the year following its sale. This being true, we do not think the doctrine of constructive receipt applies. See Howard Veit, first point decided, 8 T.C. 809.

Petitioner, in each of the years before us, returned as a part of his gross income the checks which he actually received in payment for his wheat. This being so, we think he complied with the income tax laws governing a taxpayer who keeps his accounts and makes his returns on the cash basis. . . .

NOTES

1. *Current rules.* Amend's sale of the wheat would now be an installment sale (see §453(b) (1)), and unless he elected out, he would use the installment method. Under the installment method, Amend would report his entire gain in 1945 since he received 100 percent of the payment for the wheat in 1945. So the result would not be changed.[12] If, however, Amend elected out of the installment method (pursuant to §453(d)), he would be required to report in 1944 the fair market value of the obligation of the buyer, Burrus.[13] This result is required by the present rule for sales of property not reported under the installment method. See supra page 361, Note 3, describing the adoption of new rules for the installment method and the effort to limit the "open transaction" approach of Burnet v. Logan (supra page 358), and the following language from Temporary Regs. §15a.453-1(d) (2):

> (i) Receipt of an installment obligation shall be treated as a receipt of property, in an amount equal to the fair market value of the obligation, whether or not such obligation is the equivalent of cash. An installment obligation is considered to be property and is subject to valuation, [using fair market value], without regard to whether the obligation is embodied in a note, an executory contract, or any other instrument, or as an oral promise enforceable under local law.

12. Because of the exception for farmers in §453(1)(2), Amend's sale is not a "dealer disposition," so it is not excluded from installment sale treatment under §453(b)(2)(A). The exception for inventories in §453(b)(2)(B) would not be applicable because Amend would not be required to, and presumably would not, use an inventory method of accounting. See Regs. §1.471-6.

13. An accrual method taxpayer who elects out of the installment method is required to report the total amount payable (not including interest or OID) rather than the fair market value of the obligation. Regs. §15a.453-1(d)(2)(ii)(A).

(ii) Under no circumstances will an installment sale for a fixed amount be considered an "open" transaction.

The doctrine of constructive receipt would still be relevant, however. If the payment by Burrus had been constructively received by Amend in 1944 (for example, if the contract had given Amend the legal right to demand cash payment at any time), then Amend would have been required to report the amount to which he was entitled in 1944. He could not have deferred recognition under the installment method. The installment method permits a taxpayer to avoid recognition of gain under the rule limiting open transactions, or under the cash equivalence doctrine, not under the doctrine of constructive receipt.

The installment method is available only for sales of property, not for sales of services. With respect to services, as soon will be seen (infra pages 380-386), a right to payment is not currently treated as income by a cash-method taxpayer, at least as long as it is embodied in a "mere promise to pay."

2. *Consistency and clear reflection of income.* Note the court's reference to the fact that the taxpayer had been consistent in his practice. Thus, there was no distortion of income. Had there been such distortion, the Service could have invoked the forerunner of §446(b), which allows the Service to impose a method of accounting if the taxpayer's method does not "clearly reflect income."

3. *The relevance of delivery.* Amend delivered his wheat to Burrus in 1944, but apparently he was not legally required by contract to do so. If the contract had required delivery (and transfer of title) in 1944, would the result have been different?

The next case tests the distinction between constructive receipt and economic benefit.

PULSIFER v. COMMISSIONER

64 T.C. 245 (1975)

HALL, Judge.

Respondent determined a deficiency of $2,449.41 against each of the three petitioners for 1969. The sole issue for decision is whether petitioners, who were minors in 1969, must include in gross income in 1969 their winnings from the 1969 Irish Hospital Sweepstakes which were deposited with the Irish court.

Findings of Fact

All of the facts have been stipulated and are so found.

The petitioners, Stephen W. Pulsifer, Susan M. Pulsifer, and Thomas O. Pulsifer, are brothers and sister who lived in Medford, Mass., when they filed their petitions. . . . They are the minor children of Gordon F. Pulsifer and Theodora T. Pulsifer of Medford, Mass., who together are petitioners' counsel herein.

Mr. Pulsifer acquired an Irish Hospital Sweepstakes ticket in his name and the names of his three minor children. On March 21, 1969, he and petitioners received a telegram from the Hospital Trust advising them that their ticket would be represented by Saratoga Skiddy, a horse which would run on their behalf in the Lincolnshire Handicap. Saratoga Skiddy placed second, winning $48,000.

When he applied for the winnings, Mr. Pulsifer was advised that three-fourths of the amount would not be released to him because the ticket stub reflected three minor co-owners. He was further advised that, pursuant to Irish law, the withheld portion together with interest earned to date would be deposited with the Bank of Ireland at interest to the account of the Accountant of the Courts of Justice for the benefit of each of the petitioners. The money would not be released until petitioners reached 21 or until application on their behalf was made by an appropriate party to the Irish court for release of the funds. Mr. Pulsifer was sent his share of the prize.

The amounts paid over and credited to each of the petitioners were principal of $11,925 plus interest of $250.03, or $12,175.03. Mr. Pulsifer, as petitioners' next friend and legal guardian, has since filed for release of those funds, and he has an absolute right to obtain them.[14]

Opinion

Both parties agree the prize money is income to the petitioners. The only question is in what year must it be included in income. Petitioners contend that they should not be required to recognize the Irish Hospital Sweepstakes winnings held for them by the Irish court in 1969. They reason that neither the constructive-receipt nor the economic-benefit doctrines apply, and that all they had in 1969 was a nonassignable chose in action. Respondent argues that the economic-benefit doctrine applies, thereby dictating recognition of the prize money in 1969. . . . We agree with respondent.

Under the economic-benefit theory, an individual on the cash receipts and disbursements method of accounting is currently taxable on the

14. The record does not disclose whether he had already received the funds at the time of trial.

economic and financial benefit derived from the absolute right to income in the form of a fund which has been irrevocably set aside for him in trust and is beyond the reach of the payor's debtors. E. T. Sproull, 16 T.C. 244 (1951), affd. per curiam, 194 F.2d 541 (6th Cir. 1952). Petitioners had an absolute, nonforfeitable right to their winnings on deposit with the Irish court. The money had been irrevocably set aside for their sole benefit. All that was needed to receive the money was for their legal representative to apply for the funds, which he forthwith did. See Orlando v. Earl of Fingall, Irish Reports 281 (1940). We agree with respondent that this case falls within the legal analysis set out in *E. T. Sproull,* supra.

In the *Sproull* case the employer-corporation unilaterally and irrevocably transferred $10,500 into a trust in 1945 for taxpayer's sole benefit in consideration for prior services. In 1946 and 1947, pursuant to the trust document, the corpus was paid in its entirety to taxpayer. In the event of his death the funds were to have been paid to his administrator, executor, or heirs. The Court held that the entire $10,500 was taxable in 1945 because Sproull derived an economic benefit from it in 1945. The employer had made an irrevocable transfer to the trust, relinquishing all control. Sproull was given an absolute right to the funds which were to be applied for his sole benefit. The funds were beyond the reach of the employer's creditors. Sproull's right to those funds was not contingent, and the trust agreement did not contain any restrictions on his right to assign or otherwise dispose of that interest.

The record does not show whether the right to the funds held by the Bank of Ireland was assignable. Petitioner claims they were not, but cites no authority for his position. However, the result is the same whether or not the right to the funds is assignable. See Renton K. Brodie, 1 T.C. 275 (1942) (deferred annuity contract held currently taxable even though nonassignable and without surrender value).

In order to reflect our conclusion, decisions will be entered for the respondent.

QUESTIONS

Could the court have reached the same result under the doctrine of constructive receipt? What if the funds could not be obtained until the person entitled to them reached age 21?

2. *Drescher* Revisited

Review the opinion in United States v. Drescher, supra page 79. That case was examined at the beginning of Chapter 2 as part of an inquiry into the question of *what* is income. Here, we use it as a vehicle for considering the question of *when* to tax income from personal services. Think about the following possible sets of rules for taxing the annuity in *Drescher*:

(a) Follow the approach taken by the court in the actual case by taxing Drescher on the $5,000 cost of the annuity at the time it was bought by the employer, Bausch & Lomb. Bausch & Lomb is entitled to a deduction at the same time. There is no further tax on Drescher until he begins to receive payments under the annuity contract, at which time we apply the normal rules for taxing annuities. (Drescher's investment in the contract is the $5,000 on which he was previously taxed.)

(b) No tax on Drescher at the time of the purchase of the annuity by Bausch & Lomb and no deduction by Bausch & Lomb at that time. As Drescher receives payments, the amounts received are included in his gross income in their entirety. Bausch & Lomb is entitled to deductions for amortization of its $5,000 cost, beginning when payments to Drescher begin and spread over the expected term of the payments.

(c) Include in Drescher's gross income the $5,000 cost of the annuity at the time the annuity is purchased by Bausch & Lomb, and allow Bausch & Lomb a deduction of $5,000 at that time. In addition, include in Drescher's gross income each year the increase in the value of the annuity contract (or possibly, instead, the amount set aside by the insurance company as a reserve for that contract). When Drescher starts receiving payments under the contract, apply the normal rule for taxing annuities, Drescher's investment in the contract being the total amount previously included in income.

Which of these possibilities most accurately reflects economic reality? Which makes most sense taking account of all the goals of the income tax? How important is consistency in treatment by Drescher and Bausch & Lomb?

3. Deferred Compensation

In Revenue Ruling 60-31, 1960-1 C.B. 174, the IRS set forth some basic rules for the taxation of deferred compensation (that is, compensation whose receipt is deferred to a future taxable year). One important principle stated in the ruling is that a cash-method employee is not taxable currently by virtue of an employer's "mere promise to pay" some amount of compensation in the future, even if the promise is unqualified (that is, without contingencies). Citing the *Amend* case (supra page 372), the ruling observes that "the statute cannot be administered by speculating whether the payor would have been willing to agree to an earlier payment." On the other hand, where money is set aside in a trust or an escrow account for the benefit of the employee, out of the control of the employer, the employee is taxed at the time when the money is paid by the employer to the trustee or escrow agent. The case that follows applies these principles.

MINOR v. UNITED STATES

772 F.2d 1472 (9th Cir. 1985)

The government appeals a tax refund judgment holding that contributions to a deferred compensation plan are not currently taxable. We affirm.

Ralph H. Minor is a physician practicing in Snohomish County, Washington. In 1959, he entered into an agreement with the Snohomish County Physicians Corporation (Snohomish Physicians) under which he agreed to render medical services to subscribers of Snohomish Physicians' prepaid medical plan in exchange for fees to be paid by Snohomish Physicians according to its fee schedule.

In 1967, Snohomish Physicians adopted a deferred compensation plan for its participating physicians. Under the voluntary plan, a physician who desired deferred compensation entered into a "Supplemental Agreement" in which the physician and Snohomish Physicians agree that for future services the physician would be paid a designated percentage of the fee he or she would receive under the fee schedule if not participating in the plan. The physician could elect any percentage from 10 per cent to 90 per cent. The balance would go into the deferred compensation fund. Minor's agreement with Snohomish Physicians provided that he would be paid 50 per cent of the scheduled fees through November 30, 1971, and 10 per cent thereafter.

To provide for its obligations under the Supplemental Agreement, Snohomish Physicians established a trust. Snohomish Physicians was the settlor, three physicians, including Minor, were trustees, and Snohomish Physicians was the beneficiary. The trustees, pursuant to instructions from Snohomish Physicians, purchased retirement annuity policies to provide for the payment of benefits under the plan. These benefits would become payable to the physician or to his beneficiaries when he or she retires, dies, becomes disabled, or leaves the Snohomish Physicians service area to practice medicine elsewhere. The physician agrees to continue to provide services to Snohomish Physicians patients until the benefits become payable, to limit his or her practice after retirement, to continue to provide certain emergency and consulting services at Snohomish Physicians's request, and to refrain from providing medical services to competing groups.

On his federal income tax returns for 1970, 1971, and 1973, Minor included in gross income only the 10 per cent of the scheduled fees which he actually received. The remaining 90 per cent, which Minor did not receive, went into the deferred compensation plan trust.

The IRS argues that Minor should have included in his gross income that portion of the fees Snohomish Physicians placed in trust for his future benefit. The IRS relies on the economic benefit doctrine, which is an exception to the well-settled rule that a taxpayer pays income tax only on income which is actually or constructively received by him. In this case, Minor did not actually receive the income the IRS attributes to him nor, the IRS has conceded, did he constructively receive the income. The IRS argues, however, that the economic benefit doctrine applies here because an economic benefit was presently conferred on Minor, although he did not receive and had no right to receive the deferred compensation benefits during the tax year.

Minor argues that the participants in the deferred compensation plan have no right to compel Snohomish Physicians to execute the trust agreement, or even to cause it to be created, implemented or continued. The participants have no right, title or interest in the trust agreement or any asset held by the trust. He argues that his right to receive payments of currently earned compensation in the future is contingent, and therefore does not vest any interest in him.

Recent cases from a number of courts provide useful guidelines for determining when a taxpayer is entitled to defer his tax obligations by participating in a deferred compensation plan. The cases fall into two general groups.

(1) *Constructive Receipt.* The constructive receipt doctrine holds that income, although not actually reduced to the taxpayer's possession, is constructively received by the taxpayer during any year in which it is credited to his account or otherwise set apart so that it is available to him without "substantial limitations or restrictions." Regs. §1.451-2(a) (1985). . . . If a corporation merely credits funds to an employee on its books but does not make those funds available to the employees, there has been no constructive receipt. [Regs.] §1.451-2(a). Similarly, an employer's mere promise to pay funds, not represented by notes or otherwise secured, cannot constitute constructive receipt by the employee to whom the promise is made. Rev. Rul. 60-31, 1960-1 C.B. 174, 177.

The IRS has conceded that Minor did not constructively receive the proceeds of Snohomish Physicians' deferred compensation plan. Because the IRS has acknowledged that the doctrine does not apply, we need not decide whether, under the constructive-receipt doctrine, Snohomish Physicians' promise to pay deferred compensation is anything more than a "naked, unsecured promised to pay compensation in the future." Goldsmith v. United States, 586 F.2d 810, 816, 218 Ct. Cl. 387 (1978).

(2) *Economic Benefit.* Although taxation of deferred compensation plans is generally analyzed under the constructive receipt doctrine, the

economic benefit doctrine provides an alternate method of determining when a taxpayer receives taxable benefits. Under that doctrine, an employer's promise to pay deferred compensation in the future may itself constitute a taxable economic benefit if the current value of the employer's promise can be given an appraised value. The concept of economic benefit is quite different from that of constructive receipt because the taxpayer must actually receive the property or currently receive evidence of a future right to property. . . .

The economic benefit doctrine is applicable only if the employer's promise is capable of valuation. . . . A current economic benefit is capable of valuation where the employer makes a contribution to an employee's deferred compensation plan which is nonforfeitable, fully vested in the employee and secured against the employer's creditors by a trust arrangement.

In cases where courts or the IRS have found a current economic benefit to have been conferred, the employer's contribution has always been secured or the employee's interest has been nonforfeitable. See United States v. Basye, 410 U.S. 441, 445-446 (1973) (because trust was established, partnership's interest was nonforfeitable even though individual partner's share of the trust monies was not capable of valuation); *Goldsmith,* 586 F.2d at 821 (life insurance benefits were a nonforfeitable current economic benefit although other unsecured elements of deferred compensation plan did not constitute currently taxable economic benefit); Reed v. Commissioner, 723 F.2d 138, 147 (1st Cir. 1983) (economic benefit for a cash basis taxpayer requires that taxpayer's contractual right to future payment be evidenced by an instrument which is not only nonforfeitable but also readily assignable); United States v. Drescher, 179 F.2d 863, 865 (2d Cir.) (non-assignable annuity confers an economic benefit because annuity was nonforfeitable), cert. denied, 340 U.S. 821 (1950), McEwen v. Commissioner, 6 T.C. 1018, 1026 (1946) (deferred compensation secured by trust in which employee was the beneficiary). If the employee's interest is unsecured or not otherwise protected from the employer's creditors, the employee's interest is not taxable property, see [Regs.] §1.83-3(e) (1985), so the forfeitability of the employee's interest is irrelevant.

Superficially, the Snohomish Physicians' deferred compensation plan establishes a trust arrangement which protects the plan against Snohomish Physicians' creditors but also establishes conditions upon Minor's receipt of the deferred compensation which makes his benefits forfeitable. We examine separately the trust arrangement and risk of forfeiture.

Trust Arrangement. Neither Minor nor any other participants in the deferred compensation plan has any right, title or interest in the trust which holds the annuity contract. The trust, which was established to hold the assets of the deferred compensation plan, was not established pursuant to Minor's Supplemental Agreement, but was created at the initiative of Snohomish Physicians which is both the settlor and beneficiary of the trust. Although Minor incidentally benefits from the trust, he is not a beneficiary. See Restatement (Second) of Trusts §126 (1959). Because Snohomish Physicians has not established any trust in favor of Minor or the other participants, the assets of the trust remain solely those of Snohomish Physicians and subject to the claims of its general creditors. . . .

Minor has pointed out several provisions of the trust agreement which show that the participating physicians had no vested, funded right to the assets of the trust. The IRS in response has cited Sproull v. Commissioner, 16 T.C. 244 (1951), aff'd, 194 F.2d 541 (6th Cir. 1952), in which a corporation paid over to a trustee compensation for past services rendered by petitioner. The trustee was directed to hold, invest, and pay over this sum to petitioner or his estate in two installments. The Tax Court held the entire trust fund was income to the petitioner in the year it was paid to the trustee. In *Sproull,* the settlor of the trust was the corporation and the beneficiary was the petitioner or his estate. The petitioner exercised substantial control over the money because he could assign or otherwise alienate the trust, had standing to bring an action against the trustee, if needed, and other powers under the trust. See id. at 247-248. In this case Snohomish Physicians is both the settlor and the beneficiary of the trust. Minor's only involvement is as one of the trustees. Because Snohomish Physicians' trust was not established in favor of Minor or the other plan participants, the deferred compensation plan is unfunded. Unfunded plans do not confer a present taxable economic benefit. . . .

Risk of Forfeiture. Minor's receipt of benefits under the deferred compensation plan is contingent upon his agreement to limit his practice after retirement to consulting services and to refrain from competing with Snohomish Physicians if he leaves its practice. The district court found that this restriction subjected Minor's benefits to a risk of forfeiture. The Code requires a taxpayer to include in his gross income any property transferred in connection with the performance of services unless the taxpayer's rights in such property are subject to a "substantial risk of forfeiture." §83(a) (1982). The district court did not enter a finding on the substantiality of the risk that Minor's benefits could be forfeited. See §83(c)(1) (1982).

If a recipient must perform or refrain from performing further acts as a condition to payment of benefits, the recipient's rights are regarded as forfeitable. . . . If Minor's Supplemental Agreement requires him to perform substantial post-retirement services or imposes substantial conditions upon his receipt of benefits, the economic benefit doctrine is inapplicable. . . .

From the record before us, we are unable to determine whether the restrictions on Minor's receipt of benefits satisfy the substantiality requirement of §83. We need not, however, invade the province of the trial court by inferring either substantiality or insubstantiality. We conclude that the deferred compensation plan is unsecured from Snohomish Physicians' creditors and therefore incapable of valuation. Thus, Minor's benefits do not constitute property under §83 (1982) and [Regs.] §1.83-3.

While Minor's deferred compensation plan severely stretches the limits of a non-qualified deferred compensation plan, we conclude that the Snohomish Physicians' plan is an unfunded, unsecured plan subject to a risk of forfeiture. We need not examine the substantiality of that risk.

Affirmed.

NOTES

1. *Constructive receipt.* In *Minor* it was clear that the taxpayer could have contracted for payment to him of the amounts that were in fact, pursuant to the actual contract, credited to his account in the deferred compensation fund. This being so, why was the amount set aside for the taxpayer not constructively received?

2. *The importance of looking at both sides of the transaction.* The attractiveness of deferred compensation plans of the sort approved by Rev. Rul. 60-31 is limited by the fact that the employer will not receive a deduction for the amount to be paid in the future until the year in which the employee recognizes income. See §404(a)(5). If, in a given situation, a deferred payment is not taxed to the employee until ten years from now, the deferred payment will not generate a deduction for the employer until ten years from now. If the parties are in the same tax bracket, the advantage to the employee of deferral of the income will be exactly offset by the disadvantage to the employer of deferral of the deduction for the amount to be paid.

If the employer is in a lower tax bracket than the employee, deferral can be advantageous. To understand why this is so, imagine an employee who works for a tax-exempt employer, such as a private university. Suppose the employee's marginal tax rate is 40 percent (combined federal and state) and she is able to earn a 10 percent before-tax rate of return on her money. Her after-tax rate of return is 6 percent. The employer, on the other hand, pays no tax and is able to earn a before-tax and after-tax rate of return of 10 percent. The employee obviously would be better off if she were able to invest a portion of her salary at her employer's after-tax rate of return.

In the past, employees who worked for tax-exempt institutions managed to achieve this result through deferred compensation arrangements. The amount of currently deferred compensation would be invested by the employer and would increase in value at the employer's after-tax (that is, no-tax) rate — in our example, 10 percent. Eventually, the deferred funds, together with the interest earned on the funds, would be distributed to the employee.[15]

Concern over the use of such plans led to the adoption of §457, which places dollar limitations on such plans when used by state agencies. A less strict limitation applies to charitable organizations described in §501(c)(3) (such as schools and churches) and to public educational institutions. See §403(b). An employer such as a professional sports team might be nontaxable because it has substantial tax losses, but may be sufficiently well-financed so that the promise of future payment is acceptable consideration. Employees of this kind of organization may therefore find it advantageous to defer unlimited amounts of their income, as long as the deferred arrangement meets the guidelines described in the *Minor* case.

We shall soon see (page 395 infra) that Congress has established a form of deferred compensation arrangement, known as a qualified pension or profit-sharing plan, that offers the same sort of tax advantage that is described in this note. Qualified pension and profit-sharing plans must, however, cover a broad spectrum of the employer's workforce and are subject to a number of other restrictions.

PROBLEM

Suppose you represent a superstar college football player who was selected first in the National Football League draft, by a newly established team (an "expansion" team). The team has offered to pay your client a signing bonus of $1 million, payable at the end of five years. This is in addition to salary and performance bonuses and is not contingent on any aspect of performance other than signing the contract. You are satisfied with the amount of the signing bonus, but are con-

15. A numerical example may help illuminate this point. Suppose, under the above facts, that the employee decides to save the after-tax portion of $10,000 of her salary. Since she is taxed at a rate of 40 percent, the initial amount of her after-tax investment is $6,000. If that sum is invested at an after-tax rate of 6 percent, the total amount at the end of the year is $6,360 (1.06($6,000)). Suppose instead that the employee enters into a deferred compensation agreement under which $10,000 of her salary, plus the 10 percent annual interest that the employer can earn on that amount, is deferred for one year — that is, is not paid until a year later. The amount initially in the hands of the employer, held for payment to the employee, is $10,000. At the end of a year that amount increases to $11,000. (Recall that the employer earns 10 percent and pays no tax.) At the end of the year the $11,000 is paid to the employee. The employee pays a tax at a rate of 40 percent, so the tax is $4,400 and the after-tax amount is $6,600. This $6,600 is $240 more than the $6,360 that the employee would have wound up with if she had taken immediate payment and had invested the proceeds herself for a year. In other words, the employee increases her after-tax amount by 4 percent of the $6,000 she would have received had she taken immediate payment. Her total return on that $6,000 is $600, or 10 percent.

cerned about the financial ability of the team to continue to pay the $1 million at the end of the five years, since it will presumably operate at a loss for at least five years and the losses may turn out to be greater than expected. The team is operated as a corporation. All the shares of stock of the corporation are held by a real estate tycoon who is active in management of the team and who is extremely anxious that your client sign. Your client is anxious not to pay tax on money that he has not received and wants to avoid any substantial risk of not being paid. What is your advice about each of the following possible ways of structuring the deal?

(a) The corporation buys an annuity policy from an insurance company. The policy names the player as the annuitant and provides for payment of $1 million to the player at the end of five years. The corporation pays $600,000 for the policy. It is nonassignable and the payment cannot be accelerated.

(b) The corporation contributes $600,000 to a trust. The trustee is directed to invest the $600,000 in U.S. Treasury bonds. The interest that will be earned on these bonds (and on the interest received) over the next five years will total $400,000. The trustee is directed at the end of the five years to pay the $1 million to the player. The corporation retains no interest in the trust.

(c) The facts are the same as in (b) except that at the end of the five years the $1 million is to be paid to the corporation to provide funds that it can use to meet its own contractual obligation to the player.

(d) The corporation signs an unconditional agreement to pay $1 million to the player at the end of five years. The real estate tycoon who owns all the shares of the corporation signs a guarantee of its obligation.

AL-HAKIM v. COMMISSIONER

T.C. Memo. 1987-136

In 1970, petitioner Abdul Jalil al-Hakim (al-Hakim) began to negotiate contracts for professional athletes. He operated as a sole proprietor under the name "Superstar Management, the Genius of Randy Wallace" and maintained a business checking account (business account) at Lloyd's Bank in Oakland, California. . . .

During 1977, al-Hakim represented Lyman Bostock (Bostock), a professional baseball player, and negotiated on his behalf with 18 teams, including the Minnesota Twins and the California Angels (Angels). Al-Hakim was successful in negotiating a five-year contract for Bostock with the Angels.

Bostock and the Angels signed the contract on November 21, 1977 and the American League of Professional Baseball Clubs signed it on

January 4, 1978. Under the terms of the contract, the Angels were to pay to Bostock a total of $2,250,000. Pursuant to a deferred-compensation agreement, Bostock was to receive said $2,250,000 over 12 years — $195,000 per year for the first five years, and the remaining $1,275,000 over the next seven years.

Al-Hakim's fee for negotiating Bostock's contract was $112,500, i.e., 5 percent of the $2,250,000 contract amount. Bostock was to pay the fee over ten years and in ten equal installments of $11,250 per year.

A letter from al-Hakim to Bostock stated:

> Dear Lyman,
>
> As per our conversation Jan. 1, 1978, I am sending you this letter to consummate our agreement.
>
> (A) Your fee of $112,500 due SUPER STAR MANAGEMENT upon league approval of your contract is to be paid at the rate of $11,250 a year for ten (10) years begginning [sic] July 1, 1978 and is to be paid each July 1st thereafter. You are aware that this is a ten year repayment schedule and that it is less than the paying term of your contract, however you desire it to be repaid as scheduled.
>
> (B) You are providing SUPER STAR MANAGEMENT with an interest free loan in the amount of $112,500 by Jan. 15, 1978. This loan is to be repaid at the rate of $11,250 a year for ten (10) years begining [sic] Dec. 30, 1978 and is to be paid each Dec. 30th thereafter. The intrest [sic] free loan should be sent by bank money wire to:
>
> SUPER STAR MANAGEMENT
c/o LLOYDS BANK, TEMESCAL BRANCH
4900 Telegraph Ave
Oakland, CA 94609
Attention: MARIE SILVA
(415) 653-5277
>
> Respectfully,
>
> Abdul-Jalil

In January 1978, the Angels loaned to Bostock $112,500, and on January 13, 1978, Bostock loaned to al-Hakim $112,500.

In May 1978, al-Hakim billed Bostock $11,250 for the first installment of his $112,500 fee. Al-Hakim, as payment for the $11,250 installment, reduced the amount, which was shown as a loan from Bostock to him, to $101,250 ($112,500 – $11,250) and reported $11,250 in income from Bostock on his 1978 Federal individual income tax return.

Opinion

Respondent contends that petitioner was entitled to a fee from Bostock in the amount of $112,500, and al-Hakim received said amount on January 13, 1978, the date on which Bostock "loaned" al-Hakim $112,500. Petitioner contends that the $112,500, which Bostock transferred to him, was a loan. Petitioner further contends that pursuant to his arrangement with Bostock, he was entitled to only $11,250 of his fee in 1978, and pursuant to the settlement agreement, Genius, Inc., was entitled to the remaining part of his fee which was $101,250.

In the present case, petitioner testified that the $112,500, which Bostock transferred to him, was a loan, and the letter, which al-Hakim sent to Bostock, supports al-Hakim's testimony. Pursuant to the terms of the contract between al-Hakim and Bostock, Bostock was to pay al-Hakim's fee over 10 years and in 10 equal installments of $11,250 per year. Based on petitioner's testimony and its supporting documentation, we find that the $112,500, which Bostock transferred to al-Hakim on January 13, 1978, was a loan, and not the payment of his $112,500 fee. . . .

QUESTIONS

1. *Economic reality.* Is al-Hakim's economic position in 1978 any different from what it would have been if Bostock had simply paid the $112,500 fee? Under the "loan" arrangement, al-Hakim's expected net cash flow was as follows:

	Loan Proceeds		*Fee Earned*		*Loan Repayment*		*Net Cash*
1978	$112,500	+	$11,250	−	$11,250	=	$112,500
1979	-0-	+	11,250	−	11,250	=	-0-
1980	-0-	+	11,250	−	11,250	=	-0-
1981	-0-	+	11,250	−	11,250	=	-0-
1982	-0-	+	11,250	−	11,250	=	-0-
1983	-0-	+	11,250	−	11,250	=	-0-
1984	-0-	+	11,250	−	11,250	=	-0-
1985	-0-	+	11,250	−	11,250	=	-0-
1986	-0-	+	11,250	−	11,250	=	-0-
1987	-0-	+	11,250	−	11,250	=	-0-

2. *The possibility of bankruptcy.* What would have happened to al-Hakim if, during the ten-year period of the loan, Bostock had become insolvent and had filed for bankruptcy, listing debts substantially in excess of his assets?

3. *Section 7872.* If §7872 had been part of the Code in the years in which this case arose, the effect would have been a complex imputation of income and deductions to al-Hakim and to Bostock.

4. *Other cases.* In United States v. Ivey, 414 F.2d 199 (5th Cir. 1969), a farmer entered into an agreement with a grain broker; the broker

purchased the farmer's cotton and made advances to the farmer pending final settlement when the cotton was sold. The advances were treated as loans. Accord: Rutland v. Commissioner, 36 T.C.M. 40 (1977), where a farmer could obtain advances before his crop was sold by paying interest on the advances. See also United States v. Merrill, 211 F.2d 297 (9th Cir. 1954), where a taxpayer who agreed to repay amounts erroneously paid to him was held not in receipt of income, on a loan-equivalent theory, even though repayment was not made until several years later.

COMMISSIONER v. OLMSTED INCORPORATED LIFE AGENCY

304 F.2d 16 (8th Cir. 1962)

VOGEL, Circuit Judge.

The Commissioner of Internal Revenue, petitioner herein, seeks review and reversal of a decision by the Tax Court of the United States holding that Olmsted Incorporated Life Agency, respondent, did not realize taxable income upon the receipt by it in 1956 of a contract whereby it was to be paid monthly payments for a period of fifteen years in consideration for its surrender of all rights to future renewal commissions on previously written life insurance policies.

The facts, mainly stipulated, are not in dispute. Respondent is an Iowa corporation having its principal place of business in Des Moines, its main activity, beginning June 15, 1929, being that of exclusive general insurance agent in the State of Iowa for the Peoples Life Insurance Company of Frankfort, Indiana (hereinafter Peoples). The original agency contract between respondent and Peoples was signed on respondent's behalf by Oliver C. Miller, its president and principal stockholder who died in 1957. Two or three years prior to 1956, Peoples, because of its desire to develop insurance sales in Iowa by dividing the state into smaller territories, indicated its wish to terminate its exclusive contract with respondent. Under that contract Peoples was paying more favorable commissions to respondent than it was paying to other agencies under contracts executed subsequent to 1950. Miller did not at first accept Peoples' proposal, but subsequently, because of failing health, he did enter into a new agreement whereby the old agency agreement between respondent and Peoples was cancelled as of midnight December 31, 1955. Under the terms of the new agreement, respondent assigned to Peoples all of its rights in and to renewal commissions earned and payable after January 1, 1956. Respondent and its three stockholders agreed not to sell life insurance contracts for any other than Peoples within the State of Iowa. Respondent agreed to turn over to Peoples all papers, documents and records pertaining to its business, and Peoples agreed to issue, payable to the order of respondent or to such person or persons as respondent might direct, an annuity or annuities calling for a total payment of $500 per month beginning February 1, 1956, for a total of 180 months. Peoples based the total amount of consideration it would pay to respondent under the new agreement upon the present value of respondent's renewal commissions that would be due after January 1, 1956. As a further consideration, Peoples agreed to pay the agents theretofore employed by the respondent such renewal commissions as might be required by their contracts with respondent.

In its 1956 corporate income tax return respondent reported $5,500, being the total of payments actually received that year pursuant to the new contract. The Commissioner determined a deficiency in the respondent's return for 1956 in the amount of $27,009.34, taking the position that the entire fair market value ($67,924.47) of the new contract, whereby respondent gave up its rights to future renewal commissions and received in place thereof a fixed income over a period of fifteen years, should have been included in respondent's gross income for the year 1956. The Tax Court, in 35 T.C. 429, rejected the Commissioner's contention, holding that the case was ruled by James F. Oates, 18 T.C. 570, affirmed in Commissioner of Internal Revenue v. Oates, 7 Cir., 1953, 207 F.2d 711.

In seeking review, the Commissioner claims:

> The Tax Court Erred in Holding That Taxpayer's Assignment of Its Right to Future Renewal Commissions Did Not Constitute a "Sale or Other Disposition" of Property Within the Meaning of Section 1001(a) and (b), Internal Revenue Code of 1954.

U.S.C.A. §1001(a) defines the term "gain" as meaning the "amount realized" from the "sale or other disposition of property," less the adjusted basis in the property. The Commissioner argues that respondent here has "disposed" of its rights to renewal commissions, with a basis of zero, in exchange for an annuity contract, with an undisputed fair market value of $67,924.47, and that this amount was taxable in the year the transaction was completed. . . .

In Herbert's Estate v. Commissioner, [139 F.2d 756 (3d Cir. 1943), cert. denied, 322 U.S. 752 (1944)], the court said the issue was whether there was "a disposition" under Section 1001 where one receives payment for a claim he has against another. The court answered in the affirmative. However, there the money was received. That is not the situation before us. Payment here (other than the $5,500 received in 1956 and included in respondent's report) is absent. All that has occurred is the exchange of one contract for another, the principal change therein being the rate of payment. . . .

Inasmuch as the Tax Court held this case to be controlled by *Oates,* supra, and the Commissioner seeks to distinguish that case, detailed consideration is indicated to determine its applicability.

In *Oates,* the taxpayers were general insurance agents who, at retirement, amended their agency agreement with the insurance company by providing that future renewal commissions should be paid to them in specified equal monthly amounts over a fifteen-year period irrespective of when and in what amounts the renewal commissions would have become due and payable under the original agency contract. The obvious reason was that under the taxpayers' old contracts, the bulk of their renewal commissions would be collected by them in the first years after retirement and toward the end of the ninth year collections would dwindle off to little or nothing. Thereafter, and in accordance with the election given by the amended contract, the taxpayers elected to receive their payments in equal amounts over a fifteen-year period with a provision for a lump sum final payment if anything remained in the agents' renewal commission account. The Commissioner determined that the taxpayers there were taxable on the renewal commissions as they accrued under the terms of the original agency contract prior to its amendment. In rejecting the Commissioner's contention, the Tax Court in 18 T.C. 570 said that the taxpayers

> . . . under their amended contracts which were signed prior to their retirement . . . were not entitled to receive any more than they did in fact receive and that being on the cash basis they can only be taxed on these amounts [actually received] and that the remainder will be taxed to them if and when received by them.

18 T.C. at 585.

By unanimous decision, the Seventh Circuit, in Commissioner of Internal Revenue v. Oates, supra, 1953, 207 F.2d 711, affirmed the Tax Court. In doing so, that court said that the amended contract was a novation, that the old contract was extinguished, and that the taxpayer had no right to demand any additional compensation other than that which was listed in the new contract. Then after discussing Massachusetts Mutual Life Ins. Co. v. United States, 1933, 288 U.S. 269, as support for its affirmance of the Tax Court, Judge Lindley, referring to cases relied upon by the Commissioner wherein each taxpayer had "effectually received the accrued income with which he was charged," said at pages 713-714 of 207 F.2d:

> This case is far removed from such decision. Here the parties were confronted by a situation where inconvenience and resulting dissatisfaction came to the retired agents by reason of the constantly decreasing payments made by the company under the original contract. To relieve the situation, the company and the taxpayer, after full and complete

> negotiations, before retirement of the agent, agreed to abrogate and annul the old contract, to substitute a new one and thus to improve the unsatisfactory posture of affairs. *The taxpayer did not reduce to his immediate possession or to his present enjoyment anything that might thereafter accrue to him. He made no assignment; he took no dominion over the accrued commission other than to agree to receive them in cash installments as they matured under the contract. He did nothing to charge himself with the economic benefit to be derived from the accruing commissions but, on the contrary, let them accumulate under an agreement whereby the company was to pay the same amount every month rather than constantly decreasing amounts.*

(Emphasis supplied.) We think the Tax Court shows sound basis for its reliance on *Oates,* convincingly pointing out its applicability here. Just as cogently has the Tax Court pointed out the insignificance of the distinguishing factors the Commissioner considers to be of importance. It said at pages 434-437 of 35 T.C.:

> Respondent seeks to distinguish the *Oates* case by arguing that in that case the contract was not transferable and the rights thereunder nonassignable, while here the petitioner's rights to the periodic payments were assignable. We cannot conceive what difference in principle this would make. Also in the *Oates* case the rights and interests under the contract were subject to assignment with the written consent of the insurance company, and a careful examination of the amendment to the general agent's contract indicates quite clearly that the periodic payments to the taxpayers were "subject to the rights of any assignee."
>
> Respondent also makes much of the testimony that Peoples was ready in December 1955 to pay the commuted value of the renewal commissions to petitioner in a lump-sum payment. The executive officer of Peoples testified that "We told him he could have it either way but we decided upon the annuity. We knew that Mr. Miller wanted to prolong his income." It would seem from this that Peoples decided upon the annuity. However, even if the choice were up to petitioner, it is clear that he had no *right* to demand cash as of December 1955. Nothing was due and payable at that time. The parties were simply bargaining for a suitable agreement and it is this agreement, which was bona fide and legally binding, that determined the rights of petitioner in 1956. . . .
>
> The fact that here the new contract was an annuity and in the *Oates* case it was not, points up no difference that would warrant different tax treatment. In both, the deferred payments were computed to return to the agents their future renewal commissions. The only difference is that in the *Oates* case the company set up a renewal commission account for the agents on its books and made disbursements to the agents from these accounts. . . .
>
> We hold there is no significant difference in the facts between this case and the *Oates* case and the same rule applies, to wit: The periodic payments are taxable to petitioner as ordinary income under the annuity contract when and if received. There was no "sale or other disposition" of the agent's right to renewals under the agency contract within the meaning

of section 1001(b), I.R.C. 1954, and petitioner realized no gain taxable under said statute.

We agree with the Tax Court in its conclusion that there was no "sale or other disposition" within the meaning of Section 1001, and that the new contract merely provided for a different rate or manner of payment whereby the insurance company could discharge its liability under its agency contract.

The Commissioner's alternative argument here is that even if there is found to be no sale or other disposition within the meaning of Section 1001, this is an annuity contract and that to the extent of its fair market value, such contract constituted gross income to the respondent under the provisions of Section 61. In support of his argument, the Commissioner cites [several cases, including United States v. Drescher, supra page 79]. However, analysis of those cases points up that the court, in each, relied upon a factor absent herein — in each of those cases an employer had paid out, and deducted for that year, money to an insurance company for an annuity for the employees as added compensation. The courts there held that the amount paid out in that year was for the benefit of the employee, and therefore the employee was taxable to that extent, though he had not yet received any payment under the annuity. In the case before us, there is, of course, no payment made by Peoples, no deduction claimed by Peoples, no intended compensation from Peoples to the taxpayers for employment other than what had already been earned. There is, on the other hand, consideration running both ways in that Peoples obtained a cancellation of the exclusive territorial contract held by respondent, as well as respondent's promise to sell for no one but Peoples in the State of Iowa, and respondent received the new contract with its payments distributed evenly over a fifteen-year period. All that was intended here, as found by the Tax Court, was to substitute one contract for another — in other words, a novation. At no time was respondent in a position *to demand* more than the stipulated monthly payments. It did not reduce future payments to possession. It did not assign the contract. It did nothing to indicate it had assumed dominion over the installments to be made in the future.

We hold with the Tax Court that this cash basis taxpayer is to be taxed only on the payments as it receives them in accordance with the new agreement.

Affirmed.

NOTES AND QUESTIONS

1. *Analysis.* (a) Is the decision consistent with the decision in Helvering v. Bruun, supra page 301 (inclusion in landlord's income of value of

building constructed by tenant when tenant abandoned the lease)? With Rev. Rul. 82-166, supra page 320 (exchange of gold bullion for silver bullion results in recognition of gain)? With Cottage Savings Association v. Commissioner (supra page 308) (recognition of loss on swap of loans)?

(b) Did the court distinguish United States v. Drescher, supra page 79 (value of annuity bought by employer taxable to employee), to your satisfaction? What would the outcome in *Olmsted* have been if the annuity provided to the taxpayer had been issued by an insurance company other than the employer? From the taxpayer's perspective, how much difference do you suppose that would have made apart from tax considerations?

(c) Consider the relevance of Regs. §1.1001-1(a): "Except as otherwise provided . . . , the gain or loss realized from the conversion of property into cash, *or from the exchange of property for other property differing materially either in kind or in extent,* is treated as income or as loss sustained." (Emphasis added.)

(d) What if the initial contract had provided that all compensation would be in the form of annuity contracts issued by the employer?

2. *Where's the harm?* Are you disturbed by the outcome in the case? By the precedent?

3. *Novation versus constructive receipt.* For more on the possibility of amending an existing contract to postpone the receipt of taxable income, see Pittsburgh-Des Moines Steel Co. v. United States, 360 F. Supp. 597 (W.D. Pa. 1973). In 1960, a cash-method corporate taxpayer agreed to sell stock it owned in another corporation and mailed the endorsed stock certificates to the purchaser. It then discovered it would have losses from its ordinary business operations in 1960. The gain from the stock would have been long-term capital gain and presumably the taxpayer preferred to carry its net operating loss back against prior ordinary income. The buyer and seller modified the contract to postpone part of the payment to 1961. The court, following *Olmsted,* held for the taxpayer on the basis that a novation had occurred before receipt of the money.

4. Qualified Employee Plans

Basic rules. Employers are permitted to establish qualified pension, profit-sharing, or stock bonus plans,[16] which have the following set of highly attractive tax features:

16. Generally speaking, a pension plan may be thought of as a plan under which an employer agrees to provide annual fixed retirement benefits to each employee based on factors such as the employee's preretirement salary and the number of years of employment. Under a profit-sharing plan, an employer makes fixed contributions to a trust on behalf of each employee; the amount of contributions usually is based on company profit

(a) Amounts paid into the plan (that is, paid to the plan's trustee) are not taxed to those employees who become entitled to future benefits by virtue of such payments, even if the employee rights are vested (that is, are payable even if the employee quits or is fired before retirement). Employees are taxed only when they actually receive payments on retirement.[17] Under so-called 401(k) plans (after Code §401(k), which provides the legal authority), employees are not taxable on amounts up to $7,000 per year set aside for retirement, even if they had the option to take cash.

(b) Employers are entitled to an immediate deduction for amounts paid into the plan. Thus, disregarding the tax and nontax effects on the employee, the employer should be indifferent as between a payment into a plan and a payment of an equal amount as part of the employee's current wage or salary; the employer gets the same deduction either way.

(c) Earnings on funds paid into the plan and invested by it are not taxed (except to the extent that they are taxed to employees when paid to them).

Amount of tax benefit. The following hypothetical figures illustrate the tax advantage of qualified plans. Suppose that an employer pays into a qualified defined-contribution plan, on behalf of an employee, $10,000 per year for twenty-five years, and these funds earn an annual return of 10 percent. At the end of twenty-five years, on these assumptions, the total of the contributions and the earnings will be $983,471. Assume that at this point the employee retires and begins to collect benefits for life; that his life expectancy is fifteen years; and that the amounts to be paid to him are calculated on the assumption that the funds held in the plan will continue to earn 10 percent per year. The annual payment to the employee will be $129,301,[18] all of which is taxable. Assume that

---

or employee salary. The contributions (plus any interest earned on the contributions) are distributed to the employee on retirement, often in the form of a lifetime annuity. A stock bonus plan is like a profit-sharing plan except that benefits are distributable in the form of employer stock.

17. At retirement, in some circumstances an employee may be allowed to take a lump sum payment instead of payments spread over his or her remaining life. Lump-sum payments are taxed under a special five-year averaging provision. §402(e). Under this provision, a tax is computed on one-fifth of the lump sum, using normal rates but assuming no other income. This tax is then multiplied by five. The effect is to give the taxpayer five starts at the bottom of the rate schedule. Obviously, the effect may be highly favorable compared with normal methods of tax computation, but where the amounts are large, the taxpayer may still be better off to take benefits spread out over the rest of his or her life, since such benefits are taxed only as received and the taxpayer gains from nontaxation of earnings on the amount held in reserve to fund the future payments.

18. This figure is not quite accurate. In calculating it, the assumption was made that each year of life expectancy is weighed equally. In the real world this assumption is not accurate. The deviation from reality is not important for our purposes, however, since it is relatively minor and since the same method of calculation is used in the next paragraph.

the employee pays a tax on this amount at a rate of 35 percent on the entire amount. The amount left after tax will be $84,045.

Now consider what happens if we remove all the tax benefits. The employer pays $10,000 each year to the employee as a bonus. Assume that the employee is taxed on this amount at a rate of 35 percent. After tax, the amount available for investment is $6,500. Assume that this sum is invested each year at 10 percent before tax. The after-tax rate of return will be 6.5 percent. Assuming, then, an investment of $6,500 per year with a return of 6.5 percent per year, the total accumulated at the end of twenty-five years will be $382,770. Assume that this fund is used to buy an annuity whose payout is calculated based on an assumption of a rate of return of 10 percent. Again, assume a life expectancy of fifteen years. The annual payment will be $50,324. Of this, $24,810 will be taxed.[19] Assuming a tax rate of 35 percent, the tax will be $8,684, leaving, after tax, $41,640 per year. This is 49.5 percent of the after-tax amount ($84,045) available where the qualified plan is used.[20]

Note that in this hypothetical a constant tax rate of 35 percent has been assumed and that consequently the entire advantage of the qualified plan is from deferral. The comparison probably overstates somewhat the advantage of the use of qualified plans, however, because it assumes that a taxpayer whose salary and investment returns are not sheltered by such a plan would fail to find some form of investment with a tax advantage (e.g., investment in common stocks with growth potential, where there is deferral on unrealized appreciation). Note that tax-favored returns are of no advantage in a qualified plan.

Qualification. Congress has conditioned the availability of the tax benefits associated with qualified plans on compliance with certain rules. The most important of these are rules prohibiting discrimination in favor of highly paid employees. The purpose of the antidiscrimination rules may be understood by first examining the interests of highly paid and of rank-and-file employees. Rank-and-file employees are generally in the lower tax brackets and benefit less than highly paid employees from the tax savings associated with qualified pension plans. Moreover, rank-and-file employees generally are inclined to save only a small portion of their salaries. Highly paid employees, on the other hand, benefit more substantially from the tax savings associated with qualified plans and generally are more inclined to save a higher portion of their salaries

19. See §72(e). The exclusion ratio is the investment in the contract ($382,770) divided by the expected return ($50,324 × 15 = $754,860), or 0.507. The amount excluded is 0.507 × $50,324, which is $25,514. The amount taxed is the $50,324 received, less the $25,524 excluded under §72(e), or $24,810.

20. The calculation ignores social security taxes, which would be relevant for a taxpayer whose other income is below the social security maximum. For such taxpayers, the cash bonus will be subject to the social security tax, but neither contributions to qualified plans nor retirement benefits received from such plans are. The additional social security taxes will, however, result in increased social security retirement benefits.

than are low-paid employees. Absent a rule to the contrary, highly paid employees might bargain with employers to receive a large percentage of their salaries in the form of tax-favored pension benefits while rank-and-file employees might bargain with employers for low pension benefits or none at all or might not be offered the option of taking a pension benefit in lieu of wages.

The antidiscrimination rules prevent this outcome by requiring that qualified plans must provide reasonably comparable benefits to all employees. At the heart of the antidiscrimination rules is the requirement that, in general, the ratio of pension benefits to salary for highly paid employees must be no greater than the ratio of such benefits to the wages of rank-and-file employees. Thus, if highly paid employees receive benefits equal to 50 percent of their immediate preretirement salary, rank-and-file employees must also receive benefits equal to 50 percent of their preretirement wages. This requirement tends to limit the use of qualified plans by highly paid employees, while at the same time helping to ensure that rank-and-file employees receive some form of pension benefits. It is important to understand, however, that the benefits do not necessarily represent a "gift" to rank-and-file employees. Some portion of the benefits is most likely paid for by a reduction in the cash wages received by those employees.

The other major condition for qualification is compliance with the so-called ERISA rules (after the Employee Retirement Income Security Act of 1974), which impose obligations designed to ensure the safety of investments by the plan and which impose vesting requirements. The vesting rules are designed to ensure that after specified periods of service an employee's retirement benefit becomes nonforfeitable (that is, it is not lost if the employee quits or is fired). See §§401(a)(7), 411.

The ERISA rules and the antidiscrimination rules are extremely complex; partly because of these rules, the role of adviser on qualified plans has become a full-time specialty.

The rules on qualified plans also contain provisions designed to protect the interest of an employee's spouse in the retirement benefits earned by the employee. See §§401(a)(11), 417.

Individuals. There are special rules under which self-employed individuals are permitted to set up qualified plans, called H.R. 10 (formerly "Keogh") plans. For many years, self-employed doctors, lawyers, actors, and other highly paid individuals formed corporations, of which they became the sole (or at least the major) employee, in order to take advantage of the more generous rules available to employees (as compared with self-employed individuals). The Tax Equity and Fiscal Responsibility Act of 1982 (TEFRA) removed most of the advantage of this artificial use of the corporate form, partly by increasing the maximum amount that can be set aside each year by self-employed individuals and partly by reducing to the same level the maximum amount that can be set aside in corporate plans.

Individuals may also set up for themselves qualified plans called individual retirement accounts (IRA). See §408. Up to $2,000 per year ($2,250 for a married couple with only one earner) may be set aside in an IRA account. The income earned by the account is not taxed as long as it is accumulated. The amounts put into the account each year are deductible if the taxpayer is not covered by an employer plan or, if covered, has adjusted gross income less than $25,000 (for an individual) or $40,000 (for a married couple filing a joint return), with a phaseout as income rises above these levels. Amounts ultimately withdrawn as retirement benefits are included in income, with an exclusion to take account of amounts for which there was no deduction.

5. Stock Options, Restricted Property, and Other Employee Compensation

The following case, Commissioner v. LoBue, addresses the taxation of "compensatory" or "employee" stock options — that is, options granted to an employee (usually a high-level executive) in consideration of services to a corporate employer, with the option entitling the employee to buy a specified number of shares of the employer's common stock at a specified price during or at the end of some defined period of time (usually two to five years from the date of the grant). Compensatory stock options should be distinguished from ordinary options on common stock sold by the owner of that stock to some other person in consideration of an immediate cash payment (which options are sometimes said to be "side bets," since they affect the shareholder but not the corporation itself). The question of how to tax compensatory stock options is complicated by the fact that such options generally reflect, or result in, a combination of compensation for services and return on investment in a capital asset and therefore raise issues both of timing and of capital gain versus ordinary income.

There are three major possibilities for taxing compensatory stock options (assuming the option cannot be transferred and can be exercised only at the end of its term):

(a) Tax the employee on the value *of the option* when granted (and allow the employer a corresponding deduction at that time). It must be emphasized, in support of this possibility, that a stock option is worth something even if the option price is equal to, or exceeds, the market price of the stock at the time the option is granted. For example, if *X* Corp. common stock is currently selling for $50 a share and *X* Corp. grants to its employee, *E*, an option to buy shares at $55 per share three years from the date of the grant, that option has some significant present value. *E* will receive the benefit of any increase in price above $55 at the end of the three years and suffers no loss from any decline below the present price. People pay hard cash for such options, though options available in the financial marketplace usually run for only six months and are available only for corporate stock in which there is a relatively high volume of trading. Often, however, the value of a compensatory option will be extremely difficult to determine, especially where there are restrictions on transfer or possibilities of forfeiture (for example, forfeiture if the employee quits before the option can be exercised).

Assuming that the grant of the option is treated as a taxable event, the amount included in income is ordinary income. *E* will be treated as if she had received a cash bonus equal to the value of the option and had used that cash to buy the option. *X* Corp. should be entitled to a deduction equal to the amount included in *E*'s income. If the option expires without being exercised (which *E* will allow to happen if the price of the shares does not rise above $55), *E* will be entitled to a deduction for a loss, equal to the amount previously included in income. (It will be a capital loss.) Correspondingly, *X* Corp. should realize a gain (as if it had sold an option for cash and the option had expired, leaving *X* Corp. with the cash). If, at the end of three years, the price of the shares is above $55, and *E* exercises the option, she will not be taxed on the difference between the exercise price and the market value of the shares at that time. (This is the rule for holders of ordinary stock options.) Her basis will be the exercise price ($55 per share) plus the amount previously included in income, and any spread between the exercise price and the market price at the time of exercise will show up for tax purposes only on ultimate disposition of the shares in the form of higher gain or lower loss.

To illustrate the tax consequences of this approach, suppose that *X* Corp., at a time when its shares are selling for $50 per share, grants to *E* an option to buy 100 shares at $55 per share at the end of three years. Suppose that the option is valued at $1,000. This amount would be included in *E*'s income and deducted by *X* Corp. at the time the option is granted. (It is treated as if *X* Corp. had paid *E* a salary of $1,000, in cash, and *E* had used the cash to buy the option: *E* would have income of $1,000 from the salary and an investment of $1,000 in the option; *X* Corp. would have a deduction of $1,000 for the salary; *X* Corp would not recognize gain from the sale of the option.) If at the end of three years the shares are selling for $55 or less, *E* will not exercise the option and it will expire. She will be entitled to a capital-loss deduction of $1,000 at that time — as if she had earned $1,000 and had used that money to buy the option — and *X* Corp. will report gain of $1,000. Suppose that at the end of the three years the stock is selling for $70 per share. *E* will exercise the option and will pay $5,500 for $7,000 worth of stock. No gain will be recognized at this time. *E*'s basis will be $6,500 — the $5,500 purchase price plus the $1,000 tax cost of the option. Gain (or loss) will be recognized only when the stock is ultimately sold and will be capital gain or loss. For example, if *E* sells the shares two years later for $7,700, the gain will be $1,200, all of which will be capital gain. If *E* were to sell instead for $6,000, she would have a capital loss of $500.

(b) Under the second major alternative, *E* is not taxed on the value of the option when granted, and *X* Corp. is not allowed a deduction at that time. If the option is never exercised, the grant has no tax consequences — no income to *E* or deduction by *X* Corp. If the option is exercised, *E* is taxed at that time on the difference between the exercise price and the market value. For example, if *E* is able to buy for $5,500 stock that is worth $7,000, she would be taxed on the $1,500 spread. This would be treated as ordinary income. *X* Corp. would be entitled to a deduction of the amount included in *E*'s income. *E*'s basis would be $7,000. Any subsequent gain or loss would be capital gain or loss.

(c) Under the third alternative, *E* is not taxed either on the grant of the option or on the spread at the time of exercise. Correspondingly, *X* Corp. is not entitled to a deduction. *E*'s basis is the amount paid for the shares. For example, if *E* pays $5,500 for shares worth $7,000, her basis is $5,500. Any gain on ultimate disposition would be capital gain.[21] This is likely to be the most favorable alternative for *E* since it defers gain until ultimate disposition of the shares. But the tax benefit to *E* may be less than the tax detriment to *X* Corp. associated with the fact that it is not entitled to a deduction. The net tax effect will depend on the tax rates applicable to *E* and to *X* Corp. and on how long *E* holds the stock.

It is important to note that while the *X* Corp. assets are not diminished by the grant of a compensatory stock option, or by its exercise (indeed, the exercise results in an increase in its assets), the increase in the wealth of the employee is at the expense of the shareholders, though they may get their money's worth in the form of improved services by the employee. To demonstrate this point, suppose that a person, *S*, owns 1,000 shares of the common stock of *X* Corp. and that there are no other shares outstanding; in other words, *S* is the sole shareholder. Suppose the shares are worth $100 each or a total of $100,000. Presumably that total is also the value of the corporation's assets. Now suppose that *X* Corp. sells to its employee, *E*, 100 shares for $12 per share or a total of $1,200. With the $1,200 received for the new shares, *X* Corp. should be worth $101,200. There will now be 1,100 shares outstanding and

21. Of course, if the value of the shares were to fall below $7,000 at the time of ultimate disposition, the gain recognized would be reduced accordingly, and if the shares fell in value below $5,500, there would be a loss. It is by no means obvious that the gain on ultimate disposition should be treated as capital gain rather than ordinary income. It could be viewed not as gain from holding the asset but rather as deferred compensation (at least to the extent of the $1,500 spread). But in the *LoBue* case (immediately following), the parties and the court seemed to assume that under the third alternative the entire gain (or loss) ultimately recognized would be capital gain (or loss).

each share should be worth $92. *S*'s 1,000 shares should be worth $92,000 or $8,000 less than they were previously worth. *E's* shares should be worth $9,200 or $8,000 more than she paid for them.

COMMISSIONER v. LoBUE

351 U.S. 243 (1956)

Mr. Justice BLACK delivered the opinion of the Court.

This case involves the federal income tax liability of respondent LoBue for the years 1946 and 1947. From 1941 to 1947 LoBue was manager of the New York Sales Division of the Michigan Chemical Corporation, a producer and distributor of chemical supplies. In 1944 the company adopted a stock option plan making 10,000 shares of its common stock available for distribution to key employees at $5 per share over a 3-year period. LoBue and a number of other employees were notified that they had been tentatively chosen to be recipients of nontransferable stock options contingent upon their continued employment. LoBue's notice told him: "You may be assigned a greater or less amount of stock based entirely upon your individual results and that of the entire organization." About 6 months later he was notified that he had been definitely awarded an option to buy 150 shares of stock in recognition of his "contribution and efforts in making the operation of the Company successful." As to future allotments he was told "It is up to you to justify your participation in the plan during the next two years."

LoBue's work was so satisfactory that the company in the course of 3 years delivered to him 3 stock options covering 340 shares. He exercised all these $5 per share options in 1946 and in 1947,[22] paying the company only $1,700 for stock having a market value when delivered of $9,930. Thus, at the end of these transactions, LoBue's employer was worth $8,230 less to its stockholders and LoBue was worth $8,230 more than before. The company deducted this sum as an expense in its 1946 and 1947 tax returns but LoBue did not report any part of it as income. Viewing the gain to LoBue as compensation for personal services the Commissioner levied a deficiency assessment against him, relying on . . . [§61(a)]. . . . Finding after hearings that the options were granted to give LoBue "a proprietary interest in the corporation, and not as compensation for services" the Tax Court held for LoBue. 22 T.C. 440, 443. Relying on this finding the Court of Appeals affirmed, saying: "This was a factual issue which it was the peculiar responsibility of the Tax Court to resolve. From our examination of the evidence we

22. There may be some question as to whether the first option was exercised in 1945 or 1946. See the discussion, infra, as to when the transactions were completed.

cannot say that its finding was clearly erroneous." 223 F.2d 367, 371. Disputes over the taxability of stock option transactions such as this are long-standing. We granted certiorari to consider whether the Tax Court and the Court of Appeals had given [§61(a)] too narrow an interpretation. 350 U.S. 893.

We have repeatedly held that in defining "gross income" as broadly as it did in [§61(a)] Congress intended to "tax all gains except those specifically exempted." See, e.g., Commissioner v. Glenshaw Glass Co. [supra page 126]. The only exemption Congress provided from this very comprehensive definition of taxable income that could possibly have application here is the gift exemption of [§102(a)]. But there was not the slightest indication of the kind of detached and disinterested generosity which might evidence a "gift" in the statutory sense. These transfers of stock bore none of the earmarks of a gift. They were made by a company engaged in operating a business for profit, and the Tax Court found that the stock option plan was designed to achieve more profitable operations by providing the employees "with an incentive to promote the growth of the company by permitting them to participate in its success." 22 T.C., at 445. Under these circumstances the Tax Court and the Court of Appeals properly refrained from treating this transfer as a gift. The company was not giving something away for nothing.

Since the employer's transfer of stock to its employee LoBue for much less than the stock's value was not a gift, it seems impossible to say that it was not compensation. The Tax Court held there was no taxable income, however, on the ground that one purpose of the employer was to confer a "proprietary interest."[23] But there is not a word in [§61(a)] which indicates that its broad coverage should be narrowed because of an employer's intention to enlist more efficient service from his employees by making them part proprietors of his business. In our view there is no statutory basis for the test established by the courts below. When assets are transferred by an employer to an employee to secure better services they are plainly compensation. It makes no difference that the compensation is paid in stock rather than in money. Section [§61(a)] taxes income derived from compensation "in whatever form paid." And in another stock option case we said that [§61(a)] "is broad enough to include in taxable income any economic or financial benefit conferred on the employee as compensation, whatever the form or mode by which it is effected." Commissioner v. Smith, 324 U.S. 177, 181. LoBue received a very substantial economic and financial benefit from his employer prompted by the employer's desire to get better

23. The Tax Court noted "that in practically all such cases as the one before us, both the element of additional compensation and the granting of a proprietary interest are present." 22 T.C., at 445. See also Geeseman v. Commissioner, 38 B.T.A. 258, 263.

work from him. This is "compensation for personal service" within the meaning of [§61(a)].

LoBue nonetheless argues that we should treat this transaction as a mere purchase of a proprietary interest on which no taxable gain was "realized" in the year of purchase. It is true that our taxing system has ordinarily treated an arm's length purchase of property even at a bargain price as giving rise to no taxable gain in the year of purchase. . . . But that is not to say that when a transfer which is in reality compensation is given the form of a purchase the Government cannot tax the gain under [§61(a)]. The transaction here was unlike a mere purchase. It was not an arm's length transaction between strangers. Instead it was an arrangement by which an employer transferred valuable property to his employees in recognition of their services. We hold that LoBue realized taxable gain when he purchased the stock.

A question remains as to the time when the gain on the shares should be measured. LoBue gave his employer promissory notes for the option price of the first 300 shares but the shares were not delivered until the notes were paid in cash. The market value of the shares was lower when the notes were given than when the cash was paid. The Commissioner measured the taxable gain by the market value of the shares when the cash was paid. LoBue contends that this was wrong, and that the gain should be measured either when the options were granted or when the notes were given.

It is of course possible for the recipient of a stock option to realize an immediate taxable gain. See Commissioner v. Smith, 324 U.S. 177, 181-182. The option might have a readily ascertainable market value and the recipient might be free to sell his option. But this is not such a case. These three options were not transferable and LoBue's right to buy stock under them was contingent upon his remaining an employee of the company until they were exercised. Moreover, the uniform Treasury practice since 1923 has been to measure the compensation to employees given stock options subject to contingencies of this sort by the difference between the option price and the market value of the shares at the time the option is exercised. We relied in part upon this practice in Commissioner v. Smith, 324 U.S. 177, 324 U.S. 695. And in its 1950 Act affording limited tax benefits for "restricted stock option plans" Congress adopted the same kind of standard for measurement of gains. Under these circumstances there is no reason for departing from the Treasury practice. The taxable gain to LoBue should be measured as of the time the options were exercised and not the time they were granted.

It is possible that a bona fide delivery of a binding promissory note could mark the completion of the stock purchase and that gain should be measured as of that date. Since neither the Tax Court nor the Court of Appeals passed on this question the judgment is reversed and the case is remanded to the Court of Appeals with instructions to remand the case to the Tax Court for further proceedings.[24]

Reversed and remanded.

[Mr. Justice FRANKFURTER and Mr. Justice CLARK concurred.]

Mr. Justice HARLAN, whom Mr. Justice BURTON joins, concurring in part and dissenting in part.

In my view, the taxable event was the grant of each option, not its exercise. When the respondent received an unconditional option to buy stock at less than the market price, he received an asset of substantial and immediately realizable value, at least equal to the then-existing spread between the option price and the market price. It was at that time that the corporation conferred a benefit upon him. At the exercise of the option, the corporation "gave" the respondent nothing; it simply satisfied a previously created legal obligation. That transaction, by which the respondent merely converted his asset from an option into stock, should be of no consequence for tax purposes. The option should be taxable as income when given, and any subsequent gain through appreciation of the stock, whether realized by sale of the option, if transferable, or by sale of the stock acquired by its exercise, is attributable to the sale of a capital asset and, if the other requirements are satisfied, should be taxed as a capital gain.[25] Any other result makes the division of the total gains between ordinary income (compensation) and capital gain (sale of an asset) dependent solely upon the fortuitous circumstance of when the employee exercises his option.[26]

24. [On remand, the Tax Court held that the income was realized when the taxpayer gave his notes, rather than when he paid them. LoBue v. Commissioner, 28 T.C. 1317 (1957). — Eds.]

25. Commissioner v. Smith, 324 U.S. 177, 324 U.S. 695, does not require an opposite result. In that case Smith's employer, Western, had undertaken the management of a reorganized corporation, Hawley, under a contract by which Western was to receive as compensation for its managerial services a specified amount of stock in Hawley if it was successful in reducing Hawley's indebtedness by a stated amount. Western, in turn, gave Smith, who was active in the Hawley reorganization, an option to buy, at the then-existing market price, a fixed share of any Hawley stock received under the management contract. The management contract was successfully performed, and a part of the Hawley stock received by Western — the value of which was of course substantially enhanced by the performance of the contract — was sold to Smith at the option price. Under the peculiar facts of that case — more analogous to an assignment to an employee of a share in the anticipated proceeds of a contract than to the usual employee stock option plan — the Tax Court's finding that the gain that would accrue to Smith upon the successful performance of the management contract was intended as "compensation" to him for his services was no doubt amply justified. But as the Court expressly stated in upholding that finding: "It of course does not follow that in other circumstances not here present the option itself, rather than the proceeds of its exercise, could not be found to be the only intended compensation." Id., at p.182.

26. Suppose two employees are given unconditional options to buy stock at $5, the current market value. The first exercises the option immediately and sells the stock a year later at $15. The second holds the option for a year, exercises it, and sells the stock immediately at $15. Admittedly the $10 gain would be taxed to the first as capital gain;

The last two options granted to respondent were unconditional and immediately exercisable, and thus present no further problems. The first option, however, was granted under somewhat different circumstances. Respondent was notified in January 1945 that 150 shares had been "allotted" to him, but he was given no right to purchase them until June 30, 1945, and his right to do so then was expressly made contingent upon his still being employed at that date. His right to purchase the first allotment of stock was thus not vested until he satisfied the stated condition, and it was not until then that he could be said to have received income, the measure of which should be the value of the option on that date.

Accordingly, while I concur in the reversal of the judgment below and in the remand to the Tax Court, I would hold the granting of the options to be the taxable events and would measure the income by the value of the options when granted.

NOTES AND QUESTIONS

1. *Analysis.* Did the majority pick the right time? Is the result accurate in reflecting economic reality? Is it practical (easily administered)? Given the conclusion as to when to tax, does the conclusion as to the nature of the income or gain seem appropriate?

2. *Legislative aftermath.* The rule in *LoBue,* taxing as ordinary income the spread between the purchase price and the market value at the time of purchase, proved to be sufficiently unfavorable to virtually eliminate the use of stock options. In 1950, however, after the events of *LoBue* but before the decision of the Supreme Court, Congress enacted a provision that gave corporate executives what they wanted. Under this provision, "restricted" stock options (later called "qualified" stock options) resulted in no tax until the stock was sold and then generally the tax was at capital gain rates. This provision made stock options quite popular, despite the denial of a deduction to the employer. As a result of amendments in 1964, the attractiveness of stock options was reduced and, after further restrictive changes in 1969, the provision was repealed in 1976. This left the law as it was under *LoBue.* In 1981, however, the statutory stock option was reinstated, with a new label, "incentive stock option" (ISO). §422A. The policy justification offered for the resurrection, and the basic features of the new provision, are reflected in the General Explanation of the Economic Recovery Tax Act of 1981, pre-

---

under the Court's view, it would be taxed to the second as ordinary income because it is "compensation" for services. I fail to see how the gain can be any more "compensation" to one than it is to the other.

pared by the Staff of the Joint Committee on Taxation, 97th Cong., 1st Sess., at 157 (1981):

> The Congress believed that reinstitution of a stock option provision will provide an important incentive device for corporations to attract new management and to retain the service of executives who might otherwise leave, by providing an opportunity to acquire an interest in the business. Encouraging the management of a business to have a proprietary interest in its successful operation will provide an important incentive to expand and improve the profit position of the companies involved. The provision is designed to encourage the use of stock options for key employees without reinstituting the alleged abuses which arose with the restricted stock option provisions of prior law.
>
> **Explanation of Provision**
>
> *In general.* The Act provides for "incentive stock options," which are taxed in a manner similar to the tax treatment previously applied to restricted and qualified stock options. That is, there are no tax consequences when an incentive stock option is granted or when the option is exercised, and the employee generally is taxed at capital gains rates when the stock received on exercise of the option is sold. Similarly, no business expense deduction is allowed to the employer with respect to an incentive stock option (sec. 421(a)).

A stock option must meet a number of conditions in order to qualify for the benefits of incentive stock option (ISO) status. Among other things, it must require the employee to retain the stock for at least two years after the grant of the option and one year after the transfer of the stock to him or her (§422A(a)(1)) and the option price must be no less than the fair market value of the stock at the time the option is granted (§422A(b)(4)).

3. *Forfeitability, restrictions, and §83.* Meanwhile, during the 1960s, people started to use so-called nonstatutory stock options — that is, ones that did not meet the requirements of the statute. To understand this development, one must begin with definitions of "restricted" stock and of "risk of forfeiture." Suppose an employer sells to an employee, for $5, shares of its common stock that are at the time of the sale selling on a public exchange for $30, but that the purchase by the employee is subject to two conditions: (1) If the employee is fired for cause or quits within the next two years, he must sell the shares back to the employer for $5 per share, and (2) in any event, the employee cannot sell the shares for five years. The first condition creates a risk of forfeiture; the second is a restriction on transferability. Obviously, both affect adversely the value to the employee of the shares he or she has bought.

After the attractiveness of statutory stock options was reduced in 1964, employers began increasingly to replace them with nonstatutory options and with outright transfers subject to various kinds of provisions imposing restrictions and risks of forfeiture. The employees claimed (with some initial success in the courts) that the risk of forfeiture or the restriction meant that no tax could be imposed on the employee, at least at the time of the initial transfer, because of problems of valuation. (Employers were prepared to accept their own inability to claim a deduction, just as they are with statutory options.)

Section 83, adopted in 1969, responded to this development, though its language is far more general, applying to all transfers of property as compensation for services. Under §83, if property is transferred to a person (generally, but not necessarily, an employee) as compensation for services, without restrictions or risk of forfeiture, the difference between the value of the property and the amount paid by the employee is income at the time of transfer. Subsequent gain in the value of the property is not recognized until the property is sold (and is capital gain). If an employee receives from an employer stock (or other property) that is nontransferable and subject to a substantial risk of forfeiture, the employee does not recognize income until the stock becomes transferable or nonforfeitable, at which time ordinary income is recognized in an amount equal to the difference between the value of the stock and the amount paid for it by the employee. The employee has an election, however, to recognize income at the time of the initial transfer. The effect of an election is that subsequent gain is capital gain rather than ordinary income. If the election is made, no deduction is allowed in the event that the stock is ultimately sold at a loss.[27] Thus, under present law the election will rarely have any appeal.

If an employer sells stock (or other property) to an employee subject to a restriction, the employee is taxable on the full amount of the difference between (a) the market value of the stock (or property) without any restriction and (b) the amount paid for it by the employee.[28] In Sakol v. Commissioner, 574 F.2d 694 (2d Cir.), cert. denied, 439 U.S. 859 (1978), the taxpayer was unsuccessful in an attack on this provision based on the fifth and sixteenth amendments and on the notion that she was being taxed on more than she received.

27. For example, suppose an employer transfers to an employee 100 shares of its common stock, worth $1,000, at no cost to the employee but subject to the condition that the shares must be returned if the employee terminates her employment for any reason within two years. The shares are subject to a substantial risk of forfeiture and their value need not be included in income when received. Suppose that at the end of the two years the employee is still employed by the employer and the shares are worth $2,500. At that time the employee would be required to include the $2,500 in income as ordinary income. The employee could have elected to include $1,000 in income at the time of the initial transfer, in which case the subsequent $1,500 gain would have been capital gain.

28. If, however, the restriction is one that by its terms will never lapse (e.g., a requirement that upon termination of employment, or at death, the stock must be sold to the corporation at a price to be determined by a formula), it is taken into account in valuing the stock. §83(d).

The application of §83 to options may be summarized as follows: First, if the option has a "readily ascertainable market value" (see §83(e)(3)), its tax treatment depends on whether it is transferable or forfeitable, or both.[29]

(a) If the option is either transferable (that is, there are no "restrictions" on its transfer) or nonforfeitable, then its value is included in the employee's income at the time it is granted and the employer is entitled to a deduction. There is no tax at the time of exercise. Gain or loss on disposition of the stock is capital gain or loss. Thus, the tax treatment follows the pattern described in paragraph (a) of the introductory note for this section (supra page 399).
(b) If the option is subject to a substantial risk of forfeiture (see Regs. §1.83-3(c)(2)), and is not transferable, its value is not included in income unless the employee elects inclusion. In the absence of an election, when the option becomes nonforfeitable or transferable, its value is included in income.
(c) If the option is nontransferable and is subject to a substantial risk of forfeiture, the employee may elect to include its value in income. The consequence of doing so is that gain thereafter will not be recognized until the stock is sold and will be capital gain. If, however, the outcome is a loss, no deduction is allowed. See §83(b).[30]

Second, if the option does not have a readily ascertainable fair market value (which is generally the case), then the rule of *LoBue* is still applicable: no tax at the time the option is granted and a tax at the time of exercise on the spread between the fair market value of the stock and the option price. This rule has now been incorporated into §83. See §83(a); Regs. §1.83-7.

4. *Review.* For a brief review, we can return to the three possible tax treatments of stock options described at supra pages 399-402. The first possibility (a) is consistent with the rule under §83 if the option is not an Incentive Stock Option (ISO) and has a readily ascertainable fair market value. The second possibility (b) describes the rules for an option

29. In 1976, by an ex post facto expression of "legislative intent," Congress attempted to facilitate the use of options by suggesting to the Service that it should be receptive to finding an ascertainable market value if the employee wants to be taxed. See 2 B. Bittker, Federal Income Taxation of Individuals, Estates and Gifts, ¶60.5.2 (1981).

30. Employees receiving stock options are often highly optimistic about the prospects of the firms for which they work and believe that the stock will rise dramatically in value. They are prepared to recognize a small gain at the time of issuance of the option in order to avoid recognizing what they expect will be a much larger gain at the time of exercise and are inclined to minimize the risk of any loss.

that is not an ISO and has no readily ascertainable fair market value. The basic approach is that of the *LoBue* case. The third possibility (c) is ISO treatment.

F. TRANSFERS INCIDENT TO MARRIAGE AND DIVORCE

1. Introduction

Transfers incident to marriage and divorce raise an interesting set of issues. Suppose, for example, that pursuant to a divorce, Linda transfers to her ex-spouse, Martin, stock with a basis of $40,000 and a fair market value of $100,000. One question raised by such a transfer is whether, by virtue of the transfer, Martin should be required to include $100,000 in his income and Linda should be allowed to deduct $100,000. That is the "alimony" issue, to which we will return later in this section. (The answer under current law is that Linda would not be entitled to a deduction and Martin would not be required to include any amount in his income, but it is by no means obvious that that result is consistent with sound principles of tax policy.) At this point we address the narrower question — the "recognition" question — of whether the transfer should be treated as a realization event for Linda, an appropriate time at which to recognize Linda's gain of $60,000. Should Linda be treated as if she had sold the property and transferred the proceeds? Should it matter whether the transfer is of community property? Whether the transfer is made pursuant to a divorce decree or an antenuptial agreement?

As we have just suggested, transfers incident to marriage and divorce raise income and deduction issues as well. Suppose that, in addition to the stock transfer described above, Linda makes cash alimony payments of $1,000 a month for three years to Martin. Those payments would be deductible by Linda and taxable to Martin, but we will see that there are complex rules distinguishing between alimony and other types of transfers that are not deductible by the payor and not taxable to the payee. The income and deduction issues that arise with transfers of both appreciated and nonappreciated property might be discussed in Chapter 2, in connection with other characteristics of income, or in Chapter 4, in connection with other personal deductions. Instead, in the pages that follow, we provide an introduction to all tax issues raised by transfers incident to marriage and divorce, but we begin with the recognition issue, which plainly fits in this chapter.

2. Property Settlements

a. *Transfers Incident to a Divorce or Separation Agreement*

UNITED STATES v. DAVIS

370 U.S. 65 (1962)

Mr. Justice CLARK delivered the opinion of the Court.

These cases involve the tax consequences of a transfer of appreciated property by Thomas Crawley Davis to his former wife pursuant to a property settlement agreement executed prior to divorce. . . .

In 1954 the taxpayer and his then wife made a voluntary property settlement and separation agreement calling for support payments to the wife and minor child in addition to the transfer of certain personal property to the wife. Under Delaware law all the property transferred was that of the taxpayer, subject to certain statutory marital rights of the wife including a right of intestate succession and a right upon divorce to a share of the husband's property. Specifically as a "division in settlement of their property" the taxpayer agreed to transfer to his wife, inter alia, 1,000 shares of stock in the E. I. duPont de Nemours & Co. The then Mrs. Davis agreed to accept this division "in full settlement and satisfaction of any and all claims and rights against the husband whatsoever (including but not by way of limitation, dower and all rights under the laws of testacy and intestacy). . . ."

I

The determination of the income tax consequences of the stock transfer described above is basically a two-step analysis: (1) Was the transaction a taxable event? (2) If so, how much taxable gain resulted therefrom? Originally the Tax Court (at that time the Board of Tax Appeals) held that the accretion to property transferred pursuant to a divorce settlement could not be taxed as capital gain to the transferor because the amount realized by the satisfaction of the husband's marital obligations was indeterminable and because, even if such benefit were ascertainable, the transaction was a nontaxable division of property. . . . However, upon being reversed in quick succession by the Courts of Appeals of the Third and Second Circuits, . . . the Tax Court accepted the position of these courts and has continued to apply these views in appropriate cases since that time. . . . [T]he Courts of Appeals reasoned that the accretion to the property was "realized" by the transfer and that this gain could be measured on the assumption that the relinquished marital rights were equal in value to the property transferred.

The matter was considered settled until the Court of Appeals for the Sixth Circuit, in reversing the Tax Court, ruled that, although such a transfer might be a taxable event, the gain realized thereby could not be determined because of the impossibility of evaluating the fair market value of the wife's marital rights. . . . In so holding that court specifically rejected the argument that these rights could be presumed to be equal in value to the property transferred for their release. This is essentially the position taken by the Court of Claims in the instant case.

II

We now turn to the threshold question of whether the transfer in issue was an appropriate occasion for taxing the accretion to the stock. There can be no doubt that Congress, as evidenced by its inclusive definition [in §61(a)] of income subject to taxation, i.e., "all income from whatever source derived, including . . . [g]ains derived from dealings in property," intended that the economic growth of this stock be taxed. The problem confronting us is simply when is such accretion to be taxed. Should the economic gain be presently assessed against taxpayer, or should this assessment await a subsequent transfer of the property by the wife? The controlling statutory language, which provides [§§1001 and 1002] that gains from dealings in property are to be taxed upon "sale or other disposition," is too general to include or exclude conclusively the transaction presently in issue. Recognizing this, the Government and the taxpayer argue by analogy with transactions more easily classified as within or without the ambient [sic] of taxable events. The taxpayer asserts that the present disposition is comparable to a nontaxable division of property between two co-owners,[31] while the Government contends it more resembles a taxable transfer of property in exchange for the release of an independent legal obligation. Neither disputes the validity of the other's starting point.

In support of his analogy the taxpayer argues that to draw a distinction between a wife's interest in the property of her husband in a

31. Any suggestion that the transaction in question was a gift is completely unrealistic. Property transferred pursuant to a negotiated settlement in return for the release of admittedly valuable rights is not a gift in any sense of the term. To intimate that there was a gift to the extent the value of the property exceeded that of the rights released not only invokes the erroneous premise that every exchange not precisely equal involves a gift but merely raises the measurement problem discussed in Part III [of this opinion]. Cases in which this Court has held transfers of property in exchange for the release of marital rights subject to gift taxes are based not on the premise that such transactions are inherently gifts but on the concept that in the contemplation of the gift tax statute they are to be taxed as gifts. Merrill v. Fahs, 324 U.S. 308 (1945); Commissioner v. Wemyss, 324 U.S. 303 (1945); see Harris v. Commissioner, 340 U.S. 106 (1950). In interpreting the particular income tax provisions here involved, we find ourselves unfettered by the language and considerations ingrained in the gift and estate tax statutes. See Farid-Es-Sultaneh v. Commissioner [infra page 416].

common-law jurisdiction such as Delaware and the property interest of a wife in a typical community property jurisdiction would commit a double sin; for such differentiation would depend upon "elusive and subtle casuistries which . . . possess no relevance for tax purposes," Helvering v. Hallock, 309 U.S. 106, 118 (1940), and would create disparities between common-law and community property jurisdictions in contradiction to Congress' general policy of equality between the two. The taxpayer's analogy, however, stumbles on its own premise, for the inchoate rights granted a wife in her husband's property by the Delaware law do not even remotely reach the dignity of co-ownership. The wife has no interest — passive or active — over the management or disposition of her husband's personal property. Her rights are not descendable, and she must survive him to share in his intestate estate. Upon dissolution of the marriage she shares in the property only to such extent as the court deems "reasonable." 13 Del. Code Ann. §1531(a). What is "reasonable" might be ascertained independently of the extent of the husband's property by such criteria as the wife's financial condition, her needs in relation to her accustomed station in life, her age and health, the number of children and their ages, and the earning capacity of the husband. See, e.g., Beres v. Beres, 52 Del. 133, 154 F.2d 384 (1959).

This is not to say it would be completely illogical to consider the shearing off of the wife's rights in her husband's property as a division of that property, but we believe the contrary to be the more reasonable construction. Regardless of the tags, Delaware seems only to place a burden on the husband's property rather than to make the wife a part owner thereof. In the present context the rights of succession and reasonable share do not differ significantly from the husband's obligations of support and alimony. They all partake more of a personal liability of the husband than a property interest of the wife. The effectuation of these marital rights may ultimately result in the ownership of some of the husband's property as it did here, but certainly this happenstance does not equate the transaction with a division of property by co-owners. Although admittedly such a view may permit different tax treatment among the several States, this Court in the past has not ignored the differing effects on the federal taxing scheme of substantive differences between community property and federal taxing systems. E.g., Poe v. Seaborn [infra page 745]. To be sure Congress has seen fit to alleviate this disparity in many areas, . . . but in other areas the facts of life are still with us. . . .

III

Having determined that the transaction was a taxable event, we now turn to the point on which the Court of Claims balked, viz., the measurement of the taxable gain realized by the taxpayer. The Code defines the taxable gain from the sale or disposition of property as being the "excess of the amount realized therefrom over the adjusted basis. . . ." §1001(a). The "amount realized" is further defined as "the sum of any money received plus the fair market value of the property (other than money) received." §1001(b). In the instant case the "property received" was the release of the wife's inchoate marital rights. The Court of Claims, following the Court of Appeals for the Sixth Circuit, found that there was no way to compute the fair market value of these marital rights and that it was thus impossible to determine the taxable gain realized by the taxpayer. We believe this conclusion was erroneous.

It must be assumed, we think, that the parties acted at arm's length and that they judged the marital rights to be equal in value to the property for which they were exchanged. There was no evidence to the contrary here. Absent a readily ascertainable value it is accepted practice where property is exchanged to hold, as did the Court of Claims in Philadelphia Park Amusement Co. v. United States, 130 Ct. Cl. 166, 172, 126 F. Supp. 184, 189 (1954), that the values "of the two properties exchanged in an arm's-length transaction are either equal in fact, or are presumed to be equal." . . . To be sure there is much to be said of the argument that such an assumption is weakened by the emotion, tension and practical necessities involved in divorce negotiations and the property settlements arising therefrom. However, once it is recognized that the transfer was a taxable event, it is more consistent with the general purpose and scheme of the taxing statutes to make a rough approximation of the gain realized thereby than to ignore altogether its tax consequences. . . .

Moreover, if the transaction is to be considered a taxable event as to the husband, the Court of Claims' position leaves up in the air the wife's basis for the property received. In the context of a taxable transfer by the husband,[32] all indicia point to a "cost" basis for this property in the hands of the wife [under §1012]. Yet under the Court of Claims' position her cost for this property, i.e., the value of the marital rights relinquished therefor, would be indeterminable, and on subsequent disposition of the property she might suffer inordinately over the Commissioner's assessment which she would have the burden of proving erroneous. . . . Our present holding that the value of these rights is ascertainable eliminates this problem; for the same calculation that determines the amount received by the husband fixes the amount given

32. Under the present administrative practice, the release of marital rights in exchange for property or other consideration is not considered a taxable event as to the wife. For a discussion of the difficulties confronting a wife under a contrary approach, see Taylor and Schwartz, Tax Aspects of Marital Property Agreements, 7 Tax L. Rev. 19, 30 (1951); Comment, The Lump Sum Divorce Settlement as a Taxable Exchange, 8 U.C.L.A. L. Rev. 593, 601-602 (1961).

up by the wife, and this figure, i.e., the market value of the property transferred by the husband, will be taken by her as her tax basis for the property received.

Finally, it must be noted that here, as well as in relation to the question of whether the event is taxable, we draw support from the prior administrative practice and judicial approval of that practice. See supra. We therefore conclude that the Commissioner's assessment of a taxable gain based upon the value of the stock at the date of its transfer has not been shown erroneous.

IV

[Discussion of attorney fee question omitted.]

Reversed in part and affirmed in part.

Mr. Justice FRANKFURTER took no part in the decision of these cases.

Mr. Justice WHITE took no part in the consideration or decision of these cases.

NOTES AND QUESTIONS

1. *Analysis of* Davis. (a) Assume that the general approach of the Court was correct and that the outcome of *Davis* should turn on whether Mrs. Davis owned an "interest" in property held in Mr. Davis's name, as opposed to a "mere expectancy"; on whether Mrs. Davis received property that she previously owned in some sense, as opposed to a payment in discharge of a debt owed to her by Mr. Davis. How should the issue be decided? By reference to one's common-sense judgment about how married people in Delaware are likely to think of the property rights of husbands and wives? By reference to what sociologists can tell us about the question? By trying to count the ways in which Delaware marital property law is like or unlike community property law? Or by reference to rules of law defining what is an interest in property for purposes of resolving other legal issues? Which approach did the Court adopt?

(b) Compare the outcome of this case with the rules adopted by Congress in provisions such as §§1031, 1033, 1034, and 109. What does this comparison tell you about the wisdom and fairness of the rule applied in the case?

(c) What was Mrs. Davis's basis in the property received? What is the conceptual foundation for that result? If the Court had held that the transfer did not result in the realization of gain by Mr. Davis, what should Mrs. Davis's basis have been? Under what Code provision can that result be reached?

2. *Belated congressional response.* The *Davis* decision gave rise to a substantial amount of litigation and complexity in the law. Ultimately, Congress altered the result in *Davis* and simplified the law by adopting §1041. Section 1041 provides that no gain or loss shall be recognized on transfers of property between spouses or incident to a divorce. Thus, most spousal transfers of appreciated or depreciated property are not treated as sales that generate gain or loss to the transferor. Consistent with nonrecognition treatment, the property transferred has a substituted basis in the hands of the transferee. Section 1041 works together with the alimony rule, in §71(b)(1), discussed below (see page 420), that provides that only cash transfers are considered alimony. Alimony is deductible by the payor and included in the income of the payee; other transfers incident to divorce are not deductible by the payor or included in the income of the payee. The results are that a transfer of property, other than cash, incident to divorce (a) does not result in the recognition of gain and (b) does not give rise to a deduction by the transferor or income to the transferee. This combination of rules may offend other goals of the tax system but it does simplify administration.

3. *The limits of §1041.* In Rev. Rul. 87-112, 87-2 C.B. 207, the taxpayer, *A,* transferred to the taxpayer's former spouse, *B,* U.S. Series E and EE savings bonds that had been bought in an earlier year entirely with *A*'s separate funds. *A,* pursuant to §454(c) and Regs. §1.454-1(a), had not included in income the interest on these bonds; taxpayers are allowed to defer tax on such interest until the bonds are cashed in. The Ruling holds that §1041(a) does not apply to the gain from the accrued interest and that "the deferred, accrued interest from the date of original issuance of the bonds to the date of transfer of the bonds to *B* is includable in *A*'s gross income."

4. *Unmarried couples.* Section 1041 substantially reduces the problems of dividing the economic interests of married couples. It is not available to unmarried couples who split up, no matter how long they have lived together, how deep and sincere their sharing and mutual commitment has been, and how tangled and intertwined their economic interests — and regardless of the fact that, if they were a same-sex couple, they had no legal opportunity to marry.

b. Antenuptial Settlements

FARID-ES-SULTANEH v. COMMISSIONER

160 F.2d 812 (2d Cir. 1947)

Before Swan, Chase, and Clark, Circuit Judges.

Chase, Circuit Judge. . . .

[In 1924, S. S. Kresge, in contemplation of his marriage to taxpayer (petitioner) Farid-Es-Sultaneh, transferred to her some shares of stock of the S. S. Kresge Co. worth a total of about $800,000. Shortly thereafter they entered into an antenuptial agreement under which she acknowledged receipt of the shares "as a gift . . . pursuant to this indenture, and as an antenuptial settlement" and in consideration thereof released all her dower and other marital rights, including the right to support. Kresge and Farid-Es-Sultaneh were married in 1924 and divorced in 1928. She did not claim or receive alimony. Kresge's basis for the shares transferred in 1924 was 15 cents per share; their value at that time was about $10 per share. In 1938 Farid-Es-Sultaneh sold some of the shares for $19 per share].[33]

When the petitioner and Mr. Kresge were married he was 57 years old with a life expectancy of 16½ years. She was then 32 years of age with a life expectancy of 33¾ years. He was then worth approximately $375,000,000 and owned real estate of the approximate value of $100,000,000.

The Commissioner determined [a deficiency for the year 1938] on the ground that the petitioner's stock . . . was acquired by gift . . . and [that under §1015(a) she must thus use] as the basis for determining the gain on her sale of it the basis it would have had in the hands of the donor. This was correct if [§1015(a)] is applicable, and the Tax Court held it was on the authority of Wemyss v. Commissioner, 324 U.S. 303 (1945) and Merrill v. Fahs, 324 U.S. 308 (1945).

The issue here presented cannot, however, be adequately dealt with quite so summarily. The *Wemyss* case determined the taxability to the transferor as a gift, under [§§2511(a) and 2512(b)], of property transferred in trust for the benefit of the prospective wife of the transferor pursuant to the terms of an ante-nuptial agreement. It was held that the transfer, being solely in consideration of her promise of marriage, and to compensate her for loss of trust income which would cease upon her marriage, was not for an adequate and full consideration in money or money's worth within the meaning of [§2512(b)], the Tax Court having found that the transfer was not one at arm's length made in the ordinary course of business. But we find nothing in this decision to show that a transfer, taxable as a gift under the gift tax, is ipso facto to be treated as a gift in construing the income tax law.

In Merrill v. Fahs [supra], it was pointed out that the estate and gift tax statutes are in pari materia and are to be so construed. . . . Although Congress in 1932 also expressly provided that the release of marital rights should not be treated as a consideration in money or money's

33. [After her divorce from Kresge (her second husband), the taxpayer "sailed in luxury to Europe. An extremely attractive woman who just missed beauty," she met and married Prince Farid of Sadri-Azam, a nephew of a former Shah of Iran, and acquired the title Princess Farid-Es-Sultaneh. Her marriage to the prince ended in 1936, but for the rest of her life she continued to use the name Farid-Es-Sultaneh and, despite the published declaration of the prince that she was not entitled to do so, the title "princess." N.Y. Times, Aug. 13, 1963, at 31, col. 3 (obituary). — Eds.]

worth in administering the estate tax law [see §2043(b)] and failed to include such a provision in the gift tax statute, it was held that the gift tax law should be construed to the same effect.

We find in this decision no indication, however, that the term "gift" as used in the income tax statute should be construed to include a transfer which, if made when the gift tax were effective, would be taxable to the transferor as a gift merely because of the special provisions in the gift tax statute defining and restricting consideration for gift tax purposes.[34]

In our opinion the income tax provisions are not to be construed as though they were in pari materia with either the estate tax law or the gift tax statutes. They are aimed at the gathering of revenue by taking for public use given percentages of what the statute fixes as net taxable income. Capital gains and losses are . . . factors in determining net taxable income. What is known as the basis for computing gain or loss on transfers of property is established by statute in those instances when the resulting gain or loss is recognized for income tax purposes. . . . When Congress provided that gifts should not be treated as taxable income to the donee, there was, without any correlative provisions fixing the basis of the gift to the donee, a loophole which enabled the donee to . . . take as the basis for computing gain or loss its value when the gift was made. Thus it was possible to exclude from taxation any increment in value during the donor's holding and the donee might take advantage of any shrinkage in such increment after the acquisition by gift in computing gain or loss upon a subsequent sale or exchange. It was to close this loophole that Congress provided that the donee should take the donor's basis when property was transferred by gift. . . . Because of this we think that a transfer which would be classed as a gift under the gift tax law is not necessarily to be treated as a gift income-tax-wise. Though such a consideration as this petitioner gave for the shares of stock she acquired from Mr. Kresge might not have relieved him from liability for a gift tax, had the present gift tax then been in effect, it was nevertheless a fair consideration which prevented her taking the shares as a gift under the income tax law since it precluded the existence of a donative intent.

Although the transfers of the stock made . . . to this taxpayer are called a gift in the ante-nuptial agreement later executed and were to be for the protection of his prospective bride if he died before the marriage was consummated, the "gift" was contingent upon his death before such marriage, an event that did not occur. Consequently, it would appear that no absolute gift was made before the ante-nuptial contract was executed and that she took title to the stock under its

34. [See the suggestion of Judge Jerome N. Frank that the terms "gift," "gaft," and "geft" be used, depending upon whether the gift, income, or estate tax meaning is implied. Commissioner v. Beck's Estate, 129 F.2d 243 (2d Cir. 1942). — Eds.]

terms, viz.: in consideration for her promise to marry him coupled with her promise to relinquish all rights in and to his property which she would otherwise acquire by the marriage. Her inchoate interest in the property of her affianced husband greatly exceeded the value of the stock transferred to her. It was a fair consideration under ordinary legal concepts of that term for the transfers of the stock by him. . . . She performed the contract under the terms of which the stock was transferred to her and held the shares not as a donee but as a purchaser for a fair consideration. . . .

Decision reversed.

CLARK, Circuit Judge (dissenting). . . .

It is true that Commissioner v. Wemyss and Merrill v. Fahs, supra, which would require the transactions here to be considered a gift, dealt with estate and gift taxes. But no strong reason has been advanced why what is a gift under certain sections of the Revenue Code should not be a gift under yet another section. . . . The Congressional purpose would seem substantially identical — to prevent a gap in the law whereby taxes on gifts or on capital gains could be avoided or reduced by judicious transfers within the family or intimate group.

But decision on that point might well be postponed. . . . Kresge transferred the stock to petitioner more than three months before their marriage. Part was given when Kresge was married to another woman. At these times petitioner had no dower or other rights in his property. If Kresge died before the wedding, she could never secure dower rights in his lands. Yet she would nevertheless keep the stock. Indeed the specifically stated purpose of the transfer was to protect her against his death prior to marriage. It is therefore difficult to perceive how her not yet acquired rights could be consideration for the stock. . . .

If the transfer be thus considered a sale, as the majority hold, it would seem to follow necessarily that this valuable consideration (equivalent to one-third for life in land valued at one hundred million dollars) should have yielded sizable taxable capital gains to Kresge, as well as a capital loss to petitioner when eventually she sold. I suggest these considerations as pointing to the unreality of holding as a sale what seems clearly only intended as a stimulating cause to eventual matrimony.

QUESTIONS

1. What were the tax consequences to Kresge in 1924? Note the court's statement (last paragraph of majority opinion) about the value of the rights released by Farid-Es-Sultaneh.

What would have been the tax consequences of the transfer in 1924 if §1041 had been enacted? What if the antenuptial agreement provided that the transfer would not be made until after the marriage? What do these questions suggest about negotiating and drafting antenuptial settlements?

2. Was Farid-Es-Sultaneh taxable in 1924? If not, on what theory? Whatever your theory, is it better than viewing the transfer as a gift?

3. In Marvin v. Marvin, 18 Cal. 3d 660, 557 F.2d 106, 134 Cal. Rptr. 815 (1976), the plaintiff alleged an agreement with the defendant by which they would live together as husband and wife and the plaintiff would "'devote her full time to defendant . . . as a companion, homemaker, housekeeper and cook'" and in return defendant would "'provide for all of plaintiff's financial support and needs for the rest of her life.'" 18 Cal. 3d at 666. The court held that the complaint stated a cause of action. What is the proper tax treatment of any amount ultimately recovered by the plaintiff? Is the defendant entitled to a deduction? If the final judgment were to order the defendant to transfer a house to the plaintiff, what would be the tax consequences to the defendant?

3. Alimony, Child Support, and Property Settlements

a. *The Basic Scheme*

The Code establishes a coordinated system in which, following divorce, certain payments received by the payee spouse are taxable to him or her under §71(a) and those payments become deductible by the payor spouse under §215. Other payments are not taxable to the payee spouse and are not deductible by the payor spouse. Very roughly speaking, alimony (and separate maintenance) is taxable to the payee and deductible by the payor, while child support and "property settlements" are not taxable to the payee and are not deductible by the payor. To some significant degree, however, the terms "alimony" (and separate maintenance) and "child support" have special meanings for tax purposes. The phrase "property settlement" is not used in the Code. It has some historical foundation and is used to help describe certain specific rules; the technical language is "excess front loading rules." The alimony deduction is an adjustment in arriving at AGI (adjusted gross income), so it is available to payors who do not itemize deductions. See §62(a)(10).

b. *The Rules*

"Alimony," and "separate maintenance payments," are payments that meet certain conditions specified in §71. First, the payment must be in cash. §71(b)(1). This rule jibes with the rule of §1041 (see supra page

416) that no gain or loss is recognized on certain transfers of property between spouses and former spouses. The two rules together serve the goal of simplicity. Putting aside that goal, it is difficult to see why a transfer of property in satisfaction of periodic support-type obligations should not be treated as alimony.

Second, the payment must be received under an "instrument" of divorce or separate maintenance. §§71(b)(1)(A), 71(b)(2). Oral agreements will not do. Unmarried couples are not covered.

Third, the parties must not have agreed that the payment will be nontaxable to the payee and nondeductible by the payor. This rule simply gives the parties an election as to payments that would, but for the election, be treated as alimony. Note, however, that the election goes only one way. There is no election available to treat as deductible by the payor and taxable to the payee payments that are not alimony or separate maintenance within the rules of §71.

Fourth, the parties must not be members of the same household. §71(b)(1)(C). This rule will remove some or all of the tax incentive for friendly divorces by couples who seek to take advantage of the favorable single-person (or head-of-household) rates. A tax advantage will still be available to unmarried couples (either never-married or divorced from one another) whose marginal rates on their individual incomes would be about the same. See supra page 39. But for couples with unequal incomes the advantage of the more favorable rates for single taxpayers will be offset by the disadvantage of having more income taxed at the higher end of the rate structure and they will not be able to equalize the individual incomes by alimony payments — unless they are prepared to live apart.

Fifth, the payments cannot continue after the death of the payee spouse. §71(b)(1)(D). This rule is consistent with a notion that alimony and separate maintenance are payments for support of the payee. If the payments continue after the death of the payee, they cannot have been intended purely as support; they must be in the nature of a property settlement or, at least in part, for the support of some other person. The nondeductibility of property settlements seems to be based on the idea that because such payments do not represent a diversion of income there is no justification for a deduction.

Sixth, the payments must not be for child support. The relevant provision, §71(c), attempts to ensure that substance prevails over form. Thus, a payment that is called "alimony" but terminates when a child of the marriage dies or reaches age 18 will be treated as child support. This is an important change from prior law. The idea behind the denial of a deduction for child support is that if the payor had custody of, and supported, the children, there would be no deduction for the cost of the support, so there is no justification for deduction of similar amounts when paid to a former spouse. Obviously this rule does not take account of the expense of maintaining two households. Perhaps the lack of sympathy for that circumstance is a reflection of a moral (or moralistic) sense that people should not expect the tax system to relieve them of burdens of their own making.

Finally, there is a set of rules that deals broadly, and arbitrarily, with the problem of distinguishing between alimony and cash "property settlements." Roughly speaking, §71(f) provides that only payments that are substantially equal for the first three years will be treated as alimony. This requirement of "periodicity" reflects a long-held notion of a distinction between, on the one hand, once-and-for-all settlements ("property settlements"), in one payment or a few installments, and, on the other hand, regular support payments (alimony).

Under §71(f)'s arbitrary implementation of this distinction, if the first three yearly payments are "front-loaded" — that is, unequal, with larger amounts in the first or second year — some portion of the amount paid will not be treated as alimony. (Section 71(f) does not recharacterize alimony payments that are unequal but "back-loaded" — that is, payments that increase in size over the first three years.) Specifically, if the payments in the first year exceed the average payments in the second and third years by more than $15,000, the payments initially are treated as alimony but the excess amounts are "recaptured" in the third year. "Recaptured" means that the payor must include the excess in income. A similar rule applies to the extent that the payments in the second year exceed the payments in the third year by more than $15,000. In effect the payor is required to include in income an amount previously deducted as alimony, on the ground that in retrospect, because the payments did not continue in a manner consistent with the concept of alimony, the purported alimony was in fact a property settlement. When the payor is required to include an excess amount in income, the payee, who will have taken the full amount into income in the first or second year, is allowed a deduction in the same amount.

To illustrate the mechanics of the basic rule, suppose the payor makes and deducts an alimony payment of $50,000 in the first year and makes no payments in the second and third years. The amount recaptured in the third year is $35,000 (the $50,000 payment in the first year less the $15,000 threshold amount); $35,000 of the $50,000 payment that was deducted by the payor in the first year is included in the payor's income in the third year. The payee, who has included the $50,000 first-year payment in income, is allowed a $35,000 deduction in the third year. Timing differences aside, the net effect of the payment structure is that only $15,000 of the payment is treated as alimony.

The primary and intended effect of the recapture rule is on the planning process; it deprives people of the opportunity and incentive to convert property settlements into alimony.[35] It has the potential for

35. If the payor spouse has income-producing assets, however, those assets can be

harshness, however, when payments are reduced not by design but by virtue of changed circumstances. To minimize such harshness, recapture is not required if either party dies or if the payee spouse remarries by the end of the calendar year which is two years after the payments began and payments end because of the remarriage. Also, the recapture rule does not apply to temporary support payments or to payments based on an obligation to pay a fixed portion of the payor's income for at least three years.

c. *Policy Questions*

Is the deduction for alimony a subsidy to marriage? to divorce? Can it sensibly be defended as an effort to encourage support of ex-spouses? to remove obstacles to remarriage? Or is it just part of a proper definition of income, based on notions of involuntariness and lack of consumption? In Gould v. Gould, 245 U.S. 151 (1917), involving an attempt to tax a spouse receiving alimony, the Supreme Court held that alimony was not encompassed by the phrase "gains or profits and income derived from any source whatever" as used in the Revenue Act of 1917.

d. *The Tax Incentive*

To understand the effect of the rules it is useful to begin with a sense of the tax saving that can be achieved, and shared by the payor and the payee, when a payment is treated as alimony. Suppose that the payor is taxed at a marginal rate of 35 percent (state and federal tax combined) and the payee is taxed at a marginal rate of 15 percent, and that the payor is obligated to make a payment of $2,000 that will not be treated as alimony for tax purposes. The net after-tax cost to the payor, and the benefit to the payee, obviously, will be the amount of the payment — the $2,000. Now suppose we are able to transform the payment into alimony and that we raise the amount to $2,700. The net after-tax cost to the payor will be $1,755 (65 percent of $2,700). He or she will be $245 to the good ($2,000 less $1,755). The net after-tax amount in the hands of the payee will be $2,295; he or she will be $295 to the good ($2,295 less $2,000). The total gain to the payor and the payee combined is $540 ($245 plus $295), which results from reducing the tax on $2,700

placed in trust, with the income payable to the payee spouse, for any time period desired. The income from the trust is taxable to the payee spouse. See §682. For example, assume that *A* wishes to make payments to *B* of $25,000 per year for two years and no longer and that *A* owns bonds that pay interest of $25,000 a year. *A* can create a trust with a duration of two years, with *B* as the income beneficiary and with the reversion to *A*, and fund the trust with the bonds. The $25,000 interest on the bonds will be paid, and taxed, to *B* each year for the two years and then the bonds will be returned to *A*.

by 20 percent, the difference between the payor's rate of 35 percent and the payee's rate of 15 percent.

Under the rate structure effective in 1991, the potential gain from transforming a payment from nondeductible child support or property settlement into deductible alimony is much less than it had been. The maximum difference between the rates is only 16 percentage points (from 15 percent to 31 percent). Moreover, for single individuals, the 28 percent rate begins at about $33,000 and the 31 percent rate begins at about $50,000. Many recipients will find the bulk of their alimony payments taxed at the 28 percent or 31 percent rates. In those cases, the tax benefit of the deduction to the payor will be roughly offset by the tax owed by the payee. The total tax savings available through transforming child support or property settlements into alimony will rarely rise above a few thousand dollars. That is nothing to be sniffed at, but it is scarcely in the realm of big-time tax avoidance.

e. A Final Question

Is the game worth the candle? Considering the amounts of tax saving at issue, would it be better either to (a) deny any deduction for alimony or (b) allow the parties complete freedom to decide whether any payment is alimony?

PROBLEMS

1. Suppose Manuel and Wanda have decided to dissolve their marriage. Manuel is a successful surgeon. Wanda has just finished her first year of law school. Manuel and Wanda have decided that for each of the next two years Manuel should pay Wanda $60,000, while she finishes law school; that he should pay her $5,000 per year for the succeeding two years; and that at the end of four years there should be no more payments. If the terms of this agreement are incorporated in a decree of divorce, what will be the tax consequences to Manuel and Wanda? Are these tax results objectionable? If so, what suggestion would you make?

2. Suppose the facts are the same as in Problem 1, except that Wanda has a father, Fred, who lives with Manuel and Wanda and is dependent on them, and that the agreement provides that if Wanda dies during the four-year period in which payments are required, the payments will be made to Fred. Moreover, during the four years, Manuel is required to pay for an insurance policy on Wanda's life, with Fred as beneficiary. What are the tax consequences to Manuel, Wanda, and Fred?

3. Suppose Mike and Wilma have a son, Carlos, who is two years old. Mike is a successful lawyer. Wilma was also a successful lawyer, but quit practice when Carlos was born, with the understanding that she would care for him until he reached age 12 and then would return to work. Mike and Wilma have decided to end their marriage and have agreed that Mike will pay Wilma $40,000 a year for ten years, but with the obligation to terminate if Carlos should die sooner. What will be the tax consequences to Mike and Wilma?

4. Suppose that the marriage of Nancy and John is dissolved by a judicial decree that requires that Nancy pay John spousal support (alimony) of $10,000 per year. When the payment becomes due in the first year after the decree is entered, Nancy offers to transfer to John, in settlement of her obligation to pay the spousal support, shares of stock of IBM with a fair market value of $10,000 and a basis in her hands of $1,000. Suppose that John would be legally entitled to insist on payment in cash and that no other form of payment had been contemplated at the time of the dissolution. If John accepts the IBM stock in satisfaction of Nancy's obligation, what are the tax consequences to him and to Nancy? What if the same events occur in the second year following the dissolution of the marriage? Regs. §1.1041-1T, A-7 provides that "[a] transfer of property is treated as related to the cessation of the marriage if the transfer is pursuant to a divorce or separation instrument . . . and the transfer occurs not more than 6 years after the date on which such marriage ceases."

4. Child Support Obligations in Default

Child support is not deductible by the payor and is not taxed to the payee (usually the custodial parent). Suppose that child support payments are not made, and the expense of child support is borne entirely by the custodial parent. The custodial parent is clearly poorer. Should the tax burden of the custodial parent reflect the loss?

DIEZ-ARGUELLES v. COMMISSIONER

48 T.C.M. 496 (1984)

FINDINGS OF FACT . . .

In 1972, petitioner, Christina Diez-Arguelles ("Christina"), was divorced from her former husband, Kevin Baxter, and was granted custody of their two minor children. Pursuant to a property settlement agreement, which was incorporated into the divorce decree, Mr. Baxter agreed to pay Christina $300 per month for child support. Mr. Baxter failed to make full payment of his obligation for child support during the years 1972 through 1978 and by the end of 1978 he was in arrears by the amount of $4,325.00. During 1979 he paid only $600.00 in child support and consequently at the end of 1979 was in arrears by another $3,000.00. On their 1978 return the petitioners treated the $4,325.00 then due from Mr. Baxter as a nonbusiness bad debt and deducted the amount from their gross income as a short-term capital loss. On their 1979 return they deducted the $3,000.00 in the same manner. Respondent disallowed both deductions in their entirety.

Because of Mr. Baxter's failure to meet his support obligations, the petitioners had to bear the entire support of the two children from the date of the divorce in 1972 through 1979. The amount of such support borne by the petitioners through the end of 1978 exceeded the support payments made by Mr. Baxter during that period by at least $4,325.00. The amount of such support borne by them during 1979 exceeded the support payments made by Mr. Baxter in that year by more than $3,000.00.

Over the years Christina has diligently attempted to collect the support payments from Mr. Baxter. She has returned to the divorce court on several occasions and has received judgments and supplemental orders against him but to the date of trial she had been unable to collect the amount deducted on the joint returns for 1978 and 1979.

Opinion . . .

Under section 166(d) a noncorporate taxpayer may deduct nonbusiness bad debts as a short-term capital loss in the year such debts become completely worthless. However, the nonbusiness bad debts are deductible only to the extent of the taxpayer's basis in the debts. Section 166(b); Long v. Commissioner, 35 B.T.A. 479 (1937), affd., 96 F.2d 270 (9th Cir. 1938), cert. denied 305 U.S. 616 (1938). In Long v. Commissioner, supra, the Board of Tax Appeals held that the uncollectible obligation of a taxpayer's ex-husband to pay her a fixed amount for maintenance was not deductible as a bad debt because the taxpayer was not "out of pocket" anything as the result of the ex-husband's failure to pay the support obligation. In other words, the taxpayer had no basis in the debt. Swenson v. Commissioner, 43 T.C. 897 (1965).

In the case before us, petitioners argue that they are "out of pocket" the amounts they expended for the support of Christina's children in excess of the support payments received from Mr. Baxter. We have considered and rejected this argument in similar cases. Swenson v. Commissioner, supra; Imeson v. Commissioner, T.C. Memo. 1969-180, affd. 487 F.2d 319 (9th Cir. 1973), cert. denied 417 U.S. 917 (1974).

In *Imeson* the Ninth Circuit affirmed our decision but stated by way of dictum that the taxpayer might have a basis in the debt up to the amount she had expended from her capital or income to support the children, 487 F.2d at 321. Because of this dictum we subsequently reexamined our position on this issue and concluded that the cases cited by the Ninth Circuit were distinguishable. Williford v. Commissioner, T.C. Memo. 1975-65. Consequently, our position on this issue is still the same as set forth in Swenson v. Commissioner, supra, and Imeson v. Commissioner, supra. Respondent's determination that the amounts due Christina by Mr. Baxter for child support are not deductible under section 166 as nonbusiness bad debts is sustained.

Accord, Pierson v. Commissioner, 48 T.C.M. 954 (1984).

NOTES AND QUESTIONS

1. *Analysis.* Is the result in *Diez-Arguelles* consistent with principles of taxation previously examined? Does it seem fair? In answering these questions, consider the following hypotheticals. What are the tax consequences to Ann and Bob in each? Why? In each of the hypotheticals, assume that Ann is obligated to pay Bob $10,000 pursuant to a court order for child support issued on their divorce.

(a) In lieu of $10,000 cash, Bob accepts from Ann shares of stock of IBM for which she had paid $1,000 and that are worth $10,000 at the time of transfer. Bob later sells the shares for $9,000. See §§1001, 1012. (Assume that §1041 does not apply.)

(b) Ann borrows $10,000 from Thelma and pays Bob. Ann defaults on the debt to Thelma. Bob invests the $10,000 in IBM stock, which he later sells for $9,000. What are the tax consequences not only to Ann and Bob but also to Thelma? See §166.

(c) Ann pays Bob $10,000. Two days later, pleading a medical emergency, Ann borrows the $10,000 back from Bob. Shortly thereafter, Ann dies, totally destitute (though she had a good job at the time of her death).

(d) Ann, having failed to pay Bob the $10,000 child support obligation when it became due, executes and delivers to Bob a negotiable promissory note, payable in three months and bearing interest at the market rate of 1 percent per month. Shortly thereafter, Ann dies, totally destitute.

(e) Same as (d), except that before Ann dies, Bob sells the note to Thelma for $9,000.

(f) What are the implications of the Court's statement that "the taxpayer had no basis in the debt"? Suppose, again, that Ann owes Bob $10,000 for child support. If she pays him the $10,000, it is excluded from Bob's gross income under §71(c). Basis seems to be irrelevant because of the statutory exclusion. But what if Bob sells or assigns his claim against Ann to a third party for $9,000?

2. *Public policy.* (a) In Perry v. Commissioner, 92 T.C. 470 (1989), aff'd, 912 F.2d 1466 (5th Cir. 1990), the Tax Court again rejected a claim for a bad debt deduction for nonpayment of child support. After addressing a variety of legal arguments, the court concluded with the following:

> Petitioner insists that she ought to be allowed to deduct the shortfall in Perry's support payment obligations. If this were to be viewed as an appeal to public policy, i.e., the public failed to see to it that Perry satisfied his legal obligations and so the public ought to make up for this to some extent by reducing petitioner's tax obligations, then we have two responses.
>
> Firstly, the statute for the years in issue does not embody that policy; to get that policy into the law, petitioner should go to the Congress, in which has been "vested" "All legislative Powers herein granted." U.S. Const., art. 1, §1.
>
> Secondly, since the tax benefit of such a deduction relates directly to the taxpayer's marginal tax bracket, it would appear that this claimed public policy would provide the greatest relief to those who have the greatest amount of other income and little or no relief to those who truly depended on the fulfillment of the support obligations. The Congress, of course, may enact any public policy it chooses (unless otherwise limited by the Constitution), but the policy that would be advanced by allowing such a deduction may fairly be viewed as topsy-turvy.
>
> In any event, this Court will not so legislate in the guise of filling in gaps in the statute, or whatever other judicial power it is that petitioner would have us exercise.

(b) Why does the court in the *Diez-Arguelles* case refer to Kevin Baxter as Mr. Baxter and to Christina Diez-Arguelles as Christina?

3. *A bad trip.* Compare Garber v. Commissioner, 48 T.C.M. 959 (1984), in which the taxpayer signed up for a two-year, around-the-world sailing trip with seven other people. Each of the eight contributed $16,000 toward the cost of the boat. Their agreement with the captain provided that if any of them were required to leave, there would be no refund, but if the boat were destroyed there would be a pro rata refund. The taxpayer became ill and left the boat for several months. He recovered from his illness and would have returned to the boat for the remainder of the cruise, but it was destroyed by fire. He was unable to obtain a refund and claimed a deduction for a bad debt. The court denied the

deduction, relying on Regs. §1.166-1(c), which requires a "valid and enforceable obligation to pay a fixed or determinable sum of money." The court said, "Generally, a claim which arises out of breach of contract prior to being reduced to judgment does not create a debtor-creditor relationship because the injured party has only an unliquidated claim to damages." Suppose the captain had written a letter to the taxpayer saying, "I have collected insurance proceeds from the loss of the boat and clearly I owe you $5,000. I will put a check in the mail tomorrow." Suppose the check never arrives and the captain dies following a drunken binge on which he spent all the insurance money. What if the captain had sent a check for $5,000, but it bounced (i.e., proved uncollectible)?

Was the claim in the *Diez-Arguelles* case a "valid and enforceable obligation to pay a fixed or determinable sum of money"?

4. *Legal fees.* In McClendon v. Commissioner, T.C. Mem. 1986-416, legal fees incurred to obtain child support payments were held to be nondeductible personal expenses. The court relied on United States v. Gilmore, infra page 601.

G. THEORETICAL ISSUES

Compare the tax treatment of the individuals in each of the four following situations:

(a) Charlie Carpenter last year earned $35,000. This year he reduced the number of hours he worked, earned $20,000, and devoted himself to building a house that he intends to hold for rental to others. He used $30,000 of savings from earlier years to buy the land and materials. When he completed the building of the house, for which he supplied all the labor, its fair market value was $45,000.

(b) Tom Trucker this year earned $35,000 driving a truck. He took $30,000 of savings from earlier years and $15,000 of this year's earnings and bought, for $45,000, a house that he intends to hold for rental.

(c) Ann Accountant earned $35,000 last year. This year she reduced the number of hours she worked, earned $20,000, and went to law school.

(d) Perry Player was born with exceptional coordination and by the time he graduated from UCLA this year was over seven feet tall and an all-American center on its basketball team. He has played and practiced basketball almost incessantly since he was old enough to hold the ball. Everyone agrees that he will be the number one draft choice in the National Basketball Association and will be able to sign a contract that will be certain to make him a multimillionaire. In a recent article in a leading sports magazine, a highly respected actuary estimated that the present value of Player's expected future earnings is $30 million. It has been clear since he was a senior in high school that he was an exceptional basketball player.

Under an income tax, should Player be taxed at some point in his amateur career on the expected value of his future earnings or, if you will, on the value of his genetic inheritance and the rewards for his investment of time in self-improvement? How about Carpenter? Should he be taxed on the $15,000 increment to his wealth that can be attributed to the performance of services for himself? If Carpenter is to be taxed on only $20,000, how about Trucker? If both Trucker and Carpenter are to be taxed on $35,000, what about Accountant (and other future professionals)? Is it not clear that she has invested $15,000 worth of her time in creating "human capital"? If Accountant is to be taxed on $35,000, again, how about Player? If Player is to be taxed on the benefit of what some call his "genetic windfall," should Accountant be taxed similarly — that is, on some amount reflecting the full value of her law degree, not just the value of the time she invested in it? If you think that Ann or Perry should be taxed on the value of their human capital, as reflected in their prospective earnings, how, if at all, would you take account of their prospective tax liabilities? In answering these questions, be sure to take account of the Simons definition of income (supra page 76) and the arguments in support of it. See Klein, Timing in Personal Taxation, 6 J. Legal Stud. 461 (1977).

H. CONSUMPTION TAX

We have seen that a core concept of our income tax laws, reflected in cases like Eisner v. Macomber though not in any express provision of the Code, is that unrealized gain is not taxable. Congress has extended this core concept generously in provisions like §1031. Unrealized appreciation can be thought of as a form of saving; it is a gain that has, in a sense, been reinvested in the same property. Congress has also favored other forms of saving — most notably retirement savings held in qualified pension plans. No one has ever seriously suggested that we should tax savings in the nature of investment in human capital. The tax system that we wind up with thus falls far short of a tax on income as it is defined by Simons and other purists. The result of the departure from truly comprehensive taxation of all income may be unfairness and departures from economic rationality. If one abandons hope of "reforming" the income tax by defining income more broadly, a plausible alternative may be to allow a deduction for all savings. The result would be a tax on consumption. If amounts saved are excluded from income, amounts dissaved (taken out of savings) must be included. If an amount is saved, it is ipso facto invested (assuming that investment is construed to include increments in bank balances). If savings are deducted, the assets bought with savings will all have a zero basis. When such assets are sold, income is increased by the full proceeds (though income may be reduced if those proceeds are invested elsewhere). The result is a pure cash-flow tax system. See Andrews, A Consumption-Type or Cash Flow Personal Income Tax, 87 Harv. L. Rev. 1113 (1974).

Symbolically,

$$Y = C + S,$$

where Y is income, C is consumption, and S is saving (investment). It follows that,

$$C = Y - S,$$

which tells us that a tax on consumption is the same as a tax on income minus saving, which tells us in turn that if we want to tax consumption we need not measure it directly. We can think of a consumption tax as an income tax with a deduction for an account like an IRA (see supra page 399) that has no limits on the amounts contributed or the purpose for which funds may be withdrawn. Withdrawals would be included in income, as they are now with IRAs.

To illustrate, suppose that an individual in a given year earns a salary of $100,000, borrows $50,000, and invests $85,000 in an apartment building. Under a consumption tax, the salary plus the loan, a total of $150,000, would be treated as "income." From this amount would be deducted the $85,000 invested in the apartment building, leaving a net of $65,000. The $65,000 is presumably the amount used for consumption and would be taxed (at progressive rates). Since the entire cost of the building is deducted at the time of purchase, its basis would be zero and there would be no depreciation deduction. Suppose that in the next year the building is sold for $70,000, the salary is again $100,000, and the individual's bank account increases by $50,000. The taxable amount (consumption) would be $120,000 ($70,000 + $100,000 − $50,000).

Under this system of taxation, any amounts earned by a corporation and not distributed by it would, at least from the shareholder perspective, be saved and invested. Corporations cannot have consumption; only individuals can. Thus, under a consumption tax there would be no need for a corporation income tax to prevent tax avoidance by shareholders.

To the extent that we increase opportunities for tax deductible savings (for example, through pension plans or through rapid deductions for depreciation), we move in the direction of a consumption tax. The wisdom of such moves is a hotly debated issue.

I. CASH RECEIPTS AND PAYMENTS OF ACCRUAL-METHOD TAXPAYERS

The two major systems of accounting are the cash method and the accrual method. See description supra page 53. The cash method focuses on actual receipts and disbursements, while the accrual method focuses on amounts earned (though not necessarily received) and obligations incurred (though not necessarily paid). The accrual method attempts to match income with the expense of earning it. While this method results in a more accurate annual measurement of income than does the cash method, it requires more sophisticated bookkeeping and accounting. Therefore most individuals and small businesses use the cash method if possible.

Almost all businesses of any substantial size report on the accrual method of accounting.[36] The accrual method, however, is not a matter of mathematical certainty; it has its infirmities and is constantly evolving and often controversial. Moreover, the Treasury has consistently opposed certain aspects of normal accrual accounting such as the deferral of prepaid income or accrual of estimated future expenses.

For nontax purposes a good accounting system should organize and present the underlying data of a business in a way that permits its managers to make sound decisions and investors to make sound judgments about its condition. It is by no means clear, however, that the rules that are appropriate for nontax purposes are also appropriate for tax purposes. It does seem plain that tax accounting rules can have significant effects on behavior. For example, if tax rules allow the immediate deduction of a particular investment that has an expected life of five years, people will tend to prefer that investment over one whose cost must be written off over its five-year life. If income from an activity must be reported earlier than is consistent with economic reality, the effect will be to discourage that activity as compared with other activities in which income is more accurately reported. To the extent that income for purposes of tax accounting differs from true economic income, we

36. Most large-scale firms are required to use the accrual method. See §448.

will tend to discourage some activities and encourage others, often for no good reason.[37]

Of the four cases that follow, the first three are concerned with the accrual of income and the fourth with the accrual of a deduction. The first, Georgia School-Book Depository v. Commissioner, involves income that was earned for services performed, where payment had not been received. In requiring the recognition of income despite the nonreceipt of cash, the court relies on what is now called the "all events test," under which "income is to be included for the taxable year when all the events have occurred which fix the right to receive such income and the amount thereof can be determined with reasonable accuracy." See Regs. §1.451-1(a). In the second case, American Automobile Association v. United States, the taxpayer received payment for services to be performed in the future. The Court rejects generally accepted principles of accrual accounting by holding that income must be recognized when the cash is received. In the third case, Indianapolis Power & Light Co. v. Commissioner, the taxpayer is not required to include a cash receipt in income because it is treated as a deposit rather than as an advance payment for services. In the fourth case, United States v. General Dynamics Corp., the all events test is applied to a taxpayer's claim of a deduction for payments, owed by the taxpayer, for medical services performed for employees.

37. Similarly, a system that allows deductions for depreciation at a rate faster than the actual decline in the value of the asset will favor investment in long-lived assets over short-lived assets and investment in capital (plant, machinery, etc.) over investment in current labor inputs. In other words, if an income tax is to be neutral among different types of investments and inputs, it must be accurate in its measurement of income. A deduction for depreciation greater than the actual decline in value of the asset in the taxable year introduces inaccuracy. See Samuelson, Tax Deductibility of Economic Depreciation to Insure Invariant Valuations, 72 J. Pol. Econ. 604 (1964). This is not to say, however, that an income tax is to be preferred to a consumption tax, even though a consumption tax allows an immediate write-off of all investments. It is merely a statement about neutrality once the decision has been made to adopt an income tax. Some economists believe that an income tax unduly burdens all investment and that a consumption tax is preferable for that reason. If one accepts this position, then it is the consumption tax that produces neutrality among investments, as well as between investment and consumption. In any event, all arguments based on the desirability of a neutral tax system are confounded, even trivialized, by the reality of pervasive nontax governmental intervention in the allocation of resources.

1. Delay in the Receipt of Cash

GEORGIA SCHOOL-BOOK DEPOSITORY v. COMMISSIONER

1 T.C. 463 (1943)

KERN, Judge.

The question is whether petitioner, which was on an accrual basis, should have accrued certain school book commissions at the time the books were sold by the publishers to the state, or should have returned them as income only when the books were paid for by the state, as petitioner contends.

Petitioner was a broker which received an 8 percent commission on all school books purchased by the State of Georgia through it. For this commission it performed certain services of advantage to both parties, such as executing the contracts of the state board of education with various publishers, taking care of the books as a central depository until final distribution, seeing that enough were on hand to meet the state's demands, distributing them, and collecting the moneys in payment from the state and holding them in trust until paid over to the publishers. It was responsible for the return in salable condition of any books not used. It had no title to the books at any time, and (except in the case of one publisher) posted a bond with each publisher to guarantee performance of its duties. Petitioner also carried on a somewhat similar business as a book broker of college books not on the state list and under these contracts was responsible for the collection of all accounts.

Petitioner did not accrue its commissions on the state books but did accrue its commissions on the college books at the same time that its liability for the books to the publishers was accrued. Under the contracts for state school books it was provided that petitioner should receive its brokerage "at the time of settlement" and this term is explained by the provision that the petitioner shall make quarterly reports "so as to show the exact balance due" the publisher by the petitioner, and shall remit "its pro rata share of all cash received from the collection of warrants issued by the State of Georgia for books sold to the state when and as such warrants are received."

The publishers could look for payment from the state, and, consequently, petitioner could look for its commissions only from the "Free Textbook Fund," which was renewed only from the excise laid on beer.[38]

38. [The court's findings of fact describe the textbook fund as follows:

On March 4, 1937, the State of Georgia enacted a Free Textbook Act, under which the state board of education was directed to inaugurate and administer a system of free textbooks for the public schools of Georgia, and to execute contracts therefor. The act provides that the cost of administering the free textbook system and purchasing the books shall be paid by the state from such funds as may be provided by the General Assembly for that purpose. . . . The Legislature thereupon

During the taxable years 1938 and 1939 this fund was insufficient to pay the petitioner in full. The state, in its accounting, did not treat these large deficits as present liabilities except to the extent that funds were already on hand to meet them, the remainder being considered an encumbrance on the textbook fund in the next year. The "accounts ripen," the auditor reported, "for payment when and as funds become available in the Textbook Fund."

Petitioner contends, first, that the brokerage was not earned until payment, and, secondly, that there was no reasonable expectancy that payment ever would be made; and for these reasons, it urges its ultimate contention that the commissions here involved were not properly accruable in the respective taxable years.

In so far as appears, all acts which were required of petitioner to earn its brokerage, save one, had been done in the taxable year. It had received the books from the publishers, stored them, and later distributed them to the several schools. All it had not done was to receive the money from the state and pay it out to the publishers. On this account the actual payment of the brokerage may not have been due to petitioner until this money was received, but the right to it had accrued by the performance of its duties. United States v. Anderson, 269 U.S. 422. It is the *right* to receive money which in accrual accounting justifies the accrual of money receivable and its return as accrued income.

The Supreme Court said in Spring City Foundry Co. v. Commissioner, 292 U.S. 182 (p.184):

> . . . Keeping accounts and making returns on the accrual basis, as distinguished from the cash basis, import that it is the right to receive and not the actual receipt that determines the inclusion of the amount in gross income. When the right to receive an amount becomes fixed, the right accrues. . . .

The receipt of the money from the state, the deduction of petitioner's commission, and the transmission of the balance to the publishers were the least of its duties and can not be made the criterion of the arisal of the right. Paragraph 9 of the contract assumes that the publisher's right to payment had arisen, for it requires that the quarterly reports which petitioner was to submit should "show the exact balance due the first party by the second party [petitioner]. . . ."

---

created a free textbook fund, made up solely from excise taxes on the sale of malt beverages in the state. The act provides that funds derived from taxes on malt beverages shall be apportioned as follows: Not over 3 percent shall be paid to the revenue commission for enforcing the malt beverage act and "the remainder shall be set aside and devoted for the support of the common schools of the state and used for the purpose of furnishing free textbooks to the children attending the common schools, any excess to be used for other school purposes."

— Eds.]

We pass, then, to the second question, whether there was a reasonable expectancy that the claim would ever be paid. Where there is a contingency that may preclude ultimate payment, whether it be that the right itself is in litigation or that the debtor is insolvent, the right need not be accrued when it arises. This rule is founded on the old principle that equity will not require a suitor to do a needless thing. The taxpayer need not accrue a debt if later experience, available at the time that the question is adjudged, confirms a belief reasonably held at the time the debt was due, that it will never be paid. . . . On the other hand, it must not be forgotten that the alleviating principle of "reasonable expectancy" is, after all, an exception, and the exception must not be allowed to swallow up the fundamental rule upon which it is engrafted requiring a taxpayer on the accrual basis to accrue his obligations, Spring City Foundry Co. v. Commissioner, supra. If this were so, the taxpayer might at his own will shift the receipt of income from one year to another as should suit his fancy. . . . To allow the exception there must be a definite showing that an unresolved and allegedly intervening legal right makes receipt contingent or that the insolvency of his debtor makes it improbable. Postponement of payment without such accompanying doubts is not enough. . . .

Applying these principles to the instant case, we must conclude that, despite the condition of the treasury of the State of Georgia when the free schoolbook fund was inaugurated and for several years thereafter, there was no reasonable expectation that the sums owed by the state to petitioner's publishers and, consequently, the commissions to petitioner itself, would not ultimately be paid. It would naturally take a few years to establish in full working order a system of such magnitude, but a comparison of the two years before us shows that Georgia was gradually reducing its schoolbook obligations. Georgia is a state possessing great resources and a fine record of fiscal probity, and undoubtedly it can and will meet its obligations. The fact that petitioner, on behalf of its principals, continued to sell and deliver school books to the state indicates that there was no serious doubt as to the ultimate collection of the accounts here involved.

We conclude, therefore, that petitioner's commissions on all books purchased by the state through it in the taxable years should have been accrued and returned as income in those years.

Judgment will be entered for the respondent.

NOTES AND QUESTIONS

1. *Analysis.* (a) Under *Georgia School-Book Depository,* delay in the receipt of cash in the absence of doubt about ultimate payment is not enough to prevent accrual of income. Collectibility has nothing to do

with accruability unless the obligor is insolvent. The "reasonable expectancy" language in *Georgia School-Book Depository* goes to the issue of solvency. It is important to distinguish between a contingent receivable, which will not accrue since it is uncertain whether the taxpayer has earned it as yet, and an earned determinable amount, which must be accrued even if there is some question as to whether it will ultimately be collected. In defense of its rule, the court says that if "reasonable expectancy" is interpreted too favorably to taxpayers, "a taxpayer might at his own will shift the receipt of income from one year to another as should suit his fancy." Do you agree? See §446(b).

(b) In Hallmark Cards, Inc. v. Commissioner, 90 T.C. 26 (1988), Hallmark, in order to maintain a level production schedule and to avoid warehousing costs, shipped Valentine cards to retailers in December. After the customers objected to including the cards in their inventory (which resulted, among other things, in their becoming liable for personal property taxes), Hallmark adopted a policy under which it retained title to the cards until January 1. The court held that Hallmark was not required to accrue income from the sale of the cards in December, because the "all events" test was not satisfied until title passed in January.

2. *Other accrual methods.* Section 446(c) speaks of "the" cash receipts and disbursements method of accounting for taxable income, but in sanctioning accrual accounting, it uses the more expansive phrase "an accrual method." The principal variations are the installment method of reporting income from installment sales (supra page 364) and the "completed-contract" and "percentage-of-completion" methods of reporting income from building, installation, construction, or manufacturing contracts not completed within one taxable year (supra page 198).

2. Prepaid Income

The following case involves income of an automobile club operated by the American Automobile Association. For purposes of analysis it may be helpful to refer to the following hypothetical facts.

Suppose that the club is on the calendar year and that a particular member joins on October 1 of 1982 for one year and pays upon joining a fixed fee of $60. The member is entitled, among other things, to towing services and maps, on demand. The club has hundreds of thousands of members and has kept good records of its costs. Its fixed costs (for offices, staff, etc.) are $3 per month per member and vary only insignificantly from month to month and year to year. Its variable costs (for towing, etc.) are (on average) $3 per month per member in the six months of October through March and $1 per month per member in the other six months, but they vary from member to member.

How was AAA reporting these kinds of receipts and outlays before being challenged? How was it required to report under the decision in the case? Why?

AMERICAN AUTOMOBILE ASSOCIATION v. UNITED STATES

367 U.S. 687 (1961)

Mr. Justice CLARK delivered the opinion of the Court.

In this suit for refund of federal income taxes the petitioner, American Automobile Association, seeks determination of its tax liability for the years 1952 and 1953. Returns filed for its taxable calendar years were prepared on the basis of the same accrual method of accounting as was used in keeping its books. The Association reported as gross income only that portion of the total prepaid annual membership dues, actually received or collected in the calendar year, which ratably corresponded with the number of membership months covered by those dues and occurring within the same taxable calendar year. The balance was reserved for ratable monthly accrual over the remaining membership period in the following calendar year as deferred or unearned income reflecting an estimated future service expense to members. The Commissioner contends that petitioner should have reported in its gross income for each year the entire amount of membership dues actually received in the taxable calendar year without regard to expected future service expense in the subsequent year. The sole point at issue, therefore, is in what year the prepaid dues are taxable as income.

In auditing the Association's returns for the years 1952 through 1954, the Commissioner, in the exercise of his discretion under [§446(b)], determined not to accept the taxpayer's accounting system. As a result, adjustments were made for those years principally by adding to gross income for each taxable year the amount of prepaid dues which the Association had received but not recognized as income, and subtracting from gross income amounts recognized in the year although actually received in the prior year. . . .

The Association is a national automobile club organized as a nonstock membership corporation with its principal office in Washington, D.C. It provides a variety of services to the members of affiliated local automobile clubs and those of ten clubs which taxpayer itself directly operates as divisions, but such services are rendered solely upon a member's demand. Its income is derived primarily from dues paid one year in advance by members of the clubs. Memberships may commence or be renewed in any month of the year. For many years, the association has employed an accrual method of accounting and the calendar year as its taxable year. It is admitted that for its purposes the method used is in accord with generally accepted commercial accounting principles. The membership dues, as received, were deposited in the Association's bank accounts without restriction as to their use for any of its corporate purposes. However, for the Association's own accounting purposes, the dues were treated in its books as income received ratably[39] over the 12-month membership period. The portions thereof ratably attributable to membership months occurring beyond the year of receipt, i.e., in a second calendar year, were reflected in the Association's books at the close of the first year as unearned or deferred income. Certain operating expenses were chargeable as prepaid membership cost and deducted ratably over the same periods of time as those over which dues were recognized as income.

The Court of Claims bottomed its opinion on Automobile Club of Michigan v. Commissioner, 1957, 353 U.S. 180, finding that "the method of treatment of prepaid automobile club membership dues employed [by the Association here was,] . . . for Federal income tax purposes, 'purely artificial.'" 181 F. Supp. 255, 258. It accepted that case as "a rejection by the Supreme Court of the accounting method advanced by plaintiff in the case at bar." Ibid. The Association does not deny that its accounting system is substantially identical to that used by the petitioner in *Michigan.* It maintains, however, that *Michigan* does not control this case because of a difference in proof, i.e., that in this case the record contains expert accounting testimony indicating that the system used was in accord with generally accepted accounting principles; that its proof of cost of member service was detailed; and that the correlation between that cost and the period of time over which the dues were credited as income was shown and justified by proof of experience. The holding of *Michigan,* however, that the system of accounting was "purely artificial" was based upon the finding that "substantially all services are performed only upon a member's demand and the taxpayer's performance was not related to fixed dates after the tax year." 353 U.S. 180, 189, note 20. That is also true here. . . .

Whether or not the Court's judgment in *Michigan* controls our disposition of this case, there are other considerations requiring our

39. In 1952 and 1953 dues collected in any month were accounted as income to the extent of one-twenty-fourth for that month (on the assumption that the mean date of receipt was the middle of the month), one-twelfth for each of the next eleven months, and again one-twenty-fourth in the anniversary month. In 1954, however, guided by its own statistical average experience, the Association changed its system so as to more simply reach almost the same result by charging to year of receipt, without regard to month of receipt, one-half of the entire dues payment and deferring the balance to the following year.

affirmance. . . . In 1954 the Congress found dissatisfaction in the fact that

> as a result of court decisions and rulings, there have developed many divergencies between the computation of income for tax purposes and income for business purposes as computed under generally accepted accounting principles. The areas of difference are confined almost entirely to questions of when certain types of revenue and expenses should be taken into account in arriving at net income.

House Ways and Means Committee Report, H.R. Rep. No. 1337, 83d Cong., 2d Sess. 48. As a result, it introduced into the Internal Revenue Code of 1954 §452 and §462 which specifically permitted essentially the same practice as was employed by the Association here. Only one year later, however, in June, 1955, the Congress repealed these sections retroactively. . . . [T]he repeal of the section the following year, upon insistence by the Treasury that the proposed endorsement of such tax accounting would have a disastrous impact on the Government's revenue, was . . . clearly a mandate from the Congress that petitioner's system was not acceptable for tax purposes. . . . We are further confirmed in this view by consideration of the even more recent action of the Congress in 1958, subsequent to the decision in *Michigan,* supra. In that year §455 was added to the Internal Revenue Code of 1954. It permits publishers to defer receipt as income of prepaid subscriptions of newspapers, magazines and periodicals. An effort was made in the Senate to add a provision in §455 which would extend its coverage to prepaid automobile club membership dues. However, in conference the House Conferees refused to accept this amendment. . . .

The validity of the long established policy of the Court in deferring, where possible, to congressional procedures in the tax field is clearly indicated in this case. Finding only that, in light of existing provisions not specifically authorizing it, the exercise of the Commissioner's discretion in rejecting the Association's accounting system was not unsound, we need not anticipate what will be the product of further "study of this entire problem."

Affirmed.

Mr. Justice STEWART, whom Mr. Justice DOUGLAS, Mr. Justice HARLAN, and Mr. Justice WHITTAKER join, dissenting. . . .

The effect of the Court's decision is to allow the Commissioner to prevent an accrual basis taxpayer from making returns in accordance with the accepted and clearly valid accounting practice of excluding from gross income amounts received as advances until the right to such amounts is earned by rendition of the services for which the advances were made. To permit the Commissioner to do this, I think, is to ignore the clear statutory command that a taxpayer must be allowed to make his returns in accord with his regularly employed method of accounting, so long as that method clearly reflects his income. . . .

I can find nothing in *Automobile Club of Michigan* which controls disposition of this case. And the legislative history upon which the Court alternatively relies seems to me upon examination to be singularly unconvincing.

In *Michigan* there was no offer of proof to show the rate at which the taxpayer fulfilled its obligations under its membership contracts. The deferred reporting of prepaid dues was, therefore, rejected in that case simply because there was no showing of a correlation between the amounts deferred and the costs incurred by the taxpayer in carrying out its obligations to its members. Until today, that case has been recognized as one that simply held that, in the absence of proof that the proration used by the taxpayer reasonably matched actual expenses with the earning of related revenue, the Commissioner was justified in rejecting the taxpayer's proration. . . .

As to the enactment and repeal of §452 and §462, upon which the Court places so much reliance, . . . I think that the enactment and subsequent repeal of §452 and §462 give no indication of Congressional approval of the position taken by the Commissioner in this case. If anything, the legislative action leads to the contrary impression. . . .

To my mind, this legislative history shows that Congress made every effort to dissuade the courts from doing exactly what the Court is doing in this case — drawing from the repeal of §452 an inference of Congressional disapproval of deferred reporting of advances. But even if the legislative history on this point were hazy, the same conclusion would have to be reached upon examination of Congressional purpose in repealing §452 and §462. . . . Sections 452 and 462 were repealed *solely* because of a prospective loss of revenue during the first year in which taxpayers would take advantage of the new sections. Insofar as the reporting of advances was concerned, that loss of revenue would have occurred solely as a consequence of taxpayers changing their method of reporting, without the necessity of securing the Commissioner's consent, to that authorized under §452 and §462. The taxpayer who shifted his basis for reporting advances would have been allowed what was commonly termed a "double deduction" during the transitional year. Under §462, deductions could be taken in the year of change for expenses attributable to advances taxed in prior years under a claim of right theory, as well as for reserves for future expenditures attributable to advances received and reported during that year. Similarly, under §452, pre-payments received during the year of transition would be excluded from gross income while current expenditures attributable to past income would still be deductible.

The Congressional purpose in repealing §452 and §462 — maintenance of the revenues — does not, however, require disapproval of sound accounting principles in cases of taxpayers who, like the petitioner, have customarily and regularly used a sound accrual accounting method in reporting advance payments. No transition is involved, and no "double deduction" is possible. Moreover, taxpayers formerly reporting advances as income in the year of receipt can now shift to a true accrual system of reporting only with the approval of the Commissioner. See . . . §446(e). Before giving his approval the Commissioner can be expected to insist upon adjustments in the taxpayer's transition year to forestall any revenue loss which would otherwise result from the change in accounting method. . . .

The net effect of compelling the petitioner to include all dues in gross income in the year received is to force the petitioner to utilize a hybrid accounting method — a cash basis for dues and an accrual basis for all other items. Schlude v. Commissioner, 8 Cir., 283 F.2d 234, 239. Cf. Commissioner of Internal Revenue v. South Texas Lumber Co., 333 U.S. 496, 501. For taxpayers generally the enforcement of such a hybrid accounting method may result in a gross distortion of actual income, particularly in the first and last years of doing business. On the return for the first year in which advances are received, a taxpayer will have to report an unrealistically high net income, since he will have to include unearned receipts, without any offsetting deductions for the future cost of earning those receipts. On subsequent tax returns, each year's unearned prepayments will be partially offset by the deduction of current expenses attributable to prepayments taxed in prior years. Even then, however, if the taxpayer is forbidden to correlate earnings with related expenditures, the result will be a distortion of normal fluctuations in the taxpayer's net income. For example, in a year when there are low current expenditures because of fewer advances received in the preceding year, the result may be an inflated adjusted gross income for the current year. Finally, should the taxpayer decide to go out of business upon fulfillment of the contractual obligations already undertaken, in the final year there will be no advances to report and many costs attributable to advances received in prior years. The result will be a grossly unrealistic reportable net loss.

The Court suggests that the application of sound accrual principles cannot be accepted here because deferment is based on an estimated rate of earnings, and because this estimate, in turn, is based on average, not individual, costs. It is true, of course, that the petitioner cannot know what service an individual member will require or when he will demand it. Accordingly, in determining the portion of its outstanding contractual obligations which have been discharged during a particular period (and hence the portion of receipts earned during that period), the petitioner can only compare the total expenditures for that period against estimated average expenditures for the same number of members over a full contract term. But this use of estimates and averages is in no way inconsistent with long-accepted accounting practices in reflecting and reporting income. . . .

Finally, it is to be noted that the regulations under both the 1939 and 1954 Codes permit various methods of reporting income which require the use of estimates.[40] In the absence of any showing that the estimates used here were faulty, I think the law did not permit the Commissioner to forbid the use of standard accrual methods simply upon the ground that estimates were necessary to determine what the rate of deferral should be. . . .

NOTES AND QUESTIONS

1. *Other cases.* In Schlude v. Commissioner, 372 U.S. 128 (1963), the Supreme Court held (five to four) that a dancing school was taxable in the year of receipt on amounts paid by students for lessons to be provided in the future; the school's consistent practice had been to treat such payments as deferred income, to be recognized in aliquot portions as the lessons were given or when the student's lack of activity indicated that no more lessons would be called for. The majority relied in part on its discussion in the *AAA* case of the retroactive repeal of §452 and the limited scope of the subsequently enacted §456.

A more sympathetic attitude toward the use of accrual principles (requiring deferral of prepaid but unearned income) is reflected in Artnell Co. v. Commissioner, 400 F.2d 981 (7th Cir. 1968), rev'g 48 T.C. 411 (1967). *Artnell* concerned the recognition of income from prepaid admissions to baseball games to be played in the following taxable year. The court observed that the time and extent of the future services was so specific that if the taxpayer's method clearly reflected income, the Commissioner's refusal to permit deferral would result in an abuse of his discretion under §446. The three Supreme Court decisions (*Automobile Club of Michigan, American Automobile Association,* and *Schlude*) were distinguished as follows (400 F.2d at 984):

> The uncertainty stressed in those decisions is not present here. The deferred income was allocable to games which were to be played on a fixed schedule. Except for rain dates, there was certainty. We would have no difficulty distinguishing the instant case in this respect.

The court went on to say (400 F.2d at 984-985):

> It is our best judgment that, although the policy of deferring, where possible, to congressional procedures in the tax field will cause the Su-

40. See, e.g., Treas. Reg. §1.451-3 (1975) (providing for the percentage of completion method of reporting income on long-term contracts); Treas. Reg. §1.451-4 (1957) (providing for [a] deduction for redemption of trading stamps based upon "the rate, in percentage, which the stamps redeemed in each year bear to the total stamps issued in such year"). . . .

> preme Court to accord the widest possible latitude to the commissioner's discretion, there must be situations where the deferral technique will so clearly reflect income that the Court will find an abuse of discretion if the commissioner rejects it.

On remand to determine whether the taxpayer's method did in fact clearly reflect income, the Tax Court held in favor of the taxpayer. 29 T.C.M. 403 (1970).

A similar sympathy for accrual principles is found in Boise Cascade Corp. v. United States, 530 F.2d 1367 (Ct. Cl.), cert. denied, 429 U.S. 867 (1976), where the taxpayer had performed engineering services. In some instances it performed services but was not entitled to, and did not receive, payment until later, in which case it accrued and reported the income when the services were performed. In other instances, it collected payment first and later performed the services, in which case it did not accrue and report the income until the services were performed. The Commissioner sought to require that the income be reported when the services were performed or when the payment was collected, whichever came first. This was too much for the court to swallow. In upholding the taxpayer's method, it referred to testimony by an accountant who was an expert witness for the taxpayer (530 F.2d at 1371):

> He termed [the Commissioner's] method as "hybrid" in that while it recognized the accrual method with respect to unbilled charges which were earned but not yet billable, it had the effect of imposing a cash basis method as to the billed but unearned charges. . . .

The court attempted to distinguish *American Automobile Association* and *Schlude* by saying that in *Boise Cascade* the services to be performed by the taxpayer were "in no sense . . . dependent solely upon the demand or request of its clientele." It went on to say that "the inconsistency within the Commissioner's method is strident," and that "his method would appear to the ordinary mind to distort income instead of clearly reflecting it" (530 F.2d at 1377-1378).

The result in *Boise Cascade,* though seemingly consistent with logic, common sense, and rudimentary notions of fair play, nonetheless seems inconsistent with at least the spirit of *American Automobile Association* and *Schlude.* The *Boise Cascade* taxpayer's treatment of instances where the performance of services preceded the receipt of cash seems consistent with sound principles of accrual accounting. Given that, in general, taxpayers are to be allowed to use the accrual method (see §446(c)), there is no reason for tax purposes to change that part of its method of accounting. As to instances where the receipt preceded the performance of services, to require the taxpayer to include the payments in income when received is to put it on the cash method for tax purposes for such receipts, even though for most other items of income and deduction it is on the accrual method. But that is precisely what was required of the taxpayer in *American Automobile Association* and *Schlude.*

Greater deference to the spirit of *American Automobile Association* and *Schlude* is found in RCA Corp. v. United States, 664 F.2d 881 (2d Cir. 1981), cert. denied, 457 U.S. 1133 (1982), where deferral was disallowed. In that case, the taxpayer sold service contracts for the repair of television sets, with the service available on demand. The taxpayer sold many of these contracts over the years and was able to forecast when services would be performed. Instead of reporting revenues from the sale of service contracts when payment was received, it included in income "only those service contract revenues that it estimated it had earned during the taxable year by actual performance," a method that "matched service contract revenues and related expenses with reasonable accuracy" (664 F.2d at 883). The Commissioner demanded that the taxpayer report all service contract revenues as received. The court upheld the position of the Commissioner, emphasizing that the question before it was whether the Commissioner had abused his discretion in rejecting the taxpayer's method. The court had this to say about the policy reflected in the Supreme Court decisions (664 F.2d at 887-888):

> The policy considerations that underlie *Michigan, AAA,* and *Schlude* are quite clear. When a taxpayer receives income in the form of prepayments in respect of services to be performed in the future upon demand, it is impossible for the taxpayer to know, at the outset of the contract term, the amount of service that his customer will ultimately require, and, consequently, it is impossible for the taxpayer to predict *with certainty* the amount of net income, i.e., the amount of the excess of revenues over expenses of performance, that he will ultimately earn from the contract. For purposes of financial accounting, this uncertainty is tolerable; the financial accountant merely estimates future demands for performance and defers recognition of income accordingly. Tax accounting, however, "can give no quarter to uncertainty." Thor Power Tool [v. Commissioner, 439 U.S. 522, 543 (1979), infra page 633]. The entire process of government depends on the expeditious collection of tax revenues. Tax accounting therefore tends to compute taxable income on the basis of the taxpayer's present ability to pay the tax, as manifested by his current cash flow, without regard to deductions that may later accrue. . . . By the same token, tax accounting is necessarily hostile to accounting practices that defer recognition of income, and thus payment of the tax on it, on the basis of estimates and projections that may ultimately prove unsound.

2. *The deduction side.* One of the principal objectives of accrual accounting is to match income with the costs of producing that income. The good sense of such an approach is obvious in the case of a firm

like American Automobile Association. Imagine the first year of its operations. If it reports as income the fees received during the year from members, without taking into account the cost of the services that it will be required to render to those members in the following year, it will overstate its income. Thus, assuming that the decision in the *AAA* case is controlling as to income, should the taxpayer be allowed to claim a deduction for the expected costs of providing services? In light of the opinion in the case, what do you think is the likelihood that such a deduction would in fact be allowed? This issue should be reconsidered after study of United States v. General Dynamics Corp., infra page 456, and the notes following it.

3. *Policy: income/expense symmetry.* In *Boise Cascade,* supra, the taxpayer argued in the alternative that if it were to be required to report *unearned* cash payments on the cash method (that is, as received), it should be allowed to use the cash method for *earned* income for which payment had not yet been received. That argument seems appealing. If the government's position is that it is entitled to its share of cash when the cash comes in, then perhaps it should be willing to wait for its share of cash that has not yet come in. If we push that argument far enough, it would seem to require a deduction for all cash outlays, including those for capital investments. One might think of the government as a partner that has insisted on receiving its share of cash when it comes in, that correspondingly should be required to pay its share of expenses when they are paid out in cash, and that must ante up for its share of all investments. (A deduction for cash outlays has the effect of requiring the government to bear part of the burden of that outlay, since the deduction reduces income and the government's tax revenue is correspondingly reduced, in the same proportion as its tax revenue is increased when income is increased.)

4. *The short, unhappy lives of §§452 and 462.* Accountants have frequently criticized the Treasury's attitude toward prepaid income and expense reserves; indeed, these are probably the most important departures, in computing taxable income, from conventional accounting methods. The 1954 enactment of §452 and §462, discussed by the Court in *American Automobile Association,* was therefore regarded by accountants as a great victory for "generally accepted accounting principles." But both provisions were repealed a year later, after the Treasury had expressed to Congress its alarm over the amount of revenue that it estimated would be lost in the transition years as taxpayers that had not previously deferred income began to do so. In its report on the repeal bill the Senate Finance Committee strongly recommended that substitute provisions be adopted in the near future. No such general legislation has been enacted, but some specific legislative changes have been enacted and some administrative loosening has occurred. These developments are discussed in the following two notes.

5. *The legislative sequel to the* AAA *case.* Following the decision in *American Automobile Association,* Congress enacted §456 to permit membership organizations reporting on the accrual method to elect to spread prepaid dues over the period of responsibility for the performance of services. The provision has much in common with §455 (prepaid subscription income), to which both the majority and the dissenters in the *AAA* case referred.

6. *Limited administrative deferral under Rev. Proc. 71-21 and Regs. §1.451-5.* In an effort to narrow the differences between tax and financial accounting treatment of unearned income, the Commissioner exercised his discretion under §446 and promulgated Rev. Proc. 71-21, 1971-2 C.B. 549, which provides a limited right of deferral for payments received (or due and payable) in one year for services to be rendered before the end of the following year. Instead of reporting such items when received (or when due and payable), an accrual basis taxpayer may report them in the next succeeding taxable year or when the services are performed, whichever occurs first. There are a number of qualifications and exceptions to this right, which does not in any event apply to services to be performed on property sold by the taxpayer under a service warranty unless the taxpayer also sells the same property without a service agreement. See also Regs. §1.451-5, relating to certain "advance payments."

7. *An observation.* Suppose that *T,* an individual accrual-method taxpayer, performs services for the U.S. Treasury Department and receives in return a promise by the Treasury to pay her $1,500 at the end of twenty years. Consider the implications of a rule that requires the inclusion of $1,500 in *T*'s income in the year the services are performed. Assume that *T* pays taxes at a rate of 33 percent and that as a result the Treasury collects $500 in taxes from her. Suppose that that amount is invested by the Treasury at 10 percent. At the end of twenty years it would grow to $3,364 and the Treasury would be ahead $1,864 by virtue of having incurred the obligation to pay the $1,500. Or suppose *T* decides to accept no payment for her services. She will pay $500 less in taxes in the year the services are performed. If she invests this amount at 6.7 percent after taxes, she will have $1,829 at the end of twenty years, $329 more than if she had agreed to accept payment. Compare the discussion of deduction of amounts of damages a taxpayer is obligated to pay in the future under a structured settlement, supra page 227, Note 2.

3. Deposits versus Advance Payments

COMMISSIONER v. INDIANAPOLIS POWER & LIGHT CO.

493 U.S. 203 (1990)

Justice BLACKMUN delivered the opinion of the Court.

Respondent Indianapolis Power & Light Company (IPL) requires certain customers to make deposits with it to assure payment of future bills for electric service. Petitioner Commissioner of Internal Revenue contends that these deposits are advance payments for electricity and therefore constitute taxable income to IPL upon receipt. IPL contends otherwise.

I

IPL is a regulated Indiana corporation that generates and sells electricity in Indianapolis and its environs. It keeps its books on the accrual and calendar year basis. During the years 1974 through 1977, approximately 5% of IPL's residential and commercial customers were required to make deposits "to insure prompt payment," as the customers' receipts stated, of future utility bills. These customers were selected because their credit was suspect. Prior to March 10, 1976, the deposit requirement was imposed on a case-by-case basis. IPL relied on a credit test but employed no fixed formula. The amount of the required deposit ordinarily was twice the customer's estimated monthly bill. IPL paid 3% interest on a deposit held for six months or more. A customer could obtain a refund of the deposit prior to termination of service by requesting a review and demonstrating acceptable credit. The refund usually was made in cash or by check, but the customer could choose to have the amount applied against future bills.

In March 1976, IPL amended its rules governing the deposit program. See Title 170, Ind. Admin. Code 4-1-15 (1988). Under the amended rules, the residential customers from whom deposits were required were selected on the basis of a fixed formula. The interest rate was raised to 6% but was payable only on deposits held for 12 months or more. A deposit was refunded when the customer made timely payments for either nine consecutive months, or for 10 out of 12 consecutive months so long as the two delinquent months were not themselves consecutive. A customer could obtain a refund prior to that time by satisfying the credit test. As under the previous rules, the refund would be made in cash or by check, or, at the customer's option, applied against future bills. Any deposit unclaimed after seven years was to escheat to the State. See Ind. Code §32-9-1-6(a) (1988).

IPL did not treat these deposits as income at the time of receipt. Rather, as required by state administrative regulations, the deposits were carried on its books as current liabilities. Under its accounting system, IPL recognized income when it mailed a monthly bill. If the deposit was used to offset a customer's bill, the utility made the necessary accounting adjustments. Customer deposits were not physically segregated in any way from the company's general funds. They were commingled with other receipts and at all times were subject to IPL's unfettered use and control. It is undisputed that IPL's treatment of the deposits was consistent with accepted accounting practice and applicable state regulations.

Upon audit of respondent's returns for the calendar years 1974 through 1977, the Commissioner asserted deficiencies. Although other items initially were in dispute, the parties were able to reach agreement on every issue except that of the proper treatment of customer deposits for the years 1975, 1976, and 1977. The Commissioner took the position that the deposits were advance payments for electricity and therefore were taxable to IPL in the year of receipt. He contended that the increase or decrease in customer deposits outstanding at the end of each year represented an increase or decrease in IPL's income for the year. IPL disagreed and filed a petition in the United States Tax Court for redetermination of the asserted deficiencies.

In a reviewed decision, with one judge not participating, a unanimous Tax Court ruled in favor of IPL. 88 T.C. 964 (1987). The court followed the approach it had adopted in City Gas Co. of Florida v. Commissioner of Internal Revenue, 74 T.C. 386 (1980), rev'd, 689 F.2d 943 (11th Cir. 1982). It found it necessary to "continue to examine all of the circumstances," 88 T.C., at 976, and relied on several factors in concluding that the deposits in question were properly excluded from gross income. It noted, among other things, that only 5% of IPL's customers were required to make deposits; that the customer rather than the utility controlled the ultimate disposition of a deposit; and that IPL consistently treated the deposits as belonging to the customers, both by listing them as current liabilities for accounting purposes and by paying interest. Id., at 976-978.

The United States Court of Appeals for the Seventh Circuit affirmed the Tax Court's decision. 857 F.2d 1162 (1988). The court stated that "the proper approach to determining the appropriate tax treatment of a customer deposit is to look at the primary purpose of the deposit based on all the facts and circumstances. . . ." Id., at 1167. The court appeared to place primary reliance, however, on IPL's obligation to pay interest on the deposits. It asserted that "as the interest rate paid on a deposit to secure income begins to approximate the return that the recipient would be expected to make from the use of the deposit amount, the deposit begins to serve purposes that comport more squarely with a security deposit." Id., at 1169. Noting that IPL had paid interest on the customer deposits throughout the period in question, the court upheld, as not clearly erroneous, the Tax Court's determination that the principal purpose of these deposits was to serve as security rather than as prepayment of income. Id., at 1170.

Because the Seventh Circuit was in specific disagreement with the Eleventh Circuit's ruling in City Gas Co. of Florida, supra, we granted certiorari to resolve the conflict. — U.S. — (1989).

II

We begin with the common ground. IPL acknowledges that these customer deposits are taxable as income upon receipt if they constitute advance payments for electricity to be supplied.[41] The Commissioner, on his part, concedes that customer deposits that secure the performance of nonincome-producing covenants — such as a utility customer's obligation to ensure that meters will not be damaged — are not taxable income. And it is settled that receipt of a loan is not income to the borrower. See Commissioner v. Tufts, [supra page 256] ("Because of [the repayment] obligation, the loan proceeds do not qualify as income to the taxpayer"); James v. United States, 366 U.S. 213, 219 (1961) (accepted definition of gross income "excludes loans"); Commissioner v. Wilcox, 327 U.S. 404, 408 (1946). IPL, stressing its obligation to refund the deposits with interest, asserts that the payments are similar to loans. The Commissioner, however, contends that a deposit which serves to secure the payment of future income is properly analogized to an advance payment for goods or services. See Rev. Rul. 72-519, 1972-2 C.B. 32, 33 ("[W]hen the purpose of the deposit is to guarantee the customer's payment of amounts owed to the creditor, such a deposit is treated as an advance payment, but when the purpose of the deposit is to secure a property interest of the taxpayer the deposit is regarded as a true security deposit").

In economic terms, to be sure, the distinction between a loan and an advance payment is one of degree rather than of kind. A commercial loan, like an advance payment, confers an economic benefit on the recipient: a business presumably does not borrow money unless it believes that the income it can earn from its use of the borrowed funds

41. This Court has held that an accrual-basis taxpayer is required to treat advance payments as income in the year of receipt. See Schlude v. Commissioner, 372 U.S. 128 (1963); American Automobile Assn. v. United States, [supra page 438]; Automobile Club of Michigan v. Commissioner, 353 U.S. 180 (1957). These cases concerned payments — nonrefundable fees for services — that indisputably constituted income; the issue was when that income was taxable. Here, in contrast, the issue is whether these deposits, as such, are income at all.

will be greater than its interest obligation. See Illinois Power Co. v. Commissioner, [supra page 204]. Even though receipt of the money is subject to a duty to repay, the borrower must regard itself as better off after the loan than it was before. The economic benefit of a loan, however, consists entirely of the opportunity to earn income on the use of the money prior to the time the loan must be repaid. And in that context our system is content to tax these earnings as they are realized. The recipient of an advance payment, in contrast, gains both immediate use of the money (with the chance to realize earnings thereon) and the opportunity to make a profit by providing goods or services at a cost lower than the amount of the payment.

The question, therefore, cannot be resolved simply by noting that respondent derives some economic benefit from receipt of these deposits. Rather, the issue turns upon the nature of the rights and obligations that IPL assumed when the deposits were made. In determining what sort of economic benefits qualify as income, this Court has invoked various formulations. It has referred, for example, to "undeniable accessions to wealth, clearly realized, and over which the taxpayers have complete dominion." Commissioner v. Glenshaw Glass Co., 348 U.S. 426, 431 (1955). It also has stated: "When a taxpayer acquires earnings, lawfully or unlawfully, without the consensual recognition, express or implied, of an obligation to repay and without restriction as to their disposition, 'he has received income. . . .'" James v. United States, 366 U.S., at 219, quoting North American Oil Consolidated v. Burnet, 286 U.S. 417, 424 (1932). IPL hardly enjoyed "complete dominion" over the customer deposits entrusted to it. Rather, these deposits were acquired subject to an express "obligation to repay," either at the time service was terminated or at the time a customer established good credit. So long as the customer fulfills his legal obligation to make timely payments, his deposit ultimately is to be refunded, and both the timing and method of that refund are largely within the control of the customer.[42]

The Commissioner stresses the fact that these deposits were not placed in escrow or segregated from IPL's other funds, and that IPL therefore enjoyed unrestricted use of the money. That circumstance, however, cannot be dispositive. After all, the same might be said of a commercial loan; yet the Commissioner does not suggest that a loan is taxable upon receipt simply because the borrower is free to use the funds in whatever fashion he chooses until the time of repayment. In

42. See Illinois Power Co., 792 F.2d, at 690. See also Burke & Friel, Recent Developments in the Income Taxation of Individuals, Tax-Free Security: Reflections on Indianapolis Power & Light, 12 Rev. of Taxation of Individuals 157, 174 (1988) (arguing that economic-benefit approach is superior in theory, but acknowledging that "an economic-benefit test has not been adopted, and it is unlikely that such an approach will be pursued by the Service or the courts").

determining whether a taxpayer enjoys "complete dominion" over a given sum, the crucial point is not whether his use of the funds is unconstrained during some interim period. The key is whether the taxpayer has some guarantee that he will be allowed to keep the money. IPL's receipt of these deposits was accompanied by no such guarantee.

Nor is it especially significant that these deposits could be expected to generate income greater than the modest interest IPL was required to pay. Again, the same could be said of a commercial loan, since, as has been noted, a business is unlikely to borrow unless it believes that it can realize benefits that exceed the cost of servicing the debt. A bank could hardly operate profitably if its earnings on deposits did not surpass its interest obligations; but the deposits themselves are not treated as income.[43] Any income that the utility may earn through use of the deposit money of course is taxable, but the prospect that income will be generated provides no ground for taxing the principal.

The Commissioner's advance payment analogy seems to us to rest upon a misconception of the value of an advance payment to its recipient. An advance payment, like the deposits at issue here, concededly protects the seller against the risk that it would be unable to collect money owed it after it has furnished goods or services. But an advance payment does much more: it protects against the risk that the purchaser will back out of the deal before the seller performs. From the moment an advance payment is made, the seller is assured that, so long as it fulfills its contractual obligation, the money is its to keep. Here, in contrast, a customer submitting a deposit made no commitment to purchase a specified quantity of electricity, or indeed to purchase any electricity at all.[44] IPL's right to keep the money depends upon the customer's purchase of electricity, and upon his later decision to have the deposit applied to future bills, not merely upon the utility's adherence to its contractual duties. Under these circumstances, IPL's dominion over the fund is far less complete than is ordinarily the case in an advance-payment situation.

The Commissioner emphasizes that these deposits frequently will be used to pay for electricity, either because the customer defaults on his obligation or because the customer, having established credit, chooses to apply the deposit to future bills rather than to accept a refund. When

43. Cf. Rev. Rul. 71-189, 1971-1 C.B. 32 (inactive deposits are not income until bank asserts dominion over the accounts). . . .

44. A customer, for example, might terminate service the day after making the deposit. Also, IPL's dominion over a deposit remains incomplete even after the customer begins buying electricity. As has been noted, the deposit typically is set at twice the customer's estimated monthly bill. So long as the customer pays his bills in a timely fashion, the money he owes the utility (for electricity used but not yet paid for) almost always will be less than the amount of the deposit. If this were not the case, the deposit would provide inadequate protection. Thus, throughout the period the deposit is held, at least a portion is likely to be money that IPL has no real assurance of ever retaining.

this occurs, the Commissioner argues, the transaction, from a cash-flow standpoint, is equivalent to an advance payment. In his view this economic equivalence mandates identical tax treatment.[45]

Whether these payments constitute income when received, however, depends upon the parties' rights and obligations at the time the payments are made. The problem with petitioner's argument perhaps can best be understood if we imagine a loan between parties involved in an ongoing commercial relationship. At the time the loan falls due, the lender may decide to apply the money owed him to the purchase of goods or services rather than to accept repayment in cash. But this decision does not mean that the loan, when made, was an advance payment after all. The lender in effect has taken repayment of his money (as was his contractual right) and has chosen to use the proceeds for the purchase of goods or services from the borrower. Although, for the sake of convenience, the parties may combine the two steps, that decision does not blind us to the fact that in the substance two transactions are involved.[46] It is this element of choice that distinguishes an advance payment from a loan. Whether these customer deposits are the economic equivalents of advance payments, and therefore taxable upon receipt, must be determined by examining the relationship between the parties at the time of the deposit. The individual who makes an advance payment retains no right to insist upon the return of the funds; so long as the recipient fulfills the terms of the bargain, the money is its to keep. The customer who submits a deposit to the utility, like the lender in the previous hypothetical, retains the right to insist upon repayment in cash; he may choose to apply the money to the purchase of electricity, but he assumes no obligation to do so, and the utility therefore acquires no unfettered "dominion" over the money at the time of receipt.

When the Commissioner examines privately structured transactions, the true understanding of the parties, of course, may not be apparent. It may be that a transfer of funds, though nominally a loan, may conceal an unstated agreement that the money is to be applied to the purchase of goods or services. We need not, and do not, attempt to devise a test for addressing those situations where the nature of the parties' bargain is legitimately in dispute. This particular respondent, however, conducts

45. The Commissioner is unwilling, however, to pursue this line of reasoning to the limit of its logic. He concedes that these deposits would not be taxable if they were placed in escrow, Tr. of Oral Arg. 4; but from a cash-flow standpoint it does not make much difference whether the money is placed in escrow or commingled with the utility's other funds. In either case, the utility receives the money and allocates it to subsequent purchases of electricity if the customer defaults or chooses to apply his refund to a future bill.

46. The Commissioner contends that a customer's decision to take his refund while making a separate payment for services, rather than applying the deposit to his bill, would amount to nothing more than an economically meaningless "exchange of checks." But in our view the "exchange of checks," while less convenient, more accurately reflects the economic substance of the transactions.

its business in a heavily regulated environment; its rights and obligations vis-à-vis its customers are largely determined by law and regulation rather than by private negotiation. That the utility's customers, when they qualify for refunds of deposits, frequently choose to apply those refunds to future bills rather than taking repayment in cash does not mean that any customer has made an unspoken commitment to do so.

Our decision is also consistent with the Tax Court's longstanding treatment of lease deposits — perhaps the closest analogy to the present situation. The Tax Court traditionally has distinguished between a sum designated as a prepayment of rent — which is taxable upon receipt — and a sum deposited to secure the tenant's performance of a lease agreement. See, e.g., J.&E. Enterprises, Inc. v. Commissioner, 26 T.C.M. 944 (1967).[47] In fact, the customer deposits at issue here are less plausibly regarded as income than lease deposits would be. The typical lease deposit secures the tenant's fulfillment of a contractual obligation to pay a specified rent throughout the term of the lease. The utility customer, however, makes no commitment to purchase any services at all at the time he tenders the deposit.

In Rev. Rul. 72-519, 1972-2 C.B. 32, the Commissioner relied in part on *J.&E. Enterprises* as authority for the proposition that deposits intended to secure income-producing covenants are advance payments taxable as income upon receipt, while deposits intended to secure nonincome-producing covenants are not. Id., at 33. In our view, neither *J.&E. Enterprises* nor the other cases cited in the Revenue Ruling support that distinction. See Hirsch Improvement Co. v. Commissioner of Internal Revenue, 143 F.2d 912 (2d Cir.), cert. denied, 323 U.S. 750 (1944); Mantell v. Commissioner, 17 T.C. 1143 (1952); Gilken Corp. v. Commissioner, 10 T.C. 445 (1948), aff'd, 176 F.2d 141 (6th Cir. 1949). These cases all distinguish between advance payments and security deposits, not between deposits that do and do not secure income-producing covenants.

We recognize that IPL derives an economic benefit from these deposits. But a taxpayer does not realize taxable income from every event that improves his economic condition. A customer who makes his deposit reflects no commitment to purchase services, and IPL's right to retain the money is contingent upon events outside its control. We hold

47. In *J.&E. Enterprises* the Tax Court stated: "If a sum is received by a lessor at the beginning of a lease, is subject to his unfettered control, and is to be applied as rent for a subsequent period during the term of the lease, such sum is income in the year of receipt even though in certain circumstances a refund thereof may be required. . . . If, on the other hand, a sum is deposited to secure the lessee's performance under a lease, and is to be returned at the expiration thereof, it is not taxable income even though the fund is deposited with the lessor instead of in escrow and the lessor has temporary use of the money. . . . In this situation the acknowledged liability of the lessor to account for the deposited sum on the lessee's performance of the lease covenants prevents the sum from being taxable in the year of receipt." 26 T.C.M. at 945-946.

that such dominion as IPL has over these customer deposits is insufficient for the deposits to qualify as taxable income at the time they are made.

The judgment of the Court of Appeals is affirmed.

It is so ordered.

NOTES AND QUESTIONS

1. *Planning.* Suppose you have just bought a rental apartment building. In accordance with local practice, you expect that at the time you rent an apartment you will collect the first month's rent in advance plus an amount equal to the last month's rent, with the latter intended to provide security for any damages to the apartment and for the payment of the rent. Is it possible to contract with your lessees so that the "last month's rent" will be treated as a security deposit rather than as advance rent? What might you do, both at the outset of the lease and thereafter?

2. *What kind of issue?* Why are these "deposit" cases placed here, in a chapter on timing, rather than in Chapter 2, with material on what is income? The courts, in cases like *Indianapolis Power,* frame the issue as whether the amounts received are to be treated as income, and that is certainly a useful perspective. At the same time, the taxpayer has received money and the question of how that money should be treated turns at least in part on expected obligations in the future — specifically, on whether it is likely that the money will be returned to the payor or applied to that person's benefit. Moreover, the timing issue is easy to see. If the amount is included at the outset and is later returned, a deduction will be allowed upon return. If the amount is excluded at the outset and later is applied to the payment of damages, rent, or services, it will be included in income when so applied. Thus, ultimate inclusion (disregarding timing) depends on how the money is used and the question of income versus deposit only determines when the income arises, if at all. In any event, the cases demonstrate the difficulty of separating the question "what is income?" from the question "when is it income?" and, more fundamentally, the limitations, and arbitrariness, of almost any system of classification. The cases may also suggest that there must be a better way to think about the tax issue.

3. *The claim of right doctrine.* Is the decision in this case consistent with the claim of right doctrine (which was covered earlier, at pages 201-208).

4. *The deduction issue.* In Iowa Southern Utilities Co. v. United States, 841 F.2d 1108 (Fed. Cir. 1988), the state regulatory agency allowed the taxpayer to increase its rates in order to finance the construction of a new power plant, subject to an obligation to "refund" the increase over a thirty-year period after the new plant began operating. The court

rejected the taxpayer's claim that the amounts of the increase should be treated as loans and excluded from its income. The court relied on the facts that the obligation to repay was only a "declaration of regulatory policy," not a fixed obligation, that the funds were not segregated and were not to be repaid to the same people from whom they had been collected, and that no interest was to be paid. The taxpayer also argued that if the income was not excludable, it should have been allowed to accrue (that is, claim currently) a deduction for its future obligation. The court rejected this argument on the ground that the repayments should be viewed not as costs associated with current revenues but rather as reductions in future revenues.

4. Current Deduction of Future Expenses

UNITED STATES v. GENERAL DYNAMICS CORP.

481 U.S. 239 (1987)

Justice Marshall delivered the opinion of the Court.

The issue in this case is whether an accrual basis taxpayer providing medical benefits to its employees may deduct at the close of the taxable year an estimate of its obligation to pay for medical care obtained by employees or their qualified dependents during the final quarter of the year, claims for which have not been reported to the employer.

I

Taxpayers, respondents herein, are the General Dynamics Corporation and several of its wholly-owned subsidiaries (General Dynamics).[48] General Dynamics uses the accrual method of accounting for federal tax purposes; its fiscal year is the same as the calendar year. From 1962 until October 1, 1972, General Dynamics purchased group medical insurance for its employees and their qualified dependents from two private insurance carriers. Beginning in October, 1972, General Dynamics became a self-insurer with regard to its medical care plans. Instead of continuing to purchase insurance from outside carriers, it undertook to pay medical claims out of its own funds, while continuing to employ private carriers to administer the medical care plans.

To receive reimbursement of expenses for covered medical services, respondent's employees submit claims forms to employee benefits personnel, who verify that the treated persons were eligible under the

48. Respondents filed a consolidated federal income tax return for 1972, the year at issue here. We therefore treat them as a single entity.

applicable plan as of the time of treatment. Eligible claims are then forwarded to the plan's administrators. Claims processors review the claims and approve for payment those expenses that are covered under the plan.

Because the processing of claims takes time, and because employees do not always file their claims immediately, there is a delay between the provision of medical services and payment by General Dynamics. To account for this time lag, General Dynamics established reserve accounts to reflect its liability for medical care received, but still not paid for, as of December 31, 1972. It estimated the amount of those reserves with the assistance of its former insurance carriers.

Originally, General Dynamics did not deduct any portion of this reserve in computing its tax for 1972. In 1977, however, after the IRS began an audit of its 1972 tax return, General Dynamics filed an amended return, claiming it was entitled to deduct its reserve as an accrued expense, and seeking a refund. The IRS disallowed the deduction, and General Dynamics sought relief in the Claims Court.

The Claims Court sustained the deduction, holding that it satisfied the "all events" test embodied in Treas. Reg. 1.461-1(a)(2), since "all events" which determined the fact of liability had taken place when the employees received covered services, and the amount of liability could be determined with reasonable accuracy. Thus, the court held that General Dynamics was entitled to a refund. 6 Cl. Ct. 250 (1984). The Court of Appeals for the Federal Circuit affirmed, largely on the basis of the Claims Court opinion. 773 F.2d 1224, 1226 (1985).

The United States sought review of the question whether all the events necessary to fix liability had occurred. . . .[49]

49. The United States did not seek review of whether the amount of liability in this case could be determined with reasonable accuracy. See Pet. for Cert. 13, n.2.

[The Claims Court opinion observes that the amount of liability deducted was an estimate determined as a "percentage of the payments actually made during a prior period of equal length." 6 Cl. Ct. at 252. That opinion conceded that this method "did not reflect any specific liability to particular employees who received treatment; rather, plaintiffs [General Dynamics and its subsidiaries] estimated their aggregate liability." Id. at 253. The government had argued that estimation must be done item by item, but the court held that the aggregate approach, based on expert advice, was permissible. In its petition for certiorari, the government noted that for the year 1972 the amount deducted was $5,575,289, while the amount ultimately paid was $4,583,893, or 17.8 percent less, and stated that it believed that the decision of the lower courts, allowing the use of the estimate, was in error. As the Supreme Court observes, however, the government did not seek review of that issue. Presumably the government considered that it had a strong case on the first part of the all events test ("all the events . . . have occurred") and did not want to argue the second part of the test (requiring estimation of the amount "with reasonable accuracy"), which is essentially a factual issue. The petition observed that "while the second part of the test permits a degree of computational flexibility, the Regulations emphasize that the first part of the test is absolute. . . ." — Eds.]

II

As we noted in United States v. Hughes Properties, Inc., 106 S. Ct. 2092 (1986),[50] whether a business expense has been "incurred" so as to entitle an accrual-basis taxpayer to deduct it under §162(a) is governed by the "all events" test that originated in United States v. Anderson, 269 U.S. 422, 441 (1926). In *Anderson,* the Court held that a taxpayer was obliged to deduct from its 1916 income a tax on profits from munitions sales that took place in 1916. Although the tax would not be assessed and therefore would not formally be due until 1917, all the events which fixed the amount of the tax and determined the taxpayer's liability to pay it had occurred in 1916. The test is now embodied in Treas. Reg. 1.461-1(a)(2), which provides that "[u]nder an accrual method of accounting, an expense is deductible for the taxable year in which all the events have occurred which determine the fact of the liability and the amount thereof can be determined with reasonable accuracy." Ibid.[51]

It is fundamental to the "all events" test that, although expenses may be deductible before they have become due and payable, liability must first be firmly established. This is consistent with our prior holdings that a taxpayer may not deduct a liability that is contingent. Nor may a taxpayer deduct an estimate of an anticipated expense, no matter how statistically certain, if it is based on events that have not occurred by the

50. [Eds. — In *Hughes Properties* the taxpayer operated a gambling casino that contained "progressive" slot machines. On these machines there was a jackpot that built up over time, sometimes to large amounts, as money was gambled on the machine. The progressive payoff was displayed on a "payoff indicator" on the face of the machine. The state gambling commission strictly enforced a rule prohibiting any reduction in the displayed payoff. The Court held that the all events test was satisfied and that the taxpayer was entitled to deduct the payoff amounts shown at the end of the taxable year on its progressive machines (reduced by the amounts shown, and deducted, the prior year). The government had argued that the all events test was not satisfied until a patron had won the jackpot. For years after 1985, the result in the case has been reversed by the adoption, in 1986, of §461(h) (described infra page 464). See Prop. Regs. §1.461-4(g) (8), Example 5.]

51. The regulation in force in 1972 was identical to the present version. See 26 C.F.R. §1.461-1(a)(2) (1972).

The "all events" test has been incorporated into the Internal Revenue Code by the Deficit Reduction Act of 1984, Pub. L. 98-369, 98 Stat. 598, 607, 26 U.S.C. §461(h)(4) (1982 ed. supp. III). Section 461(h) imposed limits on the application of the test, providing that "in determining whether an amount has been incurred with respect to any item during any taxable year, the all events test shall not be treated as met any earlier than when economic performance with respect to such item occurs." §461(h)(1). The pertinent portions of the 1984 amendments were retained in the Tax Reform Act of 1986.

Section 461(h) does not apply in this case. It became effective as of July 18, 1984. . . . While that statute permits a taxpayer to elect the application of §461(h) to amounts incurred on or before July 18, 1984, see §91(g)(2), there is no indication that the taxpayer here has done so. We do not address how this case would be decided under §461(h), but note that the legislative history of the Act indicates that, "[i]n the case of . . . employee benefit liabilities, which require a payment by the taxpayer to another person, economic performance occurs as the payments to such person are made." H.R. Rep. No. 98-432, pt. 2, p. 1255 (1984). . . .

close of the taxable year. Brown v. Helvering, 291 U.S. 193, 201 (1934); cf. American Automobile Assn. v. United States [supra page 438].

We think that this case, like *Brown,* involves a mere estimate of liability based on events that had not occurred before the close of the taxable year, and therefore the proposed deduction does not pass the "all events" test. We disagree with the legal conclusion of the courts below that the last event necessary to fix the taxpayer's liability was the receipt of medical care by covered individuals.[52] A person covered by a plan could only obtain payment for medical services by filling out and submitting a health expense benefits claim form. Employees were informed that submission of satisfactory proof of the charges claimed would be necessary to obtain payment under the plans. General Dynamics was thus liable to pay for covered medical services *only* if properly documented claims forms were filed.[53] Some covered individuals, through oversight, procrastination, confusion over the coverage provided, or fear of disclosure to the employer of the extent or nature of the services received, might not file claims for reimbursement to which they are plainly entitled. Such filing is not a mere technicality. It is crucial to the establishment of liability on the part of the taxpayer. Nor does the failure to file a claim represent the type of "extremely remote and speculative possibility" that we held in *Hughes,* 471 U.S., at 601, did not render an otherwise fixed liability contingent. Cf. Lucas v. North Texas Lumber Co., 281 U.S. 11, 13 (1930) (where executory contract of sale was created in 1916 but papers necessary to effect transfer were not prepared until 1917, unconditional liability for the purchase price was not created in 1916 and the gain from the sale was therefore not realized until 1917). Mere receipt of services for which, in some instances, claims will not be submitted does not, in our judgment, constitute the last link in the chain of events creating liability for purposes of the "all events" test.

The parties stipulated in this case that as of December 31, 1972, the taxpayer had not received all claims for medical treatment services rendered in 1972, and that some claims had been filed for services rendered in 1972 that had not been processed. The record does not reflect which portion of the claims against General Dynamics for medical

52. We do not challenge the Claims Court's factual conclusion that the processing of the claims was "routine," "clerical," and "ministerial in nature," 6 Cl. Ct. 250, 254 (1984). The Claims Court did not, however, make any factual findings with respect to the *filing* of claims. We conclude that, as a matter of law, the filing of a claim was necessary to create liability.

53. General Dynamics could not avoid its obligation to pay for services after they were received by, for example, discharging the employee. If an employee were terminated after receiving covered services but before filing a claim, the taxpayer would still be obliged to reimburse that employee, but *only in the event* that the employee filed a claim form. The filing of the claim is thus a true condition precedent to liability on the part of the taxpayer.

care had been filed but not yet processed and which portion had not even been filed at the close of the 1972 tax year. The taxpayer has the burden of proving its entitlement to a deduction. . . . Here, respondent made no showing that, as of December 31, 1972, it knew of specific claims which had been filed but which it had not yet processed. Because the taxpayer failed to demonstrate that any of the deducted reserve represented claims for which its liability was firmly established as of the close of 1972, all the events necessary to establish liability were not shown to have occurred, and therefore no deduction was permissible.

This is not to say that the taxpayer was unable to forecast how many claims would be filed for medical care received during this period, and estimate the liability that would arise from those claims. Based on actuarial data, General Dynamics may have been able to make a reasonable estimate of how many claims would be filed for the last quarter of 1972. But that alone does not justify a deduction. In *Brown,* supra, the taxpayer, a general agent for insurance companies, sought to take a deduction for a reserve representing estimated liability for premiums to be returned on the percentage of insurance policies it anticipated would be cancelled in future years. The agent may well have been capable of estimating with a reasonable degree of accuracy the ratio of cancellation refunds to premiums already paid and establishing its reserve accordingly. Despite the "strong probability that many of the policies written during the taxable year" would be cancelled, 291 U.S., at 201, the Court held that "no liability accrues during the taxable year on account of cancellations which it is expected may occur in future years, since the events necessary to create the liability do not occur during the taxable year." 291 U.S., at 200. A reserve based on the proposition that a particular set of events is likely to occur in the future may be an appropriate conservative accounting measure, but does not warrant a tax deduction. See American Automobile Assn. v. United States [supra].

That these estimated claims were not intended to fall within the "all events" test is further demonstrated by the fact that the Internal Revenue Code specifically permits insurance companies to deduct additions to reserves for such "incurred but not reported" (IBNR) claims. See §832(b)(5) (providing that an insurance company may treat as losses incurred "all unpaid losses outstanding at the end of the taxable year"); §832(c)(4) (permitting deduction of losses incurred as defined in §832(b)(5)).[54] If the "all events" test permitted the deduction of an estimated reserve representing claims that were actuarially likely but not yet reported, Congress would not have needed to maintain an

54. During the time that private insurance carriers provided insurance coverage for General Dynamics employees, the insurers maintained reserves for IBNR claims and deducted those reserves in the tax year in which the services were received. 6 Cl. Ct., at 252.

explicit provision that insurance companies could deduct such reserves.[55]

General Dynamics did not show that its liability as to any medical care claims was firmly established as of the close of the 1972 tax year, and is therefore entitled to no deduction. The judgment of the Court of Appeals is reversed.

Justice O'CONNOR, with whom Jusice BLACKMUN and Justice STEVENS join, dissenting.

Section 446(a) of the Internal Revenue Code of 1954 provides that taxable income "shall be computed under the method of accounting on the basis of which the taxpayer regularly computes his income in keeping his books." The Code specifically recognizes the use of "an accrual method," §446(c)(2), under which a taxpayer is permitted to deduct an expense in the year in which it is "incurred," regardless of when it is actually paid. §162(a). Under the "all events" test, long applied by this Court and the Internal Revenue Service, an expense may be accrued and deducted when all the events that determine the fact of liability have occurred, and the amount of the liability can be determined with reasonable accuracy. §1.461-1(a)(2) (1986). Because the Court today applies a rigid version of the all events test that retreats from our most recent application of that test, and unnecessarily drives a greater wedge between tax and financial accounting methods, I respectfully dissent.

This case calls for the Court to revisit the issue addressed only last Term in United States v. Hughes Properties, Inc., 476 U.S. 593 (1986). . . .

In my view, the circumstances of this case differ little from those in *Hughes Properties.* The taxpayer here is seeking to deduct the amounts reserved to pay for medical services that are determined to have been provided to employees in the taxable year, whether or not the employees' claims for benefits have been received. The taxpayer's various medical benefits plans provided schedules for the medical and hospital benefits, and created a contractual obligation by the taxpayer to pay for the covered services upon presentation of a claim. The courts below found that the obligation to pay became fixed once the covered medical services were received by the employee. Once the medical services were rendered to an employee while the relevant benefit plan was in effect, General Dynamics could not avoid liability by terminating the plan prior to the filing of a claim. Neither could General Dynamics extinguish its liability by firing an employee before the employee filed a claim for benefits.

55. Respondent has never sought to be treated as an insurance company entitled to take IBNR deductions under the provisions of Subchapter L.

It is true, of course, that it was theoretically possible that some employees might not file claim forms. In my view, however, this speculative possibility of nonpayment differs not at all from the speculation in *Hughes Properties* that a jackpot might never be paid by a casino. As we observed in *Hughes Properties,* the potential of nonpayment of a liability always exists, and it alone does not prevent accrual. The beneficiary of a liability always has the option of waiving payment, but a taxpayer is still unquestionably entitled to deduct the liability. An injured employee entitled absolutely to reimbursement for medical services under a worker's compensation statute, for example, may fail to utilize the medical services. The employer, however, has been held to be entitled to deduct the expected medical expenses because the worker's compensation law creates liability. See Wien Consolidated Airlines, Inc. v. Commissioner, 528 F.2d 735 (C.A.9 1976) (holding that accrual-basis taxpayer may deduct expected worker's compensation payments in year of injury even though injured workers may not utilize medical benefits). Similarly, any business liability could ultimately be discharged in bankruptcy, or a check might never be cashed by its recipient. There can be no doubt, however, that these remote possibilities alone cannot defeat an accrual basis taxpayer's right to deduct the liability when incurred.

The Claims Court found that the processing of the employees' claims was "routine" and "ministerial in nature," 6 Cl. Ct. 250, 254 (1984), and the majority does not question that finding. . . . Instead, the majority holds that "as a matter of law, the filing of a claim was necessary to create liability." . . . Even if, in a technical sense, the Court is correct that the filing of a claim is a necessary precondition to liability as a matter of law, the failure to file a claim is at most a "merely formal contingenc[y], or [one] highly improbable under the known facts," that this Court has viewed as insufficient to preclude accrual and deductibility. 2 J. Mertens, Law of Federal Income Taxation §12.62, p. 241 (Weinstein rev. 1985). Indeed, in the very case that first announced the all events test, United States v. Anderson, 269 U.S. 422 (1926), this Court concluded that a taxpayer should deduct a federal munitions tax before the year in which the tax was even assessed — in effect before the government had made a claim for the tax. The Court recognized that "[i]n a technical legal sense it may be argued that a tax does not accrue until it has been assessed and becomes due," but concluded that otherwise all the events that determined the liability for the munitions tax had occurred. Id., at 441. Similarly, in Continental Tie & Lumber Co. v. United States, 286 U.S. 290 (1932), the Court held that an accrual basis taxpayer should immediately include as income a federal payment to railroads created by statute, but neither claimed by the taxpayer nor awarded by the Federal Government until years later. The Court explained that although no railroad had any vested right to payments under the statute until a claim was made by the railroad and awarded by the Interstate Commerce Commission, "[t]he right to the award was fixed by the passage of the Transportation Act. What remained was mere administrative procedure to ascertain the amount to be paid." Id., at 295. Clearly, the right to reimbursement for medical benefits under any of the medical benefits plans at issue in this case arises once medical services are rendered; the filing and processing of a claim is purely routine and ministerial, and in the nature of a formal contingency, as correctly perceived by the courts below.

The holding of the Court today unnecessarily burdens taxpayers by further expanding the difference between tax and business accounting methods without a compelling reason to do so. Obviously, tax accounting principles must often differ from those of business accounting. The goal of business accounting "is to provide useful and pertinent information to management, shareholders, and creditors," while the responsibility of the Internal Revenue Service is to protect the public fisc. United States v. Hughes Properties, Inc., 476 U.S., at 603. Therefore, while prudent businesses will accrue expenses that are merely reasonably foreseeable, for tax purposes the liability must be fixed. But Congress has expressly permitted taxpayers to use the accrual method of accounting, and from its inception in United States v. Anderson, supra, the all events test has been a practical adjustment of the competing interests in permitting accrual accounting and protecting the public fisc. Unfortunately, the Court today ignores the pragmatic roots of the all events test and instead applies it in an essentially mechanistic and wholly unrealistic manner. Because the liability in this case was fixed with no less certainty than the range of expenses both routinely accrued by accrual method taxpayers and approved as deductible for tax purposes by this Court and other courts in a variety of circumstances, I respectfully dissent.

NOTES AND QUESTIONS

1. *The all events test.* Under the all events test, there are two issues: (a) whether the fact of liability has been established and (b) whether the amount of liability can be determined with reasonable accuracy. On which of these issues did the Court focus in *General Dynamics?*

2. *Five stages of the claims.* The claims process in *General Dynamics* can be divided into five stages:[56] (a) injury or illness occurs, (b) medical services performed, (c) claim filed, (d) claim approved, (e) claim paid.

56. This presentation and much of the material in the next note is based on Jensen, The Supreme Court's Misleading Footnote in General Dynamics, Tax Notes, Nov. 7, 1988, p. 665.

At which stage did the taxpayer seek to claim a deduction? At which stage was the Court prepared to allow a deduction?

3. *The effect of §§461(h) and 404. General Dynamics* arose before the adoption, in 1984, of §461(h). That provision adds to the judicially and administratively developed all events test an additional requirement of "economic performance." Under the language of §461(h), when would a deduction be allowable if the all events test is otherwise satisfied? See §461(h)(1), (h)(2)(A)(i), (h)(2)(B), and (h)(3). When would you say that the service (what service?) is provided (by or on behalf of whom?)? The bill that became §461(h) at one time included "employee benefit liabilities" along with workers' compensation and tort liabilities in the provision that became §461(h)(2)(C), but employee benefit liabilities were deleted from this provision before it became law. The House Committee Report language cited by the Court in *General Dynamics* in the last sentence of footnote 51 referred to the earlier version that was not enacted. Section 404, which applies to unfunded deferred benefit plans (see §404(b)(2)(A)), might also come into play, but analysis of that part of the law is beyond our scope. See also §419. It is enough to observe that deductions for employee benefits are now governed by a complex set of statutory provisions.

4. "*Mooney bonds.*" (a) Tax lawyers have long been captivated by the facts in Mooney Aircraft v. United States, 420 F.2d 400 (5th Cir. 1969).[57] It is a good paradigm for examining the relationship between some basic tax and financial principles. The taxpayer in *Mooney Aircraft* was in the business of manufacturing and selling a single-engine aircraft. When it sold each aircraft, it issued to the buyer a "Mooney bond," which was a promise to pay $1,000 to the bearer when the aircraft was retired from service. The taxpayer claimed a deduction for the full $1,000 at the time the aircraft was sold and the bond issued. The court denied the deduction, saying that "the most salient feature in this case is the fact that many or possibly most of the expenses which the taxpayer wishes to presently deduct will not actually be paid for 15, 20, or even 30 years," and concluding that the all events test had not been satisfied.

(b) An intriguing aspect of the case is the possibility of deducting the full amount of a future obligation rather than its present value. Deduction of the full amount is consistent with generally accepted accounting principles. (See Financial Accounting Standards Board Opinion No. 21 requiring use of present value but only in the case of "contractual rights to receive money or contractual rights to pay money on fixed or determinable dates.") With a full current deduction of the future amount, a taxpayer can be better off, after tax effects, by virtue of having incurred an obligation than it would have been with no obligation at all. For example, suppose a taxpayer incurs a debt of $1,000 payable 15 years

57. This may say more about tax practice than about the facts.

hence. Suppose the taxpayer's marginal rate is 40 percent and its after-tax rate of return on investments is 7 percent. An immediate deduction of $1,000 produces a tax saving of $400. That $400, if invested at 7 percent for 15 years will grow to $1,103. Thus, at the end of fifteen years, by incurring the debt and thereby obtaining a tax deduction, the taxpayer can accumulate $1,103, pay the $1,000, and be $103 ahead. This advantage to the obligor may, however, be offset by a corresponding disadvantage to the obligee, who may (if an accrual-method taxpayer) be required to report the entire $1,000 at the outset, when the obligor claims the deduction. See note 7, page 447.[58]

(c) The financially correct treatment is to deduct (or exclude) at the outset the present value of the future obligation and then each year deduct the amount by which the present value increases (that is, the accrued interest). For an intuitive sense of why this is the correct treatment, imagine that the taxpayer in *Mooney* decides to set aside an amount of money sufficient, with the interest that can be earned on it, to pay the $1,000 at the end of some assumed period of time — say twenty years. The amount to be set aside would be the present value of the $1,000, or, at 6 percent, $312. That should be treated as an offset to present receipts, since it is an amount of money actually set aside for future payment. The offset can be achieved either by excluding from gross income $312 of the total amount paid by the buyer or by including in gross income the total amount paid by the buyer and allowing a deduction for $312. As the set-aside fund earns interest, that interest must also be set aside for future payment and it should also be nontaxable (through either an exclusion or a deduction). It is interesting to note that this approach is consistent with treating a portion of the initial purchase price of the aircraft as a loan from the buyer to Mooney and then applying the original issue discount (OID) rules (discussed supra at page 353) to determine an annual interest deduction.

(d) The approach that Mooney claimed, unsuccessfully, it was entitled to use, a current deduction for the $1,000, is equivalent to exclusion of $1,000 of the purchase price, which is in turn consistent with treating the $1,000 as a deposit. A deposit is, in turn, equivalent in this situation to an interest-free loan. Under that view of the matter, interest might (under present law) be attributed to the buyer of the aircraft under §7872. If the aircraft were used by the buyer for business purposes, the

58. It is worth noting that items of earned income to be received in the future must be reported by an accrual-method taxpayer at their full face value. See, e.g., Rev. Rul. 79-278, 1979-2 C.B. 302. On the other hand, where a cash-method taxpayer sells property other than in the ordinary course of business and receives a promissory note or obligation in return, the amount deemed received is the fair market value of the promissory note or obligation. See Warren Jones Co. v. Commissioner, 524 F.2d 788 (9th Cir. 1975). The availability of installment reporting (supra page 364), however, may reduce the significance of rules relating to the amount of income to be accrued.

interest income would be offset by a business-expense deduction, but if the aircraft were used for personal purposes there would be no such offset.

(e) If *Mooney Aircraft* arose today, and if the Mooney bond is not treated as a loan from the buyer to Mooney, §461(h) might apply to deny a deduction until the "bond" is paid. See §461(h)(2)(B). On the other hand, the transaction might be treated as one involving the purchase of (1) an aircraft and (2) a "zero-coupon" bond, with an appropriate portion of the purchase price allocated to each element. On that view of the facts, the amount allocated to the bond (which would be equivalent to the present value of the future obligation) would be excluded from Mooney's income as a loan. Under the OID rules, the buyer would be required to report income each year and Mooney would have a corresponding deduction. This treatment is the same as the financially correct treatment outlined in (c) above.

(f) In Burnham Corp. v. Commissioner, 90 T.C. No. 62 (1988), the taxpayer, as a result of patent litigation, became obligated to pay to a Mrs. Reichhelm or her estate $1,250 per month for her life, with a minimum of forty-eight payments to be made to her or her estate. Mrs. Reichhelm's life expectancy was sixteen years. The taxpayer was allowed a deduction of the total amount expected to be paid, $240,000, in the year in which the obligation was incurred. The court emphasized that the contingency arose from a condition subsequent and concluded that the all events test for deduction had been met. The court asked for supplemental briefs on the question whether the deduction should be limited to the present value of the payments to be made. On that issue, the court stated:

> On brief respondent concedes that no statutory authority or case law exists that would require accrual basis taxpayers to discount current deductions of long-term liabilities. Respondent points to the works of several commentators which propose time value calculations in such cases. While as a theoretical policy matter, petitioner should perhaps be entitled to deduct only a discounted amount, we decide cases on the law not on theories of policy. Because of respondent's concession, we do not require petitioner to discount the estimated payments to Mrs. Reichhelm.

5. *Other applications of §461(h).* Section 461(h) contains express language denying deductions for so-called structured settlements of tort liabilities and for workers' compensation claims, if payments are made directly by the taxpayer (as opposed to the purchase by the taxpayer of an annuity that is owned by the person entitled to payment). See §461(h)(2)(c) and supra page 227, Note 3. One of the most important costs to which §461(h) applies is the cost of reclaiming land after strip mining (often in accordance with an obligation imposed by state or federal law),

but there is a special elective provision for such costs (§468). See also §468A, covering nuclear decommissioning costs.

6. *Other cases.* In Schuessler v. Commissioner, 230 F.2d 722 (5th Cir. 1956), a taxpayer who sold gas furnaces with a guarantee that he would turn the furnace on and off each year for five years was allowed to deduct the estimated cost of performing this service, on a showing that his price for furnaces was $20 to $25 more than that of his competitors, who did not undertake a similar obligation (230 F.2d at 725):

> The record below amply supports the contention of the taxpayer that there was a legal liability created in 1946, when the purchase price was paid for the gas furnaces, for the taxpayer to turn the furnaces on and off for the succeeding five years; that the cost of such service was reasonably established at a minimum of $2.00 per visit; and that the payment of $20.00 to $25.00 extra by the purchases fully proved their intention to call upon the taxpayer each year for the service. These facts authorized the setting up of a reserve out of the 1946 income to enable the taxpayer to meet these established charges in future years.

In Washington Post Co. v. United States, 405 F.2d 1279 (Ct. Cl. 1969), the taxpayer was allowed a current deduction for obligations to a fund for dealer incentives. In Pacific Grape Products Co. v. Commissioner, 219 F.2d 862 (9th Cir. 1955), the taxpayer was allowed to deduct in the year of sale of its product the estimated cost of labeling and preparing goods for shipment and related brokerage fees, even though shipment and the payment of fees would occur in the following year.

How would the deductions in these cases be treated after the adoption of §461(h)? See §461(h)(3).

7. *Reserves for bad debts.* The 1986 act repealed a provision that had allowed a deduction for reserves for bad debts. The House Report offered the following justification (H.R. Rep. 99-426, 99th Cong., 1st Sess. at 640 (1986)):

> The committee generally believes that the reserve method of accounting for bad debts should be repealed. Use of the reserve method for determining losses from bad debts results in deductions being allowed for tax purposes that statistically occur in the future. In this regard, the reserve for bad debts is inconsistent with the treatment of other deductions under the all events test. Moreover, use of the reserve method allows a deduction prior to the time that the losses actually occur. If a deduction is allowed prior to the taxable year in which the loss occurs, the value of the deduction to the taxpayer will be overstated and the overall tax liability of the taxpayer understated.

8. *Contested taxes.* Dixie Pine Products Co. v. Commissioner, 320 U.S. 516 (1944), held that the taxpayer could not deduct certain state taxes

that had been assessed but had not been paid and the liability for which the taxpayer was contesting. The Court said that before a deduction may be claimed "all the events must occur in that year which fix the amount and the fact of the taxpayer's liability . . . and this cannot be the case where the liability is contingent and is contested by the taxpayer." 320 U.S. at 519. Under §461(f), adopted after *Dixie Pine,* the taxpayer is entitled to a deduction for an asserted liability if it makes payment. This eliminates the difficult choice between contesting a liability and claiming a deduction.

9. *Use of checks and notes as payment.* In accordance with commercial expectation, a cash-basis taxpayer is treated as paying an expense upon delivery of a check, provided the check is honored when presented. See Estate of Spiegel v. Commissioner, 12 T.C. 524 (1949), acq., Rev. Rul. 54-465, 1954-2 C.B. 93. But see Rev. Rul. 67-396, 1967-2 C.B. 351 (for gift tax purposes, a gift is not consummated by delivery of the donor's own check since it can be revoked until paid, certified, or negotiated). It is also clear that for a cash-basis taxpayer issuance of a note does not give rise to a deductible expense until the note is paid. See Eckert v. Burnet, 283 U.S. 140 (1931), and Helvering v. Price, 309 U.S. 409 (1940). In Don E. Williams Co. v. Commissioner, 429 U.S. 569 (1977), the Supreme Court held that an accrual-basis taxpayer was not permitted a current deduction on the delivery of fully secured demand promissory notes to an employee pension and profit sharing plan. Section 404(a) allows a deduction for a contribution "paid," and the Court found that actual payment of cash or its equivalent is required regardless of the taxpayer's method of accounting. In distinguishing between a promissory note and a check, the Court stated:

> The line between the two may be thin at times, but it is distinct. The promissory note, even when payable on demand and fully secured, is still, as its name implies, only a promise to pay, and does not represent the paying out or reduction of assets. A check, on the other hand, is a direction to the bank for immediate payment, is a medium of exchange, and has come to be treated for federal tax purposes as a conditional payment of cash.

10. *Charges to bank credit cards as payment.* Rev. Rul. 78-38, 1978-1 C.B. 67, ruled that a charitable contribution made by a charge to a bank credit card is deductible under §170(a) in the year the charge is made regardless when the bank is repaid. This rule treats the bank charge as the equivalent of the actual use of borrowed funds to make a contribution.

J. CORPORATE TRANSACTIONS: INCORPORATIONS AND REORGANIZATIONS

In this section we will examine briefly, and only at the most rudimentary level, rules relating to the taxation of exchanges arising in the corporate context. The objective is in part to offer a glimpse into the law in this area and in part to examine, in still another context, problems of realization and recognition.

1. Incorporation

Incorporation of a sole proprietorship. Suppose that *T* owns and operates as a sole proprietorship a business whose assets have a fair market value of $100,000 and a basis of $30,000. She has decided, for a variety of reasons, that she wants to operate in corporate form. In order to incorporate, typically *T* would form the corporation (draft and file the necessary documents, etc.) and transfer to the corporation the assets of the business in exchange for shares of the corporation's common stock. She would then be the sole shareholder, but she would no longer own the assets, any more than a shareholder of IBM owns the assets of that corporation. The assets would be owned by the corporation. At least this is how the matter is perceived in our legal system, both for tax and nontax purposes. The corporation is treated as a separate entity, one having an existence separate from that of its shareholders; it is reified. Of course, *T* would have the power as sole shareholder to elect all the directors of the corporation, and the directors would have the power to control its operation. The directors might appoint *T* president of the corporation, in which case she would have day-to-day control, but in the eyes of the law (and of the tax system) her control would be as an employee, an agent of the corporation, not as an owner.

Once one appreciates the notion of the separate entity status of corporations, one can begin to grasp the realization/recognition problem. When *T* exchanges her assets for shares of common stock of the corporation, that exchange results in a realization of the gain of $70,000. Should that gain be recognized? Using our common sense and ignoring conceptualisms, we can see that all that has happened is that *T* has changed the legal form in which she is doing business. That does not seem like the kind of change that should give rise to the recognition of gain by *T*. Congress, having accepted that common-sense view, enacted a nonrecognition provision, §351,[59] and a corollary provision, §1032, under which the corporation does not recognize gain on the exchange of its shares for *T*'s assets. It is important to recognize, however, that without §351, gain would be recognized by *T* under §§61(a) and 1001(c). One must therefore look to the language of §351 to determine the circumstances in which gain is or is not recognized in the case of particular corporate formations.

Amalgamations. What happens if twenty people, all with assets used in their separate unincorporated businesses, decide to pool their assets and form a single firm, using the corporate form? Each contributes assets to the newly formed corporation and each receives in return a pro rata share of the common stock of the corporation. Now what do you think about the arguments in favor of nonrecognition? Under §351, would this be a nontaxable transaction?

Basis. Return to the initial facts, with one person, *T*, contributing to a corporation assets with a fair market value of $100,000 and a basis of $30,000. What must *T*'s basis be for her shares? If you have mastered the material in the earlier parts of this chapter, your instinct should be to suppose that *T*'s shares must take a substituted basis of $30,000. That is in fact the result dictated by the Code, in §358. The only plausible alternative would be a basis of $100,000. But if this were the rule, and if *T* had decided to sell her unincorporated business assets, she could instead incorporate and sell the shares of stock in the corporation and thereby avoid taxation on her gain.

What about the basis of the assets held by the corporation? Under §362(a) the basis is $30,000. Again, this rule is required in order to prevent tax avoidance. Suppose that the corporation's basis were $100,000. Now suppose that *T* had decided to sell her unincorporated business assets and reinvest the proceeds in a different kind of business, but that there was no nonrecognition provision (such as §1031) available that would allow her to escape tax on the gain. If the rule were that the corporation took a basis of $100,000 for the assets, she could transfer the assets to a corporation and have it sell them and reinvest in the new business, thereby escaping tax on the gain. That possibility is foreclosed by §362(a). But do §358 and §362(a), combined, go too far? What happens if *T* sells her shares and then the corporation sells the assets? What is the total amount of gain recognized? Does this seem right?

Transfer of property subject to debt. Suppose that *T*, as sole proprietor of the business, had borrowed $40,000 nonrecourse on the security of its assets and later transferred the assets, subject to the debt, to a corporation in return for its shares. We have previously seen that loan proceeds are not taxable, but that when debt is discharged gain may be

59. See also §721, which provides for nonrecognition in the case of contributions of property to partnerships.

recognized. See Chapter 2H. In the case of transfers to a corporation, a specific Code provision, §357(c), provides for recognition of gain to the extent that liabilities ($40,000) exceed basis ($30,000). *T* would recognize a gain of $10,000. Her basis for the shares would then be zero. See §358(a) and (d). The basis outcome accords with tax logic. *T* started out with a basis of $30,000; that was her investment for tax purposes. She previously received $40,000 as a loan and has put this money in her pocket, so she is ahead $10,000; that $10,000 was recognized when she transferred the assets to the corporation, but the addition to basis to which she is entitled by virtue of this recognition of gain ($10,000), plus the original basis ($30,000), must be assigned to the cash that she previously received ($40,000) and did not transfer to the corporation. See section on "boot" and basis, supra at page 327. So there is no basis left for the shares of stock of the corporation. By contrast, if she had transferred the $40,000 to the corporation, she would have that much less cash and her basis for her shares would be $40,000.

Contributions of services. Suppose that at the time she decides to incorporate, *T* decides to hire *M* to manage the business for her. Suppose further that *T* and *M* agree that *T* will contribute her assets to the corporation in return for seventy shares of common stock and *M* will serve as its manager and will receive thirty shares. What are the tax consequences to *T* and to *M*? How might *T* and *M* structure their arrangement so that *M* still winds up with 30 percent of the common shares but the tax effects are more favorable?

2. Reorganization

Changing the state of incorporation. Suppose that a corporation was initially formed in and under the laws of California but it has grown into a worldwide conglomerate and its directors have decided to shift the state of incorporation to Delaware. This cannot be done by simply writing to the authorities in each state and asking them to arrange for a transfer. In the eyes of the law, what must happen is that a new corporation must be organized under Delaware law, the assets or shares of the California corporation must be transferred to the new Delaware corporation, and the shareholders must receive shares of the Delaware corporation in exchange for their shares of the California corporation. The California corporation would probably be liquidated; it would then cease to exist. This is clearly a situation in which there should be a nonrecognition provision to relieve the shareholders from recognition of gain (and preclude recognition of loss); there is not a sufficient change in the nature of the investment to justify recognition. In fact there is, as one would expect, a nonrecognition provision. See §§354(a) and 368(a)(1)(F). Substituted basis is provided for both the shareholders and the corporation under §§358 and 362, the same provisions applying to §351 transfers.

Mergers and acquisitions (amalgamations). (a) Suppose that an individual, *A*, owns 100 shares of *X* Corp. stock, with a fair market value of $10,000 and a basis of $1,000, and another individual, *B*, owns 100 shares of *Y* Corp. stock, with a fair market value of $10,000 and a basis of $2,000. Now suppose that *A* and *B* decide to combine their investments, with each becoming an equal cotenant in the shares of each of the two corporations. That transaction would require the recognition of gain by each of the two individuals; no nonrecognition provision applies. *A* would be treated as having exchanged half her interest in *X* Corp., with a basis of $500 (for the half interest), for a half interest in *B*'s shares of *Y* Corp., worth $5,000 (for the half interest) and would recognize a gain of $4,500. *B*'s recognized gain would be $4,000.

(b) Suppose that the directors of two corporations, *X* and *Y*, with the approval of the shareholders, decide to merge them into a single corporation. This can be done in a number of ways. *X* can be merged into *Y* or vice versa; both can be merged into a newly formed corporation; shares can be exchanged for shares or assets can be exchanged for shares. No matter how it is done, if *A* and *B* receive shares of the new firm (or if one of them receives new shares and the other keeps her old shares), and if the appropriate formats have been adopted, the amalgamation can be achieved, under §354, with no recognition of gain to either *A* or *B*. This is true, moreover, even if one of the corporations is huge (a "whale") and the other is tiny (a "minnow").

(c) Can the results in the situations described in the two preceding paragraphs be reconciled according to any sound principle of tax policy? Nontax policy?

4

PERSONAL DEDUCTIONS, EXEMPTIONS, AND CREDITS

A. INTRODUCTION

1. The Mechanics of Personal Deductions

Personal deductions are subtracted from adjusted gross income to arrive at taxable income. Personal deductions include the assortment of "itemized" deductions described in this chapter: casualty losses, medical expenses, charitable donations, interest, and state and local taxes. Personal deductions also include alimony, described in the previous chapter. Individuals may elect to give up the itemized deductions (other than alimony) and instead claim the so-called standard deduction. The amount of the standard deduction varies with the status of the taxpayer. In 1993, single individuals who were not heads of households were eligible for a standard deduction of $3,700; married individuals who filed a joint return were eligible for a standard deduction of $6,200. §63(c)(2). The amount of the standard deduction is adjusted annually to reflect increases in the Consumer Price Index (CPI). §63(c)(4). In addition to itemizing or claiming the standard deduction, all taxpayers are entitled to a personal exemption deduction for themselves and for each of their dependents. §151. In 1993, the amount of the personal exemption was $2,350; that amount too is adjusted for annual increases in the CPI.

The benefits of the personal exemption are phased out as adjusted gross income rises above certain threshold amounts. For married individuals filing a joint return for the tax year 1993, personal exemptions are reduced by 2 percent for each $2,500 increment that adjusted gross income exceeds $162,700. Single taxpayers and heads of households face the same phaseout rule, though the threshold amounts are lower. The threshold amounts, too, are adjusted for increases in the CPI.

The benefits of itemized deductions are also reduced once adjusted gross income rises above a certain threshold amount. In 1993, that amount is $108,450. This threshold amount, too, is adjusted for increases in the CPI. Under §68, itemized deductions will be reduced by 3 percent of the excess of adjusted gross income over the threshold amount. Thus, an individual with an adjusted gross income of $158,450 will lose $1,500 of itemized deductions. (The excess of adjusted gross income over the threshold amount is $50,000; 3 percent of $50,000 is $1,500.) The loss cannot exceed 80 percent of the otherwise allowable itemized deductions and deductions allowable for medical care, casualty losses, and investment interest expense are not subject to the limitation.

To illustrate the mechanics of personal deductions, suppose that in 1993 Maria had an adjusted gross income of $50,000 and a single expense that could have been taken as an itemized deduction: state and local income and property taxes of $6,000. Suppose further that Maria was single and had no dependents. Maria could either have claimed the standard deduction (which was $3,700 in 1993) or deducted the $6,000 tax outlay as an itemized deduction. Obviously, she would have claimed the $6,000 itemized deduction. In addition, she would have taken the $2,350 personal exemption deduction for herself. Thus, her taxable income would have been $41,650.

For many low-income people, the standard deduction simplifies the taxpaying process and, together with the personal exemption, ensures that no tax will be imposed on income below a certain level.

2. The Role of the Personal Deduction

Personal deductions are those that have nothing to do with the production of income. They raise issues similar to the issues raised by certain exclusions, such as the exclusion of personal injury awards under §104(a)(2). See Chapter 2F. On the one hand, a deduction may be a proper allowance in arriving at a definition of income that accords with our sense of justice; it may be a proper refinement of the concept of income as a measure of ability to pay. On the other hand, a deduction may be intended not as a refinement of the concept of income so much as an express approval of, or encouragement to, particular kinds of expenditures, in which case the deduction can sensibly be analogized to a direct subsidy. The use of deductions as subsidies is often attacked on the ground that the subsidy rises as income rises, since a deduction is worth nothing to a poor person and more to a high-bracket person than to a low-bracket person. For this reason, certain personal deductions are sometimes labeled "upside-down" subsidies — subsidies that benefit most those who need them least.

One should be cautious, however, about embracing the notion of personal deductions (and exclusions, exemptions, and credits) as subsidies and the implicit argument that such deductions and exclusions, exemptions, and credits, are offensive to fairness, to economic rationality, and to simplicity. The argument may lead further than one might expect. A proponent of reform may begin with an attack on the personal deductions — for example, the deductions for interest on home mortgages, for individual state income and property taxes, for extraordinary medical expenses, and for charitable contributions. But then one is entitled to ask about such items as the deduction for alimony and the credit for child-care expenses. And what about business deductions and special investment credits (e.g., for investment in low-income housing)? Some proposals, though vaguely stated, seem to contemplate a tax on gross receipts, with no deduction for wages, rent, or even for the cost of goods sold, but short of that kind of radical change, many analysts would eliminate special depreciation deductions and all investment credits. There are long-standing arguments for taxing the interest on state and municipal bonds and employer contributions to qualified pension plans, and many tax experts are deeply concerned about imputed income from home ownership and unrealized appreciation.

The proponents of plans for base-broadening (i.e., for elimination of certain deductions, exemptions, exclusions, and credits) often have other objectives, sometimes explicit, sometimes hidden. Some reformers have seen the revenue generated by base-broadening as a means of reducing the tax burden on middle- and low-income individual taxpayers. Others have tied base-broadening to a reduction in top rates. The Tax Reform Act of 1986 combined base-broadening with a dramatic reduction in the top rates, a modest reduction in middle-income rates, and an increase in exemption levels that relieved many low-income people of the burden of paying any tax (though they had not been paying much anyway).

It is interesting and instructive to note that the Code has for a number of years contained a provision that imposes a flat-rate tax on a broader base — namely, the alternative minimum tax, in §55. See Graetz, The 1982 Minimum Tax Amendments as a First Step in the Transition to a "Flat-Rate" Tax, 56 S. Cal. L. Rev. 527 (1983) (suggesting the possibility of using this provision as a transition to a broad-based, low-rate flat tax). Section 55 is described infra at page 750.

B. CASUALTY LOSSES

We begin with the deduction under §165(c)(3) for losses from "fire, storm, shipwreck, or other casualty, or from theft." Since 1983, the deduction has been limited to losses that exceed in the aggregate, for the year, 10 percent of adjusted gross income, after reduction by a $100 "floor" for each individual loss. These limitations have substantially reduced litigation over this deduction. Many of the litigated cases involve marginal or far-fetched claims, or claims for the loss of luxury items, where the loss may arouse little, if any, sympathy. Still, casualty losses offer interesting insights to the problem of defining income and to the legislative process.

Imagine that a lawyer receives, from a client for whom he was able to obtain an acquittal in a narcotics case, a fee of $10,000, in cash, and that on the way home he is robbed of this amount. He will never have the opportunity to use the $10,000 for consumption. It is not available to pay taxes. A strong case can therefore be made for a deduction. Yet robberies are all too common. Perhaps the loss should be seen as part of the ordinary vicissitudes of life, part of the cost of living. These observations suggest a possible distinction between "casualties" and the day-to-day misfortunes that we must all learn to bear without tax relief.

DYER v. COMMISSIONER

20 T.C.M. 705 (1961)

On their income tax return for the year 1955, petitioners claimed a casualty loss deduction[1] of $100 for damages to a vase broken by their household pet, a Siamese cat. The vase was one of a pair given to Jean by her father prior to her marriage to petitioner and was bought by him in France. The vase was one of a matched pair, the pair having a value when acquired by petitioner of $250, and singly a value of $100 each. One of the vases was broken by petitioners' Siamese cat in the course of having its first fit. The cat had developed a neurosis and thereafter had other fits; within a month it was pronounced incurable by the veterinarian and had to be destroyed. Immediately after the accident the broken vase had no value at all. The broken vase was repaired at a cost of $33.49; the value of the two vases was then $133.49. The vases were insured under a comprehensive insurance policy covering loss from fire, theft, tornado, malicious mischief, etc., up to $200

1. [The taxpayer relied on §165(c)(3), which, at the time the case arose, permitted the deduction of the entire amount of the loss (but not more than the taxpayer's basis). — Eds.]

in value but the company refused to reimburse petitioners for any loss arising from damage to the vase. . . .

Manifestly, petitioners' loss was not from fire, storm, or shipwreck. They, of course, make no claim that it was. But was it a casualty loss at all? In construing the term "other casualty" the rule of ejusdem generis is applicable and in order that a loss may be deductible as a casualty loss it must appear that the casualty was of a similar character to a fire, storm, or a shipwreck. Of course, it goes without saying that it does not have to be exactly the same. The breakage of ordinary household equipment such as china or glassware through negligence of handling or by a family pet is not a "casualty loss" under section 165(c)(3) in our opinion. Petitioners do not question the soundness of the foregoing statement as a general proposition. In their brief they state as follows:

> Petitioners admit that breakage of the vase, if occasioned by its ordinary handling by their servant, or by their cat, would not entitle them to a casualty loss deduction. . . . But that was not the situation here. The breakage of the vase was not occasioned by the cat's ordinary perambulations on the top of the particular piece of furniture, but by its extraordinary behavior there in the course of having its first fit.

We are not persuaded that the distinction which petitioners endeavor to draw in the foregoing quotation from their brief is a sound one and it is, therefore, not sustained. Doubtless, petitioners' "kitty cat" was having its first fit as petitioner testified at the trial. We have no reason to doubt the truth of his testimony to that effect. We do not think, however, such fact would make the loss a "casualty loss" within the meaning of the applicable statute. . . .

[W]e hold in favor of respondent.

NOTES AND QUESTIONS

1. *The threshold of 10 percent of AGI.* The rule limiting deductions to those that exceed 10 percent of adjusted gross income has rid the courts of pesky little cases like this one. Indeed, the prior $100 threshold would have been enough to avoid this particular case. Are those thresholds enough to dispose of the "ordinary wear and tear" argument?

2. *Analysis of the case.* Was the decision in *Dyer* correct? What if the cat had recently been purchased for $1,000 and had been struck by lightning? run over by a car? died of heart failure? Do you think that a deduction is required by the statutory language in any of these situations? If the answer is yes to one or more and no to the others, is there any sensible policy justification for the difference in outcome?

3. *The "suddenness" requirement: termites, dry rot, and lost rings.* The Service has ruled that termite damage is not deductible because scientific data establishes that it does not occur "with the suddenness comparable to that caused by fire, storm, or shipwreck." Rev. Rul. 63-232, 1963-2 C.B. 97. Similarly, a deduction has been denied for damage due to dry rot. Hoppe v. Commissioner, 42 T.C. 820 (1964), aff'd, 354 F.2d 988 (9th Cir. 1965). The suddenness requirement has led to differing results in cases involving lost rings. In Stevens v. Commissioner, 6 T.C.M. 805 (1947), the taxpayer was duck hunting. While he was retrieving a decoy, his ring "slipped off his finger and dropped into muddy water several feet deep." The taxpayer recovered from his insurance company for part of the loss and claimed a casualty-loss deduction for the rest. The deduction was denied because there was no "intervention of any sudden or destructive force." In Keenan v. Bowers, 91 F. Supp. 771 (E.D.S.C. 1950), a husband and wife stayed at a motel one night. Before going to sleep the wife wrapped her diamond ring in a tissue and put it on the night stand. During the night the husband used tissues to blow his nose and in the morning gathered up all the tissues on the nightstand, including the one with the ring, and flushed them down the toilet. Held: no deduction; not sudden. In Carpenter v. Commissioner, 25 T.C.M. 1186 (1966), the wife put her diamond ring in a glass of water and ammonia for the purpose of cleaning it and placed the glass on the kitchen counter next to the sink. The husband, while washing the dishes, emptied the glass, with the ring, into the garbage disposal unit and turned it on. The ring was a total loss. Held: deduction allowed. In White v. Commissioner, 48 T.C. 430 (1967), the wife's ring was lost when the husband slammed a car door on her hand. Held: deduction allowed. And, finally, in Kielts v. Commissioner, 42 T.C.M. 238 (1981), the wife lost her diamond ring with no help from her husband. It was simply found to be missing from its setting one day. There was evidence, however, that good care had been taken of the setting and that the loss had been the result of a "sudden, unexpected, destructive blow to the ring" — though not so violent as to have been noticed by the wife. Held: deduction allowed.

Is a deduction in any of these cases consistent with the language of the statute? with sound tax policy? It appears that Congress reacted to some concrete situations and failed to develop a rule reflecting general principles. What should those principles be? If you were responsible for drafting a new provision, how would it read? If insurance was reasonably available and the taxpayer failed to buy it, should the government provide relief through the tax system when a loss occurs? On the other hand, if insurance was not reasonably available, does that tell us something about the nature of the loss that should affect our attitude toward tax relief?

4. *Effect on insurance.* The availability of the deduction discourages the purchase of insurance. For a taxpayer in the 31 percent tax bracket, the government bears almost one-third of the burden of any deductible loss, but it does not pay any portion of the premium for insurance against the loss. To put that another way, the insurance premium buys coverage against all the loss, but where there is no insurance, taxes are reduced by virtue of the deduction and part of the loss is borne by the government, not by the taxpayer; thus, the insurance premium to some extent protects against a loss to the government. Note §165(h)(4)(e), under which deductions for losses covered by insurance are allowed only if a timely claim was filed.

BLACKMAN v. COMMISSIONER

88 T.C. 677 (1987)

Findings of Fact

. . . At the time of the filing of the petition in this case, the petitioner, Biltmore Blackman, resided in Billerica, Massachusetts. He and his wife filed their joint Federal income tax return for 1980 on April 28, 1981, with the Internal Revenue Service Center, Atlanta, Georgia.

The petitioner's employer transferred him from Baltimore, Maryland, to South Carolina. The petitioner relocated his wife and children to South Carolina. Mrs. Blackman was dissatisfied with South Carolina and returned, with the couple's five children, to Baltimore. During the 1980 Labor Day weekend, the petitioner returned to Baltimore, hoping to persuade his wife to give South Carolina another chance. When he arrived at his Baltimore home, he discovered that another man was living there with his wife. The neighbors told the petitioner that such man had been there on other occasions when the petitioner had been out of town on business.

On September 1, 1980, the petitioner returned to his former home to speak to his wife. However, Mrs. Blackman was having a party; her guests refused to leave despite the petitioner's request that they do so. He returned to the house several times, repeating his request, and emphasizing it by breaking windows. Mrs. Blackman's guests did not leave the house until about 3 A.M., September 2, 1980.

Later, on September 2, 1980, the petitioner again went to his former home. He wanted to ask his wife whether she wanted a divorce. They quarreled, and Mrs. Blackman left the house. After she left, the petitioner gathered some of Mrs. Blackman's clothes, put them on the stove, and set them on fire. The petitioner claims that he then "took pots of water to dowse the fire, put the fire totally out" and left the house. The fire spread, and the fire department was called. When the firefighters arrived, they found some of the clothing still on the stove. The house and its contents were destroyed.

The petitioner was arrested later that day and charged with one count of Setting Fire while Perpetrating a Crime, a violation of Md. Ann. Code art. 27, sec. 11 (Repl. vol. 1982), and one count of Destruction of Property (Malicious Mischief), a violation of Md. Ann. Code art. 27, sec. 111 (Repl. vol. 1982). The arson charge was based on the allegation that the petitioner "had set fire to and burned . . . [the house] while perpetrating the crime of Destruction of Property" and the malicious destruction charge was based on the allegation that he "did willfully and maliciously destroy, injure, deface and molest clothing, the property of" Mrs. Blackman. The petitioner pleaded not guilty to both charges. On November 5, 1980, by order of the District Court of Baltimore County, the arson charge was placed on the "stet" docket. The petitioner was ordered to serve 24 months unsupervised probation without verdict on the malicious destruction charge.

The petitioner filed a claim for the fire damage with his insurer, State Farm Fire & Casualty Co. of Baltimore, Maryland. The company refused to honor the claim due to the cause of the fire.

On his 1980 Federal income tax return, the petitioner deducted as a casualty loss $97,853 attributable to the destruction of his residence and its contents. In his notice of deficiency, the Commissioner disallowed the deduction. . . .

Opinion

The primary issue for our decision is whether the petitioner is allowed to deduct the loss resulting from the fire started by him. Section 165(a) allows a deduction for "any loss sustained during the taxable year and not compensated for by insurance or otherwise." Section 165(c)(3) provides, in pertinent part, that in the case of an individual, the deduction allowed in subsection (a) is to be limited to "losses of property not connected with a trade or business, if such losses arise from fire, storm, shipwreck, or other casualty, or from theft." The Commissioner concedes that the petitioner sustained a loss through fire. However, the Commissioner argues that the petitioner intentionally set the fire which destroyed his home in violation of Maryland's public policy, that allowing the deduction would frustrate that public policy, and that, therefore, under the doctrine of Commissioner v. Heininger, 320 U.S. 467 (1943), and subsequent cases, the petitioner is not entitled to a deduction for the damage caused by his fire.

Courts have traditionally disallowed business expense and casualty loss deductions under section 162 or 165 where national or state public policies would be frustrated by the consequences of allowing the deduction. Commissioner v. Heininger, supra. "[T]he test of non-deductibility always is the severity and immediacy of the frustration resulting from allowance of the deduction." Tank Truck Rentals v. Commissioner, 356 U.S. 30, 35 (1958). "From the cases, it is clear that the question of illegality to frustrate public policy is, in the last analysis, *one of degree, to be determined from the peculiar facts of each case.*" Fuller v. Commissioner, 213 F.2d 102, 106 (10th Cir. 1954), aff'g 20 T.C. 308 (1953); emphasis supplied. . . .

Conviction of a crime is not essential to a showing that the allowance of a deduction would frustrate public policy. . . .

Moreover, it is well settled that the negligence of the taxpayer is not a bar to the allowance of the casualty loss deduction. . . . On the other hand, gross negligence on the part of the taxpayer will bar a casualty loss deduction. . . . "Needless to say, the taxpayer may not knowingly or willfully sit back and allow himself to be damaged in his property or willfully damage the property himself." White v. Commissioner, 48 T.C. 430, 435 (1967).

In our judgment, the petitioner's conduct was grossly negligent, or worse. He admitted that he started the fire. He claims that he attempted to extinguish it by putting water on it. Yet, the firemen found clothing still on the stove, and there is no evidence to corroborate the petitioner's claim that he attempted to dowse the flame. The fact is that the fire spread to the entire house, and we have only vague and not very persuasive evidence concerning the petitioner's attempt to extinguish the fire. Once a person starts a fire, he has an obligation to make extraordinary efforts to be sure that the fire is safely extinguished. This petitioner has failed to demonstrate that he made such extraordinary efforts. The house fire was a foreseeable consequence of the setting of the clothes fire, and a consequence made more likely if the petitioner failed to take adequate precautions to prevent it. We hold that the petitioner's conduct was grossly negligent and that his grossly negligent conduct bars him from deducting the loss claimed by him under section 165(a) and (c)(3).

In addition, allowing the petitioner a deduction would severely and immediately frustrate the articulated public policy of Maryland against arson and burning. Maryland's policy is clearly expressed. Article 27, section 11, of the Maryland Annotated Code (Repl. vol. 1982), makes it a felony to burn a residence while perpetrating a crime. The petitioner admits that he set fire to his wife's clothes, and he has not denied that the residence burned as a result of the fire started by him. The petitioner was charged with violating that section, but that charge was placed on the "stet" docket. As we understand Maryland practice, such action merely postponed any action on the charge. . . . However, the mere fact that the petitioner was never brought to trial for burning the house does not foreclose a finding by this Court that the petitioner acted in violation of that policy. . . . We are mindful, also, that Maryland has an articulated public policy against domestic violence. We refuse to encourage couples to settle their disputes with fire. We hold that allowing a loss deduction, in this factual setting, would severely and immediately frustrate the articulated public policies of Maryland against arson and burning, and against domestic violence. . . .

The remaining issue concerns the addition, under section 6653(a), for negligence or intentional disregard of rules and regulations. The Commissioner argues that the petitioner is liable for the addition because he claimed a substantial deduction to which he was not entitled and that such a claim justifies imposing the addition. We cannot agree in this case. Under the circumstances of this case, it was not negligent for the petitioner to claim a deduction for his loss by fire. . . . Imposition of the addition is therefore not warranted in this case.

QUESTIONS

1. *Ordinary versus gross negligence.* Imagine that Carol was building a cabinet in the living room of her house, left a cigarette burning while she went to answer the telephone, and returned to find that the cabinet was burning. She ran to the kitchen, filled a bucket with water, and emptied the bucket of water on the fire. Satisfied in her own mind that the fire was out, she left the house. In fact, the fire had not been thoroughly extinguished and started up again. The house burned down and was not adequately insured. Carol had invested $100,000 in the house and recovered only $40,000 from her insurance company. Is her $60,000 loss deductible under §165(c)(3)? On the question of the role of negligence in casualty loss cases, how is her situation any different from that of Blackman? What if Carol had been smoking marijuana, rather than tobacco?

2. *Public policy.* Why is it that allowing Blackman a deduction would frustrate public policy? Suppose an arsonist sets fire to a house owned by someone else. The possibility of a casualty-loss deduction for the arsonist simply does not arise; the arsonist has no casualty loss. The arsonist will presumably be subject to whatever penalties are imposed by the state for arson. Blackman, in addition to whatever penalties are imposed on him under state law, will lose his tax deduction. Is that because we assume that, for Blackman, whatever criminal penalty is imposed by the state is inadequate to effectuate its policies? Then what about the arsonist who sets fire to someone else's house?

3. *Intentional conduct.* Before the clothes-burning incident, Blackman broke some windows in his house. Suppose the house had not caught fire and burned down. Would Blackman have been entitled to deduct the loss resulting from the broken windows?

C. EXTRAORDINARY MEDICAL EXPENSES

Medical expenses are deductible to the extent that they exceed 7.5 percent of adjusted gross income. §213(a). The 7.5 percent floor or threshold seems to reflect the same kind of effort to distinguish between extraordinary misfortunes and the ordinary vicissitudes of life that is reflected in the casualty-loss deduction. See supra page 476. The threshold also reduces the number of taxpayers who are required to figure out precisely how much they spent on medical care and the resources that the Service and the courts must devote to the process of verifying medical expense deductions.

Congress has not, however, been consistent in its treatment, on the one hand, of medical expenses incurred by individuals and, on the other hand, of medical benefits supplied by employers in the form of insurance premiums or payments or reimbursements of employee medical costs. The latter are excluded from income without any threshold. §§105(b), 106. This is equivalent to including the benefits in income and allowing a full deduction. Thus, "ordinary" medical expenses that are paid or reimbursed under an employer's plan are paid with before-tax dollars while the same expenses incurred directly by an individual must be paid with after-tax dollars. Can this distinction be defended as an effort to encourage people to insist on and participate in employer plans? On the ground that employers and their insurance carriers have an incentive to monitor claims and reject more outlandish claims? Or is it evidence that most people cannot comprehend that certain forms of noncash benefits are essentially the same as cash income? Or does this distinction just indicate the degree of power held by labor unions, employers, and group insurance providers?

Most of the legal issues concerning medical expenses relate to the question of what is "medical care" as it is defined in §213(e). The cases that follow raise some puzzling aspects of that question.

TAYLOR v. COMMISSIONER

54 T.C.M. 129 (1987)

. . . Due to a severe allergy, petitioner's doctor instructed him not to mow his lawn. Petitioner in 1982 paid a total of $178 to have his lawn mowed and claimed a medical expense deduction in that amount for lawn care.

. . . Petitioner contends that since his doctor had advised him not to mow his lawn, he is entitled to a deduction for amounts he paid someone else to do his lawn mowing. Respondent contends the amounts paid by petitioner for lawn mowing are nondeductible personal expenses under section 262 rather than section 213 medical expenses.

Except as otherwise specifically provided, section 262 disallows deductions for personal, living or family expenses. Section 213, however, specifically authorizes a deduction for medical care expenses paid during the taxable year which are not compensated for by insurance or otherwise. . . .

In this case, petitioner, bearing the burden of proof . . . must establish that the apparently personal expense of lawn care is a medical expense. Petitioner has cited no authority to support his position either in general or with respect to lawn care expenses specifically. Petitioner testified that due to a severe allergy his doctor had directed him not to perform lawn care activities but there was no showing why other family members could not undertake these activities or whether petitioner would have paid others to mow his lawn even absent his doctor's direction not to do so himself.

Doctor recommended activities have been held in a number of cases not to constitute deductible medical expenses where the expenses did not fall within the parameters of "medical care." For example, in Altman v. Commissioner, 53 T.C. 487 (1969), this Court held that the expense of playing golf was not a deductible medical expense even though this activity was recommended by the taxpayer's doctor as treatment for his emphysema and provided therapeutic benefits. On this record we conclude that petitioner has not carried his burden of proof with respect to the deduction of lawn care costs as a medical expense and is thus not entitled to include the $178 expended for lawn care in his medical expense deductions.

Decision will be entered for the respondent.

OCHS v. COMMISSIONER

195 F.2d 692 (2d Cir. 1952)

Before Augustus N. Hand, Chase and Frank, Circuit Judges.

Augustus N. Hand, Circuit Judge. . . .

The Tax Court made the following findings:

> During the taxable year petitioner was the husband of Helen H. Ochs. They had two children, Josephine age six and Jeanne age four.
>
> On December 10, 1943, a thyroidectomy was performed on petitioner's wife. A histological examination disclosed [cancer]. . . . During the taxable year [1946] the petitioner maintained his two children in day school during the first half of the year and in boarding school during the latter half of the year at a cost of [$1450]. Petitioner deducted this sum from his income for the year 1946 as a medical expense under [§213].
>
> During the taxable year . . . [efforts by Helen] to speak were painful, required much of her strength, and left her in a highly nervous state. . . . Petitioner and his wife consulted a reputable physician and were advised

by him that if the children were not separated from petitioner's wife she would not improve and her nervousness and irritation might cause a recurrence of the cancer. Petitioner continued to maintain his children in boarding school [until 1948] . . . having been advised that if there was no recurrence . . . during that time his wife could be considered as having recovered from the cancer.

During the taxable year petitioner's income was between $5,000 and $6,000. Petitioner's two children have not attended private school but have lived at home and attended public school since [1948]. . . .

In our opinion the expenses incurred by the taxpayer were nondeductible family expenses within the meaning of [§262] rather than medical expenses. Concededly the line between the two is a difficult one to draw, but this only reflects the fact that expenditures made on behalf of some members of a family unit frequently benefit others in the family as well. . . . If, for example, the husband had employed a governess for the children, or a cook, the wages he would have paid would not be deductible. Or, if the wife had died, and the children were sent to a boarding school, there would certainly be no basis for contending that such expenses were deductible. The examples given serve to illustrate that the expenses here were made necessary by the loss of the wife's services, and that the only reason for allowing them as a deduction is that the wife also received a benefit. We think it unlikely that Congress intended to transform family expenses into medical expenses for this reason. . . .

The decision is affirmed.

Frank, Circuit Judge (dissenting). . . .

The Commissioner, the Tax Court, and now my colleagues, are certain Congress did not intend relief for a man in this grave plight. The truth is, of course, no one knows what Congress would have said if it had been faced with these facts. The few paltry sentences of Congressional history for [§213] do not lend strong support — indeed any support at all — to a strict construction theory:

> This allowance is granted in consideration of the heavy tax burden that must be borne by industry during the existing emergency [1942] and of the desirability of maintaining the present high level of public health and morale. . . . The term "medical care" is broadly defined to include amounts paid for the diagnosis, cure, mitigation, treatment, or prevention of disease, or for the purpose of affecting any structure or function of the body. It is not intended, however, that a deduction should be allowed for any expense that is not incurred primarily for the prevention or alleviation of a physical or mental defect or illness.[2]

2. Sen. Rep. 1631, 77th Cong., 2d Sess. 95-96 (1942).

I think that Congress would have said that this man's expense fell within the category of "mitigation, treatment, or prevention of disease," and that it was for the "purpose of affecting [a] structure or function of the body." . . . The Commissioner seemingly admits that the deduction might be a medical expense if the wife were sent away from her children to a sanitarium for rest and quiet, but asserts that it never can be if, for the very same purpose, the children are sent away from the mother — even if a boarding-school for the children is cheaper than a sanitarium for the wife. "I cannot believe that Congress intended such a meaningless distinction. . . ."[3] The cure ought to be the doctor's business, not the Commissioner's. . . .

In the final analysis, the Commissioner, the Tax Court and my colleagues all seem to reject Mr. Ochs' plea because of the nightmarish spectacle of opening the floodgates to cases involving expense for cooks, governesses, baby-sitters, nourishing food, clothing, frigidaires, electric dish-washers — in short, allowances as medical expenses for everything "helpful to a convalescent housewife or to one who is nervous or weak from past illness." I, for one, trust the Commissioner to make short shrift of most such claims. The tests should be: Would the taxpayer, considering his income and his living standard, normally spend money in this way regardless of illness? Has he enjoyed such luxuries or services in the past? Did a competent physician prescribe this specific expense as an indispensable part of the treatment? Has the taxpayer followed the physician's advice in the most economical way possible? Are the so-called medical expenses over and above what the patient would have to pay anyway for his living expenses, i.e., room, board, etc.? Is the treatment closely geared to a particular condition and not just to the patient's general good health or well-being?

My colleagues . . . would classify the children's schooling here as a family expense, because, they say, it resulted from the loss of the wife's services. . . . The Tax Court specifically found that the children were sent away so they would not bother the wife, and not because there was no one to take care of them. Ochs' expenditures fit into the Congres-

3. The Commissioner has, in the past, shown more liberal tendencies in sanctioning somewhat unorthodox kinds of treatment as contemplated by the statute: He has allowed the deduction of fees paid to chiropractors and Christian Science practitioners. I.T. 3598, 1943 C.B. 157. He should not, in this context, lag behind the progress of the medical art. Especially in this case should the Commissioner realize the growing emphasis placed by medical practitioners upon peace of mind as a major factor in the recovery of patients from what were formerly thought to be entirely organic diseases. If the wife here had been recovering from a nervous breakdown, it could not be sensibly argued that the cure did not fit the disease. Are we ready now to discount the uncontroverted evidence of the doctor in this case that peace of mind and body (it takes not only mental but physical gymnastics to keep up with two children aged four and six) was essential to recovery from, and prevention of, a throat cancer?

[See Ring v. Commissioner, 23 T.C. 950 (1955) (disallowing cost of trip to shrine at Lourdes). — Eds.]

sional test for medical deductions because he was compelled to go to the expense of putting the children away primarily for the benefit of his sick wife. Expenses incurred solely because of the loss of the patient's services and not as a part of his cure are a different thing altogether. . . . I would limit the deductible expense to the care of the children at the times when they would otherwise be around the mother. . . .

Line-drawing may be difficult here as everywhere, but that is what courts are for. See Lavery v. Purssell, 399 Ch. D. 508, 517: ". . . courts of justice ought not to be puzzled by such old scholastic questions as to where a horse's tail begins and where it ceases. You are obliged to say, this is a horse's tail at some time."

NOTES AND QUESTIONS

1. *Causation.* (a) The expenditure in *Ochs* would not have been incurred but for the illness, which suggests that it should be deductible. It is equally true, however, that the expenditure would not have been incurred but for the children, which suggests that it should not be deductible. (Cf. W. Prosser, The Law of Torts 236 (4th ed. 1971): "In a philosophical sense, the consequences of an act go forward to eternity, and the causes back to the discovery of America and beyond.") Is it relevant to ask whether Mr. and Mrs. Ochs made a conscious decision to have children; in the language of torts, whether the children were "preventable"? What about the *Taylor* case? What were the significant necessary antecedents to the expense incurred in that case?

(b) In some cases, of course, a court may reject entirely the taxpayer's claimed causative link. In Jacobs v. Commissioner, 62 T.C. 813 (1974), the taxpayer claimed a deduction under §213 for the lawyer's fees and settlement costs for his divorce, claiming that his psychiatrist had recommended the divorce after the taxpayer had experienced severe depression and suicidal tendencies. The Tax Court concluded that the divorce would have been obtained regardless of the psychiatric problems and denied the deduction. The court distinguished Gerstacher v. Commissioner, 414 F.2d 448 (6th Cir. 1969), which allowed a deduction under §213 of legal fees for a commitment proceeding that was necessary in order to render medical treatment, on the ground that there the expenses would not have been incurred but for the illness.

2. *The language of the Code.* The claim for a deduction in *Ochs* may appeal strongly to one's sense of compassion or fairness, but how strong is the statutory basis for the deduction? Was the expenditure for the "cure, mitigation, treatment, or prevention of disease, or for the purpose of affecting any structure or function of the body"? §213(d)(1)(A). Or was it only for dealing with the consequences of disease? If you

interpret §213 to allow a deduction in *Ochs,* would a deduction also be allowed in *Taylor?*

3. *Statutory drafting.* How would you draft the language of a Code provision intended to ensure a deduction in a case like *Ochs?* Would you favor extending the deduction to expenses that would have been incurred by someone like Mr. Ochs in raising his children if Mrs. Ochs had died? If so, what about the child-rearing expenses of other single parents? What about a deduction for all expenses incurred as a result of any physical or mental impairment, illness, or disability, including additional living expenses? Would such a provision promote the goal of fairness? If your answer is yes, what does that imply as to societal obligations to people with an impairment, illness, or disability and no income?

4. *Drawing the line.* (a) Rev. Rul. 75-318, 1975-2 C.B. 88, holds that a taxpayer may deduct as a medical expense the excess of the cost of braille books and magazines, for his blind child, over the cost of regular printed editions. And Rev. Rul. 64-173, 1964-1 C.B. (Pt. 1) 121, allows a deduction for the cost of hiring a person to accompany the taxpayer's blind child while at school "for the purpose of guiding the child in walking throughout the school day." The rationale is that the purpose of the outlay is to "alleviate the child's physical defect of blindness." Has the Service had a change (addition) of heart since *Ochs?*

(b) Deductions have also been allowed for face-lifts (Rev. Rul. 76-332, 76-2 C.B. 81) and for electrolysis but not for tattoos and ear piercing (Rev. Rul. 82-111, 1982-1 C.B. 48).

(c) Outlays for elevators, swimming pools in one's house, etc., are currently deductible if they are necessitated by illness, though only to the extent that they do not add to the value of the house. Regs. §1.213-1(e)(1)(iii).

(d) Sometimes Congress discharges its lawmaking function by inserting into the legislative history of a current enactment language that purports to "clarify" existing law. The attraction of this approach is that it avoids the necessity of facing the difficult task of drafting appropriate language and of cluttering up the Code. The effect may also be to delegate lawmaking discretion to the Treasury. An example is reflected in the following excerpt from Rev. Rul. 87-106, 1987-2 C.B. 67:

> In S. Rep. No. 99-313, 99th Cong., 2d Sess. 59 (1986), 1986-3 (Vol. 3) C.B. 59, and 2 H.R. Rep. No. 99-841 (Conf. Rep.), 99th Cong., 2d Sess. II-22 (1986), 1986-3 (Vol. 4) C.B. 22, Congress expressed a desire to clarify that certain capital expenditures generally do not increase the value of a personal residence and thus generally are deductible in full as medical expenses. These expenditures are those made for removing structural barriers in a personal residence for the purpose of accommodating it to the handicapped condition of the taxpayer or the taxpayer's spouse or dependents who reside there.

The Internal Revenue Service has determined that expenditures for the following purposes generally do not increase the fair market value of a personal residence and thus generally are eligible in full for the medical expense deduction when made for the primary purpose of accommodating a personal residence to the handicapped condition of the taxpayer, the taxpayer's spouse, or dependents who reside there:

1. constructing entrance or exit ramps to the residence;
2. widening doorways at entrances or exits to the residence;
3. widening or otherwise modifying hallways and interior doorways;
4. installing railing, support bars, or other modifications to bathrooms;
5. lowering of or making other modifications to kitchen cabinets and equipment;
6. altering the location of or otherwise modifying electrical outlets and fixtures;
7. installing porch lifts and other forms of lifts (Generally, this does not include elevators, as they may add to the fair market value of the residence and any deduction would have to be decreased to that extent. See section 1.213-1(e)(1)(iii) of the regulations.);
8. modifying fire alarms, smoke detectors, and other warning systems;
9. modifying stairs;
10. adding handrails or grab bars whether or not in bathrooms;
11. modifying hardware on doors;
12. modifying areas in front of entrance and exit doorways; and
13. grading of ground to provide access to the residence.

The above list of expenditures is not exhaustive.

The first six items listed in this Ruling are taken almost verbatim from the Senate Report.

5. *Policy.* (a) It seems reasonable to suppose that a significant portion of total medical deductions is for expenses that tend to be incurred only by the affluent — for example, for private-duty nurses, private rooms at hospitals, outpatient psychiatric care, orthodonture, and a variety of other benefits that tend not to be covered by insurance and that middle- and low-income people tend to find they can do without. Should the line be drawn to deny deductions for such outlays?

(b) Consider the strength of each of the following policy rationales for deductions for extraordinary medical expenses and the implications of each for the scope of the deduction:

(i) Amounts spent for extraordinary medical expenses do not provide consumption in the ordinary sense and therefore are simply not part of income.

(ii) Individuals who pay their own medical costs relieve the government of an expense that it would otherwise be obliged to bear.

(iii) The deduction is a proper encouragement to people to take good care of themselves; it is a useful subsidy for medical care.

(iv) In many instances, an injury or illness stems from work (e.g., a professional athlete's bad knee) or interferes with the ability to work (e.g., a truck driver's bad back), so the cost of medical care should be regarded as a cost of producing income.

6. *Medical expenses attributable to misfeasance.* Reconsider the *Blackman* case, supra page 479. Suppose Blackman had been badly burned in the fire he had set and had incurred substantial medical expenses. Would he be allowed to deduct those expenses? Should he be allowed to deduct those expenses?

D. CHARITABLE CONTRIBUTIONS

1. Overview

The Code allows individuals to claim as itemized deductions any "charitable contribution . . . payment of which is made within the taxable year." §170(a)(1). The term "charitable contribution" is defined to be a "contribution or gift to or for the use of" certain enumerated eligible donees. §170(c). These include the United States and any political subdivisions of it or any of the states, organizations that are "organized and operated exclusively for religious, charitable, scientific, literary, or educational purposes," and certain other enumerated donees, including veterans organizations, fraternal-lodge organizations (but only if the gift is to be used for charitable purposes), and cemetery companies. In general, these organizations must operate on a nonprofit basis, and none of their profits can "inure to the benefit of any private shareholder or individual." Either by statute or regulation, these groups are disqualified if they engage in efforts to influence legislation (with certain exceptions) or intervene in any political campaign on behalf of any candidate for public office.

Section 170 limits allowable deductions for gifts made to churches, educational organizations, medical institutions, and certain publicly supported organizations, as listed in §170(b)(1), to 50 percent of the taxpayer's "contribution base" (which is generally adjusted gross income). In the case of contributions to other organizations, principally "private foundations," and gifts "for the use of" an organization, the allowable deductions are limited to 30 percent of adjusted gross income (but are reduced to the extent that 50 percent deductions exceed 20 percent of adjusted gross income). §170(b)(1)(B). The 30 percent limit also applies to most gifts of property whose sale would have resulted in the recognition of long-term capital gain. §170(b)(1)(C). (See further discussion of such gifts infra at page 491.) Some gifts of capital-gain property are subject to a 20 percent limit. §170(b)(1)(D). If the taxpayer makes gifts that exceed any of these limits, the excess may be carried over to the succeeding five years. See §§170(d), 170(b)(1)(B), 170(b)(1)(C)(ii), and 170(b)(1)(D)(ii).

Section 170(c) specifies the organizations that qualify as recipients of deductible contributions. However, the organization's own immunity from taxation on receipts from donors, from its investments, and from its activities is determined not by §170(c), but by §§501 et seq. For some organizations, the same characteristics that permit donors to deduct contributions also serve to confer tax exemption on the organization. Thus, the charitable, religious, and educational organizations that are described by §170(c)(2) also enjoy tax exemption by virtue of identical language in §501(c)(3). However, the overlap is far from complete. Many organizations that are tax exempt under §501 (e.g., pension plans, social welfare groups, foreign charities, labor unions, social clubs, chambers of commerce, etc.) do not meet the requirements of §170(c); conversely, but much less frequently, organizations (e.g., posts of war veterans and fraternal lodges) may be qualified donees under §170(c) without meeting all of the standards for tax exemption prescribed by §501. Section 527 provides separate and detailed rules for the tax treatment of political organizations, making them taxable on their income, but excluding from their income such items as political contributions, income from fund-raising events, etc.

If an organization engages in lobbying, it may lose its status as an organization to which tax-deductible contributions may be made, though it may remain exempt from taxation. See §§170(c)(2)(D), 501(c)(3), 501(h). Some organizations have coped with the prohibition on lobbying by setting up separate but related organizations that limit their activities to such matters as nonpartisan education or litigation.

When a taxpayer makes a gift of property whose sale would produce long-term capital gain, the amount allowed as a deduction is the full fair market value of the property. If, for example, a person owns shares of common stock with a fair market value of $10,000 and a basis of $1,000, has held them for the requisite holding period (one year for property acquired after 1987) and gives them to a charitable organization, no tax is paid on the gain and the deduction is for the full $10,000 value. Obviously, then, the gift of the property itself is more advantageous than the sale of the property followed by a gift of the proceeds. In the case of a gift of property whose sale would produce short-term capital gain or ordinary income, the deduction is limited to the taxpayer's basis in the property; there is also a limit on the deductibility of the value of tangible personal property (e.g., a painting, except when given to certain kinds of organizations). §170(e)(1).

One of the major problems with charitable contributions has been the overvaluation of works of art. A good illustration is provided by the case of Isbell v. Commissioner, 44 T.C.M. 1143 (1982). The taxpayer contributed to a public television station, for its annual fund-raising auction, a Han dynasty jar with a crack on one side and a hole in its bottom (made for the purpose of converting the jar to a lamp). Isbell had received the jar as a gift. Initially he claimed a deduction of $15,000 and later, in an amended return, raised this to $50,000, based on an appraisal of all his valuables, done at his request two years before the gift, by a firm that appraised interior furnishings, that had no experience in appraising Asian art objects, whose representatives were not called as witnesses, and whose appraisal was "incorrect in several respects." The jar sold at the auction for $360. A "very impressive" expert who testified for the government placed the value at $800, which the court accepted as the fair market value. The amount of the deduction was further reduced under §170(e)(1)(B). It does not appear that the Service sought to impose fraud or negligence penalties. In response to the abuse and the enforcement difficulties suggested by this case, the Tax Reform Act of 1984 imposed a requirement that the Treasury issue regulations for substantiation of the amount of the deduction in the case of gifts of property with a value greater than $5,000 (or $10,000 in the case of nonpublicly traded stock). See §155 of the act, which was not made part of the Code. Substantiation is not required, however, for publicly traded stock. To meet the substantiation requirement, the donor must obtain a qualified appraisal and attach to his or her return a signed appraisal summary. The appraisal must come from an independent person, not, for example, the seller of the property or any person regularly employed by the seller. If the donee sells the property within two years of receipt, it must report the selling price and identify the donor.

In response to more garden variety forms of noncompliance, Congress added further substantiation provisions as part of the Revenue Reconciliation Act of 1993. Under those provisions, taxpayers who claim a deduction for any form of contribution in excess of $250 must be able to substantiate the deduction with a written acknowledgement of the donation by the donee organization. The acknowledgement must state the fair market value, if any, of any services or goods provided by the organization in return for the donation. §170(f).

For a sense of the revenue impact of the deduction for charitable contributions, see the tax expenditure budget figures, supra at page 24.

2. Policy

Review the list of possible objectives of the deduction for medical expenses, Note 5, supra page 489. Which of these objectives — or some other objective — best supports the deduction for charitable contributions? In answering this question, it may be helpful to refer to four kinds of contributions.

1. A contribution to a charity such as the United Fund, the Red Cross, the American Cancer Society, or the Boy Scouts
2. An ordinary contribution to a church or other religious organization
3. A contribution to a church by a person who feels bound by a religiously based obligation to tithe, where the person genuinely believes that 10 percent of one's income belongs not to oneself but to God
4. A contribution to New York's Metropolitan Opera by a wealthy opera lover

In Regan v. Taxation With Representation of Washington, 461 U.S. 540 (1983), the Court responded to the taxpayer's argument that the prohibition on lobbying violated its first amendment rights by asserting that the first amendment does not require Congress to grant a subsidy to lobbying. The Court treated as self-evident its assertion, "Both tax exemptions and tax-deductibility are a form of subsidy that is administered through the tax system. A tax exemption has much the same effect as a cash grant to the organization of the amount of tax it would have to pay on its income." Do you agree with the quoted statement? If so, can you defend the inclusion of religious organizations in §§170(c)(2)(B) and 501(c)(3)? See Walz v. Tax Commissioner of the City of New York, 397 U.S. 664 (1969), holding that a tax exemption for the real property of churches does not violate the first amendment. And what about Mueller v. Allen, 463 U.S. 388 (1983), upholding the allowance under Minnesota's income tax law of a deduction for tuition, textbooks, and transportation costs incurred in sending children to schools (including, but not limited to, private and parochial schools)?

Suppose we take as given the desirability of government support for the type of organizations listed in §170(c). Is a tax deduction for charitable gifts a cost effective way to support those organizations? The charitable deduction reduces tax revenues by well over fifteen billion dollars a year. See supra pages 26-27. Does the deduction stimulate charitable giving? Or is the deduction just a (deserved?) windfall to those who would give (and give the same amount) anyway? One way to answer these questions is to look at how charitable giving changes as tax rates change. A decline in the marginal tax rates of donors reduces the value of the tax deduction. If the tax deduction is an important factor in charitable giving, then donations should decline with falling marginal rates. Conversely, donations should rise as marginal rates rise, as the deduction becomes more valuable. Economists who have studied the issue have generally concluded that the "dollar efficiency" of the deduction is quite high. Deductions stimulate donations, and most studies find the dollar gain to the supported organizations equals and in some cases exceeds the dollar loss to the fisc. See Auten, Cilke, & Randolph, The Effects of Tax Reform on Charitable Contributions,

XLV National Tax Journal 266 (1993); Choe & Jeong, Charitable Contributions by Low and Middle-Income Taxpayers: Further Evidence with a New Method, XLV National Tax Journal 33 (1993); Fullerton & Goodman, The Economic Recovery Tax Act of 1981: Implications for Charitable Giving, 16 Tax Notes 1027 (1982).

3. Gifts with Private Objectives or Benefits

OTTAWA SILICA CO. v. UNITED STATES

699 F.2d 1124 (Fed. Cir. 1983)

[The taxpayer, Ottawa, was in the business of mining, processing, and marketing silica, also known as quartzite. Beginning in 1956 the taxpayer acquired various ranch properties in Oceanside, California, a town located on the ocean, north of San Diego, with a major U.S. Marine Corps base, Camp Pendleton, on its northern border. Initially Ottawa acquired properties for their quartzite deposits; those deposits were found only on a portion of the land, and the rest was of relatively little interest to Ottawa. Before many years had passed, however, it became apparent that the land would ultimately be valuable for residential or commercial development. Silica mining is a dirty process that cannot be carried on close to residential areas, so Ottawa was in no hurry with the development, but in 1965 it hired William L. Pereira & Associates to produce a plan for the use of the properties that Ottawa had acquired. On the recommendation of Pereira, Ottawa bought two additional ranches (the Jones and Talone ranches) for the purpose of permitting it to maximize its land development opportunities; these ranches contained no quartzite deposits.

In the mid-1960s it became apparent that a new high school would be needed for the school district that included Oceanside and its neighbor to the south, Carlsbad. The Oceanside-Carlsbad Union High School District (OCUHSD), after a survey of possible sites, asked Ottawa whether it would be willing to donate to it about fifty acres on a portion of its property known as the Freeman Ranch. It was plain that if the OCUHSD did build the high school on the taxpayer's site, it would be required to build access roads that would be of benefit to Ottawa. In 1970, after long negotiations, Ottawa contributed the fifty-acre site, plus twenty acres for right-of-way for two access roads, to OCUHSD, and claimed a deduction of $415,000 for the value of the property contributed. It was conceded that OCUHSD was a political subdivision of the State of California within the meaning of §170(c)(1). The government argued that no deduction was allowable because Ottawa had received a substantial benefit from the transfer of the property. The court of appeals agreed, affirming per curiam the Claims Court decision on the basis of the opinion of Judge Colaianni. Portions of that opinion follow.]

The case law dealing with this aspect of a §170 deduction makes clear that a contribution made to a charity is not made for exclusively public purposes if the donor receives, or anticipates receiving a substantial benefit in return. . . .

In Singer [Co. v. United States, 196 Ct. Cl. 90, 449 F.2d 413 (1972)], this court considered whether discount sales of sewing machines to schools and other charities entitled Singer to a charitable deduction. The court found that Singer, which at the time of the sales was in the business of selling sewing machines, had made the discount sales to the schools for the predominant purpose of encouraging the students to use and, in the future, to purchase its sewing machines, thereby increasing Singer's future sales. This purpose colored the discount sales, making them business transactions rather than charitable contributions. Accordingly, the court disallowed the deduction for the sales to the schools. The court allowed deductions for the discount sales made to other charities, however, because Singer had no expectation of increasing its sales by making the contributions and benefited only incidentally from them.

The *Singer* court noted that the receipt of benefits by the donor need not always preclude a charitable contribution. The court stated its reasoning as follows:

> [I]f the benefits received, or expected to be received, [by the donor] are substantial, and meaning by that, benefits greater than those that inure to the general public from transfers for charitable purposes (which benefits are merely *incidental* to the transfer), then in such case we feel that the transferor has received, or expects to receive, a quid pro quo sufficient to remove the transfer from the realm of deductibility under section 170.

Singer Co. v. United States, 196 Ct. Cl. at 106, 449 F.2d 423. The parties to the present case disagree as to the meaning of the above quotation. The plain language clearly indicates that a "substantial benefit" received in return for a contribution constitutes a quid pro quo, which precludes a deduction. The court defined a substantial benefit as one that is "greater than those that inure to the general public from transfers for charitable purposes." Id. at 106, 449 F.2d at 423. Those benefits that inure to the general public from charitable contributions are incidental to the contribution, and the donor, as a member of the general public, may receive them. It is only when the donor receives or expects to receive additional substantial benefits that courts are likely to conclude that a quid pro quo for the transfer exists and that the donor is therefore not entitled to a charitable deduction. . . .

Plaintiff argues that it received no benefits, except incidental ones as defined by *Singer,* in return for its contribution of the site, and it is therefore entitled to a §170 deduction for the transfer of its land to the school district. After having considered the testimony and the evidence adduced at trial, I conclude that the benefits to be derived by plaintiff from the transfer were substantial enough to provide plaintiff with a quid pro quo for the transfer and thus effectively destroyed the charitable nature of the transfer.

To begin, although plaintiff is correct in arguing that it was not the moving party in this conveyance, and that the school district sought plaintiff out for a donation of a high school site, that alone fails to justify a §170 deduction. The record clearly establishes that following the passage of a bonding referendum, which authorized the building of a new high school by the city of Oceanside in 1968, as many as nine sites had been evaluated. Because of the eastward growth of the city, Mr. LaFleur, the superintendent of the OCUHSD, felt that the ideal location for the new high school would be near El Camino Real [the road on the western boundary of plaintiff's property]. Following careful consideration, the city and school district decided that the best location for a high school would be on plaintiff's land. Thus, during the summer of 1968, John Steiger, the vice-mayor of Oceanside, and Mr. LaFleur approached Mr. Thomas Jones to see if plaintiff would consider making a site on the Freeman Ranch available for the new high school.

On September 20, 1968, Mr. LaFleur wrote to plaintiff's president, Mr. Thornton, to ask if plaintiff would be willing to donate 50 acres of its land for a school site. The record also establishes, however, that plaintiff was more than willing to oblige Mr. LaFleur on the basis of its own self-interest. Indeed, the evidence shows that on that same September 20, Mr. Jones also wrote to Mr. Thornton to advise him of the discussions he had participated in regarding a high school site. In his letter Mr. Jones stated that he had met with John Steiger and Larry Bagley, Oceanside's planning director, and had learned that the school district's first choice for a high school site was on land owned by plaintiff. In a most revealing statement, Mr. Jones went on to say:

> I was pessimistic when talking to John and Larry, but this actually could trigger and hasten the development of the whole eastern end of [the] Freeman and Jones [ranches] at no cost to us. The increase in these property values should be substantial if this should go through. . . . In any event, nothing more is to be done on this until the school board writes to you and asks to open negotiations. On the other hand, I recommend that [Ottawa] actively pursue this, since a high school in this location would probably trigger the early development of El Camino Real from the May Co. to Mission Road.

The exact meaning of Mr. Jones' statement will be better understood following a full development of the prevailing circumstances at the time of the transfer. It should be recalled that plaintiff had amassed some 2,300 acres in eastern Oceanside, but only 481 acres had silica reserves. . . . While a portion of the western boundary of the Freeman

Ranch ran along El Camino Real, its northernmost boundary was about a mile from all of the major roads. The unavailability of major roads to service the northernmost reaches of the Cubbison and Freeman Ranches ultimately led Pereira to recommend that plaintiff purchase the Jones and Talone Ranches. . . .

The only thing frustrating the implementation of the plan was the inaccessibility of the Jones Ranch from Mission Boulevard. . . .

The construction of a high school on the Freeman Ranch, however, alleviated this problem for plaintiff. State and local officials required that the high school be serviced by two separate access roads. After some discussions, the school district and plaintiff agreed on the general direction of Mesa Drive which would provide the school with access to El Camino Real, and the surrounding topography dictated that the second road run north to Mission Boulevard through the Jones Ranch and parcels of property owned by Mr. Ivey and the Mission of San Luis Rey. This road, Rancho Del Oro Drive, provided plaintiff with access to the Jones Ranch directly from Mission Boulevard. Plaintiff could not have obtained such access to Mission Boulevard on its own unless both Mr. Ivey and the fathers at the mission had agreed to convey part of their land or easements to plaintiff. There is no evidence suggesting that either party was interested in doing so. Mr. Ivey, in fact, had resisted plaintiff's overtures about selling or developing his land. . . .

It is thus quite apparent that plaintiff conveyed the land to the school fully expecting that as a consequence of the construction of public access roads through its property it would receive substantial benefits in return. In fact, this is precisely what happened. Plaintiff obtained direct access to the Jones Ranch via Rancho Del Oro Drive and ultimately sold the ranch to a developer. Plaintiff also sold two parcels of the Freeman Ranch, lying north of Mesa Drive, to other developers. . . . It is my opinion that the plaintiff knew that the construction of a school and the attendant roads on its property would substantially benefit the surrounding land, that it made the conveyance expecting its remaining property to increase in value, and that the expected receipt of these benefits at least partially prompted plaintiff to make the conveyance. Under *Singer,* this is more than adequate reason to deny plaintiff a charitable contribution for its conveyance.

NOTES AND QUESTIONS

1. *What's at stake in* Ottawa Silica Co.? Had the taxpayer won, it would have recognized a current deduction equal to the fair market value of the contributed property. Instead, the taxpayer received no current deduction and could only add the basis of the contributed property to its other land. See discussion of capital expenditures in Chapter 6, infra. The taxpayer would, in effect, be able to deduct that basis when and if

it sold its other land. The effect of the government victory was twofold. First, the taxpayer was forced to defer any tax benefit for what might turn out to be many years. Second, the eventual tax benefit would be limited to the basis of the contributed property, rather than the fair market value of the contributed property.

2. *Gifts with nonbusiness-related benefits.* (a) *The law.* The issue of private benefit comes up most commonly in the context of individual donors and nonbusiness related benefits. Consider, for example, an individual who pays $100 to attend a benefit dinner or concert sponsored by an organization described in §170(c), such as an educational institution. Is the entire $100 deductible as a charitable contribution? Or must the deduction be reduced to reflect the value of the dinner or concert? The law is plain: To the extent that the taxpayer receives something of value, there is no deduction. The taxpayer can therefore deduct only the excess of the amount paid over the fair market value of the dinner or concert. See Rev. Rul. 67-246, 1967-2 C.B. 104. In practice, of course, one suspects that the full price of the event is often deducted.

(b) *The complicitous role of some charitable organizations.* The problem of disentangling individual benefit from charitable donation is exacerbated by the tendency of many §170(c) organizations to adopt fee structures that blur the distinction between donations and the costs of services. As a result, individuals deduct amounts that might be more accurately described as nondeductible fees for services. Consider, for example, the fee structure at one west coast opera company. The nominal cost of a "Series A" box seat is $1,585. However, such seats are available only after a major donation. The amount of donation that will secure such a box is said to be $20,000 — down from $100,000 in the more prosperous 1980s. In addition, holders of Series A boxes are requested to make a "minimum contribution" of $4,500 a year. It is virtually certain that holders of Series A seats deduct the major donation necessary to get the seats and the annual minimum contribution associated with the seats. Suppose, instead, that the opera company charged (continued to charge?) what the market would bear for the seats but did not tie the seats to donations or term any of the amount paid as a donation. It would then be clear that no portion of the ticket price could be deducted. The after-tax cost of the seats would rise. This would disadvantage ticket holders. It would also make it harder to sell seats and, in that sense, disadvantage the opera company. (Indeed, the most likely result is that the opera company would have to reduce the price of the seats.)

(c) *The new substantiation and disclosure rules.* Some of the results referred to above may be altered by the substantiation and disclosure provisions of the Revenue Reconciliation Act of 1993. As noted supra, p. 492, under the sutstantiation rules, a taxpayer who wishes to itemize a charitable contribution in excess of $250 must substantiate the contribution with written acknowledgement from the donee organization. The acknowledgement must include a good faith estimate of the value of goods or services provided by the organization to the donor. In the case of any "quid pro quo contribution" in excess of $75, the 1993 Act also imposes an additional disclosure requirement on the donee organization. A quid pro quo contribution is defined under newly amended §6115 as a payment made partly as a contribution and partly in consideration for goods or services provided by the donee organization. An organization receiving such a contribution must provide the donee with a written statement that informs the donor that the amount of the contribution is limited to the excess of payment over the value of goods or services received. The organization must also provide the donee with a good faith estimate of the value of such goods and services. Thus, the onus is now on the charitable organizations to alert donors to the value of services or goods received in connection with any donation.

3. *The special case of collegiate athletics.* In Rev. Rul. 86-63, 86-1 C.B. 88, the IRS ruled on the politically sensitive issue of deductions for contributions to the athletic scholarship programs of colleges and universities, where the contributor becomes entitled to buy tickets for seating at athletic events. The holding, relying on Rev. Rul. 67-246, supra, was that where reasonably comparable seating would not have been available in the absence of the contribution, there is a presumption that the contribution was the price of a substantial benefit to the taxpayer and no deduction is allowable unless the taxpayer can establish that the amount of the contribution exceeded the value of the benefit received. After considerable whining by universities and the supporters of their athletic (and other) programs, Congress, in 1988, adopted §170(m). This provision allows a deduction for 80 percent of any amount paid to an "institution of higher learning" if the deduction would be allowable "but for the fact that the taxpayer receives (directly or indirectly) as a result of paying such amount the right to purchase tickets for seating at an athletic event in an athletic stadium of such institution." Why are athletic events treated differently from, say, musical or dramatic performances?

4. *Religious benefits and services.* Rev. Rul. 70-47, 1970-1 C.B. 49, states that "pew rents, building fund assessments, and periodic dues paid to a church . . . are all methods of making contributions to the church, and such payments are deductible as charitable contributions within the limitations set out in section 170 of the Code." Similarly, the IRS has never challenged the deductibility of specified amounts required to be paid for attendance at Jewish High Holy Day services. On the other hand, fees for attendance at parochial schools providing mostly secular education are not deductible.

In Hernandez v. Commissioner, 490 U.S. 680 (1989), the Supreme Court upheld the Commissioner's disallowance of a deduction for amounts paid by members of the Church of Scientology for individual "training" (learning of doctrine) and "auditing" (development of "spiritual awareness"). The amounts to be paid were determined by a schedule of prices based on the length of the sessions and their level of "sophistication." A central tenet of the Church was the "doctrine of exchange," under which a person receiving something must pay something in return. Free auditing or training sessions were "categorically barred." For the purposes of the case, the IRS stipulated that the Church was a bona fide religious organization, contributions to which were deductible. The IRS's argument was that the fees at issue were not "contributions." The majority concluded, "As the Tax Court found, these payments were part of a quintessential quid pro quo exchange: in return for their money, petitioners received an identifiable benefit, namely, auditing and training sessions." In reaching this result, the majority rejected the taxpayers' argument that the receipt of consideration in the form of religious or spiritual services is not inconsistent with the notion of gift or contribution. Justice O'Connor, in a dissent joined by Justice Scalia, argued that the disallowance of the deductions was inconsistent with the IRS's "70-year practice of allowing [deduction of] fixed payments indistinguishable from those made by petitioners." The majority attempted to avoid this argument by stating that the record was unclear on the precise facts in the allegedly similar situations — "for example, whether payments for other faiths' services are truly obligatory or whether any or all of these services are generally provided whether or not the encouraged 'mandatory' payment is made."

The question elided by the Court in *Hernandez* — whether Scientology's payment structure is distinguishable from the payment structures of more mainstream religions — was raised in a slightly different context in Powell v. United States, 945 F.2d 374 (11th Cir. 1991). The plaintiff in that case alleged that the IRS practice was invalid as an inconsistent application of the statute and a violation of the Establishment Clause of the First Amendment. The plaintiff's complaint was dismissed by the trial court for failure to state a claim. The Court of Appeals for the Eleventh Circuit vacated that dismissal.

The issue in *Powell* and the application of *Hernandez* to the Church of Scientology were rendered moot by a turnabout in the government's position on the matter. In Rev. Rul. 93-72, the government declared obsolete a prior ruling under which it had held that payments made in return for auditing and other services provided by the Church of Scientology were not deductible as charitable contributions. Rev. Rul. 93-73, 1993-34 I.R.B. 7; Rev. Rul. 78-189, 1978-1 C.B. 68.

5. *Voluntariness.* In Lombardo v. Commissioner, 50 T.C.M. 1374 (1985), the taxpayer pleaded guilty to a state-law charge of felonious sale and delivery of marijuana. Incident to the taxpayer's arrest, the police seized fourteen tons of marijuana, $148,000 in cash, the land (with improvements) on which he was operating, and various other

property. The taxpayer was placed on probation and was able to stay out of prison under an order that required him to pay $145,000 to the county school fund. He made the required payments, over two years, and claimed charitable deductions. His tax returns for the years at issue (during which he was on probation) showed income from "Business or Profession," without elaboration; in response to a question on the return about the nature of his business, he relied on the fifth amendment. The Tax Court upheld the Commissioner's denial of the charitable deduction. It observed that the taxpayer made the payments in order to avoid going to prison and stated, "It would strain our credulity to the breaking point to conclude that petitioner's contributions proceeded even remotely from a charitable impulse." The court viewed as irrelevant the possibility that the state court might have exceeded its authority by requiring a payment of $145,000 for violation of a statute with a maximum fine of $5,000.

6. *Psychic returns.* If an individual contributes money to a university in return for the university's agreement to name a building after him or her, it is plain that the contribution is deductible despite the quid pro quo. How can this result be reconciled with the law as described above?

4. What Is Charitable?

BOB JONES UNIVERSITY v. UNITED STATES

461 U.S. 574 (1983)

Chief Justice BURGER delivered the opinion of the Court.

We granted certiorari to decide whether petitioners, nonprofit private schools that prescribe and enforce racially discriminatory admissions standards on the basis of religious doctrine, qualify as tax-exempt organizations under §501(c)(3) of the Internal Revenue Code of 1954.

I . . .

Bob Jones University is a nonprofit corporation located in Greenville, South Carolina. Its purpose is "to conduct an institution of learning . . . , giving special emphasis to the Christian religion and the ethics revealed in the Holy Scriptures." . . . The corporation operates a school with an enrollment of approximately 5,000 students, from kindergarten through college and graduate school. Bob Jones University is not affiliated with any religious denomination, but is dedicated to the teaching and propagation of its fundamentalist Christian religious beliefs. It is both a religious and educational institution. Its teachers are required to be devout Christians, and all courses at the University are taught according to the Bible. Entering students are screened as to their religious beliefs, and their public and private conduct is strictly regulated by standards promulgated by University authorities.

The sponsors of the University genuinely believe that the Bible forbids interracial dating and marriage. To effectuate these views, Negroes were completely excluded until 1971. From 1971 to May 1975, the University accepted no applications from unmarried Negroes, but did accept applications from Negroes married within their race.

Following the decision of the United States Court of Appeals for the Fourth Circuit in McCrary v. Runyon, 515 F.2d 1082 (C.A. 4 1975), aff'd 427 U.S. 160 (1976), prohibiting racial exclusion from private schools, the University revised its policy. Since May 29, 1975, the University has permitted unmarried Negroes to enroll; but a disciplinary rule prohibits interracial dating and marriage. That rule reads:

There is to be no interracial dating

1. Students who are partners in an interracial marriage will be expelled.
2. Students who are members of or affiliated with any group or organization which holds as one of its goals or advocates interracial marriage will be expelled.
3. Students who date outside their own race will be expelled.
4. Students who espouse, promote, or encourage others to violate the University's dating rules and regulations will be expelled.

The University continues to deny admission to applicants engaged in an interracial marriage or known to advocate interracial marriage or dating.

Until 1970, the IRS extended tax-exempt status to Bob Jones University under §501(c)(3). By the letter of November 30, 1970, that followed the injunction issued in Green v. Kennedy [309 F. Supp. 1127 (D.D.C.), app. dismissed sub nom. Cannon v. Green, 398 U.S. 956 (1970)] the IRS formally notified the University of the change in IRS policy, and announced its intention to challenge the tax-exempt status of private schools practicing racial discrimination in their admissions policies.[4]

The United States District Court for the District of South Carolina held that revocation of the University's tax-exempt status exceeded the

4. Revenue Ruling 71-447, 1971-2 Cum. Bull. 230, defined "racially nondiscriminatory policy as to students" as meaning that:

> [T]he school admits the students of any race to all the rights, privileges, programs, and activities generally accorded or made available to students at that school and that the school does not discriminate on the basis of race in administration of its educational policies, admissions policies, scholarship and loan programs, and athletic and other school-administered programs.

delegated powers of the IRS, was improper under the IRS rulings and procedures, and violated the University's rights under the Religion Clauses of the First Amendment. 468 F. Supp. 890, 907 (D.S.C. 1978). . . .

The Court of Appeals for the Fourth Circuit, in a divided opinion, reversed, 639 F.2d 147 (C.A. 4 1980). Citing Green v. Connally, supra, with approval, the Court of Appeals concluded that §501(c)(3) must be read against the background of charitable trust law. To be eligible for an exemption under that section, an institution must be "charitable" in the common law sense, and therefore must not be contrary to public policy. In the court's view, Bob Jones University did not meet this requirement, since its "racial policies violated the clearly defined public policy, rooted in our Constitution, condemning racial discrimination and, more specifically, the government policy against subsidizing racial discrimination in education, public or private." Id., at 151. The court held that the IRS acted within its statutory authority in revoking the University's tax-exempt status. Finally, the Court of Appeals rejected petitioner's arguments that the revocation of the tax exemption violated the Free Exercise and Establishment Clauses of the First Amendment. The case was remanded to the District Court with instructions to dismiss the University's claim for a refund and to reinstate the Government's counter-claim. . . .

Goldsboro Christian Schools is a nonprofit corporation located in Goldsboro, North Carolina. Like Bob Jones University, it was established "to conduct an institution of learning . . . , giving special emphasis to the Christian religion and the ethics revealed in the Holy scriptures." . . . The school offers classes from kindergarten through high school, and since at least 1969 has satisfied the State of North Carolina's requirements for secular education in private schools. The school requires its high school students to take Bible-related courses, and begins each class with prayer.

Since its incorporation in 1963, Goldsboro Christian Schools has maintained a racially discriminatory admissions policy based upon its interpretation of the Bible.[5] Goldsboro has for the most part accepted only Caucasians. On occasion, however, the school has accepted children from racially mixed marriages in which one of the parents is Caucasian.

[A district court decision in favor of the government's denial of exemption was affirmed by the Fourth Circuit on the authority of *Bob Jones University*.][6]

5. According to the interpretation espoused by Goldsboro, race is determined by descendance from one of Noah's three sons — Ham, Shem and Japheth. Based on this interpretation, Orientals and Negroes are Hamitic, Hebrews are Shemitic, and Caucasians are Japhethitic. Cultural or biological mixing of the races is regarded as a violation of God's command. . . .

6. After the Court granted certiorari, the Government filed a motion to dismiss, informing the Court that the Department of Treasury intended to revoke Revenue Ruling

II

In Revenue Ruling 71-447, the IRS formalized the policy first announced in 1970, that §170 and §501(c)(3) embrace the common law "charity" concept. Under that view, to qualify for a tax exemption pursuant to §501(c)(3), an institution must show, first, that it falls within one of the eight categories expressly set forth in that section, and second, that its activity is not contrary to settled public policy.

Section 501(c)(3) provides that "[c]orporations . . . organized and operated exclusively for religious, charitable . . . or educational purposes" are entitled to tax exemption. Petitioners argue that the plain language of the statute guarantees them tax-exempt status. They emphasize the absence of any language in the statute expressly requiring all exempt organizations to be "charitable" in the common law sense, and they contend that the disjunctive "or" separating the categories in §501(c)(3) precludes such a reading. Instead, they argue that if an institution falls within one or more of the specified categories it is automatically entitled to exemption, without regard to whether it also qualifies as "charitable." The Court of Appeals rejected that contention and concluded that petitioners' interpretation of the statute "tears section 501(c)(3) from its roots." United States v. Bob Jones University, supra, 639 F.2d, at 151. . . .

Section 501(c)(3) . . . must be analyzed and construed within the framework of the Internal Revenue Code and against the background of the Congressional purposes. Such an examination reveals unmistakable evidence that, underlying all relevant parts of the Code, is the intent that entitlement to tax exemption depends on meeting certain common law standards of charity — namely, that an institution seeking tax-exempt status must serve a public purpose and not be contrary to established public policy.

This "charitable" concept appears explicitly in §170 of the Code. That section contains a list of organizations virtually identical to that contained in §501(c)(3). It is apparent that Congress intended that list to have the same meaning in both sections. In §170, Congress used the list of organizations in defining the term "charitable contributions." On

71-447 and other pertinent rulings and to recognize §501 (c)(3) exemptions for petitioners. The Government suggested that these actions were therefore moot. Before this Court ruled on that motion, however, the United States Court of Appeals for the District of Columbia Circuit enjoined the Government from granting §501(c)(3) tax-exempt status to any school that discriminates on the basis of race. Wright v. Regan, No. 80-1124 (C.A.D.C. Feb. 18, 1982) (per curiam order). Thereafter, the Government informed the Court that it would not revoke the revenue rulings and withdrew its request that the actions be dismissed as moot. The Government continues to assert that the IRS lacked authority to promulgate Revenue Ruling 71-447, and does not defend that aspect of the rulings below. [The Court appointed special counsel to argue in support of the Court of Appeals decision.]

its face, therefore, §170 reveals that Congress' intention was to provide tax benefits to organizations serving charitable purposes. The form of §170 simply makes plain what common sense and history tell us: in enacting both §170 and §501(c)(3), Congress sought to provide tax benefits to charitable organizations, to encourage the development of private institutions that serve a useful public purpose or supplement or take the place of public institutions of the same kind.

Tax exemptions for certain institutions thought beneficial to the social order of the country as a whole, or to a particular community, are deeply rooted in our history, as in that of England. The origins of such exemptions lie in the special privileges that have long been extended to charitable trusts.[7] . . .

A corollary to the public benefit principle is the requirement, long recognized in the law of trusts, that the purpose of a charitable trust may not be illegal or violate established public policy. . . .

When the Government grants exemptions or allows deductions all taxpayers are affected; the very fact of the exemption or deduction for the donor means that other taxpayers can be said to be indirect and vicarious "donors." Charitable exemptions are justified on the basis that the exempt entity confers a public benefit — a benefit which the society or the community may not itself choose or be able to provide, or which supplements and advances the work of public institutions already supported by tax revenues. History buttresses logic to make clear that, to warrant exemption under §501(c)(3), an institution must fall within a category specified in that section and must demonstrably serve and be in harmony with the public interest.[8] The institution's purpose must not be so at odds with the common community conscience as to undermine any public benefit that might otherwise be conferred.

We are bound to approach these questions with full awareness that determinations of public benefit and public policy are sensitive matters with serious implications for the institutions affected; a declaration that a given institution is not "charitable" should be made only where there can be no doubt that the activity involved is contrary to a fundamental public policy. But there can no longer be any doubt that racial discrimination in education violates deeply and widely accepted views of elementary justice. Prior to 1954, public education in many places still was conducted under the pall of Plessy v. Ferguson, 163 U.S. 537 (1896);

7. The form and history of the charitable exemption and deduction sections of the various income tax acts reveal that Congress was guided by the common law of charitable trusts. See Simon, The Tax-Exempt Status of Racially Discriminatory Religious Schools, 36 Tax L. Rev. 477, 485-489 (1981) (hereinafter Simon).

8. The Court's reading of §501(c)(3) does not render meaningless Congress' action in specifying the eight categories of presumptively exempt organizations, as petitioners suggest. See Brief of Petitioner Goldsboro Christian Schools 18-24. To be entitled to tax-exempt status under §501(c)(3), an organization must first fall within one of the categories specified by Congress, and in addition must serve a valid charitable purpose.

racial segregation in primary and secondary education prevailed in many parts of the country. See, e.g., Segregation and the Fourteenth Amendment in the States (B. Reams & P. Wilson, eds. 1975). This Court's decision in Brown v. Board of Education, 347 U.S. 483 (1954), signalled an end to that era. Over the past quarter of a century, every pronouncement of this Court and myriad Acts of Congress and Executive Orders attest a firm national policy to prohibit racial segregation and discrimination in public education.

An unbroken line of cases following Brown v. Board of Education establishes beyond doubt this Court's view that racial discrimination in education violates a most fundamental national public policy, as well as rights of individuals. . . . In Norwood v. Harrison, 413 U.S. 455, 468-469 (1973), we dealt with a nonpublic institution:

> [A] private school — even one that discriminates — fulfills an important educational function; *however, . . . [that] legitimate educational function cannot be isolated from discriminatory practices. . . . [D]iscriminatory treatment exerts a pervasive influence on the entire educational process.*

(Emphasis added.) See also Runyon v. McCrary, 427 U.S. 160 (1976); Griffin v. County School Board, 377 U.S. 218 (1964). . . .

Petitioners contend that, regardless of whether the IRS properly concluded that racially discriminatory private schools violate public policy, only Congress can alter the scope of §170 and §501(c)(3). Petitioners accordingly argue that the IRS overstepped its lawful bounds in issuing its 1970 and 1971 rulings.

Yet ever since the inception of the tax code, Congress has seen fit to vest in those administering the tax laws very broad authority to interpret those laws. In an area as complex as the tax system, the agency Congress vests with administrative responsibility must be able to exercise its authority to meet changing conditions and new problems. . . .

The actions of Congress since 1970 leave no doubt that the IRS reached the correct conclusion in exercising its authority. It is, of course, not unknown for independent agencies or the Executive Branch to misconstrue the intent of a statute; Congress can and often does correct such misconceptions, if the courts have not done so. Yet for a dozen years Congress has been made aware — acutely aware — of the IRS rulings of 1970 and 1971. As we noted earlier, few issues have been the subject of more vigorous and widespread debate and discussion in and out of Congress than those related to racial segregation in education. Sincere adherents advocating contrary views have ventilated the subject for well over three decades. Failure of Congress to modify the IRS rulings of 1970 and 1971, of which Congress was, by its own studies and by public discourse, constantly reminded; and Congress' awareness of the denial of tax-exempt status for racially discriminatory schools when enacting other and related legislation make out an unusually strong case of legislative acquiescence in and ratification by implication of the 1970 and 1971 rulings. . . .

The evidence of Congressional approval of the policy embodied in Revenue Ruling 71-447 goes well beyond the failure of Congress to act on legislative proposals. Congress affirmatively manifested its acquiescence in the IRS policy when it enacted the present §501(i) of the Code. . . .

III

Petitioners contend that, even if the Commissioner's policy is valid as to nonreligious private schools, that policy cannot constitutionally be applied to schools that engage in racial discrimination on the basis of sincerely held religious beliefs. As to such schools, it is argued that the IRS construction of §170 and §501(c)(3) violates their free exercise rights under the Religion Clauses of the First Amendment. This contention presents claims not heretofore considered by this Court in precisely this context. . . .

The governmental interest at stake here is compelling. . . . [T]he Government has a fundamental, overriding interest in eradicating racial discrimination in education[9] — discrimination that prevailed, with official approval, for the first 165 years of this Nation's history. That governmental interest substantially outweighs whatever burden denial of tax benefits places on petitioners' exercise of their religious beliefs. The interests asserted by petitioners cannot be accommodated with that compelling governmental interest, . . . and no "less restrictive means" . . . are available to achieve the governmental interest.

The judgments of the Court of Appeals are, accordingly,

Affirmed.

Justice Powell, concurring in part and concurring in the judgment. . . .

I . . . concur in the Court's judgment that tax-exempt status under §§170(c) and 501(c)(3) is not available to private schools that concededly are racially discriminatory. I do not agree, however, with the Court's more general explanation of the justifications for the tax exemptions provided to charitable organizations. . . .

With all respect, I am unconvinced that the critical question in determining tax-exempt status is whether an individual organization pro-

9. We deal here only with religious *schools* — not with churches or other purely religious institutions; here, the governmental interest is in denying public support to racial discrimination in education. . . .

vides a clear "public benefit" as defined by the Court. Over 106,000 organizations filed §501(c)(3) returns in 1981. Internal Revenue Service, 1982 Exempt Organization/Business Master File. I find it impossible to believe that all or even most of those organizations could prove that they "demonstrably serve and [are] in harmony with the public interest" or that they are "beneficial and stabilizing influences in community life." Nor am I prepared to say that petitioners, because of their racially discriminatory policies, necessarily contribute nothing of benefit to the community. It is clear from the substantially secular character of the curricula and degrees offered that petitioners provide educational benefits.

Even more troubling to me is the element of conformity that appears to inform the Court's analysis. The Court asserts that an exempt organization must "demonstrably serve and be in harmony with the public interest," must have a purpose that comports with "the common community conscience," and must not act in a manner "affirmatively at odds with [the] declared position of the whole government." Taken together, these passages suggest that the primary function of a tax-exempt organization is to act on behalf of the Government in carrying out governmentally approved policies. In my opinion, such a view of §501(c)(3) ignores the important role played by tax exemptions in encouraging diverse, indeed often sharply conflicting, activities and viewpoints. . . .

The Court's decision upholds IRS Revenue Ruling 71-447, and thus resolves the question whether tax-exempt status is available to private schools that openly maintain racially discriminatory admissions policies. There no longer is any justification for Congress to hesitate — as it apparently has — in articulating and codifying its desired policy as to tax exemptions for discriminatory organizations. Many questions remain, such as whether organizations that violate other policies should receive tax-exempt status under §501(c)(3). These should be legislative policy choices. . . . The contours of public policy should be determined by Congress, not by judges or the IRS.

Justice REHNQUIST, dissenting.

The Court points out that there is a strong national policy in this country against racial discrimination. To the extent that the Court states that Congress in furtherance of this policy could deny tax-exempt status to educational institutions that promote racial discrimination, I readily agree. But, unlike the Court, I am convinced that Congress simply has failed to take this action and, as this Court has said over and over again, regardless of our view on the propriety of Congress' failure to legislate we are not constitutionally empowered to act for them. . . .

With undeniable clarity, Congress has explicitly defined the requirements for §501(c)(3) status. An entity must be (1) a corporation, or community chest, fund, or foundation, (2) organized for one of the eight enumerated purposes, (3) operated on a nonprofit basis, and (4) free from involvement in lobbying activities and political campaigns. Nowhere is there to be found some additional, undefined public policy requirement.

I have no disagreement with the Court's finding that there is a strong national policy in this country opposed to racial discrimination. I agree with the Court that Congress has the power to further this policy by denying §501(c)(3) status to organizations that practice racial discrimination. But as of yet Congress has failed to do so. Whatever the reasons for the failure, this Court should not legislate for Congress.

NOTES AND QUESTIONS

1. *Congressional avoidance.* On February 1, 1982, R. T. McNamar, Deputy Secretary of the Treasury, appeared before the Senate Finance Committee to speak in support of a bill offered by the Reagan administration that would have amended the Code to deny exempt status to schools such as Bob Jones University and the Goldsboro School. Hearings on Legislation to Deny Tax Exemption to Racially Discriminatory Private Schools, 97th Cong., 2d Sess. 225 (1982). Consider the following statement by Mr. McNamar and the question whether the opinion of the Supreme Court in *Bob Jones* provides an adequate basis for responding to the problems that he raised (id. at 229-232).

> The Justice Department has prepared and delivered to the Treasury Department a memorandum of law which describes the legal deficiencies in the Service's position. As the Justice Department memorandum concludes, there is no adequate basis in law for the Service's position that it has the authority to select certain Federal public policies and impose these policies on tax exempt organizations. . . .
>
> The implications of continuing the policy of allowing the IRS to determine on its own those public policies denying tax exemptions was well stated by the district court in the *Bob Jones* case. There, the judge pointed out that Section 501(c)(3) does not endow the IRS with authority to discipline wrongdoers or to promote social change by denying exemptions to organizations that offend federal public policy. Voicing apprehension over such broad power, the district court observed:
>
>> Federal public policy is constantly changing. When can something be said to become federal public policy? Who decides? With a change of federal public policy, the law would change without congressional action — a dilemma of constitutional proportions. Citizens could no longer rely on the law of Section 501(c)(3) as it is written, but would then rely on the IRS to tell them what it had decided the law to be for that particular day. Our laws would change at the whim of some nonelected IRS personnel, producing bureaucratic tyranny.

For example, if we were to endorse the theory on which the Service was proceeding before the Supreme Court, what would prevent the Service from revoking the tax exempt status of Smith College, a school open only to women? Does sex discrimination violate a clearly enunciated public policy? Apparently someone in the state of Massachusetts thinks so, because litigation on this issue is currently going forward in the state courts of Massachusetts.

What about religious organizations that refuse to ordain priests of both sexes? And could the Commissioner decide that if Black Muslim organizations refuse to admit whites they should be denied a tax exempt status because they discriminate?

Further, should the IRS Commissioner be permitted — in the absence of legislation — to determine what is national policy on abortion? Should hospitals that refuse to perform abortions be denied their tax exempt status? Or, reading Federal policy another way, should hospitals that do perform abortions be denied their tax exempt status? . . .

Finally, I turn to a description of the Administration's bill, which is before the committee this morning. Section one of that bill directly addresses the issue before us. Specifically, a new Section 501(j) would be added to the Internal Revenue Code to deny 501(c)(3) treatment and 501(a) treatment if the school practices racial discrimination. . . .

New Code Section 501(j)(2) defines "racially discriminatory policy." Generally, under the bill, a school has such a policy if it refuses to admit students of all races (defined to include also color and national origin) to the rights, privileges, programs, and activities usually accorded or made available to students by that organization, or if the organization refuses to administer its educational policies, admissions policies, scholarship and loan programs, or other programs in a manner that does not discriminate on the basis of race. This definition generally conforms to that first established by the court in the *Green* litigation and carried forward by the IRS in Rev. Rul. 71-447 and subsequent pronouncements.

Additionally, Section 501(j)(2) contains an explicit provision in recognition of the legitimate interests of religious-based schools. Thus, under the bill, an admissions policy or a program of religious training or worship that is limited to, or grants preference or priority to, members of a particular religious organization or belief would not be considered a racially discriminatory policy. Thus, schools may confine admission and training to persons of a particular religion. The protection, however, will not apply if the policy, program, preference or priority is based upon race or upon a belief that requires discrimination on the basis of race. Pursuant to this rule, we expect that Bob Jones and Goldsboro would be denied their tax exempt status if they continue their past racial practices.

In the dialogue that followed Mr. McNamar's presentation, attention at one point turned to "the classic case, . . . a yeshiva, which is limited to people who believe in Judaism." Id. at 235-236. Everyone seemed to agree that such a school should not be denied exemption even if located in a community in which, as a practical matter, "all of the kids in the school would be white." Id. at 236. The key element in such a case, it was thought, was the absence of an intent to discriminate against blacks.

2. *Public policy.* Once the Court in *Bob Jones* decides that §§501(c)(3) and 170 include a public policy limitation, it turns to the question whether racial discrimination in private schools violates public policy. The Court cites Brown v. Board of Education. How is that case relevant to racial discrimination in private education? Note that if the Court had been willing to treat tax deductibility as a form of governmental support or subsidy, Brown v. Board of Education would have been not only relevant but dispositive. But what would that approach have done to the deduction for contributions to religious organizations? See the quotation from *Taxation With Representation of Washington,* supra page 493.

Norwood v. Harrison, also cited by the Court, held that the equal protection and due process rights of minority citizens were violated by a state textbook lending program for private schools to the extent that it included schools that engaged in racial discrimination. And Runyon v. McCrary, also cited, held that the protection of the right of contract under the Civil Rights Act of 1866 (now 42 U.S.C. §1981) applied to private schools.

3. *"Charitable" versus "educational."* Given the Court's interpretation of §170(c)(2)(B), does the word "educational" have any function? That is, could the provision be amended, without losing anything, to cover "charitable purposes" as opposed to "charitable or educational purposes"? See footnote 8 supra.

4. *Where there's a will.* Examine §501(i). Note its limited applicability and its failure to include discrimination based on gender. What does that tell us about public policy concerning such discrimination?

5. *Loss of exemption due to private inurement.* Bob Jones University lost its tax-exempt status because the relevant statutory provisions were held to incorporate the requirement that an organization's activities be consistent with public policy. A more common reason for loss (or denial) of tax-exempt status is that an organization benefits donors, or employees, or other persons and therefore serves a private, rather than public purpose. See §503; Regs. §1.501(c)(3).

E. INTEREST

1. The Rules

Business or investment interest — that is, interest incurred in a trade or business or for the production of income — is a proper adjustment in arriving at net income and has always been allowed as a deduction, though in recent years subject to certain limitations designed to curb tax avoidance. See §163(a), (d). We will return to business and investment interest in Chapter 6. Here we focus our attention on interest on debt incurred for personal purposes.

Before 1987, all personal interest was deductible, but in the 1986 and 1987 acts Congress substantially limited the deduction. Interest on a mortgage loan incurred after October 13, 1987, is deductible in full if it is "qualified residence interest." §163(h)(3). All other interest not incurred for business or investment purposes is nondeductible "personal interest." §163(h)(2).

For loans incurred after October 13, 1987, "qualified residence interest" is interest on loans falling within either of two categories. First, there is "acquisition indebtedness," which is debt incurred to buy, build, or improve a personal residence, and which is secured by the residence. There is a limit of $1 million on such debt. §163(h)(3)(B). Second, there is "home equity indebtedness," which is any debt secured by a personal residence, with a limit of $100,000, but not in excess of the fair market value of the residence. §163(h)(3)(C).

The following examples illustrate the new rules. In each example assume that the loan at issue was incurred after October 13, 1987, and that the house is used as the taxpayer's personal residence.

Example A. A buys a house for $1.5 million, with a down payment of $300,000 and a loan of $1.2 million. Acquisition indebtedness accounts for $1 million (which is the limit) of the loan. An additional $100,000 of the debt qualifies as home equity indebtedness. Thus, the qualified residence interest (that is, the amount of interest that can be deducted) is the interest allocable to $1.1 million of the $1.2 million loan.

Example B. B buys a house for $300,000, with a loan of $115,000 and the remaining $185,000 from her savings. A month later she borrows $125,000, secured by the house. The entire amount of the first loan ($115,000) is acquisition indebtedness. The second loan ($125,000) is a home equity loan and qualifies only up to $100,000. If *B* had borrowed the entire $240,000 at the time of the purchase of the house, the entire amount of the loan would have been acquisition indebtedness. Can you think of any sound justification for this difference in result?

Example C. C bought a house many years ago for $50,000. It is now worth $300,000. The debt incurred at the time of the original purchase was paid off several years ago. *C* takes out a loan of $140,000; the loan is secured by the house. Since the loan was not used to buy, build, or improve the house, the qualified residence interest is limited to the home equity indebtedness amount, $100,000. Note that home equity indebtedness may exceed basis. Note also that if *C* had sold her present house for $300,000 and had bought another house for the same price, but with a loan of $140,000 secured by the house, she would have wound up with $140,000 in cash from the transaction (just as if she had borrowed that amount on the security of the first house), but the entire loan would have qualified as acquisition indebtedness. (The same possibility arises in Example B.) Why would Congress create that kind of incentive?

Example D. D has a house that he bought many years ago. The house is worth $300,000 and the balance on the original mortgage was $40,000. On October 15, 1987, *D* borrowed $200,000 on the security of his house and used $40,000 of this to pay off the existing loan. To the extent of the original $40,000, the new loan is treated as acquisition indebtedness. The remaining $160,000 is home equity indebtedness and qualifies for interest deductibility only to the extent of $100,000. Thus, the total of the qualified debt is $140,000.

For loans incurred before October 14, 1987, there is no limit on the amount of acquisition indebtedness. Such loans do, however, "use up" the $1 million limit on loans incurred after October 13, 1987.

Example E. On October 1, 1987, *E* bought a house for $5 million, with a loan, secured by the house, of $4 million. The entire $4 million loan is acquisition indebtedness; the interest is fully deductible. If *E* sells the house, her buyer will be subject to the $1 million limit and she will be subject to that limit on any replacement house she might buy. Is this fair to *E*? What is the likely effect on the prices of expensive houses?

2. Policy Issues

One widely held view of interest on personal indebtedness is that it is a cost of consuming sooner rather than later, part of the cost of achieving personal satisfaction, and as such represents a form of consumption expense that should not be deductible. To this is often added the thought, sometimes expressed in pious, paternalistic, and condescending phrases, that the deduction encourages people to spend more than they should. It has also been claimed that borrowing for the purchase of individual investments such as homes and automobiles uses capital that could better be used for business investment.

Consistently with the observations made in the preceding paragraph, the Senate Finance Committee Report on the 1986 bill (S. Rep. No. 313, 99th Cong., 2d Sess. 804 (1986)), in justifying the denial of a deduction for consumer interest, states that investment in housing and other consumer durables "allows consumers to avoid the tax that would apply if funds were invested in assets producing taxable income." The Report concludes that the tax system thus provided "an incentive to consume rather than save." Do you agree? When a person buys a house for $250,000, is that $250,000 of consumption or $250,000 of saving? In any event, what's wrong with consumption?

In the same Senate Report, the favorable treatment of loans secured by personal residences is justified on the ground that "encouraging home ownership is an important policy goal." Do you agree? Are renters morally or socially defective? Why should Congress encourage people to buy homes rather than automobiles or other consumer durables, or for that matter, good, wholesome meals at their local restaurants?

Many reformers believe the home mortgage interest deduction ought to be eliminated. One difficulty with this reform is persons have purchased homes on the assumption that they would be able to deduct their mortgage interest. Such individuals might find it difficult to keep up their mortgage payments without the benefit of the tax deduction. It would be possible, of course, to grandfather persons with existing loans but repeal the deduction for new mortgage indebtedness. This more limited reform would not affect current homeowners who keep their present home and do not increase the size of their mortgage. The reform would, however, reduce the value of homes to new purchasers, who could no longer deduct mortgage interest. This in turn would reduce the price existing homeowners could get when and if they decide to sell their home. Does the reliance interests of current homeowners constitute a persuasive argument against reform? Can you think of a change in the present pattern of deductions that would not increase the tax burden on some class of individuals?

3. Tracing

The differing treatment of interest on personal and business loans raises a number of difficult tracing issues. Suppose, for example, that business property is used to secure a loan that is used for personal purposes. Is the loan a personal or a business loan? Or suppose that borrowed and nonborrowed funds are commingled and used for both business and personal purposes. Should the interest expense be allocated to the business purposes, the personal purposes, or some combination of business and personal purposes? The government's answer to these and other questions is provided in proposed Treasury Regulation §1.163-8T.

Under that regulation, interest generally is allocated according to the *use* of the loan proceeds. Thus, interest on a loan that is used for personal purposes is characterized as personal interest; the fact that the loan may be secured by business property is irrelevant. Regs. §1.163-8T(c). As noted earlier, however, special rules apply to interest incurred in connection with a principal residence.

A complicated set of rules governs situations in which borrowed and nonborrowed funds are commingled. The general ordering rule provides that expenditures from commingled funds are allocated to borrowed funds until all the borrowed funds are deemed to have been spent. Regs. §1.163-8T(c)(4). To illustrate, assume that on May 1, 1991, John deposits $200 of nonborrowed funds in a checking account; on May 2, 1991, he deposits $100 of borrowed funds in the same account. On June 3, 1991, John withdraws $100 from the account for personal use and on June 4, 1991, he withdraws $150 for business use. Under the general ordering rule, the first expenditure — here, the June 3 personal expense — is deemed to have been made out of the borrowed funds. The result would be the same if the order of the deposits had been reversed. If, on May 2, John had deposited in the checking account $150, instead of $100, of borrowed funds, then $100 of the borrowed funds would be tied to the June 3 personal expense and the remaining $50 of borrowed funds would be tied to the June 4 business expense. The basic numbers may be summarized as follows.

DEPOSITS

	Borrowed funds	*Nonborrowed funds*	*Total*
May 1	—	$200	$200
May 2	$100	—	100
			$300

WITHDRAWALS

	Personal use	*Business use*	*Total*
June 3	$100	—	$100 Borrowed funds
June 4	—	$150	150 Nonborrowed funds
			$250

Under a supplemental ordering rule, taxpayers may elect to treat any expenditure made within fifteen days of deposit of borrowed funds as made from borrowed funds. The difference between the general and the supplemental rule may be grasped by imagining a taxpayer who deposits $500 of borrowed funds and $500 of nonborrowed funds in a bank account on August 1, 1991. Suppose that the taxpayer withdraws $500 for personal purposes on August 2, 1991, and $500 for business purposes on August 3, 1991. Under the general ordering rule, the August 2 personal expense would be deemed to have been made with the borrowed funds. Under the supplemental rule, the taxpayer may elect to have the borrowed funds tied to the August 3 business expense.

The tracing rules place a premium on tax planning. We have earlier noted that a taxpayer who has $100,000 cash and wishes to spend $100,000 on a house and $100,000 on other items of personal consumption would be wise to spend the cash on the other items of personal consumption and borrow to finance the house. That way, the interest on the loan is deductible as qualified residence interest. Similar considerations apply to the taxpayer who wishes to buy both business property and items of personal consumption. Imagine a taxpayer who has $10,000 cash and wishes to spend $10,000 on her business and $10,000 on personal consumption. If the taxpayer uses the cash to buy the business property and borrows $10,000 to pay for personal consumption, interest on the loan will be personal interest. If, on the other hand, the taxpayer uses the cash on personal consumption and the loan to pay for the business property, interest on the loan will be business interest.

PROBLEMS

1. Jennifer has $50,000 in a savings account. She uses the $50,000 to buy a Mercedes and the next day borrows $50,000 to finance the purchase of a fast-food franchise that she intends to operate. Will the interest on the $50,000 loan be deductible?

2. Barbara owns her personal residence free and clear. Its value is $100,000. She borrows $50,000 on a "home equity" loan, secured by the residence. (a) She uses the proceeds to buy a Mercedes. Is the interest deductible? Under what Code section? (b) She uses the proceeds instead to buy a tax-exempt bond. Is the interest deductible? See §265(a)(2), §163(h)(2)(D), §163(a). (c) She uses the proceeds of the loan to buy taxable bonds, but at the time she holds $50,000 of tax-exempt bonds. Is the interest deductible?

3. Joe has a portfolio of stocks and bonds worth $200,000. The annual income from the portfolio is $12,000. *T* borrows $50,000 on a margin loan and uses the proceeds to buy a Mercedes. Since the proceeds are used to buy the Mercedes, the interest on the loan is personal interest. See Regs. §1.163-8T(c)(1). What might she do to achieve a better tax result?

4. What Is "Interest"?

A question of what is interest arose as lending institutions passed various costs on to the borrower, sometimes to avoid legal limits on interest and sometimes merely to take advantage of tight money markets. If the loan is personal, expenses other than interest will normally be nondeductible. The Service has ruled that points (fees for making a loan measured by a percentage of the total loan) on home loans are interest if paid "for the use of money." Rev. Rul. 69-188, 1969-1 C.B. 54. This is confirmed by §461(g)(2), enacted in 1976. Rev. Rul. 69-188 also provides that other loan costs (cost of credit reports, escrow fees, etc.) are not interest. If a bank makes no separate charges for these items and merely takes them into account in setting the total interest rate, they are deductible.

In Rev. Rul. 83-51, 1983-1 C.B. 48, the Service addressed a recently developed financing device used for purchases of personal residences, the shared appreciation mortgage (SAM). With a SAM, the borrower pays interest at a rate below the rate that would be charged on a normal loan and agrees in addition to pay to the lender a portion of any appreciation in the value of the house on sale or at the end of some specified period of time (e.g., ten years). The ruling states that the borrower has all the usual incidents of ownership, such as the right to occupy the premises, the obligation to pay taxes and other costs of ownership, and the right to sell, improve, etc. The lender does not share in any decline in value in the house. Based on these facts, the Service ruled that the borrower is entitled to deduct as interest the amount ultimately paid to the lender as the lender's share of the appreciation. The ruling cautions, however, that its conclusions

> should not be considered to apply to SAM agreements, particularly in situations in which the loan proceeds are used for commercial or business activities, in which the lender acquires greater rights with respect to the borrower or the mortgaged property than are described in the facts section of this ruling; in which the parties evidence an intention to create a relationship other than that of debtor and creditor; or if other circumstances indicate that the SAM loan represents in substance an equity interest in the mortgaged property.

5. Interest and Inflation

In a period of inflation, interest cost and interest income are overstated. For example, suppose *B* borrows $1,000 from *L* for one year at 12 percent at a time when the rate of inflation is expected to be 8 percent. Assume that the rate of inflation in fact turns out to be 8 percent. At the end of the year, when *B* pays $1,120 to *L*, after adjustment for inflation, $1,080 is a return of capital and $40 is interest. Viewing the matter from *L*'s perspective, if *L* wants to maintain his or her wealth or capital, he or she can afford to treat only $40 as income; the rest is a return of capital. It may be that the tax law should be changed to require an inflation adjustment for interest income and expense, but Congress has thus far shown no enthusiasm for the idea.

F. TAXES

Under §164, certain taxes may be claimed as itemized "personal" deductions, without regard to any business or investment connection. These and other taxes may also be claimed under §162 or §212 as allowances in arriving at adjusted gross income, if they are incurred in carrying on a trade or business or in the production of income. The most prominent of the taxes listed as personal deductions in §164 are state and local income and real property taxes. User fees, such as sewer fees, tuition at state colleges, and charges for entry to state parks, are not treated as taxes and therefore are not deductible under §164. Nor are federal taxes, including income taxes, estate and gift taxes, and the employee share of social security taxes. Foreign income taxes are deductible but generally are instead taken as credits under §901.

The policy issue presented by §164 is similar in many ways to the issue raised by other deductions considered in this chapter. Fundamentally, they all present the question whether certain outlays should be treated as reductions in arriving at a proper definition of net income and, if not, whether a deduction is a sensible device for achieving some desirable goal extraneous to the income tax system, in this case support of state and local governmental operations. On the question of properly defining income, perhaps the strongest argument for a deduction for taxes is that they are involuntary and do not buy personal consumption. This argument may seem stronger in the case of income taxes than in the case of property taxes. Even as to income taxes, however, we must bear in mind Justice Holmes's observation, "Taxes are what we pay for civilized society. . . ." Compania General de Tobacos de Filipinas v. Collector, 275 U.S. 87, 100 (1927). Do we get our money's worth? Might it be sensible to distinguish between that portion of income taxes that pays for police protection, streets, parks, trash collection, schools, etc., and that portion used for relief of poverty?

What about property taxes? To some degree they are voluntary. Moreover, they can be thought of as part of the cost of consuming. But they are voluntary only to a degree, and they add nothing to the value of the housing that we consume.[10] Are they therefore comparable to income taxes? Should they be regarded as offsets in arriving at a proper definition of income? Even if property taxes are not thought to be comparable to income taxes, there is another, related, argument for making them deductible if one begins with the premise that income taxes ought to be deductible. The argument is that different states rely on different forms of taxation and that the residents of those states that choose to raise revenues through property (or sales) taxes should not be left worse off than the residents of those states that rely on income taxes. Stated somewhat differently, it is not appropriate for the federal government to favor one form of state and local taxation over another.

Given the deductibility of income and property taxes, respect for the role of the states in our federal system argues in favor of a deduction for sales taxes, especially for taxpayers in states with no income tax. Until 1987, sales taxes were deductible. In the process of formulating the 1986 act, the Senate adopted a bill with a provision that would have allowed a deduction for 60 percent of the excess of a taxpayer's sales taxes over his or her income taxes. Tax Reform Bill of 1986 (H.R. 3838, §136, June 24, 1986). The deduction for sales taxes was a controversial issue. The Senate bill included the following language in support of its position (id., §137):

Sec. 137. Deductibility of State and Local Sales, Real and Personal Property, and Income Taxes

(a) Findings. The Senate finds that—

(1) a deduction for State and local taxes has been allowed by Federal income tax law since 1861,

(2) the deduction for State and local taxes is a cornerstone of Federalism, protecting State revenue sources from the effects of double taxation and allowing State and local governments the flexibility to develop tax structures without Federal interference,

(3) elimination of the deduction for State and local taxes would constitute an unjustified Federal intrusion into the fiscal affairs of States

10. Note that if the imputed income from home ownership were included in income, deduction of property taxes would be an appropriate allowance as part of the cost of producing that income. See the discussion of a similar point in respect of the interest deduction, supra page 512. Renters are not allowed to deduct the portion of their rent that they pay, through their landlords, as property taxes. It is not relevant that the landlord gets a deduction for payment of the tax; the landlord is best seen as a conduit. What is relevant is that the discrimination against renters stems essentially from the failure to tax the imputed income of people who own their homes. Allowing renters a deduction for part of their rent might be defended as a device for reducing the inequality in treatment stemming from this failure. But see the discussion of the indirect benefits to renters, supra page 119.

> and prejudice the right of State and local governments to select appropriate revenue measures,
>
> (4) elimination or restriction of the deductibility of some State and local taxes would encourage States to shift tax levies to taxes which continue to be deductible, increasing the tax burden of certain segments of the population and undermining the ability of State and local governments to raise revenue,
>
> (5) the deduction for State and local taxes is the single most popular deduction in the Internal Revenue Code of 1954,
>
> (6) the revenue measures selected by a State should not significantly alter the value of the Federal deduction for State and local taxes paid by its citizens,
>
> (7) sales taxes are used by some State and local governments as general purposes taxes, while other jurisdictions use income and property taxes as general purpose taxes,
>
> (8) funding for public education, the largest category of expenditure for State and local governments, would be affected by any restriction on the deduction for State and local taxes, and
>
> (9) the sales tax is the largest source of revenue for all States combined.
>
> (b) Sense of the Senate. It is the sense of the Senate that any tax reform legislation should preserve the full deduction for State and local sales, real and personal property, and income taxes.

Despite this stirring rhetoric, when the bill reached the Conference Committee of the House Committee on Ways and Means and the Senate Committee on Finance, it was amended to eliminate any deduction for sales taxes and this position ultimately became the law.

How far does the argument based on state autonomy lead? If a "taxpayer revolt" leads to a reduction of property taxes and a corresponding increase in various kinds of fees for public services, should the fees be deductible? If low taxes result in reduced public school budgets, which leads to bad public schools, which induces some people to send their children to private or parochial schools, should the tuition payments be deductible? What about amounts spent by a group of neighbors to hire a private security patrol for its neighborhood?

G. PERSONAL AND DEPENDENCY EXEMPTIONS

Section 151 grants each taxpayer a deduction for a personal exemption. The amount was $2,300 in 1992, and is annually adjusted for inflation. §151. If a joint return is filed by a married couple, there are two taxpayers and, consequently, two exemptions. If a married individual files a separate return, one personal exemption is allowed for the taxpayer and a second for the spouse if the spouse has no gross income and is not another's dependent. §151(b).

Section 151(e) provides an exemption for each qualified dependent of the taxpayer. To qualify, the person must

1. be related to the taxpayer by blood, marriage, or adoption in the ways specified by §152(a)(1)-(8) or meet the special requirements of §152(a)(9) or (10);
2. derive more than one-half of his or her support (which does not include scholarships) from the taxpayer; and
3. have a gross income of less than the exemption amount for the year in which dependency is claimed.

The gross income restriction is inapplicable, however, if the dependent is the taxpayer's child, is either under the age of 19 or a student under age 24, and, if married, does not file a joint return with his spouse.

A child of divorced or separated parents is generally treated as a dependent of the custodial parent, provided only that the parents together furnish more than one-half of the child's support. However, the custodial parent can waive the deduction in favor of the noncustodial parent. §152(e).

The personal and dependency exemptions are available in addition to the standard deduction amount. §63.

H. CREDITS BASED ON PERSONAL CIRCUMSTANCES

Section 22, providing a credit for retirement income, was initially designed to equalize the tax burden on people over 65 receiving federal social security benefits, which until 1983 were wholly tax exempt (see supra page 157), and people who provided for their own retirement with pension, annuities, or other investments. In 1976, however, the law was changed to apply the credit to income from any source, including earnings from services currently performed. Unlike §151, §22 retains in its title (though not in text) the now-suspect term "the elderly," which a sensitive person might wish to replace with "senior citizens," or, better yet, "persons who through no fault of their own have attained age sixty-five." In order to limit the credit to low-income taxpayers, §22(d) reduces the "section 22 amount" as income rises above $7,500 (single persons), $10,000 (joint returns), or $5,000 (separate return filed by married individual).

The earned income credit in §32 is another attempt to protect low-income taxpayers from the burden (and the disincentive effects) of the income tax. It is phased out as income rises above $11,840 (in 1992). Note that this credit is refundable; if it exceeds the amount of tax owed, the person entitled to the credit receives a check from the Treasury. Thus, the credit is properly thought of as a form of social welfare benefit, of the sort sometimes called a "negative income tax." It is also interesting to note that this credit is available only to people, with children, who are either married or a surviving spouse (§2(a)) or a head of household (§2(b)).

5

ALLOWANCES FOR MIXED BUSINESS AND PERSONAL OUTLAYS

The allowances examined in the previous chapter were associated with purely personal circumstances or objectives. In Chapter 6 we will examine allowances associated with purely business or investment circumstances or objectives. In this chapter we examine the somewhat perplexing intermediate ground.

There are two basic provisions under which individuals may claim deductions for expenses that may be thought of as the cost of generating income. First is §162(a), the deduction for the "ordinary and necessary expenses paid or incurred . . . in carrying on any trade or business." It is under this provision, for example, that a practicing lawyer who heads her own office would claim deductions for office expenses, salaries paid to associates, automobile expenses, entertainment expenses, etc.[1] A salaried associate in a law firm would also rely on this section for deduction of unreimbursed expenses, such as for legal periodicals, bar dues, and continuing education courses.[2] The associate, but not the self-employed lawyer who heads the office, would, however, be subject to the 2 percent threshold found in §67 (described immediately below).

The other basic deduction provision for individuals is §212,[3] which covers expenses of generating income from sources other than a trade

1. These deductions are taken in arriving at "adjusted gross income" (see §62(a)(1)) and are sometimes called "above-the-line" deductions.

2. The §162 deductions of employees are "below-the-line" deductions. That is, they are deducted from adjusted gross income to arrive at taxable income.

3. Deductions under §212 are "itemized" deductions, which are deducted from adjusted gross income to arrive at taxable income.

or business. Under this provision a person with investments in stocks and bonds would claim deductions for fees paid to investment advisors, the cost of a subscription to the Wall Street Journal, and expenses incurred in attending investment seminars, again subject to §67.

On the other side is §262, providing that "no deduction shall be allowed for personal, living, or family expenses."

Section 67, adopted in 1986, provides that certain deductions are allowable only to the extent that in the aggregate they exceed 2 percent of adjusted gross income. The most notable deductions covered by §67 are deductions claimed under §212 and deductions claimed by employees under §162. Thus, for example, a self-employed practicing lawyer or a self-employed salesperson may claim deductions under §162 without regard to §67. The §162 expenses of a lawyer or salesperson who works as an employee, however, are covered by §67, though the burden may be avoided to a considerable extent, with the cooperation of the employer, by establishing a "reimbursement or other expense allowance arrangement with [the] employer." §62(a)(2)(A).

To some extent §67 has the effect of disallowing deductions for expenses with a significant personal element — for example, the cost of subscribing to the Wall Street Journal or of entertainment of customers. At the same time, however, it disallows deductions for expenses with no personal element — for example, fees paid by an investor to an investment adviser or to agents by actors (who typically become employees in each of the separate productions for which their services are engaged).

There are also a variety of specific tax rules designed to limit or deny particular types of deductions — for example, §280A, which severely limits deductions for vacation homes and home offices. In the interests of administrability and of prevention of abuse, rules such as these may establish arbitrary criteria for deduction. The result may be unfairness in individual cases.

A. CONTROLLING THE ABUSE OF BUSINESS DEDUCTIONS

1. Hobby Losses

NICKERSON v. COMMISSIONER

700 F.2d 402 (7th Cir. 1983)

Pell, Circuit Judge.

Petitioners appeal the judgment of the United States Tax Court finding that profit was not their primary goal in owning a dairy farm. Based on this finding the tax court disallowed deductions for losses incurred in renovating the farm. The sole issue presented for our review is whether the tax court's finding regarding petitioners' motivation was clearly erroneous.

I. Facts

Melvin Nickerson (hereinafter referred to as petitioner) was born in 1932 in a farming community in Florida. He worked evenings and weekends on his father's farm until he was 17. Petitioner entered the field of advertising after attending college and serving in the United States Army. During the years relevant to this case he was self-employed in Chicago, serving industrial and agricultural clients. His wife, Naomi W. Nickerson, was a full-time employee of the Chicago Board of Education. While petitioners were not wealthy, they did earn a comfortable living.

At the age of forty, petitioner decided that his career in the "youth oriented" field of advertising would not last much longer, and he began to look for an alternative source of income for the future. Petitioners decided that dairy farming was the most desirable means of generating income and examined a number of farms in Michigan and Wisconsin. After several years of searching, petitioners bought an 80-acre farm in Door County, Wisconsin for $40,000. One year later they purchased an additional 40 acres adjoining the farm for $10,000.

The farm, which had not been run as a dairy for eight years, was in a run-down condition. What little equipment was left was either in need of repair or obsolete. The tillable land, about 60 acres, was planted with alfalfa, which was at the end of its productive cycle. In an effort to improve this state of affairs petitioners leased the land to a tenant farmer for $20 an acre and an agreement that the farmer would convert an additional ten acres a year to the cultivation of a more profitable crop. At the time of trial approximately 80 acres were tillable. The rent received from the farmer was the only income derived from the farm.

Petitioner visited the farm on most weekends during the growing season and twice a month the rest of the year. Mrs. Nickerson and the children visited less frequently. The trip to the farm requires five hours of driving from petitioners' home in Chicago. During these visits petitioner and his family either worked on their land or assisted neighboring farmers. When working on his own farm petitioner concentrated his efforts on renovating an abandoned orchard and remodeling the farm house. In addition to learning about farming through this experience petitioner read a number of trade journals and spoke with the area agricultural extension agent.

Petitioners did not expect to make a profit from the farm for approximately 10 years. True to their expectations, petitioners lost $8,668 in 1976 and $9,872.95 in 1977. Although they did not keep formal books of account petitioners did retain receipts and cancelled checks relating to farm expenditures. At the time of trial, petitioners had not yet acquired any livestock or farm machinery. The farm was similarly devoid of recreational equipment and had never been used to entertain guests.

The tax court decided that these facts did not support petitioners' claim that the primary goal in operating the farm was to make a profit. We will examine the tax court's reasoning in more detail after setting out the relevant legal considerations.

II. The Statutory Scheme

Section 162(a) of the Code allows deduction of "all the ordinary and necessary expenses paid or incurred during the taxable year in carrying on any trade or business." Section 183, however, limits the availability of these deductions if the activity "is not engaged in for profit" to deductions that are allowed regardless of the existence of a profit motive and deductions for ordinary and necessary expenses "only to the extent that the gross income derived from such activity for the taxable year exceeds [otherwise allowable deductions]." §183(b)(2). The deductions claimed by petitioners are only allowable if their motivation in investing in the farm was to make a profit.

Petitioners bear the burden of proving that their primary purpose in renovating the farm was to make a profit.[4] . . . In meeting this burden, however, "it is sufficient if the taxpayer has a bona fide expectation of realizing a profit, regardless of the reasonableness of such expectation." . . . Although petitioners need only prove their sincerity rather than their realism the factors considered in judging their motivation are primarily objective. In addition to the taxpayer's statements of intent, which are given little weight for obvious reasons, the tax court must consider "all facts and circumstances with respect to the activity," including the following:

> (1) *Manner in which the taxpayer carries on the activity.* The fact that the taxpayer carries on the activity in a businesslike manner and maintains complete and accurate books and records may indicate that the activity is engaged in for profit. . . .
>
> (2) *The expertise of the taxpayer or his advisors.* Preparation for the activity by extensive study of its accepted business, economic, and scientific prac-

4. The Code does provide a presumption that a taxpayer engaged in an activity with a bona fide profit motive when a profit is realized two of five consecutive years. §183(d). Because of petitioners' consistent losses this is not available. [The rule has now been changed from two of five to three of five consecutive years. — Eds.]

> tices, or consultation with those who are expert therein, may indicate that the taxpayer has a profit motive where the taxpayer carries on the activity in accordance with such practices. . . .
>
> (3) *The time and effort expended by the taxpayer in carrying on the activity.* The fact that the taxpayer devotes much of his personal time and effort to carrying on the activity, particularly if the activity does not have substantial personal or recreational aspects, may indicate an intention to derive a profit. . . . The fact that the taxpayer devotes a limited amount of time to an activity does not necessarily indicate a lack of profit motive where the taxpayer employs competent and qualified persons to carry on such activity.
>
> (4) *Expectation that assets used in activity may appreciate in value.* . . .
>
> (5) *The success of the taxpayer in carrying on other similar or dissimilar activities.* . . .
>
> (6) *The taxpayer's history of income or losses with respect to the activity.* . . .
>
> (7) *The amount of occasional profits, if any, which are earned.* . . .
>
> (8) *The financial status of the taxpayer.* . . .
>
> (9) *Elements of personal pleasure or recreation.* The presence of personal motives in [the] carrying on of an activity may indicate that the activity is not engaged in for profit, especially where there are recreational or personal elements involved. On the other hand, a profit motivation may be indicated where an activity lacks any appeal other than profit. It is not, however, necessary that an activity be engaged in with the exclusive intention of deriving a profit or with the intention of maximizing profits. . . .

Treas. Reg. §1.183-2(b)(1)-(9). None of these factors is determinative, nor is the decision to be made by comparing the number of factors that weigh in the taxpayer's favor with the number that support the Commissioner. Id. There is no set formula for divining a taxpayer's true motive, rather "[o]ne struggles in vain for any verbal formula that will supply a ready touchstone. The standard set by the statute is not a rule of law; it is rather a way of life. Life in all its fullness must supply the answer to the riddle." Welch v. Helvering [infra page 645]. Nonetheless, we are given some guidance by the enumerated factors and by the Congressional purpose in enacting section 183.

> The legislative history surrounding section 183 indicates that one of the prime motivating factors behind its passage was Congress' desire to create an objective standard to determine whether a taxpayer was carrying on a business for the purpose of realizing a profit or was instead merely attempting to create and utilize losses to offset other income.

Jasionowski v. Commissioner, 66 T.C. 312, 321 (1976). Congressional concern stemmed from a recognition that

> [w]ealthy individuals have invested in certain aspects of farm operations solely to obtain "tax losses" — largely bookkeeping losses — for use to

> reduce their tax on other income. . . . One of the remarkable aspects of the problem is pointed up by the fact that persons with large nonfarm income have a remarkable propensity to lose money in the farm business.

S. Rep. No. 91-552, 91st Cong., 1st Sess., reprinted in 1969 U.S. Code Cong. & Ad. News 2027, 2376. With this concern in mind we will now examine the decision of the tax court.

III. Decision of the Tax Court

The tax court analyzed the relevant factors and determined that making a profit was not petitioners' primary goal in engaging in farming. The court based its decision on a number of factors that weighed against petitioners. The court found that they did not operate the farm in a businesslike manner and did not appear to have a concrete plan for improving the profitability of the farm. The court believed that these difficulties were attributable to petitioners' lack of experience, but did not discuss the steps actually taken by Melvin Nickerson to gain experience in farming.

The court found it difficult to believe that petitioners actually believed that the limited amount of time they were spending at the farm would produce a profit given the dilapidated condition of the farm. Furthermore, the court found that petitioners' emphasis on making the farm house habitable rather than on acquiring or repairing farm equipment was inconsistent with a profit motive. These factors, combined with the consistent history of losses borne by petitioners, convinced the court that "petitioner at best entertains the hope that when he retires from the advertising business and can devote his complete attention to the farming operation, he may at that time expect to produce a profit." The court did not think that this hope rose to the level of a bona fide expectation of profit.

IV. Review of the Court's Findings

Whether petitioners intended to run the dairy farm for a profit is a question of fact, and as such our review is limited to a determination of whether the tax court was "clearly erroneous" in determining that petitioners lacked the requisite profit motive. . . . This standard of review applies although the only dispute is over the proper interpretation of uncontested facts. . . . This is one of those rare cases in which we are convinced that a mistake has been made.

Our basic disagreement with the tax court stems from our belief that the court improperly evaluated petitioners' actions from the perspective of whether they sincerely believed that they could make a profit from their current level of activity at the farm. On the contrary, petitioners need only prove that their current actions were motivated by the expectation that they would later reap a profit, in this case when they finished renovating the farm and began full-time operations. It is well established that a taxpayer need not expect an immediate profit; the existence of "start up" losses does not preclude a bona fide profit motive. . . . We see no basis for distinguishing petitioners' actions from a situation in which one absorbs larger losses over a shorter period of time by beginning full-time operations immediately. In either situation the taxpayer stands an equal chance of recouping start-up losses. In fact, it seems to us a reasonable decision by petitioners to prepare the farm before becoming dependent upon it for sustenance. Keeping in mind that petitioners were not seeking to supplement their existing incomes with their current work on the farm, but rather were laying the ground work for a contemplated career switch, we will examine the facts relied upon by the tax court.

The tax court found that the amount of time petitioners devoted to the farm was inadequate. In reaching this conclusion the court ignored petitioners' agreement with the tenant-farmer under which he would convert 10 acres a year to profitable crops in exchange for the right to farm the land. In this situation the limited amount of time spent by petitioners, who were fully employed in Chicago, is not inconsistent with an expectation of profit. . . .

The court also rested its decision on the lack of a concrete plan to put the farm in operable condition. Once again, this ignores petitioners' agreement with the tenant-farmer concerning reclamation of the land. Under this agreement the majority of the land would be tillable by the time petitioners were prepared to begin full-time farming. The tax court also believed that petitioners' decision to renovate the farm house and orchard prior to obtaining farm equipment evidenced a lack of profit motive. As petitioners planned to live on the farm when they switched careers refurbishing the house would seem to be a necessary first step. The court also failed to consider the uncontradicted testimony regarding repairs made to the hay barn and equipment shed, which supported petitioners' contention that they were interested in operating a farm rather than just living on the land. Additionally, we fail to understand how renovating the orchard, a potential source of food and income, is inconsistent with an expectation of profit.

The tax court took into account the history of losses in considering petitioners' intentions. While a history of losses is relevant, in this case little weight should be accorded this factor. Petitioners did not expect to make a profit for a number of years, and it was clear from the condition of the farm that a financial investment would be required before the farm could be profitable. . . .

The court believed that most of petitioners' problems were attributable to their lack of expertise. While lack of expertise is relevant, efforts at gaining experience and a willingness to follow expert advice should also be considered. Treas. Reg. §1.183-2(b)(2). The court here failed to consider the uncontradicted evidence that Melvin Nickerson read trade journals and Government-sponsored agricultural newsletters, sought advice from a state horticultural agent regarding renovation of the orchard and gained experience by working on neighboring farms. In addition, petitioners' agreement with the tenant-farmer was entered into on the advice of the area agricultural extension agent. To weigh petitioners' lack of expertise against them without giving consideration to these efforts effectively precludes a bona fide attempt to change careers. We are unwilling to restrict petitioners in this manner and believe that a proper interpretation of these facts supports petitioners' claims.

The tax court recognized that the farm was not used for entertainment and lacked any recreational facilities, and that petitioners' efforts at the farm were "prodigious," but felt that this was of little importance. While the Commissioner need not prove that petitioners were motivated by goals other than making a profit, we think that more weight should be given to the absence of any alternative explanation for petitioners' actions. As we previously noted the standard set out by the statute is to be applied with the insight gained from a lifetime of experience as well as an understanding of the statutory scheme. Common sense indicates to us that rational people do not perform hard manual labor for no reason, and if the possibility that petitioners performed these labors for pleasure is eliminated the only remaining motivation is profit. The Commissioner has argued that petitioner was motivated by a love of farming that stems from his childhood. We find it difficult to believe that he drove five hours in order to spend his weekends working on a dilapidated farm solely for fun, or that his family derived much pleasure from the experience. Furthermore, there is no support for this contention in the record. At any rate, that petitioner may have chosen farming over some other career because of fond memories of his youth does not preclude a bona fide profit motive. Treas. Reg. §1.183-2(b)(9). We believe that the absence of any recreational purpose strongly counsels in favor of finding that petitioners' prodigious efforts were directed at making a profit. . . .

If this were a case in which wealthy taxpayers were seeking to obtain tax benefits through the creation of paper losses we would hesitate to reverse. Before us today, however, is a family of modest means attempting to prepare for a stable financial future. The amount of time and hard work invested by petitioners belies any claim that allowing these deductions would thwart Congress' primary purpose, that of excluding "hobby" losses from permissible deductions. Accordingly, we hold that the tax court's finding was clearly erroneous and reverse.

NOTES AND QUESTIONS

1. *Hobby losses and tax losses.* Since the court in *Nickerson* holds that the Nickersons' farm activity was a business and not a hobby, the losses incurred in running the farm are deductible — that is, those losses can be used to offset the Nickersons' salary and other income. Assuming that the Nickersons reasonably and realistically viewed their cash outlays on the farm not as money down the drain (a true economic loss) but rather as an investment in what they hoped would be a valuable asset, their loss can be thought of as an artifact of the tax system, a "tax loss" that is not a true economic loss. (See further discussion of this point in Note 2 below.) The Code now contains a variety of provisions designed to limit the deductibility of tax losses, most notably §469 (adopted in 1986), which denies current deductions for certain losses from "passive activities." Under that section, an individual with a loss from a passive activity may deduct that loss only (1) to offset income from other passive activities; (2) to offset income from passive activities in later years; or (3) at the time the investment which generated the loss is sold. A passive activity is statutorily defined as a trade or business in which the taxpayer does not materially participate. §469(c). Under proposed Treasury regulations, an individual will be deemed to materially participate only if one of seven tests is met. Under one test, an individual must work at the activity for more than 500 hours a year; under another test, an individual's work on the activity must constitute substantially all of the work on the activity. Regs. §1.469-5T. If the Nickersons' farm were considered a passive activity, then the loss from the farm could be deducted only against other current or future income from passive activities, or at the time the farm were sold. If, on the other hand, the farm were considered a hobby, the loss would be a personal expense and, as such, would never be deductible. The passive activity loss rules of §469 are discussed in more detail in Chapter 6 (infra page 711).

2. *Start-up costs.* Although the Tax Court opinion in *Nickerson* does not describe the outlays that gave rise to the deductible losses, it seems clear that on the court's view of the taxpayers' primary objective, those outlays were made for the purpose of creating a productive farm; they were part of the farm's start-up costs. For purposes of normal accounting, such outlays should be treated as capital expenditures; they are part of the cost of acquisition of a productive farm, not current expenses. For tax purposes, however, the outlays are treated as deductible expenses, at least for a cash-method farmer. (The distinction between capital expenditures and current expenses is explored infra at Chapter 6A, page 613.) On the government's view of the case, the distinction between capital and current outlays was irrelevant to the outcome of the case it was litigating, since the outlays were simply the personal cost of indulging a desire to play farmer. The distinction would, however, be relevant to basis and thus to gain on disposition. If a person buys a

farm for purely personal purposes, the acquisition cost becomes the farm's basis, which affects gain or loss on ultimate disposition. Though a loss would not be deductible, a gain would be taxable. Expenses of maintaining the farm (current outlays) would not be added to basis and thus would not reduce any gain that might otherwise be realized on disposition, but even for a farm owned for personal purposes capital outlays would increase basis.

3. *Imputed income.* One other source of some possible confusion in *Nickerson* is that Mr. Nickerson appears to have performed valuable services in improving the farm. As we have seen, the value of those services is a form of imputed income that escapes taxation. See supra page 117. (In this situation, however, even if income were imputed, that income would be offset by a deduction — as if Mr. Nickerson had paid himself wages, which would then be part of the costs that the court considered he was entitled to deduct.) The value of the services was an element that made the prospect for profit better by far than it would otherwise have been and thus helped establish that the Nickersons' primary purpose was economic gain, not personal pleasure. Suppose that Mr. Nickerson had hired someone else to perform all the services that he in fact performed himself. Would that have weakened or strengthened his argument that he was seeking primarily profit rather than pleasure in operating the farm?

4. *Primary purpose.* (a) The *Nickerson* court follows the typical approach in cases involving activities with both business and personal elements: It seeks to determine the taxpayer's primary purpose. The objectively observed facts reviewed by the court are indirect evidence of purpose. The court insists, however, that the taxpayers "need only prove their sincerity rather than their realism." In other words, a person might establish a sincere intent to make a profit even though the hope or expectation of profit is unrealistic. How likely do you suppose it is that a person with an unrealistic expectation will be able to prove a sincere intent to make a profit? See infra Note 7. How important are the nine factors listed in the regulations (§1.183-2(b)) and cited by the court? See the last sentence of Regs. §1.183-2(a).

(b) Is the court's decision too trusting and generous? Why do you suppose the farm had been abandoned eight years before the Nickersons bought it?

5. *An alternative approach.* Is primary purpose the best test? Why not focus on benefit? Suppose, for example, that it could be established that the Nickersons had lost (and had expected to lose) $10,000 per year, that the farm was not as good an investment as other alternatives available to them, but that it became a good investment when they took account of the fact that it provided $6,000 worth of pleasure each year. How much deduction, if any, would you allow? What if the pleasure had been worth only $4,000 per year? Is it feasible to determine the

value of the pleasure element? Less so than to determine primary purpose? If you don't like either approach because of the difficulty of the factual determinations, what objective approach would you prefer?

6. *The role of §183.* (a) Does §183 provide much guidance with respect to the basic question of deductibility in cases like *Nickerson?*

(b) Note the presumption rule in §183(d). Where applicable, this rule overcomes the normal presumption of correctness of the Commissioner's determination. Did that presumption seem important in *Nickerson?*

(c) Section 183(b) allows income generated by a hobby venture to be offset by the expenses of that venture (after reduction of the income by the amount of any deductions, such as for interest and taxes, allowed without regard to profit-seeking motive), but, since 1987, only to the extent that those expenses, plus other miscellaneous expenses, exceed 2 percent of AGI. See §§67, 183(b).

7. *Results in other hobby cases.* Commenting on country estate and racing stable cases, long ago Randolph Paul said: "The American businessman has never appeared so indefatigably optimistic as in some of the cases on this point." Paul, Motive and Intent in Federal Tax Law, in Selected Studies in Federal Taxation 281-282 (2d ser. 1938).

Horse breeding and racing, though the sport of kings, have been held in a surprising number of cases to be the business of taxpayers. See, e.g., Farish v. Commissioner, 103 F.2d 63 (5th Cir. 1939). In that case, the possibility of geographical and occupational discrimination was suggested (103 F.2d at 65):

> It is common for a man in the oil business, of sound judgment, to expend thousands of dollars in exploring the land and drilling for oil in "wild cat" territory. Sometimes, this results in dry holes and the costs of drilling and development are totally lost. On other occasions, producing wells are brought in and the profits are enormous. The breeding of horses would not be considered merely a fad in Texas. It is not at all improbable that men in the oil business, having ample capital, would engage in the enterprises here involved with the hope and expectation of ultimately making a fair return on the investment.

In Dailey v. Commissioner, 44 T.C.M. 1352 (1982), the taxpayers, husband and wife, who were knowledgeable and experienced antique collectors, were denied deductions of $4,050 for the cost of a trip to Europe to visit museums, $926 for travel to museums in this country for the same purpose, and $201 for subscriptions to art and antique journals. The court observed (44 T.C.M. at 1353):

> Petitioners collected art and antique items for fun and profit, much like a philatelist might collect stamps, or a numismatist coins. Over a period of more than three decades, petitioners never advertised any item for sale, never offered an item for sale, and in fact never sold an item. A

> comprehensive inventory was first prepared in connection with this trial. They hoped to make a profit through appreciation, but so does the numismatist or philatelist. This floating expectation does not make the trip to Europe or to museums in this country deductible.

Do you think that the Nickersons had more than a "floating expectation" of profit? Is antique collecting basically different from farming in ways that should affect tax results? If you represented a couple like the Daileys before the Tax Court, what kind of evidence would you want to introduce?

2. Home Offices and Vacation Homes

Many people have offices in their homes, or at least claim that they do, even though their principal place of work is elsewhere. Where a person does in fact use part of his home exclusively, or even primarily, for business, the costs of that part of the home (including a pro rata share of utility bills and depreciation on that part) might properly be regarded as a deductible business expense. It is not difficult, however, to see the opportunities for abuse of any opportunity for deduction. For many years, the Service and the courts tried to curb the abuses, but that was a losing effort. The problem was that it was easy for a dishonest, or at least self-serving, taxpayer to offer his or her own testimony in support of a primary business purpose or use and difficult for the government to rebut that testimony. Not only were some taxpayers winning doubtful cases at the administrative level (within the IRS) and in the courts, but many more were playing, and winning, the audit lottery. Congress finally intervened, in 1976, adopting the stringent restrictions found in §280A. The approach of §280A is to begin with a general rule denying deductions for any use of a home for business purposes (§280A(a)) and then to list specific, concrete exceptions (§280A(c)), which you should examine briefly.

At the same time it addressed offices in the home, Congress dealt with vacation homes, again a source of considerable abuse. There are, of course, taxpayers who have bought resort-area houses and condominiums strictly as investments. Often these investments showed losses for tax purposes because deductions for interest, taxes, depreciation, utilities, condominium fees, and so forth exceeded rental returns. In other words, a resort-area house or condominium could have been acquired as a "tax shelter," with no element of personal use. The 1986 act substantially reduced the attractiveness of such investments by disallowing deductions for "passive losses." See §469, described infra page 711. People may continue to hold, or acquire, such investments despite the passive loss limitations. They should be, and are, allowed to offset any income from renting such units by claiming all the ordinary deductions, including depreciation (ACRS). But there is another tax issue. In the past many people acquired resort-area dwelling units largely for personal use, while claiming that the purpose of the acquisition was to make a profit and that the personal use was purely incidental. Since a profit-making objective depends on the investor's state of mind, the opportunity for abuse was, as with offices in the home, great. Real estate developers aggressively exploited the opportunity to sell vacation units intended for mostly personal use by pointing to the tax advantages that could be achieved by claiming investor status. Section 280A deals with this problem, with an arbitrary approach that is severe, though somewhat less so than the approach taken with respect to offices in the home.

Because §280A covers both vacation homes and offices in the home, it is not easy to follow. Moreover, the rules for both vacation homes and offices in the home are themselves complex.

(a) Vacation homes. The title of §280A refers to "vacation homes," and vacation homes presented the problem that Congress sought to cure in adopting the provision, but the language of the statute covers any "dwelling unit" that is used by the taxpayer for more than a specified amount of time during the year for personal purposes. See §280A(a) and (d). The specified amount of time is the greater of "14 days, or 10 percent of the number of days during [the] year for which [the] unit is rented at a fair rental." See §280A(d)(1).

(1) If the unit is not used at all for personal purposes, the taxpayer is allowed to deduct expenses (utilities, repairs, condominium fees, etc.), depreciation (cost recovery), interest, and taxes, subject to the limitation on deduction of passive activity losses.

(2) If the unit is used for personal purposes for more than the specified amount of time, but is rented out for less than 15 days, then the owner excludes the rental income and may not claim deductions other than for interest and taxes (which are deductible without regard to profit motive, subject to the §163(h) limits on the interest deduction). See §280A(g), (b). This is obviously intended to be a de minimis exception but has allowed tax windfalls for people who have been able to rent their homes for short periods, at high rents, during times of special events such as the Olympics in Los Angeles in 1984.

(3) If the unit is used for personal purposes for less than the specified amount of time, the disallowance rule of §280A(a) does not apply, but the deduction other than for taxes is allowed only on a pro rata basis (comparing rental and personal use) (§280A(e)) and, again, is subject to the limitation on deduction of passive activity losses. (Interest cannot be deducted without regard to profit because the unit is not a "second home," since it is occupied less than the required number of days. If a profit motive is lacking, the interest becomes "personal interest," which is not deductible. See §163(h)(1), (h)(3), and (h)(4)(A).)

(4) If the unit is used for personal purposes for more than the specified amount of time, then expenses other than interest and taxes must still be prorated, but the deduction for such prorated expenses cannot exceed the rent received, reduced by an allocable share of the interest and taxes. See §280A(c)(5). This rule is comparable to that found in §183(b), which limits deductions for hobby activities to the income from the activity (see Regs. §1.183-1(d)(3)).

(b) Offices in the home. To curb the abuse of deductions for offices in the home, Congress used broad language denying a deduction (§280A(a)), followed by a set of specific, relatively concrete exceptions (§280A(c)). Specificity in statutory language serves the laudable goal of providing clear guidance to taxpayers and of reducing the possibility of ad hoc, or even personalized, decisions by government employees. At the same time, specific rules may lead to seemingly unfair results.

PROBLEMS

1. (a) Susan is an associate at a large law firm. On nights and weekends, Susan often works at home in her study. Susan and her family also use the study for personal purposes. The use of the study is divided about equally between personal and work activities. May Susan deduct half of the cost of the study as a business expense? See §280A(c).

(b) The facts are the same as in (a) except that the study is used exclusively for work. May Susan deduct the cost of the study as a business expense?

(c) The facts are the same as in (b) except that Susan sees clients in the study. May Susan deduct the cost of the study as a business expense?

2. Sharon uses her vacation home sixty days a year and rents it out ten days a year. What portion, if any, of the depreciation and rental expenses may Sharon deduct? See §280A(g). (For this and the following questions, you may assume that otherwise deductible losses will not be limited by the passive loss rules of §469.)

3. (a) Anne uses her vacation home five days a year and rents it out ninety-five days a year. Rental income from the property is $8,000, real estate taxes are $2,000, and annual depreciation and maintenance for the property amounts to $10,000. There are no other expenses associated with the property. How much, if any, of the annual depreciation and maintenance expense may Anne deduct? See §280A(e).

(b) The facts are the same as in (a) except that Anne uses her vacation home fifteen days a year and rents it out eighty-five days a year. How much, if any, of the annual depreciation and maintenance expense may Anne deduct? See §280A(c)(5), (e).

The following case, decided in 1983, arises under §280A, but the outcome turns on whether the taxpayers were engaged in a "trade or business." The "trade or business" concept arises in a variety of contexts and has taken on increased importance recently because of the adoption in 1986 of §67. Section 67, as we have seen, imposes a 2 percent threshold on deductions for expenses claimed by investors, under §212, but not for expenses claimed, under §162, as trade or business expenses. Indeed, in the case itself there is a reference to substantial expenses that were deducted without challenge under §212 and that would now be subject to §67's partial disallowance.

MOLLER v. UNITED STATES

721 F.2d 810 (Fed. Cir. 1983)

Before KASHIWA, Circuit Judge, NICHOLS, Senior Circuit Judge, and NIES, Circuit Judge.

KASHIWA, Circuit Judge.

This is an appeal by the United States from a judgment of the Claims Court granting taxpayers, Joseph A. and Dorothy D. Moller, a tax refund for the years 1976 and 1977. 1 Cl. Ct. 25, 553 F. Supp. 1071 (1982). The Claims Court concluded that taxpayers were active investors engaged in the "trade or business" of making investments and held that taxpayers were entitled to deduct the expenses of two home offices under I.R.C. §280A. For the reasons stated below, we reverse.

FACTS

Since 1965 taxpayers have relied almost entirely on the income derived from their investments for their support. Their only other sources of income have been two small pensions and social security payments.

The Mollers' investments consist of four portfolios of stocks and bonds. Mr. and Mrs. Moller own an investment portfolio individually and each receives income from a portfolio held in trust. However, they have full management control of all four portfolios, including those held in trust.

In 1976 and 1977 taxpayers devoted their full time to their investment activities. Each spent approximately forty to forty-two hours per week in connection with these activities. They kept regular office hours and monitored the stock market on a daily basis. They made all their investment decisions on their own. The total value of the four portfolios was $13,500,000 in 1976 and $14,500,000 in 1977.

The Mollers engaged in a variety of activities in managing their portfolios. They maintained a "watch list" listing their portfolios. They maintained a "watch list" listing all stocks on the New York Stock Exchange that were considered to be potential purchases. They kept detailed records of the stocks in their portfolios. They also subscribed to and regularly studied a number of financial publications and services.

The Claims Court concluded that taxpayers engaged in 83 security purchase transactions and 41 sales transactions in 1976 and 76 purchase and 30 sales transactions in 1977. Eight of the security purchase transactions in 1976 and nine in 1977 consisted of deposits to secure shares in interest-bearing common trust accounts; three transactions in 1976 and 23 in 1977 consisted of invasions by Mrs. Moller of her trust corpus; and 14 transactions in 1976 and nine in 1977 consisted of stocks acquired through splits and dividends. Twenty-two of the sales transactions in 1976 and seven in 1977 were withdrawals from common trust accounts. The stocks which taxpayers sold in 1976 and 1977 had been held for an average of more than 3½ and 8 years, respectively.

The taxpayers did not purchase stocks for speculative purposes. They were primarily interested in long-term growth potential and the payment of interest and dividends. Interest and dividend income was over 98% of their gross income in 1976 and 1977. In 1976 their income from the sale of securities was only $612, while in 1977 their sales resulted in a loss of $223.

The taxpayers also invested in Treasury Bills but they did so to maintain liquidity and earn interest. Of the taxpayers' 46 Treasury Bill transactions in 1976 and 1977, only 7 involved bills sold before maturity.

The Mollers maintained a summer and a winter residence. Each house had quarters in which the taxpayers conducted their investment activities. The taxpayers kept regular hours and used the quarters exclusively for investment activities.

In managing their portfolios, the taxpayers incurred expenses of $22,659.91 in 1976 and $29,561.69 in 1977, and deducted these on their joint income tax returns. The expenses attributable to maintaining the taxpayers' two home-offices amounted to $7,439.65 in 1976 and $7,247.21 in 1977.[5]

The Internal Revenue Service disallowed that portion of the claimed deductions based on the home-office expenses for both offices and asserted deficiencies against the taxpayers for the years 1976 and 1977.[6] The taxpayers paid the deficiencies and filed claims for refunds. After

5. The home-office expenses included depreciation, utilities, insurance, and various maintenance expenses attributable to the offices.

6. The other investment expenses, amounting to $15,220.26 for 1976 and $22,314.48 for 1977 included subscriptions, office supplies, accounting and legal services, and other similar items. There is no dispute that taxpayers are entitled to deduct these expenses under I.R.C. §212.

these claims were disallowed, the taxpayers brought this action seeking recovery of the taxes paid, plus interest.

The Claims Court held that taxpayers were investors, not traders, but were nevertheless engaged in the trade or business of making investments and therefore entitled to deduct their home-offices expenses under section 280A of the Internal Revenue Code.

Opinion

I

Section 280A was added to the Internal Revenue Code of 1954 by the Tax Reform Act of 1976, Pub. L. No. 455, 90 Stat. 1520, to provide "definitive rules . . . governing the deductibility of expenses attributable to the maintenance of an office in the taxpayers' personal residence." S. Rep. No. 938, 94th Cong., 2d Sess. 144, 147, reprinted in 1976 U.S. Code Cong. & Admin. News 2897, 3576, 3579; H.R. Rep. No. 658, 94th Cong., 2d Sess. 157, 160, reprinted in 1976 U.S. Code Cong. & Admin. News 2897, 3050, 3053. Section 280A generally disallows all deductions for a taxpayer's use of a residence. Section 280A(c)(1)(A), however, provides an exception to this rule for that portion of the residence used as "the principal place of business for any trade or business of the taxpayer."

In order to get a deduction under section 280A, a taxpayer must conduct an activity which is a trade or business, the principal office of which is in his home.[7] Prior to the enactment of section 280A, home-office expenses could have been deducted either under I.R.C. §162(a), if incurred in carrying on a trade or business, or under I.R.C. §212 if incurred for the production of income. The legislative history of section 280A makes clear that a taxpayer can no longer take a home-office deduction for an activity where it is for the production of income within the meaning of section 212 but is not a "trade or business" under section 162. . . .

The principal question in the instant case is whether the taxpayers' investment activity was a trade or business.

II

Neither the Internal Revenue Code nor the regulations define "trade or business." However, the concept of engaging in a trade or business, as distinguished from other activities pursued for profit, has been in

7. There is also the statutory requirement that the office be "exclusively used on a regular basis." The government concedes that this requirement has been met.

the Internal Revenue Code since its inception and has generated much case law.

In determining whether a taxpayer who manages his own investments is engaged in a trade or business, the courts have distinguished between "traders," who are considered to be engaged in a trade or business, and "investors," who are not. See e.g., Levin v. United States, 597 F.2d 760, 765 (Ct. Cl. 1979). Contrary to the holding of the trial court, investors are considered to be merely engaged in the production of income. See Purvis v. Commissioner, 530 F.2d 1332 (9th Cir. 1976).

This court's predecessor, the Court of Claims, has defined a trader as one whose profits are derived from the "direct management of purchasing and selling." *Levin*, 597 F.2d at 765. The Ninth Circuit has adopted a similar test to distinguish between investment and trading accounts:

> In the former, securities are purchased to be held for capital appreciation and income, usually without regard to short-term developments that would influence the price of securities on the daily market. In a trading account, securities are bought and sold with reasonable frequency in an endeavor to catch the swings in the daily market movements and profit thereby on a short term basis.

Purvis, 530 F.2d at 1334, quoting Liang v. Commissioner, 23 T.C. 1040, 1043 (1955).

Therefore, in order to be a trader, a taxpayer's activities must be directed to short-term trading, not the long-term holding of investments, and income must be principally derived from the sale of securities rather than from dividends and interest paid on those securities. In determining whether a taxpayer who manages his own investments is a trader, and thus engaged in a trade or business, relevant considerations are the taxpayer's investment intent, the nature of the income to be derived from the activity, and the frequency, extent, and regularity of the taxpayer's securities transactions. See *Purvis,* 530 F.2d at 1334.

The Claims Court concluded that taxpayers were investors and not traders because they were primarily interested in the long-term growth potential of their stocks. We agree. Mr. Moller testified that he was looking for long-term growth and the payment of dividends. In addition, the taxpayers did not derive their income from the relatively short-term turnover of stocks, nor did they derive any significant profits through the act of trading. Interest and dividend income was over 98% of taxpayers' gross income for 1976 and 1977, and in 1976 their profit from the sale of securities was only $612, while in 1977 their sales resulted in a loss of $223.

The number of sales transactions made by the taxpayers also leads to the conclusion that they were not traders in securities. In the cases in which taxpayers have been held to be in the business of trading in securities for their own account, the number of their transactions indicated that they were engaged in market transactions on an almost daily basis. At most, the Mollers engaged in 83 security purchase transactions and 41 sales transactions in 1976 and 76 purchase and 30 sales transactions in 1977.

Moreover, taxpayers did not "endeavor to catch the swings in the daily market movements and profit thereby on a short term basis." *Purvis,* 530 F.2d at 1334. The stocks owned by taxpayers, which they sold during 1976 and 1977, had been held for an average of over 3½ and 8 years, respectively.

The Mollers were investors and not traders. The Claims Court so concluded and we agree.

III

The Claims Court, however, went on to hold that despite the fact that the Mollers were investors, they were in the trade or business of making investments. The court distinguished between passive and active investors and concluded that the Mollers were active investors engaged in a trade or business because their investment activities were regular, extensive, and continuous, and they involved the active and constant exercise of managerial and decision-making functions. We disagree.

A taxpayer who merely manages his investments seeking long-term gain is not carrying on a trade or business. This is so irrespective of the extent or continuity of the transactions or the work required in managing the portfolio. Higgins v. Commissioner, 312 U.S. 212 (1941). The fact that the Mollers spent much time managing a large amount of money is not determinative of the question whether they were engaged in a trade or business.

In *Higgins* a taxpayer who resided abroad maintained an office in the United States to handle bookkeeping and other details of his extensive security transactions. The taxpayer directed these activities from abroad. He sought primarily permanent investments but did make changes in his portfolio. Despite the fact that the taxpayer devoted a considerable amount of time to overseeing his securities, the Court held that his securities activities did not constitute a trade or business:

> The petitioner merely kept records and collected interest and dividends from his securities, through managerial attention for his investments. No matter how large the estate or how continuous or extended the work required may be, such facts are not sufficient as a matter of law to permit the courts to reverse the decision of the Board.

312 U.S. at 218.

The Claims Court, relying on Kales v. Commissioner, 101 F.2d 35 (6th Cir. 1939), distinguished the *Higgins* case on the basis that the taxpayer's activities in *Higgins* "were not at all comparable to the regular, extensive, and continuous activities of the plaintiffs in this case." In *Kales,* the Sixth Circuit held that a taxpayer was engaged in the trade or business of managing her own investments because her management activities were "extensive, varied, regular and continuous." 101 F.2d at 39. However, in a subsequent case, the Sixth Circuit recognized that "the decision in *Kales* was impliedly if not expressly disapproved in *Higgins*. . . ." Goodyear Investment Corp. v. Campbell, 139 F.2d 188, 191.

The Claims Court erred in relying on the *Kales* case. The "regular, extensive, and continuous" test is not in itself the correct test for determining whether a taxpayer is engaged in the trade or business of managing his own investments. In *Higgins,* the Court stated that continuity and extent of investment activity were not determinative of the question of whether a taxpayer who manages his own investment is engaged in a trade or business. In a subsequent case, Whipple v. Commissioner, 373 U.S. 193 (1963), the Court stated that it had established a definition of trade or business in *Higgins* and went on to explain the import of the case:

> In response to the *Higgins* case and to give relief to Higgins-type taxpayers . . . Section 23(a) (now I.R.C. §162) was amended not by disturbing the Court's definition of "trade or business" but by following the pattern that had been established since 1916 of "[enlarging] the category of incomes with reference to which expenses were deductible" . . . to include [in new §212] expenses incurred in the production of income.

373 U.S. at 200.

The Internal Revenue Code, however, does not provide that all expenses incurred in the production of income are deductible expenses. In *Whipple,* section 166, which restricts bad debt deductions to those incurred in a trade or business, as section 280A restricts home-office deductions to expenses incurred in a trade or business, was at issue. In denying the taxpayer a deduction because the bad debt was incurred in an activity entered into for profit, and not in a trade or business, the Court stated: "[w]hen the only return is that of an investor, the taxpayer has not satisfied his burden of demonstrating that he is engaged in a trade or business since investing is not a trade or business. . . ." 373 U.S. at 202.

The Court of Claims, relying on *Higgins,* has also stated: "Managing one's own investments in securities is not the carrying on of a trade or business, irrespective of the extent of the investments or the amount of time required to perform the managerial functions." Wilson v. United States, 376 F.2d 280, 293 (1967).

In the instant case, taxpayers were not engaged in a trade or business. They were active investors in that their investment activities were continuous, regular, and extensive. However, this is not determinative of the issue and it is not the correct test. What is determinative is the fact that the taxpayers' return was that of an investor: they derived the vast majority of their income in the form of dividends and interest; their income was derived from the long-term holding of securities, not from short-term trading; and they were interested in the capital appreciation of their stocks, not short-term profits. Merely because taxpayers spent much time managing their own sizeable investments does not mean that they were engaged in a trade or business.

CONCLUSION

Although taxpayers' investment activity was entered into for the production of income, it did not rise to the level of a trade or business. Section 280A restricts home-office deductions to expenses incurred in the carrying on of a trade or business. Therefore, taxpayers were not entitled to a deduction under this section.

Because we decide this case on the grounds that taxpayers were not engaged in the trade or business of making investments, we need not and do not reach the issue of whether they could deduct the expenses of both their home-offices as their "principal place of business."

Accordingly, the judgment of the Claims Court is reversed.

QUESTIONS

1. Under the *Moller* decision, deductions are allowed under §280A for traders but not for investors like the Mollers. What is the difference between a trader and an investor?

2. Does the deduction claimed by the Mollers seem to have strong personal elements? In general, are the expenses of investors more likely to be personal than those of traders?

3. Reconsider the *Nickerson* case. Why do you suppose Congress might be unwilling or unable to adopt arbitrary rules for denial of deductions for hobby farmers? Can you think of how such a rule might be framed?

NOTES

1. Specific, arbitrary rules sometimes offer clever tax advisers the opportunity to devise "creative" tax plans (also less respectfully referred

to as tax avoidance schemes or loopholes). Where the statutory language is specific and clear, judges, responding to the notion that taxpayers should be able to rely on the plain meaning of such language, may be required to validate a tax-reduction plan that seems to undercut the abuse-curbing objectives of the provision at issue. The process is illustrated in Feldman v. Commissioner, 791 F.2d 781 (9th Cir. 1986). The taxpayer in that case was an accountant and was one of the principals (a shareholder and managing director) in the incorporated accounting firm at which he performed his services. He had good business reasons for doing some of his work at home and for that purpose used one room of his house exclusively as an office. If the firm had simply made an adjustment in his salary and he had borne the cost of the office, he would not have been entitled to any deduction for his office expense (a pro rata share of utilities and other expenses and depreciation). See the plain language of §280A(c)(1). Instead, he rented the office to the firm (technically, his employer) and claimed a deduction under §280A(c)(3). The Commissioner disallowed the deduction, claiming that the taxpayer's arrangement was an artificial scheme designed to avoid the strict limitations of §280A(c)(1). The Tax Court held in favor of the taxpayer. 84 T.C. 1 (1985). The Ninth Circuit affirmed, stating that the taxpayer "draws his support from the plain meaning of the statute" and that "we are content to await the action of Congress." The wait was not long. In the 1986 act, Congress added §280A(c)(6), adopting plain language reversing the result in the case. The new provision adds to the bulk of the Code and to its apparent complexity. It does not significantly increase taxpayer compliance burdens, since its effect is simply that people will not engage in artificial transactions that only a clever person intent on reducing his taxes would have thought of in the first place. Still, it is one more provision that many lawyers and accountants will be required to be aware of.

2. Arbitrary rules can also, of course, generate harsh, seemingly unfair, and possibly unintended outcomes. In Commissioner v. Soliman, — U.S. — (1993), the taxpayer was an anesthesiologist who spent about thirty-five hours per week practicing his profession in three separate hospitals. None of the hospitals supplied him with an office. He set aside a spare room in the condominium in which he lived and used this room exclusively as an office. He spent two to three hours a day in the office, performing such tasks as "contacting patients, surgeons, and hospitals by telephone; maintaining billing records and patient logs; preparing for treatments and presentations; satisfying continuing medical education requirements; and reading medical journals and books." He claimed deductions for a portion of his condominium fees, utilities, and depreciation allocable to the office. The Court held that the deductions were not allowable because the office was not the doctor's "principal place of business" within the meaning of §280A(c)(1)(A). This

conclusion was based on the amount of time spent in the office and at the hospitals and the importance of the activity carried on at each place.

3. Office Decoration

HENDERSON v. COMMISSIONER

46 T.C.M. 566 (1983)

Petitioners, Hoke F. Henderson, Jr., and Karen L. Henderson (hereinafter petitioner), resided at Columbia, S.C., at the time the petition was filed.

Petitioner was employed in 1977 by the State of South Carolina as an assistant attorney general. As an employee of the State of South Carolina, petitioner was provided an office with furniture and furnishings that consisted of a desk, a desk chair, a work table, a telephone, a dictaphone, a bookcase, a filing cabinet, law books, and two chairs for visitors. Her duties included consulting with public officials and attorneys and others from the private sector, which at times took place in her office.

During 1977, petitioner purchased a framed print for $35 and a live plant for $35 for the purpose of decorating her office. In addition, petitioner paid a total of $180 to rent a parking space located across the street from her office. Petitioner occasionally used her automobile for business purposes when an automobile from the pool of State automobiles was not available.

In the statutory notice of deficiency, respondent disallowed the deduction for the framed print, live plant, and parking fees in their entirety.

Opinion

The only issue is whether petitioner is entitled to a deduction under section 162(a) for amounts paid for a framed print and live plant used to decorate her office, and for amounts paid to rent a parking space. Petitioner contends that the expenses were all ordinary and necessary business expenses deductible under section 162(a). Respondent counters that the expenses were not ordinary and necessary, and that the expenses are nondeductible personal expenses under section 262. We agree with respondent that the expenses constitute nondeductible personal expenses under section 262.

Section 162(a) allows a deduction for all the ordinary and necessary expenses paid or incurred during the taxable year in carrying on any trade or business. However, even assuming an expense meets the requirements of section 162(a), it still may be disallowed if the amount was expended for a personal, living, or family expense. Sec. 262. The essential inquiry here is whether a sufficient nexus existed between petitioner's expenses and the "carrying on" of petitioner's trade or business to qualify the expenses for the deduction under section 162(a), or whether they were in essence personal or living expenses and nondeductible by virtue of section 262. . . . Moreover, where both sections 162(a) and 262 may apply, the latter section takes priority over the former. . . .

We find that the amounts paid for the framed print and live plant were expended to improve the appearance of petitioner's office, a personal expense, and only tangentially, if at all, aided her in the performance of her duties as an employee of the State of South Carolina. Her employer had provided her with all the furnishings considered necessary to do her job. No evidence was presented to prove that the presence of the print and plant in her office were either necessary or helpful in performing her required services. "It is not enough that there may be some remote or incidental connection" with the taxpayer's business to support the deduction. Larrabee v. Commissioner, 33 T.C. 838, 843 (1960).

The two cases primarily relied on by petitioners, Gillis v. Commissioner, T.C. Memo. 1973-96, and Judge v. Commissioner, T.C. Memo. 1976-283, are distinguishable. In *Gillis* the Court relied on the fact that the circumstances were very unusual. In *Judge,* which involved a pediatrician who furnished his own office, the Court found that the paintings in issue were of subjects "intended to be of interest to children," the taxpayer's patients, and were used solely for the purpose of decoration of petitioner's business offices and not for any personal or non-business use. Accordingly, we deny the deduction for these two expenditures.

QUESTIONS

1. Suppose that Ms. Henderson had been in private practice and had bought the plant and the print for her office. Would she have been entitled to treat the cost as a business outlay?

2. Suppose that Ms. Henderson had installed a carpet in her office and had donated it to the state of South Carolina. Would she have been entitled to a charitable deduction? See supra pages 494-501.

4. Automobiles and Computers

The 1984 act provides special rules for "listed property," which includes computers kept in the home, automobiles, "any property of a type generally used for purposes of entertainment, recreation, or amusement," or "any other property of a type specified by the Secretary by regulations." §280F(d)(4). Where listed property is used 50 percent or less for business purposes, depreciation (as to the portion of the cost allocable to business use) is limited to straightline using the normal useful life (as opposed to the shorter life available under ACRS). §280F(b). Moreover, where an employee (such as a professor of law) acquires and uses listed property (such as a computer in his or her home), the business use requirement of this provision is not met except by use that is "for the convenience of the employer and required as a condition of employment." §280F(d)(3). Does that seem fair? Even as applied to a professor who is single and uses the computer exclusively for writing articles and books? If not, how can the denial of the deduction be justified? What about the possibility of having the university "require" that the professor buy the computer? The House Conference Report on the Tax Reform Act of 1984, H.R. Rep. No. 861, 98th Cong., 2d Sess. 1027 (1984), says that the "condition of employment" language will not be "satisfied merely by an employer's statement that the property is required as a condition of employment. The conferees intend that the principles of Dole v. Commissioner, 43 T.C. 697, aff'd, 351 F.2d 308 (1st Cir. 1965) apply." In *Dole,* the Tax Court said (at 706) that the test is "objective"; it does not turn on the employer's "state of mind." Is it likely that a law professor could show that he or she was required by objectively observable circumstances to have the tools of the teaching and writing trade in his or her home rather than at the office supplied by the law school?

B. TRAVEL AND ENTERTAINMENT EXPENSES

If a person must go to another city on business, the cost of getting there and back is deductible. If the person stays overnight, the cost of food and lodging also is deductible. In most instances these rules are easily reconciled with sound tax policy objectives, but such reconciliation can become difficult where there are significant personal as well as business benefits from the trip. We properly ignore the fact that a person traveling on business may enjoy traveling. The fact that one enjoys one's job is not a reason for denying a deduction of the costs of getting that job done; purely psychic benefits are not part of the income tax base. But suppose that a person is going to another city on business, that the person's mother happens to live there, and that the person is anxious to see her. Now we have a substantial personal benefit that is not an inextricable part of the business activity. Suppose that the air fare for the trip is $400, that the person would have been willing to pay this much for the purely business objectives, but that he or she would also have been willing to pay that amount to travel to the same place just to see his or her mother. An appealing argument can be made for including in income the value of the personal satisfaction or (what amounts to the same thing) denying a deduction for the $400. But the practical difficulty of such an approach should be obvious. The rule that the courts purport to apply is that the cost of a trip, or of other activities such as dinner with a customer at a restaurant, is deductible if the "primary purpose" is business. The primary purpose test is based on unrealistic assumptions about how people think and about the ability of the tax authorities to get at the true facts. For example, if you travel to another city on business and see your mother while you're there, do you necessarily engage in a mental process in which you weigh the value of the business objective against that of the personal objective? Of course not. And even if you did, the IRS employee who examines your return would have no practical way of verifying or challenging your assertions about that mental process. Thus, one can reasonably surmise that in practice some other test must be used. In all probability that test is that if there is a *sufficient* business justification for the trip, the deduction will be allowed. Even that test leaves considerable opportunity for cheating, since the tax authorities are properly reluctant, and limited in their ability, to challenge the business judgments of taxpayers. The following cases provide some sense of the nature of the problem, but they reflect those relatively unusual situations where the IRS happened to detect abuse, decided to attack it without compromise, and was successful (or at least partly so) in its attack. In reading the cases, think about the taxpayer attitudes that resulted in the litigation. It was that kind of attitude that led to the relatively stringent rules now found in §274 (discussed in the notes following the two cases), but the "expense account living" that is characterized by the cases is by no means a thing of the past.

1. Early Cases

RUDOLPH v. UNITED STATES

370 U.S. 269 (1962)

PER CURIAM. . . .

An insurance company provided a trip from its home office in Dallas, Texas, to New York City for a group of its agents and their wives. Rudolph and his wife were among the beneficiaries of this trip, and the Commissioner assessed its value to them as taxable income. It appears to be agreed between the parties that the tax consequences of the trip turn upon the Rudolphs' "dominant motive and purpose" in taking the trip and the company's in offering it. In this regard, the District Court, on a suit for a refund, found that the trip was provided by the company for "the primary purpose of affording a pleasure trip . . . in the nature of a bonus reward, and compensation for a job well done" and that from the point of view of the Rudolphs it "was primarily a pleasure trip in the nature of a vacation. . . ." 189 F. Supp. 2, 4-5. The Court of Appeals approved these findings. 291 F.2d 841. Such ultimate facts are subject to the "clearly erroneous" rule, cf. Comm'r v. Duberstein [supra page 130], and their review would be of no importance save to the litigants themselves. The appropriate disposition in such a situation is to dismiss the writ as improvidently granted. . . .

Mr. Justice FRANKFURTER took no part in the decision of this case.

Mr. Justice WHITE took no part in the consideration or decision of this case.

Separate opinion of Mr. Justice HARLAN. . . .

[N]ow that the case is here I think it better to decide it, two members of the Court having dissented on the merits. . . .

Petitioners, husband and wife, reside in Dallas, Texas, where the home office of the husband's employer, the Southland Life Insurance Company, is located. By having sold a predetermined amount of insurance, the husband qualified to attend the company's convention in New York City in 1956 and, in line with company policy, to bring his wife with him. The petitioners, together with 150 other employees and officers of the insurance company and 141 wives, traveled to and from New York City on special trains, and were housed in a single hotel during their two-and-one-half-day visit. One morning was devoted to a "business meeting" and group luncheon, the rest of the time in New York City to "travel, sightseeing, entertainment, fellowship or free time." The entire trip lasted one week.

The company paid all the expenses of the convention-trip . . . petitioner's allocable share being $560. . . . The District Court held that the value of the trip being "in the nature of a bonus, reward, and compensation for a job well done," was income to Rudolph, but being "primarily a pleasure trip in the nature of a vacation," the costs were personal and nondeductible.

I

Under §61 . . . was the value of the trip to the taxpayer-husband properly includable in gross income? . . .

[I]t was surely within the Commissioner's competence to consider as "gross income" a "reward, or a bonus given to . . . employees for excellence in service," which the District Court found was the employer's primary purpose in arranging this trip. . . .

II

There remains the question whether, though income, this outlay for transportation, meals, and lodging was deductible by petitioners as an "ordinary and necessary" business expense under §162. . . .

[T]he crucial question is whether . . . the purpose of the trip was "related primarily to business" or was rather "primarily personal in nature." . . . [T]hat certain doctors, lawyers, clergymen, insurance agents or others have or have not been permitted similar deductions only shows that in the circumstances of those cases, the courts thought that the expenses were or were not deductible as "related primarily to business."

The husband places great emphasis on the fact that he is an entrapped "organization man," required to attend such conventions, and that his future promotions depend on his presence. Suffice it to say that the District Court did not find any element of compulsion; to the contrary, it found that the petitioners regarded the convention in New York City as a pleasure trip in the nature of a vacation. . . .

Mr. Justice DOUGLAS, with whom Mr. Justice BLACK joins, dissenting.

I

It could not, I think, be seriously contended that a professional man, say a Senator or a Congressman, who attends a convention to read a paper or conduct a seminar *with all expenses paid* has received "income." . . . Income has the connotation of something other than the mere payment of expenses. . . .

The formula "all expenses paid" might be the disguise whereby compensation "for services" is paid. Yet it would be a rare case indeed where one could conclude that a person who gets only his expenses for attendance at one convention gets "income" in the statutory sense. If this arrangement were regular and frequent or if it had the earmarks of a sham device as a cloak for remuneration, there would be room for fact-finders to conclude that it was evasive. But isolated engagements of the kind here in question have no rational connection with compensation "for services" rendered.

It is true that petitioner was an employee and that the expenses for attending the convention were paid by his employer. He qualified to attend the convention by selling an amount of insurance that met a quota set by the company. Other salesmen also qualified, some attending and some not attending. They went from Dallas, Texas, to New York City, where they stayed two and a half days. One day was given to a business session and a luncheon; the rest of the time was left for social events.

On this record there is no room for a finding of fact that the "expenses paid" were "for services" rendered. They were apparently a proper income tax deduction for the employer. The record is replete with evidence that from management's point of view it was good business to spend money on a convention for its leading agents — a convention that not only kept the group together in New York City, but in transit as well, giving ample time for group discussions, exchanges of experience, and educational training. It was the exigencies of the employment that gave rise to the convention. There was nothing dishonest, illegitimate, or unethical about this transaction. No services were rendered. New York City may or may not have been attractive to the agents and their wives. Whether a person enjoys or dislikes the trip that he makes "with all expenses paid" has no more to do with whether the expenses paid were compensation "for services" rendered than does his attitude toward his job. . . .

III

The wife's expenses are, on this record, also deductible.[8] The Treasury Regulations state in §1.162-2(c):

> Where a taxpayer's wife accompanies him on a business trip, expenses attributable to her travel are not deductible unless it can be adequately shown that the wife's presence on the trip has a bona fide business purpose. The wife's performance of some incidental service does not cause her expenses to qualify as deductible business expenses. . . .

The civil law philosophy, expressed in the community property concept, attributes half of the husband's earnings to the wife — an equitable idea that at long last was reflected in the idea of income splitting under the federal income tax law. The wife's contribution to the business productivity of the husband in at least some activities is well known. . . . Business reasons motivated the inclusion of wives in this particular insurance convention. An insurance executive testified at this trial:

8. This case arose before the adoption of §274(m)(3), which, beginning in 1994, would expressly deny a deduction by Rudolph's employer of the travel expenses of the spouses.

Q. I hand you Plaintiff's Exhibit 15, and you will notice it is a letter addressed to "John Doe"; also a bulletin entitled "A New Partner Has Been Formed."
Will you tell us what that consists of?
A. This is a letter addressed to the wife of an agent, a new agent, as we make the contract with him. This letter is sent to his wife within a few days after the contract, enclosing this booklet explaining to her how she can help her husband in the life insurance business.
Q. Please tell us, as briefly as you can and yet in detail, how you as agency director for Southland attempt to integrate the wives' performance with the performance of agents in the life insurance business.
A. One of the important functions we have in mind is the attendance at these conventions. In addition to that communication, occasionally there are letters that will be written to the wife concerning any special sales effort that might be desired or promoted. The company has a monthly publication for the agents and employees that is mailed to their homes so the wife will have a convenient opportunity to see the magazine and read it.
At most of our convention program[s], we have some specific references to the wife's work, and in quite a few of the convention programs we have had wives appear on the program.
Q. Suppose you didn't have the wives and didn't seek to require their attendance at a convention, would there be some danger that your meetings and conventions would kind of degenerate into stag affairs, where the whole purpose of the meeting would be lost?
A. I think that would definitely be a tendency.

I would reverse the judgments below and leave insurance conventions in the same category as conventions of revenue agents, lawyers, doctors, businessmen, accountants, nurses, clergymen and all others, until and unless Congress decides otherwise.

SCHULZ v. COMMISSIONER

16 T.C. 401 (1951), acq., 1951-2 C.B. 4

ARUNDELL, J.

The respondent has disallowed as a deduction from the petitioner's 1945 taxable income the sum of [$9,300] claimed as entertainment expense, and a $400 item claimed as advertising expense. There is no serious dispute as to whether either of these sums was spent; the issue is whether they are deductible.

Entertainment expenses are allowed as a deduction from gross income only to the extent that they are "ordinary and necessary" in carrying on a trade or business. . . . The requirements that the expense must be both ordinary and necessary must be strictly complied with . . . and whether contested expenditures are ordinary and necessary is primarily a question of fact. . . . Proof is required that the purpose of the expenditure was primarily business rather than social or personal, and that business in which taxpayer is engaged benefited or was intended to be benefited thereby. . . .

During 1945, petitioner elaborately entertained buyers and others connected with the jewelry business, personally spending about $7000. In addition thereto approximately $2000 was expended by his wife and employees on luncheons, drinks, weekend visits, conventions, suppers, theaters, and nightclubs. Approximately $3400 of the $7000 expended by petitioner personally was spent on suppers, theaters, and nightclubs and other forms of evening entertainment. On these occasions petitioner would bring his wife and the party or parties he was entertaining would also bring their wives. There is little to distinguish these occasions from the usual social gatherings among friends to renew acquaintanceship and enjoy a pleasant evening. They bear little semblance to the usual gatherings of business people at restaurants or other places of entertainment which serve primarily as congenial meeting places for the discussion or negotiation of business matters. Petitioner made no attempt to show that the evening entertainment he offered his guests served this purpose or that all of it was directly related to the operations of his business.

These gatherings may have been desirable and helpful to the present and future success of petitioner's business, but this is usually true of all entertaining done by business or professional people for the purpose of acquiring or retaining the favor of patrons and clients. Such expenditures are nonetheless nondeductible absent a showing that they were ordinary and necessary to the taxpayer's business . . . [and that they] "had a direct relation to the conduct of a business or the business benefits expected." [Boehm v. Commissioner, 35 B.T.A. 1106.]

After taking into consideration the nature of the entertainment provided by the petitioner and the fact that it was undertaken at a time when he had more business than he could handle, we are not convinced that all of the expenditures in issue were made for purely business reasons. . . .

Moreover, the petitioner's attempt to deduct such nondeductible items as the cost of repairing an automobile, the cost of hotel rooms, tips, and meals on two occasions when, after a night of entertaining customers, he remained in New York after missing the train home, and the inclusion of $200 which had been placed in the petty cash fund but was not expended on entertainment, all create doubt as to the accuracy of the total deduction.

On the other hand, we are convinced that some part of the expenditures was prompted by strictly business considerations and should be characterized as ordinary and necessary expenses. Applying the rule of

Cohan v. Comm'r,[9] we have reached an approximation . . . that $5500 fairly represents the amount spent by the petitioner for ordinary and necessary business entertainment. . . .

The petitioner has included in his advertising expense the sum of $400 spent in entering his horse named "Schulztime" in a horse show and for such items as horse show programs and trophies. Petitioner has not satisfactorily shown how these expenditures were calculated to advertise or publicize his business. There is no evidence that the petitioner called the attention of those persons attending the horse shows to the fact that he was a dealer in watches by advertising in the horse show program. . . . There is an inference in the record that the name "Schulztime" was relied on by petitioner to publicize his business but if this be true the name chosen was so subtle and the entry of a horse in a show so far removed from the petitioner's business that it could not reasonably have been expected to publicize the business. In our opinion, the $400 so expended was not an ordinary and necessary business expense. . . .

2. Section 274

The requirement of the *Schulz* decision of a "direct relation" between a claimed deduction and the alleged business benefit was by no means universally applied by the courts, much less by the Service. The attitudes reflected by the claims of the taxpayers in *Schulz* and *Rudolph* and by the dissenting justices in *Rudolph* were widespread, as was the perception that many taxpayers were routinely and successfully claiming the kinds of deductions involved in the two cases. Moreover, the law, at least as administered, vested in employees of the Internal Revenue Service a

9. [In Cohan v. Commissioner, 39 F.2d 540, 543 (2d Cir. 1930), the court (per Judge L. Hand) made an approximation of the business expenses incurred by George M. Cohan under these circumstances:

> In the production of his plays, Cohan was obliged to be free-handed in entertaining actors, employees, and, as he naively adds, dramatic critics. He had also to travel much, at times with his attorney. These expenses amounted to substantial sums, but he kept no account and probably could not have done so. At the trial before the Board [of Tax Appeals] he estimated that he had spent eleven thousand dollars in this fashion during the first six months of 1921, twenty-two thousand dollars, between July 1, 1921, and June 30, 1922, and as much for his following fiscal year, fifty-five thousand dollars in all. The Board refused to allow him any part of this, on the ground that it was impossible to tell how much he had in fact spent, in the absence of any items or details. The question is how far this refusal is justified, in view of the finding that he had spent much and that the sums were allowable expenses. Absolute certainty in such matters is usually impossible and is not necessary; the Board should make as close an approximation as it can, bearing heavily if it chooses upon the taxpayer, whose inexactitude is of his own making.

The scope of the *Cohan* doctrine was much reduced by the enactment of §274(d) (relating to substantiation of travel and entertainment expenses) in 1962. — Eds.]

degree of discretion that was offensive to the principle of a "government of laws" and created far too much opportunity for corruption. In 1962, Congress, responding to these and other problems, enacted §274, which superimposes on the basic requirements of §162 additional rules for travel and entertainment (often referred to as "T and E"). Congress has amended §274 at various times since then. Section 274 is specific and detailed; the regulations, which to a considerable extent pick up ideas and language found in congressional committee reports, are even more so. The principal features of §274 are described below.

Required relationship between expense and business purpose. Section 274(a)(1)(A) allows taxpayers to deduct the cost of "any activity which is of a type generally considered to constitute entertainment, amusement, or recreation" only if the activity is "directly related" to business. This language echoes the "direct relation" requirement found in *Schulz* and is intended to rule out deductions for entertainment intended merely to establish goodwill. See Regs. §1.274-2(c). It is true, of course, that expenditures to establish goodwill might be incurred for sound business reasons, but in this instance the opportunity for abuse proved to be so great as to justify a blanket denial of deductions. The direct relationship standard of §274(a) is weakened considerably, however, by another part of that same section, which allows deductions for expenses that are "associated with" business and directly precede or follow a "substantial and bona fide business discussion." Thus, for example, not only is the cost of a dinner at which business is discussed treated as a business expense, but the cost of a dinner or sporting or other entertainment event that directly precedes or follows a business discussion is also treated as a business expense. That provides plenty of scope for expense-account living for taxpayers who are willing to stretch the truth or who genuinely believe that their entire lives are business. And it may help explain why, if you must pay your own way, with no help from the government by way of a tax deduction, you may find you cannot afford good seats at professional basketball or football games.[10]

Fifty percent limitation on meal and entertainment deduction. Section 274(n), adopted in 1986, limits the otherwise allowable deduction for meals and entertainment to 50 percent of the cost. The remaining 50 percent of the cost is treated as a nondeductible personal expense. The reasons given in Congress in 1986 for the original version of this provision, which limited the deduction to 80 percent of the amount otherwise allowable, are noted in the Report of the Senate Finance Committee

10. Some relief may be experienced by beleaguered nonbusiness sports and entertainment enthusiasts as a result of a provision adopted in 1986 that limits deductions for tickets to sports and entertainment events to the face value of the ticket (except in case of certain charitable events). §274(l)(1)(A). The 1986 act also limited deductions for the cost of renting a "skybox." §274(l)(1)(b).

in its discussion of the 1986 act (S. Rep. No. 313, 99th Cong., 1st Sess. 68 (1986)):

> The committee believes that present law, by not focusing sufficiently on the personal-consumption element of deductible meal and entertainment expenses, unfairly permits taxpayers who can arrange business settings for personal consumption to receive, in effect, a Federal tax subsidy for such consumption that is not available to other taxpayers. The taxpayers who benefit from deductibility under present law tend to have relatively high incomes, and in some cases the consumption may bear only a loose relationship to business necessity. For example, when executives have dinner at an expensive restaurant following business discussions and then deduct the cost of the meal, the fact that there may be some bona fide business connection does not alter the imbalance between the treatment of those persons, who have effectively transferred a portion of the cost of their meal to the Federal Government, and other individuals, who cannot deduct the cost of their meals.
>
> The significance of this imbalance is heightened by the fact that business travel and entertainment often may be more lavish than comparable activities in a nonbusiness setting. For example, meals at expensive restaurants and season tickets at sporting events are purchased to a significant degree by taxpayers who claim business deductions for these expenses. This disparity is highly visible, and contributes to public perceptions that the tax system is unfair. Polls indicate that the public identifies the deductibility of normal personal expenses such as meals to be one of the most significant elements of disrespect for and dissatisfaction with the present tax system.
>
> In light of these considerations, the committee bill generally reduces by 20 percent the amount of otherwise allowable deductions for business meals and entertainment. [See §274(n).] This reduction rule reflects the fact that meals and entertainment inherently involve an element of personal living expenses, but still allows an 80 percent deduction where such expenses also have an identifiable business relationship. The bill also tightens the requirements for establishing a bona fide business reason for claiming meal and entertainment expenses as deductions. [See §274(k).] The bill includes exceptions to the general percentage reduction rule for certain traditional employer-paid recreational expenses for employees, de minimis fringe benefits, promotional activities made available to the general public, costs for certain sports events related to charitable fund-raising, and meals provided as an integral part of certain business meeting programs during 1987-88.

Expenses of spouse. Where a person is on a legitimate tax-deductible business trip, no deduction is allowed for the additional travel expenses of the person's spouse (or dependent, or any other person accompanying that person), unless (i) the spouse (etc.) is an employee of the person claiming the deduction, (ii) the spouse (etc.) had a bona fide business purpose for going on the trip, *and* (iii) the additional expenses would otherwise be deductible. §274(m)(3) (added by the 1993 act). This provision overrules cases allowing deductions of a spouse's expenses if there was a valid reason for the spouse to come along (such as assisting with the entertainment of clients).

Section 274's substantiation requirements. By virtue of §274(d), no deduction may be taken for traveling expenses, entertainment, or business gifts unless the taxpayer "substantiates by adequate records or by sufficient evidence corroborating the taxpayer's own statement" the amount, the time and place of the travel or entertainment or the date and description of the gift, the business purpose of the expense, and the business relationship to the person entertained or the donee. This requirement of substantiation is intended to overrule the *Cohan* case, supra page 554, in this area. As the *Schulz* case demonstrates, the practice before 1962 of not requiring precise records encouraged taxpayers to claim generous estimates of entertainment expenditures and then to rely on the *Cohan* rule. The substantiation requirement may have been the most significant aspect of the 1962 T and E legislation.

The Treasury is authorized to dispense with some or all of the substantiation requirements, and this power has been exercised as to some expenditures. For example, the amount of expenditures under $25 (other than for lodging) need not be substantiated by receipts (Regs. §1.274-5T(c)(2)(iii)); per diem and mileage allowances paid by an employer to an employee need not be substantiated if they do not exceed maximum amounts specified from time to time by the Commissioner (Regs. §1.274-5T(g)); employees are not required to substantiate expenses to the Service if they have substantiated those expenses to their employers for purposes of obtaining reimbursement (Regs. §1.274-5T(f)(2)); and taxpayers may claim fixed per diem amounts for meals ($34 per day in high-cost cities like New York City or Chicago and $26 per day in other places) without substantiation if the time, place, and business purpose of the travel are properly substantiated (but subject to §274(n)'s 50 percent limitation on the deduction for meals). See Rev. Proc. 92-17, 92-1 C.B. 679.

Entertainment facilities. With respect to entertainment *facilities,* such as yachts, hunting lodges, country clubs, and the like, the 1962 legislation was much more stringent than it was with respect to entertainment *activities* (meals and entertainment). Even so, the perception of continuing abuse became so great that in 1978, §274(a) was amended to deny completely deductions for the basic costs (e.g., depreciation on a yacht) of facilities other than clubs. For clubs, the dues could be deducted only if the club was used "primarily for the furtherance of the taxpayer's trade or business." If, for example, a country club was used a great deal by a taxpayer's family and occasionally for entertaining the taxpayer's business guests, the taxpayer would not be heard to assert that he or she would not have joined but for the business use; a deduction for the dues was disallowed. Finally, in 1993, Congress went all the way and denied any deduction for "amounts paid or incurred for membership in any club organized for business, pleasure, recreation, or other social purpose." §274(a)(3).

Exceptions. Examine briefly §274(e), which contains exceptions that are relatively straightforward and easy to understand.

Foreign travel. Section 274(c) provides that in certain circumstances, where a person combines business and pleasure on a trip to a foreign country, the air fare is partially disallowed. This provision seems to look to benefit rather than to primary purpose or to the sufficiency of the business objective. As initially adopted in 1962 it applied to domestic as well as foreign travel but in 1964 was repealed as to domestic travel. The moral of this bit of history would seem to be that one should not underestimate the political power of the hotel and travel industry and the unions representing all the people who work in that industry.

Cruises and foreign conventions. Section 274(h) now contains rules, not part of the original 1962 legislation, that disallow deductions for conventions held outside the "North American area" unless "it is as reasonable for the meeting to be held outside the North American area as within." Again, this was a response to widespread abuses such as deduction of the expenses of attending an annual American Bar Association convention held in London and, more so, to the adverse effects of the prior law on the owners and employees of domestic hotels and restaurants. There is also a special rule for conventions and seminars on cruise ships (§274(h)(2)) and a rule, added in 1986, denying deductions for "luxury water transportation" (§274(m)(1)).

QUESTIONS AND PROBLEMS

1. The court in *Schulz* disallowed part of the taxpayer's expenses for insufficient proof. What kind of proof was lacking? Assume that the expenses in *Schulz* were incurred subsequent to the enactment of §274. Do you think it is more or less likely that the taxpayer would deduct those expenses? If the taxpayer deducted the expenses, do you think it more or less likely that the deduction would be upheld on audit or in court?

2. (a) A law firm with offices in six cities holds an annual three-day "retreat" for partners at an exclusive warm-weather resort in February. The firm sponsors the following activities: Friday and Saturday night banquets; Saturday and Sunday golf and tennis tournaments; and Sunday horseback riding. A two-hour firm meeting is held from noon to 2 P.M. on Saturday. The firm's leading partners believe that the annual meetings enable partners in different offices to become acquainted with one another and share views about the firm. Attendance

at the retreat is encouraged but not required. All expenses are paid by the firm. Are the expenses deductible? See §274(a)(1)(A), §274(e)(4), (5); Regs. §1.274-2(f)(2)(vi).

(b) The facts are the same as in (a) except that associates are also invited to the retreat and many associates believe that attendance will further their chances of making partner. Are the associates taxable on the value of the room, meals, and entertainment?

3. Lawyer Lopez's law firm invites promising law students to interview with members of the firm. After the interview, the students are taken out to dinner. Lopez often takes his wife (not a lawyer) along on such dinners. Is the cost of Lopez's wife's dinner deductible? See Regs. §1.274-2(d)(4).

4. (a) Lawyer Friedman is a partner in an urban law firm. The law firm buys season tickets for the local professional baseball team's games. Lawyers at the firm generally give the tickets to clients, or use the tickets to take clients to the games. About one-fourth of the time, however, the tickets are not claimed by lawyers who wish to give them to clients or take clients to games. In that case, the tickets are used by the firm's partners and their families and friends. Should the firm be allowed to deduct the entire cost of the season tickets?

(b) The facts are the same as in (a) except that tickets not given to clients or used to take clients to games are used by associates and their families or friends. Are the associates taxed on the value of the tickets?

The following cases illustrate the application of the substantiation rules. They also suggest the difficulty of enforcement: Imagine the number of taxpayers who claimed deductions like the ones at issue in these cases whose returns were not selected for audit.

LEVINE v. COMMISSIONER

51 T.C.M. 651 (1986)

Petitioners resided in Brockton, Massachusetts, at the time their petition was filed. As used hereinafter, petitioner in the singular refers to Paul R. Levine.

During the years in issue, petitioner was employed by and president of, C. Itoh Shoe Company, Inc. (hereinafter Cisco), a New York corporation which imported footwear. Petitioner was responsible, in part, for the development and/or approval of Cisco's annual and long-range plans and of its routine and extraordinary product lines, the approval of sales contracts in the ordinary course of business, lines of credit up to $100,000, and the terms of payment and settlement of disputes of less than $10,000 with customers and factors. He was authorized to incur, and was reimbursed for, reasonable expenses of promoting Cisco's business, including entertainment expenses. Petitioner's compensation by Cisco was $64,166.69 in 1979 and $62,082.85 in 1980.

During the years in issue, petitioner was also the owner and sole employee of Ray Levine, Inc., a Massachusetts corporation engaged in the sale of footwear and retained by Cisco as an independent sales representative. Under the terms of the Independent Sales Representative Agreement (Agreement) between these corporations, Ray Levine, Inc. was required to maintain its own sales office and pay all expenses incurred by it. The record does not indicate what percent of petitioner's time was dedicated to the business of Ray Levine, Inc. as opposed to his employment by Cisco. Petitioner reported income of $62,121.77 and $48,590 from Ray Levine, Inc. in 1979 and 1980, respectively.

[The court first considered a deduction for an office in the taxpayers' home.]

We turn now to . . . expenses for business entertainment in [the taxpayers'] home. Early in his sales career, petitioner found that it was advantageous to entertain customers and business associates in a social atmosphere in his home. Petitioner called on approximately 20 customers regularly and, during any year, he would entertain approximately 12 of these customers in his home. Additionally, executives of Cisco and other high ranking corporate officials of Taiwanese companies would be guests in petitioners' home. To create a relaxed atmosphere, petitioner would invite his customers and business associates to his home on weekends or weekday evenings and entertain them, their wives, children, and other relatives. During these weekend and evening entertainments, business was generally discussed and, at times, petitioner's customers would review his product line in the basement. While orders were written on some occasions, the record does not indicate the frequency or significance of this activity.

In order to be entitled to deduct entertainment expenses, petitioners must demonstrate that the requirements of Code sections 162 and 274 have been met. . . . Section 162 allows a deduction for ordinary and necessary business expenses. Section 274 is a disallowance provision: it operates to disallow expenses which have been shown to be deductible under another section of the Code. . . . Section 274(d)(2) provides that a taxpayer must substantiate by adequate records or sufficient evidence corroborating his or her statements the following elements of all claimed entertainment expenses, the amount, time and place, and business purpose of the expenditures as well as the business relationship to the taxpayer of the persons entertained. See sections 1.274-5(b)(3) and 1.274-5(c)(2) and (3), Income Tax Regs. These strict requirements for deductibility were intended by Congress to overrule the so-called Cohan rule (Cohan v. Commissioner, 39 F.2d 540 (2d Cir. 1930)) which enabled the Court in certain circumstances to make an approximation of a deductible expense. . . . Mere estimates of expenses and uncorroborated oral testimony are insufficient to satisfy the requirements of section 274(d). . . .

Mrs. Levine estimated business entertainment in the home including use of the family swimming pool and dinners or other refreshments, occurred approximately 60 times a year. She further estimated that an afternoon with couples at the pool would cost approximately $30 whereas a full dinner with all the embellishments involved an expense of $55 to $75. While we question the deductibility of all expenses claimed in conjunction with petitioners' home entertainment, we need not determine what percent, if any, constitutes bona fide business entertainment since petitioners have failed in any way to provide the requisite expense substantiation.[11] We also do not need to address respondent's alternative argument that petitioners' home entertainment expenses were not directly related to or associated with the active conduct of petitioner's trade or business and, therefore, would not be deductible even if substantiated.

Petitioners candidly admit that "strict compliance with record keeping requirements is not present." They argue, however, that circumstances exist which mitigate against demanding full compliance with section 274(d) substantiation requirements. According to petitioners, such circumstances include the facts that (1) the estimates of Mrs. Levine are "extremely educated recollection[s]" and "essentially the equivalent of a 'contemporaneous diary' admittedly without specific names relating to specific dates"; (2) the 60 occasions estimated were not challenged by respondent; and (3) the estimated number and per-occasion cost of $100 were reasonable. These facts do not mitigate against requiring full compliance with section 274(d) or exculpate petitioners from their failure to do so. Petitioners' reliance on Howard v. Commissioner, T.C. Memo. 1981-250, for the proposition that failure to observe the stringent requirements of section 274 is not fatal is misplaced. In that case, the taxpayers substantiated the amounts claimed as deductions, the corporate employer had explicitly adopted a policy requiring the taxpayer to entertain in the home, business dinners were held rather infrequently and usually on a weekday night after the conclusion of the day's business, the taxpayers did not seek deductions for a significant amount of their social entertainment and the surroundings in which the food and beverages were furnished were conducive to the business

11. Our skepticism as to the deductibility of all home entertainment expenses asserted is based on two factors: petitioners assert that they did not entertain socially and attempt to deduct all costs of all entertaining in the home while conceding that petitioner's customers and business associates were also his social friends. The fact that one does business with an individual does not preclude interacting with that person as on a social basis.

purpose of the function. Similar circumstances do not exist in this case. Having failed to substantiate any of the claimed home entertainment expenses, we sustain respondent's disallowance of these deductions.

QUESTIONS

1. What records should the taxpayers have kept? See Regs. §1.274-5T.

2. If the taxpayers had been good record keepers (or creators), how much, if any, of their claimed deductions do you suppose they could have sustained?

3. Do you sense that the substantiation requirement is unduly burdensome? effective? fair in its application?

CARVER v. COMMISSIONER

50 T.C.M. 444 (1985)

. . . During the years 1978 and 1979, petitioner operated a painting contracting business as a sole proprietorship. Petitioner maintained the principal office of this business in his home. During the year 1978, petitioner was away from home for 217 days in connection with his business, and during the year 1979 was away from home for 129 days in connection with his business.

. . . On his 1979 and 1978 returns petitioner deducted $5,805 and $2,646, respectively, for the cost of meals while on a job away from his tax home. . . .

Petitioner maintained no records whatsoever of his traveling expenses. His argument is that he claimed no more than $38.44 a day for meals and lodging on the days he was away from home. He argues that since the instructions with the return state that an employee who has made a satisfactory accounting for expenses to his employer may deduct up to $44 a day of traveling expenses, he should be allowed his claimed deduction. The portion of the statement petitioner specifically relies on is the following:

> If you claim a deduction for business expenses, you should attach Form 2106. Show the total of all amounts received from or charged to your employer and the nature of your occupation. Also show the amount of your business expenses broken down into broad subjects.
>
> Even if you do not claim a deduction for your business expenses, you must attach the above information to your return unless you were required to, and did make a satisfactory accounting to your employer.
>
> You are considered to have made a satisfactory accounting if:

(a) You received either a daily allowance of no more than $44, instead of actual living expenses, or the maximum per diem rate authorized to be paid by the Federal Government in the locality in which the travel is performed. . . .

Petitioner, however, was not an employee and therefore he made no accounting of any type to an employer, nor was he made an allowance for expenses by an employer.

Whether under different circumstances the statement contained in the instructions to the return would be justification for a taxpayer's failure to keep records, we need not decide. Petitioner owned and operated his own business and was required by section 274(d) to keep appropriate records. That section provides that no deduction shall be allowed under sections 162 or 212 of any traveling expenses including meals and lodging, while away from home unless the taxpayer substantiates by adequate records or by sufficient evidence corroborating the taxpayer's own statement the amount of such expenses. Section 1.274-5(c)(2)(i), Income Tax Regs. sets forth the requirement that a taxpayer shall maintain an account book, diary and documentary evidence which, in combination, are sufficient to establish each element of an expenditure with respect to expenses for meals and lodging when away from home. This regulation has been upheld as a reasonable interpretation of the statute. . . . Here, petitioner kept no records and therefore is not entitled to any deduction in excess of the deduction allowed by respondent. We therefore sustain respondent's disallowance of petitioner's claimed travel expenses in excess of the $12 per day he allowed for meals in the notice of deficiency.

NOTE AND QUESTIONS

1. *Use of per diem rate.* The rules under which no substantiation is required in the case of certain per diem amounts received from an employer are found in Regs. §1.274-5T(f), (g), and (j) and Rev. Proc. 92-17, 1992-1 C.B. 679. This is nothing but a substantiation rule. If the amount received exceeds the actual expenditure, the employee is supposed to report the excess as income. For example, the maximum per diem allowance for food and lodging for New York City in 1992 was $151 per day. If your employer pays you an allowance of $151 per day and you stay with friends and spend only, say, $61 per day, you are supposed to report the difference, $90 per day, as income. What do you imagine is the level of compliance with the obligation to report such income? What do you think of a rule that says, in effect, "You must report certain income, but if you fail to do so, we promise to take your word for the fact that you didn't have any"?

2. *Practical administration.* Note that the Commissioner allowed taxpayer Carver to deduct $12 per day for meals, without substantiation. The amount in 1992 would be $34 or $26, depending on the location. See Rev. Proc. 92-17, supra. Do these amounts seem to be about right? Note that greater amounts can be deducted if the taxpayer keeps adequate records.

3. Business Lunches

MOSS v. COMMISSIONER

758 F.2d 211 (7th Cir. 1985)

POSNER, Circuit Judge.

The taxpayers, a lawyer named Moss and his wife, appeal from a decision of the Tax Court disallowing federal income tax deductions of a little more than $1,000 in each of two years, representing Moss's share of his law firm's lunch expense at the Cafe Angelo in Chicago. The Tax Court's decision in this case has attracted some attention in tax circles because of its implications for the general problem of the deductibility of business meals. . . .

Moss was a partner in a small trial firm specializing in defense work, mostly for one insurance company. Each of the firm's lawyers carried a tremendous litigation caseload, averaging more than 300 cases, and spent most of every working day in courts in Chicago and its suburbs. The members of the firm met for lunch daily at the Cafe Angelo near their office. At lunch the lawyers would discuss their cases with the head of the firm, whose approval was required for most settlements, and they would decide which lawyer would meet which court call that afternoon or the next morning. Lunchtime was chosen for the daily meeting because the courts were in recess then. The alternatives were to meet at 7:00 A.M. or 6:00 P.M., and these were less convenient times. There is no suggestion that the lawyers dawdled over lunch, or that the Cafe Angelo is luxurious.

The framework of statutes and regulations for deciding this case is simple, but not clear. Section 262 of the Internal Revenue Code (Title 26) disallows, "except as otherwise expressly provided in this chapter," the deduction of "personal, family, or living expenses." Section 119 excludes from income the value of meals provided by an employer to his employees for his convenience, but only if they are provided on the employer's premises; and section 162(a) allows the deduction of "all the ordinary and necessary expenses paid or incurred during the taxable year in carrying on any trade or business, including — . . . (2) traveling expenses (including amounts expended for meals . . .) while away from home. . . ." Since Moss was not an employee but a partner in a partnership not taxed as an entity, since the meals were not served on the employer's premises, and since he was not away from home (that is, on an overnight trip away from his place of work, see United States v. Correll, 389 U.S. 299 (1967)), neither section 119 nor section 162(a)(2) applies to this case. The Internal Revenue Service concedes, however, that meals are deductible under section 162(a) when they are ordinary and necessary business expenses (provided the expense is substantiated with adequate records, see section 274(d)) even if they are not within the express permission of any other provision and even though the expense of commuting to and from work, a traveling expense but not one incurred away from home, is not deductible. Treasury Regulations on Income Tax §1.262-1(b)(5); Fausner v. Commissioner, 413 U.S. 838 (1973) (per curiam).

The problem is that many expenses are simultaneously business expenses in the sense that they conduce to the production of business income and personal expenses in the sense that they raise personal welfare. This is plain enough with regard to lunch; most people would eat lunch even if they didn't work. Commuting may seem a pure business expense, but is not; it reflects the choice of where to live, as well as where to work. Read literally, section 162 would make irrelevant whether a business expense is also a personal expense; so long as it is ordinary and necessary in the taxpayer's business, thus bringing section 162(a) into play, an expense is (the statute seems to say) deductible from his income tax. But the statute has not been read literally. There is a natural reluctance, most clearly manifested in the regulation disallowing deduction of the expense of commuting, to lighten the tax burden of people who have the good fortune to interweave work with consumption. To allow a deduction for commuting would confer a windfall on people who live in the suburbs and commute to work in the cities; to allow a deduction for all business-related meals would confer a windfall on people who can arrange their work schedules so they do some of their work at lunch.

Although an argument can thus be made for disallowing *any* deduction for business meals, on the theory that people have to eat whether they work or not, the result would be excessive taxation of people who spend more money on business meals because they are business meals than they would spend on their meals if they were not working. Suppose a theatrical agent takes his clients out to lunch at the expensive restaurants that the clients demand. Of course he can deduct the expense of their meals, from which he derives no pleasure or sustenance, but can he also deduct the expense of his own? He can, because he cannot eat more cheaply; he cannot munch surreptitiously on a peanut butter and jelly sandwich brought from home while his client is wolfing down tournedos Rossini followed by soufflé au grand marnier. No doubt our theatrical agent, unless concerned for his longevity, derives personal utility from his fancy meal, but probably less than the price of the meal. He would not pay for it if it were not for the business benefit; he would get more value from using the same money to buy something else; hence the meal confers on him less utility than the cash equivalent would. The law could require him to pay tax on the fair value of the meal to him; this would be (were it not for costs of administration) the economically correct solution. But the government does not attempt this difficult measurement; it once did, but gave up the attempt as not worth the cost. . . . The taxpayer is permitted to deduct the whole price, provided the expense is "different from or in excess of that which would have been made for the taxpayer's personal purposes." Sutter v. Commissioner, 21 T.C. 170, 173 (1953).

Because the law allows this generous deduction, which tempts people to have more (and costlier) business meals than are necessary, the Internal Revenue Service has every right to insist that the meal be shown to be a real business necessity. This condition is most easily satisfied when a client or customer or supplier or other outsider to the business is a guest. Even if Sydney Smith was wrong that "soup and fish explain half the emotions of life," it is undeniable that eating together fosters camaraderie and makes business dealings friendlier and easier. It thus reduces the costs of transacting business, for these costs include the frictions and the failures of communication that are produced by suspicion and mutual misunderstanding, by differences in tastes and manners, and by lack of rapport. A meeting with a client or customer in an office is therefore not a perfect substitute for a lunch with him in a restaurant. But it is different when all the participants in the meal are coworkers, as essentially was the case here (clients occasionally were invited to the firm's daily luncheon, but Moss has made no attempt to identify the occasions). They know each other well already; they don't need the social lubrication that a meal with an outsider provides — at least don't need it daily. If a large firm had a monthly lunch to allow partners to get to know associates, the expense of the meal might well be necessary, and would be allowed by the Internal Revenue Service. . . . But Moss's firm never had more than eight lawyers (partners and associates), and did not need a daily lunch to cement relationships among them.

It is all a matter of degree and circumstance (the expense of a testimonial dinner, for example, would be deductible on a morale-building rationale); and particularly of frequency. Daily — for a full year — is too often, perhaps even for entertainment of clients, as implied by Hankenson v. Commissioner, 47 T.C.M. 1567, 1569 (1984), where the Tax Court held nondeductible the cost of lunches consumed three or four days a week, 52 weeks a year, by a doctor who entertained other doctors who he hoped would refer patients to him, and other medical personnel.

We may assume it was necessary for Moss's firm to meet daily to coordinate the work of the firm, and also, as the Tax Court found, that lunch was the most convenient time. But it does not follow that the expense of the lunch was a necessary business expense. The members of the firm had to eat somewhere, and the Cafe Angelo was both convenient and not too expensive. They do not claim to have incurred a greater daily lunch expense than they would have incurred if there had been no lunch meetings. Although it saved time to combine lunch with work, the meal itself was not an organic part of the meeting, as in the examples we gave earlier where the business objective, to be fully achieved, required sharing a meal.

The case might be different if the location of the courts required the firm's members to eat each day either in a disagreeable restaurant, so that they derived less value from the meal than it cost them to buy it, . . . or in a restaurant too expensive for their personal tastes, so that, again, they would have gotten less value than the cash equivalent. But so far as appears, they picked the restaurant they liked most. Although it must be pretty monotonous to eat lunch the same place every working day of the year, not all the lawyers attended all the lunch meetings and there was nothing to stop the firm from meeting occasionally at another restaurant proximate to their office in downtown Chicago; there are hundreds.

An argument can be made that the price of lunch at the Cafe Angelo included rental of the space that the lawyers used for what was a meeting as well as a meal. There was evidence that the firm's conference room was otherwise occupied throughout the working day, so as a matter of logic Moss might be able to claim a part of the price of lunch as an ordinary and necessary expense for work space. But this is cutting things awfully fine; in any event Moss made no effort to apportion his lunch expense in this way.

Affirmed.

NOTE

In Christey v. United States, 841 F.2d 809 (8th Cir. 1988), cert. denied, 489 U.S. 1016 (1989), the court allowed a deduction for the meal expenses of a state highway patrol officer. See description of the case supra page 95. In footnote 7 of the case the court stated that the government in the *Moss* case had "conceded that meals are deductible under §162(a) when they are ordinary and necessary business expenses" but noted that the court in that case had concluded that the expenses were not "necessary."

QUESTIONS

1. Is the court's decision in *Moss* grounded on the theory that a taxpayer should only be able to deduct business meals that are more expensive than the meals the taxpayer would otherwise have consumed? On the theory that a taxpayer should only be able to deduct business meals with clients? On the theory that Congress could not have intended to allow a taxpayer to deduct lunch every day?

2. Do you agree with Judge Posner that eating with clients "reduces the costs of transacting business" by lessening the "frictions and the failures of communication that are produced by suspicion and mutual misunderstanding"? Do you think that disallowance of a deduction for all business meals would significantly reduce business efficiency? How do you suppose it would affect the restaurant business and the people employed in that activity?

3. In which, if any, of the following circumstances will the lunch be deductible?

(a) A lawyer takes her client to lunch to discuss her firm's handling of the client's case.

(b) A client takes her lawyer to lunch to discuss the lawyer's firm's handling of the client's case.

(c) A lawyer takes her client to lunch in order to retain the client's goodwill.

(d) A partner in a law firm takes an associate to lunch to discuss the associate's future with the firm.

(e) A partner in a law firm takes an associate to lunch to discuss a pending case.

(f) Two partners go to lunch once a week to talk about an ongoing case.

4. More on Entertaining Customers

DANVILLE PLYWOOD CORPORATION v. UNITED STATES

899 F.2d 3 (1990)

I. Facts . . .

Danville is a closely held Virginia corporation owned by George Buchanan, his wife, and their relatives. At all relevant times Buchanan has served as Danville's president.

Danville manufactures custom plywood for use in kitchen cabinets, store fixtures, furniture, wall panels, wall plaques, and similar items. Danville sells to wholesale distributors who in turn sell to architects, mill work houses, and cabinet shops. Each order Danville receives is filled to customer specifications and thus Danville does not maintain a fixed inventory of finished products.

During the years at issue, Danville maintained its books and filed its returns using the accrual method of accounting with a fiscal year ending November 30. On its returns for 1980 and 1981 Danville claimed deductions totaling $103,444.51[12] in connection with a weekend trip for 120 persons to the Super Bowl in New Orleans, Louisiana, from January 23 through January 26, 1981.

To decide who [sic] to invite to the Super Bowl weekend, Danville looked at the current and potential income from each customer. Danville did not invite specific individuals; instead, it sent two invitations to the selected customer and instructed the customer to decide whom to send. Buchanan asserts that Danville asked the customer to send individuals with "decision making authority." The majority of the customers sent one individual who was accompanied by that individual's spouse.

Of the people attending the Super Bowl, six were employees of Danville (including Buchanan), five were spouses of the employees, one was the daughter of a shareholder, three were Buchanan's children, and four were Buchanan's friends. The remaining individuals were 58 of Danville's customers, 38 spouses of those customers, two children of one of Danville's customers, and three customers of one of Danville's customers.

In making arrangements for the Super Bowl weekend, Danville sent a letter on June 5, 1980, to Abbott Tours, a New Orleans travel agency. In the letter Danville requested accommodations for three nights, Super Bowl tickets, banquet facilities for one night, and a Mississippi River cruise. Notably, Danville did not indicate that the trip was in any way business related and failed to request access to meeting rooms or other facilities appropriate for a business trip. As finalized, the weekend included accommodations at the Sheraton Hotel, a Saturday evening dinner in the hotel's dining room, and an outing to the French Quarter on Saturday night.

On January 13, 1981, Danville sent a letter to the selected customers stating that "Super Bowl weekend is just around the corner." This letter also failed to contain any reference to business meetings or discussions of any kind. Shortly before Super Bowl weekend, Buchanan distributed a memorandum to the Danville employees who would be going to New

12. Of this amount $27,151.00 constituted payment for Super Bowl tickets; $30,721.51 for airfare for Danville's employees and guests; $45,300.00 to a tour agency for accommodations and related services; and $272.00 to General Aviation to pick up football tickets. Of the amount claimed the Commissioner disallowed $98,297.83. Of this amount $64,467.51 was disallowed on the 1980 return and $33,380.32 on the 1981 return.

Orleans. In the memorandum, Buchanan told his employees they should promote certain types of wood, inform the customers Danville could supply 10 ft. panels, and survey the customers regarding their need for Danville to purchase a "cut-to-size" saw.

Upon arrival at the hotel, Danville's customers were met at a hospitality desk in the lobby staffed by family members of Danville's employees. Danville also displayed some of its products in an area adjacent to the lobby. During the weekend Danville's employees met informally with customers.

During the dinner on Saturday evening Danville's customers shared the dining room with other hotel guests, although the customers were segregated in one section of the dining room. There were no speakers or general announcements made at the dinner. Buchanan and Danville's other employees circulated among the tables to speak with their guests. None of the customers placed orders during the weekend although some promised to contact Danville's employees in the future. The only scheduled activity on Sunday was the Super Bowl game and by Monday the guests were preparing to leave.

During an audit of the 1980 and 1981 returns the Commissioner disallowed the deductions claimed by Danville for the expenses incurred relating to Super Bowl weekend. . . .

II. Statutory Scheme

Prior to 1961, §162 was the sole statutory provision regulating the deduction of entertainment expenses. In response to what was perceived as widespread abuse of expense accounts and entertainment expenses Congress enacted §274.[13] This provision is referred to as a "disallowance provision" and its effect is to disallow certain deductions for entertainment expenses which would otherwise be properly deductible under §162.

Under the stricter limitations of §274, no deduction for business expenses allowable under §162 shall be allowed unless the taxpayer establishes that the item was "directly related to" or "associated with" the active conduct of the taxpayer's trade or business. In the case of the latter situation the item for which the deduction is claimed must directly precede or follow a substantial and bona fide business discussion. §274(a)(1)(A).

13. See H.R. Rep. No. 1447, 87th Cong., 2d Sess. 16-19 (1962-63 Cum. Bull. 405, 423); S. Rep. No. 1881, 87th Cong., 2d Sess., U.S. Code Cong. & Admin. News 1962, p.3297 (1962-63 Cum. Bull. 707, 731). Section 274 was also enacted in response to Cohan v. Commissioner, 39 F.2d 540 (2d Cir. 1930), which allowed a taxpayer to estimate the amount of his entertainment expenses. Today, §274(d) of the code contains strict substantiation requirements. Because of our disposition of this appeal it is not necessary for us to reach the issue of adequate substantiation.

Therefore, to be deductible, an entertainment expense must meet the requirements of both §162 and §274. First, the expense must be an ordinary and necessary business expense under §162. Second, the expense must be either "directly related to" or "associated with" the active conduct of the taxpayer's business.

III. Standard of Review

The Claims Court held that the expenses surrounding the Super Bowl weekend were neither "ordinary and necessary" business expenses of Danville's trade or business under §162 nor "directly related to" or "associated with" the active conduct of Danville's business under §274. Danville acknowledges that both of these findings are factual and must be sustained on appeal unless clearly erroneous. . . .

The ruling of the Commissioner enjoys a presumption of correctness and a taxpayer bears the burden of proving it to be wrong. . . . This means that the taxpayer must come forward with enough evidence to support a finding contrary to the Commissioner's determination. . . . Even after satisfying this burden, the taxpayer must still carry the ultimate burden of proof. . . .

IV. Section 162

A. Children and Shareholder

Three of Buchanan's children and two children of Danville's customers as well as a shareholder of Danville attended Super Bowl weekend at Danville's expense. In its brief on appeal, Danville concedes that the expenses of these six individuals were not deductible and thus we need not address this class of attendees.

B. Employees' Spouses

Five spouses of Danville employees also attended Super Bowl weekend.[14] Danville argues that these individuals "manned the hospitality desk all day Saturday and Sunday morning, and otherwise assisted by handling other tasks which needed attention." Danville also argues that Buchanan was aware that a significant number of the customer representatives would bring their wives and thus he "deemed it appropriate

14. [The deductions claimed for spouses would now be disallowed under §274(m)(3). The court's discussion of prior law and of the facts of this case illustrates the potential for abuse and the problem of enforcement. — Eds.]

and helpful to have five wives of Danville employees" there to meet and entertain the spouses of the customer representatives.

Treasury regulations provide that when a taxpayer's wife accompanies him on a business trip, her expenses are not deductible unless the taxpayer can adequately show that her presence has a bona fide business purpose. The wife's performance of an incidental service does not meet this requirement. §1.162-2c(c). This regulation does not directly apply because the taxpayer here is a corporation and the deductibility involved the expenses not of the corporation president's wife, but of the wives of other employees. The principle upon which that regulation rests, however, is no less applicable to the wives of employees of a corporate taxpayer than it is to the wife of an individual taxpayer.

Under the standards of this regulation, the Claims Court concluded that the wives of Danville's employees performed at best a social function and thus their expenses were not deductible. . . .

Danville cites United States v. Disney, 413 F.2d 783, 788 (9th Cir. 1969), and Wilkins v. United States, 348 F. Supp. 1282, 1284 (D. Neb. 1972), as examples of cases which allowed a taxpayer to deduct his wife's expenses. In *Disney,* the court stated that the "critical inquiries are whether the dominant purpose of the trip was to serve her husband's business purpose in making the trip and whether she actually spent a substantial amount of her time in assisting her husband in fulfilling that purpose." *Disney,* 413 F.2d at 788. The court in *Disney* went on to state that "the result reached in an individual case is so dependent upon the peculiar facts of that case, that the decisions called to our attention are of only limited assistance." Id.

In the case at bar, Danville simply did not present enough evidence to the Claims Court to sustain its burden of establishing that the spouses of Danville's employees performed a bona fide business purpose and not merely incidental services. Meridian Wood Prod. Co. v. United States, 725 F.2d 1183 (9th Cir. 1984) (expenses of corporation's president's spouse not deductible because her primary purpose was to socialize with other wives of business associates). The record leaves one with the overall impression that the wives of the employees went along for fun and merely helped out when they could.

C. CUSTOMER REPRESENTATIVES AND SPOUSES

As stated previously, to qualify as an "ordinary and necessary" business expense under §162(a) an expenditure must be both "common and accepted" in the community of which Danville is a part as well as "appropriate" for the development of Danville's business. . . . The Claims Court found that Danville failed to carry its burden of proof to establish that the expenses for the customer representatives met these requirements. In support of this conclusion the Court cited the testimony of Will Gregory, General Manager for Central Wholesale Supply, one of Danville's customers. Mr. Gregory testified that he had attended seminars hosted by the National Building Materials Distributors Association which consisted of booths manned by vendors where the attendees could talk privately about the company's products.

Danville argues that nothing could be more "ordinary, necessary, usual, customary, common or important in a manufacturing business than efforts to promote products and increase sales." We agree that this is true as a general proposition. However, what is at issue in this case is the manner in which Danville attempted to promote its products and increase sales. The Claims Court stated that the "record inescapably demonstrates that the entertainment . . . was the *central* focus of the excursion, with all other activities running a distant second in importance." (Emphasis in original.)

We cannot say the Claims Court finding is clearly erroneous. What business discussions that occurred were incidental to the main event, i.e., entertainment for Danville's customers. Similarly, expenses for the customers of one of Danville's customers who attended Super Bowl weekend are not deductible under §162.

D. DANVILLE'S EMPLOYEES

The treasury regulations provide that only traveling expenses which are reasonable and necessary to the conduct of the taxpayer's business and which are directly attributable to it may be deducted. §1.162-2(a). The Claims Court held that Danville failed to establish that the expenses of its employees were attributable to its business, and that the trip was undertaken primarily for business purposes. The court found that none of the correspondence between Danville and Abbott Tours referred to the business nature of the trip. Furthermore, the Claims Court described the agenda distributed by Danville to its employees as little more than a "bootstrapping afterthought."

Danville argues that its employees met with customer representatives throughout the weekend and discussed business. As indicated by the Claims Court, only two of the six Danville employees who attended the Super Bowl weekend testified. Thus, the Court could not ascertain how the other four employees spent their time. In addition, the three customer representatives who testified indicated that the discussions which did occur took place "whenever we found [Buchanan] . . . and whenever we could catch him." In light of this evidence the Claims Court concluded that Danville had failed to carry its burden of proof of demonstrating that the trip was undertaken for bona fide business purposes or that the expenses were directly attributable to Danville's business.

Danville argues that these quotes of the customer representatives were taken out of context and the full quotes indicate that the representatives talked to Buchanan whenever he was not engaged in discussions with other customers. Accepting Danville's version as true, once again we must agree with the Claims Court that Danville failed to present sufficient evidence to satisfy its burden of proof. The Super Bowl weekend appears to have been little more than a group social excursion with business playing a subsidiary role.

On the narrow facts of this case, we hold that the decision of the Claims Court that Danville failed to satisfy its burden of proof that the Super Bowl expenses were "ordinary and necessary" business expenses under §162(a) of the Code is not clearly erroneous.

In view of our holding that Danville has not met its burden relative to §162(a), any discussion of §274 is unnecessary. . . .

NOTES AND QUESTIONS

1. *The ordinary and necessary test.* The court in *Danville* based its opinion in large part on the fact that the expenses in question did not meet the "ordinary and necessary" test of §162. The requirement that a deduction be "ordinary," if interpreted literally, would rule out deductions for many expenses that are deductible, and should be deductible. Suppose, for example, an urban department store suffers an unheard-of infestation of locusts. The locusts swarm around the entrance and drive away customers. The store responds by purchasing other insects to feed upon the locusts. That expense may properly be characterized as extraordinary and would not be deductible under a literal interpretation of the ordinary and necessary test. It is quite clear, however, that the expense is and should be deductible.

The requirement that a deduction be "necessary" is rarely invoked. To understand why this is so, suppose that a company decides to greatly expand its advertising budget. So long as the company purchases advertising from an unrelated party, the IRS will not inquire as to whether the expense is necessary. This seems correct. A tax deduction offsets only part of the real cost of a business expense. (For example, a taxpayer in the 40 percent combined state and federal tax bracket saves only 40 cents in taxes for every dollar spent.) It will never be worthwhile for a business to make unnecessary payments to an unrelated party. There does not seem to be any reason, then, for the IRS to second-guess the "necessity" of payments to unrelated parties.

What distinguishes *Danville* from the cases described above? Are there other tests the court might rely on to determine the deductibility of these sorts of expenses? What about primary purpose?

2. *The expense of sending customers and their spouses to the Super Bowl.* The court in *Danville* disallowed costs incurred to purchase tickets and the like for Danville's customers and their spouses. The court reasoned

that these expenses were not "ordinary and necessary." Suppose that instead of providing travel and entertainment, Danville had simply sent its customers a rebate, or lowered its prices on future goods. The rebate or price reduction would have reduced taxable income in much the same way and same amount as the cost of the Super Bowl tickets. As stated in Note 1, supra, the IRS would not have inquired as to the necessity for the rebate or reduction.

What if Danville had simply mailed its best customers Super Bowl tickets and travel vouchers for free air fare to the Super Bowl but had not sent any of its own employees to the Super Bowl? Could Danville have then deducted the expense as an advertising or promotional expense? Could Danville have argued that, because the tickets went solely to unrelated parties, it was inappropriate for the IRS to inquire as to the business necessity for the expense?

Danville argued that the expense of both customer and employee tickets should be deducted because the trip made it possible for Danville employees to pitch products to Danville customers. Under this theory, the presence of Danville employees supported the deduction for Danville customers. Consistent with this theory, Danville deducted the cost of sending its employees to the Super Bowl. It also deducted the cost of sending spouses and, in one case, children of its employees. Danville did not treat the cost as salary to the employees and thus did not withhold employment taxes from that sum or report that sum as salary to the IRS. Danville's employees in turn treated the travel and entertainment they (and their spouses and, in one case, children) received as a non-taxable — an incidental benefit received in connection with a business trip. Is it possible that the court regarded the whole affair as an excuse to provide a tax-free fringe benefit to Danville employees, and that the presence of such employees (and their relations) tainted the deduction otherwise allowable for Danville customers? Or did the cost of the travel and entertainment provided to Danville's customers simply offend the IRS and the court?

3. *The costs of sending its own employees and their spouses to the Super Bowl.* Had Danville simply given its employees cash equal to the cost of the travel and entertainment, the expense would clearly have been deducted as salary. Indeed, had Danville given its employees (and their relations) a free vacation and reported that expense as salary to the employees it is virtually certain it would have been deductible under §162. Seen from this perspective, the "offending" aspect of the Super Bowl trip was not the deduction to the employer, but the fact that the employer did not report the value of the travel and entertainment as income, and that the employees did not pay tax on that income. Provided that the employer and employees are in roughly the same tax bracket, the disallowance of the deduction has much the same effect as allowing deduction of the salary but taxing the employees on the value of the trip.

4. *Planning.* With hindsight, what advice would you have given to Danville about the conduct of the trip to the Super Bowl to increase the odds of the deduction being sustained? Would you advise that spouses of employees not be invited? See §274(m)(3). What about hiring the spouses as temporary employees of Danville?

C. CHILD-CARE EXPENSES

The case that follows arose before the adoption of express statutory provisions allowing a credit for certain child- and household-care expenses of working parents. See infra Note 4. It is still controlling on the question of deductibility of child-care expenses and interesting in that it reflects an effort to grapple with the question whether such expenses should be regarded as costs of earning income.

SMITH v. COMMISSIONER

40 B.T.A. 1038 (1939), aff'd without opinion, 113 F.2d 114 (2d Cir. 1940)

OPPER, J.

[The Commissioner] determined a deficiency . . . in petitioners' 1937 income tax . . . due to the disallowance of a deduction claimed by petitioners, who are husband and wife, for sums spent by the wife in employing nursemaids to care for petitioners' young child, the wife, as well as the husband, being employed. . . .

Petitioners would have us apply the "but for" test. They propose that but for the nurses, the wife could not leave her child; but for the freedom so secured, she could not pursue her gainful labors, and but for them, there would be no income and no tax. This thought evokes an array of interesting possibilities. The fee to the doctor, but for whose healing service, the earner of the family income could not leave his sickbed; the cost of the laborer's raiment, for how can the world proceed about its business unclothed; the very home which gives us shelter and rest and the food which provides energy, might all by an extension of the same proposition be construed as necessary to the operation of business and to the creation of income. Yet these are the very essence of those "personal" expenses the deductibility of which is expressly denied. [§262.]

We are told that the working wife is a new phenomenon. This is relied on to account for the apparent inconsistency that the expenses in issue are now a commonplace, yet have not been the subject of legislation, ruling, or adjudicated controversy. But if that is true, it becomes all the more necessary to apply accepted principles to the novel facts. We are not prepared to say that the care of children, like similar aspects of family and household life, is other than a personal concern. The wife's services as custodian of the home and protector of its children are ordinarily rendered without monetary compensation. There results no taxable income from the performance of this service and the correlative expenditure is personal and not susceptible of deduction. . . . Here the wife has chosen to employ others to discharge her domestic function and the services she performs are rendered outside the home. They are a source of actual income and taxable as such. But that does not deprive the same work performed by others of its personal character. . . .

We are not unmindful that, as petitioners suggest, certain disbursements normally personal may become deductible by reason of their intimate connection with an occupation carried on for profit. In this category fall entertainment, . . . traveling expenses, . . . and the cost of an actor's wardrobe. . . . The line is not always an easy one to draw nor the test simple to apply. But we think its principle is clear. It may for practical purposes be said to constitute a distinction between those activities which, as a matter of common acceptance and universal experience, are "ordinary" or usual as the direct accompaniment of business pursuits, on the one hand; and those which, though they may in some indirect and tenuous degree relate to the circumstances of a profitable occupation, are nevertheless personal in their nature, of a character applicable to human beings generally, and which exist on that plane regardless of the occupation, though not necessarily of the station in life, of the individuals concerned. See Welch v. Helvering [infra page 645].

In the latter category, we think, fall payments made to servants or others occupied in looking to the personal wants of their employers. . . . And we include in this group, nursemaids retained to care for infant children.

NOTES AND QUESTIONS

1. *Causation.* The court's rejection of the taxpayers' "but for" argument is not convincing: The other expenses to which the court refers would be incurred by people even if they were not employed. It is clear in the *Smith* case that the child-care expense would not have been incurred but for the job. It is equally clear, however, that the expense would not have been incurred but for the child. Where does this kind of analysis leave you? See discussion of the *Ochs* case in Note 1, supra page 487. The Smiths would have you compare them with another

couple with a child but with one parent staying home to care for it. The court would have you compare them with another couple with both spouses employed but with no children. Where does this kind of observation leave (or lead) you?

2. *The statutory language.* However appealing the taxpayers' claim may be, can their outlays sensibly be characterized as "ordinary and necessary expenses paid or incurred . . . in carrying on a trade or business"?

3. *Policy.* (a) Which of the following arguments for some sort of allowance for child-care expenses do you find most appealing?

(i) In our society, since most married people have children, children should be taken as given. From the perspective of a potential job seeker with children the return from taking a job is the amount available after deduction for unavoidable child-care expenses. "Income" must therefore be defined as the net amount after child-care expenses, both in the interests of fairness and in order to avoid distorting job-taking decisions.

(ii) Our tax system discourages job-taking by the person who is the secondary worker in a marriage. It does this by taxing the secondary worker's earned income at rates determined by piling that income on top of the income of the primary worker (see supra page 38), while at the same time imposing no tax on imputed income from performing household and child-care services (see supra page 121). The secondary worker also pays social security taxes and incurs a variety of work-related expenses. Most secondary workers are women. Thus, the system tends to discourage job-taking by women. It may at the same time impose psychological and other burdens on women by depreciating the value of services performed outside the home as compared with those performed in the home. An allowance for child-care expenses mitigates these effects.

(iii) Child-care allowances are necessary in order to permit low-income people to take jobs.

(iv) Child-care allowances will encourage people to have more children.

(v) Child-care allowances will lead to child-care jobs and will provide employment to people who might otherwise be unemployed.

(b) What implications does each of these arguments have for whether the allowance should be a deduction of the entire outlay, a deduction of some part of the outlay, or a credit?

4. *Congressional response.* (a) In 1954, Congress responded to the claims of people like the Smiths with a new deduction that had some interesting limitations, reflecting the attitudes of the time toward working mothers.

The deduction was initially limited to $600 per year. (Even in 1954 it must have been difficult at best to hire baby-sitters for $12 a week.) It was available to unmarried women, widows, and divorced men but not to unmarried men. For married couples, the deduction was phased out as income rose above $4,500 per year, apparently reflecting the view that as long as she was married, a woman's place was in the home, unless she was forced to work to maintain the family at a minimum level of income. The deduction was liberalized modestly in 1963 and 1964, more substantially in 1971, and finally in 1976 changed to a credit, which is what we find today in §21. The credit is a percentage of the amount spent for household services, up to $2,400 for one child (or other "qualifying individual") and $4,800 for two or more children (or qualifying individuals). The percentage used in determining the amount of the credit declines as income rises. In a household with a wife and husband, both employed, with a total income of $30,000, two children, and expenses of $4,800 or more, the credit (which reduces the amount of tax payable dollar-for-dollar) would be $960.

(b) Examine §21. Consider the possible rationale for each of the following features:

(i) The phase-down of the credit from 30 percent to 20 percent of expenses as income rises above $10,000 (§21(a)(2));
(ii) The importance of having in the home a "qualifying individual" (§21(a)(1) and (b)(1));
(iii) The availability for "expenses for household services" (§21(b)(2)(A)(i));
(iv) The limitation on the dollar amount of the credit (§21(c)); and
(v) The limitation of expenses that may be taken into account, in the case of a husband and wife, to the income of the lower earner (§21(d)(1)(B)).

(c) Compare §129, which permits an employer to make available to employees, free of tax, up to $5,000 per year for child-care expenses through a dependent care assistance program, or DCAP. This benefit may be part of a §125 cafeteria plan (see supra page 108), so the employee can be allowed, in effect, to treat up to $5,000 of salary as a nontaxable DCAP benefit. But under §21(c), the amount of child-care expenses that can be used to calculate the §21 tax credit is reduced by amounts paid through a DCAP and excluded under §129. Taxpayers are therefore confronted with a tax-planning choice. When the marginal rate of tax on their income is lower than the credit rate on their expenses (which, as we have just seen, ranges from 30 percent to 20 percent), they are better off to forgo the DCAP exclusion and use their expenses to claim a credit under §21. For example, suppose a couple has two children and qualified expenses of $4,000 and a taxable income of

$15,000. Their marginal rate is 15 percent. If they take the $4,000 under a DCAP plan and avoid tax on that amount, they save $600. Suppose their adjusted gross income is $19,000. The credit rate for them is 25 percent. If they forgo the DCAP exclusion and claim a credit for the $4,000 of expenses, the amount of their credit will be $1,000, or $400 more than they would save by using the DCAP. On the other hand, if their taxable income were $50,000, their marginal rate would be 28 percent and a DCAP exclusion would save them $1,120. If their adjusted gross income were $60,000, their credit rate would be 20 percent and the amount of the credit would be $800, which is $320 less than what they could save under the DCAP.

5. *What is an "employment-related" expense?* In Zoltan v. Commissioner, 79 T.C. 490 (1982), the taxpayer, who worked fifty-five hours a week as an accountant, sent her eleven-year-old son to an eight-week summer camp costing $1,100. Alternative forms of child care for the same period would have cost about the same amount. The Tax Court allowed the taxpayer to treat the entire $1,100 as a child-care expense within the contemplation of §21(c)(2)(A). After this case became a news item, Congress amended §21(b)(2)(A) to provide that "employment expenses" do not include the costs of "a camp where the [child] stays overnight." The Senate Committee on Finance explanation (see Report on the Omnibus Budget Reconciliation Act of 1987, 100th Cong., 1st Sess. 165 (1987)) states that "overnight camp expenses are a personal consumption expenditure that is not a necessary cost of being able to go to work." Do you agree?

In the *Zoltan* case the taxpayer also sent her son on a school trip to Washington, D.C., during the week of his Easter vacation. The cost, including transportation and lodging, was $116, which was less than what the taxpayer would have been required to pay for his care if he had remained home. The court disallowed all but $35 of this because of the educational value of the trip. What if the Easter trip had been to Disneyland?

D. COMMUTING EXPENSES

COMMISSIONER v. FLOWERS

326 U.S. 465 (1945)

Mr. Justice MURPHY delivered the opinion of the Court.

This case presents a problem as to the meaning and application of the provision of [the predecessor of §162(a)(2)], allowing a deduction for income tax purposes of "traveling expenses (including the entire amount expended for meals and lodging) while away from home in the pursuit of a trade or business."

The taxpayer, a lawyer, has resided with his family in Jackson, Mississippi, since 1903. There he has paid taxes, voted, schooled his children and established social and religious connections. He built a house in Jackson nearly thirty years ago and at all times has maintained it for himself and his family. He has been connected with several law firms in Jackson, one of which he formed and which has borne his name since 1922.

In 1906 the taxpayer began to represent the predecessor of the Gulf, Mobile & Ohio Railroad, his present employer. He acted as trial counsel for the railroad throughout Mississippi. From 1918 until 1927 he acted as special counsel for the railroad in Mississippi. He was elected general solicitor in 1927 and continued to be elected to that position each year until 1930, when he was elected general counsel. Thereafter he was annually elected general counsel until September, 1940, when the properties of the predecessor company and another railroad were merged and he was elected vice president and general counsel of the newly formed Gulf, Mobile & Ohio Railroad.

The main office of the Gulf, Mobile & Ohio Railroad is in Mobile, Alabama, as was also the main office of its predecessor. When offered the position of general solicitor in 1927, the taxpayer was unwilling to accept it if it required him to move from Jackson to Mobile. He had established himself in Jackson both professionally and personally and was not desirous of moving away. As a result, an arrangement was made between him and the railroad whereby he could accept the position and continue to reside in Jackson on condition that he pay his traveling expenses between Mobile and Jackson and pay his living expenses in both places. This arrangement permitted the taxpayer to determine for himself the amount of time he would spend in each of the two cities and was in effect during 1939 and 1940, the taxable years in question.

The railroad company provided an office for the taxpayer in Mobile but not in Jackson. When he worked in Jackson his law firm provided him with office space, although he no longer participated in the firm's business or shared in its profits. He used his own office furniture and fixtures at this office. The railroad, however, furnished telephone service and a typewriter and desk for his secretary. It also paid the secretary's expenses while in Jackson. Most of the legal business of the railroad was centered in or conducted from Jackson, but this business was handled by local counsel for the railroad. The taxpayer's participation was advisory only and was no different from his participation in the railroad's legal business in other areas.

The taxpayer's principal post of business was at the main office in Mobile. However, during the taxable years of 1939 and 1940, he devoted nearly all of his time to matters relating to the merger of the railroads.

Since it was left to him where he would do his work, he spent most of his time in Jackson during this period. In connection with the merger, one of the companies was involved in certain litigation in the federal court in Jackson and the taxpayer participated in that litigation.

During 1939 he spent 203 days in Jackson and 66 in Mobile, making 33 trips between the two cities. During 1940 he spent 168 days in Jackson and 102 in Mobile, making 40 trips between the two cities. The railroad paid all of his traveling expenses when he went on business trips to points other than Jackson or Mobile. But it paid none of his expenses in traveling between these two points or while he was at either of them.

The taxpayer deducted $900 in his 1939 income tax return and $1,620 in his 1940 return as traveling expenses incurred in making trips from Jackson to Mobile and as expenditures for meals and hotel accommodations while in Mobile.[15] The Commissioner disallowed the deductions. . . .

The portion of [§162(a)] authorizing the deduction of "traveling expenses (including the entire amount expended for meals and lodging) while away from home in the pursuit of a trade or business" is one of the specific examples given by Congress in that section of "ordinary and necessary expenses paid or incurred during the taxable year in carrying on any trade or business." It is to be contrasted with the provision of [§262]. [The Regulations provide] that

> Traveling expenses, as ordinarily understood, include railroad fares and meals and lodging. If the trip is undertaken for other than business purposes, the railroad fares are personal expenses and the meals and lodging are living expenses. If the trip is solely on business, the reasonable and necessary traveling expenses, including railroad fares, meals, and lodging, are business expenses. . . . Only such expenses as are reasonable and necessary in the conduct of the business and directly attributable to it may be deducted. . . . Commuters' fares are not considered as business expenses and are not deductible.

Three conditions must thus be satisfied before a traveling expense deduction may be made under [§162(a)(2)]:

(1) The expense must be a reasonable and necessary traveling expense, as that term is generally understood. This includes such items as transportation fares and food and lodging expenses incurred while traveling.

(2) The expense must be incurred "while away from home."

(3) The expense must be incurred in pursuit of business. This means that there must be a direct connection between the expenditure and the

15. No claim for deduction was made by the taxpayer for the amounts spent in traveling from Mobile to Jackson. . . .

carrying on of the trade or business of the taxpayer or of his employer. Moreover, such an expenditure must be necessary or appropriate to the development and pursuit of the business or trade.

Whether particular expenditures fulfill these three conditions so as to entitle a taxpayer to a deduction is purely a question of fact in most instances. . . . And the Tax Court's inferences and conclusions on such a factual matter, under established principles, should not be disturbed by an appellate court. . . .

In this instance, the Tax Court without detailed elaboration concluded that "The situation presented in this proceeding is, in principle, no different from that in which a taxpayer's place of employment is in one city and for reasons satisfactory to himself he resides in another." It accordingly disallowed the deductions on the ground that they represent living and personal expenses rather than traveling expenses incurred while away from home in the pursuit of business. The court below accepted the Tax Court's findings of fact but reversed its judgment on the basis that it had improperly construed the word "home" as used in the second condition precedent to a traveling expense deduction under [§162(a)(2)]. The Tax Court, it was said, erroneously construed the word to mean the post, station or place of business where the taxpayer was employed — in this instance, Mobile — and thus erred in concluding that the expenditures in issue were not incurred "while away from home." The court below felt that the word was to be given no such "unusual" or "extraordinary" meaning in this statute, that it simply meant "that place where one in fact resides" or "the principal place of abode of one who has the intention to live there permanently." 148 F.2d at 164. Since the taxpayer here admittedly had his home, as thus defined, in Jackson and since the expenses were incurred while he was away from Jackson, the court below held that the deduction was permissible.

The meaning of the word "home" in [§162(a)(2)] with reference to a taxpayer residing in one city and working in another has engendered much difficulty and litigation. . . . The Tax Court and the administrative rulings have consistently defined it as the equivalent of the taxpayer's place of business. . . . On the other hand, the decision below and Wallace v. Commissioner, 144 F.2d 407 (C.C.A.9), have flatly rejected that view and have confined the term to the taxpayer's actual residence. . . .

We deem it unnecessary here to enter into or to decide this conflict. The Tax Court's opinion, as we read it, was grounded neither solely nor primarily upon that agency's conception of the word "home." Its discussion was directed mainly toward the relation of the expenditures to the railroad's business, a relationship required by the third condition of the deduction. Thus even if the Tax Court's definition of the word "home" was implicit in its decision and even if that definition was erroneous, its judgment must be sustained here if it properly concluded that the necessary relationship between the expenditures and the railroad's business was lacking. Failure to satisfy any one of the three conditions destroys the traveling expense deduction.

Turning our attention to the third condition, this case is disposed of quickly. There is no claim that the Tax Court misconstrued this condition or used improper standards in applying it. And it is readily apparent from the facts that its inferences were supported by evidence and that its conclusion that the expenditures in issue were non-deductible living and personal expenses was fully justified.

The facts demonstrate clearly that the expenses were not incurred in the pursuit of the business of the taxpayer's employer, the railroad. Jackson was his regular home. Had his post of duty been in that city the cost of maintaining his home there and of commuting or driving to work concededly would be non-deductible living and personal expenses lacking the necessary direct relation to the prosecution of the business. The character of such expenses is unaltered by the circumstance that the taxpayer's post of duty was in Mobile, thereby increasing the costs of transportation, food and lodging. Whether he maintained one abode or two, whether he traveled three blocks or three hundred miles to work, the nature of these expenditures remained the same.

The added costs in issue, moreover, were as unnecessary and inappropriate to the development of the railroad's business as were his personal and living costs in Jackson. They were incurred solely as the result of the taxpayer's desire to maintain a home in Jackson while working in Mobile, a factor irrelevant to the maintenance and prosecution of the railroad's legal business. The railroad did not require him to travel on business from Jackson to Mobile or to maintain living quarters in both cities. Nor did it compel him, save in one instance, to perform tasks for it in Jackson. It simply asked him to be at his principal post in Mobile as business demanded and as his personal convenience was served, allowing him to divide his business time between Mobile and Jackson as he saw fit. Except for the federal court litigation, all of the taxpayer's work in Jackson would normally have been performed in the headquarters at Mobile. The fact that he traveled frequently between the two cities and incurred extra living expenses in Mobile, while doing much of his work in Jackson, was occasioned solely by his personal propensities. The railroad gained nothing from this arrangement except the personal satisfaction of the taxpayer.

Travel expenses in pursuit of business within the meaning of [§162(a)(2)] could arise only when the railroad's business forced the taxpayer to travel and to live temporarily at some place other than Mobile, thereby advancing the interests of the railroad. Business trips are to be identified in relation to business demands and the traveler's business headquarters. The exigencies of business rather than the personal conveniences and necessities of the traveler must be the motivating factors. Such was not the case here.

It follows that the court below erred in reversing the judgment of the Tax Court.

Reversed.

Mr. Justice JACKSON took no part in the consideration or decision of this case.

Mr. Justice RUTLEDGE, dissenting.

I think the judgment of the Court of Appeals should be affirmed. When Congress used the word "home" in [§162] of the Code, I do not believe it meant "business headquarters." And in my opinion this case presents no other question. . . .

Respondent's home was in Jackson, Mississippi, in every sense, unless for applying [§162]. There he maintained his family, with his personal, political and religious connections; schooled his children; paid taxes, voted, and resided over many years. There too he kept hold upon his place as a lawyer, though not substantially active in practice otherwise than to perform his work as general counsel for the railroad. . . .

I agree with the Court of Appeals that if Congress had meant "business headquarters," and not "home," it would have said "business headquarters." When it used "home" instead, I think it meant home in everyday parlance, not in some twisted special meaning of "tax home" or "tax headquarters." . . .

Congress gave the deduction for traveling away from home on business. The commuter's case, rightly confined, does not fall in this class. One who lives in an adjacent suburb or city and by usual modes of commutation can work within a distance permitting the daily journey and return, with time for the day's work and a period at home, clearly can be excluded from the deduction on the basis of the section's terms equally with its obvious purpose. But that is not true if "commuter" is to swallow up the deduction by the same sort of construction which makes "home" mean "business headquarters" of one's employer. If the line may be extended somewhat to cover doubtful cases, it need not be lengthened to infinity or to cover cases as far removed from the prevailing connotation of commuter as this one. Including it pushes "commuting" too far, even for these times of rapid transit.[16] . . .

By construing "home" as "business headquarters"; by reading "temporarily" as "very temporarily" into [§162]; by bringing down "ordinary and necessary" from its first sentence into its second; by finding "inequity" where Congress has said none exists; by construing "commuter" to cover long-distance, irregular travel; and by conjuring from the "statutory setting" a meaning at odds with the plain wording of the

16. Conceivably men soon may live in Florida or California and fly daily to work in New York and back. Possibly they will be regarded as commuters when that day comes. But, if so, that is not this case and, in any event, neither situation was comprehended by Congress when [§162] was enacted.

clause, the Government makes over understandable ordinary English into highly technical tax jargon. There is enough of this in the tax laws inescapably, without adding more in the absence of either compulsion or authority. The arm of the tax-gatherer reaches far. In my judgment it should not go the length of this case. . . .

HANTZIS v. COMMISSIONER

638 F.2d 248 (1st Cir.), cert. denied, 452 U.S. 962 (1981)

Campbell, Circuit Judge. . . .

In the fall of 1973 Catharine Hantzis (taxpayer), formerly a candidate for an advanced degree in philosophy at the University of California at Berkeley, entered Harvard Law School in Cambridge, Massachusetts, as a full-time student. During her second year of law school she sought unsuccessfully to obtain employment for the summer of 1975 with a Boston law firm. She did, however, find a job as a legal assistant with a law firm in New York City, where she worked for ten weeks beginning in June 1975. Her husband, then a member of the faculty of Northeastern University with a teaching schedule for that summer, remained in Boston and lived at the couple's home there. At the time of the Tax Court's decision in this case, Mr. and Mrs. Hantzis still resided in Boston.

On their joint income tax return for 1975, Mr. and Mrs. Hantzis reported the earnings from taxpayer's summer employment ($3,750) and deducted [under §162(a)(2)] the cost of transportation between Boston and New York, the cost of a small apartment rented by Mrs. Hantzis in New York and the cost of her meals in New York ($3,204). . . .

The Commissioner disallowed the deduction on the ground that taxpayer's home for purposes of section 162(a)(2) was her place of employment and the cost of traveling to and living in New York was therefore not "incurred . . . while away from home." The Commissioner also argued that the expenses were not incurred "in the pursuit of a trade or business." Both positions were rejected by the Tax Court, which found that Boston was Mrs. Hantzis' home because her employment in New York was only temporary and that her expenses in New York were "necessitated" by her employment there. The court thus held the expenses to be deductible under section 162(a)(2).[17]

In asking this court to reverse the Tax Court's allowance of the deduction, the Commissioner has contended that the expenses were not incurred "in the pursuit of a trade or business." We do not accept this

17. The court upheld the Commissioner's disallowance of a deduction taken by Mr. and Mrs. Hantzis on their 1975 return for expenses incurred by Mrs. Hantzis in attending a convention of the American Philosophical Association. Mr. and Mrs. Hantzis do not appeal that action.

argument; nonetheless, we sustain the Commissioner and deny the deduction, on the basis that the expenses were not incurred "while away from home." . . .

II

The Commissioner has directed his argument at the meaning of "in pursuit of a trade or business." He interprets this phrase as requiring that a deductible traveling expense be incurred under the demands of a trade or business which predates the expense, i.e., an "already" existing trade or business. Under this theory, section 162(a)(2) would invalidate the deduction taken by the taxpayer because she was a full-time student before commencing her summer work at a New York law firm in 1975 and so was not continuing in a trade or business when she incurred the expenses of traveling to New York and living there while her job lasted. The Commissioner's proposed interpretation erects at the threshold of deductibility under section 162(a)(2) the requirement that a taxpayer be engaged in a trade or business *before* incurring a travel expense. Only if that requirement is satisfied would an inquiry into the deductibility of an expense proceed to ask whether the expense was a result of business exigencies, incurred while away from home, and reasonable and necessary.

Such a reading of the statute is semantically possible and would perhaps expedite the disposition of certain cases.[18] Nevertheless, we reject it as unsupported by case law and inappropriate to the policies behind section 162(a)(2).

The two cases relied on by the Commissioner do not appear to us to establish that traveling expenses are deductible only if incurred in connection with a preexisting trade or business. . . .

Nor would the Commissioner's theory mesh with the policy behind section 162(a)(2). [T]he travel expense deduction is intended to exclude from taxable income a necessary cost of producing that income. Yet the recency of entry into a trade or business does not indicate that travel expenses are not a cost of producing income. To be sure, the costs incurred by a taxpayer who leaves his usual residence to begin a trade or business at another location may not be truly *travel* expenses, i.e.,

18. We do not see, however, how it would affect the treatment of this case. The Commissioner apparently concedes that upon starting work in New York the taxpayer engaged in a trade or business. If we held — as we do not — that an expense is deductible only when incurred in connection with an already existing trade or business, our ruling would seem to invalidate merely the deduction of the cost of taxpayer's trip from Boston to New York to begin work (about $64). We would still need to determine, as in any other case under section 162(a)(2), whether the expenses that arose *subsequent* to the taxpayer's entry into her trade or business were reasonable and necessary, required by business exigencies and incurred while away from home.

expenses incurred while "away from home," see infra, but practically, they are as much incurred "in the pursuit of a trade or business" when the occupation is new as when it is old.

An example drawn from the Commissioner's argument illustrates the point. The Commissioner notes that "if a construction worker, who normally works in Boston for Corp. *A,* travels to New York to work for Corp. *B* for six months, he is traveling . . . in the pursuit of his own trade as a construction worker." Accordingly, the requirement that travel expenses be a result of business exigencies is satisfied. Had a construction worker just entering the labor market followed the same course his expenses under the Commissioner's reasoning would not satisfy the business exigencies requirement. Yet in each case, the taxpayer's travel expenses would be costs of earning an income and not merely incidents of personal lifestyle. Requiring that the finding of business exigency necessary to deductibility under section 162(a)(2) be predicated upon the prior existence of a trade or business would thus captiously restrict the meaning of "in pursuit of a trade or business." . . .

III

Flowers [v. Commissioner, supra page 580], construed section 162(a)(2) to mean that a traveling expense is deductible only if it is (1) reasonable and necessary; (2) incurred while away from home, and (3) necessitated by the exigencies of business. Because the Commissioner does not suggest that Mrs. Hantzis' expenses were unreasonable or unnecessary, we may pass directly to the remaining requirements. Of these, we find dispositive the requirement that an expense be incurred while away from home. As we think Mrs. Hantzis' expenses were not so incurred, we hold the deduction to be improper.

The meaning of the term "home" in the travel expense provision is far from clear. When Congress enacted the travel expense deduction now codified as section 162(a)(2), it apparently was unsure whether, to be deductible, an expense must be incurred away from a person's residence or away from his principal place of business. . . . This ambiguity persists and courts, sometimes within a single circuit, have divided over the issue. . . . It has been suggested that these conflicting definitions are due to the enormous factual variety in the cases. . . . We find this observation instructive, for if the cases that discuss the meaning of the term "home" in section 162(a)(2) are interpreted on the basis of their unique facts as well as the fundamental purposes of the travel expense provision, and not simply pinioned to one of two competing definitions of home, much of the seeming confusion and contradiction on this issue disappears and a functional definition of the term emerges.

We begin by recognizing that the location of a person's home for purposes of section 162(a)(2) becomes problematic only when the person lives one place and works another. Where a taxpayer resides and works at a single location, he is always home, however defined; and where a taxpayer is constantly on the move due to his work, he is never "away" from home. (In the latter situation, it may be said either that he has no residence to be away from, or else that his residence is always at his place of employment. . . .) However, in the present case, the need to determine "home" is plainly before us, since the taxpayer resided in Boston and worked, albeit briefly, in New York.

We think the critical step in defining "home" in these situations is to recognize that the "while away from home" requirement has to be construed in light of the further requirement that the expense be the result of business exigencies. The traveling expense deduction obviously is not intended to exclude from taxation every expense incurred by a taxpayer who, in the course of business, maintains two homes. Section 162(a)(2) seeks rather "to mitigate the burden of the taxpayer who, *because of the exigencies of his trade or business, must* maintain two places of abode and thereby incur additional and duplicate living expenses." . . . Consciously or unconsciously, courts have effectuated this policy in part through their interpretation of the term "home" in section 162(a)(2). Whether it is held in a particular decision that a taxpayer's home is his residence or his principal place of business, the ultimate allowance or disallowance of a deduction is a function of the court's assessment of the reason for a taxpayer's maintenance of two homes. If the reason is perceived to be personal, the taxpayer's home will generally be held to be his place of employment rather than his residence and the deduction will be denied. . . . If the reason is felt to be business exigencies, the person's home will usually be held to be his residence and the deduction will be allowed. . . . We understand the concern of the concurrence that such an operational interpretation of the term "home" is somewhat technical and perhaps untidy, in that it will not always afford bright line answers, but we doubt the ability of either the Commissioner or the courts to invent an unyielding formula that will make sense in all cases. The line between personal and business expenses winds through infinite factual permutations; effectuation of the travel expense provision requires that any principle of decision be flexible and sensitive to statutory policy.

Construing in the manner just described the requirement that an expense be incurred "while away from home," we do not believe this requirement was satisfied in this case. Mrs. Hantzis' *trade or business* did not require that she maintain a home in Boston as well as one in New York. Though she returned to Boston at various times during the period of her employment in New York, her visits were all for personal reasons. It is not contended that she had a business connection in Boston that necessitated her keeping a home there; no professional interest was served by maintenance of the Boston home — as would have been the case, for example, if Mrs. Hantzis had been a lawyer based in Boston with a New York client whom she was temporarily serving. The home in Boston was kept up for reasons involving Mr. Hantzis, but those reasons cannot substitute for a showing by *Mrs.* Hantzis that the exigencies of *her* trade or business required *her* to maintain two homes. Mrs. Hantzis' decision to keep two homes must be seen as a choice dictated by personal, albeit wholly reasonable, considerations and not a business or occupational necessity. We therefore hold that her home for purposes of section 162(a)(2) was New York and that the expenses at issue in this case were not incurred "while away from home."

We are not dissuaded from this conclusion by the temporary nature of Mrs. Hantzis' employment in New York. Mrs. Hantzis argues that the brevity of her stay in New York excepts her from the business exigencies requirement of section 162(a)(2) under a doctrine supposedly enunciated by the Supreme Court in Peurifoy v. Commissioner, 358 U.S. 59 (1958) (per curiam).[19] The Tax Court here held that Boston was the taxpayer's home because it would have been unreasonable for her to move her residence to New York for only ten weeks. At first glance these contentions may seem to find support in the court decisions holding that, when a taxpayer works for a limited time away from his usual home, section 162(a)(2) allows a deduction for the expense of maintaining a second home so long as the employment is "temporary" and not "indefinite" or "permanent." . . . This test is an elaboration of the requirements under section 162(a)(2) that an expense be incurred due to business exigencies and while away from home. . . . Thus it has been said:

> Where a taxpayer reasonably expects to be employed in a location for a substantial or indefinite period of time, the reasonable inference is that his choice of a residence is a personal decision, unrelated to any business necessity. Thus, it is irrelevant how far he travels to work. The normal expectation, however, is that the taxpayer will choose to live near his place

19. In *Peurifoy* the Court stated that the Tax Court had "engrafted an exception" onto the requirement that travel expenses be dictated by business exigencies, allowing "a deduction for expenditures . . . when the taxpayer's employment is 'temporary', as contrasted with 'indefinite' or 'indeterminate.'" 358 U.S. at 59. Because the Commissioner did not challenge this exception, the Court did not rule on its validity. It instead upheld the circuit court's reversal of the Tax Court and disallowance of the deduction on the basis of the adequacy of the appellate court's review. The Supreme Court agreed that the Tax Court's finding as to the temporary nature of taxpayer's employment was clearly erroneous. Id. at 60-61.

Despite its inauspicious beginning, the exception has come to be generally accepted. Some uncertainty lingers, however, over whether the exception properly applies to the "business exigencies" or the "away from home" requirement. . . . In fact, it is probably relevant to both. . . .

> of employment. Consequently, when a taxpayer reasonably expects to be employed in a location for only a short or temporary period of time and travels a considerable distance to the location from his residence, it is unreasonable to assume that his choice of a residence is dictated by personal convenience. The reasonable inference is that he is temporarily making these travels because of a business necessity.

Frederick [v. United States], 603 F.2d at 1294-95 (citations omitted).

The temporary employment doctrine does not, however, purport to eliminate any requirement that continued maintenance of a first home have a business justification. We think the rule has no application where the taxpayer has no business connection with his usual place of residence. If no business exigency dictates the location of the taxpayer's usual residence, then the mere fact of his taking temporary employment elsewhere cannot supply a compelling business reason for continuing to maintain that residence. Only a taxpayer who lives one place, works another and has business ties to *both* is in the ambiguous situation that the temporary employment doctrine is designed to resolve. In such circumstances, unless his employment away from his usual home is temporary, a court can reasonably assume that the taxpayer has abandoned his business ties to that location and is left with only personal reasons for maintaining a residence there. Where only personal needs require that a travel expense be incurred, however, a taxpayer's home is defined so as to leave the expense subject to taxation. See supra. Thus, a taxpayer who pursues temporary employment away from the location of his usual residence, but has no business connection with that location, is not "away from home" for purposes of section 162(a)(2). . . .

On this reasoning, the temporary nature of Mrs. Hantzis' employment in New York does not affect the outcome of her case. She had no business ties to Boston that would bring her within the temporary employment doctrine. By this holding, we do not adopt a rule that "home" in section 162(a)(2) is the equivalent of a taxpayer's place of business. Nor do we mean to imply that a taxpayer has a "home" for tax purposes only if he is already engaged in a trade or business at a particular location. Though both rules are alluringly determinate, we have already discussed why they offer inadequate expressions of the purposes behind the travel expense deduction. We hold merely that for a taxpayer in Mrs. Hantzis' circumstances to be "away from home in the pursuit of a trade or business," she must establish the existence of some sort of business relation both to the location she claims as "home" and to the location of her temporary employment sufficient to support a finding that her duplicative expenses are necessitated by business exigencies. This, we believe, is the meaning of the statement in *Flowers* that "[b]usiness trips are to be identified *in relation to* business demands and the traveler's business headquarters." 326 U.S. at 474 (emphasis added). On the uncontested facts before us, Mrs. Hantzis had no business relation to Boston; we therefore leave to cases in which the issue is squarely presented the task of elaborating what relation to a place is required under section 162(a)(2) for duplicative living expenses to be deductible.

Reversed.

KEETON, District Judge, concurring in the result.

Although I agree with the result reached in the court's opinion, and with much of its underlying analysis, I write separately because I cannot join in the court's determination that New York was the taxpayer's home for purposes of §162(a)(2). In so holding, the court adopts a definition of "home" that differs from the ordinary meaning of the term and therefore unduly risks causing confusion and misinterpretation of the important principle articulated in this case. . . .

A word used in a statute can mean, among the cognoscenti, whatever authoritative sources define it to mean. Nevertheless, it is a distinct disadvantage of a body of law that it can be understood only by those who are expert in its terminology. Moreover, needless risks of misunderstanding and confusion arise, not only among members of the public but also among professionals who must interpret and apply a statute in their day-to-day work, when a word is given an extraordinary meaning that is contrary to its everyday usage.

The result reached by the court can easily be expressed while also giving "home" its ordinary meaning, and neither Congress nor the Supreme Court has directed that "home" be given an extraordinary meaning in the present context. . . .

NOTES AND QUESTIONS

1. Flowers *and commuting costs.* The deductions at issue in *Flowers* were in large part for the expenses of living in Mobile, but the case has been treated as authority primarily for the proposition that a person cannot deduct transportation costs incurred in commuting to and from work. The view of the majority in *Flowers* was that Mr. Flowers's trips to Mobile and back (usually via New Orleans) were just a long commute. As an employee of the railroad on which he traveled, Mr. Flowers "had a railroad pass [and] paid no train fare but did have to pay seat or berth fare." Flowers v. Commissioner, 3 T.C.M. 803, 805 (1944). The Commissioner did not treat the value of the free train fare as income to Mr. Flowers, though logic would suggest that such treatment would have been appropriate.

2. *Causative analysis.* In *Flowers,* the Court says that the expenses at issue "were incurred solely as a result of the taxpayer's desire to maintain

a home in Jackson while working in Mobile." In other words, the expenses would not have been incurred but for the personal decision to live in Jackson. It is equally clear, however, that the expenses would not have been incurred but for the business decision to take the job in Mobile. The same kind of observation may be made about the expenses in *Hantzis:* There were two necessary conditions for incurring the expenses, the job and the home. Compare the earlier discussion of "but for" analysis in connection with the deductions for medical expenses (supra page 487, Note 1) and for child-care expenses (supra page 577, Note 1). Does it help to try to identify a "proximate" cause of the expenses? Should it be relevant that the necessary business condition (the job in Mobile for Flowers or in New York for Hantzis) arose after the necessary personal condition (the home in Jackson for Flowers or in Boston for Hantzis)? (See also the discussion of the deductibility of legal expenses, infra page 606, Note 1.) As between the two necessary conditions, which seems relatively more fixed and which relatively more variable in each case? Does this depend on the strength of each of the taxpayer's marriages?

3. *The motivation in* Hantzis. Hantzis earned $3,750 and spent $3,204, which means she netted $546 for her ten weeks of work. She could have netted more working part time at a menial job in Boston. So why did she go to New York, and what does your answer tell you about how people like her should be taxed?

4. *Temporary versus indefinite jobs.* The court in *Hantzis* refers to the rule, cited by the Supreme Court in Peurifoy v. Commissioner, 358 U.S. 59 (1958) (per curiam), under which a person who takes a *temporary* job away from his or her home area is allowed to deduct travel and living costs (as, for example, would a lawyer from New York who must spend three months in Chicago trying a case). The costs are not deductible, however, where the job away from the area of the taxpayer's residence is of *indefinite* duration. A new job with an indefinite duration is treated as if it were a permanent new job, like Mr. Flowers's job in Mobile. The temporary-versus-indefinite distinction has given rise to a great deal of litigation. Many of the cases involve construction workers. The legal uncertainty that gave rise to much of this litigation was ended in 1992, when Congress, as part of comprehensive energy legislation, added the final sentence of §162(a), which limits "temporary" jobs to those lasting a year or less.

5. *Split summers.* Catharine Hantzis was not allowed to deduct the travel, meals, and lodging expenses she incurred in connection with her summer employment at a New York law firm because, for tax purposes, her "home" was considered to be the place of her principal employment, New York. Suppose Hantzis had spent the first six weeks of her summer working in New York and then had spent the last five weeks of the summer working in the Los Angeles office of the same New York law

firm. Would her expenses in connection with the Los Angeles job have been deductible? What if the job in Los Angeles had been with a firm not affiliated with the New York firm?

6. *Testing the rationale.* The usual rationale for disallowing a deduction for commuting expenses is that the taxpayer is expected to move as near as possible to the job location. If that is done, the expense is trivial. If the taxpayer chooses to live far from the job, that is regarded as a personal choice. Consider the soundness of that rationale in each of the following hypotheticals. Would a deduction be allowed in any of them (disregarding the effect of §67)? Consider whether the tax outcome in each case seems fair and how that outcome might affect family harmony, job-taking decisions by women, and the rationality of job-taking choices in general.

(a) Taxpayer *A* is a woman who lives on a farm with her husband. She drives each day to town, where she earns $50 per day teaching school. The distance is thirty miles each way and the cost of driving is $10 per day. There is no public transportation.

(b) Taxpayer *B* is a poor woman who lives in the central city and works as a maid in an affluent suburb. The distance from her home to the place where she works is twenty miles. Public transportation is available but would take about two hours each way because of the need to make several transfers and to walk substantial distances. *B*'s employer pays $10 a day to a driver of a van who picks *B* up near her home each morning and drops her off at the place where she works. Her pay is $30 per day. She supports her two young children as well as herself. For purposes of determining eligibility for Medicaid, food stamps, and other welfare, what seems to you to be the proper amount of income? What is the rule for income tax purposes? See §132(f). What do you suppose is the practice? Note that even though the worker is probably below the income threshold for paying taxes, the amount of her income is relevant to calculation of her earned income tax credit.

(c) *C* is a tax lawyer who works in the central business district and lives in the suburbs, twenty-five miles from work. When he first took his job, he lived in an apartment about two miles from the office but later decided that he preferred the ambience and the recreational opportunities in the suburbs. He earns $150,000 per year and commutes in a Mercedes that costs $20 a day to drive to and from work each day. On rare occasions he uses the car during the day to drive to a meeting with a client.

(d) *D* is a trial lawyer who lives next door to *C*, works in the same firm, earns the same amount, and drives to work in the same model car. *D* needs his car most days in order to get to the various courts in which he must make appearances or to places where he takes depositions.[20] He says that he brings the car to work only in order to have it

20. The costs of driving to court or to take depositions plainly are deductible, under

available for these business uses, but in fact he drives to work even on those days when he will almost certainly spend the entire day in the office. He could take the bus, which would add about forty-five minutes each way to his commuting time and would cost $4 per day round trip.[21]

(e) *E* is a lawyer who is just like *D* in all respects except that his reason for moving to the suburbs was the "better" schools available there. At the time he moved, a federal court had just issued a desegregation order requiring busing in the city schools. In the suburb where he lives, there are very few minority children, and there is no school busing. He denies that his move to the suburbs had anything to do with desegregation and every year contributes $100 to the NAACP Legal Defense Fund.

(f) *F* is also a lawyer, working at the same firm as *C, D,* and *E*. *F* is married to *E*. She would prefer to live in the city and to have her children go to the city schools or to a private school in the city but acquiesced in *E*'s decision to move to the suburbs. Because *E* and *F* have different schedules, they cannot drive to work together.

(g) *G* is a construction worker. He has lived in the same home, in the central city, for many years. He works at various job sites, for periods ranging from a month to a year. His commutes range in distance from ten to forty miles each way. Rarely is public transportation available, but when it is *G* takes it (largely because he is an avid reader and likes to have the time on the bus or train for reading).

(h) *H* is a construction worker who cannot find a job in the area in which he has lived and worked for the past twenty years. He takes a job in another city, 200 miles away. He expects that job to last about three months, which it does. His cost of traveling to and from the new job location is $100. His living costs while he is there, including food and lodging, are $25 per day. In addition, he spends $5 per day driving back and forth between the job site and his temporary dwelling place.

---

§162(a), as "ordinary and necessary expenses." Section 162(a)(2) is irrelevant to this expense, though even in cases where it is relevant it is only an elaboration on the basic operative rule stated in the opening clause of §162(a).

21. In the *Henderson* case, supra page 545, the court denied the taxpayer's deduction of $180 for parking across the street from her office, despite her statement that she "occasionally used her automobile for business purposes when an automobile from the pool of State automobiles was not available." The court said that "petitioner has offered no evidence to establish that her employer required her to have her car at her place of employment or that she would not have driven to work in any event." Similarly, in Fillerup v. Commissioner, 1988-103 T.C.M., where the taxpayer, a doctor, was allowed to deduct the cost of driving his car (a 6.9 Mercedes-Benz) from one hospital to another, but not from home to the first hospital or from the last hospital back home. The court in this case rested its partial disallowance on the ground that the taxpayer would have driven to work even if he had not needed the car to get from one hospital to another. In Croughan v. Commissioner, 1988-303 T.C.M., the court disallowed a deduction for commuting expenses despite its finding that if the taxpayer, a microbiologist, "had not been required to have her car available at work [to transport specimens from her place of work to other public health facilities], she would have commuted to work by bus." The court reasoned that the taxpayer was required to have a car available at work, but not to take it home at night, and that the commuting use was therefore personal.

(i) *I* is just like *H* except that the new job is expected to last three years.

(j) *J* is a civilian employee at an air force base. He is not allowed to live on the base. The nearest habitable community is twenty miles from the workplace. The cost of driving the forty miles to and from work each day in his own car is $8. No other means of transportation is available. (Held, on similar facts: no deduction. Sanders v. Commissioner, 439 F.2d 296 (9th Cir.), cert. denied, 404 U.S. 864 (1971).)

7. *Two places of employment or business.* What if Mr. Flowers had continued to practice law in Jackson after he took the job in Mobile? The Tax Court would apparently permit his expenses in Mobile to be deducted if the business activity in Jackson were substantial, even though the income therefrom was less than the Mobile income. The Service generally takes the position that the "home" of a taxpayer having two widely separated posts of duty is the "principal business" post, so that the taxpayer is not "away from home" while there but may deduct living expenses while at the minor post. See, e.g., Rev. Rul. 75-432, 1975-2 C.B. 60. This ruling is also applicable to seasonal workers such as baseball players.

8. *Moving expenses.* Examine briefly §217, which allows a deduction for the moving expenses (as defined in §217(b)) of a taxpayer who takes a new job, if, roughly speaking, the new job would add at least 50 miles to his or her commute and in the year following the move the taxpayer works at least thirty-nine weeks at the new job (§217(c)). Is it not clear that moving expenses above a minimal amount would not be incurred but for personal decisions relating to the acquisition of a family and of possessions? Where does that observation lead you?

Section 217 was in large part a response to the unfairness of prior law, under which payments or reimbursements by an employer for an employee's moving expenses were not income, but amounts paid by an employee or a self-employed person to meet such expenses were not deductible. Congress finds it easier to eliminate unfairness of this sort by extending benefits than by contracting them. Its statement of the reasons for the adoption of the provision is, however, an interesting illustration of the application of principles of tax policy. See Staff of the Joint Committee on Internal Revenue Taxation, General Explanation of the Tax Reform Act of 1969, 91st Cong., 2d Sess. 101 (1970)):

> *General reasons for change.* The mobility of labor is an important and necessary part of the nation's economy, since it reduces unemployment and increases productive capacity. It has been estimated that approximately one-half million employees are requested by their employers to move to new job locations each year. In addition, self-employed individuals relocate to find more attractive or useful employment. Substantial moving expenses often are incurred by taxpayers in connection with employment-

related relocations, and these expenses may be regarded as a cost of earning income.

The Congress believed that more adequate recognition should be given in the tax law to expenses connected with job-related moves. In addition, the Congress concluded that equity required that the moving expense deduction be made available on a comparable basis for self-employed persons who move to a new work location. Finally, it was desired to equalize fully the tax treatment for the moving expenses of new employees and unreimbursed transferred employees with the treatment accorded reimbursed employees.

Deductions under §217 are not subject to the 2 percent threshold found in §67. See §67(b)(6). Moreover, for the years after 1993, the deduction is an above-the-line item that can be claimed by people who use the standard deduction. §62(a)(15).

E. CLOTHING EXPENSES

PEVSNER v. COMMISSIONER

628 F.2d 467 (5th Cir. 1980)

JOHNSON, Circuit Judge.

This is an appeal by the Commissioner of Internal Revenue from a decision of the United States Tax Court. The tax court upheld taxpayer's business expense deduction for clothing expenditures in the amount of $1,621.91 for the taxable year 1975. We reverse.

Since June 1973 Sandra J. Pevsner, taxpayer, has been employed as the manager of the Sakowitz Yves St. Laurent Rive Gauche Boutique located in Dallas, Texas. The boutique sells only women's clothes and accessories designed by Yves St. Laurent (YSL), one of the leading designers of women's apparel. Although the clothing is ready to wear, it is highly fashionable and expensively priced. Some customers of the boutique purchase and wear the YSL apparel for their daily activities and spend as much as $20,000 per year for such apparel.

As manager of the boutique, the taxpayer is expected by her employer to wear YSL clothes while at work. In her appearance, she is expected to project the image of an exclusive lifestyle and to demonstrate to her customers that she is aware of the YSL current fashion trends as well as trends generally. Because the boutique sells YSL clothes exclusively, taxpayer must be able, when a customer compliments her on her clothes, to say that they are designed by YSL. In addition to wearing YSL apparel while at the boutique, she wears them while commuting to and from work, to fashion shows sponsored by the boutique, and to business luncheons at which she represents the boutique. During 1975, the taxpayer bought, at an employee's discount, the following items: four blouses, three skirts, one pair of slacks, one trench coat, two sweaters, one jacket, one tunic, five scarves, six belts, two pairs of shoes and four necklaces. The total cost of this apparel was $1,381.91. In addition, the sum of $240 was expended for maintenance of these items.

Although the clothing and accessories purchased by the taxpayer were the type used for general purposes by the regular customers of the boutique, the taxpayer is not a normal purchaser of these clothes. The taxpayer and her husband, who is partially disabled because of a severe heart attack suffered in 1971, lead a simple life and their social activities are very limited and informal. Although taxpayer's employer has no objection to her wearing the apparel away from work, taxpayer stated that she did not wear the clothes during off-work hours because she felt that they were too expensive for her simple everyday lifestyle. Another reason why she did not wear the YSL clothes apart from work was to make them last longer. Taxpayer did admit at trial, however, that a number of the articles were things she could have worn off the job and in which she would have looked "nice."

On her joint federal income tax return for 1975, taxpayer deducted $990 as an ordinary and necessary business expense with respect to her purchase of the YSL clothing and accessories. However, in the tax court, taxpayer claimed a deduction for the full $1,381.91 cost of the apparel and for the $240 cost of maintaining the apparel. The tax court allowed the taxpayer to deduct both expenses in the total amount of $1,621.91. The tax court reasoned that the apparel was not suitable to the private lifestyle maintained by the taxpayer. This appeal by the Commissioner followed. . . .

The generally accepted rule governing the deductibility of clothing expenses is that the cost of clothing is deductible as a business expense only if: (1) the clothing is of a type specifically required as a condition of employment, (2) it is not adaptable to general usage as ordinary clothing, and (3) it is not so worn. . . .

In the present case, the Commissioner stipulated that the taxpayer was required by her employer to wear YSL clothing and that she did not wear such apparel apart from work. The Commissioner maintained, however, that a deduction should be denied because the YSL clothes and accessories purchased by the taxpayer were adaptable for general usage as ordinary clothing and she was not prohibited from using them as such. The tax court, in rejecting the Commissioner's argument for the application of an objective test, recognized that the test for deductibility was whether the clothing was "suitable for general or personal wear" but determined that the matter of suitability was to be judged subjectively, in light of the taxpayer's lifestyle. Although the court recognized that the YSL apparel "might be used by some members of society for general purposes," it felt that because the "wearing of YSL apparel outside work would be inconsistent with . . . [taxpayer's] lifestyle," sufficient reason was shown for allowing a deduction for the clothing expenditures. . . .

[T]he Circuits that have addressed the issue have taken an objective, rather than subjective, approach. . . . Under an objective test, no reference is made to the individual taxpayer's lifestyle or personal taste. Instead, adaptability for personal or general use depends upon what is generally accepted for ordinary streetwear.

The principal argument in support of an objective test is, of course, administrative necessity. The Commissioner argues that, as a practical matter, it is virtually impossible to determine at what point either price or style makes clothing inconsistent with or inappropriate to a taxpayer's lifestyle. Moreover, the Commissioner argues that the price one pays and the styles one selects are inherently personal choices governed by taste, fashion, and other unmeasurable values. Indeed, the tax court has rejected the argument that a taxpayer's personal taste can dictate whether clothing is appropriate for general use. . . . An objective test, although not perfect, provides a practical administrative approach that allows a taxpayer or revenue agent to look only to objective facts in determining whether clothing required as a condition of employment is adaptable to general use as ordinary streetwear. Conversely, the tax court's reliance on subjective factors provides no concrete guidelines in determining the deductibility of clothing purchased as a condition of employment.

In addition to achieving a practical administrative result, an objective test also tends to promote substantial fairness among the greatest number of taxpayers. As the Commissioner suggests, it apparently would be the tax court's position that two similarly situated YSL boutique managers with identical wardrobes would be subject to disparate tax consequences depending upon the particular manager's lifestyle and "socio-economic level." This result, however, is not consonant with a reasonable interpretation of Sections 162 and 262.

For the reasons stated above, the decision of the tax court upholding the deduction for taxpayer's purchase of YSL clothing is reversed. Consequently, the portion of the tax court's decision upholding the deduction for maintenance costs for the clothing is also reversed.

NOTE

In Nelson v. Commissioner, 1966-224 T.C.M., the taxpayers, husband and wife, were allowed to deduct the cost of the clothing they wore in the television series *The Adventures of Ozzie and Harriet.* The annual costs ranged from $12,341 in 1957 to $6,037 in 1962. In the series, the taxpayers "portrayed an average American family, with certain reasonable exaggerations." While the clothing was suitable for personal use, the court found that some of it was too heavy for use in southern California, where the Nelsons lived, it was subject to heavy wear and tear in production of the show, the Nelsons worked such long hours that they had little chance to wear the clothing off the set, and in fact the personal use was de minimis.

In Mella v. Commissioner, T.C.M. 1986-594, the taxpayer was a tennis professional. He was head professional at two tennis clubs and a nationally ranked player who played in at least a dozen tournaments in the year at issue. He claimed deductions for tennis clothes and shoes. The shoes lasted only two or three weeks. The court denied the deductions, stating:

> The Court observes that it is relatively commonplace for Americans in all walks of life to wear warm-up clothes, shirts, and shoes of the type purchased by the petitioner while engaged in a wide variety of casual or athletic activities. The items are fashionable, and in some cases have the name or logo of designers that have become common in America. Indeed, at trial, it was stated that tennis professionals, such as the petitioner, are clothing style setters for their students.

In Williams v. Commissioner, T.C. Memo. 1991-317, the taxpayer rode a motorcycle in his business as an Amway distributor. He was allowed to deduct the cost of his "leather uniform," which he wore while riding the motorcycle in connection with his business, and which bore the Amway label, but not the cost of the helmet and steel-toe boots that he also wore and that the court considered to be suitable for nonbusiness use.

QUESTIONS

1. (a) Do you think the result in *Pevsner* is unfair to the taxpayer? (b) If so, can you suggest a rule that would allow her a deduction, would be feasible for the Service to administer, and would not lead to abuse?

2. Is the present rule that allows a deduction for the cost of uniforms not suitable for ordinary wear subject to significant abuse?

F. LEGAL EXPENSES

UNITED STATES v. GILMORE

372 U.S. 39 (1963)

Mr. Justice Harlan. . . .

In 1955, the California Supreme Court confirmed the award to the respondent taxpayer of a decree of absolute divorce. . . . The case before us involves the deductibility for federal income tax purposes of that part of the husband's legal expense incurred in such proceedings as is attributable to his successful resistance of his wife's claim to certain of his assets asserted by her to be community property under California law. The claim to such deduction, which has been upheld by the Court of Claims, 290 F.2d 942, is founded on [§212(2)], which allows as deductions from gross income: . . . ordinary and necessary expenses . . . incurred during the taxable year . . . for the . . . conservation . . . of property held for the production of income.

At the time of the divorce proceedings, instituted by the wife but in which the husband also cross-claimed for divorce, respondent's property consisted primarily of controlling stock interests in three corporations [General Motors dealerships]. . . . As president . . . of the three corporations, he received salaries from them aggregating about $66,800 annually, and in recent years his total annual dividends had averaged about $83,000. . . . His income from other sources was negligible.

As found by the Court of Claims the husband's overriding concern in the divorce litigation was to protect these assets against the claims of his wife. Those claims had two aspects: *First,* that the earnings accumulated and retained by these three corporations during the Gilmores' marriage (representing an aggregate increase in corporate net worth of some $600,000) were the product of respondent's personal services, and not the result of accretion in capital values, thus rendering respondent's stockholdings in the enterprises pro tanto community property under California law; *second,* that to the extent that such stockholdings were community property, the wife, allegedly the innocent party in the divorce proceeding, was entitled under California law to more than a one-half interest in such property.

The respondent wished to defeat those claims for two important reasons. *First,* the loss of his controlling stock interests, particularly in the event of their transfer in substantial part to his hostile wife, might well cost him the loss of his corporate positions, his principal means of livelihood. *Second,* there was also danger that if he were found guilty of his wife's sensational and reputation-damaging charges of marital infidelity, General Motors Corporation might find it expedient to exercise its right to cancel these dealer franchises.

The end result of this bitterly fought divorce case was a complete victory for the husband. He, not the wife, was granted a divorce on his cross-claim; the wife's community property claims were denied in their entirety; and she was held entitled to no alimony.

Respondent's legal expenses in connection with this litigation amounted to . . . a total of $40,611.36. . . . The Commissioner found all of these expenditures "personal" or "family" expenses and as such none of them deductible. [§262.] In the ensuing refund suit, however, the Court of Claims held that 80 percent of such expense (some $32,500) was attributable to respondent's defense against his wife's community property claims respecting his stockholdings and hence deductible under [§212(2)] as an expense "incurred . . . for the . . . conservation . . . of property held for the production of income." . . .

The Government['s] . . . sole contention here is that the court below misconceived the test governing [§212(1) and (2)] deductions, in that the deductibility of these expenses turns, so it is argued, not upon the *consequences* to respondent of a failure to defeat his wife's community property claims but upon the *origin* and *nature* of the claims themselves. . . . [W]e think the Government's position is sound and that it must be sustained.

I

For income tax purposes, Congress has seen fit to regard an individual as having two personalities: "one is [as] a seeker after profit who can deduct the expenses incurred in that search; the other is [as] a creature satisfying his needs as a human and those of his family but who cannot deduct such consumption and related expenditures."[22] The Government regards [§212(1) and (2)] as embodying a category of expenses embraced in the first of these roles.

Initially, it may be observed that the wording of [§212(2)] more readily fits the Government's view of the provision than that of the Court of Claims. For in context "conservation of property" seems to refer to operations performed with respect to the property itself, such as safeguarding or upkeep, rather than to a taxpayer's retention of ownership in it. But more illuminating than the mere language of [§212(1) and (2)] is the history of the provision.

Prior to 1942 [the Code] allowed deductions only for expenses incurred "in carrying on any trade or business," the deduction presently authorized by [§162(a)]. In Higgins v. Comm'r, 312 U.S. 212, this Court gave that provision a narrow construction, holding that the activities of

22. Surrey and Warren, Cases on Federal Income Taxation, 272 (1960).

an individual in supervising his own securities investments did not constitute the "carrying on of a trade or business," and hence that expenses incurred in connection with such activities were not tax deductible. . . . The Revenue Act of 1942 . . . by adding what is now [§212(1) and (2)], sought to remedy the inequity inherent in the disallowance of expense deductions in respect of such profit-seeking activities, the income from which was nonetheless taxable.

As noted in McDonald v. Comm'r, 323 U.S. 57, 62, the purpose of the 1942 amendment was merely to enlarge "the category of incomes with reference to which expenses were deductible." And committee reports make clear that deductions under the new section were subject to the same limitations and restrictions that are applicable to those allowable under [§162(a)]. Further, this Court has said that [§212(1) and (2)] "is comparable and in pari materia with [§162(a)]," providing for a class of deductions "coextensive with the business deductions allowed by [§162(a)], except for" the requirement that the income-producing activity qualify as a trade or business. Trust of Bingham v. Comm'r, 325 U.S. 365, 373, 374.

A basic restriction upon the availability of a [§162(a)] deduction is that the expense item involved must be one that has a business origin. That restriction not only inheres in the language of [§162(a)] itself, confining such deductions to "expenses . . . incurred . . . in carrying on any trade or business," but also follows from [§262], expressly rendering nondeductible "in any case . . . [p]ersonal, living, or family expenses." In light of what has already been said with respect to the advent and thrust of [§212(1) and (2)], it is clear that the "[p]ersonal . . . or family expenses" restriction of [§262] must impose the same limitation upon the reach of [§212(1) and (2)] — in other words that the only kind of expenses deductible under [§212(1) and (2)] are those that relate to a "business," i.e., profit-seeking, purpose. The pivotal issue in this case then becomes: was this part of respondent's litigation cost a "business" rather than a "personal" or "family" expense?

The answer to this question has already been indicated in prior cases. In Lykes v. U.S., 343 U.S. 118, the Court rejected the contention that legal expenses incurred in contesting the assessment of a gift tax liability were deductible. The taxpayer argued that if he had been required to pay the original deficiency he would have been forced to liquidate his stockholdings, which were his main source of income, and that his legal expenses were therefore incurred in the "conservation" of income-producing property and hence deductible under [§212(2)]. The Court first noted that the "deductibility [of the expenses] turns wholly upon the nature of the activities to which they relate" (343 U.S. at 123), and then stated (id. at 125-126):

> Legal expenses do not become deductible merely because they are paid for services which relieve a taxpayer of liability. That argument would

> carry us too far. It would mean that the expense of defending almost any claim would be deductible by a taxpayer on the ground that such defense was made to help him keep clear of liens whatever income-producing property he might have. For example, it suggests that the expense of defending an action based upon personal injuries caused by a taxpayer's negligence while driving an automobile for pleasure should be deductible. Section [212(1) and (2)] never has been so interpreted by us. . . .
>
> [T]he threatened deficiency assessment . . . related to the tax payable on petitioner's gifts. . . . The expense of contesting the amount of the deficiency was thus at all times attributable to the gifts, as such, and accordingly was not deductible.
>
> If, as suggested, the relative size of each claim, in proportion to the income-producing resources of a defendant, were to be a touchstone of the deductibility of the expense of resisting the claim, substantial uncertainty and inequity would inhere in the rule.

In Kronhauser v. U.S., 276 U.S. 145, this Court considered the deductibility of legal expenses incurred by a taxpayer in defending against a claim by a former business partner that fees paid to the taxpayer were for services rendered during the existence of the partnership. In holding that these expenses were deductible even though the taxpayer was no longer a partner at the time of suit, the Court formulated the rule that "where a suit or action against a taxpayer is directly connected with, or . . . proximately resulted from, his business, the expense incurred is a business expense. . . ." 276 U.S. at 153. Similarly, in a case involving an expense incurred in satisfying an obligation (though not a litigation expense), it was said that "it is the origin of the liability out of which the expense accrues" or "the kind of transaction out of which the obligation arose . . . which [is] crucial and controlling." Deputy v. duPont, 308 U.S. 488, 494, 496.

The principle we derive from these cases is that the characterization, as "business" or "personal," of the litigation costs of resisting a claim depends on whether or not the claim *arises in connection with* the taxpayer's profit-seeking activities. It does not depend on the *consequences* that might result to a taxpayer's income-producing property from a failure to defeat the claim, for, as *Lykes* teaches, that "would carry us too far"[23] and would not be compatible with the basic lines of expense deductibility

23. The Treasury Regulations have long provided:

> An expense (not otherwise deductible) paid or incurred by an individual in determining or contesting a liability asserted against him does not become deductible by reason of the fact that property held by him for the production of income may be required to be used or sold for the purpose of satisfying such liability.

Treas. Regs. (1954 Code) §1.212-1(m); see Treas. Regs. 118 (1939 Code) §39.23(a)-15(k).

drawn by Congress.[24] Moreover, such a rule would lead to capricious results. If two taxpayers are each sued for an automobile accident while driving for pleasure, deductibility of their litigation costs would turn on the mere circumstance of the character of the assets each happened to possess, i.e., whether the judgments against them stood to be satisfied out of income- or nonincome-producing property. We should be slow to attribute to Congress a purpose producing such unequal treatment among taxpayers, resting on no rational foundation. . . .

We turn then to the determinative question in this case: did the wife's claims respecting respondent's stockholdings arise in connection with his profit-seeking activities?

II

In classifying respondent's legal expenses the court below did not distinguish between those relating to the claims of the wife with respect to the *existence* of community property and those involving the *division* of any such property. . . . Nor is such a break-down necessary for a disposition of the present case. It is enough to say that in both aspects the wife's claims stemmed entirely from the marital relationship, and not, under any tenable view of things, from income-producing activity. This is obviously so as regards the claim to more than an equal division of any community property found to exist. For any such right depended entirely on the wife's making good her charges of marital infidelity on the part of the husband. The same conclusion is no less true respecting the claim relating to the existence of community property. For no such property could have existed but for the marriage relationship.[25] Thus, none of respondent's expenditures in resisting these claims can be deemed "business" expenses, and they are therefore not deductible under [§212(2)]. . . .

Mr. Justice Black and Mr. Justice Douglas believe that the Court reverses this case because of an unjustifiably narrow interpretation of the 1942 amendment to the Internal Revenue Code and would accordingly affirm the judgment of the Court of Claims.

24. Expenses of contesting tax liabilities are now deductible under §212(3) of the 1954 Code. This provision merely represents a policy judgment as to a particular class of expenditures otherwise nondeductible, like extraordinary medical expenses, and does not cast any doubt on the basic tax structure set up by Congress.

25. The respondent's attempted analogy of a marital "partnership" to the business partnership involved in the *Kronhauser* case, supra, is of course unavailing. The marriage relationship can hardly be deemed an income-producing activity.

NOTES AND QUESTIONS

1. *Causative analysis revisited.* (a) Is the "origins" test in *Gilmore* different from the "but for" test that we have encountered earlier in connection with deductions for medical expenses (supra page 487, Note 1), child-care expenses (supra page 577, Note 1), and commuting costs (supra page 592, Note 2)?

(b) Would and should the result in *Gilmore* have been different if Mr. Gilmore had first met Mrs. Gilmore when she came to work for his business?

(c) The Court would presumably have us compare Mr. Gilmore with a taxpayer who had the same property interests but who never married or, having married, never got divorced. Does the Court offer any explanation of why we should not compare Mr. Gilmore with a man who gets divorced but who has no property in jeopardy?

(d) What was Mr. Gilmore's "primary purpose" in incurring the expenses he sought to deduct? Would primary purpose be a better test than "origins"?

(e) Are Mr. Gilmore's fees like casualty losses? medical expenses? commuting expenses? Does the answer depend on the incidence of divorce among people like the Gilmores?

2. *The scope of* Gilmore. In a companion case, United States v. Patrick, 372 U.S. 53 (1963), the Supreme Court held nondeductible a husband's payments to his and his wife's attorneys for services in connection with another divorce where there was a private settlement of various property interests. The Court held that *Gilmore* was controlling:

> We find no significant distinction in the fact that [in *Patrick*] the legal fees for which the deduction is claimed were paid for arranging a transfer of stock interests, leasing real property, and creating a trust rather than for conducting litigation. These matters were incidental to litigation brought by respondent's wife, whose claims arising from respondent's personal and family life were the origin of the property arrangements.

372 U.S. at 57. Do you agree that *Gilmore* is controlling?

3. *Addition to basis.* In a subsequent year, Mr. Gilmore sold some of the stock that had been contested in the divorce actions. He added disallowed attorneys' fees to the basis of his stock as capitalized costs of defending title. Prior cases had allowed the addition of such costs to basis. See Gilmore v. United States, 245 F. Supp. 383, 384 (N.D. Cal. 1965). The government contended that the reasoning of the Supreme Court in United States v. Gilmore should also be applied to basis questions. The District Court held for the taxpayer, finding that costs of defending title are capital expenses whether arising in suits primarily business or personal in character. The court conceded that legal expen-

ses may not be added to basis in some personal suits because "as a factual matter, the expenses would not have been primarily to defend title." Suppose that a taxpayer is sued for alleged personal debts and a lien is placed on his personal residence, which is his only asset. May the cost of defending against the suit be added to his basis for the house?

4. *Criminal defense.* In Accardo v. Commissioner, 942 F.2d 444 (7th Cir. 1991), the taxpayer, Anthony Accardo, had successfully defended himself in a criminal prosecution for violation of the Racketeer Influenced and Corrupt Organizations Act (RICO). Accardo was "the reputed head of the Chicago organized crime family." See United States v. Guzzino, 810 F.2d 687, 690 (7th Cir. 1987), cert. denied, 481 U.S. 1030. He was accused of having taken "kickbacks from a union insurance program." Some of his co-defendants were convicted and were allowed to deduct their legal fees as ordinary and necessary business expenses, under §162. Accardo could not claim a deduction under §162 because he was acquitted. Because of the acquital he was not in the trade or business of racketeering, so his legal expenses could not be trade or business expenses. Thus, the guilty criminal defendants were treated better by the tax system than innocent defendants. In reaching this result, which it calls "paradoxical," the Seventh Circuit opinion relies in part on *Gilmore.* The deduction under §162 is considered further in Chapter 6, infra page 651.

Accardo in effect conceded that he was not entitled to a deduction under §162 and claimed instead that the cost of his legal defense was deductible under §212 as the cost of protecting certain assets from seizure by the government under provisions of RICO for forfeiture of the fruits of criminal activity. The court rejected this claim on the ground that the assets that Accardo claimed he sought to protect were not in fact traceable to any criminal activity and therefore were not subject to forfeiture. The court found Accardo's argument so lacking in merit that it sustained a penalty for negligence and a penalty for substantial underpayment of tax (two separate penalties that are now combined in §6662).

What if the government had alleged that Accardo's assets were in fact traceable to the racketeering activity of which he was accused, but, as in the actual case, he was acquitted?

G. EXPENSES OF EDUCATION

CARROLL v. COMMISSIONER

418 F.2d 91 (7th Cir. 1969)

Castle, Chief Judge. . . .

James A. Carroll (hereinafter referred to as the petitioner) was employed by the Chicago Police Department as a detective during the year in question. In his 1964 federal income tax return, he listed as a deduction $720.80 which represented his cost of enrollment in DePaul University. The course of study entered into by plaintiff was stated by him to be in preparation for entrance to law school and consisted of a major in Philosophy. The six courses in which plaintiff was enrolled included two English, two Philosophy, one History and one Political Science course. Petitioner justified the deduction under §162(a), . . . as an expense "relative to improving job skills to maintain [his] position as a detective."

During 1964, the Police Department had in effect General Order No. 63-24, which encouraged policemen to attend colleges and universities by arranging their schedules of duties so as to not conflict with class schedules. Petitioner availed himself of the benefits of this order when he enrolled in DePaul University. . . .

[Regs. §1.162-5] abolished the primary purpose test and established a more objective standard for determining whether the cost of education may be deducted as a business expense. . . . Thus, petitioner in the instant case must justify his deduction under §1.162-5(a)(1), as maintaining or improving skills required by him in his employment. . . .

While the Commissioner concedes that a general college education "hold[s] out the potential for improved performance as a policeman," he argues that petitioner has failed to demonstrate a sufficient relationship between such an education and the particular job skills required by a policeman. Thus, although a college education improves the job skills of all who avail themselves of it, this relationship is insufficient to remove the expense of such education from the realm of personal expenses which are disallowed under §262. Many expenses, such as the cost of commuting, clothing, and a babysitter for a working mother, are related and even necessary to an individual's occupation or employment, but may not be deducted under §162(a) since they are essentially personal expenditures. See Smith v. Commissioner [supra page 576]. We are of the opinion that plaintiff's educational expenditure is even more personal and less related to his job skills than the expenditures enumerated above.

Of course, not all college courses may be so classified as nondeductible. Thus, the cost of a course in Industrial Psychology was properly deducted from the income of an Industrial Psychologist, although it led to an advanced degree and the potential of new job opportunities. . . . Similarly, a housing administrator was allowed to deduct the cost of courses in housing administration, . . . and a professional harpist was allowed to deduct the cost of music lessons. . . . The difference between those cases and the instant case is that petitioner's courses were general and basically unrelated to his duties as a policeman. As the Commissioner notes in his brief, a currently employed taxpayer such as petitioner might be allowed to deduct the cost of college courses which directly relate to the duties of his employment. If such courses were taken along with other, more general courses, their cost, or that part of the tuition representing their cost, would be deductible under §162(a). In the instant case, however, petitioner does not claim that any particular course in which he was enrolled in 1964 bears any greater relationship to his job skills than the others.

Therefore, while tax incentives might be employed as an effective tool to encourage such valuable public servants as policemen, as well as others, to acquire a college education so as to improve their general competence, we feel that such a decision should be made by the Congress rather than the courts. To allow as a deduction the cost of a general college education would surely go beyond the original intention of Congress in its enactment of the Internal Revenue Code of 1954. Accordingly, we affirm the judgment of the Tax Court.

Affirmed.

NOTES AND QUESTIONS

1. *Personal expenses.* The cost of a college education, according to the orthodox rationale relied on in *Carroll,* is a personal expense. It seems even more clearly personal than the commuting and child-care costs to which the court analogizes. Of course, some philistines may go to college only to enhance their future earning capacity, but surely we cannot countenance a rule under which self-professed philistines are allowed a deduction and seekers of wisdom and culture are not. Mr. Carroll tried to avoid the rule that college expenses are nondeductible by arguing that his education was helpful to him in his job as a detective. Do you agree that this kind of argument must be rejected?

2. *Personal versus capital expenditures.* The best rationale for nondeductibility of the cost of a law school (or other professional) education is not that it is a personal expense (despite the potential personal rewards) but rather that it is a capital, as opposed to current, expenditure. That is, it creates an asset, the ability (or at least the essential credential)

to practice law, that will produce income over many years. The distinction between capital and current expenditures is examined further in the next chapter. Infra page 613. Mr. Carroll said that he went to college in order to prepare to go to law school. Should this objective take his college costs out of the category of personal expenses? See infra page 649.

3. *Travel by school teachers.* A frequent source of litigation has been the deduction by school teachers of the travel costs for trips that they claim to be useful to them in their role as teachers. For example, in Krist v. Commissioner, 483 F.2d 1345 (2d Cir. 1973), the taxpayer taught first grade and deducted the cost of a trip to Europe and the Far East while she was on sabbatical leave. Her itinerary was approved by school authorities in connection with her application for the leave. During her six months of travel she visited schools on five days. Her argument for the claimed deduction was summarized by the court as follows (483 F.2d at 1350):

> Appellee claims that if she had been on vacation, as opposed to a business trip, she would not have used freighters, would have stayed at better hotels, and her activities would have been geared to swimming and skating rather than the travel and visits she made which she said tired her each day. But the fact that she used a freighter for travel and didn't go to "the best hotels" doesn't indicate a thing one way or the other as to whether her travel was related to her teaching. Economy travel and travel accommodations are as consistent with a personal as with an educational trip. She was six weeks on one freighter trip itself, and while there did no specific reading directed toward her teaching although she did read Louis Nizer and How to Tour Japan on Five Dollars a Day.
>
> When Mrs. Krist returned from her trip she did use in her teaching some of the pictures, costumes, dolls and games that she had acquired during the trip. She also acquired one technique abroad, the use of an individual slate and abacus at each child's desk, which she learned in Japan. Mrs. Krist was also required to write a report and make a presentation to the faculty regarding her trip on her return. The superintendent of the district certified that Mrs. Krist had "completed the program for which she was granted leave" and that "[t]he travel was undertaken for professional improvement in order to enhance her teaching skills."

In upholding the Commissioner's denial of the deduction, the court said (483 F.2d at 1351):

> All travel has some educational value, but the test is whether the travel bears a direct relationship to the improvement of the traveler's particular skills. Such a relationship must be substantial, not ephemeral; the trip must be more than . . . "sightseeing." . . . We do not have to say here whether a trip abroad or two-thirds around the world for a first grade

> teacher could ever directly and substantially relate to educational skills. Suffice it to say here that taxpayer's trip in 1967 was not sufficiently so related as a matter of law.

The 1986 act added §274(m)(2), which disallows deductions for "travel as a form of education" and thereby puts an end to deductions in cases like *Krist.* Do you approve of this congressional action? Why do you suppose it was thought to be necessary? What does that tell you about tax administration? About school teachers?

6

DEDUCTIONS FOR THE COSTS OF EARNING INCOME

A. CURRENT EXPENSES VERSUS CAPITAL EXPENDITURES

ENCYCLOPAEDIA BRITANNICA v. COMMISSIONER

685 F.2d 212 (7th Cir. 1982)

POSNER, Circuit Judge.

Section 162(a) of the Internal Revenue Code allows the deduction of "all the ordinary and necessary expenses paid or incurred during the taxable year in carrying on any trade or business. . . ," but this is qualified (see §161) by section 263(a) of the Code, which forbids the immediate deduction of "capital expenditures" even if they are ordinary and necessary business expenses. We must decide in this case whether certain expenditures made by Encyclopaedia Britannica, Inc. to acquire a manuscript were capital expenditures.

Encyclopaedia Britannica decided to publish a book to be called The Dictionary of Natural Sciences. Ordinarily it would have prepared the book in-house, but being temporarily shorthanded it hired David-Stewart Publishing Company "to do all necessary research work and to prepare, edit and arrange the manuscript and all illustrative and other material for" the book. Under the contract David-Stewart agreed "to work closely with" Encyclopaedia Britannica's editorial board "so that the content and arrangement of the Work (and any revisions thereof) will conform to the idea and desires of [Encyclopaedia Britannica] and be acceptable to it"; but it was contemplated that David-Stewart would turn over a complete manuscript that Encyclopaedia Britannica would copyright, publish, and sell, and in exchange would receive advances against the royalties that Encyclopaedia Britannica expected to earn from the book.

Encyclopaedia Britannica treated these advances as ordinary and necessary business expenses deductible in the years when they were paid, though it had not yet obtained any royalties. The Internal Revenue Service disallowed the deductions and assessed deficiencies. Encyclopaedia Britannica petitioned the Tax Court for a redetermination of its tax liability, and prevailed. The Tax Court held that the expenditures were for "services" rather than for the acquisition of an asset and concluded that therefore they were deductible immediately rather than being, as the Service had ruled, capital expenditures. "The agreement provided for substantial editorial supervision by [Encyclopaedia Britannica]. Indeed, David-Stewart's work product was to be the embodiment of [Encyclopaedia Britannica's] ideas and desires. David-Stewart was just the vehicle selected by [Encyclopaedia Britannica] to assist . . . with the editorial phase of the Work." Encyclopaedia Britannica was "the owner of the Work at all stages of completion" and "the dominating force associated with the Work." The Service petitions for review of the Tax Court's decision pursuant to §7482.

As an original matter we would have no doubt that the payments to David-Stewart were capital expenditures regardless of who was the "dominating force" in the creation of The Dictionary of Natural Sciences. The work was intended to yield Encyclopaedia Britannica income over a period of years. The object of sections 162 and 263 of the Code, read together, is to match up expenditures with the income they generate. Where the income is generated over a period of years the expenditures should be classified as capital, contrary to what the Tax Court did here. From the publisher's standpoint a book is just another rental property; and just as the expenditures in putting a building into shape to be rented must be capitalized, so, logically at least, must the expenditures used to create a book. It would make no difference under this view whether Encyclopaedia Britannica hired David-Stewart as a mere consultant to its editorial board, which is the Tax Court's conception of what happened, or bought outright from David-Stewart the right to a book that David-Stewart had already published. If you hire a carpenter to build a tree house that you plan to rent out, his wage is a capital expenditure to you. See Commissioner of Internal Revenue v. Idaho Power Co., 418 U.S. 1,13 (1974).[1]

1. [In *Idaho Power* the taxpayer claimed current deductions for depreciation on the trucks and other such equipment it used in constructing capital assets such as transmission

We are not impressed by Encyclopaedia Britannica's efforts to conjure up practical difficulties in matching expenditures on a book to the income from it. What, it asks, would have been the result if it had scrapped a portion of the manuscript it received from David-Stewart? Would that be treated as the partial destruction of a capital asset, entitling it to an immediate deduction? We think not. The proper analogy is to loss or breakage in the construction of our hypothetical tree house. The effect would be to increase the costs of construction, which are deductible over the useful life of the asset. If the scrapped portion of the manuscript was replaced, the analogy would be perfect. If it was not replaced, the tax consequence would be indirect: an increase or decrease in the publisher's taxable income from the published book.

What does give us pause, however, is a series of decisions in which authors of books have been allowed to treat their expenses as ordinary and necessary business expenses that are deductible immediately even though they were incurred in the creation of long-lived assets — the books the authors were writing. The leading case is Faura v. Commissioner, 73 T.C. 849 (1980); it was discussed with approval just recently by a panel of the Tenth Circuit in Snyder v. United States, 674 F.2d 1359, 1365 (10th Cir. 1982), and was relied on heavily by the Tax Court in the present case.

We can think of a practical reason for allowing authors to deduct their expenses immediately, one applicable as well to publishers though not in the circumstances of the present case. If you are in the business of producing a series of assets that will yield income over a period of years — which is the situation of most authors and all publishers — identifying particular expenditures with particular books, a necessary step for proper capitalization because the useful lives of the books will not be the same, may be very difficult, since the expenditures of an author or publisher (more clearly the latter) tend to be joint among several books. Moreover, allocating these expenditures among the different books is not always necessary to produce the temporal matching of income and expenditures that the Code desiderates, because the taxable income of the author or publisher who is in a steady state (that is, whose output is neither increasing nor decreasing) will be at least approximately the same whether his costs are expensed or capitalized. Not the same on any given book — on each book expenses and receipts will be systematically mismatched — but the same on average. Under these conditions the benefits of capitalization are unlikely to exceed the accounting and other administrative costs entailed in capitalization.

---

lines. The Court upheld the Commissioner's disallowance of such deductions, reasoning that the cost of the trucks was simply part of the cost of creating the capital asset itself. — Eds.]

Yet we hesitate to endorse the *Faura* line of cases: not only because of the evident tension between them and *Idaho Power,* supra, where the Supreme Court said that expenses, whatever their character, must be capitalized if they are incurred in creating a capital asset, but also because *Faura,* and cases following it such as *Snyder,* fail in our view to articulate a persuasive rationale for their result. *Faura* relied on cases holding that the normal expenses of authors and other artists are deductible business expenses rather than nondeductible personal expenses, and on congressional evidence of dissatisfaction with the Internal Revenue Service's insistence that such expenses be capitalized. See 73 T.C. at 852-861. But most of the cases in question (including all those at the court of appeals level), such as Doggett v. Burnett, 65 F.2d 191 (D.C. Cir. 1933), are inapposite, because they consider only whether the author's expenditures are deductible at all — not whether, if they are deductible, they must first be capitalized. . . .

[But] we need not decide whether *Faura* is good law, and we are naturally reluctant to precipitate a conflict with the Tenth Circuit. The Tax Court interpreted *Faura* too broadly in this case. As we interpret *Faura* its principle comes into play only when the taxpayer is in the business of producing a series of assets that yield the taxpayer income over a period of years, so that a complex allocation would be necessary if the taxpayer had to capitalize all his expenses of producing them. This is not such a case. The expenditures at issue are unambiguously identified with The Dictionary of Natural Sciences. We need not consider the proper tax treatment of any other expenses that Encyclopaedia Britannica may have incurred on the project — editorial expenses, for example — as they are not involved in this case. Those expenses would be analogous to author Faura's office and travel expenses; they are the normal, recurrent expenses of operating a business that happens to produce capital assets. This case is like *Idaho Power,* supra. The expenditure there was on transportation equipment used in constructing capital facilities that Idaho Power employed in its business of producing and distributing electricity, and was thus unambiguously identified with specific capital assets, just as Encyclopaedia Britannica's payment to David-Stewart for the manuscript of The Dictionary of Natural Sciences was unambiguously identified with a specific capital asset.

It is also relevant that the commissioning of the manuscript from David-Stewart was somewhat out of the ordinary for Encyclopaedia Britannica. Now the word "ordinary" in section 162 of the Internal Revenue Code has two different uses: to prevent the deduction of certain expenses that are not normally incurred in the type of business in which the taxpayer is engaged ("ordinary" in this sense blends imperceptibly into "necessary"), . . . and to clarify the distinction between expenses that are immediately deductible and expenses that must first be capitalized. . . . (A merging of these two distinct senses of the word is a possible explanation for the result in *Faura.*) Most of the "ordinary," in the sense of recurring, expenses of a business are noncapital in nature and most of its capital expenditures are extraordinary in the sense of nonrecurring. Here, as arguably in *Idaho Power* as well — for Idaho Power's business was the production and distribution of electricity, rather than the construction of buildings — the taxpayer stepped out of its normal method of doing business. In this particular project Encyclopaedia Britannica was operating like a conventional publisher, which obtains a complete manuscript from an author or in this case a compiler. The conventional publisher may make a considerable contribution to the work both at the idea stage and at the editorial stage but the deal is for a manuscript, not for services in assisting the publisher to prepare the manuscript itself. Yet we need not consider whether a conventional publisher should be permitted to deduct royalty advances made to its authors as current operating expenses, merely because those advances are for its recurring business expenses because its business is producing capital assets. *Idaho Power,* though factually distinguishable, implies one answer to this question (no), [and] *Faura* another (yes). . . . But the principle of *Faura,* whatever its soundness, comes into play only when the expenditure sought to be immediately deducted is a normal and recurrent expense of the business, as it was not here. . . .

There is another point to be noted about the distinction between recurring and nonrecurring expenses and its bearing on the issue in this case. If one really takes seriously the concept of a capital expenditure as anything that yields income, actual or imputed, beyond the period (conventionally one year . . .) in which the expenditure is made, the result will be to force the capitalization of virtually every business expense. It is a result courts naturally shy away from. . . . It would require capitalizing every salesman's salary, since his selling activities create goodwill for the company and goodwill is an asset yielding income beyond the year in which the salary expense is incurred. The administrative costs of conceptual rigor are too great. The distinction between recurring and nonrecurring business expenses provides a very crude but perhaps serviceable demarcation between those capital expenditures that can feasibly be capitalized and those that cannot be. Whether the distinction breaks down where, as in the case of the conventional publisher, the firm's entire business is the production of capital assets, so that it is literally true that all of its business expenses are capital in nature, is happily not a question we have to decide here, for it is clear that Encyclopaedia Britannica's payments to David-Stewart were of a nonnormal, nonrecurrent nature.

In light of all that we have said, the contention that really what David-Stewart did here was to render consulting services to Encyclopaedia Britannica no different from the services of a consultant whom Encyclopaedia Britannica might have hired on one of its in-house projects, which if true would make the payments more "ordinary" in the *Faura* sense, is of doubtful relevance. But in any event, if that is what the Tax Court meant when it said that David-Stewart was not the "dominating force," its finding was, we think, clearly erroneous. We deprecate decision by metaphor. If the concept of a dominating force has any relevance to tax law, which we doubt, an attempt should have been made to operationalize it, as by computing the ratio of Encyclopaedia Britannica's in-house expenditures on The Dictionary of Natural Sciences to its payments to David-Stewart. If the ratio was greater than one, then Encyclopaedia Britannica could fairly be regarded as the dominant force in the enterprise. Although this computation was never made, we have no doubt that Encyclopaedia Britannica was dominant in the sense that, as the buyer, it was calling the tune; and it was buying a custom-made product, built to its specifications. But what it was buying was indeed a product, a completed manuscript. This was a turnkey project, remote from what is ordinarily understood by editorial consultation. While maybe some creators or buyers of capital goods — some authors and publishers — may deduct as current expenses what realistically are capital expenditures, they may not do so . . . when the expense is tied to producing or acquiring a specific capital asset.

Encyclopaedia Britannica urges, as an alternative ground for sustaining the Tax Court's decision, that the payments to David-Stewart were immediately deductible as research and experimental expenditures under §174(a). This ground was not considered by the Tax Court, and it would be premature for us to consider it without the benefit of that court's views. The Tax Court can on remand consider it and any other unresolved issues.

Reversed and remanded.

NOTES AND QUESTIONS

1. *True reflection of income.* As the court in *Encyclopaedia Britannica* observes, "The object of sections 162 and 263 of the Code, read together, is to match up expenditures with the income they generate." This objective, though often ignored both by Congress and by the courts in shaping the rules of *tax* accounting, is consistent with the basic goal of sound accrual accounting principles, which is to provide a true reflection of income. To appreciate the importance of the point, imagine that the contract in the *Encyclopaedia Britannica* case had represented a large part of the total operations of Encyclopaedia Britannica for the year at issue. If the entire cost of the contract had been treated as an expense of the year in which the payment was made, the result could well have been a huge loss for that year. Surely it would be misleading for the managers or the shareholders of the company to conclude that

in fact they had had a very bad year and that drastic changes might be required. The amounts spent are obviously the price of acquiring a capital asset, not money down the drain. It seems quite likely, therefore, that for the purposes of making investment decisions and of reporting to shareholders (assuming the item was significant), the outlay was not treated as an offset to current income.

2. *Capitalization of inventory, construction, and development costs.* The court in *Encyclopaedia Britannica* states that "if you hire a carpenter to build a tree house that you plan to rent out, his wage is a capital expenditure to you." The court cites Commissioner v. Idaho Power Co., 418 U.S. 1 (1974), which is described supra page 614, footnote 1. The principle underlying the court's tree-house metaphor, and *Idaho Power,* is now generalized in §263A, which was adopted in 1986 and is described below (page 623).

3. *Depreciation and amortization.* When an outlay is treated as the cost of acquiring a capital asset, traditional accounting principles require that that cost be recovered over the useful life of the asset — that is, over the time in which the asset is expected to contribute to the production of the firm's income. In the case of an intangible asset like a copyright for a book, the label given to the annual deductions is "amortization." In the case of a tangible asset like a factory building or a truck, the deduction has traditionally been called "depreciation." See §167. Under the present Code, the deduction is called "ACRS" (accelerated cost recovery system). See §168, which is described infra page 674. Under ACRS, the time over which deductions are claimed in some cases is shorter than the expected useful lives of the assets. This favorable tax treatment may be the result of a conscious decision to use the tax system to encourage investments in plant and equipment.

4. *Scrapping part of the manuscript.* If a taxpayer buys four trucks in a single transaction, the cost is allocated among them. If one is destroyed in a fire, the cost of that truck is deductible as a loss under §165(a). (Even though the loss is attributable to a "casualty," §165(c)(3) is irrelevant because its function is to permit deductions of certain nonbusiness losses.) On the other hand, if Encyclopaedia Britannica had scrapped a portion of the manuscript that it had acquired, presumably, as the court suggests, there would be no loss deduction. The amount paid for the original manuscript would be treated as the cost of what was ultimately used. What if a publisher commissions the preparation of a set of four books and ultimately decides to sell only three of them?

5. *Cash-method versus accrual-method of accounting.* Note that §263 applies to both cash- and accrual-method taxpayers. Thus, it is irrelevant that individual authors are likely to be cash-method taxpayers while Encyclopaedia Britannica no doubt used the accrual method.

6. *The value of deferral.* In distinguishing the *Faura* case, the court in *Encyclopaedia Britannica* observes that "the taxable income of the author

or publisher who is in a steady state . . . will be at least approximately the same whether his costs are expensed or capitalized." This is true only in the long run. Imagine an author, with income from other sources, who begins to write books in 1992 and to receive royalties in 1993. Suppose he is allowed to begin deducting research expenses in 1992, rather than in 1993, and continues this practice until he retires forty years later. He will have the advantage of deferral to the extent of one year's deductions not just for one year but for forty. That is, he will reduce his income in 1992 and the effects will not catch up with him until forty years later. To put that still another way, he has the advantage of a premature deduction of expense attributable to the next year's income not just in the first year (1992) but in every year until retirement. What is the relative burden of a tax paid now as compared with one paid forty years from now? See supra page 63. What does this tell you about the significance of the *Encyclopaedia Britannica* decision?

7. *Economic consequences.* How do you suppose the holding in *Encyclopaedia Britannica* affected the decisions of firms like Encyclopaedia Britannica about contracting out manuscript-preparation work to other firms? Was that a sensible economic outcome?

8. *Exceptions to the requirement of capitalization and some tax shelter fundamentals.* One important exception to the requirement of capitalization of expenditures expected to produce revenues in future years is §174, covering research and development (R&D) expenditures. Another important exception is found in Regs. §1.162-12, which permits expensing of the costs of developing farms, orchards, and ranches. This rule led to a substantial amount of investment by high-bracket people seeking tax shelters. For example, a person with a high income from a medical practice would buy a parcel of undeveloped land and develop an orange grove. The cost of the land itself was a capital expenditure, but most of the costs of developing the land into a productive orange grove were currently deductible. Thus, in the years before the grove reached a productive state, the investment showed losses for tax purposes. These tax losses offset income from the medical practice, though in an economic sense they were not losses but, instead, the cost of acquiring a capital asset. When the grove reached a productive state, it was sold, and the gain, which was largely attributable to deducted expenditures for development, was realized. But that gain was capital gain, so only part of it was taxed. Thus, even if the venture lost money apart from taxes, it could turn out to be profitable after taxes were taken into account. The tax avoidance possibility described here has now largely been foreclosed by the repeal of the favorable treatment of long-term capital gain, by the denial of deductions for passive activity losses (§469), and by a requirement of capitalization of the cost of property produced by a taxpayer (§263A).

9. *Prepaid expenses.* In Commissioner v. Boylston Market Association, 131 F.2d 966 (1st Cir. 1942), a cash-basis taxpayer was required to capitalize prepaid insurance premiums covering a three-year period. The court cited similar results in cases involving prepaid rent, bonuses for the acquisition of leases, and commissions for negotiating leases.

Under §461(g), a taxpayer must capitalize most forms of prepaid interest. Note, however, the special treatment of "points" in §461(g)(2).

10. *The problem is timing.* The issue presented in the *Encyclopaedia Britannica* case, and in most of the rest of the material in this chapter, is, at the broadest level, one of timing. The time when a deduction is taken obviously affects the time when a corresponding amount of income is recognized. Thus, this chapter has much in common with Chapter 3.

REVENUE RULING 85-82

1985-1 C.B. 57

Issue

May a taxpayer currently deduct, under section 162 of the Internal Revenue Code, the portion of the purchase price of farmland that is allocable to growing crops?

Facts

In August 1982, *A*, an individual, purchased a farm under a land contract that provided for a purchase price of 550*x* dollars, payable by (1) an initial payment of 65*x* dollars upon execution of the contract, and (2) 55*x* dollars in annual payments (including interest) due on December 15 of each year under the terms of the contract.

The seller of the farm did not deduct the costs of planting and raising the crops to the date of the sale. At the time of the purchase, 50 percent of the farm land was in growing crops.

A elected the cash method of accounting for the farm operation. *A* harvested the growing crops in 1982 and sold the harvested crops in 1983.

Law and Analysis

Section 61(a)(3) of the Code provides that except as otherwise provided by law, gross income means all income from whatever source derived, including dealings in property.

Section 162(a) of the Code provides that there will be allowed as a deduction all the ordinary and necessary expenses paid or incurred during the tax year in carrying on any trade or business.

Section 1012 of the Code provides that the basis of property shall be the cost of such property, except as otherwise provided. . . .

Under section 1.61-4(a) of the regulations, farmers who buy goods for resale must account for the cost of the goods when the goods are sold and, therefore, may deduct the cost of the items in the year purchased only if the goods are also sold that year. The exception to the general rule of section 1.61-4(a) that is found in section 1.162-12(a) allows a current deduction solely for "the cost of seeds and young plants that are purchased for further development and cultivation prior to sale in later years. . . ." Section 1.162-12(a) allows a deduction only to the person who purchases the seeds and young plants for further development and cultivation, that is, planting, and not to a subsequent purchaser of the already planted growing crops who does not actually or directly incur the costs specified in section 1.162-12(a). . . . [I]tems not specified in section 1.162-12(a) are not currently deductible.

In this case, *A* incurred no costs for seeds and young plants purchased for further development and cultivation within the meaning of section 1.162-12(a) of the regulations prior to sale in a later year. *A*'s cost was based on the value of the crops. This value represented the initial costs of seeds and young plants (as well as cultivation costs, etc.) that were incurred and paid by the seller of the property, not *A*, and the appreciation due to growth of the crops. Section 1.162-12(a) does not allow a deduction to *A* for such items. . . .

The costs incurred by *A* for purchase of the growing crops that are not deductible are capitalized and included in the crops' basis, as defined in section 1012 of the Code. Section 1012 provides that the basis for property will be the cost of the property, except as otherwise provided.

Holding

A may not deduct in 1982 the portion of the purchase price allocable to the growing crops, but may take into account such portion in arriving at the net farm profit or loss for 1983, the year in which the growing crops are sold.

QUESTION

The ruling assumes that part of the purchase price of the farm was for the growing crops. Thus, if the farm had been bought in the spring, before the crops were planted, the price would have been lower. The taxpayer (buyer) would then have incurred expenses in planting and raising crops. Would those expenses have been deductible currently? If so, why should the taxpayer be denied a current deduction when the expenses were incurred by the seller and in effect reimbursed by the taxpayer as part of the purchase transaction?

NOTE ON UNIFORM CAPITALIZATION RULES (§263A)

Before 1986 the rules governing capitalization of costs incurred in creating inventory or other long-lived assets were inconsistent. This inconsistency is apparent on careful reading of the *Encyclopaedia Britannica* case, supra page 613. In that case, the court held that the cost of purchasing a completed manuscript from an unrelated company must be capitalized and amortized against sales. The court noted, however, that the in-house costs of producing such a manuscript would be currently deductible. One reason why in-house publishing expenses have in the past been deductible is administrative. An in-house employee's time may be spent on many different projects. Allocating that time among projects may be quite difficult. As the court in *Encyclopaedia Britannica* concluded (supra page 617), "The administrative costs of conceptual rigor are too great." (Note, however, that allocation of costs may be vital to making sound business decisions. How can a business person decide whether a project will be or has been profitable without knowing what it cost?)

In 1986, Congress decided that conceptual rigor and, probably more important, revenue needs outweighed administrative concerns in this area, and adopted §263A, the uniform capitalization (UNICAP) rules. Under that provision, the costs of producing self-created assets, such as the in-house production of a manuscript, must be capitalized. See §263A(b); General Explanation of the Tax Reform Act of 1986, Staff of the Joint Committee on Taxation (May 4, 1987) at 509 n.58; Temp. Regs. §1.263A-1T(a)(5). These costs include not only the salaries of people writing the manuscript, but such indirect expenses as the allocable share of the salaries of supervisory and administrative people.

The UNICAP rules extend to virtually all manufacturers. All the costs of the manufacture of the inventory of goods to be sold, including such items as the cost of insurance on the manufacturing plant, must be added to the cost of the inventory and deducted at the time the inventory is sold. Temp. Regs. §1.263A-1T(b)(2). Similar rules apply to large wholesalers and retailers of inventory. For example, the salaries of purchasing agents must be allocated to inventory and recovered at the time the inventory is sold. Temp. Regs. §1.263A-1T(d)(3)(ii)(B).

Costs incurred by sellers or producers of long-lived assets that do not require capitalization include marketing and advertising costs, and costs of general and administrative expenses that do not relate to sale or production. In this latter category are costs of general business planning, costs of shareholder or public relations, and other costs removed from sale or production. Temp. Regs. §1.263A-1T(b)(2), (b)(4).

As is perhaps evident from the preceding discussion, the rules governing uniform capitalization under §263A are complicated and require many difficult determinations. For example, it will often be unclear whether a particular employee's time is spent on matters that relate to production or to general business planning. Congress has limited the scope of §263A somewhat by excluding from its ambit retailers and wholesalers with annual gross receipts of less than $10,000,000. §263A(b)(2)(B). Congress has also excluded from §263A costs incurred by freelance writers, artists, and photographers. §263A(h). Other producers and sellers will have to learn to live with the complexity (and conceptual rigor) of UNICAP.

NOTE ON THE INDOPCO *DECISION*

Cases such as *Encyclopaedia Britannica* and, more importantly, §263A, require capitalization of expenses that create or enhance long-lived assets. What about an expense that does not create an identifiable asset but instead provides long-term benefits for an organization's entire business? In the recent case of INDOPCO, Inc. v. Commissioner, 112 S.Ct. 1039 (1992), the Supreme Court held that this category of expenses, too, must be capitalized. At issue in *INDOPCO* was the treatment of legal and investment banking fees incident to a merger. The Court held that the merger produced long-term benefits to the taxpayer: It made available to INDOPCO the resources of the larger company with which it merged, eliminated a variety of shareholder-relations expenses, and provided operational synergy. The fees incurred to achieve that merger, therefore, were appropriately capitalized rather than deducted.

INDOPCO resolved a conflict among the circuits. Prior to the decision in that case, a number of courts had allowed taxpayers to deduct expenses that produced long-term benefits but did not create or enhance separate and distinct assets. See Commissioner v. Lincoln Savings & Loan Association, 403 U.S. 345 (1971); NCNB Corporation v. United States, 684 F.2d 285 (4th Cir. 1982). After *INDOPCO*, the fact that an expense does not create or enhance a separate and distinct asset is irrelevant. The general rule, which requires capitalization for expenses that produce long-term benefits, applies both to expenses that create specific assets and expenses that enhance overall business operation. We shall see in the following sections of this chapter, however, that this general rule is subject to a number of qualifications and exceptions.

B. REPAIR AND MAINTENANCE EXPENSES

MIDLAND EMPIRE PACKING CO. v. COMMISSIONER

14 T.C. 635 (1950), acq., 1950-2 C.B. 3

ARUNDELL, Judge.

The issue in this case is whether an expenditure for a concrete lining in petitioner's basement to oil-proof it against an oil nuisance created by a neighboring refinery is deductible as an ordinary and necessary expense under [§162(a)], on the theory it was an expenditure for a repair, or, in the alternative, whether the expenditure may be treated as the measure of the loss sustained during the taxable year and not compensated for by insurance or otherwise within the meaning of [§165(a)].

The respondent has contended, in part, that the expenditure is for a capital improvement and should be recovered through depreciation charges and is, therefore, not deductible as an ordinary and necessary business expense or as a loss.

[Regs. §1.162-4] is helpful in distinguishing between an expenditure to be classed as a repair and one to be treated as a capital outlay. In Illinois Merchants Trust Co., Executor, 4 B.T.A. 103, at p.106, we discussed this subject in some detail and in our opinion said:

> It will be noted that the first sentence of the article [now Regs. §1.162-4] relates to repairs, while the second sentence deals in effect with replacements. . . . To repair is to restore to a sound state or to mend, while a replacement connotes a substitution. A repair is an expenditure for the purpose of keeping the property in an ordinarily efficient operating condition. It does not add to the value of the property, nor does it appreciably prolong its life. It merely keeps the property in an operating condition over its probable useful life for the uses for which it was acquired. Expenditures for that purpose are distinguishable from those for replacements, alterations, improvements, or additions which prolong the life of the property, increase its value, or make it adaptable to a different use. The one is a maintenance charge, while the others are additions to capital investment which should not be applied against current earnings.

It will be seen from our findings of fact that for some 25 years prior to the taxable year petitioner had used the basement rooms of its plant as a place for the curing of hams and bacon and for the storage of meat and hides. The basement had been entirely satisfactory for this purpose over the entire period in spite of the fact that there was some seepage of water into the rooms from time to time. In the taxable year it was found that not only water, but oil, was seeping through the concrete walls of the basement of the packing plant and, while the water would soon drain out, the oil would not, and there was left on the basement floor a thick scum of oil which gave off a strong odor that permeated the air of the entire plant, and the fumes from the oil created a fire hazard. It appears that the oil which came from a nearby refinery had also gotten into the water wells which served to furnish water for petitioner's plant, and as a result of this whole condition the Federal meat inspectors advised petitioner that it must discontinue the use of the water from the wells and oil-proof the basement, or else shut down its plant.

To meet this situation, petitioner during the taxable year undertook steps to oil-proof the basement by adding a concrete lining to the walls from the floor to a height of about four feet and also added concrete to the floor of the basement. It is the cost of this work which it seeks to deduct as a repair. The basement was not enlarged by this work, nor did the oil-proofing serve to make it more desirable for the purpose for which it had been used through the years prior to the time that the oil nuisance had occurred. The evidence is that the expenditure did not add to the value or prolong the expected life of the property over what they were before the event occurred which made the repairs necessary. It is true that after the work was done the seepage of water, as well as oil, was stopped, but, as already stated, the presence of the water had never been found objectionable. The repairs merely served to keep the property in an operating condition over its probable useful life for the purpose for which it was used.

While it is conceded on brief that the expenditure was "necessary," respondent contends that the encroachment of the oil nuisance on petitioner's property was not an "ordinary" expense in petitioner's particular business. But the fact that petitioner had not theretofore been called upon to make a similar expenditure to prevent damage and disaster to its property does not remove that expense from the classification of "ordinary" for, as stated in Welch v. Helvering [infra page 645]:

> ordinary in this context does not mean that the payments must be habitual or normal in the sense that the same taxpayer will have to make them often. . . . [T]he expense is an ordinary one because we know from experience that payments for such a purpose, whether the amount is large or small, are the common and accepted means of defense against attack. . . . The situation is unique in the life of the individual affected, but not in the life of the group, the community, of which he is a part.

Steps to protect a business building from the seepage of oil from a nearby refinery, which had been erected long subsequent to the time petitioner started to operate its plant, would seem to us to be a normal thing to do. . . .

In American Bemberg Corporation, 10 T.C. 361, we allowed as deductions, on the ground that they were ordinary and necessary expenses, extensive expenditures made to prevent disaster, although the repairs were of a type which had never been needed before and were unlikely to recur. In that case the taxpayer, to stop cave-ins of soil which were threatening destruction of its manufacturing plant, hired an engineering firm which drilled to the bedrock and injected grout to fill the cavities where practicable. . . . We found that the cost [of the drilling and grouting] did not make good the depreciation previously allowed, and stated in our opinion:

> [T]he . . . program was intended to avert a plant-wide disaster and avoid forced abandonment of the plant. The purpose was not to improve, better, extend or increase the original plant, nor to prolong its original useful life. Its continued operation was endangered; the purpose of the expenditures was to enable petitioner to continue the plant in operation not on any new or better scale, but on the same scale and, so far as possible, as efficiently as it had operated before.

. . . In our opinion, the expenditure of $4868.81 for lining the basement walls and floor was essentially a repair and, as such, it is deductible as an ordinary and necessary business expense. This holding makes unnecessary a consideration of petitioner's alternative contention that the expenditure is deductible as a business loss. . . .

NOTES AND QUESTIONS

1. *Repairs and losses.* (a) An interesting aspect of the *Midland Empire* opinion is its reference at the beginning and end to the possible alternative of a deduction for a loss, which would be claimed under §165(a). A problem with deductions for losses is they must be "realized." There must be some identifiable event that justifies a current accounting. A decline in value due to wear and tear, to changes in the economic environment, or to other circumstances does not give rise to a loss deduction; such a decline is recognized only through ACRS (formerly, and for nontax purposes, called depreciation) or as a loss when the property is sold. Does the oil-seepage problem confronted by the taxpayer in *Midland Empire* seem to you to justify a loss deduction? If so, what is the best way to measure the amount of the loss? If no loss deduction is available, is a deduction for repair a sensible substitute?

(b) If a deduction for a loss is allowed, a deduction for any repair to restore the property to the preloss condition must be denied. See Regs.

§1.161-1 ("Double deductions are not permitted").[2] To illustrate this principle, suppose a farmer builds a new barn for $50,000. The cost is a capital expenditure, even for a cash-method farmer. See Regs. §1.162-12(a). The basis for the barn is its cost, $50,000. This cost is deducted over time through ACRS. Suppose that in the first year of its existence, the roof of the barn is destroyed by a tornado and is replaced at a cost of $10,000. The farmer has two tax alternatives. One alternative is to claim a deduction for a loss. The amount, quite plainly, would be $10,000. The loss deduction would reduce basis by $10,000, to $40,000. §1016(a)(1). The cost of the replacement, or repair, would not be deducted. It would be treated as a capital cost, increasing basis by $10,000, back to $50,000. §1016(a)(1). The other alternative is to forgo any deduction for a loss and deduct instead the cost of the repair, $10,000, as a current expense. The basis of the barn would not change. Under either alternative we get the same net result: a current deduction of $10,000 and a basis of $50,000, which properly reflects what happened.

(c) But what if the roof wears out over a period of several years, because of shoddy initial construction or because of some unusually harsh weather, or both? Is a loss deduction still available? Should the replacement be treated as a repair or as a capital expenditure? See Regs. §§1.162-4, 1.167(a)-11(d)(2), and 1.263(a)(1).

In Mt. Morris Drive-In Theatre Co. v. Commissioner, 238 F.2d 85 (6th Cir. 1956), a taxpayer, whose actions in clearing land to build a drive-in theater caused substantial increase of water drainage onto an adjacent landowner's property, installed a correction drainage system under threat of litigation. Held: The cost of the drainage system had to be capitalized since the need for it was foreseeable and was part of the process of completing taxpayer's initial investment for its original intended use. See also United States v. Times-Mirror Co., 231 F.2d 876 (9th Cir. 1956) (cost of microfilming a set of back issues as protection against loss by enemy bombing deductible; amount spent allowed "business to be operated on the same scale and not to increase"); Jones v. Commissioner, 242 F.2d 616 (5th Cir. 1957) (taxpayer reconstructed decrepit building in French Quarter of New Orleans because he could not get permission to raze it; held: costs of general rehabilitation must be capitalized).

What if a taxpayer is required to install a sprinkler system in a hotel, in order to comply with a city fire code? That issue was presented in Hotel Sulgrave v. Commissioner, 21 T.C. 619 (1954), where the court said (at 621):

2. The same conclusion seems to be supported by §263(a)(2), but Regs. §1.263(a)-1(a)(2) refers only to deductions for "depreciation, amortization, or depletion."

> We do not agree that the installation of the sprinkler system constituted a repair made "for the purpose of keeping the property in an ordinarily efficient operating condition." . . . It was a permanent addition to the property ordered by the city of New York to give the property additional protection from the hazard of fire. It was an improvement or betterment having a life extending beyond the year in which it was made and which depreciates over a period of years. While it may not have increased the value of the hotel property or prolonged its useful life, the property became more valuable for use in the petitioner's business by reason of compliance with the city's order. The respondent did not err in determining that the cost of this improvement or betterment should be added to petitioner's capital investment in the building, and recovered through depreciation deductions in the years of its useful life.

2. *Repairs and accounting theory.* Apart from the connection to a loss, what justification is there for treating any repair as a current expense, except where the amount is so small that an addition to basis would not be worth the trouble? Consider the example supra Note 1, of a farmer whose roof is destroyed by a tornado. When she decides to replace the roof, will she look to the benefits that the replacement will provide for this year only or to the benefits over many years in the future? What about the taxpayer in *Midland Empire?*

3. *Maintenance of a business versus creating a new capability.* The concept of a repair is widely recognized and fairly easily grasped. It serves therefore as a useful analogy in approaching other problems that are conceptually similar. One of these is the distinction between efforts to maintain an existing business in the face of changing conditions and efforts to expand into new, related lines of business.

C. INVENTORY ACCOUNTING

If a taxpayer buys machinery that will produce income over several years, its costs must be capitalized and depreciated over such period. If a taxpayer buys pencils, stationery, and other supplies, they are usually currently deductible even if some may last beyond the present tax year. But what of goods that the taxpayer will sell to the public? What if the owner of a clothing store buys dresses, suits, and other goods during the year, sells some, and has some on hand at the end of the year? Or what if a manufacturer of clothing buys cloth, thread, and other materials, some of which is on hand at the end of the year in its original form and some of which has been embodied in finished product that has not yet been shipped out? Inventory accounting methods are used to match costs with revenues in such cases.

The use of authorized methods of inventory accounting is required in every situation where the production, purchase, or sale of merchandise is an income-producing factor (except in farming). This means, for example, that a retailer does not simply deduct the cost of the goods and materials purchased during the year. Instead, the purchases are added to "inventory" and their cost is treated as if it were a capital expenditure; the ultimate disposition of the goods and materials, as reflected in changes in the quantity of physical goods in the inventory after taking account of additions to it during the year, is treated as the event giving rise to a deduction for that cost. See Regs. §1.471.

The inventory account includes all finished or partly finished goods and those raw materials and supplies acquired for sale or that will become part of merchandise intended for sale. Regs. §1.471-1. Merchandise is included in inventory if title to it is vested in the taxpayer, even though the merchandise may be in transit or otherwise may not be in the physical possession of the taxpayer. The accrual method of accounting is required with regard to purchases and sales whenever the use of an inventory is necessary. Regs. §1.446-1(c)(2).

Cost of goods sold. Gross profit from a business operation is found by deducting the cost of goods sold from gross receipts. The cost of goods sold is found by adding the beginning inventory to the cost of goods purchased or produced during the year and subtracting the total inventory still on hand at the end of the year. (See Table 6-1.)

The taxable income of a business is understated whenever the inventory at the end of the year is understated. If the inventory is overstated, profits will be overstated. In the example in Table 6-1, if the taxpayer reported the ending inventory as $50,000, the cost of goods sold deduction would become $190,000, and the taxable income would be understated by $10,000. Such manipulation of inventories may be accomplished by using unreasonably low market values when inventories are permitted to be valued at the lower of cost or market (discussed infra) or by understating the actual amount of the inventory. The IRS may become alerted to manipulation of inventories by comparing the profit margin the taxpayer reports with that of other competitors in the

TABLE 6-1
Illustration of Cost of Goods Sold

Beginning inventory	$ 40,000
Purchases during year	200,000
Total	240,000
Less ending inventory	60,000
Cost of goods sold	$180,000

same industry or by data indicating that the taxpayer's inventory turnover is not consistent with general industry turnover.

Valuation of inventories. It is necessary to both identify and value the particular goods in inventory so that proper costs can be applied. Regs. §1.471-2(b) states that in the valuation of inventories greater weight is to be given to consistency in practice than to any particular method of inventorying. The two common bases of valuing inventories are (1) cost (Regs. §1.471-3) and (2) cost or market, whichever is lower (Regs. §1-471-4).

When inventory is valued at cost, for merchandise on hand at the beginning of the year, cost is the amount at which it was included in the closing inventory of the preceding taxable year. For merchandise purchased after the beginning of the year, cost is invoice price plus transportation and other acquisition charges less certain trade discounts. For merchandise produced during the year, cost is the total of direct costs (e.g., raw materials, labor, and supplies) and indirect production costs (e.g., depreciation computed under the full absorption method of Regs. §1.471-11).

Any change in valuation method is a change of accounting requiring consent from the Commissioner.

Inventory cost. Inventory accounting requires that the taxpayer determine the cost of items in inventory. Often there will be many identical items in inventory, such items will have been purchased in more than one year, the cost of the items will have changed over time, and it may be impractical to determine when items now on hand were acquired. In that situation, in order to arrive at a cost figure for the items currently on hand, some assumption must be made about how items move into and out of inventory. The general rule is that a first-in-first-out (FIFO) assumption, or method, should be used. However, last-in-first-out (LIFO) may be used if the taxpayer so elects under §472.

FIFO assumes that goods first acquired are sold first and therefore the goods in the closing inventory are those most recently purchased. Either method of valuing inventory — *cost* or *cost or market, whichever is lower* — may be used with FIFO. The use of cost with FIFO often presents a profit or loss picture closest to the actual results of the physical flow of goods through a business. In a rising market there is usually no difference between cost and cost or market, whichever is lower, since market will rarely be lower than cost. But in a falling market, the lower of cost or market tends to reduce income; the value of the closing inventory is reduced to market, creating a higher cost of goods sold, resulting in lower gross income. So cost or market, whichever is lower, anticipates losses in a falling market but not additional profits in a rising market.

Under LIFO, since items purchased last are considered sold first, closing inventory is valued as if composed of the earliest purchases.

Under LIFO, inventories must be valued at cost. The Treasury has consistently opposed efforts to permit LIFO in conjunction with the lower of cost or market. Overall, the LIFO method tends to have a stabilizing effect on the measurement and reporting of income during periods of fluctuating prices, since current receipts tend to be matched with current costs. Since LIFO results in lower reported profits in a rising market, it generally produces the best tax results for taxpayers during periods of rising prices; tax liability is deferred on inventory gains as long as the firm maintains the inventory. In a period of declining prices, by the same token, LIFO would not be advantageous since losses inherent in earlier high-cost inventory are not realized.

Section 472(c) contains a requirement that LIFO must be used for reports to investors and for credit purposes if it is used for tax purposes.[3] Because LIFO reduces taxes in periods of rising prices, and because prices have risen persistently in recent decades, one might expect that almost all businesses would use LIFO. Bear in mind that choice of an accounting method does not in any way change underlying economic realities. Economic profit is the same regardless of what method of accounting is used. But managers of businesses generally are anxious to issue reports that show the highest possible profit. This may explain why many businesses still use FIFO despite the fact that their decision to do so results in their paying higher taxes than they would pay under LIFO. Is the conformity requirement of §472(c) desirable? If so, should it be extended to ACRS deductions?

PROBLEMS

1. In December 1993, Products Inc. begins business and buys 100,000 widgets for $200,000. It has no sales in 1993. In January 1994, Products Inc. buys another 100,000 widgets for $300,000. In June 1994, Products Inc. sells 100,000 widgets for $350,000. Assume that there are no costs allocable to the widget inventory under §263A. (a) Assume Products Inc. uses the LIFO method of inventory valuation. What is the cost of the goods sold and the gross profit on the June 1994 sale? (b) What is the answer to the same question if Products Inc. uses FIFO instead of LIFO?

2. In March 1993, Products Inc. begins business and buys 40,000 widgets for $120,000. In May 1993, Products Inc. sells 20,000 widgets for $80,000. Developments in the second half of 1993 cause the value of the widgets to fall. At the close of the year, the 20,000 widgets left

3. This is in contrast to accounting for depreciation, where a taxpayer may (and most do) claim a higher deduction for tax purposes than for purposes of reporting to shareholders.

in inventory have a value of $20,000. Assume that Products Inc. is able to value closing inventory at the lower of cost or market. Determine the company's 1993 cost of goods sold deduction and gross profit on widget sales.

THOR POWER TOOL CO. v. COMMISSIONER

439 U.S. 522 (1979)

Mr. Justice Blackmun delivered the opinion of the Court. . . .

Taxpayer . . . manufactures hand-held power tools, parts and accessories, and rubber products. At its various plants and service branches, Thor maintains inventories of raw materials, work-in-process, finished parts and accessories, and completed tools. At all times relevant, Thor has used, both for financial accounting and for income tax purposes, the "lower of cost or market" method of valuing inventories. See Treas. Reg. §1.471-2(c).

Thor's tools typically contain from 50 to 200 parts, each of which taxpayer stocks to meet demands for replacements. Because of the difficulty, at the time of manufacture, of predicting the future demand for various parts, taxpayer produced liberal quantities of each part to avoid subsequent production runs. Additional runs entail costly retooling and result in delays in filling orders.

In 1960, Thor instituted a procedure for writing down the inventory value of replacement parts and accessories for tool models it no longer produced. It created an inventory contra-account and credited that account with 10% of each part's cost for each year since production of the parent model had ceased. The effect of the procedure was to amortize the cost of these parts over a 10-year period.

[In 1964, it took more drastic writedowns of spare parts. The IRS did not question the writeoff of parts that were soon thereafter scrapped or sold at reduced prices.]

This left some 44,000 assorted items, the status of which is the inventory issue here. Management concluded that many of these articles, mostly spare parts, were "excess" inventory, that is, that they were held in excess of any reasonably foreseeable future demand. It was decided that this inventory should be written down to its "net realizable value," which, in most cases, was scrap value.

Two methods were used to ascertain the quantity of excess inventory. Where accurate data were available, Thor forecast future demand for each item on the basis of actual 1964 usage, that is, actual sales for tools and service parts, and actual usage for raw materials, work-in-process, and production parts. Management assumed that future demand for each item would be the same as it was in 1964. Thor then applied the following aging schedule: the quantity of each item corresponding to less than one year's estimated demand was kept at cost; the quantity of each item in excess of two years' estimated demand was written off entirely; and the quantity of each item corresponding to from one to two years' estimated demand was written down by 50% or 75%. Thor presented no statistical evidence to rationalize these percentages or this time frame. . . .

At two plants where 1964 data were inadequate to permit forecasts of future demand, Thor used its second method for valuing inventories. At these plants, the company employed flat percentage write-downs of 5%, 10%, and 50% for various types of inventory. Thor presented no sales or other data to support these percentages. . . .

Although Thor wrote down all its "excess" inventory at once, it did not immediately scrap the articles or sell them at reduced prices, as it had done with the $3 million of obsolete and damaged inventory, the write-down of which the Commissioner permitted. Rather, Thor retained the "excess" items physically in inventory and continued to sell them at original prices. The company found that, owing to the peculiar nature of the articles involved, price reductions were of no avail in moving this "excess" inventory. As time went on, however, Thor gradually disposed of some of these items as scrap; the record is unclear as to when these dispositions took place. . . .

Thor credited [the write-downs] to its inventory contra-account, thereby decreasing closing inventory, increasing cost of goods sold, and decreasing taxable income for the year by that amount.[4] . . . On audit, the Commissioner disallowed the write-down in its entirety, asserting that it did not serve clearly to reflect Thor's 1964 income for tax purposes.

The Tax Court, in upholding the Commissioner's determination, found as a fact that Thor's write-down of excess inventory did conform to "generally accepted accounting principles"; indeed, the court was "thoroughly convinced . . . that such was the case." The court found that if Thor had failed to write down its inventory on some reasonable basis, its accountants would have been unable to give its financial statements the desired certification. The court held, however, that conformance with "generally accepted accounting principles" is not enough; §446(b), and §471 as well . . . , prescribe, as an independent requirement, that inventory accounting methods must "clearly reflect income." . . .

Inventory accounting is governed by §§446 and 471 of the Code. Section 446(a) states the general rule for methods of accounting: "Taxable income shall be computed under the method of accounting on the

4. For a manufacturing concern like Thor, Gross Profit basically equals Sales minus Cost of Goods Sold. Cost of Goods Sold equals Opening Inventory, plus Cost of Inventory Acquired, minus Closing Inventory. A reduction of Closing Inventory, therefore, increases Cost of Goods Sold and decreases Gross Profit accordingly.

basis of which the taxpayer regularly computes his income in keeping his books." Section 446(b) provides, however, that if the method used by the taxpayer "does not clearly reflect income, the computation of taxable income shall be made under such method as, in the opinion of the [Commissioner], does clearly reflect income." Regulations promulgated under §446, and in effect for the taxable year 1964, state that "no method of accounting is acceptable unless, in the opinion of the Commissioner, it clearly reflects income." Treas. Reg. §1.446-1(a)(2).

Section 471 prescribes the general rule for inventories. It states:

> Whenever in the opinion of the [Commissioner] the use of inventories is necessary in order clearly to determine the income of any taxpayer, inventory shall be taken by such taxpayer on such basis as the [Commissioner] may prescribe as conforming as nearly as may be to the best accounting practice in the trade or business and as most clearly reflecting the income.

As the Regulations point out, §471 obviously establishes two distinct tests to which an inventory must conform. First, it must comply "as nearly as may be" with the "best accounting practice," a phrase that is synonymous with "generally accepted accounting principles." Second, it "must clearly reflect the income." Treas. Reg. §1.471-2(a)(2).

It is obvious that on their face, §§446 and 471, with their accompanying Regulations, vest the Commissioner with wide discretion in determining whether a particular method of inventory accounting should be disallowed as not clearly reflective of income. This Court's cases confirm the breadth of this discretion. In construing §446 and its predecessors, the Court has held that "[t]he Commissioner has broad powers in determining whether accounting methods used by a taxpayer clearly reflect income." Commissioner v. Hansen, 360 U.S. 446, 467 (1959). Since the Commissioner has "[m]uch latitude for discretion," his interpretation of the statute's clear-reflection standard "should not be interfered with unless clearly unlawful." Lucas v. American Code Co., 280 U.S. 445, 449 (1930). . . .

As has been noted, the Tax Court found as a fact in this case that Thor's write-down of "excess" inventory conformed to "generally accepted accounting principles" and was "within the term, 'best accounting practice,' as that term is used in section 471 of the Code and the regulations promulgated under that section." 64 T.C., at 161, 165. Since the Commissioner has not challenged this finding, there is no dispute that Thor satisfied the first part of §471's two-pronged test. The only question, then, is whether the Commissioner abused his discretion in determining that the write-down did not satisfy the test's second prong in that it failed to reflect Thor's 1964 income clearly. Although the Commissioner's discretion is not unbridled and may not be arbitrary we sustain his exercise of discretion here, for in this case the write-down was plainly inconsistent with the governing Regulations which the taxpayer, on its part, has not challenged.

It has been noted above that Thor at all pertinent times used the "lower of cost or market" method of inventory accounting. The rules governing this method are set out in Treas. Reg. §1.471-4. That Regulation defines "market" to mean, ordinarily, "the current bid price prevailing at the date of the inventory for the particular merchandise in the volume in which usually purchased by the taxpayer." §1.471-4(a). The courts have uniformly interpreted "bid price" to mean replacement cost, that is, the price the taxpayer would have to pay on the open market to purchase or reproduce the inventory items. Where no open market exists, the Regulations require the taxpayer to ascertain "bid price" by using "such evidence of a fair market price at the date or dates nearest the inventory as may be available, such as specific purchases or sales by the taxpayer or others in reasonable volume and made in good faith, or compensation paid for cancellation of contracts for purchase commitments." §1.471-4(b).

The Regulations specify two situations in which a taxpayer is permitted to value inventory below "market" as so defined. The first is where the taxpayer in the normal course of business has actually offered merchandise for sale at prices lower than replacement cost. Inventories of such merchandise may be valued at those prices less direct cost of disposition. . . .

The second situation in which a taxpayer may value inventory below replacement cost is where the merchandise itself is defective. If goods are "unsalable at normal prices or unusable in the normal way because of damage, imperfections, shop wear, changes of style, odd or broken lots, or other similar causes," the taxpayer is permitted to value the goods "at bona fide selling prices less direct cost of disposition." §1.471-2(c). . . .

It is clear to us that Thor's procedures for writing down the value of its "excess" inventory were inconsistent with this regulatory scheme. Although Thor conceded that "an active market prevailed" on the inventory date, it "made no effort to determine the purchase or reproduction cost" of its "excess" inventory. Thor thus failed to ascertain "market" in accord with the general rule of the Regulations. . . . The formulae governing this write-down were derived from management's collective "business expertise"; the percentages contained in those formulae seemingly were chosen for no reason other than that they were multiples of five and embodied some kind of analogical symmetry. The Regulations do not permit this kind of evidence. If a taxpayer could write down its inventories on the basis of management's subjective estimates of the goods' ultimate salability, the taxpayer would be able, as the Tax Court observed, "to determine how much tax it wanted to pay for a given year."

For these reasons we agree with the Tax Court and with the Seventh Circuit that the Commissioner acted within his discretion in deciding that Thor's write-down of "excess" inventory failed to reflect income clearly. . . .

The taxpayer's major argument against this conclusion is based on the Tax Court's clear finding that the write-down conformed to "generally accepted accounting principles." Thor points to language in Treas. Reg. §1.446-1(a)(2), to the effect that "[a] method of accounting which reflects the consistent application of generally accepted accounting principles . . . *will ordinarily be regarded* as clearly reflecting income" (emphasis added). Section 1.471-2(b) of the Regulations likewise stated that an inventory taken in conformity with best accounting practice "can, *as a general rule,* be regarded as clearly reflecting . . . income" (emphasis added). These provisions, Thor contends, created a *presumption* that an inventory practice conformable to "generally accepted accounting principles" is valid for income tax purposes. Once a taxpayer has established this conformity, the argument runs, the burden shifts to the Commissioner affirmatively to demonstrate that the taxpayer's method does *not* reflect income clearly.

. . . We believe, however, that no such presumption is present. Its existence is insupportable in light of the statute, the Court's past decisions, and the differing objectives of tax and financial accounting.

First, as has been stated above, the Code and Regulations establish two distinct tests to which an inventory must conform. The Code and Regulations, moreover, leave little doubt as to which test is paramount. While §471 of the Code requires only that an accounting practice conform "as nearly as may be" to best accounting practice, §1.446-1(a)(2) of the Regulations states categorically that "*no* method of accounting is acceptable unless, in the opinion of the Commissioner, it clearly reflects income" (emphasis added). Most importantly, the Code and Regulations give the Commissioner broad discretion to set aside the taxpayer's method if, "in [his] opinion," it does not reflect income clearly. This language is completely at odds with the notion of a "presumption" in the taxpayer's favor. The Regulations embody no presumption; they say merely that, in most cases, generally accepted accounting practices will pass muster for tax purposes. And in most cases they will. But if the Commissioner, in the exercise of his discretion, determines that they do not, he may prescribe a different practice without having to rebut any presumption running against the Treasury.

Second, the presumption petitioner postulates finds no support in this Court's prior decisions. It was early noted that the general rule specifying use of the taxpayer's method of accounting "is expressly limited to cases where the Commissioner believes that the accounts clearly reflect the net income." Lucas v. American Code Co., 280 U.S., at 449. More recently, it was held in American Automobile Assn. v. United States, supra, that a taxpayer must recognize prepaid income when received, even though this would mismatch expenses and revenues in contravention of "generally accepted commercial accounting principles." 367 U.S., at 690. . . . Indeed, the Court's cases demonstrate that divergence between tax and financial accounting is especially common when a taxpayer seeks a current deduction for estimated future expenses or losses. . . .

Third, the presumption petitioner postulates is insupportable in light of the vastly different objectives that financial and tax accounting have. The primary goal of financial accounting is to provide useful information to management, shareholders, creditors, and others properly interested; the major responsibility of the accountant is to protect these parties from being misled. The primary goal of the income tax system, in contrast, is the equitable collection of revenue; the major responsibility of the Internal Revenue Service is to protect the public fisc. Consistently with its goals and responsibilities, financial accounting has as its foundation the principle of conservatism, with its corollary that "possible errors in measurement [should] be in the direction of understatement rather than overstatement of net income and net assets."[5] In view of the Treasury's markedly different goals and responsibilities, understatement of income is not destined to be its guiding light. Given this diversity, even contrariety, of objectives, any presumptive equivalency between tax and financial accounting would be unacceptable.

This difference in objectives is mirrored in numerous differences of treatment. Where the tax law requires that a deduction be deferred until "all the events" have occurred that will make it fixed and certain, United States v. Anderson, 269 U.S. 422, 441 (1926), accounting principles typically require that a liability be accrued as soon as it can reasonably be estimated. Conversely, where the tax law requires that income be recognized currently under "claim of right," "ability to pay," and "control" rationales, accounting principles may defer accrual until a later year so that revenues and expenses may be better matched. Financial accounting, in short, is hospitable to estimates, probabilities, and reasonable certainties; the tax law, with its mandate to preserve the revenue, can give no quarter to uncertainty. This is as it should be. Reasonable estimates may be useful, even essential, in giving shareholders and creditors an accurate picture of a firm's overall financial health; but the accountant's conservatism cannot bind the Commissioner in his efforts to collect taxes. . . .

Finally, a presumptive equivalency between tax and financial accounting would create insurmountable difficulties of tax administration. Accountants long have recognized that "generally accepted accounting

5. AICPA Accounting Principles Board, Statement No. 4, Basic Concepts and Accounting Principles Underlying Financial Statements of Business Enterprises, ¶171 (1970), reprinted in 2 APB Accounting Principles 9089 (1973). . . .

principles" are far from being a canonical set of rules that will ensure identical accounting treatment of identical transactions. "Generally accepted accounting principles," rather, tolerate a range of "reasonable" treatments, leaving the choice among alternatives to management. Such, indeed, is precisely the case here. Variances of this sort may be tolerable in financial reporting, but they are questionable in a tax system designed to ensure as far as possible that similarly situated taxpayers pay the same tax. If management's election among "acceptable" options were dispositive for tax purposes, a firm, indeed, could decide unilaterally — within limits dictated only by its accountants — the tax it wished to pay. Such unilateral decisions would not just make the Code inequitable; they would make it unenforceable.

Thor complains that a decision adverse to it poses a dilemma. According to the taxpayer, it would be virtually impossible for it to offer objective evidence of its "excess" inventory's lower value, since the goods cannot be sold at reduced prices; even if they could be sold, says Thor, their reduced-price sale would just "pull the rug out" from under the identical "non-excess" inventory Thor is trying to sell simultaneously. The only way Thor could establish the inventory's value by a "closed transaction" would be to scrap the articles at once. Yet immediate scrapping would be undesirable, for demand for the parts ultimately might prove greater than anticipated. The taxpayer thus sees itself presented with "an unattractive Hobson's choice: either the unsalable inventory must be carried for years at its cost instead of net realizable value, thereby overstating taxable income by such overvaluation until it is scrapped, or the excess inventory must be scrapped prematurely to the detriment of the manufacturer and its customers."

If this is indeed the dilemma that confronts Thor, it is in reality the same choice that every taxpayer who has a paper loss must face. It can realize its loss now and garner its tax benefit, or it can defer realization, and its deduction, hoping for better luck later. Thor, quite simply, has suffered no present loss. . . .

The judgment of the Court of Appeals is affirmed.

NOTE AND QUESTIONS

To illustrate the taxpayer dilemma referred to near the end of the opinion in *Thor Power Tool,* suppose that a taxpayer has spare parts for which the cost, on its books, is $100,000; that it estimates that much of this inventory ultimately will be scrapped; that its best guess is that it will ultimately realize a total of $10,000 from the sale of the parts; that it has excess warehouse space so the cost of holding the parts is minimal; and that it would like to keep the parts for five years, largely for the sake of customer goodwill, but certainly will dispose of them at the end of that period of time. If it scraps the parts immediately, it gets a deduction of $100,000. Assuming a marginal tax rate of 34 percent (see §11(b)), this means a tax saving of $34,000. Thus, the question is whether to scrap the parts and take the $34,000 tax saving now or hold on and realize (probably) $10,000 plus a tax saving of $30,600 (34 percent of the ultimate loss of $90,000) five years from now. At an interest rate of 10 percent, the present value of $30,600 five years from now is $19,000. The present value of the $10,000 from the sale of the parts depends on when it is expected they will be sold; assume, arbitrarily, that the present value turns out to be $8,000. By retaining the inventory of parts, then, the taxpayer gives up a present tax saving of $34,000 in return for future returns with a present value of $27,000. The difference, in favor of current sale, is $7,000. To summarize:

Scrap inventory now		
Inventory book value	$100,000	
Loss deduction	100,000	
Tax saving from deduction	34,000	
Net present value		$34,000
Hold for five years		
Inventory book value	$100,000	
Ultimate sale price	10,000	
Ultimate loss deduction	90,000	
Tax saving from deduction	30,600	
Present value, sale price	8,000	
Present value, deduction	19,000	
Total present value		$27,000
Benefit of sale now		
Sale now	$34,000	
Hold for five years	27,000	
Benefit of sale now		$ 7,000

The $7,000 difference may be too high a price for preserving customer goodwill. The tax system may induce the taxpayer to follow a course of action that is unwise both for it and for its customers, a course of action that is plainly wasteful. Why is it that a rule that produces this kind of result is not an abuse of discretion by the Commissioner? Are the administrative problems of the rule that the taxpayer in *Thor Power Tool* sought to apply so severe as to compel endorsement of the economically perverse rule imposed by the Commissioner? In some circumstances, of course, the taxpayer may be able to sell the inventory of spare parts to an independent supplier and recognize the loss. Is there any good reason why the tax system should encourage such transactions?

D. RENT PAYMENT VERSUS INSTALLMENT PURCHASE

STARR'S ESTATE v. COMMISSIONER

274 F.2d 294 (9th Cir. 1959)

CHAMBERS, Circuit Judge.

Yesterday's equities in personal property seem to have become today's leases. This has been generated not a little by the circumstance that one who leases as a lessee usually has less trouble with the federal tax collector. At least taxpayers think so.

But the lease still can go too far and get one into tax trouble. While according to state law the instrument will probably be taken (with the consequent legal incidents) by the name the parties give it, the [IRS] is not always bound and can often recast it according to what the service may consider the practical realities.[6] . . . The principal case concerns a fire sprinkler system installed at the taxpayer's plant. . . . The "lessor" was "Automatic" Sprinklers of the Pacific, Inc. . . . The instrument entitled "Lease Form of Contract" (hereafter "contract") is just about perfectly couched in terms of a lease for five years with annual rentals of $1,240. But it is the last paragraph thereof, providing for nominal rental for five years, that has caused the trouble. It reads as follows:

> 28. At the termination of the period of this lease, if Lessee has faithfully performed all of the terms and conditions required of it under this lease, it shall have the privilege of renewing this lease for an additional period of five years at a rental of $32.00 per year. If Lessee does not elect to renew this lease, then the Lessor is hereby granted the period of six months in which to remove the system from the premises of the Lessee.

Obviously, one renewal for a period of five years is provided at $32.00 per year, if Starr so desired. Note, though, that the [contract] is silent as to [the] status of the system beginning with the eleventh year. . . .

The tax court sustained the [Commissioner], holding that the five payments of $1,240, or the total of $6,200, were capital expenditures

6. Thus, it shifts rental payments of a business (fully deductible) to a capital purchase for the business. If the nature of the property is wasting, then depreciation may be taken, but usually not all in one year.

and not pure deductible rental. Depreciation of $269.60 was allowed for each year. Generally, we agree. . . .

The law in this field for this circuit is established in Oesterreich v. Commissioner, [226 F.2d 798]. . . . There we held that for tax purposes form can be disregarded for substance and, where the foreordained practical effect of the rent is to produce title eventually, the rental agreement can be treated as a sale.

In this, Starr's case, we do have the troublesome circumstance that the contract does not by its terms ever pass title to the system to the lessee. Most sprinkler systems have to be tailor-made for a specific piece of property and, if removal is required, the salvageable value is negligible. Also, it stretches credulity to believe that the "lessor" ever intended to or would "come after" the system. And the "lessee" would be an exceedingly careless businessman who would enter into such contract with the practical possibility that the "lessor" would reclaim the installation. He could have believed only that he was getting the system for the rental money. And we think the commissioner was entitled to take into consideration the practical effect rather than the legal, especially when there was a record that on other such installations the "lessor," after the term of the lease was over, had not reclaimed from those who had met their agreed payments. It is obvious that the nominal rental payments after five years, of $32.00 per year, were just a service charge for inspection.

Recently the Court of Appeals for the Eighth Circuit had decided Western Contracting Corporation v. Commissioner, 1959, 271 F.2d 694, reversing the tax court in its determination that the commissioner could convert leases of contractor's equipment into installment purchases of heavy equipment. . . .

There are a number of facts there which make a difference. For example, in the contracts of Western there is no evidence that the payments on the substituted basis of rent would produce for the "lessor" the equivalent of his normal sales price plus interest. There was no right to acquire for a nominal amount at the end of the term as in *Oesterreich* and the value to the "lessor" in the personalty had not been exhausted as in Starr's case. And there was no basis for inferring that Western would just keep the equipment for what it had paid. It appears that Western paid substantial amounts to acquire the equipment at the end of the term. There was just one compelling circumstance against Western in its case: What it had paid as "rent" was apparently always taken into full account in computing the end purchase price. But on the other hand, there was almost a certainty that the "lessor" would come after his property if the purchase was not eventually made for a substantial amount. This was not even much of a possibility in *Oesterreich* and not a probability in Starr's case.

In Wilshire Holding Corporation v. Commissioner, 9 Cir., 262 F.2d 51, we referred the case back to the tax court to consider interest as a deductible item for the lessee. We think it is clearly called for here. Two yardsticks are present. The first is found in that the normal selling price of the system was $4960 while the total rental payments for five years were $6200. The difference could be regarded as interest for the five years on an amortized basis. The second measure is in clause 16 (loss by fire), where the figure of six percent per annum discount is used. An allowance might be made on either basis, division of the difference (for the five years) between "rental payments" and "normal purchase price" of $1240, or six percent per annum on the normal purchase price of $4960, converting the annual payments into amortization. We do not believe that the "lessee" should suffer the pains of a loss for what really was paid for the use of another's money, even though for tax purposes his lease collapses.

We do not criticize the commissioner. It is his duty to collect the revenue and it is a tough one. If he resolves all questions in favor of the taxpayers, we soon would have little revenue. However, we do suggest that after he has made allowance for depreciation, which he concedes, and an allowance for interest, the attack on many of the "leases" may not be worthwhile in terms of revenue.

Decision reversed for proceedings consistent herewith.

NOTES AND QUESTIONS

1. *Advance rent.* Suppose a taxpayer becomes a tenant in property, used for business, under a lease with a ten-year term and a single rental payment of $7,000 at the beginning of the term. As we have seen (see discussion of *Boylston Market,* supra page 621), the advance payment cannot be deducted in the year of payment. The taxpayer would be required to take deductions in the form of amortization at the rate of $700 per year over the ten-year term. What does this suggest as to an alternative approach to *Starr's Estate?*

2. *Distinguishing leases from installment purchases.* What are the critical elements supporting the conclusion that a transaction such as the one in *Starr's Estate* is an installment purchase rather than a true lease? The taxpayer's objective in the case was to bunch deductions as much as possible in the early years of the use of the asset.[7] How would you advise a taxpayer in similar circumstances to structure a transaction so as to be successful in this objective (bearing in mind that what the seller has in mind is pinning down a sale)?

7. In order to accomplish this objective, the taxpayer was required to pay out the cash in the year in which the deduction was sought and thereby to forgo the interest that could have been earned on part of the cash if a slower rate of payment had been called for; but presumably the value of the payments of cash (i.e., of the forgone interest) was reflected in the total amount of payments called for under the contract.

3. *Changing times.* At the time this case arose, depreciation deductions were at a rate substantially lower than what is now available under ACRS. At present, because of ACRS, the kind of transaction at issue in *Starr's Estate* would offer little, if any, advantage over ownership. These days, it may be advantageous for the seller (or some other person or entity) to purport to retain (or acquire) ownership in order to take advantage of ACRS deductions, which, for any of a variety of reasons, may not be of benefit to the user of the property. At the same time, however, the user might want the ordinary economic incidents of ownership. This state of affairs has led to complex transactions in which the user purported to lease property from the seller (or some third person) and to correspondingly complex judicial, administrative, and statutory developments, which are explored later in this chapter (infra pages 716-732).

4. *The interest element.* At the end of the opinion in *Starr's Estate,* the court points out that if the transaction is treated as an installment purchase, the taxpayer is entitled to an interest deduction, as well as depreciation. The normal selling price of the system, says the court, is $4,960. The actual payments are $1,240 per year for five years. The implicit interest rate turns out to be 7.93 percent (assuming the first payment is at the end of the first year). That means that the interest for the first year, on the $4,960, would be $393. The allowable depreciation deduction, according to the court, was $269. Thus, the total deductions should be $662. The total dollar amounts are not large, but $662 is only 53 percent of the $1,240 claimed by the taxpayer. For a tax planner, that is a dramatic difference.

5. *Substance versus form. Starr's Estate* presents one of many situations in which, in an effort to achieve tax benefits, a transaction's substance (here, an installment sale) is different from the form in which it has been cast (a lease). Why is it that here the court insists on treating the transaction for tax purposes according to its substance?

PROBLEM

Suppose Seller owns an office building (or a residence) with a basis of $100,000 and a fair market value of $1,000,000. Buyer is willing to pay $1,000,000, with an immediate cash payment of $300,000 and a promissory note (secured by a mortgage on the property) for the remaining $700,000, with interest at 10 percent (the prevailing market rate), payable one year after closing. (Thus, the total payable at the end of the year would be $770,000.) Just before Buyer and Seller are about to sign a contract of purchase and sale, Buyer's sister-in-law, Lois (an accountant who fancies herself an expert in finding loopholes in the tax law) suggests to Buyer that the promissory note be in the principal amount of $600,000, with interest of $170,000. Lois points out that Seller should have no objection to this change (since there is no longer a tax advantage for capital gain) and that Buyer will benefit by accelerating or increasing her deductions. (a) Is Lois right?[8]

(b) Suppose that Lois was able to convince Buyer that her plan would work and that the transaction was in fact structured as she suggested. A year has now passed, the promissory note has been paid in full, and Buyer asks you for your legal opinion on whether she can deduct the full $170,000 of "interest" that she has paid. What is your response? What if the interest element had been $270,000? $90,000?

E. GOODWILL AND OTHER ASSETS

WELCH v. HELVERING

290 U.S. 111 (1933)

Mr. Justice CARDOZO delivered the opinion of the Court.

The question to be determined is whether payments by a taxpayer, who is in business as a commission agent, are allowable deductions in the computation of his income if made to the creditors of a bankrupt corporation in an endeavor to strengthen his own standing and credit.

In 1922, petitioner was the secretary of the E. L. Welch Company, a Minnesota corporation, engaged in the grain business. The company was adjudged an involuntary bankrupt, and had a discharge from its debts. Thereafter, the petitioner made a contract with the Kellogg Company to purchase grain for it on a commission. In order to reestablish his relations with customers whom he had known when acting for the Welch Company and to solidify his credit and standing, he decided to pay the debts of the Welch business so far as he was able. In fulfillment of that resolve, he made payments of substantial amounts during five

8. Proposed Regs. §1.1274-1(d) provides:

> *Excessive interest.* If a debt instrument given in consideration for the sale or exchange of property calls for interest at a rate that, in light of the terms of the debt instrument and the creditworthiness of the borrower, is clearly greater than the arm's-length rate of interest that would have been charged in a cash lending transaction (that is, one not involving a sale of property) between the same two parties, the Commissioner may recharacterize a portion of the stated interest as additional purchase price. The portion of interest to be recharacterized as additional purchase price shall be determined in a manner consistent with section 1274 and may be based either on the fair market value of the property sold or on the arm's-length rate described in the preceding sentence.

Note also, however, that §1274 does not apply to certain sales, including sales of personal residences. §1274(c)(3)(B). Is there any statutory foundation for the regulation?

successive years. In 1924, the commissions were $18,000,[9] the payments $4000; in 1925, the commissions $31,000, the payments $12,000; in 1926, the commissions $21,000, the payments $13,000; in 1927, the commissions $22,000, the payments $7,000; and in 1928, the commissions $26,000, the payments $11,000. The Commissioner ruled that these payments were not deductible from income as ordinary and necessary expenses, but were rather in the nature of capital expenditures, an outlay for the development of reputation and goodwill. . . . [The Tax Court and Eighth Circuit sustained the Commissioner.]

We may assume that the payments to creditors of the Welch Company were necessary for the development of the petitioner's business, at least in the sense that they were appropriate and helpful. . . . He certainly thought they were, and we should be slow to override his judgment. But the problem is not solved when the payments are characterized as necessary. Many necessary payments are charges upon capital. There is need to determine whether they are both necessary and ordinary. Now, what is ordinary, though there must always be a strain of constancy within it, is none the less a variable affected by time and place and circumstance. Ordinary in this context does not mean the payments must be habitual or normal in the sense that the same taxpayer will have to make them often. A lawsuit affecting the safety of a business may happen once in a lifetime. The counsel fees may be so heavy that repetition is unlikely. None the less, the expense is an ordinary one because we know from experience that payments for such a purpose, whether the amount is large or small, are the common and accepted means of defense against attack. . . . The situation is unique in the life of the individual affected, but not in the life of the group, the community, of which he is a part. At such times there are norms of conduct that help to stabilize our judgment, and make it certain and objective. The instance is not erratic, but is brought within a known type.

The line of demarcation is now visible between the case that is here and the one supposed for illustration. We try to classify this act as ordinary or the opposite, and the norms of conduct fail us. No longer can we have recourse to any fund of business experience, to any known business practice. Men do at times pay the debts of others without legal obligation or the lighter obligation imposed by the usages of trade or by neighborly amenities, but they do not do so ordinarily, not even though the result might be to heighten their reputation for generosity and opulence. Indeed, if language is to be read in its natural and common meaning . . . we should have to say that payment in such circumstances, instead of being ordinary, is in a high degree extraordinary. There is nothing ordinary in the stimulus evoking it, and none in the response. Here, indeed, as so often in other branches of the law,

9. [Amounts have been rounded. — Eds.]

the decisive distinctions are those of degree and not of kind. One struggles in vain for any verbal formula that will supply a ready touchstone. The standard set up by the statute is not a rule of law; it is rather a way of life. Life in all its fullness must supply the answer to the riddle.

The Commissioner of Internal Revenue resorted to that standard . . . and found that the payments in controversy came closer to capital outlays than to ordinary and necessary expenses in the operation of a business. His ruling has the support of a presumption of correctness, and the petitioner has the burden of proving it to be wrong. . . . Unless we can say from facts within our knowledge that these are ordinary and necessary expenses according to the ways of conduct and the forms of speech prevailing in the business world, the tax must be confirmed. But nothing told us by this record or within the sphere of our judicial notice permits us to give that extension to what is ordinary and necessary. Indeed, to do so would open the door to many bizarre analogies. One man has a family name that is clouded by thefts committed by an ancestor. To add to his own standing he repays the stolen money, wiping off, it may be, his income for the year. The payments figure in his tax return as ordinary expenses. Another man conceives the notion that he will be able to practice his vocation with greater ease and profit if he has an opportunity to enrich his culture. Forthwith the price of his education becomes an expense of the business, reducing the income subject to taxation. There is little difference between these expenses and those in controversy here. Reputation and learning are akin to capital assets, like the good will of an old partnership. . . . For many, they are the only tools with which to hew a pathway to success. The money spent in acquiring them is well and wisely spent. It is not an ordinary expense of the operation of a business.

Many cases in the federal courts deal with phases of the problem presented in the case at bar. To attempt to harmonize them would be a futile task. They involve the appreciation of particular situations, at times with border-line conclusions. Typical illustrations are cited in the margin.[10]

The decree should be affirmed.

10. Ordinary expenses: Comm'r v. People's Pittsburgh Trust Co., 60 F.(2d) 187, expenses incurred in the defense of a criminal charge growing out of the business of the taxpayer; American Rolling Mill Co. v. Comm'r, 41 F.(2d) 314, contributions to a civic improvement fund by a corporation employing half of the wage earning population of the city, the payments being made, not for charity, but to add to the skill and productivity of the workmen . . . ; Corning Glass Works v. Lucas, 37 F.(2d) 798, donations to a hospital by a corporation whose employees with their dependents made up two-thirds of the population of the city; Harris & Co. v. Lucas, 48 F.(2d) 187, payments of debts discharged in bankruptcy, but subject to be revived by force of a new promise. Cf. Lucas v. Ox Fibre Brush Co., 281 U.S. 115, where additional compensation, reasonable in amount, was allowed to the officers of a corporation for services previously rendered. Not ordinary expenses: Hubinger v. Comm'r, 36 F.(2d) 724, payments by the taxpayer for the repair of fire damage, such payments being distinguished from those for wear and tear; Lloyd

NOTES AND QUESTIONS

1. *Analysis. Welch* is a famous and often-cited decision. Needlessly Delphic, it has generated considerable confusion. The issue presented by the Commissioner was simply whether the payments were capital expenditures or current expenses. This being so, what is the relevance, if any, of "uniqueness" (of litigation expenses) or of payments to establish "reputation for generosity and opulence," to "protect a family name," or to "enrich [one's] culture"? Does Justice Cardozo confuse the distinction between capital and current with the distinction between personal and business?[11] Is it clear that "one struggles in vain for any verbal formula that will apply a ready touchstone"? See the opinion in the *Encyclopaedia Britannica* case, supra page 613. If your authorities were limited to the principal cases in this chapter, on which one would you place your principal reliance if you were representing Mr. Welch? What facts would you emphasize?

2. *Other debt-repayment cases.* In Dunn & McCarthy v. Commissioner, 139 F.2d 242 (2d Cir. 1943), a corporation was permitted to deduct amounts it paid to certain employees who had lent funds to its former president; he had lost the money gambling at the race track and had died insolvent. The court did not think the payments were "extraordinary": "It was the kind of outlay which we believe many corporations would make, and have made, under similar circumstances." The *Welch* case was distinguished: "Welch made a capital outlay to acquire goodwill for a new business. In the present case the payment was an outlay to retain an existing goodwill, that is, to prevent loss of earnings that might result from destroying such goodwill by failing to recognize the company's moral obligation." In M. L. Eakes Co. v. Commissioner, 686 F.2d 217 (4th Cir. 1982), the court allowed a current deduction of the debts of a predecessor corporation that had become insolvent. The court concluded that the payments were made to establish credit and thereby preserve an existing business rather than to establish a new one and, after quoting extensively from the *Welch* discussion of "ordinary and

---

v. Comm'r, 55 F.(2d) 842, counsel fees incurred by the taxpayer, the president of a corporation, in prosecuting a slander suit to protect his reputation and that of his business; One Hundred Five West Fifty-Fifth Street v. Comm'r, 42 F.(2d) 849, and Blackwell Oil & Gas Co., v. Comm'r, 60 F.(2d) 257, gratuitous payments to stockholders in settlement of disputes between them, or to assume the expense of a lawsuit in which they had been made defendants; White v. Comm'r, 61 F.(2d) 726, payments in settlement of a lawsuit against a member of a partnership, the effect being to enable him to devote his undivided efforts to the partnership business and also to protect its credit.

11. In Commissioner v. Tellier, 383 U.S. 687, 689-690 (1966) (see infra page 661), the Court said,

> The principal function of the term ordinary in §162(a) is to clarify the distinction, often difficult, between those expenses that are currently deductible and those that are in the nature of capital expenditures, which, if deductible at all, must be amortized over the useful life of the asset. Welch v. Helvering. . . .

necessary," referred to testimony to the effect that the repayment of debts of a liquidated corporation was not unusual in the business in which the taxpayer was engaged.

3. *Recovery of cost of goodwill.* As suggested in Note 1, supra, the holding in *Welch* is best justified on the rationale that the expenditure at issue produced benefits beyond the current year and for that reason was capital in nature. If the cost of acquiring goodwill is a capital expenditure, can a taxpayer receive a deduction for amortization of that cost over the expected life of the asset? Historically, the answer to this question has been "no." Amounts paid to produce goodwill have been recoverable for tax purposes only upon sale or other taxable disposition of the business. The same treatment has applied to the portion of the purchase price paid for a business that is allocable to goodwill: No current deduction, no amortization, recovery only upon disposition of the business. Understandably, taxpayers have gone to great length to avoid characterizing expenditures for goodwill. Section 197, added to the tax law in 1993, provides for a 15-year amortization of goodwill acquired through purchase. Self-created goodwill, such as that at issue in *Welch,* is still unamortizable. See infra page 676.

4. *Advertising.* Except in unusual circumstances, the Service has acquiesced in the current deduction of advertising expenses, even in the case of institutional advertising and promotion of a new trade name or product. See I.T. 3581, 1942-2 C.B. 88, Regs. §1.263A-IT(b)(2)(v)(A). In Briarcliff Candy Corp. v. Commissioner, 475 F.2d 775 (2d Cir. 1973), one of the rare situations in which the Commissioner did challenge deduction of a promotional expense, the court allowed a current deduction for the costs of an extensive campaign by a manufacturer to have retailers sell its products in a specially designed display area, observing that "the rulings and decisions are in a state of hopeless confusion," that "practically all businesses are constantly seeking new customers and pursuing a distribution program," and that the taxpayers are "entitled to reasonably clear criteria or standards."

5. *Education.* We have already seen that the cost of a college education is nondeductible because it is a "personal" expense. See supra page 609. For education that relates more directly to the production of income, the regulations (Regs. §1.162-5) adopt a set of objective tests (as opposed to tests dependent on motive or purpose) that rely on the distinction between capital expenditures and current expenses. No deduction is allowed for the expense of meeting "the minimum educational requirements for qualification in [an] employment or other trade or business." Regs. §1.162-5(b)(2)(i). This rule is most widely applied to people who, while holding jobs as schoolteachers, complete or continue their education. Deductions are also denied for the expenses of "a program of study being pursued by [a person] which will lead to qualifying [the person] in a new trade or business." Regs. §1.162-5(b)(3)(i). This rule

precludes deductions for the cost of a law school education, even by people working as, say, engineers, accountants, or police officers, who claim that they never intend to practice law and that the law school education is intended only to enhance their performance in their present occupations.

If the taxpayer is already qualified to practice an occupation or profession but incurs expenses for additional training, the regulations allow deductions for two overlapping categories of education. The first is education that "maintains or improves skills required by the individual in his employment or other trade or business." Regs. §1.162-5(a)(1). A refresher course to bring a lawyer or doctor up to date on new developments is most typical of this category. The second is education that meets the "express requirements of the individual's employer, or the requirements of applicable law or regulations, imposed as a condition to the retention by the individual of an established employment relationship, status or rate of compensation." Regs. §1.162-5(a)(2). Covered under this category are annual graduate course credits that public school teachers are often required to obtain as a condition of retaining their positions.

Sharon v. Commissioner, 66 T.C. 515 (1976), aff'd, 591 F.2d 1273 (9th Cir. 1978), cert. denied, 442 U.S. 941 (1979), held that a lawyer could not amortize the costs of a legal education or of a bar preparation course but could (under §167) amortize registration, test, and bar admission fees over his expected life. In Kohen v. Commissioner, 44 T.C.M. 1518 (1982), the court denied a deduction of the cost of obtaining an LLM in taxation at NYU immediately following graduation from law school but before entering into practice in any way other than giving free advice to family members. Presumably the costs of a legal education cannot be deducted as a loss when one's legal career ends. See Regs. §1.162-5(b)(1), indicating that the costs "constitute an inseparable aggregate of personal and capital expenditures." Do you agree?

6. *The cost of finding a new business or job.* Rev. Rul. 77-254, 1977-2 C.B. 63, 64 holds:

> Expenses incurred in the course of a general search for or preliminary investigation of a business or investment include those expenses related to the decisions *whether* to enter a transaction and *which* transaction to enter. Such expenses are personal [!] and are not deductible under section 165 of the Code. Once the taxpayer has focused on the acquisition of a specific business or investment, expenses that are related to an attempt to acquire such business or investment are capital in nature and, to the extent that the expenses are allocable to an asset the cost of which is amortizable or depreciable, may be amortized as part of the asset's cost if the attempted acquisition is successful. If the attempted acquisition fails, the amount capitalized is deductible in accordance with section 165(c)(2). The taxpayer need not actually enter the business or purchase the investment in order to obtain the deduction.

Do you agree that the costs of a "general search" for a business or investment opportunity are personal? If not, does the language of the Code require the result that some outlays of this sort will never give rise to a deduction? Compare the treatment of the costs of a law school education. In some circumstances, the costs of investigating a business opportunity may be amortizable under §195, enacted in 1980, but this provision does not appear to be relevant to the costs of "general search."

Regs. §1.212-1(f) denies current deductions under §212 for "expenses such as those paid or incurred in seeking employment or in placing oneself in a position to begin rendering personal services for compensation. . . ." In Cremona v. Commissioner, 58 T.C. 219 (1972), acq., a taxpayer who was employed as an "administrator" paid $1,500 for job counseling and referral services that had not led to a new position by the time of hearing of the case. The Court held the expenses deductible under §162 since the taxpayer was in "the trade or business of being an administrator." Rev. Rul. 77-16, 1977-1 C.B. 37, allowed deduction of the expenses of looking for a new position in the taxpayer's present trade or business, a limit that is quite broad since the Service, like the Tax Court, recognizes such a broad trade or business as being a corporate executive or administrator. See also Rev. Rul. 78-93, 1978-1 C.B. 38, permitting the deduction of expenses for career counseling when the taxpayer, engaged in the businesses of being both a full-time practicing attorney and part-time law school lecturer, after receiving the counseling secured a position of full-time assistant professor of law. The Service held that since the taxpayer had been engaged in two trades or businesses, he was not changing his trade or business by seeking a full-time teaching job.

7. *Two percent threshold.* Business expenses of *employees,* including the cost of employment-related education, can be deducted only to the extent that in the aggregate they exceed 2 percent of adjusted gross income (AGI). See §67, which is described supra page 524.

F. "ORDINARY AND NECESSARY"

1. Extraordinary Behavior

GILLIAM v. COMMISSIONER

51 T.C.M. 515 (1986)

When the petition was filed in the instant case, petitioners Sam Gilliam, Jr. (hereinafter sometimes referred to as "Gilliam"), and Dorothy B. Gilliam, husband and wife, resided in Washington, D.C.

Gilliam was born in Tupelo, Mississippi, in 1933, and raised in Louisville, Kentucky. In 1961, he received a master of arts degree in painting from the University of Louisville.

Gilliam is, and was at all material periods, a noted artist. His works have been exhibited in numerous art galleries throughout the United States and Europe, including the Corcoran Gallery of Art, Washington, D.C., the Philadelphia Museum of Art, Philadelphia, Pennsylvania, the Karl Solway Gallery, Cincinnati, Ohio, the Phoenix Gallery, San Francisco, California, and the University of California, Irvine, California. His works have also been exhibited and sold at the Fendrick Gallery, Washington, D.C. In addition, Gilliam is, and was at all material periods, a teacher of art. On occasion, Gilliam lectured and taught art at various institutions.

Gilliam accepted an invitation to lecture and teach for a week at the Memphis Academy of Arts in Memphis, Tennessee. On Sunday, February 23, 1975, he flew to Memphis to fulfill this business obligation.

Gilliam had a history of hospitalization for mental and emotional disturbances and continued to be under psychiatric care until the time of his trip to Memphis. In December 1963, Gilliam was hospitalized in Louisville; Gilliam had anxieties about his work as an artist. For periods of time in both 1965 and 1966, Gilliam suffered from depression and was unable to work. In 1970, Gilliam was again hospitalized. In 1973, while Gilliam was a visiting artist at a number of university campuses in California, he found it necessary to consult an airport physician; however, when he returned to Washington, D.C., Gilliam did not require hospitalization.

Before his Memphis trip, Gilliam created a 225-foot painting for the Thirty-fourth Biennial Exhibition of American Painting at the Corcoran Gallery of Art (hereinafter sometimes referred to as "the Exhibition"). The Exhibition opened on Friday evening, February 21, 1975. In addition, Gilliam was in the process of preparing a giant mural for an outside wall of the Philadelphia Museum of Art for the 1975 Spring Festival in Philadelphia. The budget plans for this mural were due on Monday, February 24, 1975.

On the night before his Memphis trip, Gilliam felt anxious and unable to rest. On Sunday morning, Gilliam contacted Ranville Clark (hereinafter sometimes referred to as "Clark"), a doctor Gilliam had been consulting intermittently over the years, and asked Clark to prescribe some medication to relieve his anxiety. Clark arranged for Gilliam to pick up a prescription of the drug Dalmane on the way to the airport. Gilliam had taken medication frequently during the preceding 10 years. Clark had never before prescribed Dalmane for Gilliam.

On Sunday, February 23, 1975, Gilliam got the prescription and at about 3:25 P.M., he boarded American Airlines flight 395 at Washington National Airport, Washington, D.C., bound for Memphis. Gilliam occupied a window seat. He took the Dalmane for the first time shortly after boarding the airplane.

About one and one-half hours after the airplane departed Washington National Airport, Gilliam began to act in an irrational manner. He talked of bizarre events and had difficulty in speaking. According to some witnesses, he appeared to be airsick and held his head. Gilliam began to feel trapped, anxious, disoriented, and very agitated. Gilliam said that the plane was going to crash and that he wanted a life raft. Gilliam entered the aisle and, while going from one end of the airplane to the other, he tried to exit from three different doors. Then Gilliam struck Seiji Nakamura (hereinafter sometimes referred to as "Nakamura"), another passenger, several times with a telephone receiver. Nakamura was seated toward the rear of the airplane, near one of the exits. Gilliam also threatened the navigator and a stewardess, called for help, and cried. As a result of the attack, Nakamura sustained a one-inch laceration above his left eyebrow which required four sutures. Nakamura also suffered ecchymosis of the left arm and pains in his left wrist. Nakamura was treated for these injuries at Methodist Hospital in Memphis.

On arriving in Memphis, Gilliam was arrested by Federal officials. On March 10, 1975, Gilliam was indicted. He was brought to trial in the United States District Court for the Western District of Tennessee, Western Division, on one count of violation of 49 U.S.C. §1472(k) (relating to certain crimes aboard an aircraft in flight) and two counts of violating 49 U.S.C. §1472(j) (relating to interference with flight crew members or flight attendants). Gilliam entered a plea of not guilty to the criminal charges. The trial began on September 9, 1975, and ended on September 10, 1975. After Gilliam presented all of his evidence, the district court granted Gilliam's motion for a judgment of acquittal by reason of temporary insanity.

Petitioners paid $9,250 and $9,600 for legal fees in 1975 and 1976, respectively, in connection with both the criminal trial and Nakamura's civil claim. In 1975, petitioners also paid $3,900 to Nakamura in settlement of the civil claim.

Petitioners claimed deductions for the amounts paid in 1975 and 1976 on the appropriate individual income tax returns. Respondent disallowed the amounts claimed in both years attributable to the incident on the airplane.

Gilliam's trip to Memphis was a trip in furtherance of his trades or businesses.

Petitioners' expenses for the legal fees and claim settlement described, supra, are not ordinary expenses of Gilliam's trades or businesses.

Opinion

Petitioners contend that they are entitled to deduct the amounts paid in defense of the criminal prosecution and in settlement of the related civil claim under section 162.[12] Petitioners maintain that the instant case is directly controlled by our decision in Dancer v. Commissioner, 73 T.C. 1103 (1980). According to petitioners, "[t]he clear holding of *Dancer* is . . . that expenses for litigation arising out of an accident which occurs during a business trip are deductible as ordinary and necessary business expenses." Petitioners also contend that Clark v. Commissioner, 30 T.C. 1330 (1958), is to the same effect as *Dancer.*

Respondent maintains that *Dancer* and *Clark* are distinguishable. Respondent contends that the legal fees paid are not deductible under either section 162 or section 212 because the criminal charges against Gilliam were neither directly connected with nor proximately resulted from his trade or business and the legal fees were not paid for the production of income. Respondent maintains that "the criminal charges which arose as a result of . . . [the incident on the airplane], could hardly be deemed 'ordinary,' given the nature of [Gilliam's] profession." Respondent contends "that the provisions of section 262 control this situation." As to the settlement of the related civil claim, respondent asserts that since Gilliam committed an intentional tort, the settlement of the civil claim constitutes a nondeductible personal expense.

We agree with respondent that the expenses are not ordinary expenses of Gilliam's trade or business.

Section 162(a) allows a deduction for all the ordinary and necessary expenses of carrying on a trade or business. In order for the expense to be deductible by a taxpayer, it must be an ordinary expense, it must be a necessary expense, and it must be an expense of carrying on the taxpayer's trade or business. If any one of these requirements is not met, the expense is not deductible under section 162(a). Deputy v. du Pont, 308 U.S. 488 (1940); Welch v. Helvering, [supra page 645]; Kornhauser v. United States, 276 U.S. 145 (1928). In Deputy v. du Pont, the Supreme Court set forth a guide for application of the statutory requirement that the expense be "ordinary," as follows (308 U.S. at 494-497)[13]:

12. At trial, petitioners asserted that the amounts paid were deductible under section 162 and section 212. On brief, petitioners do not address the deductibility of the amounts paid under section 212. Whether this constitutes a concession by petitioners is unclear; however, it does not affect the analysis herein, since the same criteria apply to the deduction of expenses under section 162 and section 212. . . .

13. [In Deputy v. du Pont the taxpayer had claimed a deduction for certain expenses arising from his sale of stock in the du Pont Corporation to a group of young executives. The purpose of the sale was to give these executives a financial interest in the corporation; because the corporation was prevented by legal restrictions from doing so, the taxpayer

In the second place, these payments were not "ordinary" ones for the conduct of the kind of business in which, we assume arguendo, respondent was engaged. The District Court held that they were "beyond the norm of general and accepted business practice" and were in fact "so extraordinary as to occur in the lives of ordinary business men not at all" and in the life of the respondent "but once." Certainly there are no norms of conduct to which we have been referred or of which we are cognizant which would bring these payments within the meaning of ordinary expenses for conserving and enhancing an estate. We do not doubt the correctness of the District Court's finding that respondent embarked on this program to the end that his beneficial stock ownership in the du Pont Company might be conserved and enhanced. But that does not make the cost to him an "ordinary" expense within the meaning of the Act. Ordinary has the connotation of normal, usual, or customary. To be sure, an expense may be ordinary though it happen but once in the taxpayer's lifetime. Cf. Kornhauser v. United States, supra. Yet the transaction which gives rise to it must be of common or frequent occurrence in the type of business involved. Welch v. Helvering, supra. Hence, the fact that a particular expense would be an ordinary or common one in the course of one business and so deductible under [§162(a)] does not necessarily make it such in connection with another business. . . . As stated in Welch v. Helvering, supra, pp. 113-114: ". . . What is ordinary, though there must always be a strain of constancy within it, is none the less a variable affected by time and place and circumstance." One of the extremely relevant circumstances is the nature and scope of the particular business out of which the expense in question accrued. The fact that an obligation to pay has arisen is not sufficient. It is the kind of transaction out of which the obligation arose and its normalcy in the particular business which are crucial and controlling.

Review of the many decided cases is of little aid since each turns on its special facts. But the principle is clear. And on application of that principle to these facts, it seems evident that the payments in question cannot be placed in the category of those items of expense which a conservator of an estate, a custodian of a portfolio, a supervisor of a group of investments, a manager of wide financial and business interests, or a substantial stockholder in a corporation engaged in conserving and enhancing his estate would ordinarily incur. We cannot assume that they are embraced within the normal overhead or operating costs of such activities. There is no evidence that stockholders or investors, in furtherance of enhancing and conserving their estates, ordinarily or frequently lend such assistance to employee stock purchase plans of their corporations. And in absence of such evidence there is no basis for an assumption, in experience or common knowledge, that these payments are to be placed in the same category as typically ordinary expenses of such activities, e.g., rental of safe deposit boxes, cost of investment counsel or of investment services, salaries of secretaries and the like. Rather these payments seem to us to

---

stepped in "to the end that his beneficial stock ownership in the du Pont Company might be conserved and enhanced." — Eds.]

> represent most extraordinary expenses for that type of activity. Therefore, the claim for deduction falls, as did the claim of an officer of a corporation who paid its debts to strengthen his own standing and credit. Welch v. Helvering, supra. And the fact that the payments might have been necessary in the sense that consummation of the transaction with the Delaware Company was beneficial to respondent's estate is of no aid. For Congress has not decreed that all necessary expenses may be deducted. Though plainly necessary they cannot be allowed unless they are also ordinary. Welch v. Helvering, supra.

Petitioners bear the burden of proving entitlement to a deduction under section 162. Welch v. Helvering, 290 U.S. at 115; Rule 142(a), Tax Court Rules of Practice & Procedure. Gilliam is a noted artist and teacher of art. It undoubtedly is ordinary for people in Gilliam's trades or businesses to travel (and to travel by air) in the course of such trades or businesses; however, we do not believe it is ordinary for people in such trades or businesses to be involved in altercations of the sort here involved in the course of any such travel. The travel was not itself the conduct of Gilliam's trades or businesses. Also, the expenses here involved are not strictly a cost of Gilliam's transportation. Finally, it is obvious that neither the altercation nor the expenses were undertaken to further Gilliam's trades or businesses.

We conclude that Gilliam's expenses are not ordinary expenses of his trades or businesses.

It is instructive to compare the instant case with Dancer v. Commissioner, supra, upon which petitioners rely. In both cases, the taxpayer was travelling on business. In both cases, the expenses in dispute were not the cost of the travelling, but rather were the cost of an untoward incident that occurred in the course of the trip. In both cases, the incident did not facilitate the trip or otherwise assist the taxpayer's trade or business. In both cases, the taxpayer was responsible for the incident; in neither case was the taxpayer willful. In *Dancer,* the taxpayer was driving an automobile; he caused an accident which resulted in injuries to a child. The relevant expenses were the taxpayer's payments to settle the civil claims arising from the accident. 73 T.C. at 1105. In the instant case, Gilliam was a passenger in an airplane, he apparently committed acts which would have been criminal but for his temporary insanity, and he injured a fellow passenger. Gilliam's expenses were the costs of his successful legal defense, and his payments to settle Nakamura's civil claim.

In *Dancer,* we stated as follows (73 T.C. at 1108-1109):

> It is true that the expenditure in the instant case did not further petitioner's business in any economic sense; nor is it, we hope, the type of expenditure that many businesses are called upon to pay. Nevertheless, neither factor lessens the direct relationship between the expenditure and the

> business. Automobile travel by petitioner was an integral part of this business. *As rising insurance rates suggest, the cost of fuel and routine servicing are not the only costs one can expect in operating a car. As unfortunate as it may be, lapses by drivers seem to be an inseparable incident of driving a car. . . .* Costs incurred as a result of such an incident are just as much a part of overall business expenses as the cost of fuel. [Emphasis supplied.]

Dancer is distinguishable.

In Clark v. Commissioner, supra, also relied on by petitioners, the expenses consisted of payments of (a) legal fees in defense of a criminal prosecution and (b) amounts to settle a related civil claim. In this regard, the instant case is similar to *Clark.* In *Clark,* however, the taxpayer's activities that gave rise to the prosecution and civil claim were activities directly in the conduct of Clark's trade or business. In the instant case, Gilliam's activities were not directly in the conduct of his trades or businesses. Rather, the activities merely occurred in the course of transportation connected with Gilliam's trades or businesses. And, as we noted in Dancer v. Commissioner, 73 T.C. at 1106, "in cases like this, where the cost is an adjunct of and not a direct cost of transporting an individual, we have not felt obliged to routinely allow the expenditure as a transportation costs deduction."

Petitioners also rely on Commissioner v. Tellier, 383 U.S. 687 (1966), in which the taxpayer was allowed to deduct the cost of an unsuccessful criminal defense to securities fraud charges. The activities that gave rise to the criminal prosecution in *Tellier* were activities directly in the conduct of Tellier's trade or business. Our analysis of the effect of Clark v. Commissioner, applies equally to the effect of Commissioner v. Tellier.

In sum, Gilliam's expenses were of a kind similar to those of the taxpayers in *Tellier* and *Clark;* however the activities giving rise to Gilliam's expenses were not activities directly in the conduct of his trades or businesses, while Tellier's and Clark's activities were directly in the conduct of their respective trades or businesses. Gilliam's expenses were related to his trades or businesses in a manner similar to those of the taxpayer in *Dancer;* however Gilliam's actions giving rise to the expenses were not shown to be ordinary, while Dancer's were shown to be ordinary. *Tellier, Clark,* and *Dancer* all have similarities to the instant case, however, *Tellier, Clark,* and *Dancer* are distinguishable in important respects. The expenses are not deductible under section 162(a).

We hold for respondent.

NOTES AND QUESTIONS

1. *Precedent.* The court in *Gilliam* relies on Welch v. Helvering (supra page 645) and Deputy v. du Pont (quoted at length in the court's

opinion). Disregarding the language of those two cases, how might they be distinguished?

2. *Appropriate time and place?* Suppose Gilliam's anxiety attack had occurred while he had been lecturing to a room full of students and he had injured one of them. Would his expenses then have been deductible?

3. *Causation.* (a) Is it the assumption of the court that the anxiety attack was brought on by the business trip — that is, that it would not have occurred but for the pressures associated with that trip? Or is the assumption that it was only a coincidence that the attack occurred while Gilliam was on a business trip? Should it matter? Compare our prior encounters with the problem of causation, supra at pages 487, 577, 592, and 606.

(b) Suppose that Gilliam had hired an attendant to accompany him on the trip, to soothe and, if necessary, restrain him. Would the cost have been deductible?

4. *The scrupulous lawyer and other extraordinary taxpayers.* (a) In Friedman v. Delaney, 171 F.2d 269 (1st Cir. 1948), cert. denied, 336 U.S. 936 (1949), the taxpayer, Friedman, was a lawyer. After one of his clients had become insolvent, Friedman met with creditors to work out a settlement and finally reached an agreement under which the client would pay $5,000 to the creditors. Friedman, relying on prior representations by the client, gave his word that this money would be forthcoming, but when Friedman asked for it, the client (who had anticipated cashing in an insurance policy to produce the money) had a change of heart and refused. Thereupon, Friedman paid the $5,000 himself. Claiming that the ethics of his profession and his own conscience required that he keep his word, he deducted the $5,000 as a business loss. The court denied the deduction on the ground that the payment was "voluntary." The court said that "it is obviously no part of a lawyer's business to take on a personal obligation to make payments which should come from his client, unless in pursuance of a previous understanding or agreement to do so."

(b) On the other hand, in Pepper v. Commissioner, 36 T.C. 886 (1961), another lawyer paid up when his client misbehaved and a deduction was allowed. The taxpayer had helped a client find financing for a business by approaching other clients, friends, and business acquaintances and by drafting the necessary loan and security arrangements. On discovering that the client was engaged in fraudulent manipulations and that the business was bankrupt, the taxpayer and his law partner paid about $65,000 to the victims after concluding that the payments were "imperative" in order to save their law practice. Welch v. Helvering, supra page 645, was distinguished on the ground that there "the expenditures were made to *acquire,* and not to *retain or protect,* the taxpayer's business." *Friedman* was distinguished on the ground that in that case "there was no contention that the money involved was paid to protect or promote Friedman's business." Does this mean that if Freidman had proved that his conduct had been a response not to moral scruple, but rather to profit-maximization goals, the deduction would have been allowed? If a payment is not unlawful, if its deduction would not contravene public policy in some fashion (a problem dealt with infra at page 660), and if it is made in a taxpayer's business judgment for profit-making reasons, should a deduction be denied merely because it is unusual, extraordinary, or unique?

In Goedel v. Commissioner, 39 B.T.A. 1, 12 (1939), a stock dealer was denied a deduction for premiums paid on insurance on the life of the President of the United States, whose death, he feared, would disrupt the stock market:

> Where, as here, the expenditure is so unusual as never to have been made, so far as the record reveals, by other persons in the same business, *when confronted with similar conditions*, . . . then we do not think the expenditure was ordinary or necessary, so as to be a deductible business expense within the intendment and meaning of the statute.

In Trebilcock v. Commissioner, 64 T.C. 852 (1975), aff'd, 557 F.2d 1226 (6th Cir. 1977), a deduction was denied for the cost of hiring an ordained minister "to minister spiritually to petitioner and his employees [and to conduct] prayer meetings, at which he tried to raise the level of spiritual awareness of the participants." The court said that such "benefits . . . are personal in nature." Suppose an employer who is a physical-fitness addict hires a physical education instructor to come to her place of business each morning and lead her employees in exercises. "Ordinary"? Deductible? If not, what if the employer hates all forms of physical exercise but thinks it might make her employees work better? What if an employer hires a yoga instructor to lead his employees in meditation each morning?

2. Reasonable Compensation

Section 162(a)(1) provides expressly for the deduction of a "reasonable allowance for salaries or other compensation for personal services actually rendered." This language seems to add little, if anything, to the basic requirement of §162 that deductible payments must be for genuine business expenses. The language was originally intended to *permit* taxpayers to deduct reasonable amounts "allowed" for salaries, even though not paid, for purposes of computing the World War I excess profits tax, but it has been relied on by the Service and the courts in *denying* deductions for salaries thought to be unreasonable. The instances of denial of deductions, however, almost always involve situations in which the salary is not truly a salary but rather a nondeductible payment masquerading as a salary. Probably the most common situation giving rise to denial is that of the closely held corporation where it is found that what purports to be a deductible salary is in fact a nondeductible dividend. The recipient of the payment may be either an employee who is a principal shareholder or an employee who is a child, parent, or other relation of a principal shareholder. The purported salary in these cases is referred to as a "disguised dividend." A purported salary might also be paid by the buyer of property to the seller in lieu of a higher purchase price, in order to give the buyer a deduction for what is in reality a capital expenditure.

As one might expect, the determination of what is a reasonable amount of salary is a difficult and uncertain matter, turning on all the relevant facts and circumstances. In Mayson Manufacturing Co. v. Commissioner, 178 F.2d 115, 119 (6th Cir. 1949), the court indicated in the following language the kinds of facts that are relevant:

> Although every case of this kind must stand upon its own facts and circumstances, it is well settled that several basic factors should be considered by the Court in reaching its decision in any particular case. Such factors include the employee's qualifications; the nature, extent and scope of the employee's work; the size and complexities of the business; a comparison of salaries paid with the gross income and the net income; the prevailing general economic conditions; comparison of salaries with distributions to stockholders; the prevailing rates of compensation for comparable positions in comparable concerns; the salary policy of the taxpayer as to all employees; and in the case of small corporations with a limited number of officers the amount of compensation paid to the particular employee in previous years. The action of the Board of Directors of a corporation in voting salaries for any given period is entitled to the presumption that such salaries are reasonable and proper. . . . The situation must be considered as a whole with no single factor decisive.

In Elliotts, Inc. v. Commissioner, 716 F.2d 1241 (9th Cir. 1983), the court added the profitability of the corporation to the *Mayson* list of facts bearing on reasonableness. In *Elliotts* the taxpayer's corporation had earned 20 percent on its equity, after the payment of the disputed compensation. The court viewed this favorable return on investment as evidence in support of the taxpayer's claim that compensation had been reasonable.

The possibility of disallowance of a deduction of a salary payment to be made by a corporation presents the tax practitioner with something of a dilemma where the client would prefer to retain the funds in the corporation if there is to be no deduction. One response to this dilemma has been to provide by agreement between the corporation and the employee that any payment that is subsequently held to be nondeductible by the corporation will be repaid to the corporation by the employee (who will also, of course, be the sole, or a principal, shareholder or the object of the bounty of such a person). Rev. Rul. 69-115, 1969-1 C.B. 50, holds that the employee can deduct the amount refunded if the obligation to do so was imposed before the payments were made and is enforceable under local law. It has been suggested that a repayment agreement is evidence of the unreasonableness of the salary. Charles Schneider & Co. v. Commissioner, 500 F.2d 148, 155 (8th Cir. 1974), cert. denied, 420 U.S. 908 (1975). In light of the difficulty of predicting outcomes in this area (take our word for it), does this seem fair?

In addition to the reasonable compensation limit of §162(a)(1), deductions for compensation are subject to a number of additional limitations. Under §162(m), added to the Code in 1993, publicly held corporations cannot deduct more than $1 million a year in pay to a chief executive officer or any other of its four highest paid employees. The $1 million limit on deductible compensation does not apply to performance-based compensation. Provided certain conditions are met, the term performance-based compensation includes stock options and other stock appreciation rights.

Of somewhat lesser importance, §§280G and 4999, added in 1984, restrict deductions for so-called golden parachute payments and impose an excise tax on such payments. Roughly speaking, golden parachute payments are substantial bonuses paid to corporate executives on termination of employment following a change in control of the corporation.

3. Costs of Illegal or Unethical Activities

Pre-1970 judicial doctrine. Before 1970 the courts, generally relying on the "ordinary and necessary" language of §162(a), disallowed deductions whose allowance, it was thought or assumed, would frustrate public policy. The state of the law was uncertain and controversial. In Tank Truck Rentals v. Commissioner, 356 U.S. 30 (1958), the Court held that fines paid by a trucking company for violations of state maximum-weight laws were nondeductible. At the same time, in Commissioner v. Sullivan, 356 U.S. 27 (1958), it permitted the deduction of the rent and wages paid in operating an illegal bookmaking establishment in Chicago, Illinois, even though payment of the rent was itself an illegal act under Illinois law. Earlier, in Lilly v. Commissioner, 343 U.S. 90 (1952), the Court had permitted the deduction of payments made by an optician to a physician who prescribed the glasses the optician made and sold; the Court relied on a finding that the practice was widespread. In Commissioner v. Tellier, 383 U.S. 687 (1966), a securities dealer was allowed to deduct legal expenses incurred when he was convicted of violating the Securities Act of 1933 and mail fraud statutes. Citing United States v. Gilmore, supra page 601, the Court said that the source of the expenses was business. (Why was the source not the taxpayer's purely personal, and extraordinary, defect of character, which led him down the path of crime?) The Court observed, "No public policy is offended when a man faced with serious criminal charges employs a lawyer to help in his defense."

Tellier seemed to limit the relevance of "ordinariness" and the frustration-of-public-policy doctrine, saying (383 U.S. at 694):

> Only where the allowance of a deduction would "frustrate sharply defined national or state policies proscribing particular types of conduct" have we upheld its disallowance. Commissioner v. Heininger, 320 U.S., at 473. Further, the "policies frustrated must be national or state policies evidenced by some governmental declaration of them." Lilly v. Commissioner, 343 U.S., at 97. Finally, the "test of non-deductibility always is the severity and immediacy of the frustration resulting from allowance of the deduction." Tank Truck Rentals v. Commissioner, 356 U.S. 30, 35.

Despite the language quoted in this passage, in United Draperies v. Commissioner, 340 F.2d 936 (7th Cir. 1964), the court had disallowed the deduction (in the years 1957 through 1960) of kickbacks from a drapery company to officers and employees of customers in the business of manufacturing mobile homes. The taxpayer had been extremely successful and its practices did not violate any state law. Distinguishing the *Lilly* case on the ground that there the practice was widespread, the court stated, "As a matter of common knowledge we are convinced that the mores of the marketplace of this nation is not such that 'kick-backs' by vendor-suppliers to the officers or employees of customers, while they do occur, are an ordinary means of securing or promoting business." 340 F.2d at 938.

The Tax Reform Act of 1969 amendments to §162. In 1969 Congress responded to complaints about the murkiness of the law and about the fact that the Internal Revenue Service was making decisions about what did and did not violate public policy[14] by adding to §162 three new subsections, §162(c), (f), and (g).

Section 162(f) flatly prohibits the deduction of "any fine or similar penalty paid to a government for violation of any law."

Section 162(c) covers bribes and kickbacks. Section 162(c)(1) prohibits the deduction of any illegal bribe or kickback to a government employee and (as amended in 1982) bribes or kickbacks to employees of foreign governments "if the payment is unlawful under the Foreign Corrupt

14. Compare this objection to the objection to the decision in the *Bob Jones University* case, supra page 501. See Note 1, page 509.

Practices Act of 1977."[15] Section 162(c)(2) covers illegal payments to people other than government employees, "but only if [the] law is generally enforced." And §162(c)(3), added in 1971, disallows deductions for kickbacks, rebates, or bribes by physicians, suppliers, and other providers of services or goods in connection with Medicare or Medicaid, regardless whether the payment is illegal.

Section 162(g) disallows deductions for the punitive two-thirds portion of damages paid for criminal violations of the antitrust provisions found in the Clayton Act.

The Senate report on these amendments states that the statute "is intended to be all-inclusive" and that "[p]ublic policy, in other circumstances, generally is not sufficiently clearly defined to justify the disallowance of the deductions." S. Rep. No. 91-552, 91st Cong., 1st Sess. 274 (1969), 1969-3 C.B. 423, 597. In recommending further amendments to §162 in 1971, a Senate report stated that the "committee continues to believe that the determination of when a deduction shall be denied should remain under the control of Congress." S. Rep. No. 92-437, 92d Cong., 1st Sess. (1971), 1972-1 C.B. 559, 599. Future disputes should therefore focus largely on the statutory language. See Rev. Rul. 74-323, 1974-2 C.B. 40, holding that advertising expenses by an employment agency were deductible although in violation of the Civil Rights Act of 1964, since the public policy doctrine was preempted by §162(c), (f), and (g), which do not apply to the expenses at issue. In Max Sobel Wholesale Liquors v. Commissioner, 630 F.2d 670 (9th Cir. 1980), acq., however, the court avoided §162(c) and allowed as an exclusion from gross income, as part of the cost of goods sold, the cost of extra liquor transferred to some customers in violation of state minimum-price law. The court conceded that because of §162(c) the cost of the extra liquor would not be allowable as a deduction, but held that that provision does not affect items that are considered to constitute adjustments in the selling price. On the other hand, in Car-Ron Asphalt Paving Co. v. Commissioner, 758 F.2d 1132 (6th Cir. 1985), a deduction was denied for kickbacks by a paving subcontractor to an employee of a general contractor. The court cited, among other cases, *United Draperies,* supra, and stated that the "evidence does not in any way establish that the payment of kickbacks is common or ordinary in the construction business generally or in the paving business in particular." The court also said that the kickbacks were not necessary to the taxpayer's business, which had prospered on the basis of contracts not dependent on such payments. The court distinguished its decision in Bertolini Trucking Co. v. Commissioner, 736 F.2d 1120 (6th Cir. 1984), a case with facts

15. The pre-1982 version of this provision was in part the basis in 1976 for a large-scale and well-publicized attack by the IRS and the SEC on "questionable foreign payments" and secret "slush funds" used to make such payments.

quite similar to those in *Car-Ron Asphalt* (the person taking the bribe was the same in each case), on the ground that in that case the Commissioner has conceded that the bribe had been "necessary," whereas in *Car-Ron Asphalt* the Tax Court had found that the bribe was not "necessary" or "ordinary."

In Lincoln v. Commissioner, 50 T.C.M. 185 (1985), the taxpayer was denied a theft loss deduction where he had put up $140,000 in a scheme in which he thought he was buying $600,000 of stolen money; in fact, the scheme was a ruse devised by his confederates to bilk him of his own money.

See also §280E, denying deductions for expenses incurred in drug trafficking.

What would be the outcome under present law in each of the cases summarized supra at page 661?

Taxes paid to disfavored nations. In general, persons that pay income taxes to foreign countries but are subject to United States income tax on their worldwide income may credit the foreign tax payments against their United States income tax liability. See §901. This credit is subject to a number of limitations, but in its most simple form the credit allows United States taxpayers to reduce their tax liability by the amount of the foreign tax paid. This credit is not available, however, for taxes paid to countries the United States does not recognize, to countries with which the United States does not have current diplomatic relations, and to countries that the Secretary of State designates as supporters of international terrorism. §901(j)(2). The credit also is not available for taxes paid to South Africa, so long as that nation is not in compliance with the Comprehensive Anti-Apartheid Act of 1986. Taxes that do not qualify for the credit can still be deducted against income. A deduction, however, is worth less than a credit (which reduces taxes dollar-for-dollar).

Remaining scope for judicial development. The Service seems to have conceded that the post-1969 limitation on the frustration-of-public-policy doctrine applies to §212 as well as §162(a). See Regs. §§1.162-1(a) and 1.212-1(p). The Service continues, however, to apply that doctrine to losses deducted under §165. See Rev. Rul. 77-126, 1977-1 C.B. 47 (no deduction under §165 for loss of "coin-operated gaming devices" seized and forfeited for failure to pay wagering taxes); Holt v. Commissioner, 69 T.C. 75 (1977), aff'd, 611 F.2d 1160 (5th Cir. 1980) (no deduction under §165 for loss of truck, trailer, and one ton of marijuana, seized from taxpayer while he was engaged in his business of trafficking in marijuana); Mazzei v. Commissioner, 61 T.C. 497 (1974) (denying a theft loss to a taxpayer who was defrauded by his confederates in a scheme to make counterfeit money; although the case involved a pre-1970 year, the Service would presumably contend for the same result in later years since the deduction was claimed under §165).

STEPHENS v. COMMISSIONER

905 F.2d 667 (2d Cir. 1990)

Background

In September of 1981, Stephens and other defendants were indicted for participating in a scheme to defraud Raytheon, a Delaware corporation doing business in the United States and in foreign countries. Following a jury trial, Stephens was convicted in December of 1982 of four counts of wire fraud . . . ; one count of transportation of the proceeds of fraud in interstate commerce . . . ; and one count of conspiracy. . . .

Stephens was sentenced on December 3, 1982. . . .

In pronouncing sentence, the sentencing judge agreed [with a recommendation of the U.S. Attorney] that Stephens ought to make restitution to Raytheon. After emphasizing that she "believe[d] a period of imprisonment is absolutely necessary in this case not only for the protection of the public but because we cannot ignore the seriousness of the crimes for which you stand convicted," and "that [Stephens was among] the most culpable," the judge added, "Now, this Court does believe that Raytheon must get its money back. I'm just firmly convinced of that. . . . I can and shall require restitution from the principals of the [corporate defendant] because you, in my view, the principals . . . defrauded Raytheon. . . . I'm going to see to it that you give Raytheon its money back."

On each of the counts of wire fraud, Stephens was sentenced to a concurrent 5-year prison term and a $1,000 fine. On the conspiracy count, he was sentenced to a concurrent prison term of 5 years and a $10,000 fine. On the count of interstate transportation of the proceeds of fraud, Stephens was sentenced to a consecutive 5-year prison term and a $5,000 fine; execution of this consecutive prison term, but not the fine, was suspended, and Stephens was placed on 5 years of probation, on the condition that he make restitution to Raytheon in the amount of $1,000,000.

The $1,000,000 represented $530,000 in principal, the amount which was initially embezzled from Raytheon, and $470,000 in interest. Stephens was taxed upon his receipt of the $530,000 in 1976. In 1984, as part of a settlement agreement with Raytheon in connection with two civil actions Raytheon had brought against Stephens, Stephens turned over to Raytheon the $530,000 fund, and executed a $470,000 promissory note, representing the interest. In an Amended 1984 Tax Return, Stephens claimed as a deduction the $530,000 restitution payment. . . .

Discussion

As Stephens and the Commissioner agree, Stephens' restitution payment is deductible, if at all, pursuant to Section 165(c)(2) of the Tax Code, which permits an individual to deduct any uncompensated loss sustained during the taxable year, incurred in any transaction entered into for profit, though not connected with a trade or business. . . . Deductions under Section 165 have been disallowed by the courts, however, where "the allowance of a deduction would 'frustrate sharply defined national or state policies proscribing particular types of conduct.' . . ." Commissioner v. Tellier, 383 U.S. 687, 694 (1966) (quoting Commissioner v. Heininger, 320 U.S. 467, 473, (1943)). Thus, "the 'test of nondeductibility always is the severity and immediacy of the frustration resulting from allowance of the deduction.'" Id. (quoting Tank Truck Rentals, Inc. v. Commissioner, 356 U.S. 30, 35 (1958)).

For example, in *Tellier*, the Tax Court disallowed a deduction for expenses incurred in the successful defense of a criminal prosecution. This Court reversed, and the Supreme Court affirmed. Emphasizing that "the 'policies frustrated must be national or state policies evidenced by some governmental declaration of them,'" id. (quoting Lilly v. Commissioner, 343 U.S. 90, 97 (1952)), the Court concluded that "[n]o public policy is offended when a man faced with serious criminal charges employs a lawyer to help in his defense." Id. On the other hand, in Tank Truck Rentals, Inc. v. Commissioner, 356 U.S. 30 (1958), the Supreme Court affirmed the disallowance of a deduction of fines paid by a trucking company for violations of state maximum weight laws. Id. at 35-36. . . .

Although *Tellier* and *Tank Truck Rentals* were both decided pursuant to Tax Code provisions relating to business expenses, the test for nondeductibility enunciated in those opinions is applicable to loss deductions under Section 165. Accordingly, the issue before us is whether a deduction for Stephens' restitution payment of embezzled funds to Raytheon so sharply and immediately frustrates a governmentally declared public policy that the deduction should be disallowed.

We note at the outset that . . . taxpayers who repay embezzled funds are ordinarily entitled to a deduction in the year in which the funds are repaid. . . . Clearly, no public policy would be frustrated if a restitution payment unrelated to a criminal prosecution were at issue; Stephens would be entitled to a deduction for repaying the embezzled funds to Raytheon.

The Commissioner, however, argues that because Stephens made the restitution payment in lieu of punishment, the deduction should be disallowed. Emphasizing that the sentencing judge suspended the consecutive 5-year sentence on the condition that Stephens make restitution to Raytheon, the Commissioner contends that allowing Stephens a deduction for the restitution payment would take "the sting" out of Stephens' punishment, and therefore would sharply and immediately frustrate public policy. See *Tank Truck Rentals,* 356 U.S. at 35-36. Because Stephens has already paid taxes on the embezzled funds in his 1976 tax return, however, disallowing the deduction for repaying the funds would in effect result in a "double sting.". . . The sentencing judge made no reference to these tax consequences at the sentencing hearing. Moreover, Stephens received a stern sentence: he was sentenced to five years in prison, and fined a total of $16,000 — the $5,000 fine which accompanied the suspended consecutive sentence was not, as we have noted, suspended. We believe that allowing Stephens a deduction for his restitution payment would not severely and immediately frustrate public policy.

However, having reviewed the cases that have sought to elucidate the meaning and scope of the public policy exception under Section 165, and finding them insufficiently decisive, we turn next to Section 162, the Tax Code provision on deductibility of business expenses, as an aid in applying Section 165. Prior to the codification of the public policy exception to deductibility of business expenses, the test for nondeductibility of business expenses and losses was the same: whether the deduction would severely and immediately frustrate a sharply defined national or state policy proscribing particular types of conduct, evidenced by some governmental declaration thereof. In 1969, Congress codified this public policy exception to deductibility of expenses in Section 162 of the Code, limiting the exception to: illegal bribes, kickbacks, and other illegal payments (subsection 162(c)); fines or similar penalties paid to a government for the violation of any law (subsection 162(f)); and a portion of treble damage payments under the anti-trust laws (subsection 162(g)). Congress intended these "provision[s] for the denial of the deduction for payments in these situations which are deemed to violate public policy . . . to be all inclusive. Public policy, in other circumstances, generally is not sufficiently clearly defined to justify the disallowance of deductions." S. Rep. No. 552, 91st Cong., 1st Sess., reprinted in 1969 U.S. Code Cong. & Admin. News 2027, 2311 (hereinafter S. Rep. 552).

The public policy exception to deductibility under Section 165 was not explicitly affected by the amendments to Section 162. The Internal Revenue Service summarized its view on the impact of the amendments in a Revenue Ruling:

> Congress codified and limited the public policy doctrine in the case of ordinary and necessary business expenses by amending section 162(c) of the Code, adding section 162(f) and (g) in the Tax Reform Act of 1969 . . . , and amending section 162(c) in the Revenue Act of 1971. . . .
>
> However, the rules for disallowing a deduction under section 165 of the Code on the grounds of public policy were not limited by Congress but remain the same as they were before 1969. Therefore, disallowance

> of deductions under section 165 is not limited to amounts of a type for which deduction would be disallowed under section 162(c), (f), and (g) and the regulations thereunder in the case of a business expense.

Rev. Rul. 77-126, 1977-1 C.B. 47, 48. The Tax Court, however, announced a different view: "[t]here is some question whether the public policy doctrine retains any vitality since the enactment of sec. 162(f)." Medeiros v. Commissioner, 77 T.C. 1255, 1262 n.8 (1981). The court observed that "[i]f sec. 162(f) was intended to supplant the public policy doctrine, in all likelihood it would disallow deductions under sec. 165(c)(1) as well as sec. 162(a), as both involved an expenditure incurred in a trade or business." Id.

Though Congress, in amending Section 162, did not explicitly amend Section 165, we believe that the public policy considerations embodied in Section 162(f) are highly relevant in determining whether the payment to Raytheon was deductible under Section 165. Congress can hardly be considered to have intended to create a scheme where a payment would not pass muster under Section 162(f), but would still qualify for deduction under Section 165. It is arguable that the converse is also true, that a payment imposed in the course of a criminal prosecution that does pass muster under Section 162(f) will escape the public policy limitations of Section 165. However, we need not decide in this case whether that is so.

Reference to Section 162(f) supports our conclusion that allowing Stephens a deduction for his restitution payment would not severely and immediately frustrate public policy. Two considerations drawn from Section 162(f) and the cases construing that provision combine to support our conclusion in this case. Whether either consideration alone would suffice is a matter we need not decide.

First, Stephens' restitution payment is primarily a remedial measure to compensate another party, not a "fine or similar penalty," even though Stephens repaid the embezzled funds as a condition of his probation. . . .

Our review of the proceedings at Stephens' sentencing convinces us that Stephens' restitution payment was more compensatory than punitive in nature. . . .

Second, Stephens' payment was made to Raytheon, and not "to a government.". . .

We conclude that Stephens' restitution payment was neither a fine or similar penalty, nor paid to the government. Thus, we hold that neither the public policy exception to Section 165, precluding a deduction when it would severely and immediately frustrate public policy to allow it, nor the codification of the public policy exception to deductibility of expenses pursuant to Section 162, bars deduction of Stephens' restitution payment. Accordingly, we reverse and remand to the Tax Court for further proceedings not inconsistent with this opinion.

QUESTION

In 1992, Jim had gross income of $100,000. All of his income was realized from the sale of stolen goods. Discuss whether the following expenses are, or should be, deductible.

(a) Payment to "get-away" driver used in four burglaries

(b) Three-hundred-dollar gift to "fence" who purchases stolen goods from Jim

(c) Costs of purchasing locksmith tools from retiring burglar

(d) Bribe to local police officer

(e) Cost of gun carried on burglaries

G. DEPRECIATION AND THE INVESTMENT CREDIT

1. General Principles

The basic idea. The allowance for depreciation is an offset against revenues for the cost of assets that are used for the production of those revenues; the assets must have a useful life of more than one year but will decline in value each year because of use or obsolescence, or both.[16] For example, suppose a farmer buys a tractor that she expects to use for five years. To properly determine her income from operation of the farm, we must take account of the cost of the tractor, since it is a "wasting asset." The full cost should not be treated as a cost of earning income in the year of purchase, since the tractor will have a substantial value at the end of that year. Allowing a deduction of the full cost in the first year would result in an understatement of income. On the other hand, allowing no deduction until the year in which the tractor is disposed of (sold, exchanged, or scrapped) would result in an overstatement of income until the year of disposition and, in that year, an understatement. What is needed is some allocation of a portion of the cost of the tractor to each year of its use. If the farmer buys land, there is no deduction for depreciation because it is not expected that the land will decline in value; it is not a wasting asset.

Economic depreciation and economic incentives. The economically accurate method for allocating the cost of the tractor, or any other asset, would be to treat as a cost of each year's operations the difference between the value of the asset at the beginning of the year and the

16. No deduction is allowed for a decline in the value of an asset used for personal purposes, such as an automobile used for personal purposes or a personal residence. The decline in the value of such assets is a nondeductible personal expense.

value at the end of the year. This is often referred to as "economic depreciation." For example, suppose the farmer buys the tractor for $10,000, puts it to use on the farm, and at the end of the first year of use could sell it for $8,000. The cost of use for the year, then, would be $2,000. No other figure accurately reflects economic reality and, correspondingly, the use of any other figure will misstate income. Some economists claim that any deduction in an amount other than economic depreciation will "distort" economic choice. Such people will claim, accordingly, that a deduction greater than economic depreciation should be thought of as a "subsidy" to investment, generally with the expectation, or hope, that the word "subsidy" will evoke at least mild disapproval. The notion of depreciation as a tax "subsidy," however, relies on a fictional concept of "neutral" tax rules. The concept of a neutral tax rule or set of rules is fictional because it requires that one ignore all the other actions of government that have affected the economy. Once the government starts raising taxes and spending money, it changes economic behavior in so many ways that the consequences are impossible to identify; neutrality, in the economic sense, no longer exists. What we are left with in the case of the tax treatment of depreciation, then, is the simple idea that any allowance for depreciation that is greater or less than economic depreciation will result in an understatement or overstatement of the true economic income from an investment, for better or worse. If accuracy in the measurement of income is what you want, economic depreciation is the proper standard, but accuracy may not be what you want.

Practicality. In any event, no one has ever seriously suggested that it would be feasible to determine each year the amount by which assets have declined in value. Accountants have long taken the position that the allowance for the cost of a wasting asset should be thought of simply as a device for spreading the total cost over time in some reasonably realistic manner. This spreading, or allocation, of cost over time involves three elements: (a) the determination of useful life, (b) taking account of salvage value, and (c) the application of a method of allocating the cost, in excess of salvage value, over the useful life. For example, if the farmer buys the tractor for $10,000, expects to use it for five years and then sell it for scrap for $2,000, the useful life is five years, the salvage value is $2,000, and the amount to be allocated over the five years is $8,000. One possible method of allocation would be to assign equal amounts of $1,600 to each year; this is called the "straightline" method. Other methods are described below.

Useful lives. The basic idea of determining the expected useful life of an asset is simple enough that it requires no discussion. The application of the idea, however, has proved to be difficult, particularly in the case of certain long-lived assets (e.g., factory buildings), complex, specialized machinery and equipment, and unique assets such as customer lists.

Salvage value. Salvage value is of much less importance than useful lives and method of allocation. Under the ACRS system that now applies to all tangible assets, salvage value is disregarded; that is, salvage value is assumed to be zero. This rule obviously favors taxpayers. It sacrifices accuracy for simplicity.

Methods of allocation. As indicated above, under the *straightline* method an equal portion of the total cost of the asset is allocated to each year. The deduction can be expressed as an annual percentage: for an asset with a useful life of five years, 20 percent a year; for an asset with a useful life of ten years, 10 percent a year; and so forth. This percentage is applied to the original cost (unadjusted basis). There are various accelerated methods, by which greater amounts are allocated to early years than to later years. Most taxpayers prefer to use accelerated methods since the effect is to increase deductions, and reduce income, in the early years of the life of an asset, at the price of reduced deductions, and increased income, in the later years. The advantage is deferral.

The currently most significant accelerated method is the *declining balance* method. Under this method, the straightline percentage is determined and then this percentage is increased by a specified factor. The resulting percentage is applied to the cost of the asset reduced by the amounts previously deducted. For example, suppose an asset costs $10,000 and has an expected life of ten years and a zero salvage value. Under the straightline method, the annual deduction would be 10 percent of $10,000, or $1,000. Suppose the declining balance factor is 200 percent (which is referred to as the double, or 200 percent, declining balance method). The amount of the deduction in the first year would be double the straightline method, or 20 percent, or $2,000. The next year the same percentage is used, but it is applied to the balance of the original $10,000 cost after subtracting the $2,000 already deducted. The balance would be $8,000 and the deduction would be $1,600. The balance the next year would be $6,400 and 20 percent of that would be $1,280. And so forth. At some point, this method produces a deduction less than would be produced by straightline; and it never reaches zero. Under the present system, however, when the point is reached where the straightline amount exceeds the declining balance amount, the taxpayer switches to straightline.

The other major accelerated method is the *sum-of-the-years-digits-method.* It is no longer of much practical importance for tax purposes.[17]

17. Under this method a changing fraction is applied each year to the original cost of the asset. The numerator of the fraction for a given year is the number of years remaining in the asset's useful life, including the current year, and the denominator, which remains constant, is the sum of the numerals representing each year of the asset's useful life. For example, suppose an asset has a useful life of five years. The denominator is 15 (1 + 2 + 3 + 4 + 5). In the first year the numerator is 5; in the second year, 4; etc.

It would be possible, of course, to use a method under which deductions are lower in the early years of an asset than in the later years. In fact, if an asset produces a steady stream of income over its useful life, the method that corresponds with economic depreciation has this characteristic (that is, the characteristic of rising each year). The possibility of a "decelerated" (sometimes referred to as "sinking fund") method as a basic or general method of cost recovery is only of theoretical importance. In recent years, it has not been thought of as a serious basic alternative for tax purposes.

Other methods are also possible (and, until 1981, were authorized for tax purposes if a taxpayer could establish that they were "reasonable" (see §167(a) and (b) and §168(a), (c), and (e)), including methods based on production, on use, or on predicted income.

Rapid amortization. The Code contains a number of provisions allowing "rapid amortization" for various types of assets such as child-care facilities (§188), pollution control facilities (§169), and railroad rolling stock (§184).

The first year of service. There is a practical problem of how much of a deduction to allow for an asset that is first used during a taxable year but is not used for the whole year. The question is, just how accurate does one want to be? One possibility would be to prorate the deduction on a daily basis, but that could be more trouble than it is worth. The practical compromise under present law is described below; the rules are referred to as the "applicable convention."

Component depreciation. Another problem of practicality is how far to go in allowing, or requiring, different rates of depreciation for different components of an asset. For example, in the case of a building, should there be separate rates for the structure, the roof, the elevators, the plumbing and wiring, the air-conditioning equipment, etc.?

Basis and gain or loss on disposition. The deduction for depreciation, or cost recovery, results, for tax purposes, in a reduction of basis. In fact, the basis is reduced if depreciation is allowable, even if the deduction is not taken. See §1016(a)(2). If the depreciation deduction happens to correspond exactly with economic reality, adjusted basis will correspond exactly with market value. Otherwise there will be a gain or loss that will be reported on disposition of the asset.

Recapture. Generally, when a business asset is disposed of, any gain is treated as capital gain. See infra page 829. But the depreciation deduction is an offset to ordinary income. For example, suppose that a farmer buys a tractor for $10,000 and over the first three years of its use claims depreciation deductions of $6,000, leaving an adjusted basis of $4,000. Now suppose the tractor is sold for $5,000. The gain is $1,000. But for the "recapture" rule, adopted in 1962, that gain would be treated as capital gain. Capital gain treatment seems wrong since the gain is in a sense a recovery of what turned out to be an excess reduction of ordinary income by virtue of depreciation deductions. In the case of personal property such as tractors (and other equipment and machinery), the Code now provides that any gain on disposition is treated as ordinary income to the extent of prior deductions for depreciation. §1245. Thus, in our example, the gain of $1,000 would be treated as ordinary income. If the tractor had been sold for $11,000, the gain would consist of $6,000 of ordinary income (the amount of depreciation previously taken) and $1,000 of capital gain. The recapture rule for real property (buildings, etc.) is more complicated, but is of little continuing importance since virtually all depreciation on real property is now straightline and the amount subject to recapture for such property is the excess of accelerated over straightline depreciation. See §1250.

Investment tax credit. The depreciation deduction has been supplemented, from time to time, by a series of investment tax credits. As the term implies, an investment tax credit gives a taxpayer a one-time credit upon purchase of a qualifying asset. Perhaps the most important investment tax credit was adopted in 1981 and generally applied to tangible depreciable property other than real estate. Taxpayers purchasing such property received a tax credit equal to 10 percent of the purchase price. In effect, the government paid 10 percent of the cost of all qualifying property. (Recall that while a deduction simply reduces taxable income, a credit produces a dollar-for-dollar reduction in taxes owed. See supra page 51.)

2. History

The depreciation deduction has been part of the modern income tax since its inception. In the early years of the tax, the debate over the deduction was cast in terms of what was a realistic allowance — one that accorded with economic reality. The basic rule was that useful lives were determined on an individual basis, according to all the "facts and circumstances" relating to particular assets as they were used by each taxpayer. The tax law now deviates from that ideal in two important respects. First, the useful life of tangible assets is no longer determined on an individualized basis; instead, each tangible asset falls within a specific category of assets and must be depreciated over the recovery period applicable to that category. For example, automobiles fall within the category of five year property and are depreciated over that period. Second, and most important, for tangible assets at least, tax depreciation is no longer intended to mirror economic depreciation. Instead, Congress has deliberately provided taxpayers with a deduction in excess of the anticipated decline in value of the asset, in the hopes of thereby stimulating investment. This favorable treatment has been brought about by assigning each category of assets a useful life for tax purposes below the actual useful lives, so that, for example, an asset that might be expected to last eight years is given a five-year useful life. In addition, within the prescribed recovery period, taxpayers have been allowed to use methods of depreciation that concentrate deductions in the early years of that period. Finally, the depreciation deduction has been supplemented, from time to time, by investment tax credits, described supra page 673.

Increasingly favorable cost of recovery rules were passed in the Eisenhower, Kennedy, and Nixon administrations. The trend toward generous depreciation allowances and investment tax credits reached its zenith in the 1981 Economic Recovery Tax Act, passed in the first year of the Reagan administration. This Act combined short useful lives, accelerated methods of depreciation that concentrated the deduction in the first years of that useful life, and investment tax credits. The net effect was as favorable, for some capital investments, as a rule that allowed the taxpayer to deduct the entire amount of the investment in the first year of service. Again, the motive for the generous cost of recovery rules was the desire to stimulate investment. Since 1981, fiscal pressures have led to a scale-back of depreciation and the investment tax credit. After a series of minor downward adjustments to the cost recovery system, Congress in 1986 repealed the investment tax credit, increased the useful lives for many assets, and changed the method of depreciation to lessen the deductions available in the first few years of service. Depreciation has been the subject of further, albeit minor, reductions in more recent years.

3. Basic Rules

a. *Tangible assets depreciable under §168.* Tangible assets placed in service after 1980 are depreciated under the rules of §168, described below.

Recovery period. The useful life or (to use the statutory term) recovery period for some assets is stated directly in the statute. For example, automobiles are subject to a five year recovery period. §168(c), (e)(3). The recovery period for other assets is defined with respect to Asset Depreciation Range Class Life tables published by the Treasury Department. §168(e)(1), (i). Cost recovery begins not when property is acquired but when it is "placed in service."

Personal property: basic recovery periods. For personal property there are now recovery periods for six different classes of property — three-year property (e.g., certain special tools and racehorses more than two years old when placed in service); five-year property (e.g., computers, typewriters, copiers, trucks, cargo containers, and semiconductor manufacturing equipment); seven-year property (e.g., office furniture, fixtures and equipment, railroad tracks, and single-purpose agricultural and horticultural structures); ten-year property (e.g., assets used in petroleum refining); fifteen-year property (e.g., sewage treatment plants and telephone distribution plants); and twenty-year property (e.g., municipal sewers).

Personal property: basic method. The method prescribed for personal property is 200 percent declining balance for three-, five-, seven-, and ten-year property and 150 percent for fifteen- and twenty-year property, shifting to straightline when that produces larger deductions. A half-year convention is used for the first year of service; that is, for the first year the rate is half of what it would be for a full year (as if the asset were placed in service exactly in the middle of the year, without regard to when it was actually placed in service). If, however, more than 40 percent of all property is placed in service in the last quarter of the taxable year, a mid-quarter convention applies. A half-year's deduction is allowed in the year of disposition.

Personal property: optional recovery periods and method. Taxpayers have the option of using certain recovery periods and methods that tend to delay deductions.

Real property: basic recovery periods. The recovery periods for real property are 27.5 years for residential rental property and 39 years for other real property.

Real property: basic method. The method for real property is straightline. The first-year applicable convention is that the full-year deduction is prorated according to the number of months during which the property is in service during the year. Similarly, in the year of disposition, the deduction is prorated according to months of service. Component depreciation is not permitted; the recovery period and method used for a building as a whole must be used for all its components that are real property.

Real property: optional recovery periods and method. Taxpayers may use optional longer useful lives.

Recapture. There are complex rules for recapture for both real and personal property, but their practical significance is substantially reduced now that there is no longer any advantage to long-term capital gain. The recapture rule does, however, transform capital gain, which can be offset by capital losses, into ordinary gain, which cannot be offset by capital losses (except for $3,000 per year for individuals). See infra page 829. Recapture also remains significant in two other situations. First, recapture gain is not eligible for the installment method. §453(i). Second, the amount of recapture gain reduces the amount of the deduction in the case of a gift of property to a charity. §170(e).

Limited expensing. Up to $17,500 of the cost of certain property (roughly, all personal property) used in a trade or business may be treated as a current expense. §179. This deduction may not exceed the income from the business in which the property is used and is phased out, dollar for dollar, as total investment exceeds $200,000.

Investment credit. The investment credit was repealed in 1986.

Intangible assets. Intangible assets, such as patents and copyrights, are subject to §167 and are not eligible for the accelerated statutory methods of depreciation described above. In general, such assets must be depreciated on a straight-line basis. Intangible assets that are purchased rather than created "in-house" are generally subject to new §197, discussed immediately below.

4. Goodwill and Other Intangibles

An individual who acquires more than one asset in a single transaction must allocate a portion of the purchase price to each asset. The allocation is made on the basis of the relative fair market value of the assets as of the date of purchase. Under this rule, the purchase of a business is treated as the purchase of the individual assets of the business. In many cases, tangible assets and intangible assets such as copyrights or patents will account for the entire purchase price. In some cases, however, some portion of the purchase price will be attributable to a different sort of intangible, such as the enterprise's reputation, loyal customers, or skilled work force. These sorts of intangibles are sometimes referred to collectively as the enterprise's going concern value or goodwill. A business with a high going concern value may be worth far more than the sum of its tangible assets and discrete intangible assets, such as copyrights.

The treatment of going concern value, goodwill, and similar intangibles for purposes of depreciation has long been a bone of contention. For many years, the government has contended that such assets are nondepreciable goodwill. Taxpayers, on the other hand, have estimated useful lives for some of these assets and have depreciated the portion of the purchase price allocated to them over their useful lives. In 1993, the Supreme Court attempted to resolve a conflict among the circuits over the treatment of such assets in its decision in Newark Morning Ledger Co. v. United States, 113 S. Ct. 1670 (1993). The taxpayer in that case had paid $328 million to acquire a chain of newspapers and had allocated $67.8 million of that amount to an intangible asset denominated "paid subscribers." The $67.8 million was the taxpayer's estimate of the present value of future profits to be derived from the newspaper's current subscribers, most of whom were expected to continue to subscribe after the acquisition. The taxpayer presented experts who testified that, using generally accepted statistical techniques, they were able to estimate how long the average subscriber would continue to subscribe. The taxpayer then depreciated the $67.8 million on a straight-line basis over the estimated life of the asset. The government denied the deduction on the ground that the concept of "paid subscribers" was indistinguishable from goodwill, which had long been treated as nondepreciable. The Court (in a five to four decision) held that the taxpayer had in fact shown the asset had a determinable useful life, and allowed the deduction.

The decision in *Newark Morning Ledger Co.* threatened to embroil taxpayers, the Service, and the courts in a never-ending wave of fact-specific litigation. To understand why this is so, suppose you represent a client who in 1992 paid $2,000,000 for a well-regarded and highly successful restaurant. The restaurant's tangible assets were worth only $500,000; the remaining value was attributable to the reputation and skill of the current employees, the presumed loyalty of the current clientele, and the restaurant's reputation apart from its current employees. Under *Newark Morning Ledger Co.*, the remaining $1,500,000 is in theory depreciable. But how would one go about assigning values to the different intangibles described above? And how would one determine the useful life of those intangibles?

To end unproductive litigation, and to limit the damage to the fisc from aggressive taxpayer positions, Congress in 1993 passed §197, which provides for a 15-year amortization of a long list of intangibles. In connection with the acquisition of a business, these intangibles include goodwill, going concern value, the value of work force in place, trademarks, and the value of current relationships with customers or suppliers. Under §197, then, it no longer matters whether the premium paid in connection with a business is called by a general term such as goodwill or going concern value, or is divided among its component parts and allocated to work force in place or customer relationships. The premium will in any event be depreciable over 15 years.

Section 197 also applies to purchases of more traditional sorts of intangible assets, such as copyrights or patents (and for purchases of nonpatented or copyrighted knowhow, process, or similar items). The amortization period for such assets is now 15 years. The copyright, patent, or the like need not be purchased as part of the acquisition of a business to fall within the ambit of §197 — any purchase will do. Self-created patents or copyrights are not covered by §197, but are subject to the general rules of §167.

H. DEPLETION AND INTANGIBLE DRILLING COSTS

Cost and percentage depletion. Although the Court in the *Baltic Mining Co.* case, supra page 167, stated that an "adequate allowance . . . for the exhaustion of the ore body" resulting from mining operations is not required by the Constitution, Congress has always allowed depletion to be deducted in computing taxable income from mining and other extractive activities.

Originally, the deduction was based on the cost of the property being depleted, and cost depletion is still authorized. §611. When this method is employed, the taxpayer allocates adjusted basis equally among the estimated recoverable units and deducts an appropriate amount as the units are sold. Thus, if the cost to be allocated is $100,000 and there are 100,000 recoverable tons, the depletion allowance will be $1 per ton, deducted as the ore is sold. This method of depletion, cost depletion, may simply be viewed as another method of depreciation. The provision considered in the *Baltic Mining Co.* case, providing that the depletion allowance might not in any circumstances exceed 5 percent of gross income, was repealed in 1916.

The second method available for recovering the cost of most depletable deposits is percentage depletion. The percentage depletion method ignores both the taxpayer's cost and the number of recoverable units. Instead, the taxpayer is permitted to deduct a given percentage of gross income (but not to exceed 50 percent of taxable income calculated before depletion is taken) as a depletion allowance. This method avoids the problem in cost depletion of estimating the number of recoverable units in the deposit — an estimate that may be only the wildest of guesses.[18] For the taxpayer, percentage depletion has the special attraction of an increasing depletion allowance as income rises, which ordinarily is when the deduction will save most in taxes. But percentage depletion just keeps rolling along, even after the taxpayer's full cost has been recovered. This is not an essential feature of percentage depletion, since the total depletion deductions *could* have been limited to the tax cost of the deposit, but the statute does not contain such a limitation.

Percentage depletion rates. The percentage of annual gross income that may be deducted as depletion ranges from 22 percent for certain minerals (such as sulfur and uranium) to 5 percent for other minerals (such as clay used in the manufacture of drainage and roofing tile). §613(b). The percentage depletion rates reflect the political clout of the various extractive industries. As the political influence of an industry changes, the percentage depletion rates sometimes change. For example, soon after the oil blockade was carried out by Arab members of OPEC, percentage depletion was eliminated for major oil and gas producers, but was retained for the relatively small, independent producers and royalty owners (though even for them it was reduced from 22 percent to 15 percent). Many explanations have been given for these changes, but the most cogent appears to be that independent producers

18. Despite this, the taxpayer may have to compute depletion on a cost basis for some purposes (e.g., for purposes of the alternative minimum tax, discussed infra page 735), even though percentage depletion is used in determining taxable income.

and royalty owners were an effective lobbying group and were not as unpopular as the major oil and gas producers, whose images were tarnished by charges of collaboration with the blockading OPEC nations.

The concept of an "economic interest" in the depletable mineral. There are many problems in determining which of the many persons with a financial stake in the extraction of a mineral are entitled to a deduction for depletion. Since the grant of depletion rights to one taxpayer may deny it to another in the chain of production, many cases have been litigated. The Supreme Court early formulated the notion of an economic interest in the mineral extracted as the touchstone. To have an economic interest, the taxpayer must have acquired an interest in the mineral in place and must look only to the mineral for return of his or her capital. Palmer v. Bender, 287 U.S. 551 (1933). For example, a landowner who allows another the right to drill for and extract oil in exchange for a royalty based on production has such an economic interest. See Thomas v. Perkins, 301 U.S. 655 (1937), and Kirby Petroleum Co. v. Commissioner, 326 U.S. 599 (1946). Thus, if the gross income is $100 and the royalty is 16½ percent, the operator uses $83.50 as the base for percentage depletion while the landowner takes percentage depletion on the $16.50.

Income subject to percentage depletion. The appropriate percentage depletion rate for a mineral (other than oil or gas) is applied to the "gross income from mining" to determine the taxpayer's percentage depletion deduction. In United States v. Cannelton Sewer Pipe Co., 364 U.S. 76 (1960), the taxpayer mined clay, processed it, and manufactured clay pipes and other related products. It claimed percentage depletion on its gross income from the sale of manufactured sewer pipe. The Court found that it was entitled to a percentage depletion only on the value of the clay up to the cutoff point of processes used by a nonintegrated miner before sale. The range of choice in *Cannelton* was from $1.60 (the going price for fire clay) to $40 per ton, the value of the finished pipe product, but for some other minerals the range is even more dramatic; for example, salt worth $10 at an early point in the extractive process might be worth $1,800 after it has been purified for table use and packaged in small containers for sale to consumers.

Today, gross income from mining is defined in §613(c) to include income from certain technical processes and from transportation. Section 613(c)(4)(G) now contains an explicit statement of the processes that qualify for sewer pipe clay.

Limits on percentage depletion. Section 613 limits the percentage depletion deduction to 50 percent of the taxable income from the property. The importance of this limitation may be illustrated as follows: Suppose that *X* Corp. sells 10,000 tons of a certain mineral for $100,000; that *X* Corp. has labor and other mining costs (exclusive of depletion) of $90,000; and that the depletion percentage for the mineral is 22 percent. *X* Corp.'s gross income from mining is $100,000 and its depletion deduction would therefore be 22 percent of that amount, or $22,000. But *X* Corp.'s taxable income from mining is only $10,000 and its percentage depletion deduction is limited to half of that amount, or $5,000.

Intangible drilling costs. Section 262(c) allows taxpayers that develop an oil, gas, or geothermal deposit (as opposed to buying a deposit from someone else) to deduct as current expenses the "intangible drilling and development costs."[19] These costs, roughly speaking, include materials that are used up in the drilling or development process and labor. See Regs. §1.612-4. Section 263(c) is a dramatic exception to the general rule that the costs of acquiring a capital asset must be treated as a capital expenditure; it is an important element in the economics of the extractive industries and in tax-shelter planning. To the same general effect as §263(c) are §§616 and 617, applying to other deposits.[20]

Percentage depletion is particularly beneficial to taxpayers that take advantage of §263(c). Such taxpayers will have deducted virtually all the costs of development before production of the mineral deposit and will have a cost basis in the deposit of zero (or close to it). Cost depletion will therefore be of no value. Percentage depletion, however, will be unaffected by the low basis.

Foreign natural resource interest. While the tax benefits provided the natural resource industries are often justified on the ground that they stimulate increased supplies of such resources in the United States, the benefits in the past normally applied to foreign activities also. Increasingly, this has changed. See, e.g., limitations to U.S. deposits in §613(b)(1)(B) and (b)(2); §613A(c); §616(d); §617(h)(1); §901(e).

The environment and natural resource tax benefits. It is interesting to speculate on the effect of the tax benefits to our natural resource industries on some of our current environmental problems. For example, have these benefits led to a lower price for gasoline and encouraged the use of more and larger automobiles than would otherwise have been the case? If so, has this contributed to the demise or stillbirth of public transportation in many parts of our country and substantial reliance on automobile transportation to the detriment of the quality of our air? Has this contributed to or created patterns of suburban living that might otherwise not have occurred? Does the fact that new metals and some virgin oil receive percentage depletion make recycling of used metals or used oil relatively less economical and therefore accelerate the exhaustion of natural resources and exacerbate waste disposal problems?

19. For large, "integrated" producers, however, 30 percent of intangible drilling and development costs must be amortized over a five-year period. See §291(b).

20. In the case of foreign mines, however, exploration and development costs are recovered by either (a) ten-year straightline amortization or (b) at the election of the taxpayer, as part of basis for cost depletion. See §616(d).

As previously noted, the tax benefits to promote home ownership may also have had a role in creating some of the present living and community habits. The federal and state highway trust funds, which pour a steady stream of gasoline tax and other revenues into highway construction, must also be given a leading role in such speculation.

I. "LEGITIMATE" TAX REDUCTION, TAX AVOIDANCE, AND TAX SHELTERS

1. The Tax Shelter Problem

"Legitimate" tax reduction. People regularly make investments and engage in other activities that are motivated by, and result in, substantial tax savings. Probably the clearest example is the purchase of tax-exempt bonds. Suppose that you can buy either a U.S. Treasury bond that pays interest at a rate of 9 percent or a tax-exempt bond with virtually identical characteristics except that the interest rate is 7 percent. If you buy the tax-exempt bond, your *sole* reason must be to save taxes. Purchase of the tax-exempt would make no sense whatsoever but for tax considerations. Yet most informed people would not describe the investment in tax-exempts, pejoratively, as a "tax shelter." They might even be uncertain about use of the less pejorative, but still disapproving, term "tax avoidance." Nor would the IRS or the courts hold (as they have done with other tax-motivated investments) that the tax benefit (exemption) is lost because the sole motive was tax reduction. Much the same observations can be made about a purchase of common stocks by a person who is clear in his or her own mind that but for the tax advantages of that investment (deferral of recognition of gain and capital gain), he or she would have bought bonds. People whose employers provide them with retirement benefits under qualified plans are not thought of (at least by lay people) as engaging in "tax avoidance." Nor are corporations that claim deductions for depreciation. State and local bonds, common stock, pension plans, and the use of depreciable assets would be important features of our economy without any tax inducements. "Tax avoidance" is generally thought to require something more unusual and more consciously structured to produce tax benefits, often by generating tax losses (allowable deductions in excess of income) that are used to reduce income from other sources (e.g., salaries or the income from the practice of medicine or law). A "tax shelter" is an investment or transaction structured to achieve "tax avoidance."[21] An

21. For a more precise and more limited definition, adopted for the purpose of

"abusive tax shelter" (a phrase recently popularized by the Treasury) is a tax shelter in which the tax benefits are a relatively large part of the total return and that pushes the law to its limits or beyond. It is useful to remember, however, that people who invest in tax shelters or engage in other tax avoidance activities may achieve tax reductions no greater than those achieved by investors in tax-exempt bonds,[22] common stocks, and qualified pension plans; in the aggregate, probably far less.

Most of the tax shelters described in the following pages generate paper losses that are used to offset income from other sources. Over the years a variety of rules have been adopted to prevent such tax avoidance, culminating in 1986 in the passive activity loss (PAL) rules, described at page 711. A description of tax shelters is important, however, for an understanding of the development of the law and the role of the various limitations that one now encounters.

The elements of a tax shelter. Tax shelters attempt to achieve either (a) deferral or (b) conversion (also known as transformation or exemption), or both. Deferral consists of pushing income into the future by incurring costs that are currently deductible and receiving the corresponding return from the investment in some future year. The tax advantage arises from the use of the funds that would otherwise be paid in taxes for the period of deferral. (See supra page 61.)

Conversion consists of converting ordinary income into tax-favored income, usually by taking deductions against ordinary income for the costs of investments that produce tax-exempt income, tax-free loans on the security of property with unrealized appreciation (for example, on an insurance or annuity policy), or capital gain.

The real estate tax shelter. The operation of a typical real estate tax shelter may be illustrated by the following simplified example. Assume that, before the enactment of the anti-tax-shelter legislation described below, an investor borrowed $100,000 at 9 percent and used the proceeds to buy an apartment building. In the first year, the investor paid $9,000 interest. Assume further that during the first year, the apartment building produced net rental income of $9,000. The net rental income represented profit after taking into account all expenses except that of the $9,000 interest payment on the loan used to purchase the building. Finally, assume that the building neither increased nor decreased in value. The rental income therefore exactly offset the interest expense and left the investor's wealth unchanged. For tax purposes, the investor

---

requiring registration with the IRS, see §6611(c). For another Code definition, used in applying a penalty for "substantial understatement" of tax, see §6662(b)(2)(C)(ii).

22. A person who has wealth can shelter the income from that wealth by investing in a tax-favored investment such as tax-exempt bonds. A person with a high income from performance of services can shelter that income only by investing in a tax shelter, whose tax losses can be used to offset the income from the performance of the services. Thus, attacks on tax shelters often have the effect of limiting tax benefits to people and firms with wealth to invest.

recognized rental income and deducted interest expense. In addition, however, the investor was able to deduct approximately $12,000 depreciation. Thus, a break-even economic investment produced a $12,000 tax loss. The investor could use this loss as a deduction to offset income from other sources.

Eventually, the tax and economic consequences of the investment would converge. The $12,000 depreciation deduction taken in the first year would reduce the basis of the building to $88,000. If the building were sold on the first day of the second year for its fair market value of $100,00, the taxpayer would recognize $12,000 gain. In effect, the taxpayer was required to "give back" the $12,000 of depreciation taken in the previous year.

The investment was nonetheless advantageous because the loss in the first year allowed the investor to defer taxes payable on income from other sources. The investment was even more advantageous if, as was generally the case, the gain recognized on sale qualified for favorable capital gain treatment.

Financial and other tax shelters. Real estate was not the only source of tax-shelter investments. Many tax shelters were based on financial investments. For example, an individual might borrow at 9 percent to buy a deferred annuity (that is, an annuity policy that did not start making payments until some time in the future) that provided a return of 8 percent. The 9 percent interest would be currently deductible, while the 8 percent appreciation would not be taxed until the payments on the annuity began. The loan might be secured by the annuity and made by the company that sold the annuity. A variant of this kind of tax shelter is discussed in the *Knetsch* case, infra at page 684.

Another form of tax shelter was based on the investment tax credit, which was a credit of up to 10 percent of the amount of certain investments, such as in machinery and alternative energy sources. Taxpayers could borrow to buy these investments and receive, as it were, a rebate of up to 10 percent of the amount of the (borrowed) purchase price. In addition, taxpayers could deduct the interest on the loan and the depreciation on the equipment. In the first year, the reduction in taxes might be many times the (nonborrowed) cash investment.

Overvaluation. The attractiveness of many tax shelters depended on overvaluation of an asset and the use of nonrecourse debt. For example, Rev. Rul. 77-110, 1977-1 C.B. 58, describes a motion picture tax shelter in which the investors purported to buy the picture for $2 million with $200,000 in cash and $1.8 million in the form of a nonrecourse promissory note payable out of the proceeds of its exploitation. The promoter of this tax shelter had bought the picture a few months earlier for $200,000, and there was nothing to suggest that it was worth more than that amount. The investors presumably were little concerned about the fact that they "overpaid" for the picture; they expected to recover their investment from depreciation deductions on an asset with a claimed basis of $2 million. Eventually, of course, the investors would default on the note and recognize gain from discharge of indebtedness, but the value of deferral would nonetheless have made the transaction advantageous. The motion picture scheme was thwarted by an IRS decision that "an obligation, the payment of which is so speculative as to create [only] contingent liability, cannot be included in the basis of the property." But other, less egregious shelters based on overvaluation were more successful. The use of overvaluation in tax shelters is illustrated by the *Estate of Franklin* and *Rose* cases, infra at pages 694 and 699.

2. The Judicial Response to Tax Shelters

KNETSCH v. UNITED STATES

364 U.S. 361 (1960)

Mr. Justice BRENNAN delivered the opinion of the Court.

This case presents the question of whether deductions . . . of $143,465 in 1953 and of $147,105 in 1954, for payments made by petitioner, Karl F. Knetsch, to Sam Houston Life Insurance Company, constituted "interest paid . . . on indebtedness" within the meaning of . . . §163(a). . . .

On December 11, 1953, the insurance company sold Knetsch ten 30-year maturity deferred annuity bonds, each in the face amount of $400,000 and bearing interest at two and one-half percent compounded annually. The purchase price was $4,004,000. Knetsch gave the Company his check for $4,000, and signed $4,000,000 of nonrecourse annuity loan notes for the balance. The notes bore 31/2% interest and were secured by the annuity bonds. The interest was payable in advance, and Knetsch on the same day prepaid the first year's interest, which was $140,000. Under the Table of Cash and Loan Values made part of the bonds, their cash or loan value at December 11, 1954, the end of the first contract year, was to be $4,100,000. The contract terms, however, permitted Knetsch to borrow any excess of this value above his indebtedness without waiting until December 11, 1954. Knetsch took advantage of this provision only five days after the purchase.[23] On

23. [The following summary of the basic transaction may be helpful:

Loan to Knetsch from Ins. Co.	$4,000,000	
Interest on loan (at 3½%)		$140,000
Investment by Knetsch in annuity	4,000,000	
Tax-free return (at 2½%)*		100,000
Net before tax effects		(40,000)
Tax saving from interest deduction, at tax rate of:		

December 16, 1953, he received from the company $99,000 of the $100,000 excess over his $4,000,000 indebtedness, for which he gave his notes bearing 3½% interest. This interest was also payable in advance and on the same day he prepaid the first year's interest of $3,465. In their joint return for 1953, the petitioners deducted the sum of the two interest payments, that is $143,465, as "interest paid . . . within the taxable year on indebtedness." . . .

The second contract year began on December 11, 1954, when interest in advance of $143,465 was payable by Knetsch on his aggregate indebtedness of $4,099,000. Knetsch paid this amount on December 27, 1954. Three days later, on December 30, he received from the company cash in the amount of $104,000, the difference less $1,000 between his then $4,099,000 indebtedness and the cash or loan value of the bonds of $4,204,000 on December 11, 1955. He gave the company appropriate notes and prepaid the interest thereon of $3,640. In their joint return for the taxable year 1954 the petitioners deducted the sum of the two interest payments, that is $147,105. . . .

[Roughly the same procedure was followed in December 1955.]

Knetsch did not go on with the transaction for the fourth contract year beginning December 11, 1956, but terminated it on December 27, 1956. His indebtedness at that time totalled $4,307,000. The cash or loan value of the bonds was the $4,308,000 value at December 11, 1956. . . . He surrendered the bonds and his indebtedness was canceled. He received the difference of $1000 in cash.

The contract called for a monthly annuity of $90,171 at maturity (when Knetsch would be 90 years of age) or for such smaller amount as would be produced by the cash or loan value after deduction of the then existing indebtedness. It was stipulated that if Knetsch had held the bonds to maturity and continued annually to borrow the net cash value less $1,000, the sum available for the annuity at maturity would be . . . enough to provide an annuity of only $43 per month.

The trial judge made findings that "[t]here was no commercial economic substance to the . . . transaction," that the parties did not intend that Knetsch "become indebted to Sam Houston," that "[n]o indebted-

90%	126,000
70	98,000
50	70,000
25	35,000
Net after-tax effects at tax rate of:	
90%	86,000
70	58,000
50	30,000
25	(5,000)

*In the form of loan based on increased value of annuity.

— Eds.]

ness of [Knetsch] was created by any of the . . . transactions," and that "[n]o economic gain could be achieved from the purchase of these bonds without regard to the tax consequences. . . ." His conclusion of law . . . was that "[w]hile in form the payments to Sam Houston were compensation for the use or forbearance of money, they were not in substance. As a payment of interest, the transaction was a sham."

We first examine the transaction between Knetsch and the insurance company to determine whether it created an "indebtedness." . . . We put aside a finding by the District Court that Knetsch's "only motive in purchasing these 10 bonds was to attempt to secure an interest deduction."[24] As was said in Gregory v. Helvering [infra pages 910, 911]: "The legal right of a taxpayer to decrease the amount of what otherwise would be his taxes, or altogether avoid them, by means which the law permits, cannot be doubted. . . . But the question for determination is whether what was done, apart from the tax motive, was the thing which the statute intended."

When we examine "what was done" here, we see that Knetsch paid the insurance company $294,540 during the two taxable years involved and received $203,000 back in the form of "loans." What did Knetsch get for the out-of-pocket difference of $91,570? In form he had an annuity contract . . . which would produce monthly annuity payments of $90,171, or substantial life insurance proceeds in the event of his death before maturity. This, as we have seen, was a fiction, because each year Knetsch's annual borrowings kept the net cash value, on which any annuity or insurance payments would depend, at the relative pittance of $1,000. . . . What he was ostensibly "lent" back was in reality only the rebate of a substantial part of the so-called "interest" payments. The $91,570 difference retained by the company was its fee for providing the facade of "loans" whereby the petitioners sought to reduce their 1953 and 1954 taxes in the total sum of $233,298 [about 80 percent of the "interest deduction"]. . . .

The petitioners contend, however, . . . that §264(a)(2) denies a deduction for amounts paid on indebtedness incurred to purchase or carry a single-premium annuity contract, but only as to contracts purchased after March 1, 1954. The petitioners thus would attribute to Congress a purpose to allow the deduction of pre-1954 payments under transactions of the kind carried on by Knetsch with the insurance company without regard to whether the transactions created a true obligation to pay interest. Unless that meaning plainly appears we will not attribute it to Congress. "To hold otherwise would be to exalt artifice above reality

24. We likewise put aside Knetsch's argument that, because he received ordinary income when he surrendered the annuities in 1956, he has suffered a net loss even if the contested deductions are allowed, and that therefore his motive in taking out the annuities could not have been tax avoidance.

and to deprive the statutory provision in question of all serious purpose." Gregory v. Helvering [infra page 910]. . . .

Congress . . . in 1942 denied a deduction for amounts paid on indebtedness incurred to purchase single-premium life insurance and endowment contracts . . . "to close a loophole" in respect of interest allocable to partially exempt income.

The 1954 provision extending the denial to amounts paid on indebtedness incurred to purchase or carry single-premium annuities appears to us simply to expand the application of the policy in respect of interest allocable to partially exempt income.[25] . . .

Moreover the provision itself negates any suggestion that sham transactions were the congressional concern, for the deduction denied is of certain interest payments on actual "indebtedness." And we see nothing . . . to suggest that Congress is exempting pre-1954 annuities intended to protect sham transactions. . . .

The judgment of the Court of Appeals is affirmed.

Mr. Justice DOUGLAS, with whom Mr. Justice WHITTAKER and Mr. Justice STEWART concur, dissenting. . . .

It is true that in this transaction the taxpayer was bound to lose if the annuity contract is taken by itself. At least, the taxpayer showed by his conduct that he never intended to come out ahead on that investment apart from his income tax deduction. . . . Yet as long as the transaction itself is not hocus-pocus, the interest . . . seem[s] to be deductible . . . as respects annuity contracts made prior to March 1, 1954, the date Congress selected for terminating this class of deductions. . . . The insurance company existed; it operated under Texas law; it was authorized to issue these policies and to make these annuity loans. . . .

Tax avoidance is a dominating motive behind scores of transactions. It is plainly present here. Will the Service that calls this transaction a "sham" today not press for collection of taxes[26] arising out of the surrender of the annuity contract? I think it should, for I do not believe any part of the transaction was a "sham." . . . The remedy is legislative. Evils or abuses can be particularized by Congress. . . .

25. [In 1964, Congress acted again in this field, by enacting §264(a)(3), which disallows (subject to certain exceptions) any deduction for interest on indebtedness incurred or continued to purchase or carry a life insurance, endowment, or annuity contract pursuant to a plan which "contemplates the systematic direct or indirect borrowing of part or all of the increases in the cash value of such contract."—Eds.]

26. Petitioners terminated this transaction in 1956 by allowing the bonds to be canceled and receiving a check for $1,000. The termination was reflected in their tax return for 1956. It might also be noted that the insurance company reported as gross income the interest payments which it received from petitioners in 1953 and 1954.

NOTES AND QUESTIONS

1. *Expenses.* Knetsch failed in a later attempt to deduct out-of-pocket expenses incurred in purchasing the annuity contract as a loss under §165(c)(2) or as an expense under §212. Knetsch v. United States, 348 F.2d 932 (Ct. Cl. 1965), cert. denied, 383 U.S. 957 (1966). See also §183.

2. *Tax economics.* In the first year of the investment, 1953, Knetsch paid interest at the rate of 3½ percent, a total of about $140,000. His investment increased in value at the rate of 2½ percent, or about $100,000, which was withdrawn tax free as a loan. Thus, from an economic perspective, apart from taxes, the loss was $40,000. In 1953, the top marginal rate was 91 percent. Assuming a marginal rate of 90 percent, if the interest had been deductible, the after-tax cost of the interest payment would have been only 10 percent of the $140,000, or $14,000, and the after-tax gain would have been $86,000. The numbers increased each year, as the growth in the value of the policy increased and as Knetsch borrowed more and more to pay interest, interest on interest, etc., but the relationships remained essentially the same.

3. *Gain on disposition.* The Court appears to have misunderstood the proper tax consequence of the termination of the transaction in 1956. Knetsch's basis for the annuity contracts was his cost of $4,004,000 — $4,000 in cash and $4 million borrowed from the insurance company. Each of the loans subsequent to the initial $4 million loan was used to pay interest; the loan proceeds were not invested in the annuity and, consequently, did not lead to any increase in the basis of $4,004,000. The proceeds on disposition were the $1,000 received plus the debt discharged, $4,307,000, or a total of $4,308,000 (see supra page 685). Thus, the gain was $304,000, which should have been treated as ordinary income (see §72(e)). The Court, however, seems to have assumed that the amount included in income in 1956 was only $1,000, the cash received. According to the record before the Court, the district court seems to have concluded that in 1956 Knetsch was entitled to a deduction of $138,000, arrived at by subtracting the total loan proceeds ($307,000), and the $1,000 received in 1956, from the total amount of interest paid over the three years the policy was in force ($441,000) and the initial cash payment ($4,000). Record at 41-42. Neither the government nor the taxpayer brief before the Supreme Court discusses the tax effects in 1956. One can understand why the taxpayer might not have wanted to raise the issue. The government may have been aware of the way the disposition was treated in 1956 and the way it should have been treated and may have decided to ignore the matter to avoid embarrassment or to avoid undercutting its basic argument, or both. Might the case have been decided differently if the tax realities of 1956 had been recognized?

The observation about the proper tax treatment in 1956 reveals a serious general problem for investors in insurance-based tax-avoidance schemes. If the investor must terminate the transaction before death (for example, because his or her income, and tax rate, decline), a huge tax liability may arise (though §1035 offers some opportunities for avoiding this kind of calamity by trading the original policy for a paid-up policy). More generally, investors in tax shelters often are ignorant of the adverse tax effects at the end of the transaction. It is difficult for people not trained in tax law to understand how they can have taxable income when they have received no cash, especially when the investment has been a loser apart from taxes. Promotional literature for tax shelters has often failed to reveal adequately the adverse tax consequences on termination. There may be many taxpayers who fail to report income from discharge of debt and whose omission is never discovered by the Service.

4. *Nonrecourse obligation.* If the debt to the insurance company had been with recourse, would the result have been different? What if the loan had been made by a bank (with recourse)? Should personal liability on the debt have been a cause for significant concern to Mr. Knetsch?

5. *Economic substance.* The loans from the insurance company to Knetsch were repayable at his option at any time, with no penalty. The obligations of the insurance company under the annuity contract, on the other hand, could not be changed by it without Knetsch's consent. In other words, Knetsch was entitled to earn interest from the insurance company on his annuity at the rate of 2½ percent as long as he lived, but he was free to pay off his 3½ percent loan from the insurance company and borrow elsewhere. He was also free to terminate the arrangement at any time. Anyone who thought that there was a significant possibility of a decline in the borrowing rate to less than 2½ percent might find this to be an attractive speculative investment. Do you think such a decline was a realistic possibility? What if the year were changed to 1981 and the rates were changed to 12 percent and 15 percent? Do you suppose Knetsch himself had substantial nontax economic objectives for entering into the transaction? What do the answers to these questions tell you about the role of taxpayer motive in cases of this sort?

6. *Statutory responses.* As the Court observed, after 1954, §264 expressly denied deductions for interest on debt of the sort involved in *Knetsch.* Would §163(d), adopted in 1969, also do the job?

7. *"Sham" as an argument.* The more closely one analyzes cases like *Knetsch,* the more difficult it may be to understand the theory on which they rest. Such cases may encourage government counsel, figuratively speaking, to put on a red, white, and blue cape, run into the courtroom yelling "sham, sham, sham," and do no more. The next case reveals that that strategy will not always work.

FABREEKA PRODUCTS CO. v. COMMISSIONER

294 F.2d 876 (1st Cir. 1961)

ALDRICH, Circuit Judge.

[At the time the transactions in this case occurred, certain bonds were available that sold on the bond market at a premium above their face value but could be "called" (that is, called in for redemption by the issuer) for face value (or a trifle above that amount). For example, bonds selling on the market at $115 could be called, and paid off, at $100. The experience with these kinds of bonds was that the risk of their being called was in fact negligible; the issuers simply did not call them. Nonetheless, under the law at the time of the transactions involved in the case, the entire amount of the premium over the call price could be claimed by the purchaser as an ordinary deduction after the bonds had been held for thirty days. Typically, the purchasers used the bonds as security for loans equal to the call price. The decision in the case involved three taxpayers, each with a different clever scheme of tax avoidance based on these bonds. Fabreeka Products Co. bought the bonds at $115, with borrowed funds of $100, then after thirty days distributed the bonds, subject to the debt, to its shareholders, who promptly sold them. The shareholders had a taxable dividend equal to the net amount of $15, but the corporation had a deduction for amortization in the same amount. While dividend payments ordinarily are not deductible by a corporation, in effect these dividends were. This tax benefit was the corporation's only motive for entering into the transaction. The other two schemes involved taxpayers named Friedman and Sherman, whose cases are described by the court in the passages that follow.]

These three cases illustrate that there is nothing more conducive to disagreement than the matter of interpreting a statute whose apparent meaning would produce in the particular instance a result distasteful to the court. The common question is how far a court should go in analyzing a transaction or series of transactions literally within a statute, in the light of a finding that a taxpayer's sole motivation was tax-avoidance, and interpreting the statute to deny a claimed deduction. The *Fabreeka Products Co.* and *Sherman* cases led to five different approaches in the Tax Court; the *Friedman* case to six. *Friedman* was based principally upon the court's prior divided decision in Maysteel Products, Inc., 1960, 33 T.C. 1021, which has since been reversed by a divided court in Maysteel Products, Inc. v. Commissioner, 7 Cir., 1961, 287 F.2d 429. A majority of the Tax Court has decided against the taxpayers and they seek review. . . .

In *Sherman* an individual taxpayer purchased similar (in fact, the same) bonds at a premium, wrote off the premium in thirty days, and sold them after six months, reporting the recovered premium as a long term gain. Had he sold at the price he bought (actually he fared less well), he would have had a net deduction of one-half of the premium. [At the time the case arose, taxpayers were entitled to a deduction of 50 percent of the amount of long-term capital gain.—Eds.] Again, the court's finding that the anticipated tax saving was the sole motive for the entire transaction was amply supported.

In *Friedman* the taxpayer, instead of selling such bonds, gave them to a charity, subject to the lien for the purchase loan. The charity's subsequent sale netted the premium for itself, and the taxpayer claimed two deductions, first for the amortized premium and second for the charitable gift. The government's anguish here is understandably intense because the taxpayer's bracket is such that if she is allowed both deductions she will show an over-all profit, thereby, in its opinion, demonstrating far too tangibly the blessedness of giving.

The government admits that all petitioners have brought themselves within the literal language of the statute. Nor can it say, except with tongue in cheek, that the transactions were shams. The brightness of the motive cannot be permitted to blind our eyes to the existence of substantive events. . . . The government's charge that there was "no reality to the transaction as an investment" amounts only to saying that it was not entered into for what it describes as "investment motives." It argues that these were "sophisticated and elaborate[27] tax avoidance schemes where taxpayers [were] willing to pay money out-of-pocket or to take some measure of risk to establish a claim to tax benefits in a much larger amount." But this describes neither a sham transaction, nor one unmarked by events or risks beyond the control of the taxpayer, nor one different in substance and effect from what it appeared to be on its face. Cf. . . . Knetsch v. United States [supra page 684].

Whatever their ultimate purpose, the taxpayers made actual "investments" in the ordinary sense of the word. They purchased the bonds. During the necessary holding period they incurred fully all of the risks of ownership, both that the bonds might decline in value, a real risk, as Sherman learned to his cost, and the possibilities that during that time they might be called. This latter exposure, however negligible it may have been in fact, was the very matter for which the statute provided the deduction. The subsequent sale or other transfers were not paper proceedings, but were transactions done legitimately every day. Other taxpayers might have done exactly the same thing, and if they had left no indicia of motive, their deductions would have been unquestioned.

27. This phrase came from Gregory v. Helvering [infra page 910]. We are not sure the government likes it too well. Later it uses the characterization "crude and blatant." This contradiction may be some indication of the government's difficulties. Nor do we think a dog is to be hanged simply by giving him a bad name. . . .

We may distinguish between general motives of tax avoidance, which admittedly of themselves cannot destroy an otherwise legitimate deduction, and the affirmative motive — of "investment" — which the government claims is needed to come within this statute. Nevertheless, unless Congress makes it abundantly clear, we do not think tax consequences should be dependent upon the discovery of a purpose, or a state of mind, whether it be elaborate or simple. The limitation which the government asks us to read into the statute, even if appealing in the particular instance, might readily, as we said in another connection in Eaton v. White, 1 Cir., 1934, 70 F.2d 449, at page 452, "create difficulties and uncertainties more objectionable in their results than any seeming inequities which would be eliminated or prevented." Granting the government's proposition that these taxpayers have found a hole in the dike, we believe it one that calls for the application of the Congressional thumb, not the court's.

Judgments will be entered vacating the decisions of the Tax Court and remanding the actions for further proceedings not inconsistent herewith.

NOTE AND QUESTIONS

In Goldstein v. Commissioner, 364 F.2d 734 (2d Cir. 1966), cert. denied, 385 U.S. 1005 (1967), the taxpayer, having won $140,000 in the Irish Sweepstakes in 1958, in that year borrowed $465,000 from a bank at 4 percent and prepaid $52,000 of interest. She used the proceeds of the loan to buy (for $465,000) U.S. Treasury notes with a face value of $500,000, bearing interest at 1½ percent and due in October 1961. She also entered into another transaction of the same sort with another bank. Her projected economic loss on these two transactions, assuming the bonds were held to maturity, was $18,500. Her expected tax saving was from two sources. First, the interest deduction would reduce her income in 1958 and returns on the Treasury notes would arise in later years. Thus, she would push part of her income from the sweepstakes into later years when it would be taxed at lower rates than if it were all taxed in 1958. Second, the interest deduction was to be an offset to the ordinary income from the sweepstakes, while a large part of the return would be capital gain (the difference between the purchase price of the bonds and notes and proceeds received at maturity). The taxpayer was a retired garment worker living on a modest pension and was totally unsophisticated in financial affairs. She followed the advice of her son, a certified public accountant (whose computation of the projected $18,500 economic loss was introduced by the government). The court upheld the Commissioner's denial of an interest deduction for the loans used to finance these transactions. It refused to follow

Knetsch and characterize the transactions as "shams," pointing out that the loans were made by independent financial institutions, that the "two loan transactions did not within a few days return all the parties to the position from which they started," that the banks could demand payment at any time, and that the notes were with recourse. In holding for the Commissioner, the court relied instead on the fact that the taxpayer's sole motive (given her son's careful computation) was tax avoidance. The court said that §163 "does not permit a deduction for interest paid or accrued in loan arrangements, like those now before us, that cannot with reason be said to have purpose, substance, or utility apart from their anticipated tax consequences." The court went on to opine (364 F.2d at 741):

> In order fully to implement [the] Congressional policy of encouraging purposive activity to be financed through borrowing, Section 163(a) should be construed to permit the deductibility of interest when a taxpayer has borrowed funds and incurred an obligation to pay interest in order to engage in what with reason can be termed purposive activity, even though he decided to borrow in order to gain an interest deduction rather than to finance the activity in some other way. In other words, the interest deduction should be permitted whenever it can be said that the taxpayer's desire to secure an interest deduction is only one of mixed motives that prompt the taxpayer to borrow funds; or, put a third way, the deduction is proper if there is some substance to the loan arrangement beyond the taxpayer's desire to secure the deduction. After all, we are frequently told that a taxpayer has the right to decrease the amount of what otherwise would be his taxes, or altogether avoid them, by any means the law permits. E.g., Gregory v. Helvering [infra page 910]. On the other hand, and notwithstanding Section 163(a)'s broad scope, this provision should not be construed to permit an interest deduction when it objectively appears that a taxpayer has borrowed funds in order to engage in a transaction that has no substance or purpose aside from the taxpayer's desire to obtain the tax benefit of an interest deduction; and a good example of such purposeless activity is the borrowing of funds at 4% in order to purchase property that returns less than 2% and holds out no prospect of appreciation sufficient to counter the unfavorable interest rate differential.[28] Certainly the statutory provision's underlying purpose, as

28. [The court seemed to misconceive the facts. It says that "a good example of . . . purposeless activity is the borrowing of funds at 4% in order to purchase property that returns less than 2%." The current return (the interest payments) on the first set of bonds was 1½ percent. But the face value of the bonds was $500,000 and their cost was only $465,000. Assuming three years to maturity, the interest return from the discount is 2.45 percent. So the total return is 3.95 percent. On this view it is quite conceivable that a person might have entered into the transaction with a profit motive, though it is clear that Mrs. Goldstein's motive was tax avoidance. Looking at it another way, the total face value of the two sets of bonds bought by Mrs. Goldstein was $1 million and the projected cost (on her son's calculations) was $18,500. That might well have been an attractive speculation apart from taxes. But the court did not seem to see it that way and perhaps in interpreting the case we must take the facts as they are seen by the court. — Eds.]

> we understand it, does not require that a deduction be allowed in such a case. Indeed, to allow a deduction for interest paid on funds borrowed for no purposive reason, other than the securing of a deduction from income, would frustrate Section 163(a)'s purpose; allowing it would encourage transactions that have no economic utility and that would not be engaged in but for the system of taxes imposed by Congress. . . .

1. (a) Can *Goldstein* be reconciled with *Fabreeka Products?* (b) Does *Goldstein* leave open the possibility that another taxpayer entering into precisely the same transaction as the one described in the case would be entitled to an interest deduction? (c) What if the taxpayer's son had not so carefully documented the expected loss?

2. How would you describe the rule of law of *Knetsch,* of *Fabreeka Products,* and of *Goldstein?*

ESTATE OF FRANKLIN v. COMMISSIONER

544 F.2d 1045 (9th Cir. 1976)

SNEED, Circuit Judge.

This case involves another effort on the part of the Commissioner to curb the use of real estate tax shelters.[29] In this instance he seeks to disallow deductions for the taxpayers' distributive share of losses reported by a limited partnership[30] with respect to its acquisition of a motel and related property. These "losses" have their origin in deductions for depreciation and interest claimed with respect to the motel and related property. These deductions were disallowed by the Commissioner on the ground either that the acquisition was a sham or that the entire acquisition transaction was in substance the purchase by the partnership of an option to acquire the motel and related property on January 15, 1979. The Tax Court held that the transaction constituted an option exercisable in 1979 and disallowed the taxpayers' deductions.

29. An early skirmish in this particular effort appears in Manuel D. Mayerson, 47 T.C. 340 (1966) which the Commissioner lost. The Commissioner attacked the substance of a nonrecourse sale, but based his attack on the nonrecourse and long-term nature of the purchase money note, without focusing on whether the sale was made at an unrealistically high price. In his acquiescence to *Mayerson,* 1969-2 Cum. Bull. xxiv, the Commissioner recognized that the fundamental issue in these cases generally will be whether the property has been "acquired" at an artificially high price, having little relation to its fair market value.

> The Service emphasizes that its acquiescence in *Mayerson* is based on the particular facts in the case and will not be relied upon in the disposition of other cases except where it is clear that the property has been acquired at its fair market value in an arm's length transaction creating a bona fide purchase and a bona fide debt obligation.

Rev. Rul. 69-77, 1969-1 Cum. Bull. 59.

30. [For a description of the taxation of partners and partnerships, see supra page 60. — Eds.]

Estate of Charles T. Franklin, 64 T.C. 752 (1975). We affirm this disallowance although our approach differs somewhat from that of the Tax Court.

The interest and depreciation deductions were taken by Twenty-Fourth Property Associates (hereinafter referred to as Associates), a California limited partnership of which Charles T. Franklin and seven other doctors were the limited partners. The deductions flowed from the purported "purchase" by Associates of the Thunderbird Inn, an Arizona motel, from Wayne L. Romney and Joan E. Romney (hereinafter referred to as the Romneys) on November 15, 1968.

Under a document entitled "Sales Agreement," the Romneys agreed to "sell" the Thunderbird Inn to Associates for $1,224,000. The property would be paid for over a period of ten years, with interest on any unpaid balance of seven and one-half percent per annum. "Prepaid interest" in the amount of $75,000 was payable immediately; monthly principal and interest installments of $9,045.36 [$108,544 per year] would be paid for approximately the first ten years, with Associates required to make a balloon payment at the end of the ten years of the difference between the remaining purchase price, forecast as $975,000, and any mortgages then outstanding against the property.

The purchase obligation of Associates to the Romneys was nonrecourse; the Romneys' only remedy in the event of default would be forfeiture of the partnership's interest. The sales agreement was recorded in the local county. A warranty deed was placed in an escrow account, along with a quitclaim deed from Associates to the Romneys, both documents to be delivered either to Associates upon full payment of the purchase price, or to the Romneys upon default.

The sale was combined with a leaseback of the property by Associates to the Romneys; Associates therefore never took physical possession. The lease payments were designed to approximate closely the principal and interest payments with the consequence that with the exception of the $75,000 prepaid interest payment no cash would cross between Associates and [the] Romneys until the balloon payment. The lease was on a net basis; thus, the Romneys were responsible for all of the typical expenses of owning the motel property including all utility costs, taxes, assessments, rents, charges, and levies of "every name, nature and kind whatsoever." The Romneys also were to continue to be responsible for the first and second mortgages until the final purchase installment was made; the Romneys could, and indeed did, place additional mortgages on the property without the permission of Associates. Finally, the Romneys were allowed to propose new capital improvements which Associates would be required to either build themselves or allow the Romneys to construct with compensating modifications in rent or purchase price.[31]

31. [The expected tax benefits are revealed in the following table taken from the Tax Court opinion (64 T.C. 752, 760):

In holding that the transaction between Associates and the Romneys more nearly resembled an option than a sale, the Tax Court emphasized that Associates had the power at the end of ten years to walk away from the transaction and merely lose its $75,000 "prepaid interest payment." It also pointed out that a *deed* was never recorded and that the "benefits and burdens of ownership" appeared to remain with the Romneys. Thus, the sale was combined with a leaseback in which no cash would pass; the Romneys remained responsible under the mortgages, which they could increase; and the Romneys could make capital improvements.[32] The Tax Court further justified its "option" characterization by reference to the nonrecourse nature of the purchase money debt and the nice balance between the rental and purchase money payments.

Our emphasis is different from that of the Tax Court. We believe the characteristics set out above can exist in a situation in which the sale imposes upon the purchaser a genuine indebtedness within the meaning of section 167(a), Internal Revenue Code of 1954, which will support both interest and depreciation deductions.[33] They substantially so existed in Hudspeth v. Commissioner, 509 F.2d 1224 (9th Cir. 1975) in which parents entered into sale-leaseback transactions with their children. The children paid for the property by executing nonnegotiable notes and mortgages equal to the fair market value of the property; state law proscribed deficiency judgments in case of default, limiting

		Depreciation				
	Lease income	*Building*	*Furnishings*	*Total*	*Contract interest*	*Indicated income (loss)*
1968 (2 months)	$2,800	$8,000	$16,300	$24,300	$75,000	($96,500)
1969	48,800	47,500	92,900	140,400	31,300	(122,900)
1970	108,550	44,700	65,000	109,700	89,550	(90,700)
1971	108,550	42,000	53,600	95,600	88,250	(75,300)
1972	108,550	39,500	53,600	93,100	86,550	(71,100)
1973	108,550	37,100	44,600	81,700	84,850	(58,000)
1974	108,550	34,900		34,900	83,050	(9,400)
1975	108,550	32,800		32,800	81,050	(5,300)
1976	108,550	30,800		30,800	78,950	(1,200)
1977	108,550	29,000		29,000	76,650	2,900
1978 (10 months)	90,500	22,700		22,700	62,000	5,800

During this time period, the only cash changing hands was the $75,000 of interest in 1968; rents precisely equaled debt service (interest and principal), and the lessee paid all expenses and taxes. — Eds.]

32. There was evidence that not all of the benefits and burdens of ownership remained with the Romneys. Thus, for example, the leaseback agreement appears to provide that any condemnation award will go to Associates.

33. Counsel differed as to whether the Tax Court's decision that the transaction was not a sale, but at best only an option, is reviewable by this court as a question of law or of fact. We agree with other circuits that, while the characteristics of a transaction are questions of fact, whether those characteristics constitute a sale *for tax purposes* is a question of law. . . .

the parents' remedy to foreclosure of the property. The children had no funds with which to make mortgage payments; instead, the payments were offset in part by the rental payments, with the difference met by gifts from the parents to their children. Despite these characteristics this court held that there was a bona fide indebtedness on which the children, to the extent of the rental payments, could base interest deductions. . . .

In none of these cases, however, did the taxpayer fail to demonstrate that the purchase price was at least approximately equivalent to the fair market value of the property. Just such a failure occurred here. The Tax Court explicitly found that on the basis of the facts before it the value of the property could not be estimated. 64 T.C. at 767-768.[34] In our view this defect in the taxpayers' proof is fatal.

Reason supports our perception. An acquisition such as that of Associates if at a price approximately equal to the fair market value of the property under ordinary circumstances would rather quickly yield an equity in the property which the purchaser could not prudently abandon. This is the stuff of substance. It meshes with the form of the transaction and constitutes a sale.

No such meshing occurs when the purchase price exceeds a demonstrably reasonable estimate of the fair market value. Payments on the principal of the purchase price yield no equity so long as the unpaid balance of the purchase price exceeds the then existing fair market value. Under these circumstances the purchaser by abandoning the transaction can lose no more than a mere chance to acquire an equity in the future should the value of the acquired property increase. While this chance undoubtedly influenced the Tax Court's determination that the transaction before us constitutes an option, we need only point out

34. The Tax Court found that appellants had "not shown that the purported sales price of $1,224,000 (or any other price) had any relationship to the actual market value of the motel property. . . ." 64 T.C. at 767.

Petitioners spent a substantial amount of time at trial attempting to establish that, whatever the actual market value of the property, Associates acted in the good faith *belief* that the market value of the property approximated the selling price. However, this evidence only goes to the issue of sham and does not supply substance to this transaction. "Save in those instances where the statute itself turns on intent, a matter so real as taxation must depend on objective realities, not on the varying subjective beliefs of individual taxpayers." Lynch v. Commissioner, 273 F.2d 867, 872 (2d Cir. 1959). . . . On the other side, there existed cogent evidence indicating that the fair market value was substantially less than the purchase price. This evidence included (i) the Romneys' purchase of the stock of two corporations, one of which wholly-owned the motel, for approximately $800,000 in the year preceding the "sale" to Associates ($660,000 of which was allocable to the sale property, according to Mr. Romney's estimate), and (ii) insurance policies on the property from 1967 through 1974 of only $583,200, $700,000, and $614,000. 64 T.C. at 767-768.

Given that it was the appellants' burden to present evidence showing that the purchase price did not exceed the fair market value and that he had a fair opportunity to do so, we see no reason to remand this case for further proceedings.

that its existence fails to supply the substance necessary to justify treating the transaction as a sale ab initio. It is not necessary to the disposition of this case to decide the tax consequences of a transaction such as that before us if in a subsequent year the fair market value of the property increases to an extent that permits the purchaser to acquire an equity.[35]

Authority also supports our perception. It is fundamental that "depreciation is not predicated upon ownership of property *but rather upon an investment in property.* Gladding Dry Goods Co., 2 BTA 336 (1925)." *Mayerson,* supra at 350 (italics added). No such investment exists when payments of the purchase price in accordance with the design of the parties yield no equity to the purchaser. . . . In the transaction before us and during the taxable years in question the purchase price payments by Associates have not been shown to constitute an *investment in the property.* Depreciation was properly disallowed. Only the Romneys had an investment in the property.

Authority also supports disallowance of the interest deductions. This is said even though it has long been recognized that the absence of personal liability for the purchase money debt secured by a mortgage on the acquired property does not deprive the debt of its character as a bona fide debt obligation able to support an interest deduction. *Mayerson,* supra at 352. However, this is no longer true when it appears that the debt has economic significance only if the property substantially appreciates in value prior to the date at which a very large portion of the purchase price is to be discharged. Under these circumstances the purchaser has not secured "the use or forbearance of money." See Norton v. Commissioner, 474 F.2d 608, 610 (9th Cir. 1973). Nor has the seller advanced money or forborne its use. . . . Prior to the date at which the balloon payment on the purchase price is required, and assuming no substantial increase in the fair market value of the property, the absence of personal liability on the debt reduces the transaction in economic terms to a mere chance that a genuine debt obligation may arise. This is not enough to justify an interest deduction. To justify the deduction the debt must exist; potential existence will not do. For debt to exist, the purchaser, in the absence of personal liability, must confront a situation in which it is presently reasonable from an economic point of view for him to make a capital investment in the amount of the unpaid purchase price. . . .

Our focus on the relationship of the fair market value of the property to the unpaid purchase price should not be read as premised upon the belief that a sale is not a sale if the purchaser pays too much. Bad bargains from the buyer's point of view — as well as sensible bargains from buyer's, but exceptionally good from the seller's point of view —

35. These consequences would include a determination of the proper basis of the acquired property at the date the increments to the purchaser's equity commenced.

do not thereby cease to be sales. . . . We intend our holding and explanation thereof to be understood as limited to transactions substantially similar to that now before us.

Affirmed.

NOTES AND QUESTIONS

1. *The option theory.* How important is the difference between the Tax Court's option theory and the Court of Appeals' equity theory? Suppose that you have negotiated to buy a house for $30,000 payable at the time you take title and possession and $70,000 payable one year later. The buyer insists that the transaction take the form of a payment of $30,000 for an option to buy the house one year hence for $70,000. Is this what we would normally think of as a true option? Why?

2. *Precedent.* Could the court in *Franklin's Estate* have cited *Knetsch* (supra page 684) and forgone further analysis?

3. *Future equity.* The court leaves open the question of "the tax consequences . . . in a subsequent year [if] the fair market value of the property increases to an extent that permits the purchaser to acquire an equity." Presumably if that happens the taxpayer becomes an owner in an economic and tax sense and can begin to deduct losses. Under an option theory, when would the taxpayer become an owner? Is it only an increase in value of the property that might give rise to an equity interest? What if the market rate of interest rises?

4. *Future interest?* Might it be fair to say that the taxpayer acquired a contingent future interest? If so, what is the proper tax treatment? See the *Alstores Realty Corp.* case, supra page 367.

ROSE v. COMMISSIONER

88 T.C. 386 (1987), aff'd, 868 F.2d 851 (6th Cir. 1989)

The taxpayers (petitioners) were a married couple, James and Judy Rose. Before the years at issue, Mr. Rose had been in the coal mining and, later, the banking business. Mrs. Rose had worked for a time in the coal mining business. Neither had any training or experience in art. Mrs. Rose was, however, "interested in finding an activity that she could pursue as a business."

Jackie Fine Arts (Jackie) was in the business of marketing tax shelters involving art. Jackie had an agreement with a company controlled by Marina Picasso, the granddaughter of Pablo Picasso. In essence what Marina sold was a set of 1,000 photographs of Picasso paintings or other works of art (Images) with the right to use those photographs to produce reproductions (in various media) for sale. Jackie in turn sold to investors such as the Roses the rights to single items in the set. Jackie provided information and advice, including a list of outlets for the reproductions, advice on how to make the reproductions, legal opinions by two well-known law firms on the tax benefits of the investment, and appraisals by two purported experts. The tax benefit arose from the fact that the cash down payment was a relatively small part of the total purchase price and the taxpayers were entitled to an investment credit and deductions for accelerated depreciation. Thus, it was represented that the tax "write-off" would be at least 4 times the amount invested in the year of acquisition and 3.3 times the investment in the next year.

The petitioners' total purchase price for each of the first two "packages" (that is, the photograph, with copyright, plus the advice, etc. from Jackie) was $550,000. Of this, $40,000 was paid in cash at the closing in 1979, $40,000 was due April 1, 1980, and $20,000 was due February 1, 1981. The deferred amounts bore interest at 8 percent. Mr. Rose also executed a note for $450,000, of which $200,000 was labeled "recourse" and $250,000 was labeled "nonrecourse." This note was due January 15, 1991, with interest at 6 percent. The interest was nonrecourse. Mr. Rose also paid $5,000 in 1979 for production costs. The Roses acquired a similar package in 1980, for the same price.

In 1980 petitioners, with another investor in Picasso packages, opened an art gallery in Knoxville, Tennessee; they opened another gallery in Atlanta, Georgia in 1981. The Roses disposed of their interests in both galleries in 1983.

In 1982, Mr. Rose filed a lawsuit against Jackie and various individuals, seeking rescission and damages (including punitive).

One of the two experts supplied by Jackie valued each of the three packages at $675,000; the other expert placed the value at $750,000. Neither provided much backup information to support their valuations. One of the government's two experts provided a detailed estimate of expected sales and concluded that optimistic estimates of the revenues from the three Picasso packages were, respectively, $11,809, $3,101, and $12,491. The realistic estimates were $2,828, ($659), and $4,993. These were total net returns on investments of $555,000. The government's other expert "doubted that any market existed for the reproductions in question . . . [and] concluded . . . that the Picasso packages had no economic feasibility whatsoever."

[The Roses claimed an investment tax credit and deductions for depreciation and interest.]

Ultimate Findings of Fact

Petitioners' acquisition of Picasso packages from Jackie Fine Arts in 1979 and 1980 was motivated primarily, if not exclusively, by tax considerations. There was no reasonable possibility that items produced from the Picasso packages would generate sales sufficient for petitioners to recoup their cash investment. Petitioners were relying on recovering their cash investment by immediate tax deductions and credits.

Petitioners did not have an actual and honest profit objective in acquiring the Picasso packages, and the transactions were devoid of economic substance.

Opinion

With the exception of additional interest under section 6621(d), raised by the amendment to the answer, petitioners have the burden of proving that respondent's determinations are incorrect. . . . Particularly with respect to deductions, they must bring themselves within the terms of the applicable statutes. . . .

To qualify for the claimed depreciation deductions with respect to their acquisition of the Picasso packages, petitioners must demonstrate that the packages either were used in a "trade or business" or were held "for the production . . . of income" within the meaning of section 167(a). Under section 48(a)(1), the investment tax credit is allowable only for property with respect to which depreciation (or amortization in lieu thereof) is allowable. Thus petitioners' right to both depreciation deductions and investment tax credit depends upon their showing that their activities with respect to the Picasso packages either constituted a trade or business or were undertaken and carried on for the production of income. . . .

For the reasons set forth below, we conclude that petitioners are not entitled to the investment tax credits claimed or to any deductions other than interest actually paid on the recourse portion of the indebtedness to Jackie. . . .

This case lends itself to comprehensive analysis because (1) petitioners candidly admit that tax motives played a significant part in their decision to purchase Picasso packages; (2) respondent does not challenge petitioners' testimony concerning their reliance on Jackie and those associated with Jackie about salability of the Picasso reproduction prints and posters; (3) petitioners were not totally passive but actually engaged in post-acquisition activities regarding the assets acquired; and (4) the origin and design of the Jackie program can fairly be characterized as a tax shelter arrangement typical to the years in issue. Use of this occasion to formulate a unified approach is also justified by the necessity of re-examining our position on the deductibility of interest on recourse indebtedness in view of the reversal of our decision on that issue by the Court of Appeals for the Fourth Circuit in Rice's Toyota World, Inc. v. Commissioner, supra.

OBJECTIVE AND SUBJECTIVE TESTS

In Rice's Toyota World, Inc. v. Commissioner, 81 T.C. 184 (1983), aff'd in part and rev'd in part, 752 F.2d 89 (4th Cir. 1985), we considered whether a purchase and lease-back arrangement with a computer equipment leasing corporation entitled the taxpayers to deductions for depreciation and interest. We first concluded that the individual taxpayer had no business purpose for entering into the transaction other than tax avoidance. We then stated:

> Our analysis does not end here. Mr. Rice's failure to focus on the business or non-tax aspects of the transaction is not necessarily fatal to petitioner's claim. If an objective analysis of the investment indicates a realistic opportunity for economic profit which would justify the form of the transaction, it will not be classified as a sham.[36] In order to make this determination, we must probe beneath the labels given by the parties and view the transaction in the context of its surrounding facts and circumstances.

After applying the above test, we concluded that the transaction in question in *Rice's Toyota* was a sham and disallowed all deductions. . . .

In attempting to apply objective factors to determine subjective intent under section 183, we have said that no one factor is determinative, that the absence of a particular indicium of profit may be more significant to our determination than the superficial presence of another indicium, and that mere statements of intent will not be controlling. . . .

We have also noted that the cases decided under section 183 use such words as "basic," "dominant," "primary," "predominant," and "substantial" to describe the requisite profit motive . . . but do not demonstrate application of a precise standard. . . .

Review of those cases applying the "subjective test" (of section 183) shows common characteristics reminiscent of those in which the "objective test" (of economic substance) has been applied: (1) Tax benefits were the focus of promotional materials; (2) the investors accepted the terms of purchase without price negotiation; (3) the assets in question consist of packages of purported rights, difficult to value in the abstract

36. In Frank Lyon Co. v. United States [infra page 717] the Government argued sham, but the Supreme Court rejected that argument because it found sufficient business purpose for the transaction. Once business purpose is established, the transaction should not be classified a "sham." A finding of no business purpose, however, is not conclusive evidence of a sham transaction. The transaction will still be valid if it possesses some modicum of economic substance. . . .

Conversely, transactions devoid of economic substance are not always shams such as where a taxpayer mistakenly believes there existed a potential for profit. But, when there is a finding that the taxpayer entered into the transaction for tax reasons only, then it is proper to subject the transaction to an objective economic analysis to determine whether there could have been an opportunity for profit. [81 T.C. at 203.]

and substantially overvalued in relation to tangible property included as part of the package; (4) the tangible assets were acquired or created at a relatively small cost shortly prior to the transactions in question; and (5) the bulk of the consideration was deferred by promissory notes, nonrecourse in form or in substance. In cases having these characteristics, tax motivation is apparent. The question addressed is whether sufficient business purpose existed for the taxpayer to obtain the claimed tax benefits. Such cases, hereinafter referred to as "generic tax shelters," involve a variety of assets, such as:

(a) Books. . . .
(b) Master Recordings. . . .
(c) Lithographic materials. . . .
(d) Innovations/Inventions. . . .
(e) Mining ventures. . . .
(f) Films. . . .

In any case where a taxpayer establishes a business purpose, i.e., an actual and honest profit objective, we may still recharacterize the terms of the transactions to accord with what we perceive to be the reality of the situation. . . .

While the subjective test is thus well founded in section 183, a unified approach emphasizing objective factors is preferable in cases involving generic tax shelters, i.e., those having the characteristics listed above. . . . First, because this approach emphasizes objective factors, it is more susceptible to consistent and predictable application. Second, because it does not require weighing the objective facts against a taxpayer's statement of his intent, it should be more understandable to taxpayers who doubt our ability to determine their subjective state of mind. Third, taxpayers similarly situated will be treated the same for tax purposes. Fourth, the test allows us to separate the real economic aspects from the "financial fantasies" surrounding a transaction and to apply the tax laws accordingly, rather than to disallow all deductions (or limit them to gross income under section 183(b)(2), which in the typical case is zero). As applied below, the objective and subjective tests merge into an approach in which the objective test incorporates factors considered relevant in cases decided under section 183, as well as concepts underlying those statutes providing for the deductions (sections 162 and 167) and credits (sections 38 and 48) in dispute in this case.

ECONOMIC SUBSTANCE

The record in this case, particularly in view of petitioners' post-acquisition activities, does not support the conclusion that petitioners' acquisition of Picasso packages was "a mere paper chase or otherwise fictitious." . . . Nonetheless, the transactions will be disregarded if, applying the objective test, we find that they are devoid of economic substance consonant with their intended tax effects.

1. The Dealings Between Jackie and Petitioners

It is apparent from our findings of fact, which we will not repeat here, that the Picasso packages were sold by Jackie and purchased by petitioners as a tax shelter, without regard to the income that might be produced, the fair market value of the products, or the methods by which the products might be sold by petitioners. Based on the entire record, we conclude that petitioners engaged in the transaction primarily, if not exclusively, to obtain tax deductions and credits and thereby reduce the tax they would otherwise have to pay on their substantial income from other sources. . . .

Petitioners admit that tax considerations played a part in their decision to acquire the Picasso packages. Their adviser at the time of the initial acquisition was their tax accountant, whose records reflect that he considered his function to be advising petitioners with respect to "tax shelter." The information sought and received from Jackie focused primarily on the tax advantages to be obtained. Petitioners neither sought nor received prior to their acquisitions in December 1979 information on the manner in which they could commercially exploit the property that they were acquiring. At no time did they obtain any independent valuation information or distribution information, and they never entered into distribution agreements with anyone. The evidence indicates that they were indifferent to the real value of the Picasso packages. Petitioners were totally unbusinesslike in their initial dealings with Jackie. See sec. 1.183-2(b)(1) and (2), Income Tax Regs.

Persuasive evidence of the lack of arm's-length price negotiation is petitioners' blind acceptance of the exaggerated values of the images claimed by Jackie. The evidence of value discussed below demonstrates that an inquiry would have readily shown that the claims of value that were made to petitioners before the first acquisitions could not be supported in fact. Although they had plenty of time in 1980, before the close of that tax year, to investigate these facts before making the second acquisition, they failed to do so. By the time of the second acquisition, [a] dispute between Paraselenes S.A. [Marina Picasso's company] and VAGA [a company controlled by other, competing heirs of Picasso] was in full swing, and petitioners had not received the products that they had been promised in December 1979. Not surprisingly, they never did (and apparently never will) receive net income from the activity. See sec. 183-2(b)(1), (4), (6), and (7), Income Tax Regs.

We must acknowledge the existence of some evidence that Mrs. Rose made an effort to familiarize herself with the distribution prospects and that, after acquiring the Picasso packages, she became involved in art galleries. This evidence, however, is susceptible of various interpretations. One possibility is that, after being introduced to the Picasso packages, Mrs. Rose developed a bona fide interest in the art business. A second possibility is that these activities were undertaken primarily to protect the anticipated tax benefits of the acquisition, in accordance with the advice contained in Metry's [Jackie's salesperson] December 19, 1979, note to Krauser [the Roses' accountant]. A third possibility is that Mrs. Rose, who was looking for activities to fill the time left because of the maturity of her children, was engaging in the activity in the nature of a "hobby." We are not persuaded, in any event, that the activities with respect to the art galleries prove that petitioners had an actual and honest profit objective at the time that they acquired any of the Picasso packages. Petitioners disposed of their interests in the galleries in 1983 (about the time of the statutory notice). The activities of Mrs. Rose have not been shown to involve the time, effort, or expertise consonant with an actual profit objective. See sec. 1.183-2(b)(1), (2), (3), (5), and (9), Income Tax Regs.

2. *Relationship Between Sales Price and Fair Market Value*

Petitioners agreed to pay $550,000 for each Picasso package when, according to the best available evidence, the fair market value of the packages was negligible. We do not, however, rely on hindsight in the form of the opinions of respondent's experts in reaching the conclusion that the purchase price agreed to had no reasonable relationship to anything other than projected tax benefits.

The "Reproduction Masters" sold to petitioners as Picasso packages included the rights acquired the same month from Paraselenes S.A. for $10,000 plus 60 percent of the "gross receipts" received by Jackie to be applied against certain minimum guarantees. The guarantees would be, and were in fact, satisfied upon sale of 100 Picasso packages to purchasers and payment of $1 million to Paraselenes S.A. for 1979.

The appraisals of F. P. Rose and Rothschild [the appraisers provided by Jackie] sent to petitioners in 1980 did not explain the manner in which they arrived at values of $675,000 and $750,000, respectively. In attempting to support those appraisals at the time of trial in 1986, however, F. P. Rose projected the sale of 23,000 products of each image, at prices ranging from $12.50 for a poster to $2,000 for a signed [by Marina Picasso] and numbered print. Rothschild assumed sales of over 36,550 for each image, ranging from puzzles and calendars at $6.50 to tapestries at $4,000. Both F. P. Rose and Rothschild gave equivalent appraisals, and presumably made equivalent assumptions, for each of the Picasso packages sold by Jackie. Thus, the values that they asserted assumed the ability of investors such as petitioners to simultaneously sell literally millions of items. No expertise is necessary to recognize that such a volume of sales is improbable and, in any event, would have to be taken into account in establishing a price reflecting fair market value. . . .

Similarly, it is clear that F. P. Rose, Rothschild, and even respondent's expert, Cole, were speculating as to maximum potential revenue and not determining fair market value. Carolan [the IRS's other expert] similarly assumed that the products would sell, although she differentiated between maximum potential sales and probable gross revenues. As set forth in our findings of fact, we conclude that the opinions of F. P. Rose and Rothschild are not credible because they are unsupported by any independent evidence and can only be attributable to bias resulting from the contract between them and Jackie. . . .

We do not believe that under these circumstances the $10,000 paid to Paraselenes S.A. is indicative of a minimum fair market value. That price was paid by Jackie on the assumption that Jackie would immediately resell the rights for a cash down payment of $40,000 and production costs of $5,000, plus a promise to pay an additional $40,000 in a few months' time.

Through April 1980, petitioners paid a total of $85,000 cash in relation to each of the images acquired December 1979. On their 1979 tax return, due April 15, 1980, they claimed investment tax credit of $55,000, plus depreciation of almost $63,000 for each package, reducing income taxable at rates exceeding 50 percent. As of that time, therefore, the tax savings exceeded the cash invested. It defies reason to suggest that the amounts paid by petitioners are indicative of fair market value of the Picasso packages without regard to the anticipated tax benefits. Mr. Rose testified that he thought he might achieve sales of "up to $2 million" and that —

A. It was $800 to $1,000 per print, because they were to be signed by Marina Picasso, and because there were to be only 500 of them in the country, and we felt like it was such a limited edition that they would command at approximately $1,000 each.
Q. You mentioned that there was a price, an estimated price of the limited edition of $800; is that correct?
A. $800 to $1,000.
Q. Where did you get that information?
A. Because in —
Q. Where?
A. — Barron's article at the time, it had the lesser known artist that were bringing $500 to $600 and in articles like that, and from representations made by Mr. Metry and the others at the time.

These assumptions, of course, ignore the difference between prints actually made by the artist and the Picasso reproductions in question here. We do not believe, in any event, that a person with Mr. Rose's business acumen and experience would translate such speculation into a purchase price of $550,000. We do not believe that, absent the assurances that he requested and received concerning the anticipated tax benefits, Mr. Rose would have paid anything for the Picasso packages.

3. Structure of the Financing

As indicated above, the presence of deferred debt that is in substance or in fact not likely to be paid is an indicia of lack of or exaggeration of economic substance. . . . On the other hand, bona fide third-party debt may indicate that a transaction, or at least part of it, should be recognized. . . .

In this case, written representations of Jackie and oral testimony of Finesod confirm that the partial recourse notes were used only for tax reasons, and that the recourse portion of the notes was specifically designed to be approximately equal to the tax deductions expected to be taken during the first two years of investment. In other words, petitioners were only agreeing to be personally liable for what they expected to get back shortly after filing their tax returns reporting the transactions. In substance, therefore, prior to the due dates of the deferred notes only the public treasury was out of pocket for the amount of cash actually paid by petitioners. The balance of the debt, including interest, was subject to a contingency of actual sales of products by petitioners.

The nonrecourse debt in this case was not likely to be paid because the revenues from which it would be paid were not likely to be received. . . .

A fortiori, the interest is too unlikely to be paid to be deducted on an accrual basis. . . .

4. Perceived Congressional Intent

Petitioners suggest that they were merely taking advantage of tax incentives created by Congress. Indeed, Congress created deductions and investment tax credits to encourage certain types of activities, and the taxpayers who engage in those activities are entitled to the attendant benefits. . . . Such congressional intent is readily demonstrated with respect to identifiable tangible property . . . or property dealt with by specific statutes, such as film or videotapes. . . . When available, expressions of congressional intent will, of course, control. . . . Thus, although arrangements involving films may have the characteristics of generic tax shelters, we do not doubt that the property qualifies for depreciation and investment tax credits if other conditions are met. . . .

We are not at all persuaded that Congress intended to encourage activities such as the Jackie program, which, if successful, would at most flood the market with mass-produced reproductions that, according to respondent's expert Cole, would merely denigrate the fine print art market. There is no evidence or reason to believe that the activities engaged in by Jackie and by petitioners in this case are among those favored by Congress. To the contrary, as discussed below in our discussion of section 6621(d), it appears that the transactions in issue are in the category of those that lead to adverse congressional action.[37]

The nature of the dealings between the parties, the total disparity between the purchase price and the fair market value of the property acquired by petitioners, and the illusory nature of the financing of the transactions convince us that petitioners' acquisition of Picasso packages from Jackie is devoid of economic substance. The transactions, therefore, do not give rise to any depreciation deductions, miscellaneous deductions, or investment tax credits. . . .

NOTES

1. *Interest actually paid on notes.* The taxpayers deducted accrued but unpaid interest on the purchase money notes used to acquire the Picasso packages. The Court held that such interest was too unlikely to be paid to be deducted on an accrual basis. The taxpayers also deducted a much smaller amount of interest than had actually been paid. Under the law in effect at that time, personal interest was deductible without regard to profit motive. Consistent with this rule, the Court of Appeals allowed a deduction for that portion of the interest that was actually paid by the taxpayer.

2. *The appellate decision.* The opinion of the Court of Appeals, affirmed the tax court decision,

> Whether the taxpayers used the Picasso packages in a "trade or business" or held them "for the production of income" is a question of fact. The tax court findings of fact on this issue shall not be overturned unless clearly erroneous. . . . This court will not inquire into whether a transaction's primary objective was for the production of income or to make a profit, until it determines that the transaction is bona fide and not a sham. . . . The proper standard in determining if a transaction is a sham is whether the transaction has any practicable economic effects other than the creation of income tax losses. . . . A taxpayer's subjective business purpose and the transaction's objective economic substance may be relevant to this inquiry.
>
> We review de novo the legal standard applied by the tax court in determining whether or not a transaction is a sham. . . .

37. Overvalued lithographs acquired in tax shelter promotions and donated to charities have led to negative congressional response. See Explanation of the Senate Finance Committee, p. 444, of charges to sec. 6659 made by the Deficit Reduction Act of 1984, Pub. L. 98-369, 98 Stat. 494, 693.

The taxpayers argue that the "generic tax shelters" standard applied by the tax court is not authorized or permitted under law. Under the "generic tax shelter" test, the tax court determined whether the taxpayer's transaction was a generic tax shelter and then determined whether the transaction had economic substance. The tax court outlined several characteristics that would constitute a generic tax shelter.

We choose not to adopt the generic tax shelter test because it does not aid us in the basic inquiry as to whether the transaction had any practicable economic effect other than the creation of income tax losses. As the Ninth Circuit stated in Collins v. Commissioner, 857 F.2d [1383], 1386 [1988]:

> The case books are already glutted with tests. Many such tests proliferate because they give the comforting illusion of consistency and precision. They often obscure rather than clarify. Whether characterized as a "generic tax shelter" test or a two-prong subjective/objective analysis, the essential inquiry is whether the transaction had any practicable economic effect other than the creation of economic tax losses.

Though characterized as a generic tax shelter test, the tax court examined the taxpayers' profit motive and the economic substance of their venture. The tax court looked past the taxpayers' particular transaction involving the Picasso packages and uncovered its substance. As the tax court stated:

> [The taxpayers'] acquisition of the Picasso packages from Jackie Fine Arts in 1979 and 1980 was motivated primarily, if not exclusively, by tax considerations. There was no reasonable possibility that the items produced from the Picasso packages would generate sales sufficient for [the taxpayers] to recoup their cash investment. [Taxpayers] were relying on recovering their cash investment by immediate tax deductions and credits. The [taxpayers] did not have an actual and honest profit objective in acquiring the Picasso packages, and the transactions were devoid of economic substance.

In sum, the tax court's analysis is correct and consistent with the analysis traditionally applied by this circuit in determining whether a particular transaction is a sham. . . .

The record of the tax court is full of evidence to support its factual findings that the taxpayers had no honest profit motive and that the Picasso venture was completely devoid of economic substance. The tax court noted that the taxpayers admitted that tax considerations played a major part in their decision to acquire the Picasso packages. Their investment advisor and tax accountant at the time of the initial acquisition of the packages considered his function to be advising the petitioners with respect to tax shelters. The information sought and received from Jackie Fine Arts focused primarily on the tax advantages of purchasing the packages. Taxpayers never obtained any information on the commercial viability of the packages. At no time did the taxpayers obtain any independent art appraisals. They never entered into distribution agreements with anyone. The evidence also clearly indicates that they were indifferent to the real value of the Picasso packages. They blindly accepted the

> exaggerated values claimed by Jackie Fine Arts. Any inquiry by the taxpayers would have readily shown that the claims of value made by Jackie Fine Arts to the taxpayers before the first acquisitions were totally unsupported in fact and the only thing they bought were tax losses.
>
> Finally, as we affirm the tax court's determination that the Picasso package transaction was devoid of economic substance, the tax court was correct in holding the taxpayers liable for additional interest under §6621(d). . . .

In a later case, the Sixth Circuit again voiced its objection to the objective nature of the Tax Court's interpretation of §183. In Dean B. Smith v. Commissioner, 937 F.2d. 309 (1991), the appellate court held that the taxpayer's profit objective was sufficient to avoid not-for-profit status under §183, even if that expectation was (as an objective matter) unreasonable. The Tax Court, however, continues to apply the test as stated in *Rose* in cases appealable to other circuits. See Peat Oil and Gas Associates v. Commissioner, 100 T. C. 271 (1993).

QUESTIONS

1. Was this just a case of very bad judgment on the part of the taxpayers as to the business aspects of the investment? As to each "package," how many prints would they have been required to sell, at the most optimistic price, in order to recover their investment? How many other investors were trying to sell Picasso prints pursuant to the Jackie Fine Arts promotion?
2. What was the taxpayers' motive? What is the relevance of motive?
3. What were the taxpayers' realistic economic prospects? What is the relevance of this reality?
4. Suppose it had been established that the taxpayers realistically expected the following costs and returns, expressed in present values:

Investment	$500,000
Sales (net of costs)	450,000
Tax benefits	150,000

Would they be entitled to deduct their losses? What if the present value of the expected sales had been $510,000?

5. Suppose you are a lawyer and one night at a bar you meet a man who convinces you (you've had a few drinks) that he has a great oil drilling project. He tells you that you will get immediate tax deductions for the intangible drilling costs and that eventually, when he strikes oil, you may recover as much as ten times your initial investment. On the

spot, you write out a check for $10,000 for a 10 percent participation in the project. It turns out that the oil man is honest, but incompetent and misguided. He spends all the money on the project, but it was a foolish venture to begin with and there are no returns. Can you deduct the $10,000?

3. The Congressional Response to Tax Shelters

Losses incurred on passive investments. Over the years Congress has responded in various ways to the kinds of transactions generally thought of as tax shelters or tax-avoidance schemes. The rules that have been adopted leave many gaps and tend to display some redundancy. The most recent, and in many ways the broadest, piece of anti-tax-shelter legislation is §469, which limits deductions for passive activity losses. A passive activity loss is a loss on an investment (a) that constitutes a trade or business and (b) in which the taxpayer does not "materially participate." See §469(d)(1). A passive loss from one investment may be used to offset passive income from another investment, and net passive losses may be carried forward indefinitely and deducted when the investment that generates the loss is sold, but passive losses may not be used to offset other income from nonpassive investments or activities, wages and salaries, or "portfolio income" (dividends, interest, etc.).

The passive loss rules may be illustrated by again considering the investor who borrows $100,000 at 9 percent and uses the proceeds to buy an apartment building that appreciates at 8 percent a year. (Assume that the rental income is offset by taxes, maintenance costs, and other expenses.) Absent special limitations, in the first year the taxpayer would be able to deduct interest and depreciation. The taxpayer would not pay tax on the appreciation since it is not realized gain. If, however, the investor does not materially participate in the activity and does not qualify for special relief provisions discussed below, the loss from the building will be a passive loss. That loss will be deductible against current or future passive activity income from other sources, or from the building itself (in future years), or it may be deducted at the time the building is sold, but the loss will not be deductible against other current income such as salary or portfolio income.

The concept of material participation is central to the passive loss rules. Material participation is statutorily defined as participation that is "regular, continuous, and substantial." §469(h). Under proposed regulations, a taxpayer will be deemed to materially participate in an activity only if he or she meets one of seven tests. Under one test, the taxpayer must personally spend more than 500 hours on the activity. Under another test, the taxpayer must spend at least 100 hours on the activity and must spend at least as much time on the activity as any other individual. Under a third test, the taxpayer must have met the material participation standard, as articulated in other tests, during five of the immediately preceding ten taxable years. A fourth test is qualitative: An individual materially participates in an activity if (unspecified) facts and circumstances show material participation. Regs. §1.469-5T(a). Section 469 contains many exceptions, special rules, and exceptions to the special rules. For example, limited partnership interests and rental activities are considered passive activities. Rental activities, however, are not passive for individuals in the real property business who meet certain tests (such as performing more than 750 hours of service in connection with a real property rental activity). §469(c)(7). In addition, up to $25,000 of annual losses may be deducted from real estate rental activities of individuals who meet a lesser standard of participation, but this exemption is phased out as income rises from $100,000 to $150,000.

Limitations on the deduction of interest on "investment indebtedness." The passive loss rules only restrict losses from investments that constitute a trade or business or a rental activity. Section 163(d), which was adopted in 1969, applies a similar restriction on the deduction of interest on "investment indebtedness" — that is on debt tied to any investment, including stocks and bonds and undeveloped real estate. The role of this provision may be illustrated as follows: Assume that an investor borrows $100,000 at 10 percent and uses the proceeds to buy shares of common stock of a growing electronics company. In the first year, consistent with expectations, the shares increase in value by 15 percent but pay no dividends. There has been an economic gain, but no gain or income for tax purposes. Absent special rules, the $10,000 interest expense would be deductible. Section 163(d) prevents a tax advantage by limiting the amount of the interest deduction to "net investment income." Net investment income includes non-capital gain income from all portfolio investments, so that interest payments incurred in holding one such investment can be deducted to the extent of income from another such investment. Net investment income includes capital gain income only if the taxpayer elects to forgo the lower maximum rate on such income and, in effect, treat capital gain income as ordinary income. Interest disallowed as a deduction by reason of §163(d) may be deducted, subject to the same limitations, in succeeding taxable years. In the present example, there is no investment income, so the $10,000 interest expense would not be currently deductible.

Limitations of deductions to amount of "at risk" investment. Another broad-scale approach is the "at risk" rules of §465, first introduced in 1976 and broadened in application in 1978 and 1986. These rules are another form of attack on the leverage (use of borrowed funds) that has been vital to most tax shelters. Section 465 disallows deductions for "*losses*" (that is, the excess of deductions over income) of an investment in excess of the amount that the taxpayer has at risk in that investment. The amount at risk includes cash invested plus amounts of debt for which the taxpayer is personally liable or which is secured by assets of the taxpayer (other than assets of the tax-shelter investment). Thus, to return to an earlier example (supra page 683), if a person purports to buy a motion picture for $2 million but puts up only $200,000 in cash and signs a nonrecourse note for the balance, the maximum loss that can be deducted is $200,000. Losses not currently deductible may be carried forward and deducted against income in later years as the investment produces taxable income, or as the at-risk amount increases. Section 465 applies to all investments and business activities except that in the case of real estate it does not apply to "qualified nonrecourse financing" (which includes loans from banks and certain other loans; see §465(b)(6)). Section 465 overlaps with the passive loss rules of §469 since both may apply to investments that constitute a trade or business. Losses on trade or business investments will not be deductible unless they pass muster under both §465 and §469.

Debt used to purchase or carry tax-favored investments. One of the earliest responses to tax avoidance was to deny deductions for "interest on indebtedness incurred or continued to purchase or carry" tax-exempt bonds. §265(a)(2). See also §265(a)(1), denying deductions for certain expenses "allocable to" tax-exempt income. Absent §265(2), a taxpayer might borrow at 8 percent to buy tax-exempt bonds that pay 7 percent. Interest paid on the loan would be deductible, while the interest on the bonds would be tax-free. Under §265, the interest on the loan would be nondeductible.

In a similar vein, §264 denies deductions for interest on indebtedness "incurred or continued to purchase or carry" certain insurance and annuity policies. Section 264, among other things, now expressly covers the type of transaction engaged in by the taxpayer in the *Knetsch* case (supra page 684).

Capitalization of outlays. Denial of deductions under §264 or §265 is an extreme remedy. Another approach is to treat certain outlays as capital expenditures rather than current expenses, even for cash-method taxpayers. This approach was taken in §278(a), which related to the expenses of developing a citrus or almond grove. In 1986, §278 and other, similar provisions were replaced by the uniform capitalization rules of §263A. As explained earlier (see page 623), these rules require the capitalization or inclusion in inventory cost of certain expenses incurred in the production of property for use or for sale by the taxpayer. Left in place in 1986 was §464, which requires that in the case of a farming syndicate, "amounts paid for feed, seed, fertilizer, or other similar farm supplies" are deductible only when "actually used or consumed." See also §461(g) covering prepaid interest.

A related limitation, designed to prevent mismatching of expenses and income, is found in §448, which prohibits the use of the cash method by various entities, including "tax shelters" (as defined in §461(i)(3)).

Other anti-tax-shelter provisions. Other anti-tax-shelter provisions that have been important in the past are the recapture rule of §§1245 and 1250, which prevent the conversion of ordinary income into capital gain. See description supra page 682. Less important recapture rules include §1252 (recapture of soil and water conservation expenditures and expenditures by farmers for clearing land), §1254 (recapture of intangible drilling costs), and §1255 (recapture of excluded portion of payments under certain special government programs).

Still another broadly phrased provision is §183, which limits deductions of an "activity [that] is not engaged in for profit." The original objective of this provision was primarily to limit hobby losses (see supra page 531), but in recent years it has been used increasingly to attack tax shelters, especially where the investment has been overvalued. See, e.g., Dean v. Commissioner, 83 T.C. 56 (1984); Capek v. Commissioner, 86 T.C. 14 (1986).

In addition to all this there is the alternative minimum tax, which is described infra at page 735, and there are various anti-tax-avoidance judicial doctrines reflected in the cases we have examined (beginning supra at page 672).

Penalties since 1982. Congressional concern with tax shelters led to the adoption of a new set of enforcement tools in the 1982 act (TEFRA). In an effort to attack abusive tax shelters at their source, Congress imposed a penalty, equal to the greater of $1,000 or 10 percent of the gross income derived or to be derived from a tax-shelter activity, on promoters, organizers, or sellers who make statements that they know or have reason to know are false, about the availability of tax benefits or statements that consist of a "gross overvaluation" (more than 200 percent of the correct value). §6700.

The 1982 act also imposed a new tax equal to 20 percent of any "substantial understatement of income tax." §6662. A substantial understatement is one that exceeds the greater of 10 percent of the proper tax or $5,000. The amount of the understatement is reduced by amounts attributable to tax treatment for which there was substantial authority, but, in the case of a tax shelter, only if the taxpayer "reasonably believed that the tax treatment of [the] item . . . was more likely than not" proper. §6662(d)(2)(C)(i).

In addition to these new penalties, the 1982 act added a penalty for aiding and abetting the understatement of a tax liability (§6701), provided for injunctions against promoters of abusive tax shelters (§7408), added or increased other penalties, and added other procedural devices.

In 1984, Congress added provisions requiring that tax shelters register with the IRS (§§6111, 6707) and that an organizer of a "potentially abusive tax shelter" maintain a list of investors (§§6112, 6708). Congress also imposed a new penalty on tax-shelter promoters who provide false or fraudulent statements about tax effects or who provide a "gross valuation overstatement" (§6700).

PROBLEMS

1. (a) On January 1, 1991, Stan obtains a recourse loan of $200,000 and uses the proceeds to buy shares of common stock. Stan pays $20,000 interest on the loan in 1991 and receives $10,000 in dividends. Stan has no other investments or loans. How much, if any, of the 1991 interest payment is deductible?

(b) The facts are the same as in (a) except that Stan also receives $5,000 of dividends from another stock that he bought with nonborrowed funds. How much, if any, of the 1991 interest payment is deductible?

2. On January 1, 1992, Jamie invests $250,000 of nonborrowed funds in a widget manufacturing enterprise. Jamie does not materially participate in the enterprise, which shows a taxable loss of $50,000 for the year. Jamie is the sole owner of the enterprise.

(a) If Jamie has no other investments, how much, if any, of the loss may she deduct?

(b) Assume Jamie has another trade or business investment in which she does materially participate, and in 1992, this produces taxable income of $40,000. How much, if any, of the loss from the widget enterprise may Jamie deduct for the year?

(c) Assume Jamie has net dividend income of $20,000 from common stocks in 1992. How much, if any, of the loss from the widget enterprise may Jamie deduct?

(d) Assume that in 1993 Jamie has no income or loss from the widget enterprise, but that in 1993 she has income of $30,000 from a different trade or business in which she materially participates. How much, if any, of the 1992 loss from the widget enterprise may Jamie deduct?

3. On January 1, 1991, Rafael borrows $200,000 and uses the proceeds to buy a restaurant. The loan is nonrecourse and does not require repayment of any of the principal until 1994. Rafael rents the building in which the restaurant operates. In 1991, the restaurant shows a net loss of $40,000. In 1992, the restaurant shows a net income of $25,000. Also in 1992, Rafael obtains a recourse loan of $10,000 and uses the proceeds to improve the restaurant. In all years, Rafael materially participates in the management of the restaurant. Is any portion of the 1991 loss deductible? When?

4. On January 1, 1991, Sarah obtains a recourse loan of $100,000 and uses the proceeds to buy Fly Co. common stock. In 1991, Sarah pays $10,000 interest on the loan and the stock pays dividends of

$15,000. Sarah pays $10,000 interest on the loan in 1992 and in 1993. The stock pays no dividends in 1992 and dividends of $15,000 in 1993. Sarah has no other investments. What portion, if any, of Sarah's $30,000 interest expense is deductible? When?

4. Sale and Leaseback Transactions

Overview. The favorable depreciation rules are designed to, and do, stimulate business investment. Suppose, though, that a taxpayer in a low bracket (or one that pays no tax at all) wishes to expand a trade or business and requires additional depreciable property. Is there any way such a taxpayer can take advantage of the generous depreciation allowance?

One alternative for the low-bracket taxpayer is to lease the depreciable property from a high-bracket taxpayer. The high-bracket taxpayer will enjoy the tax advantages associated with the investment and can pass on part of those advantages to the low-bracket taxpayer in the form of lower rent.

In some cases, finding a high-bracket lessor of the desired property is difficult. In that situation, the low-bracket taxpayer may itself buy or construct the depreciable property. Before the property is placed in service, however, a suitable high-bracket lessor may be found, in which case the property may be sold to the high-bracket taxpayer, which in turn leases it back to the low-bracket taxpayer. The high-bracket taxpayer receives the tax benefits of ownership and the low-bracket taxpayer receives either some up-front cash in addition to the amount of its investment or rental payments that are less than they would otherwise be.

The following simplified example may help illustrate the sale-leaseback transaction. Suppose Yaba Company requires $1 million of depreciable property for its business. Yaba has past operating losses that can be carried over to present and future years; as a result, Yaba is in a zero percent marginal tax bracket and will not benefit from the depreciation deduction on the new investment. Yaba buys the property for $1 million and then sells it to Xenon Corporation for $1 million. Xenon pays $200,000 cash and gives Yaba a note for the remaining $800,000. Xenon then leases the property back to Yaba at an annual rent that is exactly equal to the payments Xenon must make on the $800,000 purchase note. The only money that ever changes hands between Yaba and Xenon is the $200,000 purchase payment.

When the smoke has cleared, Xenon has paid $200,000 for the legal ownership of $1 million of business property. Xenon must make payments on its $800,000 purchase money note, but those payments will be offset by the rental payments it receives from Yaba. If the transaction is respected for tax purposes, Xenon will receive the tax benefits associated with the property. Yaba, on the other hand, receives the property it needs for a net outlay of $800,000 instead of $1 million. Yaba will be required to make annual rental payments to Xenon, but these will be offset by the payments to which it will be entitled on the purchase money note.

Will the transaction be respected for tax purposes? As the following case and discussion indicate, the answer to that question will depend on many considerations, including the motivation of the parties and the incidents of ownership borne by the purported lessor.

FRANK LYON CO. v. UNITED STATES

435 U.S. 561 (1978)

Mr. Justice Blackmun delivered the opinion of the Court.

This case concerns the federal income tax consequences of a sale-and-leaseback in which petitioner Frank Lyon Company (Lyon) took title to a building under construction by Worthen Bank & Trust Company (Worthen) of Little Rock, Ark., and simultaneously leased the building back to Worthen for long-term use as its headquarters and principal banking facility. . . .

Lyon is a closely held Arkansas corporation engaged in the distribution of home furnishings, primarily Whirlpool and RCA electrical products. Worthen in 1965 was an Arkansas-chartered bank and a member of the Federal Reserve System. Frank Lyon was Lyon's majority shareholder and board chairman; he also served on Worthen's board. Worthen at that time began to plan the construction of a multistory bank and office building to replace its existing facility in Little Rock, about the same time Worthen's competitor, Union National Bank of Little Rock, also began to plan a new bank and office building. Adjacent sites on Capitol Avenue, separated only by Spring Street, were acquired by the two banks. It became a matter of competition, for both banking business and tenants, and prestige as to which bank would start and complete its building first.

Worthen initially hoped to finance, to build, and to own the proposed facility at a total cost of $9 million for the site, building, and adjoining parking deck. This was to be accomplished by selling $4 million in debentures and using the proceeds in the acquisition of the capital stock of a wholly owned real estate subsidiary. This subsidiary would have formal title and would raise the remaining $5 million by a conventional mortgage loan on the new premises. Worthen's plan, however, had to be abandoned for two significant reasons:

1. As a bank chartered under Arkansas law, Worthen legally could not pay more interest on any debentures it might issue than that then specified by Arkansas law. But the proposed obligations would not be marketable at that rate.

2. Applicable statutes or regulations of the Arkansas State Bank Department and the Federal Reserve System required Worthen, as a state bank subject to their supervision, to obtain prior permission for the investment in banking premises of any amount (including that placed in a real estate subsidiary) in excess of the bank's capital stock or of 40% of its capital stock and surplus. . . . Worthen, accordingly, was advised by staff employees of the Federal Reserve System that they would not recommend approval of the plan by the System's Board of Governors.

Worthen therefore was forced to seek an alternative solution that would provide it with the use of the building, satisfy the state and federal regulators, and attract the necessary capital. In September 1967 it proposed a sale-and-leaseback arrangement. The State Bank Department and the Federal Reserve System approved this approach, but the Department required that Worthen possess an option to purchase the leased property at the end of the 15th year of the lease at a set price, and the federal regulator required that the building be owned by an independent third party.

Detailed negotiations ensued with investors that had indicated interest, namely, Goldman, Sachs & Company; White, Weld & Co.; Eastman Dillon, Union Securities & Company; and Stephens, Inc. Certain of these firms made specific proposals.

Worthen then obtained a commitment from New York Life Insurance Company to provide $7,140,000 in permanent mortgage financing on the building, conditioned upon its approval of the titleholder. At this point Lyon entered the negotiations and it, too, made a proposal.

Worthen submitted a counterproposal that incorporated the best features, from its point of view, of the several offers. Lyon accepted the counterproposal, suggesting, by way of further inducement, a $21,000 reduction in the annual rent for the first five years of the building lease. Worthen selected Lyon as the investor. After further negotiations, resulting in the elimination of that rent reduction (offset, however, by higher interest Lyon was to pay Worthen on a subsequent unrelated loan), Lyon in November 1967 was approved as an acceptable borrower by First National City Bank for the construction financing, and by New York Life, as the permanent lender. In April 1968 the approvals of the state and federal regulators were received.

In the meantime, on September 15, before Lyon was selected, Worthen itself began construction.

B

In May 1968 Worthen, Lyon, City Bank, and New York Life executed complementary and interlocking agreements under which the building was sold by Worthen to Lyon as it was constructed, and Worthen leased the completed building back from Lyon.

1. *Agreements between Worthen and Lyon.* Worthen and Lyon executed a ground lease, a sales agreement, and a building lease.

Under the ground lease dated May 1, 1968, App. 366, Worthen leased the site to Lyon for 76 years and 7 months through November 30, 2044. The first 19 months were the estimated construction period. The ground rents payable by Lyon to Worthen were $50 for the first 26 years and 7 months and thereafter in quarterly payments:

12/1/94 through 11/30/99 (5 years)	$100,000 annually
12/1/99 through 11/30/04 (5 years)	$150,000 annually
12/1/04 through 11/30/09 (5 years)	$200,000 annually
12/1/09 through 11/30/34 (25 years)	$250,000 annually
12/1/34 through 11/30/44 (10 years)	$10,000 annually

Under the sales agreement dated May 19, 1968, . . . Worthen agreed to sell the building to Lyon, and Lyon agreed to buy it, piece by piece as it was constructed, for a total price not to exceed $7,640,000, in reimbursements to Worthen for its expenditures for the construction of the building.[38]

Under the building lease dated May 1, 1968, . . . Lyon leased the building back to Worthen for a primary term of 25 years from December 1, 1969, with options in Worthen to extend the lease for eight additional 5-year terms, a total of 65 years. During the period between the expiration of the building lease (at the latest, November 30, 2034, if fully extended) and the end of the ground lease on November 30, 2044, full ownership, use, and control of the building were Lyon's, unless, of course, the building had been repurchased by Worthen. . . . Worthen was not obligated to pay rent under the building lease until completion of the building. For the first 11 years of the lease, that is, until November 30, 1980, the stated quarterly rent was $145,581.03 ($582,324.12 for the year). For the next 14 years, the quarterly rent was $153,289.32 ($613,157.28 for the year), and for the option periods the rent was $300,000 a year, payable quarterly. . . . The total rent for the building over the 25-year primary term of the lease thus was $14,989,767.24. That rent equaled the principal and interest payments

38. This arrangement appeared advisable and was made because purchases of materials by Worthen (which then had become a national bank) were not subject to Arkansas sales tax. . . . Sales of the building elements to Lyon also were not subject to state sales tax, since they were sales of real estate. . . .

that would amortize the $7,140,000 New York Life mortgage loan over the same period. When the mortgage was paid off at the end of the primary term, the annual building rent, if Worthen extended the lease, came down to the stated $300,000. Lyon's net rentals from the building would be further reduced by the increase in ground rent Worthen would receive from Lyon during the extension.[39]

The building lease was a "net lease," under which Worthen was responsible for all expenses usually associated with the maintenance of an office building, including repairs, taxes, utility charges, and insurance, and was to keep the premises in good condition, excluding, however, reasonable wear and tear.

Finally, under the lease, Worthen had the option to repurchase the building at the following times and prices:

11/30/80 (after 11 years)	$6,325,169.85
11/30/84 (after 15 years)	$5,432,607.32
11/30/89 (after 20 years)	$4,187,328.04
11/30/94 (after 25 years)	$2,145,935.00

These repurchase option prices were the sum of the unpaid balance of the New York Life mortgage, Lyon's $500,000 investment, and 6% interest compounded on that investment.

2. *Construction financing agreement.* By agreement dated May 14, 1968, . . . City Bank agreed to lend Lyon $7,000,000 for the construction of the building. This loan was secured by a mortgage on the building and the parking deck, executed by Worthen as well as by Lyon, and an assignment by Lyon of its interests in the building lease and in the ground lease.

3. *Permanent financing agreement.* By Note Purchase Agreement dated May 1, 1968, . . . New York Life agreed to purchase Lyon's $7,140,000 6-3/4% 25-year secured note to be issued upon completion of the building. Under this agreement Lyon warranted that it would lease the building to Worthen for a noncancelable term of at least 25 years under a net lease at a rent at least equal to the mortgage payments on the note. Lyon agreed to make quarterly payments of principal and interest equal to the rentals payable by Worthen during the corresponding primary term of the lease. . . . The security for the note was a first deed

39. This, of course, is on the assumption that Worthen exercises its option to extend the building lease. If it does not, Lyon remains liable for the substantial rents prescribed by the ground lease. This possibility brings into sharp focus the fact that Lyon, in a very practical sense, is at least the ultimate owner of the building. If Worthen does not extend, the building lease expires and Lyon may do with the building as it chooses.

The Government would point out, however, that the net amounts payable by Worthen to Lyon during the building lease's extended terms, if all are claimed, would approximate the amount required to repay Lyon's $500,000 investment at 6% compound interest. . . .

of trust and Lyon's assignment of its interests in the building lease and in the ground lease. . . . Worthen joined in the deed of trust as the owner of the fee and the parking deck.

In December 1969 the building was completed and Worthen took possession. At that time Lyon received the permanent loan from New York Life, and it discharged the interim loan from City Bank. The actual cost of constructing the office building and parking complex (excluding the cost of the land) exceeded $10,000,000.

Lyon filed its federal income tax returns on the accrual and calendar year basis. On its 1969 return, Lyon accrued rent from Worthen for December. It asserted as deductions one month's interest to New York Life; one month's depreciation on the building; interest on the construction loan from City Bank; and sums for legal and other expenses incurred in connection with the transaction.

On audit of Lyon's 1969 return, the Commissioner of Internal Revenue determined that Lyon was "not the owner for tax purposes of any portion of the Worthen Building," and ruled that "the income and expenses related to this building are not allowable . . . for Federal income tax purposes." . . . He also added $2,298.15 to Lyon's 1969 income as "accrued interest income." This was the computed 1969 portion of a gain, considered the equivalent of interest income, the realization of which was based on the assumption that Worthen would exercise its option to buy the building after 11 years, on November 30, 1980, at the price stated in the lease, and on the additional determination that Lyon had "loaned" $500,000 to Worthen. In other words, the Commissioner determined that the sale-and-leaseback arrangement was a financing transaction in which Lyon loaned Worthen $500,000 and acted as a conduit for the transmission of principal and interest from Worthen to New York Life.

All this resulted in a total increase of $497,219.18 over Lyon's reported income for 1969, and a deficiency in Lyon's federal income tax for that year in the amount of $236,596.36. The Commissioner assessed that amount, together with interest of $43,790.84, for a total of $280,387.20. . . .

After trial without a jury, the District Court, in a memorandum letter-opinion setting forth findings and conclusions, ruled in Lyon's favor and held that its claimed deductions were allowable. . . .

The United States Court of Appeals for the Eighth Circuit reversed. 536 F.2d 746 (1976). It held that the Commissioner correctly determined that Lyon was not the true owner of the building and therefore was not entitled to the claimed deductions. It likened ownership for tax purposes to a "bundle of sticks" and undertook its own evaluation of the facts. It concluded in agreement with the Government's contention, that Lyon "totes an empty bundle" of ownership sticks. Id., at 751. It stressed the following: (a) The lease agreements circumscribed Lyon's right to profit from its investment in the building by giving Worthen the option to purchase for an amount equal to Lyon's $500,000 equity plus 6% compound interest and the assumption of the unpaid balance of the New York Life mortgage. (b) The option prices did not take into account possible appreciation of the value of the building or inflation. (c) Any award realized as a result of destruction or condemnation of the building in excess of the mortgage balance and the $500,000 would be paid to Worthen and not Lyon. (d) The building rental payments during the primary term were exactly equal to the mortgage payments. (e) Worthen retained control over the ultimate disposition of the building through its various options to repurchase and to renew the lease plus its ownership of the site. (f) Worthen enjoyed all benefits and bore all burdens incident to the operation and ownership of the building so that, in the Court of Appeals' view, the only economic advantages accruing to Lyon, in the event it were considered to be the true owner of the property, were income tax savings of approximately $1.5 million during the first 11 years of the arrangement. The court concluded, . . . that the transaction was "closely akin" to that in Helvering v. Lazarus & Co., 308 U.S. 252 (1939).

> In sum, the benefits, risks, and burdens which [Lyon] has incurred with respect to the Worthen building are simply too insubstantial to establish a claim to the status of owner for tax purposes. . . . The vice of the present lease is that all of [its] features have been employed in the same transaction with the cumulative effect of depriving [Lyon] of any significant ownership interest.

536 F.2d, at 754. . . .

This Court, almost 50 years ago, observed that "taxation is not so much concerned with the refinements of title as it is with actual command over the property taxed — the actual benefit for which the tax is paid." Corliss v. Bowers, 281 U.S. 376, 378 (1930). In a number of cases, the Court has refused to permit the transfer of formal legal title to shift the incidence of taxation attributable to ownership of property where the transferor continues to retain significant control over the property transferred. . . . In applying this doctrine of substance over form, the Court has looked to the objective economic realities of a transaction rather than to the particular form the parties employed. The Court has never regarded "the simple expedient of drawing up papers," Comm'r v. Tower, 327 U.S. 280, 291 (1946), as controlling for tax purposes when the objective economic realities are to the contrary. "In the field of taxation, administrators of the laws, and the courts, are concerned with substance and realities, and formal written documents are not rigidly binding." Helvering v. Lazarus & Co., 308 U.S. 252, 255

(1939). . . . Nor is the parties' desire to achieve a particular tax result necessarily relevant. . . .

In the light of these general and established principles, the Government takes the position that the Worthen-Lyon transaction in its entirety should be regarded as a sham. The agreement as a whole, it is said, was only an elaborate financing scheme designed to provide economic benefits to Worthen and a guaranteed return to Lyon. The latter was but a conduit used to forward the mortgage payments, made under the guise of rent paid by Worthen to Lyon, on to New York Life as mortgagee. This, the Government claims, is the true substance of the transaction as viewed under the microscope of the tax laws. Although the arrangement was cast in sale-and-leaseback form, in substance it was only a financing transaction, and the terms of the repurchase options and lease renewals so indicate. It is said that Worthen could reacquire the building simply by satisfying the mortgage debt and paying Lyon its $500,000 advance plus interest, regardless of the fair market value of the building at the time; similarly, when the mortgage was paid off, Worthen could extend the lease at drastically reduced bargain rentals that likewise bore no relation to fair rental value but were simply calculated to pay Lyon its $500,000 plus interest over the extended term. Lyon's return on the arrangement in no event could exceed 6% compound interest (although the Government conceded it might well be less, Tr. of Oral Arg. 32). Furthermore, the favorable option and lease renewal terms made it highly unlikely that Worthen would abandon the building after it in effect had "paid off" the mortgage. The Government implies that the arrangement was one of convenience which, if accepted on its face, would enable Worthen to deduct its payments to Lyon as rent and would allow Lyon to claim a deduction for depreciation, based on the cost of construction ultimately borne by Worthen, which Lyon could offset against other income, and to deduct mortgage interest that roughly would offset the inclusion of Worthen's rental payments in Lyon's income. If, however, the Government argues, the arrangement was only a financing transaction under which Worthen was the owner of the building, Worthen's payments would be deductible only to the extent that they represented mortgage interest, and Worthen would be entitled to claim depreciation; Lyon would not be entitled to deductions for either mortgage interest or depreciation and it would not have to include Worthen's "rent" payments in its income because its function with respect to those payments was that of a conduit between Worthen and New York Life.

The Government places great reliance on Helvering v. Lazarus & Co., supra, and claims it to be precedent that controls this case. The taxpayer there was a department store. The legal title of its three buildings was in a bank as trustee for land-trust certificate holders. When the transfer to the trustee was made, the trustee at the same time leased the buildings back to the taxpayer for 99 years, with option to renew and purchase. The Commissioner, in stark contrast to his posture in the present case, took the position that the statutory right to depreciation followed legal title. The Board of Tax Appeals, however, concluded that the transaction between the taxpayer and the bank in reality was a mortgage loan and allowed the taxpayer depreciation on the buildings. This Court, as had the Court of Appeals, agreed with that conclusion and affirmed. It regarded the "rent" stipulated in the leaseback as a promise to pay interest on the loan, and a "depreciation fund" required by the lease as an amortization fund designed to pay off the loan in the stated period. Thus, said the Court, the Board justifiably concluded that the transaction, although in written form a transfer of ownership with a leaseback, was actually a loan secured by the property involved.

The *Lazarus* case, we feel, is to be distinguished from the present one and is not controlling here. Its transaction was one involving only two (and not multiple) parties, the taxpayer-department store and the trustee-bank. The Court looked closely at the substance of the agreement between those two parties and rightly concluded that depreciation was deductible by the taxpayer despite the nomenclature of the instrument of conveyance and the leaseback. . . .

The present case, in contrast, involves three parties, Worthen, Lyon, and the finance agency. The usual simple two-party arrangement was legally unavailable to Worthen. Independent investors were interested in participating in the alternative available to Worthen, and Lyon itself (also independent from Worthen) won the privilege. Despite Frank Lyon's presence on Worthen's board of directors, the transaction, as it ultimately developed, was not a familial one arranged by Worthen, but one compelled by the realities of the restrictions imposed upon the bank. Had Lyon not appeared, another interested investor would have been selected. The ultimate solution would have been essentially the same. Thus, the presence of the third party, in our view, significantly distinguishes this case from *Lazarus* and removes the latter as controlling authority.

It is true, of course, that the transaction took shape according to Worthen's needs. As the Government points out, Worthen throughout the negotiations regarded the respective proposals of the independent investors in terms of its own cost of funds. It is also true that both Worthen and the prospective investors compared the various proposals in terms of the return anticipated on the investor's equity. But all this is natural for parties contemplating entering into a transaction of this kind. Worthen needed a building for its banking operations and other purposes and necessarily had to know what its cost would be. The investors were in business to employ their funds in the most remunerative way possible. And, as the Court has said in the past, a transaction must be given its effect in accord with what actually occurred and not in accord with what might have occurred. . . .

There is no simple device available to peel away the form of this transaction and to reveal its substance. The effects of the transaction on all the parties were obviously different from those that would have resulted had Worthen been able simply to make a mortgage agreement with New York Life and to receive a $500,000 loan from Lyon. Then *Lazarus* would apply. Here, however, and most significantly, it was Lyon alone, and not Worthen, who was liable on the notes, first to City Bank, and then to New York Life. Despite the facts that Worthen had agreed to pay rent and that this rent equaled the amounts due from Lyon to New York Life, should anything go awry in the later years of the lease, Lyon was primarily liable. No matter how the transaction could have been devised otherwise, it remains a fact that as the agreements were placed in final form, the obligation on the notes fell squarely on Lyon. Lyon, an ongoing enterprise, exposed its very business well-being to this real and substantial risk.

The effect of this liability on Lyon is not just the abstract possibility that something will go wrong and that Worthen will not be able to make its payments. Lyon has disclosed this liability on its balance sheet for all the world to see. Its financial position was affected substantially by the presence of this long-term debt, despite the offsetting presence of the building as an asset. To the extent that Lyon has used its capital in this transaction, it is less able to obtain financing for other business needs.

In concluding that there is this distinct element of economic reality in Lyon's assumption of liability, we are mindful that the characterization of a transaction for financial accounting purposes, on the one hand, and for tax purposes, on the other, need not necessarily be the same. . . . Accounting methods or descriptions, without more, do not lend substance to that which has no substance. But in this case accepted accounting methods, as understood by the several parties to the respective agreements and as applied to the transaction by others, gave the transaction a meaningful character consonant with the form it was given.[40] Worthen was not allowed to enter into the type of transaction which the Government now urges to be the true substance of the arrangement. Lyon and Worthen cannot be said to have entered into the transaction intending that the interests involved were allocated in a way other than that associated with a sale-and-leaseback. . . .

The Court of Appeals acknowledged that the rents alone, due after the primary term of the lease and after the mortgage has been paid, do not provide the simple 6% return which, the Government urges,

40. We are aware that accounting standards have changed significantly since 1968 and that the propriety of Worthen's and Lyon's methods of disclosing the transaction in question may be a matter for debate under these new standards. . . .

Lyon is guaranteed, 536 F.2d, at 752. Thus, if Worthen chooses not to exercise its options, Lyon is gambling that the rental value of the building during the last 10 years of the ground lease, during which the ground rent is minimal, will be sufficient to recoup its investment before it must negotiate again with Worthen regarding the ground lease. There are simply too many contingencies, including variations in the value of real estate, in the cost of money, and in the capital structure of Worthen, to permit the conclusion that the parties intended to enter into the transaction as structured in the audit and according to which the Government now urges they be taxed.

It is not inappropriate to note that the Government is likely to lose little revenue, if any, as a result of the shape given the transaction by the parties. No deduction was created that is not either matched by an item of income or that would not have been available to one of the parties if the transaction had been arranged differently. While it is true that Worthen paid Lyon less to induce it to enter into the transaction because Lyon anticipated the benefit of the depreciation deductions it would have as the owner of the building, those deductions would have been equally available to Worthen had it retained title to the building. The Government so concedes. . . .

As is clear from the facts, none of the parties to this sale-and-leaseback was the owner of the building in any simple sense. But it is equally clear that the facts focus upon Lyon as the one whose capital was committed to the building and as the party, therefore, that was entitled to claim depreciation for the consumption of that capital. The Government has based its contention that Worthen should be treated as the owner on the assumption that throughout the term of the lease Worthen was acquiring an equity in the property. In order to establish the presence of that growing equity, however, the Government is forced to speculate that one of the options will be exercised and that, if it is not, this is only because the rentals for the extended term are a bargain. We cannot indulge in such speculation in view of the District Court's clear finding to the contrary. We therefore conclude that it is Lyon's capital that is invested in the building according to the agreement of the parties, and it is Lyon that is entitled to depreciation deductions, under §167. . . .

In short, we hold that where, as here, there is a genuine multiple-party transaction with economic substance which is compelled or encouraged by business or regulatory realities, is imbued with tax-independent considerations, and is not shaped solely by tax-avoidance features that have meaningless labels attached, the Government should honor the allocation of rights and duties effectuated by the parties. Expressed another way, so long as the lessor retains significant and genuine attributes of the traditional lessor status, the form of the transaction adopted by the parties governs for tax purposes. What those attributes are in any particular case will necessarily depend upon its facts. It suffices to say that, as here, a sale-and-leaseback, in and of itself, does not necessarily operate to deny a taxpayer's claim for deductions.

The judgment of the Court of Appeals, accordingly, is reversed.

Mr. Justice WHITE dissents and would affirm the judgment substantially for the reasons stated in the opinion in the Court of Appeals for the Eighth Circuit. 536 F.2d 746 (1976).

Mr. Justice STEVENS, dissenting.

In my judgment the controlling issue in this case is the economic relationship between Worthen and petitioner, and matters such as the number of parties, their reasons for structuring the transaction in a particular way, and the tax benefits which may result, are largely irrelevant. The question whether a leasehold has been created should be answered by examining the character and value of the purported lessor's reversionary estate.

For a 25-year period Worthen has the power to acquire full ownership of the bank building by simply repaying the amounts, plus interest, advanced by the New York Life Insurance Company and petitioner. During that period, the economic relationship among the parties parallels exactly the normal relationship between an owner and two lenders, one secured by a first mortgage and the other by a second mortgage. If Worthen repays both loans, it will have unencumbered ownership of the property. What the character of this relationship suggests is confirmed by the economic value that the parties themselves have placed on the reversionary interest.

All rental payments made during the original 25-year term are credited against the option repurchase price, which is exactly equal to the unamortized cost of the financing. The value of the repurchase option is thus limited to the cost of the financing, and Worthen's power to exercise the option is cost free. Conversely, petitioner, the nominal owner of the reversionary estate, is not entitled to receive *any* value for the surrender of its supposed rights of ownership. Nor does it have any power to control Worthen's exercise of the option.

"It is fundamental that 'depreciation is not predicated upon ownership of property *but rather upon an investment in property.*' No such investment exists when payments of the purchase price in accordance with the design of the parties yield no equity to the purchaser." Estate of Franklin v. Commissioner [supra page 694] (emphasis in original). Here, the petitioner has, in effect, been guaranteed that it will receive its original $500,000 plus accrued interest. But that is all. It incurs neither the risk of depreciation,[41] nor the benefit of possible appreciation. Un-

41. Petitioner argues that it bears the risk of depreciation during the primary term of

der the terms of the sale-leaseback, it will stand in no better or worse position after the 11th year of the lease — when Worthen can first exercise its option to repurchase — whether the property has appreciated or depreciated.[42] And this remains true throughout the rest of the 25-year period.

Petitioner has assumed only two significant risks. First, like any other lender, it assumed the risk of Worthen's insolvency. Second, it assumed the risk that Worthen might *not* exercise its option to purchase at or before the end of the original 25-year term. If Worthen should exercise that right *not* to repay, perhaps it would *then* be appropriate to characterize petitioner as the owner and Worthen as the lessee. But speculation as to what might happen in 25 years cannot justify the *present* characterization of petitioner as the owner of the building. Until Worthen has made a commitment either to exercise or not to exercise its option,[43] I think the Government is correct in its view that petitioner is not the owner of the building for tax purposes. At present, since Worthen has the unrestricted right to control the residual value of the property for a price which does not exceed the cost of its unamortized financing, I would hold, as a matter of law, that it is the owner.

I therefore respectfully dissent.

NOTES AND QUESTIONS

1. *Transaction generated by nontax considerations.* (a) Would (and should) the outcome have been different if Worthen had been free under the banking laws to own the building but had decided to enter into the

---

the lease because the option price decreases over time. . . . This is clearly incorrect. Petitioner will receive $500,000 plus interest, and no more or less, whether the option is exercised as soon as possible or only at the end of 25 years. Worthen, on the other hand, does bear the risk of depreciation, since its opportunity to make a profit from the exercise of its repurchase option hinges on the value of the building at the time.

42. After the 11th year of the lease, there are three ways that the lease might be terminated. The property might be condemned, the building might be destroyed by act of God, or Worthen might exercise its option to purchase. In any such event, if the property had increased in value, the entire benefit would be received by Worthen and petitioner would receive only its $500,000 plus interest. . . .

43. In this case, the lessee is not "economically compelled" to exercise its option. . . . Indeed, it may be more advantageous for Worthen to let its option lapse since the present value of the renewal leases is somewhat less than the price of the option to repurchase. See Brief for United States 40 n.26. But whether or not Worthen is likely to exercise the option, as long as it retains its unrestricted cost-free power to do so, it must be considered the owner of the building. See Sun Oil Co. v. Commissioner, 562 F.2d 258, 267 (C.A.3 1977) (repurchase option enabling lessee to acquire leased premises by repaying financing costs indicative of lessee's equity interest in those premises).

In effect, Worthen has an option to "put" the building to petitioner if it drops in value below $500,000 plus interest. Even if the "put" appears likely because of bargain lease rates after the primary terms, that would not justify the present characterization of petitioner as the owner of the building.

transaction with Frank Lyon Co. because the tax benefits of ownership were more beneficial to Frank Lyon Co. than to Worthen? (b) Does the Court mean to imply that the result turns on motive? If so, whose motive should be relevant? (c) Do you suppose Lyon (or any of the other bidders) would have been interested in the transaction were it not for the tax benefits? (d) The Court says that "the Government is likely to lose little revenue" by virtue of the decision because the tax benefits gained by Lyon are sacrificed by Worthen. This observation is inaccurate because when this case arose banks like Worthen generally could avoid paying taxes by investing in tax-exempt bonds and in fact in "the first full year for which it would have been entitled to interest and depreciation deductions, Worthen was not subject to federal income tax because it had no taxable income." Wolfman, The Supreme Court in the *Lyon*'s Den: A Failure of Judicial Process, 66 Cornell L. Rev. 1075, 1095 (1981). How are revenue effects relevant? Should the results in otherwise identical cases of this sort turn on the tax status of the parties? Given its tax status, why did Worthen initially want to own the building?

2. *Three-party transaction.* The Court distinguishes the *Lazarus & Co.* case on the ground that that case involved a two-party transaction while the present case involves three parties. Does this distinction make sense? "If Lyon had had available cash of $7,640,000, not just $500,000, it could have invested the full building cost without the intervention of New York Life. Would that have made the case a harder one for Lyon? The Court seems to say so." Wolfman, supra, at 1087. What if Worthen itself, rather than New York Life, had made the loan to Lyon?

3. *The burden on Lyon.* The Court says that the transaction can be expected to affect Lyon's ability "to obtain financing for other business needs." Why so? Would Lyon's financing ability have been less seriously constrained if the form of the transaction had been a loan of $500,000 by Lyon to Worthen and a guarantee by Lyon of a debt by Worthen to New York Life for $7,140,000?

4. *Risks and benefits to Lyon.* What are the prospects for Lyon's recovering more or less than its $500,000 plus interest? In other words, realistically, what were Lyon's risks and its opportunities for profit? What did the Court think about this issue? Is this the critical issue in the case? If so, do you think it was wise of the Court to have granted certiorari?

The safe-harbor leasing experiment. During the 1970s, the IRS and the courts developed rules for determining what was a genuine sale and leaseback as opposed to a financing arrangement. *Frank Lyon Co.* is the leading case of that era. In the 1981 act, Congress adopted "safe-harbor leasing" provisions, which allowed arrangements to be treated as leases even though the substance of ownership (by the lessor) was plainly lacking. Under the safe-harbor leasing rules, the transaction between Yaba and Xenon, described in the first part of this section, would have been treated as a genuine sale and leaseback. The effect of this law was to permit firms that did not pay tax (e.g., Chrysler Corp., which had suffered huge operating losses) to gain the advantage of accelerated depreciation and the investment credit by arranging for a firm with a profit (e.g., IBM) to buy the assets that the no-tax firm needed and lease those assets to the no-tax firm. The tax benefits of ownership by the profit firm (IBM) were passed on to the no-tax firm (Chrysler) (at least in large part, depending on the outcome of the bargain between the parties) in the form of relatively low rent payments by the latter. The effect was akin to a sale of tax benefits, which was the characterization given to these transactions in newspaper accounts. Huge deals were reported, and the public became outraged. Do you think the outrage was justified? If Congress wanted to allow no-tax firms to be able to take advantage of incentives to investment, is safe-harbor leasing the best way to do it?[44] In any event, in 1982 Congress repealed the 1981 rules.

Current law. The repeal of the safe-harbor leasing rules left the treatment of lease transactions in substantially the same position as that set forth in *Frank Lyon Co.,* and the treatment has remained in that position in the years following the repeal. In general, a sale-leaseback will be respected notwithstanding tax considerations so long as the transaction has a bona fide business purpose and the lessor retains sufficient burdens and benefits of ownership.

In *Frank Lyon Co.,* the Court focused on the business purpose of the lessee in structuring the transaction. In other cases, courts have focused on the business purpose of the lessor. Where the transaction is motivated entirely by tax considerations, and the lessor has no chance of earning a before-tax profit, courts have disallowed depreciation deductions

44. It would be possible to provide that where a firm is not subject to taxation, the investment credit (or even the ACRS deduction) would entitle the firm to a check from the Treasury. This possibility has been referred to as refundability. The arguments against it are summarized in the following passage from Sunley, Safe Harbor Leasing, 43 Tax Found. Tax Rev. 17 (April 1982):

> Refundability would tend to increase further the enormous power of the tax-writing committees. Refundability also might further erode the perception that the tax system is fair, since some companies will be paying what will be viewed as a negative income tax. Nonrefundability may also help keep the investment credit from entities not subject to the income tax, such as state and local governments, charities, and schools. Finally, the business community may fear that if the investment credit is made refundable, Congress will view it not as a reduction in tax, but as a subsidy program for business, thereby endangering the basic credit itself.

Refundability of the investment tax credit would not be as generous as leasing, since the ACRS benefits would not be cashed out. . . .

taken by the lessor. See Hilton v. Commissioner, 74 T.C. 305 (1980), aff'd per curiam, 671 F.2d 316 (9th Cir. 1982); James v. Commissioner, 87 T.C. 905 (1986).

As the *Frank Lyon Co.* case demonstrates, the determination of whether the lessor retains the benefits and burdens of ownership is factually complex. Where the rental payments are equal to the purchase price, plus interest, and the lessee is granted the option to purchase or to renew the lease at a nominal price, courts have tended to treat the lessee, rather than the lessor, as the owner of the property for tax purposes. See Oesterreich v. Commissioner, 226 F.2d 798 (9th Cir. 1955); Estate of Starr v. Commissioner, supra page 641.

The IRS has promulgated guidelines under which it will issue advance rulings that certain equipment leases will be respected for tax purposes. These guidelines are set forth in Revenue Procedures 75-21, 1975-1 C.B. 715, and 75-28, 1975-1 C.B. 752. The guidelines are not intended to represent the IRS's position on audit and do not apply to many forms of leases, such as the leases of real property. Nonetheless, the guidelines are generally taken into account when structuring a lease transaction. The guidelines have been summarized as follows by the Joint Committee on Taxation (General Explanation of the Revenue Provisions of the Tax Equity and Fiscal Responsibility Act of 1982 — Safe Harbor Leasing, 97th Cong., 2d Sess. 45-63 (1982)):

> 1. *Minimum investment.* The lessor must have a minimum 20 percent unconditional at-risk investment in the property. This rule represents an attempt to ensure that the lessor suffers some significant loss if the property declines in value.
>
> 2. *Purchase options.* In general, the lessee may not have an option to purchase the property at the end of the lease term unless, under the lease agreement, the option can be exercised only at fair market value (determined at the time of exercise). This rule precludes fixed price purchase options, even at a bona fide estimate of the projected fair market value of the property at the option date. In addition, when the property is first placed in service by the lessee, the lessor cannot have a contractual right to require the lessee or any other party to purchase the property, even at fair market value (a put).
>
> The fair market value purchase option requirement fulfills three purposes related to the determination of the economic substance of the transaction. First, it ensures that the lessor bears the risk implicit in ownership that no market will exist at the end of the lease. The owner of depreciable property is the person who bears any decline in value of the asset. Second, it ensures that the lessor has retained an equity interest in the property. Any fixed price option represents a limitation on the lessor's right of full enjoyment of the property's value. Third, it limits the ability of the parties to establish an artificial rent structure to avoid the cash flow test (described below). However, several courts have held that the mere existence of a fixed price purchase option does not prevent lease treatment

so long as the lessor retains other significant burdens and benefits of ownership.

3. *Lessee investment precluded.* Neither the lessee nor a party related to the lessee may furnish any part of the cost of the property. The rationale is that a lessee investment may suggest that the lessee is in substance a co-owner of the property.

4. *No lessee loans or guarantees.* As a corollary to the prior rule, the lessee must not loan to the lessor any of the funds necessary to acquire the property. In addition, the lessee must not guarantee any lessor loan.

5. *Profit and cash flow requirements.* The lessor must expect to receive a profit from the transaction and have a positive cash flow from the transaction independent of tax benefits. As mentioned previously, a profitability requirement is based on the requirement that lease transactions must have a business purpose independent of tax benefits.

6. *Limited use property.* Under Revenue Procedure 76-30, 1976-2 C.B. 647, property that can be used only by the lessee (limited use property) is not eligible for lease treatment. The rationale is that if the lessee is the only person who could realistically use the property, the lessor has not retained any significant ownership interest.

5. The Role of the Tax Lawyer

Most tax shelters require the services of a tax lawyer. The tax lawyer helps structure the transaction and often issues an opinion to investors that describes the probable tax consequences of the investment. In some cases, the tax benefits of the investment are unambiguous, and the work of the tax lawyer is noncontroversial. In other cases, however, the tax benefits might be uncertain, or overstated by the promoters of the tax shelter. May the tax lawyer write a narrowly drafted opinion that ignores this uncertainty? In 1984, after much debate and some compromise, the Treasury adopted a rule on tax-shelter opinions that requires the tax lawyer to opine on each material issue raised by the tax shelter and make inquiry as to all the facts that are relevant to its tax consequences. The rule (31 C.F.R. §10.33) is set forth below:

> (a) *Tax shelter opinions and offering materials.* A practitioner who provides a tax shelter opinion analyzing the Federal tax effects of a tax shelter investment shall comply with each of the following requirements:
>
> (1) *Factual matters.*
>
> (i) The practitioner must make inquiry as to all relevant facts, be satisfied that the material facts are accurately and completely described in the offering materials, and assure that any representations as to future activities are clearly identified, reasonable and complete.
>
> (ii) A practitioner may not accept as true asserted facts pertaining to the tax shelter which he/she should not, based on his/her back-

ground and knowledge, reasonably believe to be true. However, a practitioner need not conduct an audit or independent verification of the asserted facts, or assume that a client's statement of the facts cannot be relied upon, unless he/she has reason to believe that any relevant facts asserted to him/her are untrue.

(iii) If the fair market value of property or the expected financial performance of an investment is relevant to the tax shelter, a practitioner may not accept an appraisal or financial projection as support for the matters claimed therein unless:

(A) The appraisal or financial projection makes sense on its face;

(B) The practitioner reasonably believes that the person making the appraisal or financial projection is competent to do so and is not of dubious reputation; and

(C) The appraisal is based on the definition of fair market value prescribed under the relevant Federal tax provisions.

(iv) If the fair market value of purchased property is to be established by reference to its stated purchase price, the practitioner must examine the terms and conditions upon which the property was (or is to be) purchased to determine whether the stated purchase price reasonably may be considered to be its fair market value.

(2) *Relate law to facts.* The practitioner must relate the law to the actual facts and, when addressing issues based on future activities, clearly identify what facts are assumed.

(3) *Identification of material issues.* The practitioner must ascertain that all material Federal tax issues have been considered, and that all of those issues which involve the reasonable possibility of a challenge by the Internal Revenue Service have been fully and fairly addressed in the offering materials.

(4) *Opinion on each material issue.* Where possible, the practitioner must provide an opinion whether it is more likely than not that an investor will prevail on the merits of each material tax issue presented by the offering which involves a reasonable possibility of a challenge by the Internal Revenue Service. Where such an opinion cannot be given with respect to any material tax issue, the opinion should fully describe the reasons for the practitioner's inability to opine as to the likely outcome.

(5) *Overall evaluation.*

(i) Where possible, the practitioner must provide an overall evaluation whether the material tax benefits in the aggregate more likely than not will be realized. Where such an overall evaluation cannot be given, the opinion should fully describe the reasons for the practitioner's inability to make an overall evaluation. Opinions concluding that an overall evaluation cannot be provided will be given special scrutiny to determine if the stated reasons are adequate.

(ii) A favorable overall evaluation may not be rendered unless it is based on a conclusion that substantially more than half of the material tax benefits, in terms of their financial impact on a typical investor, more likely than not will be realized if challenged by the Internal Revenue Service.

(iii) If it is not possible to give an overall evaluation, or if the overall evaluation is that the material tax benefits in the aggregate will not be realized, the fact that the practitioner's opinion does not constitute a favorable overall evaluation, or that it is an unfavorable overall evaluation, must be clearly and prominently disclosed in the offering materials.

(iv) The following examples illustrate the principles of this paragraph:

Example (1). A limited partnership acquires real property in a sale-leaseback transaction. The principal tax benefits offered to investing partners consist of depreciation and interest deductions. Lesser tax benefits are offered to investors by reason of several deductions under Internal Revenue Code section 162 (ordinary and necessary business expenses). If a practitioner concludes that it is more likely than not that the partnership will not be treated as the owner of the property for tax purposes (which is required to allow the interest and depreciation deductions), then he/she may not opine to the effect that it is more likely than not that the material tax benefits in the aggregate will be realized, regardless of whether favorable opinions may be given with respect to the deductions claimed under Code section 162.

Example (2). A corporation electing under subchapter S of the Internal Revenue Code is formed to engage in research and development activities. The offering materials forecast that deductions for research and experimental expenditures equal to 75% of the total investment in the corporation will be available during the first two years of the corporation's operations, other expenses will account for another 15% of the total investment, and that little or no gross income will be received by the corporation during this period. The practitioner concludes that it is more likely than not that deductions for research and experimental expenditures will be allowable. The practitioner may render an opinion to the effect that based on this conclusion, it is more likely than not that the material tax benefits in the aggregate will be realized, regardless of whether he/she can opine that it is more likely than not that any of the other tax benefits will be achieved.

Example (3). An investment program is established to acquire offsetting positions in commodities contracts. The objective of the program is to close the loss positions in year one and to close the profit positions in year two. The principal tax benefit offered by the program is a loss in the first year, coupled with the deferral of offsetting gain until the following year. The practitioner concludes that the losses will not be deductible in year one. Accordingly, he/she may not render an opinion to the effect that it is more likely than not that the material tax benefits in the aggregate will be realized, regardless of the fact that he/she is of the opinion that losses not allowable in year one will be allowable in year two, because the principal tax benefit offered is a one-year deferral of income.

Example (4). A limited partnership is formed to acquire, own and operate residential rental real estate. The offering material forecasts gross income of $2,000,000 and total deductions of $10,000,000, resulting in net losses of $8,000,000 over the first six taxable years. Of the total deductions, depreciation and interest are projected to be $7,000,000, and other deductions $3,000,000. The practitioner concludes that it is more likely than not that all of the depreciation and interest deductions will be allowable, and that it is more likely than not that the other deductions will not be allowed. The practitioner may render an opinion to the effect that it is more likely than not that the material tax benefits in the aggregate will be realized.

In Formal Opinion 346 (Revised), 68 A.B.A.J. 471 (1982), the ABA Committee on Ethics and Professional Responsibility focuses on situations in which a lawyer's legal opinion on a tax-shelter investment will be presented by the lawyer's client (the promoter), in "offering materials," to nonclient investors, who "may be expected to rely upon the tax-shelter opinion in determining whether to invest in the venture." In this setting, the opinion offers, as a "guideline," the view that a lawyer should make a good faith effort to ensure that the facts presented to the investors are accurate and that all material legal issues have been addressed. In addition, a lawyer should:

6. Where possible, provide an opinion as to the likely outcome on the material tax issues addressed in the offering materials.

7. Where possible, provide an overall evaluation of the extent to which the tax benefits in the aggregate are likely to be realized.

Compare these guidelines with the standard of conduct prescribed in Formal Opinion 85-352 (supra page 44, footnote 86) for giving tax advice to a client ("some realistic possibility of success").

6. The Alternative Minimum Tax

The alternative minimum tax (AMT) imposes a tax at a reduced rate on a broader base. Its original objective was to ensure that a taxpayer (corporate or individual) could not take advantage of certain preferences (deductions, exclusions, accounting methods, etc.) to avoid all tax liability. This objective is achieved, roughly speaking, by taking taxable income, adding to it the amount of the preferences, and imposing a tax on this amount,[45] at a reduced rate (presently 26 to 28 percent for individuals and 20 percent for corporations); but the resulting tax is payable only to the extent that it exceeds the normal tax. To the extent that the amount of the AMT tax attributable to timing rules (as opposed to exclusions such as tax-exempt interest) exceeds the regular tax, the excess is treated as a credit that can be used in subsequent years to reduce the excess of the regular tax over the AMT. The credit provides relief where an AMT timing rule (e.g., the rule relating to the completed-contract method) results in an item being included in AMT income in one year and the same item is included in regular income under the regular-tax rules in a later year.

The AMT reflects an uneasy compromise over the role of tax preferences. Preferences are not part of the tax law by accident and their revenue costs are substantial. Congress seems prepared to accept the fact that they may be used by certain taxpayers to save millions of dollars in taxes. Yet Congress refuses to allow a taxpayer to use one or more preferences to reduce taxes too far, even though the total tax saving for that taxpayer may be only a few thousand dollars rather than millions.[46]

While originally conceived of as a device for preventing overuse of certain preferences, the AMT has been broadened (particularly in 1986) to the point where it may now be thought of as creating a second concept of taxable income that operates alongside the basic concept of the normal tax. The concept of the normal tax is narrow; it allows a wide variety of preferences. Since Congress is not entirely confident of that concept, it adopts the AMT, which defines a broader one, with fewer preferences. But Congress reflects its continuing, though uncertain, fidelity to the narrower concept by imposing a tax on the broader base only at a lower rate and collecting that tax only to the extent it exceeds the tax imposed on the narrower base. While the AMT represents an attack on preferences in general, it may deflect attention from particular preferences, and the objectives served by each, since the tax imposed

45. There is, however, an exemption of $40,000 for corporations and $45,000 for married taxpayers filing a joint return ($33,750 for single taxpayers). This exemption is phased out at the rate of 25 cents per dollar as alternative minimum taxable income (AMTI) rises above $150,000 ($112,500 for single taxpayers).

46. The AMT was first adopted in 1969 after the Treasury had brought to public attention a small number of cases of individuals with substantial incomes who had used various preferences to reduce their taxable incomes to zero and thereby avoid paying any tax. It was never made clear why one should be concerned about a few people saving relatively small amounts of taxes, when the source of their saving was a set of provisions that cost the Treasury billions of dollars each year and that Congress seemed to consider essential to the well-being of the economy. Nonetheless, the thought of rich people paying no taxes seemed to be sufficiently disturbing to force Congress to take some action.

under the AMT is a function of the aggregate effect of all listed preferences.

By no means all tax provisions that might be regarded as sources of deviation from an accurate definition of income are treated as preferences under the AMT. For example, some, but not all, tax-exempt interest is treated as a preference. As one can easily imagine, the legislative process for prescribing tax preferences for purposes of the AMT involves intense lobbying and debate and the resulting list may tell us more about political power than it does about sound principles of taxation.

The preferences are not entirely the same for individuals and corporations. The preferences for both individuals and corporations include the following:

1. *Depreciation on real property.* The preference amount for real property placed in service after 1986 is the excess of the amount allowed under the normal ACRS rules over the amount computed using a forty-year life (and the straightline method).

2. *Depreciation on personal property.* For property placed in service after 1986, the preference is computed by using the 150 percent declining balance method (as opposed to the 200 percent method under the normal tax) and a longer useful life. For both personal and real property, in computing AMT gain or loss from the disposition of the property, basis is adjusted using the depreciation allowed for AMT purposes.

3. *Tax-exempt interest.* The interest on certain newly issued private activity bonds is a preference.

4. *Percentage depletion.* The amount of the percentage depletion allowance in excess of cost depletion is a preference.

5. *Intangible drilling costs.* The preference is the excess of expensing over ten-year amortization or cost depletion, to the extent in excess of 65 percent of net oil and gas income.

6. *Accounting methods.* The benefits of the installment method and the completed-contract and other long-term-contract methods are preferences.

7. *Others.* Other preferences relate to sixty-month amortization of pollution control facilities; incentive tax credits; expensing of mining exploration and development costs; excludable income earned abroad by U.S. citizens; foreign tax credits; and net operating losses.

Preferences for individuals only include the following:

1. *Research and experimentation expenses.* The preference is the excess of the amount claimed as a current expense over the amount allowable with ten-year amortization.

2. *Incentive stock options.* The preference is the spread between the fair market value of the stock and the exercise price, at the time of exercise.

3. *Passive losses.* The preference is the amount of passive losses still allowable because of transition rules or special exceptions.

4. *Itemized deductions.* The amount of the preference is determined by disallowing certain itemized deductions, including the deduction for state and local taxes, and by limiting the deduction for medical expenses to the excess over 10 percent of AGI (as opposed to 7.5 percent for the normal tax).

5. *Circulation expenses.* The excess of expensing of circulation expenses of newspapers, magazines, etc. over three-year amortization is a preference.

6. *Half the amount of gain excluded under §1202.* (Section 1202 allows taxpayers to exclude 50 percent of gain on the sale of certain small business stock. See infra page 832.)

The preferences for corporations only include the following:

1. *Bad-debt reserves.* The allowance for bad-debt reserves (for small banks and thrifts, which are still permitted such reserves for normal tax purposes) is a preference.

2. *Alternative accounting methods.* There is an adjustment designed to capture part of the difference between income for tax purposes and income determined under an alternative method of accounting that generally includes more income and allows fewer current deductions and is thought to be closer to a true economic income.

3. *Others.* Other preferences relate to capital construction funds for shipping companies and certain specialized deductions for Blue Cross/Blue Shield and similar organizations.

4. *Planning.* The AMT creates opportunities for tax advisers to earn their fees by recommending tax-minimization strategies. For example, suppose a corporation in the current year will have normal income of $1 million and alternative minimum taxable income (AMTI) of $5 million, but expects that in the next year its normal income and its AMTI will both be $5 million. Suppose that the income expected for next year includes a $1 million fee for services and that it may be possible to arrange for advance payment of that fee, so that it can be included in the current year's income. At what rate will the fee be taxed if it is received in the current year? At what rate will it be taxed if it is received in the next year? Do you get the point? Suppose there is a repair expense that can be incurred this year or deferred until next year. What do tax considerations suggest should be done?

5. *Illustration.* The application of the AMT is illustrated in Table 6-2.

TABLE 6-2
Illustration of Individual Alternative Minimum Tax (§55)

Assume an individual, single taxpayer in 1994 with an adjusted gross income of $150,000; medical expenses (not reimbursed by insurance) of $20,000 (so the deduction, after allowing for the special 10 percent floor, is $5,000); and other deductions listed below; and the following items of tax preference for that year:

Adjusted gross income		$150,000
Plus: Preference items:		
ACRS deduction (in excess of amount permitted for AMT)	$50,000	
Bargain element of incentive stock option	15,000	
Total		$65,000
Less: Permissible deductions:		
Charitable contributions	$25,500	
Interest on home mortgage	12,000	
Medical expenses	5,000	
Total		$42,500
Alternative minimum taxable income		$172,500
Less: Exemption amount (after partial phase-out)		18,750
Amount subject to AMT		153,750
AMT tax (at 26 percent)		39,975
Regular tax (assumed arbitrarily for example)		33,390
Additional tax		$6,585

7

THE SPLITTING OF INCOME

For many purposes, families or households act as economic units, sharing income and other resources and assuming mutual obligations. Legal ownership of property and rights to income often has little or no effect on how funds are used. For income tax purposes, however, individual members of families or households, other than husband and wife, are, generally speaking, treated as separate taxpaying units and legal rights, rather than economic reality, often determine tax results. For example, if, within a household, a parent and his or her minor child both have income, two tax returns will be filed and the total income may enjoy the tax benefit of two starts at the bottom of the rate structure and a standard deduction for the child even if the parent claims itemized deductions. Before 1987 this advantage was available for the child's unearned, as well as earned, income. It was also possible for two personal exemptions to be claimed for the child, one by the parents and one by the child. Much tax planning was devoted to efforts to exploit the opportunities created by this system for defining taxpaying units. The effort is often referred to as the "splitting" or "shifting" of income or, when unsuccessful for tax purposes, as "assignment of income." The effect of the more compressed rate structure introduced by the 1986 act and of changes in the rules relating to the standard deduction and the personal exemption, and to the taxation of unearned income, was to remove much of the tax advantage of income splitting with children.

Since the incentive to split income arises from the Code's treatment of individuals within a family or household (other than husband and wife) as separate taxable units, one might think that there is an easy solution: require aggregation of all the household income on a single tax return. On examination, however, aggregation of income is a troublesome idea, even as to husband and wife. Some sense of the nature of the problem may be gained by thinking about how one should tax two households. The financial characteristics of the five people living in the first household are as follows:

	Husband	*Wife*	*Wife's mother*	*Daughter age 24*	*Son age 16*
Income from:					
Wages	$50,000	$25,000	-0-	$15,000	$1,000
Separate property	2,000	3,000	$10,000	-0-	-0-
Community property	5,000	5,000	-0-	-0-	-0-
Trust	-0-	-0-	-0-	5,000	5,000
Pension	-0-	-0-	8,000	-0-	-0-
Total	$57,000	$33,000	$18,000	$20,000	$6,000

Total household income: $134,000

The other household is the same except that all of the income of $134,000 is from the salary of the husband.

Taxpayers have sought to shift income not only to other individuals but also to entities such as trusts and corporations.

A. INCOME FROM SERVICES: DIVERSION BY PRIVATE AGREEMENT

Our first case, Lucas v. Earl, arose at a time when there was only one rate schedule used by all taxpayers and when husband and wife were treated as separate taxpayers. Since 1948 we have had a system of joint returns and split income for husband and wife (see supra page 38) and as a result no advantage can be achieved (except in rare circumstances) by shifting income from one spouse to another, but the legal principles developed in early husband/wife cases are still relevant to efforts to shift income to other family members and to entities.

LUCAS v. EARL

281 U.S. 111 (1930)

Mr. Justice HOLMES delivered the opinion of the Court.

This case presents the question whether the respondent, Earl, could be taxed for the whole of the salary and attorney's fees earned by him in the years 1920 and 1921, or should be taxed for only a half of them in view of a contract with his wife which we shall mention. The Commissioner of Internal Revenue and the Board of Tax Appeals imposed a tax upon the whole, but their decision was reversed by the Circuit Court of Appeals, 30 F.2d 898. . . .

By the contract, made in 1901, Earl and his wife agreed

> that any property either of us now has or may hereafter acquire . . . in any way, either by earnings (including salaries, fees, etc.), or any rights by contract or otherwise, during the existence of our marriage, or which we or either of us may receive by gift, bequest, devise, or inheritance, and all the proceeds, issues, and profits of any and all such property shall be treated and considered, and hereby is declared to be received, held, taken, and owned by us as joint tenants, and not otherwise, with the right of survivorship.

The validity of the contract is not questioned, and we assume it to be unquestionable under the law of the State of California,[1] in which the parties lived. Nevertheless we are of opinion that the Commissioner and Board of Tax Appeals were right.

The Revenue Act of 1918 . . . imposes a tax upon the net income of every individual including "income derived from salaries, wages, or compensation for personal service . . . of whatever kind and in whatever form paid," [§61(a)]. . . . A very forcible argument is presented to the effect that the statute seeks to tax only income beneficially received, and that taking the question more technically the salary and fees became the joint property of Earl and his wife on the very first instant on which they were received. We well might hesitate upon the latter proposition, because however the matter might stand between husband and wife he was the only party to the contracts by which the salary and fees were earned, and it is somewhat hard to say that the last step in the performance of those contracts could be taken by anyone but himself alone. But this case is not to be decided by attenuated subtleties. It turns on the import and reasonable construction of the taxing act. There is no doubt that the statute could tax salaries to those who earned them and provide that the tax could not be escaped by anticipatory arrangements and contracts however skillfully devised to prevent the salary when paid from vesting even for a second in the man who earned it. That seems to us the import of the statute before us and we think that no distinction can be taken according to the motives leading to the arrangement by which the fruits are attributed to a different tree from that on which they grew.

Judgment reversed.

1. [Under the community property law of California at the time this case arose, Mrs. Earl's rights in Mr. Earl's salary and fees were less substantial than the rights she acquired under the contract. In 1927, in response to Poe v. Seaborn, infra page 745, California changed its law to give wives greater community-property rights. — Eds.]

NOTES AND QUESTIONS

1. *Fruit and tree.* The fruit-and-tree metaphor in the last sentence of Justice Holmes's opinion is widely known among tax experts and is frequently cited but, like many metaphors, is more colorful than helpful. For example, if two unrelated lawyers form a partnership and agree to split equally any net income, the income will be taxed according to the rights created by the agreement, regardless whose efforts happen to generate the income. The fruit-and-tree metaphor is simply inaccurate as applied to such a case. In other cases, it is often more puzzling to try to figure out what is tree and what is fruit than to reach a decision by using more direct analysis.

2. *Mrs. Earl's tax status.* Was Mrs. Earl also taxable on the income in question? Why?

3. *Tax avoidance.* Was *Earl* a tax avoidance case?

4. *Theory of the case.* (a) Is it fair to say that in the era of male supremacy in which this case arose, Mr. Earl probably gave up nothing of significance when he entered into the contract with Mrs. Earl? Would the result have been different if the agreement had been for the life of Mr. Earl rather than "during the existence of [the] marriage"? If the income in question had gone into a trust for the benefit of impoverished relatives of Mrs. Earl, to be selected by her, would it still have been taxable to Mr. Earl?

(b) What if Mrs. Earl had paid for Mr. Earl's legal education, his law library, etc., in return for an assignment of 50 percent of his professional earnings either for a stated period or for life? Would the income then be taxed to Mr. Earl? See Hundley v. Commissioner, 48 T.C. 339 (1967), in which the taxpayer, a teenager, agreed in 1958 in exchange for his father's coaching, business management, and agent services, to share with his father equally any bonus he might receive for signing a professional baseball contract. The taxpayer signed with a professional team in 1960 and was allowed to deduct as a business expense $55,000 (one-half of his $110,000 bonus) paid to his father. But compare Allen v. Commissioner, 50 T.C. 466 (1968), aff'd per curiam, 410 F.2d 398 (3d Cir. 1969), where a similar effort failed since the taxpayer shared his bonus with his mother, whom the Tax Court found to be ignorant of baseball.

(c) In some instances splitting may be attempted by creation of a partnership between, say, a father and his sons. This possibility is explored later in this chapter (page 791).

5. *Gratuitous performance of services.* Suppose that a famous actress plays the lead role in a movie produced by her son and is not paid for her services. Should and would the mother be taxed on some reasonable compensation? How would you determine the appropriate amount? It may be difficult to draw the line between this kind of service performed

for one's child and other, presumably nontaxable, benefits that a parent may bestow on a child, such as investment advice by an investment adviser or legal advice by a lawyer.

When it comes to services performed for charities, the rules are more generous to taxpayers than the rules relating to services performed for an employer, customer, or client. Ordinarily any income that might be attributed to a taxpayer from performance of services for a charity would be offset by a deduction of the same amount. The issue becomes significant, however, where the deduction would be limited by the percentage limitations in §170, by the phaseout of §68, or by the alternative minimum tax. The regulations provide that no income arises where services are rendered directly to a charitable organization (Regs. §1.61-2(c)), and this includes services rendered to a charity as promoter of public entertainment (G.C.M. 27026, 1951-2 C.B. 7). But despite the scorn expressed by Justice Holmes for "attenuated subtleties," the regulations distinguish between services rendered directly to the charity and services rendered to a third person with payment going to the charity. This is the kind of distinction that invites manipulation of the forms of transactions to achieve desirable tax results.

It may be difficult to work up concern about the shifting of income to charities. The principles applied to charities have been extended, however, to services rendered for the benefit of political organizations. See Rev. Rul. 68-503, 1968-2 C.B. 44, issued during the heat of the 1968 presidential campaign and holding that a featured performer at a political fund-raising event, for which admission was charged, was not taxable on any amount of income. Is this result consistent with *Earl?* with sound principles of taxation? with sound principles of campaign funding? If income should be taxed to the performer at a political fund-raising event, what if a famous actor appears in a television "spot" on behalf of a candidate (with no direct effort to raise money)?

B. INCOME FROM SERVICES: DIVERSION BY OPERATION OF LAW

POE v. SEABORN

282 U.S. 101 (1930)

Mr. Justice ROBERTS delivered the opinion of the Court.

Seaborn and his wife, citizens and residents of the State of Washington, made for the year 1927 separate income tax returns. . . .

During and prior to 1927 they accumulated property comprising real estate, stocks, bonds and other personal property. While the real estate stood in [the husband's] name alone, it is undisputed that all of the property real and personal constituted community property and that neither owned any separate property or had any separate income.

The income comprised Seaborn's salary, interest on bank deposits and on bonds, dividends, and profits on sales of real and personal property. He and his wife each returned one-half the total community income as gross income and each deducted one-half of the community expenses to arrive at the net income returned.

The Commissioner of Internal Revenue determined that all of the income should have been reported in the husband's return. . . .

The case requires us to construe Sections 210(a) and 211(a) of the Revenue Act of 1926,[2] and apply them, as construed, to the interests of husband and wife in community property under the law of Washington. These sections lay a tax upon the net income of every individual. The Act goes no farther, and furnishes no other standard or definition of what constitutes an individual's income. The use of the word "of" denotes ownership. . . .

The Commissioner concedes that the answer to the question involved in the cause must be found in the provisions of the law of the State, as to a wife's ownership of or interest in community property. What, then, is the law of Washington as to the ownership of community property and of community income including the earnings of the husband's and wife's labor?

The answer is found in the statutes of the State, and the decisions interpreting them.

These statutes provide that, save for property acquired by gift, bequest, devise or inheritance, all property however acquired after marriage, by either husband or wife, or by both, is community property. On the death of either spouse his or her interest is subject to testamentary disposition, and failing that, it passes to the issue of the decedent and not to the surviving spouse. While the husband has the management and control of community personal property and like power of disposition thereof as of his separate personal property, this power is subject to restrictions which are inconsistent with denial of the wife's interest as co-owner. The wife may borrow for community purposes and bind the community property. . . . Since the husband may not discharge his separate obligation out of community property, she may, suing alone, enjoin collection of his separate debt out of community property. . . . She may prevent his making substantial gifts out of community property without her consent. . . . The community property is not liable for the husband's torts not committed in carrying on the business of the community. . . .

2. [These sections provided that the normal tax and the surtax "shall be levied, collected, and paid for each taxable year upon the net income of every individual." Substantially the same language now appears in §1(a) of the Code. — Eds.]

Without further extending this opinion it must suffice to say that it is clear the wife has, in Washington, a vested property right in the community property, equal with that of her husband; and in the income of the community, including salaries or wages of either husband or wife, or both. . . .

The taxpayer contends that if the test of taxability under Sections 210 and 211 is ownership, it is clear that income of community property is owned by the community and that husband and wife have each a present vested one-half interest therein.

The Commissioner contends, however, that we are here concerned not with mere names, nor even with mere technical legal titles; that calling the wife's interest vested is nothing to the purpose, because the husband has such broad powers of control and alienation, that while the community lasts, he is essentially the owner of the whole community property, and ought so to be considered for the purposes of Sections 210 and 211. He points out that as to personal property the husband may convey it, make contracts affecting it, may do anything with it short of committing a fraud on his wife's rights. And though the wife must join in any sale of real estate, he asserts that the same is true, by virtue of statutes, in most States which do not have the community system. He asserts that control without accountability is indistinguishable from ownership, and that since the husband has this, quoad community property and income, the income is that "of" the husband under Sections 210, 211 of the income tax law.

We think, in view of the law of Washington above stated, this contention is unsound. The community must act through an agent. . . .

The reasons for conferring such sweeping powers of management on the husband are not far to seek. Public policy demands that in all ordinary circumstances, litigation between wife and husband during the life of the community should be discouraged. Law-suits between them would tend to subvert the marital relation. The same policy dictates that third parties who deal with the husband respecting community property shall be assured that the wife shall not be permitted to nullify his transactions. The powers of partners, or of trustees of a spendthrift trust, furnish apt analogies.

The obligations of the husband as agent of the community are no less real because the policy of the State limits the wife's right to call him to account in a court. Power is not synonymous with right. Nor is obligation coterminous with legal remedy. The law's investiture of the husband with broad powers, by no means negatives the wife's present interest as a co-owner.

We are of opinion that under the law of Washington the entire property and income of the community can no more be said to be that of the husband, than it could rightly be termed that of the wife. . . .

The Commissioner urges that we have, in principal [sic], decided the instant question in favor of the Government. He relies on United States

v. Robbins, 269 U.S. 315; Corliss v. Bowers, 281 U.S. 376; and Lucas v. Earl [supra page 742].

In the *Robbins* case, we found that the law of California, as construed by her own courts, gave the wife a mere expectancy and that the property rights of the husband during the life of the community were so complete that he was in fact the owner. . . .

The *Corliss* case raised no issue as to the intent of Congress, but as to its power. We held that where a donor retains the power at any time to revest himself with the principal of the gift, Congress may declare that he still owns the income. While he has technically parted with title, yet he in fact retains ownership, and all its incidents. But here the husband never has ownership. That is in the community at the moment of acquisition.

In the *Earl* case a husband and wife contracted that any property they had or might thereafter acquire in any way, either by earnings (including salaries, fees, etc.), or any rights by contract or otherwise, "shall be treated and considered and hereby is declared to be received held taken and owned by us as joint tenants. . . ." We held that, assuming the validity of the contract under local law, it still remained true that the husband's professional fees, earned in years subsequent to the date of the contract, were his individual income, "derived from salaries, wages, or compensation for personal services." . . . The very assignment in that case was bottomed on the fact that the earnings would be the husband's property, else there would have been nothing on which it could operate. That case presents quite a different question from this, because here, by law, the earnings are never the property of the husband, but that of the community. . . .

The District Court was right in holding that the husband and wife were entitled to file separate returns, each treating one-half of the community income as his or her respective income, and its judgment is affirmed.

NOTES AND QUESTIONS

1. *Strategy.* In Poe v. Seaborn the government relied on United States v. Robbins, a California case that it had won, and on the notion of the husband's control of the property. With the advantage of hindsight one can suggest that the government might have done better to emphasize that part of the income had been the husband's salary, to attempt to tax only that part, and to invoke Justice Holmes's fruit-and-tree metaphor from Lucas v. Earl. One might take some comfort in the fact that the government may have lost because of overreaching, but the outcome has had profound, and probably unfortunate, consequences for the development of our tax structure. See infra Note 4.

2. *Reconciliation with Lucas v. Earl.* What do you think of the Court's effort to distinguish Lucas v. Earl?

3. *Diversions to comply with the law.* Suppose that a politician is offered a bribe and declines to accept it on the ground that bribes are illegal, but suggests that payment to his wife might be appropriate. If the money is then paid to the wife, who is taxable? Would it matter if, somehow, the payment to the wife were legally permissible and the politician argues, "I could not legally take the money, so it cannot be my income"? In Commissioner v. First Security Bank of Utah, 405 U.S. 394 (1972), the taxpayer bank had been earning sales commissions equal to 40 to 55 percent of the premiums paid by its borrowers on credit life, health, and accident insurance business generated by the bank. After having been advised by counsel that it could not lawfully earn such commissions, the bank set up another corporation, which it owned and which in effect received the fees that had previously been received by the bank. This new arrangement apparently was lawful because the subsidiary was regarded as a separate entity, and it, rather than the parent bank, was viewed as the seller of the policies. The Commissioner sought to tax the profits of the subsidiary to the bank under §482. (Section 482 is, roughly speaking, a statutory embodiment of the assignment of income doctrine that originated in cases like Lucas v. Earl. See section K of this chapter.) The Court held in favor of the bank, saying, among other things (405 U.S. at 403), "We know of no decision of this Court wherein a person has been found to have taxable income which he did not receive and which he was prohibited from receiving." On the other hand, consider United States v. Scott, 660 F.2d 1145 (7th Cir. 1981), cert. denied, 455 U.S. 907 (1982). In that case the taxpayer, Scott, in 1972 was Attorney General of Illinois and had regulatory and enforcement powers over various businesses owned by a man named Wirtz. Scott called Wirtz and asked Wirtz to find a job for his friend Cooper, a woman whom Scott later married. Wirtz put Cooper on the payroll of one of his corporations, but it was established that Cooper performed no services for the corporation or for any other of Wirtz's businesses. Wirtz also made some payments directly to Scott. The court held Scott taxable on payments of about $11,000 received by Cooper from Wirtz's corporation. The court was not required to consider whether the payments, if made directly to Scott, would have been bribes, though it is difficult to imagine any more appropriate description.

4. *Subsequent events: joint returns and the marriage penalty.* After the decision in Poe v. Seaborn, couples in community property states enjoyed a significant tax advantage compared with couples in common-law property states. Spouses in common-law property states could split income by transfers of income-producing property but not by diversions of earnings from the performance of services. In the years following the decision in *Seaborn,* particularly as rates rose before and during

World War II, some common law states reacted by adopting the community property system. Congress could have eliminated most of the disparity among the states by rejecting *Seaborn* and taxing spouses on their own salaries, wages, fees, etc., regardless of the effects of community property law; *Seaborn* was based on statutory language, not on the Constitution. But rejecting *Seaborn* would have meant taking away from couples in community property states a benefit to which they had become accustomed, and Congress followed the more politically palatable course of extending the benefit of income splitting to all married couples. It did this, in 1948, by allowing married couples in all states to file joint returns and compute the total tax by first computing a tax on half of the total and then doubling that amount, thereby providing two starts at the bottom of the rate structure, regardless of how income was earned and regardless of legal claims to it.

The effect of the 1948 introduction of joint returns and income splitting was to treat all couples alike regardless not only of where they lived but also of the portions of the income contributed by each spouse. Single-earner families paid the same tax as families with the same total income earned half by each spouse. In other words, the principle was that equal-income couples paid equal taxes. This meant in turn that taxes generally were reduced by marriage; if a high-income individual married a person with little or no income, the total tax liability declined substantially. As time passed and social structure and mores changed, single people began increasingly to complain of this effect, pointing out that married individuals whose income was the same as theirs were paying substantially less tax. They complained of what might be called a "singles penalty." In 1969 Congress responded to this complaint by reducing the rates for single people by 20 percent, thereby reducing, though not eliminating, the singles penalty. But Congress was unwilling to make this new rate structure available to married couples wishing to file separate returns. If it had done so, it would have reintroduced the pre-1948 disparity between community-property and common law states, unless it had been willing to reject Poe v. Seaborn and tax each spouse on his or her own income regardless of community property rules. But that possibility would have required rejection of the principle, by then firmly embedded, that equal-income couples should pay the same tax regardless who produces the income.

The 1969 introduction of the single-person rate schedule, together with the denial of this rate schedule to married persons filing separate returns, produced the "marriage penalty" described in Chapter 1 (page 40). There was no way to avoid this unfortunate effect without abandoning either the favorable rate structure for single people or the principle that all married couples with the same income should pay the same tax. To illustrate the marriage penalty and its sources, imagine four households. In household *A* is a single person with a taxable income of $100,000. Her tax is $26,876 (using the 1991 rate schedule). Household *B* consists of a married couple. The wife earns a taxable income of $100,000 and the husband earns nothing. Their tax is $24,116. In household *C* we find another married couple, with a total taxable income of $100,000, of which $50,000 is earned by the husband and $50,000 by the wife. Household *D* consists of a man and a woman who are not married to each other but are living together in an intimate, sharing, long-term relationship. Each has a taxable income of $50,000 and pays a tax of $11,376. These facts are summarized in Table 7-1.

If the two individuals in household *D* marry each other, their tax increases by $1,365. Suppose Congress decides to eliminate this marriage penalty by raising the tax for each of them so that their total tax is $24,116, the same as that of couple *C*. This means raising the single-person rate. If that is done, it becomes necessary to raise the rate for single person *A* as well. But then *A* would compare herself with wife *B;* this is the kind of complaint that led to the adoption in 1969 of the single-person rate schedule. Let's return, then, to couple *D* and couple *C*. Suppose Congress allows husband *C* and wife *C* to file separately and pay a tax of $22,751. This eliminates the marriage penalty, but now couple *B* cries "foul," on the theory that married couples with the same total income should pay the same tax, a theory that seems to be popular in Congress and consistent with community property law (see Poe v. Seaborn) and with modern notions of the role of the stay-at-home spouse in generating family income. In short, if you want a progressive rate structure and at the same time (a) you want to impose equal amounts of tax on married couples with the same total income, regardless of which spouse performs the services that directly produce the income, and (b) you want to mitigate the disparity between single person *A* and couple *B,* then you cannot avoid a system that produces a marriage penalty.[3]

TABLE 7-1
Illustration of the "Marriage Penalty"
1988

Taxpayer(s)	*Taxable Income*	*Tax*
A. Single person *A*	$100,000	$26,876
B. Husband *B*	-0-	
Wife *B*	100,000	
Total	100,000	24,116
C. Husband *C*	50,000	
Wife *C*	50,000	
Total	100,000	24,116
D. Single man *D*	50,000	11,376
Single woman *D*	50,000	11,376
Total	100,000	22,751

3. The aspect of the marriage penalty that seems to bother people most is not the

C. INCOME FROM SERVICES: MORE ON DIVERSION BY PRIVATE AGREEMENT

ARMANTROUT v. COMMISSIONER

67 T.C. 996 (1977), aff'd per curiam, 570 F.2d 210 (7th Cir. 1978)

. . . Hamlin, Inc., a Delaware corporation (Hamlin), is engaged in the business of manufacturing, distributing, and selling electronic components. During the taxable years 1971 through 1973, petitioner Richard T. Armantrout was employed by Hamlin as vice president in charge of marketing. . . .

Educo, Inc. (Educo), a Delaware corporation, is engaged in the business of designing, implementing, and administering college education benefit plans for corporate employers.

Sometime in 1969, petitioner Llewellyn G. Owens noticed an advertisement in the Wall Street Journal which outlined, in a general way, the potential benefits of the Educo plan. Upon subsequent investigation, Mr. Owens suggested that such a plan be implemented by Hamlin, Inc.

On September 2, 1969, Hamlin entered into an agreement with Funds for Education, Inc., a Delaware corporation. Subsequently, on November 17, 1969, Funds for Education changed its corporate name to Educo, Inc.

Pursuant to the agreement, Educo undertook to administer an Educo education plan to provide funds for college expenses for the children of certain key employees of Hamlin. Hamlin, upon becoming a participant of the Educo plan, agreed to make contributions to the Continental Illinois National Bank & Trust Co. of Chicago which acted as trustee under a trust agreement entered into with Educo on December 9, 1969.

Pursuant to the Educo plan, children of Hamlin's key employees named in the enrollment schedules which formed a part of the plan would be entitled to receive sums from the trustee to defray college education expenses. Upon receipt of the appropriate information from Hamlin, Educo would direct the trustee to pay, in accordance with the

increase in tax that occurs where two single people meet, marry, and then begin to live together. In that case a significant change in circumstances has occurred, which might justify a change in tax liability. What is most bothersome is the increase that occurs where two people who have been living together for some time decide to marry. It has been suggested that this form of the marriage penalty could be eliminated by treating single people who are cohabitating as if they were married. See Blumberg, Cohabitation without Marriage: A Different Perspective, 28 U.C.L.A. L. Rev. 1125, 1158-1159 (1981). Presumably such a proposal contemplates married-person status only for those single people living together in some degree of intimacy, not just as roommates or as renter and boarder. But how would the government test for the required degree of intimacy? If the proposal is to impose the married-person rate on any person who shares living space with another person, the incentive effects seem intolerably perverse.

enrollment schedule, the expenses incurred by the employees' children in attending a college or university, trade or vocational school. . . .

The Educo plan as implemented by Hamlin provided for a maximum of $10,000 to be made available to the children of any one employee with an upper limit of $4,000 available to any one child. Payments to or on behalf of a child enrolled in the plan were limited during any one year to one-fourth of the total amount scheduled for that child; however, the unused funds of a prior year could be used to defray expenses in a subsequent academic year. Children otherwise qualified who did not utilize any of the available funds before reaching age 21 or within 2 years after completing the 12th grade would be ineligible to participate in the plan.

In adopting the Educo plan, it was Hamlin's intention to make available sufficient funds to enable at least two children of each key employee to attend college. Consonant therewith, the plan was in general administered so that $4,000 was scheduled to be received by each of the employee's two eldest children while $2,000 would be provided to a third younger child; funds not utilized by the older children were in turn made available to younger children, thus it was possible that more than three children of each key employee could ultimately participate in the plan. However, this administrative policy was not required by the terms of the plan and, moreover, prior to the adoption of the first enrollment schedule the employee-parents were given the opportunity to allocate the available funds within the maximum allowed by the plan to their children in amounts different from those described above. . . .

If any child covered by the Educo plan did not utilize the funds scheduled for his benefit within the period prescribed by the plan, Hamlin could enroll a replacement child of the same or younger age to use any unused funds. Moreover, Hamlin could allocate the unused funds to children already enrolled in the plan or it could apply the funds toward the reduction of its future obligation to make payments to the Educo trust. . . .

The Hamlin Educo plan was adopted, in part, to relieve Hamlin's most important employees from concern and trepidation about the cost of providing a college education for their children and, thus, enable those employees to better perform their duties as employees of Hamlin. Moreover, it was felt by Hamlin that the Educo plan was a benefit which the key employees wanted it to provide. The cost of higher education would be defrayed by the Educo trust for all the children enrolled in the plan without regard to any objective scholastic criteria such as admissions test scores, rank in high school class, or financial need.

Children eligible to participate in the Educo plan were those whose parents were regarded as key employees in the Hamlin organization and although the selection of such employees bore a rough correlation to salary, the determinative factor was the employees' value to the company. Compensation of key employees who did not have children was not increased to counterpoise the effect of the Educo plan on those employees with children. Children of lesser employees could be included as the value of the parents to Hamlin increased.

The employees whose children participated in the Educo plan had no right or claim to the benefits which flowed from the trustees in discharge of their children's educational expenses as outlined in the plan. It was, moreover, impossible for the parent of any child enrolled in the plan to receive benefit from any unused portion of the available funds not expended by their children.

Under the terms of the plan, benefits were payable in accordance with the applicable enrollment schedule to defray the costs incurred by the employee's child in attending college. However, should an employee-parent cease to be employed by Hamlin, the plan would become inoperable for each of his children except that education expenses incurred prior to the termination of the parent's employment would continue to be eligible for payment in accordance with the terms of the Educo plan.

Considering the Educo plan to be a unique benefit made available to its most important employees, Hamlin would describe in a general way the nature and advantages offered by the plan to prospective employees. The existence of the plan has enabled Hamlin to be successful in recruiting and retaining key employees and to do so without the assistance of higher salaries competitive with those in larger urban areas.

By statutory notices of deficiency issued to the respective taxpayers in the cases consolidated herein, the Commissioner determined that the amounts distributed by the Educo trust were scholarships which formed a part of the employees' compensation and were directly related to each employee's pattern of employment and, therefore, compensation for services includable in gross income.

Opinion

Respondent contends that the amounts distributed by the Educo trust in discharge of certain of the educational expenses of petitioners' children constitute taxable income to petitioners because the payments were attributable to petitioners' employment relationship with Hamlin rather than on the basis of any competitive criteria such as need, motivation, or merit.

Petitioners in essence argue, however, that while the amounts distributed by the Educo trust were perhaps "generated" by their efforts as employees of Hamlin, they do not constitute gross income because they were neither beneficially received by them nor did they have the right to receive such distributions and, moreover, because they did not possess an ownership interest in such amounts. In addition, petitioners assert that the mere realization of some familial satisfaction is not sufficient to occasion the recognition of income. For reasons which will hereinafter be expressed, we hold that the distributions from Educo trust to petitioners' children were in the nature of deferred compensation to petitioners and, therefore, includable in their gross income according to the provisions of section 83.

Proper analysis of this issue must begin with the notion often called "the first principle of income taxation: that income must be taxed to him who earns it." Commissioner v. Culbertson, 337 U.S. 733, 739-740 (1949). It is also important to recall that the income tax consequences of a particular transaction are not to be accorded by reference to "anticipatory arrangements" or "attenuated subtleties" but rather income must be attributed to the tree upon which it grew. Lucas v. Earl [supra page 742]. In addition, in apportioning the income tax consequence of a particular factual pattern, it is the substance of the transaction which must govern. Gregory v. Helvering [infra page 910]. . . .

While we might agree with petitioners that mere realization of some "familial" satisfaction is perhaps not sufficient to occasion a tax, we must nevertheless take cognizance of the context in which such a benefit accrues. When such a benefit is created in an employment situation and in connection with the performance of services, we are unable to conclude that such a benefit falls outside the broad scope of section 61. . . . This view is especially compelling herein because there is a specific, additional, and identifiable cost incurred by petitioners' employer.

We find Kohnstamn v. Pedrick, 153 F.2d 506 (2d Cir. 1945), to be inapposite to the issue presented. In *Kohnstamn,* the Commissioner sought to charge the husband with income earned on investments made by his wife from income which was paid to her by a trust to support and maintain their children. The Government's theory was that because the mother consulted him in the management of the income, he "generated" it and was, therefore, taxable on that income. The court held that the amounts earned on the trust earnings were not taxable to the husband because the realization of some familial satisfaction, without more, was not sufficient to occasion a tax burden. In our view, the *Kohnstamn* rationale does not extend to amounts paid to family members which are clearly attributable and related to the performance of services by another family member. . . .

In any event, we do not understand respondent's position to be that the mere "generation" of income is sufficient to occasion a tax. Instead, respondent argues that the amounts paid by the Educo trust were "generated" by petitioners in connection with their performance of services for Hamlin and were, therefore, compensatory in nature. We find this view to be amply supported by the record. . . .

Employees eligible to participate were selected on the basis of their value to the company; selection was thus inexorably linked to the quality of the employee's performance of services. Moreover, the eventual payment of benefits by the Educo trust was directly related to petitioners' employment. This is illustrated quite graphically by the fact that only those expenses incurred by petitioners' children while the parent was employed by Hamlin were covered by the plan.

In recruiting new employees, Hamlin would describe the benefits accorded by the plan and how an employee could become entitled to participate upon attaining a level at which he was sufficiently valuable to the company. The plan was successful in aiding the recruitment and retention of key employees. Moreover, the utilization of the Educo plan at the corporate level was clearly a substitute for salary because it enabled Hamlin to compete with employers in more populated areas which paid higher salaries.

It is fundamental that anticipatory arrangements designed to deflect income away from the proper taxpayer will not be given effect to avoid tax liability. United States v. Basye, 410 U.S. 441 (1973) [infra page 819]; Lucas v. Earl [supra page 742]. In substance, by commencing or continuing to be employed by Hamlin, petitioners have allowed a portion of their earnings to be paid to their children. Petitioners have acquiesced in an arrangement designed, at least in part, to shift the incidence of tax liability to third parties unconnected in any meaningful way with their performance of services.

Petitioners arduously suggest, however, that the doctrine of Lucas v. Earl, supra, can have no application herein because they neither received nor possessed a right to receive the amounts distributed to their children by the Educo trust. In support of this contention, petitioners rely on Commissioner v. First Security Bank of Utah, 405 U.S. 394 (1972), and Paul A. Teschner, 38 T.C. 1003 (1962).

In *First Security Bank of Utah,* a holding company organized a subsidiary corporation to engage in the insurance business (Life); another subsidiary corporation was a national bank (Bank). Bank originated credit life insurance which was placed with an independent insurance company; however, pursuant to a treaty of reinsurance, the independent company reinsured the business with Life. The Commissioner sought to allocate a portion of Life's premium income to Bank as compensation for originating and processing the credit life insurance. Court decisions construing 12 U.S.C. section 92, however, prohibited a national bank from acting as an insurance agent, thus distinguishing cases in which the taxpayer had actually received funds in violation of the law, see, e.g., James v. United States, 366 U.S. 213 (1961). The Court held that the assignment-of-income doctrine and section 482 could have no application where a taxpayer has no right as a matter of law to receive the income in question.

The rationale was that a taxpayer who did not actually receive any income did not possess sufficient dominion and control to occasion a tax where he was prevented by law from actual receipt of the income. The factual pattern in *Teschner* is analogous and much the same kind of analysis was applied. The taxpayer entered a contest by submitting two statements on a form supplied by the sponsor of the contest. The contest rules provided that only persons under age 17 were eligible to receive any prize; contestants over that age were required to designate a person under age 17 to receive the prize. The taxpayer, an adult, designated his daughter as recipient should either of his entries be selected. The taxpayer's inability to win a prize for himself was due to the contest rules and was in no way attributable to any action taken by him. One of the taxpayer's entries was selected and a prize was awarded to his daughter. The Commissioner contended that the prize was includable in the taxpayer's gross income under the principles of Lucas v. Earl, supra. This Court held that the taxpayer's mere power to direct the distribution of the prize was not sufficient to tax its value as income to him because he did not possess a right to receive the prize under the contest rules; thus, it was not includable in his gross income.

While the facts in these cases are analogous to those presented herein, there are crucial distinctions which mandate a different result.

Hamlin and petitioners were acting at arm's length in an employment situation. By accepting employment or continuing to be employed by Hamlin, cognizant of the trust payments, petitioners in effect consented to having a portion of their earnings paid to third parties. There is no evidence to indicate that petitioners were unable to bargain with Hamlin about the terms of their employment and the available avenues of compensation. Hamlin could have made available a direct salary benefit to those employees who so desired, and by supplemental enrollment schedule continued to make available the Educo plan to others. We also think significant petitioners' power, whether exercised or not, to designate which of their children would be enrolled in the Educo plan. Under the facts of this case, such power lends substantial compensatory flavor to the Educo arrangement. Petitioners were in a position to influence the manner in which their compensation would be paid; choosing to acquiesce in the payments to the Educo plan was in our view tantamount to an "anticipatory arrangement" prohibited by Lucas v. Earl, supra. By contrast, in neither *First Security Bank of Utah,* supra, nor in Paul A. Teschner, supra, did such a potential for "arm's-length" negotiation exist. Moreover, the prohibition on petitioners' receipt of the payments in this case was not imposed by a rule of law as in *First Security Bank of Utah,* or as the result of a rule imposed by an independent third party as in *Teschner.* Petitioners herein were not prohibited from receiving income within the meaning of *First Security Bank of Utah* or *Teschner.*

To find the rationale of these cases controlling here would be to ignore the consensual nature of the method of compensation adopted by Hamlin and the economic realities existing in an employer-employee situation. It is clear that a taxpayer may not avoid taxation by entering into an anticipatory assignment of income; to allow petitioners to enter into such an arrangement through the back door simply by allowing the employer to make the necessary arrangements would be highly anomalous and inconsistent with the rationale of Lucas v. Earl, supra, and United States v. Basye [supra]. We can only conclude that this arrangement provided petitioners with additional and deferred compensation as determined by the Commissioner and should have been so reported; the plan was, in effect, a clever and skillfully designed arrangement which cannot be given effect for tax purposes. . . .

Although the legislative history is somewhat vague and the parties have chosen not to argue this case based upon interpretation of section 83, we must point out that our decision is supported by the specific language of section 83 which provides:

> (a) GENERAL RULE. If in connection with the performance of services, property is transferred to *any person* other than the person for whom such services are performed the excess of — . . . shall be *included in the gross income of the person who* performed such services. . . .[Emphasis added.]

Accordingly, we hold that the amounts paid by the Educo trust constituted additional compensation to petitioners and, therefore, are includable in gross income.

Decisions will be entered for the respondent.

NOTES AND QUESTIONS

1. *The theory.* Which is the better theory in support of the decision, assignment of income (Lucas v. Earl) or noncash benefit (§83, described supra page 407)?

2. *Time for inclusion.* Under each of the two possible theories, what is the proper time for taxation — when funds are paid to the trustee by Hamlin or when funds are paid by the trustee to a child? How does the choice of time for taxation affect the amount to be taxed? When is Hamlin (the employer) entitled to a deduction? See §§404(a)(5), 83(h), 419. In Grant-Jacoby, Inc. v. Commissioner, 73 T.C. 700 (1980), on facts like those in *Armantrout,* the court held that the employer could take a deduction for amounts contributed to its educational trust only when distributions from the trust were includable in the employee's income. The court reasoned that the distributions are deferred compensation, which are normally deductible only when actually paid over to the employee under §404(a)(5). In Greensboro Pathology Associates, P.A. v. United States, 698 F.2d 1196 (Fed. Cir. 1982), however, the court held that amounts paid by an employer into a trust under a plan for

college scholarships for the children of employees were deductible under §162 and Regs. §1.162-10 (which governs employee welfare plans) when paid irrevocably into the trust, rather than later, when benefits became taxable to the employee, as required by §404(a)(5) (which governs deferred compensation). In drawing the line, the court said that not all fringe benefits are deferred compensation and emphasized that under the plan of this employer benefits were available to the children of all employees and were not linked to employee salaries. The case arose before the adoption of §419.

3. *Reconciliation with earlier decisions.* Possibly the result in *First Security Bank of Utah* (discussed by the court in *Armantrout* and in Note 3, supra page 749) can be defended on the authority (such as it is) of Poe v. Seaborn (supra page 745). But what about *Teschner,* also discussed in *Armantrout?*[4] Do you agree that it is more like *Seaborn* and *First Security Bank of Utah* than it is like *Earl* and *Armantrout?*

4. *Implications.* Suppose that the plan adopted by Hamlin were modified to make benefits available to the children of all executives with salaries above a given level after they had been employed for five years and with the benefits not contingent on continued employment by Hamlin after the transfer of the relevant amounts into the trust. Would the result be different? Would Hamlin still be likely to find the plan attractive?

5. *Equal protection.* In Wheeler v. Commissioner, 768 F.2d 1333 (Fed. Cir. 1985), the taxpayer was taxed on funds provided for his children's college expenses under a plan virtually identical to that in *Armantrout.* The court rejected the taxpayer's argument that, in light of the favorable treatment of employees of educational institutions under Regs. §1.117-3(a), now embodied in Code §117(d), this outcome led to a denial of his constitutional right of equal protection.

6. *Funds received as agent for another.* Suppose a person manages an apartment building, collects rents in cash, and turns over the sums collected, less a 10 percent commission, to the owner of the building. The amounts turned over to the owner are not included in the income of the manager. The legal rationale generally is that the manager receives those amounts as agent for the owner. Similarly, suppose an associate for a law firm performs services for a client of the firm, the client pays cash to the lawyer, and the lawyer turns the money over to the firm, as she is required to do by her implied contract with the firm. Again, the lawyer is not taxable on the payment received as agent for the firm. In Schuster v. Commissioner, 84 T.C. 764 (1985), aff'd, 800 F.2d 672 (7th Cir. 1986), the taxpayer was a member of a religious order of the Roman Catholic Church. Part of her agreement with and com-

4. The lawyer for the taxpayer in *Armantrout* was Paul A. Teschner, who was the taxpayer, and represented himself, in *Teschner.*

mitment to the order was a vow of poverty, which required, among other things, that she turn over to the order any amounts she received for performing services. She was a nurse-practitioner (midwife) and took a job with a clinic funded by the federal government. Before taking the job, she was required to receive approval from the order. She was paid for her services by checks from the clinic and endorsed the checks over to the order. The Tax Court, sitting en banc and dividing ten to seven, held that she was taxable on the amounts received from the clinic. The majority relied on the fact that the obligation to provide services to the clinic was that of the taxpayer, not of the order; that in providing the services the taxpayer did not act as agent for the order; and that the checks satisfied a legal obligation to the taxpayer, not to the order. The majority noted that if the taxpayer had worked in a clinic operated by the order, amounts received from patients in payment for her services would not have been taxable to her, since in that situation the legal obligation of the payor would be to the order. The dissenting opinion, relying in part on Poe v. Seaborn, argued that the taxpayer, consistent with her vow of poverty, in fact acted as agent for the order when she contracted with the clinic and when she received payment from it. In other words, the dissent focused on the relationship between the taxpayer and the order, not on the triangular relationship of the taxpayer, the order, and the clinic. The dissent concluded by accusing the majority of a "blind and indiscriminating application of Lucas v. Earl" (supra page 742). 84 T.C. at 789.[5]

The Seventh Circuit majority accepted the Tax Court majority's result in *Schuster* but rejected as too narrow its "agency triangle" theory, which stresses the relationship (or lack of it) between the payor and the alleged principal of the payee. The appellate court looked to a number of facts indicating that the taxpayer had earned her wages in an individual capacity rather than as an agent, including the facts that she was free to withdraw from the order at any time, that she was not under its day-to-day control, and that she endorsed the paychecks over to the order. The dissenting judge focused on the order's right to control and direct the taxpayer's activities, on her vow of poverty, and on the fact that her activities were of a type within the mission or purpose of the order.

Both the majority and dissent in the Seventh Circuit drew on the approach of the Federal Circuit in Fogarty v. United States, 780 F.2d 1005 (1986). In that case the taxpayer was a Jesuit priest who became

5. The taxpayer was entitled to a charitable deduction for the amounts paid to the order, but the deduction is subject to the 50 percent (of AGI) limit in §170(b)(1)(A). At one time, under a rule popularly known as the "Philadelphia nun" provision, an unlimited deduction was allowed to people who contributed substantially all of their income to charities for an extended period of time. This special rule was repealed, however, after it came to be used, often in combination with other deductions and exclusions, by many wealthy people, not members of religious orders, to reduce their tax liability to zero.

an associate professor at the University of Virginia, where he taught courses in religious thought, development, and history. Like the taxpayer in *Schuster,* he had taken a vow of poverty. Checks for his salary were made payable to him but at his direction were deposited to an account of his order. The court said that the "facts present a very close case" and held that the taxpayer was taxable on amounts paid to the order. Like the Seventh Circuit, the court rejected the "triangle" theory, instead holding that the "question whether a member of a religious order earns income in an individual capacity, or as an agent of the order, is a question of law based on general rules of agency to be established by considering all the underlying facts." Among the facts the court deemed relevant were the degree of control exercised by the order, the purposes or mission of the order and the type of work performed by the member, the dealings between the member and the payor (including "circumstances surrounding job inquiries and interviews, and control or supervision exercised by the employer"), and dealings between the employer and the order.

Recall the statement by Justice Holmes in Lucas v. Earl that the issue of who is to be taxed "is not to be decided by attenuated subtleties." How do you suppose he would have decided *Schuster* and *Fogarty?* How would you decide them? Suppose you are asked by the head of a religious order whether the order should give up on the tax issue or try to change the way in which the orders proceeded in cases like *Schuster* and *Fogarty* and try again. What advice would you give?

D. TRANSFERS OF PROPERTY AND INCOME FROM PROPERTY

Generally, income from property is treated for tax purposes as owned by the owner of the property and is taxed to that person, at that person's rate. One notable limitation, added by the 1986 act, provides that the unearned income of a child under age 14 is taxed at his or her parents' marginal rate. §1(i). Putting that aside, in applying the principle that income from property is taxed to the owner of that property we are confronted with the question of what is meant by "property." It will be seen in the cases that follow that the courts have sometimes answered this question in legalistic or metaphysical ways.

The next two cases can be viewed from a formalistic perspective as efforts to distinguish between gifts of property and gifts of income from property. From a more realistic perspective the two cases can be seen as efforts to draw the line between diversions of income from property that are respected for tax purposes and those that are not, which should depend, in large part at least, on the economic characteristics of what was given away and what was retained. In the first case (*Blair*), the taxpayer had a limited interest (a life estate), but gave away a portion for its entire duration (i.e., part of the income for his life). In the second (*Horst*), the taxpayer owned the entire property (a bond), and gave away a limited interest (the interest income for a brief period of time); he gave away what has come to be called a "carved out" income interest.[6] The challenge in reading the cases is to figure out why the first taxpayer won and the second lost.

BLAIR v. COMMISSIONER

300 U.S. 5 (1937)

Mr. Chief Justice HUGHES delivered the opinion of the Court.

This case presents the question of the liability of a beneficiary of a testamentary trust for a tax upon the income which he had assigned to his children. . . .

The trust was created by the will of [the petitioner's (taxpayer's) father and called for payment of all income to petitioner during his life]. In 1923, . . . petitioner assigned to his daughter . . . an interest amounting to $6,000 for the remainder of that calendar year, and to $9,000 in each calendar year thereafter, in the net income. . . . At about the same time, he made like assignments of interest, amounting to $9,000 in each calendar year, in the net income of the trust to [two other children]. . . . In later years, by similar instruments, he assigned to these children additional interests. . . . The trustees accepted the assignments and distributed the income directly to the assignees. . . .

[After holding that a judgment in an earlier proceeding involving the same trust was not conclusive in this proceeding as res judicata and that the assignments were valid under local law, the Supreme Court turned to the third issue in the case.]

Third. The question remains whether, treating the assignments as valid, the assignor was still taxable upon the income under the federal income tax act. That is a federal question.

Our decisions in Lucas v. Earl [supra page 742] and Burnet v. Leininger, 285 U.S. 136, are cited. In the *Lucas* [sic] case . . . [w]e were of the opinion that the case turned upon the construction of the taxing act. We said that "the statute could tax salaries to those who earned them and provide that the tax could not be escaped by anticipatory arrangements and contracts however skillfully devised to prevent the

6. An assigned interest that is coextensive in time with the assignor's interest is sometimes called a "horizontal" division or "horizontal slice," as contrasted with an interest for a fixed number of years shorter than the assignor's interest, called a "vertical slice."

same when paid from vesting even for a second in the man who earned it." That was deemed to be the meaning of the statute as to compensation for personal service and the one who earned the income was held to be subject to the tax. In Burnet v. Leininger, supra, a husband, a member of a firm, assigned future partnership income to his wife. We found that the revenue act dealt explicitly with the liability of partners as such. The wife did not become a member of the firm; the act specifically taxed the distributive share of each partner in the net income of the firm; and the husband by the fair import of the act remained taxable upon his distributive share. These cases are not in point. The tax here is not upon earnings which are taxed to the one who earns them. Nor is it a case of income attributable to a taxpayer by reason of the application of the income to the discharge of his obligation. . . . There is here no question of evasion or of giving effect to statutory provisions designed to forestall evasion; or of the taxpayer's retention of control. . . .

The Government points to the provisions of the revenue acts imposing upon the beneficiary of a trust the liability for the tax upon the income distributable to the beneficiary.[7] But the term is merely descriptive of the one entitled to the beneficial interest. . . . If under the law governing the trust the beneficial interest is assignable, and if it has been assigned without reservation, the assignee thus becomes the beneficiary and is entitled to rights and remedies accordingly. We find nothing in the revenue acts which denies him that status.

The decision of the Circuit Court of Appeals turned upon the effect to be ascribed to the assignments. The court held that the petitioner had no interest in the corpus of the estate and could not dispose of the income until he received it. Hence it was said that "the income was *his*" and his assignment was merely a direction to pay over to others what was due to himself. The question was considered to involve "the date when the income became transferable." 83 F.(2d), p.662. The Government refers to the terms of the assignment, — that it was of the interest in the income "which the said party of the first part now is, or may hereafter be, entitled to receive during his life from the trustees." From this it is urged that the assignments "dealt only with a right to receive the income" and that "no attempt was made to assign any equitable right, title or interest in the trust itself." This construction seems to us to be a strained one. We think it apparent that the conveyancer was not seeking to limit the assignment so as to make it anything less than a complete transfer of the specified interest of the petitioner as the life beneficiary of the trust, but that with ample caution he was using words to effect such a transfer. That the state court so construed the assign-

7. [The provisions stated in general terms that the "beneficiary" of a trust was taxable on the income distributable to him. See §§652(a) and 662(a). — Eds.]

ments appears from the final decree which described them as voluntary assignments of interests of the petitioner "in said trust estate," and it was in that aspect that petitioner's right to make the assignments was sustained.

The will creating the trust entitled the petitioner during his life to the net income of the property held in trust. He thus became the owner of an equitable interest in the corpus of the property. . . . By virtue of that interest he was entitled to enforce the trust, to have a breach of trust enjoined and to obtain redress in case of breach. The interest was present property alienable like any other, in the absence of a valid restraint upon alienation. . . . The beneficiary may thus transfer a part of his interest as well as the whole. See Restatement of the Law of Trusts, §§130, 132 et seq. The assignment of the beneficial interest is not the assignment of a chose in action but of the "right, title, and estate in and to property." . . . See Bogert, Trusts and Trustees, vol. 1,9185, pp. 516, 517; 17 Columbia Law Review, 269, 273, 289, 290.

We conclude that the assignments were valid, that the assignees thereby became the owners of the specified beneficial interests in the income, and that as to these interests they and not the petitioner were taxable for the tax years in question. . . .

HELVERING v. HORST

311 U.S. 112 (1940)

Mr. Justice Stone delivered the opinion of the Court.

The sole question for decision is whether the gift, during the donor's taxable year, of interest coupons detached from the bonds, delivered to the donee and later in the year paid at maturity, is the realization of income taxable to the donor.[8]

In 1934 and 1935 respondent, the owner of negotiable bonds, detached from them negotiable interest coupons shortly before their due date and delivered them as a gift to his son who in the same year

8. [Coupon bonds, which were far more common in earlier days than they are now, are "bearer" obligations (that is, payable to the bearer, or holder). The obligation is reflected in a large, sturdy piece of paper, part of which states the borrower's obligation to pay the principal amount on a given date and part of which is divided into segments called coupons, each of which states the borrower's obligation to pay a fixed amount of money, the interest payment, on a particular interest-payment date, with one coupon for each interest payment. Each coupon is a separate negotiable instrument. Ordinarily, the holder of the bond collects interest by cutting off ("clipping") coupons as they mature and cashing them in, usually at a bank, but, as this case reveals, any other holder of the coupons can cash them in on their due date. These days, most corporate bonds are registered; the owner's name is registered with the debtor company, and the interest payment goes in the mail by check to the registered owner. Since 1983, most bonds are in effect required to be registered. See §§103(d), 163(f), 165(j), 1232(d), and 4701. — Eds.]

collected them at maturity. The Commissioner ruled that under [§61(a)], the interest payments were taxable, in the years when paid, to the respondent donor who reported his income on the cash receipts basis. . . .

The court below thought that as the consideration for the coupons had passed to the obligor, the donor had, by the gift, parted with all control over them and their payment, and for that reason the case was distinguishable from Lucas v. Earl [supra page 742] and Burnet v. Leininger, 285 U.S. 136, where the assignment of compensation for services had preceded the rendition of the services, and where the income was held taxable to the donor.

The holder of a coupon bond is the owner of two independent and separable kinds of right. One is the right to demand and receive at maturity the principal amount of the bond representing capital investment. The other is the right to demand and receive interim payments of interest on the investment in the amounts and on the dates specified by the coupons. Together they are an obligation to pay principal and interest given in exchange for money or property which was presumably the consideration for the obligation of the bond. Here respondent, as owner of the bonds, had acquired the legal right to demand payment at maturity of the interest specified by the coupons and the power to command its payment to others which constituted an economic gain to him.

Admittedly not all economic gain of the taxpayer is taxable income. From the beginning the revenue laws have been interpreted as defining "realization" of income as the taxable event rather than the acquisition of the right to receive it. And "realization" is not deemed to occur until the income is paid. But the decisions and regulations have consistently recognized that receipt in cash or property is not the only characteristic of realization of income to a taxpayer on the cash receipts basis. Where the taxpayer does not receive payments of income in money or property realization may occur when the last step is taken by which he obtains the fruition of the economic gain which has already accrued to him. . . .

In the ordinary case the taxpayer who acquires the right to receive income is taxed when he receives it, regardless of the time when his right to receive payment accrued. But the rule that income is not taxable until realized has never been taken to mean that the taxpayer, even on the cash receipts basis, who has fully enjoyed the benefit of the economic gain represented by his right to receive income, can escape taxation because he has not himself received payment of it from his obligor. The rule, founded on administrative convenience, is only one of postponement of the tax to the final event of enjoyment of the income, usually the receipt of it by the taxpayer, and not one of exemption from taxation where the enjoyment is consummated by some event other than the taxpayer's personal receipt of money or property. . . . This may occur when he has made such use of disposition of his power to receive or control the income as to procure in its place other satisfactions which are of economic worth. The question here is, whether because one who in fact receives payment for services or interest payments is taxable only on his receipt of the payments, he can escape all tax by giving away his right to income in advance of payment. If the taxpayer procures payment directly to his creditors of the items of interest or earnings due him, see Old Colony Trust Co. v. Commissioner, 279 U.S. 716; Bowers v. Kerbaugh-Empire Co., 271 U.S. 170; United States v. Kirby Lumber Co. [supra page 235], or if he sets up a revocable trust with income payable to the objects of his bounty, Corliss v. Bowers, 281 U.S. 376, he does not escape taxation because he did not actually receive the money. . . .

Underlying the reasoning in these cases is the thought that income is "realized" by the assignor because he, who owns or controls the source of the income, also controls the disposition of that which he could have received himself and diverts the payment from himself to others as the means of procuring the satisfaction of his wants. The taxpayer has equally enjoyed the fruits of his labor or investment and obtained the satisfaction of his desires whether he collects and uses the income to procure those satisfactions, or whether he disposes of his right to collect it as the means of procuring them. . . .

Although the donor here, by the transfer of the coupons, has precluded any possibility of his collecting them himself he has nevertheless, by his act, procured payment of the interest, as a valuable gift to a member of his family. Such a use of his economic gain, the right to receive income, to procure a satisfaction which can be obtained only by the expenditure of money or property, would seem to be the enjoyment of the income whether the satisfaction is the purchase of goods at the corner grocery, the payment of his debt there, or such non-material satisfactions as may result from the payment of a campaign or community chest contribution, or a gift to his favorite son. Even though he never receives the money he derives money's worth from the disposition of the coupons which he has used as money or money's worth in the procuring of a satisfaction which is procurable only by the expenditure of money or money's worth. The enjoyment of the economic benefit accruing to him by virtue of his acquisition of the coupons is realized as completely as it would have been if he had collected the interest in dollars and expended them for any of the purposes named. . . .

In a real sense he has enjoyed compensation for money loaned or services rendered and not any the less so because it is his only reward for them. To say that one who has made a gift thus derived from interest or earnings paid to his donee has never enjoyed or realized the fruits of his investment or labor because he has assigned them instead of collecting them himself and then paying them over to the donee, is to affront common understanding and to deny the facts of common experience. Common understanding and experience are the touchstones for the interpretation of the revenue laws.

The power to dispose of income is the equivalent of ownership of it. The exercise of that power to procure the payment of income to another is the enjoyment and hence the realization of the income by him who exercises it. We have had no difficulty in applying that proposition where the assignment preceded the rendition of the services, Lucas v. Earl, supra; Burnet v. Leininger, supra, for it was recognized in the *Leininger* case that in such a case the rendition of the service by the assignor was the means by which the income was controlled by the donor and of making his assignment effective. But it is the assignment by which the disposition of income is controlled when the service precedes the assignment and in both cases it is the exercise of the power of disposition of the interest or compensation with the resulting payment to the donee which is the enjoyment by the donor of income derived from them.

This was emphasized in Blair v. Commissioner [supra page 762], on which respondent relies, where the distinction was taken between a gift of income derived from an obligation to pay compensation and a gift of income-producing property. In the circumstances of that case the right to income from the trust property was thought to be so identified with the equitable ownership of the property from which alone the beneficiary derived his right to receive the income and his power to command disposition of it that a gift of the income by the beneficiary became effective only as a gift of his ownership of the property producing it. Since the gift was deemed to be a gift of the property the income from it was held to be the income of the owner of the property, who was the donee, not the donor, a refinement which was unnecessary if respondent's contention here is right, but one clearly inapplicable to gifts of interest or wages. Unlike income thus derived from an obligation to pay interest or compensation, the income of the trust was regarded as no more the income of the donor than would be the rent from a lease or a crop raised on a farm after the leasehold or the farm has been given away. . . .

The dominant purpose of the revenue laws is the taxation of income to those who earn or otherwise create the right to receive it and enjoy the benefit of it when paid. . . . The tax laid by the 1934 Revenue Act upon income "derived from . . . wages, or compensation for personal service, of whatever kind and in whatever form paid . . . ; also from interest . . ." therefore cannot fairly be interpreted as not applying to income derived from interest or compensation when he who is entitled to receive it makes use of his power to dispose of it in procuring satisfactions which he would otherwise procure only by the use of the money when received.

It is the statute which taxes the income to the donor although paid to his donee. Lucas v. Earl, supra; Burnet v. Leininger, supra. True, in those cases the service which created the right to income followed the assignment and it was arguable that in point of legal theory the right to the compensation vested instantaneously in the assignor when paid although he never received it; while here the right of the assignor to receive the income antedated the assignment which transferred the right and thus precluded such an instantaneous vesting. But the statute affords no basis for such "attenuated subtleties." The distinction was explicitly rejected as the basis of decision in Lucas v. Earl. It should be rejected here, for no more than in the *Earl* case can the purpose of the statute to tax the income to him who earns, or creates and enjoys it be escaped by "anticipatory arrangements . . . however skillfully devised" to prevent the income from vesting even for a second in the donor.

Nor is it perceived that there is any adequate basis for distinguishing between the gift of interest coupons here and a gift of salary or commissions. The owner of a negotiable bond and of the investment which it represents, if not the lender, stands in the place of the lender. When, by the gift of the coupons, he has separated his right to interest payments from his investment and procured the payment of the interest to his donee, he has enjoyed the economic benefits of the income in the same manner and to the same extent as though the transfer were of earnings and in both cases the import of the statute is that the fruit is not to be attributed to a different tree from that on which it grew. See Lucas v. Earl, supra.

Reversed.

The separate opinion of Mr. Justice McReynolds.

. . . The unmatured coupons given to the son were independent negotiable instruments, complete in themselves. Through the gift they became at once the absolute property of the donee, free from the donor's control and in no way dependent upon ownership of the bonds. No question of actual fraud or purpose to defraud the revenue is presented. . . .

The Chief Justice and Mr. Justice Roberts concur in this opinion.

NOTES AND QUESTIONS

1. *Rationale:* Blair. The Court says that Mr. Blair was "the owner of an equitable interest in the corpus of the property." So what? Is the characterization relevant because of language in the Code? Because of

tax policy objectives? Does it help make the law more predictable? If so, at what cost?

2. *Rationale:* Horst. (a) Is realization a problem in *Horst?* (b) What is the relevance of the fact that Mr. Horst may have obtained some satisfaction from the enjoyment of the income by the son? If Mr. Horst had given the entire bond to the son, would his satisfaction in the son's enjoyment of the income over the next several years have been less? Would the father have been taxed on the interest payments received by the son? (c) What if the father had removed some of the coupons and given them to the son and given the rest of the coupons and the bond itself (that is, the claim to the terminal payment at maturity) to his daughter? Who would be taxed on what? See Irwin v. Gavit, supra page 188. (d) Suppose that the father had cut off all the coupons and given them to the son, at the same time had given the bond itself to his daughter, and thereafter the son had given all the coupons to his son (the grandson). Now who is taxed on the interest: son, daughter, or grandson? Should it matter whether the coupons are called "property" or "an equitable interest in the corpus of the property"? (e) What *is* the proper rationale for *Horst?*

3. *Financial analysis.* Suppose that *F* (father) owns a bond with a face value (the amount due at maturity) of $1,000, due in three years, with interest payable annually at the rate of 12 percent or $120 per year, and that the market rate of interest on such bonds is 12 percent and remains at this level throughout the remaining three-year term. *F* assigns the right to collect the interest for the remaining three years to *S* (son). Immediately after the assignment, the value of *S*'s claim to the interest is $288 (the present value of the right to $120 per year for three years, discounted at 12 percent) and the value of *F*'s claim to the $1,000 payable at maturity is $712. These relationships change over time in the manner suggested by the figures in Table 7-2.

Perhaps the most accurate system of taxation would be one in which *S* is taxed each year on the amounts in row (e) and *F* is taxed each year on the amounts in row (f) (assuming that neither *S* nor *F* sells his interest during the remaining three-year term of the bond). Note that the total income taxed each year under this approach would be $120, which is the correct total amount. *S* can be compared to the holder of a life estate and *F* with the holder of a remainder. We have seen that where a life estate (or term of years) and a remainder have been created by a transfer from a third party, the life tenant (or holder of the term interest) is taxed on the entire payment received each year and the holder of the remainder reports no income until he or she starts collecting income on the termination of the life estate. See, again, Irwin v. Gavit, supra page 188. That approach may not be accurate, but it appeals to one's sense of practicality. In the present example, practicality may dictate that since the lion's share of the gain each year is *F*'s, *F*

TABLE 7-2
Illustration of Assignment of Bond Interest

		Start	*End year 1*	*End year 2*	*End year 3*
(a)	Value of *F*'s claim	$712	$797	$893	$1,000
(b)	Value of *S*'s claim	288	203	107	-0-
(c)	Interest payment	—	120	120	120
(d)	Decline in value of *S*'s claim	—	85	96	107
(e)	Economic gain to *S**	—	35	24	13
(f)	Increase in value of *F*'s claim	—	85	96	107

*The difference between the interest payment received and the decrease in the value of *S*'s claim during the year.

should pay tax on all the income. What does this imply as to the limits of *Horst*? If we assume a bond with a remaining life of ten years and an interest rate of 12 percent, and an assignment of the interest payments from *F* to *S* for the entire ten-year term, then immediately after the assignment *S*'s claim is worth $678 and *F*'s claim is worth $322. The economic gain to *S* in the first year is $81, and the increase in the value of *F*'s interest is $39. For the last three years of the ten-year assignment, the relationships would be the same as in the table below.

4. *Unrealized appreciation.* Can the result in *Horst* be reconciled with the rule approved in Taft v. Bowers (supra page 159) and reflected in §1015, that the donee, rather than the donor, is taxed on the unrealized gain on property transferred by gift? See also the discussion of income in respect of a decedent, supra page 163.

E. SERVICES TRANSFORMED INTO PROPERTY

HELVERING v. EUBANK

311 U.S. 122 (1940)

Mr. Justice STONE delivered the opinion of the Court.

This is a companion case to Helvering v. Horst [supra page 764], and presents issues not distinguishable from those in that case.

Respondent, a general life insurance agent, after the termination of his agency contracts and services as agent, made assignments in 1924 and 1928 respectively of renewal commissions to become payable to him for services which had been rendered in writing policies of insurance under two of his agency contracts.[9] The Commissioner assessed the renewal commissions paid by the companies to the assignees in 1933 as income taxable to the assignor in that year under [§61].

No purpose of the assignments appears other than to confer on the assignees the power to collect the commissions, which they did in the taxable year. The Government and respondent have briefed and argued the case here on the assumption that the assignments were voluntary transfers to the assignees of the right to collect the commissions as and when they became payable, and the record affords no basis for any other.

For the reasons stated at length in the opinion in the *Horst* case, we hold that the commissions were taxable as income of the assignor in the year when paid. The judgment below is reversed.

The separate opinion of Mr. Justice McReynolds. . . .

The court below declared —

> In the case at bar the petitioner owned a right to receive money for past services; no further services were required. Such a right is assignable. At the time of assignment there was nothing contingent in the petitioner's right, although the amount collectible in future years was still uncertain and contingent. But this may be equally true where the assignment transfers a right to income from investments, as in Blair v. Commissioner, [supra page 762], and Horst v. Commissioner, 107 F.2d 906 (C.C.A. 2), or a right to patent royalties, as in Nelson v. Ferguson, 56 F.2d 121 (C.C.A. 3), certiorari denied, 286 U.S. 565. By an assignment of future earnings a taxpayer may not escape taxation upon his compensation in the year when he earns it. But when a taxpayer who makes his income tax return on a cash basis assigns a right to money payable in the future for work already performed, we believe that he transfers a property right, and the money, when received by the assignee, is not income taxable to the assignor.

Accordingly, the Board of Tax Appeals was reversed; and this, I think, is in accord with the statute and our opinions.

The assignment in question denuded the assignor of all right to commissions thereafter to accrue under the contract with the insurance company. He could do nothing further in respect of them; they were entirely beyond his control. In no proper sense were they something either earned or received by him during the taxable year. The right to

9. [The commissions were assigned to a corporate trustee. The opinion of the Supreme Court and of the lower courts and the record before the Supreme Court all fail to reveal the purposes of the trust or the relationship of the beneficiaries to Mr. Eubank. The record (at page 6) does, however, establish that the assignment was gratuitous. For purposes of analysis, it seems reasonable to treat the case as if the assignee had been Mr. Eubank's wife or children. — Eds.]

collect became the absolute property of the assignee without relation to future action by the assignor.

A mere right to collect future payments, for services already performed, is not presently taxable as "income derived" from such services. It is property which may be assigned. Whatever the assignor receives as consideration may be his income; but the statute does not undertake to impose liability upon him because of payments to another under a contract which he had transferred in good faith, under circumstances like those here disclosed. . . .

The general principles approved in Blair v. Commissioner, . . . are controlling and call for affirmation of the judgment under review.

THE CHIEF JUSTICE and Mr. Justice ROBERTS concur in this opinion.

HEIM v. FITZPATRICK

262 F.2d 887 (2d Cir. 1959)

Before SWAN and MOORE, Circuit Judges, and KAUFMAN, District Judge.

SWAN, Circuit Judge.

This litigation involves income taxes of Lewis R. Heim, for the years 1943 through 1946. On audit of the taxpayer's returns, the Commissioner of Internal Revenue determined that his taxable income in each of said years should be increased by adding thereto patent royalty payments received by his wife, his son and his daughter. . . .

Plaintiff was the inventor of a new type of rod end and spherical bearing. In September 1942 he applied for a patent thereon. On November 5, 1942 he applied for a further patent on improvements of his original invention. Thereafter on November 17, 1942 he executed a formal written assignment of his invention and of the patents which might be issued for it and for improvements thereof to The Heim Company.[10] This was duly recorded in the Patent Office and in January 1945 and May 1946 plaintiff's patent applications were acted on favorably and patents thereon were issued to the Company. The assignment to the Company was made pursuant to an oral agreement, subsequently reduced to a writing dated July 29, 1943, by which it was agreed (1) that the Company need pay no royalties on bearings manufactured by it prior to July 1, 1943; (2) that after that date the Company would pay specified royalties on 12 types of bearings; (3) that on new types of bearings it would pay royalties to be agreed upon prior to their manufacture; (4) that if the royalties for any two consecutive months or for any one year should fall below stated amounts, plaintiff at his option

10. The stock of The Heim Company was owned as follows: plaintiff 1%, his wife 41%, his son and daughter 27% each, and his daughter-in-law and son-in-law 2% each.

might cancel the agreement and thereupon all rights granted by him under the agreement and under any and all assigned patents should revert to him, his heirs and assigns; and (5) that this agreement is not transferable by the Company.

In August 1943 plaintiff assigned to his wife "an undivided interest of 25 per cent in said agreement with The Heim Company dated July 29, 1943, and in all his inventions and patent rights, past and future, referred to therein and in all rights and benefits of the First Party [plaintiff] thereunder. . . ." A similar assignment was given to his son and another to his daughter. Plaintiff paid gift taxes on the assignments. The Company was notified of them and thereafter it made all royalty payments accordingly. As additional types of bearings were put into production from time to time the royalties on them were fixed by agreement between the Company and the plaintiff and his three assignees. . . .

The appellant contends that the assignments to his wife and children transferred to them income-producing property and consequently the royalty payments were taxable to his donees, as held in Blair v. Commissioner [supra page 762]. Judge Anderson, however, was of opinion that [151 F. Supp. 576]: "The income-producing property, i.e., the patents, had been assigned by the taxpayer to the corporation. What he had left was a right to a portion of the income which the patents produced. He had the power to dispose of and divert the stream of this income as he saw fit." Consequently he ruled that the principles applied by the Supreme Court in Helvering v. Horst [supra page 764], and Helvering v. Eubank [supra page 770], required all the royalty payments to be treated as income of plaintiff. . . .

In the present case more than a bare right to receive future royalties was assigned by plaintiff to his donees. Under the terms of his contract with The Heim Company he retained the power to bargain for the fixing of royalties on new types of bearings, i.e. bearings other than the 12 products on which royalties were specified. This power was assigned and the assignees exercised it as to new products. Plaintiff also retained a reversionary interest in his invention and patents by reason of his option to cancel the agreement if certain conditions were not fulfilled. This interest was also assigned. The fact that the option was not exercised in 1945, when it could have been, is irrelevant so far as concerns the existence of the reversionary interest. We think that the rights retained by plaintiff and assigned to his wife and children were sufficiently substantial to justify the view that they were given income-producing property.

In addition to Judge Anderson's ground of decision appellee advances a further argument in support of the judgment, namely, that the plaintiff retained sufficient control over the invention and the royalties to make it reasonable to treat him as owner of that income for tax purposes. Commissioner v. Sunnen, 333 U.S. 591, is relied upon. There a patent was licensed under a royalty contract with a corporation in which the taxpayer-inventor held 89% of the stock. An assignment of the royalty contract to the taxpayer's wife was held ineffective to shift the tax, since the taxpayer retained control over the royalty payments to his wife by virtue of his control of the corporation, which could cancel the contract at any time. The argument is that, although plaintiff himself owned only 1% of The Heim Company stock, his wife and daughter together owned 68% and it is reasonable to infer from depositions introduced by the Commissioner that they would follow the plaintiff's advice. Judge Anderson did not find it necessary to pass on this contention. But we are satisfied that the record would not support a finding that plaintiff controlled the corporation whose active heads were the son and son-in-law. No inference can reasonably be drawn that the daughter would be likely to follow her father's advice rather than her husband's or brother's with respect to action by the corporation. . . .

For the foregoing reasons we hold that the judgment should be reversed and the cause remanded with directions to grant plaintiff's motion for summary judgment.

So ordered.

NOTES AND QUESTIONS

1. *Analysis.* (a) In *Eubank,* the majority relied on *Horst.* Was there a better case to rely on? The dissent relied on *Blair.* As between *Blair* and *Horst,* which seems more in point? (b) In *Heim,* the lower court relied on *Horst* and *Eubank.* Again, was there a better case?

(c) We encountered renewal commissions earlier in Commissioner v. Olmsted Incorporated Life Agency, supra page 390. In that case the taxpayer surrendered rights to renewal commissions in return for an annuity of $500 per month for 15 years. The court rejected the Commissioner's argument that the exchange should have been treated as a taxable disposition. It relied heavily on Commissioner v. Oates, 207 F.2d 711 (7th Cir. 1953). In that case the taxpayer had been entitled to renewal commissions and exchanged that right for a right to payments extending over a longer period of time than the expected duration of the renewal commissions. The Commissioner in *Oates* relied in part on Lucas v. Earl (page 742), on Helvering v. Horst (page 764), and on *Eubank.* The court distinguished those cases by observing that in each of them the "taxpayer had effectually received the income" in that "by assigning it, he took dominion over it, converted it to his own use and treated it as a property right, thus realizing its full economic benefit." What was the economic benefit in *Earl,* in *Horst,* and in *Eubank?* Why was there no similar economic benefit in *Blair* (page 762) or in *Heim?*

2. *The pattern.* (a) *A,* an engineer who spends all her time working for herself on ideas for inventions, creates and patents an invention, then gives (assigns) the patent to her son, who licenses it and receives royalties. As is clear from *Heim,* the son, not the mother, is taxable on the royalties.

(b) *B,* an investor, buys a patent from the inventor and gives the patent to her son, who licenses it and receives the royalties. Plainly, the son, not the mother, is taxable on the royalties.

(c) *C,* a lawyer, assists *N,* an inventor, in obtaining financing for *N*'s invention, which *N* patents. *N* licenses the patent to *X* and, in return for *C*'s services, assigns to *C* a portion of the royalties to be paid by *X*. *C* then assigns her rights to the royalties to her son. In a closely analogous case, the Second Circuit, relying on *Earl* and *Eubank,* and on the fact that the assignor (the *C* counterpart) did not receive any part of the patent itself or any right to control its disposition, held that the royalties were taxable to the assignor. Strauss v. Commissioner, 168 F.2d 441 (2d Cir. 1948), cert. denied, 335 U.S. 858, rehearing denied, 335 U.S. 888 (1948).

(d) *D,* an author, copyrights her book and then assigns the copyright to her son, who licenses it and receives royalties. The royalties are taxable to the son. See Rev. Rul. 54-599, 1954-2 C.B. 52.

(e) Do the outcomes in these hypothetical cases form a consistent pattern? a sensible one?

(f) *F,* an architect, agrees with a client to design a building but refuses to set a price for the job. When the plans are completed, *F* gives them to her son, who sells them to the client for a share of the rents from the building for the next twenty years. Who is taxable on the share of the rents received by the son? When?

3. *The interest element.* In *Eubank* the commissions received by the assignees were a form of deferred compensation and must have included an element of interest on the amount initially earned. Suppose that immediately after writing a group of policies, Mr. Eubank had assigned the renewal commissions to a person who paid him the full market value of the rights, $1,000. How would Mr. Eubank have been taxed? What about the assignee? See Chapter 2D. What, if anything, does this tell us about how the amounts collected by the assignee in the actual situation in *Eubank* should be taxed? Should the *amount* taxable to Mr. Eubank be the value of the renewal commissions at the time of the assignment? If so, at what *time* should this amount be taxed, and how should the assignee be taxed?

F. TRUSTS

1. Overview

In the foregoing cases, the courts had to determine which of *two* parties should be taxed on the income. We now turn to more complex situations in which *three* (or more) parties are potential taxpayers: The owner of property (grantor) transfers it to a trustee to administer, with instructions for distributing the income, currently or at a later date, to one or more beneficiaries. Who — the grantor, the trust, or one of the beneficiaries — is taxed on the income? Occasionally there is another possibility: A person who under the trust instrument can get the income or corpus on demand.

To gain a sense of the nature of the problem, suppose George (the grandfather) is a wealthy man with a daughter, Peggy (the parent), who is a lawyer working in the office of the U.S. Attorney, and who is divorced, with two children, Carol (age 19) and Chris (age 15). George establishes a trust, with his friend Tom as trustee, for the benefit of Carol and Chris. The trust provides that the trustee may, at his discretion, accumulate the income or may use it to provide for the "education, support, or welfare" of Carol or Chris, with the principal and any accumulated income to be distributed to them in equal shares, or to the survivor, ten years hence. Assume that the income is substantial; part of it is used to pay for Carol to go to a private college and to buy her a car. Part of it is used to send Chris to a private boarding school and to summer camp and to pay for his tennis lessons. The rest is accumulated. How should the income be taxed? Should George be taxed on the theory that he has not yet sufficiently severed his ties to the property placed in trust? What if he dies? Should Peggy be taxed on the amounts paid out of the trust for Carol and Chris on the theory that she is the effective beneficiary (bearing in mind that George could have given the property to her and allowed her to pay the bills for Carol and Chris, except that such an approach, natural as it might seem, would have resulted in higher taxes than if the income were taxed to Carol and Chris)? Should Carol and Chris be taxed on the income used for their benefit, on the simple theory that it is legally their income from their property? What about the income accumulated by the trust? Should it be taxed to the trust? At what rate? If it is taxed to the trust, what should happen when it is later distributed? Or should it be taxed to Carol and Chris as earned? These are some of the basic issues addressed by the rules described below.

In the ordinary case, where the trust is irrevocable and the grantor reserves little or no control over it, the trust income will be taxed either to the trust or to the beneficiaries.[11] Trusts of this character, ordinary

11. Section 102(a), providing that gifts are not included in the donee's gross income,

trusts, are governed by §§641 through 668 of the Code. However, a grantor who retains power over the economic benefits of the trust property may be taxed as the "substantial owner" thereof. These trusts, sometimes called grantor trusts, are governed by §§671 through 677 of the Code, examined infra pages 781-790. Finally, a third person who has the right to get the income or corpus of the trust on demand may be taxed as the substantial owner of the income under §678. Trusts of this type are sometimes called Mallinckrodt trusts, after a leading case (see infra page 786).

Special rules tax the U.S. grantor of a foreign trust on its income where there is a U.S. beneficiary. §679. Special rules also govern employees' pension and similar trusts, §501(a); certain tax-exempt organizations in trust form, §501(c); alimony trusts, §682; and certain other trusts.

2. Tax Treatment of (Ordinary) Simple Trusts

The statutory provisions governing ordinary trusts are exceedingly complex. In an effort to make the statutory scheme less formidable, the Code distinguishes between *simple trusts* (those that are required to distribute all income currently, that have made no distributions of corpus, and that claim no charitable deduction in the taxable year) and *complex trusts* (all others). The statutory provisions applicable to simple trusts are found in Subpart B of Subchapter J, §§651-652; those applicable to complex trusts in Subparts C and D of Subchapter J, §§661-668.

A simple trust is nominally subject to tax on its income. In computing its income, however, a simple trust deducts all the income that is required to be distributed currently. §651. Since a simple trust is defined as one that is required to distribute all its income currently, a simple trust generally pays no tax.[12] Instead, the income of the trust is taxed to the beneficiary. §§61(a)(15), 652(a). A simple trust is sometimes described as a mere conduit. The conduit principle extends to the characterization of trust income. Section 652(b) provides that distributed income shall have the same character in the hands of the beneficiary as in the hands of the trust. Thus, tax-exempt interest and capital gains preserve their special character when distributed to the beneficiary. If

---

does not protect the beneficiary of trust income because of the last sentence of §102(b). Thus, the distinction between gifts, which can be received tax free under §102(a), and gifts of income from property, which are taxable to the recipient, is delegated, so far as trust income is concerned, to the rules of Subchapter J.

12. A simple trust may be taxed on capital gain that is not treated as income for trust purposes and that is retained by the trust. In that case, the trust will be subject to the same rate bracket, and generally subject to the same limitations on personal deductions, etc., as are described below for complex trusts.

there is more than one beneficiary, each receives an appropriate share of these items, unless they are allocated differently by local law or the trust instrument. See Regs. §1.652(b)-1, (b)-2.

3. Tax Treatment of (Ordinary) Complex Trusts

A complex trust is any trust that is not a simple trust. A complex trust is subject to taxation on its income under a rate schedule similar to that for individuals, but with the brackets changing at much lower income levels, with the result that the 39.6 percent bracket applies to income over $7,500. (Simple trusts are subject to the same rate schedule on their taxable income, but, as noted above, seldom have taxable income.)

The taxable income of a complex trust is computed in about the same manner as an individual's taxable income. The principal differences are that (a) in lieu of the personal exemption and dependency deductions, a trust is allowed a deduction of either $100 or $300 per year (§642(b)); (b) the trust is not allowed a standard deduction; and (c) the trust is not subject to the §170 20-30-50 percent limits on charitable deductions.[13] Most important, a complex trust, like a simple trust, is allowed a deduction for current income distributed to beneficiaries.

Beneficiaries generally are subject to tax on the lesser of the amount of trust distributions and the amount of the trust's "distributable net income." Distributable net income is generally equal to current taxable income and is often referred to as DNI. See §643(a). However, under a complicated system of "throwback rules," a beneficiary who receives income that has been accumulated by the trust is taxed on that income when it is distributed in later years. The tax that the beneficiary must pay is reduced by the taxes already paid on that income by the trust. See the last sentence of §667(b)(1), §668(b). Distributed income has the same character in the hands of the beneficiary as in the hands of the trust.

The operation of the rules for complex trusts is illustrated by the following examples. Suppose a complex trust distributes all of its DNI in its first taxable year. In that case, the trust is entitled to a deduction for the distribution and the deduction is equal to the income, so there is no tax. The income is taxed only once, at the beneficiary's rate.

Suppose, instead, that the first-year distributions of the trust exceed the trust's DNI. In that case, the trust again pays no tax, because it is entitled to deduct the distribution from its income. The beneficiary is taxed only on the lesser of the DNI or the amount of the distribution.

13. The same differences apply to simple trusts that have taxable income after distributions to beneficiaries.

The excess of the distribution over the DNI is a tax-free recovery of corpus. Here, again, the income of the trust is taxed only once, and at the beneficiary's rates.

Suppose, finally, that the trust accumulates income during its first taxable year and distributes that income and the trust corpus on the first day of the following year. The trust is taxed on the income during the first year, and under the throwback rules, the beneficiary is taxed again on the income when it is distributed in the second year. However, the tax the beneficiary must pay on the income is reduced by the tax the trust has paid on that income during the previous year. The trust thus acts as sort of withholding agent for the beneficiary.[14] (But if the tax paid by the trust is greater than the tax owed by the beneficiary, the difference is not refunded to the beneficiary or credited against other taxes owed by the beneficiary.) Here, again, the effect of the rules is to tax the trust income only once, and, provided that the beneficiary is not in a lower bracket than the trust, at the beneficiary's rates. If the trust has accumulated income for more than one year, the same basic result applies, although the rules for taxation of the beneficiary are more complex.

The throwback rules were designed to prevent a taxpayer from achieving substantial tax avoidance in an era when the rate schedule applied to trusts taxed more income at low rates than does the rate schedule applicable since 1987. Without the throwback rules, a beneficiary's income could be accumulated by the trust and taxed at low rates and then distributed free of tax. Even with the rules, taxpayers sometimes found it advantageous to accumulate income in the trust, at its lower rates, since the additional tax on the income when it was distributed to the beneficiary was deferred. No interest was (or is) payable on an accumulation distribution. The modest potential advantage of the deferral of part of the tax on accumulated trust income is still available under current rules, but only if the accumulation is small. A modest advantage from accumulation is also available by virtue of the fact that the throwback rules do not apply to amounts accumulated for a beneficiary before age 21 or birth. §665(b). In general, though, the fact that trusts are now subject to rates equal to the maximum individual tax rates on relatively low amounts of income removes any advantage from accumulation.

14. In order to tax the beneficiary on the entire amount of the trust income, the distribution must be "grossed up" by the amount of the tax paid by the trust. For example, suppose a complex trust earns and accumulates income of $10,000, pays a tax of $2,000, and in the next year distributes the accumulated income of $8,000. The $8,000 income is grossed up by the $2,000 tax. The beneficiary is treated as having received the entire $10,000 and as having paid a tax of $2,000 on that distribution. This tax treatment follows the same pattern as the taxation of wages subject to withholding. If you earn $10,000 and your employer withholds tax of $2,000 and pays you $8,000, you report income of $10,000 and are entitled to a tax credit of $2,000.

4. The Use of Multiple Trusts

It is sometimes necessary to determine whether a single trust instrument creates several trusts or only one, since each trust is entitled to its own \$100 or \$300 deduction and to a separately calculated tax. The Service may wish to consolidate the income of two or more trusts and tax the combined income to a single entity. The issue may arise, for example, if a grantor creates two (or ten or 100) trusts all in identical terms and for the benefit of the same beneficiary, in an effort to obtain a \$100 or \$300 exemption for each trust and to compute the tax on each trust's taxable income separately. The courts tended to uphold the use of multiple trusts against the Commissioner's attack. See, e.g., Morris Trusts v. Commissioner, 51 T.C. 20 (1968), aff'd per curiam, 427 F.2d 1361 (9th Cir. 1970), in which each of ten separate declarations of trust was held to create two separate trusts or a total of twenty trusts for the same beneficiaries. However, §667(c), adopted in 1976, substantially eliminates the advantage of multiple trusts by providing that where there are accumulation distributions to a beneficiary for any prior year from more than two trusts, the taxes paid by the third trust are not imputed to the beneficiary and he or she receives no credit for those taxes. This provision overrides the normal exemption for accumulations before a beneficiary is born or reaches age 21. And §643(e), added in 1984, gives the Treasury broad rule-making powers to prevent the use of multiple trusts for tax-avoidance purposes.

G. GRANTOR TRUSTS

1. Revocable Trusts

As we have seen, a person who is willing to make an outright gift of property succeeds in shifting income for tax purposes to the donee. But many people whose objective is to shift income are unwilling, or at least reluctant, to make no-strings-attached gifts. In an early decision, the Supreme Court held that a taxpayer who had established a trust to pay the income from property to his wife and at her death to his children, but who had retained the power to revoke the trust (and thereby regain the corpus) at any time, was taxable on the income as if he had made no gift. Corliss v. Bowers, 281 U.S. 376 (1930). This outcome is now reflected in the Code in §676,[15] which goes further and nullifies the

15. Technically, a grantor with a power of revocation is "treated as the owner" of the trust. This language leads into §671, under which a person is taxed on the income of a trust of which he or she is treated as owner.

trust, for tax purposes, if the power to revoke (and thereby shift the assets back to the grantor) is held by any "nonadverse party." A nonadverse party is defined in §672(b) as one who is not an "adverse party," which §672(a) defines as one "having a substantial beneficial interest in the trust which would be adversely affected by the exercise or nonexercise of the power which he possesses respecting the trust." Thus, if a grantor transfers property to a trust with the income payable to his or her child for life and retains the power to revoke, the grantor is taxable on the income, even though the child is legally entitled to receive it, and the same is true if the power to revoke is given to the grantor's lawyer or a friend. But if the child (the income beneficiary) is given the power to revoke, since the child would plainly be an adverse party (that is, one whose interest would be adversely affected by revocation), the grantor would not be taxable under §676. Since the donee of an outright gift can always return the gift property to the donor, the rule allowing an adverse party to have a power of revocation seems to make sense. Under §676(b), §676(a) does not apply to a power of revocation whose effect might be to restore property to the donor only at such time as he or she would be permitted without adverse tax consequences to have a reversionary interest. (See §673, described infra page 782.)

2. Totten Trusts and Similar Arrangements

In Rev. Rul. 62-148, 1962-2 C.B. 153, the Service ruled that the income from funds deposited in a savings account in the depositor's name "as trustee" for another person is taxable income of the depositor if under local law the transaction creates only a revocable trust (sometimes called a Totten trust in New York, also called a tentative trust or a savings bank trust). Income of custodial accounts under state custodial and uniform gifts to minors acts (see infra page 790), however, is taxed to the child and not to the parent-custodian, on the theory that these funds are the property of the child and may not be taken back by the custodian, even though the funds may be available for support of the child (and if so used may result in income to the parent).

3. Trusts for the Benefit of the Grantor

Consistent with the notion reflected in §676(a) that a shifting of income requires a transfer that genuinely deprives the donor of the beneficial enjoyment of the property, §677(a) taxes to the grantor trust income that is, or may be, used for the benefit of the grantor or the grantor's spouse. Section 677(b) relieves the grantor of taxation on income that *might be* used to support his or her children "in the discretion of another person, the trustee, or the grantor acting as trustee or co-trustee." Such income is taxable to the grantor only to the extent actually used to discharge his or her obligation of support. On the question of what is a part of the obligation of support and what is not, see Brooke v. United States, infra page 793.

4. Reversions

Before 1987 a grantor to whom the trust corpus was to revert was not taxable on the income if, at the time the trust was established, the reversion could not take effect for at least ten years (or upon the death of the income beneficiary, if sooner). This rule gave rise to the proliferation of ten-year trusts, also known as "Clifford" trusts.[16] The 1986 act repealed the rule allowing reversions at the end of ten years (or on the death of the income beneficiary) and substituted a rule taxing the grantor on the income of a trust in which he or she has a reversionary interest whose value is greater than 5 percent of the value of the trust (with an exception for reversions after the death of a minor lineal descendant). §673.

5. Powers of Control

Section 674(a) lays down the general rule that the grantor is to be treated as owner of any portion of a trust if its "beneficial enjoyment" is subject to a "power of disposition," exercisable by the grantor alone, by a nonadverse party, or by the grantor and a nonadverse party acting together, without the approval or consent of any adverse party. Typical provisions covered by §674(a) are a retention by the grantor of the power to add beneficiaries to those named in the trust instrument, to vary the proportions in which corpus or income is to be paid to specified beneficiaries, or to accelerate or postpone the time when distributions are to be made.

Section 674 contains some important exceptions to the basic rule of §674(a) that any power of disposition results in the grantor being treated as owner. Section 674(b) contains a list of powers that can be retained by anyone, including the grantor. Among the powers permitted by §674(b) are the power to withhold income temporarily (§674(b)(6)) and

16. The label came from Helvering v. Clifford, 309 U.S. 331 (1940), in which the Supreme Court, in a case arising before the adoption of the grantor trust rules (§§671-679), held that the income of a five-year trust for the benefit of the grantor's wife was taxable to the grantor. After the case was decided, the Treasury issued regulations that contained safe-harbor rules for trusts with reversions to grantors. Those regulations are the source of the present statutory scheme.

to distribute corpus (§674(b)(5)). Under §674(c) the grantor may vest in an *independent* person an unfettered "sprinkle" or "spray" power as to both income and corpus — that is, a power to choose which of several beneficiaries will receive income or corpus. And under §674(d) *any* person other than the grantor or the grantor's spouse may have the sprinkle power over income if the power is limited by a "reasonably definite external standard." The regulations provide that standards such as "reasonable support and comfort"; "education, maintenance, or health"; and enabling the beneficiary "to maintain his accustomed standard of living" all qualify as "reasonably definite." See Regs. §1.674(d)-1 and §1.674(b)-1(b)(5). With a cooperative holder of the power and a sufficiently large class of beneficiaries, the effect of the §674 exceptions is to allow the grantor very substantial control over the use of the trust income. See infra Section 7.

The powers of disposition permitted under §674 need not be held by the trustee. For example, a grantor can be the trustee (and thus, among other things, make investment decisions) and still have some other person hold the sprinkle powers permitted under §674(c) or (d).

6. Administrative Powers

Section 675(1) and (2) provide that the grantor is to be treated as owner of the trust property if certain unusual powers (e.g., to purchase trust property for less than adequate consideration) may be exercised by the grantor, a nonadverse party, or both, without the consent of any adverse party. Moreover, §675(3) treats a grantor who has borrowed from the trust as the owner of the trust property unless the loan was repaid before the beginning of the taxable year or was authorized by an independent trustee and provision was made for adequate interest and security. Finally, certain powers of administration (e.g., the power to vote stock of a corporation in which the holdings of the grantor and trust are significant to voting control) are fatal under §675(4) if exercisable by anyone acting in a nonfiduciary capacity, unless the consent of a person in a fiduciary capacity is required.

The trustee, who may be the grantor, can have broad discretion in making investment decisions. This means that the grantor, within reasonable limits, can choose to invest in common stocks whose dividend yield is quite low or in bonds that pay a high rate of interest. Of course, there is always the possibility that the beneficiaries (e.g., the grantor's children) might take the grantor to court for abuse of discretion. But the beneficiaries may hesitate to do so out of respect, affection, or fear of loss of inheritance or other tangible benefits that the grantor is in a position to bestow on those who remain, by virtue of their good behavior, the natural objects of his or her bounty and affection.

7. The Obligation of Support

In Braun v. Commissioner, 48 T.C. Mem. 1984-285, a taxpayer who was a New Jersey resident established a trust for the benefit of his children. The income was used in part to pay for the children's college educations. The court held that under New Jersey law the taxpayer had an obligation to provide his children with college educations and that consequently the amounts of trust income used for that purpose were includable in his income under §677. (This was an alternative holding. The court also found that the taxpayer had a "sprinkle" power that made him taxable under §674.) What if the trust had been created by the taxpayer's father (that is, by the children's grandfather)? See §§652(a), 662(a); Regs. §§1.662(a)-4, 1.652(a)-1.

In Stone v. Commissioner, T.C. Mem. 1987-454, *aff'd without opinion*, 867 F.2d 613 (9th Cir. 1989), the taxpayers, who were California residents, established a trust for the benefit of their minor children. The court held the parents taxable on amounts of trust income used to pay the children's tuition at private schools, on the theory that under California law affluent parents in circumstances such as those found in the case were legally obligated to provide the private school education and that, consequently, they were taxable under §677. One significant fact bearing on the obligation, according to the court, was that the parents had sent the children to the private schools for several years before the trust began to pay the tuition. The idea seems to have been that once parents start to send their children to private schools, they may have a legal obligation to continue to do so.

In Sharon v. Commissioner, T.C. Mem. 1989-478, the tax court again addressed the obligation of support under California law. Income from property given by parents to their two daughters was used to pay for "private high school and private college tuition, camps, foreign travel, and other items." The court had no difficulty in rejecting the notion that any of the items other than the private high school tuition were part of the obligation of support. As to the college tuition, it was able to rely on Cal. Civ. Code §196.5, under which the parental obligation of support ends when a child reaches age 19 or completes the twelfth grade, whichever occurs first. As to the private high school tuition, the court summarized the *Stone* decision, supra, as follows:

> If a child had special needs that would only be met by a private school, that would be an item of support. Similarly, if a child had been attending a private school prior to a divorce, continuing the private education could be an item of support. Also important in determining whether private high school tuition is a support item are the parents' financial ability to pay tuition and the background, values, and goals of parents and child.

In the case before it, the court, in support of its conclusion that the private high school tuition was not part of the obligation of support, observed that the father had begun transferring property to the daughters when they were infants. In addition:

> It cannot be said that [the father] transferred property for the specific purpose of using it to pay [the daughters'] private high school tuition. In fact, [the father] testified that the money was [the daughters'] to do with as they pleased. Had they not used the money for private high school tuition, they could have used it for other things.

8. Example

G, who has assets worth several million dollars, intends to transfer $300,000 to a trust for the benefit of his children, *S* (age 12) and *D* (age 14). The trustee is to be *B, G*'s brother. The trustee is given discretion either to accumulate income or to distribute it to either child, or both, for "their reasonable comfort or support or for their education, health, or maintenance." The trust is to terminate at the end of ten years, at which time the corpus and any previously undistributed income is to be distributed in equal shares to the two children. *B* is given broad discretion as to the kinds of investments to be held by the trust. *G* contemplates that at least initially the corpus will be invested in bonds, which should yield income of about $24,000 per year. He anticipates that each year *B* will make distributions sufficient to pay private school tuition for each of the children, plus the cost of summer camp, music lessons, ski trips, and the like. Income not used for this purpose will be accumulated and held for future distribution to the children for their college educations or upon termination of the trust. (a) Will it work? (b) Suppose that each of the children has exhibited a streak of rebelliousness and *G* wants to be able to cut off either of them without a penny if he or she fails to conform to *G*'s (and *B*'s) ideas about proper behavior (mostly relating to respect for one's elders). What can he do? (c) What if he were to include as potential (discretionary) beneficiaries his mother and father or an impecunious cousin? (d) What, if anything, might be gained by appointing *F, G*'s friend, as trustee and giving *F* unfettered discretion to distribute income or corpus to either of the children? (e) If you were *F,* would you accept this kind of power? What if you were *G*'s lawyer and *G* asked you to hold such a power?

9. Assignments of Income by Trust Beneficiaries

In Harrison v. Schaffner, 312 U.S. 579 (1941), the income beneficiary of a trust was held taxable on income that she assigned to her children for the next year only. In 1955, the Service ruled that it would not seek to tax the income beneficiaries of a trust if they assigned the income for ten years or more, provided they did not retain any strings that would be fatal under the Clifford regulations if retained by the grantor of a trust. Rev. Rul. 55-38, 1955-1 C.B. 389. Presumably the same approach would be employed, for post-1986 assignments, if the assignor does not retain any strings that would be fatal under the present law.

10. Nongrantors with Power to Demand Trust Income or Corpus

Under §678 persons other than the grantor may be taxable on the income of a trust if they have the power to demand the income or corpus or have partially released such a power, retaining such control over the trust as would, if they were grantors, cause them to be treated as its owner under the grantor trust provisions (§§671-677). A typical trust affected by §678 would be one set up by a person with her grandchildren as the income beneficiaries but with her children having the right to demand that the income be paid to them instead. These trusts are sometimes called "demand trusts" or "Mallinckrodt trusts" (after a pre-1954 case, Mallinckrodt v. Nunan, 146 F.2d 1, 5 (8th Cir.), cert. denied, 324 U.S. 871 (1945)). Note that §678 applies only to powers vested solely in the person to whom the income or corpus may be paid. Thus, if a person has the power to vest the income of a trust in his or her spouse, that power does not result in taxation of either spouse, except to the extent that income is actually distributed to the potential beneficiary spouse. Moreover, it appears that in order to result in taxation under §678, a power must be unrestricted, as opposed to a power limited by a standard such as "support" or "needs," at least if the standard imposes, as a practical matter, a substantial constraint on the holder of the power. See 3 B. Bittker and L. Lokken, Federal Taxation of Income, Estates, and Gifts ¶80.8.1 (2d ed. 1991).

REVENUE RULING 87-127

1987-2 C.B. 156

Facts

Generally, state law provides that a decedent's estate or spouse has a legal obligation to pay for the decedent's funeral. A pre-need funeral is a funeral that has been arranged for, and purchased by, the decedent prior to the decedent's death. In a pre-need funeral arrangement, the purchaser of the funeral enters into a contract with the seller, which is usually a funeral home. The purchaser selects the desired merchandise and services and agrees to pay for them in a lump sum or in installments.

The merchandise and services are delivered upon death by the seller.

Most states have laws or regulations that govern pre-need funerals. These laws and regulations protect the purchaser and provide for the investment of the money transferred to the seller. Usually, the seller is required to deposit a percentage of the money into a pre-need funeral trust for the use, benefit and protection of the purchaser; the money is invested and held by the trust until the seller performs. Based upon the purchaser's life expectancy, the present value of the right to use the deposit to pay for the purchaser's funeral exceeds 5 percent of the amount of money deposited in the trust at its inception.

Although the terms of the trust agreements may vary from seller to seller and the provisions of state law may vary from state to state, there are four pre-need funeral trust arrangements that are commonly used. Each of the following situations describes one of these arrangements.

Situation 1. The purchaser can cancel the contract with the seller at any time. Income earned on the money deposited in the trust is accumulated. Upon performance, the seller receives all of the purchaser's money that was deposited in the trust and the accumulated income. If the purchaser cancels the contract with the seller, all money deposited in the trust and the accumulated income is received by the purchaser.

Situation 2. The purchaser can cancel the contract with the seller at any time. Income earned on the money deposited in the trust is paid annually to the seller. Upon performance, the seller receives all of the purchaser's money that was deposited in the trust. If the purchaser cancels the contract with the seller, all money deposited in the trust is returned to the purchaser.

Situation 3. The purchaser can cancel the contract with the seller at any time. Income earned on the money deposited in the trust is accumulated. Upon performance, the seller receives all of the purchaser's money deposited in the trust and the accumulated income. If the purchaser cancels the contract, the purchaser is not entitled to receive any money from the trust but is only entitled to select a new seller to provide the funeral.

Situation 4. The purchaser can cancel the contract with the seller at any time. Income earned on the money deposited in the trust is accumulated. Upon performance, the seller receives all of the purchaser's money that was deposited in the trust and the accumulated income. If the purchaser cancels the contract with the seller, all the money deposited in the trust is returned to the purchaser, and the accumulated income is paid to the seller.

LAW . . .

In Rev. Rul. 73-140, 1973-1 C.B. 323, the taxpayer contracts with a funeral home for prepaid funeral services. State law provides that a seller of prepaid funeral services must deposit 90 percent of all funds collected under contracts to provide funeral services into a trust fund for the use, benefit and protection of the purchasers. The purchaser of the contract is considered to be the grantor of the trust. Since the grantor can at any time withdraw the portion of the grantor's payments paid into the trust fund, together with any interest earned thereon, the grantor is considered the owner of the trust under section 676(a) of the Code. The ruling concludes that the purchaser must include in gross income the interest earned on amounts in the trust fund for the year in which such interest is earned by the trust. . . .

Analysis and Holdings

(1) In each of the four situations, the purchaser is treated for federal income tax purposes as the grantor of the trust for the following reasons. The money that funds the trust comes from the purchaser. . . . Although the purchaser's money is paid to the seller, under state law the seller does not have dominion and control over it and is not free to dispose of it except to place the money in trust. . . . The placement of the money into the trust usually occurs soon after the purchaser's money is received by the seller. . . . Once it is in trust, the disposition of the money, and the income earned on it, reflects the wishes of the purchaser more than those of the seller. . . .

(2) In each of the four situations, the purchaser is treated under section 671 as the owner of the entire trust.

Situation 1. Because the purchaser can cancel the contract at any time and receive the money deposited into the trust and the accumulated income, the purchaser has the power to revoke the trust. Therefore, under section 676(a) of the Code the purchaser is treated as the owner of the entire trust and the income of the trust is includible in the purchaser's gross income in the year in which it is earned by the trust. Rev. Rul. 73-140.

Situation 2. This trust differs from the trust in Situation 1 in that income of the trust is paid annually to the seller. Because the purchaser can cancel the contract at any time and receive the money deposited in the trust, the purchaser has the power to revoke the trust. Therefore, under section 676(a) of the Code, the purchaser is treated as the owner of the entire trust and the income of the trust is includible in the purchaser's gross income in the year in which it is earned by the trust. The income paid annually by the trustee to the seller is a payment for merchandise and services and is includible in the seller's gross income in the year received or properly accrued depending upon the seller's method of accounting.

Situation 3. In those states in which the purchaser's estate has a legal obligation to pay for a funeral, the purchaser has a reversionary interest in the trust because the money deposited into the trust and the income earned thereon will relieve the estate of such obligation. . . . The value of this reversionary interest exceeds 5 percent of the value of that portion of the trust that includes the money deposited into the trust as of the inception of that portion. Because the value of this reversionary interest exceeds 5 percent of the value of the money deposited in the trust, the purchaser is treated under section 673(a) as the owner of the entire trust and the income of the trust is includible in the purchaser's gross income in the year in which it is earned by the trust.

In those states in which the purchaser's spouse has a legal obligation to pay for a funeral, the income earned on the money deposited into the trust may be applied in discharge of this obligation. Therefore, under section 677(a) of the Code the purchaser is treated as the owner of the entire trust and the income of the trust is includible in the purchaser's gross income in the year in which it is earned by the trust.

Situation 4. In this trust the income is accumulated. However, unlike the trust in Situation 1, the seller will receive the income even if the contract is cancelled by the purchaser. Because the trust is revocable, the purchaser is treated as the owner of that portion of the trust that includes the money deposited into the trust. Therefore, under section 676(a) of the Code the income earned on this portion is includible in the purchaser's gross income in the year in which it is earned by the trust. The income earned on the accumulated income is not subject to revocation and is paid to the seller. However, as in Situation 3, this income will benefit the purchaser's estate or spouse. Therefore, under either sections 673(a) or 677(a), the purchaser is the owner of that portion of the trust that includes the accumulated income, and, thus, the income earned on the accumulated income is includible in the purchaser's gross income in the year in which it is earned by the trust.

(3) In each of the four situations the purchaser has contracted with the seller for certain merchandise and services and the money is deposited into the trust to pay for the merchandise and services. Accordingly, any payment received by the seller from the trust is a payment for merchandise and services and under section 61 of the Code is includible in the seller's gross income in the year received or properly accrued depending upon the seller's method of accounting. . . .

QUESTIONS

1. This Ruling should be compared with "deposit" cases such as *Indianapolis Power & Light*, supra page 448. Which seems to produce tax results that are consistent with economic reality?

2. Does application of the approach of the Ruling require the existence of an arrangement that would be recognized in nontax law as a "trust"? What is a trust?

H. GIFTS TO MINORS UNDER UNIFORM ACTS

REVENUE RULING 59-357

1959-2 C.B. 212

. . . Uniform laws have been adopted in many states to facilitate gifts to minors. Generally, these laws eliminate the usual requirement that a guardian be appointed or a trust set up when a minor is to be the donee of a gift. Under the Model Gifts of Securities to Minors Act, a donor may appoint either himself or a member of the minor's family as custodian to manage a gift of securities. The Uniform Gifts to Minors Act[17] provides that money as well as securities may be the subject of a gift to a minor and that a bank, trust company, or any adult may act as custodian. When a gift is made pursuant to the model or uniform act the property vests absolutely in the minor. The custodian is authorized to apply as much of the income or principal held by him for the benefit of the minor as he may deem advisable in his sole discretion. Income and principal not so applied are to be delivered to the donee when he reaches the age of 21 or, in event of his prior death, to his estate. . . .

Revenue Ruling 56-484, C.B. 1956-2, 23, holds that income, which is derived from property transferred under the Model Gifts of Securities to Minors Act and which is used in the discharge or satisfaction, in whole or in part, of a legal obligation of any person to support or maintain a minor, is taxable to such a person to the extent so used, but is otherwise taxable to the minor donee. . . .

The provision of the Uniform Gifts to Minors Act regarding the powers of the custodian as to distributions differs from the comparable provision of the Model Gifts of Securities to Minors Act in only three respects. First, the "model" act authorizes the custodian to apply so much of the income from the securities

> as he may deem advisable for the support, maintenance, general use and benefit of the minor in such manner, at such time or times, and to such extent as the custodian in his absolute discretion may deem suitable and proper, without court order, without regard to the duty of any person to support the minor and without regard to any funds which may be applicable or available for the purposes.

17. [The Uniform Gifts to Minors Act has been succeeded, and replaced in most states, by the Uniform Transfers to Minors Act, which is broader in scope. — Eds.]

The "uniform" act does not use the term "absolute discretion," but this provision is otherwise virtually identical.

Second, the "uniform" act differs from the "model" act in that, in lieu of the latter part of the language quoted above, it provides that the income can be applied by the custodian for the minor's support without regard to the duty of himself or of any other person to support the minor or his ability to do so. Thus, the custodian, who may be legally obligated to support the minor, has power to use custodianship income for such support even though he may have adequate funds for this purpose.

Third, the "uniform" act contains a provision not found in the "model" act which gives a parent or guardian of the minor, or the minor himself after he reaches the age of 14, the right to petition the court to order the custodian to spend custodial property for the minor's support, maintenance or education. This provision, coupled with the "uniform" act's omission of the term "absolute" with reference to the discretion vested in the custodian, suggests the existence of a limitation on the custodian's otherwise uncontrolled power to withhold enjoyment of the custodial property from the minor, at least as to a portion of such property. Nevertheless, the custodian's power to withhold enjoyment is not substantially affected by such limitation.

In view of the foregoing, it is the opinion of the Internal Revenue Service that neither these nor other variations between the "model" act and the "uniform" act warrant any departure from the position previously published in . . . Revenue Ruling 56-484, supra, . . . in regard to gifts made under the "model" act. . . .

Income derived from property so transferred which is used in the discharge or satisfaction, in whole or in part, of a legal obligation of any person to support or maintain a minor is taxable to such person to the extent so used, but is otherwise taxable to the minor donee. . . .

QUESTION

Is the tax treatment of transfers under the Uniform Gifts to Minors Act (now the Uniform Transfers to Minors Act) consistent with the tax treatment of similar transfers using trusts?

I. FAMILY PARTNERSHIPS

Unlike the trust, the partnership is not a separate taxable entity. A partnership return must be filed for the Treasury's information, reporting all partnership income and deductions, but the firm's net income is taxed to the partners individually, whether withdrawn or not, in accordance with their respective interests. §§701-704. Losses and credits of the firm are similarly allocated among the partners and deducted by them on their individual returns.

With the increase in restrictions on the use of the trust for tax splitting came, fortuitously or not, the rise of the family partnership. Typically, the head of the family, doing business as an individual proprietor, would make gifts of portions of his business capital to children or other relatives. Then a partnership would be formed with these relatives, usually with the income of the enterprise to be distributed among the partners according to their interests in the firm's capital. Ordinarily the new partners took no part in the management of the firm, though occasionally they served in clerical or other minor capacities. Sometimes the donor would reserve a salary for his or her own services, to be deducted before the profits accruing to capital were calculated. The highwater mark in this area is Tinkoff v. Commissioner, 120 F.2d 564 (7th Cir. 1941), involving an accountant who took his son into his accounting firm as a partner on the day the boy was born.

In Commissioner v. Culbertson, 337 U.S. 733 (1949), the Supreme Court attempted to resolve the problematic use of family partnerships to shift income by issuing a set of criteria with which to determine whether a partnership "is real within the meaning of the federal revenue laws." These criteria included relationship of the parties, their respective abilities and capital contributions, and the actual control of income. The *Culbertson* criteria produced considerable uncertainty as to the treatment of any given partnership, leading Congress in 1951 to adopt what is now §704(e).

Under §704(e), a partner in a partnership in which capital is a material income-producing factor is free to give some or all of his interest in the partnership to a family member. The family member, not the donor, will be taxed on the income attributable to that interest. Thus, a parent with an interest in a partnership that owns an apartment building may give that interest to his or her child and the child will be taxed on the partnership income. This result is consistent with the tax principles discussed earlier in this chapter. As noted supra page 761, taxpayers may shift income from property by transferring ownership of the property. The gift of a partnership interest in which capital is a material income-producing factor represents a gift of the underlying capital of the partnership. On the other hand, suppose a parent gives his or her newborn infant an interest in his or her law partnership in the hope of shifting the income from that partnership. The attempt will fail because capital is not a material income-producing factor in a law partnership. Here it is income from services, rather than property, that the taxpayer is attempting to shift.

Even in cases in which capital is a material income-producing factor, the amount of income shifted is limited by the requirement that the donor receive reasonable compensation for services rendered to the partnership. The statute and accompanying regulations also contain rules designed to ensure that a partner is able to shift partnership income only by making an actual transfer of the partnership interest that is the source of that income. An individual may not, for example, retain voting rights or other indicia of ownership with respect to a partnership interest and succeed in shifting income from that interest through a putative transfer of the interest to a low-bracket family member.

J. GIFT AND LEASEBACK

BROOKE v. UNITED STATES

468 F.2d 1155 (9th Cir. 1972)

The taxpayer is a physician who practices medicine in Missoula, Montana. His family in 1959 included six children from ages 6 to 14. His income during the years in issue varied between $26,000 and $30,000. As a gift he deeded to his children real estate which was improved by a pharmacy, a rental apartment, and the offices of his medical practice. Following the conveyance the Montana State Probate Court appointed the taxpayer as guardian of the children. In this capacity the taxpayer collected rents from the pharmacy and apartment. Without a written lease, he also paid to himself as guardian for his children the reasonable rental value of his medical offices. The rents so collected were applied to the children's insurance, health and education. Expenditures were made for private school tuition, musical instruments, music, swimming and public speaking lessons. The taxpayer also purchased an automobile for his oldest child, and paid travel expenses to New Mexico for his asthmatic child.

The fundamental issue presented involves the sufficiency of the property interest transferred. The transfer of a sufficient property interest justifies the taxation of the donees and the deduction of the rental payments under §162(a)(3) as ordinary and necessary business expenses by the donor.

In analyzing gift and leaseback cases, several factors must be considered: (1) the duration of the transfer; (2) the controls retained by the donor; (3) the use of the gift property for the benefit of the donor; and (4) the independence of the trustee. . . . None of the above factors prevents the income from being shifted in the instant case.

No issue is presented here as to the duration of the transfer — it was absolute and irrevocable; it was by warranty deed, unconditioned and unencumbered. . . . The absolute nature of the transfer distinguishes this case from those urged as controlling by the Government. See, e.g., Helvering v. Clifford 309 U.S. 331 (1940) (five year trust). . . .

The taxpayer in this instance retained few, if any, controls over the trust property. He was obligated to and did pay the reasonable rental value of his medical offices. The fact that there was no written lease dispels any argument that the tenancy actually amounts to a reversion; the guardianship could at any time terminate the month to month tenancy. Likewise the taxpayer could at any time be terminated as guardian. Other controls retained over the trust property were consonant with possession as a tenant. Accordingly the findings of the District Court regarding both the irrevocable nature of transfer and the necessity of making rental payments are not clearly erroneous. This is in marked contrast with Commissioner v. Sunnen, 333 U.S. 591 (1948), where the taxpayer who assigned royalty agreements to his wife retained corporate control over the royalty agreements with the power to determine the amount of interest paid to his wife.

It is also apparent that trust benefits have not inured to the taxpayer as donor. The rental payments were expended solely for the insurance, health and education of the children. As discussed later, the taxpayer was not legally obligated to provide these benefits for his children.

Many decisions pivot on the issue of the independence of the trustee. . . . The necessary independence of the trustee is achieved in a guardianship. The Montana Probate Court administers a guardianship with the same requisite independence of any court-administered trust. See Mont. Rev. Codes §§91-4507, 4510, 4520 and 4522. Under the scrutiny of the court rental obligations must be met and accountings made. Mont. Rev. Codes §91-4907. Guardianship property cannot be sold without court approval. Mont. Rev. Codes §91-4518. Without belaboring the point there should be no lack of confidence in the supervision by our courts. A court appointed trustee — even though the taxpayer — offers sufficient independence.

If the taxpayer should at some future date breach his fiduciary duty toward his children, the government might well renew its challenge to the validity of the gift.

It must be emphasized that this transfer is not a sham or fraud. The Government adamantly asserts that this transfer lacks a business purpose, which therefore disqualifies it for a business deduction. Several leading cases employ such language. See, e.g., Gregory v. Helvering [infra page 910]. . . . Other cases require only that the transfer be grounded in substantial economic reality. . . .

The non-tax motives, as borne out by the record, are abundant and grounded in economic reality. The taxpayer desired to provide for the health and education of his children; avoid friction with partners in his medical practice; withdraw his assets from the threat of malpractice suits; and diminish the ethical conflict arising from ownership of a medical practice with an adjoining pharmacy. Neither substance nor impact denies this transfer professional or economic reality. This finding by the District Court is not clearly erroneous.

The Government further argues that even if deductions under §162(a) are allowable, expenditures for the children's benefit merely serve to satisfy the taxpayer's legal obligations to support them imposed by §677(b) and therefore are not allowable. The District Court determined that Rev. Rul. 56-484, 1956-2 Cum. Bul. at 23, establishes the applicability of local law in construing the meaning of support in Section 677(b). Montana law provides:

> The parent entitled to the custody of a child must give him support and education suitable to his circumstances.

Mont. Rev. Codes §61-104. The District Court held that the expenditures made were not the legal obligations of the taxpayer under Montana law. The only authority cited by the Government which suggests the contrary, Refer v. Refer, 102 Mont. 121, 56 F.2d 750 (1936), is entirely limited to its facts.

The last issue in this appeal is raised by the taxpayer: Does a court administered guardianship constitute a trust under §677(b)? Section 677 (or any regulation thereunder) does not refer to guardianships. However, the meaning of "trusts" is very broad and is specifically found in Section 641. Montana law, as interpreted by the District Judge, 292 F. Supp. at 572-573, includes guardianships within the meaning of "trusts." While a guardianship does not possess all trust requisites, for the purposes of taxation under Section 677, it must be considered a trust.

Affirmed.

Ely, Circuit Judge (dissenting).

I vigorously, although respectfully, dissent. The majority's opinion disturbs me for two principal reasons. First, I think it disregards the fundamental consideration that we are bound by prior decisions of our very own. See Etcheverry v. United States, 320 F.2d 873, 874 (9th Cir. 1963). Secondly, by creating yet another legal standard under which to assess the tax consequences of "gift and leaseback" transactions, the majority, in my judgment, adds further inconsistency to an area of tax law that is already fraught with too much semantic confusion.

Our decision controlling the tax treatment of a gift and leaseback transaction is Kirschenmann v. Westover, 225 F.2d 69 (9th Cir.), cert. denied, 350 U.S. 834 (1955), wherein we held

> Tax consequences are determined not from the formal aspect of a transaction, but from the actual substance of a piece of business. What is found

> here lacks *business meaning* for tax purposes. This court's decision in Shaffer Terminals, Inc. v. Commissioner, 9 Cir., 194 F.2d 539 [1952], is controlling.

225 F.2d at 71 (emphasis added).

In *Shaffer Terminals,* which involved a sale and leaseback transaction, we affirmed the Tax Court's disallowance of rental deductions, relying on the decision of the Tax Court and the then recently pronounced decisions of our Brothers of the Second and Fifth Circuits in White v. Fitzpatrick, 193 F.2d 398 (2d Cir. 1951), cert. denied, 343 U.S. 928 (1952) (gift and leaseback), and W. H. Armston Co. v. Commissioner, 188 F.2d 531 (5th Cir. 1951) (sale and leaseback); accord, Van Zandt v. Commissioner, 341 F.2d 440 (5th Cir.), cert. denied, 382 U.S. 814 (1965) (gift and leaseback). The prior law in our Circuit, therefore, as in the Second and Fifth Circuits, has been that both a sale and leaseback and a gift and leaseback transaction will be subjected to scrutiny under the "business purpose" test. Under that test, rentals cannot be treated as a valid business expense under Section 162 unless there is a legitimate business purpose motivating the transfer of the leased property. I have found no subsequent case in this Circuit that eschews the business purpose test, nor have I perceived its erosion in the other Circuits which follow the same standard. . . . Hence, since the District Court here found as a fact that "[t]he transfer did not serve any substantial business purposes" I would, unlike the majority, reverse on the basis of the binding effect of our prior decision in Kirschenmann v. Westover, supra. See Etcheverry v. United States, supra.

Having stated the primary ground for my concern, I would not ordinarily feel compelled to comment further on the composition of the majority's opinion. Yet, I do feel so compelled in this instance. While I do not share their view, I can understand my Brothers' reluctance to apply the business purpose test to a gift and leaseback transaction. Early cases adopting the business purpose test for a gift and leaseback transaction failed to recognize that a gift, unlike a sale of business property, is not motivated by a business purpose. Yet this distinction is important only if the gift and subsequent leaseback are viewed as separate and independent transactions. The bifurcation approach adopted by the majority does find some support in the decisions of other courts. . . . Therefore, I cannot honestly dismiss my Brothers' position on this point as being wholly unreasonable, even though I am convinced that the better approach requires an integration of the gift and leaseback transactions, at least in cases in which the donor-lessor was an occupant of the premises at the time the gift was made. When the transactions are thus integrated, it becomes obvious that the allowance of rental deductions requires satisfaction of the business purpose test at the inception of the transaction, the time when the gift was made. . . .

Even conceding the reasonableness of the majority's acceptance of the bifurcated transaction approach, I cannot acquiesce in its proposal of yet another test under which to judge a gift and leaseback. As I read the majority opinion, the standard formulated is that in order for the transaction to be recognized for tax purposes, the gift must be founded upon economic reality and must divest the donor of substantial control over the property. Such a test is unique in several respects. While my Brothers purport to rely on the Tax Court's rejection of the business purpose test, they do not adopt that court's formulation of the controlling legal standard:

> The mere transfer of legal title to property, however, is not conclusive for Federal income tax purposes, for the "sale" that lacks economic reality and business purpose, and the "gift" that leaves the donor with substantially the same control over the property that he had before, will simply be disregarded.

Penn v. Commissioner, 51 T.C. 144, 149-150 (1968).

In fashioning its new legal standard, the majority has excised one critical element from the appropriate test for the ascertainment of the validity of a sale and leaseback transaction — economic reality. Moreover, the majority directs its crucial inquiry not to the degree of control *retained* by the donor, as required by the Tax Court's analysis in Penn v. Commissioner, supra, but to the amount of control the donor *surrendered* in making the transfer. Here, the taxpayer, as sole guardian, had complete managerial powers over the property. He set the amount of the rentals, determined the terms, if any, of the unwritten lease, and decided when, if ever, the rentals were to be paid. He retained the power to mortgage, sell, or otherwise encumber or convey the property, the only impediment being that any such action on his part required, at some time, the approval of the court which had appointed him as the guardian of the estates of his children. I therefore find the majority opinion wholly at odds with the Tax Court's analysis in *Penn*. Viewed realistically, the situation here is that the taxpayer has retained "substantially the same control over the property that he had before." I cannot stretch my imagination so far as to believe that the taxpayer had an independent role, apart from his fatherhood and consistent occupancy and control, simply by virtue of some speculative degree of state court supervision over his supposed fiduciary operations.

The two standards which I recognize as being applicable to a case of this nature — the business purpose test, which should have bound us, and the standard relating to the donor's retention of control, which is applicable in the Tax Court — represent judicially imposed restrictions on the availability of a gift and leaseback transaction to effectuate a tax avoidance scheme premised upon intra-family income splitting. As I view these standards, they are interrelated. If a transaction is grounded upon economic reality and business purpose, then perhaps the majority's view as to the minimal independence of the fiduciary could, by some, be accepted. If, however, more leeway is given in the first instance by requiring only economic reality to support the transfer, then a much greater degree of independence should be required of the fiduciary. In my opinion, the necessary independence cannot exist when all managerial powers are retained by the transferor-lessor. See, e.g., Penn v. Commissioner, supra at 153-154. It seems obvious to me, under the facts of this case, that neither of the two recognized tests can be applied to the taxpayer's advantage.

NOTES AND QUESTIONS

1. *Guardianship versus other arrangements.* How much, if any, importance should be attached to the fact that a court-appointed guardian is subject to judicial supervision? In the case of a custodianship under the Uniform Gifts to Minors Act, there is no judicial involvement whatsoever, except in the extremely unlikely event that the child (or someone acting on behalf of the child) challenges the actions of the custodian. The same is generally true for trustees of ordinary trusts. Do you suppose that Dr. Brooke used a guardianship, rather than the more convenient device, a trust, in order to ensure that there would be judicial supervision?

The decision in the case was in favor of Dr. Brooke, but it was close. If Dr. Brooke had set up a trust with an independent trustee, he would have been on much safer ground. Do you suppose that this approach would have imposed significant burdens or created barriers to accomplishing the intended objectives?

2. *Nontax motives.* What is the relevance of nontax motives? Is the desire "to provide for the health and education of his children" a proper nontax motive? a proper business motive? If such a motive is sufficient, will there ever be a case in which a well-advised taxpayer fails to meet the motive test?

3. *Substance.* Did the father in *Brooke* substantially change his, and his children's, economic position (apart from taxes) by making the arrangements for the gift and leaseback?

4. *Property used in the business.* Should it matter that the property was used in the father's business? Suppose that an executive of IBM who owns $1 million worth of IBM common shares puts those shares in trust for the benefit of his children but appoints himself as trustee, with the power to vote the shares. How would the dissenting judge react to such a situation?

5. *A trust?* Was the court on sound ground in relying on the rules for taxation of trusts? In Rev. Rul. 56-484, 1956-2 C.B. 23, cited in Rev. Rul. 59-357, supra page 790, the Service ruled that a donor is taxable under §61 on income used to discharge his or her obligation of support.

6. *Subsequent holdings.* In Rosenfeld v. Commissioner, 706 F.2d 1277 (2d Cir. 1983), the taxpayer had established a trust for the benefit of his children and had contributed to it a building that he owned and that he occupied in conducting his medical practice. The court, after citing conflicting cases in other circuits, concluded that the test of substantial change in the parties' rights and economic interests had been satisfied and refused to uphold the Commissioner's denial of a deduction for rent paid to the trust. The court rejected the theory that there must be a business purpose for the gift and leaseback together, saying that a business purpose for the leaseback alone is sufficient. The court also indicated that it was important that there was an independent trustee and pointed out that the taxpayer did have a nontax motive in establishing the trust — namely, to guarantee his children's financial well-being.

K. SHIFTING INCOME THROUGH AND TO CORPORATIONS

1. Shifting Income through a Corporation

If one concentrates on economic substance rather than on legal forms, it is hard to see why efforts to shift income to children or other dependents by use of ordinary corporations should be dealt with differently from similar efforts involving partnerships or S corporations. But the intellectual tradition of treating corporations as separate entities has exerted a strong influence on tax law. Moreover, a taxpayer who uses the ordinary corporation as a vehicle for shifting income must pay a price: a tax at the corporate level. For example, suppose that a person operates in corporate form a business that generates a net income of $250,000 per year, $200,000 of which is attributable to her services; gives 40 percent of the shares of stock of the corporation to her children, retaining the other 60 percent; and takes no compensation for her services. In effect, $80,000 worth of income from the performance of services (40 percent of $200,000) is diverted to the children, in apparent violation of the principle of Lucas v. Earl that income from the performance of services must be taxed to the one who earns it. The income ultimately realized by the children may take the form of dividends and at a highly conceptual level one might argue that their income is from "property" (the shares of common stock that they own) rather than from services. This ignores underlying economic reality, as §1375(c) recognizes for S corporations, but in the case of ordinary corporations the reality is likely to be ignored; the income is not likely to be attributed to the parent. As suggested, however, the price of achieving the shift in income in our example is a corporation income tax, not just on the $80,000 diverted to the children but on the entire $250,000, plus the individual income tax on dividends paid by the corporation from the amount of corporate earnings left after the corporation income tax.[18] The corporate-level tax can be reduced by paying a deductible salary to the parent, but to that extent the objective of shifting income is defeated. Perhaps this explains why the Service has been so tolerant of shifting of the sort contemplated by our example. There are, however, limits of tolerance, as the following case illustrates.

FOGLESONG v. COMMISSIONER

621 F.2d 865 (7th Cir. 1980)

CUDAHY, Circuit Judge. . . .

This is an appeal from a decision of the United States Tax Court, 35 T.C.M. 1309 (1976), determining that the bulk of the commission income of a personal service corporation, Frederick H. Foglesong Co., Inc. (the "Corporation"), set up by a steel tubing sales representative, Frederick H. Foglesong (the "taxpayer"), was taxable to the taxpayer and not to the Corporation. The Tax Court for various reasons, which will appear, chose essentially to disregard the corporate form and, under Section 61 of the Internal Revenue Code and the assignment of income doctrine of Lucas v. Earl [supra page 742], to treat the bulk of the commission income as having been earned by, and as taxable to, the taxpayer. . . . We reverse and remand.

I

The facts here are not in substantial dispute. Frederick H. Foglesong, the taxpayer, was a sales representative for the Plymouth Tube division of the Van Pelt Corporation ("Plymouth Tube") and for the Pittsburgh

18. Section 541, imposing an additional 70 percent tax on the undistributed income of personal holding companies, or §531, imposing an additional tax at 27.5 percent of the first $100,000 and 38.5 percent of the excess of income accumulated beyond the reasonable needs of the business, may force the payment of dividends. In any event, if the objective is to put money in the hands of the children, dividends must be paid unless the children can borrow against appreciation in the value of their shares arising from the retention of earnings.

Tube Company ("Pittsburgh Tube"), two manufacturers of cold drawn steel tubing. . . . There was evidence that taxpayer had an impressive reputation as a salesman, and this was one of the principal reasons he was retained as a sales representative by Plymouth Tube and Pittsburgh Tube.

On August 30, 1966, taxpayer incorporated his business as Frederick H. Foglesong Company, Inc. He, his wife and his accountant were listed as the incorporators on the certificate of incorporation. Of the one hundred shares of common stock issued by the Corporation (for a total subscription price of $1,000), taxpayer held 98 shares and his wife and accountant held 1 share each. The Corporation paid no dividends on its common stock during the taxable years in question, 1966 through 1969.

The Corporation also issued preferred stock to the taxpayer's four minor children (for which the total subscription price was $400). The four children received dividends totaling $32,000 over the period beginning September 1, 1966 and ending December 31, 1969. . . . The Corporation made its first salary payment to taxpayer on January 9, 1967, and he received a regular monthly salary after that date during the years which are relevant here. Taxpayer's salary income from the Corporation during calendar year 1967 was $56,500. In that year and in the succeeding relevant calendar years, he reported no personal income from any business as a sole proprietor. The respective net receipts of the Corporation from sales commissions and its deductions for compensation paid to taxpayer for the four taxable years in question are as follows:

Taxable year ending	*Net receipts from commissions before payment of compensation to taxpayer*[19]	*Compensation to taxpayer deducted*
August 31, 1967	$148,486.70	$41,500.00
August 31, 1968	100,482.23	55,000.00
August 31, 1969	99,429.35	65,000.00
August 31, 1970	121,018.24	73,700.00

After the formation of the Corporation, all commissions from Plymouth Tube and Pittsburgh Tube were paid to the Corporation. But a

19. These figures show the total net commission income (before payment of compensation to taxpayer) as reported by the Corporation on its tax returns for the taxable years in issue. They thus include the income generated on certain sales made within the Corporation's exclusive sales territories, but without any selling effort on taxpayer's part. Approximately two percent of the total commissions received by the Corporation during the taxable years in question resulted from these exclusive territorial arrangements.

written agreement with Pittsburgh Tube was not executed until May 19, 1969, or with Plymouth Tube until January 1, 1971.

Taxpayer testified that he wished to incorporate his business in order to obtain the limited liability protection afforded by a corporate structure and also to provide a better vehicle for his planned expansion into several new business ventures. Subsequent to the formation of the Corporation, taxpayer interviewed a prospective salesman to help him in the New England area, but these negotiations were unsuccessful. The Corporation did, however, employ a secretary during its taxable years ending August 31, 1969 and 1970, paid her a salary and took corresponding deductions. Taxpayer asserted that he had unsuccessfully attempted to expand his sales business into other areas such as steel warehousing, transportation of steel tubing and the exporting of steel tubes to Europe but produced no documentation of these efforts.

The Corporation paid taxpayer a regular salary as a salesman, paid all of taxpayer's expenses incurred in connection with his sales activities, maintained a bank account, carried its own insurance coverage, maintained a company automobile and complied with all the formalities required of corporations in the state of New Jersey. The Corporation adopted bylaws, held an initial meeting of incorporators, at which the board of directors was elected, and conducted periodic board of directors' and stockholders' meetings as required by its bylaws. Taxpayer served as chairman of the board of directors as well as president and treasurer of the Corporation.

During the years in question here taxpayer did not enter into any written employment contracts with the Corporation nor did he enter into a covenant not to compete with the Corporation.

During these years taxpayer's only gainful activity was as an employee of the Corporation. He had no legal rights under the representation contracts with Plymouth Tube and Pittsburgh Tube subsequent to the formation of the Corporation. Taxpayer testified that during the period at issue he did not engage in any business activity other than as an employee of the Corporation.

The Tax Court, inter alia, concluded on balance that, although there was no attempt by taxpayer to form a corporation to take advantage of losses incurred by a separate trade or business, tax avoidance considerations "far outweighed any genuine business concerns taxpayer may have had in setting up [the Corporation]." Nonetheless, the Commissioner conceded, and the Tax Court found, that the Corporation was a viable, taxable entity and not a mere sham during the years in issue.

But, in spite of its finding of viability (and strongly influenced by the apparent flagrancy of the tax avoidance), the Tax Court, in effect, substantially disregarded the Corporation for tax purposes. It found that during the years in question control over 98% of the commission income remained with taxpayer so as to cause such income to be taxable to him (as the person who earned it through his personal sales efforts) and not to the Corporation. The Tax Court based this result on Section 61 of the Code and the assignment of income doctrine of Lucas v. Earl, supra. With respect to those commissions which were received by taxpayer solely because of the exclusive territorial rights assigned to the Corporation under its agreements with Plymouth Tube and Pittsburgh Tube (amounting to approximately 2% of the total), the Tax Court held that the Corporation, not the taxpayer, was the party earning this income, and, hence, such commissions should be taxed to it.

The Tax Court found it unnecessary to reach the question whether the Commissioner was authorized to allocate the commission income to taxpayer under Section 482 of the Internal Revenue Code, which permits the Commissioner to reallocate income and expenses among commonly controlled "organizations, trades or businesses."

Personal service corporation tax cases reveal a tension between "the principle of a graduated income tax . . . and the policy of recognizing the corporation as a taxable entity distinct from its shareholders in all but extreme cases." Rubin v. Commissioner, 429 F.2d 650, 652 (2d Cir. 1970). The impact of the graduated income tax is eroded when income is split artificially among several entities or over several tax years. The assignment of income doctrine under Section 61 (as formulated in Lucas v. Earl) seeks to recognize "economic reality" by cumulating income diffused among several recipients through "artificial" legal arrangements. The attribution of income to its "true earner" is simply a species of recognizing "substance" over "form." See *Rubin*, supra, at 653.

But, if the issue is one of attributing the income of a corporation to its sole stockholder-employee who "really" earned it, we encounter the important policy of the law favoring recognition of the corporation as a legal person and economic actor. As Mr. Justice Holmes said in Klein v. Board of Supervisors, 282 U.S. 19, 24 (1930):

> But it leads nowhere to call a corporation a fiction. If it is a fiction it is a fiction created by law with intent that it should be acted on as if true. The corporation is a person and its ownership is a nonconductor that makes it impossible to attribute an interest in its property to its members.

In the instant case, the following circumstances, among others, are present: (1) the Corporation and not the taxpayer is the party to the contracts under which services are performed, (2) the Corporation is recognized to be a viable, taxable entity and not a mere sham, (3) nontax business purposes are present even though tax avoidance is apparently a major concern,[20] (4) the Corporation has not been formed for

20. Actual or potential purposes served by the Corporation here included the provision of limited liability and the furnishing of a vehicle for subsequent expansion of the business.

the purpose of taking advantage of losses incurred by a separate trade or business, (5) the corporate form (and the status of the Corporation as an actual operating enterprise) has been consistently honored by the taxpayer and other parties to the transactions giving rise to the income, (6) the taxpayer does not render services as an employee to any entity other than the Corporation, (7) the Corporation is not disqualified from performing the Services required of it by contract because the law requires these services to be performed by an individual, (8) the entities paying or providing the income are not controlled or dominated by the taxpayer, and (9) as will appear, other and more appropriate legal bases exist for attacking apparent tax avoidance than broad-scale disregard of the corporate form through application of assignment of income theory. We note especially that the Tax Court did not find the Corporation to be a pure tax avoidance vehicle.

Under the circumstances of the instant case, we think it inappropriate to attempt to weigh "business purposes" against "tax avoidance motives" in a determination whether the assignment of income doctrine of Lucas v. Earl should apply, in effect, to substantially disregard the corporate form. Ostensibly this inquiry has been made in order to question the validity of a *transaction* purportedly entered into by a corporation, rather than the validity of the corporation itself. . . . But to apply Lucas v. Earl in this fashion under the circumstances present here is effectively (and more realistically) to nullify the determination that the Corporation is a viable, taxable entity and not a sham. . . .

The instant case is not unlike the early case of Fontaine Fox v. Commissioner, 37 B.T.A. 271 (1938), where a cartoonist transferred to his corporation his cartoon copyrights and various contracts pursuant to which he earned royalties and entered into an agreement with the corporation to render his services exclusively to it for a fixed salary. The corporation, in turn, made a contract with a distributor, who made payments to the corporation based on the percentage of sales of newspapers carrying taxpayer's cartoons. In *Fontaine Fox,* the Board of Tax Appeals distinguished Lucas v. Earl on the grounds that, rather than an assignment of income, *Fox* involved an assignment of property (the contracts with distributors); subsequent income arising from such property was income not of the assignor but of the assignee. Accord, Laughton v. Commissioner, 40 B.T.A. 101 (1939), rem'd, 113 F.2d 103 (9th Cir. 1940).

Although we do not regard the point as decisive, the Tax Court here found that, with respect to the contracts to perform sales services for Plymouth Tube and Pittsburgh Tube, there had been not only an assignment but a novation, with the corporation's becoming the sole party obligated to perform sales services and entitled to be compensated for such performance. Hence, this case is in essential concept quite distinguishable from Lucas v. Earl, where only income was assigned, and cannot be plausibly distinguished from *Fontaine Fox,* where the service contracts were assigned. Here not only the fruit but the tree itself was transferred to the Corporation.

In Rubin v. Commissioner, 51 T.C. 251 (1968), the Tax Court held that income was taxable to an individual who owned a 70% interest in a personal service corporation, which performed management services for another company. The same individual also controlled the company for which services were to be performed. The Tax Court attempted to analyze the problem both as one in which form differed from substance (the individual being held to work "directly" for the company) and in which the earning of the income was controlled by the individual rather than his corporation and was, therefore, taxable to the individual under the doctrine of Lucas v. Earl. In *Rubin,* the Tax Court suggested that the difference between the form over substance analysis and the assignment of income approach was only semantic. Thus it attempted to determine whether the form of the transaction, involving the personal service corporation, served any economic purpose and also whether the individual, in fact, controlled the earning of the income. The Tax Court found, first, that the income was properly taxable to the individual and distinguished both *Fox* and *Laughton* on the grounds that in *Rubin* the taxpayer was not contractually bound to (and in fact did not) render services exclusively to the personal service corporation (as he was bound to and did in *Fox* and *Laughton*). Second, in *Rubin,* the taxpayer controlled not only the personal service corporation, but also the corporation to which services were rendered; in *Fox* and *Laughton* only the personal service corporations themselves were controlled.

On the second point — taxpayer's control of the company receiving services — the instant case is like *Fox* and *Laughton* in that taxpayer here had no control over Plymouth Tube and Pittsburgh Tube. On the first point, although taxpayer here was not contractually bound to render services exclusively for the Corporation, he did in fact do so.

Rubin was later reversed on appeal by the Second Circuit, through Judge Friendly, who was of the view that "references to 'substance over form' and the 'true earner' of income merely restate the issue in cases like this: Who is the 'true earner'? What is substance and what is form?" Rubin v. Commissioner, 429 F.2d 650, 653 (2d Cir. 1970). Judge Friendly felt that Section 482 (providing for reallocation of the gross income of controlled taxpayers) was a more appropriate tool for use in this kind of case than "common law" tax doctrines such as assignment of income under Lucas v. Earl. In any event, Judge Friendly believed that the two bases on which the Tax Court distinguished *Fox* (and *Laughton*) were not relevant with respect to §61.

We think that the Tax Court determination in *Rubin* might be easily distinguished here on the grounds that the taxpayer in the instant case worked exclusively for his personal service corporation (although he was not under contract to do so). Further, he did not own or control Pittsburgh Tube or Plymouth Tube, the entities to which services were rendered. Fundamentally, however, we believe that both *Rubin* and the instant case are more like *Fox* and *Laughton* than they are unlike those leading cases. In the resolution of the instant case we accord considerable deference to Judge Friendly's holding in *Rubin*. . . .

Roubik v. Commissioner, 53 T.C. 365 (1969), on which the Tax Court also relies, involved a professional corporation consisting of four radiologists, where the question raised was whether the business of the four principals was carried on by the corporation or outside it. In *Roubik,* the individual radiologists, not the corporation, maintained contractual relationships with the institutions for which services were rendered. The corporation did not own equipment nor did it incur the great bulk of operating expenses. It did not assign its shareholders to institutions or to tasks. In short, the corporate form was repeatedly flouted. . . .

The Tax Court here also places much emphasis on the absence of a written employment contract and/or a covenant not to compete between taxpayer and the Corporation. The elevation of form over substance in this analysis is manifest. If there were an employment contract and/or a covenant not to compete (in a single employee situation) and the employee-shareholder wished to withdraw his services from the corporate engagement, he could simply (as corporate officer) rescind the contract or covenant or decline to enforce it. There is no way of establishing an enforceable legal obligation which would require the sole shareholder-employee in a personal service corporation to work exclusively for the corporation. In the instant case, the employee-shareholder has in fact so worked exclusively. This fact is more significant than any paper obligation which might have been created. We note also that in the essentially meaningless corporate arrangements of *Roubik,* there was a covenant not to compete, which apparently had no realistic impact. *Roubik,* supra.

We believe that, where the issue is application of the assignment of income doctrine to effectively set aside the corporation, under the particular circumstances of this case (which we have carefully delineated), an attempt to strike a balance between tax avoidance motives and "legitimate" business purposes is an unproductive and inappropriate exercise. Such an approach places too low a value on the policy of the law to recognize corporations as economic actors except in exceptional circumstances. This is true whether the analysis used to dismantle the corporation pursues the rubric of assignment of income or substance over form. Here there are other more precise devices for coping with the unacceptable tax avoidance which is unquestionably present in this case. But there is no need to crack walnuts with a sledgehammer. . . .

In the instant case, Section 482 of the Internal Revenue Code appears available to allocate among controlled taxpayers "gross income, deductions, credits, or allowances" to prevent evasion of taxes or to clearly reflect the income of the controlled taxpayers. Other statutory provisions and "common law" doctrines, structured for more limited application, may also be available to remedy potential tax abuse. Thus, the dividends paid to taxpayer's children, . . . may . . . be subject to attack via . . . the assignment of income doctrine. . . . We think that the very aggressive tax avoidance measures which taxpayer employed here are vulnerable, but we express no opinion as to what statutory provisions or "common law" principles may properly address them. . . .

We, therefore, remand to the Tax Court for consideration of the issues surrounding the Commissioner's claim under Section 482 and other claims if available. For those purposes we do not disagree with the Tax Court's basic findings of fact in this case. But we do not intimate any conclusive view on what specific results with respect to these claims should be.

Reversed and remanded.

Wood, Circuit Judge, dissenting.

As both sides of the issue are fully and fairly set forth in the majority opinion, little need be added in registering my dissent. Although I view it as a close case, I prefer in general the view of the United States Tax Court. In the alternative, I believe Section 482 of the Internal Revenue Code applies.

This corporation is nothing more than a few incorporating papers lying in a desk drawer of no significance except when a tax return is due. Mr. Foglesong continued to conduct his original one-man sales representative business as he always did, except he has become insulated by those incorporating papers from the taxes he should have been paying. For a subscription price of $400 for all the preferred stock, this "should-be" taxpayer accomplished, among other things, the diversion to his children of at least $8,000 of his own income for each of the four taxable years. His make-believe corporation is too transparent for me to accept for tax purposes under Section 61 of the Code. I respectfully dissent.

NOTES AND QUESTIONS

1. *Aftermath.* On remand, the Tax Court applied §482 and again allocated 98 percent of the income to Mr. Foglesong. 77 T.C. 1102 (1981). Again the taxpayer appealed and again the Court of Appeals reversed and remanded, with the following explanation of the inapplicability of §482 (691 F.2d 848, 851-852 (1982)):

> Virtually all of the cases upholding the application of section 482, many of which the appellee and the Tax Court rely upon to support their position, have done so either in situations involving an attempt to offset the profits of one business with the losses of another or in situations in which the individual performed work other than that he did on behalf of the corporation. A case involving both situations is Borge v. Commissioner, 405 F.2d 673 (2d Cir. 1968), cert. denied, 395 U.S. 933. In that case, the taxpayer was a successful entertainer who also ran a poultry farm that suffered losses. He organized a corporation and transferred to it all of the assets of the poultry business. He then entered into an agreement to work for the corporation as an entertainer and thereby offset the poultry farm's losses by entertainment profits.
>
> The court held that the section 482 dual business requirement was satisfied because despite the entertainment contract between Borge and his corporation, Borge in fact remained in a separate business. Instead of putting all of his entertainment revenues into the corporation, he put in only a percentage. "[Taxpayer] was not devoting his time and energies to the corporation; he was carrying on his career as an entertainer, and merely channeling a part of his entertainment income through the corporation." Id. at 676. An indicium that Borge, not the corporation, was running the entertainment business was that the parties seeking his services as an entertainer required that he, not the corporation, guarantee the contracts. Id. at 675. The court concluded that the only purpose of the arrangement between the taxpayer and his corporation was to offset poultry business losses with profits from the entertainment business. Id. at 677.
>
> The instant case is markedly different. The taxpayer and his corporation were engaged in the identical business and Foglesong worked exclusively for the corporation. He did no consulting on the side nor did he engage in any other business. Furthermore, he instructed everyone to pay the corporation, not him. Finally, there was no attempt to evade taxes by offsetting the profits of one business against the losses of another.

That was not, however, the end of the story. The Court of Appeals remanded "for a consideration of whether assignment of income principles may be employed to allocate dividends and preferred stock received by Foglesong's children to Foglesong." 691 F.2d at 853. And in Haag v. Commissioner, 88 T.C. 604 (1987), the Tax Court reaffirmed its position that §482 applies to one-person personal service corporations. The court noted that an appeal in *Haag* would go to the Eighth Circuit Court of Appeals, which, according to the Tax Court, in Wilson v. United States, 530 F.2d 772, 777 (1976), "implied" its support of the Tax Court rule. 88 T.C. at 614, note 4.

2. *Assignment of income doctrine versus ignoring the corporate entity.* Do you agree with the majority in *Foglesong* that application of Lucas v. Earl would be tantamount to disregard of the separate existence of the corporation? Did the decision of the Supreme Court in *Earl* make Mrs.

Earl a nonperson? In his dissenting opinion in the Tax Court in Keller v. Commissioner, 77 T.C. 1014, 1042 (1981) aff'd, 723 F.2d 58 (10th Cir. 1983) (discussed infra page 815), Judge Wilbur says, "Mere existence — either of Mrs. Earl or petitioner's corporation — does not carry automatic immunity from the assignment of income doctrine."

3. *Motive.* Determination of the motives of a particular individual for engaging in a particular transaction is, of course, a difficult and dangerous undertaking. A rule that makes motive relevant tends to reward and encourage deceit, or at least disingenuousness. Is there an acceptable alternative: an inquiry into rational business basis (that is, whether a rational person might have entered into the transaction for nontax reasons)? In situations of the sort illustrated by *Foglesong,* what effect would such a test be likely to have?

4. *Formalities.* What do you think, judging from the opinion in *Foglesong,* about the importance of observing corporate formalities such as generating minutes of corporate meetings and maintaining a separate corporate bank account? See infra page 810, footnote 21.

5. *Duration.* To what extent was Mr. Foglesong committed to the corporate arrangement? How difficult would it have been for him to terminate his relationship with the corporation? If he had done that, what would have been left for the children? Did Mr. Foglesong in effect have a power of termination that would have been fatal under §676 if he had used a trust rather than a corporation?

6. *The employment contract.* If you were advising someone like Foglesong, would you recommend a written contract between that person and his or her corporation? Is it important that the person agree to work exclusively for the corporation? Why?

7. *"Property."* The court's discussion in *Foglesong* of the *Fontaine Fox* case should be compared with the material earlier in this chapter on assignment of income from copyrights, patents, etc. See supra page 775, Note 2.

2. Shifting Income to a Corporation

Many of the doctrines and precedents encountered in cases like *Foglesong,* involving efforts to shift income *through* a corporation to members of one's family, are also encountered in cases where the effort is to shift income from an individual *to* his or her wholly owned corporation. The *Foglesong* opinion discusses several of such cases. In recent years, the primary objective of shifting income to a corporation has been to take advantage of the fact that qualified pension plans available to employees were far more attractive than those available to the self-employed and that employees cannot set up qualified pension plans for themselves. Most doctors and lawyers and many other professionals have traditionally been self-employed. (Partners are considered to be self-employed.) Entertainers and athletes usually earn most of their income as employees but often want to set aside for retirement amounts of money far in excess of any amounts that might be contributed by their employers to the employers' plans. A person may be an employee of his or her wholly owned corporation even if the corporation has no other employees. This means that, in substance, a person can be an employer (through his or her corporation) of himself or herself, which means in turn that an employee-type qualified pension plan can be established. Suppose that a doctor earns $200,000 per year and wants to set aside funds in a qualified pension plan. As a self-employed individual the most that he could set aside before 1982 was $7,500 per year. The maximum that could be set aside for an employee of a corporation was far greater. Suppose, then, that the doctor were to form a corporation, all of whose stock he owned, and that he were then to agree to perform services exclusively for the corporation. His patients would become legally obligated to make their payments to the corporation. The doctor would be required to engage in legal rituals such as producing corporate minutes and having a separate bank account for the corporation,[21] but there would be no significant change in the substance

21. A good sense of the kinds of formalities that a careful lawyer would insist on observing is conveyed by the following passage describing the facts in Keller v. Commissioner, 77 T.C. 1014, 1016-1017 (1981) (discussed infra at page 815):

> On December 3, 1973, petitioner caused a professional corporation, Dan F. Keller, M.D., Inc. (Keller, Inc.), to be organized under the Oklahoma Professional Corporation Act. At the organizational meeting, petitioner, who was the sole shareholder, was duly elected as sole director. Pursuant to that meeting, Keller, Inc., also adopted corporate bylaws; elected petitioner president-treasurer and his wife, petitioner Marilyn F. Keller, secretary; appointed a bank in Oklahoma City as the official depository bank; adopted a section 1244 stock plan (relating to losses on "Small Business Stock"); set petitioner's annual salary; adopted an employees medical expense reimbursement plan; adopted an employees wage continuation plan; adopted a defined benefit pension plan and trust; and approved an employment contract between petitioner and Keller, Inc., which was dated the date of the meeting.
>
> As stated above, petitioner was the sole shareholder of Keller, Inc., having subscribed for and purchased on December 3, 1973, 500 shares of the common stock. Such shares constituted all of the then-issued and outstanding stock. Petitioner ceased to be a partner of MAL, and Keller, Inc., was substituted as a partner pursuant to a written agreement executed by petitioner, all the other partners of MAL, and Keller, Inc. Pursuant to the agreement between petitioner and the MAL partners, petitioner also personally agreed to guarantee all obligations arising out of the relationship between Keller, Inc., and the partnership.
>
> Under the aforesaid employment contract, petitioner agreed to render his services as a pathologist to Keller, Inc., in return for an annual salary of $60,000.
>
> Within 2 months after its creation, Keller, Inc., opened a checking account with a bank in Oklahoma City; it maintained and used that account during all of 1974 and 1975. On or about July 31, 1975, Keller, Inc., also opened a savings account with a savings and loan association in Oklahoma City.
>
> Shortly after December 3, 1973, Keller, Inc., applied to the Internal Revenue Service for an employer identification number. In addition, petitioner's name was

of the doctor's activities or in his relationships with patients. For tax purposes, as long as the proper formalities were observed, the corporation would be treated as a separate entity and the doctor as its employee. The doctor could cause the corporation to pay himself, say, $150,000 as salary and to put the remaining $50,000 into a qualified pension plan. The corporation could deduct the salary and the pension contribution, so it would have no income for tax purposes. The doctor would report as income only the $150,000 salary.

After some struggle, the Service in 1969 conceded that this kind of plan was effective for tax purposes. Such is the vitality of the notion of the corporation as a separate entity. As time passed, use of this vehicle for pension planning proliferated. For all practical purposes, self-employed people were able to avoid the rules designed for them as long as they were willing to pay the legal and accounting fees and other expenses required in order to operate in corporate form — which all sensible people recognized to be a charade and a waste. Finally, in 1982, Congress significantly reduced (beginning in 1984) the advantages of the corporate plans by reducing their contribution limits, increasing the limits for plans for the self-employed, and making various other changes in the rules relating to such matters as coverage of other employees and borrowing from the plan. These changes have removed most of the tax advantage of the so-called professional corporation,[22] and one can hope that such entities will become a curious relic of an era when employees received far more favorable tax treatment than similarly situated self-

---

removed from the entrance door to the MAL facility and the name "Dan F. Keller, M.D., Inc." was substituted for petitioner's name. A similar substitution was effected on the letterhead of the various laboratory test report and consultation report forms which MAL uses in its practice.

Keller, Inc., filed an initial franchise tax return with the State of Oklahoma, regularly filed annual franchise tax returns in 1974 and 1975, and received annual corporate licenses from the State of Oklahoma for 1974 and 1975. Keller, Inc., filed annual certificates of professional corporation with the Oklahoma secretary of state in 1974 and 1975, and also, for both of those years, filed appropriate returns with the Oklahoma Employment Security Commission and paid the contributions thereunder (relating to unemployment compensation coverage).

22. Many professionals who had incorporated before 1982 will find it advantageous to continue to operate in that form rather than dissolve the corporation. Moreover, use of the corporate form by people such as entertainers and screenwriters continues to offer substantial advantages. The so-called loan-out corporations used by such people allow them to establish pension plans that would not otherwise be possible. If they are employed by their own corporations, which "loan out" their services to various other firms, their corporations can establish substantial pension plans for them. If they do not incorporate and work directly for a series of employers, they are allowed to contribute only modest amounts to IRA pension plans; they are not considered to be self-employed and cannot take advantage of the more generous pension plans (sometimes called "Keogh" plans) available to the self-employed. There are other advantages to operating in corporate form, including more favorable rules relating to the operation of the pension plan than the rules applicable to a person doing business directly (that is, without incorporating) and the availability of certain fringe benefits.

employed people and when, in response to this disparity, and in a triumph of form over substance, of magic over reality, tax-motivated incorporations became a flourishing business. The rise of the professional corporation does, however, dramatize an important issue of tax theory: Why is a person not taxable on the income that is generated by his or her services and is deflected to a corporation? The answer to that question may be, as the opinion in *Foglesong* suggests, that the notion of the corporation as a separate entity is too firmly embedded in our legal traditions, and in our subconscious, to be cast aside in the absence of conscious legislative action or intolerable abuse. But that conclusion leaves the question of the limits of the notion that income from personal services may be diverted to one's corporation. Three recent cases test those limits.

(a) In Johnson v. Commissioner, 78 T.C. 882 (1982), aff'd without opinion, 734 F.2d 20 (9th Cir.), cert. denied, 469 U.S. 857 (1984), the taxpayer was a professional basketball player with the San Francisco Warriors. He entered into a contract with Corporation *P,* his tax-planning vehicle. In this contract he agreed to perform services exclusively for *P.* The expectation was that *P* would then enter into a contract with the Warriors under which *P* would agree to supply Johnson's services to the Warriors. Typically, the athlete or entertainer would then guarantee the obligation of *P.* This is a common kind of tax-planning device for entertainers and athletes. The corporations are called "loan-out" corporations, since they loan out (for a fee) the services of the athlete or entertainer. Unfortunately for Johnson, the representatives of the Warriors were unwilling to contract with *P;* they insisted on a contract directly with Johnson. He therefore signed a contract with the Warriors and then assigned to *P* his rights to salary payments from the Warriors under that contract. The Tax Court held that the salary payments were taxable to Johnson, explaining its conclusion as follows (78 T.C. at 890-892):

> [T]he realities of the business world prevent an overly simplistic application of the Lucas v. Earl rule whereby the true earner may be identified by merely pointing to the one actually turning the spade or dribbling the ball. Recognition must be given to corporations as taxable entities which, to a great extent, rely upon the personal services of their employees to produce corporate income. When a corporate employee performs labors which give rise to income, it solves little merely to identify the actual laborer. Thus, a tension has evolved between the basic tenets of Lucas v. Earl and recognition of the nature of the corporate business form.[23]

23. That tension is most acute when a corporation operates a personal service business and has as its sole or principal employee its sole or principal shareholder. In those cases where sec. 482 applies, resort to general sec. 61 principles usually is not necessary since

> While the generally accepted test for resolving the "who is taxed" tension is who actually earns the income, that test may easily become sheer sophistry when the "who" choices are a corporation or its employee. Whether a one-person professional service corporation or a multi-faceted corporation is presented, there are many cases in which, in a practical sense, the key employee is responsible for the influx of moneys. Nor may a workable test be couched in terms of for whose services the payor of the income intends to pay. In numerous instances, a corporation is hired solely in order to obtain the services of a specific corporate employee.[24]
>
> Given the inherent impossibility of logical application of a per se actual earner test, a more refined inquiry has arisen in the form of who controls the earning of the income. . . . An examination of the case law from Lucas v. Earl hence reveals two necessary elements before the corporation, rather than its service-performer employee, may be considered the controller of the income. First, the service-performer employee must be just that — an employee of the corporation whom the corporation has the right to direct or control in some meaningful sense. . . . Second, there must exist between the corporation and the person or entity using the services a contract or similar indicium recognizing the corporation's controlling position. . . .
>
> In the case before us, we accept arguendo that the . . . agreement [between Johnson and *P*] was a valid contract which required the payments with respect to [Johnson's] performance as a basketball player ultimately to be made to [*P*]. We also accept arguendo that the . . . agreement [between Johnson and *P*] gave *P* a right of control over [Johnson's] services, although respondent maintains the agreement's control provisions systematically were ignored. . . . Thus, the first element is satisfied. However, the second element is lacking, and that is what brings this case within Lucas v. Earl rather than the cases relied on by petitioner.

In other words, if you want to take advantage of a formalistic structure, all the formalities must be strictly observed. That is the law, but does it make sense? Should substantial tax advantages depend on whether an employer is willing to accept an obligation of the employee's corporation, as many employers (including some NBA teams) have been willing to do, rather than insisting on a direct obligation of the employee, as the Warriors did?

(b) In Achiro v. Commissioner, 77 T.C. 881 (1981), Achiro and his brother-in-law, Rossi, each owned 50 percent of the stock of Tahoe City

---

sec. 482 provides a smoother route to the same "who is taxed" result. See Pacella v. Commissioner, 78 T.C. 604 (1982); Keller v. Commissioner, 77 T.C. 1014 (1981), appeal filed (10th Cir., Apr. 2, 1982). However, see Rubin v. Commissioner, 51 T.C. 251 (1968), rev'd and remanded 429 F.2d 650 (2d Cir. 1970), decided on remand 56 T.C. 1155 (1971), aff'd per curiam 460 F.2d 1216 (2d Cir. 1972), wherein application of secs. 61 and 482 led to different results.

24. Such instances are commonplace in personal service businesses such as law, medicine, accounting, and entertainment.

Disposal, a corporation operating a successful scavenger and landfill-management business. Achiro and Rossi formed a new corporation, A&R, to provide management services to Tahoe City Disposal. The management services were those of Achiro and Rossi. The A&R stock was owned 24 percent each by Achiro and Rossi and 52 percent by Achiro's brother (Rossi's brother-in-law), who had no significant operating role in the venture. Tahoe City Disposal paid substantial fees to A&R. A&R in turn paid salaries to Achiro and Rossi and made contributions to a pension plan for each of them. After these payments, A&R had very little income left, so it paid trivial amounts of income tax. The advantage sought by this arrangement was to avoid compliance with nondiscrimination rules relating to qualified plans, under which any plan set up by Tahoe City Disposal would have been required to provide coverage for all of its employees, not just Achiro and Rossi. The Tax Court responded to the government's §482 argument as follows (77 T.C. at 897-900):

> In the context of the present case, respondent may utilize section 482 to insure that the charges among the controlled entities represent arm's-length amounts. Instead of making such an allocation, respondent chose to allocate all of A&R's income and deductions to Tahoe City Disposal and Kings Beach Disposal. The evidence in the present case indicates that A&R received the arm's-length value of the services it rendered to Tahoe City Disposal and Kings Beach Disposal. In addition, respondent has essentially conceded that the payments reflect arm's-length charges by agreeing that if the payments are not allowed as deductible management fees to A&R, they will be allowed almost in their entirety to Tahoe City Disposal and Kings Beach Disposal as deductible salary payments. . . .
>
> Moreover, the cases respondent relies on do not support his position that without showing an arm's-length price for the services rendered, he may reallocate the entire price of such services from one corporation to another. . . .
>
> In Borge v. Commissioner, 405 F.2d 673 (2d Cir. 1968), aff'g a Memorandum Opinion of this Court, also relied on by respondent, entertainer Victor Borge formed a corporation to which he transferred the assets of an unprofitable poultry business. In addition, Borge entered into an employment agreement with the corporation pursuant to which he agreed to perform entertainment services for the corporation in exchange for an annual salary of $50,000. The $50,000 salary was far less than the amount Borge's entertainment activities produced each year, and it was found that Borge would not have made a similar agreement in an arm's-length transaction. Accordingly, respondent properly allocated a larger amount of Borge's entertainment earnings directly to him. . . .
>
> The fact that petitioners in the present case chose to incorporate A&R for the primary purpose of obtaining the benefits of its retirement plans does not justify respondent's section 482 allocations. In addition, none of the cases relied on by respondent support his sweeping reallocation of all

> service income from A&R to Tahoe City Disposal and Kings Beach Disposal. Accordingly, section 482 is inapplicable.

After also rejecting the government's effort to deny Tahoe City Disposal a deduction for the management fees, the court went on to hold that the common stock ownership of Achiro's brother in A&R should be ignored for purposes of the application of §414(b), so Achiro and Rossi were treated as owning 50 percent each. Thus, under §414(b) Tahoe City Disposal and A&R were treated as a single entity for purposes of testing compliance with the rules for qualified plans, A&R's plan failed to qualify, and contributions to the plan were currently taxable to Achiro and Rossi under §§402(b) and 83(a). Does this result show that Congress knows how to disregard corporate shells when it wants to and that, in the absence of express provisions like §414(b), separate corporate existence should be respected?

(c) In Keller v. Commissioner, 77 T.C. 1014 (1981), aff'd, 723 F.2d 58 (10th Cir. 1983) (see supra page 810, footnote 21), the Tax Court upheld the use of personal service corporations by members of personal service partnerships. The taxpayer, a pathologist, had been a member of a partnership consisting of eleven pathologists. He organized a one-man corporation, Keller, Inc., which became a member of the partnership in his place. The partnership income thereafter paid to Keller, Inc., was in part paid by it to Keller as salary and in part contributed to a qualified pension plan for his benefit. The majority held that §482 was applicable (a conclusion at odds with the later decision of the Seventh Circuit in *Foglesong*, supra page 800), but that no reallocation was called for where the salary and benefits paid by the corporation to its shareholder/employee equalled (as they did in Keller's case and would in most circumstances) the amounts that he would have earned by performing services directly. The majority also rejected the Commissioner's arguments based on lack of business purpose, substance over form, and assignment of income.

In a dissenting opinion, Judge Wilbur described the one-man corporation in this case as, among other things, "a small and barely discernible shadow on a thin edge of the partnership." 77 T.C. at 1036. The challenge for Judge Wilbur was to distinguish between Keller's situation and that of the typical professional corporation that is not a member of a partnership. His argument begins with a concession as to the latter (77 T.C. at 1040-1041):

> [A] brief review of history will show [that a] service business could always incorporate, but the incorporation of a professional service business presented unique ethical and policy problems. The States resolved the problems by permitting the incorporation of a professional practice or

> business, subject to certain constraints, the most important preserving individual liability for malpractice. This greatly restricted the limited liability normally associated with the corporate form. After considerable litigation over the proper classification of these organizations, the Service in Rev. Rul. 70-101, 1970-1 C.B. 278, conceded they were corporations. But that concession, like the cases litigated and the professional service corporation statutes enacted, focused on the incorporation of a professional business — a physician or several physicians incorporating their practice, with the assets, contracts, goodwill, books and records, accounts receivable and payable, medical facilities, equipment and supplies, physical facilities, and employees normally associated with that practice. As to these organizations, the dust has settled, and any further changes — if any are appropriate — will have to emanate from Congress. Respondent's concession clearly was confined to that type of creature. . . .

Attempting to show the insignificance of Keller's corporation, Judge Wilbur stated (77 T.C. at 1037-1039):

> Keller, Inc., "did not own any equipment, incur any debts for rent, office or medical supplies or services or for salaries, except the salaries of the petitioner." It had no expenses — petitioner continued to practice with the same facilities at the same locations owned or leased by [the partnership].
>
> It had no medical records, business records, or any other item or paraphernalia of business of any kind whatsoever. It supervised no employees and had no contracts with hospitals or contacts with primary care physicians — these all belonged to and were completely controlled by [the partnership]. "The maintenance of these records for tax purposes appears to be the only real business activity engaged in by the corporation."
>
> The partnership has both the contracts with the hospitals and the contacts with other customers. The partnership establishes every essential element of the business — from fees charged and customers served to the division of the income among the 11 partners in accordance with the partnership agreement. The partners, using the adjunct facilities, equipment, and employees of [a related corporation], earned this income by providing comprehensive pathological services to all of its customers. . . .
>
> The partnership controlled all of the elements that determined the income earned by the collective efforts of the partners. Petitioner was subject to these constraints to the same extent as the other partners, and he remained personally liable to the partnership in fulfilling his obligations as a partner. He simply assigned his share of the earnings and his salary from the [related] corporation to his corporate shell.

Are you convinced that Keller's corporation is more an empty charade than the thousands of corporations formed by individual doctors? If solo practitioners are to be permitted to gain tax advantages by elevating form over substance, why not practitioners who are members of partnerships? Is it persuasive to say that the floodgates must be kept closed? Consider the following observation by Judge Wilbur (77 T.C. at 1039-1040):

> The majority opinion produces strange results indeed, for as I read it, each individual partner could incorporate. We would have . . . the partnership and 11 corporate arms extending out in different directions, each a hollow prosthetic device without offices, a laboratory, equipment, facilities, employees, medical records, or any other items normally used in the practice of pathology. The sole function of this paper octopus would be to serve as an incorporated pocketbook, enabling each physician to have a pension plan and fringe benefit package tailored to his own preferences without regard to the quite different preferences of each of his partners and whether or not the employees of the business were provided anything at all.[25] After this decision, anyone may form a corporation, paper the file a little, and market his services with his salary being paid to his corporation. If Dr. Keller can do this, so can the technicians . . . working by his side. And nurses, teachers, pilots, truck drivers, and virtually any other employee one can think of, for this is the logical and practical consequence of the majority opinion. This may be a good idea, but I never thought it was the law until today.

Would it be a good idea? Congress thought not. In 1982 it enacted §269A, which applies to corporations whose principal activity is the performance of personal services for or on behalf of one other corporation or a partnership or other entity. Section 269A was consciously intended to "overturn the results in cases like Keller v. Commissioner, 77 T.C. 1014 (1981), where the corporation served no meaningful business purpose other than to secure tax benefits which would not otherwise be available." Joint Committee on Taxation, General Explanation of the Revenue Provisions of the Tax Equity and Fiscal Responsibility Act of 1982, H.R. 4961, 97th Cong., 2d Sess. 326 (1982).

The importance of §269A has been substantially diminished, however, by the adoption, for years after 1984, of provisions under which self-employed individuals, in creating qualified retirement plans, achieve no significant advantage by using the corporate form. Thus, in Letter Ruling 8737001, the Service ruled, in the case of a one-doctor corporation, that "in applying section 269A . . . , Congress intended that a personal service corporation's qualified pension or retirement

25. For the years in question, neither sec. 414(b) or (c) nor the applicable decisions would interfere with this. . . . For plan years subsequent to 1980, sec. 414(m) would appear to circumscribe the discrimination involved as to pensions, and sec. 105(h)(8) as to medical reimbursement. This simply demonstrates that each time Congress has spoken, it has unmistakably expressed its displeasure at the transparent manipulations involved. For the years in issue, the majority holding also permits petitioner (through his medical reimbursement plan) to funnel his share of net fees through his corporate shell, insulating him from the 3-percent floor on medical deductions so nettlesome to the patients who paid these fees.

plan will not be taken into account." The ruling goes on to note that, on the facts before it, other tax advantages of incorporation were "relatively insignificant" and that the corporation did serve the nontax purpose of protecting the doctor from "various liabilities of the partnership" for which the doctor performed services. The ruling concludes that, consequently, the facts did not "establish a principal purpose of tax avoidance."

In Sargent v. Commissioner, 93 T.C. 572 (1989), the Tax Court adopted a new approach that would seem to rule out the use of personal-service corporations for tax purposes by professional athletes in team sports and by other people whose jobs require that they be subject to the detailed control of the organization or person to whom the services are delivered. In *Sargent*, the taxpayer was a member of the Minnesota North Stars hockey team. He set up a personal-service corporation and went through all the proper legal ritual designed to make him an employee of that corporation, which in turn purported to supply his services to the team. The tax court concluded, however, that the team had substantial control over the manner in which team members perform their tasks and that therefore the taxpayer was, under common law rules relating to the employer-employee relationship, an employee of the team. Having reached this conclusion, it had no difficulty in taxing the individual on the amounts paid for his services by the team, under "classic assignment of income" doctrine (§61) or under §482. The court pointed out that the theory on which it relied (common law rules defining the employer-employee relationship) had not been invoked in earlier cases, which suggests that under its new approach those cases might now be decided differently.

On appeal, however, the Eighth Circuit Court of Appeals, rejected the Tax Court's "team" theory and reversed. 929 F.2d 1252 (1991). The appellate court opinion observes that almost all employment involves work for a "team" of sorts, and thus notes what it considers an inconsistency between the unfavorable ruling against Sargent and a subsequent favorable ruling in a case involving an actress, the formal terms of whose contractual arrangements were essentially the same as Sargent's. The opinion also rejects application of the assignment of income doctrine and §482. Although the case arose before the adoption of §269A, the opinion states that Sargent's personal service corporation was "established for a legitimate purpose," though it is not clear what that purpose (other than tax reduction) might have been.

The IRS quickly responded to the Eighth Circuit decision by issuing a statement that it disagrees with that decision and "warns that it will continue to litigate . . . based on the Tax Court's conclusions and will defend its position in all circuits except the Eighth Circuit." AOD 1991-022.

L. PENSION TRUST

UNITED STATES v. BASYE
410 U.S. 441 (1973)

Mr. Justice Powell delivered the opinion of the Court. . . .

Respondents, each of whom is a physician, are partners in a limited partnership known as Permanente Medical Group, which was organized in California in 1949. Associated with the partnership are over 200 partner physicians, as well as numerous nonpartner physicians and other employees. In 1959, Permanente entered into an agreement with Kaiser Foundation Health Plan, Inc., a nonprofit corporation providing prepaid medical care and hospital services to its dues-paying members.

Pursuant to the terms of the agreement, Permanente agreed to supply medical services for the 390,000 member-families, or about 900,000 individuals, in Kaiser's Northern California Region which covers primarily the San Francisco Bay area. In exchange for those services, Kaiser agreed to pay the partnership a "base compensation" composed of two elements. First, Kaiser undertook to pay directly to the partnership a sum each month computed on the basis of the total number of members enrolled in the health program. That number was multiplied by a stated fee, which originally was set at a little over $2.60. The second item of compensation — and the one that has occasioned the present dispute — called for the creation of a program, funded entirely by Kaiser, to pay retirement benefits to Permanente's partner and nonpartner physicians.

The pertinent compensation provision of the agreement did not itself establish the details of the retirement program; it simply obligated Kaiser to make contributions to such a program in the event that the parties might thereafter agree to adopt one.[26] As might be expected, a separate trust agreement establishing the contemplated plan soon was

26. The pertinent portion of the Kaiser-Permanente medical service contract states:

Article H
Base Compensation to Medical Group

As base compensation to [Permanente] for Medical Services to be provided by [Permanente] hereunder [Kaiser] shall pay to [Permanente] the amounts specified in this Article H. . . .

Section H-4. Provision for Savings and Retirement Program for Physicians. In the event that [Permanente] establishes a savings and retirement plan or other deferred compensation plan approved by [Kaiser], [Kaiser] will pay, in addition to all other sums payable by [Kaiser] under this Agreement, the contributions required under such plan to the extent that such contributions exceed amounts, if any, contributed by Physicians. . . .

executed by Permanente, Kaiser, and the Bank of America Trust and Savings Association, acting as trustee. Under this agreement Kaiser agreed to make payments to the trust at a predetermined rate, initially pegged at 12 cents per health plan member per month. Additionally, Kaiser made a flat payment of $200,000 to start the fund and agreed that its pro rata payment obligation would be retroactive to the date of the signing of the medical service agreement.

The beneficiaries of the trust were all partner and nonpartner physicians who had completed at least two years of continuous service with the partnership and who elected to participate. The trust maintained a separate tentative account for each beneficiary. As periodic payments were received from Kaiser, the funds were allocated among these accounts pursuant to a complicated formula designed to take into consideration on a relative basis each participant's compensation level, length of service, and age. No physician was eligible to receive the amounts in his tentative account prior to retirement, and retirement established entitlement only if the participant had rendered at least 15 years of continuous service or 10 years of continuous service and had attained age 65. Prior to such time, however, the trust agreement explicitly provided that no interest in any tentative account was to be regarded as having vested in any particular beneficiary.[27] The agreement also provided for the forfeiture of any physician's interest and its redistribution among the remaining participants if he were to terminate his relationship with Permanente prior to retirement.[28] A similar forfeiture and redistribution also would occur if, after retirement, a physician were to render professional services for any hospital or health plan other than one operated by Kaiser. The trust agreement further stipulated that a retired physician's right to receive benefits would cease if he were to refuse any reasonable request to render consultative services to any Kaiser-operated health plan.

The agreement provided that the plan would continue irrespective either of changes in the partnership's personnel or of alterations in its organizational structure. The plan would survive any reorganization of the partnership so long as at least 50% of the plan's participants remained associated with the reorganized entity. In the event of dissolu-

27. The trust agreement states:

> The tentative accounts and suspended tentative accounts provided for Participants hereunder are solely for the purpose of facilitating record keeping and necessary computations, and confer no rights in the trust fund upon the individuals for whom they are established. . . .

28. If, however, termination were occasioned by death or permanent disability, the trust agreement provided for receipt of such amounts as had accumulated in that physician's tentative account. Additionally, if, after his termination for reasons of disability prior to retirement, a physician should reassociate with some affiliated medical group his rights as a participant would not be forfeited.

tion or of a nonqualifying reorganization, all of the amounts in the trust were to be divided among the participants entitled thereto in amounts governed by each participant's tentative account. Under no circumstances, however, could payments from Kaiser to the trust be recouped by Kaiser: once compensation was paid into the trust it was thereafter committed exclusively to the benefit of Permanente's participating physicians.

Upon the retirement of any partner or eligible nonpartner physician, if he had satisfied each of the requirements for participation, the amount that had accumulated in his tentative account over the years would be applied to the purchase of a retirement income contract. While the program thus provided obvious benefits to Permanente's physicians, it also served Kaiser's interests. By providing attractive deferred benefits for Permanente's staff of professionals, the retirement plan was designed to "create an incentive" for physicians to remain with Permanente and thus "insure" that Kaiser would have a "stable and reliable group of physicians."[29]

During the years from the plan's inception until its discontinuance in 1963, Kaiser paid a total of more than $2,000,000 into the trust. Permanente, however, did not report these payments as income in its partnership returns. Nor did the individual partners include these payments in the computations of their distributive shares of the partnership's taxable income. The Commissioner assessed deficiencies against each partner-respondent for his distributive share of the amount paid by Kaiser. Respondents, after paying the assessments under protest, filed these consolidated suits for refund.

The Commissioner premised his assessment on the conclusion that Kaiser's payments to the trust constituted a form of compensation to the partnership for the services it rendered and therefore was income to the partnership. And, notwithstanding the deflection of those payments to the retirement trust and their current unavailability to the partners, the partners were still taxable on their distributive shares of that compensation. Both the District Court and the Court of Appeals disagreed. They held that the payments to the fund were not income to the partnership because it did not receive them and never had a "right to receive" them. . . . They reasoned that the partnership, as an entity, should be disregarded and that each partner should be treated simply as a potential beneficiary of his tentative share of the retirement

29. The agreed statement of facts filed by the parties in the District Court states:

> The primary purpose of the retirement plan was to create an incentive for physicians to remain with [Permanente] . . . and thus to insure [Kaiser] that it would have a stable and reliable group of physicians providing medical services to its members with a minimum of turn-over. . . .

fund.[30] Viewed in this light, no presently taxable income could be attributed to these cash basis[31] taxpayers because of the contingent and forfeitable nature of the fund allocations. . . .

We hold that the courts below erred and that respondents were properly taxable on the partnership's retirement fund income. This conclusion rests on two familiar principles of income taxation, first, that income is taxed to the party who earns it and that liability may not be avoided through an anticipatory assignment of that income, and, second, that partners are taxable on their distributive or proportionate shares of current partnership income irrespective of whether that income is actually distributed to them. The ensuing discussion is simply an application of those principles to the facts of the present case.

II

Section 703 of the Code, insofar as pertinent here, prescribes that "[t]he taxable income of a partnership shall be computed in the same manner as in the case of an individual." §703(a). Thus, while the partnership itself pays no taxes, §701, it must report the income it generates and such income must be calculated in largely the same manner as an individual computes his personal income. For this purpose, then, the partnership is regarded as an independently recognizable entity apart from the aggregate of its partners. Once its income is ascertained and reported, its existence may be disregarded since each partner must pay a tax on a portion of the total income as if the partnership were merely an agent or conduit through which the income passed.[32]

In determining any partner's income, it is first necessary to compute the gross income of the partnership. One of the major sources of gross income, as defined in §61(a)(1) of the Code, is "[c]ompensation for

30. The Court of Appeals purported not to decide, as the District Court had, whether the partnership should be viewed as an "entity" or as a "conduit." 450 F.2d 109, 113 n.5, and 115. Yet, its analysis indicates that it found it proper to disregard the partnership as a separate entity. After explaining its view that Permanente never had a right to receive the payments, the Court of Appeals stated: "When the transaction is viewed in this light, the partnership becomes a mere *agent* contracting on behalf of its members for payments to the trust for their ultimate benefit, rather than a *principal* which itself realizes taxable income." Id., at 115 (emphasis supplied).

31. Each respondent reported his income for the years in question on the cash basis. The partnership reported its taxable receipts under the accrual method.

32. There has been a great deal of discussion in the briefs and in the lower court opinions with respect to whether a partnership is to be viewed as an "entity" or as a "conduit." We find ourselves in agreement with the Solicitor General's remark during oral argument when he suggested that "[i]t seems odd that we should still be discussing such things in 1972." Tr. of Oral Arg. 14. The legislative history indicates, and the commentators agree, that partnerships are entities for purposes of calculating and filing informational returns but that they are conduits through which the taxpaying obligation passes to the individual partners in accord with their distributive shares.

services, including fees, commissions, and similar items." §61(a)(1). There can be no question that Kaiser's payments to the retirement trust were compensation for services rendered by the partnership under the medical service agreement. These payments constituted an integral part of the employment arrangement. The agreement itself called for two forms of "base compensation" to be paid in exchange for services rendered — direct per-member, per-month payments to the partnership and other, similarly computed, payments to the trust. Nor was the receipt of these payments contingent upon any condition other than continuation of the contractual relationship and the performance of the prescribed medical services. Payments to the trust, much like the direct payments to the partnership, were not forfeitable by the partnership or recoverable by Kaiser upon the happening of any contingency.

Yet the courts below, focusing on the fact that the retirement fund payments were never actually received by the partnership but were contributed directly to the trust, found that the payments were not includable as income in the partnership's returns. The view of tax accountability upon which this conclusion rests is incompatible with a foundational rule, which this Court has described as "the first principle of income taxation: that income must be taxed to him who earns it." Commissioner v. Culbertson, 337 U.S. 733, 739-740 (1949). The entity earning the income — whether a partnership or an individual taxpayer — cannot avoid taxation by entering into a contractual arrangement whereby that income is diverted to some other person or entity. Such arrangements, known to the tax law as "anticipatory assignments of income," have frequently been held ineffective as means of avoiding tax liability. The seminal precedent, written over 40 years ago, is Mr. Justice Holmes' opinion for a unanimous Court in Lucas v. Earl. . . . There the taxpayer entered into a contract with his wife whereby she became entitled to one-half of any income he might earn in the future. On the belief that a taxpayer was accountable only for income actually received by him, the husband thereafter reported only half of his income. The Court, unwilling to accept that a reasonable construction of the tax laws permitted such easy deflection of income tax liability, held that the taxpayer was responsible for the entire amount of his income.

The basis for the Court's ruling is explicit and controls the case before us today:

> [T]his case is not to be decided by attenuated subtleties. It turns on the import and reasonable construction of the taxing act. There is no doubt that the statute could tax salaries to those who earned them and provide that the tax could not be escaped by anticipatory arrangements and contracts however skillfully devised to prevent the salary when paid from vesting even for a second in the man who earned it. That seems to us the import of the statute before us and we think that no distinction can be

> taken according to the motives leading to the arrangement by which the fruits are attributed to a different tree from that on which they grew.

Id., at 114-115. The principle of Lucas v. Earl, that he who earns income may not avoid taxation through anticipatory arrangements no matter how clever or subtle, has been repeatedly invoked by this Court and stands today as a cornerstone of our graduated income tax system. . . . And, of course, that principle applies with equal force in assessing partnership income.

Permanente's agreement with Kaiser, whereby a portion of the partnership compensation was deflected to the retirement fund, is certainly within the ambit of Lucas v. Earl. The partnership earned the income and, as a result of arm's-length bargaining with Kaiser,[33] was responsible for its diversion into the trust fund. The Court of Appeals found the *Lucas* [sic] principle inapplicable because Permanente "never had the right itself to receive the payments made into the trust as current income." 450 F.2d, at 114. In support of this assertion, the court relied on language in the agreed statement of facts stipulating that "[t]he payments . . . were paid solely to fund the retirement plan, and were not otherwise available to [Permanente]. . . ." Ibid. Emphasizing that the fund was created to serve Kaiser's interest in a stable source of qualified, experienced physicians, the court found that Permanente could not have received that income except in the form in which it was received.

The court's reasoning seems to be that, before the partnership could be found to have received income, there must be proof that "Permanente agreed to accept less direct compensation from Kaiser in exchange for the retirement plan payments." Id., at 114-115. Apart from the inherent difficulty of adducing such evidence, we know of no authority imposing this burden upon the Government. Nor do we believe that the guiding principle of Lucas v. Earl may be so easily circumvented. Kaiser's motives for making payments are irrelevant to the determination whether those amounts may fairly be viewed as compensation for services rendered.[34] Neither does Kaiser's apparent insistence upon payment to the trust deprive the agreed contributions of their character as compensation. The Government need not prove that the taxpayer had complete and unrestricted power to designate the manner and form in which his income is received. We may assume, especially in view of the relatively unfavorable tax status of self-employed persons with respect to the tax treatment of retirement plans, that many partnerships would eagerly accept conditions similar to those prescribed by this trust

33. The agreed statement of facts states that the contracting parties were separate organizations independently contracting with one another at arm's length.

34. Respondents do not contend that such payments were gifts or some other type of nontaxable contribution. . . .

in consideration for tax-deferral benefits of the sort suggested here. We think it clear, however, that the tax laws permit no such easy road to tax avoidance or deferment.[35] Despite the novelty and ingenuity of this arrangement, Permanente's "base compensation" in the form of payments to a retirement fund was income to the partnership and should have been reported as such.

III

Since the retirement fund payments should have been reported as income to the partnership, along with other income received from Kaiser, the individual partners should have included their shares of that income in their individual returns. §§61(a)(13), 702, 704. For it is axiomatic that each partner must pay taxes on his distributive share of the partnership's income without regard to whether that amount is actually distributed to him. Heiner v. Mellon, 304 U.S. 271 (1938), . . . articulates the salient proposition. After concluding that "distributive" share means the "proportionate" share as determined by the partnership agreement, id., at 280, the Court stated: "The tax is thus imposed upon the partner's proportionate share of the net income of the partnership, and the fact that it may not be currently distributable, whether by agreement of the parties or by operation of law, is not material." Id., at 281. Few principles of partnership taxation are more firmly established than that no matter the reason for nondistribution each partner must pay taxes on his distributive share.

The courts below reasoned to the contrary, holding that the partners here were not properly taxable on the amounts contributed to the retirement fund. This view, apparently, was based on the assumption that each partner's distributive share prior to retirement was too contingent and unascertainable to constitute presently recognizable income. It is true that no partner knew with certainty exactly how much he would ultimately receive or whether he would in fact be entitled to receive anything. But the existence of conditions upon the actual receipt by a partner of income fully earned by the partnership is irrelevant in determining the amount of tax due from him. The fact that the courts below placed such emphasis on this factor suggests the basic misappre-

35. Respondents contend in this Court that this case is controlled by Commissioner v. First Security Bank of Utah, 405 U.S. 394 (1972), decided last Term. [See supra page 749.] We held there that the Commissioner could not properly allocate income to one of a controlled group of corporations under §482 where that corporation could not have received that income as a matter of law. The "assignment-of-income doctrine" could have no application in that peculiar circumstance because the taxpayer had no legal right to receive the income in question. Id., at 403-404. In essence, that case involved a deflection of income imposed by law, not an assignment arrived at by the consensual agreement of two parties acting at arm's length as we have in the present case. See supra n.32.

hension under which they labored in this case. Rather than being viewed as responsible contributors to the partnership's total income, respondent-partners were seen only as contingent beneficiaries of the trust. In some measure, this misplaced focus on the considerations of uncertainty and forfeitability may be a consequence of the erroneous manner in which the Commissioner originally assessed the partners' deficiencies. The Commissioner divided Kaiser's trust fund payments into two categories: (1) payments earmarked for the tentative accounts of *nonpartner* physicians; and (2) those allotted to *partner* physicians. The payments to the trust for the former category of nonpartner physicians were correctly counted as income to the partners in accord with the distributive-share formula as established in the partnership agreement. The latter payments to the tentative accounts of the individual partners, however, were improperly allocated to each partner pursuant to the complex formula in the retirement plan itself, just as if that agreement operated as an amendment to the partnership agreement. 295 F. Supp., at 1292.

The Solicitor General, alluding to this miscomputation during oral argument, suggested that this error "may be what threw the court below off the track." It should be clear that the contingent and unascertainable nature of each partner's share under the retirement trust is irrelevant to the computation of his distributive share. The partnership had received as income a definite sum which was not subject to diminution or forfeiture. Only its ultimate disposition among the employees and partners remained uncertain. For purposes of income tax computation it made no difference that some partners might have elected not to participate in the retirement program or that, for any number of reasons, they might not ultimately receive any of the trust's benefits. Indeed, as the Government suggests, the result would be quite the same if the "potential beneficiaries included no partners at all, but were children, relatives, or other objects of the partnership's largesse."[36] The sole operative consideration is that the income had been received by the partnership, not what disposition might have been effected once the funds were received.

IV

In summary, we find this case controlled by familiar and long-settled principles of income and partnership taxation. There being no doubt

36. Brief for United States 21. For this reason, the cases relied on by the Court of Appeals, 450 F.2d, at 113, which have held that payments made into deferred compensation programs having contingent and forfeitable features are not taxable until received, are inapposite. . . . Indeed, the Government notes, possibly as a consequence of these cases, that the Commissioner has not sought to tax the *nonpartner* physicians on their contingent accounts under the retirement plan. Brief for United States 21.

about the character of the payments as compensation, or about their actual receipt, the partnership was obligated to report them as income presently received. Likewise, each partner was responsible for his distributive share of that income. We, therefore, reverse the judgments and remand the case with directions that judgments be entered for the United States.

It is so ordered.

Mr. Justice DOUGLAS dissents.

NOTES AND QUESTIONS

1. *Partnership taxation.* To illustrate the tax treatment required by the decision in *Basye,* suppose that Permanente had five doctor partners, with ten nonpartner doctors working as employees of the partnership. Suppose that Kaiser paid to the retirement trust $500 for the partners ($100 per person) and $500 for the nonpartner doctors ($50 per person); that, as in the actual case, none of the doctors had a vested interest in the trust (because all retirement benefits would be forfeited if he or she were to quit before retirement); and that each of the five partners had an equal 20 percent interest in the partnership. Under the holding of the case, the partnership would have income of $1,000 when that amount was paid into the trust by Kaiser; there would be no deduction for the contingent liabilities to the nonpartner doctors; and each partner would be taxable on his or her $200 pro rata share of the partnership's income.

2. *Entity versus aggregate.* There are two possible views of partnerships such as Permanente. Under the entity view, the partnership is, like a corporation, a separate entity, with an existence of its own. Under this view, the partnership can be thought of as the earner of income, as if it were a person. The income of the partnership is then passed along pro rata to the partners, however, so the partners are taxable on it, not the partnership. The entity view of partnerships appears to have been adopted by the *Basye* Court, despite its disparagement of the entity/conduit distinction (see supra footnote 32). It seems also to be consistent with the fact that the partners were cash method taxpayers while the partnership used the accrual method (see footnote 31).

Under the aggregate view (which many people find difficult to understand), the partnership has no separate identity. It can be thought of as an abstract concept used as a shorthand device to reflect an agreement among the partners to act collectively, through designated representatives, in such matters as bargaining with Kaiser over compensation and keeping books and records. Under this view, which was adopted by the Court of Appeals in *Basye,* the partnership itself does not have income; it merely keeps track of the amounts received by some administrator on behalf of the doctors.

3. *Entity theory.* If one adopts the entity perspective, which of the following is the best theory or concept in support of the conclusion that the amounts paid into the trust are taxable currently? (a) Income has accrued, under standard principles of accrual accounting; (b) cash equivalence (see supra page 55); (c) constructive receipt (see supra page 54); (d) assignment of income, under cases like Lucas v. Earl; or (e) §83 (see supra page 407).[37]

4. *Aggregate theory.* If one adopts the aggregate view of partnerships, what result does one reach on each of the theories or concepts listed in Note 3? In connection with the assignment-of-income concept, does it matter whether the trust is viewed as the agent of Kaiser, rather than the agent of Permanente? See Note 5.

5. *Characterization of the trust.* Suppose that it had been clear that the idea for setting up the retirement trust had originated with Kaiser, which wanted to ensure continuity of service by the doctors; that the doctors had resisted the use of the trust and would have preferred to take all their compensation in present payments; that the trustees had been selected by Kaiser; and that the documents relating to the establishment of the trust had stated that the trust is "an agent of Kaiser to receive certain payments for the benefit of individual doctors who are associated with Permanente." How would that have affected the Court's reliance on Lucas v. Earl? Would the result have been different? Compare Commissioner v. Olmsted Incorporated Life Agency, supra page 390.

6. *A problem in the use of trusts.* Suppose that a world-class amateur track star agrees with a beer company that his picture and name may be used in its commercials. The Athletic Congress (TAC), which is the governing body for amateur track and field athletics (other than collegiate), does not permit athletes to accept direct payment for such commercial services without losing their amateur status. TAC does, however, permit an arrangement in which the beer company, the athlete, and TAC agree that 10 percent of the agreed-on amount is paid by the sponsor to TAC and the rest is set aside in a trust. The trust instrument provides that the athlete may withdraw from the trust amounts to be used for his expenses in training for and competing in amateur events, plus any interest earned by the trust on the amounts set aside for him. Any funds not withdrawn as expenses or as earnings are held for future distribution to the athlete if and when he abandons his amateur status. Suppose that in 1990 the beer company pays $20,000 into a trust for the athlete and the athlete withdraws $5,000 for expenses (all verified by receipts) and $1,600 in interest earned. What are the tax consequences to the beer company, the trust, and the athlete?

37. Section 83 was adopted in 1969, after the years at issue in *Basye.* Note that under §83(h) amounts set aside for employees are not deductible by the employer until they become taxable to the employee. Cf. §404(a)(5). Such a restriction is irrelevant to a nontaxable, nonprofit organization like Kaiser. See Note 2, supra page 385.

8

CAPITAL GAINS AND LOSSES

A. BACKGROUND

Throughout most of the history of income taxation in this country, a distinction has been drawn between ordinary income (e.g., salaries, interest, dividends, and profits from running a business) and capital gain (gain from the sale or exchange of property such as real estate, stocks, and bonds). Before 1986, taxpayers were allowed a deduction for 60 percent of net long-term capital gain. ("Long-term" gain means gain from the sale of assets held more than one year.[1]) Given the high (by current standards) maximum marginal rates that then prevailed, the capital gain preference was quite significant. At one time, the maximum marginal rate on nonpersonal service income was 70 percent. The 60 percent exclusion ratio lowered the effective rate on capital gain income to 28 percent. The present advantage to long-term capital gain is less dramatic, but significant nonetheless. The maximum rate on capital gain remains at 28 percent while ordinary income is now subject to a maximum marginal rate (after taking into account the ten percent surtax) of 39.6 percent.

There is an additional advantage, apart from the favorable tax rates, to characterization of income as capital gain. Capital gain is gain from the sale of property. If a transaction is characterized as one involving the sale of property (as opposed, for example, to the rental of property), not only is the gain capital in nature, but before the gain is calculated

1. For assets acquired between June 22, 1984, and January 1, 1988, however, the holding period for long-term gain and loss is six months.

a deduction is allowed for the basis of the property. In other words, cases focusing on the capital gain issue often decide implicitly what may be a difficult timing question — namely, whether some of the amount received should be treated as a recovery of investment (basis).

In sharp contrast to the favorable treatment accorded long-term capital gain, the tax treatment of capital loss (both short and long-term) is decidedly unfavorable. Capital losses can be used only to offset capital gain plus (for individuals but not for corporations) $3,000 of ordinary income. Unused losses carry over to future years, subject to the same limitation on deductibility.

B. THE STATUTORY FRAMEWORK

Capital gain or loss arises from the "sale or exchange of a capital asset." See various parts of §1222. Note that there are two elements, "sale or exchange" and "capital asset." Most of the problems in distinguishing between capital gain and ordinary income involve interpretation of "capital asset."

"Capital asset" is defined in §1221 as all "property," with five listed exceptions. "Property" is, of course, a broad and vague term. We will see that the courts have interpreted "property" narrowly in an effort to avoid extending capital gain treatment to transactions for which such treatment seems plainly inappropriate. See infra sections E, F, and G. The major function of the five exceptions is to deny capital gain treatment for the ordinary gains and losses from operating a trade or business. The five statutory exceptions (paraphrased) are:

1. The inventory, or stock in trade, of a business (either retail or manufacturing), and property held primarily for sale to customers in the ordinary course of a trade or business;
2. Real property or depreciable property used in a trade or business;
3. Copyrights and similar property held by their creators (but not copyrights purchased from the creator or patents);
4. Accounts receivable acquired in the ordinary course of a trade or business; and
5. U.S. government publications held by someone who received them free or at reduced cost (e.g., a member of Congress).

There is, however, a limitation on §1221(2) that virtually swallows it up. The limitation is found in §1231, which seems more a response to economic or political forces than to tax logic. The rule embodied in

§1221(2) seems logically correct since it is hard to see any good reason for distinguishing, for tax purposes, between gains or losses arising from normal business operations and gains or losses from disposing of assets used in the business. Nonetheless, at the beginning of World War II, Congress became concerned that people were being compelled to sell property for wartime uses, which subjected them to high income and excess-profits taxes on their gains. Apparently it was thought unfair to impose these high taxes on windfalls generated by wartime conditions, at least when other taxpayers were able to escape such taxes by not selling. Moreover, it was feared that the potential tax liability would inhibit people from selling property such as factory buildings, machinery, and ships to others who might be able to put them to better use in the war effort. These concerns led to the adoption of the predecessor of §1231, which preserves the §1221(2) taxpayer benefit of ordinary loss treatment where the taxpayer has a net loss but provides for capital gain treatment where there is a net gain. All sales or exchanges of assets described in §1221(2) (depreciable property and real property used in a business), plus certain other transactions, are covered by §1231. There is a complex set of rules for netting out of §1231 gains and losses and for a carryover of losses.

To recapitulate, a capital asset is "property," with five listed (plus some "common law") exceptions, including §1221(2)'s exception for depreciable or real property used in a business. There is an exception to §1221(2) in §1231, which transforms net gain into capital gain, but there are limitations on this exception in the recapture rules of §§1245 and 1250 and in the loss carryover provision of §1231(c).

Various other provisions govern whether certain specified assets or transactions are accorded capital-gain or capital-loss treatment. For example, §1244 provides that loss on the sale of "small business stock" is treated as an ordinary loss even though it is plain that such stock is a capital asset within the contemplation of §1221 and therefore any gain on its sale is capital gain. Section 631 provides capital-gain treatment for the proceeds of certain sales of timber and coal, and §1232 provides that gain from original-issue discount is ordinary income. See also §§1237 and 1241, plus the provisions referred to in section J of this chapter, where the "sale or exchange" requirement is examined.

Sections 165 and 166 contain special provisions dealing with loans made by the taxpayer. If a loan is evidenced by a bond, the bond is a capital asset under §1221, so its sale gives rise to capital gain or loss. Section 1232 ensures that the result is the same where the bond is retired by the issuer, and §165(g) does the same where the bond becomes worthless. But suppose that the loan does not take the form of a bond. Suppose, for example, that an individual who is not in the finance business lends money to the corner grocer, as an investment. That is a "nonbusiness debt," and if it is not repaid, the loss is treated as a short-term capital loss under §166(d). If, on the other hand, a wholesaler sells produce to the grocer on credit and that debt is not repaid, the loss is from a business debt and is treated as an ordinary loss.

Of perhaps greater interest, §1202, added to the Code in 1993, allows taxpayers to exclude from income 50 percent of gain from certain small business stock. The stock must be acquired on initial issuance by the company or its underwriter (rather than from another stockholder) and must be held for more than five years. A small business corporation is defined, generally, as a company with no more than $50 million in assets. Stock in companies engaged in accounting, law, health, farming, banking, mining, and a variety of other activities does not qualify for the benefits of §1202. The 50 percent exclusion comes in addition to the 28 percent maximum rate applicable to capital gain, reducing the effective rate of tax on the sale of such stock to 14 percent.

Gains and losses are divided into short-term and long-term. A long-term gain is one from the sale or exchange of an asset held "*more than* one year." See §1222(3) (emphasis supplied). There is a set of rules of netting out short-term and long-term gains and losses, the effect of which is to ensure that capital gains first offset capital losses; any remaining long-term capital gain is then subject to a maximum tax rate of 28 percent. The operation of these rules, unfortunately, is somewhat complex. Under the netting rules, a taxpayer first nets short-term capital gains against short-term capital losses and long-term capital gains against long-term capital losses. If the result is short- and long-term capital gain, or short- and long-term capital loss, no further netting is required.

To illustrate this first round of netting, suppose that a taxpayer with no capital gain or loss carryovers from any previous year has a long-term capital gain of $30,000, a long-term capital loss of $25,000, and a short-term capital gain of $20,000. The taxpayer nets the long-term gain against the long-term loss and ends up with a net $5,000 long-term capital gain (subject to the maximum rate of 28 percent) and a $20,000 short-term capital gain. Note that without a system of netting, the taxpayer would be required to pay tax on the $30,000 long-term capital gain but (because of the unfavorable treatment of capital losses) would be allowed to deduct in the present year only $3,000 of the long-term capital loss.

Suppose the first round of netting results in a long-term capital gain and a short-term capital loss. In that case, the long-term gain is offset against the short-term loss. If the long-term gain is greater, the result is long-term gain; if the short-term is greater, the result is a short-term loss. The same operation is required if the first round of netting results in a long-term capital loss and a short-term capital gain. To illustrate this second round of netting, let us suppose a taxpayer with no capital gain or loss carryovers from any previous year has a long-term capital gain of $30,000 and a short-term capital loss of $20,000. The gain is offset by the loss to produce a net long-term capital gain of $10,000.

C. POLICY

1. Rationale for Favorable Treatment of Capital Gain

Here is a brief description of the major arguments that have been used to justify favorable treatment of capital gain, with similarly brief responses to each. It should be apparent that some of the arguments had more force in past years when the maximum marginal rate exceeded 50 percent.

Bunching. Capital gains often accrue over many years. The effect of taxing the entire gain in one year may be to subject all, or almost all, of it to the maximum rate even though it might have been taxed at a lower rate if realized ratably during the entire period of ownership of the asset. This argument still has little force because under the current rate structure most individuals and corporations realizing substantial capital gains will have been paying tax at the maximum rate at all relevant times.

Lock-in. A tax on capital gains tends to induce people to hold assets when they might otherwise sell and reinvest the proceeds in some other way. This effect is exacerbated by §1014, under which basis is stepped up to fair market value at death, which has the effect of eliminating the potential tax liability on such gain. Suppose, for example, an elderly entrepreneur owns a business with a fair market value of $1 million and a basis of $10,000. In the absence of taxation, the business might be worth more to another person than the entrepreneur. The entrepreneur might wish to sell her business, use some of the proceeds to purchase an annuity, and give the remainder of the proceeds to her children. Another person might have better ideas (or think she has better ideas) on how to manage the business and might be willing to put more time in the business. Present law, of course, discourages sale, since it triggers a tax that can be entirely avoided if the entrepreneur holds onto the business until her death. The lock-in effect leads to immobility of capital and inefficient uses of capital, with assets not being held by those who will put them to best use. Some supporters of preferential treatment for capital gain believe the lock-in effect is so strong that a reduction in tax rates would actually increase tax revenue by dramatically increasing the number of investors who chose to sell appreciated assets.

Inflation. Favorable treatment of capital gain mitigates the possible unfairness of taxing gains that are attributable to inflation and are therefore not "real" gains. Capital-gain treatment is, however, an inaccurate solution to the inflation problem. It provides relief in some cases where inflation may have had little, if any, impact and fails to provide relief in other cases where inflation may have taken a heavy toll. A better solution is indexing — that is, increasing the basis of assets to reflect increases in an index of prices.

General incentive. Favorable rates of taxation of capital gains reduce the aggregate tax burden on returns on investments and thus provide an incentive, or reduce the disincentive, to saving, investment, and economic growth. Of course, to provide constant tax revenue, other forms of taxes must be raised, and these taxes may reduce economic growth. For example, a cut in the capital gain tax rate may require an increase in the tax rate on labor income, and that increase might reduce work effort. See discussion, supra page 28. Supporters of favorable rates of taxation on capital income believe that the efficiency gains from reducing the tax on investment gains outweigh such efficiency losses. Again, there appear to be other, more accurate (and perhaps fairer) solutions to the problem (if it is one) of excessive tax burdens on returns on investments. Moreover, it may be that collectively we should save and invest less rather than more. Increased saving necessarily implies decreased consumption. This trade-off implies a transfer of consumption from the current generation to subsequent generations. The consumption that is forgone might be the private consumption of taxpayers or that of poor people to whom welfare payments might be made; or it might be public consumption for park services, public television, crime prevention, or national defense; or it might be any other private or public consumption.

Incentive to new industries. Since new industries tend to generate capital gain, favorable treatment of such gain will tend to stimulate such industries, and many people seem to take it for granted that such stimulation is a good thing. One can question whether new industries that need special tax breaks in order to flourish ought to be encouraged. It is one thing to say that the tax structure is too onerous for business and quite another to say that it is too onerous for new businesses and not for established businesses. Moreover, the capital gain preference is not in fact limited to new industries. If such industries do warrant favorable tax treatment, a more narrowly designed measure would be preferable. (In fact, such a measure exists: the §1202 exclusion for small business stock, discussed supra page 832.)

Unrealized gains are not taxed. The favorable rate of taxation of capital gains reduces the disparity in treatment of realized and unrealized gains. If that disparity is the problem, however, the more appropriate solution would be an expansion of the provisions allowing tax-free exchanges, which takes us down a path that ultimately seems to lead to a consumption tax. See supra page 430.

Double-tax on corporate earnings. Corporate income is in some sense taxed twice: once when earned by the corporation, and once when repatriated to the shareholders in the form of dividends or corporate repurchase of shares. The rationale for this unfavorable tax regimen is unclear. A capital gain preference reduces the tax paid by shareholders on sale of their stock. Many observers support maintaining or expanding the break shareholders get on stock sale as an indirect way of ameliorating the double-tax on corporate income. One difficulty with this argument is that the capital gains preference is not limited to investments in corporate stock, but applies to individual investments in land and other assets.

2. Rationale for the Limitation on Deduction of Capital Losses

As noted above, capital losses are subject to an unfavorable set of tax rules. Individuals may deduct capital losses from capital gain, but individuals with capital losses in excess of capital gain may deduct only $3,000 of such losses in any year. Corporations may only deduct capital losses from capital gain.

The fact that capital losses are treated unfavorably when capital gains are treated favorably may seem odd. The limitation on deductibility of capital losses certainly works against some of the policy goals that support the favorable treatment of capital gain. For example, the limitation on deductions of capital losses presumably discourages, rather than encourages, capital investment, especially in new, innovative, and risky activities. But see §1244.

Three explanations for the limitation on deduction of capital losses may be suggested. The first explanation, which relates to the realization requirement for recognition of gain or loss, is that the limitation is necessary to prevent taxpayers from manipulating the recognition of gains and losses to recognize "false" losses. Absent the limitation, a taxpayer could buy two sets of investments that are expected to move in opposite directions. For example, the taxpayer could buy some investments (such as gold) that are expected to rise with inflation and other investments (such as long-term bonds) that are expected to decline with inflation. If inflation rose, the decline in the value of one set of investments would be offset by the rise in the value of the other set of investments and the taxpayer would suffer no economic loss. However, the taxpayer could sell the investments that declined in value and retain the appreciated investments and therefore recognize a tax loss. The offsetting gain on the appreciated investments would not be recognized until those assets were sold. One obvious objection to using the capital loss restrictions to prevent manipulation of the realization requirement is that the loss restrictions apply even in cases where the taxpayer owns no appreciated assets and the manipulation of the realization requirement is therefore not possible.

A second explanation, related to the first, is also based on the realization requirement. Suppose a taxpayer has invested over the years in a diversified portfolio of common stocks and that some have risen in value while others have declined. Without the limitation on the deduction of losses, the taxpayer would have a strong incentive to sell the loss assets and retain the gain assets. In the aggregate, over the long run, the result would be a substantial advantage to investors and a corresponding disadvantage to the Treasury (that is, to other taxpayers, who would be required to pick up the slack). By imposing a limitation on the deduction of losses, Congress in effect says to taxpayers, "If you want to recognize your losses, you should also recognize a similar amount of gains." The difficulty with this explanation, as with the previous explanation, has to do with the effects of the limitation on taxpayers who have losses and no gains. For such taxpayers, the government is in a "heads-I-win-tails-you-lose" position: the government shares in gains but bears none of the burden of losses.

A third, more cynical explanation for the capital loss limitations is that the unrestricted allowance of deductions for capital losses would decrease tax revenue and these days members of Congress are more concerned about revenue than they are about fairness or economic rationality.

D. PROPERTY HELD "PRIMARILY FOR SALE TO CUSTOMERS"

1. Sale to "Customers"

VAN SUETENDAEL v. COMMISSIONER

3 T.C.M. 987 (1944), aff'd, 152 F.2d 654 (2d Cir. 1945)

HARRON, Judge. . . .

During the taxable years, and for some years prior thereto, the petitioner was primarily engaged in buying and selling securities. Approximately 90 percent of the securities purchased by him were interest-bearing bonds and the other 10 percent consisted of preferred and common stock. His income was derived principally from interest on the bonds purchased and from interest on bank deposits. . . . He was not a member of any stock exchange. His name was listed in several statistical financial publications as a dealer in securities. . . . He also listed offerings to buy or sell securities at a certain price in the National Daily Quotation Service. . . . This service was circularized among investment and trading houses in the United States. Petitioner has registered with the Securities and Exchange Commission, the State of New York, and the Bureau of Internal Revenue as a broker or dealer in securities. . . . He has also written to individuals, banks, and insurance companies offering securities at stated prices. . . .

During the taxable years, petitioner maintained separate accounts with [brokerage firms with stock exchange memberships]. . . .

In reporting the transactions of the sales of securities in each year on his return, petitioner took the view that all of the securities sold were non-capital assets. . . .

The respondent, in determining the deficiencies, held that the securities sold by petitioner were capital assets, and he therefore applied the limitations of [§1211(b)]. . . . On brief, [taxpayer] argues that the entire case resolves itself to the one question of whether he was engaged in business as a dealer in securities. That, however, is not the issue. The phrase "dealer in securities" is not defined in the statute, although it is defined in [Regs. §1.471-5]. The only issue for determination here is whether the securities sold by petitioner during the taxable years were capital assets under [§1221]. . . .

Under [§1221], all property is to be treated as capital assets unless the taxpayer is able to bring himself within one of the stated exceptions in the definition of capital assets. As far as this proceeding is concerned, the only possible exceptions which petitioner could rely upon are that the securities sold were [as contemplated by §1221(1)] . . . stock in trade or property subject to inventory in his hands . . . held by him primarily for sale to customers in the ordinary course of his business. . . . This is probably the reason why petitioner has placed such stress upon the contention that he was a dealer in securities since securities in the nature of stock in trade held primarily for sale to customers are held only by dealers in securities. . . . However, there may be many sales of securities by so-called dealers in securities which do not come within the exceptions set forth in the definition of capital assets. The fact that petitioner had a teletype machine, four telephones and statistical financial publications in his office, was listed as a "dealer" in certain publications, and advertised himself as willing to buy or sell securities is not determinative of the issue. The subject matter of the cited sections is property and it must be shown that the property itself comes within the exceptions stated in the definition of capital assets. . . .

From an analysis of the schedule showing all of petitioner's transactions in securities during these years, we cannot find as a fact that petitioner held the securities sold by him during the taxable years *primarily* for sale to customers in the ordinary course of his business. The facts are just as consonant with the theory that petitioner held the securities for speculation or for investment. . . . One who holds securities in the nature of stock in trade primarily for resale to customers is regularly engaged in the purchase of securities at wholesale. . . . He is a middleman in distributing the securities and he does not resell to the same class of persons from whom he buys. . . . Here, petitioner did not make wholesale purchases of securities. The securities purchased were in relatively small quantities and were diversified. In this respect, he acted no differently from an ordinary purchaser. Most of the securities purchased by petitioner were resold to or through the same brokers from whom they were bought. Here again, petitioner acted in the same manner as an ordinary purchaser having an account with a broker. . . . These brokers or their clients cannot be considered as petitioner's customers. . . . Over 92 percent of the securities sold by petitioner to or through [the brokers] had been previously acquired by him from the same two brokerage houses. Many of the securities were resold by petitioner at a profit on the same day on which he purchased them or a short time thereafter. . . . Petitioner could not have intended to purchase these securities for resale to "customers" as that word is used in the statute. . . . Although petitioner did make efforts to sell some of the securities through channels other than brokers and dealers, and actually did sell a small amount of the securities to other parties, we cannot find even as to those securities that they were purchased primarily for resale to customers. . . .

Respondent points out that during the taxable years, petitioner's principal source of income was derived from interest on the bonds owned by him and that the great proportion of his losses resulted from securities which he had held for a long period of time. He argues that petitioner, during each of the taxable years, selected securities which he had held for a long time and which were then unprofitable to him and disposed of those securities at the best possible price to anyone who would buy them in order that the loss sustained thereon should offset his income from the interest-bearing bonds held by him. . . . Respondent also argues that as to the securities held for a long period, petitioner did not hold them for resale to customers, but for the income which he might derive therefrom. The facts apparently support respondent's contentions. . . .

We think that a reasonable conclusion from all of the facts is that petitioner intended to sell the securities in any way he could and to any purchaser regardless of whether or not the purchaser could be deemed a "customer" within the meaning of the statute. It is therefore held that the securities sold by petitioner during the taxable years were capital assets and subject to the limitations of gain and loss set forth in [§1211(b)]. Respondent's determination is sustained. . . .

NOTES AND QUESTIONS

1. *Current relevance.* Note that in *Van Suetendael,* because the taxpayer had sustained losses that he wanted to treat as ordinary losses, he argued that his investments were not capital assets. Under current law a person might want to take the same position in order to achieve the same result. Suppose a person like Mr. Van Suetendael asks your advice on what he might do to achieve ordinary loss treatment in the future, but makes clear to you that he likes his present mode of operation and hopes to change it as little as possible. What would you say?

2. *"Traders" and "dealers."* In affirming the Tax Court's decision, the Court of Appeals observed, 152 F.2d 654, 655 (2d Cir. 1945): "[W]ith respect to some of the securities sold the taxpayer may have been a dealer and with respect to others a trader, investor or speculator. In his returns he made no attempt to distinguish one sale from another; nor did he present sufficient evidence to enable the Tax Court to do so." In Commissioner v. Burnett, 118 F.2d 659 (5th Cir. 1941), it was held that a "trader" in securities and commodities, whose trading averaged over $10 million per year, did not hold these assets "primarily for sale to customers in the ordinary course of his trade or business."

Should a "trader" in securities be treated differently from a dealer, either when he has gains or when he suffers losses?

The requirement that property, to be excluded from capital asset treatment, be held for sale "to customers" came into the statute in 1934. It was designed to prevent "a stock speculator trading on his own account" from claiming ordinary losses on his transactions and thus canceling out his income from dividends, interest, etc., by what were apparently thought by Congress often to be economically insignificant transactions. H.R. Rep. No. 1385, 73d Cong., 2d Sess., 1939-1 C.B. (Pt. 2) 627, 632. In enacting the restriction, Congress seems to have overlooked the possibility that, in another part of the business cycle, "traders" might realize profits and would be able to report them as capital gains.

3. *Investment securities held by dealers.* Section 1236 provides that if a securities dealer segregates securities in an investment account, those securities are treated as capital assets. This provision was obviously designed to allow firms dealing in securities to take advantage of the favorable treatment of capital gain. May a firm anxious to escape the capital loss restrictions avoid capital asset treatment simply by avoiding compliance with §1236? Even if it is clear that some securities are held

as investments for the benefit of the members of the firm? What advice would you give to securities dealers on how to handle the firm's investments? See Stephens, Inc. v. United States, 464 F.2d 53 (8th Cir. 1972), cert. denied, 409 U.S. 1119 (1973), holding that an investment company was not a dealer when it acquired shares of corporations, drew off large cash dividends, then sold the stock at a loss because it had reduced the net assets of the companies by the dividends. The court found that the investment house was not entitled to an ordinary loss deduction on the sale of the stock.

4. *Is §1221(1) redundant?* In *Van Suetendael,* the court says that the taxpayer's securities "cannot be classified as stock in trade or property subject to inventory in his hands unless they were held by him primarily for sale to customers in the ordinary course of his business." Does this imply that "stock in trade" is indistinguishable from "inventory property" and that both coincide completely with "property held for sale to customers" — with the result that §1221(1) embraces not two or three categories of property, but only one? In Gilbert v. Commissioner, 56 F.2d 361 (1st Cir. 1932), the court denied that §1221(1) was redundant and held that shares of stock received by a construction company as compensation were held for sale in the ordinary course of business (the term "to customers" had not yet been added to the statute) even though they were not "stock in trade" or "inventory property." The regulations provide that the taxpayer's inventory "should include all finished or partly finished goods and, in the case of raw materials and supplies, only those which have been acquired for sale or which will physically become a part of merchandise intended for sale." Regs. §1.471-1. Is this provision applicable not only to §471 (use of inventories in determining income) but also to §1221(1)? If a business sells an excess stock of supplies that were not to be physically incorporated in its merchandise (e.g., office supplies, cleaning materials, or repair parts for machinery), do they come within §1221(1)? Should the fact that their cost was deducted (from ordinary income) as a business expense be relevant in determining whether a sale produces ordinary income or capital gain?

2. "Primarily for Sale"

BIEDENHARN REALTY CO. v. UNITED STATES

526 F.2d 409 (5th Cir.), cert. denied, 429 U.S. 819 (1976)

[Before the court, en banc, thirteen judges — seven agreeing with the majority opinion, one concurring, and five dissenting.]

Goldberg, Circuit Judge.

I

[The facts, much abbreviated, are as follows: Taxpayer corporation, organized in 1923 to hold and manage family investments, held in the relevant years substantial investments in commercial real estate, a stock portfolio, a motel, warehouses, a shopping center, residential real property, and farm property. Among the last was a plantation purchased for $50,000 in 1935, totaling 973 acres, which was said to have been bought for farming and as a good investment. It was farmed for a few years and then leased for farming. The land was close to Monroe, Louisiana, and from 1939 through 1966, three basic residential subdivisions covering 185 acres were carved from the plantation. Although the plantation was named "Hardtimes," for the Biedenharn Realty it was a good investment; 208 lots were sold in 158 separate sales at an $800,000 profit. In a pre-1964 settlement with the government it was apparently agreed that 60 percent of the gain would be reported as ordinary income and 40 percent as capital gain for the years of the settlement. The taxpayer then reported its gains for the years 1964 through 1966 on the same basis. The IRS asserted a deficiency, arguing that all the gains were ordinary income, and the taxpayer filed for refund claiming all the gains to be capital.

In addition to the subdivision sales, the taxpayer also sold approximately 275 other acres from the plantation in twelve separate sales starting in 1935. From other land that it owned, the company in the years 1923 through 1966 sold 934 lots, 249 before 1935 and 477 in the years 1935 through 1966. Improvements — streets, drainage, water, sewerage, and electricity — were made in the plantation subdivisions, at an aggregate cost of about $200,000.

The District Court found that the plantation was originally bought for investment and that the intent to subdivide arose later when the city of Monroe expanded in the direction of the plantation. Sales by the taxpayer largely resulted from unsolicited approaches by individuals, except that in the years 1964 through 1966 about 75 percent of the sales were induced by independent brokers with which the company dealt. The issue before the court as to all of the 1964 through 1966 sales from the subdivisions was whether the lots constituted property held by the taxpayer primarily for sale to customers in the ordinary course of its trade or business under §1221(1)].

II . . .

The problem we struggle with here is not novel. We have become accustomed to the frequency with which taxpayers litigate this troublesome question. . . . The difficulty in large part stems from ad-hoc application of the numerous permissible criteria set forth in our multitudinous prior opinions.[2] Over the past 40 years, this case by case approach with its concentration on the facts of each suit has resulted in a collection of decisions not always reconcilable. . . .

Assuredly, we would much prefer one or two clearly defined, easily employed tests which lead to predictable, perhaps automatic, conclusions. However, the nature of the congressional "capital asset" definition and the myriad situations to which we must apply that standard make impossible any easy escape from the task before us. . . .

Yet our inability to proffer a panaceatic guide to the perplexed with respect to this subject does not preclude our setting forth some general, albeit inexact, guidelines for the resolution of many of the §1221(1) cases we confront. . . . [W]e more precisely define and suggest points of emphasis for the major *Winthrop* delineated factors[3] as they appear in the instant controversy. . . .

III

We begin our task by evaluating in the light of Biedenharn's facts the main *Winthrop* factors — substantiality and frequency of sales, improvements, solicitation and advertising efforts, and brokers' activities — as well as a few miscellaneous contentions. A separate section follows discussing the keenly contested role of prior investment intent. Finally we consider the significance of the Supreme Court's decision in Malat v. Riddell 383 U.S. 569 (1966).

A. FREQUENCY AND SUBSTANTIALITY OF SALES

Scrutinizing closely the record and briefs, we find that plaintiff's real property sales activities compel an ordinary income conclusion. In ar-

2. One finds evidence of the vast array of opinions and factors discussed therein by briefly perusing the 24 small-type, double column pages of Prentice-Hall's Federal Taxation ¶32,486 which lists the cases involving subdivided realty. See also 33 Mertens, The Law of Federal Income Taxation §§22.138-22.142 (Malone Rev.). The Second Circuit has called these judicial pronouncements "legion." Gault v. Comm'r, 2 Cir. 1964, 332 F.2d 94, 95.

3. In U.S. v. Winthrop, 5 Cir. 1969, 417 F.2d 905, 910, the Court enumerated the following factors:

(1) The nature and purpose of the acquisition of the property and the duration of the ownership; (2) the extent and nature of the taxpayer's efforts to sell the property; (3) the number, extent, continuity and substantiality of the sales; (4) the extent of subdividing, developing, and advertising to increase sales; (5) the use of a business office for the sale of the property; (6) the character and degree of supervision or control exercised by the taxpayer over any representative selling the property; and (7) the time and effort the taxpayer habitually devoted to the sales.

The numbering indicates no hierarchy of importance.

riving at this result, we examine first the most important of *Winthrop*'s factors — the frequency and substantiality of taxpayer's sales. Although frequency and substantiality of sales are not usually conclusive, they occupy the preeminent ground in our analysis. The recent trend of Fifth Circuit decisions indicates that when dispositions of subdivided property extend over a long period of time and are especially numerous, the likelihood of capital gains is very slight indeed. . . .

On the present facts, taxpayer could not claim "isolated" sales or a passive and gradual liquidation. . . .

The frequency and substantiality of Biedenharn's sales go not only to its holding purpose and the existence of a trade or business but also support our finding of the ordinariness with which the Realty Company disposed of its lots. These sales easily meet the criteria of normalcy set forth in *Winthrop*, supra at 912.

Furthermore, . . . one could fairly infer that the income accruing to the Biedenharn Realty Company from its pre-1935 sales helped support the purchase of the Hardtimes Plantation. Even if taxpayer made no significant acquisitions after Hardtimes, the "purpose, system, and continuity" of Biedenharn's efforts easily constitute a business. . . .

[T]he District Court sought to overcome this evidence of dealer-like real estate activities and property "primarily held for sale" by clinging to the notion that the taxpayer was merely liquidating a prior investment. We discuss later the role of former investment status and the possibility of taxpayer relief under that concept. Otherwise, the question of liquidation of an investment is simply the opposite side of the inquiry as to whether or not one is holding property primarily for sale in the ordinary course of his business. In other words, a taxpayer's claim that he is liquidating a prior investment does not really present a separate theory but rather restates the main question currently under scrutiny. . . .

B. IMPROVEMENTS

Although we place greatest emphasis on the frequency and substantiality of sales over an extended time period, our decision in this instance is aided by the presence of taxpayer activity — particularly improvements — in the other *Winthrop* areas. Biedenharn vigorously improved its subdivisions, generally adding streets, drainage, sewerage, and utilities. . . .

C. SOLICITATION AND ADVERTISING EFFORTS

Substantial, frequent sales and improvements such as we have encountered in this case will usually conclude the capital gains issue against taxpayer. Thus, on the basis of our analysis to this point, we would have little hesitation in finding that taxpayer held "primarily for sale" in the "ordinary course of [his] trade or business." "[T]he flexing of commercial muscles with frequency and continuity, design and effect" of which *Winthrop* spoke, supra at 911, is here a reality. This reality is further buttressed by Biedenharn's sales efforts, including those carried on through brokers. Minimizing the importance of its own sales activities, taxpayer points repeatedly to its steady avoidance of advertising or other solicitation of customers. Plaintiff directs our attention to stipulations detailing the population growth of Monroe and testimony outlining the economic forces which made Hardtimes Plantation attractive residential property and presumably eliminated the need for sales exertions. We have no quarrel with plaintiff's description of this familiar process of suburban expansion, but we cannot accept the legal inferences which taxpayer would have us draw.

The Circuit's recent decisions . . . implicitly recognize that even one inarguably in the real estate business need not engage in promotional exertions in the face of a favorable market. As such, we do not always require a showing of active solicitation where "business . . . [is] good, indeed brisk." . . . In cases such as *Biedenharn,* the sale of a few lots and the construction of the first homes, albeit not, as in *Winthrop,* by the taxpayer, as well as the building of roads, addition of utilities, and staking off of the other subdivided parcels constitute a highly visible form of advertising. Prospective home buyers drive by the advantageously located property, see the development activities, and are as surely put on notice of the availability of lots as if the owner had erected large signs announcing "residential property for sale." We do not by this evaluation automatically neutralize advertising or solicitation as a factor in our analysis. This form of inherent notice is not present in all land sales, especially where the property is not so valuably located, is not subdivided into small lots, and is not improved. Moreover, inherent notice represents only one band of the solicitation spectrum. Media utilization and personal initiatives remain material components of this criterion. When present, they call for greater Government oriented emphasis on *Winthrop*'s solicitation factor.

D. BROKERAGE ACTIVITIES

In evaluating Biedenharn's solicitation activities, we need not confine ourselves to the . . . *Winthrop* theory of brisk sales without organizational efforts. Unlike in . . . *Winthrop* where no one undertook overt solicitation efforts, the Realty Company hired brokers who, using media and on site advertising, worked vigorously on taxpayer's behalf. We do not believe that the employment of brokers should shield plaintiff from ordinary income treatment. . . . Their activities should at least in discounted form be attributed to Biedenharn. To the contrary, taxpayer argues that "one who is not already in the trade or business of selling real estate does not enter such business when he employs a broker who acts as an independent contractor. Fahs v. Crawford, 161 F.2d 315 (5 Cir. 1947); Smith v. Dunn, 224 F.2d 353 (5 Cir. 1955)." Without presently entangling ourselves in a dispute as to the differences between an agent and an independent contractor, we find the cases cited distinguishable from the instant circumstances. In both *Fahs* and *Smith,* the taxpayer turned the entire property over to brokers, who, having been granted total responsibility, made all decisions including the setting of sales prices. In comparison, Biedenharn determined original prices and general credit policy. Moreover, the Realty Company did not make all the sales in question through brokers as did taxpayers in *Fahs* and *Smith.* Biedenharn sold the Bayou DeSiard and Biedenharn Estates lots and may well have sold some of the Oak Park land. In other words, unlike *Fahs* and *Smith,* Biedenharn's brokers did not so completely take charge of the whole of the Hardtimes sales as to permit the Realty Company to wall itself off legally from their activities.

E. ADDITIONAL TAXPAYER CONTENTIONS

Plaintiff presents a number of other contentions and supporting facts for our consideration. . . . Taxpayer emphasizes that its profits from real estate sales averaged only 11.1% in each of the years in controversy, compared to 52.4% in *Winthrop.* Whatever the percentage, plaintiff would be hard pressed to deny the substantiality of its Hardtimes sales in absolute terms (the subdivided lots alone brought in over one million dollars) or, most importantly, to assert that its real estate business was too insignificant to constitute a separate trade or business.

The relatively modest income share represented by Biedenharn's real property dispositions stems not from a failure to engage in real estate sales activities but rather from the comparatively large profit attributable to the Company's 1965 ($649,231.34) and 1966 ($688,840.82) stock sales. The fact of Biedenharn's holding, managing, and selling stock is not inconsistent with the existence of a separate realty business. . . .

Similarly, taxpayer observes that Biedenharn's manager devoted only 10% of his time to real estate dealings and then mostly to the company's rental properties. This fact does not negate the existence of sales activities. Taxpayer had a telephone listing, a shared business office, and a few part-time employees. Because, as discussed before, a strong seller's market existed, Biedenharn's sales required less than the usual solicitation efforts and therefore less than the usual time. Moreover, plaintiff . . . hired brokers to handle many aspects of the Hardtimes transaction — thus further reducing the activity and time required of Biedenharn's employees.

Finally, taxpayer argues that it is entitled to capital gains since its enormous profits (74% to 97%) demonstrate a return based principally on capital appreciation and not on taxpayer's "merchandising" efforts. We decline the opportunity to allocate plaintiff's gain between long-term market appreciation and improvement related activities. . . . Even if we undertook such an analysis and found the former element predominant, we would on the authority of *Winthrop*, supra at 856, reject plaintiff's contention which, in effect, is merely taxpayer's version of the Government's unsuccessful argument in that case.

IV

The District Court found that "[t]axpayer is merely liquidating over a long period of time a substantial investment in the most advantageous method possible." 356 F. Supp. at 1336. In this view, the original investment intent is crucial, for it preserves the capital gains character of the transaction even in the face of normal real estate sales activities.

The Government asserts that Biedenharn Realty Company did not merely "liquidate" an investment but instead entered the real estate business in an effort to dispose of what was formerly investment property. Claiming that Biedenharn's activities would result in ordinary income if the Hardtimes Plantation had been purchased with the intent to divide and resell the property, and finding no reason why a different prior intent should influence this outcome, the Government concludes that original investment purpose is irrelevant. Instead, the Government would have us focus exclusively on taxpayer's intent and the level of sales activity during the period commencing with subdivision and improvement and lasting through final sales. Under this theory, every individual who improves and frequently sells substantial numbers of land parcels would receive ordinary income.[4]

While the facts of this case dictate our agreement with the Internal Revenue Service's ultimate conclusion of taxpayer liability, they do not require our acquiescence in the Government's entreated total elimination of *Winthrop's* first criterion, "the nature and purpose of the acquisition."

We reject the Government's sweeping contention that prior investment intent is always irrelevant. There will be instances where an initial investment purpose endures in controlling fashion notwithstanding con-

4. The Government suggests that taxpayer can avoid ordinary income treatment by selling the undivided, unimproved tract to a controlled corporation which would then develop the land. However, this approach would in many instances create attribution problems with the Government arguing that the controlled corporation's sales are actually those of the taxpayer. . . . Furthermore, we are not prepared to tell taxpayers that in all cases a single bulk sale provides the only road to capital gains.

tinuing sales activity. We doubt that this aperture, where an active subdivider and improver receives capital gains, is very wide; yet we believe it exists. We would most generally find such an opening where the change from investment holding to sales activity results from unanticipated, externally induced factors which make impossible the continued preexisting use of the realty. . . . Acts of God, condemnation of part of one's property, new and unfavorable zoning regulations, or other events forcing alteration of taxpayer's plans create situations making possible subdivision and improvement as a part of a capital gains disposition. . . .

The distinction drawn above reflects our belief that Congress did not intend to automatically disqualify from capital gains bona fide investors forced to abandon prior purposes for reasons beyond their control. At times, the Code may be severe, and this Court may construe it strictly, but neither Code nor Court is so tyrannical as to mandate the absolute rule urged by the Government. However, we caution that although permitting a land owner substantial sales flexibility where there is a forced change from original investment purpose, we do not absolutely shield the constrained taxpayer from ordinary income. . . .

Clearly, under the facts in this case, the distinction just elaborated undermines Biedenharn's reliance on original investment purpose. Taxpayer's change of purpose was entirely voluntary and therefore does not fall within the protected area. Moreover, taxpayer's original investment intent, *even if* considered a factor sharply supporting capital gains treatment, is so overwhelmed by the other *Winthrop* factors discussed supra, that that element can have no decisive effect. However wide the capital gains passageway through which a subdivider with former investment intent could squeeze, the Biedenharn Realty Company will never fit.

V

The District Court, citing Malat v. Riddell, supra, stated that "the lots were not held . . . primarily for sale as that phrase was interpreted . . . in *Malat*. . . ." 356 F. Supp. at 1335. Finding that Biedenharn's primary purpose became holding for sale and consequently that *Malat* in no way alters our analysis here, we disagree with the District Court's conclusion. *Malat* was a brief per curiam in which the Supreme Court decided only that as used in Internal Revenue Code §1221 (1) the word "primarily" means "principally," "of first importance." The Supreme Court, remanding the case, did not analyze the facts or resolve the controversy which involved a real estate dealer who had purchased land and held it at the time of sale with the dual intention of developing it as rental property or selling it, depending on whichever proved to be the more profitable. . . . In contrast, having substantially abandoned its investment and farming intent, Biedenharn was cloaked primarily in the garb of sales purpose when it disposed of the 38 lots here in controversy. With this change, the Realty Company lost the opportunity of coming within any dual purpose analysis. . . .

VI . . .

We cannot write black letter law for all realty subdividers and for all times, but we do caution in words of red that once an investment does not mean always an investment. A simon-pure investor forty years ago could by his subsequent activities become a seller in the ordinary course four decades later. The period of Biedenharn's passivity is in the distant past; and the taxpayer has since undertaken the role of real estate protagonist. The Hardtimes Plantation in its day may have been one thing, but as the plantation was developed and sold, Hardtimes became by the very fact of change and activity a different holding than it had been at its inception. No longer could resort to initial purpose preserve taxpayer's once upon a time opportunity for favored treatment. The opinion of the District Court is reversed.

[Four judges joined in a dissent written by Judge Gee stating that the majority summarily discounted a critical trial court fact finding that taxpayer was still farming a large part of the land, that neither the plaintiff nor the court claimed any dual purpose, and that the majority placed preeminent emphasis on sales activities and improvements, effectively eliminating the other factors in *Winthrop*.]

NOTES AND QUESTIONS

1. *Standard of review.* In *Biedenharn,* the Fifth Circuit treated the "ultimate" issue of holding purpose as a question of law. In Byram v. United States, 705 F.2d 1418 (1983), however, responding to the Supreme Court decision on standard of review in Pullman-Standard v. Swint, 456 U.S. 273 (1982), the Fifth Circuit changed its position and held that the question of holding purpose is one of fact, subject to the "clearly erroneous" standard of review. In *Byram,* the court sustained a district court judgment for the taxpayer, who had, "during a three-year period, sold 22 parcels of real estate for over $9 million, netting approximately $3.4 million profit." In the taxpayer's favor, the court cited these facts:

> Byram made no personal effort to initiate the sales; buyers came to him. He did not advertise, he did not have a sales office, nor did he enlist the

aid of brokers. The properties at issue were not improved or developed by him. The district court found that Byram devoted minimal time and effort to the transactions.

2. *Condominium conversion.* In Gangi v. Commissioner, 1987-561 T.C. Memo., Gangi and Maginn had been partners in the ownership of an apartment building. After a period of time in which they rented out the apartments, they converted the building to a condominium and sold the units. The court held that the gain on the sales of the units was capital gain. Its reasoning is reflected in these excerpts from its opinion:

> We conclude that Gangi and Maginn did not hold the building "primarily" for sale to customers in the ordinary course of business. They purchased the land and built the building as a retirement investment, and for 8 to 9 years rented the units in accordance with their initial investment motive. When for business and personal reasons they determined it was in their best interest to sell, a business judgment was made to convert the building to condominiums. This decision was made in connection with their investment in real estate, and not in the ordinary course of a business. While we are aware that the purpose for which a taxpayer originally holds the property is not determinative of how the gain from a subsequent sale will be treated for tax purposes, it is nevertheless an important factor to be considered. . . . Thus, while we concede that Gangi and Maginn "sold" the condominium units, we do not think that this activity rises to the level of holding property "primarily" for sale to customers. Petitioners' original intent is relevant for our purposes under all the facts and circumstances.
>
> . . . [W]e also determine that Gangi and Maginn were not selling units in the ordinary course of their trade or business. . . .
>
> Respondent urges us to conclude that Gangi and Maginn sold the units in the ordinary course of their trade or business. . . . Respondent points to petitioners' activities in connection with the conversion including the substantial sales, the advertising to increase the sales, the model condominium unit, and the overall involvement of the partnership with the conversion process.
>
> Specifically, respondent notes that 1) the partnership sold twenty-six units to twenty-six different purchasers during 1979 and two units to two purchasers in 1980; 2) the partnership expended $129,384.44 to convert the building into condominium units; 3) the partnership advertised the sale of the condominium units in a local newspaper; 4) the partnership opened a model unit 6 days a week from noon to 5 P.M. to facilitate the sales; and, finally, 5) that the partnership received more money as a result of the conversion of the building into condominium units than it would have received had the building been sold intact. Respondent thus argues that Gangi and Maginn's efforts to sell the units rise to the level of producing sales in the ordinary course of a trade or business.
>
> Petitioners view the transaction differently. In 1970, Gangi and Maginn formed a partnership, which constructed the building for investment purposes. From November 1970 to August 1978, the property was held

solely as rental property. In June 1977, petitioners no longer wished to remain as partners, and they concluded that a conversion to condominiums would be the most profitable way for them to liquidate their investment. Maginn testified that the Glendale real estate market for rental real property had declined. Moreover, the building was "showing a relatively poor return. . . ." Confronted with the desire to terminate the partnership and a poor market to sell rental real estate, they decided the additional expenditures to convert the building were worthwhile. . . .

In Heller Trust v. Commissioner, 382 F.2d 675, 680 (9th Cir. 1967), the court held that where the facts clearly indicated that the taxpayer held his property as rental/investment property and that "this purpose continued until shortly before the time of a sale, and that the sale is prompted by a liquidation intent, the taxpayer should not lose the benefits provided for by the capital gain provisions."

In *Heller,* the taxpayer sold 169 duplexes (which formerly had been rented) between the years 1955 and 1958. He hired a staff, advertised the sale and opened a model unit in connection with the sales. The Ninth Circuit noted that the situation had changed between the time the taxpayer originally acquired the investment and the time the duplexes were sold. There was a decline in the taxpayer's health and in the economic conditions of the area in general.

The court commented that if it followed the lower court's treatment of the duplexes as being for sale in the ordinary course of business, the court could not conceive of "how persons with an investment such as we have here could bring themselves within the purview of the capital gains provisions of the statute where . . . they had to abandon a disappointing investment by means of a series of sales." The court stated that they did not "believe that such a harsh treatment is warranted under the applicable law and the facts of this case." Heller v. Commissioner, supra at 680.

We find that petitioners' motives were equally as strong for abandoning their investment. Just as declining health is unanticipated, so is the disintegration of a business relationship between two partners. Moreover, from the testimony of Maginn, it is evident that there was a decline in interest for rental buildings in the Glendale real estate market at the time Gangi and Maginn decided to terminate the partnership and sell the building. . . .

. . . Gangi and Maginn placed advertisements in only one newspaper, the Glendale News Press. The extent of the partnership's advertising to promote the sales totalled $4,437. This amount is minimal compared to the gross sales price of the units of $2,114,295. Moreover, petitioners paid a low brokerage commission of 1¾ percent. . . . Gangi and Maginn were not substantially involved with the sales end of the condominiums.

It must also be noted that the majority of the improvements made to the building prior to sale consisted of maintenance such as painting and carpeting that would have been necessary even if petitioners continued to hold the building as rental/investment property. No structural changes were made to the units themselves and no state or local permits were required prior to the conversion. We do not find that these activities rise to the level of being in the ordinary trade or business of holding condominium units for sale to customers. . . .

3. *Real estate "dealers."* (a) Compare the taxpayer in *Biedenharn* with the taxpayer in *Van Suetendael.* Is there any reason of policy why one should realize ordinary income and losses while the other has capital gains and losses? If the persons to whom Biedenharn sold land were "customers," as that term is used in §1221(1), why were not the persons who bought securities from Van Suetendael also "customers"? Neither taxpayer had a regular clientele of the kind enjoyed by a department store or other dealer in merchandise. How do the taxpayers in each of these two cases compare with a television manufacturer that sells to distributors? with the distributors, which sell to retailers? with an importer of television sets, which buys from distributors in Japan and sells to distributors in the United States?

(b) While the relevance of most of the factors discussed by the court in *Biedenharn* is easy enough to see, the effect of the use of agents may be puzzling. To what extent should the activities of others be attributed to the owner? What if the owner of the property enters into a contract with a real estate firm in which the latter is paid a fixed fee plus a percentage of gain above a certain level and is given complete control of selling price and methods, with permission to subdivide and make improvements out of its fee? What if the owner subdivides and improves and then contracts with an agent to sell the lots, with the owner to receive a fixed price for each lot, regardless of the selling price? See Fahs v. Crawford, 161 F.2d 315 (5th Cir. 1947), distinguished in *Biedenharn* as a case where the broker made all sales and was given full responsibility over the project so that the taxpayer could wall himself off legally from the activities of the broker; Voss v. United States, 329 F.2d 164 (7th Cir. 1964), where the owner of farm land authorized a real estate dealer to arrange for subdividing and selling property for a fee; held, capital gain.

(c) All of the leading real estate development cases are like *Biedenharn* in that the taxpayer realized gain and argued for status as an investor rather than a dealer. For the tax planner, the challenge before 1987 was to figure out how far one could go with development and sales activities without becoming a dealer. Roughly speaking, the answer was not far at all. Under present law, capital gain is only moderately favored, and capital loss quite disfavored. For the future, advisers to real estate investors often will want to know how much activity is necessary in order to qualify as a dealer so that losses will be ordinary. Suppose you represent a group of investors who bought a parcel of farm land several years ago and intended to hold it for investment until it became attractive to developers. Unfortunately, the value of the land has declined.

They are ready to sell. The investors are doctors, lawyers, and other such professionals who have no inclination to become involved in the business of development and sales. Yet they would like to be able to treat their losses as ordinary losses. What advice would you give them?

E. TRANSACTIONS RELATED TO THE TAXPAYER'S REGULAR BUSINESS

While Congress, in §1221, broadly defined capital assets as *all* "property," the word "property" cannot be given a broad, or even a plain-language, definition without violating informed notions of the congressional purpose in providing special treatment for capital gain or loss, however dimly perceived that purpose may be. For example, even though a landlord's rights to receive rent under a lease or an insurance agent's rights to renewal commissions might be thought of as "property," most knowledgeable people would agree that the landlord's sale of the leasehold or the insurance agent's sale of the rights to the renewal commissions should not produce capital gain. The cases that follow in this section, and most of the cases in the remainder of the chapter, reflect the efforts of the courts to narrow the concept of "capital asset."

The first case is Corn Products Refining Co. v. Commissioner, which appears immediately below. For the purpose of understanding and discussing the case, consider the following hypothetical and its description of the use of corn futures contracts. Suppose that *CP* is in the business of manufacturing corn syrup, which is made from corn, and that *CP* is committed to the sale of $1.2 million worth of syrup six months hence. Suppose further that the price at which the syrup will be sold, the $1.2 million, will not vary with the price of corn but the price of the corn itself may change considerably between now and five months from now, when it must be acquired in order to make the syrup. *CP* is anxious to avoid the risk associated with a possible rise in the price of corn. Fortunately for *CP*, there is an active market in corn "futures." A corn future is a contract for the purchase (and delivery) of a specified amount of corn at a specified date in the future for a specified price. A person who buys a contract for such future delivery of corn is said to buy futures (that is, corn futures contracts) or to be "long" in futures. The seller of the contract is sometimes said to have taken a "short" position. (The holder of the short position could be a speculator who anticipates a decline in the price of corn or a person who is hedging against such a decline.) Suppose that *CP* buys futures contracts for the amount of corn it needs, that the price to be paid on delivery is

$800,000, and that the cost of buying these contracts, plus all other expenses of manufacture of the syrup, will be $220,000, so the total costs of production are $1.02 million and *CP* can expect to make a profit of $180,000. Now suppose that five months later, when the time has come for *CP* to take delivery of the corn and make the syrup, the price of corn for immediate delivery on the market — the so-called spot price — is $980,000. *CP* can follow either of two routes. Under Route *A*, *CP* would take delivery of the corn that it has contracted to buy under its futures contracts, paying $800,000. The result would be a total cost of $1.02 million and a profit of $180,000, which plainly would be ordinary income, from its normal operations. Under Route *B*, *CP* would not take delivery on the corn but would instead sell the futures contracts. Ordinarily this is the more convenient way to do business. The profit on the sale of the corn futures contracts should be $180,000 — the difference between the spot price of the corn ($980,000) and the price at which the corn can be bought by a person holding the contracts ($800,000). Having sold the contracts, *CP* would buy the corn it needs on the spot market for $980,000. Disregarding the profit on the sale of the futures contracts, the production of the corn syrup would now be a break-even activity. See Table 8-1.

TABLE 8-1
Illustration of Use of Corn Futures Contracts

Route A (*CP* takes delivery under futures contracts)		
Revenue		$1,200,000
Costs		
Corn	$800,000	
Other	220,000	1,020,000
Net profit		$ 180,000
Route B (*CP* sells contracts and buys spot corn)		
Revenue		$1,200,000
Costs		
Corn	$980,000	
Other	220,000	
		$1,200,000
Net profit, operations		-0-
Gain from sale of futures contracts		$ 180,000
Total gains and profits		$ 180,000

CORN PRODUCTS REFINING CO. v. COMMISSIONER

350 U.S. 46 (1955)

Mr. Justice CLARK delivered the opinion of the Court.

This case concerns the tax treatment to be accorded certain transactions in commodity futures. In the Tax Court, petitioner Corn Products Refining Company contended that its purchases and sales of corn futures in 1940 and 1942 were capital-asset transactions under [§1221]. . . .

Petitioner is a nationally known manufacturer of products made from grain corn. It manufactures starch, syrup, sugar, and their byproducts, feeds and oil. Its average yearly grind of raw corn during the period 1937 through 1942 varied from thirty-five to sixty million bushels. Most of its products were sold under contracts requiring shipment in thirty days at a set price or at market price on the date of delivery, whichever was lower.

In 1934 and again in 1936 droughts in the corn belt caused a sharp increase in the price of spot corn. With a storage capacity of only 2,300,000 bushels of corn, a bare three weeks' supply, Corn Products found itself unable to buy at a price which would permit its refined corn sugar, cerealose, to compete successfully with cane and beet sugar. To avoid a recurrence of this situation, petitioner, in 1937, began to establish a long position in corn futures "as a part of its corn buying program" and "as the most economical method of obtaining an adequate supply of raw corn" without entailing the expenditure of large sums for additional storage facilities. At harvest time each year it would buy futures when the price appeared favorable. It would take delivery on such contracts as it found necessary to its manufacturing operations and sell the remainder in early summer if no shortage was imminent. If shortages appeared, however, it sold futures only as it bought spot corn for grinding.[5] In this manner it reached a balanced position with reference to any increase in spot corn prices. It made no effort to protect itself against a decline in prices.

In 1940 it netted a profit of $680,587.39 in corn futures, but in 1942 it suffered a loss of $109,969.38. . . . It now contends that its futures

5. The disposition of the corn futures during the period in dispute were as follows:

	Sales of futures thousand bushels	*Delivery under futures thousand bushels*
1938	17,400	4,975
1939	14,180	2,865
1940	14,595	250
1941	2,545	2,175
1942	5,695	4,460

were "capital assets" under [§1221] and that gains and losses therefrom should have been treated as arising from the sale of a capital asset. In support of this position, it claims that its futures trading was separate and apart from its manufacturing operations and that in its futures transactions, it was acting as a "legitimate capitalist." U.S. v. New York Coffee & Sugar Exchange, 263 U.S. 611, 619. It denies that its future transactions were "hedges" or "speculative" dealings as covered by the ruling of General Counsel's Memorandum 17322, XV-2 C.B. 151, and claims that it is in truth "the forgotten man" of that administrative interpretation.

Both the Tax Court and the Court of Appeals found petitioner's futures transactions to be an integral part of its business designed to protect its manufacturing operations against a price increase in its principal raw material and to assure a ready supply for future manufacturing requirements. . . .

We find nothing in this record to support the contention that Corn Products' futures activity was separate and apart from its manufacturing operation. On the contrary, it appears that the transactions were vitally important to the company's business as a form of insurance against increases in the price of raw corn. Not only were the purchases initiated for just this reason, but the petitioner's sales policy, selling in the future at a fixed price or less, continued to leave it exceedingly vulnerable to rises in the price of corn. Further, the purchase of corn futures assured the company a source of supply which was admittedly cheaper than constructing additional storage facilities for raw corn. Under these facts, it is difficult to imagine a program more closely geared to a company's manufacturing enterprise or more important to its successful operation.

Likewise the claim of Corn Products that it was dealing in the market as a "legitimate capitalist" . . . exercising "good judgment" in the futures market, . . . ignores the testimony of its own officers that in entering that market the company was "trying to protect a part of [its] manufacturing costs"; that its entry was not for the purpose of "speculating and buying and selling corn futures" but to fill an actual "need for the quantity of corn [bought] . . . in order to cover . . . what [products] we expected to market over a period of fifteen or eighteen months." It matters not whether the label be that of "legitimate capitalist" or "speculator"; this is not the talk of the capital investor but of the far-sighted manufacturer. For tax purposes, petitioner's purchases have been found to "constitute an integral part of its manufacturing business" by both the Tax Court and the Court of Appeals, and on essentially factual questions the findings of two courts should not ordinarily be disturbed. . . .

Petitioner also makes much of the conclusion by both the Tax Court and the Court of Appeals that its transactions did not constitute "true hedging." It is true that Corn Products did not secure complete protection from its market operations. Under its sales policy petitioner could not guard against a fall in prices. It is clear, however, that petitioner feared the possibility of a price rise more than that of a price decline. It therefore purchased partial insurance against its principal risk, and hoped to retain sufficient flexibility to avoid serious losses on a declining market.

Nor can we find support for petitioner's contention that hedging is not within the exclusions of [§1221]. Admittedly, petitioner's corn futures do not come within the literal language of the exclusions set out in that section. They were not stock in trade, actual inventory, property held for sale to customers or depreciable property used in a trade or business. But the capital-asset provision of [§1221] must not be so broadly applied as to defeat rather than further the purpose of Congress. Burnet v. Harmel, 287 U.S. 103, 108. Congress intended that profits and losses arising from the everyday operation of a business be considered as ordinary income or loss rather than capital gain or loss. The preferential treatment provided by [§1221] applies to transactions in property which are not the normal source of business income. It was intended "to relieve the taxpayer from . . . excessive tax burdens on gains resulting from a conversion of capital investments, and to remove the deterrent effect of those burdens on such conversions." Burnet v. Harmel, 287 U.S., at 106. Since this section is an exception from the normal tax requirements of the Internal Revenue Code, the definition of a capital asset must be narrowly applied and its exclusions interpreted broadly. This is necessary to effectuate the basic congressional purpose. This Court has always construed narrowly the term "capital assets" in [§1221]. See Hort v. Commissioner [infra page 867].

The problem of the appropriate tax treatment of hedging transactions first arose under the 1934 Tax Code revision. Thereafter, the Treasury issued G.C.M. 17322, supra, distinguishing speculative transactions in commodity futures from hedging transactions. It held that hedging transactions were essentially to be regarded as insurance rather than a dealing in capital assets and that gains and losses therefrom were ordinary business gains and losses. The interpretation outlined in this memorandum has been consistently followed by the courts as well as by the Commissioner. While it is true that this Court has not passed on its validity, it has been well recognized for 20 years; and Congress has made no change in it though the Code has been re-enacted on three subsequent occasions. This bespeaks congressional approval. . . . Furthermore, Congress has since specifically recognized the hedging exception here under consideration in the short-sale rule of §1233(a) of the 1954 Code.[6]

6. Section 1233(a) provides that gain or loss from "the short sale of property, other

We believe that the statute clearly refutes the contention of Corn Products. Moreover, it is significant to note that practical considerations lead to the same conclusion. To hold otherwise would permit those engaged in hedging transactions to transmute ordinary income into capital gain at will. The hedger may either sell the future and purchase in the spot market or take delivery under the future contract itself. But if a sale of the future created a capital transaction while delivery of the commodity under the same future did not, a loophole in the statute would be created and the purpose of Congress frustrated.

The judgment is affirmed.

Mr. Justice HARLAN took no part in the consideration or decision of this case.

ARKANSAS BEST CORPORATION v. COMMISSIONER

485 U.S. 212 (1988)

Justice MARSHALL delivered the opinion of the Court.

The issue presented in this case is whether capital stock held by petitioner Arkansas Best Corporation (Arkansas Best) is a "capital asset" as defined in §1221 of the Internal Revenue Code regardless of whether the stock was purchased and held for a business purpose or for an investment purpose.

I

Arkansas Best is a diversified holding company. In 1968 it acquired approximately 65% of the stock of the National Bank of Commerce (Bank) in Dallas, Texas. Between 1969 and 1974, Arkansas Best more than tripled the number of shares it owned in the Bank, although its percentage interest in the Bank remained relatively stable. These acquisitions were prompted principally by the Bank's need for added capital. Until 1972, the Bank appeared to be prosperous and growing, and the added capital was necessary to accommodate this growth. As the Dallas real estate market declined, however, so too did the financial health of the Bank, which had a heavy concentration of loans in the

---

than a hedging transaction in commodity futures," shall be treated as gain or loss from the sale of a capital asset to the extent "that the property, including a commodity future, used to close the short sale constitutes a capital asset in the hands of a taxpayer." The legislative history recognizes explicitly the hedging exception. H.R. Rep. No. 1337, 83d Cong., 2d Sess., p. A278; S. Rep. No. 1622, 83d Cong., 2d Sess., p.437: "Under existing law bona fide hedging transactions do not result in capital gains or losses. This result is based upon case law and regulations. To continue this result hedging transactions in commodity futures have been specifically excepted from the operation of this subsection."

local real estate industry. In 1972, federal examiners classified the Bank as a problem bank. The infusion of capital after 1972 was prompted by the loan portfolio problems of the bank.

Petitioner sold the bulk of its Bank stock on June 30, 1975, leaving it with only a 14.7% stake in the Bank. On its federal income tax return for 1975, petitioner claimed a deduction for an ordinary loss of $9,995,688 resulting from the sale of the stock. The Commissioner of Internal Revenue disallowed the deduction, finding that the loss from the sale of stock was a capital loss, rather than an ordinary loss, and that it therefore was subject to the capital loss limitations in the Internal Revenue Code.[7]

Arkansas Best challenged the Commissioner's determination in the United States Tax Court. The Tax Court, relying on cases interpreting Corn Products Refining Co. v. Commissioner, [supra page 854], held that stock purchased with a substantial investment purpose is a capital asset which, when sold, gives rise to a capital gain or loss, whereas stock purchased and held for a business purpose, without any substantial investment motive, is an ordinary asset whose sale gives rise to ordinary gains or losses. . . . The court characterized Arkansas Best's acquisitions through 1972 as occurring during the Bank's "'growth' phase," and found that these acquisitions "were motivated primarily by investment purpose and only incidentally by some business purpose." . . . The stock acquired during this period therefore constituted a capital asset, which gave rise to a capital loss when sold in 1975. The court determined, however, that the acquisitions after 1972 occurred during the Bank's "'problem' phase," . . . and, except for certain minor exceptions, "were made exclusively for business purposes and subsequently held for the same reasons." . . . These acquisitions, the court found, were designed to preserve petitioner's business reputation, because without the added capital the Bank probably would have failed. . . . The loss realized on the sale of this stock was thus held to be an ordinary loss.

The Court of Appeals for the Eighth Circuit reversed the Tax Court's determination that the loss realized on stock purchased after 1972 was subject to ordinary-loss treatment, holding that all of the Bank stock sold in 1975 was subject to capital-loss treatment. 800 F. 2d 215 (1986). The court reasoned that the Bank stock clearly fell within the general definition of "capital asset" in Internal Revenue Code §1221, and that the stock did not fall within any of the specific statutory exceptions to this definition. The court concluded that Arkansas Best's purpose in

7. Title 26 U.S.C. §1211(a) states that "[i]n the case of a corporation, losses from sales or exchanges of capital assets shall be allowed only to the extent of gains from such sales or exchanges." Section 1212(a) establishes rules governing carrybacks and carryovers of capital losses, permitting such losses to offset capital gains in certain earlier or later years.

acquiring and holding the stock was irrelevant to the determination whether the stock was a capital asset. We granted certiorari . . . and now affirm.

II

Section 1221 of the Internal Revenue Code defines "capital asset" broadly, as "property held by the taxpayer (whether or not connected with his trade or business)," and then excludes five specific classes of property from capital-asset status. Arkansas Best acknowledges that the Bank stock falls within the literal definition of capital asset in §1221, and is outside of the statutory exclusions. It asserts, however, that this determination does not end the inquiry. Petitioner argues that in Corn Products Refining Co. v. Commissioner, supra, this Court rejected a literal reading of §1221, and concluded that assets acquired and sold for ordinary business purposes rather than for investment purposes should be given ordinary-asset treatment. Petitioner's reading of *Corn Products* finds much support in the academic literature and in the courts.[8] Unfortunately for petitioner, this broad reading finds no support in the language of §1221.

In essence, petitioner argues that "property held by the taxpayer (whether or not connected with his trade or business)" does not include property that is acquired and held for a business purpose. In petitioner's view an asset's status as "property" thus turns on the motivation behind its acquisition. This motive test, however, is not only nowhere mentioned in §1221, but it is also in direct conflict with the parenthetical phrase "whether or not connected with his trade or business." The broad definition of the term "capital asset" explicitly makes irrelevant any consideration of the property's connection with the taxpayer's business, whereas petitioner's rule would make this factor dispositive.[9]

8. See, e.g., Campbell Taggart, Inc. v. United States, 744 F.2d 442, 456-458 (C.A.5 1984); Steadman v. Commissioner, 424 F.2d 1, 5 (C.A.6), cert. denied, 400 U.S. 869 (1970); Booth Newspapers, Inc. v. United States, 157 Ct. Cl. 886, 893-896, 303 F.2d 916, 920-921 (1962); W. W. Windle Co. v. Commissioner, 65 T.C. 694, 707-713 (1976).

9. Petitioner mistakenly relies on cases in which this Court, in narrowly applying the general definition of capital asset, has "construed 'capital asset' to exclude property representing income items or accretions to the value of a capital asset themselves properly attributable to income," even though these items are property in the broad sense of the word. United States v. Midland-Ross Corp., 381 U.S. 54, 57 (1965). See, e.g., Commissioner v. Gillette Motor Co., 364 U.S. 130 (1960) ("capital asset" does not include compensation awarded taxpayer that represented fair rental value of its facilities); Commissioner v. P. G. Lake, Inc., [infra page 878] ("capital asset" does not include proceeds from sale of oil payment rights); Hort v. Commissioner, [infra page 867] ("capital asset" does not include payment to lessor for cancellation of unexpired portion of a lease). This line of cases, based on the premise that §1221 "property" does not include claims or rights to ordinary income, has no application in the present context. Petitioner sold capital stock, not a claim to ordinary income.

In a related argument, petitioner contends that the five exceptions listed in §1221 for certain kinds of property are illustrative, rather than exhaustive, and that courts are therefore free to fashion additional exceptions in order to further the general purposes of the capital-asset provisions. The language of the statute refutes petitioner's construction. Section 1221 provides that "capital asset" means "property held by the taxpayer[,] . . . but does not include" the five classes of property listed as exceptions. We believe this locution signifies that the listed exceptions are exclusive. The body of §1221 establishes a general definition of the term "capital asset," and the phrase "does not include" takes out of that broad definition only the classes of property that are specifically mentioned. The legislative history of the capital asset definition supports this interpretation, see H.R. Rep. 704, 73d Cong., 2d Sess., 31 (1934) ("[T]he definition includes all property, except as specifically excluded"); H.R. Rep. 1337, 83d Cong., 2d Sess., A273 (1954) ("[A] capital asset is property held by the taxpayer with certain exceptions"), as does the applicable Treasury regulation, see 26 C.F.R. §1.1221-1(a) (1987) ("The term 'capital assets' includes all classes of property not specifically excluded by section 1221").

Petitioner's reading of the statute is also in tension with the exceptions listed in §1221. These exclusions would be largely superfluous if assets acquired primarily or exclusively for business purposes were not capital assets. Inventory, real or depreciable property used in the taxpayer's trade or business, and accounts or notes receivable acquired in the ordinary course of business, would undoubtedly satisfy such a business-motive test. Yet these exceptions were created by Congress in separate enactments spanning 30 years.[10] Without any express direction from Congress, we are unwilling to read §1221 in a manner that makes surplusage of these statutory exclusions.

In the end, petitioner places all reliance on its reading of Corn Products Refining Co. v. Commissioner, [supra page 854] — a reading we believe is too expansive. In *Corn Products*, the Court considered whether income arising from a taxpayer's dealings in corn futures was entitled to capital-gains treatment. The taxpayer was a company that converted corn into starches, sugars, and other products. After droughts in the 1930's caused sharp increases in corn prices, the company began a program of buying corn futures to assure itself an adequate supply of corn and protect against price increases. . . . The company "would

10. The inventory exception was part of the original enactment of the capital-asset provision in 1924. See Revenue Act of 1924, ch. 234, §208(a)(8), 43 Stat. 263. Depreciable property used in a trade or business was excluded in 1938, see Revenue Act of 1938, ch. 289, §117(a)(1), 52 Stat. 500, and real property used in a trade or business was excluded in 1942, see Revenue Act of 1942, ch. 619, §151(a), 56 Stat. 846. The exception for accounts and notes receivable acquired in the ordinary course of trade or business was added in 1954. Internal Revenue Code of 1954, §1221(4), 68A Stat. 322.

take delivery on such contracts as it found necessary to its manufacturing operations and sell the remainder in early summer if no shortage was imminent. If shortages appeared, however, it sold futures only as it bought spot corn for grinding." . . . The Court characterized the company's dealing in corn futures as "hedging." . . . As explained by the Court of Appeals in *Corn Products,* "[h]edging is a method of dealing in commodity futures whereby a person or business protects itself against price fluctuations at the time of delivery of the product which it sells or buys." 215 F.2d 513, 515 (C.A.2 1954). In evaluating the company's claim that the sales of corn futures resulted in capital gains and losses, this Court stated:

> Nor can we find support for petitioner's contention that hedging is not within the exclusions of [§1221]. Admittedly, petitioner's corn futures do not come within the literal language of the exclusions set out in that section. They were not stock in trade, actual inventory, property held for sale to customers or depreciable property used in a trade or business. But the capital-asset provision of [§1221] must not be so broadly applied as to defeat rather than further the purpose of Congress. Congress intended that profits and losses arising from the everyday operation of a business be considered as ordinary income or loss rather than capital gain or loss. . . . Since this section is an exception from the normal tax requirements of the Internal Revenue Code, the definition of a capital asset must be narrowly applied and its exclusions interpreted broadly. . . .

The Court went on to note that hedging transactions consistently had been considered to give rise to ordinary gains and losses, and then concluded that the corn futures were subject to ordinary-asset treatment. . . .

The Court in *Corn Products* proffered the oft-quoted rule of construction that the definition of capital asset must be narrowly applied and its exclusions interpreted broadly, but it did not state explicitly whether the holding was based on a narrow reading of the phrase "property held by the taxpayer," or on a broad reading of the inventory exclusion of §1221. In light of the stark language of §1221, however, we believe that *Corn Products* is properly interpreted as involving an application of §1221's inventory exception. Such a reading is consistent both with the Court's reasoning in that case and with §1221. The Court stated in *Corn Products* that the company's futures transactions were "an integral part of its business designed to protect its manufacturing operations against a price increase in its principal raw material and to assure a ready supply for future manufacturing requirements." . . . The company bought, sold, and took delivery under the futures contracts as required by the company's manufacturing needs. As Professor Bittker notes, under these circumstances, the futures can "easily be viewed as surrogates for the raw material itself." 2 B. Bittker, Federal Taxation of

Income, Estates and Gifts para. 51.10.3, p. 51-62 (1981). The Court of Appeals for the Second Circuit in *Corn Products* clearly took this approach. That court stated that when commodity futures are "utilized solely for the purpose of stabilizing inventory cost[,] . . . [they] cannot reasonably be separated from the inventory items," and concluded that "property used in hedging transactions properly comes within the exclusions of [§1221]." . . . This Court indicated its acceptance of the Second Circuit's reasoning when it began the central paragraph of its opinion, "Nor can we find support for petitioner's contention that hedging is not within the exclusions of [§1221]." . . . In the following paragraph, the Court argued that the Treasury had consistently viewed such hedging transactions as a form of insurance to stabilize the cost of inventory, and cited a Treasury ruling which concluded that the value of a manufacturer's raw-material inventory should be adjusted to take into account hedging transactions in futures contracts. . . . This discussion, read in light of the Second Circuit's holding and the plain language of §1221, convinces us that although the corn futures were not "actual inventory," their use as an integral part of the taxpayer's inventory-purchase system led the Court to treat them as substitutes for the corn inventory such that they came within a broad reading of "property of a kind which would properly be included in the inventory of the taxpayer" in §1221.

Petitioner argues that by focusing attention on whether the asset was acquired and sold as an integral part of the taxpayer's everyday business operations, the Court in *Corn Products* intended to create a general exemption from capital-asset status for assets acquired for business purposes. We believe petitioner misunderstands the relevance of the Court's inquiry. A business connection, although irrelevant to the initial determination of whether an item is a capital asset, is relevant in determining the applicability of certain of the statutory exceptions, including the inventory exception. The close connection between the futures transactions and the taxpayer's business in *Corn Products* was crucial to whether the corn futures could be considered surrogates for the stored inventory of raw corn. For if the futures dealings were not part of the company's inventory-purchase system, and instead amounted simply to speculation in corn futures, they could not be considered substitutes for the company's corn inventory, and would fall outside even a broad reading of the inventory exclusion. We conclude that *Corn Products* is properly interpreted as standing for the narrow proposition that hedging transactions that are an integral part of a business' inventory-purchase system fall within the inventory exclusion of §1221.[11] Arkansas

11. Although congressional inaction is generally a poor measure of congressional intent, we are given some pause by the fact that over 25 years have passed since Corn Products Refining Co. v. Commissioner, [supra], was initially interpreted as excluding

Best, which is not a dealer in securities, has never suggested that the Bank stock falls within the inventory exclusion. *Corn Products* thus has no application to this case.

It is also important to note that the business-motive test advocated by petitioner is subject to the same kind of abuse that the Court condemned in Corn Products. The Court explained in Corn Products that unless hedging transactions were subject to ordinary gain and loss treatment, taxpayers engaged in such transactions could "transmute ordinary income into capital gain at will." . . . The hedger could garner capital-asset treatment by selling the future and purchasing the commodity on the spot market, or ordinary-asset treatment by taking delivery under the future contract. In a similar vein, if capital stock purchased and held for a business purpose is an ordinary asset, whereas the same stock purchased and held with an investment motive is a capital asset, a taxpayer such as Arkansas Best could have significant influence over whether the asset would receive capital or ordinary treatment. Because stock is most naturally viewed as a capital asset, the Internal Revenue Service would be hard pressed to challenge a taxpayer's claim that stock was acquired as an investment, and that a gain arising from the sale of such stock was therefore a capital gain. Indeed, we are unaware of a single decision that has applied the business-motive test so as to require a taxpayer to report a gain from the sale of stock as an ordinary gain. If the same stock is sold at a loss, however, the taxpayer may be able to garner ordinary-loss treatment by emphasizing the business purpose behind the stock's acquisition. The potential for such abuse was evidenced in this case by the fact that as late as 1974, when Arkansas Best still hoped to sell the Bank stock at a profit, Arkansas Best apparently expected to report the gain as a capital gain. . . .

III

We conclude that a taxpayer's motivation in purchasing an asset is irrelevant to the question whether the asset is "property held by a taxpayer (whether or not connected with his business)" and is thus within §1221's general definition of "capital asset." Because the capital stock held by petitioner falls within the broad definition of the term "capital asset" in §1221 and is outside the classes of property excluded from capital-asset status, the loss arising from the sale of the stock is a capital loss. Corn Products Refining Co. v. Commissioner, supra, which

assets acquired for business purposes from the definition of capital asset, see Booth Newspapers, Inc. v. United States, [supra], without any sign of disfavor from Congress. We cannot ignore the unambiguous language of §1221, however, no matter how reticent Congress has been. If a broad exclusion from capital-asset status is to be created for assets acquired for business purposes, it must come from congressional action, not silence.

we interpret as involving a broad reading of the inventory exclusion of §1221, has no application in the present context. Accordingly, the judgment of the Court of Appeals is affirmed.

It is so ordered.

Justice KENNEDY took no part in the consideration or decision of this case.

NOTES AND QUESTIONS

1. *What is an inventory substitute?* (a) In United States v. Rogers, 286 F.2d 277 (6th Cir.), cert. denied, 366 U.S. 961 (1961), a taxpayer who was in the livestock business on a large scale claimed an ordinary loss on transactions in various other commodity futures on the ground that he bought and sold the commodity futures in an effort to protect against losses in the livestock business (largely from uncollectible accounts receivable), rather than for investment or speculation. The court held that the transactions produced capital losses because there was not a close enough link between the risks in the taxpayer's regular business and the price movements in the commodities on which the losses were incurred. One judge dissented, arguing that the taxpayer's practice of selling commodity futures short would produce a gain in the event of an economic decline and that this gain would offset the credit losses that might result from the impact of the same economic decline on his livestock customers.

(b) What if the taxpayer in *Corn Products* had been unwilling for some reason to buy corn futures and, as an alternative hedge against a rise in the price of corn, had bought contracts for some other commodity, such as hogs, whose price fluctuations were closely correlated to fluctuations in the price of corn?

(c) What if the taxpayer had concluded that the price of corn futures contracts was low and had bought contracts for more corn than it normally used in its operations?

(d) To come within §1221(1), how closely must the taxpayer match the delivery time under the futures contracts and the need for raw material inventory? For example, what if the taxpayer in *Corn Products* normally used corn in the months of April through June and bought futures contracts calling for delivery of corn in August (even though contracts for delivery in earlier months were available)?

2. *Source of supply cases.* Some of the cases applying the *Corn Products* doctrine, or similar analysis, to allow ordinary deductions for losses on investments involved investments made to ensure a source of supply. For example, in *Booth Newspapers,* cited by the Court in *Arkansas Best,* the taxpayer, a newspaper publisher, bought shares of stock of a paper manufacturer to protect its source of newsprint in a time of shortage. Do source-of-supply investments fit within the inventory ex-

ception so that cases like *Booth Newspapers* come out the same after *Arkansas Best?* In approaching this question should a court ask whether source-of-supply investments generally turn out to be losers? How would a court, or a taxpayer, get data on this issue?

3. *Hedges that are not inventory substitutes.* The decision in *Arkansas Best* provides clear and sensible rules for taxpayers who hedge inventory risks by purchasing securities or by other means. Since the gain and loss on the inventory would be ordinary, the gain or loss on the hedge is also ordinary. The decision does not, however, give much guidance to taxpayers who attempt to ensure a certain level of operating income by hedging other sorts of risk. Consider, for example, a United States taxpayer who sells goods on January 1 with payment to be made in yen on March 1 of that same year. Under current exchange rates, the yen received under the contract will be worth $3,000,000 and the contract will produce operating income of $1,000,000. The taxpayer believes, however, that the value of the yen relative to the dollar may fall by as much as 10 percent prior to payment. If that occurs, the yen received under contract will be worth only $2,700,000. The taxpayer, seeking to lock in its $1,000,000 profit, enters into a currency hedge that protects it against any decline in the value of the yen prior to March 1. Suppose the value of the yen then in fact declines by 10 percent relative to the dollar. The taxpayer receives yen worth only $2,700,000 and so realizes only a $700,000 profit under the contract. On the other hand, the taxpayer recognizes $300,000 of income from its currency hedge. Neither the currency hedge nor the underlying contract is inventory. Is the transaction therefore outside the ambit of the *Corn Products* doctrine as set forth in *Arkansas Best?* Does the taxpayer recognize capital gain on its currency hedge? This issue is discussed (and on an administrative level resolved) in the Proposed Regulations described in the Treasury Decision that follows.

TREASURY DECISION 8493

Filed October 18, 1993

Background

This document contains temporary regulations amending the Income Tax Regulations (26 CFR part 1) under section 1221 of the Internal Revenue Code (Code) (relating to the definition of capital asset). . . .

Paragraph (a)(1) of §1.1221-2T provides that property that is part of a hedging transaction, as defined in the regulations, is not a capital asset. . . .

A hedging transaction generally is a transaction that a taxpayer enters into in the normal course of the taxpayer's business primarily to reduce the risk of interest rate or price changes or currency fluctuations. Thus, the regulations do not provide ordinary treatment for gain or loss from the disposition of stock where, for example, the stock was acquired to protect the goodwill or business reputation of the acquirer or to ensure the availability of goods.

The definition of a hedging transaction covers most, but not all, common business hedges. . . .

Hedges of property within the exceptions to section 1221 and property that produces ordinary gain or loss . . . generally come within the definition of the term "hedging transaction." The Service believes that it is inappropriate, however, to have a loss on a hedge treated as ordinary when gain on the item or items being hedged could be treated as capital gain. Thus, a hedge of a section 1231 asset or a hedge of the ordinary income produced by a capital asset is excluded from the definition. Hedges of non-inventory supplies are also excluded because they are capital assets, notwithstanding the fact that they give rise to ordinary deductions when they are consumed in the taxpayer's business.

QUESTIONS

1. The operating income of airlines is highly dependent upon the price of fuel oil. Suppose an airline believes that the price of fuel is likely to rise. The airline can guard against this result and lock in a certain level of operating income by purchasing and storing fuel oil. Suppose the airline instead hedges that risk through the purchase of options. Under the regulations described above, would the gain or loss from those options be capital in nature? (See the last sentence quoted above.)
2. How would the source of supply cases, discussed in Note 2 following *Arkansas Best,* be treated under the proposed regulations?

F. SUBSTITUTES FOR ORDINARY INCOME

The next two cases (*Hort* and *McAllister*) focus on the question of whether the taxpayer is entitled to a recovery of basis, but also are treated as authority on the issue of capital gain versus ordinary income.

1. Payment for Cancellation of a Lease

HORT v. COMMISSIONER

313 U.S. 28 (1941)

Mr. Justice MURPHY delivered the opinion of the Court.

We must determine whether the amount petitioner received as consideration for cancellation of a lease of realty in New York City was ordinary gross income as defined in [§61(a)], and whether, in any event, petitioner sustained a loss through cancellation of the lease which is recognized in [§165(a)].

Petitioner acquired the property, a lot and ten-story office building, by devise from his father in 1928. At the time he became owner, the premises were leased to a firm which had sublet the main floor to the Irving Trust Co. In 1927, five years before the head lease expired, the Irving Trust Co. and petitioner's father executed a contract in which the latter agreed to lease the main floor and basement to the former for a term of fifteen years at an annual rental of $25,000, the term to commence at the expiration of the head lease.

In 1933, the Irving Trust Co. found it unprofitable to maintain a branch in petitioner's building. After some negotiations, petitioner and the Trust Co. agreed to cancel the lease in consideration of a payment to petitioner of $140,000. Petitioner did not include this amount in gross income in his income tax return for 1933. On the contrary, he reported a loss of $21,494.75 on the theory that the amount he received as consideration for the cancellation was $21,494.75 less than the difference between the present value of the unmatured rental payments and the fair rental value of the main floor and basement for the unexpired term of the lease. He did not deduct this figure, however, because he reported other losses in excess of gross income.

The Commissioner included the entire $140,000 in gross income, disallowed the asserted loss, made certain other adjustments not material here, and assessed a deficiency. The Board of Tax Appeals affirmed. 39 B.T.A. 922. The Circuit Court of Appeals affirmed per curiam on the authority of Warren Service Corp. v. Commissioner, 110 F.2d 723. 112 F.2d 167. Because of conflict with Commissioner v. Langwell Real Estate Corp., 47 F.2d 841, we granted certiorari limited to the question whether, "in computing net gain or loss for income tax purposes, a taxpayer [can] offset the value of the lease canceled against the consideration received by him for the cancellation." 311 U.S. 641.

Petitioner apparently contends that the amount received for cancellation of the lease was capital rather than ordinary income and that it was therefore subject to [the provisions of the Code] which govern capital gains and losses. Further, he argues that even if that amount must be reported as ordinary gross income he sustained a loss which [§165(a)] authorizes him to deduct. We cannot agree.

The amount received by petitioner for cancellation of the lease must be included in his gross income in its entirety. . . . [Section 61(a)] reached the rent paid prior to cancellation just as it would have embraced subsequent payments if the lease had never been canceled. It would have included a prepayment of the discounted value of unmatured rental payments whether received at the inception of the lease or at any time thereafter. Similarly, it would have extended to the proceeds of a suit to recover damages had the Irving Trust Co. breached the lease instead of concluding a settlement. . . . That the amount petitioner received resulted from negotiations ending in cancellation of the lease rather than from a suit to enforce it cannot alter the fact that basically the payment was merely a substitute for the rent reserved in the lease. So far as the application of [§61(a)] is concerned, it is immaterial that petitioner chose to accept an amount less than the strict present value of the unmatured rental payments rather than to engage in litigation, possibly uncertain and expensive.

The consideration received for cancellation of the lease was not a return of capital. We assume that the lease was "property," whatever that signifies abstractly. Presumably the bond in Helvering v. Horst [supra page 764] and the lease in Helvering v. Bruun [supra page 301] were also "property," but the interest coupon in *Horst* and the building in *Bruun* nevertheless were held to constitute items of gross income. Simply because the lease was "property" the amount received for its cancellation was not a return of capital, quite apart from the fact that "property" and "capital" are not necessarily synonymous in the Revenue Act of 1932 or in common usage. Where, as in this case, the disputed amount was essentially a substitute for rental payments which [§61(a)(5)] expressly characterizes as gross income, it must be regarded as ordinary income, and it is immaterial that for some purposes the contract creating the right to such payments may be treated as "property" or "capital."

For the same reasons, that amount was not a return of capital because petitioner acquired the lease as an incident of the realty devised to him by his father. Theoretically, it might have been possible in such a case to value realty and lease separately, and to label each a capital asset. . . . But that would not have converted into capital the amount petitioner received from the Trust Co., since [§102(b)(1)] would have required him to include in gross income the rent derived from the property, and that section, like [§61(a)], does not distinguish rental payments and a payment which is clearly a substitute for rental payments.

We conclude that petitioner must report as gross income the entire amount received for cancellation of the lease, without regard to the claimed disparity between that amount and the difference between the present value of the unmatured rental payments and the fair rental value of the property for the unexpired period of the lease. The cancellation of the lease involved nothing more than relinquishment of the right to future rental payments in return for a present substitute payment and possession of the leased premises. Undoubtedly it diminished the amount of gross income petitioner expected to realize, but to that extent he was relieved of the duty to pay income tax. Nothing in [§165(a)] indicates that Congress intended to allow petitioner to reduce ordinary income actually received and reported by the amount of income he failed to realize. . . . We may assume that petitioner was injured insofar as the cancellation of the lease affected the value of the realty. But that would become a deductible loss only when its extent had been fixed by a closed transaction. Regulations [§1.165-1(b)]. . . .

The judgment of the Circuit Court of Appeals is affirmed.

NOTES AND QUESTIONS

1. *Background: prepaid leases.* (a) Suppose *L* buys land for $100,000 and can rent it out for $10,000 per year net of all expenses. For the sake of simplicity, assume further that there is no inflation, that the rent is expected to remain $10,000, and the value of the land $100,000, for the foreseeable future. If *L* rents the land for one year and receives a rent payment of $10,000 at the end of that year, plainly the $10,000 is fully taxed as ordinary income. Note that there are two elements in this statement of tax consequences. First, no part of *L*'s basis is offset against the $10,000 receipt. This is as it should be, since at the end of the year she still has the land, which is not a wasting asset and which is therefore presumed for tax purposes still to be worth $100,000. (If the land in fact changes in value, that change is *unrealized* gain or loss.) Second, the $10,000 is ordinary income. It is rent, not the proceeds of the sale of property.

(b) Suppose that *L* rents the land for two years with the tenant paying $17,355 in advance. ($17,355 is the present value of the right to receive $10,000 at the end of each year for two years, discounted at the rate of 10 percent. Assume here and in the subsequent questions in this note that 10 percent is the appropriate market rate.) Is the entire amount taxable at the time received? Is it still ordinary income?

(c) What if the lease is for ten years and the advance payment is $61,000 (the approximate present value of $10,000 at the end of each year for ten years, discounted at 10 percent)? If the value of the leasehold is $61,000, the value of the reversion should be $39,000. As time passes, the value of the leasehold declines and the value of the reversion rises. Cf. Note 1 following Irwin v. Gavit, supra page 191, showing changes in the values of term of years and remainder. Does this observation help to explain why it may be appropriate to treat the receipt of the advance rent as income, with no basis offset? Does it help explain why the amount received is ordinary income rather than capital gain?

(d) What if the lease is for ninety-nine years and the advance payment is $99,992 (the present value, at a 10 percent discount rate). Compare Regs. §1.1031(a)-1(c) (leasehold for thirty years or more is like a fee for purposes of like-kind exchange rules).

(e) By way of review, what are the tax consequences for the tenant in each of the above situations, assuming the property is used in the tenant's business? See Chapter 6A.

(f) If the property is depreciable, how is *L*'s deduction for depreciation affected by the fact that *L* receives two or more years' rent in advance?

2. *The legal doctrine of* Hort. Is the holding of *Hort* that there was no "sale or exchange" or that what was sold was not a "capital asset" (that is, "property" not within one of the exceptions of §1221)?

3. *Inherited property.* Suppose that *L* owns property worth $100,000, leases it for $10,000 per year (payable at the end of each year) for ten years, and immediately dies, leaving the property, subject to the lease, to her son, *S*. At the time of *L*'s death the leasehold is worth $61,000, and the remainder $39,000. Before any time passes, *S* talks the tenant into paying $60,000 to *S* in full payment for the use of the property for the remaining ten years of the lease. What are the tax consequences to *S* under *Hort*? Is that result consistent with sound tax policy? Suppose *S* argues that he inherited a leasehold worth $61,000, sold it immediately for only $60,000, resulting in a loss of $1,000.[12] How would you respond?

4. *Premium leases.* Suppose that *L,* the owner of land worth $100,000, leases it for $10,000 per year for ten years and that a year later the value of the land has fallen to $60,000 and the rent that could be earned if now leased for nine years would be $6,000 per year. The existing lease for $10,000 per year is a valuable asset; it calls for a premium rent and is called a premium lease. The value of the premium is the present value of the difference, for nine years, between the rent payment called for in the lease ($10,000) and the rent that could be earned if the

12. In essence this was the position taken by the taxpayer in *Hort.* The taxpayer claimed that the right to receive rent of $25,000 per year for the remaining thirteen years of the lease was worth $257,000, that he received a cash payment of $140,000, plus the right to the use of the property for the fourteen years (worth $96,000), so he gave up $257,000 and received a total of only $236,000 and was entitled to deduct the difference of $21,000. To this, the Court of Appeals (112 F.2d 167 (2d Cir. 1940)) responded by citing its earlier decision in Warren Service Corp. v. Commissioner, 110 F.2d 723 (1940), in which it had said that the taxpayer's claimed loss was "merely a diminution of expected income," which produces "no loss of property in the income-tax sense." 110 F.2d at 724. This may dispose of the taxpayer's claim to a loss deduction but does not resolve the question of how the receipt of the $140,000 should be treated. Apart from the defect in the taxpayer's position noted by the Court of Appeals in *Hort,* it is not the value of the property sold but rather its *basis* that determines the amount of a gain or loss. See §1001(a).

property were rented at market rates ($6,000). That difference on our facts is $4,000 per year. The present value of $4,000 per year for nine years, discounted at 10 percent, is approximately $23,000. Thus, *L*'s wealth includes the land, independent of the lease, worth $60,000,[13] plus the premium value of the lease, worth $23,000, or a total of $83,000. Suppose that *L* dies and leaves the land, subject to the lease, to her son, *S*. The property, with the lease, is worth $83,000. At the end of the remaining nine-year term of the lease it will be worth only $60,000 (all other things equal). The premium lease is a wasting asset. A forceful argument can therefore be made that *S* should treat the premium value of the lease as a separate asset with a basis of $23,000, to be taken into account in determining gain or loss on disposition, or through a deduction for amortization if *S* retains the property and collects the annual rent. But see Schubert v. Commissioner, 286 F.2d 573, 580 (4th Cir. 1961), cert. denied, 366 U.S. 960 (1961) (discussing a conflict in other circuits and denying a deduction for failure of proof of premium). The position of a purchaser of property subject to a premium lease is different. See World Publishing Co. v. Commissioner, 299 F.2d 614 (8th Cir. 1962), where the taxpayer bought property subject to a lease with twenty-eight years remaining and a building constructed by the lessee, with a useful life less than twenty-eight years and a value of $300,000. The taxpayer's purchase price was $700,000, and there was testimony that the land was worth $400,000. The court allowed depreciation on the building, with a basis of $300,000. The court commented sympathetically on the alternative possibility, not urged by the taxpayer, that a deduction for the premium value of the lease should be allowed. In any event, in *Hort* it seems unlikely that the lease was a premium lease at the time the property was inherited by the taxpayer.

5. *Leases as capital assets of lessees.* We now turn our attention from the lessor with an advantageous (premium) lease to the lessee with an advantageous (premium) lease.

(a) Suppose *T* is the tenant under a lease calling for annual rental payments of $10,000 and having a remaining term of ten years and that *T* is able to sell the leasehold interest to a third person for $25,000. Is the $25,000 capital gain? The answer is yes, regardless whether the property has been used for personal purposes and is therefore covered by §1221 or has been used in the taxpayer's business and thus is §1231 property. See Rev. Rul. 72-85, 1972-1 C.B. 234. How can this result be

13. The $60,000 can be divided into two segments, one consisting of the right to $6,000 per year for nine years (worth $34,554), and the other consisting of the right to $60,000 at the end of nine years (worth $25,446). Adding to this the $23,000 (approximate) present value of the right to the $4,000 premium for nine years, we arrive at the total value of $83,000.

reconciled with *Hort*? What if *T* had sold the next three years of the remaining ten years of use of the leasehold for $10,000?

(b) Suppose *T* pays $60,000 in advance for the use of the land for ten years and one year later sells the leasehold interest for $75,000. What is the amount of gain? Is it capital gain? What if the leasehold had been sold for $40,000? Does the result depend on whether the property was used in *T*'s business? Rev. Rul. 72-85, supra, states that a tenant's leasehold interest in land is "real property."

6. *The relevance of §61(a).* The reliance in the *Hort* opinion on the fact that §61(a)(5) "expressly characterizes [rental payments] as gross income" reflects a common misunderstanding about capital gain and the meaning of gross income. Section 61(a) defines gross income. Capital gain is part of gross income; §61(a)(3) expressly includes in gross income "gains derived from dealings in property." Section 61(a) provides no guidance in distinguishing between capital gain and ordinary income.

7. *The "substitute for ordinary income" theory.* The suggestion in the *Hort* opinion that an amount can be characterized as ordinary income because it is a "substitute for" ordinary income such as rental payments is also misguided. If Mr. Hort had sold his entire interest in the land, the amount he received would be a substitute for the rents he otherwise would have received in perpetuity. A fundamental principle of economics is that the value of an asset is equal to the present discounted value of all the expected net receipts from that asset over its life.

What, then, is the rule of the *Hort* case?

8. *Payment for a temporary taking.* In Commissioner v. Gillette Motor Transport, 364 U.S. 130 (1960), the taxpayer claimed that compensation received for the temporary requisition of its facilities by the government during World War II was taxable as capital gain. The Court held that it was not (364 U.S., at 135):

> While a capital asset is defined in [§1221] as "property held by the taxpayer," it is evident that not everything which can be called property in the ordinary sense and which is outside the statutory exclusions qualifies as a capital asset. . . .
>
> In the present case, respondent's right to use its transportation facilities was held to be a valuable property right compensable under the requirements of the Fifth Amendment. However, that right was not a capital asset within the meaning of [§§1221 and 1231]. To be sure respondent's facilities were themselves property embraceable as capital assets under [§1231]. Had the Government taken a fee in those facilities, or damaged them physically beyond the ordinary wear and tear incident to normal use, the resulting compensation would no doubt have been treated as gain from the involuntary conversion of capital assets. . . . But here the Government took only the right to determine the use to which those facilities were to be put.
>
> That right is not something in which respondent had any investment, separate and apart from its investment in the physical assets themselves.

> Respondent suggests no method by which a cost basis could be assigned to the right; yet it is necessary, in determining the amount of gain realized for purposes of [§1222], to deduct the basis of the property sold, exchanged, or involuntarily converted from the amount received. [§1001(a).] Further, the right is manifestly not of the type which gives rise to the hardship of the realization in one year of an advance in value over cost built up in several years, which is what Congress sought to ameliorate by the capital-gains provisions. . . . In short, the right to use is not a capital asset, but is simply an incident of the underlying physical property, the recompense for which is commonly regarded as rent.

With the first two sentences in the above extract, compare Regs. §1.1221-1(a): "The term 'capital assets' includes all classes of property not specifically excluded by section 1221."

2. Sale of Interest in a Trust

McALLISTER v. COMMISSIONER

157 F.2d 235 (2d Cir. 1946), cert. denied,
330 U.S. 826 (1947), acq.

Before SWAN, CLARK, and FRANK, Circuit Judges.

CLARK, Circuit Judge. This petition for review presents the question whether the sum of $55,000 received by petitioner on "transfer" or "surrender" of her life interest in a trust to the remainderman constitutes gross income under [§61(a)], or receipts from the sale of capital assets as defined in [§1221]. . . . Petitioner contends that the life estate was a capital asset, the transfer of which resulted in a deductible capital loss, leaving her with no taxable income for the year. A majority of the Tax Court agreed with the Commissioner that the receipt in question was merely an advance payment of income. . . .

The will of Richard McAllister established a trust fund of $100,000, the income of which was to be paid to his son John McAllister for life and, on the latter's death without children, to John's wife, the petitioner herein. On her death, the trust was to terminate, the residue going to the testator's wife and his son Richard. The testator died in 1926, his widow in 1935, and John in 1937. Except for stock in the R. McAllister corporation, not immediately salable at a fair price, John left assets insufficient to meet his debts; and in order to obtain immediate funds and to terminate extended family litigation according to an agreed plan, petitioner brought suit in the Court of Chancery of New Jersey to end the trust. The parties then agreed upon, and the court in its final decree ordered, a settlement by which the remainderman Richard, in addition to taking over the stock for $50,000, was to pay petitioner $55,000, with accumulated income and interest to the date of payment, in consideration of her release of all interest in the trust and consent to its termination and cancellation. For the year 1940, she reported a capital loss on the transaction of $8,790.20, the difference between the amount received and the value of the estate computed under [Regs. §1.1014-5].[14]

The issue, as stated by the Tax Court and presented by the parties, reduces itself to the question whether the case is within the rule of Blair v. Commissioner [supra page 762], or that of Hort v. Commissioner, [supra page 867]. In the *Blair* case, the life beneficiary of a trust assigned to his children specified sums to be paid each year for the duration of the estate. The Supreme Court held that each transfer was the assignment of a property right in the trust and that, since the tax liability attached to ownership of the property, the assignee, and not the assignor, was liable for the income taxes in the years in question. The continued authority of the case was recognized in Helvering v. Horst [supra page 764], although a majority of the Court thought it not applicable on the facts, and in Harrison v. Schaffner, 312 U.S. 579 (1941), where the Court very properly distinguished it from the situation where an assignor transferred a portion of his income for a single year. We think that its reasoning and conclusion support the taxpayer's position here. . . .

Petitioner's right to income for life from the trust estate was a right in the estate itself. Had she held a fee interest, the assignment would unquestionably have been regarded as the transfer of a capital asset; we see no reason why a different result should follow the transfer of the lesser, but still substantial, life interest. As the Court pointed out in the *Blair* case, the life tenant was entitled to enforce the trust, to enjoin a breach of trust, and to obtain redress in case of breach. The proceedings in the state chancery court completely divested her of these rights and of any possible control over the property. The case is therefore distinguishable from that of Hort v. Commissioner, supra, where a landlord for a consideration cancelled a lease for a term of years, having still some nine years to run. There the taxpayer surrendered his contractual right to the future yearly payments in return for an immediate payment of a lump sum. The statute expressly taxed income derived from rent [§61(a)(5)]; and the consideration received was held a substitute for the rent as it fell due. It was therefore taxed as income.

What we regard as the precise question here presented has been determined in the taxpayer's favor on the authority of the *Blair* case by the Eighth Circuit in Bell's Estate v. Commissioner, 8 Cir., 137 F.2d 454, reversing 46 B.T.A. 484. . . .

The Tax Court and the government have attempted to distinguish both the *Bell* and the *Blair* cases on grounds which seem to us to lack

14. [See infra page 877, Note 2. The court apparently uses "value of the estate" to mean "basis." — Eds.]

either substance or reality. The principal ground seems to be the form the transaction assumed between the parties. Thus the Court says that petitioner received the payment for "surrendering" her rights to income payments, and "she did not assign her interest in the trust, as did petitioners in the *Bell* case." But what is this more than a distinction in words? Both were cases where at the conclusion of the transaction the remaindermen had the entire estate and the life tenants had a substantial sum of money. . . .

Setting the bounds to the area of tax incidence involves the drawing of lines which may often be of an arbitrary nature. But they should not be more unreal than the circumstances necessitate. Here the line of demarcation between the *Blair* and the *Hort* principles is obviously one of some difficulty to define explicitly or to establish in borderline cases. Doubtless all would agree that there is some distinction between selling a life estate in property and anticipating income for a few years in advance. . . . The distinction seems logically and practically to turn upon anticipation of income payments over a reasonably short period of time and an out-and-out transfer of a substantial and durable property interest, such as a life estate at least is. See 57 Harv. L. Rev. 382; 54 Harv. L. Rev. 1405; 50 Yale L.J. 512, 515. Where the line should be finally placed we need not try to anticipate here. But we are clear that distinctions attempted on the basis of the various legal names given a transaction, rather than on its actual results between the parties, do not afford a sound basis for its delimitation. More rationally, to accept the respondent's contention we ought frankly to consider the *Blair* case as overruled, 50 Yale L.J. 512, 518, a position which, as we have seen, the Supreme Court itself has declined to take.

The parties are in conflict as to the valuation of the life estate; and we are returning the case to the Tax Court for computation, without, of course, assuming that there will necessarily be some tax.

Reversed and remanded.

Frank, Circuit Judge (dissenting). . . .

We must . . . ascertain the intention of Congress expressed in those provisions — especially [§1221] — in the light of the language it employed and the policy there embodied. . . .

My colleagues avoid a direct discussion of that problem. Instead, they rely on Blair v. Commissioner, which they hold to be controlling. But the court in the *Blair* case had no occasion to, and did not, consider [§1221]. . . . The only question was whether thereafter the donor, notwithstanding the gift, should be regarded, under [§61(a)], as the recipient annually of that part of the income which was the subject of the gift and, consequently, should be taxed each year thereon. In other words, no capital gain or loss was involved, and the one issue was whether the donor or donee was annually taxable.

The policy of the capital gains provisions is not in doubt: Congress believed that the exaction of income tax on the usual basis on gains resulting from dispositions of capital investments would undesirably deter such dispositions. To put it differently, Congress made an exception to [§61(a)], in order to give an incentive to the making of such transfers. Having regard to that purpose, the courts have been cautious in interpreting the clauses creating that exception. They have refused to regard as "capital" transactions for that purpose divers sorts of transfers of "property," especially those by which transferors have procured advance payments of future income.

Those cases and Hort v. Commissioner, seem to me to render it somewhat doubtful whether any transfer of a life estate for a valuable consideration is within [§1221]. The consideration paid for such a transfer is a substitute for future payments which would be taxable as ordinary income, and resembles the advance payment of dividends, interest or salaries. . . .

I think it most unlikely that Congress intended by [§1221] to relieve such a taxpayer of the ordinary tax burdens to supply an incentive for the demolition of such a trust. . . .

NOTES AND QUESTIONS

1. *Treatment of the life tenant.* The court decided two issues in *McAllister:* first, that a life estate is a capital asset falling within the general statutory definition of §1221, and second, that a life tenant has basis in a life estate. In accord with the characterization of a life estate as a capital asset is Allen v. First National Bank & Trust Co., 157 F.2d 592 (5th Cir. 1946), which held *Hort* not applicable because the taxpayer in *Hort* did not sell all his rights in the property he owned.

Recall that under the rule applied in Irwin v. Gavit, supra page 188, if Mrs. McAllister had retained her life estate and collected the income, she would have been taxable on the entire amount received; no part of the basis of the property held in trust would have been allocated to her in this situation. On the other hand, under the *McAllister* decision, when she in fact sold, part of the basis in the property was allocated to her (see infra Note 2) and she reported a loss. She could then have taken the $55,000 and used it to buy an annuity for her life. Disregarding the costs of servicing the annuity, the payments she should receive under it should be about the same as the payments she would have received from the life estate. But part of the payments received under the annuity would be excluded from income. Meanwhile, the purchaser of the life estate would be entitled to amortize, over Mrs. McAllister's life, the cost of buying it from her,[15] even if the purchaser was also the holder of

15. If the life estate continued past the expected life, the purchaser's entire basis would

the remainder interest. See Bell v. Harrison, 212 F.2d 253 (7th Cir. 1954), and Rev. Rul 62-132, 1962-2 C.B. 73 (acquiescence in Bell v. Harrison, limited to transactions that are bona fide and not for tax avoidance purposes). Even though part of the basis for the property had been used by the life tenant, when the life estate ultimately terminated, the remainder holder's basis would be the entire basis for the property, so the effect is a double use of part of the property's basis. This set of rules gave rise to tax avoidance opportunities that were ended in 1969 with the adoption of §1001(e), which provides that where a life tenant sells the life interest, unless the remainder holder sells at the same time, the basis for the life interest is zero. Thus, under present law, Mrs. McAllister would have recognized a gain of $55,000. It would still have been capital gain.

2. *Uniform basis.* At the time of *McAllister,* and under present law if the life tenant and the remainder holder sell at the same time, to allocate the total basis in the property between the life interest and the remainder interest, one starts with the adjusted basis for the property (the uniform basis) and allocates that basis between the two interests in accordance with the relative actuarial values of each at the time of sale. Thus, the basis of the life estate declines as the life expectancy of the life tenant declines and the basis of the remainder rises correspondingly. See Regs. §1.1014-5. The same rule determines the basis for the remainder where the remainder holder sells his or her interest, regardless of whether the life tenant sells at the same time.

3. *The consequences of accelerating income.* Under present law, if a life tenant sells a life interest in a trust and the remainder holder does not sell, the entire amount of the proceeds is taxable, at the capital-gain rate. Suppose that a life tenant sells because of a concern for the nature of the investment held by the trust, and uses the proceeds to buy a life annuity. If the rate of return of the trust and of the company selling the annuity are comparable, it would take the full amount of the proceeds of the sale of the life interest to buy an annuity with annual income equal to the income of the trust. But the proceeds of the sale of the trust will be reduced by the tax on those proceeds, so the life tenant who changes the source of his or her income stream will experience a reduction in income, both before and after tax.[16] Does this outcome argue for allowing the exchange of a life interest for an annuity to be accomplished tax free under a provision like §1031 (see supra page 304)? If not, does it argue for a favorable rate of taxation of the proceeds of the sale of the life interest?

---

be exhausted, and the full amounts received would be taxable. If, on the other hand, the life estate terminated before the entire cost had been recovered through amortization deductions, the purchaser would be entitled to a deduction for the remaining basis.

16. This effect will be mitigated but not eliminated by the fact that the annuity will have a basis equal to its cost and, consequently, part of each annuity payment will be nontaxable (see supra page 179).

4. *Sale of a payment from the life estate.* Suppose that in return for a present payment of $30,000, Mrs. McAllister had "sold" the right to the next $30,000 worth of income from the trust plus an increment equal to 5 percent of the unrecovered balance. Assuming that §1001(e) applies, her gain would be $30,000. Should that be treated as ordinary income or capital gain? Reserve a decision on this question until you have read the next case.

3. Oil Payments

COMMISSIONER v. P. G. LAKE, INC.

356 U.S. 260 (1958)

Mr. Justice DOUGLAS delivered the opinion of the Court.

We have here, consolidated for arguments, five cases involving an identical question of law. . . . The cases are here on petitions for certiorari which we granted because of the public importance of the question presented. 353 U.S. 982.

The facts of the *Lake* case are closely similar to those in the *Wrather* and *O'Connor* cases. Lake is a corporation engaged in the business of producing oil and gas. It has a seven-eighths working interest[17] in two commercial oil and gas leases. In 1950 it was indebted to its president in the sum of $600,000 and in consideration of his cancellation of the debt assigned him an oil payment right in the amount of $600,000, plus an amount equal to interest at 3 percent a year on the unpaid balance remaining from month to month, payable out of 25 percent of the oil attributable to the taxpayer's working interest in the two leases. At the time of the assignment it could have been estimated with reasonable accuracy that the assigned oil payment right would pay out in three or more years. It did in fact pay out in a little over three years.

In its 1950 tax returns Lake reported the oil payment assignment as a sale of property producing a profit of $600,000 and taxable as a long-term capital gain.[18] . . . The Commissioner determined a deficiency,

17. An oil and gas lease ordinarily conveys the entire mineral interest less any royalty interest retained by the lessor. The owner of the lease [that is, the lessee] is said to own "the working interest" because he has the right to develop and produce the minerals.

In Anderson v. Helvering, 310 U.S. 404, we described an oil payment as "the right to a specific sum of money, payable out of a specified percentage of the oil, or the proceeds received from the sale of such oil, if, as and when produced." Id., at 410. A royalty interest is "a right to receive a specified percentage of all oil and gas produced" but, unlike the oil payment, is not limited to a specified sum of money. The royalty interest lasts during the entire term of the lease. Id., at 409.

18. [It would seem that the proceeds of the sale of the oil payment would be the amount of debt discharged (see supra, pages 232-237) rather than the amount to be received by the assignee. For purposes of analysis, one can assume that the taxpayer sold the oil payment for $600,000 cash. The taxpayer's treatment of the entire $600,000 as

ruling that the purchase price (less deductions not material here) was taxable as ordinary income, subject to depletion.

[The Court here describes the facts in the companion cases, all of which present the same issue raised by the *P. G. Lake* facts.]

[A]s to whether the proceeds were taxable as long term capital gains . . . or as ordinary income subject to depletion, [t]he Court of Appeals started from the premise, laid down in Texas decisions, . . . that oil payments are interests in land. We too proceed on that basis; and yet we conclude that the consideration received for these oil payment rights (and the sulphur payment right) was taxable as ordinary income, subject to depletion.

The purpose of [the capital gains provisions] was "to relieve the taxpayer from . . . excessive tax burdens on gains resulting from a conversion of capital investments, and to remove the deterrent effect of those burdens on such conversions." See Burnet v. Harmel, 287 U.S. 103, 106. And this exception has always been narrowly construed so as to protect the revenue against artful devices. See Corn Products Refining Co. v. Commissioner [supra page 854].

We do not see here any conversion of a capital investment. The lump sum consideration seems essentially a substitute for what would otherwise be received at a future time as ordinary income. The pay-out of these particular assigned oil payment rights could be ascertained with considerable accuracy. Such are the stipulations, findings, or clear inferences. In the *O'Connor* case, the pay-out of the assigned oil payment right was so assured that the purchaser obtained a $9,990,350 purchase money loan at 3 1/2 percent interest without any security other than a deed of trust of the $10,000,000 oil payment right, he receiving 4 percent from the taxpayer. Only a fraction of the oil . . . rights were transferred, the balance being retained.[19] . . . [C]ash was received which

---

capital gain raises the question of why there was no reduction for the adjusted basis of the property. Presumably the answer is that the basis had started out small because of the deduction of intangible drilling costs, and what there was had been exhausted by depletion allowances. — Eds.]

19. Until 1946 the Commissioner agreed with the contention of the taxpayers in these cases that the assignment of an oil payment right was productive of a long-term capital gain. In 1946 he changed his mind and ruled that "consideration (not pledged for development) received for the assignment of a short-lived in-oil payment carved out of any type of depletable interest in oil and gas in place (including a larger in-oil payment right) is ordinary income subject to the depletion allowance in the assignor's hands." G.C.M. 24849, 1946-1 C.B. 66, 69. This ruling was made applicable "only to such assignments made on or after April 1, 1946," I.T. 3895, 1948-1 C.B. 39. In 1950 a further ruling was made that represents the present view of the Commissioner. I.T. 4003, 1950-1 C.B. 10,11, reads in relevant part as follows:

> After careful study and considerable experience with the application of G.C.M. 24849, supra, it is now concluded that there is no legal or practical basis for distinguishing between short-lived and long-lived in-oil payment rights. It is, therefore, the present position of the Bureau that the assignment of any in-oil payment right (not pledged for development), which extends over a period less than the life

was equal to the amount of the income to accrue during the term of the assignment, the assignee being compensated by interest on his advance. The substance of what was assigned was the right to receive future income. The substance of what was received was the present value of income which the recipient would otherwise obtain in the future. In short, consideration was paid for the right to receive future income, not for an increase in the value of the income-producing property.

These arrangements seem to us transparent devices. Their forms do not control. Their essence is determined not by subtleties of draftsmanship but by their total effect. See Helvering v. Clifford, 309 U.S. 331; Harrison v. Schaffner, 312 U.S. 579. We have held that if one, entitled to receive at a future date interest on a bond or compensation for services, makes a grant of it by anticipatory assignment, he realizes taxable income as if he had collected the interest or received the salary and then paid it over. That is the teaching of Helvering v. Horst [supra page 764] and Harrison v. Schaffner, supra; and it is applicable here. As we stated in Helvering v. Horst, [supra page 764], "The taxpayer has equally enjoyed the fruits of his labor or investment and obtained the satisfaction of his desires whether he collects and uses the income to procure those satisfactions, or whether he disposes of his right to collect it as the means of procuring them." There the taxpayer detached interest coupons from negotiable bonds and presented them as a gift to his son. The interest when paid was held taxable to the father. Here, even more clearly than there, the taxpayer is converting future income into present income. . . .

NOTES AND QUESTIONS

1. *Analysis.* (a) Note that the Court cites *Horst* (supra page 764), in which a father gave bond coupons to his son, and not *Hort* (supra page

---

of the depletable property interest from which it is carved, is essentially the assignment of expected income from such property interest. Therefore, the assignment for a consideration of any such in-oil payment right results in the receipt of ordinary income by the assignor which is taxable to him when received or accrued, depending upon the method of accounting employed by him. Where the assignment of the in-oil payment right is donative, the transaction is considered as an assignment of future income which is taxable to the donor at such time as the income from the assigned payment right arises.

Notwithstanding the foregoing, G.C.M. 24849, supra, and I.T. 3935 supra, do not apply where the assigned in-oil payment right constitutes the entire depletable interest of the assignor in the property or a fraction extending over the entire life of the property.

The pre-1946 administrative practice was not reflected in any published ruling or regulation. It therefore will not be presumed to have been known to Congress and incorporated into the law by reenactment. . . . Moreover, prior administrative practice is always subject to change "through exercise by the administrative agency of its continuing rule-making power." See Helvering v. Reynolds, 313 U.S. 428, 432.

867). Which of the two cases seems to you to be more relevant? In its brief (at page 30), the government cited *Hort* (and other cases) for the proposition that "in any case where the lump sum consideration is essentially a substitute for what would otherwise be received in the future as ordinary income, the lump sum consideration is taxable as ordinary income even though, in a sense, a transfer of 'property' is involved." Does this statement go too far? Earlier in its brief (page 25) the government describes *Horst* as holding that even though the coupons given to the son were "property," they were a type of property that "amounted only to a right to receive future income from the income-producing property (the bond)," that the label attached by the state law of property should not be controlling for tax purposes, and that the state-law characterization of oil payments as "interests in land" should be irrelevant for tax purposes. Is this argument sound? Is it dispositive?

(b) Suppose a taxpayer owns a farm whose boundaries are formed in part by streams and ridges and whose size is about 1,000 acres. The taxpayer sells a rectangular portion of the central part of the farm, consisting of 600 acres. Plainly, the taxpayer has sold a capital asset, with the consequence that any gain is treated as capital gain and the taxpayer is entitled to offset against the proceeds of the sale some portion of his or her total basis in the property. (See supra page 170.) If the taxpayer's oil interest in *P. G. Lake* had been valued at $1 million and the taxpayer had sold an undivided 60 percent share in that oil interest for $600,000, the transaction would no doubt have been treated as a sale of a capital asset. How do these transactions differ from the actual transaction in the case?

(c) Suppose a taxpayer owns the right to take half of the water flowing along a river and sells this right for the next ten years for a lump sum payment of $60,000. Has the taxpayer sold a capital asset? How does this case differ from *P. G. Lake?*

(d) Suppose a taxpayer pays $60,000 for the right to use as lessee certain business premises for ten years and then subleases those premises for six years for $40,000 paid in advance. What are the tax consequences? How does this case differ from *P. G. Lake?*

2. *Advantages to taxpayers from* P. G. Lake *and the enactment of §636.* In certain situations, the *P. G. Lake* decision proved advantageous to taxpayers. For example, if a taxpayer with a producing mineral property had a net loss from other transactions or was restricted in the amount of percentage depletion it could claim by reason of the 50 percent of taxable income limit (§613), it could boost current depletable income by carving out and selling an oil payment.

Another taxpayer ploy was called the *ABC* transaction. *A*, the owner of a mineral property, would sell *B* the entire interest less a carved-out, retained mineral payment, which *A* would then sell to *C*. *A* would have capital gain, having disposed of all that he or she owned. The amounts received by *C* were treated as *C*'s income, but *C* was entitled to offset the receipts with an amortization deduction. The payments to *C* were not treated as *B*'s income and, to that extent, *B* was able, in effect, to acquire the property with before-tax dollars.

Under §636, enacted in 1969, these taxpayer opportunities are eliminated by treating the transactions in most instances as a financing device, with the buyer of the oil payment treated as a lender. Thus, in the *ABC* transaction, *B* is treated as the purchaser of both the working interest and the oil payment, with the latter used as security for a nonrecourse loan from *C*.

4. Bootstrap Sale to Charity

In the next case, the narrow legal issue is one of capital gain versus ordinary income, but the broader issue is substance versus form or, somewhat less broadly, when is a transaction that purports to be a sale not a sale for tax purposes? The case is important, and frequently cited, for its treatment of the broader issue and for that reason remains worthy of study despite the diminished importance of the special tax status of capital gain.

COMMISSIONER v. BROWN

380 U.S. 563 (1965)

Mr. Justice White delivered the opinion of the Court.

In 1950, when Congress addressed itself to the problem of the direct or indirect acquisition and operation of going businesses by charities or other tax-exempt entities, it was recognized that in many of the typical sale and leaseback transactions, the exempt organization was trading on and perhaps selling part of its exemption. . . . For this and other reasons the Internal Revenue Code was accordingly amended in several respects, of principal importance for our purposes by taxing as "unrelated business income" the profits earned by a charity in the operation of a business, as well as the income from long-term leases of the business.[20] The short-term lease, however, of five years or less, was not affected and this fact has moulded many of the transactions in this field since that time, including the one involved in this case.

The Commissioner, however, in 1954, announced that when an exempt organization purchased a business and leased it for five years to another corporation, not investing its own funds but paying off the purchase price with rental income, the purchasing organization was in

20. [The Revenue Act of 1950 added what are now §§501(b) and 511 to 515. The Tax Reform Act of 1969 further amended these sections. See Note 4, infra page 894. — Eds.]

danger of losing its exemption; that in any event the rental income would be taxable income; that the charity might be unreasonably accumulating income;[21] and finally, and most important for this case, that the payments received by the seller would not be entitled to capital gains treatment. Rev. Rul. 54-420, 1954-2 C.B. 128.[22] . . . The basic facts are undisputed. Clay Brown, members of his family and three other persons owned substantially all of the stock in Clay Brown & Company, with sawmills and lumber interests near Fortuna, California. Clay Brown, the president of the company and spokesman for the group, was approached by a representative of California Institute for Cancer Research in 1952, and after considerable negotiation the stockholders agreed to sell their stock to the Institute for $1,300,000, payable $5,000 down from the assets of the company and the balance within 10 years from the earnings of the company's assets. It was provided that simultaneously with the transfer of the stock, the Institute would liquidate the company and lease its assets for five years to a new corporation, Fortuna Sawmills, Inc., formed and wholly owned by the attorneys for the sellers.[23] Fortuna would pay to the Institute 80% of its operating profit without allowance for depreciation or taxes, and 90% of such payments would be paid over by the Institute to the selling stockholders to apply on the $1,300,000 note. This note was noninterest bearing, the institute had no obligation to pay it except from the rental income and it was secured by mortgages and assignments of the assets transferred or leased to Fortuna. If the payments on the note failed to total $250,000 over any two consecutive years, the sellers could declare the entire balance of the note due and payable. The sellers were neither stockholders nor directors of Fortuna but it was provided that Clay Brown was to have a management contract with Fortuna at an annual salary and the right to name any successor manager if he himself resigned.[24]

The transaction was closed on February 4, 1953. Fortuna immediately took over operations of the business under its lease, on the same premises and with practically the same personnel which had been employed by Clay Brown & Company. Effective October 31, 1954, Clay Brown resigned as general manager of Fortuna and waived his right to name his successor. In 1957, because of a rapidly declining lumber market, Fortuna suffered severe reverses and its operations were terminated.

21. [Section 504, dealing with accumulations, was repealed in 1969, but a tougher rule relating only to private foundations was added to the Code. See §4942. — Eds.]

22. [This rule was declared obsolete by Rev. Rul 77-278, 1977-2 C.B. 485. — Eds.]

23. The net current assets subject to liabilities were sold by the Institute to Fortuna for a promissory note which was assigned to sellers. The lease covered the remaining assets of Clay Brown & Company. Fortuna was capitalized at $25,000, its capital being paid in by its stockholders from their own funds.

24. Clay Brown's personal liability for some of the indebtedness of Clay Brown & Company, assumed by Fortuna, was continued. He also personally guaranteed some additional indebtedness incurred by Fortuna.

Respondent sellers did not repossess the properties under their mortgages but agreed they should be sold by the Institute with the latter retaining 10% of the proceeds. Accordingly, the property was sold by the Institute for $300,000. The payments on the note from rentals and from the sale of the properties totaled $936,131.85. Respondents returned the payments received from rentals as the gain from the sale of capital assets.[25] The Commissioner, however, asserted the payments were taxable as ordinary income and were not capital gain. . . .

In the Tax Court, the Commissioner asserted that the transaction was a sham and that in any event respondents retained such an economic interest in and control over the property sold that the transaction could not be treated as a sale resulting in a long-term capital gain. A divided Tax Court, 37 T.C. 461, found that there had been considerable good-faith bargaining at arm's length between the Brown family and the Institute, that the price agreed upon was within a reasonable range in the light of the earnings history of the corporation and the adjusted net worth of its assets, that the primary motivation for the Institute was the prospect of ending up with the assets of the business free and clear after the purchase price had been fully paid, which would then permit the Institute to convert the property and the money for use in cancer research, and that there had been a real change of economic benefit in the transaction.[26] . . .

Having abandoned in the Court of Appeals the argument that this transaction was a sham, the Commissioner now admits that there was real substance in what occurred between the Institute and the Brown family. . . .

Whatever substance the transaction might have had, however, the Commissioner claims that it did not have the substance of a sale within the meaning of §1222(3). His argument is that since the Institute invested nothing, assumed no independent liability for the purchase price and promised only to pay over a percentage of the earnings of the company, the entire risk of the transaction remained on the sellers. . . .

To say that there is no sale because there is no risk-shifting and that there is no risk-shifting because the price to be paid is payable only from the income produced by the business sold, is very little different from saying that because business earnings are usually taxable as ordinary income, they are subject to the same tax when paid over as the purchase price of property. This argument has rationality but it places an unwarranted construction on the term "sale," is contrary to the policy

25. [Currently, the transaction would result in original issue discount under §1272, and, in the absence of §1272, part of the payments would be treated as interest income under §483. — Eds.]

26. The Tax Court found nothing to indicate that the arrangement between the stockholders and the Institute contemplated the Brown family's being free at any time to take back and operate the business.

of the capital gains provisions of the Internal Revenue Code, and has no support in the cases. We reject it.

"Capital gain" and "capital asset" are creatures of the tax law and the Court has been inclined to give these terms a narrow, rather than a broad, construction. Corn Products Co. v. Commissioner [supra page 854]. A "sale," however, is a common event in the non-tax world; and since it is used in the Code without limiting definition and without legislative history indicating a contrary result, its common and ordinary meaning should at least be persuasive of its meaning as used in the Internal Revenue Code. . . .

As of January 31, 1953, the adjusted net worth of Clay Brown & Company as revealed by its books was $619,457.63. This figure included accumulated earnings of $448,471.63, paid in surplus, capital stock and notes payable to the Brown family. The appraised value as of that date, however, relied upon by the Institute and the sellers, was $1,064,877, without figuring interest on deferred balances. Under a deferred payment plan with a 6% interest figure, the sale value was placed at $1,301,989. The Tax Court found the sale price agreed upon was arrived at in an arm's-length transaction, was the result of real negotiating and was "within a reasonable range in light of the earnings history of the corporation and the adjusted net worth of the corporate assets." 37 T.C. 461, 486.

Obviously, on these facts, there had been an appreciation in value accruing over a period of years . . . and an "increase in the value of the income-producing property." . . . This increase taxpayers were entitled to realize at capital gains rates on a cash sale of their stock; and likewise if they sold on a deferred payment plan taking an installment note and a mortgage as security. Further, if the down payment was less than 30% (the 1954 Code requires no down payment at all) and the transactions otherwise satisfied [§453] the gain itself could be reported on the installment basis.

In the actual transaction, the stock was transferred for a price payable on the installment basis but payable from the earnings of the company. Eventually $936,131.85 was realized by respondents. This transaction, we think, is a sale, and so treating it is wholly consistent with the purposes of the Code to allow capital gains treatment for realization upon the enhanced value of a capital asset.

The Commissioner, however, embellishes his risk-shifting argument. Purporting to probe the economic realities of the transaction, he reasons that if the seller continues to bear all the risk and the buyer none, the seller must be collecting a price for his risk-bearing in the form of an interest in future earnings over and above what would be a fair market value of the property. Since the seller bears the risk, the so-called purchase price *must* be excessive and *must* be simply a device to collect future earnings at capital gains rates. . . .

[The argument] denies what the tax court expressly found — that the price paid was within reasonable limits based on the earnings and net worth of the company; and there is evidence in the record to support this finding. . . .

[T]he Commissioner ignores as well the fact that if the rents payable by Fortuna were deductible by it and not taxable to the Institute, the Institute could pay off the purchase price at a considerably faster rate than the ordinary corporate buyer subject to income taxes, a matter of considerable importance to a seller who wants the balance of his purchase price paid as rapidly as he can get it. . . .

Furthermore, risk-shifting of the kind insisted on by the Commissioner has not heretofore been considered an essential ingredient of a sale for tax purposes. In Le Tulle v. Scofield, 308 U.S. 415, one corporation transferred properties to another for cash and bonds secured by the properties transferred. The Court held that there was "a sale or exchange upon which gain or loss must be reckoned in accordance with the provisions of the revenue act dealing with the recognition of gain or loss upon a sale or exchange," id., at 421, since the seller retained only a creditor's interest rather than a proprietary one. "[T]hat the bonds were secured solely by the assets transferred and that, upon default, the bondholder would retake only the property sold, [did not change] his status from that of a creditor to one having a proprietary stake." Ibid. . . . To require a sale for tax purposes to be to a financially responsible buyer who undertakes to pay the purchase price from sources other than the earnings of the assets sold or to make a substantial down payment seems to us at odds with the commercial practice and common understanding of what constitutes a sale. The term "sale" is used a great many times in the Internal Revenue Code and a wide variety of tax results hinge on the occurrence of a "sale." To accept the Commissioner's definition of sale would have wide ramifications which we are not prepared to visit upon taxpayers, absent congressional guidance in this direction.

The Commissioner relies heavily upon the cases involving a transfer of mineral interests, the transferor receiving a bonus and retaining a royalty or other interest in the mineral production. . . . Thomas v. Perkins [301 U.S. 655] is deemed particularly pertinent. There a leasehold interest was transferred for a sum certain payable in oil as produced, and it was held that the amounts paid to the transferor were not includable in the income of the transferee but were income of the transferor. We do not, however, deem either Thomas v. Perkins or the other cases controlling.

First, "Congress . . . has recognized the peculiar character of the business of extracting natural resources." . . .

Second, Thomas v. Perkins does not have unlimited sweep. The Court in Anderson v. Helvering, [310 U.S. 404], pointed out that it was still possible for the owner of a working interest to divest himself finally and completely of his mineral interest by effecting a sale. In that case the owner of royalty interest, fee interest and deferred oil payments contracted to convey them for $160,000 payable $50,000 down and the balance from one-half the proceeds which might be derived from the oil and gas produced and from the sale of the fee title to any of the lands conveyed. The Court refused to extend Thomas v. Perkins beyond the oil payment transaction involved in that case.[27] . . .

There is another reason for us not to disturb the ruling of the Tax Court and the Court of Appeals. In 1963, the Treasury Department, in the course of hearings before the Congress, noted the availability of capital gains treatment on the sale of capital assets even though the seller retained an interest in the income produced by the assets. The Department proposed a change in the law which would have taxed as ordinary income the payments on the sale of a capital asset which were deferred over more than five years and were contingent on future income. Payments, though contingent on income, required to be made within five years would not have lost capital gains status nor would payments not contingent on income even though accompanied by payments which were. . . .[28]

27. Respondents place considerable reliance on the rule applicable where patents are sold or assigned, the seller or assignor reserving an income interest. In Rev. Rul. 58-353, 1958-2 C.B. 408, the Service announced its acquiescence in various Tax Court cases holding that the consideration received by the owner of a patent for the assignment of a patent or the granting of an exclusive license to such patent may be treated as the proceeds of a sale of property for income tax purposes, even though the consideration received by the transferor is measured by production, use, or sale of the patented article. The government now says that the Revenue Ruling amounts only to a decision to cease litigating the question, at least temporarily, and that the cases on which the rule is based are wrong in principle and inconsistent with the cases dealing with the taxation of mineral interests. We note, however, that in Rev. Rul. 60-226, 1960-1 C.B. 26, the Service extended the same treatment to the copyright field. Furthermore, the Secretary of the Treasury in 1963 recognized the present law to be that "the sale of a patent by the inventor may be treated as the sale of a capital asset," Hearings before the House Committee on Ways and Means, 88th Cong., 1st Sess., Feb. 6, 7, 8, and 18, 1963, Pt. I (rev.), on the President's 1963 Tax Message, p.150, and the Congress failed to enact the changes in the law which the Department recommended.

These developments in the patent field obviously do not help the position of the Commissioner. Nor does I.R.C. 1954, §1235, which expressly permits specified patent sales to be treated as sales of capital assets entitled to capital gains treatment. We need not, however, decide here whether the extraction and patent cases are irreconcilable or whether, instead, each situation has its own peculiar characteristics justifying discrete treatment under the sale and exchange language of §1222. Whether the patent cases are correct or not, absent §1235, the fact remains that this case involves the transfer of corporate stock which has substantially appreciated in value and a purchase price payable from income which has been held to reflect the fair market value of the assets which the stock represents.

28. It did, however, accept and enact another suggestion made by the Treasury Department. Section 483, which was added to the Code, provided for treating a part of the purchase price as interest in installment sales transactions where no interest was specified. The provision was to apply as well when the payments provided for were

Congress did not adopt the suggested change but it is significant for our purposes that the proposed amendment did not deny the fact or occurrence of a sale but would have taxed as ordinary income those income-contingent payments deferred for more than five years. If a purchaser could pay the purchase price out of earnings within five years, the seller would have capital gain rather than ordinary income. The approach was consistent with allowing appreciated values to be treated as capital gain but with appropriate safeguards against reserving additional rights to future income. In comparison, the Commissioner's position here is a clear case of "overkill" if aimed at preventing the involvement of tax-exempt entities in the purchase and operation of business enterprises. There are more precise approaches to this problem as well as to the question of the possibly excessive price paid by the charity or foundation. And if the Commissioner's approach is intended as a limitation upon the tax treatment of sales generally, it represents a considerable invasion of current capital gains policy, a matter which we think is the business of Congress, not ours.

The problems involved in the purchase of a going business by a tax-exempt organization have been considered and dealt with by the Congress. Likewise, it has given its attention to various kinds of transactions involving the payment of the agreed purchase price for property from the future earnings of the property itself. In both situations it has responded, if at all, with precise provisions of narrow application. We consequently deem it wise to "leave to the Congress the fashioning of a rule which, in any event, must have wide ramifications." American Automobile Association v. United States, [supra page 438, 367 U.S. at 697].

Affirmed.

Mr. Justice HARLAN, concurring.

Were it not for the tax laws, the respondents' transaction with the Institute would make no sense, except as one arising from a charitable impulse. However the tax laws exist as an economic reality in the businessman's world, much like the existence of a competitor. Businessmen plan their affairs around both, and a tax dollar is just as real as one derived from any other source. The Code gives the Institute a tax exemption which makes it capable of taking a greater after-tax return from a business than could a nontax-exempt individual or corporation. Respondents traded a residual interest in their business for a faster payout apparently made possible by the Institute's exemption. The respondents gave something up; they received something substantially

---

indefinite as to their size, as for example "where the payments are in part at least dependent upon future income derived from the property," S. Rep. No. 830, 88th Cong., 2d Sess., p.103. This section would apparently now apply to a transaction such as occurred in this case.

different in return. If words are to have meaning, there was a "sale or exchange." . . .

One may observe preliminarily that the Government's remedy for the so-called "bootstrap" sale — defining sale or exchange so as to require the shifting of some business risks — would accomplish little by way of closing off such sales in the future. It would be neither difficult nor burdensome for future users of the bootstrap technique to arrange for some shift of risks. If such sales are considered a serious abuse, ineffective judicial correctives will only postpone the day when Congress is moved to deal with the problem comprehensively. Furthermore, one may ask why, if the Government does not like the tax consequences of such sales, the proper course is not to attack the exemption rather than to deny the existence of a "real" sale or exchange.

The force underlying the Government's position is that the respondents did clearly retain some risk-bearing interest in the business. Instead of leaping from this premise to the conclusion that there was no sale or exchange, the Government might more profitably have broken the transaction into components and attempted to distinguish between the interest which respondents retained and the interest which they exchanged. The worth of a business depends upon its ability to produce income over time. What respondents gave up was not the entire business, but only their interest in the business' ability to produce income in excess of that which was necessary to pay them off under the terms of the transaction. The value of such a residual interest is a function of the risk element of the business and the amount of income it is capable of producing per year, and will necessarily be substantially less than the value of the total business. Had the Government argued that it was that interest which respondents exchanged, and only to that extent should they have received capital gains treatment, we would perhaps have had a different case. . . .

Mr. Justice GOLDBERG, with whom THE CHIEF JUSTICE and Mr. Justice BLACK join, dissenting. . . .

. . . In essence respondents conveyed their interest in the business to the Institute in return for 72% of the profits of the business and the right to recover the business assets if payments fell behind schedule.

At first glance it might appear odd that the sellers would enter into this transaction, for prior to the sale they had a right to 100% of the corporation's income, but after the sale they had a right to only 72% of that income and would lose the business after 10 years to boot. This transaction, however, afforded the sellers several advantages. The principal advantage sought by the sellers was capital gain, rather than ordinary income, treatment for that share of the business profits which they received. Further, because of the Tax Code's charitable exemption and the lease arrangement with Fortuna,[29] the Institute believed that neither it nor Fortuna would have to pay income tax on the earnings of the business. Thus the sellers would receive free of corporate taxation, and subject only to personal taxation at capital gains rates, 72% of the business earnings until they were paid $1,300,000. Without the sale they would receive only 48% of the business earnings, the rest going to the Government in corporate taxes, and this 48% would be subject to personal taxation at ordinary rates. In effect the Institute sold the respondents the use of its tax exemption, enabling the respondents to collect $1,300,000 from the business more quickly than they otherwise could and to pay taxes on this amount at capital gains rates. In return, the Institute received a nominal amount of the profits while the $1,300,000 was being paid, and it was to receive the whole business after this debt had been paid off. In any realistic sense the Government's grant of a tax exemption was used by the Institute as part of an arrangement that allowed it to buy a business that in fact cost it nothing. I cannot believe that Congress intended such a result. . . .

In dealing with what constitutes a sale for capital gains purposes, this Court has been careful to look through formal legal arrangements to the underlying economic realities. Income produced in the mineral extraction business, which "resemble[s] a manufacturing business carried on by the use of the soil," Burnet v. Harmel, [287 U.S. 103], at 107, is taxed to the person who retains an economic interest in the oil. Thus, while an outright sale of mineral interests qualifies for capital gains treatment, a purported sale of mineral interests in exchange for a royalty from the minerals produced is treated only as a transfer with a retained economic interest, and the royalty payments are fully taxable as ordinary income. . . .

In Thomas v. Perkins, 301 U.S. 655, an owner of oil interests transferred them in return for an "oil production payment," an amount which is payable only out of the proceeds of later commercial sales of the oil transferred. The Court held that this transfer, which constituted a sale under state law, did not constitute a sale for tax purposes because there was not a sufficient shift of economic risk. The transferor would be paid only if oil was later produced and sold; if it was not produced, he would not be paid. The risks run by the transferor of making or losing money from the oil were shifted so slightly by the transfer that

29. This lease arrangement was designed to permit the Institute to take advantage of its charitable exemption to avoid taxes on payment of Fortuna's profits to it, with Fortuna receiving a deduction for the rental payments as an ordinary and necessary business expense, thus avoiding taxes to both. Though unrelated business income is usually taxable when received by charities, an exception is made for income received from the lease of real and personal property of less than five years. See I.R.C. §514. . . . Though denial of the charity's tax exemption on rent received from Fortuna would also remove the economic incentive underlying this bootstrap transaction, there is no indication in the Court's opinion that such income is not tax exempt. . . .

no §1222(3) sale existed, notwithstanding the fact that the transaction conveyed title as a matter of state law, and once the payout was complete, full ownership of the minerals was to vest in the purchaser.

I believe that the sellers have retained an economic interest in the business fully as great as that retained by the seller of oil interests in Thomas v. Perkins. . . .

Moreover, in numerous cases this Court has refused to transfer the incidents of taxation along with a transfer of legal title when the transferor retains considerable control over the income-producing asset transferred. See e.g., . . . Helvering v. Clifford 309 U.S. 331 (1940), Corliss v. Bowers, [281 U.S. 376 (1930)]. Control of the business did not, in fact, shift in the transaction here considered. Clay Brown, by the terms of the purchase agreement and the lease, was to manage Fortuna. Clay Brown was given power to hire and arrange for the terms of employment of all other employees of the corporation. The lease provided that "if for any reason Clay Brown is unable or unwilling to so act, the person or persons holding a majority interest in the principal note described in the Purchase Agreement shall have the right to approve his successor to act as general manager of Lessee company." Thus the shareholders of Clay Brown & Co. assured themselves of effective control over the management of Fortuna. Furthermore, Brown's attorneys were the named shareholders of Fortuna and its Board of Directors. The Institute had no control over the business.

I would conclude that on these facts there was not a sufficient shift of economic risk or control of the business to warrant treating this transaction as a "sale" for tax purposes. . . . Moreover, the entire purchase price was to be paid out of the ordinary income of the corporation, which was to be received by Brown on a recurrent basis as he had received it during the period he owned the corporation. I do not believe that Congress intended this recurrent receipt of ordinary business income to be taxed at capital gains rates merely because the business was to be transferred to a tax-exempt entity at some future date.[30] . . .

. . . Even if the Court restricts its holding, allowing only those transactions to be §1222(3) sales in which the price is not excessive, its decision allows considerable latitude for the unwarranted conversion of ordinary income into capital gain. Valuation of a closed corporation is notoriously difficult. The Tax Court in the present case did not determine that the price for which the corporation was sold represented its true value; it simply stated that the price "was the result of real negotiating" and "within a reasonable range in light of the earnings history of the cor-

30. The fact that respondents were to lose complete control of the business after the payments were complete was taken into account by the Commissioner, for he treated the business in respondents' hands as a wasting asset, see I.R.C., 1954, §167, and allowed them to offset their basis in the stock against the payments received.

poration and the adjusted net worth of the corporate assets." 37 T.C., at 486. The Tax Court, however, also said that "[i]t may be . . . that petitioner [Clay Brown] would have been unable to sell the stock at as favorable a price to anyone other than a tax-exempt organization." 37 T.C., at 485. Indeed, this latter supposition is highly likely, for the Institute was selling its tax exemption, and this is not the sort of asset which is limited in quantity. Though the Institute might have negotiated in order to receive beneficial ownership of the corporation as soon as possible, the Institute, at no cost to itself, could increase the price to produce an offer too attractive for the seller to decline. . . .

Although the Court implies that it will hold to be "sales" only those transactions in which the price is reasonable, I do not believe that the logic of the Court's opinion will justify so restricting its holding. If this transaction is a sale . . . because it was arrived at after hard negotiating, title in a conveyancing sense passed, and the beneficial ownership was expected to pass at a later date, then the question recurs, which the Court does not answer, why a similar transaction would cease to be a sale if hard negotiating produced a purchase price much greater than actual value. The Court relies upon Kolkey v. Commissioner, 254 F.2d 51 (7th Cir.), as authority holding that a bootstrap transaction will be struck down where the price is excessive. In *Kolkey,* however, the price to be paid was so much greater than the worth of the corporation in terms of its anticipated income that it was highly unlikely that the price would in fact ever be paid; consequently, it was improbable that the sellers' interest in the business would ever be extinguished. Therefore, in *Kolkey,* the Court, viewing the case as one involving "thin capitalization," treated the notes held by the sellers as equity in the new corporation and payments on them as dividends. Those who fashion "bootstrap" purchases have become considerably more sophisticated since *Kolkey;* vastly excessive prices are unlikely to be found and transactions are fashioned so that the "thin capitalization" argument is conceptually inapplicable. Thus I do not see what rationale the Court might use to strike down price transactions which, though excessive, do not reach *Kolkey*'s dimensions, when it upholds the one here under consideration. Such transactions would have the same degree of risk-shifting, there would be no less a transfer of ownership, and consideration supplied by the buyer need be no less than here.

Further, a bootstrap tax avoidance scheme can easily be structured under which the holder of any income-earning asset "sells" his asset to a tax-exempt buyer for a promise to pay him the income produced for a period of years. The buyer in such a transaction would do nothing whatsoever; the seller would be delighted to lose his asset at the end of, say, 30 years in return for capital gains treatment of all income earned during that period. It is difficult to see, on the Court's rationale, why such a scheme is not a sale. . . .

NOTES AND QUESTIONS

1. *The* Clay Brown *case's impact on definition of capital gains transaction.* (a) As noted by the Court, the government finally rested its attack on the ground that a capital gains transaction requires the transfer of a risk-bearing economic interest to the transferee. Even though the Court rejected the government's argument in *Clay Brown* that there is no sale if the purchase price is to be paid from the earnings of the asset that is sold, the government again advanced that argument in Boone v. United States, 470 F.2d 232 (10th Cir. 1972), where shareholders in a closely held insurance company sold stock for an agreed price that, after a down payment, was payable by the purchasing company only from net premium income on the transferred policies. The court held *Clay Brown* dispositive and in light of the factual evidence found that a sale had occurred.

(b) Would acceptance of the government's theory in *Clay Brown* have invalidated the capital gains eligibility of many real estate sales where the buyer takes subject to — without assuming — an existing mortgage or where under state law there is no personal liability for a purchase money obligation? If *A* sells property to *B*'s newly formed corporation, thus insulating *B* from personal liability for the purchase price, is there a transfer of risk?

(c) In considering these questions, which made the Court hesitate about accepting the government's theory, it should be noted that the government's brief indicated that a down payment or acceptance of personal liability were not the only ways in which a transfer of risk could occur. For example, the performance of significant services by a buyer or other significant changes in his circumstances might have been a sufficient commitment to shift risk.

2. *Transactions where the price is not reasonable.* The *Clay Brown* majority limited its holding that a sale had occurred to transactions in which the purchase price was reasonable. Justice Goldberg, writing for the dissent, was concerned that, under the logic of the majority opinion, this restriction might not be enforceable. On the *Clay Brown* facts, was there any nontax reason why another charity might not have been willing to pay twice the price that was set by the parties in that case? If you had represented the taxpayer in the case, would you have been willing to have your client accept the higher offer? See Frank Lyon Co. v. United States, supra page 717, and Estate of Franklin v. Commissioner, supra page 694. In Berenson v. Commissioner, 507 F.2d 262 (2d Cir. 1974), the court considered a transaction similar to the one in *Clay Brown* but concluded that the price was excessive (more than double what would have been paid by a nonexempt purchaser) and that the seller was entitled to capital gain treatment only to the extent of what a nonexempt purchaser would have paid, with the excess treated as ordinary income.

(The proceedings following remand are reported at 612 F.2d 695 (2d Cir. 1980)).

As to the reasonableness of the price in *Clay Brown,* note that the transaction called for deferred payments without interest. As a matter of sound financial analysis, it is clear that part of those payments should be treated as interest, but at the time the case arose there was no authority for such treatment for tax purposes. If the market rate of interest on high-quality loans was around 5 percent, what would have been a realistic rate for the purported loan in *Clay Brown,* which was nonrecourse, with a principal amount of $1.3 million and a down payment of $5,000?

3. *The IRS response to* Clay Brown. In Rev. Rul. 66-153, 1966-1 C.B. 187, the Service announced that it would "continue to resist what is in substance an attempt to convert future business profits to capital gains" but would limit its attacks to cases in which the purchase price was "excessive."

4. *The legislative aftermath.* The Tax Reform Act of 1969 made several changes that eliminated some of the tax advantages available in the tax-exempt bootstrap transactions. Section 514 expanded the definition of unrelated trade or business income, which is taxable to an exempt organization, to include debt-financed income. Under §514, income is taxed in the proportion in which property is financed by debt, notwithstanding that it otherwise would not be unrelated business income (e.g., dividends, interest, rents, etc.). As the debt is reduced, the percentage taxed diminishes. The provision does not apply to property related in use to the organization's exempt function. The rental income earned by the charity from the operating company in *Clay Brown* would have been taxed under this new provision and the ability of the exempt organization to pay the purchase price considerably impaired as a result. Section 511(a) was also amended to subject churches to the tax imposed on unrelated business income. Charitable organizations that are private foundations are effectively prohibited through severe penalties from owning a controlling interest in a business in any form. §4943.

G. OTHER CLAIMS AND CONTRACT RIGHTS

1. Theatrical Production Rights

COMMISSIONER v. FERRER

304 F.2d 125 (2d Cir. 1962)

FRIENDLY, Circuit Judge.

This controversy concerns the tax status of certain payments received by José Ferrer with respect to the motion picture "Moulin Rouge" portraying the career of Henri de Toulouse-Lautrec. The difficulties Mr. Ferrer must have had in fitting himself into the shape of the artist can hardly have been greater than ours in determining whether the transaction here at issue fits the rubric "gain from the sale or exchange of a capital asset held for more than 6 months," [§1221(3)], as the Tax Court held, 35 T.C. 617 (1961), or constitutes ordinary income, as the Commissioner contends. We have concluded that neither party is entirely right, that some aspects of the transaction fall on one side of the line and some on the other, and that the Tax Court must separate the two.

In 1950 Pierre LaMure published a novel, "Moulin Rouge," based on the life of Toulouse-Lautrec. He then wrote a play, "Monsieur Toulouse," based on the novel. On November 1, 1951, LaMure as "Author" and Ferrer, a famous actor but not a professional producer, as "Manager" entered into a contract, called a Dramatic Production Contract, for the stage production of the play by Ferrer.

The contract was largely on a printed form recommended by the Dramatists Guild of the Authors League of America, Inc. However great the business merits of the document, which are extolled in Burton, Business Practices in the Copyright Field, in C.C.H., 7 Copyright Problems Analyzed (1952) 87, 109, for a court, faced with the task of defining the nature of the rights created, it exemplifies what a contract ought not to be. Its first six pages include eleven articles, some introduced by explanatory material whose contractual status is, to say the least, uncertain. Here the last of these pages was preceded by three single-spaced typewritten pages of "Additional Clauses," one with a still further insert. Finally come 15 pages of closely printed "Supplemental Provisions," introduced by explanatory material of the sort noted. We shall thread our way through this maze as best we can.

By the contract the Author "leased" to the Manager "the sole and exclusive right" to produce and present "Monsieur Toulouse" on the speaking stage in the United States and Canada, and gave certain rights for its production elsewhere. Production had to occur on or before June

1, 1952, unless the Manager paid an additional advance of $1500 not later than that date, in which event the deadline was extended to December 1, 1952. Five hundred dollars were paid as an initial advance against Author's royalties; the Manager was required to make further advances of like amount on December 1, 1951, and January 1, 1952. Royalties were to be paid the Author on all box-office receipts, on a sliding scale percentage basis.

Article Seventh said that "In the event that under the terms hereof the Manager shall be entitled to share in the proceeds of the Motion Picture and Additional Rights hereafter referred to, it is agreed that the Manager shall receive" 40% for the first ten years and diminishing percentages thereafter. Among the additional rights so described were "Radio and Television."

For the beginning of an answer whether the Manager would be so entitled, we turn to Article IV, §2, of the Supplemental Provisions. This tells us that "In the event the Manager has produced and presented the play for the 'Requisite Performances and Terms,' the Negotiator shall pay the Manager" the above percentages "of the proceeds, from the disposal of the motion picture rights." Article VI, §3, contains a similar provision as to payment by the Author of the proceeds of the "additional rights" including radio and television. . . .

Further provisions put flesh on these bones. Article IV, §1(a), says that "The title" to the motion picture rights "vests in the Author, as provided in Article VIII hereof." Article VIII says, even more broadly, "The Author shall retain for his sole benefit, complete title, both legal and equitable, in and to all rights whatsoever (including, but not by way of limitation, the Motion Picture Rights . . . Radio and Television Rights . . .)," other than the right to produce the play. . . .

Finally, . . . [an] "Additional Clause" prescribes that "All dramatic, motion picture, radio and television rights in the novel MOULIN ROUGE shall merge in and with the play during the existence of this contract," and if the Manager produces and presents the play for a sufficient period, "throughout the copyright period of the play."

Shortly after signature of the Dramatic Production Contract, John Huston called Ferrer to ask whether he would be interested in playing Toulouse-Lautrec in a picture based upon "Moulin Rouge." On getting an affirmative indication, Huston said he would go ahead and acquire the motion picture rights. Ferrer replied, in somewhat of an exaggeration, "When you get ready to acquire them talk to me because I own them."

Both Huston and Ferrer then had discussions with LaMure. Ferrer expressed a willingness "to abandon the theatrical production in favor of the film production, provided that, if the film production were successful, I would be recompensed for my abandoning the stage production." On the strength of this, LaMure signed a preliminary agreement with Huston's corporation. In further negotiations, Huston's attorney insisted on "either an annulment or conveyance" of the Dramatic Production Contract. LaMure's lawyer prepared a letter of agreement, dated February 7, 1952, whereby Ferrer would cancel and terminate the Contract. Ferrer signed the letter but instructed his attorney not to deliver it until the closing of a contract between himself and the company that was to produce the picture; the letter was not delivered until May 14, 1952.

Meanwhile, on May 7, 1952, Ferrer entered into a contract with Huston's company, Moulin Productions, Inc. ("Moulin"), hereafter the Motion Picture Contract. This was followed by an agreement and assignment dated May 12, 1952, whereby LaMure sold Huston all motion picture rights to his novel, including the right to exploit the picture by radio and television. Under this agreement LaMure was to receive a fixed sum of $25,000, plus 5% and 4% of the Western and Eastern Hemisphere motion picture profits, respectively, and 50% of the net profits from exploitation by live television.

The Motion Picture Contract said that Romulus Films Limited, of London, proposed to produce the picture "Moulin Rouge," that Moulin would be vested with the Western Hemisphere distribution rights, and that Moulin on behalf of Romulus was interested in engaging Ferrer's services to play the role of Toulouse-Lautrec. Under clause 4(a), Ferrer was to receive $50,000 to cover 12 weeks of acting, payments to be made weekly as Ferrer rendered his services. Ferrer's performance was to begin between June 1 and July 1, 1952. By clause 4(b), Ferrer was to receive $10,416.66 per week for each additional week, but this, together with an additional $50,000 of salary provided by clause 4(c), was "deferred and postponed" and was payable only out of net receipts. Finally, clauses 4(d) and (e) provided "percentage compensation" equal to stipulated percentages of the net profits from distribution of the picture in the Western and Eastern Hemispheres respectively — 17% of the Western Hemisphere net profits until Ferrer had received $25,000 and thereafter 12¾% (such payments to "be made out of sixty-five (65%) percent of the net profits," whatever that may mean), and 3¾% of the Eastern Hemisphere net profits. If Ferrer's services were interrupted by disability or if production of the picture had to be suspended for causes beyond Moulin's control, but the picture was thereafter completed and Ferrer's "acts, poses and appearances therein" were recognizable to the public, he was to receive a proportion of the compensation provided in clauses 4(c), (d) and (e) corresponding to the ratio of his period of acting to 12 weeks. The same was true if Ferrer failed to "conduct himself with due regard to public conventions and morals" etc. and Moulin cancelled on that account. The absence of any similar provision with respect to termination for Ferrer's wilful refusal or neglect to perform services indicates that all his rights, except that for compensation already due under clause 4(a), would be forfeited in that event. Over objections by the Commissioner, Ferrer offered testimony by Huston's attorney, who was also president of Moulin, that in the negotiation "it was said that the ultimate percentage payment to be made to Ferrer would be his compensation for giving up his interest in the dramatization guild," and a letter from the same attorney, dated March 3, 1953, confirming that in the negotiations with Ferrer's attorney "for the sale of the dramatic rights held by you to the property entitled 'MONSIEUR TOULOUSE' and the novel 'MOULIN ROUGE,' it was understood that the consideration for such sale price was the payments due, or to become due, to you under Clause 4(d) and Clause 4(e)," and also that LeMure "refused to sell the motion picture rights for the production of the motion picture known as 'MOULIN ROUGE' unless you sold the aforesaid dramatic rights." Ferrer's agent testified, again over objection, that the largest salary Ferrer had previously received for a moving picture appearance was $75,000.

Moulin's books showed $109,027.74 as a salary payment to Ferrer in August, 1953, and $178,751.46 at various later dates in 1953 as the payment of "Participating Interests" under clause 4(d). Ferrer's 1953 return reported the former as ordinary income, and the latter, less expenses of $26,812.72, as a long-term capital gain. The Commissioner determined a deficiency on the basis that the difference, $151,938.74, constituted ordinary income; from the Tax Court's annulment of that determination he has taken this appeal.

Section . . . 1221 tells us, not very illuminatingly, that "capital asset" means property held by the taxpayer (whether or not connected with his trade or business), but does not include four (now five) types of property therein defined. However, it has long been settled that a taxpayer does not bring himself within the capital gains provision merely by fulfilling the simple syllogism that a contract normally constitutes "property," that he held a contract, and that his contract does not fall within a specified exclusion. . . . This is easy enough; what is difficult, perhaps impossible, is to frame a positive definition of universal validity. Attempts to do this in terms of the degree of clothing adorning the contract cannot explain all the cases, however helpful they may be in deciding some, perhaps even this one; it would be hard to think of a contract more "naked" than a debenture, yet no one doubts that is a "capital asset" if held by an investor. Efforts to frame a universal negative, e.g., that a transaction can never qualify if the taxpayer has merely collapsed anticipation of future income, are equally fruitless; a lessor's sale of his interest in a 999 year net lease and an investor's sale of a perpetual bond sufficiently illustrate why. . . .

Two issues can be eliminated before we do this. We need no longer concern ourselves, as at one time we might have been obliged to do, over the alleged indivisibility of a copyright; the Commissioner is now satisfied that sales and exchanges of less than the whole copyright may result in capital gain. . . . Neither do we have in this case any issue of excludability under . . . §1221(1); Ferrer was not in the "trade or business" of acquiring either dramatic production rights or motion picture rights.

When Huston displayed an interest in the motion picture rights in November, 1951, Ferrer was possessed of a bundle of rights, three of which are relevant here. First was his "lease" of the play. Second was his power, incident to that lease, to prevent any disposition of the motion picture rights until June 1, 1952, or, on making an additional $1500 advance, to December 1, 1952, and for a period thereafter if he produced the play, and to prevent disposition of the radio and television rights even longer. Third was his 40% share of the proceeds of the motion picture and other rights if he produced the play. All these, in our view, Ferrer "sold or exchanged," although the parties set no separate price upon them. To be sure, Moulin had no interest in producing the play. But Ferrer did, unless a satisfactory substitute was provided. Hence Moulin had to buy him out of that right, as well as to eliminate his power temporarily to prevent a sale of the motion picture, radio and television rights to liquidate his option to obtain a share of their proceeds.

(1) Surrender of the "lease" of the play sounds like the transactions held to qualify for capital gain treatment in [Commissioner v. Golonsky, 200 F.2d 72 (3d Cir. 1952), cert. denied, 345 U.S. 939 (1953); Commissioner v. McCue Bros & Drummond, Inc., 210 F.2d 752 (2d Cir.), cert. denied, 348 U.S. 829 (1954)], see §1241. Such cases as Wooster v. Crane & Co., 147 F. 515 (8 Cir. 1906), . . . are a fortiori authority that courts would have enjoined LaMure, or anyone else, from interfering with this, unless the Dramatic Production Contract dictated otherwise. None of its many negations covered this basic grant. Ferrer thus had an "equitable interest" in the copyright of the play.

The Commissioner did not suggest in the Tax Court, and does not here, that this interest or, indeed, any with which we are concerned in this case, fell within . . . §1221(3), excluding from the term "capital asset" "a copyright; a literary, musical, or artistic composition; or similar property; held by — (i) a taxpayer, whose personal efforts created such property. . . ." He was right in not doing this. In one sense the lease of the play was "created" simply by the agreed advance of $1500. If it be said that this is too narrow an approach and that we must consider what Ferrer would have had to do in order to make the lease productive, the result remains the same. Although the Dramatic Production Contract demanded Ferrer's personal efforts in the play's production, much else in the way of capital and risk-taking was also required. Yet the legislative history, . . . shows that [§1221(3)] was intended to deal with personal efforts and creation in a rather narrow sense. . . . Ferrer's role as producer, paying large sums to the theatre, the actors, other personnel, and the author, is not analogous to that of the writer or even the "creator" of a radio program mentioned by the Committee. Moreover, the dramatic producer does not normally "sell" the production to a single purchaser, as an author or radio program "creator" usually does — he offers it directly to public customers.

We see no basis for holding that amounts paid Ferrer for surrender of his lease of the play are excluded from capital gain treatment because receipts from the play would have been ordinary income. The latter is equally true if a lessee of real property sells or surrenders a lease from which he is receiving business income or subrentals; yet *Golonsky* and *McCue Bros. & Drummond* held such to be the sale or exchange of a capital asset, as §1241 now provides. Likewise we find nothing in the statute that forbids capital gain treatment because the payment to Ferrer might be spread over a number of years rather than coming in a lump sum; although prevention of the unfairness arising from applying ordinary income rates to a "bunching" of income may be one of the motivations of the "capital gains" provisions, the statute says nothing about this. . . . Finally, with respect to the lease of the play, there was no such equivalence between amounts paid for its surrender and income that would have been realized by its retention as seems to lie at the basis of the Tenth Circuit's recent refusal of capital gain treatment in Wiseman v. Halliburton Oil Well Cementing Co., 301 F.2d 654 (1962), a decision as to which we take no position.

(2) Ferrer's negative power, as an incident to the lease, to prevent any disposition of the motion picture, radio and television rights until after production of the play, was also one which . . . would be protected in equity unless he had contracted to the contrary, and would thus constitute an "equitable interest" in this portion of the copyright. . . . As a practical matter, this feature of the Dramatic Production Contract "clouded" LaMure's title, despite the Contract's contrary assertion. Huston would not conclude with LaMure and LaMure would not conclude with Huston unless Ferrer released his rights; Huston's attorney testified that a contract like Ferrer's "imposes an encumbrance on the motion picture rights." Ferrer's dissipation of the cloud arising from the negative covenant seems analogous to the tenant's relinquishment of a right to prevent his landlord from leasing to another tenant in the same business, held to be the sale or exchange of a capital asset in *Ray*. What we have said in (1) with respect to possible grounds for disqualification as a capital asset is a fortiori applicable here.

(3) We take a different view with respect to the capital assets status of Ferrer's right to receive 40% of the proceeds of the motion picture and other rights if he produced "Monsieur Toulouse."

We assume, without deciding, that there is no reason in principle why if the holder of a copyright grants an interest in the portion of a copyright relating to motion picture and other rights contingent on the production of a play, or, to put the matter in another way, gives the producer an option to acquire such an interest by producing the play, the option would not constitute a "capital asset" unless the producer is disqualified by . . . §1221(1). Although the copyright might not be such an asset in the owner's hands because of that section or . . . §1221(3)(A), the latter disqualification would not apply to the producer for reasons already discussed, and the former would not unless the producer was a professional. However, it is equally possible for the copyright owner to reserve the entire "property" both legal and equitable in himself and agree with the producer that a percentage of certain avails shall be paid as further income from the lease of the play — just as the lessor of real estate might agree to pay a lessee a percentage of what the lessor obtained from other tenants attracted to the building by the lessee's operations. In both instances such payments would be ordinary income. If the parties choose to cast their transaction in the latter mold, the Commissioner may take them at their word.

Here the parties were at some pains to do exactly that. LaMure was to "retain for his sole benefit, complete title, both legal and equitable, in and to all rights whatsoever" other than the right to produce the play. Ferrer was to "have no right, title or interest, legal or equitable, in the motion picture rights, other than the right to receive the Manager's share of the proceeds"; even as to that, he was to have "no recourse, in law or in equity" against a purchaser, a lessee, or the Negotiator, but only a right to arbitration against the Author. We cannot regard all this as mere formalism. The Contract is full of provisions designed to emphasize the Negotiator's freedom to act — provisions apparently stemming from a fear that, without them, the value of the motion picture rights might disintegrate in controversy. . . .

It follows that if Ferrer had produced the play and LaMure had sold the motion picture, radio and television rights for a percentage of the profits, Ferrer's 40% of that percentage would have been ordinary income and not the sale or exchange of a capital asset. The decisions in *Hort* [supra page 867] and [Holt v. Commissioner, 303 F.2d 687 (9 Cir. 1962) (producer receives profit percentage in return for future services; liquidation of claim for lump sum payment treated as ordinary income)] point to what would seem the inevitable corollary that if, on the same facts, Ferrer had then sold his rights to a percentage of the profits for a lump sum, that, too, would have been ordinary income. . . . The situation cannot be better from Ferrer's standpoint because he had merely a contingent right to, or an option to obtain, the 40% interest. . . .

The situation is thus one in which two of the rights that Ferrer sold or exchanged were "capital assets" and one was not. Although it would be easy to say that the contingent contract right to a percentage of the avails of the motion picture, radio and television rights was dominant and all else incidental, that would be viewing the situation with the inestimable advantage of hindsight. In 1952 no one could tell whether the play might be a huge success and the picture a dismal failure, whether the exact opposite would be true, whether both would succeed or both would fail. We cannot simply dismiss out of hand the notion that a dramatic production, presenting an actor famous on the speaking stage and appealing to a sophisticated audience, might have had substantial profit possibilities, perhaps quite as good as a film with respect to a figure, not altogether attractive and not nearly so broadly known then as the success of the picture has made him now, which presumably would require wide public acceptance before returning production costs. At the very least, when Ferrer gave up his lease of the play, he was abandoning his bet on two horses in favor of a bet on only one.

In such instances, where part of a transaction calls for one tax treatment and another for a different kind, allocation is demanded. . . . If it be said that to remand for this purpose is asking the Tax Court to separate the inseparable, we answer that no one expects scientific exactness; that however roughly hewn the decision may be, the result is certain to be fairer than either extreme; and that similar tasks must be performed by the Tax Court in other areas. . . .

Still we have not reached the end of the road. The Commissioner contends that, apart from all else, no part of the payments here can qualify for capital gain treatment, since Ferrer could receive "percentage compensation" only if he fulfilled his acting commitments, and all the payments were thus for personal services. [T]he Commissioner says it was error for the Tax Court to rely on extrinsic evidence to vary the written contract.

Although the parties have taken opposing positions on the applicability of the "parol evidence rule" to a dispute involving a stranger to the contract, . . . no such issue is here presented. No one argued the contract provided anything other than what was plainly said. Huston's attorney did not assert that Ferrer would become entitled to the percentage compensation without fulfilling his acting commitment; what the attorney said in his testimony, as he had earlier in his letter, was that Ferrer was selling two things to Moulin — his services as an actor and his rights under the Dramatic Production Contract — and that the parties regarded the payments under clauses 4(a), (b) and (c) as the consideration for the former and those under clauses 4(d) and (e) as the consideration for the latter.

On the basis of this evidence the Tax Court found that the percentage compensation was not "to any extent the consequence of, or consideration for, petitioner's personal services." In one sense, this is hardly so. Under the Motion Picture Contract, Ferrer would receive no percentage compensation if he wrongfully refused to furnish acting services, and none or only a portion if, for reasons beyond his control, he furnished less than all. Since that must have been as plain to the Tax Court as to us, we read the finding to mean rather that Ferrer and Moulin adopted the percentage of profits formula embodied in clauses 4(d) and (e) as an equivalent and in lieu of a fixed sum payable in all events for the release of the Dramatic Production Contract. If they had first agreed on such a sum and had then substituted the arrangement here made, it would be hard to say that although payments under their initial arrangement would not be disqualified for capital gain treatment, payments under the substituted one would be. Ferrer was already bound to play the role of Toulouse-Lautrec, at a salary implicitly found to constitute fair compensation for his services; adoption of a formula whereby his receipt of percentage compensation for releasing his rights was made contingent on his fulfilling that undertaking does not mean that the percentage compensation could not be solely for his release of the Contract. The Tax Court was not bound to accept the testimony that this was the intent — it could lawfully have found that the percentage compensation was in part added salary for Ferrer's acting services and in part payment for the release. However, it found the contrary, and we cannot say that in doing so it went beyond the bounds to which our review of its fact findings is confined [under] §7482(a). Since, on the taxpayer's own evidence, the percentage compensation was for the totality of the release of his rights under the Dramatic Production Contract, allocation is required as between rights which did and rights which did not constitute a "capital asset."

We therefore reverse and remand to the Tax Court to determine what portion of the percentage compensation under clauses 4(d) and (e) of the Motion Picture Contract constituted compensation for Ferrer's surrendering his lease of the play and his incidental power to prevent disposition of the motion picture and other rights pending its production, as to which the determination of deficiency should be annulled, and what part for the surrender of his opportunity to receive 40% of the proceeds of the motion picture and other rights as to which it should be sustained. . . .

NOTES AND QUESTIONS

1. *Fragmentation.* Why did the court break up the set of rights for which Ferrer had bargained? Does it seem likely that Ferrer himself saw the rights as independent of one another?

2. *Drafting around the decision.* Could the contract between Ferrer and LaMure have been written so that all of Ferrer's gain would have been capital gain? Would that have required significant changes in LaMure's

substantive rights? Would such changes have had any adverse tax effect for LaMure?

3. *The significance of profit sharing.* Note that the fact that Ferrer was to receive a share of the profits of the film, rather than a fixed amount, did not preclude a finding of a "sale" for purposes of allowing capital-gain treatment. This result is consistent with the position taken by the Service (after a long battle) as to licenses of patents (Rev. Rul. 58-353, 1958-2 C.B. 408)[31] and copyrights (Rev. Rul. 60-226, 1960-1 C.B. 26, regardless of whether the amounts "are payable over a period generally coterminus with the grantee's use of the copyrighted work").

4. *Other favorable contracts.* Perhaps the most intriguing case cited in *Ferrer* is Commissioner v. Pittston Co., 252 F.2d 344 (2d Cir.), cert. denied, 357 U.S. 919 (1958), where the taxpayer had entered into two transactions with Russell. In order to enable Russell to install a coal mining plant on Russell's coal property, it loaned Russell $250,000 and, at the same time, under a second contract, Russell agreed to sell to the taxpayer all of the coal produced by the plant for a period of ten years at a discount below fair market price. Parts of the payments for the coal were to be applied to repay the loan. Russell paid off the loan in four years, and a year later Russell paid the taxpayer $500,000 in consideration of the taxpayer's surrender of its rights under the coal purchase agreement. The taxpayer reported the $500,000 as long-term capital gain and was upheld by the Tax Court. The Circuit Court viewed the two contracts separately and reversed. It held that there was no sale or exchange, but merely the release of "naked" contract rights, which were not property. The court bolstered its position by stating that since Russell could break the contract and respond in damages only, there was no property right that could be specifically enforced; it therefore found that payment was more in the nature of future income (i.e., income Pittston would otherwise earn by buying Russell's coal at a discount and selling it at a higher price) paid in a lump sum. The dissent, viewing the two transactions, the loan and coal purchase agreement, together, concluded that the taxpayer had a property right rather than a mere contract right; that the agreement could have been specifically enforced; that the payment was analogous to payments made to a lessee for voluntary termination of a leasehold prior to expiration; that the payment was not anticipated income because it bore no relationship to future income; and that a surrender of the rights was similar to a sale or exchange. The earlier Second Circuit cases of Commissioner v. Starr Bros., 204 F.2d 673 (2d Cir. 1953) (which found ordinary income on cancellation of an exclusive distributorship), and General Artists Corp.

31. Section 1235, enacted in 1954, allows royalties received by the inventor or other "holder" to be treated as capital gains.

v. Commissioner, 205 F.2d 360 (2d Cir.), cert. denied, 346 U.S. 866 (1953) (which found ordinary income on release of exclusive agency rights), had been distinguished by the Tax Court as cases where a contractual right was not "sold or exchanged" but was "released" and merely vanished.

In Commercial Solvents Corp. v. United States, 427 F.2d 749 (Ct. Cl.), cert. denied, 400 U.S. 943 (1970), a case similar to *Pittston,* the cancellation of a contract giving the taxpayer the right to buy all the production of a certain chemical plant was held to give rise to ordinary income because of the nature of the contract ("a naked contract right"). The government had stipulated that the cancellation of the contract was a sale or exchange.

2. Right of Privacy or of Exploitation

MILLER v. COMMISSIONER

299 F.2d 706 (2d Cir.), cert. denied, 370 U.S. 923 (1962)

Before WATERMAN, KAUFMAN and MARSHALL, Circuit Judges.

KAUFMAN, Circuit Judge. Petitioner is the widow of Glenn Miller, a band leader who achieved world fame about twenty-five years ago. Although Glenn Miller died in 1944, petitioner has been able to engage in a number of enterprises actively exploiting his continuing popularity. . . .

Thus, in 1952, she entered into a contract with Universal Pictures Company, Inc. (Universal) in connection with the production of a motion picture film entitled "The Glenn Miller Story"; and in the calendar year 1954, she received $409,336.34 as her share of the income derived from that theatrical venture. According to the terms of the 1952 contract, petitioner had purportedly granted to Universal "the exclusive right to produce, release, distribute and exhibit . . . one or more photoplays based upon the life and activities of Glenn Miller throughout the world"; and had warranted that she was "the sole and exclusive owner of all the rights" conveyed by her.

Petitioner now contends that the payment . . . should be considered . . . "gain from the sale or exchange of a capital asset held for more than 6 months. . . ." [T]he conflict is narrowed to the meaning of the word "property" for purposes of [§1221].

The Internal Revenue Code does not define "property" as used in §1221. . . . Therefore, we must look outside the eight corners of the Code for some elucidation. The ordinary technique is to refer to principles of state property law for, if not an answer, at least a hint. Since ultimately it is the Congressional purpose which controls, such nontax definitions are certainly not binding on us. . . . On the other hand, Congress may be presumed to have had ordinary property concepts in mind so they are relevant to our inquiry.

Most people trained in the law would agree that for many purposes one may define "property" as a bundle of rights, protected from interference by legal sanctions. Cf. Restatement, Property §§1-5. This concept is behind one prong of petitioner's attack. She cites several cases, claiming they indicate that if Universal had made its motion picture without contracting with her, it would have been the victim of a substantial lawsuit.

Even if this were so, those cases would not compel this court to recognize, for income tax purposes, a "property right" in Glenn Miller himself if he were still alive. However, it is not necessary for us to reach a determination upon such an assertion. Those cases do not even remotely bear on the question whether such a property right, if it existed, could pass to the sole beneficiary under his will; and certainly they lend no support to petitioner's theory that the reputation or fame of a dead person could give rise to such "property rights." In fact, in the only case cited in which the rights of a dead man were considered at all, the court held against the claimant. . . .

Undeterred by her failure to find case authority which would substantiate the existence of "property rights" petitioner invokes the authority of logic. With considerable ingenuity, she argues:

(1) Universal paid petitioner $409,336.34 in 1954, which is a great deal of money.

(2) Universal was a sophisticated corporate being to which donative intent would be difficult to ascribe.

(3) If there was no danger in free use of Glenn Miller material, why did Universal pay?

Petitioner appears to find this question unanswerable unless it is conceded that there was a sale of "property right." Petitioner is wrong.

It is clear to this Court, at least, that many things can be sold which are not "property" in any sense of the word. One can sell his time and experience, for instance, or, if one is dishonest, one can sell his vote; but we would suppose that no one would seriously contend that the subject matter of such sales is "property" as that word is ordinarily understood. Certainly no one would contend that such subject matter was inheritable. We conclude, therefore, that not everything people pay for is "property."

In the instant case, "something" was indeed sold. And the expedient business practice may often be to sell such "things." But the "thing" bought, or more appropriately "bought off," seems to have been the chance that a new theory of "property" might be advanced, and that a lawsuit predicated on it might be successful. . . . Because Universal feared that it might sometime in the future be held to have infringed a property right does not mean, however, that a court presently considering whether that property right *did* exist in 1952 must realize Universal's worst fears. That does not mean that Universal's payment was foolish or illusory. It got what it contracted for in 1952 and what it later paid Mrs. Miller for: freedom from the danger that at a future date a defensible right constituting "property" *would* be found to exist. But it didn't pay for "property."[32]

It may be helpful to compare this situation with one which involves the settlement of a tort claim, e.g., a negligence lawsuit. No one doubts the existence of a legal principle creating liability for negligence. If the facts are as a plaintiff contends, and they come within that principle, the defendant's liability exists. Even if they do not, the defendant, for his own reasons, may agree to make a payment in settlement of his alleged liability. Moreover, the Commissioner, for purposes of taxation, may accept that settlement as an implied affirmation that the *facts* were substantially as the plaintiff contended, and treat the recovery accordingly. But no two individuals can, by agreement between themselves, create a *legal* principle, binding upon everyone else, including the Commissioner, where none existed before. This is the exclusive domain of the legislature and the courts as repository of the public will. . . . Petitioner concedes that at the time of the "sale" there had been no authoritative decision holding that a decedent's successors had any "property right" to the public image of a deceased entertainer; and therefore it follows that their bargain was not, at that time, a bargain that both parties knew involved a "property right." . . .

"[I]t is evident that not everything which can be called property in the ordinary sense and which is outside the statutory exclusions qualifies as a capital asset. . . ." Commissioner v. Gillette Motor Transport, Inc., 364 U.S. 130, 134 (1960). . . . Gains which result from the sale or exchange of capital assets receive preferential tax treatment. Therefore, "The definition of a capital asset must be narrowly applied," Corn Products Refining Co. v. Commissioner [supra page 854], in order to effectuate the basic Congressional purpose "to relieve the taxpayer from . . . excessive tax burdens on gains resulting from a conversion of capital investments, and to remove the deterrent effect of those burdens on such conversions." Burnet v. Harmel, [287 U.S. 103, 106 (1932)]; Corn Products Refining Co. v. Commissioner, supra. We do not believe that for income tax computation purposes beneficiaries of the estate of a deceased entertainer receive by descent a capitalizable "property" in the name, reputation, right of publicity, right of privacy or "public image"

32. One must remember that, the techniques of advertising and promotion being what they are, timing is very important and a successful motion for a preliminary injunction made by one who *claims* a "property right" might be as disastrous as a final award of damages. One can easily find wisdom in this payment by Universal without finding that it paid for "property."

of the deceased; or that in this case the petitioner, for tax purposes, owned any "property" which came into existence after Glenn Miller's death. Therefore, income received by Mrs. Miller from contractual arrangements made by her with Universal dealing with deceased's intangible rights of the nature above specified is "ordinary" income as opposed to capital gain or loss under §1221.

Affirmed.

QUESTIONS

Suppose that at the time of the decision in the *Miller* case there had been clear precedent that a person like Glenn Miller has the exclusive right to exploit his own name and fame and that this right is enforceable by injunction and passes by inheritance to his heirs at his death.[33] Would the result in *Miller* have been different? Should it be? Would Mrs. Miller be entitled to capital gain treatment even if Mr. Miller would not have been? Compare the treatment of holders of copyrights, discussed in the next section.

3. Patents and Copyrights

Before 1950, a patent or copyright was treated as a capital asset if the taxpayer could show that it was neither property held for sale to customers in the regular course of trade or business nor depreciable property used in his or her business. In general, capital-gain treatment was confined to "amateur" authors, and inventors, who had not made more than one or two sales. In 1950, Congress added §§1221(3) and 1231(b)(1)(C), depriving authors of the possibility of capital-gain treatment for the fruits of their efforts. This rule does not apply, however, to a person who has bought the copyright. These rules are consistent with the notion that gains from one's efforts are ordinary income while gains or losses from passive investments are capital gains or losses. The

33. In Lugosi v. Universal Pictures, 25 Cal. 3d 813, 160 Cal. Rptr. 323, 603 P.2d 425 (1979), the California Supreme Court held that the heirs of Bela Lugosi did not have any protected rights in his special depictions of the character Dracula, despite the fact that he might have had such rights during his lifetime. In 1984, the California legislature added Cal. Civ. Code §990, which provides a cause of action for damages for unauthorized commercial use of "a deceased person's name, voice, signature, or likeness" and stating that the rights established are "property rights, freely transferable." Cal. Civ. Code §3344 provides a similar cause of action in respect of living persons. Compare Factors, Etc., Inc. v. Creative Card Co., 444 F. Supp. 279 (S.D.N.Y. 1977); Factors, Etc., Inc. v. Pro Arts, Inc., 44 F. Supp. 288 (S.D.N.Y. 1977); and Memphis Dev. Found. v. Factors, Etc., Inc., 441 F. Supp. 1323 (W.D. Tenn. 1977) — all recognizing property rights in the name and likeness of Elvis Presley; the rights had been exploited by him during his lifetime and survived his death.

"letter or memorandum" language was added to §§1221(3) and 1231(b)(1)(C) in 1969, apparently in an effort (in conjunction with §170(e)(1)(A)) to prevent politicians from claiming charitable deductions for contributions of their papers to libraries, museums, etc. The addition of this language helped bring about the impeachment of President Richard Nixon, who, having signed the legislation, later filed a tax return claiming a deduction based on backdated documents of transfer of his own papers.

The reference in §1221(3) to "similar property" includes "theatrical productions, a radio program, a newspaper cartoon strip, or any other property eligible for copyright protection but . . . does not include a patent, or an invention, or a design which may be protected only under the patent law and not under the copyright law." Regs. §1.1221-1(c)(l). The term "similar property" has also been applied to the format of a radio quiz program "Double or Nothing," on which participants could progressively double their winnings by electing to answer an additional question. Cranford v. United States, 338 F.2d 379 (Ct. Cl. 1964). Even if not entitled to copyright protection, the idea was held to be similar to the items explicitly listed in §1221(3) because it was a type of artistic work resulting from personal effort and skill. The same fate befell the author of "Francis," a talking army mule figuring in a series of novels, when he sold his rights to the character and the novels to a motion-picture company. Stern v. United States, 164 F. Supp. 847 (E.D. La. 1958), aff'd per curiam, 262 F.2d 957 (5th Cir.), cert. denied, 359 U.S. 969 (1959).

The 1950 amendment did not change the treatment of inventors and in 1954 Congress added §1235, which, when applicable, ensures that income from the transfer of patents will be taxed as long-term capital gain even if received by a professional inventor.

H. BAIL-OUT OF CORPORATE EARNINGS

As we have seen before, people sometimes try to use a tax provision to accomplish an objective other than what one would have assumed was intended by the drafters of the statute. Often this kind of effort depends on the use of unnatural and cumbersome legal forms — forms that no sensible lawyer would have used except in the hope of achieving a tax advantage. A notable example of this phenomenon is the set of transactions engaged in by the taxpayer in Starker v. United States (page 336) (delayed multiple-party like-kind exchange). In that case, the taxpayer was successful; form prevailed over substance. In many instances, substance will prevail, and a lawyer must always be sensitive to this possibility, even though reliable prediction of outcomes may be impossible. The case that follows, Gregory v. Helvering, is a classic, taxing the transaction according to its substance while preserving at least an appearance of fidelity to the statutory language by interpreting "reorganization" to require a business purpose for the transaction. The taxpayer owned shares of stock of a corporation that had assets that could have been paid out as a dividend. Dividends, however, are ordinary income. The taxpayer adopted a complex scheme by which she sought to "bail out" the assets in a manner that would produce capital gain rather than ordinary income.

GREGORY v. HELVERING

293 U.S. 465 (1935)

Mr. Justice SUTHERLAND delivered the opinion of the Court.

Petitioner in 1928 was the owner of all the stock of United Mortgage Corporation. That corporation held among its assets 1000 shares of the Monitor Securities Corporation. For the sole purpose of procuring a transfer of these shares to herself in order to sell them for her individual profit, and, at the same time, diminish the amount of income tax which would result from a direct transfer by way of dividend, she sought to bring about a "reorganization" under [a predecessor of §386(a)(1)(D)]. To that end, she caused the Averill Corporation to be organized under the laws of Delaware on September 18, 1928. Three days later, the United Mortgage Corporation transferred to the Averill Corporation the 1000 shares of Monitor stock, for which all the shares of the Averill Corporation were issued to the petitioner. On September 24, the Averill Corporation was dissolved, and liquidated by distributing all its assets, namely, the Monitor shares, to the petitioner. No other business was ever transacted, or intended to be transacted, by that company. Petitioner immediately sold the Monitor shares for $133,333.33. She returned for taxation, as capital net gain, the sum of $76,007.88, based upon an apportioned cost of $57,325.45. . . .

The Commissioner of Internal Revenue, being of opinion that the reorganization attempted was without substance and must be disregarded, held that petitioner was liable for a tax as though the United Corporation had paid her a dividend consisting of the amount realized from the sale of the Monitor shares. . . .

Section 112 of the Revenue Act of 1928 deals with the subject of gain or loss resulting from the sale or exchange of property. Such gain or loss is to be recognized in computing the tax, except as provided in that section. The provisions of the section, so far as they are pertinent to the question here presented, follow:

> Sec. 112. . . . (g) *Distribution of Stock on Reorganization.* If there is distributed, in pursuance of a plan of reorganization, to a shareholder in a corporation a party to the reorganization, stock or securities in such corporation or in another corporation a party to the reorganization, without the surrender by such shareholder of stock or securities in such a corporation, no gain to the distributee from the receipt of such stock or securities shall be recognized. . . .
>
> (i) *Definition of Reorganization.* As used in this section . . .
>
> (1) The term "reorganization" means . . . (B) a transfer by a corporation of all or a part of its assets to another corporation if immediately after the transfer the transferor or its stockholders or both are in control of the corporation to which the assets are transferred. . . .

It is earnestly contended on behalf of the taxpayer that since every element required by the foregoing subdivision (B) is to be found in what was done, a statutory reorganization was effected; and that the motive of the taxpayer thereby to escape payment of a tax will not alter the result or make unlawful what the statute allows. It is quite true that if a reorganization in reality was effected within the meaning of subdivision (B), the ulterior purpose mentioned will be disregarded. The legal right of a taxpayer to decrease the amount of what otherwise would be his taxes, or altogether avoid them, by means which the law permits, cannot be doubted. . . . But the question for determination is whether what was done, apart from the tax motive, was the thing which the statute intended. The reasoning of the court below in justification of a negative answer leaves little to be said.

When subdivision (B) speaks of a transfer of assets by one corporation to another, it means a transfer made "in pursuance of a plan of reorganization" (section 112(g)) of corporate business; and not a transfer of assets by one corporation to another in pursuance of a plan having no relation to the business of either, as plainly is the case here. Putting aside, then, the question of motive in respect of taxation altogether, and fixing the character of the proceeding by what actually occurred, what do we find? Simply an operation having no business or corporate purpose — a mere device which put on the form of a corporate reorganization as a disguise for concealing its real character, and the sole object and accomplishment of which was the consummation of a preconceived plan, not to reorganize a business or any part of a business, but to transfer a parcel of corporate shares to the petitioner. No doubt, a new and valid corporation was created. But that corporation was nothing more than a contrivance to the end last described. It was brought into existence for no other purpose; it performed, as it was intended from the beginning it should perform, no other function. When that limited function had been exercised, it immediately was put to death.

In these circumstances, the facts speak for themselves and are susceptible of but one interpretation. The whole undertaking, though conducted according to the terms of subdivision (B), was in fact an elaborate and devious form of conveyance masquerading as a corporate reorganization, and nothing else. The rule which excludes from consideration the motive of tax avoidance is not pertinent to the situation, because the transaction upon its face lies outside the plain intent of the statute. To hold otherwise would be to exalt artifice above reality and to deprive the statutory provision in question of all serious purpose.

Judgment affirmed.

NOTE

The following paragraph from the opinion of Judge Learned Hand in the Court of Appeals in the principal case provides another approach (69 F.2d 809, 810-811 (2d Cir. 1934)):

> We agree with the Board and the taxpayer that a transaction, otherwise within an exception of the tax law, does not lose its immunity, because it is actuated by a desire to avoid, or, if one choose, to evade, taxation. Any one may so arrange his affairs that his taxes shall be as low as possible; he is not bound to choose that pattern which will best pay the Treasury; there is not even a patriotic duty to increase one's taxes. . . . Therefore, if what was done here, was what was intended by section 112(i)(1)(B), it is of no consequence that it was all an elaborate scheme to get rid of income taxes, as it certainly was. Nevertheless, it does not follow that Congress meant to cover such a transaction, not even though the facts answer the dictionary definitions of each term used in the statutory definition. It is quite true, as the Board has very well said, that as the articulation of a statute increases, the room for interpretation must contract; but the meaning of a sentence may be more than that of the separate words, as a melody is more than the notes, and no degree of particularity can ever obviate recourse to the setting in which all appear, and which all collectively create. The purpose of the section is plain enough; men engaged in enterprises — industrial, commercial, financial, or any other — might wish to consolidate, or divide, to add to, or subtract from, their holdings. Such transactions were not to be considered as "realizing" any profit, because the collective interests still remained in solution. But the underlying presupposition is plain that the readjustment shall be undertaken for reasons germane to the conduct of the venture in hand, not as an ephemeral incident, egregious to its prosecution. To dodge the shareholders' taxes is not one of the transactions contemplated as corporate "reorganizations."

I. FRAGMENTATION VERSUS UNIFICATION OF COLLECTIVE ASSETS

WILLIAMS v. McGOWAN

152 F.2d 570 (2d Cir. 1945)

Before L. Hand, Swan, and Frank, Circuit Judges.

L. Hand, Circuit Judge. . . .

Williams, the taxpayer, and one Reynolds, had for many years been engaged in the hardware business in the City of Corning, New York. On the 20th of January, 1926, they formed a partnership, of which Williams was entitled to two-thirds of the profits, and Reynolds, one-third. . . . The business was carried on through the firm's fiscal year, ending January 31, 1940, in accordance with this agreement, and thereafter until Reynolds' death on July 18th of that year. Williams settled with Reynolds' executrix on September 6th in an agreement by which he promised to pay her $12,187.90, and to assume all liabilities of the business. . . . On September 17th of the same year, Williams sold the business as a whole to the Corning Building Company for $63,926.28 — its agreed value as of February 1, 1940 — "plus an amount to be computed by multiplying the gross sales of the business from the first day of February, 1940 to the 28th day of September, 1940," by an agreed fraction. This value was made up of cash of about $8100, receivables of about $7000, fixtures of about $800, and a merchandise inventory of about $49,000 less some $1000 for bills payable. To this was added about $6000 credited to Williams for profits under the language just quoted, making a total of nearly $70,000. Upon this sale Williams suffered a loss upon his original two-thirds of the business, but he made a small gain upon the one-third which he had bought from Reynolds' executrix; and in his income tax return he entered both as items of "ordinary income," and not as transactions in "capital assets." This the Commissioner disallowed and recomputed the tax accordingly; Williams paid the deficiency and sued to recover it in this action. The only question is whether the business was "capital assets" under [§1221].

It has been held that a partner's interest in a going firm is for tax purposes to be regarded as a "capital asset." . . . We too accepted the doctrine in McClellan v. Commissioner, 2 Cir., 117 F.2d 988, although we had held the opposite in Helvering v. Smith, 2 Cir., 90 F.2d 590, 591, where the partnership articles had provided that a retiring partner should receive as his share only his percentage of the sums "actually collected" and "of all earnings . . . for services performed." Such a payment, we thought, was income; and we expressly repudiated the notion that the Uniform Partnership Act had, generally speaking, changed the firm into a juristic entity. . . . If a partner's interest in a going firm is "capital assets" perhaps a dead partner's interest is the same. . . . We need not say. When Williams bought out Reynolds' interest, he became the sole owner of the business, the firm had ended upon any theory, and the situation for tax purposes was no other than if Reynolds had never been a partner at all, except that to the extent of one-third of the "amount realized" on Williams' sale to the Corning Company, his "basis" was different. . . . We have to decide only whether upon the sale of a going business it is to be comminuted into its fragments, and these are to be separately matched against the definition in [§1221], or whether the whole business is to be treated as if it were a single piece of property.

Our law has been sparing in the creation of juristic entities; it has never, for example, taken over the Roman "universitas facti";[34] and indeed for many years it fumbled uncertainly with the concept of a corporation. One might have supposed that partnership would have been an especially promising field in which to raise up an entity, particularly since merchants have always kept their accounts upon that basis. Yet there too our law resisted at the price of great and continuing confusion; and even when it might be thought that a statute admitted, if it did not demand, recognition of the firm as an entity, the old concepts prevailed. . . . And so, even though we might agree that under the influence of the Uniform Partnership Act a partner's interest in the firm should be treated as indivisible, and for that reason a "capital asset" within [§1221], we should be chary about extending further so exotic a jural concept. Be that as it may, in this instance the section itself furnishes the answer. It starts in the broadest way by declaring that all "property" is "capital assets," and then makes three exceptions. The first is "stock in trade . . . or other property of a kind which would properly be included in the inventory"; next comes "property held . . . primarily for sale to customers"; and finally, property "used in the trade or business of a character which is subject to . . . allowance for depreciation." In the face of this language, although it may be true that a "stock in trade" taken by itself should be treated as a "universitas facti," by no possibility can a whole business be so treated; and the same is true as to any property within the other exceptions. Congress plainly did mean to comminute the elements of a business; plainly it did not regard the whole as "capital assets."

As has already appeared, Williams transferred to the Corning Company "cash," "receivables," "fixtures" and a "merchandise inventory." "Fixtures" are not capital because they are subject to a depreciation allowance; the inventory, as we have just seen, is expressly excluded. So

34. "By universitas facti is meant a number of things of the same kind which are regarded as a whole; e.g., a herd, a stock of wares." Mackeldey, Roman Law §162.

far as appears, no allowance was made for "good-will"; but, even if there had been, we held in Haberle Crystal Springs Brewing Company v. Clarke, Collector, 2 Cir., 30 F.2d 219, that "good-will" was a depreciable intangible.[35] It is true that the Supreme Court reversed that judgment — 280 U.S. 284 — but it based its decision only upon the fact that there could be no allowance for the depreciation of "good-will" in a brewery, a business condemned by the Eighteenth Amendment. There can of course be no gain or loss in the transfer of cash; and, although Williams does appear to have made a gain of $1072.71 upon the "receivables," the point has not been argued that they are not subject to a depreciation allowance.[36] That we leave open for decision by the district court,[37] if the parties cannot agree. The gain or loss upon every other item should be computed as an item in ordinary income.

Judgment reversed.

FRANK, Circuit Judge (dissenting in part). . . .

I do not agree that we should ignore what the parties to the sale, Williams and the Corning Company, actually did. They did not arrange for a transfer to the buyer, as if in separate bundles, of the several ingredients of the business. They contracted for the sale of the entire business as a going concern. Here is what they said in their agreement:

> The party of the first part, agrees to sell and the party of the second part agrees to buy, *all of the right, title and interest* of the said party of the first part *in and of the hardware business* now being conducted by the said party of the first part, *including* cash on hand and on deposit in the First National Bank & Trust Company of Corning in the A. F. Williams' Hardware Store account, in accounts receivable, bills receivable, notes receivable, merchandise and fixtures, including two G.M. trucks, good will and all other assets of every kind and description used in and about said business. . . . Said party of the first part agrees not to engage in the hardware business within a radius of twenty-five miles from the City of Corning, New York, for a period of ten years from the 1st day of October 1940.

To carve up this transaction into distinct sales — of cash, receivables, fixtures, trucks, merchandise, and good will — is to do violence to the realities. I do not think Congress intended any such artificial result. . . . Where a business is sold as a unit, the whole is greater than its parts. Businessmen so recognize; so, too, I think, did Congress. Interpretation of our complicated tax statutes is seldom aided by saying that taxation is an eminently practical matter (or the like). But this is one instance where, it seems to me, the practical aspects of the matter should guide

35. [Goodwill is now a nondepreciable intangible. — Eds.]
36. [Section 1221(4) would now cover receivables. — Eds.]
37. [The decision on remand is reported at 70 F. Supp. 31 (W.D.N.Y. 1947). — Eds.]

our guess as to what Congress meant. I believe Congress had those aspects in mind and was not thinking of the nice distinctions between Roman and Anglo-American legal theories about legal entities.

NOTES AND QUESTIONS

1. *Analysis.* In Williams v. McGowan, Judge Hand relies on legal history and precedent in approaching the question whether a proprietorship should, for tax purposes, be thought of as an entity. (See the discussion of the entity/aggregate distinction at page 827, Note 2, following the *Basye* case.) Judge Frank, dissenting, relies instead on his perception of how the ordinary business person would think. Which approach seems most likely to be consistent with congressional purpose? with promoting sound tax-policy objectives?

2. *Partnerships and partners; corporations and shareholders.* If a partnership sells the assets of a business it operates (or, if you sympathize with Judge Frank's view in Williams v. McGowan, if it sells "a business") the sale is governed by the fragmentation principle of Williams v. McGowan. If, on the other hand, an individual partner sells his or her interest in the partnership, that sale produces capital gain or loss, except to the extent that the proceeds are attributable to unrealized receivables, recapture property, substantially appreciated inventory items, or certain other ordinary-income property. See §§741 and 751. Similarly, a sale of business assets by a corporation is governed by Williams v. McGowan, while a sale of shares by a shareholder ordinarily is treated as the sale of a single capital asset.

3. *Allocation of purchase price.* Where a business is bought and sold for a lump sum and the rule of Williams v. McGowan must be applied, the lump sum must be allocated among the elements. Obviously, allocation can be a difficult task. An analogous problem that is a source of frequent dispute between taxpayers and the IRS is allocation of a single payment between the goodwill of a business and the owner's personal covenant not to compete. Goodwill is a capital asset for the seller, and ordinarily its cost cannot be amortized by the buyer; a covenant not to compete produces ordinary income for the seller, and its cost can be amortized by the buyer. The problem of separation is particularly vexatious where, as is often the case, the sole purpose of the covenant not to compete is to protect the goodwill. Generally, if the parties agree on an allocation and use it consistently, the Service will not challenge that allocation, but may do so when the circumstances of the parties are such that an advantage is given to one party at no cost to the other.

J. CORRELATION WITH PRIOR RELATED TRANSACTIONS

MERCHANTS NATIONAL BANK v. COMMISSIONER

199 F.2d 657 (5th Cir. 1952)

STRUM, Circuit Judge. . . .

On January 1, 1941, the petitioner held notes of Alabama Naval Stores Company, representing loans made by the bank to the Naval Stores Company, on which there was an unpaid balance of $49,025.00. In 1941 and 1943, at the direction of national bank examiners, the bank charged these notes off as worthless, thereafter holding them on a "zero" basis. Deductions for the charge-offs, as ordinary losses, were allowed in full by the Commissioner on petitioner's income tax returns in 1941 and 1943. In 1944, petitioner sold the notes to a third party for $18,460.58, which it reported on its return for 1944 as a long term capital gain and paid its tax on that basis. The Commissioner held this sum to be ordinary income. . . .

The rule is well settled, and this Court has held, that when a deduction for income tax purposes is taken and allowed for debts deemed worthless, recoveries on the debts in a later year constitute taxable income for that year to the extent that a tax benefit was received from the deduction taken in a prior year. . . .

When these notes were charged off as a bad debt in the first instance, the bank deducted the amount thereof from its ordinary income, thus escaping taxation on that portion of its income in those years. The amount subsequently recovered on the notes restores pro tanto the amount originally deducted from ordinary income, and is accordingly taxable as ordinary income, not as a capital gain. When the notes were charged off, and the bank recouped itself for the capital loss by deducting the amount thereof from its current income, the notes were no longer capital assets for income tax purposes. To permit the bank to reduce its ordinary income by the amount of the loss in the first instance, thus gaining a maximum tax advantage on that basis, and then permit it to treat the amount later recovered on the notes as a capital gain, taxable on a much lower basis than ordinary income, would afford the bank a tax advantage on the transaction not contemplated by the income tax laws.

The fact that the bank sold these notes to a third party, instead of collecting the amount in question from the maker of the notes does not avoid the effect of the rule above stated. . . .

As the recoveries in question were ordinary income, not capital gains, the 1944 deficiency was properly entered.

Affirmed.

ARROWSMITH v. COMMISSIONER

344 U.S. 6 (1952)

Mr. Justice BLACK delivered the opinion of the Court.

. . . In 1937 two taxpayers, petitioners here, decided to liquidate and divide the proceeds of a corporation in which they had equal stock ownership. Partial distributions made in 1937, 1938, and 1939 were followed by a final one in 1940. Petitioners reported the profits obtained from this transaction, classifying them as capital gains. They thereby paid less income tax than would have been required had the income been attributed to ordinary business transactions for profit. About the propriety of these 1937-1940 returns, there is no dispute. But in 1944 a judgment was rendered against the old corporation. . . . The two taxpayers were required to and did pay the judgment for the corporation, of whose assets they were transferees. . . . Classifying the loss as an ordinary business one, each took a tax deduction for 100% of the amount paid. Treatment of the loss as a capital one would have allowed deduction of a much smaller amount. . . . The Commissioner viewed the 1944 payment as part of the original liquidation transaction requiring classification as a capital loss, just as the taxpayers had treated the original dividends as capital gains. . . .

[Section 165(f)] treats losses from sales or exchanges of capital assets as "capital losses" and [§331(a)(1)] requires that liquidation distributions be treated as exchanges. The losses here fall squarely within the definition of "capital losses" contained in these sections. Taxpayers were required to pay the judgment because of liability imposed on them as transferees of liquidation distribution assets. And it is plain that their liability as transferees was not based on any ordinary business transaction of theirs apart from the liquidation proceedings. It is not even denied that had this judgment been paid after liquidation, but during the year 1940, the losses would have been properly treated as capital ones. For payment during 1940 would simply have reduced the amount of capital gains taxpayers received during that year.

It is contended, however, that this payment which would have been a capital transaction in 1940 was transformed into an ordinary business transaction in 1944 because of the well-established principle that each taxable year is a separate unit for tax accounting purposes. United States v. Lewis [supra page 205], North American Oil Consolidated v. Burnet [supra page 201]. But this principle is not breached by considering all the 1937-1944 liquidation transaction events in order properly to classify the nature of the 1944 loss for tax purposes. Such an examination is not an attempt to reopen and readjust the 1937 to 1940 tax returns, an action that would be inconsistent with the annual tax accounting principle. . . .

Affirmed.

Mr. Justice DOUGLAS, dissenting.

I agree with Mr. Justice JACKSON that these losses should be treated as ordinary, not capital, losses. There were no capital transactions in the year in which the losses were suffered. Those transactions occurred and were accounted for in earlier years in accord with the established principle that each year is a separate unit for tax accounting purposes. See United States v. Lewis [supra]. I have not felt, as my dissent in the *Lewis* case indicates, that the law made that an inexorable principle. But if it is the law, we should require observance of it — not merely by taxpayers but by the Government as well. We should force each year to stand on its own footing, whoever may gain or lose from it in a particular case. We impeach that principle when we treat this year's losses as if they diminished last year's gains.

Mr. Justice JACKSON, whom Mr. Justice FRANKFURTER joins, dissenting.

This problem arises only because the judgment was rendered in a taxable year subsequent to the liquidation.

Had the liability of the transferor-corporation been reduced to judgment during the taxable year in which liquidation occurred, or prior thereto, this problem, under the tax laws, would not arise. The amount of the judgment rendered against the corporation would have decreased the amount it had available for distribution, which would have reduced the liquidating dividends proportionately and diminished the capital gains taxes assessed against the stockholders. Probably it would also have decreased the corporation's own taxable income.

Congress might have allowed, under such circumstances, tax returns of the prior year to be reopened or readjusted so as to give the same tax results as would have obtained had the liability become known prior to liquidation. Such a solution is foreclosed to us and the alternatives left are to regard the judgment liability fastened by operation of law on the transferee as an ordinary loss for the year of adjudication or to regard it as a capital loss for such year.

I find little aid in the choice of alternatives from arguments based on equities. One enables the taxpayer to deduct the amount of the judgment against his ordinary income which might be taxed as high as 87%, while if the liability had been assessed against the corporation prior to liquidation it would have reduced his capital gain which was taxable at only 25% (now 26%). The consequence may readily be characterized as a windfall (regarding a windfall as anything that is left to a taxpayer after the collector has finished with him).

On the other hand, adoption of the contrary alternative may penalize the taxpayer because of two factors: (1) [limitations on the deductibility of capital losses against ordinary income]; and (2) had the liability been discharged by the corporation, a portion of it would probably in effect have been paid by the Government, since the corporation could have taken it as a deduction, while here the total liability comes out of the pockets of the stockholders.

Solicitude for the revenues is a plausible but treacherous basis upon which to decide a particular tax case. A victory may have implications which in future cases will cost the Treasury more than a defeat. This might be such a case, for anything I know. Suppose that subsequent to liquidation it is found that a corporation has undisclosed claims instead of liabilities and that under applicable state law they may be prosecuted for the benefit of the stockholders. The logic of the Court's decision here, if adhered to, would result in a lesser return to the Government than if the recoveries were considered ordinary income. Would it be so clear that this is a capital loss if the shoe were on the other foot?

Where the statute is so indecisive and the importance of a particular holding lies in its rational and harmonious relation to the general scheme of the tax law, I think great deference is due the twice-expressed judgment of the Tax Court . . . [which] is a more competent and steady influence toward a systematic body of tax law than our sporadic omnipotence in a field beset with invisible boomerangs. I should reverse, in reliance upon the Tax Court's judgment more, perhaps, than my own.

NOTE

In United States v. Skelly Oil Co., 394 U.S. 678 (1969), the taxpayer was required to refund amounts that it had received in an earlier year from the sale of natural gas and that had been the basis for a 27½ percent depletion allowance. The Court held that the deduction for the refund was limited to 72½ percent of the amount refunded, since it was only this amount that had been taxed. In reaching this result, the Court referred to the problems created by the principle of annual accounting (see supra page 55) and, citing *Arrowsmith,* said that "the annual accounting concept does not require us to close our eyes to what happened in prior years." 394 U.S. at 684. The Court went on to say (at 685):

> The rationale for the *Arrowsmith* rule is easy to see; if money was taxed at a special lower rate when received, the taxpayer would be accorded an unfair tax windfall if repayments were generally deductible from receipts

taxable at the higher rate applicable to ordinary income. The Court in *Arrowsmith* was unwilling to infer that Congress intended such a result.

Four Circuit Court decisions have addressed the tax problem that arises from the repayment of insider profits. In each case, an employee stockholder made a profit on employer stock purchased and sold (or sold and purchased) allegedly in violation of the securities laws regarding trading restrictions on insiders. None of the employees admitted liability, but each decided to repay the profits to the corporation to preserve his business position and reputation. In all four cases, the Tax Court held the amount repaid was a deduction from ordinary income rather than a capital loss since the taxpayers made the sales in their capacities as shareholders rather than as employees, while the repayments arose from their status as employees. The Circuit Courts reversed all four decisions and held that the deduction must take its character from the income item in which it had its genesis, which was the purchase and/or sale of a capital asset. Mitchell v. Commissioner, 428 F.2d 259 (6th Cir. 1970), cert. denied, 401 U.S. 909 (1971); Anderson v. Commissioner, 480 F.2d 1304 (7th Cir. 1973); Cummings v. Commissioner, 506 F.2d 449 (2d Cir. 1974), cert. denied, 421 U.S. 913 (1975); Brown v. Commissioner, 529 F.2d 609 (10th Cir. 1976).

K. REQUIREMENT OF A SALE OR EXCHANGE

HELVERING v. HAMMEL

311 U.S. 504 (1941)

Mr. Justice Stone delivered the opinion of the Court. . . .

Respondent taxpayers, with other members of a syndicate, purchased "on land contract" a plot of land in Oakland County, Michigan, for the sum of $96,000, upon a down payment of $20,000. The precise nature of the contract does not appear beyond the fact that payments for the land were to be made in installments, and the vendor retained an interest in the land as security for payment of the balance of the purchase price. Before the purchase price was paid in full the syndicate defaulted on its payments. The vendor instituted foreclosure proceedings by suit in equity in a state court which resulted in a judicial sale of the property, the vendor becoming the purchaser, and in a deficiency judgment against the members of the syndicate. Respondents' contribution to the purchase money, some $4000, was lost. . . .

It is not denied that it was the foreclosure sale of respondents' interest in the land purchased by the syndicate for profit, which finally liquidated the capital investment made by its members and fixed the precise amount of the loss which respondents seek to deduct as such from gross income. But they argue that the "losses from sales" which by [§165(f)] are made deductible only to the limited extent provided by [§1211(b)] are those losses resulting from sales voluntarily made by the taxpayer, and that losses resulting from forced sales like the present not being subject to the limitations of [§1211(b)] are deductible in full like other losses under [§165(c)(2)].

To read this qualification into the statute respondents rely on judicial decisions applying the familiar rule that a restrictive covenant against sale or assignment refers to the voluntary action of the convenantor and not to transfers by operation of law or judicial sales in invitum. . . . But here we are not concerned with a restrictive covenant of the taxpayer, but with a sale as an effective means of establishing a deductible loss for the purpose of computing his income tax. The term sale may have many meanings, depending on the context, see Webster's New International Dictionary. The meaning here depends on the purpose with which it is used in the statute and the legislative history of that use. . . .

As will presently appear, the legislative history of this definition shows that it was not chosen to exclude from the capital assets provisions losses resulting from forced sales of taxpayers' property. And, if so construed, substantial loss of revenue would result under the 1934 Act, whose purpose was to avoid loss of revenue by the application of the capital assets provisions. . . . It accordingly reduced the tax burden on capital gains . . . and permitted the deduction, on the same scale, of capital losses, but only to the extent that there are taxable capital gains, plus $2000. In thus relieving capital gains from the tax imposed on other types of income, it cannot be assumed, in the absence of some clear indication to the contrary, that Congress intended to permit deductions in full of losses resulting from forced sales of the taxpayers' property, from either capital gains or ordinary gross income, while taxing only a fraction of the gains resulting from the sales of such property. . . .

Congress thus has given clear indication of a purpose to offset capital gains by losses from the sale of like property. . . . This purpose to treat gains and deductible losses on a parity but with a further specific provision provided by [§1211(b)], permitting specified percentages of capital losses to be deducted from ordinary income to the extent of $2000, would be defeated in a most substantial way if only a percentage of the gains were taxed but losses on sales of like property could be deducted in full from gross income. This treatment of losses from sales of capital assets in the 1924 and later Acts and the reason given for adopting it afford convincing evidence that the "sales" referred to in the statute include forced sales such as have sufficed, under long accepted income tax practice, to establish a deductible loss in the case of non-capital assets. Such sales can equally be taken to establish the loss in the case of capital assets without infringing the declared policy of the statute to treat capital gains and losses on a parity. . . .

It is not without significance that Congress, in the 1934 Act, enlarged the scope of its provisions relating to losses from sales of capital assets by including within them losses upon the disposition of the taxpayer's property by methods other than sale and without reference to the voluntary action of the taxpayer. It thus treats as losses from sales or exchanges the loss sustained from redemption of stock, retirement of bonds, losses from short sales, and loss sustained by failure of the holder of an option to exercise it [§§331(a)(2), 1232, 1233, and 1234], although none of these transactions involves a loss from a sale. . . .

The scope of the capital loss provisions was still further enlarged by [§165(g)], which provides that if securities, which are capital assets, are ascertained to be worthless and are charged off within the taxable year the loss, with an exception not now material, shall be considered as a loss arising from a sale or exchange. These provisions disclose a consistent legislative policy to enlarge the class of deductible losses made subject to the capital assets provisions without regard to the voluntary action of the taxpayer in producing them. We could hardly suppose that Congress would not have made provision for the like treatment of losses resulting from a forced sale of the taxpayer's property acquired for profit either in the 1934 or 1938 Act, if it had thought that the term "sales or exchanges" as used in both acts did not include such sales of the taxpayer's property.

Respondents also advance the argument . . . that the definitive event fixing respondents' loss was not the foreclosure sale but the decree of foreclosure which ordered the sale and preceded it. But since the foreclosure contemplated by the decree was foreclosure by sale and the foreclosed property had value which was conclusively established by the sale for the purposes of the foreclosing proceeding, the sale was the definitive event establishing the loss within the meaning and for the purpose of the revenue laws. . . .

Reversed. . . .

NOTES

1. *Relation of "sale or exchange" to requirement of a "closed transaction."* Does the Court imply that every "closed transaction" involving a capital asset is a "sale or exchange" of the asset? If so, it soon repudiated that implication by holding in Helvering v. William Flaccus Oak Leather Co.,

313 U.S. 247, 249 (1941), that the taxpayer had not engaged in a "sale or exchange" when its plant was destroyed by fire and it recovered compensation for the loss from its insurance company:

> Generally speaking, the language in the Revenue Act, just as in any statute, is to be given its ordinary meaning, and the words "sale" and "exchange" are not to be read any differently. Compare Helvering v. Hammel. . . . Neither term is appropriate to characterize the demolition of property and subsequent compensation for its loss by an insurance company. Plainly that pair of events was not a sale. Nor can they be regarded as an exchange, for "exchange" . . . implies reciprocal transfers of capital assets, not a single transfer to compensate for the destruction of the transferee's asset.

Note that §1231 now provides that such conversions are to be treated as sales or exchanges.

The possibility should be kept in mind that in deciding that a particular transaction with a capital asset is not a "sale or exchange," the courts may be focusing on the question of whether the transaction is "closed," rather than on the issue of whether the taxpayer's gain or loss is capital or ordinary. In such a case, the capital gain and loss provisions are inapplicable not because there was no "sale or exchange" within the meaning of §1222, but because there was no "sale or other disposition" within the meaning of §1001(a), so that the transaction is not "closed" and the taxpayer may not offset his basis for the property against the amount received. Thus, if a purported "sale" is held to be a "lease," the taxpayer's receipts will be taxed in the same manner (ordinary income, offset by depreciation) whether the property in question is a capital asset or not. It would be more accurate in such a case to hold that there has been no "sale or other disposition"; to say that the transaction does not constitute a "sale or other exchange" may imply, erroneously, that the transaction constitutes a "sale or other disposition" and fails to qualify for capital gain (or loss) treatment only because it does not satisfy the more exacting standards implicit in the term "sale or exchange." Compare the government's arguments in the *Brown* case, supra page 882. See also discussion of open versus closed transactions, supra page 358.

It has sometimes been suggested that the term "sale or exchange" was deliberately chosen by Congress to encompass a more limited range of transactions than the term "sale or other disposition" in §1001(a) (providing that gain or loss "from the sale or other disposition of property" is the difference between its adjusted basis and the amount realized), but one might infer, to the contrary, that the difference in language was accidental from the fact that the recognition provision — §1001(c) — also uses the phrase "sale or exchange" yet is usually said to embrace *all* closed transactions. At a number of points the Code explicitly provides that transactions shall be treated as sales or exchanges even though they clearly or arguably would not otherwise qualify,[38] and in the *William Flaccus Oak Leather Co.* case, supra, the Court implied that Congress has thereby provided an exclusive list of the "ambiguous transactions" that are to be treated as sales or exchanges.

2. *Worthless securities §165(g).* Section 165(g)(1) provides that if a "security" (defined to include stock, as well as bonds and other evidences of indebtedness) that is a capital asset becomes worthless during the taxable year, the loss shall be treated as though it had arisen on a sale or exchange. The reason is that a sale of the security just before it became worthless would have created a capital loss. There is no good reason to treat the taxpayer differently if he sells the security a month before it becomes totally worthless for a dollar or holds it until it is worthless. But the statutory parallelism between holding and selling is not perfect.

(a) Section 165(g)(1) applies only to securities issued by corporations or political bodies. A loan to an individual or to a partnership will give rise to a bad debt deduction when it becomes worthless, although a sale before it became worthless may have produced capital loss. This disparity is reduced if the worthless obligation is a "non-business debt" within the meaning of §166(d), but even if it is, the taxpayer gets a short-term capital loss, whereas a sale would have produced either a long-term or a short-term capital loss, depending upon the holding period.

(b) Even if the borrower is a corporation or political body, §165(g)(1) does not apply to loans if there is no "evidence of indebtedness" or if the evidence of indebtedness is not coupon-bearing or in registered form.

(c) When §165(g)(1) applies, the worthless security is treated as though it had been sold on the last day of the taxable year (presumably because it is difficult enough to determine the year of worthlessness, without endeavoring to pinpoint the day), but this may give the taxpayer a long-term capital loss, although a sale a few days earlier would have resulted in a short-term loss.

38. See §§331(a)(2), 1232, 1233, and 1234, all cited in *Hammel,* and §§631(a), 631(c), 1235, and 1241.

TABLE OF CASES

Italic type indicates principle cases.

TABLE OF INTERNAL REVENUE CODE PROVISIONS

TABLE OF TREASURY REGULATIONS

TABLE OF REVENUE RULINGS

Italic type indicates rulings that are reprinted.

TABLE OF MISCELLANEOUS IRS PRONOUNCEMENTS

Italic type indicates opinions that are reprinted.

INDEX